THE GREAT WAR

VOLUME 3

This Volume Combines Volume 3 & Volume 4
of an Original 13 Volume Set.

Reprinted 1999 from the 1915 editions
TRIDENT PRESS INTERNATIONAL
Copyright 1999

ISBN 1-582790-26-4 Standard Edition

Printed in Croatia

From the Painting by C. M. Sheldon

Frontispiece. Vol. III THE GREAT WAR.

The Capture of the German Trenches at Neuve Chapelle

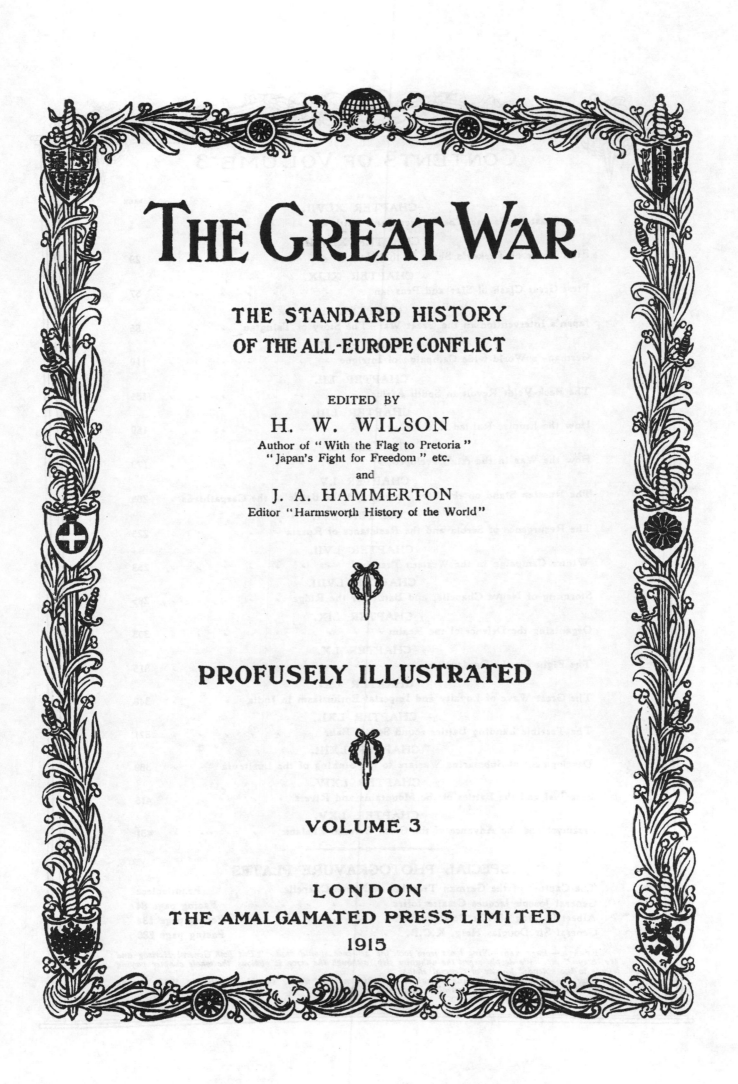

THE GREAT WAR

THE STANDARD HISTORY
OF THE ALL-EUROPE CONFLICT

EDITED BY

H. W. WILSON

Author of "With the Flag to Pretoria"
"Japan's Fight for Freedom" etc.

and

J. A. HAMMERTON

Editor "Harmsworth History of the World"

PROFUSELY ILLUSTRATED

VOLUME 3

LONDON
THE AMALGAMATED PRESS LIMITED
1915

CONTENTS OF VOLUME 3

SPECIAL PHOTOGRAVURE PLATES

ERRATA.—Page 149.—Nine lines from foot, the sentence should read: " But both General Hertzog and Mr. Steyn," etc. We deeply regret the unhappy slip, although the error is obvious, the whole chapter paying tribute to the splendid loyalty of General Botha.
Page 166.—Photograph showing arrival of troopship in home waters should be entitled: " The coming of the Australians. Arrival of Australian Reservists at Plymouth."

THE GREAT WAR

THE STANDARD HISTORY OF THE ALL-EUROPE CONFLICT

VOLUME 3

CHAPTER XLVII.

EAST COAST RAIDS AND THE DOGGER BANK BATTLE.

First Vain Attempt on Yarmouth—German Armoured Cruiser Sunk by German Mines—Fog Saves the Raiders from Our Fleet—
Scarborough and Whitby Massacres—Attack on the Hartlepools—The Third Raid upon the British Coast—Sir David
Beatty Catches the Hostile Squadron—Derfflinger Set on Fire and Battered—German Admiral's Flagship Half-Sinking—
The Terrible End of the Blücher—The Lion Damaged at Bows—Action Broken Off as Enemy Ships are Nearly Sunk.

IT was on Monday, November 2nd, 1914, that the German Admiralty received news of the victory of their China Squadron over the Good Hope and Monmouth in the action off Coronel. It was then decided to launch the battle-cruiser squadron at once across the North Sea, and to bombard the East Coast of England, with a view to increasing the panic among the civil population of our country. The Staff of the German Admiralty took it for granted that the loss of the chief ships in Admiral Cradock's squadron would produce a panic, and it was hoped that the bombardment of Yarmouth and Lowestoft would increase violently the perturbation of the British people.

It was also expected that our battle-cruiser squadron, under Sir David Beatty, would try to engage the raiding warships under Rear-Admiral Funke. So a new mine-field was laid between Heligoland and Jahde Bay, where Wilhelms-haven is situated. The idea was to draw the counter-attacking British ships into the minefield, where a large flotilla of German submarines was also acting. For nine years this plan of provoking a naval engagement with the fast wing of the British Navy had been elaborated. Each German vessel designed for the operation had been provided with an unusual number of stern guns of large calibre. The Blücher, vainly planned in 1906 to counter

ADMIRAL FRIEDRICH VON INGENOHL.
Former Commander of the German High Seas Fleet,
superseded for lack of dash and initiative.

our first battle-cruisers, was able to bring six large guns to bear astern. Then the first true German battle-cruiser, the Von der Tann, also had a stern fire of six large guns. The Moltke and Goeben were still more heavily gunned for a retreating fight, for they had each eight 11 in. guns astern, and only six ahead. The heavy armament of the Seydlitz was arranged in the same manner.

All these ships, in short, were built to run away, and yet fight terrifically while they were running, and lure the British squadron into a minefield.

Being well aware of the cool and even fighting temper of the ordinary British admiral, the Germans looked about for some means of working our seamen up to a heat of blind passion, in which such a thing as a minefield at the end of a long fighting chase might be overlooked.

The bombardment of some of our coast towns was selected as the best means to this end. It would rouse our sailors to anger, as well as create a feeling of widespread uncertainty and apprehension in our civil population.

So, as evening fell on Monday, November 2nd, a German squadron of three armoured cruisers and three battle-cruisers came out of Wilhelmshaven, and threaded the minefield around Jahde Bay, and then tore at high speed due west for the East Anglian coast. There they arrived at dawn on Tuesday morning, November 3rd. One of

THE "SMOKE BLANKET" WHICH SAVED THE HALCYON.
When, about seven o'clock on the morning of November 3rd, 1914, a German squadron appeared off the Yarmouth coast, the only British warship on view was the old gunboat Halcyon. The great German ships rained shells on the little vessel, but she was only hit eight times; and a British destroyer arriving on the scene, sent up a screen of thick smoke, behind which the battered but uncrippled Halcyon got safely away.

Meanwhile, the bombardment of Yarmouth proceeded with much noise and fury, but with no damage. For the Admiralty had thoughtfully anticipated German tactics by providing the raiders with a minefield at the end of their outward journey. Nearly all the German shells fell with a mighty splash into the sea some two miles from the famous Yarmouth beach, where holiday-makers used to resort, as it was dangerous for the attackers to come much closer. For nearly an hour flashes of flame were visible along the seaward horizon, and the murderous missiles sent up towering cascades as they approached the shore. Nearer and nearer sounded the firing, and it was gravely feared that the town at last would suffer. But a little before eight o'clock, after a hundred shots had been uselessly fired, the hostile squadron disappeared into the haze.

Their destroyers, scattered northward and southward, had got into touch with the outer guard of our advancing battle-cruiser squadron. A wireless message came to the German admiral, and learning that a far superior force was closing down upon him, he turned for home at top speed, and escaped having to fight by getting into a thick mist. Some of his ships also started dropping mines as soon as they left Yarmouth Roads. As the result of this mine-dropping there was a chapter of accidents to some British vessels. About ten o'clock in the morning a steam-drifter, the Fraternal, was blown up eight miles off the coast, midway between Lowestoft and Yarmouth. She sank slowly, and her crew were rescued by other steam-drifters. Then the Copious, arriving from the herring-grounds, was struck, and sank quickly with the loss of most of her men. A few minutes afterwards two British submarines, moving in pursuit of the Germans, came in sight. One of them was submarine D5, a boat of 630 tons, built in 1910. She was travelling on the surface, with Lieut.-Commander Godfrey Herbert in charge, and the skipper of a Yarmouth trawler spoke him, and told him of the danger of mines. But as D5 shot over to the other submarine to carry the warning to her, she herself struck one of the mines. Her bow went up in the air, and she sank immediately, nearly all her crew of twenty men being lost.

Loss of Submarine D5

our steam-trawling fleets, fishing about eight miles off Lowestoft, saw the warships steam by just at dawn, all lights out and no ensigns flying. A skipper of a steam-drifter was so sure that they were British boats that he waved his teapot at them as a morning greeting. He got in reply a line of shaking fists and angry faces on the deck of the nearest enemy ship.

About seven o'clock the bombardment began. The only British warship in view of the Germans was the old gunboat the Halcyon, lying ten miles off the English coast on fishing patrol duties. The great German ships rained shells upon the gunboat, which had only two 4·7 in. and four 6-pounder guns. She could scarcely do eighteen knots, being more than twenty years old; but her captain, running her on a zigzag course, only had his boat hit eight times. Then a British destroyer arrived, and sent up a screen of thick smoke, behind which the battered but uncrippled little Halcyon got safely away.

But what we lost on this occasion by German mines was little in comparison with what the raiders themselves lost. For the thick fog that saved the hostile squadron from the attack of our battle-cruisers was a death-trap to the modern armoured cruiser the Yorck. Built just before the Scharnhorst and Gneisenau, she was sister-ship to the Roon, having an armament of four 8·2 in. guns and ten 6 in. guns, with a 4 in. armoured belt and 6 in. turrets.

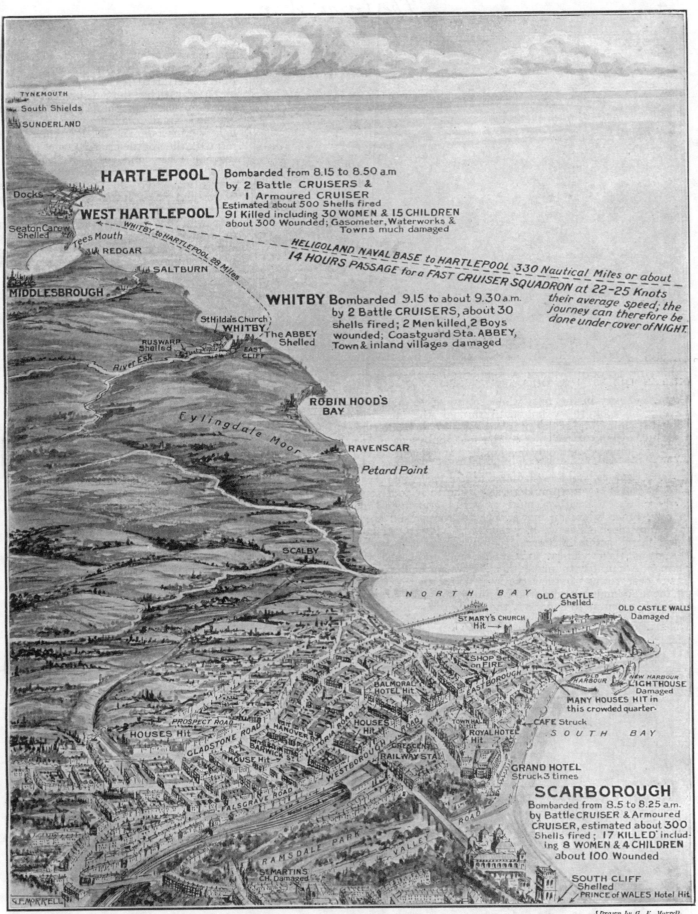

Within the image:

TYNEMOUTH
South Shields
SUNDERLAND

Docks

HARTLEPOOL
Seaton Carew Shelled
Tees Mouth
REDGAR
WEST HARTLEPOOL

Bombarded from 8.15 to 8.50 a.m.
by 2 Battle CRUISERS &
1 Armoured CRUISER
Estimated about 500 Shells fired
91 Killed including 30 WOMEN & 15 CHILDREN
about 300 Wounded; Gasometer, Waterworks &
Towns much damaged

WHITBY to HARTLEPOOL 28 Miles

HELIGOLAND NAVAL BASE to HARTLEPOOL 330 Nautical Miles or about
14 HOURS PASSAGE for a FAST CRUISER SQUADRON at 22-25 Knots
their average speed; the journey can therefore be done under cover of NIGHT.

SALTBURN
MIDDLESBROUGH
St Hilda's Church
WHITBY
RUSWARP Shelled
The ABBEY Shelled
EAST CLIFF
River Esk

WHITBY Bombarded 9.15 to about 9.30 a.m.
by 2 Battle CRUISERS, about 30
shells fired; 2 Men killed, 2 Boys
wounded; Coastguard Sta. ABBEY,
Town & inland villages damaged

Eylingdale Moor

ROBIN HOOD'S BAY

RAVENSCAR
Petard Point

SCALBY

NORTH BAY
OLD CASTLE Shelled
OLD CASTLE WALLS Damaged
St MARY'S CHURCH Hit
SHOP Set on FIRE
EAST BOROUGH
NEW HARBOUR
OLD HARBOUR
LIGHTHOUSE Damaged
MANY HOUSES HIT in this crowded quarter.
BALMORAL HOTEL Hit
PROSPECT ROAD
HOUSES Hit
GLADSTONE ROAD
HANOVER ROAD
VICTORIA ROAD
HOUSES Hit
CAFE Struck
HOUSES HIT
BARWICK ST.
HOUSE Hit
WESTBOROUGH
CRESCENT
RAILWAY STA.
TOWN HALL
ROYAL HOTEL Hit
SOUTH BAY
FALSGRAVE ROAD
PARK
GRAND HOTEL Struck 3 times
RAMSDALE PARK
VALLEY
ROAD
St MARTIN'S CH. Damaged

SCARBOROUGH
Bombarded from 8.5 to 8.25 a.m.
by Battle CRUISER & Armoured
CRUISER, estimated about 300
Shells fired; 17 KILLED' including 8 WOMEN & 4 CHILDREN
about 100 Wounded

SOUTH CLIFF Shelled
PRINCE of WALES Hotel Hit

G.F.MORRELL

[Drawn by G. F. Morrell.

BARBARIC KULTUR: GERMAN NAVY'S BOMBARDMENT OF OUR EAST COAST HOLIDAY RESORTS.

The bombardment by German warships of Scarborough, Whitby, and the Hartlepools, on the morning of December 16th, 1914, was described by a German paper as affording " further proof of the gallantry of the German Navy." The exploit, so graphically recalled to us in the above pictorial plan of the bombarded coast-line, supplied, rather, evidence that the German people had forgotten the lesson of their own Thirty Years' War, that the conventions of civilised warfare are based not merely on humane sentiment, but on sound general common-sense. In the three towns named above German shells killed, altogether, seventy-eight women and children, and wounded two hundred and twenty-eight.

ON THE LOOK-OUT FROM A SPLINTER-PROOF TRENCH
ON THE EAST COAST.

occasion they prepared to risk the whole fighting power of their Fleet. For they brought out their latest, swiftest, and most powerful battle-cruiser, the Derfflinger, and used with her the Seydlitz, the Moltke, the Von der Tann, the Blücher, and two of their small remaining stock of fast lighter cruisers. The chief of these ships formed the battle-cruiser wing of the German Fleet, and on them would fall in a general fleet action the task of preventing the envelopment of the slower and more unwieldy battleships by our swift battle-cruisers.

It will thus be seen that the German Admiralty was taking a tremendous risk merely for the sake of killing and wounding a few hundred children, women, and

Losing her way in the mist while returning to Wilhelmshaven, she took the wrong path through the minefield, exploded a mine, and sank just in the entrance to Jahde Bay, thereby blocking it. Owing to the fog, the rescue of her crew was impeded, and only one hundred and seventy-seven men out of a complement of six hundred and twenty-nine were saved. She was a more modern ship than the Good Hope, with a more powerful armament, and in regard merely to ship power, her destruction did much to restore the balance we had temporarily lost three days before in the action off Coronel.

Yorck blown up by mines

And as their victory at Coronel had provoked the German Admiralty to make their first vain raid on our East Coast towns, so their crushing defeat in the Battle off the Falkland Islands aroused them to make a more desperate attempt to carry out the scheme for which their battle-cruiser wing had been designed. On this second

EXTERIOR VIEW OF THE ABOVE SPLINTER-PROOF.

GUARDING THE CABLE STATION AT CUNARD BAY, ISLE OF WIGHT.

Admiral Jellicoe, in reply to certain alarmists, stated that the Isle of Wight was "the safest place in the world." Certainly, when this statement was published, in March, 1915, the island had so far escaped injury. The other photographs on this page illustrate the work of men of our new armies in trench-digging at home, either for practice or in view of the possible if not probable German invasion of these islands.

non-combatant men in certain towns on our East Coast. In actual matter of fact, the roles of Germans and Britons in the proposed stern-chase action across the North Sea had been already reversed from the original intention of the German Staff. The leaders of the British Navy were just as cool and as scientific in both their strategical dispositions and their manner of handling their ships in action as they had been at the outbreak of the war. It was the German admirals who had been worked up into such a passion of rage, and subjected to such political and social pressure, that they had ceased to calculate forces or to try to organise a victory. Not only were the fighting seamen of Germany losing their spirit, but the long inaction of the High Seas Fleet was one of the

A NOVEL SIGHT ON THE CLIFFS OF OLD ENGLAND.

factors of depression upon the minds of the overtasked German soldiers. Something striking had to be done to revive the courage of every German.

Therefore, about five o'clock in the evening of Tuesday, December 15th, the great German battle-cruiser fleet steamed out of Wilhelmshaven, and for fourteen hours made at a speed of twenty-five knots for part of the Durham and Yorkshire coast which was known to be unprotected by a minefield.

Of course, it seemed very negligent of our Admiralty not to have mined the approaches to the busy commercial port of the Hartlepools. But our entire coast could not be defended by mines without hampering our Navy and crippling our commerce. Certain risks had to be taken, but we were prepared to strike, if our risks tempted the Germans to cross the sea. It was all planned by the subtlest and most brilliant mind in our Navy—by the man who had won his position as Commander

The sea-raiders' second venture

ANOTHER VIEW OF A SPLINTER PROOF ON THE EAST COAST.

BRITISH CAVALRY PATROL ON THE SANDS AT SCARBOROUGH AFTER THE RAID.

The murders at Scarborough began a little after eight o'clock in the morning. The Moltke, with her 11 in. shells, and an armoured cruiser firing 6 in. shells, came up in the mist, and opened fire at close range, the smaller vessel steaming up to within a quarter of a mile of the beach. The bombardment lasted about twenty minutes. Four children, eight women, and five men were killed, and some hundred were wounded.

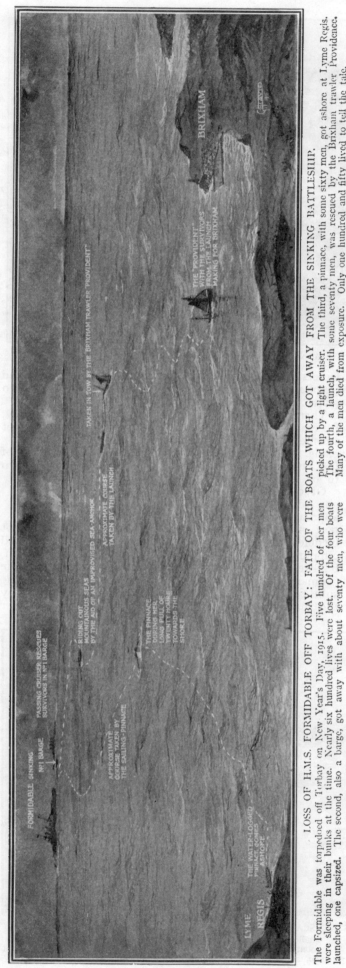

FORMIDABLE SINKING. N°I BARGE

PASSING CRUISER RESCUES SURVIVORS IN N°I BARGE

APPROXIMATE COURSE TAKEN BY THE SAILING-PINNACE

THE WATER-LOGGED PINNACE COMES ASHORE

LYME REGIS

THE PINNACE DURING HER LONG PULL OF TWENTY MILES TOWARDS THE SHORE

RIDING OUT MOUNTAINOUS SEAS BY THE AID OF AN IMPROVISED SEA-ANCHOR

APPROXIMATE COURSE TAKEN BY THE LAUNCH

TAKEN IN TOW BY THE BRIXHAM TRAWLER "PROVIDENT"

THE "PROVIDENT" WITH THE SURVIVORS FROM THE LAUNCH MAKING FOR BRIXHAM

BRIXHAM

LOSS OF H.M.S. FORMIDABLE OFF TORBAY: FATE OF THE BOATS WHICH GOT AWAY FROM THE SINKING BATTLESHIP.

The Formidable was torpedoed off Torbay on New Year's Day, 1915. Five hundred of her men were sleeping in their bunks at the time. Nearly six hundred lives were lost. Of the four boats launched, one capsized. The second, also a barge, got away with about seventy men, who were picked up by a light cruiser. The third, a pinnace, with some sixty men, got ashore at Lyme Regis. The fourth, a launch, with some seventy men, was rescued by the Brixham trawler Providence. Many of the men died from exposure. Only one hundred and fifty lived to tell the tale.

of our Grand Fleet through never having been beaten in any battle manœuvres in which he took a leading part. Sir John Rushworth Jellicoe divined generally what the German Admiralty intended to do. He divined exactly how far the scope of the German Intelligence Department would reach. In fact, he may have allowed it to reach as far as the knowledge that there was no minefield protecting the Hartlepools. But by a curious coincidence, as soon as the German battle-cruiser squadron left Wilhelmshaven on its night voyage to the Durham coast, there was a stir of activity throughout our Grand Fleet. Not only did our First and Second Battle-Cruiser Squadrons put out to sea, but, on a remote point of the northern British coast, eight of our fastest super-Dreadnought battleships got up steam and turned southward.

It was all done in absolute silence. No easily decoded wireless messages could be picked up by spies in Norway, or by adventurous German boats scouting round Scotland. The British counter-stroke was arranged with so absolute a mastery that it is the greatest **The British counter-stroke** stroke of pure ill-luck in the history of naval strategy it did not come off. It reminds one of Huxley's satirical definition of a tragedy according to Herbert Spencer—a beautiful theory, killed by a wicked fact. It was a beautiful battle-plan, prepared with subtle genius and arranged with admirable skill. A tremendous array of forces was exquisitely adjusted for the rapid and complete annihilation of the raiding warships, but at the critical moment a heavy fog blanketed the scene of action, and allowed the enemy to escape.

Meanwhile, the surprised and stricken townspeople of Scarborough, Whitby, and the Hartlepools had to bear the brunt of the raiders' murderous attack. Of the three towns, only the Hartlepools—East and West, lying in a crescent on the Durham coast, with their tidal basins, docks, and shipbuilding yards—were legally liable to bombardment, for they were defended by forts. The case was entirely different in regard to Whitby and Scarborough. In Whitby was merely a coastguard look-out, with a signalling apparatus. At Scarborough was preserved as a curiosity a Russian 64-pounder captured in one of the old wars, and as useful against modern warships as a bow and arrow. The old garrison batteries had been dismantled when Lord Haldane provided the Volunteer Artillery with field-guns.

Moreover, in both the ancient fishing town and the picturesque watering-place, the enemy ships were able to approach quite close to the shore. Thus there was no minefield putting them technically among fortified places. The bombardment of them, and the killing and wounding of babes, children, women, and civilian men, was not an act of war. It was piracy.

The murders began at Scarborough a little after eight o'clock in the morning. The Moltke, with her 11 in. shells, and an armoured cruiser firing 6 in. shells, came up in the morning mist, and opened fire at close range, the smaller vessel steaming up to within a quarter of a mile of the beach. The first shell tore up the promenade and foreshore. Then the Grand Hotel and other prominent buildings were struck. The walls of the ancient castle, ten feet thick, were shattered in places, and the **Scarborough under fire** keep was also damaged. Happily, the old barracks on Castle Hill, at which the Germans continually aimed, were unoccupied. Naturally some of the churches were shelled, for no German gunner could see a Christian temple without wanting to destroy it in the interests of Deutsche Kultur.

It was a dark morning, and most people were either just getting up or breakfasting by gaslight. Women, barefooted, with wraps thrown over their nightdresses, ran into the streets, carrying their frightened children in their arms, with the only thought of getting out of the firing zone. A servant-girl was killed while cleaning a doorstep, a postman, who was about to deliver a letter at the same house being also blown to bits. Children with their mothers were killed with terrible suddenness in their wrecked homes, while fancying that the noise of the firing was only a thunderstorm. The bombardment lasted for about twenty minutes, and at times ten shells fell every minute. In all, four children, eight women, and five men were killed outright, and over a hundred were wounded. It was rather a small result for the expense of ammunition and the risk to the German battle-cruiser and her consort, for sufficient shells were used to have sunk a British battleship if they had all got well home. Far from terror-ising the Yorkshire people by this act of piracy, the Germans only increased the population of the beau-tiful shattered water-ing-place, producing a special bombardment season in the dullest part of the winter, when thousands of

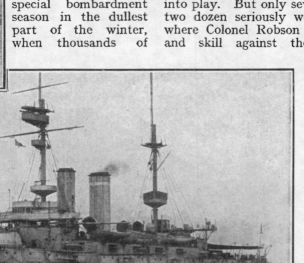

THRILLING EPISODE OF HEROISM AT SEA.
Heroism characteristic of the finest traditions of the sea marked the conduct of Captain Loxley and the crew of the Formidable after she had been torpedoed ; and the same remark applies to the captain and crew of the trawler Providence, which was instrumental in saving some seventy lives. Above is a photograph of the lost battleship. Inset : (1) The trawler ; and (2) the crew of the little craft—left to right, back row : W. Carter, Captain W. Pillar, J. Clark ; front row : Dan Taylor, L. Pillar.

visitors came to see with their own eyes what the baby-killers had done.

It was the same at Whitby, where a coastguard and a vanman were killed and two boys wounded by two battle-cruisers firing 11 in. shells. They opened fire a little after nine o'clock, half a mile south of the Whitby Bell Buoy, and nearly opposite the point **The baby-killers at** on the reef where the hospital-ship **Whitby** Rohilla had struck in the previous October. The old Abbey of St. Hilda and the parish church were injured, and some women and children were wounded. At Whitby the fire was directed chiefly upon the signal station ; but the general intention of the baby-killers was to slay as many non-combatants as possible, and to do the utmost damage to private property. This is quite clear from the number of rounds they fired, and from the manner in which they swept Scarborough, especially in the most crowded parts of the town.

At the Hartlepools the bombardment began at the same time as at Scarborough. The weather was very

hazy, and the three enemy ships are said to have come in under the British flag, and to have fired first out to sea and signalled that a German squadron was approaching. This was a trick of war which, owing to the sea mist, apparently deceived the forts until the ships opened fire. The three battle-cruisers got within a range of about four thousand yards. But except for one shot that destroyed the gas-holders, little military damage was done. The coast batteries, though dominated by the heavier naval guns, maintained an artillery duel all the time, and inflicted some loss on the enemy. The shipbuilding yards were **Homes shattered** not hit, and three small British vessels **at Hartlepool** that engaged the enemy were not sunk. They were the light cruiser Patrol, with nine 4 in. guns, and two destroyers, the Doon and the Hardy, with a few guns of a similar calibre. The destroyers made a gallant and desperate attempt to get near enough to the great hostile battle-cruisers to torpedo them, but were, naturally, unsuccessful. Only on a dark night and by a surprise attack can frail destroyers sufficiently elude observation to bring their torpedo-tubes into play. But only seven sailors were killed and about two dozen seriously wounded. In the land batteries, where Colonel Robson performed prodigies of bravery and skill against the overpowering, longer-ranged ordnance of the enemy, six men of the Durham Light Infantry were killed, and seventeen of the Durhams, the Yorkshire Regiment, and the Royal Engineers were wounded.

The slaughter of non-combatants in this seaport, however, was serious. A hundred children, women, and men were killed, while nearly four hundred and fifty were wounded. Altogether, in the three towns, the men, women and children killed or wounded numbered six hundred and seventy-one. One dauntless little innocent mite set out for school, careless of the rain of shells, saying, " I must get that medal, mother." It was the medal for regular attendance she desired to win, but she was blown to pieces in Crimdon Street. Babies of six and fourteen months perished in agony. Three frightened children, running out into the street, were killed by a single shell, and kindly working women, trying to carry their neighbours' children to a place of safety, were slain with their frail, living burdens during the bombardment which a Berlin newspaper proclaimed to be " a further proof of the gallantry of the German Navy."

Scores of homes in the old town of Hartlepool were blown into fragments. Roofs were lifted off, the walls thrown down, and all that remained of them was, here and there, a heap of broken bricks and plaster, from which protruded portions of bedsteads and other pieces of domestic furniture. The German gunners were well informed as to the lie of the town. After trying to blow down the dock-basin gates they swept the sea front, and then shelled the gasworks, the railway-stations, the electricity works, the waterworks, and the shipbuilding yards. But only the gasworks and Messrs. Furness, Withy & Co.'s works

SURVIVORS OF THE FORMIDABLE BEING TAKEN ON
BOARD THE PROVIDENCE.

After being in their open cutter for nearly twelve hours, two officers and
some seventy men of the torpedoed battleship Formidable were rescued by
the Brixham trawler Providence.　Inset: Sectional view of the side of the
Formidable, showing the point probably struck by torpedoes.

The principal conventions of civilised warfare are not based on simple, humane feeling. They are based on the common interests of the combatants. The Germans first learned this in their terrible Thirty Years' War, when the armies starved through the ill-treatment of non-combatants, resulting in the country through which the soldiers moved becoming an uncultivated and foodless waste. It was for the soldiers' sake that non-combatants were afterwards spared in ordinary civilised land warfare. In the same way the British and French, in the old days, worked out in long practice the humane conventions of naval warfare. At first the fleets raided each other's coast towns. Then gradually they saw that this was folly. The fleet that wasted costly ammunition, carried abroad with much trouble, on damaging property and slaying non-combatants, left itself so much the weaker when it faced the rival fleet on the seas. Therefore the contending admirals learned to keep strictly to business, and to save their powder and shot for naval action.

But the Germans, being without experience in the exercise of sea-power, went back at once to the foolish barbarism of the ancient days. The Goeben and Breslau began it in the Mediterranean, by wasting their ammunition in bombarding Algerian coast towns soon after the outbreak of hostilities, when there were powerful French and British squadrons seeking an action with them. The same ships adopted a like policy afterwards in the Black Sea. If the Germans had any clear idea of obtaining any definite military advantage by the wanton massacre of civilians, it could only have been that at which the Assyrians used to aim when they impaled prisoners outside a besieged town in order to frighten the garrison.

We have learned at first-hand in this war something that Danes and Frenchmen knew a full generation ago. There has been revealed to us all the parvenu quality of German civilisation—all that was concealed in those pedantic efforts at culture which are traceable even in Goethe's career. For a hundred and fifty years the Germans imitated, painstakingly imitated, the veritable leaders of

appear to have suffered severely, and in addition Messrs. Richardson, Westgarth & Co.'s engineering works were somewhat damaged. In all, about five hundred houses in the Hartlepools were hit, in a bombardment at close range lasting some forty minutes.

It was not good gunnery. Taking into consideration the number of shells fired by the three hostile warships, the loss of life was much less than might have been expected, and the damage to the seaport was not as great as it might have been. Seeing that one of the vessels

Wild German gunnery

attacking Hartlepool with 12 in. shells was the latest German battle-cruiser, the Derfflinger, which, at the range she fired, should have been able to sink a ship of her own weight, size, and armament in a quarter of an hour or less, the Germans must have fired wildly. Either the men were thoroughly ashamed of the work which they were doing, or they were disturbed by the risks they ran.

In regard to the bombardment of Whitby and Hartlepool, it was something worse than a crime—it was a blunder.

European life. But they did not grasp the vital wisdom in the old, rich traditions they so earnestly at times endeavoured to vainly absorb. They were learned barbarians. The wars for territory between their petty dynasties, which followed on the religious movement of the Reformation, left them stripped of culture while Western Europe was building up modern civilisation. Their efforts to acquire by study what they lacked in experience made them only uninspired pedants. When they were thrown back on their own stock of ideas and feelings, in the sudden stress of a supreme national struggle for dominion, they at once let go all that was to them mere convention. They then displayed that cruel stupidity, still innate in their minds, which had hitherto been masked by their docile and snobbish imitativeness.

Thereupon it remained for their opponents to teach them anew the forgotten lessons of their Thirty Years' War. They had to be shown that the conventions of civilised warfare were based, not merely on humane sentiment, which a conqueror might on occasion afford to disregard, but on sound, general common-sense. For if our modern civilisation, the best on the whole yet seen in the world, were merely founded on good feeling, its progress would not be sure. Happily, it is built on reason and experience. Therefore it can resist even the terrible organised attack of all the resurgent forces of ancient savagery, directed by a feudal militarism, clad in the armour-plate of industries.

SCENE OUTSIDE THE WRECKED BAPTIST CHAPEL AT WEST HARTLEPOOL DURING THE SECOND BOMBARDMENT OF OUR EAST COAST.

A German shell, after going clean through the chapel, rebounded from the roadway into the first-floor bed-room of the house seen on the right. One woman was struck down. A Territorial, rushing to her assistance, had his rifle blown out of his hand. The scene outside the chapel was piteous in the extreme. People came rushing from the adjacent houses, through a haze of dust, and all the windows in the vicinity were shattered.

the latest technical

In the present case the badly-needed lesson was prepared by Sir John Jellicoe. For when the last vessels of the German cruiser squadron steamed away from Whitby, about 9.30 o'clock on Thursday morning, December 17th, a considerable part of the Grand Fleet was waiting for all the raiders. There was some brilliant manœuvring by certain British admirals, and then the desired positions were obtained, amid the uncertainty of the drifting fog-banks. On one side of the German squadron was Sir David Beatty with our First Battle Cruiser wing. On the other side of him was our Second Battle Squadron wing, with eight of our super-Dreadnought battleships, all ready for instant attack. It was as complete a trap as our fighting seamen of any period have ever got an enemy into. Our Second Battle Squadron suddenly saw the Germans about eight miles away, coming out of a fog-bank. Our fire-control officers marked the ranges, and the loaded guns were laid on the mark. Then just when our ships were about to open fire, the fog came down again heavily and entirely hid the enemy. Apparently the Germans saw the British ships, and altered course as they sped away through the fog. For nothing more could be seen of them. But they did not escape quite without hurt. For as the battle-cruiser the Von der Tann was fleeing fast in the thick fog she rammed the light cruiser the Frauenlob,

Accidents to the raiders

damaging herself badly in the bows, as well as half sinking the lighter vessel.

The Von der Tann was a newish ship, completed in 1909, with a displacement of 21,000 tons and an armament of eight 11 in. guns and 7 in. armour amidships. Her injuries were to prove a serious factor in the naval engagement in the North Sea, which the Germans were provoking and yet eluding. The Frauenlob, a light cruiser, built in 1902, with ten 4·1 in. guns, and a crew of 264, was most seriously damaged, increasing the weakness of the German Navy at its weakest point. All this, however, was no compensation for the befogging of our Grand Fleet at the critical moment off our East Coast. But for the extraordinary stroke of ill-luck in regard to weather conditions, the Grand Fleet would have sunk every German ship that had taken part in the raid. So terrific were the odds that Sir John Jellicoe had brought against the enemy that there would not have been a battle but a rapid and overwhelming annihilation. However, this was not to be.

Vengeance delayed by fog

"The best-laid schemes o' mice and men
Gang aft agley."

And with all his skill in battle manœuvres, Sir John Jellicoe was unable to control the winter fogs of the North Sea. It was reported that all the officers of the German raiding squadron and a number of the men were given the Iron Cross on returning to Wilhelmshaven. In a way the baby-killers deserved the cheapened decoration which had

B

THE GERMAN BOMBARDMENT OF HARTLEPOOL.
Shells falling on the battery at the end of the pier.

THE PIER AND LIGHTHOUSE, HARTLEPOOL.

VIEW OF HARTLEPOOL DOCKS.

been distributed wholesale among the land forces of Germany. For they certainly had had a narrower escape from total destruction than had most German soldiers.

But their luck was apparently unfailing. For when they were next sent forth to cross the North Sea, only one of their armoured cruisers met the full fate again prepared by the British admiral for the entire squadron. For the third time, on Saturday afternoon, January 23rd, 1915, the remaining battle-cruisers of the High Seas Fleet of the German Empire put out to sea. First the destroyer flotilla steamed out in fan formation beyond the minefields in the Bight of Heligoland. Then, as twilight was falling, a line of long, narrow shapes—six light cruisers—threaded their way between the mines to support the destroyers, While the last glimmer of daylight lasted the destroyers

and light-cruisers continued their work of months by hunting about for some sign of a British submarine. But none was visible. So as the early winter night drew on, the defences of Wilhelmshaven opened, and four vast grey fighting ships, with the sharp bows of ocean racers, came out at full speed, under the guard of the wide-flung destroyers.

The Von der Tann, the flagship of Rear-Admiral Funke—a curious name in the circumstances—had, as we have seen, been temporarily put out of action during her flight from our Second Battle-Cruiser Squadron. On the third raid Rear-Admiral Hipper, the senior officer in the German cruiser squadrons, with his flag in the Seydlitz, led the line, consisting of his flag-ship the Derfflinger, the Moltke, and **The enemy's third** the Blücher. Owing to the incom- **attempt** pletion of the new battle-cruiser the Lützow, the loss to the German Navy of the sister-ship of the Moltke, the Goeben, and the injury to the Von der Tann, the four ships which Admiral Hipper led on this raid represented all that Germany could bring out to face our battle-cruisers.

For even her latest battleships were too slow for anything like a running fight, and their armament was so inferior in range that our swifter ships would have them at our mercy. We had available seven battle-cruisers of the Dreadnought and super-Dreadnought type, with speeds varying between twenty-eight and thirty knots.

Germany, in her supreme effort at a fast running action, could only bring up three battle-cruisers, with smaller guns than ours, together with one misbegotten, would-be battle-cruiser of the Dreadnought type—the Blücher. In the year 1906, when Lord Fisher was working out his plan for a fleet of all-big-gun capital ships, the German Admiralty heard a rumour of the creation of a British ship of the new type—the battle-cruiser. With much trouble and expense the Intelligence Department of the German Admiralty obtained a forecast of the plan of our Invincible. On this plan the design of the Blücher was carefully modelled with the same draught of about 15,500 tons as the British ship would possess. She was armed with what was thought to be an overpowering armament for a cruiser—twelve

Valentine.

THE QUEEN OF NORTHERN WATERING-PLACES—TWO VIEWS OF SCARBOROUGH—YORKSHIRE'S FASHIONABLE SPA.

8·2 in. guns—and engines were made to give her a speed of a little over twenty-six knots. But all the information obtained at considerable cost by German spies was false. The Blücher was laid down in October, 1906, and was not completed until September, 1909. In the meantime our first three battleships of the Invincible class were completed in 1908. They were not cruisers in the old sense of the word, but racing battleships, with two and a-half knots more speed than the Blücher, a tonnage of 17,250 tons, and—the grand surprise—eight 12 in. guns apiece. The best existing German battleship at the time had only 11 in. guns. Our battle-cruisers, with superior speed and longer range, could outfight any of them. Such is the story of the ill-fated Blücher that now steamed out on her last voyage.

Photochrom.
SCARBOROUGH CASTLE RUINS.

Admiral Hipper made full preparations for a running fight. He laid a new minefield north of Heligoland, and arranged for the Zeppelins on that island to come out and drop bombs, with the assistance of a squadron of seaplanes, laden with smaller shells. He also concentrated a large flotilla of submarines between the minefield and the Dogger Bank, with a view to torpedoing his possible pursuers, while his own ships were threading the mine area. All this, however, was only a precautionary measure, like the entrenchments along the Aisne heights which General von Kluck made in his rear when he advanced to attack the French in the valley of the Marne. Admiral Hipper seems to have hoped to have been able to start a different operation at some distance from the northern

SHELLS FROM GERMAN WARSHIPS BURSTING OVER SCARBOROUGH SEA-FRONT.

According to the Berlin "Lokalanzeiger," defenceless, pleasure-loving Scarborough is "the most important harbour on the East Coast of England between the Humber and the Thames." The "Berliner Tageblatt" also described Scarborough as being an important port!

11

British coast, during which one or more of his fastest battle-cruisers would be able to slip out on to the trade routes, while the British squadron was being hammered in an unexpected way. The minefield, submarines, Zeppelins and flying machines were arranged to protect the weakened but successful squadron as it turned homeward after the accomplishment of the first part of the design.

But by the same curious coincidence as marked the second German sea-raid, as Admiral Hipper left Wilhelmshaven in the Seydlitz, Sir David Beatty left a certain port in Scotland in his flagship the Lion. He took with him the Tiger, commanded by Captain Henry B.

A fateful Sunday morning — Pelly; the Princess Royal, under Captain Osmond de Beauvoir Brock; the New Zealand, flying the flag of Rear-Admiral Sir Archibald Moore, and commanded by Captain Lionel Halsey; and the Indomitable, under Captain Francis W. Kennedy. This magnificent battle-cruiser squadron was accompanied by four light cruisers of the town class—the Southampton, the Nottingham, the Birmingham, and the Lowestoft. They steamed on the port beam of the big ships, on the left-hand side looking forward from the flagship. Then, far ahead of the squadron, were our destroyers with their mother ships of the fleetest and

wind swept sea and sky clear of mist, and allowed a long vision over the grey-foam-flecked waste of waters. At half-past seven the German squadron was sighted from our flagship. It was seen leftward, on the port bow, about fourteen miles away, steaming fast, and steering towards the south-east.

The tail-end ships of the enemy's line were preparing to drop contact mines in their wake, on the chance of blowing up some of the pursuing British vessels. But this simple trick was easily countered, for the first thing Sir David Beatty did, on receiving the report of the enemy's position, was to steer his ships outside the enemy's track, getting on their quarter. In other words, he so altered his course as to pursue them on a line parallel to theirs, instead of following directly behind the hostile squadron. Thus the course of the fugitives and the line of the pursuers formed two parallel lines at least six or seven miles distant from each other. No mines dropped by the enemy could drift anywhere near the attacking squadron. All this, of course, was merely the usual battle tactics of every British squadron. Nevertheless, the hopeful Germans seemed to have brought quite a heavy cargo of floating mines. If they could not damage our fighting ships with them, there was at least a chance of sinking some neutral merchant-ship or fishing-smack, and generally increasing the perils of commerce in the North Sea.

The British squadron settled down to a long, stern chase, all the battle-cruisers working up their speed until they reached a pace of thirty-two ordinary miles an hour. This was an easy speed for the new ships, the Lion, Tiger, and Princess Royal. They were, indeed, able to add another couple of miles an hour to it. But for the Indomitable, a battle-cruiser of the oldest type, it was a great excess over her normal rate of movement. She would have tailed away out of the line, but for the tremendous exertions of her black squad. Her engineers and stokers sent her along in a way that excited the admiration of the entire squadron, and Sir David Beatty expressed the general feeling when he signalled: " Well

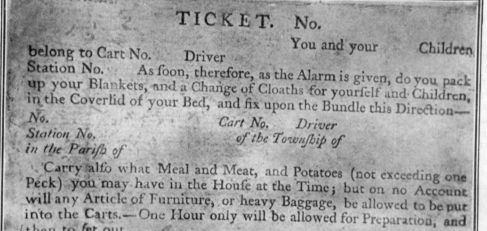

TICKET. No.

You and your Children

belong to Cart No. Driver
Station No. As soon, therefore, as the Alarm is given, do you pack up your Blankets, and a Change of Cloaths for yourself and Children, in the Coverlid of your Bed, and fix upon the Bundle this Direction—

No.
Station No.
in the Parish of

Cart No. Driver
of the Township of

Carry also what Meal and Meat, and Potatoes (not exceeding one Peck) you may have in the House at the Time; but on no Account will any Article of Furniture, or heavy Baggage, be allowed to be put into the Carts.—One Hour only will be allowed for Preparation, and then to set out.

AN INTERESTING SOUVENIR OF THE NAPOLEONIC SCARE.
Facsimile of a ticket issued to the inhabitants of North Shields in the days of Napoleon.

newest cruiser class—the Arethusa, the Aurora, and the Undaunted.

The Aurora, under Captain Wilmot Nicholson, led, and about seven o'clock on Sunday morning, January 24th, her look-out sighted the leading German light cruisers near the Dogger Bank. At twenty minutes past seven the Aurora opened fire with her two 6 in. guns, and wirelessed her flagship that she was engaging the enemy. Sir David Beatty at once altered course towards the direction of the gun flashes, which were south-south-east, ordered all his battleships to increase speed, and commanded the light cruisers and destroyers to get in touch with the enemy.

But there was no need for this last command. For as soon as the Germans had been seen, all our scouting force had flung forward on to the enemy. Admiral Hipper had been steering north-west. Without waiting to see clearly what he had to meet, he at once turned his ships about, and went full speed on a south-east course. Meanwhile the British light cruisers kept closely in touch with the hostile ships and wirelessed all their movements to Sir David Beatty. Our battle-cruiser squadron was working up to full speed, and was steering south-eastward to close with the enemy. The weather this time was extremely favourable from the British point of view. A north-east

done, Indomitable stokers ! " Even the New Zealand, completed in 1912, four years after the Indomitable, had some difficulty in keeping up with the three leading ships. For while the Tiger could do over thirty knots, the Princess Royal thirty knots, and the Lion nearly thirty knots, the older New Zealand could only do a fraction over twenty-nine knots at her best. But her black squad also drove her along at a pace that kept her fairly in line.

It was a battle between British engineers and stokers and German engineers and stokers in the first place. The Germans had fourteen miles start, which our engine-room men had to wipe out long before the danger spot was reached. The speed **Our " black squad's "** of the newly completed Derfflinger was **grand work** not known, but it was certainly less than that of our latest battle-cruisers. The speed of the Seydlitz, a 1913 ship, was about equal to that of our Princess Royal, a 1912 ship. The Moltke, completed in 1911, was just a little faster than the New Zealand, completed a few months later. And the Blücher, with an actual sea speed of about twenty-five knots, was quite out of the running. It was a blunder to have brought her out on a fast-raiding action. For the speed of a squadron that holds together is naturally that of its slowest ship.

It only took our sailors eighty-two minutes to close

Damage wrought by a German shell to the rear of a house in Hunter Street.

At the gasworks shells penetrated two gasometers, and the engine-house was hit. The escaping gas caught fire, and eight workmen were injured.

The first of these photographs gives another view of the Baptist chapel, shown on page 9. In the house in William Street (on the right) four children were killed and two injured. The third photograph is of fragments of shell fired from the German warships.

Two houses in Cleveland Road which were completely demolished. The bombardment of the Hartlepools levied a total of nearly a hundred lives.

Private dwelling-houses, the upper parts of which were shattered by German shells.

CAMERA RECORDS OF THE SEA HUNS' VISIT TO THE HARTLEPOOLS.

Interior of All Saints' Church, Scarborough, showing the wreckage which was caused by a shell that came through the roof.

The historic Church of St. Hilda, showing damage to the roof.

What a boarding-house on St. Nichol companion cru

Gap in the wall of the Town Hall, made by a shell which passed through the Council Chamber.

A corner of the Royal Hotel, showing damage caused by a German shell during the bombardment.

The Harbour Lighthouse at Scarboroug the German gunners availed

Scarborough's "fortifications." Gaps in the walls of the ancient castle caused by the German shell fire. Dating from the reign of King Stephen, the castle was dismantled by Cromwell.

looked like after the Moltke and her
steamed away.

A house in Commercial Street which
was wrecked by a German shell.

The walls of the ancient castle, ten feet thick, were shattered in places, and the
keep was also damaged by the bombardment.

Where a family perished. House in Wykeham Street, where
Mrs. Barnett and two children were killed.

Photograph showing the work of the Sea Huns on a house
in Lonsdale Road.

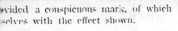

vided a conspicuous mark, of which
selves with the effect shown.

The Grand Hotel, one of the most prominent buildings from the sea, was struck by three shells. Our photograph
shows the destruction caused in the restaurant and buffet.

The ancient ruins of St. Hilda's Abbey, standing near the cliff's edge, afforded congenial "sport" for the German gunners.

The damage caused by German shell-fire to these two houses suggests that the cellars were not invariably the safest of hiding-places.

The ancient Abbey of St. Hilda, the torn shell of which is famous wherever the English language is known, stands on the site once occupied by the monastery of Streonshalh. This, according to Bede, was established in 657, when Hilda became abbess, building her abbey on ground granted by King Oswy. It was during the reign of Hilda that Whitby became the cradle of English poetry. Of the two smaller views inset, the upper one shows the damage done to the old abbey, and the lower one the wreckage of Whitby coastguard station,

DEVASTATION WROUGHT IN ANCIENT WHITBY, THE CRADLE OF ENGLISH POETRY.

within twenty thousand yards of the rear German ship. At this distance the Lion fired a single ranging shot, but it fell short. The enemy at this time were steaming in single line ahead, with their six light cruisers tearing away in front of them, and a large number of their destroyers on their starboard beam—that is, on the right-hand side.

First shell on doomed Blucher At nine minutes past nine, when the ships were about ten miles apart, the Lion got her first shell home on the Blücher. A terrific mass of high explosive and hardened steel, weighing more than half a ton, screamed through the air at a speed of more than a mile in two seconds, and crashed on the armour of the doomed Blücher. A blue light showed where steel struck on steel, and then came the smoky explosion of the lyddite tearing open the six-inch thickness of Krupp armour-plate. Eleven minutes afterwards shells from the Tiger also began to fall on the Blücher. Seeing this, the chief gunnery lieutenant of the Lion took another target, and, with the help of his fire-control officers, dropped the shells from his four bow guns on to the third ship in the German line, the Derfflinger, and struck her with salvo after salvo, from a distance of eighteen thousand yards.

The British gunnery was of unparalleled excellence. Much credit was, of course, due to the designer of our superb 13·5 in. naval gun, and to the directors of the ordnance factories who constructed it in its exquisite trueness and incomparable strength. But, after all, the best weapon of war can be impaired or enhanced by the men who handle it in the battle. And the way our men fought their guns was a revelation in warlike efficiency. Everybody worked with high and yet cool energy, many of them thinking at times of the massacred women and children of Scarborough. To Gunnery-Lieutenant-Commander Gerald F. Longhurst, of the Lion, Gunnery-Lieutenant-Commander Evan Bruce-Gardyne, of the Tiger, and to Gunnery-Commander Roland C. S. Hunt, of the Princess Royal, fell the most important work of the action; for their twelve forward guns mainly decided the action.

The position at thirty-five minutes past nine was that the Blücher had dropped astern, and had come within the range of the four forward 12 in. guns of the New Zealand, where Lieutenant-Commander Cecil B. Prickett was gunnery officer. The unfortunate Blücher had been terribly bombarded in turn by the Princess Royal the Tiger and the Lion. They had crippled her, set her on fire, and even knocked one of her gun turrets out of its holdings, and hurled it with its guns and its crew into the sea.

Now the three leading British battle-cruisers passed over the doomed rear ship of the enemy's line, and steaming ahead on their parallel course, attacked the more powerful and swifter German vessels. Our flagship had gained so much on the enemy that she could now straddle the German flagship, the Seydlitz, leading the enemy's line. To straddle an enemy vessel means to pitch a number of shells at her simultaneously, some of them perhaps falling short or going over, but some of them hitting. She is not straddled unless the middle shells, at least, get home on her armour, turrets, funnels, and conning-tower or fighting top. The Tiger also massed her guns on the Seydlitz, while the Princess Royal continued to batter the Derfflinger, the third ship in the German line.

Only the second German ship, the Moltke, escaped much damage. The reason for this was that she was, during the earlier part of the fight, hidden in smoke. Smoke was the great trouble that our gunners had to contend against. When the action opened, our flotilla cruisers, the Arethusa, Aurora, and Undaunted, with their destroyers, were steaming ahead of our line. They

PROBABLE ROUTES TAKEN BY GERMAN SUBMARINE RAIDERS.
This sketch indicates the probable course of German submarines in their attacks on British vessels in the opening weeks of 1915.

immediately dropped back so as not to foul our range with their smoke. At a distance of about ten miles, when the Lion first got home on the Blücher, the target was extremely small. The principal German ships were from six hundred to six hundred and fifty feet long, and about ninety-five feet wide amidships. On the skyline they make a mark that could be covered by a large pin's point. **Perpetually changing targets** Hold a lead pencil by the point, one and a half feet from the eye, and the small black centre of it will more than cover the target presented by the whole German battle-cruiser squadron. Naturally, therefore, any drift of smoke between this remote target and the fire-control stations on our leading battle-cruisers seriously interfered with the aim of our gunnery officers.

They were moving at something over thirty miles an hour, and the enemy's ships were driving along at nearly that pace. Thus the calculations for throwing a shell at a pin's-point target ten to eight miles away were continually changing. The battle was really fought by mathematicians, armed with various kinds of range-timing and range-finding instruments. In most cases the man who actually aimed and fired the great guns never saw the guns he fired or the mark at which he aimed. Other men supplied him with visual information, and all he had to do was to make his rapid calculations, then give his guns the right elevation and traverse, and fire them by an electrical signal when his chronometer marked the fraction of a second to which he had calculated.

Getting a gun on the mark is now a fairly easy matter with modern telescopic sights and range-finders. The trouble is to calculate the elevation at which the shot

shall be pitched into the air, so that, at the end of its curve, it shall plump down right on the mark. A gun may be truly brought into line with the target, but if the elevation is not correct the shell will pitch harmlessly into the sea, either in front or behind the enemy's ship. At a distance of ten miles, a 13·5 in. shell would be about twenty seconds making its aerial voyage. During this time, a twenty-nine or thirty knot target would have shifted an appreciable distance. So the shell has to be pitched at the spot a vessel will reach in about a third of a minute. To make quite sure of hitting it, all the attacking guns are fired at once by the chief officer of the fire-control, with the result that if his calculations are correct he straddles his target, and gets at least one terrible wrecking shell full on the mark.

Both the British and the German squadron began the action under the best conditions for good gunnery effects, for each of the principal opposing ships presented only her bow or stern at the target as a mark. This

Conditions for good gunnery meant that each ship could be more easily hit by the opposing guns than if it had shown one of its long sides to the enemy. This is a curious paradox, well known to all fighting seamen, but scarcely understood by the general public. When a ship shows only its bow or stern, leaving merely the beam of ninety to ninety-five feet clear on the skyline, it is easy to shell it. If a ship fights broadside-on, showing its long grey side, six hundred to six hundred and fifty feet in

length, it is extremely difficult to hit. The explanation lies in the old problem of raising the gun to its right elevation. When a fleeing ship is fighting bows-on or stern-on the entire length of its deck comes under fire. A shell pitched at its bow, but falling short, will strike amidships or aft. In the same way, a shell pitched at its stern, and falling over the mark, will strike amidships or forward. In short, when a ship fights broadside-on, there is only the narrow breadth of her deck as a **The odds against Hipper** target. When she fights a running action, showing her bow or stern, the entire length of her deck forms a receptacle for the enemy's shells.

For this reason a fighting admiral will not usually run away when he meets the foe, but will turn and engage in a sound, regular broadside action. In so doing he exposes his ships less to the enemy's fire than if he ran away. He puts spirit and courage into his men, and if he wins the victory it is an absolutely decisive one. To steam away, trying to escape at full speed, and expose the entire length of the ships' decks to the salvos of a confident enemy, exhilarated by the feeling of mastery, is to ride for a fall.

THE WAR AT SEA THROUGH GERMAN EYES.

The upper picture is an essay in imagination on the part of Professor Paul Teschinsky, of Hamburg, and purports to represent German torpedo-boats attacking British coast defence ships. The other picture is from a painting by Professor W. Malchin, and was painted to show the German people how their " gallant " Navy bombarded Scarborough.

Rear-Admiral Hipper had four ships against five, and thirty-six big guns against forty. His guns were all of smaller calibre than the British. The odds in gun-power were, we may admit, fully two to one against him. But this is only a paper calculation. It was up to him, by skilful manœuvring, to get certain massed fire effects, which would give him the advantage. Nelson was always ready to fight against heavy odds, and yet, by his genius in handling his ships, to bring superior forces to bear on the enemy at the critical point. Only a few weeks before, Admiral Cradock, with only two large old guns, had gallantly faced an enemy with eight times his gun-power. He attempted the impossible, perhaps, but Admiral Hipper was offered a fighting chance that any British squadron would have gladly taken. His precipitate flight looked like being both a bad move from the German

The German Press, the German people, and the German Navy appear to have been immensely satisfied with their wild work on our East Coast. This illustration is taken from a picture based by Professor F. Lindner on a sketch by a German naval officer who took part in the bombardment of Scarborough. British feeling was faithfully expressed by Mr. Winston Churchill, who wrote: " Whatever feats of arms the German Navy may hereafter perform, the stigma of the baby-killers of Scarborough will brand its officers and men while sailors sail the seas."

The above picture, by Professor Höger, of " The Panic at Scarborough," was painted to commemorate the bombardment of our East Coast towns. The deaths numbered over one hundred, and over five hundred were wounded, many severely. A large number of the victims were women and children, and all but a few dozen were unarmed civilians. The effect of this example of German "frightfulness" was to give a remarkable impetus to recruiting in London and many other parts of the country, and this impetus would have been more marked had the time not been so near Christmas. Lord Kitchener expressed his pleasure at the calmness and absence of panic among troops and civilians.

GERMAN ARTISTS' VIEWS OF THE EFFECTS OF " FRIGHTFULNESS " AT SCARBOROUGH.

THE LION LEADS THE LINE: SIR DAVID BEATTY'S BOLD AND DARING PLAN OF ACTION.

When on January 24th, 1915, the German raiding squadron under Admiral Hipper was caught unawares and turned in frantic haste for home, Sir David Beatty took a bold and daring line of action. Leaving the New Zealand and the Indomitable to get along and support him as fast as they could, he put the Lion along at her top speed, and, followed by the Tiger and the Princess Royal, faced all the guns the Germans could bring to bear upon him. The Lion got her first shell home on the Blücher when the ships were about ten miles apart. Our picture is from a drawing by Charles Dixon, R.I.

point of view and an additional dishonour to the squadron of baby-killers. It seemed to mark more clearly than anything which had occurred on land or sea up to that time how low the fighting spirit of Prussia had declined since the days of Frederick the Great. But, as we shall afterwards see, there is just a possible explanation of his apparent want of fighting energy. He may have been trying to lure Sir David Beatty into a trap.

The only other manœuvre of importance that Admiral Hipper attempted was to sacrifice his destroyers in the hope of saving his battle-cruisers. This movement began at a quarter to ten, when our two leading ships were pounding the flaming Seydlitz, while the Princess Royal was hammering the flaming Derfflinger, and the New Zealand was crippling the Blücher. Our flotilla cruisers and destroyers had previously withdrawn from the front to the left of our line, to prevent their smoke from obscuring the chief targets, and the enemy's destroyer flotillas now swept away from their battle-cruisers and charged across at our leading ships. In answer to this movement the lieutenant-commander in charge of the destroyer Meteor, steamed out to meet the enemy's mosquito attack, backed by the M Division of our destroyers, handled with splendid ability by Captain the Hon. H. Meade.

All through the critical period of the remaining part of the action the position of the little Meteor was terrifying. She was clean in the line of fire, shells whistling over and all around her, with now and again an enemy's broadside aimed directly at her. Try to imagine a frail little vessel, steaming thirty-five knots, with four battle-cruisers on either side belching forth flame and smoke continually, and the screech of the projectiles flying overhead seeming to tear the air into ribbons. Twelve and 11 in. shells, dropping perilously near, sent columns of water a hundred feet above the sea, just a few yards away from her deck, and the descending spray drenched every man. All around was the awful crashing noise of the great guns, the yellow explosions, the blue flashes, as the shells struck the armour-plate, with massive tongues of fire shooting up, and dense clouds of black or yellow smoke, which obliterated the whole ship from view when the shells burst upon her.

The terrible grandeur of the scene made the men on the destroyer forget their personal danger. For sublimely spectacular interest, their position was worth the peril they ran. They were hit twice without suffering any material damage, though most of the crew continually missed death by inches. It seemed as though they possessed a charmed life, until they tried to torpedo the Blücher. She had at last fallen out of the line, a raging furnace amidships, helpless, and the German admiral left her to her fate. She had been battered by the 13·5 in. guns of our three leading ships. Then the New Zealand turned her 12 in. guns upon her; and lastly the heroic stokers of the Indomitable brought up their vessel in time to do the final killing.

This was about noon. To hasten the job, the little Meteor circled round the doomed ship that was settling down, though still on an even keel. But

The Blucher's last shot even then she was not dead. For, firing her last round, she sent an 8·2 in. shell into the Meteor, which killed four men wounded another. What next happened is not clear. On the one hand the Meteor, two minutes after the shell struck her, discharged her torpedo. On the other hand, the Arethusa had also approached the stricken enemy ship, with the same idea of finishing her off, and of releasing the Indomitable for more important work. The Arethusa likewise discharged a torpedo. As at this time

the poor old Blücher was almost stationary, it is possible that both torpedoes got home, for the crew of the Arethusa admit that the doomed ship had a terrible list before they fired their first torpedo. The Arethusa used her second torpedo quite close, steaming up within two hundred yards of her prey before she delivered her blow.

The German crew was game to the last. They lined up to the taffrail, standing rigidly to attention, and in this attitude they would have met their death if a British sailor had not warned them. But one of the officers of the Arethusa took up a megaphone and shouted to them to jump if they wanted to save their lives. **Airmen bomb drowning seamen**
They understood him, and after gallantly waving their caps and cheering as their ship went down, they all took headers into the water.

In the meantime the last torpedo got home. The explosion was appalling, and the Blücher slowly turned over on her port side, showing her starboard side. Then for some minutes she floated bottom upwards, and at

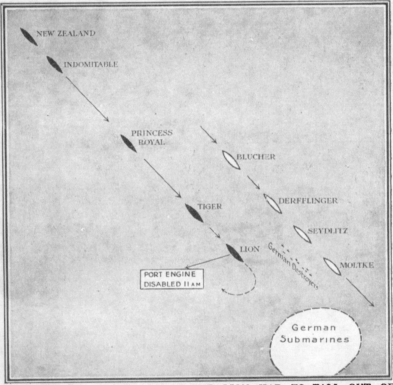

SKETCH PLAN SHOWING WHEN THE LION HAD TO FALL OUT OF LINE.

In the above plan are indicated the approximate positions of the British and German battleships in the Dogger Bank Battle, when one of the enemy vessels got a shot in on her bow, which damaged the feed tank, stopped the port engine, and made it necessary for her to turn.

last sank slowly, leaving the survivors of her crew struggling in the water. Most of the Germans wore india-rubber airbags, fitting in front of their chests, and these floats kept over a hundred and twenty-five of them up in time to be rescued. More would have been saved; but while our boats were picking up the survivors, a Zeppelin airship and a German seaplane soared above the scene of rescue and began dropping bombs upon the men who were being given their lives. One bomb fell among the drowning men, and blew four of them to pieces as they were clinging to one of the hundreds of planks which the British sailors had thrown overboard to help them till the boats came along. It is unlikely that even German airmen would deliberately kill their own defeated men as they were struggling in the water. In the distance they must have mistaken the Blücher, which had been battered out of all recognition, for a sinking British ship, thus giving rise to the extraordinary report

Courtesy of " The Daily Mail."

THE BURNING BLÜCHER, ABANDONED TO HER FATE, SANK LIKE A TIN CAN FILLED WITH WATER.

The above unique photograph, taken from a British cruiser, shows the Blücher at the moment when the great ship was about to take the final plunge. The bow of the leviathan is on the right of the picture. A remnant of the ill-fated crew clustered astern, and many slid down the ship's side in the hope of being picked up from the sea. The shattered tripod mast is observable on the right. Four 8·2 in. and two 6 in. guns are to be seen pointing passively skywards. The fore-shortened mainmast appears abaft two of the 8·2 in. guns, but both funnels had disappeared under the deadly British fire.

THE CRIPPLED BLÜCHER, A RAGING FURNACE AMIDSHIPS, WAS GAME TO THE LAST.

Reproduced by permission of "The Illustrated London News."

Fought to a standstill as the Blücher was, her crew were game to the last. They lined up at attention, and in this attitude would have met their death, had not an officer of the Arethusa shouted to them to jump to save their lives. Over one hundred and twenty-five of them were rescued.

afterwards made by the German Admiralty, that a British battle-cruiser had been seen to sink. In any case it was not chivalrous of the German airmen to bombard drowning seamen, and the fact that these seamen were their own countrymen, with whose rescue they interfered, was in a way a providential punishment for their national manner of warfare. The conduct of the Zeppelin, in regard to warlike operations, was visible. For when two shots had been fired at her, she made off with frantic haste, amidst the derisive cheers of our fighting seamen.

Screen of enemy destroyers While the affair of the Blücher was proceeding, the enemy's destroyer flotillas got between the opposing battle-cruiser lines, and emitted vast columns of smoke to screen their beaten and flying remaining big ships. Then, under cover of the thick drifting curtain of smoke, the three German battle-cruisers turned northward in order to increase their distance from our Lion and Tiger. But the manœuvre was at once discerned by Sir David Beatty, and he ordered his squadron also to alter course, form a line bearing north-north-west, and drive on at utmost speed.

Thereupon the commander of the German destroyer flotillas attempted a very brave but impossible thing. He sent his frail small boats full steam ahead at the two leading British battle-cruisers, with the intention of closing for a torpedo attack. On a dark cloudy night with a little mist, these mosquito tactics might produce an important result. It was for such work in the darkness that destroyers were partly designed. But to attempt it on a clear bright winter morning, in an air of extreme visibility, was not gallantry, but utter desperation. For the battle-cruisers had each a broadside of eight 4 in. guns, directed by a special subsidiary system of fire-control, for beating off destroyers. The small guns on the German destroyers were useless, and for **A brave but desperate effort** two reasons. In the first place they had to be laid in the old-fashioned way simply by a gunlayer, as there is no room on a destroyer for a proper system of fire-control. In the second place, the destroyer guns could not send a shell of sufficient size and penetrative power to get through the armour-plate of our new big ships. So when the Lion and the Tiger both opened fire on the enemy's mosquito craft, the effect was so overwhelming that all the German destroyers withdrew from the tempest they had drawn down upon themselves, and resumed their original course alongside their own battle-cruiser line.

Reproduced by permission of "The Illustrated London News."

THE BLÜCHER GOES TO HER DOOM: ANOTHER VIEW OF THE SINKING LEVIATHAN.

At the moment when the above striking photograph was taken the fore-turret of the great German cruiser had gone by the board, the funnels had been battered out of place, and the hull was holed from stem to stern. On the left of the photograph a British torpedo-boat destroyer is seen waiting to pick up survivors. In firing her last round the Blücher sent an 8.2 in. shell into the Meteor, killing four men and wounding another.

BOATS FROM THE ARETHUSA RESCUING MEN FROM THE SINKING BLÜCHER.

Most of the German sailors wore india-rubber airbags, fitting in front of their chests, and these kept up over one hundred and twenty-five of them from drowning before help arrived. More would have been saved, but while our boats were picking up the survivors a Zeppelin airship and a German seaplane soared above the scene of rescue and began dropping bombs among the men who were struggling in the water, one bomb blowing four of them to pieces. The airmen apparently were under the impression that the battered and now unrecognisable Blücher was a sinking British vessel.

H.M.S. LION, VICE-ADMIRAL BEATTY'S FLAGSHIP, GOING INTO ACTION.

But soon after they withdrew, about six minutes to eleven, when the Blücher was a fiery, shapeless wreck, a new source of danger to our squadron was observed. Enemy submarines were reported to be steering under water towards our cruisers from the starboard bow—that is, coming forward on the right of our line. Sir David Beatty personally observed the wash of a periscope two points on the starboard bow of his flagship. He immediately had his ship swerved round to the other side to escape the invisible torpedo. The peril of this underwater attack, however, was not great in the circumstances. For our leading ships were then being driven along at a pace of thirty-two miles an hour. No sub-

Peril of under-water attack marine was quick enough in action to get a torpedo on a target going at this speed. Sir David had already met and evaded a hostile torpedo attack in misty weather in the Bight of Heligoland. In the present Battle of the Dogger Bank the air was clear and the water calm enough for even the wash of hostile periscopes to be discerned.

Everything was going excellently from the British point of view. From 9.20 o'clock to 11 o'clock the Lion had been hurling her terrible shells at the three German battle-cruisers From 9.45 o'clock the Tiger and the Princess Royal had also been hammering the Seydlitz, Moltke, and Derfflinger; and the New Zealand had also brought her 12 in. guns to bear on the rear enemy ships. For the last seventy-five minutes the Seydlitz and the

Derfflinger had been continually on fire, and the Moltke, which had first been obscured by the drifting smoke of her flagship, had also become a clear target. There were more than a thousand men dead and wounded in the three ships, and some of their guns were out of action. An hour more and the three of them would have been at the bottom of the sea.

But the luck which had enabled the raiders to escape from Sir John Jellicoe in person again favoured them, but not to the same extent.

The enemy's concentrated fire was especially directed upon our flagship, which therefore suffered the most in Sir David Beatty's squadron. Owing, however, to her armour and to the great range at which she fought, the Lion suffered no material damage, though a **Action suddenly broken off** few of her men were wounded. One of the crew afterwards remarked that the noise of the falling German shells was like the rattle of peas on a corrugated-iron roof. The distance was too great for the German gun fire to take effect.

But at three minutes past eleven, as the Lion was going at her topmost speed, firing as she went, her bow lifted high out of the water as it tore through the seas, one of the enemy's ships, by a stroke of luck, got a shot in on her bow, which damaged the feed tank, and thus stopped the port engine.

Materially it was only a slight injury that could soon be repaired in a shipbuilding yard. But the immediate

AFTER THE BATTLE: THE INDOMITABLE TOWING THE LION BACK TO PORT.

THE DOGGER BANK BATTLE: SIR DAVID BEATTY ON THE BRIDGE OF THE TORPEDO-BOAT DESTROYER ATTACK.

During the Dogger Bank Battle on January 24th, 1915, it was reported to Admiral Sir David Beatty at about 11.3 a.m. that the injury to his flagship the Lion was incapable of immediate repair. He then directed the Lion to shape course N.W. At 11.20 he called the destroyer Attack alongside, shifting his flag to her at about 11.35 a.m. He then proceeded at utmost speed to rejoin the battle-cruiser squadron, and met them at noon retiring N.N.W. He then boarded and hoisted his flag in the Princess Royal at about 12.20 p.m., amidst the enthusiastic cheering of the crew. Admiral Beatty paid a notable tribute to the good seamanship of Lieut.-Commander Cyril Callaghan, of the Attack. The above remarkable photograph shows the gallant admiral on the bridge of the Attack approaching the battle-cruiser Princess Royal.

effect was that it reduced the speed of the flagship and compelled her to fall out of the line under a guard of destroyers. Though Sir David Beatty at once transferred his flag to one of these fast little boats, the Attack, it was some time before he could rejoin and lead his squadron. In fact, he did not shift his flag to the Princess Royal until about twenty minutes past twelve. Meanwhile, the other British cruisers pursued their flaming foes for some minutes as they fled eastward.

Then the action was suddenly broken off and the British squadron withdrew under the orders of Rear-Admiral Sir Archibald Moore. Of the three enemy battle-cruisers, one was seriously damaged, and the other two, according to German reports, were able to make good their injuries. Some damage was also done to the German destroyers, and one of their light cruisers of the town class,

the Kolberg, was engaged by our light cruiser the Aurora, and much battered. It was at first thought that she had been sunk, but the Berlin authorities denied this. Our loss in lives was very slight. Six men were severely wounded in the Lion, but none killed. In the Tiger, Engineer-Captain Taylor and nine men were killed, and four men lost their lives on the destroyer Meteor.

At two o'clock in the afternoon the Germans had one slight final chance of partly redressing the balance against them. For the starboard engine of the Lion then began to give trouble. Owing to priming, it gradually stopped, and at thirty-eight minutes past three the Indomitable was ordered to take the Lion in tow. Under difficult circumstances this task was accomplished in a seamanlike manner, and the former flagship was brought safely to port.

Rival accounts of the battle — This description of the semi-decisive battle-cruiser action in the North Sea, which partly crippled the fast wing of the German High Seas Fleet, is necessarily incomplete, for no official information has been published concerning the reason why Sir Archibald Moore, in the temporary absence of Sir David Beatty, broke off the action while we still had the odds in ships and guns on our side.

The unofficial report, issued by the Press Bureau soon after the battle, stated that the action had been broken off because of the vicinity of German submarines and minefields. On the other hand, the later British official despatches did not give this explanation, and the German

naval authorities asserted that the fight ended some seventy miles from their minefields and Heligoland. The German Admiralty, however, went on to allege that the action was broken off because the British squadron had lost a battle-cruiser and two destroyers.

Entirely false was the enemy's statement that we lost any ships. But it is impossible to deny that when Sir David Beatty, owing to the injury to his flagship, had to leave, at the critical moment, the handling of the squadron to Sir Archibald Moore, the battle ended **Admiral Moore and the critics** a few minutes afterwards, though the Germans were badly beaten and in dire distress many miles from their minefields. No clear explanation has yet appeared of the reason why the battered enemy ships were allowed to escape from our still much superior force.

Nelson used to say that if he had sunk ten ships and allowed the eleventh to escape, he should not think he had done well. If this remark is in any way applicable to the leadership of our First Battle Cruiser Squadron at the critical moment, Sir David Beatty at least cannot come under any censure. For while he was in the destroyer the Attack, the handling of the squadron had to be left to Sir Archibald Moore in the New Zealand.

There was, however, a rumour that the battle-cruiser action off

GERMAN SUBMARINES IN DOCK AT WILHELMSHAVEN.
The submarines seen in the above photograph are of the 1910-12 class, and we get a clear view of the position of the twin torpedo-tubes at the stern. In the earlier types the torpedoes were discharged only from tubes in the bow. Inset: The British submarine D5, sunk by a mine laid by one of the German cruisers returning after the raid on Yarmouth.

the Dogger Bank was only part of a possible larger operation, in which Admiral von Ingenohl with his battleships intended to engage. It was reported that the German main fleet came out eastward, and tried to close round our First Battle Cruiser Squadron, while Admiral Hipper was luring our ships towards Heligoland.

This movement by Ingenohl, it was said, was countered by the unexpected appearance of the advance guard of destroyers of our Battle Fleet, whereupon Ingenohl turned at full speed for his base. It was then alleged that in the brief interval between the promise and non-fulfilment of the hope of a general fleet action, our First Battle Cruiser Squadron, under the temporary command of Sir Archibald Moore, hesitated just for ten minutes between the larger and smaller force of enemy ships, and thus allowed the

DIAGRAM ILLUSTRATING THE WORK OF OUR 12 IN. GUNS AT FIFTEEN MILES RANGE.
Owing to the distance at which the battle-cruisers fought on January 24th, 1915, the shells from the British 12 in. guns had to take a curved path, reaching a very high point before beginning to fall towards their objectives. Admiral Sir Percy Scott has estimated that in firing at a range of fifteen miles the shot would attain an altitude of 22,500 feet, or some 6,000 feet over the summit of Mont Blanc.

Seydlitz, Moltke, and Derfflinger to escape. All this, however, was mere rumour, and a long time may pass before the full facts are made public.

It is worthy of note, however, that soon after the action Admiral von Ingenohl was superseded from the command of the German High Seas Fleet. This looked as though Rear-Admiral Hipper had played well the part assigned to him, but had failed to receive proper support from his chief. Somewhere about the same time Sir John Rushworth Jellicoe was promoted. These two changes of command and rank in regard to the contending leaders of the opposing fleets were fairly indicative of the results of the British and German naval operations at the end of the first six months of the war. The German commander had failed; the British commander had succeeded. So extreme then

REAR-ADMIRAL HIPPER.
Commanding German battle cruiser squadron.

REAR-ADMIRAL FUNKE.
Second in command to Rear-Admiral Hipper.

was the desperation of the German Admiralty that it designed the extraordinary plan of trying to torpedo, in submarine attack, all the neutral ships trading to our shores. The barbaric, lawless, murderous nature of this last piratical venture of the enemy was a fair measure of the results of the Dogger Bank action. The battle had definitely established our superiority in gunnery, and for this reason it was decisive.

"This combat between the finest ships of both navies," said Mr. Winston Churchill on February 15, "is of immense significance and value, in the light it throws upon rival systems of design and armament. Although the German shell is a most formidable instrument of destruction, the bursting, smashing power of the heavier British projectile is decidedly greater, and—this is the great thing—our shooting is *at least* as good as theirs!"

OFFICERS OF H.M.S. LION. VICE-ADMIRAL SIR DAVID BEATTY (MARKED WITH AN x) IN CENTRE OF THE GROUP.

CHAPTER XLVIII.

THE FIRST PHASE OF TURKEY'S SHARE IN THE WAR.

By A. H. Trapmann, Special War Correspondent in the Balkan Wars.

The Too Gentle Treatment of the Sublime Porte—Mission of the Goeben and Breslau—Festive Reception of German Sailors in Turkish Waters—Dilemma of the Young Turks—Germany's "Happy Expedient"—Goeben's Commander Threatens to Bombard Constantinople—Enver Pasha and his Co-Plotters—The Balkan Wars and Turkish Intrigues with Bulgaria—British Naval Missions in Greece and Turkey—Enver Engineers the Proclamation of a Jehad—Loyalty of Indian and Egyptian Mohammedans to the British Raj—Faulty Turkish Mobilisation—German's Short-Sighted Policy and Turkish Armaments—The Modernised Turkish Army—The Ottoman Fleet—Isolation of the Turkish Empire—Armenian and Arabian Factors—The Egyptian Campaign—Turkish Disaster in the Caucasus—Invasion of Persia—The Allies Knocking at the Gates of the Dardanelles.

O N November 5th, 1914, Great Britain declared war upon Turkey, and thus Asia Minor and North-East Africa became potential areas for the waging of the Great War, which hitherto had been confined to Europe and the immediate vicinity of German colonies. The declaration of war came as a surprise to no one; indeed, the only surprise was that the Porte had been allowed to defy for so long the first international principles of neutrality. The patience displayed by the Entente Powers under the most exasperating circumstances did more credit to their desire for peace than to their knowledge of the workings of the Oriental mind. Incident after incident of an unfriendly, and even of a directly hostile nature, was allowed to pass with little more than a gentle diplomatic protest. Such action was construed by the Sublime Porte as an admission of weakness.

The incidents referred to were of a sufficiently unusual nature to occasion as much surprise as annoyance. The declaration of war between the Entente and Germanic Powers found two German warships in the Mediterranean—the Goeben and the Breslau.

The Goeben was one of the latest Dreadnought cruisers. Completed in October, 1912, she had a displacement of 23,000 tons and a main armament of ten 11 in. guns. On her steam trials she attained a speed of 27 knots per hour, but she had

since attained a speed of 28·4 knots on several occasions. The Breslau was a light cruiser completed in April, 1912, with a displacement of 4,550 tons, carrying twelve 4·1 in. guns, and was capable of steaming 27·5 knots.

These two swift cruisers had been allotted the task of cruising the Indian Ocean and holding up the British main steam routes to the East beyond the Suez Canal in the event of Britain joining the Entente Powers in the war. Owing to the miscalculation of German statesmanship these vessels were still in the Western Mediterranean on their way to the Suez Canal when Britain declared war on Germany.

In the Straits of Messina they were nearly run to earth in August by a British squadron commanded by Admiral Sir A. Berkeley Milne and Rear-Admiral Troubridge. The Goeben and Breslau, thanks to their superior speed, managed to effect their escape after making a somewhat dramatic exit from the straits, which they left with decks cleared for action, crews piped to stations, and the ships' bands playing "Die Wacht am Rhein" and "Deutschland über Alles."

It was common knowledge that the Goeben, at least, was manned entirely by a crew of skilled ratings and petty-officers. Her stokehold was worked exclusively by chief stokers, and her boats' crews consisted entirely of petty-officers. It had been the intention of the Goeben to put the majority of her crew ashore at Smyrna and there pick

MEHMED V., SULTAN OF TURKEY.
Born on November 3rd, 1844, he was proclaimed Sultan on April 27th, 1909, after the deposition of his brother Abdul Hamid II.

THE BRITISH CRUISER GLOUCESTER IN ACTION.
Photograph of the second-class protected cruiser Gloucester firing a broadside while going at full speed. The gun crew is almost obscured by the spouts of water from a burst hose-pipe. Hose-pipes were laid along the decks, keeping them constantly wet, as a safeguard against fire. The Gloucester was in pursuit of the Goeben when that vessel sought safety in the Dardanelles.

up a substitute crew of less skilled German sailors who had been sent out in two merchant vessels beforehand for the purpose. The skilled ratings were then to have proceeded to the Golden Horn and staffed the whole Turkish Fleet.

The German battle-cruiser, however, was obliged to alter her programme. Chased by the British fleet she raced at her highest steaming power for the Dardanelles, and, with her little consort, gained the protection of the Turkish forts just in time to give her wash to the British pursuing squadron on August 10th. In exchanging shots with H.M.S. Gloucester the Goeben had been seriously damaged, and had sustained several casualties.

The Turkish military authorities stage-managed a most cordial reception for the two fugitive war vessels. The captain of the Goeben was received in special audience by the Sultan, and the crews were fêted (by order) by the whole population, military and civil, of the Turkish capital.

For three days the German crews gave themselves up to the delights of Oriental festivity, while the Ambassadors of the various Powers to the Sublime Porte wrangled over the point of international law raised by the vessels' stay in Turkish

30

THE TURKISH CRUISER HAMIDIEH.
The Hamidieh bombarded Novorossisk, in the Black Sea, on October 28th, 1914. Inset: Captain Rauoff.

waters. As usual the Porte was prolific with excuses and procrastinations. After the exchange of many terminological inexactitudes, Turkey eventually announced to a disbelieving world that she had arranged to purchase the two vessels and to intern their crews. It was soon apparent that this announcement was nothing but a mere subterfuge, for the vessels still continued to be manned by German officers and men wearing Turkish uniforms and flying the Turkish flag. In order still further to complicate the situation, the Goeben held up various British, French, and Italian vessels in a most arbitrary manner. Note after Note was exchanged between Britain and the Porte, but with no tangible effect. Finally, on October 28th, 1914, the Goeben, Breslau, and Hamidieh bombarded the Russian coast at Theodosia and Odessa, causing inconsiderable damage it is true, but placing the remedy of the situation beyond the reach of diplomacy. The Entente Powers delivered an ultimatum simultaneously, the terms of which were not complied with, and Britain, Russia, and France declared war upon the Sublime Porte, the Ambassadors having already left Constantinople on November 2nd.

Mobilisation scene near Constantinople. Once the finest of fighting men, the Turks fared badly in the Balkan War. Under German officers they rallied again in October, 1914, against the cause of civilisation in Europe.

Recruits from Anatolia leaving a steamer at Constantinople. Formerly only the Moslem Turk was liable for military service, but the Young Turks instituted a law making every Turkish subject liable to be called up.

Turkish Lancers leaving the Ottoman capital on their way to the front. Our photograph is eloquent of the change in uniform and equipment brought about by the German military mission. But the change did not extend very far. When Turkey threw in her lot with the cause of Kaiser Wilhelm, the arrangements for providing the troops with clothing broke down entirely, and one result was that the men had to undertake a winter campaign in cotton summer garments, and suffered terribly, especially in the Caucasus. Inset : Turkish infantry on the march.

THE "SICK MAN OF EUROPE" RALLIES AT THE KAISER'S CALL.

Germany, Turkey hoped no doubt to be able to threaten Greece with war unless Greece abandoned the lost Ægean Islands, while at the same time the astute Turk hoped to sail a middle course between the two groups of belligerent Powers—borrowing money from Germany, while putting off the Entente Powers with endless prevarications and subterfuges.

When the German officers, who doubtless had very definite instructions from Berlin, found that the Turk was disinclined to make common cause with the Germanic Alliance, they hit on the happy expedient of compromising him by bombarding the Crimean coast with the vessels which they themselves commanded, flying the Crescent from the masthead. The Entente Powers demanded an ample apology, and terms which included the interning of the Goeben and Breslau as well as the dismissal of all German officers from the Turkish Navy.

Persian leader in Constantinople announcing the Sultan's proclamation of a "Holy War." Inset: Prayer meeting, led by the Sultan (on left), and attended by German and Turkish officers, for the success of the Turkish arms.

It is now known that the Turkish executive during this period was upon the horns of a dilemma. With that love of intrigue which is the backbone of Oriental diplomacy, the Young Turk Party had flirted and coquetted with Imperial Germany to such an extent that at the crucial moment it was unable to extricate itself from the Kaiser's clutches. By allowing thousands of German officers, soldiers, and sailors to take up duties in the Ottoman Army and Fleet, and by purchasing vast supplies of war material from

Even in the Turkish Cabinet this ultimatum gave rise to two distinctly opposite views, and the fate of Turkey hung in the balance until the commander of the Goeben intimated to the Turkish Cabinet that unless they rejected the ultimatum he would at once proceed to bombard Constantinople itself, commencing with the Sultan's palace. The situation was too strong for the Turkish Cabinet. The waverers followed the line of least resistance, and preferred to offend their quondam friends beyond the gate rather than their new-found ally-enemy who had so firmly established himself in the very citadel of the Empire.

The history of the world has few more tragic moments to offer to the consideration of posterity than those dramatic hours when those who had banished Sultan Abdul Hamid, and

Mass meeting in the Turkish capital after the announcement that Turkey had taken the side of Germany in the Great War. The flag bearing the device of a lion and a drawn sword is Persian.

SULTAN MEHMED'S PROCLAMATION OF A "HOLY WAR."

usurped the reins of power under the thin disguise of setting up a constitutional government, eventually found themselves outwitted and helpless, obliged to do the bidding of a German naval officer.

To this end Enver Pasha, the arch-schemer, had undoubtedly plotted, so that the situation came as no surprise to him nor to the narrow circle of astute but unscrupulous men who for close upon a decade had controlled the suicidal foreign policy of the Ottoman Empire, but to all those who did not enjoy Enver's confidence—and at least half the members of the Cabinet must be included in this category—the blow was an exceedingly bitter one, shattering all their day-dreams of a revivified Turkey and replacing them with the worst fears of a black

Arrival of H.H. Prince Hussein Kamel Pasha in Cairo on the occasion of his proclamation as Sultan of Egypt on December 18th, 1914. His Highness was described as the eldest living prince of the family of Mehemet Ali.

nightmare. Ever since the so-called Party of Union and Progress (the " Young Turk " Party, as it was familiarly known) came into power, and by a military coup de main deposed Sultan Abdul Hamid, the Ottoman Empire had commenced to travel downhill at a greater rate than had ever been attained hitherto. Abdul Hamid, with all his wicked ways, his callous massacres of Armenians and oppression of Macedonians, his outrageous dishonesty and admitted shiftiness, was at least a ruler who had known how to keep the Ottoman Empire intact, and by skilfully playing upon the jealousies of the Great Powers had managed to misgovern his disjointed Empire without undue interference from the outside world.

When he wanted money, which was a chronic obsession, he found little difficulty in obtaining it

Hoisting the flag of the new Sultan of Egypt at the Abdin Palace, Cairo. Inset: The new Sultan, accompanied by his Prime Minister, H.E. Sir Hussein Ruchdi Pasha, on their way to the Abdin Palace.

PROCLAMATION OF PRINCE HUSSEIN KAMEL PASHA. THE NEW SULTAN, AT THE ABDIN PALACE, CAIRO.

in Paris or London by hypothecating revenues and granting monopolies. When he got into trouble with either of the groups of Great Powers, he invariably played his cards in such a manner that the other group came to his rescue. So that while Europe wrangled and Christian Ottomans suffered,

Diplomacy of the Sublime Porte

Abdul Hamid continued duly to mis-govern the land. While he amassed personal wealth, it must be admitted that by his brilliant diplomacy he invariably managed to maintain the prestige and integrity of the Ottoman Empire.

The Young Turk Party came into power, like most oppositions, with fine-sounding promises of reform. They would, so they declared, make Turkey into a modern European State, with all the advantages of Western civilisation grafted upon an inexhaustible Oriental imagination. Whether at first the Young Turks were sincere in their protestations it is difficult to say, but the fact remains that the moment they had usurped the power they fell into the same faults which have ever characterised Oriental government. It is possible to change rulers frequently, but to change the character of a nation is a process that requires centuries.

The new men at the helm committed all the old, flagrant errors of their predecessors, besides inventing a completely new set of their own. The diplomacy of the Sublime Porte was framed not by one master diplomat, as hitherto, but by a caucus of infinitely less astute men, each of whom was jealous of his neighbour, and desired more his own personal advancement than that of the Ottoman Empire. In quick succession followed the war against Italy, when Turkey lost Tripoli and Cyrenaica as the result of a year of war; and before peace had been declared with Italy, the Balkan League —Bulgaria, Serbia, Greece,

THE EX-KHEDIVE ABBAS HILMI.
Who threw in his lot with Germany.

and Montenegro—had declared war on Turkey on October 13th, 1912. In that campaign the Porte lost nearly the whole of her European provinces, including Crete, and only retained the narrow strip of territory in advance of the Chataldja lines, sufficient to safeguard Constantinople itself from a surprise attack.

The outbreak of war between the Balkan Allies on July 2nd, 1913, when Bulgaria treacherously attacked her former allies, was a heaven-sent opportunity to the Young Turk to re-establish his vanishing prestige. To do him credit he made the most of it. Hastily gathering together an army of 150,000 picked troops, Enver Pasha marched on Adrianople and, scarcely firing a shot, retook that most important city and fortress. The armistice, which began on July 31st, ended in the signing of the Treaty of Bucharest, which gave Eastern Thrace back to Turkey. It is now known that during the early summer of 1913 Turkey was intriguing with Bulgaria to enter into a war against Greece and Serbia. Turkey demanded as her share of a possibly successful campaign the restitution of Adrianople and of Albania. Bulgaria was only willing to agree to Turkey retaking Albania if the European Powers would allow it, wherefore Turkey broke off these somewhat delicate negotiations and made war on Bulgaria. It is characteristic of Ottoman policy, however, that before entering upon this campaign entirely on her own account, she offered an alliance to Greece, which

Greco-Turkish "incidents"

M. Venizelos, the Greek Premier, refused on the ground that it would be unseemly to unite with so recent an enemy to make war upon a former ally—a sentiment which perhaps was more honourable than profitable, as the sequel tended to prove; for hardly had the Treaty of Bucharest been signed than Turkey began to make trouble with Greece. The islands of Chios and Mitylene were two of the stumbling-blocks. "Incidents" were frequent. The Porte applied

SIR FRANCIS WINGATE.

GENERAL LIMAN VON SANDERS.
The German Commander-in-Chief of the Turkish Army. The portrait of Sir Francis Reginald Wingate, in supreme command of the Egyptian Army, is given in the centre of this page.

the screw of massacre and oppression upon the Greek inhabitants of Thrace and Asia Minor, and daily relations became more and more strained. The two countries vied in their endeavours to outbid each other for the purchase of two Dreadnought battleships from South American republics at fancy prices, until it was obvious to all intelligent spectators that the danger of war was very imminent.

An interesting feature of the Greco-Turkish situation was that the navies of both countries were being trained by British naval missions. Early in 1914 the Turkish Government signed a contract with a combination of British armament firms to build and maintain a dock and arsenal at Constantinople capable of dealing with the largest types of battleships afloat, while two British admirals, assisted by a well-chosen staff of naval officers, were devoting all their energies to reorganising the Turkish Fleet and dockyards. At the same time, another large British naval mission, consisting of no fewer than nineteen officers under Rear-Admiral Mark Kerr, C.B., had for several months taken in hand the reorganisation of the Greek Navy.

Into this eddy of Balkan politics fell the bombshell of the Great European War. The greater issue drowned all minor strife, but the population and bureaucracy of the Ottoman Empire were incensed against the British Government because on the outbreak of hostilities the British, according to their declared rights, commandeered all war craft building in British dockyards for

foreign Governments. Now among these were two Dreadnought battleships building for Turkey, the first instalments on the price of which had been paid by Turkey out of "voluntary" contributions subscribed by private individual citizens of the Ottoman Empire. As a matter of fact, the vast majority of the sum thus "voluntarily" collected consisted of six months' pay stopped from the salaries and wages of all Turkish Government employees, both military and civil; and these shorn lambs knew only too well that, although Great Britain would refund the money to Turkey, the Turkish Government would never reimburse the subscribers.

Enver gambling for high stakes

Once the Entente Powers had declared war upon Turkey the die for her was cast. None knew better than Enver Pasha the vital issues at stake. Success might bring a recrudescence of Turkish power, and a rehabilitation of her sovereignty over the Balkans and Northern Africa; while defeat would mean the dissolution of the Ottoman Empire into its component parts of Greek, Armenian, Circassian, Syrian, and Arab. Enver was gambling for the highest possible stakes, but so far as he himself was concerned it was a gamble well worth the risk. In the blackest days of the Balkan Wars he had rallied all the polyglot fragments of the patchwork Empire around the Crescent by an appeal to Ottoman patriotism. He invited Syrian, Jew, and Christian alike to forget their diverse creeds and to concentrate their whole energies on winning back from Bulgaria the fair

TURKEY'S EVIL GENIUS.
Enver Pasha, the leader of the Young Turks. He threw himself heart and soul into the quarrel which was forced upon Turkey by her German masters, and it was he who induced the Sultan to proclaim a Jehad, or "Holy War," against the British Empire.

DEFEATED IN THE CAUCASUS.
Shukri Pasha, commander of the Turkish troops in the Caucasus, a badly-defeated general. Inset (left): The eldest son of the Sultan of Turkey and (right) Colonel Halil Bey, commander of the Constantinople garrison.

OPENING STAGES OF THE WAR WITH TURKEY—BRITISH RAID AT THE MOUTH OF THE SHAT-EL-ARAB, PERSIAN GULF.

On November 8th, 1914, the British Admiralty announced a successful operation against Fao, at the force from India, covered by H.M.S. Odin (Commander Cathcart R. Wason), the armed launch Sirdar, a mouth of the Shat-el-Arab, a waterway which, formed by the junction of the Euphrates and the Tigris, force of Marines with a Maxim-gun party, and a boat from the Ocean. The enemy's guns were silenced falls into the Persian Gulf about sixty miles below Basra. The operation was conducted by a military after an hour's resistance, and the town was occupied by the troops and the naval brigade.

lands of the Maritza valley. In part the appeal succeeded, and when the recapture of Adrianople came to flatter this first effort, Enver found his personal prestige—which had been sadly in need of a stimulant—go soaring once more into the zenith. Prestige, however, of this kind is only fed on victory. To maintain his political ascendancy in Constantinople it was necessary for Enver to be able to boast of some new conquest biennially. He was plotting a victorious war against Greece when the German intrigues suddenly pitched him into the seething cauldron of the Great European War. He was far too astute a man to miss his opportunity. War of some kind, against somebody—it mattered not whom—was essential to h'm personally; he threw himself heart and soul into the quarrel which Turkey had had forced upon her.

In view of the fact that Enver completed his military studies in Germany, it is probable that there was a good deal of reality in the warmth with which he espoused the cause of the new Triple Alliance. **Proclamation of a "Holy War"** On the other hand, clever man as he was, he readily realised that the adversary from whom Turkey had most to fear, or most to gain in the event of final victory, was Britain. It was against Britain, therefore, that expediency and strategy combined to suggest that he should make his greatest effort. It may be imagined how cordially such a strategic doctrine was welcomed by his German ally. Since at first he was powerless to strike at Great Britain effectively either by land or by sea, he determined to strike at her morally. In a moment of exuberant optimism he induced the Sultan to proclaim a Jehad, or Holy War, against the British Empire.

Whether Enver was hypnotised by the political miscalculations of Germany (who throughout the war proved herself as impotent in diplomacy and appreciation of national character as she showed herself capable in military organisation), or whether he was merely risking a false lead in the hope that it would draw a trump, it is impossible to conjecture, but there can be no doubt that in fomenting a holy war Enver placed the seal of finality upon the crumbling destinies of the Ottoman Empire. Religious fanaticism is not a force which can be lightly invoked; when once aroused it is calculated to carry all before it, overstepping, as it does, all considerations of nationality, race, and language. So long as the Sultan of Turkey did not mix politics with his religion he remained the head of the Moslem world; and no matter what might befall the Ottoman Empire the Sultan would have always retained a great power in the world as head and leader of the Mohammedan faith, just as the Vatican still has a large voice in the council of nations despite the fact that the Empire of Rome has long since crumbled into the dust.

Had the Sultan, when proclaiming a Jehad, been able to rally the faithful to his standard by calling a war on Christianity, the move might have proved a feature of great strength, but all that he could do was to proclaim that as the ally of two Christian Empires he proposed to make war upon a group of Christian States, one of which—Britain—ruled over a vast Mohammedan Empire in India, and had nursed ten million Moslems in Egypt into a state of prosperity and religious freedom which **Moslem loyalty to the British Raj** they had never enjoyed under Turkish rule. Not unnaturally the Jehad was a fiasco. The Moslems of India and Egypt saw through the shallow device and refused to be entrapped into a pseudo-religious fanaticism against their benefactors. All the great Moslem institutions and societies throughout Egypt and the British Empire hastened to assure the British Government of their unswerving loyalty to the Raj, and openly deplored the fact that the Sultan, the chief of the Moslem faith, should have dragged their sacred religion into so sordid a political intrigue.

Thereafter, it was clear that by his folly in proclaiming a Jehad, the Sultan had lost the confidence of his co-religionists throughout the world, and that in future Mohammedans would look elsewhere for their spiritual guidance. The Sultan had let his mantle of sanctity fall away from him. It will fall upon the shoulders of a prince or rajah subject to the British throne.

In the bad old days of Abdul Hamid only the Moslem Turk was liable for military service, but the Young Turk Party altered the conscription laws, making every Turkish subject liable to be called up, irrespective of creed or race. The war against the Balkan League showed the utter futility of this new régime, for it was found that only a small percentage of the Armenian and other Christian races answered the mobilisation summons, while the vast majority of those who actually joined the colours seized the first possible opportunity to desert or to go over to the enemy. Again, another cause which contributed even more potentially to the collapse of the Turkish armies was their faulty mobilisation scheme. In order the better to make clear the vital importance to a nation of having a carefully thought out scheme of organisation, it may be as well to describe roughly the process of mobilisation. In peace time it is the object of the army organiser to maintain the largest number possible of skeleton formations, which in war time can be clothed with reservists, and thus made into a complete fighting machine; but these skeleton formations must be able to train men in peace time as well as providing a nucleus in war time. For instance, if it is desired to have a battalion of 1,200 bayonets in time of war, a conscript country need only maintain some three hundred of the men in peace time. When mobilisation takes place these three hundred are medically examined, and those who are unfit, under age, or insufficiently trained are left behind at the depot, while the battalion is brought up to war strength by calling up the various classes of reservists. Any surplus that is still left over remains at the depot and is drafted out to replace the casualties. Now, in all European countries since the Franco-Prussian War, this process of mobilisation is completed before any attempt is made to send the unit on service. A unit does not leave its mobilisation centre until it is complete to the last detail in men, arms, equipment, stores, ammunition, and transport. This, however, was not the case with the Turkish Army in the autumn of 1912. Units were sent direct from their peace stations to the firing-line, their reservists and stores being sent out to join them at the front.

To give an example. The 23rd Independent Division, stationed at Janina, in Albania, had a war strength of some 15,000 men. In peace time it actually numbered about 6,000 all told, one-third of whom had less than one year's service. The reservists, stores, and equipment for this division were supposed to come from Smyrna, in Asia Minor, and as a matter of fact never reached their destination—which is hardly surprising.

Remodelling the Turkish Army

Ever since January, 1913, the Turks under German guidance had been making desperate efforts to put their house in order, to remodel and equip their Army, to replenish their military stores, and to ·recast their entire mobilisation scheme. Each of the Active (Nizam) Divisions was allotted a mobilisation centre. At these centres the Nizam units were brought up to war strength and fully equipped, and to each Nizam Division a Redif (or Reserve) Division was affiliated. It was part of Germany's commercial policy to discourage the Turks from creating a large arsenal capable of constructing guns or ammunition on a big scale, since the firm of Krupp wished to sell such warlike stores to Turkey. But the Germans had reason to regret their short-sighted policy, for as soon as war broke out it became impossible to ship further ordnance stores from Essen to Constantinople; there was a great shortage of guns and artillery material in the new Turkish Army. The arrangements for providing the troops with clothing broke down entirely, with the result that the men had to undertake a winter campaign in cotton summer garments. This was their foretaste of the joys of German organisation

Short-sighted German policy

The modernised Turkish Army of 1914 was organised as follows:

The Army on a peace footing was to consist of twenty-five Nizam (or Regular) Divisions each, consisting of thirteen battalions of infantry, twenty-four guns, one squadron of cavalry, and various details. In all about 15,500 men.

VISIT OF THE SULTAN'S HEIR TO POTSDAM.
An interesting record of the Turco-German entente. The fourth figure in the group is Youssouf Izzedin, heir-apparent to the Turkish throne. Mustapha Pasha is the bearded man in the dark overcoat.

Five of these divisions (i.e., two at Adrianople, one at Constantinople, one in Turkish Caucasia, and one in Arabia) were to be maintained at full strength. The remaining twenty divisions, however, while kept nominally at about half strength were, for one reason or another, allowed to fall to anywhere from one-third to one-quarter of the established strength. On mobilisation all these divisions were to be brought up to full strength by drafts of reservists who had recently left the colours, or by men supposed to be serving, but who were actually on permanent leave; and, moreover, the strength of each battalion was to be augmented from a nominal 1,000 to an actual 1,250. Thus it was contemplated that the twenty-five Nizam Divisions of about 19,000 men each would muster 475,000 men. It was, moreover, schemed to add one Redif (Reserve) Division to each Nizam formation, each pair making an army corps; the men of the Redif formations being either middle-aged reservists who had finished their service or younger men who, by hook or by crook, had escaped the net of conscription. The army corps were to be grouped into five armies, each consisting

E

GERMANY'S TURKISH ALLIES IN TRAINING FOR THE FIELD.

Our first photograph shows a number of Turkish soldiers engaged in fixing wire entanglements. They are wearing their new military head-dress, half fez and half helmet. In the lower picture we see some of the Sultan's troops digging trenches. It was reported at the time that the men went about their work under German supervision with a marked lack of enthusiasm.

of five Nizam Divisions, five Redif Divisions, a mixed Cavalry Division composed of regulars, reservists, and irregulars, and two regiments (forty guns) of artillery, both light and heavy. This organisation was calculated to bring the effective field armies up to about 1,150,000, the remaining 50,000 men being accounted for in garrison artillery and gendarmerie.

There is reason to believe, however, that the utmost Turkey could hope actually to arm and muster during the present war would be the following:

It must be borne in mind and emphasised that the Redif organisations were of little military value, and their numbers were in many cases fictitious.

The troops of the Nizam and those of the five Redif Divisions raised in Anatolia were fine fighting material if any time and money had ever been spent on their training; but the days were now past when sheer courage alone sufficed to make a good soldier. Some ninety-five per cent. of the Turkish rank and file were illiterate and of low intelligence; their musketry was inferior, and their knowledge of entrenching most elementary. The vast majority of the officers had very little education, either military or otherwise. There were, however, some 1,500 officers in the Turkish Army who had either studied abroad or completed their military education under German instructors. These officers for the most part were very intelligent and eminently capable. Before the war had progressed far the old régime of incompetent pashas had been done away with, and bright westernised young officers of the new school held those superior commands which the Germans had not reserved for themselves.

The chief characteristic of the Turk as a fighting man is his wonderful doggedness in defence, even when vastly

ESTIMATED TOTAL STRENGTH OF THE TURKISH ARMIES.				
				MEN.
The Army of Europe (Adrianople)	5 Nizam Divisions, 2 Redif Divisions, and 3,000 Cavalry		.. ..	say 140,000
The Reserve Army (Constantinople)	5 Nizam Divisions (under strength)	say	70,000	
	3 Redif Divisions (under strength)	„	35,000	
	Irregular Cavalry		2,000	
				say 110,000
The Caucasian Army (with part of Smyrna Army)	8 Nizam Divisions (under strength)		120,000	
	8 Redif Divisions (under strength)		80,000	
	Mixed Cavalry		5,000	
				say 210,000
Arabian Garrison	2 Nizam Divisions (1 under strength)		30,000	
	2 Redif Divisions (probably unarmed, and very doubtful if they would mobilise at all	say	10,000	
				40,000
Smyrna Garrison	1 Nizam Division (under strength and badly armed)..	„	12,000	
	3 or, perhaps, 4 Redif Divisions (under strength and badly armed	„	40,000	
	Cavalry and Details	„	8,000	
				60,000
Available against Egypt	4 Nizam Divisions (under strength)	„	60,000	
	1 strong Redif Division (for lines of communication)	„	20,000	
				80,000
		TOTAL AVAILABLE		640,000

outnumbered. His tactics are clumsy and devoid of originality, and he is terribly slow in seizing an opportunity.

Taught by the bitter experience of the Balkan League War, Turkey had at last realised the value of sea-power, and had determined to create a fleet which would at least secure her own home waters, and keep open the fairway through the Ægean Sea. During the campaign of 1912-13, the Greek Fleet had kept the Turkish Navy

Turkey's bid for sea-power mewed up in the Sea of Marmora, an impotent onlooker, while Greek shipping furrowed the narrow seas and Greek warships effectively blockaded the Turkish coasts. Turkey had suffered bitterly by reason of her inability to dispute the mastery of her own home waters, and she had determined not to be caught napping again. Under the guidance of the British naval mission at Constantinople, she had bought or laid down two Dreadnoughts, and these were being completed by the Armstrong and Vickers yards when war broke out between Great Britain and Germany, and the British authorities promptly took over the two battleships. These were :

The Sultan Mehmet Rechad V. (now H.M.S. Erin), 23,000 tons, ten 13·5 in. and sixteen 6 in. guns, designed for a speed of twenty-one knots; and the Sultan Osman (ex-Rio de Janeiro and now H.M.S. Agincourt), 27,500 tons, fourteen 12 in. and twenty 6 in. guns, designed for a speed of twenty-two knots.

Thus the two principal units that Turkey had counted upon were not available; but by way of consolation the German vessels Goeben and Breslau (previously described in detail) were henceforth to form part of the Turkish Fleet, which consisted of the following obsolete units :

The battleships Barberossa and Torgud Reis, built in 1891 for the German Navy, and sold by Germany under the Naval Law to Turkey in 1910, of 10,000 tons, with six 11 in., and eight 4·1 in. guns each, and probably capable of steaming seventeen knots on occasion.

The Messudiyeh, built in 1874, and reconstructed in Genoa in 1903, was of 9,250 tons displacement, could steam sixteen knots, and carried two 9·4 in guns as her main armament, and twelve 6 in. guns in her secondary battery. The Messudiyeh was sunk by a British submarine which, passing under five minefields in the Dardanelles, torpedoed the ship while riding at anchor, and in imagined security. This was one of the most daring and unique naval enterprises of the war, and was performed by Lieutenant Holbrook in the B11.

The Muin-i-Zaffir, built in 1869 and refitted in 1907, was really little better than a gunboat. Of 2,400 tons displacement, she could only steam twelve knots, and was armed with four 6 in. guns.

The light cruisers Hamidieh and Medjidieh, of 3,500 tons, could only steam twenty-two knots, and carried each two 6 in., and eight 4·7 in. guns. Fifteen obsolescent gunboats, four modern destroyers and older ones, together with fifteen torpedo-boats, completed the Turkish Navy.

As a fighting force it was entirely a negligible quantity, since had it been possible to coax it into a fight in the open, one British cruiser of the armoured class would have sufficed to sink the **A weird collection** whole weird collection of scrap-iron **of scrap-iron** in a very short space of time.

Nothing could have been less sound than was the Turkish strategical situation. On all sides Turkey was isolated and surrounded by superior hostile elements. In the Black Sea she was face to face with a Russian squadron which made up in efficiency for what it lacked in paper strength. Outside the Dardanelles was concentrated a vastly superior Franco-British naval force. In European Turkey the Balkan situation was so unstable that Turkey had of necessity to keep a large army ready in order to cope with any recrudescence of a Balkan coalition. The Balkan States fully realised that should the Germanic Alliance come victorious out of the war, Turkey would be paid for her

THE ARABIAN FACTOR IN THE GREAT WORLD WAR.

For centuries the Arab has suffered under Turkish domination, and for generations he has striven by local rebellions to discard the yoke. When Turkey formally yielded to Teutonic pressure, she called upon her Arabian troops to mobilise. Our illustration shows a party of these soldiers of the desert, distinguished still by their traditional head-dress, but wearing European uniforms, and carrying German-made bugles and drums.

aid at the expense of the other Balkan Powers. So long as the Allies of the Entente continued to hold their own, so long would Rumania and Greece remain neutral, but a successful Austrian invasion of Serbia would automatically bring Greece, Rumania, and perhaps Bulgaria into the field to drive the Austrians out of Balkania

Although Turkey had to keep at least 300,000 men under arms in the vicinity of Constantinople, in order to deal with the Balkan political situation and

Turkey's hopeless isolation

to safeguard the capital against a sea-borne expeditionary force, this army could not hope in any way to co-operate with those of Turkey's allies in Europe. Turkey was left entirely to work out her own salvation, or to march in lonely solitude to her doom.

In the Caucasian area she was called upon to put into the field an army capable not only of holding back any Russian invading force, but also of maintaining Turkish suzerainty over the Armenian Christian population, long since seething with revolt. In this one theatre of war alone Turkey had more than enough to occupy all her remaining resources, for Russia could put in the field the whole of her Caucasian army of three-quarters of a million of men, troops

of a new Arabian Empire, with Arabic as its official language, Mohammedanism as its official religion, and King George as its official protector, would be welcomed throughout the length and breadth of that vast tract known to geographers as Arabia; and since every Arab is a born irregular soldier, Turkey would have found her south-eastern provinces over-run by an Arab army which would have needed at least a quarter of a million men to oppose it.

We have thus seen that the strategical situation of the Ottoman Empire was hopelessly unsound. An Empire with an extensive seaboard, she had no fleet capable of opposing serious naval operations, while all her greatest cities were on the coast. In the Black Sea she was faced by a very powerful Russian fleet, and in the Mediterranean by a still more powerful Franco-British fleet, while in the Red Sea, the Indian Ocean, and the Persian Gulf she was at the mercy of the British or Japanese navies.

All her land frontiers were also menaced, with the possible exception of the Persian frontier. Inspired by her German advisers, Turkey determined to forestall her troubles, and, applying the axiom that a vigorous offensive is the best defence, she prepared two armies of invasion. The one, based on Erzerum, was to cross the Caucasus and invade Russian territory; the other, based on Damascus, was to cross the Sinai Desert and invade Egypt. Both of these ambitious expeditions were fore-doomed to failure, but the fact that they should ever have been undertaken at all is strong testimony of the wonderful driving power of the German officers attached to the Ottoman Army.

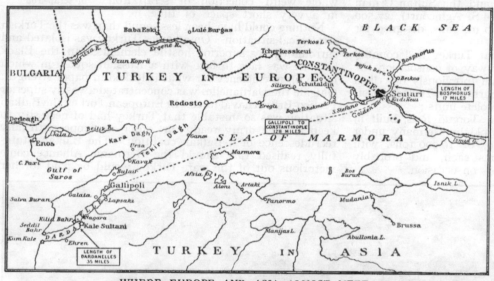

WHERE EUROPE AND ASIA ALMOST MEET.
Sketch map indicating the relationship of the Dardanelles to the Sea of Marmora and the Bosphorus, and the route by which it was hoped ships trading between Russia and her Allies in the Great War would be able to pass to and from the Black Sea.

The Egyptian campaign had these ostensible reasons:

1. A vigorous offensive by land was necessary to counter-balance the Allies' predominance of sea-power in Near Eastern waters.

2. To strike at the very spring of British trade, wealth, and power—the Suez Canal.

3. By extending the authority of the Turkish Raj over a Moslem Egypt, the holy war might be partially justified in practice.

that otherwise would not have been drawn into the maelstrom of Armageddon.

Again, in the Arabian theatre of hostilities was a huge sub-continent, all the important cities of which were at the mercy of a sea-borne army or of a naval power; and here again, as in Armenia, there was a local population only too anxious to throw off the hated yoke of the Turkish tax-collector. The Arab had little in common with the Turk, under whose domination he has suffered for many centuries all the hardships of misgovernment and over-taxation. The one sentiment Turk and Arab shared in common was the religion of Mohammed, but the fact should not be lost sight of that Mohammed himself was an Arab, and it was the Arabs who built up the great Empire of which Constantinople was the centre.

For many generations local rebellions had strived, and sometimes succeeded, in shaking off the Turkish yoke both in Africa, Asia Minor, and Arabia. Had Disraeli been alive in October, 1914, we can imagine him humbly petitioning King George to proclaim himself Emperor of the Arabs, much as he persuaded Queen Victoria to assume the Imperial crown of India. Those who know the Arab well, who know his language and his aspirations, who are aware of the immense prestige enjoyed by Britishers amongst Arab populations, will agree that the proclamation

The real reasons of the ambitious invasion were dictated, not by a council of war, but by a council of political schemers in Constantinople who had become the tools of the Kaiser. The true reasons for the invasion of Egypt may be summarised as follows:

1. Every British soldier retained to garrison Egypt would mean one man less on the Allies' line in Belgium and France, and therefore would set free a Prussian soldier to march on Warsaw and to liberate Eastern Prussia from the heel of the invading Russian host.

2. The war was already sufficiently unpopular in Turkey, and if a revolution were to be avoided, then an early success for Turkish arms was essential. Although the prospects of success in Egypt were extremely meagre,

Decision to invade Egypt

there was at least a faint possibility of achieving some military feat of arms; while in the only other area of war available to Turkish armies—the Caucasus—there was no possibility of success whatever, owing to the rigours of the climate in winter and the known superiority of the Russian armies both in organisation and numbers.

Having once decided upon the invasion of Egypt, it must be admitted the Turco-German Staff set about their task in a most businesslike manner. All Turkish officers suspected of political intrigue against the Young Turk

SINKING OF THE TURKISH BATTLESHIP MESSUDIYEH BY SUBMARINE B11.

On December 13th, 1914, the British submarine B11 (Lieutenant-Commander Norman D. Holbrook, R.N.) entered the Dardanelles, and, in spite of the current, dived under five rows of mines and torpedoed the Turkish battleship Messudiyeh, which was guarding the minefield. Although pursued by gun fire and torpedo-boats, B11 returned safely, after being submerged on one occasion for nine hours. Lieutenant-Commander Holbrook was awarded the V.C. on December 21st, just a year after he had been appointed to the command of the B11 at Malta.

Inspired by her German advisers, Turkey determined to forestall her troubles; and, applying the axiom that a vigorous offensive is the best defence, she prepared two armies of invasion. The one, based on Erzerum, was to cross the Caucasus and invade Russia; the other, based on Damascus, was to cross the Sinai Desert and invade Egypt. Both of these ambitious expeditions were foredoomed to failure. For the Caucasian venture three armies were formed, each of about 55,000 men. The campaign was planned to allow two columns to advance, while a third was kept two days' march in the rear to act as a

general reserve. Snow was already thick on the uplands when a start was made, and owing to faulty staff work and the appalling climatic conditions, one of the columns outdistanced the other. In turn both were driven back in hopeless disorder, pursued by the victorious Russians, who struggled waist-deep through the mountain snowdrifts. The arrival of the Turkish reserves synchronised with a terrific snowstorm; and during this the remnants of the Turkish army of invasion, reduced to about one-quarter of its original effectives, managed to find their way back to their base at Erzerum.

Lieutenant-Commander Norman D. Holbrook being invested by a brother officer with an "Iron Cross" on board H.M.S. Indefatigable. It will be noticed, on comparing the bottom photograph with the small one, that the gallant commander of B11 had grown a beard during his daring exploit in the Dardanelles.

After the ceremony on board the Indefatigable. Lieutenant-Commander Holbrook displaying his "Iron Cross." A few days after the humorous interlude above depicted, the King was pleased to signalise Lieutenant-Commander Holbrook's conspicuous act of heroism by bestowing upon him the V.C.—the first award of this coveted distinction to a naval officer during the Great War.

"IRON CROSS" FOR THE COMMANDER OF B11: HUMOROUS INTERLUDE AT SEA.

Party were drafted to the army of Syria, while those who were known to have Anglophile tendencies were drafted to the army of the Caucasus. It is impossible to obtain definitely detailed information regarding the troops told off to form the army of Egypt, but the following estimate is approximately correct :

ADVANCE GUARD.—A Redif Division from Arabia, consisting chiefly of Arab Bedouins, who had no

Bedlam of nomad irregulars

military training whatever, and no organisation save on paper —about eight to ten thousand. This bedlam of nomad irregulars was concentrated between Jerusalem and Akabah, and it is estimated that at least fifty per cent. of them deserted before the advance even began.

MAIN BODY.—Four Nizam Divisions, drawn from Asia Minor, consisting of the best fighting material in the Turkish Army, but considerably under strength. These Divisions were numerically strengthened but morally weakened by attaching to each certain Redif formations, raised in Syria and Palestine. This combined force, amounting to about 60,000 Nizam (regulars) and 10,000 Redifs, were concentrated at Smyrna and Damascus, and were moved forward, when completed, by successive half-divisions along the Hedjaz railway, through Jerusalem, and thence by steady marching toward the Sinai Peninsula, where, on the confines of the desert wastes, an immense camp was formed during the middle of December, 1914.

From then onwards the Turkish army came under the almost daily supervision of the British reconnoitring aircraft. The movements of the Bedouin camelry and horsemen were watched also by patrols of the Egyptian and Bikanir Camel Corps. During December and January two very minor skirmishes took place between the opposing desert riders, the advantage in each case being ludicrously to the advantage of the British.

The Turco-German army commenced a general forward movement from its rest camp at the end of December, striking out into the wilderness on the march that Moses had taken forty years to accomplish, but which, with modern organisation, was completed in as many days.

Petrograd to London

via Archangel – 3,400 miles

via Black Sea & Dardanelles – 4,600 miles

via Transiberian Ry. Vladivostock & Suez Canal – 12,700 miles

ANGLO-RUSSIAN COMMUNICATIONS.
Map showing the three routes between Russia and Great Britain, with distances in miles between Petrograd and London.

Some features of the German arrangements are worthy of being placed on record. The guns and limbers of the artillery were equipped with cast-iron wheels, some six inches wide on the tread, in order to distribute the weight of the guns on the sand of the desert. Some two thousand draught animals, other than the six thousand baggage-camels employed in carrying food and ammunition, were utilised in dragging sand-sledges. A Turkish bridging train of thirty-six galvanised-iron pontoons, German Army pattern, was intended for bridging the Suez Canal. These pontoons, somewhat resembling an iron punt, pointed at one end, were nineteen feet by four-feet-six, and could be used either as boats or as floating piers for the construction of a bridge, or bridges, wherewith to span the Suez Canal. Each pontoon was furnished with wide rollers to act as wheels on uneven ground ; but where the surface of the sand was smooth, the rollers were unshipped, and the pontoon with its iron bottom slid like a sledge across the desert behind its team of draught animals. The pontoons were also used for the transport of stores, and thus served the double purpose of cart and boat —a thoughtful economy of matériel.

Fortune at first appeared to favour the Turkish venture. During the months of November, December, and January there had been plentiful rains—in fact, the best rainfall that had occurred for seven years— and the water-holes (or wells) of the desert were unusually well sup-

Season of plentiful rains

plied with precious liquid, vegetable in taste, gritting to the teeth, café au lait in colour, which people in this part of the world call water.

A well in the desert is very different from what we are accustomed to call a well in Western Europe. The desert " well " may belong to either one of two varieties. The visible well, or waterhole, is reminiscent of an English horse-pond, and is the result of innumerable generations of industrious digging on the part of desert wayfarers and of long-forgotten convict gangs in the days of the Pharaohs. Usually with a steep bank at one end and steps reaching down to the waterside, the water level may be six to sixteen feet below the level of the bank. At the other end, however, a shelving ramp runs down to the water, so as to enable

RAILWAYS CHIEF ROADS FORTRESSES PASSES SCALE 0 20 40 MILES

TO THE MAIN CHAIN OF THE CAUCASUS AT THE DARIEL PASS.

TO THE DARIEL PASS

Kutais

Poti

Orpiri

R. Rion

BLACK SEA

R. Kur

Gori

TIFLIS

Batúm

Achalzich

THE WHOLE COUNTRY IS A TABLELAND CROSSED BY HIGH MOUNTAIN RIDGES

Achalkalaki

Ardahan

Rise

Alexandropol

R. Chorok

Soghanlu Mts

Kars

TO TIFLIS

Olti

Barduz

Schmahin

THE PASSES ROUND ERZERUM ARE DEFENDED BY FORTS

Sonomer

Sarykamish

Erivan

Khordsan

R. Aras (Araxes)

Erzerum

Kupri Keui

M. Ararat 16911

R. Euphrates

Bajesid

THE TURKISH INVASION OF THE CAUCASUS.
Key map of the passes by which the Turkish forces invaded Russian territory. They suffered utter rout at Sarykamysch (or Sarykamish), and at Ardahan.

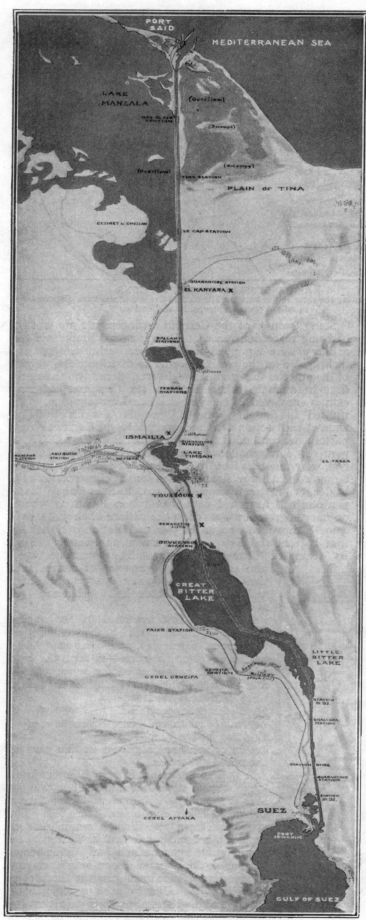

THE TURKISH ATTACK ON EGYPT.
In the above diagrammatic plan are clearly seen the points against which Djemal Pasha directed his attack—El Kantara, Ismailia, Toussoum, and Serapeum.

beasts of burden to drink. A large well will be sometimes as big as a tennis-lawn, with four or five feet of water in it after heavy rains; but in summer time this same well will be reduced to the size of a dining-room table, in which eight to ten inches of water does its best to boil under the scorching rays of the sun. The other, the invisible variety of " well," is nothing more nor less than the damp surface of an underground streamlet. In order to obtain water, it is necessary to dig down anywhere between two and twelve feet, when the supply will be fairly constant but very small in quantity. A trench six feet in length by three feet broad, for instance, will not yield water, as a rule, at a greater rate than about a half a pint a minute. In the rainy season, however, these hidden streams will often run above ground for twenty-four hours or so after a down-pour. The comparatively copious rainfalls at the end of 1914 and in January, 1915, greatly facilitated the invidious task of the invading army, and solved their principal administrative problem—transport.

Night attack in a sandstorm

During the early spring there is a desert wind that blows at times for a period of two or three days at a stretch. It comes charged with all the intolerable heat and minute sand particles of the surrounding desert, and is called the khamsin (fifty), because from its first to its last visit is supposed to be a compass of fifty days. When this hell-breath blows the atmosphere is superheated and is surcharged with sand. Even though there is no cloud in the sky, it is impossible even to guess the direction of the brilliant Egyptian sun, so thick is the sand fog. To face the gale, which often reaches a velocity of fifty miles an hour, is an impossibility, unless eyes and mouth be firmly closed.

On February 2nd, 1915, the first khamsin of the New Year blew in from the east by south, and that night the Turkish forces coming from the north-east determined to test the defences of the Suez Canal, trusting, no doubt, to the darkness and noise of the sandstorm to hide their approach, and to the biting sand particles to serve as their allies.

The British force in Egypt, under General Maxwell, at this time consisted of a strong force of Indian troops, with a fine Lancashire Territorial division. The latter were somewhat weedy and only partially trained when they first arrived in early September, but had grown into as fine a body of well-disciplined, lusty manhood as might be wished.

There was also a very strong contingent from the Antipodes, splendid specimens of manhood from Australia and New Zealand. Splendid though these men were in physique, they had not, however, at this time been sufficiently trained to that iron discipline which is essential in modern warfare to serve in garrison on the canal. They were held in reserve in the garrisons of Cairo, Alexandria, Mansourah, Tanta, and Zagazig.

To complete the truly Imperial nature of this composite force, the native Egyptian Army also furnished a not inconsiderable quota of its effectives to the force either holding the canal or immediately in reserve. Thus, along the western bank of the canal, in trenches which had been carefully prepared and strengthened for months previously, was a British force of about 50,000 men, with another 40,000 men behind it as a reserve.

Foredoomed to failure

It was against this highly-trained army, perfectly equipped in every detail, completely entrenched and serenely confident, that Djemal Pasha, the Turkish commander, launched his attack at dawn on February 3rd, 1915, under cover of a khamsin sandstorm. The issue was never in doubt for a moment, for even had the Turkish general obeyed the first rules of tactics and strategy instead of setting them at defiance, he could have hardly hoped to have overcome the obstacle of the Suez Canal and take

THE FORT OF SEDDEL BAHR, AT THE MOUTH OF THE DARDANELLES.

ONE OF THE HILL FORTS GUARDING THE ENTRANCE TO THE DARDANELLES.

CONSTANTINOPLE, WITH THE FAMOUS MOSQUE OF SULEIMAN SHOWING AGAINST THE SKY.

Rarely within living memory has the narrow channel separating Europe from Asia, known to us as the Dardanelles and to the ancients as the Hellespont, ceased to occupy the world's attention. Both sides were strongly fortified, and the safety of the Ottoman capital depended on the power of the Turks to defend the forty-mile strait. Xerxes and Alexander crossed the Dardanelles in 480 and 334 B.C., the first named to enter Europe, and the last named to enter Asia. Tradition has it that Leander, to visit Hero, nightly swam across, and Byron actually performed the feat.

PICTURESQUE SCENES ALONG THE SHORES OF THE STORIED HELLESPONT.

THE OPERATIONS IN EGYPT: OUR INDIAN TROOPS REPELLING A NIGHT ATTACK BY THE TURKS ON TOUSSOUM.

The Turkish force, advancing from the direction of Bir Murra, attempted unsuccessfully to launch boats across the canal under cover of their artillery fire. On the Egyptian side of the canal was an entrenched force of Punjabis. The main effort of the enemy was directed against the defences between Toussoum and Serapeum, where it culminated in a disastrous retreat.

the British trenches with the ill-clad, march-weary army at his disposal. As it was, however, he neglected two fundamental principles, either because he underrated his adversary, or else, as is far more probable, because there were dissensions between the Turkish and German officers. When on February 1st he arrived within striking distance of the Suez Canal, the obvious thing for him to have done would have been to push forward reconnoitring columns to ascertain the strength of the British positions. He could hardly hope to take these by surprise, since British aeroplanes had dogged his footsteps across the desert. If, on the **Aeroplanes over the desert** other hand, rejecting this obvious precaution, he was determined to attack at all costs, he should have struck with all his available force. He did neither. He blundered up against the British defences with his advance division, a second division being some three miles in rear as a support, and the rest of his army might just as well have never left Syria for all the assistance they afforded.

It seems extremely probable that the German Staff officers, for reasons which will be easily appreciated in Berlin, urged Djemal to attack at once in the sandstorm without making a preliminary reconnaissance, but trusting rather to their luck, and hoping for a laxity in British vigilance. It may well be that Djemal was over-persuaded to fall in with these views, but, not wishing to risk his whole army in such a hazardous adventure, he decided to compromise and attack with a part of his strength only. Like most military compromises the effort was foredoomed to failure. The battle itself, if battle it can be called, offers very few points of interest. The British force allowed the enemy to come on well within close range before they opened fire upon them with murderous precision. At one point, indeed, the Turks were actually allowed to bring two of their pontoons up to the canal bank and to launch them on the water before the defenders started to massacre them. The Turks fought pluckily, as is their wont, but they had no chance from the very first.

At Serapeum, where the main Turkish attack culminated in a disastrous retreat, a Turkish 6 in. gun opened a fairly effective fire upon the British position and some of the war vessels lying in Lake Timsah, off Ismailia. The Indian Marine Service vessel Hardinge was struck twice by shells; a gallant old pilot of the Canal Company, Captain Carew, was standing on the bridge piloting the ship when a great **Heroism of Captain Carew** 6 in. shell burst on the bridge, tearing off his leg and wounding him in no less than nineteen places. With that heroic devotion to duty and sublime fortitude that has always characterised the sailors of Britain, he called down to those who were still alive amongst the debris: " Bring me a chair, and I'll take her into port!" The spirit was willing, but, alas! the flesh was weak, and he was carried below in a fainting condition. It is pleasing

Line of entrenchments along the Egyptian side of the Suez Canal. These trenches were prepared and carefully strengthened months before Djemal Pasha, under Teuton tutelage, launched his ill-starred attack on the night of February 2nd, 1915.

British battleship in the Suez Canal, with decks cleared for action and sand-bag barricades fixed up to defend the crew from stray shots. The Indian Marine Service vessel Hardinge was hit twice by shells, and Captain Carew was severely wounded.

A British encampment. There was a British force estimated at about 50,000 along the western bank of the Suez Canal, while some 40,000 were held in reserve. The native Egyptian Army contributed a not inconsiderable quota to the defensive forces under General Maxwell.

THE DEFENCE OF EGYPT AGAINST THE TEUTONISED TURKS.

A FORCE OF GURKHAS—THE HIGHLANDERS OF INDIA—TAKING PART IN EGYPT'S DEFENCE.
A camera impression of our warlike Gurkhas resting, but on the alert and eager to try conclusions with " the unspeakable Turk."

to reflect that this grand specimen of Britain's mercantile marine recovered from his terrible injuries.

A short while afterwards, however, one of the warships on Lake Timsah took an ample revenge on the Turkish gun, killing the crew and silencing the gun with a well-aimed salvo from its 12-pounder guns, while the old French battleship Requin shelled the enemy's positions with 10'8 in. guns.

By six o'clock, as night was falling, the enemy's reserves were also in full retreat, but it was not considered advisable to follow them up into the desert. However, after nightfall, sniping broke out from the eastern bank of the canal, and two companies were sent across the canal next morning to round up the snipers. These were met by a quite unexpected fire from a deep trench which had been well screened from view. The two companies sat tight and fought well until further reinforcements were

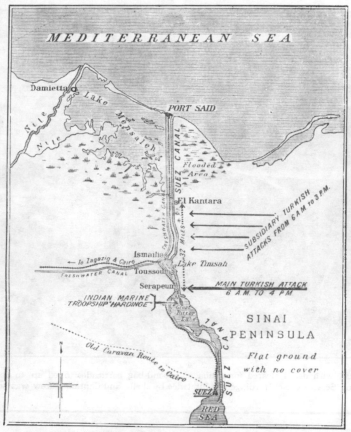

PLAN OF THE TURKISH ATTACK ON EGYPT.
Specially drawn to show the direction in which the attempts were made to test the defences of the Suez Canal.

brought up, when the trench was cleared with the bayonet. All who remained of the original occupants were captured, some two hundred and fifty prisoners, all of whom were picked men. It will never be known what losses the Turks actually incurred in the battle of the canal, for many hundreds of fugitive soldiers must have been lost in the subsequent retreat; but, in any case, their losses were not less than four thousand officers and men in killed, wounded, and prisoners, while the British casualties barely totalled threescore.

It is interesting to note that four Turks actually succeeded in swimming across the canal, and were discovered the following day hiding miserably in the vicinity of El Ferdan. Perhaps the most bitter blow of all to the Turks was the loss of practically the whole of their bridging train, which was partly destroyed and partly captured, for they did not make any attempt to save it. The

WITH OUR INDIAN TROOPS BEHIND SAND-BUILT BARRICADES IN THE EGYPTIAN DESERT.
Sikhs holding an entrenched outpost commanding one of the desert roads to the Suez Canal.

INDIAN TROOPS MARCHING ACROSS THE DESERT NEAR SUEZ.

In their first encounter with the Turks near Suez our gallant Indian troops scored a notable success. Advance parties of Indians and Turkish soldiers came into touch in the desert, and the result was entirely to the advantage of the Indians.

EGYPTIAN CAMEL CORPS GALLOPING ACROSS THE DESERT.

This splendid force formed a part of the native Egyptian Army which fought side by side with their British and Indian fellow-subjects in defending their country against the German-Turkish raiders from across the Sinai Peninsula. Long journeys across the vast Eastern sand wastes would be impossible but for the services of " the ship of the desert."

CAVALRY AND INFANTRY OF OUR EGYPTIAN ARMY ON PARADE.

Lord Kitchener's work in Egypt and the Soudan has borne wonderful fruit in the loyalty and fitness of one of the most efficient native forces in the world. Horse and foot, the Egyptian Army affords remarkable evidence of the British genius for turning coloured races into first-rate soldiers.

A UNIQUE REVIEW NEAR THE PYRAMIDS.
Sir George Reid, High Commissioner for Australia, reviewing the Australian troops as they marched past the motor-car in which he is seen acknowledging the salute.

THE RALLY FROM NEW ZEALAND.
With their Australian comrades the New Zealand contingent were halted at Egypt on their journey to Europe, to complete their training and, if necessary, to take part in the fighting against the Turks.

loss of these pontoons precluded the possibility of any further Turkish attack upon the canal for many a long week, even if the Turks had stomach for more fighting.

In the same bright, optimistic way that characterised the Egyptian Expedition, the

Turk, urged on by his German masters, sallied forth blissfully to invade Russia across the Caucasus Mountains in midwinter. By some miracle of their German taskmasters the Turks managed to mobilise between Erzerum and Van an army consisting of eight Nizam Divisions

ARRIVAL OF THE BRITISH HIGH COMMISSIONER AT CAIRO.
Sir Henry McMahon, the new High Commissioner for Egypt, arriving at Cairo on January 9th, 1915, with General Sir John Maxwell. They are seen leaving the railway-station by the Royal entrance, followed by Sir Milne Cheetham, Governor of Alexandria. In the foreground is Lewa Herbert Pasha, the commander of the Egyptian garrison in Cairo. Inset: Examination of passports at Port Said.

AUSTRALIANS IN CAMP IN THE LAND OF THE PHARAOHS.

The contingents from Australia and New Zealand were splendid specimens of manhood. They were held in reserve in the garrisons of Cairo, Alexandria, Munsourah, Tanta, and Zagazig.

A GLIMPSE OF THE ARID WASTES OF THE SINAI DESERT.

Our photograph affords a graphic impression of the plain of El Tih, near Tor. This was the scene of one of the early skirmishes between British scouting parties and advanced troops of the enemy.

FORT OF ABOUKIR, NEAR ALEXANDRIA, NOW A BRITISH NAVAL BASE IN THE MEDITERRANEAN.

TURKISH ARTILLERYMEN.
They are seen wearing their new campaign uniform.

TURKISH GUN IN ACTION.
The Turkish field artillery are armed with 7·5 cm. Krupp guns.

and eight Redif Divisions. The mobilisation was hopelessly incomplete owing to the difficulties of transport and communication and to the disinclination of fifty per cent. of the men to answer the summons. The exact numbers mustered are not known, nor are they ever likely to be, but eventually three armies were formed, each consisting of two Nizam **Turkish debacle** Divisions and one **in Caucasia** composite Redif Division, and numbering about 55,000 men each. The remainder of this group of Divisions, mustering about 15,000 of the Nizam and 25,000 of the Redif, were retained at Erzerum and used on the lines of communication. The plan of the campaign, if such it may be termed, was to advance simultaneously upon the Russian frontier in two columns, a third column being retained two days' march in rear to act as a general reserve.

The Russians, out of an available Caucasian army of three-quarters of a million men,

contented themselves with pushing up 200,000 men towards the passes and awaiting the results of the Turkish offensive. The two Turkish columns had been timed to advance simultaneously over an exceedingly difficult country where already, in November, the snow lay thick on the uplands. Owing to faulty staff work and the appalling climatic conditions one of **Waist-deep in** the Turkish col- **snowdrifts** umns outdistanced the other. The Russian advance guard drew back, luring the enemy onwards, which is a time-worn trick of Russian strategy. The Turks fell into the trap, and having for two days announced a wondrous victory in optimistic telegrams to Europe, they struck, on the third day, the real Russian main body. A disastrous action followed; over 20,000 Turks were slain on the battlefield or were lost in the subsequent rout, and the remainder fell back in hopeless disorder. The second Turkish column met with no better success

CHEWING THE CUD OF BITTER REFLECTION: TURKISH PRISONERS IN EGYPT.
On another page is given a tabular statement of the units of the Sultan's Army. From this it appears that the total force available numbered 640,000 men. The above photograph is a souvenir of the disastrous attempt of Djemal Pasha to invade Egypt, and shows Turkish prisoners in the hands of the British. Inset: Prisoners being assisted by native railway guards to board the hospital train on their way to Cairo.

and an almost exactly similar fate. Both columns fell back in hopeless disorder, hotly pursued by the victorious Russians, who struggled waist-deep through the mountain snowdrifts. At the critical moment the Turkish reserves came up. Their junction with the fugitive columns synchronised with a snowstorm of unusual violence, during which the remnants of the Turkish army of invasion, reduced to about one-quarter of its original effectives, managed to effect their escape to Erzerum, while the Russians contented themselves by consolidating their positions and going into winter quarters.

In the meanwhile a subsidiary Turkish column had, with Teutonic disregard of international rights, invaded North-Western Persia and entered Tabriz. When the general Turkish retreat set in, a Russian cavalry force marched on Tabriz and, with very little difficulty, drove the Turkish invaders before them, being assisted thereto by the Persian mountain robbers of the vicinity, who joined in right merrily in the pillage of the convoys and transports which the Turks were obliged to abandon in their retreat. At the end of February the allied fleets were heard knocking at the door of the Dardanelles.

TURKISH INVASION OF NORTH-WESTERN PERSIA.

While the Germanised Turkish forces were making their way across the Sinai Peninsula and into the heights of the Caucasus, a subsidiary column, with utter disregard of international rights, entered Tabriz, the capital of the Persian province of Azerbijan. But with very little difficulty a Russian cavalry force drove out the invaders, being assisted in this enterprise by the native mountaineers, who were rewarded by the pillage of the convoys and transports which the Turks were obliged to abandon in their retreat. Inset. A Bedouin on his steed.

NIGHT OF A GERMAN DEFEAT: INVADERS OF POLAND MARCHING INTO CAPTIVITY.

A column of German infantry taken prisoners by the Cossacks after a Russian advance into Poland. A vigorous and impressive picture of the appalling devastation of war under modern conditions. The picture from which our illustration was taken is the work of M André Devambez, and its exhibit in the French capital attracted crowds of spectators.

CHAPTER XLIX.

FIRST GREAT CLASH OF SLAV AND PRUSSIAN.

How France Helped Russia—Russians only Faced by Inferior German Troops—Russia Half Crippled by Lack of Guns, Rifles, and Munitions—Closing of Dardanelles Cuts Off her War Supplies—Hindenburg's Rise to Power—The Kaiser Comes to Graievo to Watch Triumph of his Siege Guns—Hindenburg's Essay in Grand Strategy—Tries to Conquer Main Russian Armies by Cutting their Railway Line—General Situation of the Two Teutonic Empires—Russian Recoil from the Niemen Front—Battle of the Augustovo Forest—How the Cossacks Ringed and Routed their Enemies—Victory at Raczka—Siege of Osoviec—Russian Cavalry's Magnificent Charge against Siege Guns—Hindenburg Alters his Plan and Attacks Warsaw and Ivangorod—How the German Spies Helped the Russians—The Battle of Warsaw—Retreat of Northern German Army—The Battle of Kozienice—The Defence of Ivangorod—How the Austrians were Outplayed—General Defeat of the Entire Austro-German Armies.

FTER the first-line armies of Austria-Hungary had been thrown back confused and dispirited from Poland the position of Germany became insecure. She had about twenty-two army corps round her eastern frontier, but the number of these troops was more remarkable than their quality. All the first-line soldiers of Germany were retained before the French, British, and Belgian lines, and there they remained for many months. The early rumours of the movement of large bodies of the best German troops from France to Prussia or Poland were afterwards proved to be misleading. These rumours were put about by German agents with the intention of deceiving the French Military Staff as to the strength with which the Allies in France were still opposed. It was not until the early spring of 1915 that the presence of a single first-line German army corps was clearly traced by the Russians amid the hosts facing them.

In the original design of a defensive league between Russia and France, it was supposed by both parties that the mighty forces of the Tsar would protect the French nation from their aggressive and traditional enemy. But as things worked out, it was the smaller but more progressive and inventive Republic of Western Europe which protected the vast Russian Empire. The Russians never felt the full weight of the German military machine. For the French

fought with such amazing vigour and unrelenting tenacity that the German Great Staff was never able to swing its best armies into the eastern theatre of war. Germany at no time had more than her left hand free to deal with Russia. She had engineered the war directly against Russia, with a view to extending the Teutonic Empire to Constantinople, and from thence to the undeveloped wheat-lands of Mesopotamia. France was not directly threatened. The struggle was the final clash of Slav and Teuton in regard to Constantinople, the prospect of which had disturbed Europe for two hundred years.

In former days the strife and intrigue over the heritage of the declining Ottoman Turks had been chiefly confined to Austrians and Russians, with Napoleon I. and Napoleon III. intervening, and Great Britain keeping a watchful eye upon the situation. In the opening years of the twentieth century Austria still remained nominally Russia's competitor for the succession to Constantinople. But everybody except the Austrians themselves was well aware that the House of Hohenzollern had become the principal opponent of the claims of the House of Romanoff. The strong, upstart, enterprising Prussian Emperor was merely using the Hapsburgs as a battering-ram, with a view to absorbing both the conquering Austrian and the conquered Turk in a mighty Teutonic Empire, stretching from the North Sea to the Persian Gulf. It was because the Russians were resolved to perish rather than permit

KAISER WILHELM'S MISPLACED CONFIDENCE.
Just as the German Emperor visited the outskirts of Nancy fully confident that he would be able to witness the fall of that place, so he went east to see the fall of Osoviec—again to be bitterly disappointed. He is the figure on the left of the above photograph, the officer in the centre facing the camera being General von Mackensen. The Emperor's motor-car stands in readiness on the left.

PREPARING FOR THE WINTER CAMPAIGN.
Scene outside a store in East Prussia. Germans fitting themselves with waterproofs and oilskins.

Germany to take, through Austria, the first important step to dominate Constantinople by the possession of the Serbian river valley running towards Salonica, that the Great War broke out.

France was dragged into it as a matter of honour, through a treaty at first intended merely for her protection. But the aid which she gave to her mighty ally was of incomparable value. Germany went into the long-deferred struggle for Empire between Slav and Teuton with her right arm rendered absolutely useless. Six weeks after the war broke out the ally on whom she had strongly relied for help was shrilly clamouring for assistance. For the main Austro-Hungarian armies had been shattered, and were being shepherded into the river marshes of the San and the

Vistula by the victorious Russians. At that time Germany herself was in considerable difficulty. For all her first-line armies in France had been repulsed, and were retreating before the French and British troops. Had Russia been as strong as she seemed, the war might then have come to an end quickly. Germany was in such a position that she could not do more for Austria than she had arranged to do. Her twenty-two army corps of troops of only second and third quality, concentrated round her eastern frontier, were alone available. They covered the retreat of the Austrians and Hungarians, provided officers who reorganised the beaten armies of the House of Hapsburg, and took over the entire control of these re-formed troops and of the new formations. Otherwise not a man or a gun could be spared from the western theatre of the war.

German aid for beaten Austria

In spite of this fortunate condition of affairs, the Russian Commander-in-Chief could not press home the advantage he had won. For months afterwards the most he could do was to hold his own. He had trained men in overwhelming numbers and an abundance of food for them. But, in the circumstances, millions of these men were practically

RETREAT OF THE KAISER'S TROOPS IN EAST PRUSSIA.
German troops resting, during their retreat, in a town that had suffered severely from Russian bombardment. Inset: German supply column passing through a deserted town in East Prussia.

useless at the critical time. The war-machine of Russia was too small to absorb them. There were no rifles for them, no cartridges. Vast parks of field-guns and immense stores of shell and shrapnel were needed to form the absolutely vital artillery power of the great unemployed new Russian armies. So long as the ports of Archangel and Vladivostok remained free from ice and the Dardanelles was open to our cargo steamers, it was possible for Great Britain to set some of her factories working for her ally. To some extent, also, military stores could be obtained from the armament and ammunition firms of the United States and from Japan. But our country had also to assist France in the production of munitions of war, and to build up likewise a great machine for our army of two millions or more. As a matter of fact, our newly-raised troops went for some time without actual musketry training, because we were so busy supplying the fully-trained and ready troops of France and Russia that our own raw levies had to wait for their arms.

Russia's lack of war stores

Slowly but carefully the Russians began to extend their

COMMANDEERING BREAD FOR THE KAISER'S TROOPS.
Detachment of the German commissariat corps making a bread levy from a bakery in East Prussia.

military machine; but before they could bring the whole weight of their men to bear upon the Teutons and Magyars there was a complete interruption in the armament supplies by a telling stroke of policy that greatly prolonged the war. The Germans succeeded in dragging the Turks into their camp, and thus closing the Dardanelles all through the winter. Soon afterwards the northern Russian port of Archangel, with very feeble railway communication, was closed by ice.

Russia—being mainly an Empire of agriculturists, lacking the great, costly, and slowly built-up plant needed in making guns and rifles rapidly in large quantities—was half crippled by the closing of the Dardanelles. Her existing

EAST PRUSSIAN CONVENT AS A SUPPLY STORE.
Convoy of supplies arriving at German headquarters and being stored in a convent. Inset: German field kitchens that, with other impedimenta, fell into the hands of the Russians during the German retreat from Warsaw.

GERMAN TRENCH ON THE ANGERAP RIVER, IN EAST PRUSSIA.
Camera record of the operations near Darkehmen, East Prussia. The
Prussians were armed with mitrailleuses.

hundreds of German generals included in
" Wer Ist's "—the German "Who's Who."
He was one of the laughing-stocks of the
modern fashionable soldiers who took part
in the Kaiser manœuvres. All he was
known for was his curious hobby for
keeping the wild Masurian Lakes region
in East Prussia in its original state of un-
cultivation. The only thing that moved
him to leave his Hanoverian café and go
to Berlin, in the days
before the war, was a **Problem of the**
politician's proposal **Masurian Lakes**
for the drainage and
cultivation of the Masurian Lakes. He
called on deputies, he called on party
leaders, he pleaded before committees;
and when all these efforts of his proved
vain he went to the Emperor and begged
that the scheme for reclaiming the lakes
should be abandoned.

The ruling German military school
regarded the old man as a nuisance and
a fool, and as somewhat of a coward. They
agreed with the administrators who
wanted to drain the lakes, and thus to
open up to cultivation and to inhabi-
tation an immense region which had been
unproductive from the primeval age of
the world. Over the drained and populated ancient waste of marsh and water
the German Staff intended to march their
armies across the Niemen River and cut
the railway communication between

factories were barely sufficient to keep her field armies
supplied with raw material, and to continue the construction
and munitioning of her new fleet. The result was that the
Grand Duke Nicholas had to continue to fight the Teutons
with the odds still heavy against him.

All through the first seven or eight months of the war the
Russian field armies were inferior in numbers and artillery
power to the hosts opposed to them. Germany was able
to give a million rifles to the new Austrian levies and to help
to fit them out with field-guns. She had collected enormous
stores of armament in preparation for the great struggle.
As Russia, like France and Britain, had kept her military
stores at the ordinary low level, she also was taken at a
general disadvantage. Like her western allies, she had to
fight for time, and to look forward to
Where the Prussians a defensive action throughout the
were stronger winter. Only in the spring of 1915, when
she would at last be well supplied with
rifles and guns and ammunition, could she seriously undertake a grand offensive movement. Meanwhile, the Russian
steam-roller could not get up full steam.

All this, of course, was well known to the German Great
Staff. They were weakest at the point at which the
Russians were strongest, and strongest at the point at
which the Russians were weakest. All their infantry
in the eastern field of battle was of inferior quality, but
they had more ammunition and more weapons, and what
was of still more importance, they had a commander with
a genuine talent for war. More by luck than by skill
in selection, the circle of courtiers and intriguers gathered
about the Emperor Wilhelm and constituting the directing
minds of his Great Staff hit on a good man for the
command of their eastern armies. This man was
General von Hindenburg. His name is not given among

DEVASTATING EFFECT OF A GERMAN BOMB ON A RUSSIAN
RAILWAY TRACK.
Prussian airmen successfully dropped a bomb which shattered the rails
and burrowed deeply into the permanent way.

Warsaw and St. Petersburg. But, moved by the entreaties
of the old warrior, Kaiser Wilhelm stopped the scheme for
draining the lakes, and in the ancient watery wilderness
Hindenburg continued to spend his holidays every year.

Nobody in authority remembered him, even when the
Emperor and his Staff were thrown into deep perturbation
by General Rennenkampf's sudden raid into East Prussia.
The command of the new army of defence would have
been entrusted to another untried courtier-general who
had succeeded in pleasing the Emperor but for the
patriotism of General von Ludendorff, a fairly able man of
the younger generation connected with the Great Staff.
He is said to have urged the claim of his old master in
military studies, with the result that Hindenburg was
given all the forces he required for his long-thought-out
operations in the Masurian Lakes. There, towards the

end of August, as already related, the old general trapped the Russian army under General Samsonoff and captured one corps with a large number of guns.

The grizzled, bull-necked old fighting man at once became the darling of all the Teutonic peoples. The popularity of the Kaiser, the Crown Prince, Kluck, Moltke, and Heeringen paled before that of the saviour of Prussia. Meanwhile, Rennenkampf with his cavalry forces, outstretched between Königsberg and Kovno, continued a stubborn rearguard action all through the month of

OBSERVATION WORK IN A RUSSIAN
TRENCH IN EAST PRUSSIA.
While his comrades kept a sharp look-out, the soldier with the notebook entered the results of his observations for the use of the Staff.

September, with Hindenburg vainly trying to force the main Russian army of invasion into the lakes and marshes. Rennenkampf was greatly outnumbered in both men and guns, for his opponent had nearly half a million troops, with their artillery corps increased by guns worked by part of the garrison forces of Thorn and Graudenz.

So sure was the German commander of victory that the Kaiser Wilhelm left the western theatre of war, where he had been sadly disappointed, and came in his special train to Lyck, amid the Masurian Lakes, to watch the great triumph over the Russians. From Lyck the Emperor advanced to Graievo, over the Russian frontier, immediately behind his only successful army. Just

The Kaiser at Graievo fourteen miles southeast of Graievo was the Russian river fortress of Osoviec, guarding the high, dry road across the marshlands of the Bobr River. This was the critical point in all the dispositions of Russian troops made by the General Commander-in-Chief, the Grand Duke Nicholas, and by his Chief of Staff, General Sukhomlinoff.

Something like two million Russian troops, operating far away on the southern reaches of the Vistula against the main eastern forces of Germany and Austria, depended for food and ammunition chiefly on their railway-head at Warsaw. Warsaw in turn depended on its railway communication with Petrograd, and as the line to Petrograd ran close to Osoviec, and actually touched the River Bobr a few

miles northward at the town of Grodno, where the Bobr flows into the Niemen, there was good reason for the interest which the Kaiser took in the attack upon Osoviec. Hindenburg was no mean strategist. Early in life he had seen that the Masurian Lakes system, which extends far into Russia to the banks of the Niemen and Bobr, was the key to Russian Poland. By cutting the Russian railway at Osoviec or Grodno he could win Warsaw, and throw the main Russian armies back from Silesia and Posen without a battle. For if the railways were cut, starvation and lack of ammunition would force all the Russian troops in the bend **Von Hindenburg's** of the Vistula to retire towards the new **railway strategy** railway-heads of Siedlce and Brest Litovsk. And even before they could withdraw, the Siedlce line, close to the Warsaw line, could also be cut. Without a general battle the main Russian forces could be thrown back on Brest Litovsk, nearly two hundred and forty miles from the German frontier.

It will thus be seen that, in his fierce and ceaseless attacks upon Rennenkampf's Cossacks, maintained all through the month of September in the swamps and woods and waters of the Masurian Lakes system, Hindenburg aimed at more than freeing East Prussia from the invader. It was no wonder that the Kaiser melted in pride and gratitude for the one man among his millions of men who appeared to possess a gift for grand strategy. It seemed as though

"MUSIC HATH CHARMS"—BUT NOT TO SOOTHE THE PRUSSIAN BREAST.
German troops in a trench on the Angerap, singing national songs during a lull in the fighting.

SCENE OF THE GREAT STRUGGLE BETWEEN SLAV AND TEUTON IN THE WILD MASURIAN LAKES REGION.—THE LAND OF THE DISMAL SWAMP.
The whole of this region is dotted with lakes, and the roads between them are comparatively few and unreliable. This immense tract of country has been unproductive since the primeval age of the world. A proposal for draining this watery wilderness was vetoed by the Kaiser at the earnest request of General von Hindenburg, who had long ago studied its defensive possibilities.

the road to Petrograd, along which the Kaiser had never hoped to travel, would be more easy of access than the road to Paris. If General Joffre would only have allowed it, the original German war plan, drawn up by the elder Moltke, might have been reversed. The French, British, and Belgian forces would merely have been held by an immense line of entrenchments, while the chief immediate effort of conquest would have been directed by Hindenburg against the Russians.

As we have seen, General Joffre would not allow this to be done, but continued to make rapid outflanking attacks on all the first-line German armies, till the opposing **Allies in close co-operation** fronts stretched to the North Sea, and half a million new German formations had to be railed westward to keep Sir John French from breaking through between Ypres and Lille. As a matter of fact, neither General Joffre nor the Grand Duke Nicholas was fighting for his own hand by the third week in September. Both the allied Commanders-in-Chief then began to act in closer co-operation, and many an important stroke of war in France or Belgium was aimed directly at Hindenburg. In the same way many a stroke of war by the Russians, though apparently directed at Hindenburg, was aimed at Falkenhayn and struck him in Flanders. This close and intimate co-operation was born of the loyalty, the comradeship, and the superb skill in strategy which marked the operations of the Allies.

There were no separate fields of struggle in Europe. One immense connected battle raged in and around the lands of the Teutonic Empires. The allied front stretched from Holland to Courland and the marshes of Eastern Prussia. **Situation of the** In the middle it **Teutonic Empires** was broken by the neutral territories of Switzerland and Italy; but to the west of Italy the Serbian advance formed another part of the besiegers' front, with a lessening gap between it and the Russian columns which had invaded the Hungarian plain. Then from the Carpathian heights the main Russian armies stretched through Galicia and Poland to the Niemen River. At sea the British fleet under Sir John Jellicoe cut Germany off from the food-producing countries of America, while Admiral de Lapeyrère, operating in the Adriatic with a Franco-British fleet, cut off Austria and Hungary

REFRESHMENT BY THE WAY.
Prussian cavalry patrol about to sample some refreshment at a stall in a Polish village.

RUSSIAN RED CROSS TRAIN IN POLAND.
Soldiers of the Tsar, wounded in the fighting against the Prussians, returning by train to a base hospital.

from the Suez and Mediterranean supply routes. The naval power of the Allies was also exerted in an increasing stringency of examination into the destination of cargoes in neutral vessels. By this means the points of contact which the besieged Empire had with the neutral territories of Scandinavian, Dutch, Swiss, Italian, and Rumanian Powers were lessened in importance.

No attempt was made to counter Hindenburg's attack on the Warsaw-Petrograd railway line and recover the ground lost in Prussia. Instead, the Russian Chief of Staff sent up another army to hold the line of the Niemen and Bobr Rivers, and there retain Hindenburg as long as he cared to continue attempting vainly to break through. Russia, in short, began that process of stonewalling every German and Austro-German attack, which marked her strategy all through the winter and into the spring.

Russian feint and counter-stroke

Remarkable as was the talent for war of Hindenburg, he was powerless to make any progress against the new scheme of operations which the Russian Chief of Staff rapidly organised on the Niemen and Bobr river-fronts. General Rennenkampf extricated his troops at Stallupöhnen by the end of September, and withdrew towards Kovno. But this withdrawal was only a feint. The Russian commander only moved two miles from the German frontier in order to get into touch with a large reinforcement awaiting him. Then he swung back with a force as heavy and unexpected as that with which Hindenburg had originally swung forward. The German tried to hold the Russians in the north and to counter at three distant points farther south. He sent one strong army through the Forest of Augustovo, a second still stronger force

against Osoviec, and a third unusually large force was concentrated at Mlava, to the north of Warsaw.

The new battle began about the end of September on a front of about two hundred miles. It extended from the point at which the Niemen enters Prussia to the point at which the Ukra River, a tributary of the Narew, flows out of the district of Plock. All along this line of attack the Warsaw-Petrograd railway line continued to occupy the mind of Hindenburg. In the northern section, amid the woods and swamps of the Suwalki Government, Rennenkampf turned on his pursuer, with a terrible surprise for him. His Cossack forces had been sadly wanting in artillery power, but they were now provided, not only with an abundance of ordinary field artillery, but with heavy siege-guns from Kovno.

The German Landwehr and Landsturm troops were lured, in close formation, to attack the entrenched Cossacks

Hindenburg held on desperately to the important town of Suwalki by reason of its railway connections north and south with the Warsaw line. But dearly did he pay for his inability to admit the complete defeat of his plans.

South of Suwalki was the great dense Forest of Augustovo, a primeval waste of lakelets and morasses. There were no roads, but only a few narrow winding passages, running between water and bog, with all the approaches screened by the autumnal foliage of brushwood and trees. Only a few hundred Russian woodsmen knew all the safe ways through this prehistoric wilderness, where herds of aurochs, the cattle of the stone ages, used to roam down to modern times.

The Battle of Augustovo

Led by the woodsmen, the Cossacks and their artillerymen with light guns threaded the unmapped wilderness where the Germans had entrenched on the principal paths. This was the sort of fighting the Cossack liked. By woodcraft and scouting tactics he quietly discovered the enemy's positions. The Russian guns were hauled up and trained on the forest defences, while companies of Cossacks worked round by unknown ways and got on the flank and rear of the enemy. They were Don Cossacks, the fighters in the Augustovo Forest, men who reckoned themselves the flower of the Russian forces. They were opposed by four to five times the number of Germans; but these were mostly Landwehr and Landsturm men, the latter being often either seventeen to eighteen years old or over forty. Many of them were armed with rifles dating back to 1880 or to 1899, and they had only had a few weeks' musketry practice before they were entrained for the defence of East Prussia.

There is no need to describe what happened, for only the slaughter of the new formations at Ypres can compare

A HUMBLE SERVITOR OF THE ALLIES.
The donkey seen in the above photograph, in charge of a Russian infantryman, is helping to convey supplies to an outpost patrol.

close to the concealed positions of the new guns. At the same time Russian aviators, working with their gunners, reconnoitred for advancing columns of German supports behind the attacking line. Then the unexpected bombardment began. The Germans broke and fled, with shrapnel bursting over them for eight miles of their flight. The light German field artillery which Hindenburg used in this section of the lake country was completely overmastered by the heavy Russian guns, which had taken a week or more to haul into position in the arranged ambush.

As the guns cleared their path, the Cossacks, heading their reinforcements, drove again towards the hostile frontier. The hottest fighting took place on September 30th and October 1st at Mariampol and Kalvaria. Here the Germans were driven back two days' march nearer their own country than they had been at the beginning of the week. Their retreat was conducted in a heavy and continual rainstorm, which, in the swamp country, made the worst possible conditions for fighting against men so practised in guerilla methods of warfare as the Cossacks. In spite, however, of the adverse conditions,

SIDELIGHTS ON THE MUSCOVITE POSTAL SERVICE.
Sleigh heavily laden with postal packages for the Russian troops in the field. Probably never before have the postal services of great armies attained such huge proportions as in the British, French, Russian, and German commands during the Great War; and the transport difficulties that had to be surmounted by the Russian officials in Poland were even greater than those confronting the others.
Inset: A soldier of the Tsar posting a letter home.

GIVING THE POPULATION OF EAST PRUSSIA A TASTE OF BELGIUM'S SUFFERINGS.

In East Prussia alone, during the first six months of the war, was Germany made to feel the terror of invasion. Our picture is of a street in an East Prussian town which was wrecked by Russian guns. But the damage done was in the main confined to buildings, and even here restraint was exercised, the Tsar's artillerymen making a point of sparing the churches. And non-combatants were treated with a consideration never shown to their victims by the German invaders of Belgium and Northern France.

with it. Mile by mile the Cossacks worked through the forests, avoiding the easy known paths in their advance, and ambushing rearguard after rearguard, bivouac after bivouac. It was hard, slow work, scouting for the enemy and encircling him, but the actual fighting was a fairly safe and easy job. By the end of the first week in October the Don Cossacks had reached the village of Raczka, close to the German border. The river separated them from the forest where a brigade of German troops had retired, with two batteries of guns and eight armoured motor-cars.

Cossacks over the German border

In the night the Cossacks swam the river on horseback, and made a turning movement against the hostile brigade, and then at daybreak they charged into their lines at the rear. They took three thousand prisoners, together with the batteries and all the armoured cars. This left a breach in the defences of the German frontier, and the Cossacks, sweeping over the border, seized the German town of Biala on October 7th. Three days afterwards, the more important town of Lyck was captured by General Rennenkampf, by an outflanking movement on both sides of a German force to the north, which had held too long on to Suwalki.

Meanwhile, the principal German attack, conducted against the fortress of Osoviec under the eyes of the Kaiser, had not prospered. The Germans advanced by a single narrow road running alongside the railway line, with marshes on either hand. They posted their heavy artillery about five miles from the chain of forts, and their infantry entrenched some three miles closer to the threatened fortress. For four days the forts were bombarded night and day by 11 in. and 12 in. howitzers. But nothing happened. Russian fortress engineers had had a little experience at Port Arthur, and they had not designed Osoviec in the manner of Liège, Namur, and Maubeuge. The fortress was scarcely injured by the thousands of great shells hurled at it, and the Russian commander patiently waited until all the German forces available for the operation were concentrated against him, and comfortably entrenched and sited.

He knew exactly what was happening. For a Russian artillery officer, Colonel Martinoff, was hidden with a telephone near the German lines, watching all their movements, and directing the artillery fire of the fortress. When everything was ripe for the Russian counter-move, the colonel, who had not slept for eighty hours, telephoned his final observations. In the darkness of night, in a violent downpour of rain, two strong columns of Russian infantry advanced into the swamp on either side of the road held by the Germans. Guided by shepherds, who used the dry parts of the morasses as pastures, the soldiers picked their way over the winding track of firm land. When daylight came they were well on the flank of the enemy, but still hidden from observation. As they moved out to attack, a superb force of Russian cavalry crossed the bridge over the Bobr River at Osoviec, and gathering

The defence of Osoviec

RUSSIAN CAVALRY IN ACTION: BRILLIANT CHARGE BY THE FINEST HORSE-SOLDIERS IN THE WORLD.

A German artist's impression of an engagement between a body of Russian cavalry, some of the gallant men who crossed the Carpathians from Galicia, and a force of Germany's Austrian allies. In the early days of November, 1914, to the east of Neidenburg, near the station of Muschaken, about two miles from the East Prussian frontier, the Tsar's redoubtable horsemen routed a German detachment which was guarding the railway, captured their transport, and blew up some bridges. In the same month a German cavalry division, supported by rifles, was driven back towards Kalisz.

RUSSIA'S OLDEST VOLUNTEER.
Ivan Trufanoff, aged sixty-two, a Cossack, who has taken part with distinction in three wars.

INTERESTED SOLICITUDE FOR THE PRISONER.
A Siberian prisoner in the hands of Germans, who, after supplying him with food, are anxiously putting questions, the answers to which they hope to turn to their advantage.

RUSSIA'S YOUNGEST VOLUNTEER.
Constantin Malafeef, aged fifteen, promoted sergeant on the field, and for his bravery made a knight of the military order of St. George.

IN THE HANDS OF THE ENEMY.
Prisoners hailing from remote districts of Siberia captured in the early days of the fighting round the beleaguered fortress of Przemysl.

PRAYING FOR RUSSIA'S SUCCESS.
A Jew, of Bukovina, inspired by new hope for his race, praying for a Russian victory.

by the flanking infantry attack the Russian horsemen got halfway to the guns before the German foot soldiers were ready to oppose them. Meanwhile, the alarmed gunners tried to shatter the charging squadrons. But a siege-gun is not a rifle. It takes some time to alter its range. The first salvo of shells flew over the Cossacks. The second salvo was aimed too hurriedly and fell short. By this time the Cossacks were fully halfway to the batteries. The hostile artillerymen did not try a third salvo, but bent all their energies to getting their guns safely away by motor traction. Their infantry moved forward to hold off the cavalry. But it was too late. For the two flanking Russian infantry movements culminated at this minute as the Russian cavalry reached the foremost guns. Three pieces of ordnance were captured, and the force sent to defend the guns was killed or taken. Then, breaking through this rearguard, the Cossacks swept for ten miles along the road, overtaking the motor-vehicles with the guns and limbers.

A wonderful cavalry charge

The extraordinary success of this wonderful cavalry charge against siege artillery is indicated by the fact that not one horseman was killed. There were only sixteen casualties, and most of the wounds were slight. The two flanking infantry attacks across the swamps completely shattered the nerve of the Germans. Their gunners, with a five-mile field of fire to work over, could not place one shell or case-shot amid the advancing squadrons. In all some forty heavy guns, and a far larger number of

speed as they went through the town, swept between their own forts and charged the German siege-guns.

In the confusion caused by the

light quick-firers and machine-guns, were taken on the East Prussian front between October 1st and October 7th. The Battle of Augustovo began on September 25th and ended on October 4th. The siege of Osoviec began on September 26th and ended on October 1st. An attempt to pierce the Niemen defences at Drusskeniki, eastward of the town of Suwalki, was made on September 26th, but it failed, too. In less than a week the victorious Russian forces were again operating in East Prussia.

Thus, in spite of the preliminary success of Hindenburg at Tannenberg against the wing of the Russian invading force, the acclaimed saviour of Prussia had not been able to save his country from invasion. He had come up against Rennenkampf with numbers, railways, and artillery in his favour. But far from trapping the main Russian army of invasion, he had been completely defeated himself, and had had to give ground in his own country before the new victorious advance of his opponents.

Hindenburg has to give ground

Hindenburg, however, was not personally responsible for the series of German defeats around the Niemen River, for he had left all these operations to a subordinate general soon after the affair with Samsonoff. Hindenburg was an able man. It is not saying too much to credit him with the strength and force of character of Blücher and the skill in strategy of Gneisenau, but in the Grand Duke Nicholas he met a man superior to himself in ability and in the efficient force which he wielded.

Hindenburg did not have things all his own way as Moltke did. He had better communications, superior artillery, and larger numbers

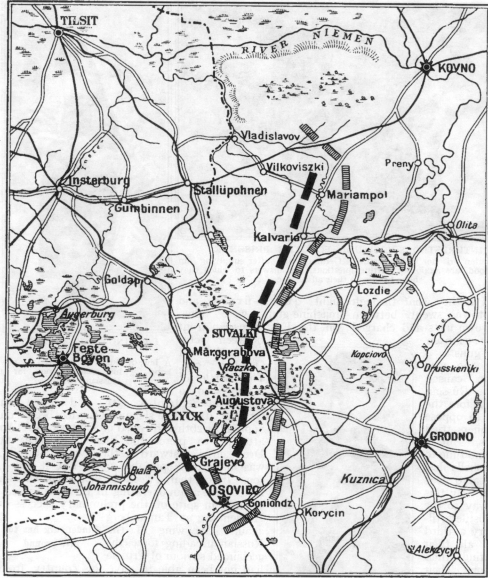

MAP OF THE TERRITORY BETWEEN THE NIEMEN AND THE MASURIAN LAKES.
Showing the area of the fighting which ended in the Russian victories at Augustovo and Osoviec, the relative positions of the opposing armies being represented by solid black lines for Germans and shaded lines for Russians.

the Grand Duke Nicholas, Ivanoff, and Russky. The important consequence was that all the chief moves of Hindenburg were continually anticipated by the Russian Staff, and that preparations were made against them. Early in October it was known to the Russians that the attack on their Niemen defences was partly a distraction intended to have the effect of inducing them to make a very great concentration of troops to protect their railway line of communication between Warsaw and Petrograd. Hindenburg was ready to push home his offensive in this region so long as it promised success. But when he found, in the first week in October, that his men were very firmly held, he adopted another plan of attack.

Leaving in the Masurian Lakes district what seemed to be a sufficient force of troops to continue a swaying battle with the Russians, he drew off about half his forces and railed them down to Thorn. Some weeks before this he had been strengthening his main force on the Warta River in Russian Poland. There he had brought up new formations from Central Germany, and reorganised the Austro-Hungarian armies at Cracow and the Galician heights. Only General Dankl was allowed to retain a veritable power of high command over part of the beaten armies of the Southern Empire. There was a wholesale dismissal or reduction in rank of officers, and in many cases the subjects of the Emperor Francis Joseph were displaced by men who owed allegiance to the Emperor William. Only the Hungarian officers escaped from this Prussianisation of the war-machine of the Hapsburg house.

The Northern Teutons treated the Hungarians as comrades, but dealt with the Austrians as with serfs. But it must be admitted that this sudden, rigorous, and thorough absorption and reorganisation of the Austrian forces by the German Great Staff was an effective and businesslike measure. It put a new power both of attack and resistance into the battered and broken armies of Austria-Hungary, and it is an achievement on which the Germans can justly pride themselves. It was mainly the enormous store of war material which the German Great Staff had prepared, when it decided on an aggressive attempt to dominate Europe, that enabled this achievement in reorganisation to be carried out on the spur of the moment.

Reorganisation of Austrian forces

By the first week in October Germany had a million and a quarter of her own men on the Polish front, with a quarter of a million Austrian troops immediately joining with them in front of Cracow. Fully another million of Austrian and Hungarian effectives were working against the Russian lines on the Galician battle-front, concentrating towards the upper course of the Vistula and the San Rivers. There were also a million troops of the third line collecting in the Hungarian plain for action against the Russian raiders

of troops than had the Russian commander. But, on the other hand, the Russians possessed more experience of war under modern conditions, troops of a finer quality, and somebody with a very high genius for strategy —probably the Chief of Staff, General Sukhomlinoff.

In addition, the chief Russian armies were commanded by men like Russky, Dimitrieff, Brussiloff, and Ivanoff, all of proved strength of character and genius of mind. Then the Grand Duke Nicholas had shown himself as remarkable an exception to the rule regarding the warlike ability of princely leaders as the young Austrian Archduke Charles did in 1796, when he beat both Jourdain and Moreau in the Wars of the Revolution. It will be seen that we have to go back fairly far into history to find some parallel to the emergence of an Imperial captain of the stamp of the Grand Duke Nicholas. Having threshed the weak elements of command out of her armies during the Manchurian campaign, Russia was immeasurably stronger than Germany and Austria in regard to leadership.

Emergence of an Imperial captain

Hindenburg was a very good man faced by still better men. In the main area of the struggle there were always at least four prime minds against his—those of Sukhomlinoff,

OPENING OF THE WINTER CAMPAIGN IN RUSSIAN POLAND.
Russian soldiers at work breaking ice on a Polish river.

THE GERMAN ADVANCE ON THE CAPITAL OF RUSSIAN POLAND.
Troops of the Kaiser, confident of victory, advancing over the East Prussian border to be broken against the Russian defences west of Warsaw.

German transport column in a Polish quagmire and attacked by Siberian horsemen. In his desperate effort to get his army back to his own frontier, the German commander buried many guns and quantities of stores. But he found the Siberians more deadly in attack than in defence. The retreating Teutons threw out strong rearguards, but one half of the German northern army had to be sacrificed to save the other half in the harassed retreat from Warsaw

During General von Hindenburg's attack on Warsaw a force of German cavalry was sighted by a Cossack patrol. To avoid a fight at close quarters, the Teutons dismounted and opened fire with their carbines. On came the Cossacks, and as they got nearer, one after the other, adopting their favourite manœuvre, dropped beneath the girths of their steeds. Thinking they had killed their adversaries, the Germans mounted, with a view to capturing

to the Warta. The pursuit was planned so that each Russian attack was made by fresh bodies of troops, and by the end of October, 1914, mounted Cossacks were threatening the frontier of German Poland at Kolo. Hindenburg's retreat was very like that of Napoleon from Moscow in 1812, and their tactics in 1914 demonstrated that the Tsar's soldiers retained many of the characteristics of their forefathers a hundred odd years ago.

what they supposed to be riderless horses. As they approached the latter, however, the Cossacks suddenly reappeared, and attacking the Germans with great fury, cut them to pieces. The Cossacks, like the Arabs, are superb horsemen, and their horses are as highly trained as the riders themselves. The Cossack lives for battle, and to him is due the Russian conquest of the whole of Northern Asia.

WATCHING THE FLAMES RISE FROM A BURNING VILLAGE IN NORTHERN POLAND.

The Russian general seen in the above photograph is watching a necessary, but to him regrettable, of the Tsar in their struggle with General von Hindenburg's forces in Northern Poland and East work of destruction. Only where it was imperative were villages committed to the flames by the soldiers Prussia, though the Germans proved as lustful of destruction in Russian territory as in Belgium.

who had crossed the Carpathians and had occupied Munkacs, Ungar, and other Hungarian towns. In both Hungary and Eastern Prussia the Russians were pressing against the flanks of the two Teutonic Empires. The obvious answer to these side pressures was a strong thrust against the Russian centre in Poland.

Against this centre the Germans had, in fact, concentrated at the opening of the war. They had crossed the border and had captured Czestochowa and Kalisz, and entrenched along the Warta River. Their position formed a long flat curve in Russian territory menacing Warsaw and Ivangorod. The Russian commander had scarcely 50,000 bayonets and 10,000 sabres operating in the rolling Polish plain—an immense region dappled and belted with forests, scantily provided with good roads, and served only by few railways. The Russian horsemen, with their infantry and light artillery supports, were little more than a reconnoitring and patrolling force, in just sufficient strength to discover any serious forward movement by the enemy. The Russian General Staff, indeed, deliberately left its line weak and yielding immediately in front of the main German armies. And the pressure that the Russians exerted on both their enemy's wings was also designed to induce the Germans to take the line of least resistance, and to attack from their centre in Poland.

So when Hindenburg advanced in the required direction he was only obeying his masters in strategy—the Russian Staff. The fact was, the Russians could not afford to attack the Germans on the Warta entrenchments. The Russian railway lines from Warsaw and Ivangorod were not sufficiently developed to supply a Russian army operating near the German frontier. In particular, there was no cross-country railway running parallel with the frontier by which the Russians could shift their troops swiftly and thus concentrate them for a series of feints and frontal attacks. The Germans, on the other hand, had two parallel railway systems running close to the Russian frontier. These railways were designed by the elder Moltke for the purpose of a border campaign with Russia. As a consequence the Grand Duke Nicholas refused to fight near the German frontier railways. He kept his main armies nearly a hundred and forty miles east of Moltke's battle-railway tracks. He left all Poland up to Warsaw and Ivangorod open to the enemy, merely occupying the country with reconnoitring forces based on the two Polish railway systems in the bend of the Vistula.

Moltke's battle-railway tracks

All this was known to Hindenburg. The manner in which he dealt with the situation is a fair measure of his powers. He made a remarkably swift attack, and so provided against possible defeat that when he was defeated he got away without losing any notable number of guns.

MAP OF THE COUNTRY EAST OF THE WARTA.
Illustrating the relative positions of Warsaw, Ivangorod, and Cracow. The black lines show the approximate positions of the German forces, and the shaded lines the Russian, when Hindenburg's army made its futile effort to reach the Polish capital.

"The Great War" copyright.

His first campaign on the Vistula was a tiger's leap, and though the tiger struck against a stone wall, he at least escaped from the pit dug for his doom. For Russia, six weeks after mobilisation, could not put into the field sufficient armed men to win the full advantage of her superior strategical position. She had millions of fairly well-trained troops waiting for rifles, artillery, and munitions. The Siberian railway formed the line of communication with ordnance works and ammunition factories in Japan and the United States. But it was choked with troops and Russian stores, and before American material reached it this material had to cross the American continent and the Pacific Ocean.

Russia, therefore, lacked the strength to hit back hard, even when she was apparently in a position to do so. Her Commander-in-Chief and Chief of Staff were occupied all the autumn and winter in solving the difficult problem of using three million fine troops to counter a series of attacks by four million soldiers of inferior quality. Considerable genius was required to divine where the two enemies would concentrate their forces, so as to be able to meet them without delay before they could break through the comparatively weak line of the Russian defences.

Russian front of 1,100 miles

THE "LAVA": A UNIQUE AND FAVOURITE METHOD OF ATTACK USED BY THE COSSACK CAVALRY.

Of all the distinctively racial methods of warfare the Cossack "lava" remains unique, and it was used with terrible effect against the Teutonic cavalry. The Cossacks allow the enemy to make the first move. Then they advance, three squadrons ahead extended in line, and two squadrons massed in close formation in the rear. This advance is made at a pace which renders any necessary turning movement to be carried out with ease and celerity. When some two hundred yards from the enemy, the pace is quickened to a gallop, and the front line divides into two sections, each of which swings outwards and spreads rapidly in file to attack the flanks of the foe. Coincidently the rear squadrons, now in the centre, engage the enemy in front.

From Memel on the Baltic to Czernovitz near the Rumanian border the Russians had to hold a front of about eleven hundred miles against the two Teutonic Empires. At any point along this immense line there was the constant danger of an unexpected concentration in overwhelming force by the enemy. The wonder is not that the Russians did not advance, but that they were able to hold on to their recovered province of Galicia, and to compel Hindenburg to attack them at the time and the place that they selected. In his first Vistula campaign Hindenburg divided his forces into four groups. The first army, formed of men drawn from East Prussia, worked up from Thorn, by the left bank of the Vistula. The second came from Kalisz and moved eastward through Lodz. These two armies concentrated against Warsaw. The third army, starting **Hindenburg's four** from Breslau, passed through Czestochowa, **invading armies** and following the southern bank of the Pilica River, turned towards the Ivangorod region. The fourth army, consisting of Austrians and Germans based on Cracow, moved up towards Kielce and Radom, and advanced north-eastward by the left bank of the Vistula.

Up till October 3rd the movement was a strategic deployment rather than an offensive attack. At this date the main Teutonic forces occupied a line running through Kutno, Lodz, Petrokoff, and Kielce. This was rather more than half-way between the German frontier and the Russian positions on the Vistula. At this time the German offensive movement against the right Russian flank on the Niemen was being defeated. But, as the Russian commander knew, his victory on his right wing denoted a withdrawal of the enemy's force for a stupendous attack against his centre. There then arose a ticklish problem for the Russian Staff. They had to foresee the point at which Hindenburg would hurl his main force. Would he try to cross the Vistula by the bridge at Warsaw or by the bridge at Ivangorod? At one place there would be a strong demonstration; at the other a long and desperate battle, where Hindenburg in person would launch some three-quarters of a million men on a wide front, strongly supported by artillery.

A victory at Ivangorod would be the more decisive; it would give a larger range for future operations against the Russian forces, and allow a turning movement against Warsaw, and another against the Russian position southward in Galicia. For this and other reasons the Russian Staff decided rightly that Ivangorod would be the critical point in their line of defence. But the trouble was that the troops which they were withdrawing from the Niemen front, in answer to the similar withdrawal of Hindenburg from this part of the battle-field, were collecting at Warsaw. This was their nearest point of concentration, and as the light railway between Warsaw and Ivangorod was heavily loaded with war traffic, the new reinforcement would have to march for a week to get into action at the decisive spot.

It was a situation of extreme difficulty; but the Grand Duke Nicholas coped with it by means of a very simple but yet effective trick. Nearly all the Jews in Russian Poland were eager for their country to be conquered by the Germans. In their view, there was more to be hoped for men of their creed from the Empire in which brilliant Jews like Ballin, Dernberg, Rathenaus, and hundreds of Jewish bankers and manufacturers had risen to eminence and power, than from the Russian rule that still prac- tically confined Jews in a pale, and prevented **German-Jewish** them from fully developing their gifts for **secret agents** finance and politics. The majority of the peasantry of true Polish race favoured the Russian cause, looking confidently to the re-establishment of the ancient kingdom of Poland under the suzerainty of the Tsar. The majority of the Jews, however, regarded this prospect with deep fear, and many of them became passionately willing to act as Secret Service agents of the invaders.

This condition of things seemed to add to the difficulties of the Russian Commander-in-Chief. But, by a stroke of genius, he transformed the German-Jewish system of espionage into a splendid instrument of Russian strategy. Warsaw was prepared for evacuation. Many of the Government officials left the city, and the troops, thrown out in front to entrench and guard the bridge, looked like a forlorn hope. About October 17th German aeroplanes began to soar over Warsaw. At first they dropped pamphlets in Polish, telling the people that the armies of redemption were at hand, and that Poland would soon be recovered from Russian tyranny. The Germans did not go on to state that all Russian Poles would then be treated as kindly as were

Civilian panic in their countrymen in Prussian **Warsaw** Poland. The Poles were left to draw this conclusion for themselves when the German airmen returned and began to throw bombs on the town. Women, children, and peaceful townsmen were killed, but no Russian soldier, for there were practically no Russian soldiers in Warsaw. The people, frightened by their defenceless condition, were swept by a terrible panic and poured out eastward to escape from the coming struggle. Nothing more hopeless than the appearance of Warsaw at this time was seen in any other field of the war. It was a combination of Paris, when the French Government was removing to Bordeaux, and Antwerp.

Naturally, everything that went on at Warsaw was soon known to Hindenburg and his Headquarters Staff. It led them to change their plan of attack somewhat, and to weaken their main offensive against Ivangorod, by detaching the second column to co-operate with the first, in a veritable attempt to carry Warsaw by storm. Nearly a quarter of a million men were assigned to this purpose, and what had only been intended as a demonstration was transformed into a real attack.

With the idea of making the most by this change in his plan, Hindenburg launched his two armies swiftly on the capital of Russian Poland before he began to threaten Ivangorod. By this means he hoped to distract the Russian Commander-in-Chief, and to induce him to attempt at the last moment to reinforce Warsaw at the expense of Ivangorod. The Grand Duke Nicholas must have smiled when he learned this last essay in strategy on the part of the enemy. For, as we have seen, Hindenburg had done everything that the Russians had wanted him to do. His army of spies in and around Warsaw pursued their work and communicated with the Germans, under the fostering attention of the Russian secret police. Every facility but one was placed in their way. It was only when they left the city in an easterly direction, and tried to find if anything were behind the crowd of fugitives, that their careers were suddenly closed. The country north

"An immense Blue- and east of the Bug River **beard's chamber"** was an immense Bluebeard's chamber, from which spies were not allowed to return. For in this region and on the Petrograd railway running through it was the Siberian army, with Cossacks and infantry from the Niemen front and wild, warlike Moslem horsemen from the steppes.

Unaware of the immense ambush before them, the quarter of a million Germans opened the battle with a series of skirmishes on Sunday, October 11th. The weak Russian

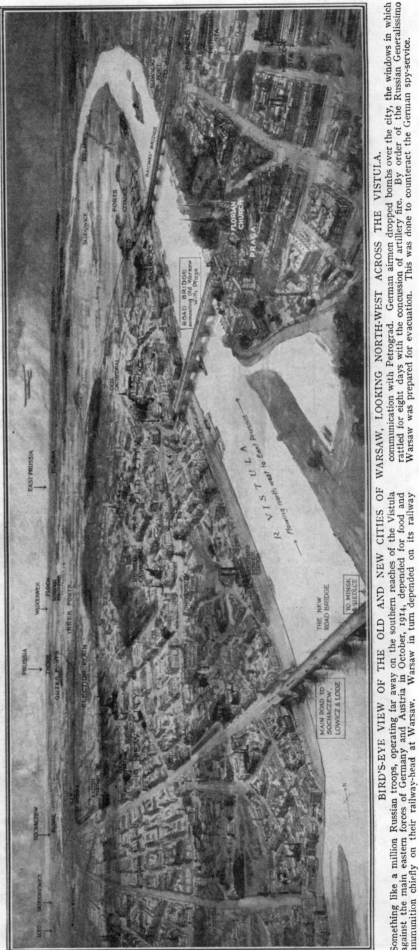

BIRD'S-EYE VIEW OF THE OLD AND NEW CITIES OF WARSAW, LOOKING NORTH-WEST ACROSS THE VISTULA.

Something like a million Russian troops, operating far away on the southern reaches of the Vistula communication with Petrograd. German airmen dropped bombs over the city, the windows in which against the main eastern forces of Germany and Austria in October, 1914, depended for food and rattled for eight days with the concussion of artillery fire. By order of the Russian Generalissimo ammunition chiefly on their railway-head at Warsaw. Warsaw in turn depended on its railway Warsaw was prepared for evacuation. This was done to counteract the German spy-service.

WHERE HINDENBURG WAS CHECKED.
Portion of railway track marking the spot where General von Hindenburg
was compelled to retreat.

advance guard fell back, continually fighting, between the Vistula and the northern bank of its tributary the Pilica. The Russian force was first composed of masses of cavalry, supported by infantry detachments; but at every stand they made the infantry and artillery power increased, especially on their northern wing.

The enemy, however, was always thrusting forward with remarkable impetuosity to find the weak section in the Russian line. This section they discovered far away from Warsaw, by the northern bank of the Pilica. Here they drove in till they passed the town of Varka, and reached the Vistula at the point where the Pilica flows into it. It was rainy weather; the roads were in a terrible state; the rivers were in flood and their valleys turned into morasses. It was not a river but a great lake to which the northern German army was allowed to penetrate with its southern wing. There it was permitted to rest, while the decision was being fought out round Warsaw—some days' march northward. There, backed by a converging system of railways and with the only bridge across the river in his hands, the Russian commander played with the enemy; for on his right was Novo Georgievsk, one of the strongest fortresses in Russia, worth an army for the support it gave to the right flank of the Russians.

The Russian advance guard continued to retire till its lines swung back a few miles from Warsaw. It entrenched at just sufficient distance from the city to prevent the large German field-guns from bombarding the Polish capital. The Russian artillery had already been sited in sufficient number and power to engage on at least equal terms the guns which the Germans were

The Battle of Warsaw

GERMAN ENGINEERS INSPECTING A DAMAGED RAILWAY LINE ON THE ROAD TO WARSAW.
The single-track line shown in the above photograph is apparently that running between Warsaw and Kalisz, a branch of which runs into Lodz. It had been torn up by the Russians and was repaired by the Germans. Inset: Destruction on the main Russian Kalisz-Lodz-Warsaw line.

GERMANS IN WARSAW—BUT NOT AS THEY EXPECTED TO BE.
Marching German prisoners through the streets of the Polish capital.

hauling forward. As the Germans brought up their guns and their ten or eleven infantry divisions, there was a remarkable hardening of the Russian resistance. Every night large bodies of Russians crossed the Vistula bridge and took up their positions in the trenches. The Germans were never allowed to slacken in their attack. If they tried to do so, there followed a tremendous infantry charge against their positions, which compelled them to counter-attack with all available forces. For eight days the windows of Warsaw rattled with the concussion of artillery fire, and the thunder of the neighbouring batteries rolled over the picturesque, historic city.

The Germans fall back The Russians made their first attack in the middle of October. This brought the Germans out of their trenches in massed formation on Saturday and Sunday, October 17th and 18th. Swept by shrapnel, mowed down by rifle fire, and at last driven in by the bayonet of the Siberian troops, the Germans fell back. To strengthen their lines before Warsaw, their commander was obliged to call in part of the army corps resting on the Pilica and the Vistula. He did this on the night of Monday, October 19th. About the same time a very strong Russian column marched south along the right bank of the Vistula, while the Germans were marching north on the left bank. The Russian column reached Goura-Kalvaria, a little more than half-way between Warsaw and Pilica River. Bringing up guns to dominate the crossing of the broad, swirling waters of the Vistula, the troops made a pontoon bridge on Monday night, October 19th. On Tuesday morning men and guns crossed the river and attacked the weakened wing of the German northern army. At the same time another Russian column was sweeping northward round by Novo Georgievsk, and menacing the right wing of the Russian army.

A WAYSIDE LUNCH IN RUSSIAN POLAND.
Russian generals partaking of a frugal meal during the operations along the Vistula.

ON THE TRACK OF THE FLYING FOE.
Cossacks examining some empty barrels left in a Polish village by the retreating Germans.

RECONSTRUCTING A BROKEN RAILWAY BRIDGE IN POLAND.
German engineers reconstructing the railway bridge at Sieradz, east of Kalisz. The gap has been temporarily filled by pontoons.

The effect of these two movements was to bring the German attack upon Warsaw to an abrupt end; for on the night of October 20th the enemy began to evacuate his position on the Goura-Kalvaria front, and to prepare a general retirement. The elaborate scheme of fortifications, intended to hold the Russians across the Vistula during the winter campaign, was abandoned without a struggle. All that the German commander **Fate of Northern German Army** then hoped and worked for was to get his army back to his own frontier with little loss. He buried many guns and stores of shells as he withdrew. But he could not avoid terrible losses in men, for the Siberians were even more deadly in attack than they were in defence. Like most of the colonial troops of the white races, they were the picked spirits of their mother country, distinguished from the stay-at-home population by their initiative, enterprise, and venturesomeness. Born sharpshooters, and as fond of the bayonet as the French, they were irresistible in attack. And as the Russian artillery skilfully and thoroughly prepared the ground for them, they worked forward very quickly.

Two German army corps—the 17th and 18th—tried to make a stand at the villages of Bloni and Pasechno, the first sixteen miles west of Warsaw and the second twelve miles south of it. There were 60,000 German bayonets holding the two villages, and fed and munitioned by the railway from Skernievice. But the Siberians got on their left flank, operating from the fortress of Novo Georgievsk. Then came the slaughter. There was only one way for the German commander to prevent his retreat from becoming a rout. He had to throw out continually strong rearguards to enable his heavy guns to be buried or got away before the Cossack horsemen got in front of the batteries. In fact, half the northern German army had to be sacrificed to save the other half and the guns. For the Russians were in such force, and were moving so quickly over the rolling prairies and forests, that a continual enveloping movement went on against each German rearguard.

Every village which the Germans tried to hold was shattered by the light field artillery of the pursuers. And while the shells were falling, the Russian impi—infantry in the centre and horse at the horns—advanced, and began to lock round the smaller hostile force. It was something more than a retreat and something less than a rout. It was a race for the **Surrender of Lodz and Lowicz** German entrenchments on the Warta. Between this river and the Vistula there was only one river-line on which the Germans could have made a stand—the line of the Bzura River, running through Lodz. But the trouble was that Lodz was a rich, industrial town, financed by the Germans, and run by them and by their Jewish sympathisers. So Lodz and Lowicz had to be surrendered without a struggle for the sake of German commercial interests. Moreover, the Cossack cavalry still continued to ride down the Vistula on its flanking movement. There

GUARDING THE RUSSIAN FLAG.
Armed escort of the Tsar's soldiers bringing in colours to the Russian Headquarters. Inset : Austrian prisoners in Galicia, on their way to a Moscow concentration camp.

were many places where German sappers prepared extremely elaborate positions along the ridges of the rolling country, with deep trenches, abatis of felled forest trees, and gun-sites with a clear sweep for fire as far as field artillery could carry. Yet the rearguard did not stay one day at many of these points. At the first **From Warsaw to** threat of an outflank- **the Warta** ing movement they fled to save the guns.

The general method of the Russians in these rearguard actions could be studied at the pretty little Polish city of Skernievice. On a ridge six and a half miles from the town were the German fortified lines; they had been abandoned without a struggle. Half a day's march farther west was another ridge near a forest. A Russian infantry brigade crept forward under the cover of its guns, took the forest at the point of the bayonet, and then turned the German trenches. The victorious troops rested for a day on the field they had won, while another brigade took up the pursuit, with the Russian cavalry spread out before it. In this way each Russian attack was made by fresh bodies of soldiers always on the march. At the same time the more fatigued, victorious brigades and divisions also advanced after a brief rest, in case the enemy should attempt a general stand. But this the Germans did not do, and by the end of October the mounted Cossacks were threatening the frontier of German Poland.

While the northern German army was thus being defeated and pursued from Warsaw to the Warta, the main central German force attacked Ivangorod. The general situation was very interesting. Swift and overwhelming as had been the defeat of the German northern wing before Warsaw, this did not bring about the retirement of the whole German front. The stronger central army of invasion, massed against Ivangorod, still hoped to retrieve the situation by forcing the passage of the Vistula and wedging itself between the Russian lines.

In this part of the field the Russian troops were commanded by General Russky, the victor of Lemberg. His army held more than a hundred and fifty miles of the winding course of the Vistula, from the point where the Pilica falls into it to the point where the Kamienna flows into the great river near Jozefov. These geographical details are of vital importance, for the distance from Russky's left wing to the battlefield of Warsaw was equal to seven days' hard marching. That is to say, Hindenburg had a week's grace in his operations round Ivangorod, in which **Battle for the** he could attempt to **Central Vistula** force the Vistula with no fear of any attack on his rear by part of the conquering Russian force from the Warsaw section. If Hindenburg won, the retreat of his northern wing would be an affair of no importance. He would still be master of the whole of Russian Poland, Warsaw being his to take when he liked to concentrate upon it, and the Russians of the southern reaches of the Vistula and the San Rivers would be at his mercy.

As a matter of fact, a strong Russian

NEWSPAPER CORRESPONDENTS' "WAR SPECIAL" IN THE EAST.
A number of war correspondents were allowed to follow the Russian armies in the field. Among those invited was Professor Pares, of Liverpool University.

A WELCOME GIFT FROM A FRIENDLY SLAV.
Russian soldier providing a German prisoner with "something to smoke," much to the interest of the onlookers. Inset: A bombarded town in Galicia, where the church was spared.

ENEMIES UNITE IN AIDING
THE WOUNDED.
Russian and Austrian Red Cross doctors
attending a wounded Austrian soldier.

column had set out from
Warsaw to reinforce General
Russky's army. Marching
through the rain and mud at
an amazing speed, it came up
at the critical point in the
central battle, and took the
enemy by surprise. An un-
paralleled vigour of movement
in bad weather over bad roads
enabled this column to beat
Hindenburg at his own game of
unexpectedly swift concentration. But whereas the Germans relied on the handling of
railways in these strategic
feats, the Russians trusted to their feet.
It was their physique that enabled them
to get the winning move.

Meanwhile the battle for the Central
Vistula was conditioned by the dense
forests in this region. There were only
three large open spaces of nearly level
country available for army operations with
a clear field for gun fire. The chief of
these open spaces was the plain of
Kozienice, running fourteen miles along
the Vistula, with a breadth of less than
six miles. It was about a day's march
from Ivangorod. Beyond it, in the
direction of Warsaw,
German semicircle was the open space of
round Ivangorod Glovachev, with a clear
battle-plain fifteen
miles long by ten miles broad. Then south
of Ivangorod was the open space of
Politchna. In all three heavy Russian
guns were placed on the opposite side
of the Vistula, while troops entrenched on
the plains to hold back the enemy. The
Germans moved forward under the cover
of the forests on the southern bank of
the Pilica. They occupied the town of
Glovachev and the larger town of Radom,

and deployed until their forces formed a
mighty semicircle round Ivangorod. Their
intention was to clear the plains of
Glovachev and Kozienice of Russian
troops, and then to force the passage of
the Vistula at these points and envelop
Ivangorod from the north, while making
also a frontal attack and a southern
enveloping movement from Radom. Here
the open space of Politchna by the Vistula
was the principal scene of struggle.

The battle opened with a series of small
successes for the Germans. Each of the
three open spaces was held by only small
bodies of Russian troops, the main defending armies being drawn up on the other
side of the great river. The idea was to
hold the open spaces as
bridge-heads, where the **Fierce fighting in**
principal Russian forces **forest paths**
could cross by pontoons
when the army of invasion had been forced
to reveal its attacking dispositions and had
been shaken by bombardments from the
numerous concealed Russian
batteries firing over the river.
But small though the Russian
advanced bodies were, they did
not act passively and simply wait
to be attacked. In all the forest
paths were fierce and desperate
encounters with each thrusting
wedge of Hindenburg's armies.
With Maxim, rifle, and bayonet
the Russians continually kept
the enemy off, until the Germans brought up their field-guns
and shelled the Russians out of
their positions.

Then at Kozienice the Russian
troops entrenched and the battle
was joined in a general fury.
The small line of advanced

A TOUCH OF NATURE IN LEMBERG.
When the Russians captured Lemberg they allowed their prisoners to be visited by their
friends. We are able to give above an interesting camera record of this act of kindliness
on the part of the victorious Muscovites. Inset: Homely interlude in a Russian trench;
cheery Slav soldiers preparing a meal.

troops became a bait to the mighty attacking force, and for nearly fourteen days it had to fight, like our 7th Division at Ypres, against a continual bombardment of shells, varied by infantry attacks in dense, deep lines. But about Thursday, October 22nd, reinforcements began to arrive from the opposite bank of the Vistula. The resisting Russian line lengthened out and thickened, and began to threaten a flank attack on the enemy. The Germans retired from the open space into the

The Battle of Kozienice forest, which was so dense with trees and underwood that a man could hardly see fifty feet around him. In this jungle the Germans had about forty-two guns to the mile, and every possible path was defended by rifle pits, with machine-guns and abatis defences. The Russian artillery was no longer able to support its infantry, as it was only wasting shell and shrapnel to try and search for the hostile positions. All that the Russian commander could do was to send his foot soldiers into the forest to poke the enemy out with the bayonet. Day after day brigade after brigade of Russians entered the tangle of trees and vanished from sight. Companies, regiments, battalions lost touch with each other, and in places brigade was cut off from brigade. Few Russian colonels there knew what was going on anywhere, except in the patch of ground on which their men were fighting. But every Russian knew that the only thing required of him was to push the enemy out. This he did yard by yard, and hour by hour, in one of the fiercest hand-to-hand struggles in his-

RUSSIAN CHARITY IN GALICIA.
Russian priest, assisted by soldiers, distributing money to poor children in Galicia.

tory. It was a soldiers' battle, won by bullet and bayonet—mainly the bayonet.

The Germans left 16,000 of their dead in the woods and thickets of Kozienice when they broke and fled on Monday, October 26th. On this day the German retreat from Ivangorod was general. At Glovachev their Twentieth Army Corps and Reserve Corps of the Guards were defeated and driven along the southern bank of the Pilica. In the centre the Russians carried the forest villages at the bayonet point. At Politchna, on the left wing, the enemy's defences were stormed, thousands of prisoners were taken with many guns, and the invading army thrown back to Radom.

While this frontal attack by the Teutons upon the Ivangorod bend of the Vistula was being repulsed, still more interesting things were happening farther south up the river at Jozefov. Here the Austro-Hungarian army, under General Dankl, was opposed by part of the southern Russian army, under the Bulgarian General Dimitrieff. Farther away was General Brussiloff, holding Lemberg and the greater part of Galicia, with part of Hungary, against the attacks of the new **Austria's new** militia forces of the **formations broken** Dual Monarchy. General Brussiloff had especially to protect the railway line, running from Lemberg to Kieff, by which his troops were provisioned and munitioned. He was greatly outnumbered by the new Austrian and Hungarian levies operating in the extreme south. Yet he had to hold Lemberg and the railway line against them, and at the same time help to defeat General Dankl's

A MEAL A LA RUSSE IN THE OPEN.
Russian soldiers snatch a hasty meal on the Galician plain while one of their number keeps a look-out. Inset: Russian officer making observations in Galicia.

BRIDGE DESTROYED BY THE GERMANS BEFORE LODZ.
The invading army under General von Hindenburg made strenuous but unsuccessful efforts to intercept the Russian railway communication at this point.

forces on the Vistula. He split his armies up. About half of the troops were left in Galicia under the personal direction of Brussiloff; the other half was sent up towards the Vistula, under the command of Dimitrieff. Brussiloff abandoned the siege of Przemysl, retired from Jaroslav, and, entrenching between these towns and Lemberg, he held out against all the assaults of the new armies of the southern Teutonic Empire. South of Przemysl, on October 27th, one of these new armies attempted a flank attack on the Russian line. The battle took place fifteen miles south of the town of Sambor, in a hollow plain amid the foot-hills. But the Russians also had newly-formed regiments, railed from Kieff, to counter the enemy's new formations. The Russian recruits shepherded their foes into the river valley and then rushed up the heights, from which they poured a terrible fire, until the Austro-Hungarian force was practically annihilated. Only a few hundreds escaped, in small squads, by the paths used by the mountain sheep. All their guns and convoys were captured. While breaking the enemy up in this manner in the valleys, General Brussiloff continued **Cossacks over the** to send raiding brigades of Cossacks over **Carpathians** the passes of the Eastern Carpathians to menace the Hungarian wheat-plains of the Danube, and to force the enemy to concentrate against him all along the mountains. His scheme of operations completely succeeded; for though the Russian raiders had at last to draw back to the mountain passes, they continued for months to detain large forces of the enemy in the ravines and high valleys. Meanwhile Lemberg was safely and firmly held until the siege of Przemysl could be renewed.

This magnificent and stubborn defence, conducted by the extreme southern wing of the Russian forces, allowed the neighbouring army, under the Bulgarian General Dimitrieff, to act more freely. Dimitrieff, who had led the Bulgarians in their victories against the Turks, and was acting as Bulgarian Minister in Petrograd on the outbreak of war, had accepted a Russian command, though he was promptly disgraced by the Bulgarian Government. His glorious achievements, performed for his brother Slavs, were one of the principal factors in swaying the minds of the Bulgarian democracy away from Austria towards Russia. Dimitrieff was engaged in the preliminary operations for the siege of Cracow until Hindenburg attempted to get the whole line of the Vistula as a base for a winter campaign. The Russians then had to retire, leaving the upper reaches of the Vistula in the hands of the enemy.

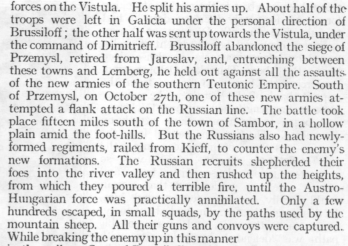

THE MOBILISATION IN SIBERIA: COSSACKS IN MODERN SERVICE UNIFORM.
Inspection of a squadron of Cossacks in a little Siberian town prior to their departure for the battle-front in Poland. Inset: A Russian battery working under the direction of an observation officer, who is locating the enemy's position from a field-ladder.

RUSSIAN ARTILLERY IN ACTION DURING THE PRUSSIAN
ATTACK ON WARSAW.

RUSSIAN RED CROSS WORKERS REMOVING WOUNDED
AUSTRIANS FROM A GALICIAN BATTLEFIELD.

Apparently the strength of the defending forces was over-taxed by the great numbers brought against them, for there was a gap of more than sixty miles along the Vistula and the San Rivers. All that Dimitrieff left was a thin cavalry screen to test the strength of the enemy's movement and watch the course of their advance. The Austro-German troops might have made things difficult for the Bulgarian general had they tried to curve round him from the north. But, as he had rightly divined, they used the gap, under the direction of Hindenburg, to strike at the more important objective of Ivangorod. They crossed the Vistula near Jozefov, the last point held by the Russians in strength. Meeting with no opposition, for the Russian cavalry retired as they advanced, the Austrians marched northward through the Lublin district, with the intention of taking the main Russian army gathered about Ivangorod suddenly in the rear.

The extraordinary success of their manœuvre must have been very exhilarating to them. Alone of all the invading armies they had crossed the Vistula, practically without a struggle, and there remained no obstacle between them and the Russian forces entrenched farther down the river, around whom they were curving. But the alluring gap through which they had first passed was only a mouse-trap on a large scale. At the southern end of the gap General Dimitrieff was in wireless communication with the Russian commander at Nova Alexandria, some fifteen miles south-west of Ivangorod. As the trapped Austrian army moved northward, Dimitrieff followed them and closed the gap ; and at the same time a strong Russian force moved south from Ivangorod.

The long-prepared surprise occurred with fine exactitude on the fatal Monday, October 26th, when Hindenburg's main army was being pushed back to Radom. The Austrians across the Vistula were marching hard to time with the already defeated movement by the German Commander-in-Chief. After a long stretch of level country with squashy, parish roads, varied by patches of marsh, the troops making the turning movement came, weary and yet unsuspecting, to the hilly country near Nova Alexandria. There they struck against a considerable force of Russians, who had done their marching the day before, and were well rested, well fed, and eager for the fight. The Russian guns were posted on the heights, with all the ranges nicely marked beforehand. Under the cover of a furious shrapnel fire the defending infantry

The long-prepared surprise

attacked with the bayonet. So swift and fierce was the onset that the Austrians were killed before they could make up their minds to surrender. Every one of them fell, and their guns and train were taken.,

As this action opened, Dimitrieff, farther up the river near Jozefov, crossed the Vistula and advanced along its tributary, the Kamienna, towards the Polish mountain range of Lysa Gora. This long line of heights extends in front of the city of Kielce, and Dimetrieff designed to forestall the main German army by occupying the heights and the rivers north and south of them—the Kamienna and the Nida. His extraordinary situation, some forty miles in the rear of the retreating main forces of Hindenburg, is evidence of the assured skill and reliant foresight with which the Russian operations were planned. By letting through the doomed Austrian force without a struggle, he co-operated in closing the trap on it, and at the same time, by sweeping across the Vistula in turn, he unexpectedly arrived behind the main army of invasion on its day of defeat.

So great was the menace of this move against his rear that Hindenburg had to withdraw from the line of the Vistula and huddle his troops westward along the southern bank of the Pilica. And there, amid the forests, they were harried by Russky's men. Some of the troops of the main Russian army got behind a wood in which one of Hindenburg's rearguards was entrenched with artillery, and fired it in four places while a strong wind was blowing. Few of that rearguard escaped from the most terrible of deaths. They died in thousands from suffocation or from fire.

It was in these circumstances that Hindenburg took a

step which is likely to sully his fame, and to prevent the Catholic Teutons and Magyars from ever forming again a warlike federation with the Protestants of Prussia. For in the terrible week of the first great retreat from Russian Poland the Prussian Commander-in-Chief deliberately sacrificed the Austrians and Hungarians in tens of thousands in order to give his own countrymen an opportunity of escaping. It is quite likely that Hindenburg found that the Austrians were already so much shaken by their early defeats that their fighting value was of **Rearguard action** small importance. But even so, it was **round Kielce** hardly fair to weed them out of his army for continual rearguard actions, in which they scarcely won a day's respite for the fugitive forces of Germany.

The chief rearguard action of this sort took place round Kielce on the night of Monday, November 2nd. The Austrian army, under General Dankl, held a long line of heights, with woods screening them from artillery fire and streams moating their positions. But the Russians under General Dimitrieff did not trouble about clearing their path with shrapnel. They had been driving the enemy along for a week at the speed of fifteen or twenty miles a day. The hero of Kirk Kilisse was well acquainted with the feeling of demoralisation in the ranks of an opponent. When evening fell he sent his troops forward in open order with fixed bayonets. Under the deepening darkness they crept close to the enemy's lines, and groping for him in the night they stabbed their way through his trenches and broke his front. When dawn came, and General Dankl was able to gather clearly what had occurred, no orderly retreat was possible. His entire line had been crumpled up. It was a rout. The last troops of the enemy left the city of Kielce at ten o'clock the following morning. Before noon the Russian soldiers were marching into the square. For hours they swung through the streets in their dirty grey coats, stained with the mud of trench and battlefield. Then, as daylight began to fade, the rumble of artillery fire came from the south. Dimitrieff and his men were working southward amid the hills and woods of the Nida to the upper reaches of the Vistula by Cracow. They entrenched on a southern tributary of the great river which they were to make famous by their long swaying movement of attack and defence against the troops holding Cracow.

The tributary they held was the Dunajec, which runs by the city of Tarnow, to Neu Sandez, in the Eastern Carpathians. There the remnants of what was once one of the main Austrian armies was now reduced to three army corps. Strengthened by a German division, it formed the eastern garrison force of Cracow. Eight miles beyond it were two 16·5 in. siege-guns of Krupp manufacture, and

closer to the Russian trenches were some hundreds of 6 in., 8 in., and 12 in. howitzers. On some days a thousand shells were pitched into the Russian lines. But Dimitrieff did not lose many men. So well were the Russian shell-proof trenches constructed that it took on the average a hundred Austrian shells to kill one Russian soldier.

All through the winter and far into the spring the strange siege went on. It was difficult at times to discover whether Dimitrieff was besieging the Austrians in Cracow or whether the Austrians were besieging him on the Dunajec. General Dimitrieff, however, had no doubt in the matter. He professed himself ready to carry the Austrian trenches and to break open the gate into Silesia at the word of command from the Grand Duke Nicholas. But the Russian Commander-in-Chief preferred to keep the enemy attacking through the mud of the Polish plain and the marshland of the lake region round the Prussian frontier. Russia was not ready to strike her great blow until arms and ammunition for her new armies arrived in the late spring of 1915. Meanwhile, scope was allowed to Hindenburg to make another attempt on Warsaw, and to maintain an offensive movement in the long, terrible, wearing Russian winter weather, in which the forces of Nature operated on the side of the hardy, enduring, patient, armed peasantry of the great agricultural Empire. Being practically in a state of siege, with an almost complete deadlock in the western theatre of the war, Germany and her unfortunate ally could not allow the Russians also to hem them in. The pressure on them was so great that they had to attempt sorties on a tremendous scale. Thus, under favouring conditions for the Powers of the Triple Entente, the struggle went on through the winter, with Russian Poland, the Masurian Lakes, and the snow-covered passes of the Carpathians as the chief scenes of conflict.

In the western theatre of war the Allies had definitely won the initiative, and, while holding the enemy all the winter, the French and British armies were improving their artillery.

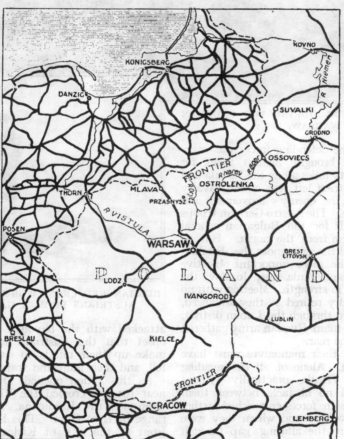

THE SECRET OF GERMANY'S MILITARY MOBILITY.
Even the best maps of the military areas do not show all the railways with which Germany, in pursuance of her long-established intention of making war, had covered her frontiers. This sketch map shows all the known strategic railways and branch lines on her eastern frontier, and it will be seen at a glance how terribly handicapped the Russians were in concentrating against the German forces, whereas Germany could swing her armies about from any part of the frontier.

In the eastern theatre of war the Russians could not reduce the fortress of Przemysl, which was relieved by the Austrian forces during Hindenburg's first vain advance against Warsaw and Ivangorod. But when Dimitrieff swung down again towards Cracow, Brussiloff also closed once more round **The siege of** Przemysl, and entrusted the task of **Przemysl** reducing the fortress to one of his best subordinate officers, General Selivanoff, a veteran of the Turco - Russian War. Early in November General Selivanoff entrenched his troops on a thirty-mile circle round Przemysl, out of range of the fortress, and waited. He had a more terrible weapon than a gun—famine. It was slow but deadly sure.

General Joseph Jacques Césaire Joffre.
Commander-in-Chief of the French Army.

JAPANESE ARTILLERY | CHAPTER L. | AT SHANTUNG.

JAPAN'S INTERVENTION IN THE GREAT WAR: THE STORY OF TSINGTAU.

By F. A. McKenzie, Author of "From Tokyo to Tiflis," "The Unveiled East," etc.

Facts Behind the Ultimatum to Germany—How the Japanese People Nursed their Wrongs and Prepared for Reprisals—Rise of the City of Tsingtau, "The Brighton of the Far East"—Terms of the Ultimatum—The Imperial Rescript—Japanese Moderation—Strength and Weakness of the Japanese Army—The Kaiser's Message: "Defend to the Last Man"—Chinese Coolies Pressed into German Service—Combined Naval and Military Operations—Perils of Mine-Sweeping—Position of China—Landing of the British Force under General Barnardiston—A British Officer's Impressions of Trench Work—The Bombardment—Experiences of Civilians—The Fall of Tsingtau—Rejoicings in Japan—Congratulatory Messages—Germany's Threat of Vengeance—General Kamio's Appointment—The British General in Tokyo—Work of the Japanese Navy.

EARLY in August, 1914, before the actual outbreak of war, the Japanese Government announced that it was prepared to do its part to aid Great Britain, as laid down in the Anglo-Japanese Alliance. The Japanese Army and Navy made ready, and on August 15th an ultimatum was presented to Germany requiring her withdrawal from the Far East. No reply being received, war was declared, and a Japanese expedition set out to capture the German protectorate of Kiao-chau, in China.

In the days to come, when the world has reshaped itself under its new conditions, historians may well regard this Japanese intervention as one of the vital points in the struggle of the nations. Its results will be as far-reaching in Asia as will be the overthrow of German militarism in Europe. To understand its real meaning and purpose it is necessary to go back for a few years in the history of the Far East.

Less than half a century ago Japan was a mediæval land. For hundreds of years her people had shut themselves altogether apart from foreigners. When at last Commodore Perry, the American naval officer, broke down the barriers of exclusion, Europeans were still regarded with suspicion and distrust. Had anyone foretold in 1871,

THE EMPEROR OF JAPAN.
Yoshihito, born August 31st, 1879; succeeded his father Mutsuhito, July 30th, 1912.

when Germany concluded her triumphant peace with France, that in the years to come Japan would humiliate and defeat the forces of Germany, it would have seemed as fantastic as if anyone to-day were to say that fifty years hence the South Sea Islanders would be in a position to attack and defeat Great Britain.

Once the Japanese people came in contact with the West they were clever enough to realise that their civilisation could not stand before ours, any more than men with arrows and spears can fight Maxim guns. They set themselves to learn from Europe and America. At first the West refused to take them seriously. When Gilbert wished to pick a land of absurdity and fantasy he selected Japan, and his generation laughed with him at the drolleries of "The Mikado." Europe heard of Japan modernising her Army, buying a Navy, and hiring distinguished men to teach her people the arts of peace and war. But it was not until 1894-5 that the world began to realise what all this meant. In 1894 Japan declared war upon China. Men expected the Mikado and his people to be swallowed up like a mouthful by the fierce and hungry Chinese giant. In place of that, the Japanese Navy wiped out the Chinese Fleet, and the Japanese armies defeated the great Chinese hosts with a celerity and a precision which few European troops could have equalled and none surpassed. China was glad to make peace on terms dictated by Japan herself, paying an indemnity of two hundred million taels (thirty-three millions sterling) and handing over large sections of territory to Japan, including the south of Manchuria, Port Arthur, and the great island of Formosa.

In the very hour of Japan's triumph, Russia, France, and Germany intervened and robbed her of the fruits of victory. They sent their warships to the Yellow Sea, cleared them for action, and advised her "in the interests of peace" to restore the territory she had taken on the Chinese mainland. They refused to allow her to retain the great fortress of Port Arthur, which she had captured

GENERAL NATHANIEL W. BARNARDISTON, M.V.O.
The commander of the British Expeditionary Force at Tsingtau with two officers of his Staff.

after a brilliant siege. The people of Japan were furious, but the Japanese Government recognised that to risk a war with Russia, Germany, and France would be to invite its own destruction. It gave way, but it gave way reluctantly, bitterly, and resolute on revenge.

Great Britain had refused to join the three Powers in coercing Japan, although they did their utmost to persuade her. Germany and her partners defended their action on the plea that they were guarding the integrity of China. They were soon to prove the insincerity of their claim. Two years afterwards the Germans found an excuse in the murder of some German missionaries in Shantung to demand territory for themselves. A German force was landed in China, and Prince Henry of Prussia was sent to the Far East with a fleet. Germany put forward a series of demands, of which the chief was the occupation of Kiao-chau and the recognition of Shantung as a German sphere of influence. Everyone, even in Germany itself, recognised that the plea of inflicting punishment for the murder of the missionaries was merely an excuse to obtain a foothold in China. The German Press frankly declared that it was necessary for the German Fleet to secure a Chinese Gibraltar and for

The "mailed fist" in Shantung

German commerce to have a Chinese Hamburg. The town, harbour, and district of Kiao-chau were formally transferred to Germany on a ninety-nine years' lease in March, 1898, and were made a German protectorate. Shortly afterwards Russia took possession of the very fortress of Port Arthur from which she and her allies had ousted Japan.

The Japanese people nursed their wrongs. They increased their fighting forces and entered into a formal alliance with Great Britain, the Power which had refused to join the others in despoiling them. In 1904-5 they took their revenge against Russia, defeated her armies, sank her fleet, and wrested Port Arthur from her. They still had a score to pay off against Germany. Their statesmen believed that the real hand in the operations against them after the Chinese War was the Kaiser himself. Little was said. A new policy of friendship was adopted towards Russia, and Japan conserved her resources and made ready for the next struggle.

Japan's first act of revenge

Germans regarded the seizure of Kiao-chau by their Government with great satisfaction. The spot was carefully chosen. There was a good harbour, with an entrance about two miles wide, which could be well defended from the high hills around. The whole protectorate had an area of about two hundred miles. It was a natural outlet for the trade of Shantung, one of the richest provinces in China. The seizure of Kiao-chau was among the first moves in the new policy of Imperial world-expansion adopted by the German Government. Men who had dreamed of a great German Empire, rivalling in extent the British Empire, now came to the fore. The occupation

LADY BARNARDISTON IN TOKYO.
The wife of the British General, accompanied by the wives of two officers of his Staff, who took part in the attack on Tsingtau, and a Japanese lady.

of this Chinese port was made an excuse for building a larger navy. The benefits that would be reaped from it were the subject of thousands of articles and speeches throughout Germany. In other words, when Germany seized Kiao-chau she set out on the road that led her finally to war with Great Britain.

Everything was done to make Kiao-chau an example of what Germany could accomplish in Imperial colonisation. It was placed under the command of the German Navy and vast sums were spent on it each year. It became the headquarters of an important group of Chinese railways and the centre for spreading German ideas, German authority, and German products throughout the Far East. The little old town of Kiao-chau itself, on the inside of the bay, was made secondary to Tsingtau, a modern city which the Germans erected at the harbour

LIEUTENANT-GENERAL KAMIO, THE "GENERAL FRENCH" OF JAPAN, AND GENERAL BARNARDISTON.
General Kamio was in command of the Japanese Expeditionary Force at Tsingtau, of which place he was afterwards appointed Governor-General.

mouth. Tsingtau became one of the show places of China. It was a delightful holiday resort, with fine bathing sands, and was known as the "Brighton of the Far East." It was kept distinctively European. Poorer class Chinese were not allowed to stay in it at nights, but had to go beyond the city limits. The houses were in European style. All the luxuries of civilisation abounded, from the best hotel in Asia to model schools. The place was in excellent sanitary condition, a great gain in Asia, it had electric light and pure water; there were—as in every white settlement in the Far East—good clubs. The trade of Tsingtau grew by leaps and bounds. Factories and works began to arise. The harbour was improved, with breakwaters and dry docks, repairing yards, floating docks, and as good a mechanical equipment for the loading and unloading of ships as could be found east of Suez. The bare hills around the city were planted with trees, and nursery establishments flourished, sending trees and bushes by the thousand throughout China.

"The Brighton of the Far East"

In the early summer of 1914 the Germans were very proud of what they had done at Tsingtau. Here was a model city, with wide streets, fine public buildings, abundant gardens, and comfortable houses. Tsingtau had been built on a system. It was as orderly, as exact. as mechanically perfect as any new town in Germany itself. Above all the place was a fortress. It was under the command of a naval governor, Captain Meyer-Waldeck, and the chance visitor was almost overwhelmed by the numbers of officers everywhere. Every second man one met in certain circles had his rank—kommandant or hauptmann, intendant or oberleutenant, or the like. There were two strong forts, called after the Kaiser and Bismarck, on the hills overlooking and commanding the city. Bomb-proof batteries and concealed entrenchments abounded, making the place a fortified zone. The Germans claimed afterwards —apparently correctly—that apart from the two main forts, many of the gun positions held only weapons of an older type. In addition to the land fortifications, there were naval works, and there were almost always several warships in the harbour.

Fortifications of Tsingtau

When Great Britain declared war against Germany, Japan realised that her hour for vengeance had come. The Japanese ultimatum was presented to Germany on August 15th, demanding the immediate withdrawal of German warships from Chinese waters, and the handing over to Japan of the complete territory of Kiao-chau for eventual restoration to China. The Japanese, as though to remind Germany that they had not forgotten past wrongs, drew

up their note in exactly the same style and with the same phraseology as the note delivered to Japan by the three Powers in 1895.

The text of the ultimatum was as follows:

We consider it highly important and necessary in the present situation to take measures to remove the causes of all disturbance of peace in the Far East, and to safeguard general interests as contemplated in the agreement of alliance between Japan and Great Britain.

In order to secure problems for Great Britain. For some years the commercial and political policy of Japan has been a source of uneasiness to the British community in China, and to the people of Australia, New Zealand, and Western Canada. A strong anti-Japanese sentiment has developed in recent years in Western America. It was feared that the entry of Japan into the fighting ranks might be used to alienate American sympathy from the Allies, and to kill the ardour of the Canadian and Australasian peoples for the war. It was recognised that German propagandists might use it to inflame **Formal statement by** fears of Japan forcing herself to a place **Great Britain** where she could despoil China and dictate the future of the Far East. To lessen such alarms the British Government made a formal statement, soon after the ultimatum was issued, that Great Britain and Japan had been in communication with each other, and were of opinion that it was necessary for each to take action to protect the general interests in the Far East contemplated by the Anglo-Japanese Alliance, keeping specially in view the independence and

MAJOR-GENERAL YAMADA, AT THE ENTRANCE TO HIS "DEN" IN THE JAPANESE LINES. ABOVE: VICE-ADMIRAL YASHIRO, JAPANESE NAVAL MINISTER.

firm and enduring peace in Eastern Asia, the establishment of which is the aim of the agreement, the Japanese Government sincerely believes it to be its duty to give advice to the German Government to carry out the following two propositions:

1. To withdraw immediately from Japanese and Chinese waters the German warships and armed vessels of all kinds, and to disarm at once those which cannot be withdrawn.

2. To deliver on a date not later than September 15th to the Japanese authorities, without condition or compensation, the entire leased territory of Kiao-chau, with **Japan's ultimatum** a view to the eventual restoration of the same **to Germany** to China.

The Japanese Government announces at the same time that in the event of its not receiving by noon on August 23rd an answer from the German Government signifying unconditional acceptance of the above advice offered by the Japanese Government, Japan will be compelled to take such action as it may deem necessary to meet the situation.

The intervention of Japan in the war created special integrity of China. "It is understood," the official communication continued, "that the action of Japan will not extend to the Pacific Ocean beyond the China Seas, except in so far as it may be necessary to protect Japanese shipping lines in the Pacific, nor beyond Asiatic waters westward of the China Seas, nor to any foreign

LIEUTENANT-GENERAL OKA, JAPANESE MINISTER OF WAR.

ONE OF THE JAPANESE SIEGE-GUNS THAT HELPED TO BRING ABOUT THE FALL OF TSINGTAU.
The men of the artillery detachment are receiving orders by telephone from Headquarters, preparatory to opening the bombardment.

JAPANESE SIEGE-GUN IN ACTION AGAINST THE GERMANS.
The dense, black smoke rising in the background is from one of the oil-tanks set on fire in the bombardment of Tsingtau.

THE JAPANESE IN TSINAN-FU.
Japanese advance guard arriving on trolley and trailer at the West Station, Tsinan-fu, on the Shantung Railway.

BRINGING UP SHELLS FOR THE JAPANESE GUNS.
Japanese artillerymen hauling shells for the siege-guns by means of a light railway, specially laid down for the purpose.

territory except territory in German occupation on the continent of Eastern Asia." This British declaration did much to allay uneasiness, particularly in the United States. Washington had confidence in the word of Great Britain.

At the expiration of the time given in the ultimatum, no reply having been received, war was declared. The Imperial Rescript declaring war was an interesting document. It has been summarised already (see Vol. II., p. 72), but may be given here *in extenso* :

"We, by the Grace of Heaven, Emperor of Japan, on the throne occupied by the same Dynasty from time immemorial, do hereby make the following proclamation to all Our loyal and brave subjects.

"We hereby declare war against Germany and We command Our Army and Navy to carry on hostilities against that Empire with all their strength, and We also command all Our competent authorities to make every effort in pursuance of their respective duties to attain the national aim within the limit of the law of nations.

"Since the outbreak of the present war in Europe, the calamitous effect of which We view with grave concern, We, on our part, have entertained hopes of preserving the peace of the Far East by the maintenance of strict neutrality, but the action of Germany has at length compelled Great Britain, Our Ally, to open hostilities against that country, and Germany is at Kiao-chau, its leased territory in China, busy with warlike preparations, while her armed vessels, cruising the seas of Eastern Asia, are threatening Our commerce and that of Our Ally. The peace of the Far East is thus in jeopardy.

"Accordingly, Our Government, and that of His Britannic Majesty, after a full and frank communication with each other, agreed to take such measures as may be necessary for the protection of the general interests contemplated in the Agree-

ment of Alliance, and We on Our part, being desirous to attain that object by peaceful means, commanded Our Government to offer, with sincerity, an advice to the Imperial German Government. By the last day appointed for the purpose, however, Our Government failed to receive an answer accepting their advice.

"It is with profound regret that We, in spite of Our ardent devotion to the cause of peace, are thus compelled to declare war, especially at this early period of Our reign and while we are still in mourning for Our lamented Mother.

"It is Our earnest wish that, by the loyalty and valour of Our faithful subjects, peace may soon be restored and the glory of the Empire be enhanced."

The Japanese people behaved at the opening of the war with the greatest correctness and moderation. There were few displays of noisy patriotism. Germans living in Japan were left unmolested. Immediately the ultimatum was issued, every Japanese subject in Germany itself was arrested and kept in prison, the German Government explaining that this was done for their protection. The Japanese Government money deposited in the Deutsche Bank in Berlin was seized. The Japanese attempted no reprisals. German money was untouched and German subjects walked freely about Japan. The German Ambassador in Tokyo evidently expected **Treatment of Germans** that his Embassy might be attacked by a **in Japan** mob, as the British Embassy in Berlin was attacked by Germans. His fears only made him seem somewhat ridiculous. Instructions were issued that German subjects in Japan were not to be injured in any way so long as they conducted themselves properly. The people of Tokyo were informed by the chief of police that although the two Governments had entered into hostilities for good reasons, the people individually were not to cultivate animosity, but were to treat the Germans who chose to continue among them with kindness. The German Ambassador remained in Tokyo until August 30th, when he sailed away with his staff and other officials. A number of Germans had left Japan previously to join the defenders at Tsingtau. A certain number of others elected to live on in Japan itself, and were allowed to continue their work there. "Of twenty-four German teachers in Government employ," says one writer, "only three left to join the colours at Tsingtau. Over fifty German teachers remained in private employ, and no students or classes showed disrespect or turbulence. No German property was injured, no German molested. No one's

German governess, valet, or employee of any kind was interfered with or imprisoned. Germans naïvely wrote their names in the lists for tennis tournaments, unconscious of the fact that not a British woman or child would tread the same court with them."

The Japanese plan of campaign was twofold—to drive the German warships from Eastern waters and to capture Tsingtau. The latter would give the Army once more an opportunity to prove its mettle.

The Japanese Army had showed its right, in the operations during the Boxer trouble in 1900 and in the war against Russia in 1904-5, to rank among the great armies of the world. The bravoes and fighting men who rallied around the clan chiefs in the middle of the nineteenth century, the heroes with their two-handed swords, the men in armour, the picturesque Oriental warriors with bows and arrows, disappeared long ago as completely as though they had never existed. But the spirit of supreme courage, of personal discipline, of self-sacrifice, and of unquestioning obedience to superiors, the loyalty of the clansmen for their chiefs, the splendid simplicity of the life of the Samurai—all these factors have gone to the making and the strengthening of Japan's modern Army. Strong in numbers, up to date in equipment, keen in professional zeal, the Japanese Army reveals in marked fashion both the strength and the weakness of the nation. Its routine side, its armament, transport, uniforms, medical service, are models of their kind. Every military movement is carried out with the mechanical precision of a perfect machine. The individual soldier has the ideal spirit for a fighting man. He is full of initiative and exceedingly brave. The retention of the old clan spirit maintains a friendly rivalry between different

Strength of the Japanese Army

regiments, which often leads the men to accomplish the apparently impossible. The whole Army is fired with an intense, burning patriotism. The weak points of the Army are twofold. The first is the lack of good cavalry, a lack due mainly to Japan being a rice-growing country and consequently unsuitable for much hard riding. The second and more serious drawback of the Japanese Army is a certain lack of boldness in the higher generalship. The Japanese soldier individually is willing to take any risks; the Japanese general plans above all things to ensure the safety of his operations.

WIRE ENTANGLEMENTS IN FRONT OF THE FIRST LINE OF THE GERMAN DEFENCE.
At a quite early stage of the bombardment of Tsingtau the barbed-wire entanglements in front of the first line of the German defence were scattered into fragments by the Japanese shells. Inset. A quaint Japanese sentry-box at Tsingtau.

At the first sign of war orders were issued for all German reservists in the Far East to report themselves at Tsingtau. Not all of them obeyed. Many women and children left, and before the final bombardment the remainder were sent out of the place, and very few civilians remained. The garrison numbered between 5,000 and 6,000 men, all told, including the new arrivals and the crews of some gunboats and destroyers in the harbour. The position had been planned more for defence against sea attack than against land attack, and the German authorities afterwards admitted that they had not anticipated hostile Japanese action. The Kaiser sent messages bidding the place defend itself to the last. "God be with you," was his last message. "I shall bear you in remembrance in the imminent hard struggle. Defend to the last man."

The Kaiser's message to Tsingtau

The garrison prepared to obey orders. Partial reports received in Europe immediately after the surrender caused some doubts to be cast at first on the stubbornness of the defence. Europe understood the place to be much stronger than it actually was, and was surprised at the briefness of its resistance. But, as the facts became better known, it was seen that the Tsingtau garrison defenders were not lacking in courage. They were overwhelmed by superior force, superior numbers, and superior artillery. That, however, is anticipating.

The entire waters for a

SPADE-WORK IN THE FAR EAST.
Japanese soldiers actively engaged digging trenches.

radius of eight miles around the place were thoroughly mined. All tall structures in the protectorate which might afford assistance to an attacking fleet by giving them sighting-points were dynamited. The railway bridge at the boundary of the German territory was blown up, and all houses or woods offering shelter to an enemy approaching from the land side were razed to the ground. Feverish work was begun on three lines of defence works. Thousands of Chinese coolies were pressed into service and set to work digging fresh emplacements and strengthening old ones. The countryside was mined. Barbed-wire entanglements were erected at many spots and were attached to the local electric works, so that they could be charged with fatal current whenever necessary. The ladies turned the houses into hospitals and made ready to nurse the wounded. When the Japanese called for the surrender of the place the Governor, Captain Meyer-Waldeck, replied: "Never shall we surrender the smallest bit of ground over which the German flag is flying. From this place we shall not retreat. If the enemy wants Tsingtau he must come and fetch it."

The Governor's "No Surrender"

The Japanese professed to look upon the order of the Kaiser to the garrison to defend itself to the last as inhuman, although doubtless they would have acted in the same way in similar circumstances. They let it be known at the start that they did not propose to make any spectacular assaults upon the town, such as those which caused such heavy losses at Port Arthur. The operations against Tsingtau were to be slow, gradual, cautious, and were to be carried out with a view of minimum loss to either side.

The Japanese were willing, and it is believed desired, to undertake the fighting against Tsingtau by themselves, but it was thought better that the operations should be carried out by a combined Japanese-British force. Two British vessels, the battleship Triumph and the destroyer Usk, shared in the sea fighting in co-operation with a number of Japanese ships. The Japanese expeditionary

JAPANESE BLUEJACKETS.

A CAPTURED GERMAN TRENCH.
One of the German trenches at Tsingtau, captured by the Japanese troops who are seen occupying it. Centre: Japanese bluejackets lending a hand with the spade outside the besieged city.

force numbered 22,890 officers and men and 142 guns. It was under the command of Lieutenant-General Kamio, with Major-General Yamanashi as Chief of Staff. The force was mainly composed of the 18th Division, the 29th Brigade of Infantry, the Siege Artillery Corps, Marine Artillery, and a Flying Corps. The British force under Brigadier-General Nathaniel W. Barnardiston, M.V.O., commander of the British troops in North China, included 910 South Wales Borderers and 450 men of the 36th Sikhs.

The day that the ultimatum expired the Japanese were ready to advance upon Tsingtau. The blockading fleet took up position on August 25th, and a blockade of the coast was declared as from August 27th. It was hoped to bottle up the German fleet in the harbour, but some of the ships slipped out. Several vessels, however, were left behind, including five gunboats, a destroyer, and a minelayer. The Austrian light cruiser Kaiserin Elisabeth was

Opening phases of the attack ordered to join the force at Tsingtau, and succeeded in doing so.

The first task of the attackers was to clear the seas of mines in order that the allied ships might approach. A number of Japanese women shell-divers from the province of Ise begged that they might be permitted to join in the work of mine-searching. These women, who are accustomed to stay for some minutes under water while searching for pearls, could undoubtedly have accomplished good work. But Japan is not the land of the New Woman, and the offer was emphatically and instantly rejected. The mine-clearing was done in much the same way as mine-clearing

around the British coast, the waters being swept by vessels moving in pairs some three hundred yards apart and pulling thick wire ropes stretched between them, wire ropes which sweep the waters and indicate, if they do not instantly explode, any mine on their path. Work like this is among the most dangerous known in modern war, and before Kiao-chau Bay, as around the North Sea, many a mine-sweeper paid the price of the search with his own life. The danger of the work made it the more attractive to many Japanese, and the crew of one boat, when applying to be engaged, wrote the letter in their own blood, as a sign of their resolution.

Heroism of the mine-sweepers

The early operations of the fleet were greatly hampered by the minefields. The Japanese suffered some losses in attempting to get near the coast, and two torpedo-boats and one cruiser were unofficially reported as blown up or

A ROUGH-AND-READY MEAL AFTER THE TAKING OF GERMANY'S PROTECTORATE IN THE FAR EAST.
The hardy Japanese soldiers, who, like the allied troops in France and Flanders, had to undergo the rigours of flooded roads and rain-filled trenches, are seen in the above photograph regaling themselves with rice-balls. Above: A luncheon more at leisure.

L

JAPANESE RED CROSS
WORKERS.

mines useless, and destroyed much of the results of their work of careful preparation.

Laichow is Chinese territory, and is therefore nominally neutral. The Japanese, however, knowing that China was in no position to resist, swept Chinese neutrality on one side. Their troops advanced to the town of Weihsien, and from there spread through a large part of the province, even taking possession of the town of Tsinan-fu. They seized the Shantung Railway, and dealt with a large part of the Chinese province as though it were conquered territory occupied and held by their troops. Yuan Shi-kai, the Chinese President, and his Cabinet were powerless to do anything else **Chinese protests** than protest. **disregarded** They consented to the Japanese control of the railway between Weihsien and Tsinan-fu, but declared themselves opposed to any occupation of Tsinan-fu Station itself. When Tsinan-fu was occupied, despite the objection, the Chinese Cabinet requested Japan to withdraw her troops. Japan took no notice. Chinese telegraph and post-offices were taken over; Chinese military establishments were used for Japanese soldiers; armed guards were placed at every railway-station. The German Government

sunk. When, however, the ships got within reasonable range they maintained a constant fire on the forts and on some outlying redoubts. People inside Tsingtau during the siege declared that most of the ships' fire was ineffective because the great distance —about nine miles— at which the ships mainly lay prevented good marksmanship. This criticism is not altogether borne out, however, by some of the known facts. The naval guns succeeded in destroying a 4 in. gun on the fortification at Mount Iltis, one of the most **Destructive work** important points, **of naval guns** and a lucky shot destroyed another gun, killing most of its crew. It was reported during the siege that the Triumph put the Bismarck fort out of the fight with seven well-directed shells.

The Japanese expeditionary force landed at Laichow Bay, to the north of the Shantung Peninsula, and advanced through Chinese territory on to Kiao-chau. Their progress was exceedingly difficult owing to phenomenal floods—heavier, it was said, than Shantung had known for sixty years. The floods hindered the landing of the heavy guns and supplies, and made it impossible to move them forward quickly. They were bad also for the Germans, for they filled their trenches, rendered many of their

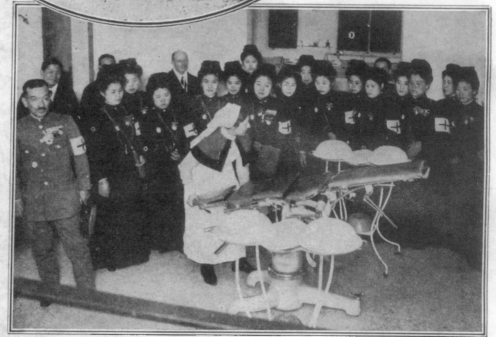

EXPLAINING THE MECHANISM OF THE OPERATING-TABLE.
Nurse of the 4th Divisional Hospital explaining to a group of Japanese nurses the working of the operating-table. Inset: Red Cross nurses departing for Tsingtau. The Japanese Red Cross Society, one of the most highly-organised institutions of its kind in the world, dates from 1877, and was originally called "The Society of Benevolence" (Hakuaisha).

BRITISH-INDIAN AMMUNITION TRAIN CROSSING A RIVER ON THE WAY TO THE FRONT.

WOUNDED JAPANESE SOLDIERS BEING TAKEN TO THE REAR ACROSS THE BESHA RIVER.

THE JAPANESE EXPEDITIONARY FORCE LANDING AT LAICHOW.

The first division of the Japanese force landed at Laichow Bay, to the north of the Shantung Peninsula, and advanced through Chinese territory on to Kiao-chau, taking possession of Weihsien and Tsinan-fu. The advance was rendered difficult by extraordinary floods—heavier, it was said, than Shantung had known for sixty years. This condition of affairs limited the rate of advance to eight miles a day.

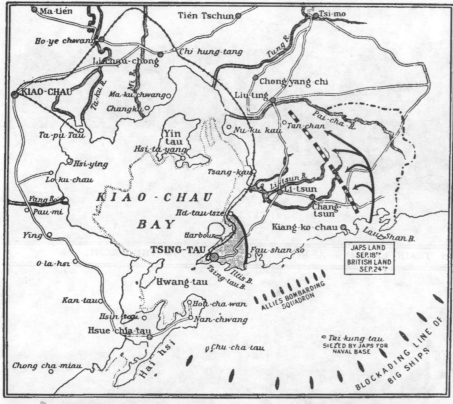

SKETCH-MAP OF THE ATTACK ON THE GERMAN STRONGHOLD.
The early operations of the fleet were greatly hampered by minefields. When, however, the ships got within reasonable range they maintained a constant and deadly fire on the forts and on some outlying redoubts.

now turned on the unhappy Chinese, and declared that since they had allowed their territory to be used against them, Germany would consider herself free to deal as she pleased with China at the end of the war.

The beginning of the end The Germans threw out scouting parties at various points beyond Tsingtau in order to discover the Japanese approach. The Japanese advance guard at times scarce succeeded in marching eight miles a day. Streams were swollen to torrents impossible to cross ; fields were turned into seas of mud ; there was nothing to do but to wait for a few days. By September 13th, however, the Japanese scouts reached and attacked the railway-station of the little town of Kiao-chau itself, twenty-two miles from Tsingtau. Japanese aeroplanes began to soar over the German positions. Day after day they dropped bombs on the fortifications, the electric-light works, and the harbour.

A battle started on September 26th. Guns were hurried into position, and a very heavy bombardment opened on the German front. Three Japanese warships —the Suwo, Iwami, and Tango— assisted by the British battleship Triumph, bombarded Tsingtau from the sea, and then came an advance on land. The Japanese set themselves to clear the outer works of Tsingtau, and completely succeeded. Point after point was stormed. Two gunboats in the

harbour—the Jaguar and the Kaiserin Elisabeth—poured shell fire on the Japanese troops as they rushed forward. At one or two points the Japanese were caught by heavy machine-gun fire, and in one case, according to German accounts, a large body of them were swept down as they came unexpectedly under enfilading fire. The Germans estimated the Japanese loss that day at a thousand, an absurdly excessive estimate, as was proved by the total casualties later. By the morning of the 28th the Germans had been driven right into their inner fortified position in Tsingtau, behind the line of hill forts. Here it was that they were to make their real defence on a comparatively small peninsula, roughly triangular in shape, with the sea on one side, Kiao-chau Bay on the other, and the land on the third, their defences centring around the Moltke, Bismarck, and Iltis Hills.

On September 30th the Germans made a desperate attempt to drive the Japanese back, attacking from land, sea, and air. Their effort was altogether vain. Their troops were driven in, one of their destroyers was sunk, and it was clear that they were completely held. The Japanese were now content to wait for a few days while some of their heaviest siege-artillery was brought up into position. At the first approach of the Japanese the Germans opened a very heavy artillery fire which was maintained day after day. Occasionally a Japanese position was located by means of the German aeroplanes, and was promptly bombarded. But much of the gun fire was mere aimless shooting. Every independent observer agreed that the big-gun ammunition was thrown away in the most reckless and careless fashion. Thus in twenty-four hours alone, early in October, the forts on the three hills fired 2,015 shells, and correspondents with the Japanese force

German waste of ammunition

WITH THE JAPANESE RED CROSS IN THE FIELD.
Bringing in the wounded. One section of the Japanese army paid a heavy price for the victory.

LANDING-PARTY OF JAPANESE BLUEJACKETS AT TSINGTAU.

In the long siege of Tsingtau, carried out deliberately in order that the loss of life might be reduced to the minimum, an important part was played by the Japanese Navy. Our photograph shows a number of sailors from the warship in the offing approaching the shore.

JAPANESE INFANTRY STORMING A HILL POSITION.

A vivid camera-picture of one of the charges that carried the German positions before Tsingtau. At dawn on November 7th, 1914, the Japanese made ready for a grand final assault, but before the whole line moved forward a white flag fluttered from the observatory. The Germans had surrendered.

Mine and hand-grenades captured from the Germans at Tsingtau. The first task of the attacking force was to clear the seas for the approach of the warships.

Japanese artillery landing for the bombardment of the German port. The heavy guns got to work on October 31st, 1914, the birthday of the Emperor of Japan. Our ally had one hundred and forty two guns in position, guns of a calibre more than sufficient to deal with the heaviest pieces of ordnance

Japanese and British landing at Laoshan Bay. While the first Japanese landing took place at Laichow Bay, the second, with the British troops, disembarked on the south of the Shantung Peninsula. The British force included 910 South Wales Borderers and 450 men of the 36th Sikhs.

Tsingtau on fire. Almost every German po[st] stood, was knocked to bits by the bombard[ment] The electric-light works were destroyed, and fo[r]

Of the four illustrations at the foot of the page, the first, taking the views from left to right, is of a heavy gun taken from the Germans at the foot of Moltke Hill. In the second a section of Japanese infantry is seen advancing across a river in the attack on Tsingtau. One man is carrying

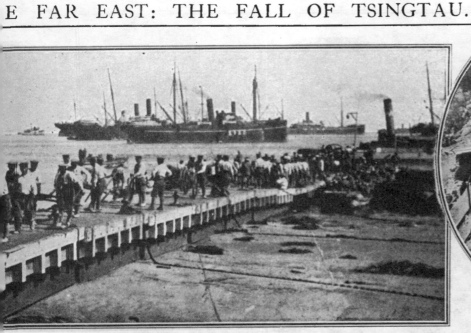

n the German forts. They had every range, and they knew exactly where to hit. The bombardment pened at dawn, and one of the first shells set fire to enormous oil-tanks in the naval docks, sending p a pillar of smoke that spread like a pall over the city.

A corner of the shattered Bismarck fortress. This, with the fortified position at Iltis, fell into the hands of the Allies with the minimum of opposition.

the bomb-proof casements in which the guns s from Japanese aeroplanes fell everywhere, days the people had nothing but candle light.

Shell-shattered oil-tanks at Tsingtau. The tanks of the Standard Oil Company and the Asiatic Petroleum Company caught fire. Most of their contents had been run off before the bombardment, but enough oil was left in them to add flame and smoke to the surrounding conflagration.

bicycle. Our third picture is of the formal entry of the victorious troops into the surrendered ty, the camera being exposed at a moment when Japanese infantry were marching past the ommander and his Staff. The last photograph displays a ruined cupola and dismounted gun.

WHERE THE "MAILED FIST" WAS BROKEN AND THE HUN HUMBLED IN THE DUST.

All that was left of one of the German fortresses at Tsingtau after the Japanese siege-guns had done their work. From the first hour the major operations began it became evident that the German resistance would be smashed by mere weight of metal. The Germans replied bravely but vainly, and when they had fired their last shot they destroyed their guns with explosives. Ammunition gave out before the food supply.

THE VICTORS INSPECTING ONE OF THE FALLEN GERMAN FORTS.

By September 13th, 1914, the Japanese were attacking the railway-station, twenty-two miles from Tsingtau. Then their aeroplanes began to soar over the German positions. Three Japanese warships and a British battleship took part in the bombardment. By the 28th the Germans had been driven right into their inner fortified position. Thence they maintained a heavy but largely futile artillery fire day after day.

declare that the entire firing during that twenty-four hours inflicted no damage on the Japanese whatever. This waste of ammunition is difficult to explain, and undoubtedly was a leading factor in the early surrender of the place, for before many days were over the shells for many of the guns ran short. The besiegers noticed in the second week of October that artillery fire fell off in surprising fashion; some forts that had formerly been keeping up an almost incessant bombardment now allowed hours to go by without a single shot. One battery of guns in

30th the Japanese opened a heavy fi.. on a dismantled gunboat, the Tiger, which lay anchored outside. One shell took her funnel away, and the others 'l all around her, inflicting serious loss.

When their heavy siege-guns were ready, the Japanese circulated a message to the defenders of Tsingtau. It was printed in German on handbills, and was dropped by the thousand from an aeroplane on to the forts in the town. It read as follows:

Aeroplane protest to the defenders

"To the honoured officers and men in the fortress.

"It is against the will of God, as well as the principles of humanity, to destroy and render useless arms, ships of war, merchantmen, and other works and constructions, not in obedience to the necessity of war, but merely out of spite, lest they fall into the hands of the enemy.

·"Trusting as we do that, as you hold dear the honour of civilisation, you will not be betrayed into such base conduct, we beg you, however, to announce to us your own view as mentioned above.—THE BESIEGING ARMY."

The British 'contingent under General Barnardiston left Tientsin on September 19th, and after calling at Wei-hai-wei for transport mules, landed in Shantung on the 21st. Our authorities were careful to select a point of landing in the German protectorate in order that no question of violating Chinese neutrality might arise. The weather was very trying, a strong

GERMAN PRISONERS UNDER JAPANESE GUARD.
The top circular photograph is of Captain Meyer-Waldeck, the German Governor of Kiao-chau, which was a naval command; and the lower shows that officer on his arrival in Tokyo.

particular, that had specially annoyed the Japanese, did not fire a single shot for three days. The attackers not unnaturally imagined that this was some trick of war on the part of the Germans, calculated to trap them.

A story was told in China early in October that when the Japanese had fixed their siege-guns in position and were ready to begin the more serious operations, they first shelled the warships in the harbour, and put them out of action without touching a slate in the town. Then they gave twenty-four hours' notice for the real bombardment to begin and for non-combatants to clear out. When the notice expired they signalled: "Are you now quite ready, gentlemen?" "The reply," said one, "came in the shape of a whizzing bullet which took three hairs out of the signalman's moustache, leaving eight remaining."

Prinz Heinrich Hill captured

The difficulty, however, in accepting this story, widely as it was circulated at the time, is that at the date the description was written the real bombardment of Tsingtau had not yet begun.

The Japanese captured with comparative ease a position, Prinz Heinrich Hill, from which they could mount their guns to bombard the forts. During the latter part of October the Japanese hold on the city steadily increased, and the artillery fire grew daily in intensity. The Japanese and British warships maintained a constant fusillade on the forts and on the infantry works near the sea. On the

southerly gale blowing, heavy rain falling, and a very heavy sea running. It seemed, when the troops landed, as though earth and sea and sky had contrived to make their work as difficult as possible. They set out on a forty-mile march, and came up behind the Japanese as they were driving' in the German advance positions. It was intended that they should participate in this attack, but the German resistance at this point was so slight that their help was not wanted. On October 30th the entire British force moved up to the front.

The British now occupied one part of the allied front, a front extending to about five miles, and there they took part with the Japanese troops in the work of digging an approach by sapping right up to the German redoubts. Night after night officers and men worked with feverish energy, digging their zigzag trenches in the direction of the enemy. It was exceedingly dangerous and trying work. The Germans constantly fired star shells, illuminating the entire position, and as they saw the allied soldiers at work, immediately opened fire on them with shells of every kind and with machine-guns. Day by day the Japanese and the British, notwithstanding all resistance, made their way like moles towards the doomed city.

In a letter to "The Times," a British officer in the expeditionary force gave a vivid description of his experiences in this work. "I left Headquarters and took over a double company," he wrote. "That night we were working in trenches along a river-bed at the bottom of the slope, where the others had been wounded, and *sans doute* most darnation close to the enemy. A beginning had been made on this trench the night before, so there was a little cover. The two redoubts were about eight hundred yards on our right and left respectively, the enemy's trenches about three hundred and fifty yards to our front. Well, for the first hour after getting down we were left severely alone. Then they started throwing star rockets and sort of Roman candle things which lit up the place like day, and at the same time they peppered us with Maxims, pom-poms, and rifle fire from all three places. We had some men hit farther back in the communication trench, but, funnily enough, none in the forward line. **British officer's experiences** The Borderers left early, and we were working by ourselves for about an hour. Then, in a lull, I withdrew to what was called the 'first position of attack,' a similar line of trenches about a thousand yards up the slope, where my double company was in position during the day. We were entertained to a certain amount of shell fire during the rest of the night. Next night we were due to leave for the forward trenches, at dusk, to carry on, having had our usual entertainment in the afternoon from the Germans, when suddenly they began throwing shrapnel at our trench. For about half an hour it was all over us, and I'm blest if I know why nobody was hit. It was the overhead cover, I fancy, that saved us this time. We came out like a lot of rabbits when it was over, and proceeded to get down below. The Japanese artillery was supporting us that night, as we were working on the enemy's side of the river, within two hundred yards

JAPANESE WARSHIPS WHICH TOOK PART IN OUSTING GERMANY FROM CHINA.
The above photograph was taken from a Japanese battleship. Among the vessels of our Far Eastern ally taking part in the operations off Tsingtau were the pre-Dreadnoughts Suwo (laid down in 1898), Iwami (1900), and Tango (1892). They were assisted by the British pre-Dreadnought battleship Triumph (upper photograph), which was acquired by purchase from Chili in 1903, and the destroyer Usk.

HYDROPLANE EMPLOYED IN SCOUTING AND RANGE-FINDING
FOR THE JAPANESE-BRITISH FORCES.

ANTI-AIRCRAFT GUN MOUNTED ON A BRITISH WARSHIP.

of their advance trenches. Never have I felt a more
comforting sensation than when watching those Japanese
shells bursting just over our heads, a little in advance, the
shrapnel from them going slap into the Germans every
time. I must say it was a magnificent sight when the
Japanese guns were going, the German rockets, etc., and
their machine-guns and rifles joining in when they could
get their heads up. One had to shout to make oneself
heard, and those who saw it from the top of Heinrich Hill
in rear said it was very fine."

The bombardment with the heavy siege-artillery opened
on October 31st, the birthday of the Emperor of Japan.
Everything had been arranged for the occasion. The
Japanese had one hundred and forty-two guns in position,
guns of a calibre more than adequate to deal with the
heaviest guns on the Tsingtau forts.

The heavy guns   They had every range, and they knew
     open fire   exactly where they meant to hit. There
                was no wasteful firing here. From Prinz
Heinrich Hill, where the staff of the Japanese and British
expeditionary forces had betaken themselves, it was possible
to see the operations like a great panorama spread out
under one's feet. That morning Japanese and British
cruisers lay out at sea, waiting for the signal to begin.
The British and Japanese troops held their entrenched
positions, and at every point concealed great guns were
directed on to Tsingtau itself. The bombardment opened
at dawn. One of the first shells set fire to enormous
oil-tanks in the naval docks, sending up a pillar of smoke
that spread like a pall over the city. Then shells burst
over the forts, and under the almost ceaseless rain of
heavy metal the gun emplacements seemed to melt and
to crumble. The barbed-wire entanglements were
scattered into fragments; the trenches were broken,
filled in here, expanded there, and blurred elsewhere
by the high-explosive shells constantly falling among
them. Under the shelter of this fire the infantrymen
continued to push up their saps and trenches. While
the artillery were at their deadly work from the shore,
the naval guns of both the Allies were pouring their
messengers of death on the town from the sea. It was
evident from the first hour the major operations began
that the German resistance would be smashed by the
mere weight of metal.

The Germans replied bravely, but vainly. A Japanese
observation balloon overhead signalled the positions and
the result of the firing. The tanks of the Standard Oil
Company and the Asiatic Petroleum Company caught
fire. Most of their contents had been run off before,
but enough was left to add to the blaze. "The noise
of the whistling and exploding shells was tremendous,"
wrote one observer. "They covered the summits of the
hills with dust and smoke."

The artillery fire was incessantly maintained for seven days, night and day. Non-combatants in the town herded themselves in cellars to escape the bursting explosives. The wounded were taken from their wards into the cellars and cared for there. The men in the German bomb-proof casements replied till all their shells had gone. Almost every German position, save the bomb-proof casements in which the guns stood, was knocked to bits. The ground was everywhere pitted and torn. The troops in the trenches between the forts were in many cases wiped out by the rain of bursting shrapnel and high explosives. Meanwhile the Japanese and British infantry had advanced by means of their trenches to

bombardment, at dinner-time, one shell struck in the street in front of the favourite café, the Kronprinz, two in the side street next to it, and two more a hundred yards from the club. " There was just a sign of uneasiness among a few at a table, but when the final crash came near by someone lifted his glass and started a scrap of a song, which was taken up around his table and had a decidedly heartening effect."

During the last days the streets were **Water scarce but** practically deserted. A few men hurried **beer plentiful** along on necessary errands. The people stopped the windows of the cellars in which they slept with bags of sand, or in some cases even with newspapers. While the supply of running water ceased in the middle of October, there was an abundant stock of beer which lasted amply until the very end. News from the outside world came through until November 5th, news that usually told of the ruin of England. " I remember one evening the roar of laughter that went up in the German Club when the news was read that England had asked Portugal for assistance. For two or three days it looked, according to the news, that the British Empire was going to pieces. We heard of revolutions in India, riots in Alexandria, mutiny and martial law in South Africa, and even disaffection in Sarawak and North Borneo."

It became clear to everyone inside that the end was drawing

JAPANESE SIEGE-GUNS IN ACTION.

points right under the forts. Here they lay watching, and picking off any man who in the least exposed himself. To add to the horrors in the place, Japanese aeroplanes were constantly soaring overhead, dropping bombs on every possible position. The Japanese fire destroyed the electric light works, so that for the last few days the people had nothing but candle light. The wireless apparatus was rendered useless. Life in Tsingtau for those few days was a concentration of all possible horrors.

What were the experiences of the few civilians left in the place ? Happily we are able to answer this question from the very vivid despatches of Mr. A. M. Brace, the staff correspondent of the Associated Press, who was the only foreign correspondent in Tsingtau itself. At first, he says, in spite of the fact that the city was almost empty, the **Civil life during** life of those who remained was quite **the siege** normal. There were enough shops open where purchases could be made. Cafés continued business, and tiffin and dinner were served without interruption at the German Club throughout the whole siege, although towards the end the number who came to the club dwindled to a few of the administrative officers and civilians. On the second day of the heavy

very near. The warships in the harbour were blown up and sunk in order that they might not fall into Japanese hands. The big guns in the forts were fired many of them to the last shot, and then the gunners, acting under orders, destroyed them with explosives. There was no shortage of food, and when the city was captured provisions were found there sufficient to feed five thousand persons for three months. But provisions without ammunition were of no use.

Bismarck Fort, one of the most powerful of all, had been destroyed at the beginning of November, as was told

A NOVELTY IN MILITARY COSTUME.
British soldiers wearing "shorts"—and attracting thereby the noticeable interest of their Japanese allies.

earlier, by the British battleship Triumph. Other forts became more and more silent. On the night of November 6th some troops advanced to attack a redoubt, and entered it with comparatively little difficulty. Encouraged by this success, the Japanese Commander ordered a general advance. Japanese and British battalions crept up silently in the darkness to point after point. The two great mountain positions of Iltis and Bismarck fell into the hands of the Allies with a minimum of opposition. At one ridge they came on a small party of Germans in charge of a searchlight. They did not fire on them, for to do

BRITISH AND JAPANESE IN ARMS AGAINST THE COMMON ENEMY.
A British field kitchen at work not far from Tsingtau. The circular photograph was taken after the fall of the city, and shows a British and a Japanese officer on their way to Headquarters.

so would be to betray themselves, but they fell on them with spades and pickaxes and killed them. At other parts they took up positions covering the exits of the forts, so that should any Germans try to emerge they could shoot them down. How the Japanese were allowed to advance that night as they were across the elaborate land defences of the Germans, practically without resistance, remains to this day a mystery. They expected to have to make a grand assault and lose possibly thousands of men. They found, so to speak, the door left open for them to enter at their ease. Were the Germans stupefied and deadened by the continuous hail of shell fire? It was said at the

THE BATHING BEACH AT TSINGTAU.

time that Captain Meyer-Waldeck was wounded a few hours before the end. The feeble resistance before the Japanese final advance is inexplicable.

When dawn broke the Japanese found themselves in command of some of the forts dominating the city. Now was the moment for a grand final assault. They made ready, but before the whole line moved forward a white flag was seen fluttering from the observatory, followed by white flags raised at other points. The Germans were going to surrender. It may safely be said that no one was so much surprised at this inglorious final collapse as the Japanese themselves.

It was seven o'clock in the morning when the white flag was raised, and as the little Japanese soldiers saw it they set up a loud shout of "Banzai! Let great Japan live for ever!"—the national cry. As they looked around their ranks they saw that even though the capture of the city had been very much easier than they expected, yet some parts of the Army had paid a heavy price. Thus the company that attacked Redoubt 2 had been caught under the fire of machine-guns, and out of two hundred and fifty men only eighty-seven were left. This was the heaviest loss of any, the total Japanese casualties in the final assault being four hundred and fifty killed and wounded. The British casualties were slight.

Casualties in the final assault

Much regret was felt over one accident. The Governor had resolved to surrender the place at six in the morning, and sent Major von Kayser, his adjutant, to approach the Japanese and to negotiate terms. Major von Kayser, accompanied by a trumpeter and another officer, left the staff headquarters bearing a white flag. The white flag was not observed, and as they got into the region of fire the trumpeter was killed and the major's horse shot under

him. According to the letters of some of the officers sent home at the time the major himself was shot.

The formal surrender of the place was arranged. The Japanese immediately took possession, and on November 16th a ceremonial entry was arranged, when a memorial service was held for the dead. The Germans before surrender had done all they could to spoil supplies likely to be of use. The warships had been sunk and the great guns damaged or destroyed. The trophies of war that were taken included 2,500 rifles, 100 machine-guns, 30 field-guns, some ammunition, cash to the amount of £1,200, 15,000 tons of coal, 40 motor-cars, and a considerable quantity of provisions. The prisoners taken numbered 4,043, including the Governor, 201 German officers, and 3,841 non-commissioned officers and men. The Japanese casualties were 236 killed and 1,282 wounded. The British casualties were 2 officers wounded, 12 men killed, and 61 wounded. These figures were surprisingly small. The Germans estimated their losses during the siege at about 1,000 men.

Rival gains and losses

The fall of the city was naturally the occasion for great rejoicing throughout Japan. The capital was decked out with flags, the Union Jack alongside of the Rising Sun. Lantern processions, a very picturesque Japanese form of rejoicing, were held in towns and villages and cities alike, where long lines of men marched in their native dress through the streets of bamboo-sided houses, bearing paper lanterns and waving banners.

Numerous congratulatory messages were received. Lord Kitchener sent his felicitations to the Japanese Minister of War at Tokyo: "Please accept my warmest congratulations on the success of the operations against Tsingtau. Will you be so kind as to express my felicitations to the

UP IN THE HILLS BEHIND GERMANY'S LOST COLONY.

Japanese forces engaged? The British Army is proud to have been associated with its gallant Japanese comrades in this enterprise." The Board of Admiralty also sent heartiest congratulations "on the prosperous and brilliant issue of the operations." The Emperor of Japan sent a message to the Japanese forces telling his appreciation of "the faithful discharge of their duties." He further sent a message to the British forces "deeply appreciating the brilliant deeds of the British Army and Navy which, co-operating with the Japanese, have fought for and bravely achieved one of the objects of the war."

The Germans tried to explain away their loss. Captain Meyer-Waldeck, interviewed when removed as a prisoner

GERMAN HOTEL AT TSINGTAU.

THE PRUSSIAN PASSION FOR MONUMENTS.
This is exemplified in the Imperial insignia which was found cut in the rock on the heights above Tsingtau.

of war to Japan, said that many of the guns at Tsingtau were old, and the Germans had not calculated on having to resist the Japanese Army. Dr. Kaempf, the President of the Reichstag, sent a telegram to the German Emperor condoling with him on the surrender, and expressing the hope that the day might come when German civilisation would reoccupy its place in the Far East. The Germans circulated an account in their Chinese subsidised newspapers in which they stated that the fortress of Tsingtau was not stormed at all but capitulated voluntarily, on receipt of orders from the Kaiser, to obviate the useless shedding of Japanese blood. The account added that the Kaiser intended, after peace had been established, to extract an enormous indemnity from Japan. The Berlin "Lokalanzeiger" threatened vengeance: "Never shall we forget the bold deed of violence of the yellow robbers or of England that set them on to do it. We know that we cannot yet settle with Japan for years to come. Perhaps she will rejoice over her cowardly robbery. Here our mills can grind but slowly. Even if the years pass, however, we shall certainly not often speak

of it, but as certainly always think of it. And if eventually the time of reckoning arrives, then as unanimously as what is now a cry of pain will a great shout of rejoicing ring through Germany, ' Woe to Nippon.' "

General Kamio was appointed Governor-General of Tsingtau. The Japanese started clearing the land and sea of mines and preparing the city for fresh life under the new administration. The prisoners were moved to concentration camps in Japan. **British General** A new series of problems now arose, **in Tokyo** problems connected with the permanent occupation of Tsingtau and the future relations between Japan and China. These matters, however, hardly come within the scope of this history.

General Barnardiston, the Commander of the British Forces, visited Tokyo early in December, and his visit was made the occasion of a great national demonstration. When he reached the Japanese capital the station was decorated and thousands of school children were waiting to greet him. Dense crowds lined the entire roadway to his hotel, and a week of entertainment was mapped out for him in the lavish fashion which the Japanese understand so well. He was received in audience by the Emperor, dined by the municipality, and treated as Great Britain's representative who had helped to seal closer the Anglo-

THROUGH GERMAN EYES: IMPRESSION OF THE FIGHTING AT TSINGTAU.
A striking picture by a German war artist representing the final phase of the fighting before the surrender of Tsingtau. It will be noticed that the caps worn by the sailors on the right of the drawing bear the name of the Austrian light cruiser Kaiserin Elisabeth.

FUNERAL OF THE CAPTAIN AND OFFICERS OF THE TORPEDOED JAPANESE CRUISER TAKACHIHO.

The Takachiho was one of the two oldest cruisers in the Japanese Navy. She was sunk off Tsingtau by a German torpedo. Her commander (Captain Ito) and seven other officers were accorded a naval funeral, which, as may be gathered from the remarkable photograph we are able to give of a part of the procession, was of a most solemn and impressive character.

Japanese Alliance. Military bands had not played in Tokyo since the death of the Dowager-Empress until he arrived, when "See the Conquering Hero Comes" was played for him.

The Japanese have helped the Allies in two other ways. It is well known that at the beginning of the war there was a considerable shortage of rifles and guns among the Allies, and sufficient weapons could not be manufactured in time to supply the suddenly raised armies. The Japanese arsenals aided the Allies, and tens of thousands

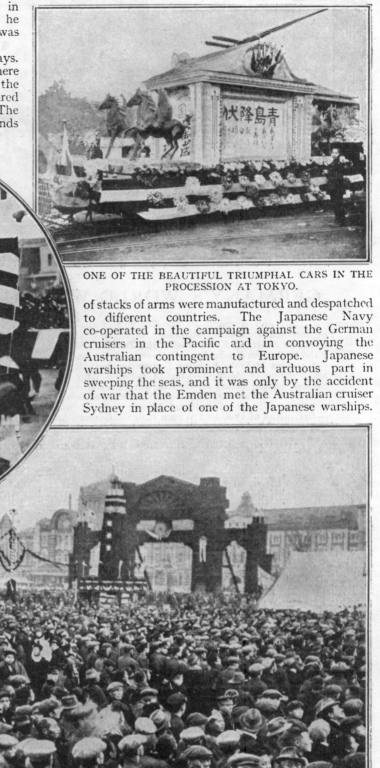

ONE OF THE BEAUTIFUL TRIUMPHAL CARS IN THE PROCESSION AT TOKYO.

of stacks of arms were manufactured and despatched to different countries. The Japanese Navy co-operated in the campaign against the German cruisers in the Pacific and in convoying the Australian contingent to Europe. Japanese warships took prominent and arduous part in sweeping the seas, and it was only by the accident of war that the Emden met the Australian cruiser Sydney in place of one of the Japanese warships.

"IO TRIUMPHE!" JAPAN'S ENTHUSIASTIC WELCOME HOME TO GENERAL KAMIO.

Perusal of the opening paragraphs of Mr. F. A. McKenzie's account of Japan's grievance against Germany will explain the joy which spread throughout Nippon on the receipt of the news of the surrender of Tsingtau. The return of General Kamio to Tokyo was made the occasion of a general holiday all over the Empire. With the Japanese Commander, General Barnardiston was received in special audience by the Emperor. The fervour of the popular reception of the victors is shown in the remarkable photographs given above of the processions through the streets of the capital.

CHAPTER LI.

GERMANY'S WORLD-WIDE CAMPAIGN OF INTRIGUE.

Influence of Italy and Rumania on the Conduct of the War—Bülow's Intrigues with the "Black" Families—Prussia as the Mainstay of the Anti-Democrat Movement throughout the World—The Pro-German Belgian Nuncio and Cardinal Mercier—Signor Giolitti's Startling Revelation of the Teutonic War Plot—Rivalry of Signor Salandra and Signor Giolitti—Bülow at Last Makes a Bid for Italian Friendship—Discovery of German Mischief-Makers in the Tripoli Risings—Italy at the Crisis of Her Destiny—Rumania Makes a Fighting Convention with Russia—Why the Rumanians Hesitated all the Winter—Conflict between Tsar and Premier of Bulgaria—Conflict between King and Premier of Greece—Disadvantage of Foreign Dynasties in the Balkan States—People Ready for Action, but Checked by their Rulers—Greece Loses her Great Chance—Bulgaria Becomes Half Inclined to Act against Turks—The General Position of Neutral Countries in Europe—United States Protests against Stopping and Searching of Ships—Convincing Answer by Sir Edward Grey—Mr. Bryan Rebukes American Partisans of Germany and Austria—Difficulties of President Wilson with the German-American League—Financial Alliance of the Powers of the Triple Entente.

THERE is often seen around a great whirl of the forces of the air a series of minor disturbances which gradually become involved in the central vortex. So it was in the Great War. Around the vast scene of actual conflict was a series of smaller disturbances, nearing the point at which thunder and lightning would appear while they now approached, and now receded from, the great centre of collision. All through the autumn and winter of 1914 and the opening months of 1915 the intricate and subtle play of the smaller outer forces of disturbance continued.

There was a gathering storm centre in Italy, and influenced by it was a movement for war in Rumania. Then, balancing Rumania to some extent, was a small reverse vortex in Bulgaria, which also had a strong effect upon the clashing currents of feeling in Greece. Across the Atlantic was another system of cyclone and anticyclone in the United States. All these outer movements of warlike currents exerted considerable pressure upon the course of the fighting on the battlefields. Indeed, some of the principal strategical moves of the rival commanders-in-chief were conceived with a view to swaying Italy and Rumania, Bulgaria and Greece. Field-Marshal von Hindenburg, especially, fought through the autumn, winter, and early spring

with one eye on Italy and Rumania and another on Russia. The unexpected movement of his southern wing into Bukovina and to the Rumanian frontier was aimed as much at the hesitating Rumanians as at the alert and unperturbed Russians. In the same way, the second disastrous invasion of Serbia by the Austrians was intended to shake and demoralise the Greeks and reassure the Bulgarians, and force them into an alliance with the Turks, while putting the entire Serbian Army out of action. And the later Franco-British bombardment of the forts of the Dardanelles was a movement against the Teutonic party in Bulgaria, as well as a stroke against Turkey, and an attempt to force a warm-water passage for the munitioning of Russia.

Had the Powers of the Triple Entente desired in the late autumn of 1914 to obtain military help at any cost, they could undoubtedly have purchased it; for Italy and Rumania were eager to take the field against Austria-Hungary on certain large conditions. The recovery of their unredeemed territories in Austria and Hungary did not at the time seem to them to be sufficient compensation for the heavy sacrifices in men and treasure which they would be compelled to make. Rumania desired also some voice in shaping the future of Constantinople and the Dardanelles. Italy had magnificent ambitions in regard to her position as one of the chief Mediterranean Powers.

PRINCE VON BÜLOW.
Leaving the German Embassy in Rome.

The Russian Commander-in-Chief could perhaps have induced the Rumanians to take the field by greatly strengthening his southern wing, and holding Bukovina strongly while pressing down upon the Hungarian plain.

Instead of doing so, he kept strictly to the purely military aspect of the conduct of the campaign, and manœuvred his troops as though Rumania and Italy were as steadfastly neutral in feeling as Denmark and Holland. The explanation was perhaps that Russia was so confident of her strength, and felt so capable of bearing the burden of a long war, that she would not relinquish in advance any of the fruits of victory for the sake of a quicker end to the struggle. Now that Turkey had entered the field against the Triple Entente, Russia had her eyes fixed upon Constantinople and the Dardanelles, and upon her future new and higher position as one of the great Sea Powers of the Mediterranean. At the cost of a longer war, and even of another **Russia and** million men, she was re- **Constantinople** solved to realise at last the plan of all her great Tsars, and to establish herself in the seat of Constantine and Justinian.

Italy was then left to come to a decision in her own interests without any pressure at all from Russia, Britain, and France. This was the opportunity for which Prince von Bülow had been waiting. Under the skilful direction of this brilliant ex-Chancellor of the German Empire, all the forces of reaction in Italy were organised in favour of the Teutonic cause. The first stroke that came from Italy against the Powers of the Triple Entente was in appearance a small and unimportant matter. Soon after the fall of Antwerp, the Papal Nuncio to Belgium gave a banquet to some of the generals and officers of the German armies in Belgium. When Cardinal Mercier of Malines was arrested on January 2nd, 1915, for writing his famous pastoral letter to his stricken and downtrodden people, the Papal Nuncio misrepresented this noble act in the confidential advice which he sent to the Vatican.

Then, when the Belgian Government brought about the dismissal of the Nuncio, and obtained the appointment of a more impartial representative of the Vatican, the chief organ of the Vatican itself, the "Osservatore Romano," republished, in a translation, a German newspaper article in which the new Nuncio was fiercely attacked because he was not a partisan of Protestant Germany. It will thus be seen that,

THE CONFLICT BETWEEN TSAR FERDINAND AND HIS PRIME MINISTER.

The top photograph is of Dr. V. Radoslavoff, the Bulgarian Premier; and immediately underneath is a photograph of Tsar Ferdinand. The large view is of Sofia, looking towards the Djumaia Pass (some forty-five miles away), from the front of the Parliament House, and showing the monument to Alexander II., at the foot of which on March 13th, 1915, Dr. Radoslavoff publicly laid a wreath in memory of "the Liberator's" death-day. The pro-German ruler of Bulgaria, like King Constantine of Greece, opposed the anti-Turkish policy of his Prime Minister.

temporarily at least, the Vatican became the active ally of the megalomaniac Protestant German Emperor, who, in some of his wilder speeches during the war, had claimed to be God's representative on earth. Pope Benedict himself tried to preserve a neutral attitude, but the Vatican as a whole was of Teutonic sympathies.

Allied with the ecclesiastical intriguers, against whom the British Cardinal Gasquet stubbornly, but apparently vainly, fought, were most of the descendants of the nobles that had wrecked Italy in the fifteenth and sixteenth centuries. These "black" families, as they are called, had for some centuries exercised the chief control over

LIEUT.-GENERAL CADORNA.
Chief of Staff of the Italian Army.
Inset: Baron Sonnino, Italian Foreign Minister.

standing with Prince von Bülow in regard to the temporal government of the world. They agreed to support the Germanic cause, and to assist by all means in their power the spread of the caste system of government for which Prussia stood. "You are aristocrats, and we are aristocrats," said Prince von Bülow in effect, "and we must work together to combat any democratic movement either in politics or in religion." As in Germany, so in Italy, some of the most powerful leaders in the fields of finance and industry were admitted into the camp of the new feudalists. And, what was more remarkable still, an apparently considerable body of Italian Socialists was induced to side, at least passively, with all the forces of reaction.

Having thus gathered, by his remarkable skill in intrigue, a great party round his Roman villa, Prince von Bülow tried to come to terms with those leaders of Italian political opinion who held the supreme power in the Government independently of both the ecclesiastical and Socialistic parties. He had to deal chiefly with both Signor Salandra and Signor Giolitti, the first the Prime Minister, and the second the leader of the largest party in the Chamber of Deputies. On November 6th Signor Salandra's position was strengthened by the appointment of Baron Sonnino, a Liberal aristocrat, to the position of Foreign Minister. Salandra and Giolitti were rivals for the control of the destinies of their country. Salandra was in office, and possessed, therefore, some means of controlling the General Election in the way usual in Italy. When menaced by an adverse vote from Giolitti's majority, he was able to reply by the threat of dissolution. In this manner he retained his position and power, and showed an impregnable front against the intrigues of Prince von Bülow.

Bülow openly made approaches to Giolitti. But the result was such a fierce movement of warlike patriotism in the general body of the Italian people that Giolitti himself drew back from anything that looked like an understanding with the German intriguer. The upshot was that Bülow found he could make no impression upon the ruling parties in the Government of Italy. He had made large promises of helping Italy at the expense of Austria. But these promises had only evoked some very plain criticism from the statesmen of Italy. They reminded Bülow that in 1866 Bismarck's agent in Rome, Usedom, had officially declared that: "If Italy resists the pressure of France, I am authorised to assure her in a confidential and precise manner that my Government will support her claim to the Southern Tyrol." And they reminded him of the insulting answer Bismarck is said to have made when asked by Italy to fulfil his promise.

Von Bülow's intrigues in Italy

THE WAR SPIRIT IN ITALY.
Scene in the Cathedral Square at Milan, where a demonstration in favour of Italian intervention in the war was held in check by Bersaglieri and Lancers.

SIGNOR SALANDRA.
Italian Prime Minister.

SIGNOR GIOLITTI.
The Italian leader who revealed the war plot of 1913.

BARON SONNINO.

the affairs of the Roman Catholic Church, and in recent years they had quashed a movement for the development of representative government in the Church which originated among the Catholics in the United States. In the winter of 1914 they came to an under-

FINANCE MINISTERS OF THE TRIPLE ENTENTE DISCUSS THE PROBLEM OF THE "SILVER BULLETS."

In February, 1915, at the French Ministry of Finance in Paris, the Finance Ministers of the Allies—M. Bark, M. Ribot, and Mr. Lloyd George (seen from left to right)—met in conference, when it was agreed that the Allies should unite their financial equally with their military resources in order to carry the war to a successful conclusion.

Long had the Italians waited for their revenge for this double act of treachery and insult. But Bülow paid to the full on January 6th, 1915, for the act of bad faith by Bismarck in 1866. Then Signor Giolitti himself—the more pro-German in appearance of the two political leaders of Italy—went out of his way to reveal to the world the fact that the Germans had plotted to make the Great War in 1913, but that the plot then temporarily failed owing to the refusal of Italy to co-operate in an aggressive action directed through Serbia at Russia. This revelation was intended to shock Bülow into sincerity. It had that effect. By this time Italy had a million first-line troops ready for war, and it was plainly hinted that she was only waiting for the snow to melt on the Alpine passes in order to recover by force the lands of her people still held by the last and worst of all the conquerors of her territory in the days of her weakness—Austria. Bülow then ceased to promise, and began to make definite offers of the

THE QUEEN OF HOLLAND IN AMSTERDAM.
Her Majesty's German consort (Prince Henry of Mecklenburg-Schwerin) is seen taking his seat on her left.

immediate cession of ancient Italian territory. He entered into negotiations with Count Tisza, the Hungarian who was almost in the position of dictator in Austria-Hungary. He arranged with the count that Italy should receive the Trentino, in the Southern Tyrol, together with an increase of frontier towards the great seaport of Trieste. The Italians insisted on Trieste itself being included. "Impossible!" Bülow at first replied. "Trieste does not belong to Austria now. It is a vital outlet for Germany."

Signor Salandra said nothing, but accelerated his military preparations, and in some of his speeches to his own people he continued to say nothing, but to hint a great deal. Meanwhile the clever but baffled German intriguer pretended that the Emperor Francis Joseph would not hear even of the cession of the Trentino, but that Germany was still trying to induce her ally to arrive at a fair compromise with Italy. Then came the thunderclap of the Queen Elizabeth's guns at the gate of the Dardanelles. This was the kind of action which Italian statesmen could well appreciate after months of grappling with the phantasmal promises of Teutonic friendship. By the middle of March, 1915, both Germany and Austria-Hungary were eager to come to terms with Italy. They made the following offer: " 1. The cession of the Trentino, and of all the frontier territory completing the basin of the Isonzo, including the new railway. 2. The concession to Trieste and the surrounding district of the modified form of self-government that existed at

CONSTANTINE I.
King of the Hellenes.

Fiume before this was withdrawn by the Hungarians. Fiume to have her rights restored. 3. Renunciation by Austria of all interference in the Italian control of Albania. 4. An agreement between Austria and Italy in regard to their respective influences in the Adriatic. A more effective co-operation of the two naval forces. A common opposition to any Serbian expansion on the Albanian coast.

Italy thus arrived, after the war had gone on for seven and a half months, at the hour of crisis in her history which would determine all her future development. The Teutons had apparently made their final offer, and the snow was beginning to melt in the mountain passes of the

German Plot to delude Italy

Trentino. It was then that the Custom-house officers at Venice made a little discovery with some great political consequences. In some barrels about to be shipped through a German firm to the rebellious Arabs at Tripoli was found a large consignment of rifles of French manufacture. The Germans had aimed at bringing down two birds with one stone. They wished to increase Italy's Colonial troubles by arming the rebels; but seeing that

M. VENIZELOS.
Greek Premier during the first phase of the Great War.

MR. WILLIAM JENNINGS BRYAN.
Secretary of State, U.S.A.

SENATOR GENERAL HORACE PORTER.
Formerly United States Ambassador to France.

these rebels would at last be conquered, weapons in hand, they sent them French rifles, with a view to involving France in difficulties with Italy The flagrant exposure of the plot in the critical days of the middle of March was as helpful to the Powers of the Triple Entente as a great victory in Bukovina would have been.

The hesitating position of Rumania during the winter of 1914 was partly due to the immobility of Italy in that period. After the death of King Carol, on October 10th, 1914, the Rumanian people became eager to fight. But they wanted, if possible, to time their sweep into the Hungarian territory of Transylvania occupied by their race with the Italian advance into the Trentino and Trieste. By attacking the common foe together, during a renewal of the Serbian offensive movement, the

Apprehensions at Bucharest

Rumanians would have only a distracted foe to face, especially if the southern Russian army were attacking the Austrians and the Hungarians at the same time. When Italy held back, and the southern Russian army was forced away from Bukovina, exposing the Rumanian frontier to an Austro-German attack, the statesmen of Bucharest became apprehensive; for it was then well known that Rumania had entered into a fighting treaty with Russia. The negotiations had taken place towards the end of October, 1914, and had ended in a convention signed towards the close of the following month. One of the clauses of this conven-

CARDINAL GASQUET.
An opponent of German ecclesiastical intrigue.

tion was to the effect that: " In return for the neutrality of Rumania, Russia consents to her annexing, by occupying them, the territories of Austria-Hungary peopled in larger part by Rumanian populations." The terms are somewhat curious, but the real significance of this clause is not obscure.

The last military preparations of Rumania were completed. Her Army had not fought since its glorious campaign of 1877-78 against the Turks of Osman Pasha, but it had continually developed in strength. With

BARON STEPHAN DE BURIAN.
Austro-Hungarian Foreign Minister.

SIGNOR GIUSEPPE MOTTA.
President of the Swiss Confederation.

A BIVOUAC IN THE BRUSHWOOD: FRENCH ADVANCE GUARD ENJOYING A TEMPORARY REST AT THE FRONT.

FRENCH ARTILLERY IN A WOOD.
The guns are cleverly hidden, the chimneys shown serving the double purpose of disguise and exit for the gases after firing.

INSPECTING A NEW TRENCH.
French officer making a final tour of inspection of a newly-constructed trench at an advanced point in the firing-line.

MAKING THE BEST—AND THE MOST—OF IT: A MEAL IN THE OPEN AIR.
When the above photograph was taken the weather was the reverse of congenial; but with characteristically French regard for the *convenances* of the table, this little detachment of soldiers had their refreshments in as much style as the means at their disposal would permit.

CLEANING UP: FRENCH SOLDIERS FIND A CONVENIENT SPOT FOR A LITTLE LAUNDRY WORK AFTER A HARD SPELL OF MARCHING AND FIGHTING.

feverish activity it had prepared for the great war of liberation. In number and in machinery Rumania had created the most notable military organisation of Europe, after those of the Great Powers. There was a first-line Rumanian Army of 400,000 men, well-organised and well-led, and to these, at the end of two or three months, another quarter of a million soldiers would be added. Both the Austrians and the Germans were well aware of Rumania's remarkable strength. For this reason they refrained from any act of hostility when they reached the frontier in their first successful advance through Bukovina. In the meantime the Rumanians went on increasing their stores of ammunition with the help of Italian armament firms.

Rumania's great military strength

The fact was that the Rumanians wanted to see the Russian troops firmly established on their frontier before they moved. Their great fear was that if they swept into Hungary while the Russian southern army was still being pressed back the Tsar of Bulgaria would attack them from the south. In 1913, 300,000 Rumanian troops had crossed the Danube, and by invading Bulgaria had brought the second Balkan War to a close quickly. Rumania had then taken an important tract of Bulgarian territory, to cover her expenses of mobilisation and military action. So it was only to be expected that the Bulgarians might now strike back if an opportunity offered.

The position of Bulgaria during the winter of 1914 and the spring of 1915 was extremely delicate. The people were angry with the Serbians and the Greeks for having deprived them of the rich province of Macedonia, where the finest kinds of Turkish tobaccos are grown. This region, with its port of Kavalla, was peopled by Bulgarians, who were being, it was said in Sofia, oppressed by their new Christian masters. If Serbia and Greece could have been induced to give up their share of Macedonia, there would have been a solidarity of interests among the Balkan States. But apparently the representatives of the Powers of the Triple Entente could not bring about this arrangement. In the meantime the domestic politics of Bulgaria were as complex and troubled as those of Greece. In both kingdoms the King and the Court party favoured the cause of the Teutons, while the people were ready to fight on the side of Russia, Britain, and France. The Premier of Bulgaria, M. Radoslavoff, co-operated with the Premier of Greece, M. Venizelos, in preparing to act against the Turkish Army in Europe, and to thus win a place of power in the council chamber of the Allies when the partition of the Ottoman Empire was being decided.

But Tsar Ferdinand and King Constantine did not agree with the views of their respective Premiers. The German Tsar of Bulgaria, having lost Constantinople in the first Balkan War through listening to the treacherous voice of Austria, was still apparently more inclined to side with his betrayers than with the natural allies of his people. It was Austria and Germany who had induced him in 1913 to shatter his Army against the forces of Greece and Serbia. And now the inveterate intriguer of the House of Coburg still placed his hopes upon the eventual success of the Teutons. He had been promised a share of Serbian territory—a share of the body of the small heroic nation which had fought faithfully with him against the Turks, until he had tried to destroy it at the bidding of Austria. His great general, Radko Dimitrieff, was winning new victories for Russia against the men who had deceived, betrayed, and broken his own country. Yet Tsar Ferdinand continued to oppose the wishes of his people and of their constitutional representatives.

The German Tsar of Bulgaria

116

WITH THE GERMAN ARMY IN POLAND.

General von Gropp, with his Chief of Staff. In the trench is a mitrailleuse which had been abandoned by the Russians.

AN ENEMY PATROL IN THE FLOODED AREA OF THE YSER.

German Lancer scout, armed with lance, sword, and rifle, looking over the waste of waters in a corner of Flanders. The circular view is of Prussian Hussars using the backs of their horses from which to survey the position of the foe.

FRENCH " 75 " WITH SHELTER FOR THE GUNNERS IN A WOOD IN THE ARGONNE.

FRENCH ARTILLERYMAN BRINGING UP A SHELL FOR A HIDDEN " 75."
The smaller photograph is entitled by our French photographer "The Passing of Winter," a title suggesting not only the life beyond the grave and the approach of spring, but the advent of eventual victory.

It was in this critical period of their history that many of the Balkan States recognised the disadvantage of their foreign dynasties, all more or less accessible to the subtle and pervasive influences of Berlin and Vienna. It was a notorious fact that the German Emperor regarded the German monarchs of Bulgaria and Rumania, and the German-Danish King of Greece, as energetic and friendly vassals. It was their duty, from the German point of view, to prepare the way for the extension of the Teutonic Empire to Constantinople and the Persian Gulf. King Carol of Rumania had been bound to the Hohenzollerns ; only his death liberated his people from the alternative of a revolution or a national decline. Greece and Bulgaria remained till the spring of 1915 in the sphere of Germanic influence.

The position of things was extremely unfortunate for the Greeks. For they had in M. Venizelos the greatest national leader since Pericles. This Cretan shepherd and guerilla soldier had fought his way to high command in his native island, and then had sailed to Athens and become the main force in the Balkan League, which would have turned the Turk out of Europe in 1913 if the **A great** Germans, Austrians, and Italians had **Cretan patriot** not interfered. After breaking with his too-ambitious ally, the Tsar of Bulgaria, Venizelos had turned to the Germanic marionettes in his own national court, and, in spite of the efforts of King Constantine, the King's four sons, and his Prussian wife, sister to Kaiser Wilhelm II., had practically banished them. Unhappily, M. Venizelos allowed them to return when the Great War broke out, in the hope of arriving at a complete national unity. But by intriguing with some of the chiefs of the Army the Prussian Court party brought about the overthrow of the great Cretan patriot, at the very moment when he was about to take measures to build his country up into one of the great Mediterranean Powers.

All through the winter Greece had been watching Bulgaria in the interests of Serbia. Had Tsar Ferdinand attempted to attack the Serbians when they were hard pressed by the Austrians, Greece would have come to the rescue of her ally. In the spring a new arrangement of the Balkan problem was worked out by Russia and Britain. While waiting to enter the Great War, Rumania took over the task of protecting the Serbians. This left Greece with her hands free. A representative of the British Government then consulted with M. Venizelos, and in February, 1915, it was arranged that when the Franco-British fleet had opened the gateway of the Dardanelles, and had wrecked some of the chief forts in the Narrows, Greece would provide part of the landing-force for operations against the Turkish troops holding the Gallipoli Peninsula.

There remained only the apparently formal act of getting the consent of King Constantine to the policy arranged by his constitutional Premier. Then it was that the Kaiser and his sister, with his nephews, were well repaid for all the trouble they had taken to win over the chiefs of the Greek Army. King Constantine refused to send a single soldier to co-operate with the allied fleet in forcing the passage of the Dardanelles. The principal generals of the Greek Army agreed with their foreign King. M. Venizelos —surprised, consternated, bewildered—resigned. One of the chiefs of the Epirote clans tried to assassinate the King. He failed. In the meantime France prepared a large Mohammedan force in her North African dominions to supply the place of the Greek Army, and Great Britain also organised in Egypt an army of invasion for transport to the Dardanelles. At the same time Russia prepared to launch a very considerable force north of Constantinople. By the end of March the Powers of the Triple Entente were

All King Constantine effected well able to do without help from either the Bulgarians or the Greeks in the operations against Turkey. All that King Constantine effected was to delay for two or three weeks the Franco-British fleet's attack upon the forts in the narrowest part of the Dardanelles.

The general position at the opening of the spring campaign around the great central battlefield was that nearly three-quarters of a million of first-rate Rumanian soldiers were ready to invade Hungary. Italy had a full million troops of the first line seemingly waiting for the snows to melt in the Trentino in order to march into Austria. The old Austrian Emperor, who had once reigned over Lombardy, said that he would rather surrender the Duchy of Galicia to the Russians, and make a separate peace with the Triple Entente, than yield any more territory to the Italians. On the other hand, it was reported that the people of Austria-Hungary were anxious for the Italians to take the field, and thus quicken the ending of the war. They did not mind who won, so long as the terrible struggle was brought abruptly to a conclusion. It is thus that we see, more clearly in the field of diplomacy than in the field of battle, the progress made by the Allies after seven months of warfare.

To all appearance the opposing fronts were held as strongly as ever. But there was a large crack between the two Teutonic Empires. Germany was in such difficulties that she was eager to sell her fighting ally Austria

BELGIAN RECRUITS IN TRAINING IN THE ENVIRONS OF PARIS.

KING ALBERT'S NEW ARMY AT DRILL IN THE VICINITY OF THE FRENCH CAPITAL.
While Lord Kitchener's new army was getting into form in various parts of the United Kingdom, and new classes of the French Army were preparing for active service, Belgian recruits were in training in France. Our smaller view shows a section of them being reviewed by M. Carton de Wiart.

to Austria's deadliest enemy—Italy. To counter this move, Austria was almost ready to come to a separate arrangement with Germany's deadliest enemy—Russia. The war had been started directly with a view to enlarging Austria's power in the Adriatic Sea. But Germany had now given up all idea of a Byzantine-Ottoman extension of her Empire. She was ready to tear up another scrap of paper—her treaty with Austria—in the hope of being able to save herself at the expense of her partner in international crime.

This act of German faithlessness was worth more than a smashing victory to the Powers of the Triple Entente, for it was something that would tell on the future relations between the Northern and Southern Teutons for several generations. It would be very long before an Austrian would again trust the word of a Prussian.

There was also a wide division between the people of Vienna and the people of Budapest. The resignation of the Austrian Foreign Minister, Count Berchtold, on January 14th, 1915, was followed by the appointment of a Hungarian magnate, Baron Burian. It was well known that Burian was only an automaton controlled by his masterful fellow-countryman Count Tisza. The count

directed all the affairs of Austria-Hungary, and the Kaiser dealt with him in every important matter, instead of arranging things with the Emperor Francis Joseph. It was really Hungary that was trying to sell Austria to Italy.

The Hungarians were dominated by fear of the Rumanians. As masters of the Southern Teutonic Empire, they first insisted upon Germany sending soldiers to help in the defence of their country against the Russians. When this was done, they proposed to stave off the Italian attack at the expense of Austrian territory, in order that Rumania should not have any co-operating force if she persisted in attempting an invasion. The result of all these involved intrigues upon the deserted and betrayed Austrian populace was that many of them became ready to make peace with Russia, and even looked forward to the success of the **Austrians ready** Rumanians with a malicious joy. **to make peace** Mutinies became more frequent in the Austrian armies, and only the Hungarian forces continued to show any resolute courage. Even the Hungarians sometimes thought of breaking away from Germany and making a separate peace.

In fact, Count Tisza hinted this tendency of his countrymen to the Kaiser and his Staff in order to induce them to send special reinforcements into Hungary to throw the Russians back from the Carpathians. Tisza was a master in making menaces of this sort, and by means of them he kept the Germans faithful to the cause of Hungary during the winter and spring. As a matter of fact, his position in his own country was not secure. There was a very powerful movement for independence among the Hungarian magnates. The leaders of this movement proposed to make peace with Russia and to leave Austria to her doom.

It was this movement that told upon the Rumanians, for they knew that they would lose Transylvania if the Hungarians first concluded negotiations with Russia. This was why the Russian-Rumanian arrangement was signed early in the winter of 1914. Rumania was resolute

FRENCH SAPPERS ERECTING TEMPORARY TELEGRAPH WIRES IN THE NORTH OF FRANCE.
In the upper view are to be seen Belgian soldiers on guard by a famous old mill near Furnes.

EN ROUTE: STRIKING VIEW IN THE CHAMPAGNE COUNTRY.

THEIR LAST FIGHT: TRIBUTE OF RESPECT TO THE FALLEN FOE.

German dead in a field on the banks of the Oise. The young Frenchman, the only living being seen in the above pathetic camera-record of the wastage of war, is crossing the stricken field with bared head. The centre picture is of the new French cannon, a weapon with a calibre of a little over six inches. It is fitted with wheel-pads to facilitate transport over rough, roadless country.

PRESIDENT POINCARE, WITH SOME OFFICERS, AT
THE FRENCH HEADQUARTERS.

By the middle of March it looked as though the German loan would be spent in buying ammunition for use against Germany's latest ally. The Turk grew apprehensive of his northern neighbour, and began to concentrate troops around Adrianople. Altogether, the prospect, from the Teutonic point of view, was very gloomy in the field of diplomacy. On March 13th, the anniversary of the death of Alexander II. of Russia, the Tsar of the Liberation, the Bulgarian Premier publicly laid a wreath on the statue of the great Romanoff to whom Bulgaria owed her redemption from Turkish tyranny. It was a very significant act, especially on the part of the leader of the Government that had lately received a large sum of money from Germany.

In other countries of Europe there was little change of policy from the autumn of 1914 to the spring of 1915. What change occurred was not to the advantage of the spoilers of Belgium. Even the German-Swiss began to

FRENCH INFANTRY ON THE MARCH.

to be first in the field on the side of the Triple Entente. Her claim to Transylvania was practically admitted by our Government on January 27th, 1915, when a British loan of £5,000,000 was made to her. Germany tried to counter this British move by making a similar loan to Bulgaria, for it was on Bulgaria that the Hungarians relied to prevent the Rumanian attack. The German loan was no doubt arranged by Count Tisza with this end in view.

Bulgaria temporises But by this time the Bulgarian Premier, M. Radoslavoff, was inclined to imitate the policy of Venizelos, of Greece. The reversion to Adrianople tempted him, as well as the tract of fertile land on the southern border of Bulgaria. When Greece drew back from the plan of co-operating in forcing the passage of the Dardanelles, M. Radoslavoff became still more tempted to let bygones be bygones in regard to Serbia, and to launch a Bulgarian army once more against the Turks.

FRENCH RED CROSS WORKER RENDERING FIRST-AID TO A WOUNDED SOLDIER IN THE FIRING-LINE.

hesitate in their blind admiration for the men of their Prussianised race on the other side of the Rhine. There was an increasingly loud revolt of opinion against the Prussian methods of many of the officers of the Swiss Army, and the Swiss President, Herr Haffmann, of German stock, was replaced by a man of Italian stock, Signor Motta, from Southern Switzerland. The Swiss censorship, which at first had been grossly biased to the German cause, was also modified. By the spring Switzerland as a whole was inclined to look with more sympathy at Belgium, and to preserve a veritable neutral attitude.

The new Swiss President

In Sweden, the only other democratic country in Europe, which showed at first a strong sympathy with Germany, a similar revolution of feeling gradually took place in the winter months. While in Persia some of the Swedish gendarmerie were actively helping the Germans to arm certain of the tribes around the Persian Gulf to enable them to attack our friendly sheikhs there, and to raid our camp, the Swedes at home became less inclined to make trouble on the Russian frontier. There was a certain incident in November, 1914, which seemed to show that some Swedish sailors were ready to go further against us than even the Swedish gendarmerie were going in the Persian Gulf. But the nation generally became more averse from any understanding with Germany.

Naturally, this aversion was not diminished when Germany instituted her extraordinary submarine campaign against all neutral ships trading to ports in the United

NEW USE FOR LACE.
The guns in the above photograph were covered with lace curtains to hide them from aerial observation. Inset: British officers at the entrance to their bomb-proof shelter.

Kingdom. In fact, this murderous measure left Germany without a friend among the democracies of Europe. Only the monarchs of Bulgaria and Greece and the reactionary aristocratic and clerical parties of Italy and Spain continued to favour the Teutonic cause. The curious condition of things in Spain, where the King and Queen stood out for the Allies against their own Court, with only part of the Spanish democracy siding with them, attracted the notice of the Portuguese Republicans. It may have been with a view to reviving the old Republican movement in Spain that the Portuguese Parliament became eager to

"SHELLS, MORE SHELLS!" THE INSATIABLE APPETITE OF THE GUNS.
Unloading ammunition immediately behind the line of fire. As the spring of 1915 approached it became more and more evident that the progress of operations depended on an increased supply of ammunition for the guns. The official French review of the first six months of the war frankly stated that the consumption of projectiles was so enormous as to cause for a moment an ammunition crisis, but that this had been completely overcome. Anxiety in Great Britain on this score was accentuated by labour disputes attributed in part to German agency.

PHOTOGRAPHIC PROOF OF THE DETERIORATION OF GERMAN EXPLOSIVES.

Extreme interest attaches to these camera-records of German gunfire. They were sent to us by a French artillery officer. In the left-hand photograph, taken in January, 1915, a 15-cm. German explosive is seen bursting at a distance of two hundred metres in front of the battery. The haziness of the view is caused by the mass of débris hurled over the earthworks on the right. Great damage was done, and the good quality of the German ammunition is shown by the quantity of smoke. Contrast this with the effect to be seen in the second photograph, of a 15-cm. German shell exploding at only thirty metres' distance from the camera. This second photograph was taken some weeks later. Had our correspondent attempted to take his first photograph at thirty metres, we should not have been able to place these interesting records before our readers.

send its Army into the battlefield of France. On November 24th the Portuguese deputies authorised their Government to support Great Britain in accordance with the old alliance between the two nations. It was a gallant gesture on the part of the Portuguese, but for reasons which are still obscure it did not result in any active measures of a warlike kind. Probably the continual disturbances which had followed the revolution had left Portugal with so empty an exchequer that she could not, even to put to shame the reactionary Spanish parties, raise the money to equip an army for the field. Still the will to fight in the great struggle for the principle of freedom was there, though the means may for the time have been lacking.

The greatest of all democracies in the world—the United States of America—continued to be divided in its sympathies. The native-born American, who owed his national independence largely to France and the greater part of his culture to the islands whose language he inherited, had to walk warily. His chief representative, President Woodrow Wilson, son of a Scots Presbyterian minister, seemed inclined to bear openly against the contraband policy of the Allies. With that peculiar conscientiousness of the Anglo-Celtic temperament, he was more troubled about the mote in Britain's eye than about the beam in the Teutonic vision. So, at least, it appeared on December 30th, 1914, when the American Note to Great Britain in regard to neutral shipping was presented in London. The Note contended that American ships, and neutral vessels carrying American cargoes, should not be taken into British ports and detained there for the purpose of search, unless our warships had, before they stopped each vessel, sufficient evidence to justify belief that contraband goods were being carried. The American Note also protested against the seizure of contraband articles consigned to neutral countries,

America's Note to Great Britain

even in cases where it was fairly patent that the neutral importers would forward the goods to Germany or Austria.

The manner in which the Note was first published, in a short, sharp résumé printed in American newspapers before the complete document was seen by Sir Edward Grey, helped to increase the bad impression made in our country. The tragic year of 1914 closed in gloom. For it looked as though President Wilson had adopted the method of President Cleveland in the former dispute about Venezuela, and was about to put us in the difficult position of resigning our proper rights or drifting into war with the United States.

The doctrine of continuous voyage

What especially saddened British feeling was the fact that we were conducting our search for contraband in accordance with the principles established by the United States. Abraham Lincoln and his advisers, in their blockade of the Southern States, gave a remarkable extension to the doctrine of continuous voyage, which had first been heard of in the French revolutionary war. Under this doctrine goods which were shipped to a neutral port, but which were intended ultimately to reach the enemy, were to be regarded as if on one continuous voyage to the enemy's ports or frontiers, and were therefore liable to seizure in neutral ships. Thus the American courts ruled that goods shipped to the Mexican port of Matamoras were liable to seizure, if those goods were intended for the Southern States, and they admitted suspicion as sufficient evidence of such a destination. There can be no doubt that the doctrine of continuous voyage was established justly, and it seemed extremely unfair that President Wilson should seek to hinder our Navy from adopting the instrument that Abraham Lincoln had once used rightly against our own shipping. For a few days there was a tendency in

IN THE ALLIES' TRENCHES BEFORE YPRES.

"THE PATHS OF GLORY LEAD BUT TO THE GRAVE."

That "there is no moderation in arms" is a thought as old as Seneca. But the above camera-picture of a handful of Frenchmen compelled to take their part in repulsing the enemy over graves and by the side of a shattered mortuary is calculated to send an icy chill to the hearts of the least impressionable of those who look at the conflict from afar. In one case the Germans actually dug deep trenches among graves.

MEN OF DESTINY: THE TWO LEADERS OF THE ALLIES IN THE WEST.

An artist's impression of a consultation between the French Generalissimo and the Commander-in-Chief of the British Forces in France. President Poincaré, in presenting General Joffre with the Military Medal, referred in glowing words to his "force of soul that nothing disturbed," and his "serenity, the salutary exam of which spread confidence and hope everywhere." The confidence of his coun men in Sir John French is only equalled by that of the French people in General Jo

THE BRITISH UNDER FIRE—AND ALMOST UNDER WATER.

During the incessant rain in Flanders the lot of our men in the trenches was such that they had to be relieved as quickly as possible. Rubber boots and leggings were but slight palliatives, and coke braziers, while they cast a ruddy glow around, gave comparatively little warmth. Where this could be done, corrugated-structures were used for protection, and the ground was covered with brushw and straw. Sometimes it was possible to pump out the water.

SCENE AT A BLUE CROSS RECEIVING DEPOT IN NORTHERN FRANCE.

terinary doctors attached to the Blue Cross service receiving a wounded war-
rse for treatment. In dealing with casualties among our four-footed friends,
e Blue Cross organisation developed on lines identical with those adopted by the
Red Cross workers on behalf of the men. First-aid having been rendered, the
wounded animals were drafted to depots for surgical and medical attention. Later
the horses were placed in meadows, to complete their recovery there.

IN THE THICK OF A BITTER CONTEST IN THE ARGONNE.

ercely contested hand-to-hand fighting went on in the forest region of the Argonne
roughout the winter. The trench shown in the above drawing was fought for
ain and again. Brilliant work on the part of our brave ally had to be followed
by yet more desperate encounters with the determined foe. The situation was one
of prolonged strain, through which, however, the survivors emerged with smiling
faces if tired frames. The struggle in the vicinity of Verdun was most exacting.

BIG GUNS USED BY THE BRITISH IN THE YSER DISTRICT—CAREFULLY SCREENED FROM BOMB-DROPPING
ENEMY AIRCRAFT.

ANOTHER EXAMPLE OF THE METHOD ADOPTED BY BRITISH GUNNERS TO CONCEAL THEIR PIECES FROM
HOSTILE OBSERVATION.

Britain to regard the modern American nation, as represented by the activities of its responsible Government, as a purely commercial community, eager to overthrow its own contribution to international law as soon as this law was found to interfere with its pursuit of wealth at any cost. But, as we shall see in the course of this chapter, this view of American policy did not cover all the facts of the case.

Meanwhile, Sir Edward Grey prepared to reply to the American Note. His preliminary answer was sent to the American Ambassador in London on January 7th, 1915.

He began by pointing out that the figures in regard to American trade, which he had seen, did not show that commerce with neutral countries had been affected by our process of searching ships. In November, 1913, the exports from New York to Denmark were worth 558,000 dollars.

In November, 1914, Denmark was taking over 7,100,000 dollars' worth of goods. In the same way, Sweden increased her New York imports from 377,000 dollars to 2,858,000 dollars; Norway from 477,000 dollars to 2,318,000 dollars; Italy from 2,971,000 dollars to 4,781,000 dollars. The increase of American copper exports to the neutral countries of Europe was very striking. Italy received more than double the amount she had done in 1913; and, with the exception of Holland and Italy, the other European states received in 1914 *nearly five times the amount of American copper* which they had taken in 1913. Sir Edward Grey pointed out that there was a very strong presumption that the bulk of American copper consigned to Norway, Sweden, Denmark, and Switzerland was intended for use in Germany and Austria. Our Government had, in fact, at the time of writing, positive evidence that four copper and aluminium consignments, then on **Copper to Germany** the way from the United States to **via Sweden** Sweden, were definitely destined for Germany. This American copper, it must be remembered, was being employed by the Germans and Austrians to make shells for the slaughter of Belgians, Serbians, Frenchmen, Russians, and British troops. In conclusion Sir Edward Grey stated:

"We are confronted with the growing danger that neutral countries contiguous to the enemy will become, on a scale hitherto unprecedented, a base of supplies for the armed forces of our enemies and for materials for manufacturing armament. The trade figures of imports show how strong this tendency is, but we have no complaint to make of the attitude of the Governments of those countries, which, so far as we are aware, have not departed from proper rules of neutrality. We endeavour, in the interest of our own national safety, to prevent this danger by intercepting goods really destined for the enemy, without interfering with those which are bona fide neutral.

"Since the outbreak of the war the Government of the United States have changed their previous practice, and have **America's** prohibited the publication of manifests **shipping policy** till thirty days after the departure of vessels from the United States ports. We had no locus standi for complaining of this change, and did not complain. But the effect of it must be to increase the difficulty of ascertaining the presence of contraband, and to render necessary, in the interest of our national safety, the examination and detention of more ships than would have been the case if the former practice had continued.

"Pending a more detailed reply, I would conclude by saying that his Majesty's Government do not desire to contest the general principles of international law on which they understand the Note of the United States to be based, and desire to restrict their action solely to interference with contraband destined for the enemy."

The reply of Sir Edward Grey was friendly in tone, but masterly in argument. It swayed the minds of a large number of American people who were not anxious to fight on the side of Germany against Britain, France, Russia, and Japan. Soon after it was received in America, President Wilson and his Secretary for Foreign Affairs consulted together in regard to the charges made by German-Americans about their shipping policy. A letter of inquiry had been received from Senator Stone, who had a large German

AS THE SOLDIER SEES THE BATTLEFIELD.
These photographs, sent to the Editor by soldiers in the front trenches, are most interesting. They are snapshots taken through the loopholes of the trenches. In the first a battle is raging. Note the distant smoke, while the dim figures in the foreground are dead Germans who fell in attacking the trench days before. The second shows a row of houses held by Germans, towards which the French engineers had stealthily sapped and mined; and in the third we have the same scene after the mine was fired— the whole of the houses destroyed and the German position made untenable

electorate in St. Louis, the chief city of his State. He was chairman of the Committee on Foreign Relations, and he stated in his letter of inquiry that many of his electorate sympathised with Germany and Austria, and believed

THE PRICE OF THE TRENCH: CHARGE OF TURCOS OVER FIRE-SWEPT OPEN COUNTRY.

In Champagne the French offensive was taken part in by Zouaves, Colonial infantry, Algerian sharpshooters, and Turcos. Our artist depicts a charge by the last-named. The Moroccans have taken one trench, and, leaving their dead and wounded with dead and dying Germans, are advancing under shell and shrapnel fire across the coverless country, to be engulfed again in another trench melée farther on. In addition to the awful price in flesh and blood paid for a slight advance, the ground between the trenches was ploughed and scarred by the tempest of fire and flame, which had also levelled any trees that formerly stood between the opposing armies. One observer tells us that in the intervals of artillery firing "larks could be heard singing continuously in joyous chorus."

130

PAY DAY ON THE BATTLEFIELD.
German infantry being paid in notes. In the circular photograph we see a French soldier assisting an unhappy German who was found practically naked in a captured trench.

WINTER FASHIONS IN THE KAISER'S ARMY.
German soldier of the Landsturm wearing a fur coat with a Medici collar.

that the United States Government was showing partiality to Britain, France, and Russia.

The letter from Senator Stone brought to a head the German-American agitation against the munitioning of the Allies by American armament firms. It was a notorious fact, for example, that the Bethlehem Steel Works were making 16 in. guns for Britain, and a considerable amount of the shells used against the German front in the western theatre of the war came from America. Something like twenty million men, women, and children of Teutonic stock, settled in the United States, looked at this position of affairs with much anger and bitterness. But in the letter in reply, drawn up by the President and the Foreign Secretary, and signed by the latter, it was pointed out that the situation was simply the inevitable sequel to the British control of the sea.

Mr. Bryan's reply to agitators

"If," said Mr. Bryan, "any American citizens who are partisans of Germany and Austria-Hungary feel that this Administration is acting in a way injurious to the cause of those countries, this feeling results from the fact that on the high seas German and Austro-Hungarian naval power is thus far inferior to the British. It is the business of a belligerent operating on the high seas, not the duty of a neutral, to prevent contraband from reaching the enemy.

"Those in this country who sympathise with Germany and Austria-Hungary appear to assume that some obligation rests upon this Government in the performance of its neutral duty to prevent all trade in contraband, and thus to equalise the difference due to the relative naval strength of the belligerents. No such obligation exists. It would be an unneutral act—an act of partiality on the part of this Government —to adopt such a policy, if the Executive had the power to do so."

Mr. Roosevelt also intervened in the discussion with considerable effect. He remarked that any restriction of the export of armaments and ammunition would weaken his country. The Government factories were inadequate to supply American needs in case of war, and it was only by allowing American business men to develop their plant for supplying any foreign nation able to maintain a sea-borne traffic that the United States

INDIAN TROOPS IN ACTION—CAUTIOUS ADVANCE OF A MAXIM-GUN DETACHMENT.

could grow in warlike strength with no increase of taxation for military purposes.

But some German-Americans were still eager to work mischief between America and the Powers of the Triple Entente and Japan. Chief among them was Mr. Edward

Breitung, a German-American trust magnate of Michigan. He purchased the steamship Dacia, of the Hamburg-Amerika Line, and prepared to send her out under the American flag with a cargo of cotton to Germany or Holland. It was expected that a British warship would seize the vessel, and that in due course she would be sold as a prize. Then Breitung, and the men working with him, hoped to work the **The case of** American people into a state of indigna- **the Dacia** tion over the insult to the flag. If, on the other hand, our Government were so daunted by the threat of trouble with America as to let the Dacia pass, it was intended to transfer all German merchant ships sheltering in American ports to German-American capitalists. When, however, the Dacia at last appeared near the English Channel, she was captured by a French warship and taken to Brest. By this very simple method our Government avoided all complications with the American people, and prevented the pro-German intriguers

INDIAN INFANTRY ON THEIR WAY TO THE FIGHTING-LINE IN NORTHERN FRANCE.
The smaller photograph is of members of the Sirhind Brigade of the British Indian troops in France. These sturdy fighting men were specially mentioned in Sir John French's despatches.

from arousing the ancient jealousy of the great Trans-Atlantic Republic in regard to our mercantile marine.

By this time the leaders of the Teutonic agitation in the United States began to attract seriously the attention of the loyal American people. At a conference held in Washington by fifty-eight representative German-Americans under the leadership of Richard Bartholdt, of Missouri, a nation-wide organisation was created on January 30th, 1915, to act in a partisan way in American politics. Chief among the leaders of the new party were five congressmen, Bartholdt, Vollmer, Barthfeld, Lobeck, and Porter. In addition were Dr. C. J. Hexamer, president of the German-American National Alliance of Phila-

The Teuton menace in America delphia, claiming a membership of two millions; Professor W. R. Shepherd, of Columbia; Professor Von Mach, of Harvard; Professor Faust, of Cornell; Mr. John Devoy, editor of the New York "Gaelic-American"; and many editors of German-American papers connected with German-American societies. The organisation claimed to represent some twenty million German-Americans, with certain Irish-American sympathisers.

Their main published programme was: " 1. We demand a free and open sea for the commerce of the United States, and unrestricted traffic in non-contraband goods, as defined by international law; 2. We favour, as a strictly American policy, the immediate enactment of legislation prohibiting the export of arms and munitions of war; 3. We pledge ourselves, individually and collectively, to support only such candidates for public office, irrespective of party, who will place American " (*sic*) " interests above those of any other country, and who will aid in eliminating all undue foreign influences from American life."

The immediate object of the organisation was to bring about an alliance between the German-American and German-Irish voters, and to defeat the native Americans in the approaching Presidential primaries and the 1916 campaign. It was intended to overthrow President Wilson and any other Democratic, Republican, or Progressive leader who refused to place

"HINDRANCES TO PROGRESS."
A field of stakes in front of a German position, designed to impale cavalry in case of a charge.

A DEVICE OF GERMAN MANUFACTURE.
Hundreds of these horrible implements were found on a road along which it was expected British cavalry would have to pass.

the insane German-American desire to provoke a war with Britain above the true interests of the peaceful, friendly majority of voters in the United States. The plan of action had been foretold by military writers in Germany, and it was notorious that the ex-German Minister, Dr. Dernburg, was the master-hand working in the background and weaving the plot. At times even the threat of another Civil War was uttered by some of the German-American hot-heads.

It was this movement that partly accounted for the Notes sent to our Government by President Wilson with regard to American shipping. The President inclined to state the American case over-strongly, in order to show that he was fighting with all his power for the true interests of all neutral nations. It did not matter much to him if, in his eagerness to champion the rights of neutrals, he laid himself open to an overpowering reply from Sir Edward Grey.

What he wanted chiefly to do **President Wilson's** was to show his countrymen **attitude** that he had gone as far as man could rightly go in trying to abate the rigour of search exercised by the British and French Navies. In short, he was preparing his case against the German-American organisation. If there were to be a fight at the next election, he intended to come into it with scrupulously clean hands, and, if necessary, to call for the co-operation of all loyal Americans to defeat the machinations of the German intriguers against their peace.

In spite of the great show of numbers of the Pro-Prussian League, it was doubtful if it could become a main force in American politics. Most of the

IN SEARCH OF A SPY.
An incident in Poland. A German officer and some of his men are searching a farmhouse in which they were led to believe a Russian spy had taken refuge.

older German emigrants to the United States had left their Fatherland in search of liberty after the overthrow of the German Liberal movement and the establishment of a policy of military aggression by Bismarck. For the last thirteen years the Kaiser had made great efforts to win over these fugitives from his scientific system of reactionary government. But only the latest multitude of German emigrants

The Kaiser and the fugitives

to America, who had mainly been attracted by the wealth rather than the freedom of the great Republic of the West, were inclined to listen to Prince Henry of Prussia and the other Ambassadors of Teutonic militarism who visited the States to inspire and organise the great intrigue.

Certain plutocrats of German and German-Jewish origin may have been won over, together with some of the younger generation of German-Americans, dazzled by the personality of the Kaiser, and swayed by the prestige of German achievements in technical industries and university education. Many of the older men of German stock, however, remembered very clearly the reason why they had left their country, and had no desire whatever to help towards the world-wide triumph of the principles of the Junker class, against which they had fought vainly in their unhappy Fatherland. For these and other reasons it was with a considerable amount of confidence in the ultimate issue that the true Americans faced the menace of the so-called German-American Neutrality League. It was generally reckoned that the result of the elections would be to bring odium and confusion upon the chief intriguers and upon all who stood with them. Indeed, it was the common belief that any show of hostility by the German-American organisation against a candidate would be sufficient to enable that candidate to win. For though the American people kept very quiet about the matter, their quietness was only that calm that sometimes goes before a storm. In the meantime the United States continued to protest about our interference with their shipping, and to supply the Powers of the Triple Entente with an enormous amount of war material.

The German intriguers then tried to make mischief in another direction. In January, 1915, Japan began to press China somewhat vigorously to make various large and profitable concessions. The United States was then urged by the German party to take warlike steps for the conservation of Chinese integrity, and challenged Great Britain in regard to the scope of the British-Japanese treaty. It was hoped either to make trouble with Britain's ally, or to detach the two island Powers of Europe and Asia from further co-operation. President Wilson, however, continued to negotiate calmly regarding all the difficulties exaggerated by the German-American Neutrality League.

In the domestic affairs of the British Empire during the autumn and winter campaign there was little of importance directly bearing

BAFFLING THE ENEMY SNIPERS.
The invention of the trench periscope, one of the innovations brought about by the war, made outlook work a matter of comparative safety except from shell fire.

upon the course and duration of the war, with the exception of the financial position of our country. The State still continued to play the part of the rich uncle. There had been guarantees to the railways, the banks, and the Stock Exchange, and on November 3rd, 1914, it was announced that help would be given to traders with foreign debts which they could not collect. Solvent traders, with moneys due from foreigners, were enabled to realise immediately fifty per cent. of the amounts owing to them. Like the other measures of financial support undertaken by the British Government, this scheme helped to prevent the widespread bankruptcy of industrial firms and the closing of factories.

On January 19th, 1915, further measures for the organisation and conservation of our financial resources were put into force. No company thenceforward was allowed to obtain fresh capital, and no new companies were permitted to obtain public subscriptions, unless in each case our Government approved the intended use of the capital. Furthermore, no capital was allowed to go abroad for the financing of foreign concerns.

Early in February Mr. Lloyd George **Financial conference** and the Governor of the Bank of England **in Paris** went to Paris to hold a conference with M. Ribot and M. Bark, the Finance Ministers of France and Russia. The outcome of this conference was one of extraordinary importance and originality. The three Powers of the Triple Entente resolved to unite their financial resources equally with their military resources for the purpose of carrying the war to a successful conclusion. With this aim in view, they decided to take over in equal shares all present and future advances to friendly countries which were then fighting with them or intending soon to do so. Financial measures were adopted for facilitating Russian exports, and for establishing, so far as possible, the par of exchange between Russia and her Allies.

It was expected that by December 31st, 1915, the combined expenses of the Allies would be about two thousand million pounds. The greatest expenditure would fall upon the British Empire, which had to maintain a huge Navy, and to create and maintain a new army of three million or more troops. Happily, as Mr. Lloyd George pointed out, Britain and France were the great bankers of the world. Merely out of the proceeds of our investments abroad we could pay for our huge war expenditure for five years, while allowing a substantial sum for depreciation. France could carry on the war for three years at least out of the proceeds of her foreign investments ; and both countries would still have something to spare to advance to their Allies. At the time when the financial alliance between Britain, France, and Russia was made, the Allies were fighting the whole mobilised strength of Germany with less than one-third of their own strength. Hence the importance of the new agreement.

Presented with "THE GREAT WAR." Part No. 37 From the Painting by Charles M. Sheldon.

Albert I King of the Belgians.

CHAPTER LII.

THE BACK-VELDT REVOLT IN SOUTH AFRICA.

South Africa and the German Ambitions—How General Botha Worked for a Permanent Settlement—German South-West Africa the Centre of Intrigue—General Beyers at Berlin—Arrangements Made for Prussianisation of South Africa—General Hertzog Breaks with General Botha—Racial Ascendancy *versus* Union of Boer and Briton—Interventionists and Neutralists—Prophecies of Van Rensburg—Botha and Smuts Stand for Swift and Active Measures—Triumph of Loyalists in Union Parliament—Beyers Plots an Outbreak of Rebellion—Puts Maritz in Command on German Frontier—Death of Delarey Stops First Revolt at Potschefstroom—General Botha's Great Speech—Maritz Betrays Loyal Forces and Opens the Rebellion—Defeat of Maritz—De Wet and Beyers Revolt—Botha Takes the Field and Breaks Up Beyers's Forces—Pursuit and Capture of De Wet—Death of Beyers.

VER since Bismarck remarked that South Africa would be the grave of Britain's greatness, the fourth-rate Machiavellis of the German Foreign Office had regarded the Cape as the clay foot of the Colossus of the British Empire. It was at this point that they began the process of undermining our Imperial power, which they afterwards vainly continued in India and in Egypt. It was mainly their machinations that brought about the South African War. Their secret service men were behind the Afrikander Bund, and President Kruger was encouraged to resort to the arbitrament of arms, in the quarrel over the rights of the Uitlanders, by receiving promises of help from the agents of the German Emperor. How sadly President Kruger was deceived, when he went in person to Germany to plead with the Kaiser to help him, is a matter of history. The President of the Transvaal was then merely a broken tool of German intrigue. There had never been any intention of helping his country, save in so far as damage could be done thereby to the British Empire, with no risk to the position of Germany.

After the generous and magnificent settlement of South African problems made by Sir Henry Campbell-Bannerman and his Cabinet in 1906, there seemed little room for any further German intrigue of a serious and widespread kind. The pacific

GENERAL LOUIS BOTHA AND HIS SONS.
The Premier of South Africa, with Captain Louis Botha, John Botha (who joined the Cape Town Highlanders), and Philip Botha, the General's youngest son.

settlement of the racial difficulties of the two white peoples was still further established by the result of the Union elections. These gave the Dutch party a working majority, with a Boer as Prime Minister. There was a considerable outcry from South Africans of British stock over the power that had been entrusted to the men with whom they had been fighting barely eight years before. But, happily, the unparalleled policy of magnanimity prevailed, and the Dutch and British parties were left to work together, without interference from Britain, and to grow by use and kindly intercourse into a combined nationality such as French and British Canadians had developed after a century of conflict

Had the Union of South Africa been as secluded from hostile outside intrigue as was the Dominion of Canada, all might have gone well. The solvent of free government and the recurring need for co-operative efforts in solving all kinds of social and industrial difficulties would gradually have grouped the nations together by classes, interests, and principles, cutting across the racial distinctions. For by the bounty of Providence the chief power had fallen into the hands of a man of noble character and enlightened mind—General Louis Botha. Eight years before he had been one of the ablest of Britain's enemies, and by his skill in war and the strength of his personality he had become the commander-in-chief of the

Boers. But after the settlement, and his rise to the Premiership, he took a wide and long view of the destinies of his country, and worked with the single purpose of reconciling both races in a harmonious union. Born in Natal in 1863, he knew the Briton as well as the Boer. He had a generosity of soul and a largeness of mind similar to that of the Liberal British statesman who had suddenly transformed South Africa into the greatest of all experiments in democratic government. General Botha resolved that the experiment should not fail, while he controlled affairs, for want of fairness, goodwill, and foresight.

Naturally, this did not suit the views of the Governor of German South-West Africa. His colony had **German strategical railways** been provided with strategical railways for the invasion of Cape Colony. The railways ran from the ports of Swakopmund and Lüderitzbucht and connected with a central track that ended near the Orange River. The nearest line in the South African Union was over three hundred and fifty miles away, while the intervening country was thinly populated and poorly provided with roads. Their railways of invasion gave the Germans a somewhat similar advantage over the South Africans to that which they possessed, on the eastern frontier of their Fatherland, over the Russians. Of course, the expensive railway system of German South-West Africa, which did not pay for itself in a commercial way, was not planned merely to waste money. But the money would certainly have been wasted if the Dutch and British stocks in South Africa had been allowed to settle down in peaceful co-operation for the development of their country.

A war with Boer and Briton combined, with the British Navy in practical control of the seas, would result in overwhelming disaster for the Germans. They

GENERAL SMUTS.

would lose their only dependency in Africa suited to colonisation by the white races, with its rich grass-lands in the north, its recently discovered diamond-fields by the shore, and its unexplored mineral resources. The Germans, therefore, resumed their old schemes of intrigue. Their intention was to set Boer and Briton again to fight

GENERAL MARITZ.

each other for German ends.

The Germans definitely began to prepare their colony north of the Orange River as a

GENERAL HERTZOG.

base of operations against British South Africa in 1908. The Germans had then been occupied for five years in a war with the natives of German South-West Africa, among whom the nomad cattle-breeders, the Hereros, were eminent. A very capable force of Boer auxiliaries had been employed in the native war. Some of them were men still unpropitiated by the grant of self-government to the Transvaal and Orange River Colony. The discontent of the irreconcilables of the back veldt was remarked by the German Governor of South-West Africa. He had formerly been German Consul-General at Cape Town, directing there the web of intrigue by which the agents of the Kaiser tried to keep the Boers ready for revolt at the word of command from Berlin.

GENERAL CHRISTIAN DE WET.
(In circle: GENERAL BEYERS.)

When the Herero war drew to an end, many of the 19,000 German troops were retained as farmers. Most of their guns were kept, with huge stores of ammunition and food, and in 1913 the preparations were fairly complete. The Germans scarcely troubled to conceal the fact that they intended to combine the South African Union with German South-West Africa into a vassal colony under the control of the Prussian bureaucracy. It was not made clear what advantage the **General Beyers and** Boers would derive from ex-**the Kaiser** changing their status as a self-governing Dominion in a loose federation of progressive and liberal powers for the rule of the Hohenzollerns. But certain Boers were shown that they would profit by the success of the Prussians.

In the autumn of 1913 General Beyers, the Commandant-General of the Union Defence Force, went with his wife to Switzerland to study the manœuvres of the Swiss militia army. Kaiser Wilhelm II. also attended these manœuvres. Naturally, the two men met. Beyers had married a German lady remarkable for the intensity of her patriotism, and, like many of the women of her country, she was more embittered by the outcome of the South African War than were the Boers themselves. Beyers was a tall, manly, handsome man, with a strong, magnetic personality. The Kaiser was delighted with him, and some time after the Swiss manœuvres he was invited to Berlin, and there feasted and flattered by the Court, until by some means he was won over.

Mere bribery was not likely to have undermined the honesty of character of this quiet, dignified man, for he was already rich ; but he was vain, and it was upon his vanity that the Kaiser and his ministers played. He was apparently offered the position of President of the Great South African Republic which was to be established under German " protection." He returned to Cape Town with his heavy black moustache turned up in the Kaiser style and the ideas of the Kaiser running in his head.

At that time the Germans intended to provoke the Great War immediately. As Signor Giolitti revealed in a speech which he made at the beginning of 1915, the attack on Serbia was first timed to take place in 1913. It was only because Italy refused at the last moment to join in the aggressive act of conflagration that Great Britain escaped being drawn into the war about the time when General Beyers first began to plot with the Germans. Meanwhile the policy of General Botha's party became troubled by the revival of a renewed movement for racial ascendancy.

General Hertzog's new party The movement originated among some of the leaders of the Dutch people of the Orange River Colony. Chief among them was General Hertzog, who had to leave the Cabinet, owing partly to a difference of opinion with General Botha concerning the Imperial responsibilities of South Africa. As a matter of fact, General Hertzog was moved largely by personal animosity to his more powerful colleague. But on breaking from him he gave his animosity a political colouring, and started a new Dutch party which aimed at racial ascendancy ending in absolute independence. General Hertzog was not prepared

to declare war against the rest of the British Empire. He thought that South Africa might remain nominally part of the Empire, until the time came for her to lapse, without any show of violence, from the British Crown. This would occur, in his view, whenever the interests of South Africa were likely to be sacrificed to the common cause of the Empire, as in the case of a war with Germany.

General Botha, on the other hand, took a high and honourable view of the obligations of his people. He intended to hold by the spirit as well as by the letter of the grant of free government. Quite likely the result **The ruling mind in the Union** of the treacherous intrigues of the Germans in the days of President Kruger weighed in the decision to which the South African Prime Minister came in 1913. Besides being the ruling mind in the Union, he was also the old commander-in-chief of the Boers. He had the patience and the tenacity of the race that produced Tromp, De Ruyter, and William of Orange. He knew well what were the intentions of Germany in regard to South Africa, and his efforts to reconcile Boer and Briton in the new Commonwealth were animated with a military purpose as well as with a generosity of view. As a Boer he had an account to settle with the Kaiser, who refused to see President Kruger in Berlin in the autumn of 1900. With fine Dutch patience, he did not go out of his way to seek a quarrel. But, as was seen in his break with Hertzog and De Wet, when he saw that the quarrel would be forced upon him, he began to prepare in 1913 to meet it with all the stubborn valour of his race.

He foresaw everything except the downright treachery of Beyers. There was an extremely difficult task before him and before his capable colleague, General Smuts, but

REPRESENTATIVE GROUP OF LOYAL BOERS WHO RESPONDED TO THE PATRIOTIC APPEAL OF GENERAL BOTHA AND RALLIED TO THE FLAG OF THE EMPIRE.

their courage only rose with their difficulties. The prorogation of Parliament on July 7th, 1914, was a stroke of good luck. For when war broke out the next month, the Government was able to arrange its plan of action in silence. The position in some of the country districts was disturbing. For in those places the agents of Germany had long been spreading the idea that when the time came for the downfall of the British Empire by German hands, a larger South African Republic would be created with the help of the Teutons. In the Western Transvaal some of the back-veldt Boers were ready to rise, and the rumour ran that the Germans had invaded the Union, and that the burghers were being called out on commando to act with them.

At one place in the Western Transvaal a mass of armed Boers collected for action. But General Delarey hastened to the spot and spoke sternly to his countrymen, and induced them to go back home. Only in the large towns was there an instant and passionate demonstration of loyalty to the Empire. In districts where settlers of Dutch stock prevailed, the general attitude of the people was that of bewildered expectancy. They were waiting

TRANSVAAL SCOTTISH PREPARING FOR THE ROLL-CALL AT THE
WANDERERS' CLUB.

to see what action their Government would take. Meanwhile a fierce and decisive struggle was going on between General Botha and General Smuts on the one side, and General Hertzog and ex-President Steyn on the other side. Between them was General Delarey, with Christian de Wet and Beyers trying to win Delarey over to active rebellion. The situation was much complicated by personal feelings of disappointed ambition on the part of General Hertzog and De Wet. Hertzog was working to establish a Hertzog Cabinet, and his chief end was to overthrow Botha rather than to

Complications and a mystery provoke armed rebellion. But if he did not actively incite traitors like Beyers and fools like De Wet, he was not displeased to watch them proceed to shed the blood of British settlers. The greater the trouble gathering round the Botha Cabinet, the greater was the chance of General Hertzog getting all the power of government into his hands. What Hertzog intended to do, when he was controller of the destinies of South Africa with the German nominee Beyers as the nominal head of his party, is a mystery. We shall perhaps know more about this when Christian de Wet speaks. At the time of writing the only important

request that the famous old guerilla leader is said to have made is that, before he was punished for his treason, he might have a quarter of an hour and a rifle alone with Hertzog.

While the party politics of the Dutchmen of South Africa were in this confused condition, the Imperial Government was troubled about German South-West Africa. It was absolutely necessary to attack this enemy colony. **Peril to British shipping** Its mighty wireless station at Windhoek, and its port of Swakopmund, made it a great danger to our shipping. It was known that a system for coaling German commerce raiders had been arranged at Cape Town, where German agents had a carrier-pigeon scheme of communication with German South-West Africa. The large number of soldiers retained in German territory, many of them having settled down as soldier-farmers in the old Roman manner, was fair proof of German intentions. The German plan was to keep their colony safe from attack, while using it as the organising centre for the intrigues of rebellion in South Africa.

Much as the Imperial Government would have liked to allow German South-West Africa to remain undisturbed till its fate was decided on the battlefields of Europe, this could not be done. For though the Empire might thereby have been enabled to content awhile the honestly-mistaken section of Afrikanders, the premature explosion of the combined forces of intrigue and invasion might have been disastrous. The proximity of a large German military force was having a demoralising effect upon the border folk of the Union. An attack had to be made upon this force.

It was only a question whether the operations should be conducted by the Imperial Government with British, Australian, New Zealand, and Indian troops, or whether the South African Government would undertake the conquest of the neighbouring hostile territory. There was an Indian army corps almost ready to sail, and composed largely of hardy men, accustomed to the kind of desert warfare that would be waged in German South-West Africa. And if the Indians had afterwards been encouraged to settle on the land they had won, the neutralists of the Union would have had no ground of complaint in the matter. This was the critical position, as General Botha afterwards pointed out to a great gathering of his constituents in the Transvaal. If the Boer was not willing to co-operate with the Briton in striking against the intriguer who intended to ruin their Commonwealth, there were other fighting races in the British Empire who would rejoice at the opportunity of conquering the finest of all German colonies.

General Botha did not hesitate. Some Boers afterwards said that he should have first of all asked permission of the people of South Africa; but, as he replied scornfully, what was the good of a Government which was not prepared to accept responsibility? He rejoiced in the power constitutionally put into his hands, and brought to the task of a fine statesman the swift decision and instant action of a military genius. To him it had suddenly been given to shape the destiny of a United South Africa. German ambition and German intrigue, he saw, could be transformed into a consolidating influence on the Union, producing in the course of months a veritable sentiment

"FIRST-LINE TRANSPORT" OF THE RAND RIFLES: SLEIGHING OVER THE SAND IN SOUTH-WEST AFRICA.

GETTING A "LONG TOM" INTO POSITION: UNION ARTILLERY ON SERVICE IN SOUTH-WEST AFRICA.

WITH THE SOUTH AFRICAN UNION FORCES AT SWAKOPMUND: IN THE TRENCHES FACING THE GERMAN POSITION.

139

of common nationality not to be developed in peace time for several generations. The hammer directed at South Africa should be turned into an anvil, on which a greater South Africa could be swiftly fashioned—a South Africa including the German colony, and perhaps Rhodesia and part of German East Africa. From Table Bay to the source of the Nile, Briton and Boer could extend their sway, with an Imperial railway linking the Empire's ports on the Mediterranean with Egypt, the Soudan, Uganda, the Zanzibar hinterland, Rhodesia, and the Union of South Africa.

Botha had to deal with the most difficult people on earth—the last of the stern, passionately narrow, and fiercely ignorant race of Calvinists. They were men of the type of the old Scottish Covenanters, and **Van Rensburg's prophecies** even superior in the vigour of their fighting fanaticism to the Cameronians. They came from the two principal persecuted stocks of the European wars of religion—the Calvinists of the Netherlands and the Huguenots of France. Two hundred and fifty years of toleration and enlightenment in Europe had not affected them. Left to themselves they would have burnt a Darwinian with more readiness than Calvin burned Servetus. The back-veldt Boers especially were quite unchanged in mind and character from their ancestors. Except a man spoke to them in the terms of their own creed, they recognised no human authority. And the trouble was that they had a famous prophet, Van Rensburg, who lived at Lichtenburg, near General Delarey. He had won renown towards the end of the South African War by inducing Delarey to attack Lord Methuen, with the result that the Boers gained a remarkable victory. It was by a prediction, in which he actually named the day on which the movement should be conducted, that Van Rensburg brought about the capture of Lord Methuen. After this he made other prophecies, some of which did not fall out as he foretold, but his one great success made him a power among the back-veldt Boers.

As soon as war broke out Van Rensburg began again to see visions and to make prophecies. In one vision there was an ocean, and across the ocean five great bulls were fighting, and a blue bull gored a great hole in a red bull. The red bull was Britain, while the blue bull was Germany. In another vision some commandos of burghers were trekking across the Orange River into the desert northward. There they met the German troops, and talked with them, and came back home without firing a shot. This, being interpreted, meant that the soldiers of the Kaiser intended not only to restore the old Republic, but to add Natal and the Cape to it.

It was on Delarey that the prophet of Lichtenburg chiefly worked, and when the famous general came down to attend a special war session of Parliament, his friends found him in a state of mind bordering on religious mania. Delarey was a well-balanced, enlightened man of strong personality; and seeing what an effect the prophet of Lichtenburg produced on him, it is easy to calculate how profound and disturbing was the influence the preacher of rebellion exercised upon the narrow, ignorant country Boers. If the policy of neutrality had been maintained for some months, men like Van Rensburg and active intriguers like Beyers might have completely undermined the settlement between Boer and Briton and created a terrible struggle, with German troops and Imperial forces intervening.

In these circumstances of extreme perplexity and danger General Botha, with the help of General Smuts, started a policy of extraordinary audacity. Nearly all their fellow-countrymen were inclined to draw together in a common aversion to any expedition against German South-West Africa. The majority of Botha's own followers were disinclined to take up arms against the Teutons. Even the Boers who were not willing to co-operate with the Germans in attacking British settlers were averse from letting any Boer blood be shed in the interests of the British Empire. Had General Botha been content to be merely the index to Boer sentiment, he would have tried to keep South Africa out of the war, and to prevent both loyalists and traitors from involving the Union in a conflict. But, as we have seen, Botha was not a follower of public opinion, but a director of the popular mind. When he saw that a majority of his countrymen were tending in the wrong direction, he rallied them by a magnificent stand for the honour, the true interests, and the right development of South Africa. On his own responsibility he entered into an agreement with the Imperial Government for the withdrawal of the Imperial troops, and undertook that the South Africans would out of their own resources launch an expedition into German territory.

General Botha was well aware of the intrigues going on about him. He did not suspect that the Commandant-General of the Union was a complete traitor, but he knew that he and various other men of position were hesitating over the course which they should adopt. So he gave a clear, bold, resolute lead, calculated to bring the domestic situation at once to a crisis that could immediately be dealt with. He revealed his plan on the opening of Parliament on September 9th, 1914. He moved a resolution to convey an address to King George, assuring him of the loyal support of the **Botha's bold and** Union, and of the determination of the **resolute lead** South Africans to co-operate in maintaining the security and integrity of the Empire. His speech, already touched upon in Chapter XXXVI., was something more than a challenge : it was a declaration of war against the pro-German party.

It must be remembered that he was speaking to men of a race of born fighters, whose minds were still deeply coloured by the tragic events of a long and terrible campaign, in which they had been overpowered by the superior numbers and superior organisation of their traditional opponents. As an example of the literature of power, his words are of high historic interest. After relating the agreement made with the Imperial Government for the invasion of German South-West Africa, General Botha said :

" To forget their loyalty to the Empire in this hour of trial would be scandalous and shameful, and would blacken South Africa in the eyes of the whole world. Of this South Africans were incapable. They had endured some of the greatest sacrifices that could be demanded of a people, but they had always kept before them ideals, founded on Christianity, and never in their darkest days had they sought to gain their ends by treasonable means. The path of treason was an unknown path to Dutch and English alike.

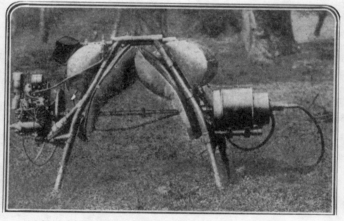

A MARCONI OUTFIT FOR MOUNTED CONVEYANCE.
Two of these sets of wireless for mounted conveyance, with equipment and operators, were offered by the Marconi Company to General Botha to present to the force under Brigadier-General Duncan Mackenzie. They were accepted, and proved of great value.

SOUTH AFRICA'S PATRIOTIC PREMIER TAKES THE FIELD.

One of the brightest features of the war in Africa was the splendid stand of General Botha against German aggression and Back-Veldt disaffection. He told his countrymen that to forget their loyalty to the Empire would blacken South Africa in the eyes of the whole world, and declared that the path of treason was an unknown path to Dutch and English alike. He then took the field in person.

"Their duty and their conscience alike bade them be faithful and true to the Imperial Government in all respects in this hour of darkness and trouble. That was the attitude of the Union Government; that was the attitude of the people of South Africa. The Government had cabled to the Imperial Government at the outbreak of war, offering to undertake the defence of South Africa, thereby releasing the Imperial troops for service elsewhere. This was accepted, and the Union Defence Force was mobilised."

In answer to this speech, General Hertzog moved an amendment to the effect that any act that would lead to an attack on German territory in South Africa would conflict with the interests of the Union and the Empire. In the speeches moved by members of the Hertzog party in support of this amendment doubts were cast on the justice of the British cause, bitter personal attacks were made on General Botha, and memories of the South African War were revived with a view to provoking racial hatred. General Botha's Government, however, **Beyers' letter of resignation** won a decisive victory by a majority of ninety-two votes against twelve votes. Of the seventeen members from the Free State, which was the Hertzog stronghold, only nine, including General Hertzog himself, voted for the amendment, and one of the nine afterwards recanted publicly.

So deep and widespread was the effect of the speeches of Generals Botha and Smuts that the leaders of the revolt became desperate. General Beyers, having more courage than General Hertzog, immediately took action. Parliament rose on Monday, September 14th, and on the following day Beyers wrote a letter of resignation of his position of Commandant-General of the Defence Force. The letter was written the day before it was dated, and a copy was given for immediate publication, so that it would be read by the people before the original letter reached General Botha and General Smuts in Cape Town. But by means of the Press censorship the Government prevented the publication of the letter until September 21st, when it was published together with the reply of General Smuts as Minister of Defence.

The letter of Beyers was not a mere resignation of his office and rank, but a practical declaration of war against the British Empire. It ran as follows:

Pretoria, September 15th.

Honourable Sir,—You are aware that during the month of August last I told you and General Botha by word of mouth that I disapproved of the sending of commandos to German South-West Africa for the purpose of conquering that territory. I was on the point then of resigning, but, hearing that Parliament would be called together, I decided to wait, hoping that a way out of the difficulty would be found. To my utmost surprise, however, Parliament confirmed the resolution adopted by the Government, namely, to conquer German South-West Africa without any provocation towards the Union from the Germans. The Government must be aware that by far the great majority of the Dutch-speaking people of the Union decidedly disapproved of our crossing the frontier, and that two conferences of commandants recently held at Pretoria bore eloquent testimony to this. I challenge the Government by an appeal to the people, without making use of compulsion, to obtain another result.

A challenge to the Government

It is said that Great Britain has taken part in the war for the sake of right and justice in order to protect the independence of smaller nations, and to comply with treaties. But the fact that three Ministers of the British Cabinet have resigned shows that even in England there is a strong minority who cannot be convinced of the righteousness of a war with Germany. History teaches us, after all, that whenever it suits her interests Great Britain is always ready to protect smaller nations; but, unhappily, history also relates instances in which the sacred rights of independence of smaller nations have been violated and treaties disregarded by that same Empire.

In proof of this I have only to indicate how the independence of the South African Republic and Orange Free State was violated, and of what weight the Sand River Convention was. It is said that war is being waged against the barbarity of the Germans. I have forgiven, but not forgotten, all the barbarities perpetrated in this our own country during the South African War. With very few exceptions all farms—not to mention many towns—were so many Louvains, of which we now hear so much. At this critical moment it is made known in Parliament that our Government was granted a loan of £7,000,000 by the British Government. This is very significant. Anyone can have his own thoughts about this. In the absence of legitimate grounds for the annexation policy of the Government, you endeavour to intimidate the public by declaring that Government possesses information showing that Germany has decided, should opportunity arise, to annex South Africa.

My humble opinion is that this will be hastened if from our side we invade German territory without having been provoked thereto by the Germans. And as to the alleged German annexation scheme, this is nothing more than the result of the

The alleged German scheme

usual national suspicion attending such matters. The allegations made in Parliament —namely, that the Germans have already violated our frontier—are ungrounded. See the official report of the Information Bureau, corroborated by Lieutenant-Colonel Maritz and his officers, who are on and near the frontier.

Apparently Government longed for some transgression by the Germans of German South-West Africa, but have been disappointed in this, for so far not a single German soldier has crossed our frontier. As you know very well, the report is perfectly correct regarding an involuntary transgression of the frontier some time ago and the tendering of an apology for so doing. Whatever may happen in South Africa, the war will be decided in Europe in any case; so if Germany triumphs and should decide to attack us, then, even if Great Britain should be unable to help us, we shall at least have a sacred and clean cause in defending our country to the utmost, provided we stay inside our borders meanwhile. In case we are attacked our people will arise as one man in defence of its rights.

Besides, I am convinced that a commando of about 8,000 Germans, as at present stationed in German territory, will not be so foolish as to attempt an attack on our country. I have always said, and repeated at Booysens recently, that if the Union is attacked, Boer

A BIVOUAC IN THE ARID SOUTH-WEST AFRICAN SAND WASTES.
In their advance in German South-West Africa the Union forces had to cross country described as a heart-numbing ocean of soft white sand billows, rising in places to a height of one thousand feet or more. Our photograph shows troops in bivouac after a period of weary "sand-jamming" over this dry and dusty country.

and Briton will defend this country side by side, and in such case I will deem it a great honour and privilege to take up my place at the head of our forces in defence of my Fatherland. I accepted the post of Commandant-General under our Defence Act, the first section of which provides that our forces can only be employed in defence of the Union. My humble opinion is that this section cannot thus be changed by informal resolution in Parliament, such being contrary to Parliamentary procedure. So the Defence Act does not allow us to go and fetch the enemy over the frontier and to light the fire in this way, but should the enemy penetrate into our country it will be our duty to drive him back and pursue him in his own territory.

In his speech General Botha speaks about the help we had from the Belgians and French after the South African War. That assistance is still appreciated by us and by all our people, but we must not forget that the Germans also were not behindhand and have always been well disposed towards us. So why should we deliberately make enemies of them? As circumstances are, I see no way of taking the offensive, and as I sincerely love my country and people, I must strongly protest against the sending of the Union Citizen Forces over the frontier. Who can foretell when the fire the Government has decided to light shall end? For the reasons enumerated above I feel constrained to resign my post as Commandant-General, as also my commissioned rank. For me this is the only way of faith, duty, and honour towards our people,

of which mention was made by General Botha, I have always tried to do my duty according to my best convictions, and it sorely grieves me that it must end in this way.—I have, etc.,

(Signed)   C. G. L. BEYERS.

To this treacherous letter, with its calculated appeal to racial animosity, General Smuts made a telling, historic reply :

Pretoria, September 19th.

Sir,—It was with regret that I received your letter of the 15th inst., tendering your resignation as the Commandant-General, Union Defence Forces, and as an officer of the Union. The circumstances under which that resignation took place and the terms in which you endeavour to justify your action tend to leave a very painful impression.

It is true that it was known to me that you entertained objections against the war operations in German South-West Africa, but I never received the impression that you would resign. On the contrary, all the information in possession of the Government was communicated to you, all plans were discussed with you, and your advice was followed to a large extent. The principal officers were appointed on your recommendation and with your concurrence, and the plan of operations which is now being followed is largely the one recommended by yourself at a conference of officers.

My last instructions to you before I left for Cape Town to attend the special session of Parliament were that in my absence you should visit certain regiments on the German border, and it was well understood between us that immediately the war operations were somewhat further advanced and co-operation among the various divisions would be practicable, you should yourself undertake the chief command in German South-West Africa.

The attitude of the Government after this remained unchanged, and was approved by Parliament after full discussion. One would have expected that that approval would make the matter easier for you, but now I find that you anticipated that Parliament would disapprove of the policy of the Government, and that your disappointment in this became the reason for your unexpected action. In order to make your motives clearer, the reasons for your resignation were explained in a long political argument, which was immediately communicated to the Press and came into the hands of the Government long after publication.

I need not tell you that all these circumstances in connection with your resignation have made a most unpleasant impression on my colleagues and myself. But this unpleasant impression has even been aggravated by the allegations contained in your letter. Your bitter attack on Great Britain is not only entirely baseless, but is the more unjustifiable coming as it does in the midst of a great war from the Commandant-General of one of the British Dominions. Your reference to barbarous acts during the South African War cannot justify the criminal devastation of Belgium, and can only be calculated to sow hatred and division among the people of South Africa.

You forgot to mention that since the South African War the British people gave South Africa her entire freedom under a Constitution which makes it possible for us to realise our national ideals along our own lines, and which, for instance, allows you to write with impunity a letter for which you would without doubt be liable in the German Empire to the extreme penalty.

As regards your other statements, they have been answered and disposed of in Parliament. From these discussions it will be apparent that neither the British Empire nor South Africa was the aggressor in this struggle. War was in the first instance declared by Austria-Hungary, and thereafter by Germany, under circumstances in which the

General Smuts' historic reply

British Government employed its utmost powers to maintain the peace of Europe and to safeguard the neutrality of Belgium.

So far as we ourselves are concerned, our coast is threatened, our mail boats are arrested, and our borders are invaded by the enemy. This latter does not occur, as you say, in an involuntary manner and with an apology, which latter, at any rate, was never tendered to the Government.

Under these circumstances it is absurd to speak about aggressive action on the part of the Union, seeing that, together with the British Empire, we have been drawn against our wish and will and entirely in self-defence into this war. As regards your insinuation concerning the loan of £7,000,000 which the British Government

SOUTH AFRICAN TROOPERS ATTEND A CHURCH SERVICE BEFORE JOINING IN THE PURSUIT OF THE REBELS.
An animated scene outside the Dutch Reformed Church at Pretoria where a special service was held prior to the departure of the troops in pursuit of Beyers and De Wet. One of the officers is accompanied by a lady, evidently a privileged relative anxious to be by his side as long as possible.

BRITISH FORCE ENTERING GERMAN SOUTH-WEST AFRICA AT A POINT NEAR RAMAN'S DRIFT.
Shortly after the above photograph was taken there was a skirmish, as the result of which the enemy were driven from their positions. The nature of the ground and the conditions of the atmosphere are indicated by the rising dust, though the pace at which the troops were moving was a slow one.

THE MOTOR CHASE OF CHRISTIAN DE WET.
Special motor-car squadron of the Union forces passing through Vryburg. They played a most active part in the pursuit of Christian de Wet, and were especially praised by General Smuts.

CAPTURED AT LAST.
General de Wet knocking the ashes from his pipe on the mudguard of the motor-car in which he was conveyed part of the way to Johannesburg.

was kind enough to grant us, and for which the public of the Union, as evidenced recently in Parliament, are most grateful, it is of such a despicable nature that there is no necessity to make any comment thereon   It only shows to what extent your mind has been obscured by political bias.

You speak about duty and honour. My conviction is that the people of South Africa will in these dark days, when the Government as well as the people of South Africa are put to the supreme test, have a clearer conception of duty and honour than is to be deduced from your letter and action. For the Dutch-speaking section in particular I cannot conceive anything more fatal and humiliating than a policy of lip loyalty in fair weather and of a policy of neutrality and pro-German sentiment in days of storm and stress.

It may be that our peculiar internal circumstances and our backward condition after the Great War will place a limit on what we can do, but nevertheless I am convinced that the people will support the Government in carrying out the mandate of Parliament, and in this manner, which is the only legitimate one, fulfil their

144

duty to South Africa and to the Empire, and maintain their dearly-won honour unblemished for the future.
Your resignation is hereby accepted.
(Signed)   J. C. SMUTS.

But before this correspondence was published General Beyers made his first open stroke against the Government and failed.   He had been actively engaged in organising rebellion weeks before he resigned his command.   In the plan of operations which he drew up for the Government, and through the officers he appointed to carry out these pretended plans, he was treacherously arranging a large concerted scheme of operations in which the German force was to take part. His chief difficulty was to win over General Delarey, the leader of the Boers of the Western Transvaal.   About a thousand armed Boers of Delarey's district were encamped at Potchefstroom, and as General Delarey returned from Cape Town on September 15th, **How Delarey was** he met General Beyers and **shot** arranged to motor with him that night and visit the camp of the Boers of the Western Transvaal.

The two generals left Pretoria by motor-car about seven o'clock in the evening, and took the road that led them through the mining city of Johannesburg. It happened that a gang of bandits, known as the Jackson gang, had been terrorising for several days the Witwatersrand Reef committing burglaries, and shooting at sight any one who interfered with them. On the afternoon of September 15th they had been traced to a house in the suburbs by some detectives ; but on an attempt being made to arrest them, they shot dead one of the detectives and escaped in a motor-car. The armed police patrols were then ordered out on all the highways leading to Johannesburg, and instructed to stop and examine all motor-cars, and fire at once if their challenge were ignored. After nightfall a motor-car resembling that of the Jackson gang was

REBELS ON THEIR WAY TO PRISON.
Men of General de Wet's rebel commando being escorted through Vryburg by mounted loyalists, on their way to captivity.

challenged at the east end of the city, as it went along at high speed with a powerful headlight. Again it was challenged twice as it flashed through the western end of the town. For a fourth time it was challenged by the western boundary. One of the policemen then fired at the wheel of the car in order to disable it, but the bullet ricochetted and struck General Delarey, killing him instantly. Almost at the same time a well-known doctor on the East Rand, Dr. Grace, was shot dead by the eastern boundary by the police while travelling in another car resembling that of the Jackson gang.

Probably the reason why General Beyers did not answer the challenges of the armed patrol was that he thought his plot had been discovered, and that he was to be arrested for treason. As a matter of fact, both Generals Botha and Smuts were unsuspicious of his immediate purpose.

The plot at Potchefstroom Beyers had intended to start the rebellion with the thousand men in Potchefstroom Camp, who had just come in from their three weeks' training. Colonel Kemp had won over their officers, and these had harangued the troops that morning on parade, and had urged them to refuse to volunteer for German South-West Africa. All loyalists who objected were jeered at, and Kemp collected what ammunition he could lay hands upon, storing it in his tent. In the afternoon the loyalists sent a warning message to General Smuts by a native runner, while the conspirators gathered in a house in Berg Street and sat there all night waiting for the sound of Beyers's car. Beyers's plan was to confront General Delarey with the accomplished fact of the opening of the rebellion in the Western Transvaal, and by shock tactics to win him over to the rebels.

But the death of Delarey completely unnerved and cowed the arch-traitor. No doubt he wondered if the shot had been meant for him, and if he would be arrested and put on his trial. All night he waited in extreme anxiety,

PIET DE WET GIVING INFORMATION.
Christian de Wet's loyalist brother Piet, telling Colonel Brits how his brother looted his horses. The loyalists wore white armlets.

doubtful whether to hush everything up, or to go to Potchefstroom and fight to the death. At three o'clock in the morning he telephoned to his fellow-conspirators, reporting the accident to Delarey, and explaining that he could not come. There was something like a panic amid the plotters, and dawn broke without the Vierkleur, the old Transvaal flag, floating over Potchefstroom.

Colonel Kemp, who had sent in his resignation at the same time as General Beyers, was so frightened that he withdrew his resignation. Over the grave of Delarey, and in the presence of General Botha, Beyers, lying to save himself, proclaimed that he had no intention of causing or advising rebellion. Yet the next day the forsworn traitor, acting with General de Wet and other conspirators, held a meeting at Lichtenburg, where Delarey had lived and had exercised wide authority, and tried to win over the country people—the country Boers who had come to the funeral of their dead leader. Beyers and De Wet began by condemning in violent language the policy of General Botha. Then they went on to create a sort of mutiny by passive resistance; for they advocated that all their fellow-countrymen serving in the Defence Force should refuse to go on active service if the commandos were called out in accordance with the Defence Act.

Botha's call for volunteers

At this time none of the loyal Dutchmen would admit that Beyers and De Wet were engaged in any intrigue against the Union. At most it was thought that they were striving with General Hertzog to overthrow the Botha Cabinet, by making the utmost difficulties over the intended campaign against German South-West Africa. Had the Prime Minister let things drift, the conspirators would soon have organised a strong party on their new policy of passive resistance, and would then have suddenly swept most of their supporters into a plan of open rebellion by means of some dangerous incident. But General Botha was well

THE LEADER OF THE REVOLT IN THE ORANGE RIVER COLONY.
General Christian de Wet (in centre) ; a photograph taken just after his capture. He headed the rebellion in the Orange River Colony on October 21st, 1914, and surrendered at Waterburg on December 1st.

aware of the perils of the situation. The old generalissimo of the Boer forces kept to his plan of audacious and quick action, with a view to forcing a solution of the issue and compelling the conspirators to cease conspiring or take the field.

On the day when Beyers and De Wet began to preach their subtle scheme of passive resistance, General Botha called for volunteers, and announced that he would lead the South Africans against the Germans in person. By this brilliant masterstroke he rallied the whole British population and a large majority of the Dutch to the support of the Government. By his gift for grasping difficult situations and doing the thing that carried people with him, he turned the position of his opponents. To the men who had been his commandants in the former war his return to the battlefield was a flaming challenge, and stilled all doubts. The vehement activity of their old leader was a heartening influence, compared with which the underground intrigues of the hesitating rebel leaders were of no avail.

His speech on this occasion was a finer effort of persuasion and direction than his Cape Town declaration. He spoke at Bank to five thousand of his own people, among whom was a strong commando of burghers. The Prime Minister

asked his constituents to speak out freely and straightforwardly. He wanted to know once and for all what was the good of talking as some people did and trying to create hostility against Great Britain. That could only provoke ill-feeling between Briton and Boer. Neutrality for South Africa was an utter impossibility. If a German warship came to Durban and imposed a levy of five millions on them, it would help them very little to say they were neutral. Would it be noble or honest to act as some people suggested that South Africa should act after the undertakings they had given in the past ? What would hostility to Great Britain mean to South Africa ? Ruin !

He was animated by a true and sincere love of his people, and yielded to no man in his patriotism to South Africa, and he wished them to understand clearly that there were only two courses open—the one that of loyalty and help, and the other that of disloyalty and treason. There was no middle course, and whoever said there was was trying to mislead them. Now, which course did they intend taking ? They must give him a straightforward answer. (Loud cries : " We want the loyal course. You have done the right thing.")

General Botha said he had information regarding German ambitions concerning South Africa which would make their hair stand on end. The fact of the matter was, General Botha declared, amid tremendous cheers, that the Kaiser wanted to go down to posterity as a second Napoleon. Incidentally he wanted a place to which to send Germany's surplus population, and South Africa appealed to him as a suitable place. German agents with their seditious talk were already doing a great deal of harm in South Africa. Surely the Government was there not to shirk responsibility, but to take responsibility, and to give the people a lead. People who shirked were people of no significance. The stain of treason had never touched South Africans, and would not now. To-day South Africa must prove to the British Empire, which was watching them, that they were worthy, and still more worthy, of trust. By doing so they would create for themselves a greater future than would ever otherwise be possible.

General Botha emphasised the importance of the gathering. He wanted them to speak with no uncertain voice. Their decision would have great influence throughout South Africa, and would go forth to the whole Empire. (Cries of " We support you.") Though the Dutch South African could not be expected to be so enthusiastic as the British South African, still he was loyal, and they did not want lip loyalists or fair-weather patriots. The people they wanted must be true patriots, men willing to do something and to make sacrifices. " The British Government must be able to look straight into our eyes and see what is in our minds." (Great cheering lasting several minutes.)

Lip loyalists not wanted

General Botha then referred directly to General Beyers. He said he was grieved that his old comrade, with whom he had gone through the South African war, should have taken up such an attitude. He had shaken the discipline of the Defence Force. He had issued a letter which was simply a political manifesto, evil in its effect, and by his conduct had greatly hurt him.

TEAM OF FORTY OXEN DRAWING A BRITISH GUN IN GERMAN SOUTH-WEST AFRICA.

General Botha continued : " But in all these difficulties I realise that God rules and will inspire the people to do what is right. Knowing and believing this, I said I shall assume responsibility and take command—(prolonged cheers)—and I ask you to strengthen my hands so that justice may be supreme." (Renewed cheers.)

After paying a moving tribute to General Delarey, General Botha said in conclusion that he wanted to serve his people. His time here might not be long, his hair was growing grey, and his health was not good, but he would continue to the end to do what he thought was in the true interest of the nation. In the past they had a clean and noble history ; let them continue so ; let there be no treason ; let them stand by the Government.

For some weeks the conspirators made no outward sign of their intention to take the field against General Botha and General Smuts. But Beyers, at least, was secretly acting in a vigorous manner against the constitutional Government of the Union. On September 26th a small force of South African Rifles, with a section of the Transvaal Horse Artillery, under Colonel Grant, was operating at Sandfontein by the German border. They had marched to a water-hole, through a narrow defile, into a valley surrounded by kopjes. Here both rifles and artillery were trapped by a couple of German battalions, who placed their guns on the ring of heights dominating the saucerlike basin in which the water-hole lay. The South African gunners fought till every man of both gun crews was either killed or wounded, and their ammunition had run out. Then, when the guns were put out of action by our men to render them useless to the enemy, the gallant little body of Britons and Boers surrendered.

Trapped by the Germans

The high-explosive shells from ten German guns on the surrounding kopjes wrought most of the slaughter. General Lukin, who had vainly tried to relieve the little trapped force, remarked at the time that no blame attached to Colonel Grant, who had fallen wounded into the hands of the enemy. It was afterwards discovered that the disaster had been brought about by the treachery of a Boer leader, who had been placed by General Beyers in command of the Union forces in the north-west territory. The traitor was Lieutenant-Colonel S. G. Maritz. He had distinguished himself in the South African War, and had then served under the Germans in the Herero campaign, but he came back in the guise of a loyalist, professing a detestation of his Teutonic neighbours. There was no doubt that he had been won over by a large sum of money, and the suspicion of him was so common that had it not been for the influence Beyers exerted on his behalf, he would never have been appointed to an important command on the German frontier. It was he who arranged that Colonel Grant's force should be trapped and slaughtered at Sandfontein, and as soon as this was suspected General Smuts ordered the traitor to give up his command and to report himself to headquarters. Maritz thereupon issued an impudent ultimatum, dated October 8th, in which he demanded to meet General Hertzog, General de Wet, General Beyers, Kemp, and Müller. He stated that if he were not allowed to receive instructions from these men he would attack Colonel Brits's force and invade the Union. He added that, in addition to his own troops, he had German guns and German soldiers, and that he had signed an agreement with the Governor of German South-West Africa, ceding Walfish Bay and other portions of the Union territory in return for a guarantee of the independence of the South African Republic.

Maritz won over by money

General Botha's reply was a proclamation of martial law throughout the Union. Maritz had arrested all his officers and men who were unwilling to join the Germans, and had sent them as prisoners into German territory. Colonel Brits, with the Imperial Light Horse, at once flung himself on the traitor, and the civil war opened on October 15th with an engagement at Ratedraai, ten miles

SOUTH AFRICAN TROOPS MOVING OFF IN THE ARDUOUS PURSUIT OF CHRISTIAN DE WET.

THE LAST CROSSING: TRAGIC END OF THE REBEL BEYERS WHILE TRYING TO CROSS THE VAAL RIVER.

General Beyers, who led the revolt in the Western Transvaal, met with a terrible end. Having divided his party into two groups, he fled with one of these in the direction of the Vaal. At daybreak on December 9th, 1914, they were trapped in the angle between the Zandspruit and the Vaal, and after a sharp fight Beyers, who was wounded, tried to swim his horse across the river. He and his companions were fired on, and it was seen that Beyers fell from his horse, but managed to grasp another animal by the tail. He was heard to cry for help, but was drowned before anybody was able to rescue him. In the above drawing he is seen in the water, with a guide who was shot. Near the river bank the remnant of Beyers' followers are holding up their hands in token of surrender.

SOLDIERS OF BRITISH
BORNEO IN KHAKI UNIFORM.

A TYPICAL FIJIAN IN
NATIVE DRESS.

south of Upington, in which seventy rebels were taken prisoners. On October 22nd Maritz attacked the post of Keimos, between Kakamas and Upington. There were only 150 loyalists at Keimos, and Maritz had 1,000 rebels and 70 German gunners. He advanced at dawn, but the small garrison held out till reinforcements arrived, and then the rebels were so severely handled that Maritz offered to surrender if a free pardon were granted. He was wounded, and fled into German territory. Two days afterwards some of the rebels with German gunners were again defeated at Kakamas. Maritz fell into disgrace with his German masters, who began to suspect he was ready to reverse the rôle he had played at Sandfontein, and lead German troops into a trap in the hope of being able in this manner to make peace with the South African Government.

The way in which Maritz's operations were defeated was extremely significant. Colonel Van de Venter, with one Staff officer, went to the town of Calvinia, in Northern Cape Colony. He called for loyalists to come out on commando for the sake of the honour and good name of the Dutch. In a few days there were two thousand men ready to take the field. Many of them were fathers and brothers of the rebels. Under Colonel Van de Venter they co-operated with the Imperial Light Horse and the Transvaal Horse, under Colonel Brits, and beat Maritz over the German frontier.

A sinister silence

Meanwhile a friend of General Botha and General Hertzog tried to get the two leaders to co-operate to end the revolt of Maritz. There can be little doubt that if General Hertzog had at once publicly repudiated the action of the traitor, the disruptive warlike movement among the Dutch would have been checked. But General Hertzog and Mr. Steyn, the former President of the Orange Free State, after closely consulting together, refused to denounce the rebellion. General Smuts even allowed Beyers afterwards to pass through the lines of the Government forces, and spend a night at Mr. Steyn's house outside Bloemfontein, with a view to giving the ex-President an opportunity of bringing the arch-traitor to his senses. But both General Botha and Mr. Steyn continued to maintain

a sinister silence at a time when a few strong words from them would have prevented Dutchmen from shedding Dutch blood.

General Smuts, in a speech at Johannesburg, made a direction allusion to the overtures which went on for a fortnight after Maritz's ultimatum. " The rebels had their own leaders, leaders to whom the people looked, and the Government were anxious to give these leaders every chance to show their patriotism and their powers of leadership in this great crisis. Efforts were being made, very serious efforts, by very important gentlemen to see whether it was not possible to bring the rebellion to a close without bloodshed." This was a plain reference to General Hertzog and Mr. Steyn, and the refusal of these two men to do what they could to prevent the rebellion from spreading entailed on them a passive responsibility for subsequent events.

Hertzog and Steyn

It was General Hertzog who, for two years, had set Beyers and De Wet in jealous opposition to General Botha and General Smuts. It was General Hertzog who had created the intense personal malevolence with which De Wet regarded his former companions-in-arms. De Wet had never reconciled himself to the advantages which Botha and Smuts had won over him. Starting, like himself, as simple farmers, they had become the leaders of a great nation, while he, after an unsuccessful term of office as Minister of Agriculture, had retired into the obscurity of the back veldt. Thus there was a deep feeling of bitterness in his mind, upon which General Hertzog was able to act, when trying to organise a party strong enough to overturn the Botha Cabinet. Then Beyers came along, with a plan for open warlike action that caught the fancy of De Wet. The famous old guerilla captain seems to have fancied

MEN OF THE FIJIAN CONTINGENT ON PARADE.

SOME OF THE MAORIS WHO VOLUNTEERED FOR SERVICE IN EGYPT.

that General Hertzog was behind the movement of rebellion, and being already himself compromised by Maritz's reference to him, he gathered a commando, and broke out in revolt on October 21st, 1914. He invaded Vrede, a town in the Northern Free State, and there he issued an amazing manifesto, in which he said:

"I signed the Vereeniging Treaty, and swore to be faithful to the British flag, but we have been so downtrodden by the miserable and pestilential English that we can endure it no longer. His Majesty King Edward VII. promised to protect us, but he has failed to do so, and has allowed a magistrate to be placed over us (he is one of the miserable and pestilential English) who is an absolute tyrant, and has made it impossible for us to tolerate it longer. I was charged before him with beating a native boy. I only did it with a small shepherd's whip, and for that I was fined five shillings."

This wildly ridiculous statement of the grounds of rebellion was a fair measure of De Wet's capacity for politics. The Vrede magistrate, "the absolute tyrant," who fined De Wet the sum of five shillings for an assault to which he had pleaded guilty, was a brother-in-law of Mr. Steyn, the former President of the Orange Free State. He had been appointed to his position at Vrede by General Hertzog, largely through the influence of Mr. Steyn. His act in fining De Wet a small sum for ill-treating a native boy was something less than justice—it was rather a favour to the fierce old Boer general. To start a great rebellion on such a ground was farcical. But, at the same time, De Wet, though ridiculous, was at least honest. For instead of trying to trump up a high-sounding case against the Union Government and the Imperial authorities, he frankly stated that his only cause of discontent was the slight measure of protection given by a magistrate to a black boy. His manifesto greatly helped to save the Union. It was believed at the time that two-thirds of the population in the Free State were either lukewarm or ready to rebel. In the Transvaal one-third of the population, drawn mainly from the Western Transvaal, were in a similar condition of ferment. But few of

De Wet's motive for rebellion

GENERAL GODLEY ADDRESSING THE MAORIS UNDER HIS COMMAND. INSET: CAPT. PITT, A MAORI OFFICER.

them were willing to rise in arms because De Wet had been fined five shillings for beating a black boy, and though Beyers at once acted with De Wet, and tried to remedy matters by a more high-flown proclamation, the movement did not increase in a formidable way.

Three members of the Union Parliament came out in arms, and a member of the Defence Council, Mr. Wessel-Wessels, went over to the rebels, together with several ministers belonging to the seceders from the Dutch Reformed Church. The rebel leaders had about 10,000 men in detached groups in the Western Transvaal and the Northern Free State. In their original plan, Beyers, De Wet, and Kemp were to converge with

MAORI CHIEFS. TOP PHOTOGRAPH: MEN OF THE SAME VIRILE RACE TAKING PART IN A WAR-DANCE AT AUCKLAND BEFORE THEIR DEPARTURE FOR EGYPT.

their commandos, effect a junction, and then march westward and join with a force under Maritz from German South-West Africa. The Germans arranged to bring the artillery and ammunition, in which the rebels were deficient. After being properly munitioned, organised, and reinforced by some thousands of German troops, the rebel army was to march on Pretoria.

From a military point of view the situation was a serious one. Politically, however, the position of the rebels was very weak. For the traitors had completed failed to make the right sort of appeal to the fanatical section of their countrymen. Had it not been for the remarkable influence exercised by the prophecies of Van Rensburg over the back-veldt Boers, Beyers and De Wet would have made a feebler show of force than they did.

All the genius in statesmanship and the power of passionate appeal resided in the Government party. The extraordinary personal influence

TYPES OF MAORI WARRIORS IN BRITISH UNIFORMS.

of Botha and the energy and resource of Smuts enabled them to command the situation. In a few weeks they had 40,000 men in the field. Of these a few thousand were part of the little army sent to occupy the coast towns of German South-West Africa, and recalled when the rebellion broke out. But by far the larger number were commandos of burghers, who came forth to fight their own kith and kin for the sake of an Empire against which they had been fighting only twelve years previously side by side with the same kith and kin.

The strain on the loyal Boers was appalling. In the course of the campaign complaints were made here and there by South Africans of British stock that they were bidden to hold their fire—while the rebels were shooting them down—to the last moment. There is no doubt that the Dutch generals and commandants were anxious to spare the lives of their own kinsmen. The loyal Boers themselves often remained for a long time under fire without shooting in reply, in the hope that the rebels would be surrounded and forced to surrender. The loyalists of both races at times suffered heavy casualties, owing to the forbearing way in which they conducted their operations. But the blood that the Boer and Briton shed side by side in the common cause of honour was worth shedding. Their comrades, who often fell while holding back their fire, were something higher even than heroes in a righteous fight. They were martyrs for the Union. They died so that the two white races of South Africa should grow into one nation, united by a common tradition of self-sacrifice and of forbearance in the hour of victory.

The rebels were never able to link up their forces. General Botha proved that he still retained the qualities by which he had won the chief command in the old days. He never gave the traitors a moment's rest. General Beyers with his commando was acting round Rustenburg on Tuesday, October 27th. General Botha in person came up in the morning and drove the rebels in headlong rout the whole day.

By October 29th Beyers was a fugitive, and some of his scattered commandos were defeated southward at Lichtenburg by Colonel Alberts. There was another action at Zuitpansdrift on November 5th, in which the rebels were again scattered. By this time the rebellion in the Western Transvaal was practically crushed. Kemp, who had been

arms. The world-wide fame which he had won in the old days as a guerilla captain inclined him to overestimate his ability, and to underestimate that of General Botha. If his rival had been commander-in-chief of the forces of the Transvaal in the old days, he, De Wet, had been commander-in-chief of the forces of the Orange Free State. And he still thought himself the more skilful fighter. Nothing but the stern ordeal of battle could bring him to his senses.

The battle at Marquard

He opened his campaign on November 7th by an action at Winburg, in which by superior numbers he managed to defeat a small loyalist commando under Cronje. One of his sons was killed in the fight. Then came the main battle between General Botha and General

NEW ZEALANDERS IN EGYPT. WASHING-
UP AFTER DINNER.

de Wet in person. It took place on November 12th at Marquard, about twenty-four miles east of Winburg. General Botha had arrived at Winburg the day before with his Transvaal commando, and by a splendid forced night march he came up with the forces of the rebel leader, and surrounded them in a north-eastern and easterly direction. At the same time Colonel Brandt, with another commando, also marched from Winburg towards Hoenderkop, where the men under De Wet were hemmed in. Then General Lukin and Colonel Brits moved from the west in order to complete the envelopment of the enemy.

If the operations had been carried out on the time-table drawn up by General Botha, the entire forces of De Wet would have been captured. But General Lukin and Colonel Brits were not able to take up their position at the appointed time. Meanwhile General Botha's commando attacked the rebels and defeated them with great loss, while Colonel Brandt also closed in on them. It was a smashing victory. The entire laager of De Wet was captured, with its stores of food and munitions, and a hundred carts, waggons, and motor-cars. In addition, two hundred and fifty prisoners were taken.

acting with Beyers, now separated, and moved with the larger force westward towards German South-West Africa, pursued by Colonel Alberts. Beyers, with a commando, tried to get into touch with De Wet, and leaving the Transvaal at Bloemhof, he crossed the Vaal River and entered the Orange Free State. He was pursued by a strong loyalist force under Colonel Lemmer. Colonel Lemmer attacked Beyers's commando near the Vet River on November 7th. The engagement occurred south-east of the Bloemhof diamond diggings, and though Beyers in person led the rebels, he was heavily defeated, three hundred and sixty-four of his men being captured, and some twenty killed and wounded. Most of the fugitives went on to Hoopstad, from which town Beyers tried to join De Wet.

By this time the poorly-organised forces that De Wet had collected in the northern districts of the Orange Free State were the only source of anxiety to the South African Government.

Rebels in the Orange Free State But every centre of revolt had been masked by strong Union forces, concentrated with remarkable speed and secrecy by General Botha. For some days negotiations went on between De Wet and other Free State leaders, while the Government refrained from action in the hope of avoiding more bloodshed. De Wet, however, was too much inflated with pride in his own talent for war to lay down his

NEWS FROM HOME.
A New Zealand trooper gets news from his far-away home. The charger by his side seems equally interested.

De Wet fled up the Vet River, with a strong Boer commando pursuing him. Then he turned south, where the pursuit was continued by another loyal commando. The rebel leader at Boshof divided his diminishing force into two divisions. With one of these he doubled back north, and reached the Vaal River with only twenty-five men out of the two thousand he had commanded at the Battle of Marquard. He was beaten back by a loyal outpost, but on November 21st he got across the Vaal,

SIR GEORGE REID, HIGH COMMISSIONER FOR AUSTRALIA, INSPECTING A CONTINGENT FROM THE GREAT ISLAND CONTINENT.

AUSTRALIAN LIGHT HORSE RETURNING TO CAMP AFTER BREAKING IN REMOUNTS FOR ACTIVE SERVICE.

INSPECTION OF CANADA'S FIRST CONTINGENT PRIOR TO EMBARKATION.
The Duke of Connaught is passing down the lines.   Top centre : His Royal Highness leaving the parade ground after the inspection.

THE AUSTRALIAN CONTINGENT ON THE SOIL OF THE MOTHERLAND.
Stalwart sons of Australia marching past the saluting point during an inspection at Romsey, Hampshire, by Sir George Reid, the High Commissioner, before leaving for active service.

MAJOR-GENERAL SAM HUGHES ADDRE
A scene at Toronto, the "City of Homes," assembly was composed of

AUSTRALIAN INFANTRY RETURN FROM A SKIRMISH BY THE SUEZ CANAL.
The men are crossing the Nile Bridge, on their return to camp after a brush with the Turkish raiders along the eastern bank of the Suez Canal.

EMPIRE RALLY FROM OVERSEAS.

GRAND MARCH-PAST OF CANADIAN TROOPS JUST BEFORE THEIR DEPARTURE FROM HOME.
When the photograph was taken the Duke of Connaught was taking the salute as these stalwart sons of Empire passed before him.

RECRUITS OF THE TORONTO DIVISION.
second great city is familiarly known.   The
second Canadian Contingent.

THE KING'S UNCLE TAKES THE ROYAL SALUTE.
The Duke of Connaught is seen taking up his position at the saluting base as the Royal Standard was being unfurled.
As Governor-General and Commander-in-Chief, he took the liveliest interest in the Dominion rally.

LADS OF THE RED ROSE AND SONS OF THE WATTLE.
A company of sturdy " Lancashire lads " marching past a guard composed of Australian troops at a spot in the vicinity of the Egyptian capital.

CITIZEN SOLDIERS OF AUSTRALIA'S SMALLEST STATE—VICTORIA—ON A ROUTE MARCH.

A CONTRAST IN IMPERIAL UNITY—ARABS UNLOADING SACKS OF CRUSHED BARLEY ON THE OUTSKIRTS OF THE NEW ZEALANDERS' CAMP IN THE EGYPTIAN DESERT.

NEW ZEALAND TROOPS ON FATIGUE DUTY.

followed by Commandant Dutoit with a special motor-car contingent from Witwatersrand.

So severe was the motor-car chase that De Wet's following was soon reduced to four men. But he managed to join another small commando of rebels, consisting mainly of fugitives from the Western Free State, who had gathered at Schweizer Reneke. With this force De Wet started westward, intending to follow Kemp and to join with Maritz in German South-West Africa. Fortune at first favoured him. For a series of heavy rainstorms reduced the roads to so bad a condition that the pursuing motor-cars could not keep up with him. On November 25th he crossed into Bechuanaland, over the railway line by Devondale. Here, however, another fresh loyalist force, under Commandant Brits, took up the pursuit. At the end of two days' chase about half of the fugitive force was captured. Then, on December 1st, Commandant Brits surrounded De Wet and the rest of the small commando at a farm at Waterburg, between the Molopo River and the Morokweni Reserve, about a hundred miles west of Mafeking. The rebel party, numbering fifty-two men, surrendered without firing a shot, and the former commander-in-chief of the Orange Free State forces was confined in prison pending his trial for high treason.

The capture of De Wet

General Beyers came to a more terrible end. He remained in the northern districts of the Orange Free State with about seventy men, while loyal commandos harried him from every side and tried to force on an action, from which he continually escaped by scattering his force. At last, after an engagement near Bothaville on December 7th, he split his party into two small groups. With one of these he fled towards the Vaal River along the tributary stream of the Zandspruit.

He was pursued by Captain Uys and Field-Cornet Deneker, with a small loyalist force. At daybreak on December 9th the rebels were trapped in the angle between the Zandspruit and the Vaal, and after a

ARABS CLIPPING HORSES IN THE NEW ZEALAND CAMP IN EGYPT.

sharp fight of fifteen minutes Beyers with some of his men tried to swim their horses across the Vaal to the Transvaal. They were fired on, and it was seen that Beyers fell from his horse, but managed to grasp another animal by the tail. This horse was swimming back to the Free State side. Beyers began to cry for help; but fighting was still going on between the loyalists and some of the rebels, and the arch-traitor was drowned before anybody was able to rescue him.

His death, following on the capture of De Wet and the flight of Maritz and Kemp, practically brought the rebellion to a close. During the first week in December General Botha continued to conduct operations in the northern district of the Orange Free State, where fogs and heavy rains veiled the movements of the last main forces of the revolt. But in a few days the rebels were hemmed in on all sides, five hundred and fifty being captured, and two hundred surrendering to a single loyalist, Commandant Kloppers, who had been previously taken prisoner and released.

One of the chief reasons for the extraordinary speed with which a rebellion of ten thousand armed men, under famous and experienced leaders, was broken up was the amnesty offered to all rebels who surrendered voluntarily by November 21st. This merciful measure, in combination with the swift and wide-driving operations of General Botha, completely undermined the apparently formidable forces of Beyers and De Wet.

By Christmas the warrior Prime Minister of South Africa was able to enjoy a week's holiday at his farm, in preparation for the arduous and difficult campaign in German South-West Africa. From a military point of view the delay caused by the rebellion was fortunate. As originally

The Burgher Forces trained afresh

planned, the expedition was dangerously inadequate in numbers; many of the men were imperfectly trained; they had not sufficient artillery, and were entirely without aircraft. All these defects, partly due, perhaps, to the treachery of General Beyers as Commandant-General of the Union Forces, were made good by General Botha and General Smuts. The members of the first expedition consisted almost exclusively of South Africans of British extraction.

But on January 5th, 1915, the burgher forces reassembled, and thousands of Boers, trained afresh for war by their recent operations against their misguided fellow-countrymen, began to encamp on Green Point Common, on the way to German South-West Africa. All that German gold, German intrigue, and German lies had accomplished was to consolidate the Union of South Africa and raise a strong Boer army, under the greatest of Boer generals, for the invasion of the only German colony suitable for white settlers. The ultimate result of a generation of German intriguers in South Africa is one of the grand ironies of history. The Germans dug their own graves as a colonising race. They thought the feet of the British Colossus were made of clay. But the Imperial Government did not build on clay; it built on the honour, the conscience,

and the virile integrity of the embattled farmers of the veldt.

And one of these farmers proved to be a statesman of supreme genius as well as a warrior of the finest Dutch type. Noble were the words he uttered at Pretoria when he went back to his farm: " For loyalist Boers in these later days it has been a tragic ordeal to hunt down and fire upon men—some of them their relatives, and many of them their friends—who were once their comrades-in-arms. The Dutch loyalists have discharged a painful duty out of a stern sense of honour, and they regard the whole rebellion as a lamentable business upon which the curtain should be rung down with as little declamation, as little controversy, as little recrimination as possible. For myself, personally, the last three months have provided the most sad experiences of all my life. I can say the same for General Smuts, and indeed for every member of the Government. The war—our South African War—is but a thing of yesterday. You will understand my feelings, and the feelings of loyal commandos, when, among rebel dead and wounded, we found from time to time men who had fought in our ranks during the dark days of that campaign. The loyal commandos have had a hard task to perform. They have performed it. The cause of law and order has been, and is being, vindicated. Let that

General Botha's noble speech

be enough. This is no time for exultation or for recrimination. Let us spare one another's feelings. Remember, we have to live together in this land long after the war is ended."

Thus spoke General Botha, the man who saved South Africa for both Boer and Briton. Let his words close the strangest, the most tragic, and yet the most glorious chapter in the history of the mighty Commonwealth that had suddenly been welded into a true nation, ripe for a great and happy destiny.

VISITING DAY IN THE CAMP OF THE VICTORIAN CONTINGENT JUST BEFORE EMBARKATION.

MARCH-PAST OF NEW ZEALANDERS AT A REVIEW NEAR CAIRO. AT THE SALUTING-BASE (LEFT TO RIGHT): GENERAL GODLEY, SIR THOMAS MACKENZIE, AND GENERAL SIR JOHN MAXWELL.

NEW ZEALAND TROOPS PASSING SHEPHEARD'S HOTEL, THE FAMOUS FASHIONABLE RENDEZVOUS IN CAIRO. INSET: NEW ZEALANDERS ARRIVING AT CHELSEA BARRACKS.

CHAPTER LIII.

HOW THE EMPIRE RALLIED TO THE FLAG.

Dissensions in the British Empire Calculated Upon by Germany—What the Potsdam Plotters Failed to See—The Question of the Empire as a Whole—Canada's Magnificent Rally to the Call—Her Splendid Contributions of Men and Material—Arrival of the First Canadian Contingent in England—In Training on Salisbury Plain—The "Patricia's" in Flanders—General Alderson's Message to the Dominion Troops at the Front—Praise from Sir John French—Second Contingent at Shorncliffe—The Australian Commonwealth's Fine Response—The First Contingent from "Down Under"—An Exciting Voyage—New Zealand's Noble Part—A Maori Incident—The Australasians Win Golden Opinions in Egypt.

GERMAN statesmen, in estimating their chances in a war against Britain, placed much weight on the advantages that would come to them from expected dissensions within the British Empire. As soon as Britain was engaged in a life-and-death struggle her subject races would, these critics believed, throw off their yoke. There would be risings in Calcutta and Bombay; while from Nairobi to Singapore, and from Khartoum to Port Elizabeth, nations would seize the chance of slaying their British administrators and returning to their old, primitive freedom. Uganda and Ceylon, Basutoland and the Straits Settlements, the solemn marches under the shadow of the Himalayas, and the fever-haunted jungles of Central Africa were alike to witness the quick, savage revolt of their people against the British oppressors.

Nor was this all. Canada would refuse to bear the burden of a war of whose origin she knew nothing, and cared less; Australia would quietly "cut the painter," and secure at a stroke her independence, and her freedom from war's burdens; while in South Africa the Boers would raise the standard of rebellion again and sweep every Briton into the sea.

This was the dream of Germany. It seemed impossible to her precise and philosophic Empire-builders that an Empire that has grown like ours, without plan or premeditation, should stand a great strain. Even those Germans who knew something of Greater Britain and of our dependencies failed to comprehend the real strength of our position. They were ever dwelling on our disputes and differences. These, they declared, were bound to split the Empire.

AT THE CANADIAN REMOUNT DEPOT.
Canadian Rough-rider showing his horsemanship.

They knew all about the line of cleavage between French Canadians and British Canadians; they were well informed of the differences in opinion between various political parties in the Dominions and at home on the question of naval defence; they had precisely recorded all the minor squabbles that must arise where independent and free peoples are working out their destiny.

What the German observers did not understand was that the differences were on the surface, and that underneath them lay a great fundamental unity. They did not realise that the French Canadians in Quebec, the British settlers in British Columbia, the Dutchmen in Cape Town, and even descendants of Germans in South Australia were one in their love of the freedom of British institutions.

Behind them stood men of a hundred nations, with skins of every hue, bound to the British rule, not by compulsion, but by their experience of generations of honest, capable, sincere, and disinterested administration.

Early in August, 1914, crowds gathered at every city in the Empire, day by day, waiting for news. Every phase was then followed with strained attention—the declaration of war upon Russia by Germany on August 1st, the invasion of French territory by German troops on August 2nd, and the mobilisation of the British Fleet on August 3rd.

When, on the evening of August 4th, war was declared between Great Britain and Germany the response was immediate. From end to end of the Empire controversies were forgotten, differences passed out of sight, and men united in one plea—"What can we do in this, *our* war?" This response has been the subject of incidental reference in Chapters Twenty-five, Thirty, Thirty-three, and

FAREWELL MARCH OF CANADA'S SECOND CONTINGENT THROUGH THE STREETS OF MONTREAL.

WINNIPEG RIFLES CROSSING A PONTOON BRIDGE OVER THE JACQUES CARTIER RIVER.
Note how the lumber has been held up by the bridge, testing the work of the Canadian Engineering Corps.

GROUP AT THE DIVISIONAL HEADQUARTERS,
FIRST CANADIAN CONTINGENT.
Lieut.-General E. A. H. Alderson, C.B., in centre.

OFFICERS OF THE DIVISIONAL HEAD-
QUARTERS STAFF, FIRST CANADIAN
CONTINGENT.

Thirty-six, but demands more extended
and particular treatment. Canada and
Australia and New Zealand began to raise
their armies to send to Europe; South
Africa rallied her sons for fighting nearer
to hand; the Indian princes mobilised
their forces and offered their armed men,
with themselves and their fortunes, to their
King. Basuto and Zulu, Kanaka and
Maori, Negro and Cingalese, clamoured to
serve. Men in the heart of Africa, and in
tiny Pacific Islands whose names were
scarcely known to a handful of people in
Britain, men who had never in their lives
seen Great Britain or met more than a
score or two of Britons, were found preparing themselves to fight for the Flag and
Empire they had learnt to love. "Why
should I, the King's servant, stand idle when
the King is fighting his enemies?" asked one Basuto chief.
And that was the question of the Empire as a whole.

In the dark days of early August, when Great Britain
suddenly found herself confronted with her armed and
well-prepared antagonist, the silver lining to the black
clouds that hung over us was the splendid consistency
of the people of the Empire. Everyone in Great Britain
who knew anything of Greater Britain knew that the
Dominions would be loyal and true. But even those who
knew Greater Britain best could hardly have believed that

BRIGADIER-GENERAL LAWRENCE.
Appointed to assist General Alderson in
the command of the Canadian Contingent.

at the first cry of danger to the Motherland old
foes would sink ancient controversies, old antagonists would clasp hands, and men from East
and West would flock to the Flag as Britain's
sons did. The world had seen
nothing like it before. **Canada's**
Even the seers who had **great lead**
visions, and the dreamers of
dreams, had failed to imagine anything so great
as what actually took place. From
August 4th it was no longer a case of
the people of Greater Britain helping
Great Britain in her war. It was the
people of Greater Britain taking their
share in their own war, making common
purpose and finding common strength
in their unity.

The people in the Dominion of
Canada regard theirs as the premier
Dominion of the Empire, and they
were resolved now to lead the way in
Imperial zeal. The Government did not
wait until war was declared. As soon
as it became evident that Great Britain
was likely to be dragged into the
struggle, the Duke of Connaught, the
popular and able Governor-General, then
touring the west, started for Ottawa, and
the Dominion Cabinet met to take action.

German cruisers were traversing the
seas, and it was thought possible that
some of these might attempt attacks on
certain vulnerable Canadian points.
There were large German colonies in the
United States, and smaller ones in Canada
itself. Would some of these Germans
seek to open guerilla war on Canada, or
try, by destroying bridges, blowing up
cities, or damaging ships, to injure the
Empire? All these things had to be guarded against.
Canada had not given much time or care to military defence
in the past. There was, it is true, a Department of
Militia responsible for military matters, and at its head was
a very active officer, Colonel (afterwards Major-General)
Sam Hughes. But Colonel Hughes's power was limited
until the approach of war by the apathy of the people.
There were numerous militia regiments, and a small
regular force, but the average young man had not thought
it worth while to trouble to do militia training. The

militia were little more than skeleton corps. But they were found, at the moment of emergency, to supply an invaluable groundwork on which a military organisation could be built up quickly.

As it became clear that war must come, steady processions of men poured from every point to the different militia headquarters offering their services. Farmers drove in twenty and thirty miles or more, cowboys left their prairies, city men, clerks and bank cashiers, owners of prosperous businesses and mechanics—young men, middle-aged, and old—moved by one common purpose, offered themselves. The militia officers found themselves suddenly overwhelmed. There were so many recruits that they could barely record their names. Soldiering, yesterday the amusement of a few, became to-day the settled work of the nation as a whole.

A truce to party strife

Party politics usually burn with a fierce heat in Canada, and the line of cleavage between Government and Opposition, both in the Dominion and the provinces, has always been clearly marked. Now, however, divisions were obliterated. Sir Wilfrid Laurier, the venerable ex-Premier and Leader of the Opposition, called his chief adherents together, and after consulting them, publicly announced that the Liberal Party would lend its support without reserve to all measures deemed necessary by the Government. "There should be a truce to party strife," said he, and he saw that the truce was declared. The statesmen of the different provinces echoed the same sentiment. The Duke of Connaught, who was to prove himself now, more than ever, a fitting leader for the

Canadian people, summarised the national position— "Canada stands united from the Pacific to the Atlantic in her determination to uphold the honour and traditions of the Empire."

Parliament was assembled, and it unanimously resolved to raise an expeditionary force of 22,000 men, fully equipped, for despatch to Europe. The Dominion Government had already placed the two Canadian cruisers, the Niobe and the Rainbow, at the services of the Admiralty. The Government paid the cost of a hospital for the French wounded in Paris, and when news came from England that there was likely to be distress among the poor in the Motherland, it sent over a gift of a million bags of flour of ninety-eight pounds each to the people of the United Kingdom.

A great outburst of public and private generosity was witnessed. Provinces, cities, banks, business organisations, and individuals vied with each other in the extent of their gifts for the Empire. Less than eight weeks after war was declared a list was drawn up of what had been offered and given. Among the provinces, Alberta gave half a million bushels of oats to England, and her civil servants set apart five per cent. of their salaries up to £300 a year, and ten per cent. beyond that, for the Patriotic Fund. British Columbia gave 25,000 cases of tinned salmon, Manitoba 50,000 bags of flour, New Brunswick 100,000 bushels of potatoes, Nova Scotia offered 100,000 tons of coal (afterwards changed to £20,000 in cash), Ontario 250,000 bags of flour, Prince Edward Island 100,000 bushels of oats, also cheese and hay, Quebec 4,000,000 pounds of

Canada's gifts in kind

SUPPORT FROM BRITAIN'S OLDEST COLONY; SECOND CONTINGENT OF NEWFOUNDLAND VOLUNTEERS AND RESERVISTS PARADING IN GOVERNMENT HOUSE GROUNDS, ST. JOHN'S.

The Colony of Newfoundland, as was specially noted in the King's message to his Overseas Dominions, doubled the numbers of its branch of the Royal Naval Reserve, and in addition contributed a force of two hundred and fifty men to take part in the operations at the front.

cheese, and Saskatchewan 1,500 horses. Then the cities made their presents : Montreal, £30,000 to the Patriotic Fund and a battery of quick-firing guns ; Ottawa, £10,000 to the Patriotic Fund, and £60,000 for a machine-gun section ; Toronto, £10,000, and other gifts. Calgary sent 1,000 men for the Legion of Frontiersmen. These were typical. The women of Canada were building, equipping, and maintaining a Canadian women's hospital of a hundred beds to supplement the British naval hospital at Haslar, near Portsmouth. They had raised altogether within between two and three weeks close on £60,000, partly as presents to the War Office for hospital purposes,

were as keen as those of British descent. Americans living in Canada clamoured to serve. Towns mainly inhabited by German emigrants led the way in loyalty. The white men were not alone. American Indians brought their gifts, of money and in kind, and offered themselves as scouts, boatmen, and woodmen.

Canada was undoubtedly handicapped at the beginning of the war by her absence of naval and military preparations. The Canadian people had for some time recognised that it was their duty to take part in the defence of the seas, but they had been unable to agree on **The Canadian Navy** their naval policy. The Government of Sir Wilfrid Laurier proposed to build a Canadian Navy, as Australia was building an Australian Navy. Preliminaries were being actively discussed when the Liberals were defeated, and the Conservatives, under Sir Robert Borden, returned to power. Sir Robert Borden and his Ministry, acting under the advice and with the support of the British Admiralty, proposed not to build, for the time, a separate Dominion Navy, but to provide a certain number of ships to form part of the regular British Navy. An ambitious

A GIFT TO THE FIRST NEW-
FOUNDLAND REGIMENT.
Mr. R. G. Reid, of the Reid-Newfoundland
Co., with one of the two guns presented
to the First Newfoundland Regiment by
Mr. W. D. Reid.

and partly for their own hospital. The Canadian Red Cross raised vast sums. The banks gave donations to the Patriotic Fund, from £2,000 from the Montreal City and Districts Savings Bank to £20,000 from the Bank of Montreal.

The public teachers of Winnipeg sent £6,000. The individual gifts of many rich Canadians were on a princely scale. Thus, Mr. J. K. L. Ross, of Montreal, presented £100,000 to the Patriotic Fund, paid the cost of taking the 5th Royal Highlanders to England, and gave a steam-yacht. Mr. Hamilton Gault, another millionaire, raised and equipped at his own cost a regiment—Princess Patricia's Light Infantry—soon to win wide fame. Crowds of rich men came together and raised many hundreds of thousands of dollars **Princess Patricia's Regiment** to purchase machine-guns and armoured motor-cars for the troops. The Canadian Pacific Railway gave £20,000, and the men on the line gave another £20,000, in addition to promising one day's pay monthly during the war.

It was not alone the rich who gave. Canada was at this time passing through a trying period of industrial depression. Many of her business men were having a desperate fight, and at the time that the war broke out the streets of many cities were full of unemployed. Yet the poorest managed to find something for King and Empire. French Canadians

NEWFOUNDLANDERS LEAVING ST. JOHN'S.
The s.s. Stephano, with two hundred and fifty men of the First Newfoundland Regiment and nearly
one hundred for the Navy, leaving their island home for Europe.

programme was drawn up, but the Government was unable to carry it through the Senate. There was an exceedingly bitter and sustained controversy, and in the end a deadlock ensued.

Hence at the outbreak of the war the Royal Canadian Navy consisted of two training ships—the Niobe and the Rainbow. The work of raising the first contingent, and of completing its equipment, was made much harder by the smallness of the Dominion military establishment, useful as that small establishment was. Despite this, the speed with which the contingent was equipped surprised the world. Canada determined to make up for lost time, and set itself with its whole heart to become a nation in arms.

It was soon found that the first contingent could not be kept within the 22,000 originally intended In a few weeks

NEW ZEALAND GUN TEAM: INSPECTION DAY IN THE CAMP NEAR CAIRO.
Men, horses, and guns were found to be in the very pink of condition.

SUPPLY WAGGON OF THE NEW ZEALAND ARMY SERVICE CORPS IN EGYPT.
Even in the photograph one can see how well the horses were selected and cared for.

A CHURCH SERVICE IN THE LAND OF THE PHARAOHS.
A remarkable camera picture of one of the many striking contrasts brought about in Egypt by the Great War.

an army of 33,000 men was raised. The different regiments of militia immediately placed their services at the disposal of the Government. The wave of passionate loyalty that swept over the country gathered strength day by day. The determination of the people showed itself, not so much in great meetings and in public demonstrations, but in strenuous preparations and willing self-sacrifice. Two quotations from Canadian newspapers, written before war was actually declared, will testify the feeling of the nation. The first is from the Toronto "Globe," a leading Opposition journal :

THE COMING OF THE CANADIANS.
Landing of the First Canadian Contingent at Plymouth.

WITH THE FORCES IN AUSTRALIA.
Guarding a river bridge in New South Wales.

If Canada is called upon to speak in the midst of the wild war babel, let her voice be strong, responsible, and authoritative —the voice of the whole Parliament of Canada. Of one thing let there be no cavil or question ; if it means war for Great Britain, it means war also for Canada. If it means war for Canada, it means also the union of Canadians for the defence of Canada, for the maintenance of the Empire's integrity, and for the preservation in the world of Great Britain's ideals of democratic government and life. When that issue is raised all differences of party and race merge into one positive and unwavering unity. Before the world Canadians are not divided. With Great Britain and all the British dominions we stand, whatever needs to be done. Sir Robert Borden may be confident that the Canadian people are not only loyal to their obligations, but soberly and resolutely ready to do their solemn duty as citizens and as a nation.

The next is from "Canada," a French Liberal newspaper published in Quebec :

When the country is in danger the time for political quarrels, for the conflict of interests or classes is past, and everyone must rally around the one who holds the national Flag. In England the country comes before parties, and we approve with all our hearts. We are certain it will be the same in Canada, and if the occasion presents itself the Liberal party will second all measures which patriotism can dictate to Sir Robert Borden. When the country is in danger political arguments must cease, and if now the danger is come Canada will be found united in this sentiment.

Country before parties

A message from the King, explaining how Great Britain

had been forced into war, brought forward fresh demonstrations of loyalty.

The various regiments raised throughout the Dominion were assembled at a newly-created camp, Valcartier, outside Quebec. Valcartier was a marvel of its kind, a camp built up from nothing in a very few weeks, with permanent buildings, shower-baths, electric light, a good water supply throughout the lines, and conveniences lacking in many camps that have been established for years. The army that arrived here had features of its own.

The camp at Valcartier

There were regiments of regulars, cavalry like the Royal Strathcona Horse and the Royal Dragoons, largely composed of veterans from the South African War. There were Highland regiments drawn from cities like Toronto, Montreal, and Vancouver, regiments affiliated with famous Highland corps in the United Kingdom—Seaforths, Gordons, and Camerons—full of the pride of tradition and race. There were scouts from the west, plainsmen trained to pioneer work in the desolate lands of the north, cowboys accustomed to life in the saddle, trappers and hunters, and farmers. There were many townsmen, but the Canadian townsman, as a rule, sees much more of the open air than the townsman in Europe, and possesses much more initiative. A very large proportion of the men were British born, young fellows who had gone out to Canada, lived there for some years, and had, at the first call of duty, volunteered to return and fight for the land of their birth.

The Dominion Government resolved that the first contingent was to be completely equipped in a way surpassed by no other army in the world. No money was to be spared. Accordingly, the personal equipment of the men was brought to a point of excellence that excited general admiration on their arrival in Europe. They were amply provided with machine-guns, their artillery was abundant in quantity and of the best. They had a splendid park of motor-transports, and the mechanical equipment was as good as could be.

The hospitals of Canada had been searched to select a strong corps of trained nurses to accompany the army. There was a complete medical department, chaplains were given military rank, and—at that time an unusual feature—secretaries to the Y.M.C.A. were given rank as officers and attached to the regular forces.

By the end of September the expeditionary force was complete, from a very carefully chosen Intelligence

BRITISH BULLDOGS IN EGYPT.
Corporal and private of the Australian Contingent in Egypt with their bulldog pets, in which the natives displayed a sympathetic interest.

Canadians, and Plymouth and Devonport thereupon set out to give the unexpected new comrades a right royal reception. The Canadians had thought they would have a cordial greeting when they reached England, but as they one and all admitted afterwards, they had never dreamed of such a demonstration as awaited them.

The coming of the Canadians was felt throughout Britain to be something more than the mere addition of some tens of thousands to our armies, important as that was. It was the visible evidence that in her great world-struggle Britain did not stand alone. Her sons had rallied to her side. "We know that they indeed come of the right breed," said "The Times," voicing the national sentiment, as it welcomed them. "If they did not, they would not have flocked of their own free will to the Flag, as they have done, and as they are still doing with unabated ardour. We remember their work and the work of their brothers from Australia and from New Zealand in South Africa. There, for the first time, the troops of the daughter nations proved their valour and their skill in a common Imperial enterprise. Now they are about to prove their soldiership for the first time in a great European war. We welcome their assistance with gratitude and with pride. We welcome it for the addition which it brings to our numbers in the field, and for the exceptionally fine quality of the troops which it gives us. We are deeply sensible of its high military worth. But we welcome it far more for the incalculable moral support which it lends us in this great struggle. Our enemies thought that a war would divide us. They have been foolish enough to utter their thoughts, and even to base their calculations upon these vain imaginings. All of us, whether at home or beyond the seas, knew that nothing could do so much as war to reveal

Department to the hospital orderlies. Then one day the men heard the bugle calling them to attention. They set out as though on a route march, but this time their steps were directed towards the St. Lawrence, and they did not look back.

A fleet of great ships had been assembled there, the expeditionary force marched aboard, its guns and supplies were slung into place, and it sailed for Europe.

The voyage of the contingent across the Atlantic was watched with anxiety by the people on both sides of the ocean. Would the raiding German cruisers succeed in attacking them en route? A complete veil had been drawn over the movements of the troops. For some weeks no Canadian newspapers were allowed to be circulated abroad. No word was breathed of where, **How the Canadians** or how, or when the Canadians **came to England** had started.

Early in October a report was circulated in England that the contingent had landed at Southampton. People rushed down to give them a great greeting. The report turned out to be false. Then, on October 14th, the people of Plymouth were surprised in the early morning to see transport after transport arrive in the Sound, and drop anchor there. The people, looking across the waters, could hear singing and shouting and cheering from the boats, and could see thousands of khaki-clad men on the ships' sides looking towards the shore. The word went round the town that the men on the crowded decks were

A CANADIAN GUN FOR THE FRONT.
Field-piece being hoisted on board a transport at Montreal.

our real unity and to foster it. We have been right, as we were sure we should be right. The coming of the Colonial troops is the proof that the peoples of this Empire understand each other better than all the spies and investigators whom Germany has sent out to study them."

A group of camps had been arranged for the contingent on Salisbury Plain, and the men were immediately moved there. The young recruits hoped to proceed to the front within a week or two. The British military authorities

SAND ARTISTS IN THE DESERT.
Queenslanders inscribe the arms of their State in the sands of Egypt.

had other ideas for them, and gave them an exceedingly hard course of training, which, starting in October, continued well on into February. It had been intended to transfer the troops before the winter weather came on from their tents to huts, but the shortage of labour in England and other causes prevented the completion of the huts, and most of the troops were still under canvas when the New Year opened. The life of the Canadian troops during those weeks on Salisbury Plain was, it must be admitted, wearisome and trying. The camps were one great sea of mud. It was an unusually wet winter. The roads had not been made to stand the strain of the heavy military traffic that fell on them, and in places they became **Wearisome and** almost impassable. The camps were **trying work** miles away from any villages, and fourteen miles from a town, in the loneliest, most exposed, and dullest part of England. The soldiers had nothing to do during the long winter nights but crouch in the semi-darkness in their tents, listening to the unceasing rain outside, unless they were able to get into the Y.M.C.A. marquee, which would not hold them all. They had plenty of money, the private soldier receiving

about five shillings a day, including allowances, but there were few or no rational ways of spending it.

The young recruits found it hard to understand military discipline. The result was that in a short time the Canadian Contingent was the object of some criticism. Those who knew the Canadians well knew that the faults, such as they were, were all on the surface. In the hasty enlistment of so many men a **The King and the** small proportion of unsuitable recruits, **Canadians** not more than five per cent. of the whole, had been accepted. Some of these were not physically fit, others had not the moral stamina. The weeks of waiting and of preparation on Salisbury Plain enabled the authorities to weed these out, and relentlessly weeded out they were.

Lieut.-General E. A. H. Alderson was given command of the contingent shortly after its arrival. The King visited the camp on November 4th, accompanied by the Queen, Lord Kitchener, and Lord Roberts, and was greeted with immense enthusiasm. Lord Roberts, as Colonel-in-Chief of the Colonial Forces, paid a special visit by himself to the Canadians, and made a speech, which was long remembered. "We have arrived at the most critical moment of our history, and you have generously come to help us in our hour of need," he told the assembled soldiers. "I need not urge you to do your best, for I know you will, for you will be fighting in the greatest of all causes —the cause of right, of justice, and of liberty."

By early in February the time of preparation in England was finished. Those who saw the troops on their arrival at Plymouth, and who saw them shortly before their departure for France, could

AUSTRALIAN FIELD ENGINEERS AT WORK.
Laying a field telegraph.

not fail to be struck by the difference. They had now experienced four months of the most rigorous military life and discipline. They had lived under surroundings of the greatest hardships, exposed to the worst weather possible, with few comforts and few conveniences, in their isolated camp on Salisbury Plain. They had been tried, hardened, and strengthened. No man of military knowledge who walked through the Canadian camps at the beginning of February could doubt but that here were men who, given opportunity, would bring glory to the Dominion and victory to the British arms.

SMART WORK OF THE NEW ZEALANDERS IN EGYPT: BRIDGE-BUILDING NEAR THE NILE.

The contingent had been accompanied on the journey to Europe by a special regiment, Princess Patricia's Light Infantry, largely composed of veteran British soldiers. Four hundred and fifty men in the ranks had the right to wear war medals. Its commander was Colonel Farquhar, D.S.O., who went to Canada as Military Secretary to the Duke of Connaught in 1913, and Mr. Gault who, as has been already stated, paid the cost of raising and equipping the regiment, served as an officer under Colonel Farquhar. The Patricias were named after the Duke of Connaught's daughter, and they were quickly nicknamed " Princess Pat's." They remained a short time with the first contingent, and then in November were transferred to Winchester, and from there were sent in December to Northern France. They were at once moved up to the fighting zone, and were first given a spell of very heavy work, digging one of the rear line of trenches. Then they set out for the fighting front.

Princess Patricia's Regiment

The arrival of the Patricias in Flanders was watched with keen interest in all parts of the Empire, for they were the first troops from the Dominions to take part in Continental fighting. At first nothing was heard of them, and then rumour after rumour spread through England and America of their fate. Mysterious stories arose, no one knew how, of how they had been wiped out in the fighting, of how they set out in charges in hundreds and returned in tens. One newspaper published a story of how, at the first opportunity, their slouch-hatted ranks had charged the German trenches with a shout " For God and Canada !" and had captured large sections of the German lines.

What actually happened to them was this. After finishing their work at trench-digging, they had two days of heavy marching of sixteen miles each day over broken, muddy roads. Then, at half-past ten one night, they were led quietly into the front line of trenches, relieving French troops there. The following description, written at the time in the " Toronto Star " by Mr. F. A. McKenzie, who saw something of their life, tells their experience :

It was pitch dark, with heavy rain. The darkness was frequently illuminated by German star shells, which fell along the front, making the position as light as daytime. Some soldiers could not immediately realise the absolute necessity of dead silence while advancing, and the noise of their movements brought a heavy, but futile, German bombardment on the lines. The first and second companies occupied the front trenches, the third and fourth companies supporting in secondary lines. The trenches were mud-holes holding from fifteen inches to three feet of water, and at some points deep, concealed cavities, into which the men plunged up to their chests in water. The Canadians took up their positions without lights, commands being whispered along the line. Some men occupied observation points ahead, crouching in the mud, searching through the darkness for any signs of a German advance. Others crouched behind parapets ready for instant action.

Face to face with the foe

Amid pauses in the almost incessant din of artillery fire they could hear Germans conversing and baling water out of their trenches scarcely a stone's throw away. The artillery on both sides kept on during the night. There was an occasional ping of a single rifle shot, which told of the activity of snipers.

Star shells fell frequently. Several times the men, believing the Germans were approaching, opened a rapid rifle fire into the darkness. Here and there along the trenches were rough tops of tarpaulins or tarred paper, beneath which some stood to escape the rain. Others were busy baling water from the trenches. It was a night none there will ever forget. The next morning gave the Canadians a fuller view of their position. They were occupying long, hidden lines in a sea of mud. The German lines, scarcely visible, were from fifty to one hundred and fifty yards away. Between both fronts were wire entanglements. The soldiers had hoped when approaching the trenches that they would have an

A GLIMPSE OF THE NEW ZEALANDERS' STIRRING CAMP NEAR CAIRO.

Johnson." A man who fell into it could not release himself, but had to be dragged out, his comrades standing at the side, and putting their rifles so that he could clutch hold and be pulled up. The drinking water was brackish, making some of the men ill with stomach troubles. Frost-bite, the terrible frost-bite of the trenches, took its toll of the Canadians. It was found, however, that they stood the exposure better than most troops, and the proportion of sick among them was below the average. The first period in the trenches was not spectacular. It was a time of waiting and endurance.

The Patricias did not appreciate the work of the German snipers, and they quickly formed their own corps of snipers, who, creeping around, repaid the Germans with interest. Then came duels between the individual snipers on either side. In February, when again in the trenches, the Patricias found an opportunity to make a gallant dash and to capture a German trench. A storming party, consisting of the corps of snipers and thirteen picked men, started out at midnight to explore the German position. They crept up until they were within twenty yards of the enemy's trench, fixing their bayonets as they approached. Then, as the order was given to charge, they leaped right into the German trenches, bayoneting the men still left there. There was fierce fighting with picks and shovels, and whatever came first to hand. Hand bombs were thrown on either side. The Germans counter-attacked with a fresh force, but the Patricias held their own, losing, however, a number of men, Major Hamilton Gault himself being one of the wounded. A few days after this, in further fighting, Colonel Farquhar was killed. The Patricias had by this time won their reputation with the British Army. They had been widely **Colonel Farquhar** chaffed at first because of their name **killed** and because of the Canadian tendency to magnify their doings. The British soldiers found, however, that they were of the right stamp, hard-bitten fighting men.

To return to the first contingent. Early in February the word was passed that the time of departure was approaching. The King paid another visit to Salisbury Plain, this time a visit of farewell. Nothing was said in the Press about the coming departure of the troops, and even the King's visit

opportunity of charging the enemy's position and driving them back. One glance showed that an advance either by the Germans or ourselves was at this point practically impossible. The contested space between the lines was a morass of mud, into which any man attempting to cross would instantly sink.

Scouts and sharpshooters on either side instantly fired upon any indication of human life. It was impossible for a man to raise his head above the trenches without a quick bullet coming. The Germans evidently knew the position of every British dug-out. They had rifles so fixed as to cover them exactly, enabling the trigger to be pulled without taking time to aim.

A fatal deed of heroism Two of the most popular officers in the regiment—Captain Newton and Captain Fitzgerald—were killed in the early fighting. Captain Newton, like Colonel Farquhar, had been formerly attached to the Duke of Connaught's staff. Soon after the Patricias arrived at the front he was moving around the trenches at night time, inspecting the lines. It was pitch dark, and a heavy storm made it scarce possible to observe anything around. Newton lost his way in the darkness in going from one trench to another, and stumbled to a place in front of our own lines. A sentry challenged him, and receiving no reply, shot him. The officer was brought in, and died some hours afterwards. Captain Fitzgerald, a former officer in the regular British Army, had won early the goodwill of all by his cheerfulness, his daring, and the careful way he looked after the men under him. One soldier had been shot by a German sniper, and his dead body lay in the trenches outside. Fitzgerald declared that he was not going to see one of his comrades lying there. He made a dash to pick up the body, but before he could grasp hold of it, a German bullet got him, and killed him. " He was a hero, and he died a hero's death," said the soldiers, as they told afterwards of how he had fallen.

Life in the trenches in these early days in January was trying and arduous. It was the custom then to keep the troops for forty-eight hours in the front line, then forty-eight hours in the reserve lines, and afterwards to send them back for a rest. The trenches were horrible. The air was charged with the sickly odour of bodies of men who had fallen weeks before, lying in spots where it was impossible to get to them. There was mud everywhere, mud sometimes up to a man's knees, sometimes up to his waist. Here and there was a deep mud-hole, caused by the explosion of a " Jack

THE FLEETING SOLACE OF A HASTY GAME DURING AN INTERVAL IN CAMP.

was not allowed to be mentioned for some weeks afterwards. The Canadians themselves understood that they were going to Rouen, where they were, they thought, to spend some weeks before proceeding to the front. Their expectation was, however, disappointed.

German submarines were very active in the Channel at this time, and it was well known that the Germans particularly aimed at destroying some of the Canadians on their way across. They entertained a particular hatred for them, for they had disappointed German hopes by taking part in the war. The British Admiralty took ample precautions to guard the sea-way. The Canadians embarked at Avonmouth and set out—not as they had expected for a trip of a few hours across the narrow waters, but towards the Atlantic Ocean. A few ships, carrying some part of the heavy military train, dodged the waiting submarines and reached Havre. Most of the vessels never tried for Havre, but made for St. Nazaire, hundreds of miles away, on

AN ARAB BOY ENJOYS THE LIGHTER SIDE OF EUROPEAN CAMP LIFE.

NEW ZEALANDERS IN EGYPT AT SIGNALLING WORK ON THE ROOF OF THEIR "DINING-HALL."

the west coast of France. There was to be no more waiting now. As the troops stepped ashore they found officials in attendance, with great stacks of fur coats, mountains of big gloves, and other equipment for the front. The men were fitted with their new garments on the spot, and at once started off for a railway journey from the extreme west to the far northeast of France. Three days later they stepped out of their trucks at their destination, somewhere in the neighbourhood of Ypres. They were where they had long wanted to be—at the actual front.

Here they settled down to the everyday work of war, taking their turn in the trenches, after first going through a preliminary course with older troops. The Canadians soon won a character for themselves with the British Army, and a character wholly good. Their one difficulty at first was a certain recklessness. The boys off duty would start and keep on with a football match, for example, under heavy German artillery fire. While they were in the trenches

it was hard for them to realise the necessity of keeping under cover. The Germans, with their amazing intelligence service, learned this characteristic of the Canadians, and on the first night they were in the trenches they tried by taunts and cries to draw them out to their death. " Come out, you Canadians ! Come out and fight ! " they called.

But the Canadians soon learned to abide by war conditions. The Dominion soldiers were filled with admiration for the British Tommies, whose trenches they shared. Letter after letter sent back to Canada was charged with praise of the British. " These English regulars are just fine," wrote one young Canadian, in a typical letter. " They're full of notions, they have all sorts of devices ; they joke over the hardest luck ; they never grumble. I tell you, when I thought of how I had grumbled over the mud of Salisbury Plain, and when I saw what they had gone through without a kick, I just felt ashamed of myself." The British were as emphatic in their praise of the Canadians.

General Alderson's message

General Alderson, who commanded the Canadian Division at the front, as he had done at Salisbury Plain, circulated a soldierlike message to the troops before they first occupied their own line of trenches :

ALL RANKS OF THE CANADIAN DIVISION.—We are about to occupy and maintain a line of trenches. I have some things to say to you at this moment, which it is well that you should consider. You are taking over good, and, on the whole, dry trenches. I have visited some myself. They are intact, and the parapets are good. Let me warn you first that we have already had several casualties while you have been attached to other divisions. Some of those casualties were unavoidable, and that is war. But I suspect that some—at least a few—could have been avoided. I have heard of cases in which men have exposed themselves with no military object, and perhaps only to gratify curiosity. We cannot lose good men like this. We shall want them all if we advance, and we shall want them all if the Germans advance.

Do not expose your heads, and do not look round corners, unless for a purpose which is necessary at the moment you do it. It will not often be necessary. You are provided with means of observing the enemy without exposing your heads. To lose your life without military necessity is to deprive the State of good soldiers. Young and brave men enjoy taking risks. But a soldier who takes unnecessary risks through levity is not playing the game, and the man who does so is stupid, for whatever be the average practice of the German Army, the individual shots whom they employ as snipers shoot straight, and screened from observation behind the lines, they are always watching. If you put your head over the parapet without orders, they will hit that head. There is another thing. Troops new to the trenches always shoot at nothing the first night. You will not do it. It wastes ammunition, and it hurts no one. And the enemy says, "These are new and nervous troops." No German is going to say that of the Canadian troops.

"The Canadians never budge" You will be shelled in the trenches. When you are shelled, sit low and sit tight. This is easy advice, for there is nothing else to do. If you get out you will only get it worse. And if you go out the Germans will go in. And if the Germans go in, we shall counter-attack and put them out, and that will cost us hundreds of men instead of the few whom shells may injure. The Germans do not like the bayonet, nor do they support bayonet attacks. If they get up to you, or if you get up to them, go right in with the bayonet. You have the physique to drive it home. That you will do it, I am sure, and I do not envy the Germans if you get among them with the bayonet.

There is one thing more. My old regiment, the Royal West Kent, has been here since the beginning of the war, and it has never lost a trench. The Army says: "The West Kents never budge." I am proud of the great record of my old regiment. And I think it is a good omen. I now belong to you and you belong to me; and before long the Army will say: "The Canadians never budge." Lads, it can be left there, and there I leave it. The Germans will never turn you out.

Sir John French, in an emphatic message to the Duke of Connaught, praised the Canadians:

The Canadian troops having arrived at the front, I am anxious to tell your Royal Highness that they have made the highest impression on us all. I made a careful inspection the week after they came to the country, and was very much struck by the excellent physique which was apparent throughout the ranks. The soldierly bearing and steadiness with which the men stop in the ranks on a bleak, cold, and snowy day are most remarkable. After two or three weeks' preliminary education in the trenches, they have now taken over their own line, and I have the utmost confidence in their capability to do valuable and efficient service.

The Princess Patricias arrived a month earlier, and since then have performed splendid service in the trenches. When I inspected them also, in pouring rain, it seemed to me that I had never seen a more magnificent-looking battalion, Guards or otherwise. Two or three days ago they captured a German trench with great dash and energy. I am **Sir John French's tribute** writing these few lines because I know how deeply indebted we all are to the untiring and devoted efforts your Royal Highness has personally made to ensure the despatch in the most efficient condition of this valuable contingent.

From now on, the work of the Canadian Contingent proceeded with that of the regular forces, the troops being first attached for training for a few days to brigades in the 3rd Corps' trenches. The Canadian artillery took part in the fighting around Neuve Chapelle, and the infantry were in the trenches. Although they did not share in the main attack, they rendered valuable help by keeping the enemy engaged in front of their trenches. The Princess Patricias shared in the battle around St. Eloi. Everywhere the Canadians won high praise for their physique, and their splendid soldiery. "If we're good enough to fight by the side of the British soldiers at the front, we're proud," said they.

Sir John French, in his despatch of April 5th, 1915, describing the Battle of Neuve Chapelle, told how he inspected the Canadian Division a few days after it arrived at the front. "They presented a splendid and most soldierlike appearance on parade. The men were of good physique, hard and fit. I judged by what I saw that they were able to take their places in the line of battle. Since then the division has justified the good opinion

SIDELIGHTS ON THE CAMP LIFE IN EGYPT OF OUR KINSMEN FROM OVERSEAS.

PONTOON-BUILDING UNDER THE
SHADOW OF THE PYRAMIDS.

I formed of it. All the soldiers of
Canada serving in the army under
my command have so far splendidly
upheld the traditions of the Empire,
and will, I feel sure, prove to be a
great source of additional strength
to the forces of this country."

While the first contingent was
completing its training, a second and
a third contingent were formed. The
second contingent arrived in England
in March, and was given headquarters
at Shorncliffe. A distinguished Canadian officer, General Sam Steele, who
took a prominent part in the Boer
War, was chosen to command it. It
was easily observable that the

REMOVING WOUNDED FROM THE SUEZ CANAL FRONT TO THE HOSPITAL TRAIN.

authorities had learned much from their first experience.
Shorncliffe was a much better site for the troops than
Salisbury Plain, and there was no whisper of disorder
from the start with the second contingent. By the middle
of April Sir Robert Borden was able to say that Canada
had 101,000 men under arms. Her people were standing,
to their last shot and their last dollar, if need be, behind
the Motherland.

At the beginning of the war the Commonwealth of
Australia had one great advantage over Canada. The
people of each of the great sister nations were equally
loyal, equally eager to help, equally
Australia's advantage determined to sacrifice all they had, if
over Canada necessary, for victory. But Canada
started her real preparations for war
when war began, while Australia had been preparing for
close on ten years.

A generation ago Australia was the least military of
nations. Her people, placed by their geographical position
out of the current of European controversies, had felt no
necessity for arming themselves. Then the developments
of the world, the rising of the new Asia, and the partitioning
of the Pacific, made every thoughtful citizen from Cape
York to Greenbushes realise that Australia must be ready
to defend herself. The flood of emigration from China,
from India, and from Japan set in southwards, and
Australia built barriers against it. The Japanese Fleet
sailed into Sydney Harbour, and held manœuvres around
the northern coasts of Western Australia. Men were
quick to realise that Australia had no defences of her
own against Japan. As a result Australia started to build
a navy, and to establish universal military training for
her young men. At the outbreak of the war the Royal
Australian Navy consisted of one battle-cruiser, five light
cruisers, two gunboats, six destroyers, and two submarines.
In November the Minister for Defence was able to
declare that Australia had a total of 164,631 men under
arms.

There was no question of what Australia should do.
"Our duty is quite clear," said the Federal Premier. On
the Monday preceding the declaration of war the Governor-
General of Australia sent on behalf of the Commonwealth
Government the following offer to Great Britain. " In the
event of war the Commonwealth of Australia is prepared
to place the vessels of the Australian Navy under the
control of the British Admiralty, if desired. It is further
prepared to despatch an expeditionary force of twenty
thousand men of any suggested composition to any destination desired by the Home Government, the force to be
at the complete disposal of the Home
Government. The cost of the despatch **The Commonwealth's**
and maintenance would be borne by this **generous offer**
Government. The Australian Press has
been notified accordingly." Mr. Harcourt, the British
Secretary for the Colonies, replied: " His Majesty's
Government greatly appreciate the prompt readiness of
your Government to place their naval forces at the disposal
of the Admiralty and their generous offer to equip and
maintain an expeditionary force. I will telegraph further
on the latter point."

Shortly after the outbreak of war there was a general
election in Australia, the Cook Ministry was overthrown
and a Labour Government, under Mr. Andrew Fisher,
succeeded it. Apprehension was entertained in some
quarters in Australia lest the Labour Government should
be less keen on giving assistance in the war than its predecessor. This fear was wholly groundless. The Labour
leaders during the election pledged themselves in the
most complete fashion. Mr. Andrew Fisher declared at
the beginning of the war that Australia should support
Great Britain with her last man and her last shilling.
When he became Prime Minister he acted on the declaration. Senator Pearce, who had done very much to create
and to mould the new defence movement in Australia,
was made Minister of Defence in the Labour Cabinet,
and showed himself the right man for the place.

There was absolutely no division of opinion in the country. Even the descendants of German settlers met to declare their unswerving loyalty and affection to the King and their determination to sacrifice, if necessary, their property and lives for the welfare of the British Empire. Private and public philanthropy were active.

Australia's active philanthrophy

Hundreds of thousands of pounds were raised for war funds, and enormous sums were given for medical and charitable purposes. Thus the Commonwealth Government gave £100,000 to the Belgian Relief Fund, and various State Governments contributed. Gifts of food were sent to England, scores of thousands of carcases of mutton, great quantities of port wine, butter, bacon, cheese, condensed milk, and the like. One newspaper sent three shiploads of foodstuffs. Sydney raised £20,000 for the Belgian Relief Fund; £50,000 was raised in a comparatively short time for the British Red Cross. These are typical cases.

The first Australian contingent consisted of 20,338 men, trained in equal proportions according to population, from the different cities of the Commonwealth. Arrangements were made to send regular monthly reinforcements of between 2,000 and 3,000 each to make up for casualties and wastage, and no sooner was the first con-

transports was kept as secret as possible. But it was impossible to suppress the overwhelming enthusiasm of the people in Melbourne and elsewhere as the boys marched down to the front. When Brigadier-General Bridges, who was responsible for the expeditionary force until it was later on taken over by General Birdwood, left Melbourne with his Staff on Trafalgar Day, he was given a reception that kings might have envied. Senator Pearce, the Minister for Defence, sent a formal message to the troops: "Upon the force devolves the honour and responsibility of representing Australia, and of performing Australia's share in the great Imperial effort in the interests of justice, honour, and international integrity. The ultimate issue of that undertaking can never be in doubt, but its attainment demands steadfast display of the British qualities of resolution and courage, which are yours by right of heredity. The people of Australia look to you to prove in battle that you are capable of upholding the traditions of the British arms. I have no fear that you will worthily represent the Commonwealth's military forces. Your presence among the Imperial forces has, however, a wide significance, as representing the solidarity of the Empire and the Imperial spirit of loyalty to the King."

Brigadier-General Bridges sent a message to the people of Australia: "I hope to report that the conduct of the Australian troops, both in camp and on the field, is worthy of the trust imposed upon them by the people of the Commonwealth. The men are a fine lot, soldierly and patriotic. I am grateful to the soldiers and citizens for the help they have given me in organising and preparing the force now about to do its part for the good of the Empire. I venture to express the hope that, no matter how great the demands on their patience, the Australian people will see to it that there is no diminution of their determination to face their responsibility. This spirit cannot fail then to pervade the troops."

A PEEP BEHIND THE SCENES: AUSTRALIAN FIELD KITCHEN IN EGYPT.

tingent ready than a second contingent of over 10,000 was prepared. Then in October the Commonwealth Government offered another brigade of light horse with brigade train and field ambulance, and the offer was gratefully accepted by the Army Council.

The work of preparing the first contingent proceeded automatically. Every man was a volunteer, for soldiers of the citizens' army cannot be called upon to serve outside the Commonwealth unless they wish. The soldiers were paid what would seem to the British "Tommy" on a princely scale, starting with 6s. a day and 1s. allowance. General Birdwood, a well-known British officer who had served with Kitchener in India, was given charge of the contingent. The first force, when it left Australia, was made up as follows. There was a light horse brigade, consisting of three regiments of cavalry, a field artillery battery, and an ammunition column, signal troop, and train and field ambulance. There was a division composed of three infantry brigades, two light horse squadrons, headquarters divisional artillery, three field artillery brigades, engineers and the accompanying train of ammunition column, signal company, field ambulance, etc. There were 9,000 horses and seventy guns.

The embarkation of the division began on October 17th and lasted five days. Nothing was allowed to be published outside Australia concerning it, and the departure of the

Much uneasiness had been caused by the presence of the Emden and other German cruisers in the Pacific Ocean, and it was believed, not without reason, that they intended to attempt a raid upon the expeditionary force on its way to Europe. The Royal Australian Navy at the outset of the war had been handed over by the Commonwealth Government to work in co-operation with the British Navy under the Admiralty, and it was already operating in the Pacific. British ships, Japanese ships, and Australian ships manœuvred to convoy and protect the vessels bearing the troops. The voyage was not to pass, however, without some excitement.

The rendezvous of the transports was Albany, Western Australia. Here not only the Australians, but also the New Zealanders arrived. "It is the most wonderful sight an Australian ever saw," said one who witnessed it. The long line of transports set out, a great string of ships,

Memorable scene at Albany

each keeping its distance behind the other, a couple of cables' lengths away, moving on, a steady, unceasing procession, the pace of all being fixed at the pace of the slowest. Around were the guardian warships. Mr. A. B. Paterson the well-known Australian writer, described the scene: "Away ahead of the whole fleet, just in sight on the edge of the horizon, is a pillar of smoke—a cruiser is clearing the way for us, setting the pace, giving the direction, and keeping a watchful eye out for enemies. Far away to

A GRAND PARADE AT MENA.
March-past of Australians before General Sir Ian Hamilton.

VOLUNTEERS OF THE GREAT COMMONWEALTH IN TRAINING FOR THE FRONT.

their silent way scarce out of hearing of the gunshots in her final battle.

The Australian contingent believed that it was going to Europe. Great was the surprise, when the ships arrived at the Suez Canal, to find that orders had come for them to disembark there, to complete their training in Egypt, and to help to guard that country from the coming attack by the Turkish army that even then was crossing the desert.

New Zealand, like Australia, was in the fortunate position of being ready by land and by sea for war. There had been for some time before the outbreak of war compulsory military training for all male citizens between the ages of twelve and twenty-five, and there was a fine defence force thoroughly trained, armed, and organised, with ample guns, transports, and scientific corps. Australia had elected to keep her Navy under her own control in times of peace, New Zealand had chosen to pool her resources with those of the Mother Country. Many people in the Dominion would gladly have seen their battle-cruiser New Zealand around their own waters; but it was with the British Fleet, helping to guard other seas at the outset of the war.

New Zealand's defence force

Some days before war was declared, the Prime Minister of New Zealand, Mr. Massey, declared that the Government intended, if necessary, to offer an expeditionary force to the Imperial Government, and an understanding already had been arrived at concerning the number and constitution of that force. The announcement was made the occasion for a remarkable display of enthusiasm. For

starboard, just visible on the skyline, is another pillar of smoke and a dimly-seen, low-lying vessel on the horizon to port shows where a cruiser is day and night keeping her watch over our movements. So we move across the ocean like a large regatta of great steamships, always the same order being inflexibly kept. It is sometimes hard to believe that a hundred and twenty miles have been covered since one saw them last—they seem to be so exactly in the same place."

As the contingent was passing the Keeling Cocos Islands word went round that an attack was imminent, and the troops were to be prepared. The men were paraded on deck, bare to the waist, with trousers rolled up to the knees and lifebelts donned.

Meanwhile, the Australian battle-cruiser Sydney was that very day seeking out the Emden not a hundred miles away. Had there been a little less care, a little less precaution, the Emden might have cut into the convoy and possibly sunk several of the ships. As it was, the Emden herself went to her doom, while the transports passed on

AWAITING THE ORDER TO ADVANCE AGAINST THE TURKISH RAIDERS: STRIKING CAMERA PICTURE OF THE AUSTRALIAN CAMP NEAR THE THREATENED BANK OF THE SUEZ CANAL.

once Parliamentary etiquette was forgotten, and every-one in the House of Representatives, whether member, visitor, or official, cheered to the echo. The leader of the Opposition, Sir Joseph Ward, declared, as soon as silence was secured, that the entire Opposition would co-operate with the Government in the defence of the Empire. The news of the declaration of war was made in dramatic fashion. The Governor appeared on the steps of Parliament House on the great afternoon and read a cablegram from the King thanking the Dominions for their loyal messages. Then he proceeded, almost as though by an afterthought: "I have yet another message—England and Germany are now at war."

The usual features familiar in other parts of the Empire followed. Men everywhere volunteered for service. The well-to-do gave their gifts of money and supplies. One of the most notable of national gifts was £20,000 divided between the National Relief Fund and the Belgian Relief Fund. In April, 1915, the Postmaster-General was able to announce that the total contribution to the Belgian Fund was £133,000 in cash, and goods and produce worth £65,000. The cash and produce sent for the poor of Great Britain and Ireland amounted to £138,000. The Maori people demanded that they should be allowed to share with the white races in the defence of the Flag. They offered to raise some thousands of men, and when news came that the British Government had decided to employ Indian soldiers in the war, it was impossible to refuse the Maoris the opportunity of doing their share.

In a very short time an expeditionary army of 8,000 was ready, and on September 24th the troops went on shipboard for Europe. "Time was, not very long ago," said Lord Liverpool, the Governor, "when the sight of a troopship in the New Zealand harbour denoted the arrival of troops from the Old Country. To-day the position is reversed. England has need of all her sons to-day, and the young Dominion is sending home to the Motherland of her best."

Lord Liverpool did not exaggerate. The young men who had volunteered for service in Europe were the very pick of the manhood of the Dominion. One found in the ranks university graduates, a large proportion of public schoolboys, the sons of statesmen and responsible business men. New Zealand, like the other parts of the Empire, gave her best.

New Zealand's splendid tribute

The expedition was timed to sail on September 25th, but probably on account of the activity of the German cruisers in the Pacific, the sailing was postponed at the last moment. The troops and horses were landed, and waited another twenty days. Then they got away.

The New Zealand Government made ample arrangements to keep the first contingent up to full strength. Shortly afterwards a further body of troops left for the front, and in February a third party sailed. The third party was notable on account of a corps of five hundred Maoris in its ranks—magnificent and eager fighting men. The Maori mothers and sisters, who came down to see them off, sent them to the front with every sign of cheerful courage. "Be brave. Do your duty. Kaiora" (farewell), one Maori mother telegraphed to her son. "No tangi"

PRINCESS PATRICIA'S CANADIAN LIGHT INFANTRY IN CAMP ON SALISBURY PLAIN.
Distribution of cigarettes to the men. In circle: Captain H. C. Buller, of the Rifle Brigade, who was appointed Lieutenant-Colonel in command in succession to Colonel Farquhar, killed in action at Neuve Chapelle.

NOT THEIR OWN ROLLING PRAIRIE.
Canadian troops engaged in field operations on the Wiltshire uplands.

A HALT BY THE WAY.
Men of the First Canadian Contingent: A photograph taken during a halt on the way to the railway-station shortly after their disembarkation in England.

(no lamentation), said another mother. "Only too glad that my sons are serving the King."

One little incident may serve to show that this spirit was not confined to the people of the greater isles. Niue (Savage Island) is one of the Cook group, annexed to New Zealand in 1901. It has a population of about 4,000, nearly all natives. These could talk no English, and had seen very few Europeans. But when the news of war came they collected £164, and counted their young men. Two hundred of their picked youths were ready to go. So they sent the gift of money to Wellington, and the offer of their two hundred sons in a letter signed by twelve chiefs. Here is a translation of their message:

"To King George V., all those in authority, and the brave men who fight.

"I am the small island of Niue, a small child that stands up to help the King to stand fast.

"There are two portions we offer—(1) Money, (2) Men."

The Australians and New Zealanders landed along the Suez Canal and camped, many of them right at the foot of the Pyramids. He would have been dull, indeed, whose spirit was not stirred, and whose emotions were not aroused by the sight of these men, strong sons of the newest of white nations, coming their many thousands of miles to stand between the oldest of nations, Egypt, and its ancient Turkish oppressor.

The Colonial troops in Cairo The Australasians won golden opinions during their stay on account of their giant stature, their fine equipment, and their orderliness. General Sir John Maxwell, the commander of the troops in Egypt, said after he inspected them that it would be impossible to find better material than this. "The Colonial troops are, as a whole, a really fine body of men," wrote one who saw them in Cairo. "Broad of shoulder, deep in the chest, and sun-burnt to a rich dark brown, they are the picture of rude health, and chock-full of animal spirits, which even the climate of Egypt cannot eliminate."

When Abbas Hilmi Pasha was deposed from the Khedivate of Egypt, and Prince Hussein appointed Sultan of Egypt, under the protectorate of the British, the presence of the Australasians helped to force the friends of Abbas to silence. On the day of the accession of the new Sultan a large number of the Australians and New Zealanders formed part of the forces for the military review. The Australian and New Zealand Light Horse, the New Zealand artillery, and the infantry made a deep impression by their splendid bearing on Europeans and natives alike.

The tale of how the Australasians, their work in Egypt done and well done, left for England, will belong to a latter part of this history.

The people of New Zealand witnessed with the greatest interest the departure of a small force, working in co-operation with the Australian Navy, for the capture of German islands in the Southern Pacific. New Zealanders had long regretted that Germany was ever allowed to acquire a foothold in Samoa. Now New Zealand troops quietly occupied Samoa, destroyed German wireless stations, and raised the **Fine work in the** British flag. The Australian Navy, **Southern Pacific** having co-operated with New Zealand in this removal of an unwanted neighbour, went on to island after island under German rule, raising the British flag everywhere. How they succeeded, the record of the useful work of the Australian Fleet, and its moral for the Empire at large belong to the naval sections of this book.

Australia and New Zealand felt, as they witnessed the triumphs of their ships and the advance of their armies, that they had stepped at last into full nationhood. They had reason for their pride and exultation. The community of sentiment in the Overseas Dominions was emphasised by the congratulatory message received from General Botha by the new Australian Premier, who in turn congratulated the General on taking the field against "the common enemy."

Elliott & Fry.

COMMANDER CHARLES RUMNEY SAMSON, D.S.O., R.N.
Commanding the Aeroplane and Armoured Motor Support, Royal Naval Air Service of the British Expeditionary Force.

CHAPTER LIV.

HOW THE WAR IN THE AIR DEVELOPED.

How Kluck's Swerve from Paris was Observed—France Brings Her Brave Civilian Pilots to the Front—German Supremacy in Aerial Fire-Control Tactics—How Our Private Aeroplane Makers Saved the Situation—Defects of Our Royal Aircraft Factory—The Small, Swift Machine of British Aerial Victories—French Invent the Terrible Air-Arrow—Losing a German Army Corps in the Woods—German Airmen Search for British Reinforcements—Sudden Improvement in German Airmanship—Due to Use of Newly-Built Machines—Our Hard and Long Struggle to Recover Aerial Supremacy—Insufficient Number of British Airmen at the Front—How Our Men were Overworked—Adventures with "Archibald" and "Cuthbert"—"Mother" and the British Aviator—Part Played by the Wind—Duels in the Air—German Airmen Commanded to Avoid Fights—Achievements of the Crack French Airmen—The Significance and Aims of the Air Raiders—Superiority of the Aerial Observation Officers—Airmanship at Neuve Chapelle—The Vital Work of the Naval Air Patrol—Air Raids on Zeppelin Sheds, Aircraft, Factories, and Submarine Bases—The Combined Operations off Cuxhaven.

IN the first month of the war the military use of aircraft was in an experimental stage. The Germans had the advantage in material, numbers, and organisation. Their airmen co-operated with their field batteries in a practised manner during the retreat of the allied troops from the Sambre to the Marne. It was largely owing to the great number of German aerial observers that the heavy German field artillery dominated many of the early battlefields.

At the opening of the campaign the military aviation system of France was sadly defective. It was not until the dashing and superbly-trained civilian air pilots of France came to the front that the German airmen were held in check by our Allies. Then General Hirschauer, a strong and businesslike reformer, was given control over the aviation system, and he soon raised the general standard of French military airmanship by a wholesale dismissal of men who had joined the flying branch of the French Army for other reasons than a liking and talent for flying.

In our own Royal Flying Corps there were happily no defects of personnel to be remedied. Our men were magnificent. It was they who discovered on September 4th that the main columns of General von Kluck's army had swerved from Paris, and had moved in a south-easterly direction towards the Marne River in an attempt to turn or break the Fifth French Army. And it was this achievement that elicited General Joffre's message of high praise for the work done by our pilots and observers. In the subsequent German retreat to the Aisne our airmen reconnoitred the movements of the enemy, and by the mastery obtained over their flying foes they managed to prevent the hostile aerial scouts from discovering the movements of our troops. During this happy turn in the fortunes of the Franco-British army, the crack French civilian aviators were allowed to go to the front and supplement the efforts of the somewhat small number of efficient French military pilots. When the heroes of French aviation got to work on either side of our small but deadly Flying Corps, the German airmen lost the command of the sky all along the western front of the war.

The results of this aerial supremacy of the Allies were not at first apparent, for the military airman only does his best work when he is harnessed to a battery of powerful pieces of ordnance. At least, such was the condition of affairs when the lengthy campaign of trench warfare opened on the Aisne. So long as the British and French armies had only their ordinary artillery corps firing against the great siege train which the Germans brought from Maubeuge to reinforce their magnificent field-guns and howitzers, the allied airmen worked at a disadvantage; for often when they discovered the enemy's chief gun positions,

WARDERS OF THE SEAS.
Navy men keeping a bright look-out for enemy aircraft.

179

OUTWITTING THE ENEMY: THRILLING INCIDENT OF THE AIR RAID ON CUXHAVEN.
One of our seaplanes coming down short of its rendezvous, a British submarine shipped the pilot, destroyed the damaged machine, and dived, its captain gaining time by waving his hat to the crew of the Schütte-Lanz airship hovering aloft, and so making them think he was a German capturing a British airman. Immediately the submarine was submerged those on board felt the shock of bomb dropped by the disappointed enemy. Our picture is from a sketch made by an officer who took part in the action.

as little successful in aeronautics as in dye-making. But several private manufacturers in our country struggled on under severe discouragement from our official organisation. Prevented for a time from assisting our Army, they yet impressed, by the uncommon merits of their machines, some enlightened men in our Admiralty. A little Admiralty work enabled them to carry on, and continue their progress in construction, with the result that they produced at last the finest flying machines in existence.

One of the most important instruments of British aerial supremacy was the small, high-speed scouting aeroplane manufactured by the Sopwith and Bristol companies. Then there was the pretty, fast Manchester-built aeroplane, the Avro, with various other swift makes by other private British firms, such as the Short, Wight, and Martinsyde. In addition, the Vickers and Sopwith companies constructed splendid gun-carrying biplanes. These machines beat the Germans in speed, which was what our French comrades were at first generally unable to do, owing to the slowness of their "'buses." The French aviators were very plucky, and, as was well known before the war, they were incomparably skilful. But for some time their machines were not fast enough to enable them to fight air duels with as much success as our men. Happily, the new Voisin biplane and the Caudron machine lifted the French aviator, in regard to material, on a level with his foemen, and at the beginning of October the new French types of aircraft seemed to be superior to anything possessed by the Germans. Their production was a striking instance

their own gunners lacked the weapons to smash the enemy. Meanwhile, our artillery and that of our Allies had a hard fight against the German airmen. In all cases the guns of the Allies had to be hidden from aerial observation with extreme ingenuity and care. When a hostile air-scout appeared above our lines it was usually dangerous for our gunners to try to bring it down with shrapnel. For, thereby, they only revealed their emplacement, and the German flier signalled this to one of his distant batteries of great howitzers, which at once began to shell our guns. The situation was mainly saved by the fighting of our flying men, and by the excellent qualities of some of their machines. Indirectly, it was the inventiveness and the tenacity of character of a score or two of men connected with several private British firms manufacturing flying machines that defeated the great organised effort made by the Germans to obtain the control of the air.

Our official centre of aeronautic research and construction—the Royal Aircraft Factory—was in many ways behind the German aircraft organisation. Some of the machines it first produced seemed to show that the direction of scientific industries by our Government was

of the manner in which the French mind, when encompassed with dangers, can improvise a brilliant achievement, eclipsing all that the plodding, patient, organising talent of the Teuton has accomplished after years of preparation.

As the Allies improved both the material and the organisation of their aircraft, the increasing power of their artillery enabled their airmen to show to more advantage. The work of the aerial scouts went on incessantly. They preceded both armies in the long race to the sea which began west of the Aisne in the third week in September and ended on the Yser in the second week in October.

Aerial observers behind each front

For a hundred miles or more behind each front the aerial observers of the opposite camp watched the movement of columns of troops and trains, the collection of rolling-stock, and the crawling lines of motor-vehicles.

They studied the size and situation of the enemy's bivouacs, parks, supply depots, and other facts giving a clue to the intentions of the hostile commanders. All this was aerial strategical reconnaissance, by far the most important part of the airmen's work. Then they had to make tactical observations. These were confined to a

THE PICTURESQUE EFFECT OF SHELLING AN AERIAL MARAUDER.

Almost as remarkable as the triumph of the aeroplane has been the ingenuity in devising anti-aircraft weapons. In the above, sketched at the front by Mr. Seppings-Wright, the well-known war artist, a German "Taube" is speeding away from the too close attention of an anti-aircraft gun, which fires shells so rapidly that they burst in a long stream, and are effective at a height of between four and six thousand feet.

The great things anticipated of German Zeppelin airships when they would first come into touch with British warships failed entirely to materialise on Christmas Day, 1914, when seven British naval seaplanes, escorted by a light cruiser and destroyer force, together with submarines, made their famous attack on German warships lying in Schillig Roads, off Cuxhaven. To quote the offic despatch relating to that episode: " As soon as the ships were seen by the Germa

1 Heligoland, two Zeppelins, three or four hostile seaplanes, and several hostile marines attacked them. It was necessary for the British ships to remain in neighbourhood in order to pick up the returning airmen, and a novel combat ensued between the most modern cruisers on the one hand and the enemy's aircraft and submarines on the other. By swift manœuvring the enemy's submarines were avoided, and the two Zeppelins were easily put to flight."

NECESSITY TO SHELTER FROM AERIAL ATTACK IS THE MOTHER OF INVENTION.

In this photograph from the front, what looks at first glance a harmless haystack, with a ladder laid against it, contains a door beneath the ladder, and this door leads into a fair-sized farmhouse, the whole of which has been ingeniously covered by British soldiers with hay to disguise it from enemy aircraft. The farmhouse within was made to serve as an important intelligence post, with telephone connections.

A BRITISH GUN IN ACTION IN THE NORTH OF FRANCE.

The above particularly clear and very interesting photograph shows on the right a British gun in firing position, while to the left is its caisson, from which one of the gunners is withdrawing shells, while the sergeant stands by calmly giving orders. There is no evidence of warlike excitement; yet the photograph was taken while the gun was in action at a severely contested portion of the British front.

BRITISH AEROPLANE FLYING OVER A VILLAGE
IN NORTHERN FRANCE.

IN READINESS FOR ENEMY AIRCRAFT.
British anti-aircraft guns on a motor-lorry cunningly concealed by the side of a haystack.

small area, which perhaps was about to be assailed, or from which an attack was expected. The flying observers had to locate the enemy's trenches, gun emplacements, reserves, headquarters, supply parks, and railheads. In some cases they took photographs of the hostile positions. Then there was the unceasing work of directing the fire of our artillery. Now and then, when occasion offered, the airmen came out in large machines, carrying a store of bombs, with which they tried to injure the railway communications of the foe. They also worried any mass of hostile troops, the French airmen having small boxes of steel arrows for dropping on the enemy.

This new aerial weapon, introduced by the French in October, was a terrible thing. It was a piece of steel rod a third of an inch in diameter, and about seven inches long. One end was pointed like a pencil for an inch or so, while the other end was machined out for five inches like the feathers of an arrow. They were packed in boxes of fifty, and released by the aviator opening the bottom of the box with a string.

The terrible aerial arrow Then the speed at which the aeroplane was travelling distributed the arrows thoroughly, while the force of gravity endued the missiles, as they fell from a great height, with horrible power. The effect on infantry, when in close formation or when lying behind low trenches, was far more deadly than the same weight of bombs.

By lying flat on the ground a fighting man could escape the effect of a bomb unless it made a direct hit, which was extremely unlikely. But men lying flat, or even crouching, beneath a shower of aerial arrows, only exposed more surface to the missiles. The effect on cavalry was worse than on infantry, for there was a larger surface to hit. Altogether, it was a horrible weapon. But it was not more horrible than long-range gun fire, against which infantry was quite as defenceless, and its wounds were no worse than those made by shell splinters. Some of our officers of the Royal Flying Corps, however, objected to the employment of these air arrows, as they thought the use of them was unsportsmanlike. As the French airmen were not fighting for sport, but to free their country from a decivilised, inhuman race of invaders, notorious for the murder of thousands of non-combatants, they proceeded to develop the use of their new weapon.

Meanwhile, the allied aerial scouts continued their work of reconnaissance around the advancing armies. They

were not always successful. An extraordinary case of an entire German army corps being lost by our airmen took place in the movement towards Arras. Two hostile army corps were seen marching through the forest at Vermand. A sharp look-out was kept on their movements. One corps was traced as it went to reinforce the German troops at St. Quentin. The other, however, vanished in a mysterious manner. A similar disappearance of a German army corps under the eyes of aeroplane scouts occurred some time before at Compiègne. In both cases it is supposed that the large mass of men, 40,000 to 50,000, concealed themselves in the forest, where their movements could not be observed by the aerial scouts. Then they left the woods in small numbers at different times, and collected at a prearranged rendezvous. But the fact that the Germans had to undertake this lengthy and difficult operation of marching an **Telling example of** army corps to a forest and scattering it, **aerial efficiency** and then arranging for it to join together again by a time-table, after a long night march, is a telling example of the way in which the aerial reconnaissance of the Allies increased the difficulties of the enemy.

Towards the middle of October there was a series of German aeroplane raids on St. Omer, Dunkirk, Calais, and Boulogne. But though the popular mind was struck by the murderous bomb-dropping exploits of the enemy fliers, this was only an amusement of the barbarians. Their real business was the reconnaissance of the approaching movements of British troops. It is clear that the German General Staff expected the landing of a stronger British reinforcement than the 7th Division and the 3rd Cavalry Division under Sir Henry Rawlinson. It was feared that a considerable number of our Territorials would at once be transported and help in strengthening the seaward front. Hence the far-ranging activities of the German airmen, who also went bomb-dropping to Paris while reconnoitring for General Joffre's reserve forces.

Improvement in German aircraft It was about this time that a German cavalry division was defeated by a few airmen, as has already been related. The large force of horsemen were pursued and harassed from the sky during the whole of October 15th, and as evening drew on a well-aimed bomb completed their discomfiture. The allied airmen, however, did not have another amazing success of this sort. For on the same day a chase occurred at St. Omer, in which three of our aeroplanes tried to hunt down one German machine. It was expected that the enemy would be overtaken and put out of action. But two of our machines proved to be slower than the Germans', and the other one met with an accident and had to give up the chase.

This was the first significant sign of a general improvement in German aeroplanes, that caused the allied commanders a considerable amount of trouble in the early part of the winter. Several things seemed to show that the superiority in the air, won by us at the beginning of the war, was partly due to the fact that our opponents, drawn from the frontier air-stations, were at first using machines they had kept there for six, twelve, or eighteen months. They had mainly old-type Taube monoplanes, Aviatik biplanes, early-type Albatross, L.V.G. biplanes, and Jeannin monoplanes. These machines were heavy and slow, and many of them had only four-cylinder engines of 70 h.-p., instead of the 100-h.-p. six-cylinder engines of the new type.

But in the middle of October a large supply of superior machines arrived in the western German lines. Some of them had been building before the war, others had been completed after the great struggle opened. The effect of this sudden and important improvement in the most useful kind of the enemy's aircraft was soon remarked. Our pilots were surprised to discover that many of the German airmen began to climb better and fly more quickly than they used to. We had, in fact, only a few machines that could keep up with them. Our main problem in aerial warfare

then rested with our manufacturers. Fortunately we had various new makes of aeroplanes capable of overtaking the best of the newest German types. The Germans had largely recovered their lost ground by modelling their new machines on ours. Their latest type of tractor biplanes were almost indistinguishable from ours by an untrained observer. The Ago tractor resembled our Sopwiths or Avros, the new Aviatik, Albatross, and L.V.G. looked like our B.E.'s. The popular chart, contrasting the silhouettes of German and British machines, and issued with the authority of our Government, was therefore misleading in regard to modern types. The old-fashioned Taube especially, so continually mentioned in our newspapers, was rarely employed by the enemy. The new Aviatik seems to have been the common German machine.

But while the Germans were imitating our inventive manufacturers, progress in construction had continued in our country. We had the Sopwith Scout, the Bristol Scout, the remarkable Avros, so light and yet so strong, and the new Martinsyde Scout, possessing some fine qualities. Then the Royal Aircraft Factory had developed out of the Sopwith and Bristol Scouts a small machine with the enormous speed of one hundred and fifty miles an hour. It was indeed so fast that it was hard to find pilots for it. One expert reckoned that there were only two men in the world who could manage it safely.

Thus, in combination with French makers, our aeroplane manufacturers were able to maintain a superiority against the better-organised efforts of the German aviation authorities. It was the old contest between the loose, free-branching activities of our muddling and yet finely-gifted race and the careful, comprehensive, and efficient system of Government control on which the Germans have relied for the last hundred years. We continued to retain the defects of our virtues. For no attempt was made to transform the Royal Aircraft Factory into a general centre of aircraft **The better-organising Teuton** research and construction, in which all the brilliant minds in our enterprising private firms could co-operate. Though Sir John French pointedly asked for greater efforts in providing our growing armies with an overwhelming superiority in the machinery of the new arm, there was no complete and really efficient organisation of the splendid resources we possessed. We still went

Flight-Commander F. E. T. Hewlett. Flight-Commander D. A. Oliver. Flight-Lieut. A. J. Miley. Flight-Commander C. F. Kilner. Flight-Sub.-Lieut. V. G. Blackburn. Flight-Commander R. P. Ross. Flight-Lieut. C. H. K. Edmonds.

A GROUP OF INTREPID BRITISH AIRMEN.

WONDERFUL CAMERA RECORD OF A FRENCH AEROPLANE PURSUING A GERMAN AIRSHIP.

This unique view was developed from a " snapshot " taken from a second aeroplane, and the incident thus recorded took place after one of the German airship raids on Paris. The aeroplane shown, in which two men can be discerned quite plainly, was in reality a considerable distance from its quarry. The distance can be gauged by the relative sizes of the two rivals for the dominion of the air. The airship is ascending and turning away from the camera, hence the foreshortening of the rear part of the immense craft, which here seems smaller than it is in reality.

along in the old free-and-easy way, managing on the whole to keep about level with the less inventive but better-organising Teuton.

The work of our Army pilots and observers was less spectacular than the raiding expeditions of our naval airmen ; but the work which our soldier fliers did was more laborious and more important. The number of pilots we had was really very small, but they made

Contrasts in aerial fire-control up in skill, courage, and endurance for their scanty numbers. It was reckoned that in the first month of the war their air mileage amounted to 87,000 miles—an average of 2,000 miles a day. Had we possessed a hundred pilots, the official figures given would have meant that each of them had only been in the air about half an hour a day. But, as a matter of fact, our men were overworked. So it is easy to see that they numbered much less than a hundred pilots.

The result was that we had not at first sufficient airmen with our Expeditionary Force to establish a general system of aerial fire-control for the batteries of our two army corps. The Germans, on the other hand, were excellently equipped on the Aisne, and the subsequent trench warfare, for the aerial control of their guns. They had a sausage-shaped balloon, known as the Parseval-Siegfeld, which was ridiculous in appearance, but admirable for observation purposes. The Germans protected their balloons from any aeroplane attack by posting a battery of anti-aircraft guns near them, often with airmen defenders. The anti-aircraft guns, however, were not very effectual against our dashing and adventurous flying men, who nicknamed them " Archibald " and " Cuthbert." Some of " Cuthbert's " shells burst at the

tremendous height of 22,000 feet. It was impossible to execute reconnaissance work and escape from their range.

But our men were not daunted by " Archibald " and " Cuthbert." The German gunmaker had been very ingenious. Both the gun and the shrapnel shells which it fired were masterpieces of Teutonic science. The gun was semi-automatic ; it let off one shell, in which was a sort of parachute. When the shell burst, this parachute floated out in the air, making a conspicuous mark by which the gunner could correct his range and the timing of his fuse. Then, with startling rapidity, six more shells followed. Often the Germans arranged their aircraft guns in a triangular formation. When one of our machines appeared above their line, a gunner at the nearest point of the triangle fired a shell, making a burst of red smoke. From this red smoke, and from the flying machine, the second gunner got a more exact range, and tried a shell giving out a black smoke. If this missed, the third gunner had three marks from which to calculate his aim, so he tried a third test shot, and then the triangle of guns shot up their stream of shells by their semi-automatic device.

The trouble was that the German gunners were not sportsmen. They acted like amateur game-shots, who shoot at a bird, instead of **Work of the** aiming at the position the bird will occupy **German gunners** when the shot arrives. After a good deal of practice, the Teutons did get to understand what a game-shot was. Instead of firing at our machine, they fired at the place the machine would occupy if it continued flying in the same direction at the same height. But, naturally, our airmen were somewhat more intelligent than a pheasant.

IN THE FORWARD "GONDOLA" OF A ZEPPELIN AIRSHIP.
The pilot and his assistants were accommodated in the forward end of the front "gondola," being in telephonic communication with the captain in the centre cabin. The windows were made of some flexible, transparent substance, such as mica, which was strong, thin, and light.

heavy pieces of ordnance, enabled our force to cope with the siege-artillery brought against our lines from Antwerp. At the same time an increase in the number of our aviators at the front enabled General Henderson to detach single machines for duty with artillery. We, in fact, then began to progress to that desirable stage of development in the use of aircraft when each artillery brigade would have its own aviators permanently attached to it. The pilots would be artillery officers in flying machines, and not merely Royal Flying Corps officers who happened to know something about guns.

A splendid beginning was made by attaching an aeroplane observer to our remarkable 9·2 in. howitzer, which our soldiers affectionately called their " Mother." It was their protection against the heavy siege-artillery of the enemy, from which they had suffered since the German stand above the Aisne. One aviator working with this great piece was at last able to direct it on a train moving behind the German lines eight miles away. The artillerymen simply loaded and fired according to wireless instructions, and got a direct hit on a moving mark far beyond their field of vision. Before the increasing use of wireless communication between the flying officer and the hidden guns which he controlled, the work of observing targets was signalled by means of smoke bombs, coloured lights with rocket tails, and other visible devices.

The artillerymen had to have an observation officer near their emplacement, watching their aeroplane observer with special instruments ; for it was mainly from the study of the position of the aeroplane giving the visible signal that the situation of the hostile target could be calculated. But early in November the winter fog began to veil the Flemish plain. The dense, grey clouds sagged lower and lower, so that the machines on both sides had to dive close to the ground for the purpose of a reconnaissance. "Archibald" became very busy, and it was assisted by rifle and machine-gun fire from the German trenches. Our darting, swerving, dancing aeroplanes were often screened by mist or cloud from the eyes of our artillerymen. Visible signalling became very chancy, with the happy result that the more scientific and exact method of wireless communication was developed.

Wireless communication developed

The military aerial work performed by our Army in the winter of 1914–15 was of supreme importance. The sodden, boggy condition of the ground between the two opposing fronts was a boon to the Allies. For in conjunction with their increasing power in artillery aircraft, it enabled them to beat back with little loss any further offensive movement by the enemy. Thus the great

As soon as "Archibald" spoke, they dived, soared, or swerved, and even altered their speed. All our machines were hit by shrapnel bullets or rifle fire, but it was very seldom that either "Archibald" or "Cuthbert" brought them down. Our men relied mainly upon the high speed of their machines. The slowest of our " 'buses" went at a mile a minute; the quickest of our " scouts" did well-nigh three miles a minute. The pilot and observer usually sat on a shield of bullet-proof steel, and though many holes were made in the planes of their machines they were rarely compelled to descend within the enemy's lines. Even when their petrol tank or some more vital part was injured, when they were making attacks or reconnaissances, they usually managed to volplane down to their own lines.

By the beginning of November, when we were at last holding the Germans firmly from Ypres to La Bassée, the co-operation between our airmen and artillery was perfected. The arrival of " Mother," our new great howitzer, and other

deadlock in the western theatre of war came about. The Germans had been so severely handled in all their vain attempts to break through that they resigned themselves to a defensive position. The Allies, on the other hand, were not yet strong enough to resume in turn their attacking movement. They needed some months' time to train their new army, to improve still further their artillery, and to increase their munitions of war. If the ground had been firm, the Germans could have worried them continually, and have compelled them at least to make frequent costly counter-attacks. But owing to the state of the soil there were few movements of importance on either side till the porous, chalky ground of Champagne began to recover from the winter rain.

The winter campaign was extremely arduous, both for the men in the air and for those in the pits and trenches.

The cold at high altitudes

The cold at high altitudes was occasionally intense, fifty degrees of frost being marked in some early morning flights. At times the pilot and observer had to be lifted from their seats when they came down. They were quite numbed by the cold, in spite of the fact that they were very warmly clad. But it was not so much the cold as the high wind that troubled our airmen. On one occasion a pilot was going at full speed in a fast machine when he found himself returning to his own lines at the pace of ten miles an hour. He had flown into a tempest which was so overpowering that it annulled the power of his engine and blew him back. It was this reduction of speed by adverse winds that made aerial reconnaissance dangerous. At times our speediest scouts could only crawl along against a gale like lumbering, old-fashioned "buses," and they then became an easy target for their dear old friend "Archibald."

On the whole, however, the wind was more favourable to the Allies than to the Germans. The prevailing wind was westerly, so it usually increased the speed of our machines on their outward journey. The German pilots, on the other hand, often had the wind against them when they came over our lines, and the slackening of their speed enabled them to be brought down in greater numbers than were our own men. In addition to this, our remarkably swift scouting machines enabled many of our men to maintain a rapid flight even against a fairly strong head wind.

The direction of the wind was often one of the decisive factors in the aerial duels that took place. The Germans usually waited until a strong wind was blowing from their lines to ours. This gave them a very rapid flight over the area of danger. Our attacking pilot then had to rise, at a disadvantage, with the enemy above him and firing at him. There was a thrilling duel of this kind about a week or so before Christmas. A fast German biplane of a new type flashed in a northerly wind above our lines. One of our pilots rose to meet him on an Avro. The German used rifle and revolver without effect, for the British airman got on the same level as his foeman. The German then tried to make for home. But the gale, which at first befriended him, now brought about his downfall. He could not make any headway against it, while the Avro machine steadily gained upon him, the British pilot shooting as he came on. The German dodged from side to side, planed down and swerved, reminding one of the twisting trail of a beaten fox. Our man countered every move. He was like a hawk circling round a crow. At last the German gave in, and, descending into our lines, was taken prisoner. He was not wounded, but utterly beaten in spirit. As our airmen put it in their expressive slang: " He came down through cold feet." There were many other duels in the air, in which the enemy was either shot or brought down by damage to his machine. But this fight was especially remarkable in that it was the nerve of the German pilot that gave way.

As a matter of fact, the German airmen appeared to have received a general order to avoid fights in the air. In the circumstances this was simply a businesslike precaution on the part of the commander of the hostile air corps. His trained men were more useful to him in scouting and in gunfire-control than in direct operations against our airmen. We had proved ourselves the better aerial fighters early in the war. It may have been due to our qualities as a nation of islanders, with fine seamanship traditions and an instinct for dangerous sports. The air was only another sort of sea, and though the Germans began with thirteen hundred aeroplanes against a hundred machines capable of service in our country, while the French had only a few hundred really effective aeroplanes,

HOW THE RAIDING ZEPPELIN KEPT IN TOUCH WITH BERLIN.
View of the silence room in the centre cabin of a Zeppelin. The aerial telegraph line consists of 750 feet of phosphor-bronze wire which, when not in use, is wound round the wheel seen in the picture. At night, when the wireless waves have their fullest efficiency, a Zeppelin over England would be well in touch with the wireless stations in Germany.

the result was similar to that of the great Armada against the small ships of Sir Francis Drake. Our men had more zest for chancy, daring fighting than the cautious, calculating Teuton. He excelled in long, patient preparatory work, being bred up in blind reliance on his all-pervading State organisation. Naturally, some sense of sportsmanship marked the Germans who took to flying before the war; and the splendid records they made in the length of their flights and the altitudes they attained proved that they had an uncommon ability in the handling of their machines. But fighting in the skies from aeroplanes did not stir their sense of adventure. At least it ceased to do so when they met the still more daring Briton and found themselves outclassed.

The French aviators had the same zest for aerial warfare as our men, and on their improved machines they harried the enemy almost continuously at times. For instance, on September 18th, 20th, 21st, and 22nd they chased the German pilots on their front and compelled them to land. M. Pegoud, the famous inventor of the "looping the loop" operation, was one of the lords of the air. He took to night flying over the German lines, doing terrible damage in the darkness, and using a petrol flash on returning to land behind his own trenches. Sergeant Louis Noel, the well-known Hendon flier, also became remarkable for his nocturnal flights. The whole of his squadron followed his example in habitually flying at night, much to the

annoyance of the Germans, who would not imitate him. Noel, in the winter of 1914, was working on the Rheims section, where he achieved a great success. For it was by his efforts that the German fortress of heavy guns west of the cathedral city was put out of action.

Some weeks before this a combined squadron of British and French airmen made an attack upon the old forts of Lille. On November 4th they blew up Fort Englos;

the next day they destroyed Fort Carnot. The forts were being used as magazines by the enemy and were important as points of support in the enemy's line of entrenchments. Their sudden destruction by aerial bombardment was an affair of some significance. Marksmanship in bomb-dropping was one of the peculiarities of the allied aviators. It was born of the same qualities as made them the victors in most of the aerial duels. They had more imperturbable daring than their opponents; they swooped lower to get well on their target; in short, they risked their lives more frequently, and at the same time they lessened the risk by the brilliance with which they handled their machines.

MILITARY AIRMEN OVER THE CLOUDS.
The remarkable photographs on this page, taken from an aeroplane over the clouds, help us to realise the difficulties of the airmen, whose observation while at a great altitude was limited to the brief glimpses they could get between the cloud-drifts of the enemy's positions on the ground below.

The air raids of the flying men of the French and British armies were seldom so spectacular in interest as the expeditions of some of our Naval Air Service aviators. They worked for the most part against the railway communications of the enemy, dropped bombs upon the motor transport columns of the German army, or attacked the German headquarters—striking at the brains of the enemy's forces. At the beginning of the war little or nothing was done by the Allies in these directions. What machines they had were urgently needed for other purposes, and the small experimental bombs first employed did not do enough damage. But when the battle of the trenches reduced modern warfare to strange new conditions, the quick-minded French had a machine ready for air raids on the enemy's communications. It was a large metal-built biplane, with a motor of 200 h.-p. It carried only a couple of very heavy bombs, charged with a new secret explosive. In the first experiment one of them made a hole in the ground ten yards wide and five feet deep. They were used for breaking down railway bridges and attacking trains. They were also employed in breaking up the permanent way in such a manner as to delay for days the supply of food and ammunition to the German front.

These great bombs weighed about one hundred and thirty pounds. A smaller bomb of twenty pounds weight could

New secret explosive

THE WAR ZONE AS SEEN BY THE AIRMAN.

Two wonderful photographs indicating in each case how great an exercise of judgment is called for on the part of the airman, whether his mission be bomb-dropping, reconnoitring, or range-indicating. In the upper view, taken somewhere in France, a squadron of cavalry is seen passing. The lower photograph, taken from an aeroplane somewhere in Flanders, shows the flat nature of the country, every object being clearly detailed.

SECTION OF GERMAN SHRAPNEL
SHELL FOR AERIAL USE.

be carried in larger numbers — in fact, most of the light and very swift machines could only take a few of the small missiles. The damage they did could quickly be repaired by the German engineers. But when a squadron of these light bomb-throwers attacked a certain important point, in a circular movement to and from their base of supplies and their point of attack, the continual aerial bombardment became an important affair. When the Germans got their new machines, about the middle of October, 1914, they adopted the same tactics. In the middle of November especially they devoted much attention to our Army Service Corps, killing some of our men and transport horses. It seemed as though we had then lost for awhile our supremacy of the air through not having enough fast and powerful aeroplanes to attack all the German pilots who approached our lines. In the first week of December the German airmen were again very active. They attacked the town of Hazebrouck, hoping to destroy one of our headquarters, but only killed three children and three adult civilians. More effectual was their bombardment on December 7th of the junction of the Armentieres-Dunkirk and Ypres-Calais railway line. Their bombs were small, and the damage they did was slight, but the operation was well planned. It showed, at least, that the Germans grasped the lesson

**Narrow escape of
the Kaiser**

of the Allies' repeated attacks upon their communications. We had previously attacked the German headquarters at Thielt on November 1st, when it was reported that the Kaiser narrowly escaped death from the thirty-two bombs thrown on the building in which he met his generals.

All the military air raids on either side, however, did no more than annoy and worry the respective enemy. Owing, perhaps, to the lack of machines and pilots, no men could be spared from reconnaissances and artillery direction duties in order to make a grand air attack on some point of importance. As cavalry reconnaissance was prevented on both sides by the barrier of the trenches, only the spy and the airman could obtain any information as to the

movements of the enemy. The airman, therefore, became exceedingly valuable. It is not too much to say that he dominated the battlefield. In fact, he gave modern trench warfare its extraordinary character. It was to escape his observation that the life of the artillerymen became a laborious round of digging holes and hiding from sight. The entrenched infantry had continually to burrow deeper, and to conceal their burrows by all manner of devices in order to escape the notice of the airman. His bombs and air arrows were of small importance. What made him so terrible was the fact that he was the eye of distant batteries of hidden howitzers.

**Aerial control of
howitzer fire**

Without aerial fire-control, the indirect fire of the howitzer would not have been the main influence upon the later western battlefields. The trench protected the soldier fairly well from the direct fire of ordinary guns. If he could have also avoided the almost vertical bombardment of high-explosive howitzer shells, the character of the fighting would have been changed. In particular, the French would probably have won the first turning movement they made under General Castelnau towards the end of September. It was the heavy German guns and howitzers, directed by aerial observers, which saved the enemy's main line of railway communications at St. Quentin and east of Cambrai. And then, when the trenches along the Aisne were prolonged to Arras, Lille, and Nieuport, the long-range howitzer and its flying controller, with his range-finding instruments and camera, still remained the master-spirit of the campaign.

BOMBS DROPPED
FROM A ZEPPELIN ON
ENGLISH SOIL.

His vision reached a hundred miles or more over the opposing front. The war became to him an intellectual pursuit of absorbing interest. If he had a genius for his work, he could read the mind of a hostile commander from the size and position of the bivouacs and the direction of the long string of motor-vehicles.

No reconnoitring cavalry or scouts on motor-cycles could have accomplished what he accomplished. Beneath his eagle eye the fog of war was dissipated. The old grand, decisive element in strategy—the use of new large forces in unexpected times or places —became impracticable. The Germans effected one overwhelming thing of this sort at the opening of the war in the west by their vast, swift concentration of armies from the Sambre and Meuse. And the British army afterwards took

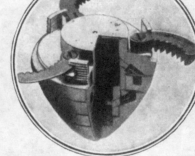

SECTION OF THE NOSE (FUSE) OF
AERIAL SHRAPNEL SHELL.

General von Kluck by surprise by hiding in the forest near Paris, and chasing away his aeroplane scouts. But with these two exceptions, and the evasion of certain German army corps from aerial reconnaissance by scattering in thick woods, the mystery of war no longer obtained in the western field of struggle.

General Joffre knew what General Falkenhayn was doing in a large way, and also what he intended to do in the immediate future. General Falkenhayn was in a similarly enlightened position in regard to his opponent. From the point of view of strategy, each commander knew what cards his opponent had in his hand. It was only by small tactical man-œuvrings of troops, conducted under cover of night, that the surprise attacks could be made. These had only a local import-ance, and by openly bringing up reinforcements the opposing com-mander always stopped the for-ward movement of the enemy.

This remarkable simplification of the art of war was the supreme achievement of the military airmen during the first nine months of the campaign. Next to it was the increased importance of long-range howitzer fire, and the general improvement in the destructive power of artillery due to fire direction from aeroplanes. In the third place came the long-range power over the enemy lines of communication, derived from the bomb-dropping art of the airmen. This line of development in the use of the new arm was not, however, followed up, for reasons already given. The best example of it was seen in the part played by our Royal Flying Corps during the attack on Neuve Chapelle in March, 1915.

This was, in plan at least, the first classic airmen's battle. But for an accident it might have resulted in the breaking of the German front and the recapture of Lille. Much time was spent in preparation. The enemy's trenches were minutely studied and photographed from the air.

ZEPPELIN HOLDING UP A MERCHANT VESSEL IN THE NORTH SEA.
Several Zeppelins took part in the German " blockade " of the British coasts ; and some of them came to grief, two (the L3 and L4) being wrecked in a storm off Denmark. Near the Haaks Lighthouse a Zeppelin came close to a Dutch steamer, the Helena, but on seeing the Dutch flag, reascended.

The artillerymen had simply to calculate the elevation of their howitzers, so as to drop an enormous number of high-explosive shells into the German line. While the guns and munitions were being secretly accumulated, the outpost duties of our airmen became very rigorous, for, naturally, no German aerial scouts could be permitted to make a reconnaissance. Each hostile flying man had to be met as soon as he appeared, and prevented from crossing our line, or brought down if he did so.

Then, when the terrific bombardment opened, and our infantry advanced, our Royal Flying Corps was used, probably for the first time in the history of warfare, in a masterly manner. They flew behind the enemy's lines and bom-barded the railway station at Don and the railway bridge at Menin, by which reinforcements could have been sent to the breaking-point of the German front. The idea was superb, and marked a new and highly-important advance in general strategy. Our airmen got behind the fighting German force and attempted to isolate it from the rest of the German army. They were not in sufficient number to control all the roads, but they seriously interfered with the working of any railway transport of fresh guns or munitions. When a grand

An advance in strategy

army counts its airmen in tens of thousands instead of in scores, this aerial bombardment of the enemy's rear, in co-operation with an artillery and infantry attack on his front, will be widely employed. The engagement at Neuve Chapelle thus marked a new era in modern warfare. In it was developed the design of interrupting the enemy's communications, in the heat of an action, which our Allies had been employing a few weeks before in their attack upon the enemy's lines at Perthes, in Champagne. By this time both General Henderson and General Hirschauer had fully worked out the tactics of the new arm. It was only their lack of thousands of airmen and of thousands of machines which prevented them from dealing the enemy a series of terrific blows from the air.

Happily, the Germans were in no better condition than the Allies in regard to the number of men and machines on the front. The continual air raids which the Germans made upon Dunkirk in January, 1915, were only a sign of the growing weakness of German airmen. About this time they were concentrating the greater part of their aerial force in Champagne and Lorraine, being apprehensive that General Joffre would make his grand offensive movement in the spring from one of the sides of Verdun. Then, to mask this withdrawal of pilots and machines from the westernmost sectors of their lines, the Germans began to make furious raids upon our provisioning base at Dunkirk.

But none of these raids was successful. On January 22nd, for instance, a squadron of twelve German aeroplanes attacked Dunkirk, and only Captain F. V. Holt, of the Oxford and Bucks Light Infantry, was on patrol duty.

Air duel at Dunkirk

But, on his little Martinsyde Scout, Captain Holt chased and fired at the two leading German machines and drove them off. By the time the other ten German aeroplanes came up, two more officers of our Royal Flying Corps, Captain Mills and Lieutenant Morgan, had ascended to a height of 6,000 feet, at which the action was taking place. Our three airmen then attacked the German machines, each of which had two men aboard. One enemy aeroplane was brought down by a bullet through one of its cylinders, and the pilot and observer were captured, with eight unexploded bombs, the observer being armed with a double-barrelled pistol for firing chain-shot. Having regard to the heavy odds against them, the achievement of Captain Holt and his two assistants was a remarkable example of the personal ascendency established by our

AIR - SCOUTING OVER THE DARDANELLES.
British seaplane, after a flight, about to be taken in tow by a ship's cutter.

SEAPLANE BEING HOISTED ON BOARD A CRUISER.
The machine had been on a flight over the Turkish positions in the Dardanelles. The pilot (seen standing) was French and the observer British.

men. Captain Holt was appointed a Companion of the Distinguished Service Order, in recognition of his gallantry and skill.

It was reckoned that from November, 1914, to February, 1915, our Army airmen flew altogether a hundred thousand miles. They always attacked any enemy craft which they sighted, except on the occasions when they were on some special duty from which they could not turn aside just for a sporting fight. Had we but possessed more machines and men, the ascendancy over the enemy would have been far more completely maintained. As it was, our overworked men did the best they could to interrupt continually the reconnaissance work of the enemy, and

by a fortunate chance their efforts were, to some extent, helped by the enlightened policy of our Admiralty.

As an organiser in war, Mr. Winston Churchill was not without defects, but he certainly had some inspiriting qualities of dash and originality. Early in the campaign, under his direction, the Royal Naval Air Service proved to be as efficient as the other branches of our naval force. This may partly have been due to the fact that the Admiralty relied less upon the Royal Aircraft Factory than our War Office did, and kept our enterprising private aeroplane makers going by Admiralty orders. Many of the best machines of the Sopwith Company and the Avro Company were taken up by the Naval Air Service and put to excellent use. The Admiralty also had, though it did not advertise the fact, a superb fleet of air destroyers, manned by men who were very anxious to try conclusions with the craft of Count Zeppelin. Our air destroyers were, indeed, the finest in the world.

But it is not yet possible to discuss the part which they played in the Great War. This is one of the things of which full details will only appear when the great struggle is over. Our naval aircraft patrolled the east coast of the North Sea and the Strait of Dover by daylight. The airships often kept aloft twelve hours, and, with the assistance of seaplanes working from a carrier steamer, the naval airmen kept continually under observation all the waters off the enemy's western coasts.

This laborious, unending, unspectacular reconnaissance work, carried out, as the war proceeded, in bitter, dangerous weather, constituted the most important achievement of the men of our Naval Air Service. Public attention was naturally fixed upon a few happy naval officers engaged in air raids. But these men were only able to be spared for picturesque and exciting work through the steady, silent, unnoted, but more important labours of their comrades.

On both sides the airship became, in regard to North Sea operations, a great auxiliary of the fleets. The Zeppelin and other large airships were soon found to be ineffectual in land warfare. The French brought the first Zeppelin down in a wood near Epinal on August 20th, 1914. No special anti-aircraft gun was necessary. The rigidly-built composite balloon was wrecked by a 3 in. shrapnel shell from one of the light French field-guns. Several of the rigid and semi-rigid German airships were destroyed by French and Russian soldiers, while our army never caught a glimpse of a Zeppelin or Parseval.

1915, in a nocturnal voyage to Yarmouth and certain Norfolk villages. They dropped bombs in water-butts and other places. A shoemaker and an aged woman were killed at Yarmouth; a lad of fourteen and a soldier's widow were murdered at King's Lynn; and one soldier at Yarmouth, belonging to the Essex Regiment, was wounded, being the first military victim of hostile aircraft in the British Isles. The affair **Night flight over** was of no importance whatever. It took **Norfolk villages** place on a rainy, foggy, night, when our naval air patrol was impeded by the weather from observing the advance of enemy aircraft. But the fog that prevented the Germans from being seen also hindered their operations. The few deaths and injuries of innocent non-combatants in East Anglia were a loss that might have occurred in an every-day street accident.

Apparently the intention of the Zeppelin commander was to recover the prestige lost by the German airships in the North Sea on Christmas Day, when they failed against our combined air and sea raid off Cuxhaven. The proper course for the Germans would have been to make a similar attack on our great ship-yards or war manufacturing centres. The latest Zeppelins were

WRECKED IN A SNOWSTORM.
The German Airship L3, which came to grief in a snowstorm on the Danish island of Fanoe. Its size may be judged by that of the two men seen standing on the left of the wreck.

The airships were at last withdrawn into their sheds, and the German land forces worked almost entirely with the speedier and handier flying machines. A night raid on a French coast town, a voyage to Paris, and a little bomb-dropping at Antwerp and round the eastern French frontier constituted the sum of activities of the Zeppelins in regard to land warfare in the western theatre of battle. The huge dirigible balloons were but huge failures. Their construction was an extremely laborious task, and also **Failure of the** highly expensive having regard **Zeppelins** to the results obtained. Large

INGLORIOUS END OF ANOTHER "AERIAL DREADNOUGHT."
The framework of this aerial monster, which met with disaster on French soil, was cut up by French soldiers. Pieces of the aluminium frame were on sale in Paris as souvenirs of the German raids.

aeroplanes, carrying each a couple of heavy bombs, were much speedier, much safer in all weathers, and much less costly in life, labour, and treasure. A single pilot, combining great daring and great skill and **Failure of the** using a scouting machine travelling at **Zeppelins** a hundred and fifty miles an hour, was likely to be able to wreck a Zeppelin. So the Zeppelins, Parsevals, and other German airships retired from the battle-front.

Some of them were preserved as bogies, intended to frighten nervous people in London. One or two of them seem to have at last reached our country on January 19th,

capable of a flight of thirty hours at their full speed of fifty miles an hour. Their range of action, in favourable weather, was therefore about twelve hundred miles, allowing for loss of power against wind on part of the journey. There was no part of the British Isles they could not have reached, partly by daylight travel; and even between evening and dawn they could have flown at full speed from Heligoland or the German coast sheds, bombarded some of our larger towns, and returned through the veil of darkness.

But they made no attack on any important centre of warlike activity, such as our Naval Air Service had continually selected in Germany. They dared not, in their first raids at least, take the risk of facing the various means of defence and offensive-defence concentrated at British places of national importance. All they attempted was an easy reconnaissance in force over an unprotected area of no military importance, where they could cheaply re-establish their prestige in their own country by a little bomb-dropping on England, with little danger to themselves.

The Zeppelins seem to have left their base about 11.30 a.m. on Tuesday, January 19th, 1915, and arrived over the East Anglian coast about 8.30 p.m. They used only half their power, for fear of encountering later either adverse air conditions or our naval airmen. As a matter of fact, they had a favouring wind on their return, and went back faster than they came. The airships appear to have travelled together towards Mundesley, and then separated, one going to Yarmouth and another to Cromer. At 8.30 p.m. Cromer was missed, but Beeston was bombarded without result, and another bomb was dropped at Sheringham, but it did not explode. The same airship seems to have travelled on past Hunstanton at 10.30 o'clock, and whirred over

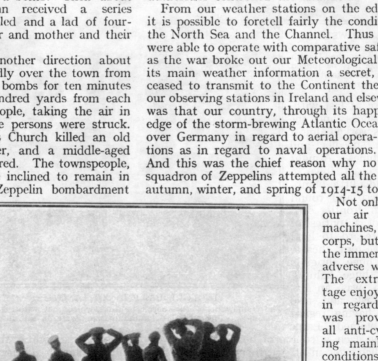

BRITISH SEAPLANE IN FLIGHT DURING THE RAID ON CUXHAVEN.

Heacham, where a water-butt received a shell, and on to Snettisham, where the village church was missed by sixty yards by a bomb. Then about 11 o'clock at night King's Lynn received a series of bombs, a soldier's widow was killed and a lad of fourteen was slain in his bed, his father and mother and their baby child being injured.

Airship attack on Yarmouth

Yarmouth was attacked from another direction about 8.30 p.m. The airship passed rapidly over the town from south to north, the crew throwing bombs for ten minutes at points all in a line about a hundred yards from each other. The streets were full of people, taking the air in the winter evening, but only three persons were struck. Two bombs thrown by St. Peter's Church killed an old lady who was fetching her supper, and a middle-aged shoemaker, while a soldier was injured. The townspeople, far from being panic-stricken, were inclined to remain in the streets, looking at the first Zeppelin bombardment of Britain; but the borough engineer cut off the lighting, as a measure of precaution against the return of the raider. This was well done, for about midnight the whir of an airship was again heard from the sky, but the hostile craft turned out to sea without attempting more slaughter or damage.

It is doubtful if the reported presence of King George and Queen Mary at Sandringham led to the second airship raiding southward from Hunstanton. The bomb may have been dropped at Snettisham in mistake for Sandringham. But, as a matter of fact, their Majesties had left Sandringham, without public

notice, so there was no danger to them—though the foe may have intended to follow the tactics of the Zeppelin raid on Antwerp, when the Royal palace was attacked, in the hope of killing King Albert and Queen Elisabeth of Belgium.

To achieve the insignificant results of the Norfolk aerial raid, the German airships, in their journeys over the waters, had to run grave risks. What these risks were was more clearly seen in the third week of February, when a Zeppelin and a Schütte-Lanz were wrecked by a storm in the North Sea. One came down, on February 17th, 1915, on Fanoe Island, and was there burned, the officers and men being arrested and interned by the Danish authorities. On the same day another German naval airship was wrecked off the west coast of Jutland, four of the crew being saved and eleven drowned.

This double disaster was a matter of supreme significance to the people of the British Isles. The two airships seemed to have been overtaken by a snowstorm. The snow that fell on their coverings, amounting perhaps to a ton in weight, pressed them down, and led to the wrecking of them. The direct cause of the disaster was a lack of knowledge of the probable weather conditions on February 17th. Our meteorological authorities controlled the situation.

From our weather stations on the edge of the Atlantic it is possible to foretell fairly the conditions of the air in the North Sea and the Channel. Thus our naval airships were able to operate with comparative safety. But as soon as the war broke out our Meteorological Department kept its main weather information a secret, and in particular ceased to transmit to the Continent the facts gathered in our observing stations in Ireland and elsewhere. The result was that our country, through its happy position on the edge of the storm-brewing Atlantic Ocean, was as supreme over Germany in regard to aerial operations as in regard to naval operations. And this was the chief reason why no squadron of Zeppelins attempted all the autumn, winter, and spring of 1914-15 to bombard London.

Our supremacy in weather-lore

Not only had they to face our air destroyers, flying machines, and anti-aircraft corps, but they had to take the immense risk of meeting adverse weather conditions. The extraordinary advantage enjoyed by our country in regard to weather-lore was providential. Nearly all anti-cyclones, representing mainly stable weather conditions, spread from the European continent to our islands. Nearly all cyclones, representing weather disturbances, sweep across the Atlantic and affect our country a day before they spread to the Continent. Thus it looks as though Britannia need not fear the coming era of aerial warfare.

TROOPERS ENDEAVOURING TO FOLLOW A DUEL IN THE AIR BETWEEN A BRITISH AEROPLANE AND A GERMAN AVIATIK.

ARMED BRITISH BIPLANE STARTING FROM HEADQUARTERS NEAR HOLLEBEKE.
The Union Jacks on the under side of each of the upper planes were for the guidance of the gunners in the allied lines. The gun in front of the observer was a Colt automatic. The bombs, suspended independently at the side of the car, were released by pulling a cord and thus withdrawing a pin in the neck of each missile. Our illustration was made from photographic material received from a British officer.

The British supremacy in weather lore was the main factor in the success of our Naval Air Service. The German airships were superior to ours in range of action. When the weather seemed to be quite settled they could venture far out into the North Sea, and there, at a height beyond the reach of our destroyers' guns, they could watch the movements of our ships and telegraph their observations by wireless to the German naval base.

German airship superiority Our smaller patrolling craft, with a less range of flight, could not operate from our coast and keep all the waters between Denmark and Holland under constant observation. We had to use steamers fitted up as aircraft carriers in order to approach the German naval bases and to watch what went on round there. It was really our knowledge of coming weather conditions that enabled us to cope with the better-equipped German naval reconnaissance officers.

Count Zeppelin had served his country well. Though his dirigible balloons were ineffectual in land warfare, they were superb instruments of reconnaissance in naval operations. In fair weather they were able to watch over five hundred or more miles of sea. Floating at a high altitude above the Dogger Bank, they could prevent any daylight surprise by our battle squadrons. If we had also possessed a large fleet of Zeppelins, employed in accordance with our knowledge of weather conditions, the task of our naval patrol would have been greatly facilitated. Yet in spite of their inferior material our men also kept good watch and ward. The result was that the preliminary movements of both fleets usually took place at night. Our raid into the Bight of Heligoland and the German raids on our East Coast were both conducted in darkness. Such was the effect of the new aerial arm upon naval manœuvres.

Our Admiralty recognised the sterling worth of the Zeppelin by directing Wing-Commander Samson to bombard some of the airship sheds along the Rhine. We have already related the first attack on the airsheds at Düsseldorf and Cologne. This was only in the nature of a preliminary reconnaissance, and a more effectual operation was conducted from Antwerp on October 8th. Squadron-Commander Grey and Lieutenant Marix, on Sopwith Scouts, and Lieutenant Sippe went to Antwerp when the siege began. When they started on the raid Lieutenant Sippe's engine gave trouble, being an example of Royal Aircraft Factory adaptation. He was unable to complete the journey, while the two other men on their fast, private-built machines reached their mark.

It was not an easy expedition, as the country was veiled by thick weather. When Lieutenant Marix came down to discover where he was, he found himself only a hundred feet above some tree-tops. On reaching the Rhine Lieutenant Marix dived five hundred feet at the airshed, and released his bombs amid the heavy fire of high-angle guns and rifles. He set the shed alight and destroyed the Zeppelin inside it. Meanwhile, Squadron-Commander Grey whirred higher up the Rhine to Cologne. But all over this city the mist was so thick that the aviator could not find the position of the airship shed. So after circling above the city, much to the amusement of the townspeople, who did not imagine he was an enemy, he launched his bombs on the central railway-station, and considerably damaged this main centre of the German line of communications.

Squadron-Commander Grey got back safely to Antwerp, but Lieutenant Marix had to alight in Belgium, through his supply of petrol running out. A Ghent newspaper at the time reported that the Belgian patrol saw a **Marix's exciting adventure** machine alight and hurried to the spot. There they found a young man, who thought he had fallen into the hands of the German soldiers and was coolly waiting for death. He was taken in an armed motor-car to Antwerp by the admiring Belgians, just in time to escape with the Belgian Army and the British Naval Division.

The next base of our raiders of the Royal Naval Air Service was Belfort. There, on November 21st, Squadron-

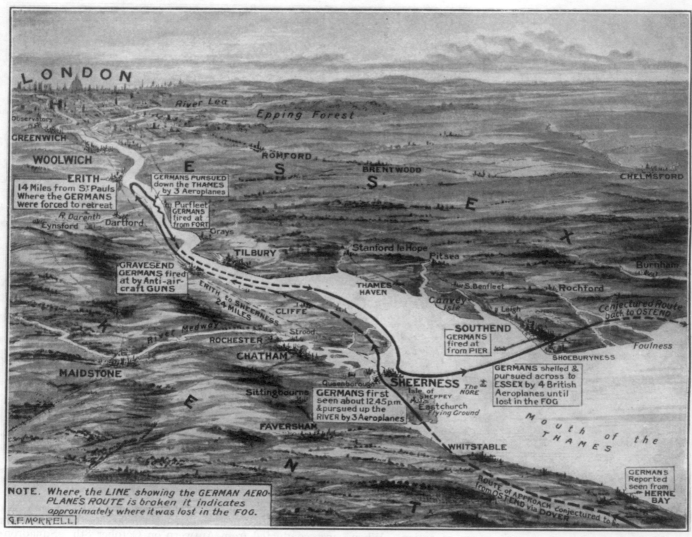

GERMANY'S CHRISTMAS DAY AIR RAID ON LONDON.

Owing to fog, the German aeroplane which flew over the Thames to within fourteen miles of St. Paul's Cathedral, on December 25th, 1914, escaped from its British pursuers. The flight, with Woolwich perhaps as its objective, caused some excitement, but no damage was done.

Commander E. F. Briggs, with Flight-Commander Babington and Lieutenant Sippe, set out on Avro machines on a round voyage of two hundred and fifty miles towards the centre of the Zeppelin industry. The three airmen had to cross the mountainous tract of the Black Forest in thick weather, and to fly over the misty waters of Lake Constance to the lakeside town of Friedrichshafen. At Schaffhausen Commander Briggs lost sight of his companions in the fog.

He was the first to arrive at the Zeppelin factory, where he dived through the fire of the machine-guns and quick-firers and dropped his bombs. Commander Babington and Lieutenant Sippe came out of the mist, and also attacked through a heavy fire. Most of the bombs were skilfully aimed at the Zeppelin works, but one or two dropped on the airshed and damaged the latest Zeppelin. The gasworks were exploded, sending up gigantic flames into the sky, and for an area of seven hundred square yards in and around the Zeppelin works considerable damage was done. The machine of Squadron-Commander Briggs was badly injured by the enemy's fire, forcing the naval aviator, who was wounded, to alight. An attempt seems to have been made to lynch him when he landed, and a German soldier attacked him; but he

Briggs' daring courage was rescued by an officer and taken to the hospital, some of his foes being full of admiration for the daring courage which he had displayed. Commander Babington and Lieutenant Sippe had each a dozen holes in their machines, but the fuselage and important fittings were untouched, and both officers got back safely to their starting-point.

The next air raid was conducted by French aviators. They also selected one of the principal aircraft construction works in Germany. The best German aeroplane was the Aviatik, which had been manufactured at Mulhouse at the beginning of the war. But when the French Army entered Alsace, and threatened to capture Mulhouse, the aeroplane works were removed across the Rhine to Freiburg in the Black Forest. Here they were repeatedly bombarded by French aviators, **Repeated raids on Freiburg** the first raid taking place in the first week in December. Considerable damage was done, and the German Government had the impudence to protest that, as Freiburg was an open town, the aerial bombardment was contrary to international law. This protest was made after German airmen had for months been busy killing civilians, mainly women and children, with the sole object of creating a panic among the French people. Important centres of military activities like Freiburg or Friedrichshafen were regarded by the Germans as sacrosanct, while quiet villages in Norfolk and un-fortified historic towns in France were treated as the proper objects of German bomb-throwers. The way in which the new barbarians combined a screaming foolish-ness in regard to attacks on their own country and a cold-blooded lust for murder of Belgian, British, and French children and women can be explained.

The explanation was obtained from Düsseldorf. There the German civil population was terrified by the success of our naval airmen. Many well-to-do families left their homes after the destruction of the Zeppelin shed and Zeppelin and settled in Central Germany. The General in command, Baron von Bissing, issued a long proclamation, in which he stated that the British raid " produced in certain circles of the population a feeling not in accordance

THE ANTI-AIRCRAFT CORPS IN ACTION: "WINGING" A GERMAN TAUBE NEAR YPRES.

Ten Anti-Aircraft men were out scouting near Ypres with an anti-aircraft gun mounted on a motor-chassis. Immediately the Taube appeared they opened fire, with the result that the machine, spouting flame and smoke, zigzagged to earth about a mile away, where it was captured.

BIRD'S-EYE VIEW OF CUXHAVEN HARBOUR, AT THE MOUTH OF THE RIVER ELBE.

Scene of the daring exploit by seven British naval airmen, assisted by H.M.S. Arethusa and Undaunted and submarines, on December 25th, 1914, when many enemy warships were attacked.

with the active and vigorous character of the German people." He went on to say that " the German people has been partly spoiled by the successes of the German armies, so that many of them suffer nerve shock when the enemy obtains some slight success anywhere in Germany." He concluded by praising the strictly censored newspapers for not showing " the same excitement and nervousness as the **Civilian terror in** great part of the **Düsseldorf** people of Düsseldorf."

Thus it looked as though we were fighting an empire of cowards, dragooned into a warlike attitude by an aristocracy of bullies.

What especially made the German people nervous was the fact that they were able to see with their own eyes the destruction of the most acclaimed and cherished part of their great war-machine—the Zeppelins. They had been told that London would be completely paralysed by a terrific aerial bombardment by a mighty fleet of Zeppelins. Children of well-to-do German families had been provided with a toy London, which they were able to destroy, with the slaughter of millions of lives, by means of a fleet of toy Zeppelins. Merely a slight attack upon certain military points of importance at Düsseldorf, Cologne, Friedrichshafen, and Freiburg made the great, brave German people feel that two could play at the aerial war-game ; and those two, it seemed to them, were Britain and France. No wonder then that Baron von Bissing had to issue a stern proclamation, even at a time when no German civilian had been killed by accident in our first raids.

By way of heartening their people the Germans sent one or two airmen on aeroplanes to attack Dover, and if possible to reach London. The most important attempt of this kind was baffled by an air patrol at Dunkirk ; and none of the large squadron of German flying men even managed to cross the Channel.

At Christmas a single **Christmas raider** raider came up the **up the Thames** Thames as far as Erith, but was chased away by our naval airmen.

On the same day our Admiralty gave the Germans a lesson in the proper handling of a small naval air force engaged in reconnaissance work. Our Navy was anxious to know what the Germans were doing in the Schillig Roads, off Cuxhaven, and as our submarine scouts could not obtain full information, our naval patrol took the matter in hand. Seven seaplanes, piloted by Flight-Commanders Oliver, Hewlett, Ross, Kilner, Miley, and Flight-Lieutenants Edmonds and Gaskell Blackburn, sailed with their machines to a spot near Heligoland.

WANTON DESTRUCTION TO MAKE A GERMAN HOLIDAY: EFFECT OF BOMB-DROPPING IN A STREET IN KING'S LYNN, NORFOLK, ON JANUARY 19TH, 1915.

The carrier steamers were convoyed by a light cruiser and destroyer force, with submarines in attendance. The attack was delivered in daylight, and as soon as our ships were seen by the look-out on Heligoland Island, two Zeppelins and three or four German seaplanes, with several hostile submarines, were ordered to counter-attack.

Reconnaissance off Cuxhaven Our seaplanes were slung outboard and lowered with their pilots and observers at daybreak. With a rush the planes were off, and quickly climbed to a height of over 2,000 feet. As they approached the shore the land batteries and warships opened fire. But our men sailed on through the low-hung clouds, and then dived to extraordinarily low positions. This made it easier for them to strike their targets, and it did not really increase their danger, for their high-speed machines were as hard to hit when low as when high up. Our airmen made a valuable reconnaissance and bombarded the German fleet. But one flier, having used his last bomb on a big battleship, met another when he was quite out of ammunition. Throttling his engine, he dived straight to the ship's deck as if to ram it, and just before he used his control and soared upward he hurled at the enemy ship the only throwable thing within reach—a large woolly golliwog which he had carried as a mascot.

After studying the condition of things in Heligoland and Cuxhaven, and doing considerable damage in a round flight of three hours, our men returned to their

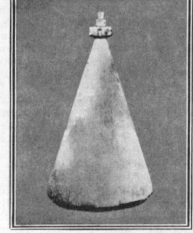

A BOMB THAT DID NOT EXPLODE. Found at Yarmouth in January, 1915.

carrier steamers. Three of the seven airmen got back to their machines. Three others, returning later, had their machines sunk, and were picked up by our submarines. Commander Hewlett was rescued by a Dutch trawler, after losing his way in a fog and floating about the sea for six hours, when his motor went wrong.

While the airmen were enjoying **Commander Hewlett's rescue** themselves at the first historic bombardment of battleships by seaplanes, their protectors — the British light cruisers and the flotillas of destroyers and submarines—had an interesting time with the enemy aircraft. The two vast, silvery Zeppelins came floating over the British vessels, appearing in and out of the clouds. But there was no fight in the airship crews. Our cruisers opened on them with common shell from their 6 in. guns. One of our seaplanes also interrupted its special work in order to have an interview with a Zeppelin. But, as the pilot remarked, "Zeppy almost sat on her tail with fright when she was attacked." That is to say, the immense airship put up her nose, and began to climb for dear life. The seaplane, being unable to spare the time for a long manœuvring fight, whirred away towards Cuxhaven. Our ships then had to face their aerial enemies with no help from our Naval Wing. Some of the seaplane-carriers had a difficult time of it. They were attacked by aircraft and submarines. But they dodged the bombs by skilful seamanship, and our destroyers helped to keep off the German underwater craft.

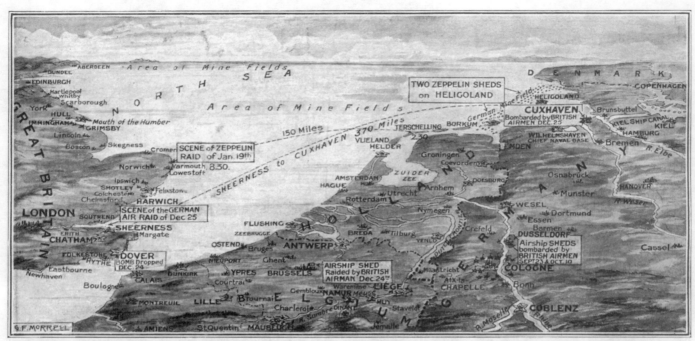

DIAGRAMMATIC MAP OF THE AREAS CHOSEN RESPECTIVELY FOR THE BRITISH AND GERMAN AIRCRAFT RAIDS IN SEPTEMBER—DECEMBER, 1914, AND JANUARY, 1915.

The hottest work was done by Lieut.-Commander Nasmyth, commanding submarine E11. He was watching inshore, to assist any seaplane which might get into difficulties. Towards him descended the airmen Oliver, Miley, and Blackburn, who had run short of petrol. The submarine officer rose and went to their help, but one of the Zeppelin look-outs saw him and the three floating aviators, and the great airship shot overhead and began dropping bombs. But by his coolness and resource Lieut.-Commander Nasmyth rescued the three pilots, and all our ships and men got safely back to the East Coast after one of the greatest adventures of the war.

The reconnaissance work accomplished was of high military value. Then, in addition to the **British bombs on Zeebrugge** damage done, the experience gained in the novel combined operation by light cruisers, destroyers, seaplane-carriers, and submarines was of importance. Commodore Reginald Tyrwhitt, well known for his work in the Battle of the Bight, was in command of the ships, and Commodore Roger Keyes directed the submarines. Lieut. Erskine Childers, of the Naval Volunteer Reserve, acted as one of the aerial reconnaissance officers, a position which this author had earned by his close study of the German coast in times of peace. Flight-Commander Kilner and Flight-Lieut. Edmonds, with Chief Petty-Officers Bell and Budds, especially distinguished themselves. The two officers were made companions of the Distinguished Service Order, while the two chief petty-officers received the Distinguished Service Medal.

The last work of importance by the Royal Naval Air Service, undertaken during the period covered by this chapter, was directed against the increasing activities of enemy submarines. On January 22nd, 1915, in answer to a German air raid on Dunkirk, Squadron-Commander Davies and Flight-Lieut. Peirse flew to Zeebrugge, the seaport of Bruges, which the Germans were using as a submarine base. They found two submarines in harbour, one of which they destroyed by bombs. They also dropped bombs on the heavy batteries on Zeebrugge Mole, and killed or wounded many of the guns' crews. Squadron-Commander Davies was wounded in the thigh on his flight towards Zeebrugge, but proceeded to his objective, carried out his work, and returned without further injury.

On February 12th a larger aerial operation was conducted against Zeebrugge and other hostile positions on the Belgian coast. Thirty-four naval aeroplanes and seaplanes set out under the command of Wing-Commander

202

Samson. Another submarine was damaged at Zeebrugge, and several batteries near the fort were put out of action. Railway communications along the coast were temporarily deranged by the destruction of the track in places, and the bombardment of the railway-stations at Ostend and Blankenberghe. A Zeppelin shed with its contents was reported to have been completely destroyed, and the electricity works at Zeebrugge had to be repaired before any more electricity could be produced.

On February 16th another strong air raid was conducted by forty aeroplanes and seaplanes. The German batteries along the Belgian coast were again bombarded; the Mole at Zeebrugge, already breached by our airmen, was further damaged; the locks of the sea canal between Bruges and the sea were partly blown up; and German mine-sweeping trawlers in the harbour were attacked. During this coast raid the German aeroplane centre at Ghistelles was bombarded by French airmen, who thus prevented the German aircraft from attempting to cut off our machines. We lost no men in these operations, though two of our airmen got out to sea, where they were picked up.

On March 7th another air attack was made on Ostend, where the German submarine repair base was bombarded. On April 1st the townspeople of Antwerp were gladdened by a break in the monotony of their lives as temporary subjects of the Kaiser. An outburst of gun fire in the morning brought them to their windows. Flight-Sub-Lieut. Frank Andreae was attacking the German submarine factory at Hoboken, near Antwerp, while the German anti-aircraft guns vainly **The attack on Hoboken** tried to frighten him away or bring him down. According to a delighted eyewitness, the aviator dived within fifty yards of the shipyard, and dropped three or four bombs on two completed submarines and on two others in a half-constructed state. Not only were they all destroyed, but a fire broke out in the shipbuilding works, and there were numerous dead or wounded men among the band of expert German mechanics engaged in submarine construction. The people of Antwerp cheered the aviator, especially when they saw him make his daring low dive to launch his bombs. On the same day Flight-Lieut. Wilson, reconnoitring over Zeebrugge, observed two submarines lying alongside the Mole. He dropped two bombs on each of them with happy results. But the vital achievements in airmanship were performed by the anonymous officers and men directing the fire of the artillery, scouting over the enemy's territory, and patrolling our coast, the Channel, and the North Sea.

THE BRITISH NAVAL AIR RAID ON THE GREAT GERMAN PORT OF CUXHAVEN.
An impression of the scene as it might have been witnessed from the foredeck of H.M.S. Undaunted when its guns and those of H.M.S. Arethusa (seen in centre of picture) drove the German aircraft back to Heligoland.

START OF THE FIRST OF THE BRITISH AIR RAIDS ON THE ZEEBRUGGE-OSTEND COASTLINE.
Squadron of naval aero-planes and seaplanes crossing the sea for the first great air raid in history, under the direction of Commander Samson, on February 12th, 1915. The object of the Admiralty was the preventing of the establishment of submarine bases at Zeebrugge and vicinity.

Railways thus
Roads "
Canals "

Copyright

First Russian Front: ••••••• ▬ ▬ ▬ ▬ *Last Russian Front.*

The Great War

MAP OF MAIN EASTERN THEATRE OF WAR IN NOVEMBER AND DECEMBER, 1914.

Showing the position of Russian armies after their pursuit of first invading force, and their later position on the river system of defences after Hindenburg's second lunge at Warsaw.

| CHAPTER LV. |

THE RUSSIAN STAND ON THE FIVE RIVERS AND THE BATTLE OF THE CARPATHIANS.

Russian Advance to the Gate of Silesia—Germany in Danger of being Half Crippled—Russky and Ivanoff Try to Force a Decisive Conflict before Cracow—How Hindenburg Evaded the Conflict and Forced Ivanoff to Retreat—Germans Make a Sudden and Powerful Lunge at Warsaw—Heroic Stand by Russians Round the Marshes of the Bzura—Terrible Struggle for the Causeway of Piontek—Germans Break Through and Half Envelop the Central Russian Army—Russky's Struggle for Life—Abrupt Transformation of the Field of Battle—Victorious German Force Cut Off and Encircled—Failure of General Rennenkampf to Carry Out His Orders—General von Mackensen again Breaks the Russian Line and Releases His Trapped Troops—General Russky Withdraws from Lodz—General Ivanoff Retires from Cracow—All the Russian Armies Entrench Behind a Formidable System of River Defences—Ghastly Scenes of Slaughter on the Bzura and Rawka Rivers—Würtemberg Brigade Forces a Passage only to be Annihilated—Magnificent Fighting Qualities of the Siberian Riflemen—Battles of Bolimoff and Inovlodz—Austrians Broken and Captured on the Nida—General Dimitrieff's Decisive Victory on the Dunajec—Russians on Dukla Pass Threatening to Invade Hungary—Opening of the Battle of the Carpathians—Hindenburg's Attempt to Avoid the Mountain Conflict.

BY the middle of November, 1914, the German offensive had exhausted much of its strength. The retreat of the Teutonic armies of invasion in Poland and the repulse of the Prussian Guard in Belgium were full of menace for Germany and Austria-Hungary. Had the Teutonic and Hungarian peoples then had any means of knowing the situation and controlling it, they might have asked for terms of peace. Of the two allies in the terrible war of aggression, Germany had suffered the less, owing to her incomparable war-machine and her superb body of one hundred and twenty thousand well-trained and masterful non-commissioned officers. The war-machine of Austria-Hungary had been shaken, and nearly all the first-line armies and a part of the second-line forces had been disintegrated. The casualties of the Dual Alliance amounted to at least two million men. The loss had fallen most heavily on the first-line armies.

Germany's best troops were indeed almost as shattered as those of Austria. But the German war-machine still worked as well as ever, and the Ersatz and Landwehr soldiers were drafted into the framework of the fighting armies and turned, by working with the remaining veteran troops, into good first-line material. Into the German war-machine the new levies of Austria-Hungary were also poured, and reorganised there into what afterwards proved to be an admirable fighting force. Yet all this was but a glittering stucco façade masking the ruin of the striking

GENERAL RADKO DIMITRIEFF.

power of two mighty empires. The Teutons were no longer living upon the income of their vital energies, upon the annual increase of their population, upon the savings and profit of their labours. They had already spent much of the capital of their vital energies. Germany, it was reckoned by an impartial American observer, had crippled her national life for generations to come.

To sue for peace, however, was to overthrow the power of the aristocracies in Germany, Austria, and Hungary. It was well known what terms the Allies would demand, and peace on those terms would have resulted in the overthrow of the governing classes in the Teutonic and Hungarian countries. Their rule had only been suffered, during the growing influence of democratic forces in neighbouring nations, because the majority of people in the two empires were gratified by the supposedly invincible military power they derived from their modern feudalistic form of policy. The acceptance of peace with defeat would have been an act of suicide by the governing parties.

Being made of mortal clay, with all their human frailties increased by the irresponsible exercise of power, the leaders of Germany and Austria-Hungary resolved to sacrifice their peoples in the hope of saving their class and dynastic interests. An attempt was made to detach France from the Triple Entente. The French nation was offered part of Alsace, and, if necessary, part of Belgium, in return for its recognition of the German annexation of Flanders and Liège.

But, as the French themselves remarked at the time, the Germans, having no sense of honour themselves, thought that other peoples were in the same condition.

Then an attempt was made to convince the Russian Court that the Germanic principle of aristocratic and Imperial government was the only safeguard for Russia against the spread of democratic ideas of a revolutionary sort. But as the Russians were beginning to see at last that their empire was an experiment in communism, with the communes organised for defence under a hereditary dictator or imperator, the Tsar was not moved by the Kaiser's sudden renewal of interest in his domestic politics. It is said that the Tsar sent the German proposal, without a word of explanation, to the Grand Duke Nicholas. The Grand Duke returned it with the remark that all his troops would mutiny and turn into armed revolutionaries if an easy peace were made with the foes against whom they were waging a Holy War of liberation.

A Holy War of liberation

As a matter of fact, the Tsar himself was most resolute to fight to a finish, and thus settle all the outstanding difficulties in Russian foreign affairs. For the possession of Constantinople, in particular, the Tsar and his

November, 1914, the Russians were sweeping towards the German frontier at Rypin, between Thorn and Graudenz, in the north, and in the south they were close against Cracow. The Austro-Hungarian army had ventured too far in its movement on the San River, supporting Hindenburg's movement against Warsaw and Ivangorod. By the capture of Sandomir the Russians had cut off part of the Austrian forces, and then in a swift northward advance they had driven a wedge into the Teuton-Magyar army round Cracow.

The position was then a paradoxical one. Austria had lost most of Galicia, and Hungary was in danger

A GERMAN SLEIGH AMBULANCE.
Horse-drawn sleigh used by Germans on the Russian frontier in taking wounded to hospital in the winter of 1914-15.

RUSSIAN INFANTRY ADVANCING THROUGH THE SNOW BEFORE CRACOW.
This striking photograph demonstrates the perilous nature of such an advance. The men made startlingly prominent targets for the enemy's fire, their figures standing out like silhouettes on the surface of the snow.

of invasion. Yet Austria and Hungary were comparatively strong. Their immediate situation was merely uncomfortable. Germany had lost only a few miles of territory in East Prussia, and she still possessed a large, rich, and important part of Russian soil, most strongly held by entrenched lines along the Warta River. Yet it was Germany who was in immediate and dire peril.

From the beginning the position of the German Empire had been remarkably curious. It resembled a great, powerful creature of a mythical kind, which could survive repeated stabs through the heart, but would die if its skin were pricked in a certain place. Let us put it that Germany had two lungs from which her supply of oxygen was derived. One of these lungs was the western frontier land of Westphalia, and particularly the Black Country stretching from Düsseldorf to Dortmund, with the iron mines of Lorraine. The other lung was the eastern frontier land of the Black Country of Silesia, that extended into Russian territory above Cracow. No advance to Berlin was necessary to overthrow the Germans. The occupation of Silesia would half cripple th m, and, if followed by the occupation of Westphalia,

Germany's two vital points

peasants were ready to fight, if need be, for a lifetime. Its possession would crown the long, painful, wonderful efforts made by the Russian village communities, under the leadership of men of the House of Rurik, for a thousand years. Throughout this period Constantinople had been their Holy City. Thirty years of war would not be too high a price to pay for it. Yet Germany and Austria were intriguing for a patched-up peace, when it was becoming clear that they could not resist longer than two years at the most.

So the war went on. By the end of the first week in

AN INCIDENT IN THE CARPATHIANS: VIENNA-BOUND TRAIN HELD UP BY COSSACKS.

it would probably reduce them to helplessness. They would lack the means for carrying on the war. It was for this reason that the Russian Commander-in-Chief threw only a couple of army corps towards Posen, on the road to Berlin, in the second week of November, while he massed his two chief armies against Silesia.

It was expected that a tremendous battle for Silesia would take place along the frontier rivers, the Warta and Przemsza. Such appears to have been the belief of General Russky and General Ivanoff, commanding the central Russian armies. But General von Hindenburg showed an undoubted talent in the manner in which he countered the impending Russian offensive movement.

Hindenburg's advantages

He had the fatigued, disappointed, and somewhat mangled army of invasion which had retreated towards the Warta River. He had also the large new formations, which had been training since the outbreak of hostilities, less the multitude of recruits slaughtered at Ypres and elsewhere before they had been made into good soldiers. He had also large bodies of fresh Hungarian and Austrian Territorials, fired with high courage by the imminence of invasion.

His forces considerably outnumbered those at the disposal of Generals Russky and Ivanoff. What was still more important, he possessed, close to the rear of his lines, the finest system of strategical railways in the world. It was with these railways that he fought. At the beginning of the second week in November large bodies of men were withdrawn from the German lines, and reinforced by fresh troops. They were formed into some seven army corps, under the command of General von Mackensen, and were railed up towards Thorn. It was arranged for further army corps to follow them as soon as possible, bringing up Mackensen's strength to nearly three-quarters of a million men. Hindenburg's plan was a simple one. Instead of fighting a defensive battle for Silesia in front of Cracow, he swiftly recovered the offensive by lunging out again at Warsaw. In withdrawing from his first movement of invasion he had thoroughly destroyed the few railway lines running across the territory which the Russians reoccupied. This had been done with a view to the execution of the plan which Hindenburg was now carrying out.

He had placed the victorious Russians in considerable difficulty. For their supplies they had to rely entirely upon strings of country carts, crawling over bad, swampy tracks. All movements of troops had to be carried out by marching through Polish mud. Hindenburg could move his armies by railways, which bent in a semicircle round the advancing Russians like a gigantic net. At need, the Russian soldiers could march thirty miles a day, but the German soldiers could move two hundred miles a day by train, and come absolutely fresh into the fight.

The power of manœuvring, therefore, rested entirely with the Germans, and everything favoured their strategy. The fighting-line extended from the north of Tilsit to the south of Czernovitz. With all its curves and irregularities it was about a thousand miles long. It was impossible for either side to entrench its troops on this tremendous front. Neither Teuton nor Slav had then sufficient men to garrison trenches of such a length. So in the eastern theatre of war the battles of manœuvres in the open field went on. On each side there were gaps between the main concentrations of forces, and in these gaps the reconnoitring mounted troops were continually skirmishing against each other. The Russians, of course, expected a grand counterstroke from the enemy, but they could not concentrate in advance for it, because they did not know at what point Hindenburg would launch his railway-speeded attack. All they could do was to try to force on the great decisive battle at the place where their own troops were most numerous. And this, as we have seen, they did by driving in upon Cracow. But it was at a spot nearly two hundred miles north of Cracow that Hindenburg again took the field.

Odds against the Russians

Mackensen's army swung forward from Thorn and Kalisz. It had a scissorlike action. One blade worked along the Vistula and the other along the Warta River. Some part of the advanced guards of Russians was caught between the blades of the scissors and destroyed. From November 11th to November 13th the Germans won a series of successes at Wloclat, Wloclawec, and Kutno. It was at the last-named town that the main battle was fought. Two Russian army corps were faced by seven German army corps. The odds against the Russians in both men and guns were terrible. But they could not retreat. The entire strategy of all the allied commanders, and of the Grand Duke Nicholas in particular, was opposed to anything like a retreat under such conditions. The outnumbered and almost enveloped Russians had to stand their ground till they were completely destroyed as a fighting corps.

The action took place on the Bzura River, between the towns of Lowicz and Lencysca. From Lowicz to Lencysca, a distance of thirty-five miles, there **Battle of the marsh** stretched a great river marsh, which con- **at Kutno** tinued for nearly another twenty miles beyond Lencysca. There were only two causeways over this marsh, one being at Piontek, nearly midway between Lencysca and Lowicz. The small Russian army lined out along the marsh in front of the causeways, and just behind the town of Kutno. They had to hold the causeways until General Russky, with the main Russian forces, could come to their assistance. This was the only way in which the Russians could fight the German railway system of manœuvring. They lacked the mechanical means of transport necessary for the constant countering of Hindenburg's terrific rushes. In France, Joffre could work his railways as quickly as—and sometimes more quickly than—Falkenhayn.

Each German rush there was stopped before it went more than a few miles. But, in Russian Poland, Russian flesh and blood had to recover the advantages won by German trains and railway tracks. The Germans had always the advantage of surprise, and to win time Russian commanders had often to lose a great number of men.

So it was in the battle of the marsh at Kutno. The Germans won an easy victory in front of the town, and the Russian troops retired behind the long river marsh midway between Thorn and Warsaw. Their way of fighting was peculiar, and it overthrew the German plan. According to German ideas conscript troops had to be handled very carefully.

It was disastrous, on the German theory, to try to make them fight for long against superior numbers and superior artillery. So Napoleon's method of sacrificing a tenth or more of an army in order to hold an enemy was impossible under modern conditions. But it was just this impossibility which the Russians on the Bzura, like the British at Ypres, turned into an accomplished fact.

The Russian troops fought magnificently. In the end they held up the Germans until first General Russky, then the commander of the Warsaw reinforcements, and lastly General Rennenkampf brought their armies, by forced marches over the muddy plain, to their help. The struggle in the marsh went on for a week. The stretch of bog, with its islands of dry land, extended for nearly sixty miles, and formed a better defence than a river—for you cannot bridge a bog with pontoons. The guns could only advance behind the infantry, over the

narrow causeways, where the Russians were able to concentrate against them, while carrying on a series of semi-disconnected fights on all the patches of firm ground.

In these circumstances, the Russian Commander-in-Chief used the most extraordinary tactics. He did not reinforce his small, battered advance army, desperately struggling to hold the marsh. But as Russky's troops marched up from the south, and new formations poured eastward from Warsaw, he drew them up in a line stretching from Sochachev, on the Bzura, through Lowicz, and then along the railway to Zgierz, and other smaller towns west and south-west of Lodz. Through lack of time to connect the converging Russian armies, a gap was left behind the Russian troops fighting in the marshes. After tremendous efforts and terrible sacrifices of life, General von Mackensen succeeded in capturing the Piontek causeway on November 19th. Thereupon the Germans poured in a broad avalanche through the gap. They took the roads to Strykof, Bresiny, and Koluszki. This last small town was right behind the Russian front at Lodz, and close to it was the main railway junction, where three Russian-Polish railways connected. It seemed as though the Germans were winning the grandest victory in the war. Round Lodz they were outflanking the principal Russian army under General Russky, who had been suddenly stricken with illness. South of Lowicz and Skernievice they were turning the northern Russian armies. At the same time another main German force had advanced from Kalisz, and was engaged in turning General Russky's southern flank at Lask. The situation was extremely critical. It was almost as critical as the position in France after the Battles of Charleroi and Mons. Never was Hindenburg so near to a grand Napoleonic success. But dangerous as was the position of General Russky, he kept his head. He threw his reserves northward from Petrokof to Tusyn. There they stopped the main German movement of envelopment, and forced the enemy to

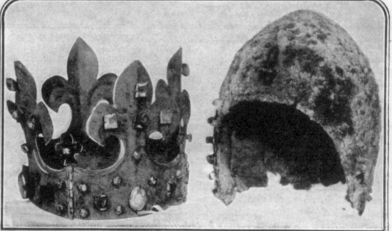

RELICS OF A GLORIOUS PAST.
The ancient crown of the Polish kings, and the iron helmet in which it was found under an old oak-tree in a Polish village about four years ago. The crown, which is in four parts and adorned with sixty-five precious stones, is preserved at Cracow.

stand on the defensive. At the same time Russky's active troops at Lask fell upon the second German army and flung the hostile columns back in disorder. Then came the mighty counterstroke, engineered by the Grand Duke Nicholas in person. He ordered General Rennenkampf to march with all haste to the decisive scene of conflict, and wheeled the army defending Warsaw from Lowicz and Skernievice south-westward. The army used Lowicz as a pivot, and swung over the hills of Central Poland for twenty-five miles till it reoccupied **Russky's advance** Strykof and Bresiny. While this move- **from Lodz** ment was going on, General Russky advanced westward from Lodz, and inflicted terrible losses on Hindenburg's central army, and forced it to withdraw back towards the Warta and entrench.

By November 23rd the situation in the eastern theatre of war had undergone a most remarkable change. The two German army corps which had forced the passage of the marshes, and almost enveloped General Russky's force, had their lines of communication cut. They were being bottled up in the region of Bresiny, some miles *behind* the Russian front. The Russians had opened and let the attackers through, and then had joined together again,

Russell & Sons.

Lieut.-General W. P. Pulteney, K.C.B., D.S.O., Commanding Third Army Corps.

Austrian General Steger Steiner and Staff watching operations in Galicia.

Russian Infantrymen entrenched on outskirts of wood in Galicia.

Twenty=eight ton Austrian siege=howitzer which fires a thousand=pound projectile.

Where Austrian trenches faced Russian across a morass in East Galicia.

Stubborn fighting on the heights carried by the Russians south of Dukla in the Carpathians.

snapping off a mass of Germans as large as the British Expeditionary Force at Mons.

The trap was as complete as a thing of man's shaping could be. But for some reason which is not yet clearly known, General Rennenkampf did not carry out his part of the operation. He delayed to march his men to the scene of action at the time when General von Mackensen was speeding up reinforcements to rescue his entrapped army corps. General Rennenkampf had been always unfortunate in his operations, though the Russian Chief of Staff had given him some of the most brilliant of Russian troops and had designed his course of action with the greatest care. Rennenkampf was one of the German barons in the Russian Empire who fought well against the Japanese, but seemed incapable of winning in any circumstances against men of his own original stock. Twice in East Prussia the Russian offensive movement had failed in a most curious manner. The troops under Rennenkampf's immediate command had been extricated with some difficulty from Hindenburg's and Eichhorn's attacks, but the Russian generals acting with Rennenkampf had on each occasion been strangely trapped in the Masurian Lakes. Now, at the Battle of Strykof, Rennenkampf himself failed to co-operate with the Russian generals in inflicting a tremendous defeat upon the Germans.

Owing to the slowness with which Rennenkampf moved, the action failed, and he was relieved of his command. From November 23rd to November 26th General von Mackensen's main army hammered fiercely and continually at the Russian line between Lowicz and Strykof. The desperate German attacks went on night and day, and as Rennenkampf's army did not arrive in time to reinforce the Russians, the final closing-up of the ring around the trapped German army corps was prevented. Mackensen succeeded in reopening the gap, and flinging in two more corps, which rescued the entrapped columns. The Germans got out, but in doing so they had to force a passage under cross-fire from the Russian machine-guns and rifles, and retreat through an area almost enclosed by Russian troops. Many of the German battalions lost three-fourths of their men; and the remnant of the columns, when they at last reached their own lines, were completely demoralised as a fighting force. They were withdrawn from the front of the battle, to be filled up with new drafts and reorganised.

After Sedan military experts concluded that a large force entirely enveloped by an enemy would do wrong to surrender. It was calculated that if courageously led and strongly handled it could cut its way out with a loss of two-thirds of its number. This is what the Germans did, and their additional losses, bringing up their casualties to two hundred and ten bayonets out of two hundred and eighty in a company, seem to have been due to their early casualties at Piontek. It will be remembered that the Second Austrian Army under General Auffenberg was surrounded by Russky and Ivanoff between the Vistula and Bug Rivers towards the middle of September, 1914. But it

Costly German retreat

also cut its way out through the marshes of the San, with a similar loss of about two-thirds of its effectives.

Altogether, the extraordinary Battle of Strykof was a grave disaster to Hindenburg's main army. The German commander had to ask for more reinforcements, and another six army corps, with five more divisions of cavalry, were thrown into the German lines. It was this arrival in mass, which began on November 25th, that enabled Mackensen to rescue the remnant of his attacking columns at Strykof, and to continue to beat against the Russian front on the Bzura and Lodz line.

The Battle of Strykof

Farther south, at Czestochowa, the Russian front continued between the Warta and Pilica, and from hence on towards Cracow and Tarnov and the Carpathian Mountains. Then far away in the north it ran from the Vistula, some forty or fifty miles in front of Warsaw, and skirted the German frontier of East Prussia at Mlava, and continued through the Masurian Lakes region to the Baltic coast.

By reason of his railway system Hindenburg could make surprise concentrations against any point or points in this far-stretched line. That he intended at any cost to obtain a decision was perfectly apparent; for some part of his new reinforcements had been obtained from the western theatre of war. The German lines in Belgium and France had at last been weakened in order to obtain a decisive result in Russia. There had been rumours of this transfer throughout the war, and Rennenkampf's first campaign in East Prussia had been reported to have caused the Kaiser to alter his plan of campaign. But this was a false statement put about by the German General Staff in order to delude the French Commander-in-Chief. Joffre, as we know, was not deluded; but about the middle of December, 1914, he received information from the Russian Staff that the Germans contemplated weakening the

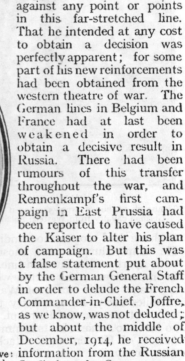

BEHIND A PRUSSIAN BARRICADE.
The Germans in Poland constructed barricades of wood. In the above photograph the German officer is seen about to look through his field-glasses over the barricade for signs of the Russian troops.

forces on his front, and he was also warned that the Russians had found on the field of battle the bodies of men in first-line German units which had apparently formed part of army corps on the Franco-Belgian front. The result was that in mid-December General Joffre published an order indicating his intention of opening a general offensive. This order he cleverly permitted to fall into the enemy's hand. Its effect was remarkable. It stopped the transfer of troops from west to east and held the first-line German armies on the western front.

Hindenburg could not fairly complain of any insufficiency in his forces in the circumstances. He had considerably more men than the Grand Duke Nicholas, and he had his railway system, designed by the elder Moltke for the struggle that was now taking place. But his only strength was his strength of character; he had no constructive imagination, no interplay of intuition and intellect. His one method of attack was a bull-like rush from some point on his railway system.

The fighting that followed the German defeat at Strykof was wild, confused, and disorderly. Hindenburg seemed

GERMAN TRANSPORT ON PACK-HORSES CROSSING THE SNOW-COVERED PLAINS OF POLAND.
Thousands of horses were employed in this arduous service in the winter of 1914-15 with the result that there was a marked disappearance of German cavalry from Western Poland. Our picture was drawn by Mr. Charles W. Simpson, R.I., from the description supplied by an eye-witness.

to have had no method indicating a co-ordinated plan. He simply lunged in a most desperate way at points wide apart on the Russian line. One day he would thrust in on the Bzura ; the next he would lunge out at Prasnysch, a village to the north of Warsaw ; and then, hundreds of miles away, he would try to break the Russian front at Czestochowa, or Petrokof. The Russian Staff went so far as to remark, in its communiqués, on the disconnected nature of Hindenburg's attacks. He was throwing his men away in tens of thousands with no clear aim in view.

It seems as if the iron nerves of the old German drunkard were giving out under the strain of repeated failure. It was, indeed, his Chief of Staff, Ludendorff, who supplied him with the brains for the Russian-Polish campaign. And Mac-

Mackensen as Kaiser's favourite kensen, the leader of the Ninth Army, fighting on the Bzura, became the Emperor's favourite, owing to the unexpected and brilliant way in which he rescued his trapped army corps from Russky's net. But no unexpected and brilliant stroke of strategy could avail Mackensen in the position in which he was. Along the Bzura, and in front of Lodz, the situation was similar to that in the western theatre of war.

The two great armies were now entrenched against each other, on a flat, marshy, muddy country, with their batteries behind them, directed by aeroplanes and observation balloons. The Russians had no occasion to move ; they were defending Warsaw and their lines of communication, and being mostly peasants accustomed to hard winter work, directed by officers with abundant experience of trench warfare in Manchuria, they were, on the whole, more comfortable than any of their Allies. It was for the Germans, if they wished to capture Warsaw,

to advance, and come under the tempest of shrapnel shell and bullets from the Russian line.

Mackensen made continually a series of infantry charges across the muddy No Man's Land between the trenches. In some places the Germans got within two hundred paces of the Russian lines, and hauled their guns within eight hundred yards of the opposing trenches. Their pluck and their determination were magnificent, but, unfortunately for them, the armed peasantry of Russia rose to a height of heroism that even the German in the supreme moment of his valour could not equal. Each attempt at a German advance along the front between Lowicz and Lodz was checked at once by a counter-charge of an incomparable kind.

The state of mind of the fighting peasantry of Russia was abnormal and unique. Nearly all of them were very sincere Christians, with an uncommon humility of soul. They had little or nothing of the aggressive spirit of the ordinary fanatic warrior—of the Arab **Russia's fighting peasantry** fighting under the Sword of God, or of the English Brownist fighting under Cromwell. There was nothing about them of the feudal Crusader, though, like him, they were fighting for their Holy City—Constantinople. These strange peasants, with their kindly communal ways, were a most peculiar mixture of a Christian martyr and a common-sense infantryman. They wanted to die in their grand Holy War, but they did not want to perish before they brought down one or two enemies. Under shell fire they were wonderfully patient, praying most of the time. They did not often joke about " Jack Johnsons " and " saucepans," as the British and French soldiers did, though the Germans brought 11 in. howitzers against the Russian positions on the Bzura. They were very serious and very prayerful, and they did not budge. When the order came to rise and charge, they went forth rather to seek death than to win a victory; but, as they used their rifles with great skill at the same time, they usually accomplished the task set them.

Only at Lask, in the first week of December, did they give ground. Here they were suddenly assaulted by dense columns of Germans secretly concentrated by Hindenburg's Staff. The Russians held out till the afternoon, but were at last forced to retire towards Lodz. But, in the meantime, the Russian Staff had prepared an unusual kind of counter-attack. As night fell, a squadron of armoured motor-cars with machine-guns and quick-firers rushed southward and penetrated the enemy's new line. From their modern war chariots the Russians poured a hail of shrapnel shell and bullets into the German troops and scattered them in all directions. Then the Russian infantry arrived and reoccupied the position.

Within gunshot of Cracow

At the beginning of December, however, the chief Russian armies were still in an awkward position. General Ivanoff won an important victory on the Upper Vistula, which brought him within gunshot of Cracow. With one more great blow he could have opened the gate to Silesia, and compelled Hindenburg's main armies to withdraw and defend their own country. The Russian Commander-in-Chief was therefore inclined to continue the pressure against Cracow, feeding and supplying Ivanoff's troops from Ivangorod. But the tremendously increased pressure of the German forces on the Bzura endangered the Russian scheme. The immediate risk to Warsaw was nothing. Warsaw could be held firmly just a few miles in front of the city, as had been done in October. It was Ivanoff's army which was in peril. If Russky's men had to give ground suddenly — as was quite a likely thing — the Germans would be able to get between Russky and Ivanoff and cut Ivanoff's communications.

The surrender of Lodz

For this reason Russky, in the first week of December, suddenly surrendered Lodz to the enemy without a fight, and withdrew by a night march to a fresh position nearer Warsaw. This was only a veritable strategical retreat. It was carried out in co-operation with General Ivanoff's right flank, before the grand German attack was made. Huge new German forces had been felt on the Bzura, indicating at last clearly what Hindenburg's plan was. He was attacking Russky with the intention of smashing

AT GRIPS WITH DEATH ON THE BZURA: GHASTLY WORK WITH THE BAYONET.
During the German attacks on Warsaw the bayonet fighting was of the most desperate character. Many of the combatants were found locked together in pairs, the one transfixed by the weapon of his opponent. The above picture was drawn by Mr. Charles W. Simpson, R.I., from details given by an eye-witness.

HISTORIC CRACOW: BIRD'S-EYE VIEW OF THE ANCIENT CAPITAL OF THE POLES SHOWING THE DIRECTION OF THE RUSSIAN ADVANCE ON THE CITY.

Ivanoff. The feeble resistance offered to Ivanoff around Cracow was intended to lull him into security until he could be attacked unexpectedly on the right flank, or even taken in reverse.

What made all this manœuvring on a vast scale very difficult was the state of the ground. Though muddy on the surface, it was frozen hard at a depth of a foot. The troops on either side could only make kneeling trenches on the battlefield. It was thus inadvisable to leave a well-prepared and deeply dug position— and, after surrendering **German attack** Lodz, the Russians **near Lowicz** were inclined to stand firm. By December 8th their situation seemed to have improved, so Hindenburg struck out in a fresh direction, and swung two army corps from East Prussia against the railway line connecting Warsaw with Petrograd. This was a further menace to the main line of communications of the Russian army. But when the German force reached Prasnysch it was so fiercely attacked that it was forced to entrench, and then its trenches were stormed, and it was thrown back over the Prussian frontier at Soldau.

All this, however, was only a diversion. It masked the further reinforcement of Mackensen's army on the Bzura-Lodz front; and at the beginning of the second week in December the Germans made a terrific attempt to break through the Russian lines near Lowicz. On some days there were seven attacks in twenty-four hours, delivered by columns in solid formation, advancing at point-blank range of the Russian position. The terrible onsets continued, day and night, for more than a week, and on December 17th Berlin and Vienna were beflagged, and German school children had a holiday. It was announced that, after a most desperate battle, the Russians were everywhere retreating and being vigorously pursued.

A few days afterwards, however, the German General Staff, which had sent the news of the great victory, rebuked the German and Austrian public for rejoicing before the battle was won. All **Rearrangement** that had really hap- **of Russian lines** pened was that the Grand Duke Nicholas had begun to rearrange the Russian lines on a purely defensive system. The threat to General Ivanoff's line of communication had become more apparent. For more than a week an army of peasants, directed by Russian engineers, had been digging into the frozen ground beneath the Polish mud. The new lines ran from the Bzura along its tributary the Rawka. Thence they continued over some hills to the Pilica River, and from the Pilica they extended to the Nida stream, and then across the Vistula to the Dunajec.

AUSTRIA'S COMMANDER-IN-CHIEF.
General Conrad von Hoetzendorf in the field, in conversation with a German officer.

Most of the Russian armies were thus moated as well as entrenched against the invaders. It was no wonder that the German Staff discounted the victories it had announced when the strength of the Russian position was seen. By giving up the attack on Cracow and withdrawing towards Ivangorod, General Ivanoff linked up at last strongly with Russky's troops on his right and Radko Dmitrieff's men on his left. Hindenburg had lost his chance. The Russians were now even more strongly entrenched than their Allies in the western theatre of war.

Their vast river system of defences, stretching from Ilov on the Lower Vistula to Tarnov in Galicia, was the most formidable series of military works ever constructed in the heat of action. It was to cost the Germans and Austrians half a million men merely to discover that the Russian lines were impregnable.

All the principal disadvantages now lay with the Germans. They were farther away from their railway-heads and struggling in a land of mud and rain. When they attacked they had to entrench feverishly before the Russian positions, and while they were digging at the hard ground the Russian guns slaughtered them. In addition to their slow and laborious cartage of food and munitions, they needed bridging

material at many of the points where they attacked, and the men fell in such large numbers that the army doctors and nurses could not tend the wounded. At the fording places on the Polish river front the streams were often dammed by the dead bodies of the invaders. The ghastly horrors and searing miseries of Hindenburg's troops in the winter of 1914 were unparalleled in modern history. To the Kaiser the second Russian campaign must have been almost as terrible as Napoleon's retreat from Moscow.

But the Germans could not retreat. They had to fight on until they were exhausted. For the confessed failure of a retreat would at once have brought Rumania and Italy into the field. The extreme desperation of the efforts made by the German commanders to obtain a decision was indicated by the appearance of the Divisions of Death. The best German regiments were picked out and brigaded into forlorn hopes, every man in them knowing that he was practically doomed. And they died heroically, but in vain. Our officers and men at Ypres had remarked upon the extraordinary access of courage in their attackers. **The " Divisions of** They ceased to fight with the prudence **Death "** and individual skill that usually distinguish the civilised man. Instead, they came on in lines in a dervish-like charge, trying to choke our rifles and guns in a blind, gregarious, maddened rush. It was a sort of disciplined mob-valour, in which the real spirit of modern Germany, created by the all-absorbing machinery of State organisation, was fully displayed. Most of the regular troops, carefully trained to individual effort by manœuvres in which a battalion was taught to go on fighting when all its officers were out of action, had been shattered. The principal fighting forces of Germany now consisted of troops of the second and third line, who were moved by the instinct to collective action which had been fostered by their semi-socialistic system of government.

This way of fighting had been a special Russian characteristic. The armed moujik, with his traditions of village communism, had always fought at his best when he felt his neighbour close to him. He was not so formidable when fighting in widely-extended formation as when packed behind a trench two to a yard, or when closing for a desperate charge. He still used the bayonet more frequently than did the

AUSTRIAN AMMUNITION SLEIGH.
The whiz of a bullet had come so near the shaggy-haired pony just before the photograph was taken that the animal was quivering with fear. The sleigh was taking ammunition to the Austrian trenches.

COSSACKS IN ACTION TAKING COVER BEHIND THE BODIES OF THEIR HORSES.
Cossacks train their horses to lend all possible aid in warfare and to remain motionless under gun fire.

Sochachev, where they defended the high-road and railway to Warsaw.

Before them was the stream of the Bzura, one hundred and fifty feet wide, running between clay banks thirty feet high, with wooded shores. On the night of December 22nd the Germans simultaneously attacked at six points along the river, and at five places their columns, wading through the fords or crossing by pontoons, were destroyed, with the loss of thousands of men. But at Sochachev a brigade of Würtembergers, brought from the Yser in Flanders, got across the river, and drove the two new Russian regiments back along the Warsaw road. The little Russian force divided; one regiment crept forward on the right, the other crept forward on the left. They were no longer soldiers; they were hunters. They caught the Würtembergers on both flanks and shot them down; those who were not shot or bayoneted were drowned in the river. Little more than five hundred of the Würtembergers remained alive when the Russian infantryman and the Russian gunner had done

British soldier, instead of relying upon the deadlier—if well-directed—stream of bullets from his magazine rifle.

But along the Bzura, where the Divisions of Death tried to break through all Christmas week, there was a new type of Russian—the Siberian. This splendid rifleman was, so to speak, the Canadian or Australian of the Russian Empire. He had the individuality and self-reliance of the adventurous colonial and backwoodsman. The ancient traditions of village communism had no hold upon him; he stood on his own feet and saw things with his own eyes, the practical result of which was that he was a magnificent rifleman. Associated with him were marksmen from the hunting region of Russia. At one spot on the Bzura there were two regiments of recruits from the sporting district of Pskoff. They had only just completed their training and came fresh into the battle near

Siberia's splendid riflemen

WITH THE AUTOMOBILE SECTION OF THE RUSSIAN ARMY.
A rest and a meal by the way in a pleasant corner of Poland before the winter set in. The smaller view shows graves of Russian soldiers of the Greek and Roman Catholic Churches and the different crosses afford interesting evidence of religious toleration on the part of our Slav Allies. The Greek symbol has three cross-pieces.

with them. Those who escaped with their lives only did so by becoming prisoners.

At the same time a tremendous conflict raged incessantly farther up the Bzura, at Bolimoff on the Rawka, and at Inovlodz on the Pilica, a few miles below Tomaszov. When the main effort failed on the Bzura, the struggle at Inovlodz became extremely violent. It can only be compared with the battle at Ypres at the close of October. The forces engaged were larger on both sides at Inovlodz than at Ypres, and the unmitigated fury of attack and counter-attack continued for a longer period, for each side threw in fresh troops as the men in the fighting-line became worn out. In this section of the battlefield the German attempts to obtain a decision went on fiercely to the end of December. Inovlodz

GERMAN SOLDIERS IN A SNOW-COVERED TRENCH IN POLAND.
The centre man was about to fire at the moment the photograph was taken.

was the connecting-point between the army of Russky and the army of Ivanoff. This was why the Germans assailed it with such terrible persistency, pouring out fresh troops for the attack from Kalisz. At the same time the main front of Ivanoff's force was also assailed, and he was forced to give ground at Kielce at the close of the month.

But there was no break in the Russian lines. On the contrary, the Grand Duke Nicholas recovered the power of offensive on the Bzura. Towards the end of December he had a large force on the German side of the river, and there can be little doubt that if he had so wished he could then have forced the Germans to retreat; for the enemy had lost from 150,000 to 200,000 men on the Bzura section alone. And the German troops there knew they were defeated, for they had received, direct from the Kaiser, the **"Give us Warsaw! Or take Berlin!"** order to take Warsaw by Christmas. It was nearly a week after Christmas; they could see with their own eyes the shattered condition of their ranks, and their feelings were well known to the Russians. In their last despairing attack they had screamed as they ran: "Give us Warsaw! Or take Berlin!" They wanted the war to end, and they did not much care how it ended.

Yet the Grand Duke Nicholas refrained from a grand counter-attack. He had got the Germans where he wanted

COSSACK OUTPOST IN ACTION IN THE SNOW-COVERED GALICIAN PLAINS.
In the small photograph we get another interesting glimpse of the way in which rifle ammunition was conveyed during the winter to the Russian trenches along the Galician battle-front.

them to remain for months—in the middle of Poland, far away from their railheads, with a difficult series of rivers to cross. He did not want as yet to get to Thorn, Posen, or Berlin; more particularly he did not want to force the main German army back again on its railways, while his own troops lengthened the distance between themselves and their railway-head at Warsaw. So he left the exhausted

Dankl's army driven back

Germans in comparative peace, having immobilised them for the winter under very harsh, wearing conditions, mitigated only by the use the Germans were able to make of the Lower Vistula for river transport service.

It was at the Austrians that the Russian Commander-in-Chief struck. On December 28th General Dankl's army attempted to help the exhausted main German forces by crossing the Nida near its junction with the Upper Vistula above Tarnov. But at this point the Russians were suddenly reinforced by a number of very gallant troops, who swam the icy stream, caught the attacking army on the flank, and drove it back with heavy loss, ten thousand Austrians being captured. About this time, when Radko Dimitrieff was operating thus successfully round Tarnov, General Brussiloff resumed his aggressive movement in Galicia. His army was fed and munitioned from Kieff, and nearly all the railway system of Galicia was at his

LAYING A NEW MOTOR-TRACK.
The motor-track illustrated was made over the mud by the automobile section of the Russian Army. The pine-logs forming the surface of the track were brought up in the special carts seen in the background.

still farther eastward, General Brussiloff's army held out against a large Austro-Hungarian force, under the command of an Arab general—Ben Ermolli.

Ben Ermolli's main offensive movement was directed in December towards the relief of Przemysl. He reached Grybov, Krosno, Sanok, and Lisko, his lines running through these towns, forming a wedge driven in between the army of Dimitrieff and that of Brussiloff. At the same time he assailed Dimitrieff furiously from the east along the line of the Dunajec and the Biala. But the hero of Bulgaria was more than a match for the Teutonised Arab. He broke him on the Dunajec in Christmas week in the most brilliant of the smaller actions in the eastern theatre of war. Nearly thirty thousand Austrian and Hungarian troops were taken prisoners, with many of their guns; and by the opening of the New Year the Russian armies in Galicia were ready for the aggressive action planned by the Grand Duke Nicholas and his Staff.

Cracow had become practically impregnable. The gate-

RUSSIAN SEARCHLIGHT CAR UNDERGOING REPAIRS.
Specially-designed searchlight cars were employed in the Russian Army. The particular car shown in the above photograph was dismantled for temporary repairs to be made. Its complicated appearance suggests the great strain placed by active service upon the mechanicians responsible for its efficiency.

service for troop manœuvres and the distribution of supplies. He had only about a quarter of a million men, but their fighting value was enhanced by the service of railways, and General Brussiloff was able to detach a large force under General Selivanoff for the investment of Przemysl.

Przemysl, however, was of no immediate importance. It commanded the railway leading past Tarnov to Cracow, and if Radko Dimitrieff's army at Tarnov had been attacking Cracow the railway would have been badly needed. But General Ivanoff's army had been compelled to retire some fifty miles north of Cracow, so the smaller force under Radko Dimitrieff could not do anything against Cracow from the east. It withdrew from the upper course of the Dunajec River and entrenched along its more westerly tributary, the Biala. From the Biala the Russian line stretched to the Dukla Pass in the snow-covered Carpathian Mountains. All along the lower valleys of the Carpathians,

way to Silesia was closed. Thus Hindenburg had achieved one of his main objects. He had forced the central Russian armies back, and prevented Germany being half crippled by the loss of one of her two mining and industrial centres. It had cost him 600,000 men merely to produce a deadlock of trench warfare about midway in the vast bend of the Vistula. Terrible as was the price for a half success of this sort, it may have been worth it from the German point of view. For there can be little doubt that if General Ivanoff and General Russky had fought and won the battle for Silesia in November, 1914, on the field they selected in front of Cracow, their continued forward movement would have brought Italy and Rumania into the struggle. Austria and Hungary would have been assailed by overwhelming forces from three sides, and when Austria-Hungary fell, the overthrow of Germany would have been imminent.

Hindenburg had at least prevented all **Hindenburg's grand** this, and though his grand counter- **counter-attack** attack had failed to break the Russian lines, it had political consequences of high importance.

One consequence was that the Russian Commander-in-Chief selected Hungary as the next object of attack. His new plan was to bring direct pressure to bear upon Vienna and Budapest, and force first the Hungarians and then the Austrians to sue for peace. If they did not accept the terms of the Triple Entente, the Russian action would have the effect of moving Italy and Rumania to invade the territory of their traditional enemies.

In these circumstances opened the long, terrible, and extraordinary Battle of the Carpathians, which remained for many months the crisis of the Great War. The Russians began with numbers against them but with a favourable position. They advanced on the Dukla Pass on Christmas Day, when the Austrians were still reeling from the blows delivered against them on the Dunajec and the Nida. The Russians only reached the mouth of the pass, but this was sufficient for their immediate purpose. All the way from the Dukla valley westward they then had Ben Ermolli's troops at a disadvantage. The Austro-Hungarian Army had first driven over the mountains the Cossack raiders who had begun to ravage the Hungarian plain. Then the main force of the enemy had won most of the passes and debouched from the

AUSTRIAN PRISONERS AND THEIR RUSSIAN GUARDS FRATERNISING AT LEMBERG.

FRIENDLY WRESTLING MATCH BETWEEN RUSSIAN SOLDIERS AND AUSTRIAN PRISONERS OF WAR.

of Galician railways at his service. From his new depot towns of Tarnopol and Lemberg he had two trunk lines with a series of cross-country tracks, each leading to the principal valley passes. To him the task of suddenly collecting artillery munition for a surprise attack at any point was an easy affair. It could be carried out in a few hours. In the same way his troops could be manœuvred by train over long distances and come fresh into the fight, while the Austro-Hungarian columns were separated from each other by inaccessible mountains.

Battle of the Carpathians

They could not concentrate quickly or manœuvre. The attacking front could only be strengthened slowly by reinforcing it from the Hungarian plain.

So long as General Brussiloff had fewer men than his opponent commanded he was loath to advance to the summits of the Carpathians. Had he done so he would have lost the advantage of his railway system, and been compelled to divide his troops into columns, wedged for the most part in the mountain valleys. His chief object in the first six weeks of the Battle of the Carpathians

valleys as far as the line on which the towns of Sanok and Lisko stood.

General Brussiloff withdrew his men without offering battle, and allowed Ben Ermolli to occupy the foothills. This occurred on December 21st, with the result that when General Brussiloff resumed the offensive at the end of the month the Austro-Hungarian troops were in great difficulties. For between them and their depots of supplies was the high barrier of the wintry Carpathians. All their food and munitions had to be conveyed from Hungary over the passes. When they lost the low, easy Dukla Pass on Christmas Day, the provisioning of the troops became a slow and arduous business. The Russians had, naturally, destroyed the mountain railways during their raid in the autumn, and in some places there were six feet of snow in the river gorges that cut through the mighty wall of rock.

General Brussiloff, on the other hand, had the well-articulated system

SOME OF THE TSAR'S MILLIONS ABOUT TO ENTRAIN FOR THE FRONT.

RUSSIAN GUNS AWAITING TRANSPORT TO THE FIRING-LINE.
The guns and their limbers were swathed in straw to hide them from the eyes of enemy aviators, and the snow helped to make the disguise more effective.

was to disturb the Hungarians with the threat of invasion, while continuing to fight mainly on the Galician slopes of the mountains, with his railways immediately behind him.

Here it was that the famous fortress of Przemysl (pronounced *Pshemissle*, "rz" standing for "sh") served the turn of the Russians. There were in it 130,000 Austrian, Hungarian, and German troops, under General von Kusmarek. They had more than 2,000 pieces of artillery, many of which could have been used in field warfare, and their stores of munitions were enormous. Thus the relief of Przemysl would have brought into the battlefield of Galicia a very powerful Teuton-Magyar force, which was being wasted in defending a single railway junction which had become of secondary importance. Being well acquainted with all these facts, General Brussiloff made no attack upon the fortressed garden city of the Carpathians.

Investment of Przemysl

Under his orders General Selivanoff entrenched the Russian troops on a circle of hills, beyond the range of the 12 in. howitzers of Przemysl. The Russian commander could have obtained in January, 1915, a siege train of heavy howitzers from Russia. But he did not want them. They were kept for use in Russia until the beginning of March. The army of investment relied entirely upon its ordinary

INHABITANTS OF A POLISH VILLAGE WATCHING THE BURSTING OF A GERMAN SHELL.
A Russian soldier is pointing to the spot where the shrapnel is bursting. Inset: An open-air granary by the side of a strategic railway. The bags contained flour destined to form rations for part of the Russian forces.

RUSSIAN GUNS IN ACTION NEAR WARSAW.
Some of the gunners are seen holding their hands over their ears to lessen the effect of the concussion.

field artillery which it directed, not at the forts of the fortress city, but at all the valley paths by which the garrison could attempt a sortie.

Famine was the weapon of reduction which the Russian commander employed.. All his trenches and gun positions were solely designed to drive the garrison back to the city whenever they attempted to escape. Extraordinary as the statement may seem, General Brussiloff did not appear to want Przemysl to fall during the winter months. He had fixed its fall for the spring, and until then the Russian siege train could be used to strengthen Osoviec and other weak spots on the Polish front of the Russian armies.

When March came, the Russians were certain of receiving large and continual supplies of munitions and general war equipment. This would enable them to put another million or more men into the field, and also to prosecute their attack with more vigour. Then it would be possible to advance from the Galician railway system and engage in the decisive struggle on the summit of the Carpathians. But until the Russians were fully equal in number and war material to their enemies, it was necessary for them to keep the Austrians fighting on the Galician slopes. So Przemysl was held out as a lure to the Austro-Hungarian Army. All through the winter and into the spring the enemy had to assail the Russian lines, under increasing difficulties as to the transport of their supplies over the mountain

TRYING TO KEEP THEMSELVES WARM.
Russian soldiers clad in heavy coats with hoods over their heads and straw around the trenches to temper the bitter cold of the wind and snow.

passes. Every movement they made was easily countered by General Brussiloff and General Radko Dimitrieff. The Austrian Commander-in-Chief maintained communications with Przemysl by means of daily aeroplane flights, and usually arranged for the garrison to make a sortie whenever the relieving army swept down the mountain valleys in an attempt to pierce the Russian line. But though the Przemysl garrison lost forty thousand men in trying to break through the ring of General Selivanoff's hill trenches, not a battalion cut its way through.

Losses of the Przemysl garrison

The slaughter of the relieving forces was more dreadful and equally vain. Neither from the Cracow side, where General Dimitrieff barred the way, nor from the southward side, where General Brussiloff dammed every mountain valley, could the Austro-Hungarian armies break through to the relief of Przemysl.

WITH THE RUSSIAN RED CROSS SERVICE IN WINTER.
Like the Germans, the Russians utilised sleighs in Poland for the purpose of conveying wounded to the hospital bases.

By the end of January the situation of Austria-Hungary had become difficult. The troops of the Dual Monarchy were exhausted by the dreadful severity of winter mountain warfare. Their transport service over the heights was often disarranged by snowstorms, and the condition of many of the wounded was horrible in the wild, desperate scenes of struggle far removed from the Hungarian railway system. Seldom in the history of warfare has the advantage of position been used to better account than by General Brussiloff when he left the Austrians in possession of most of the passes of the Carpathians in order to check, endanger, and slacken their supplies of food and munitions. Whenever they weakened

Budapest talks to Berlin in attack he pushed his light artillery forward from the railway and bombarded the mouths of the mountain passes. This forced them to counter-attack to prevent the invasion of Hungary. Then, as winter softened into spring, the clamour for help from Przemysl increased, as the store of food there grew smaller and smaller. The Austrians, therefore, had to maintain a series of attacks over the mountain rampart, until the continual heavy attrition of their forces incapacitated them from any further attempt.

This condition of things was reached about the first week in February. As it approached there was much intercourse between the leading statesmen of Budapest and Berlin. Count Tisza had a long interview with the Kaiser Wilhelm, and the Kaiser Wilhelm travelled to Schönbrunn Castle to talk matters over with Kaiser Franz Josef. Count Tisza, the Hungarian Dictator, was the dominating figure in all the discussions. What he wanted was half a million first-rate German troops to continue the Battle of the Carpathians and defend the Hungarian plain, with its immense stretches of winter wheat, from invasion. His view was that if Germany would not or could not help in the protection of Hungary, after wasting the flower of Hungarian chivalry in the plains of Poland, then the Hungarians would be compelled to save the food resources of their country by making terms with Russia.

In regard to the Austrians, whose interests were also represented by Count Tisza, they were in a similar situation.

By making terms with Russia they would not only save their land from ravage, but they would escape loss of territory to Italy. In fact, as things stood, with Rumania ready to pounce upon Hungary, and Italy ready to pounce upon Austria, a separate peace with the Powers of the Triple Entente was the best expedient in the circumstances. Some hundreds of thousands of Austrians and Hungarians had fallen in defence of the Prussian territory of Silesia —a Prussian territory, by the way, which had been taken by force from an Austrian Empress by a Prussian King.

The Germans hesitated. In the first week of September they sent a few army corps to the Carpathian front, but some time passed before they despatched the great number of fresh troops needed to resist the increasing pressure of General Brussiloff's army. In the meantime Field-Marshal von Hindenburg, who naturally disliked having to meet the Russians at a disadvantage in the mountains, tried to force the issue, on ground of his own choosing, by a new plan of attack.

His scheme was simple and effective in principle. The lines of the main Russian armies ran in a large curve from Warsaw towards Czernovitz. The Russians attacked from the central parts of this curve. It was in the centre that they were strongest. At the ends of the curve, near Warsaw and near Czernovitz, were vital railway communications, where a blow against them would tell most heavily. In the struggle on the Bzura Hindenburg had tried to take Warsaw by **Attack on Prasnysch** a frontal attack. His new plan was to **and Stanislav** make a swerving movement against both ends of the Russian lines. The village of Prasnysch, north of Warsaw, and the railway junction of Stanislav, south-east of Lemberg, were the points he aimed at. He sent an army into East Prussia to advance in two columns past Prasnysch, force the passage of the Narew, cross the Bug River, and cut the trunk railway between Warsaw and Petrograd. About the same time he launched another army over the easternmost Carpathians into Bukovina, on the Rumanian frontier, to fight its way towards Stanislav. This new operation was conducted while the main battle in the Carpathians raged with increasing fury.

NOVEL FORM OF AMBULANCE USED BY THE RUSSIAN RED CROSS SERVICE.
Where sleighs were unprocurable the Russians removed their wounded by means of a kind of sledge made of some half-dozen ski-sticks lashed together, with layers of straw or twigs on top. These ski-sledges were drawn by stout leathern thongs fastened to the belts of the bearers.

CHAPTER LVI.

THE RESURGENCE OF SERBIA AND THE RESISTANCE OF RUSSIA.

How the Austrian Second Army of Invasion Failed—Siege Warfare Along the Frontier Heights—Serbian Artillery Munitions Give Out—Retreat to the Central Mountains—Serbians Half Demoralised for Lack of a Helping Hand—France to the Rescue—Arrival of Ammunition and More Guns—Austrian Commander Over-confident and Neglectful—Brilliant Strategy of General Putnik and His Staff—General Mishitch Attacks Unexpectedly with a Beaten Army—Austrian Centre Surprised and Routed—Serbs Envelop the Austrian Centre and Southern Wing—Panic Flight of 150,000 Invaders—Most of them Killed or Taken—Serbs Concentrate Against Northern Austrian Wing—The Battle of Belgrade—How the Hungarian Division was Captured—New Austro-Hungarian Army Collected—Russia Interferes and Attracts this New Hostile Force—Battles in Bukovina—How the Divisions of Death Went to Their Doom—Great German Army Sweeps from East Prussia—Magnificent Stand by Russian Twentieth Corps—The Encirclers Encircled at Prasnysch—Defeat of Hindenburg's Plan and Resumption of Carpathian Battle.

WHILE the great struggle was going on between Slav and Teuton in Poland and Galicia, the position of the Serbians became of great importance to the Russians. For it was largely owing to a magnificently successful diversion made by the little Serb nation in December, 1914, that the great Slav Empire was able to make headway against the furious, desperate efforts of Germany and Austria - Hungary. On the other hand, the Russians were also able to help the Serbs at the most critical moment in Serbian history, in spite of the fact that they were hundreds of miles away from Serbia. On no field of the conflict was the subtle and comprehensive system of co-operation among the Allies so clearly displayed as in the central Serbian mountains at midwinter in 1914.

The entry of Turkey into the war, in the first week of November, 1914, endangered the position which the Serbians had heroically maintained. Twice had the Austrians attempted to conquer them. The first invasion in August had ended in the terrible Austrian defeat on the Drina, which we have already fully described. The second invasion began on September 8th, when six Austrian army corps were held up in the mountains and marshes west of the Drina, and round the

KING PETER OF SERBIA.
A portrait taken in January, 1915.

mountain of Matchkokanen, a few miles south of the town of Krupanje. At a cost of over thirty thousand men the splendid fighting peasantry of Serbia repulsed the invaders on Matchkokanen, or Cat's Leg Mountain, which was lost and regained eight times before it was at last firmly held by the defending army. Grave as were the Serbian losses, they were less than those inflicted upon the Austrians, and the second invasion ended in the Austrians entrenching by the Drina and maintaining a system of trench warfare similar to that which the Germans had started on the Aisne heights. The Austrians had only two footholds on Serbian territory, while the left wing of the Serbian forces was operating in Bosnia, on a mountain range to the north of the fortress town of Sarajevo.

The series of heavy defeats which the small Serbian nation inflicted upon its mighty adversary, who had brought about the Great War by an attempt to rob Serbia of the advantages she won fairly in the Balkan struggle, were bitter blows to the pride of the Hungarian aristocracy and to all the Teutonic people of Austria. Nothing more clearly revealed to the world the military weakness of the large, uncemented mosaic of empire known as Austria-Hungary. The smashing victories won by Russia in Galicia and in the Lublin district could be explained on the ground of the

SERBIAN CONTINGENT CROSSING THE RIVER SAVE NEAR BELGRADE.

THE WATCH ON THE RIVER SAVE, ON SERBIA'S NORTHERN FRONTIER.

overwhelming numbers of the Russian armies. But in regard to the disasters in Serbia, nothing could be said to explain them away. *Res ipsa per se vociferat ;* the fact itself shouted its meaning. And the German openly despised his ally by reason thereof.

So when Turkey entered the war, and Hindenburg planned his great counter-offensive against Warsaw for the protection of Silesia, measures were taken with a view to wiping out the shame of Shabatz, and settling the entire problem of the Balkans. The intention was to launch an overwhelming force in a third invasion of Serbia and conquer all the country. Then, from the valley of the Morava, the railway to Salonica would be acquired, and, with a little pressure on Greece, the forces of Turkey would be able to unite with those of Austria-Hungary. Bulgaria would be won over completely, with the result that the Rumanians would also be terrorised into a benevolent neutrality.

Serbia was thus the key to all the problems of the Balkans, and the overthrow of its heroic little people would be a deadlier stroke for Russia than the occupation of Belgium was for France and Britain. So important, indeed, was the success of the third invasion that a large number of troops was detached for the operation, at a time when every Austrian and Hungarian soldier was needed against the Russian armies. General Potiorek, the Austro-Hungarian Commander, was

226

given 300,000 troops for action against the Serbians. Bosnia was almost stripped of its garrisons, an army corps was removed from the Italian frontier, and fresh drafts were sent to the troops on the Drina.

The condition of the fatigued and battered Serbian Army was such as to justify the wildest hopes of the enemy. The Serbs had been caught unprepared for war. They had barely enough rifles for their men in the fighting-line, and their reserves only came into action as the rifles of their dead and wounded comrades were available. The Serbian light field artillery was excellent in wearing quality and in handiness, but it was dominated by the heavy siege-guns of the Austrians brought up along the Drina. The main trouble with the little Serbian Army was ammunition. In the last four years the Army had fought first against Turkey, then against Bulgaria, and twice against Austria-Hungary. It had not had time to recover from the Balkan wars before it was attacked by one of the great military empires of the world. Its small arsenal could not meet the strain, and during the trench warfare on the Drina, in September and October, 1914, the Serbian supply of ammunition completely ran out.

Serbian Army's main trouble

It was this fact that stimulated the twice-beaten Austro-Hungarians to make a supreme effort to conquer the Serbian Army, and crush the Serbian people by systematic

THE SPIRITED DEFENCE OF BELGRADE.
Serbian artillery about to fire on the attacking Austrians from an entrenched position on the outskirts of the Serbian capital.

AT WORK IN A SERBIAN FIELD HOSPITAL.

atrocities eclipsing all that the Germans had done in Belgium and Northern France. In vain did the British Government attempt to help their weakened and almost disarmed little ally, by inducing Greece to come to the help of Serbia. Sir Edward Grey offered the Greek Premier large territories in Asia Minor, including the coast from behind Chios to Rhodes, when the resettlement was made after the war. But the King of the Hellenes was too much afraid of what Turkey would do before it was dismembered, to dare to fight for his old comrades-in-arms, the Serbs, and for a future Greek Empire in Asia Minor. The extraordinary generosity of the British proposal was indeed regarded generally as a sign of the extreme desperation of the Powers of the Triple Entente. It only lent deeper colour to the wild rumours concerning the effect that the entry of Turkey into the war was having upon the fortunes of the Allies.

Britain's offer to Greece

All that France and Britain could do they did. Their own campaign in the western theatre of war was slackened, some time after the repulse of the Germans at Ypres, in order to save ammunition for the use of the Serbs. Large supplies of French material of war were shipped across the Mediterranean and sent up from the Balkan coast to Nish, arriving on the front in the first week of December. Meanwhile the Serbian Commander-in-Chief, General Putnik,

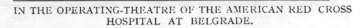

IN THE OPERATING-THEATRE OF THE AMERICAN RED CROSS HOSPITAL AT BELGRADE.

and his tattered and outworn army tasted to the full the bitterness of an approaching overwhelming national defeat. For six weeks the Serbs had been holding nearly all their frontier line, including the rich and fertile plain of Machva, between the Drina and the Save. With the coming of winter their trenches in the Machva plain became full of water, and their thin line, outstretched far beyond its strength, could not resist the pressure of the new forces brought against it.

General Putnik was compelled to order a retreat to the mountains, especially as there was no ammunition for the guns. The retreat was not carried out in good order. The Serbian infantryman was one of the finest in Europe; but he had been put to an ordeal beyond his strength. Owing to the overwhelming power of the Austrian artillery and the incessant charges of the Austrian infantry in the last weeks of the trench warfare, the Serbian soldiers had had to fight day and night without sleeping For their reserves still lacked rifles, and the 300,000 Austrians attacked furiously all along the frontier from Orsova to Visegrad. The Serb could have died where he stood, but when he was ordered to rise and make a long march back to the mountains he completely lost heart.

DR. DONNELLY AND SIR THOMAS LIPTON AT A SERBIAN VILLAGE HOSPITAL.
Dr. Donnelly, a heroic American, died of typhus while trying to relieve the sick.

His rearguards could not hold back the enemy. They swept over the frontier and converged upon the important town of Valievo, commanding the roads to Belgrade Obrenovac, and other strategical points. By the capture of Valievo, on November 11th, the Austrian commander surmounted the first series of mountain barriers which formed the natural defences of Serbia, and planted the centre of his great army in the middle of the Serbian highlands. At the same time he swung his right wing over the heights far to the south, where his mountain brigades outflanked the Serbian wing. Ridge after ridge was lost by the Serbs, who grew more demoralised as the superior numbers and irresistible artillery power of the enemy pressed them back continually.

All along the line the Serbs gave way. Their centre was thrown back on the Kolubara River on November 20th, and on November 28th the great part of the mountain defences, including the passes of the Suvobor heights, were stormed or turned by the invaders. Belgrade, the capital of Serbia, had fallen, and the line of the Austrian advance stretched for seventy miles from the Danube towards Cacac, or Chachak, in the Western Morava valley.

On December 1st the weakening Serbian Army held only the rocky wedge between the Morava valleys. In the middle of this wedge was the arsenal town of Kragujevatz, defended on the north-west by the Rudnik ridge, with peaks rising from 3,000 to 4,500 feet. Some fifteen miles westward of the Rudnik ridge was another high and snow-buried tract of mountain, the Maljen ridge. Then between the Rudnik and the Maljen extended the lower heights of Suvobor, over which ran the passes to Cacac and Kragujevatz.

The disaster of Suvobor

The ground at Suvobor rose in fold after fold to a height of 2,000 feet. It was the gateway into the central highlands of Serbia, and the First Serbian Army had surrendered it to the enemy almost without a blow and withdrawn to the lower slopes. All the ridges of Maljen westward were also lost to the Serbs on November 25th, and the Fourth Army was retreating up the valley of the Western Morava. Far to the south, along the railway leading to Salonica, by which the Serbians usually received their supplies, armed bands of Moslems and other insurgents broke their line of communication with the outer

world, preparatory to an advance by the Turks and Bulgarians against their helpless and stricken common foe of former days.

In these circumstances the Serbian peasant began, by a marvellous power of recoil, to recover his confidence. The weakness of the First Army had led to the grave disaster of Suvobor. But the soldiers were only worn out by want of sleep and dismayed by lack of ammunition, after holding the marshlands of Machva against the heavy Austrian artillery. During their retreat they had at least been able to sleep off their physical weariness; for the Austrian advance over the mountains had been remarkably slow. With this restoration to ordinary fitness, the astonishing character of the Serbian people in the hour of their apparent doom was fully displayed.

They were the least Slavlike of all the Slav races. In their ancient descent into the Balkans they had absorbed a large number of Celts occupying the highlands. The result was that they lost the stolidity that marks the Russian and Bulgarian, and acquired a natural light-heartedness and vivacity which made them the Irishmen of the Balkans. They had also quite an Irish zest for fighting. First of all the Christian people of the Balkans they had risen in open revolt against the Turks, in 1804, winning their independence after a terrible struggle that lasted thirteen years. They gained their freedom with their own hands, and all that the great Powers of Christendom afterwards did for them was to rob them of territory to increase the dominions of the German Prince of Bulgaria, and to block their trade routes and fight them down with tariff walls.

Serbia's power of recoil

Serbia had thus learnt, for a hundred and ten years, to rely only on her own strength of soul. Her peasants had a well-founded contempt for the veneer of good manners of the great neighbouring Christian nations. When they had a bad king and a bad queen they killed them without formality, and found in the exiled survivor of their older dynasty, King Peter, the military leader they needed in their difficult situation. In our country the rough-and-ready regicides of the Balkans were for

IF ENGLAND WERE INVADED—WHAT SHE MIGHT SUFFER AT THE HANDS OF THE HUN.
Serbia's sufferings are comparable to those of Belgium. The soldiers of the Emperor Franz Josef rivalled the troops of the Prussian Kaiser in their ruthless brutality. Save for the bodies of massacred civilians lying in the foreground, the above photograph might be of a peaceful English village. Actually it is a camera-record of the trail of death left by the Austrians in their retreat from Belgrade.

WITH THE SERBIAN ARMY IN THE FIELD—AN INTERVAL OF NEEDED REST.

The soldier in the centre of the photograph is displaying a Hungarian flag, a trophy of a recent engagement in which it was captured from the 32nd Regiment. Seated on the ground are some soldiers of that regiment who had been taken prisoners by the Serbians. These men do not appear much concerned as to their fate

some years regarded as the scandal of the world. We could not appreciate the perils of Austrian domination from which the Serbs had temporarily escaped by a sudden stroke at their bad king. Russia was ready to advance the cause of the independent mountaineers when they had freed themselves from Austrian influence, but the Russians could not give the Serbians the aid they needed. It was the Republicans of France who helped most, and by financing Serbia and supplying her with first-rate artillery had done much to ensure her triumph over the Turks and the Bulgarians. The admirable light French guns greatly assisted in the first smashing defeat of the Austrians, and, until the fall of Belgrade, the capital of Serbia was defended by a few French heavy guns worked by French artillerymen. To France the Serbians looked for aid in the days of their extreme peril in November 1914, and by a masterly effort some new batteries and twenty thousand shells

How France saved Serbia

were transported from France to the Adriatic coast, and thence to the Serbian highlands in the last days of November.

By this means France saved Serbia. For though the Serbian Army of 200,000 men was ravaged by typhus and other infectious diseases, and the few hospitals were so choked with wounded that injured soldiers went home with their wounds undressed to perish, or died in the streets, the fighting spirit of the heroic highlanders was not broken. The roads along which they fought and manœuvred were blocked by hundreds of thousands of fugitives, terrorised by the awful atrocities committed by the victorious armies of invasion. The winter weather in the mountains was very rigorous and severely tried the retreating Serbian troops, when their supply columns were put out of working order by the block of fugitives and by the sudden and unexpected movements of the defeated troops.

But the Serb had a remarkable strength of physique

and a still more remarkable resilience of soul. When the rumour ran through the ranks that the guns had been supplied with French ammunition, the infantry took heart and resolved to die fighting. Old King Peter came into the foremost firing-line in front of the Suvobor ridge, in order, if need be, to fall in the foremost line of the defence. It was a fine, picturesque act on the part of the King, who knew his people well, and understood the effect his attitude would have upon them. He was the grandson of Black George, the Serb shepherd, who had freed his country in 1804. When King Peter in his old age showed himself ready to die in the front trenches, battling against the new oppressors of Serbia, his attitude fired his soldiers with a flame of heroism that nothing else could have kindled.

The leaders of the Serbian forces were men of tried genius, able to take full advantage of the great and unexpected resurgence of spirit among their troops. The Commander-in-Chief, General Putnik, was a great strategist of the Napoleonic school. With him worked Colonel **Two great Serbian leaders** Pavlovitch, the son of a farm labourer, who had won a series of scholarships, enabling him to study at Berlin, and master the art of war. He had directed the military operations in the struggle against Turkey and Bulgaria, and he was doing the same thing under his old chief, General Putnik, in the struggle against Austria-Hungary. He was now struck by the slowness with which the armies of the enemy were moving. They had lost a week since their capture of the ridges of Maljen and Suvobor.

Colonel Pavlovitch came to the conclusion that the Austro-Hungarian armies were in the same condition as the Serbian forces—starving by reason of the disorganisation of their transport columns, and half demoralised by lack of food, the rigour of the wintry weather in the mountains, and the general hardships of the campaign. This view was well

229

founded. The Austrian Staff was incompetent, and yet exceedingly hopeful. It thought that, with the forcing of the Suvobor ridges, the resistance of the Serbians had been completely broken, and that it was only a matter of rounding up a shattered and demoralised mob of fugitives. News of the supposed complete Austrian victory had been sent to Vienna, and Kaiser Franz Josef, in honour of the grand event, had instituted a new military decoration, which was bestowed upon General Potiorek.

General Potiorek fully shared in the illusion of his Staff. Besides the 300,000 troops with which he was operating, there seem to have been another 150,000 men at his disposal, if necessary; for the complete conquest of Serbia was a matter of extreme urgency to Austria-Hungary, and both of her allies, Germany and Turkey, required her to carry it out at any sacrifice of life. The Russian armies, however, were then pressing strongly upon Cracow from the north and the east, and a large reinforcement was badly wanted to hold up the Russians on the Dunajec River and

the Dukla Pass. In fact, the Russian Commander-in-Chief was exerting all the pressure he could, by means of the three armies of Generals Brussiloff, Dimitrieff, and Ivanoff, with a view to forcing the Hungarians to put more men in the field against him. All this was done in the hope of relieving the terrible pressure which was being brought to bear upon Serbia. And the plan succeeded. For, owing mainly to the grave weakness displayed by the Serbian troops, Potiorek dispensed with the use of his three additional army corps, which were railed at once against the menacing Russian front.

This left the Serbians with about three to one against them. But General Putnik was a superb master of the art of strategy. In retiring his troops, he had got into such a position that he was able to work on short interior lines, while the enemy had to make large and arduous movements in trying to envelop the Serbian position.

The Serbians held, with their Second and Third Armies, the western slopes of the **Potiorek's text-book plan** Rudnik Mountains. Then, more southward, the First Serbian Army was entrenched in front of its lost position below the Suvobor ridge. Still farther southward, the Fourth Serbian Army, thrown back from the chaos of mountains by the Bosnian frontier, defended the lower reaches of the Western Morava.

General Putnik had to decide where the hostile commander would place his strongest forces. This was a question depending on the character of General Potiorek, and as he was known to be an uninspired, unoriginal man, with a firm faith in the routine methods of the Moltke school of war, it was not difficult to foresee what he would do. As a matter of fact, he followed out the text-book plan customary in the situation in which he was placed. Having broken the Serbian resistance on his centre—the Suvobor ridge—

SERBIAN INFANTRY GOING INTO ACTION AT ROJAGNE, TAKING ADVANTAGE OF THE COVER OF TREES ON THE HILLSIDE.
The photograph was taken by a Serbian officer. The circular view shows a section of the Serbian trenches, whence heavy artillery bombarded the Austrian position.

AUSTRIAN OFFICERS AS PRISONERS IN BELGRADE.

AUSTRIAN PRISONERS AT A STATION IN GALICIA.

he held this ridge with only one army corps, and placed two army corps on each of his wings. His idea was to drive round in the greatest force by the north of the Rudnik ridge, and along the valley of the Western Morava, and thus envelop the Serbian forces on both sides, and achieve a new Sedan.

But while his troops were moving with great difficulty through the deep snow on the mountains in order to get into the dumb-bell formation, General Putnik struck. One of his most brilliant Staff officers—General Mishitch—took command of the First Serbian Army, displacing the

General Mishitch in command

general who had badly conducted the retreat from the river marshes. General Mishitch was a peasant's son, who had fought his way to the front rank and acted as lieutenant to General Putnik in the three great modern wars from which his country had emerged victorious. Like his fellow-worker on the staff, Colonel Pavlovitch, the peasant general was a brilliant thinker, who had directed other commanders without taking the field himself. It was now given to him to show that he could conduct a battle as brilliantly as he could arrange one. Acting with him was General Sturm, commanding the Third Army, entrenched on the slopes of the Rudnik range.

Mishitch's plan was quite simple. He intended a surprise attack against the single Austro-Hungarian army corps holding the Suvobor ridge. While he launched the First Army against it in front, Sturm would sweep down westward from the Rudniks with the Third Army, and take

the enemy on the flank. Then, as this was being done, the two other Serbian armies would have to hold back the two very powerful wings of the invading force.

General Mishitch, with the First Army, had halted on the little mountain stream—the Dicina. He suddenly advanced in a general attack, on the morning of December 3rd, 1914, and completely surprised the Austrians. He caught them leisurely moving along the valley paths. Capturing the overlooking hills, the Serbs shot the hostile columns down, while the Austrians were still wondering where they should place their artillery. Naturally, the Serbs knew every fall and rise of the ground, for Mishitch himself had been born and bred by the Suvobor, and his gun sites, skilfully captured by sudden strokes, commanded

HAPPY THOUGH CAPTIVE—AUSTRIANS RESTING UNDER GUARD ON A SERBIAN FARM.
In the smaller photograph we have evidence that the Serbians put their Austrian prisoners to serviceable but legitimate employment.

the paths along which he was driving the enemy. So overwhelming was the unexpected recoil of the nation of highlanders, that Potiorek and his Staff thought all the Serbian armies had been massed for the attack on the Suvobor. The Austrian commander, therefore, attempted in the heat of the action to alter entirely his dispositions for battle. He ordered both his wings to send large reinforcements to his centre. But the movement of large bodies of troops through snowstorms in the mountain chaos of the Balkans, intersected only by a few rough roads, was not a quick or easy matter. The guns were also held up, with the supply waggons, and most of the Austro-Hungarian troops had nothing to eat for two days or more. And this at a time when the searching coldness of the high altitudes, in which they were operating in midwinter, hourly lowered their vitality.

The Serbian artillerymen were at the top of their form. As soon as their infantry had rushed a good gun position for them, they got their pieces up by severe and yet enjoyable labour, and then opened with shrapnel on the enemy, bunched up in the valley, and plainly outlined against the snow. All the targets were large and extraordinarily clear, and with their long experience of mountain warfare, the Serbian artillerymen, with guns firing twenty rounds a minute, wrought terrible havoc. It was the remarkable increase in the destructive power of the Serbian artillery which made the Austrian Staff conclude that all the forces of Serbia were concentrated in front of Suvobor.

At the end of ten hours of fierce, incessant conflict, the Austrian first line was thrown back with the loss of some of its mountain howitzers. The troops retired on the positions defended by their heavy siege-guns. But the Serbians, exhilarated by their preliminary success, wanted no sleep or food. Onward they swept in the darkness, gaining ground over which it would have been impossible for them to advance in daylight in the teeth of the long-range Austrian guns. After midnight they snatched a little sleep, and ate what food could be brought up; and long before the slow winter dawn broke they had hauled their light guns closer to the enemy. Then came the grand attack, carried out with an impetuosity and tenacious fighting power unparalleled even in Serbian history.

The leadership of the company officers was magnificent. After a short struggle the enemy's front was broken, and his well-entrenched positions were enfiladed and captured. Line after line of rising crests, each commanding the other, and all with a wide field of fire dominated the ground which the Serbians approached. Each assault up the slopes, against machine-guns, artillery, and rifle fire, was an arduous business, and if the snow on the ground had not been trampled into mud by the retreating invaders, the

GENERAL BULGAROFF.
Commander of heroic Twentieth Russian Army Corps.

GENERAL POTIOREK.
Commander of Austrian Armies in Serbia.

GENERAL VON BULOW.

GENERAL STEPHANOVITCH.
Victorious Serbian General.

GENERAL VON EICHHORN.
Commanded German Armies in East Prussia.

storming parties could have been marked down miles away. But the mountaineers went up in widely extended order, throwing up little mounds at the end of every rush. Then, as their guns in the rear beat down the fire from the heights, the troops closed to the final charge, and broke through on the rise.

The end came near Gorni Toplitza, where the road runs round a great height, overhanging the river valley. On the edge of the mountain the Austrians had a battery of field-guns in a plum orchard. In the road below was a string of ammunition waggons, from which the guns were served. The Serbian artillerymen hauled up their guns on the flank of this position and poured on it a devastating enfilading fire. The torrent of shrapnel shot down men and horses, and the high-explosive shells which followed wrecked the batteries, limbers, and ammunition carts. Some men tried to escape, throwing away their packs as they made for the shelter of a neighbouring ravine. But they were all caught before they reached it. The French guns used by the Serbians had a semi-automatic device for slaughtering men in thousands, or tens of thousands, by a progressive movement in a given direction.

After the slaughter at Gorni Toplitza the central Austrian army became a terrorised rabble. All that the troops thought of was to get beyond the range of the Serbian guns. They did not stay even to put their own abandoned artillery out of action. They left their machine-guns and their unexhausted stores of ammunition in the trenches, and the paths over which they ran were marked by the trail they left behind them. It was a litter of accoutrements of every kind. There was one very significant incident. A pursuing Serb battery could not get its guns up quickly enough to help the infantry against an Austrian rearguard. The artillery officer ordered his men to leave their guns and charge with the riflemen. In about half an hour they had captured the Austrian battery opposed to them, and, hauling the guns round, they poured upon the fugitives round after round of Austrian shells.

At Valievo there was at last a rally of the best regiments of the Fifteenth Army Corps, and the several brigades of the Sixteenth Corps brought up to reinforce it. There were Hungarian regiments also, sent hurriedly down from the neighbourhood of Belgrade to stop the rout. The Hungarians and Austrians entrenched along the main road from the Suvobor region, and got their guns into position. The Serbs could be seen slowly advancing against them along the road. But a considerable time passed before an attack was made. Then it was an overwhelming surprise. For the Serbs who could be seen along the road were only a reserve, waiting to pursue the

UNIQUE WAR-TIME PHOTOGRAPH OF PRINCE ALEXANDER OF SERBIA.

The above photograph was taken during the bombardment of Belgrade by the Austrians, and shows Prince Alexander near a waterfall close to the forts, watching the result of the Serbian shells on the Austrian position. The photograph affords a glimpse of the picturesque beauty of the scenery in the vicinity of Belgrade.

BRITISH HONOUR FOR SERBIA'S PRINCE REGENT.
At Nish on March 19th, 1915, the Order of the Bath was conferred on Prince Alexander of Serbia by General Sir Arthur Paget, in the name of King George. Our photograph shows a group of officers who were present at the investiture. Left to right: Anto Mitrovitch, Colonel Harrison (British Attaché), and Colonel Yivko Pavlovitch (Governor-General).

enemy when he was broken. The main force had crept over the mountains; they attacked on the flank and threatened the rear, with the result that the battle did not take place. Only the rout was intensified.

When the First Serbian Army, under Mishitch, was winning one of the best-handled battles in the Great War, the Third Army, under Sturm, and the Second Army, under Stephano-vitch, came down from the slopes of the Rudniks. Sturm's men worked through the turned flank of the central Austrian forces on December 5th, 1914, and then broke off a large part of the enemy's northern wing by a night attack in which thousands of prisoners were taken. At the same time Stephanovitch, with the Second Army, drove hard into the middle of the Austrian northern wing, and caught it as it was still extended in its vain circling movement round the Rudniks towards Kragujevac.

But though the powerful northern wing of the Austrian Army was severed from its centre, and thrown back violently, no overwhelming victory against it was achieved. This was all according to the plans of General Putnik. Being much outnumbered, he could not spare the forces necessary to rout the enemy's strong northern force. Having

broken the centre of Potiorek's front, the Serbian commander gave his chief attention to capturing the Austrian southern wing, operating in the Western Morava valley.

Here the Fourth Serbian Army, usually known from its base town as the Ushitza Army, was striding across the river valley above Cacac. For some days the Serbians in this sector of the front could only hold their own by a great effort against superior forces brought against them.

But when General Mishitch stormed the Suvobor ridges, the Austrian southern wing, connected by wireless with its centre, knew that it was in peril. So it began to withdraw on December 5th, but as the commander of the Fourth Serbian Army was even better acquainted with the general situation, he did not allow the withdrawal to take place in an orderly manner. Waiting till nightfall, when he knew the roads would be choked with the enemy's heavy artillery, he delivered an attack at midnight. As dawn came the Austrians were in full retreat. They threw out rearguards in the river valley, but the highlanders knew the mountain tracks, and dropped down behind the entrenchments, making continual hauls of guns and prisoners.

On December 7th some of Mishitch's men captured the summit of Maljen. Then, linked with the advancing edge of the Fourth Army that was curling south around Ushitza, they achieved the enveloping operation which the Austrian commander had vainly hoped to accomplish. The three

A SERBIAN OUTPOST ON THE DANUBE.
The condition of the fatigued and battered Serbian Army was such as to justify the wildest hopes of the enemy. But the astonishing recuperative qualities of the people were fully displayed after the earlier stages of the Austrian attack, and all that Britain and France could do to help they did. General Putnik was a great strategist of the Napoleonic school.

PREPARING THE DEFENCES OF BELGRADE.
Serbian soldiers completing trenches and putting up wire entanglements around the forts of their threatened capital.

fugitive army corps, which had constituted the centre and southern wing of the invading force, were cut off from the northern wing and shepherded to destruction. There was little fighting. It was merely a race towards the Drina and Save Rivers, through the labyrinth of mountains in North-West Serbia. The Austrians kept to the valley roads, and the Serbians cut them off in thousands by using the straighter mountain paths. The fact that these paths were buried in snow did not **Through mountain** seriously trouble the mountaineers, who **labyrinths** had pastured their sheep there since boyhood. They could work their way across them in the dark. By November 10th Sturm with the Third Army was nearing Obrenovac, on the Save, a few miles below Belgrade. Far in the west the Fourth Army and the First Army were collecting a miscellaneous mob of the various races peopling the Empire of Franz Josef—Austrians, Hungarians, Bosnians, Mohammedans, Serbians, Bohemians, Moravians, Slovenes, Rumanians, and Russians. The captives were all starving, and two Serbian soldiers were a strong enough force to guard a column of two thousand of them. For captivity was welcome—

IN THE TRENCHES NEAR THE RIVER DRINA.

it meant food and shelter. In between the convoys straggled men who had fallen out by the way, most of them footsore creatures, paddling along through the freezing slush till they reached some place where they could get food, or till they dropped dead by the roadside.

Meanwhile, eastward, General Potiorek was trying to retain Belgrade with his detached northern wing. Formed of the Eighth and a mixed Army Corps, this force

SERBIAN PEASANT WOMEN BY THE GRAVES OF THEIR DEAD.
The photograph is of an improvised Serbian cemetery, and the women are seen paying a tribute of homage and respect to the fallen brave.

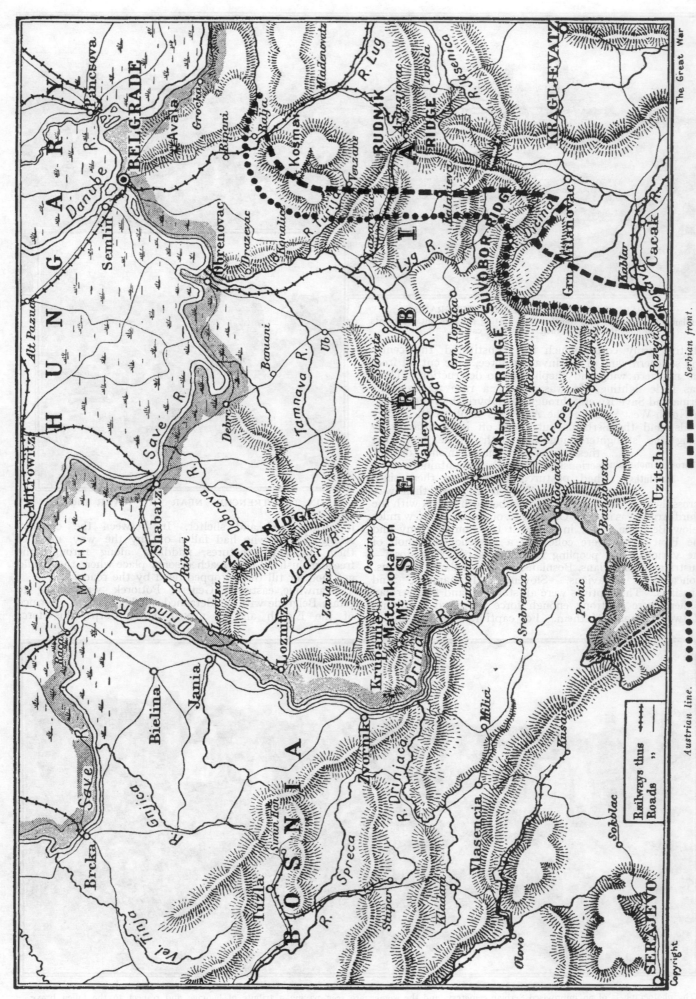

MAP OF THE THIRD AUSTRO-HUNGARIAN CAMPAIGN IN SERBIA.

Shewing the position of the invading army and that of the Serbian troops just before the attack that broke the enemy's centre.

Austrian line. ●●●●●●   Serbian front. ▬ ▬ ▬ ▬

Railways thus ━┼━┼━
Roads   „   ━━━━━

Copyright

Russian outpost going on duty carrying wood for fuel.

Russian officer testing the food at a travelling army kitchen.

Remarkable photograph of Austrian trenches near Jasionna, showing in l

...round entrance to bomb=proof, and on the right communicating trenches.

Prussian Cavalry against Cossacks of the Don: Fierce encounter on the Dniester.

240

had checked the advance of the Second Serbian Army, under General Stephanovitch, and had pressed hard against the garrison of Belgrade. This garrison, on the fall of the Serbian capital, had retired to the mountain of Kosmai, north of the Rudnik range. Here it was attacked by part of the Austrian northern wing on December 7th, 8th, and 9th. On the last day, however, the complete

THE AGONY OF SERBIA.
Stricken soldier of the suffering little kingdom refused admission to hospital because it was already overcrowded with typhus patients.

overthrow of the main forces of the enemy enabled General Putnik to rearrange his forces. He moved part of his Third Army towards the Save, some twenty miles south of Belgrade. Another part he attached to his Second Army, and added his cavalry to it, and also the Belgrade garrison. This combined force was placed under the command of General Stephanovitch, famous for his victories in earlier campaigns.

By September 10th, when Stephanovitch assumed full command of the eastern operations, the Austrian forces had been bent back from the Rudnik ridge and the
Austrian invaders shattered. height of Kosmai. Their front stretched from Grocka on the Danube to Konatice on the Kolubara River. Some fifteen miles behind them was the city of Belgrade, which they were endeavouring to retain for the honour and prestige of their empire. The failure of the movement of invasion was patent to the world. General Potiorek sorely needed the possession of Belgrade to palliate the overthrow of the third Austrian plan of conquest of Serbia.

General Putnik reckoned on this. The loss of Belgrade had become a gain to him. By means of his lost capital he was able, not merely to shatter the centre and southern wing of the invading armies, but also to make a new concentration of force against the powerful remnant of the enemy's strength. Right in the centre of the Austrian front was a hill through which ran the railway from Salonica to Vienna. General Stephanovitch brought his heavy guns up by this railway on the night of December 10th, and then at dawn he flung his troops forward, under the cover of his gun fire, and stormed the hill. At the same time his left wing advanced up the

Kolubara River towards its junction with the Save, some eight miles behind the Austrian front. The enemy had to draw back, for fear of being suddenly taken in the rear, and sent two monitors up the river to check the Serbian Cavalry Division, which was trying to work over the marshes and cut off the entire Austrian force.

But this movement of the Serbian left wing was only a feint. It was intended simply to make the Austrian line waver. While Potiorek was manœuvring his troops in answer to the feint, Stephanovitch made another frontal attack. Then for three days there was a most violent, swaying battle along the base of the little triangle of Serbian soil that ended in a point at Belgrade. The Austrians fought manfully, and, indeed, gave the Serbians one of the best fights in their long and warlike history. Instead of merely clinging to their hill entrenchments, they made fierce and tenacious attempts to break the Serbian front. But it was in one of these counter-attacks, near the central height where the railway entered a tunnel, that the resistance of the Austrians was broken. After the Serbian riflemen, with their machine-guns, had thrown back the enemy, the Serbian artillery caught the retiring troops.

This produced a panic in the dense retreating column, and the Serbian infantry left their trenches at a run, and formed into two streams, flowing on either side of the column of fugitives in the river valley. And as these streams ran uphill more quickly than the grey-blue flood moved, the Austrian rearguards, composed of heavy forces entrenched on strong positions, were turned. By December 14th the Serbians approached the line of

WAR-WORN, BUT BY NO MEANS BROKEN.
Mountain gun battery leaving Monastir for the front. The Serbian troops had been through two wars already, also a campaign against Albanian insurgents. But they responded cheerfully to the further call against the Austrian oppressor when it came to them.

hills forming the southern defence of Belgrade. Here General Potiorek had constructed a system of earthworks, consisting of deep trenches with shrapnel cover, and well-concealed gun positions, with numerous heavy howitzers and field-pieces. He intended to stand an indefinite siege on this fragment of Serbian territory, holding Belgrade as a bridge-head for another advance along the main Morava valley. In this way a rag of prestige would be saved from the debacle, enabling the campaign to be represented as a reconnaissance in force, similar to Hindenburg's first advance against Warsaw.

But his troops had received so terrible a punishment that they could not garrison the siege defences. The Serbians, steeled by victory after victory, and absolutely reckless of death as they drove in upon their capital, with their old King, the grandson of Black George, moving through their

THE FORTIFICATIONS OF BELGRADE.
The river in the foreground is the Danube, which forms a natural barrier between Hungary and Serbia.

EFFECT OF SHELL FIRE ON A BRIDGE NEAR THE SERBIAN FRONTIER.

foremost ranks, charged up in the ring of hills. On the central height of Torlak, on the evening of December 14th, they shot and bayoneted two Austrian battalions. Then moving in the darkness they captured all the heights.

No Serbians slept that night. They dragged or man-handled their guns towards Belgrade, and placed them on heights commanding the pontoon bridges, by which the enemy were fleeing over the Save. At dawn, on the happiest day in Serbian history—December 15th,

1914—the pontoon bridge was destroyed by shell fire. A cloud of fog and rain veiled the scene, but the gunners knew the position of their mark, and, breaking down the bridge, they cut off the retreat of the remnant of the two Austrian army corps. The rearguard outside the city was destroyed, and then the Serbian cavalrymen, accompanied by King Peter, swept from the height of Torlak, and entered the streets of the capital, killed a detachment of Hungarians who would not surrender, and began to round up the prisoners to the number of ten thousand. As the **King Peter gives thanks** street fighting between the cavalrymen and the Hungarians was going on, King Peter entered the cathedral of his capital to give thanks for the almost miraculous salvation of his small, heroic nation.

Of the army of 300,000 invaders who crossed the Drina and Save Rivers nearly half was put out of action. More than 41,500 prisoners were taken, together with 133 guns, 71 Maxims, 386 ammunition waggons, 3,350 transport waggons, and more than 3,250 horses and oxen. The

ANOTHER VIEW OF THE DEFENCES OF BELGRADE.
General view showing the fortress of Belgrade and the Austrian position round Semlin.

TRAGEDY IN THE HOUR OF TRIUMPH.

A realistic photograph from the Serbian battlefield. Serbian gunners left dead at their posts while their comrades were pursuing the surprised and humiliated Austrians after the latter's brief occupation of Belgrade.

WHERE PRISONERS OF WAR ENJOYED COMPARATIVE LIBERTY.

Austrian prisoners purchasing cooking utensils at a popular store in Nish. They were allowed to enter the town to buy provisions and other necessaries.

AUSTRIAN PRISONERS ARRIVING AT NISH.
When Belgrade was bombarded the Serbians made Nish their temporary capital.

A MOVING STORY.
Wounded Austrian prisoner telling the story of the Battle of Mount Tyser to Serbian soldiers near Nish.

number of dead and wounded Austro-Hungarians left on the battlefields exceeded 60,000. These were only put out of action during the retreat and rout of the invading forces, when the enemy could not stay to bury his own dead and tend his wounded. His losses during the early part of the campaign were not known, but reports from Hungarian sources went to show that one-half at least of the entire fighting force had been destroyed, captured, or disabled.

In importance, the achievement of the Serbians ranks immediately after the Battle of the Marne and the Battle of Turobin, in which latter battle the first-line armies of Austria-Hungary were overthrown. For had Serbia fallen, the Teutonic Empires would have been **The Allies' debt** united with little delay to the Ottoman **to Serbia** Empire, with Bulgaria as their new ally, Greece reduced to vassalage, and Rumania and Italy definitely intimidated. Any operation to force the Dardanelles would then have become, not merely a hard task, but a practical impossibility, and the difficulties of the entire campaign of the Powers of the Triple Entente would have been greatly increased. The Dardanelles would have become an important submarine base for Germany and Austria, and the transport of troops and the movement of shipping along the Mediterranean and through the Suez Canal might have been very gravely impeded.

In any case the Balkans would have been dominated by the enemy, and transformed into a land bridge between Turkey and the Teutonic countries. But all this was prevented by the wonderful efforts of the small race of mountaineers, exhausted by three great wars, ravaged by deadly infectious diseases, and reduced to extreme poverty. A few thousand Britons recognised what they owed to Serbia, and came forward in the spring of 1915 with offers of money, clothing, medicine, and aid in doctoring and nursing. One London hospital, in particular, sent out a capable staff of surgeons and nurses. But up to the time of writing (May, 1915), the general British public, saved from

the horrors and miseries of invasion by a strong Fleet, had shown no practical appreciation of the achievement by which Serbia had shortened the war at an, as yet, untold sacrifice of the lives of her finest men, and of the health of half or more of her people.

The Austrians and Hungarians themselves were staggered by the extraordinary power of the Serbs. Their last disaster, indeed, left them half-stunned. Then a gust of desperate anger swept over them. Calling the Germans to their aid, they began to collect, in January, 1915, a new army of 400,000 troops of good quality—Bavarians, Hungarians, and German Austrians—who were ranged close to the Serbian frontier. **Austria's call for** It is, however, impossible to say whether **German aid** these preparations were seriously meant at the outset, and were subsequently overruled by Hindenburg, or whether the Prussian Commander-in-Chief completely controlled the situation from the beginning of the new movement, and used the new menace to Serbia as a feint. However this may be, the Russian commander of the south-west armies saw to it that the hard-pressed, over-

NOVEL SERBIAN GUN TEAM.
Oxen hauling a big gun along a rough cart-track across the fields.

BRINGING UP AMMUNITION BY HAND.
Owing to the difficult nature of the country, shells for the Serbian guns had frequently to be carried by hand. In circle: Serbian artillery entrained for the front.

THE TERRIBLE QUICK-FIRING GUNS WITH WHICH THE SERBS BROKE THE POWER OF THE INVADER.
These mobile field-pieces were made on the same principle as the famous French "75."

wrought, but victorious Serbians were given breathing space.

This was accomplished by bringing pressure to bear upon Hungary. On January 5th a Russian Division, equipped with mountain guns, came down from Galicia and captured Czernovitz, and began to work its way through Bukovina. By January 13th nearly the whole of Bukovina was in the hands of the Russians, and they were advancing by the Kirlibaba Pass over the Carpathian Mountains, which rise to a great height by the Rumanian frontier. Here the Russians attacked the last Austrian fortress guarding the path to Transylvania.

At the same time the main Russian armies in Galicia, under the command of General Brussiloff, **Russia's advance into Hungary** a man of genius and courage, stormed certain of the Carpathian passes, two hundred miles north-west of the Bukovina Pass. Brussiloff had to give up for the time his easy method of fighting with the Galician railway system immediately behind his line, and send several of his army corps over the snow-buried summits. In spite of the difficulties of their enterprise, they hurled back the great Austrian army, with its first reinforcement of three German army corps. The Dukla Pass and the Uzsok Pass were captured, and an advance was made into Hungary along the river valley leading to the town of Ungvar. In conjunction with the advance towards the Kirlibaba Pass, the Russian movement threatened to sweep over all the Hungarian plain to the east of Budapest. So no troops could be spared for another invasion of Serbia, and on January 23rd, 1915,

the new Austro-German army, gathered near the Danube, was sent up into the Carpathian Mountains.

Brussiloff then had all the work and excitement he wanted. Half his forces were entrenched around Przemysl, patiently waiting for it to fall by famine. This left him with about a quarter of a million men, and with them he had to meet and hold up the whole Austrian forces on the Carpathians, not less in number than his troops, reinforced by 400,000 fresh soldiers, many of them being first-rate German fighting men, with more tenacity of character than the light, gay, artistic Austrians. The Germans advanced towards the end of January on the Uszok and Beskiden Passes, and captured them. On this section of the front Brussiloff was compelled to fall back on the Galician slopes, where he could use **A month's fighting in Bukovina** his railways. He also withdrew from the Kirlibaba Pass the single division operating there. It slowly retired, fighting in the upland forest against two army corps which were trying to reach General Brussiloff's railway communications at Stanislav. The Russian Division had to fight for time, by ambushing the advance guards of Hungarian troops, and generally impeding the enemy's advance. This it did in a month's incessant fighting in the Bukovina, that only cost the Russians in dead, wounded, and prisoners 1,007 men.

Meanwhile, Hindenburg prepared in a very able manner for his more important attack on the Russian line of communication behind Warsaw. The Russians had four army corps, under General Baron von Sieviers, operating by the East Prussia frontier. It was Hindenburg's intention

OUTPOSTS ON A SNOW-COVERED SERBIAN HILLSIDE IN THE DEPTH OF WINTER.

AUSTRIAN PRISONERS OF WAR ENGAGED IN FARM WORK AT USKUB, IN SERBIA.

SOME OF THE MEN WHO DEFEATED THE AUSTRIANS: SERBIAN SHARPSHOOTERS IN ACTION.

to overwhelm this small army by a sudden superior concentration of force in the Masurian Lakes region. Then he designed to sweep across the Niemen and the Narew Rivers and cut the line of supplies for all the Russian troops in the bend of the Vistula. The German commander had first to make sure that no important part of the Warsaw army or of Russky's army was detached to reinforce the East Prussian front. The means by which he accomplished this end was dreadfully simple.

On January 31st, 1915, seven "Divisions of Death," composed of picked troops who did not expect to return from the attack, massed behind the troops holding the German line in front of Sochachev on the Bzura and Bolimoff on the Rawka. At the same time an unusual number of heavy and light batteries were concentrated on this section of the front, and the Kaiser came to Hindenburg's **Germany's** headquarters at Kutno to watch the great **explosive bullets** offensive. The German ordnance authorities even went so far as to issue supplies of cartridges with explosive bullets to the 84,000 infantrymen designated to make the terrible demonstration. Then on the last day in January, after the Russian lines had been bombarded most heavily with high-explosive shells, many of them of 11 and 12 in. calibre, the attack was made.

Every German infantryman taking part in it went forth with high courage to die. He came on with his comrades in close formation and with strong supports, and bridged the Bzura in three or four places, and advanced on the eastern villages of Sucha, Borzimov, and Gumine, between Sochachev and Bolimoff. The Russians were forced back from the Bzura into the forest stretching to Warsaw. For a week the fight went on, with desperate tenacity and intensity. So long as the Divisions of Death retained their cohesion, they went forward, but at the edge of the forest the Russian guns caught them in dense masses, and broke them up. Then the Siberian riflemen swept down and recaptured their trenches, and by the middle of the week they won back the important position of Volya Shidlovska, near Gumine. Neither explosive bullets nor chlorine-gas bombs, both of which the Germans used freely, could stay the Russian counter-attack. At night the Russian searchlights revealed the last of the Divisions of Death marching to the support of their comrades ; but the columns were dispersed by field-guns and machine-guns, and by February 6th 45,000, out of the original 84,000 bayonets composing the seven divisions, were put out of action. Thereupon the most costly demonstration ever made in the history of war came to an end.

It may have been intended for more   **Russians held** than a demonstration. But though   **before Warsaw** it failed as an attack, it certainly succeeded in holding all the Russian armies before Warsaw, and thus facilitated Hindenburg's main plan. On the day it ended, the more important battle of East Prussia began. In three broad columns the great north-eastern German army, under General von Eichhorn and General von Bülow, advanced in the rear of Warsaw. The first column, containing an army corps of first-line troops railed from the French front, operated against Grodno. The second column advanced against the Russian fortress town of Osoviec and the important railway junction of Bielostok. The third column marched on Prasnysch, immediately north of Warsaw.

At the beginning of the struggle the main battle raged round the forest town of Augustovo, and extended to the line of the Niemen. One Russian army corps was threat-

A TRAP FOR THE ENEMY: MOTOR-CYCLISTS IN AMBUSH AT A TURN OF THE ROAD.

MOTOR RECONNOITRING PARTY PASSING OVER ROUGH
GROUND.

ened by an enveloping movement, and hurriedly retired
on Kovno. It had formed the extreme right wing of the
Russian force, and its hasty retreat exposed the neighbouring Russian army corps at Augustovo to the fate from
which it had itself narrowly escaped. This was the Twentieth
Army Corps under General Bulgaroff.

The northern German column swerved southward and
half encircled Bulgaroff's men in the trackless wilderness
of wood and water round Augustovo. Then, as the Russians
were fighting their way out, another German column
crossed the frontier still more to the south, and engaged
them on the other side, completely cutting their line of
communications. There were six German army corps
against the single Russian army corps. The Russians
were entirely encircled, and compelled to fight incessantly
on four fronts. In an ordinary way they might have been
annihilated in twenty-four hours, but the ground favoured

**Six army corps
against one**

them. It was a wilderness of lakes,
swamps, and dense brushwood, above
which rose the gaunt boughs of the
great forest trees and the sombre everlasting foliage of the pines. In this spot a force of
Cossacks had annihilated a large section of the former
German army of invasion in the autumn of 1914.

Bulgaroff still retained many of the Russian woodsmen
of the district who had guided the troops in the former
victory. This gave him a notable advantage in the use
of the difficult and intricate system of paths across the
swamp lands. Happily, there were no dominating heights
from which the enemy could bring to bear his overwhelming number of field-guns. The Twentieth Army Corps
was clearly doomed, but this fact did not disturb the
Russian commander. To General Bulgaroff had fallen
the same task as that which the Russian commander of
the two army corps at Kutno had carried out in the same
circumstances of peril. He had to put up so fierce,
stubborn, and long a resistance that when he fell the
victorious enemy would be checked by the arrival of
stronger Russian forces. He had to fight for time, to
enable the Russian Commander-in-Chief to alter his main
dispositions, and bring up a great army to defend the
Warsaw-Petrograd railway.

This Bulgaroff accomplished. As late as February
24th battalions of the heroic Twentieth Corps were cutting their way through the German ring and rejoining the
main Russian forces. Detachments continued to fight
their way out of the forest, after a struggle lasting three
weeks. Most of the corps fought on until their ammunition

RUSSIAN MOTOR SCOUTS IN TOUCH WITH THE GERMAN
COLUMNS.

was exhausted, and then surrendered. The Germans
exaggerated this small success in a very extravagant way.
They claimed that they had overthrown and routed all
the four Russian army corps defending the East Prussian
front, and that they had rounded up the remnant in the
Forest of Augustovo. But, as a matter of fact, General
Bulgaroff, by his long and splendidly-
handled defence, had saved the situation. **The fall of**
By the time he was captured, the **Prasnysch**
Russian line along the Niemen and Narew
Rivers had been so greatly strengthened that Hindenburg's
last attempt to obtain a decision was verging upon disaster.

The disaster occurred at the village of Prasnysch. Here
the third force of invasion, operating in two streams from
Soldau and Willenberg, swept down towards Warsaw.
By Saturday, February 20th, a brigade of Russian troops
holding Prasnysch were partly forced back. The Germans
did not at first directly attack them, but swept in two strong
lines southward on either side of the village, in an encircling

RUSSIAN CAVALRY IN PURSUIT OF THE AUSTRIANS ACROSS THE SNOW-BOUND UZSOK PASS.

When Austria's invasion of Galicia was turned into a precipitate retreat back into Hungary, by way of the panic-stricken soldiers of the Dual Monarchy were followed by Cossack horsemen, who attacked them the Uzsok Pass, in the Eastern Beskid range of the Carpathians, in the bitter winter of 1914-15, in flank and rear, inflicting heavy losses and taking many prisoners.

movement. A third German force marched still more southward to capture a ridge on which part of the Russian brigade was retiring.

But though Prasnysch was about to fall, the men on the ridge, overlooking an endless waste of snow, held out with as desperate a valour as the heroes of the Twentieth Corps. One German column attacked them on the west, while another column tried to storm them from the east. Their food supplies began to run out, and the ammunition for their small number of field-guns got low. But from their dominating position they held out against terrible odds from February 20th to February 24th. It was on the last date that Prasnysch fell, with half the brigade involved in its fall. But the ridge was still defended by about a thousand Russians, with their dead and wounded lying near them, and all the slopes around strewn with the bodies of their enemies. For one day and one night more the band of heroes had to stand to their work. Just twenty miles away were the two Russian army corps that had escaped defeat, in spite of the resounding falsehoods of the German Staff. These two Russian corps were extended along the River Narew, where they were greatly reinforced by the new army brought up to defend the frontier rivers.

Their general was using the remnant of the heroic brigade on the Prasnysch ridge to lure the enemy onward. When the village of Prasnysch fell, he crossed the Narew and advanced up the Orzec, and thence in a swift night march on Thursday, February 25th, he cut off the leading

A thousand Russian heroes

German army corps. The encirclers were encircled. The German commander tried to retrieve the position by swinging the whole of his force on the line of the Orzec. But the Russians were too strong for him. They captured half his first army corps and killed a great part of the other half. Then they turned upon the main German force, and fought it back from the Orzec River to the hills of Prasnysch, in an incessant battle of four days, and on March 1st their full victory was achieved.

Hindenburg had sacrificed in vain his seven Divisions of Death on the Bzura River. For the surprise he had thereby hoped to accomplish against the Warsaw line of communications had completely failed. His strongest column, with the first-line Twenty-first Army Corps from the French frontier, had forced the passage of the Niemen beyond Suwalki, but could do no more than make a bridge-head, from which it was unable to advance against the distant railways. The second column of invaders was entirely held up in front of the fortress of Osoviec, the garrison of which fought with magnificent skill as well as with superb courage.

Hindenburg's ineffective sacrifice

With the defeat of the Germans at Prasnysch, and their containment at Osoviec and the Niemen line, Hindenburg's first main attempt to create a diversion from the Battle of the Carpathians came to an end. Meanwhile, Przemysl was still holding out, and men were falling in hundreds of thousands on the high rampart of snow-covered rocks, defending the illimitable stretches of winter wheat in the Hungarian plain.

AUSTRIAN MACHINE-GUN IN ACTION IN THE SNOW.
The gun, which was of the Maxim type, was fitted with sleigh-runners so that it could be drawn along rapidly by hand.

PRUSSIAN "FRIGHTFULNESS" IN POLAND: HUNS WATCHING THE BURNING OF A VILLAGE THEY HAVE GIVEN OVER TO THE FLAMES.

It was announced in Petrograd in March, 1915, that the Germans had laid waste three-quarters of Russian Poland, ninety-five towns and large villages having been ruined, while 4,500 smaller villages were demolished, a thousand being burnt to ashes. The damage was estimated at over £100,000,000.

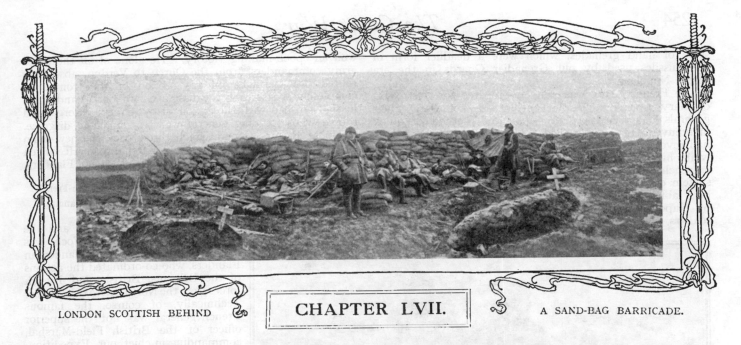

CHAPTER LVII.

THE WINTER CAMPAIGN IN THE WESTERN TRENCHES.

The Bog Between the Trenches in France and Flanders—Winter Campaign Immobilised by State of Ground—How the Allied Armies Profited by the Standstill—France Acquires a Heavier Armament—Four Million French Troops under Arms, and another Half a Million Training—Reversion to Old-Fashioned Methods and Weapons of Warfare—The British Admiralty Provides the British Soldier with a " Mother "—Germany Tries to Shift her First-Line Armies from France to Russia—General Joffre's Subtle Countermove—Gives Orders for a Grand Offensive Movement—How the Germans were Outmanœuvred and Held Up—The Strategy of the Allied Trench Attacks—The Battle of the Vosges—Reverse at Soissons—Action at Givenchy, and the Feat of Sergeant O'Leary—The Battle of Champagne—The Battle of Neuve Chapelle.

AFTER their heavy losses in the Battle of Ypres the Germans were obliged to stand on the defensive all through the winter. They were still more powerful in numbers and armament than the Allies. We had, for instance, only about 84,000 British bayonets in the field, just one more division than the little, reorganised Belgian Army mustered on our left flank. By the middle of November the French had to bring up round Ypres and Dixmude somewhat more men than we had put into the field, in order to save our line from being broken and enabling the enemy to capture Calais. Our Indian Army Corps, with 24,000 bayonets, lost ground around La Bassée, and had to be strengthened by our small body of overworked British troops. The position all along the western front at the end of the autumn campaign was still critical. Had the ground been firm and hard between the opposing lines and the air clear, the Germans might have been able to resume their offensive with some hope of success.

What chiefly checked them was the state of the soil between the hostile trenches and the pressure which the Russians were exerting against Silesia and Hungary. The ground in Flanders, after the soaking autumn rains and the mild, moist winter weather, was a bog. Any attack from either side ended in the storming party sinking up to its knees, hope-

GENERAL GOURAUD.
The youngest General in the French Army. It was announced in May, 1915, that he had succeeded General d'Amade in command of the French forces in the Dardanelles in consequence of the last-named officer's illness.

lessly entrapped, and being shot down by its enemies. In conjunction with our French reinforcements, we tried to resume a vigorous offensive from Ypres about the middle of November, 1914, but the movement was checked by the Germans without much difficulty.

Sir John French, thereupon, resolved to remain upon the defensive until the spring winds dried the ground. He would not be even tempted into a counter-attack when he lost a trench or two south of Ypres. He made the enemy pay a severe price on every occasion for every few yards they slowly won, and drew back from Zandvoord, and even from Hill 60, and strengthened his lines and awaited more men, more guns, and more ammunition. This he had to do because the Germans were better prepared for trench warfare than were the Allies. The German Staff had been deeply struck by the lesson of Mukden, in the Manchurian campaign, and for years they had been arming their forces against such an occasion as now arose in the western field of war. They had an abundant supply of special weapons for trench fighting, most of which were a revival and improvement upon the instruments used in the old-fashioned war of earthworks in the days of Marlborough. They had numerous modern trench mortars for pitching huge bombs a few hundred yards into neighbouring hostile lines; they had peculiar steel catapults fulfilling the same purpose, and a vast store of hand-grenades, which were a deadlier form of the missiles used by our Grenadier Guards in the era before Napoleon.

The French Army was quite unprepared for this extraordinary reversion to the ancient way of war. Their generals had relied entirely upon the method of quick manœuvring in the open field, by means of which Napoleon had revolutionised the art of war and won rapid decisions, while his opponents were considering where they should entrench. Only Wellington, keeping to the old-fashioned system of long lines of earthworks at Torres Vedras, had been able to resist the new method of manœuvring used by Napoleon's brilliant marshals. Great modern French soldiers, such as General Foch, had studied the lesson of

OFFICERS AND MEN OF THE CAMERONIANS' 1st BATTALION IN WINTER ATTIRE BEHIND THEIR SNOW-COVERED DEFENCES.

Mukden from a point of view different from that of the Germans. Foch and his disciples had hoped to revive and extend the battle of open manœuvres, by rapidly handling hundreds of thousands of troops in railway trains. They kept their artillery as light and as mobile as possible, with a view to massing it with great rapidity. And though General Joffre just before the outbreak of war reluctantly came to the conclusion that France would have to spend some thirty million pounds on heavy, slow field artillery, hostilities suddenly opened before the French Chamber, as thrifty as the peasants it mainly represented, could be induced to vote the expense of the additional national armament.

General Foch justified all the ideas he had preached in regard to the extension of Napoleonic tactics. In spite of his fame as a professor of strategy he had only a small command in August, 1914, being the commander of a Lorraine army

General Foch's promotion corps of some 40,000 men, operating round Nancy. First he had rescued from an overwhelming attack the broken French force trapped and routed by the Bavarians in the mountains. Then with his two divisions of infantry, including the famous Division of Iron, he had held the Grand Couronné de Nancy against the attack by the whole Bavarian army, directed in person by the Kaiser. Thereby he did more than any other one man to save France, and General Joffre rewarded him by giving him the command of the strongest French army, the new Ninth Army, holding the French centre in the Battle of the Marne. There General Foch again

won an epoch-making victory. He alone of all the allied army commanders, from the Ourcq to Verdun, absolutely routed the Germans on his section of the front. He completely shattered the Prussian Guard Corps, and when he had finished with the Saxon army it was a disorganised rabble whose leading general was sent home in disgrace. Again at Rheims General Foch threw back the new main German army with which Field-Marshal von Heeringen tried to resume the offensive. Later the Battle of Flanders, from Nieuport to La Bassée, was won by the allied troops, acting under the general control of the brilliant Lorraine commander.

The Foch-French understanding

All through the autumn and winter of 1914 and the spring of 1915 General Foch was practically the high commander in Flanders, who co-ordinated the actions of the Belgians, British, and French forces from the North Sea to below Lille. Technically, of course, the famous French general was not the superior officer of the British Field-Marshal, commanding-in-chief our Expeditionary Force. But Sir John French and General Foch admired and understood each other, as did also General D'Urbal, directing the Belgian army corps. The troops of the three allied nations moved

PART OF A TRENCH OCCUPIED BY CAMERON HIGHLANDERS, THE SNOW REMINDING THEM OF A REAL OLD HIGHLAND WINTER.

as one machine of war along their front; they lent each other guns; they were even brigaded together at times, and always acted in complete and loyal harmony.

Until the Allies were as fully armed for trench warfare as was their common enemy, there was little movement of importance in the western theatre of war. The advantage at first rested with the Germans, who inflicted small but continual losses on the allied troops by means of short-range bomb-throwers and hand-grenades. Their sniping operations, performed by men with special rifles fitted with telescopic sights, were also a considerable annoyance. Some of our Indian troops retaliated by getting close to the German lines at night with the knife,

REMARKABLE CAMERA-PICTURE OF A BRITISH ENTRENCHED
POSITION AT THE FRONT.

and doing some quick, silent slaughter. In a general way
what little progress was made was affected by sapping.
This was a complete return to the slow, old-fashioned
method of warfare, such as is vividly described by Lau-
rence Sterne in his scandalously amusing novel of the days
of Queen Anne, "Tristram Shandy." All the strange
terms of war used by Uncle Toby and Corporal Trim
became full of meaning—ravelins, covered ways, approaches, saps, traverses, and the rest of the old glossary.

From the North Sea to Switzerland four million or
more men were living like human moles. There were
three to four thousand miles of excavated earthworks,
curiously constructed to prevent more than a few yards
of trench in any part being useful to an enemy who had
captured it. The vast battlefield was a
strange, empty desert. Not a living thing
was visible on it. Even the heavy guns,
far in the rear of the firing-line, were
placed in large earthen cellars, from which only their muzzles
protruded, and these were usually hidden by an artificial
hedge or mass of brushwood. Most of the four million
soldiers, when on duty in the trenches, rested and slept
in subterranean caves. Their only glimpse of the battlefield was caught through the loophole in the parapet of
the trench, from which they fired their rifles. As the
intensity of sniping operations increased, even a peep
through the rifle-hole became perilous in many places,
and the ordinary work of observation was conducted
usually by means of trench periscopes. The top mirror
was often shattered, but it cost less than the human eye
or the brain behind and far below it.

The ingenious Germans sometimes employed gigantic
telescopes in searching for targets and watching for signs
of activity on the allied lines. One of these mighty
instruments of astronomy was set up near Lille, with a
sweeping vision over the British front near the Lys. It
was also near this place that a battalion of French or
British marksmen always came out at night, and swept
with their fire a certain place behind the German firing

**Four million
human moles**

LIVERPOOL SCOTTISH TERRITORIALS IN THE TRENCHES.

trench. Our heavy howitzers had smashed up the main
communication trench of the Germans, compelling them
to do the work of bringing up supplies and changing the
trench garrison in the darkness. Now and then a volley
from our lines would catch a large body of Germans as
they were creeping at night out in the open.

Meanwhile the engineers from both sides drove tunnels
through the enemy's front trenches, and then ran a side
shaft under them and filled the shaft with dynamite.
The result was an explosion, often followed by the capture
of the wrecked trench. The enemy would then have to
come out in the open, generally at night after a bombardment, and make a costly counter-attack. A subtler
way was to mine one's own front trench, especially when
it had been badly sited and was difficult
to hold. The enemy was allowed to capture it and alter the parapets. A feint
was made to attack him in his new posi-
tion. Consequently, he packed more men into the ground he
had proudly won, in preparation for the coming attempt
to retake it by storm. Then there would be an explosion,
and the allied troops would charge the moment after their
engineer fired the mine. In the Argonne section especially
a captured trench became regarded as a thing not worth
having by either side. It was usually a mined trap.

**Trenches as
mined traps**

255

BRITISH PIONEERS AT WORK WITH PICK AND SHOVEL "SOMEWHERE IN FRANCE."

The French were particularly good at this mole warfare. They drove their mining tunnels under many important points of support of the German lines at Vermelles, near Arras, at the Perthes furnaces in Champagne, and near the height of Eparges leading towards Metz. All this subterranean activity, however, had no large result. A few well-placed, large, high-explosive howitzer shells did as much damage in a minute as the sappers could do in a month.

Up to the middle of December, 1914, the two opposed and invisible armies practically marked time, doing what little work they safely could to keep each other occupied. All this was to the advantage of the Allies. It afforded them breathing space, during which they brought their heavy armament to an equality with that of the enemy, and then proceeded to surpass him in the general range and power of their howitzer fire. Our War Office was assisted by our Admiralty, from its stock of naval guns.

The arrival of "Mother"

Then came the arrival of that modern pet of the British soldier — his "Mother." This admirable heavy field-howitzer, with its calibre of 9·2 in., has already been described in connection with the wireless aeroplane service that found its target and directed its fire. Even heavier howitzers were brought up, christened by the soldiers "Grandmother."

The 9·2 had a range of more than eight miles; it was handier than the very heavy German howitzers, and much more formidable than their ordinary field-pieces. As a trench-breaker and an interrupter of hostile lines of communication, this gift of the British Navy to the British Army was a memorable thing. Like the naval 4·7 in. gun, used in a former war, it showed

how the superb organisation of British sea-power could be made to tell quickly and directly in land warfare.

Small as our Army originally was, it had in artillery, at least, an important source of additional strength in our great naval arsenals. And Admiral Sir Percy Scott, renowned for his skill in mounting naval guns for action on land, was again at hand to help the British soldier in the day of difficulty.

The great French gunmakers were equally alert for the needs of the new situation. Since the Balkan War of 1912 they had proved to the world by the ordeal of battle that their guns were superior to those of Krupp. All the self-advertisement and intrigue of the German firm could not palliate the failure of their guns in the Turkish armies trained by German officers. The French gunmakers were able to increase their plant owing to the prestige they had won. The result was that, when the war opened, France possessed in the works of Creusot, Schneider, and other armament firms, a system of organised machinery for the production of ordnance which rivalled, if it did not eclipse, the German plant.

French gun-plant increased

Each French battalion soon received an additional machine-gun, with an extra machine-gun party, and preparations were made to increase still further the war machinery of each battalion in this direction. At the same time large and increasing numbers of heavy howitzers were produced, with trained crews to work them, and railed to the front.

By the time the ground was dry enough for attack and counter-attack, General Joffre had two and a half million men at the front, another million and a half in the depots, and about half a million of new recruits training in camp. All the artillery corps had been strengthened by the addition of numerous long-range heavy cannon and heavy howitzers. The new pieces resembled the heavy artillery of the German Army, but the new French artillery was of a later and improved model, with special excellencies such as had distinguished the French 3 in. gun from its German imitation. The entire military forces of France had also been trained in new defensive tactics, without in any way diminishing their fine Gallic spirit of vehement attack.

All things considered, the comparative stagnation of the winter campaign in the western field of war was a boon to the Allies and a ban upon the Teutons. For it gravely diminished the fighting strength of Germany, by giving France and Britain time to build up a war-machine almost as formidable as the German organisation for battle. But as we have already seen in the study of the operations in Russia, the Great Staff of the Teutonic Empires made an attempt to profit by the bogged condition of the western front. They regarded the standstill as the temporary equivalent to a victory over the Franco-British-Belgian forces, and reverted the plan of the elder Moltke. It was their intention to garrison their trenches in France and Flanders with troops of inferior quality, and rail a large part of their first-line armies against Russia. By this means they hoped to win Warsaw, Ivangorod, and all the line of the Vistula by the spring of 1915. They thought that Galicia also might possibly be conquered by their first-line armies, whose power the Russians had never yet fully felt. Then in the spring they designed to entrench along the Niemen, Narew, and Vistula, and hold this front with troops of the second class, while they

A boon to the Allies

swung back their first-line armies for operations on the wind-dried ground of Flanders and France.

Such was the situation on December 15th, 1914. But General Joffre was equal to it. As we have explained, he loudly proclaimed that France and Britain must, at all costs, advance to the help of Russia. In spite of the mud, mist, and snow of winter, a grand offensive movement had to be undertaken against the German lines. In certain places, a hundred thousand French soldiers were massed on a narrow section of the front, with a tremendous artillery power behind them, in order to cut a way through the German trenches at the cost of all their lives. The number of the British Expeditionary Force was doubled, and afterwards trebled for the great event. A general order was issued to the allied troops, and, by a sad accident, copies of it were found by the Germans on men taken prisoners in some of the preliminary attacks intended to feel the strength of their front. But the whole thing was a feint. General Joffre never meant to advance. All he wanted to do was to disconcert and alarm his opponent, General von Falkenhayn, by the threat of a grand offensive that might sweep the Germans out of Northern France and Belgium. The affair was a magnificent bluff. Its success was extraordinary.

Joffre's magnificent bluff

By the winter of 1914 the Germans had formed sixty-nine army corps. Of these there were fifty-two army corps on the western front. So in the eastern field of battle Hindenburg had only seventeen German army corps, composed mainly of troops of the second and third line. After the wastage of the autumn campaign, these troops did not amount to half a million men. Naturally, Hindenburg wanted more, and especially more first-line

USED UP IN HEAVY MARCHING: DISCARDED RELICS OF MANY A WEARY MARCH.

troops. But little more than 180,000 first-line troops were removed from the Flemish and French front. Most of them were taken from the Yser line, where the inundations protected both sides from a sudden, serious attack. As the Germans did not know whether General Joffre was in earnest, and indeed thought he was so, they did not dare to weaken their forces in front of the French and British troops. Thus, without a battle, the French master of high strategy defeated the intentions of his enemy and imposed his will upon him.

It all sounds very simple when the main outlines of the great winter campaign are represented in this elementary fashion. But the execution of General Joffre's subtle and deceitful plan needed a master's hand to give it full effect.

DEVELOPMENT OF THE ARMOURED TRAIN.
The armoured train, vastly improved since the South African War, was used largely by the rival forces on the Continent. Our centre photograph is of a British armoured train firing its big guns while running at a high speed. Top and bottom are shown respectively one of these Dreadnoughts on wheels passing through a wayside station, and two waggons of a French armoured car in action.

Mere talk and the issuing of orders were not sufficient to throw the German commander off his balance. He had to be made to feel the pressure of Franco-British forces, superior in number and armament to those of his command. The ostentatious collection of four million Frenchmen immediately at the front or in depots; busy movements and concentrations of trucks and engines at the manœuvring centres of the French railway system; the buying of large quantities of munitions from America, and their accumulation at places within quick reach of the firing-line—all these delusive devices were employed, with a pretty shrewd guess at their effect upon the Intelligence Department of the Great Staff of Germany.

Shaking the German front

Then began the more expensive pretence of searching for an opening for the grand attack. All the comparatively weak points in the German line from Ypres to Perthes, in Champagne, and from the hills round St. Mihiel, between Verdun and Toul, to the heights of the Vosges near Mulhouse, were continually tested and shaken. It is scarcely worth while relating in detail all the steps which General Joffre

took just to shake the German front. Sometimes the British troops sprang out of their trenches and waded through the mud and drove the Germans in at St. Eloi, a village between Ypres and Lille; or they made an assault against Neuve Chapelle, or a position near La Bassée. In almost every case they were unable to advance more than a few hundred yards. Often, indeed, they lost the short stretch of trench they captured, and had to draw back to their old position. For by weakening the German line in other places, and hurrying strong reinforcements up to the threatened point by railway train or motor-vehicles, the German commander was always able to stop the gap that had been made. But when he had thus made a concentration in the north, the Chasseurs Alpins, fighting on the heights and in the valleys of the Vosges far to the south, would mass and carry some small but important position in Alsace. Again the Germans had to rail up troops in order to outnumber and master the French attackers. By this time the Germans had strengthened both ends of their lines. So the next assault would be made somewhere near their centre—in the Aisne valley, in Champagne, or east of Verdun.

Testing the German reserves

And the trouble was that the German Staff knew exactly what General Joffre was doing. He was trying to find out if the Germans had an important reserve of troops, which they were using to stop the little gaps, or whether they had to weaken their line continually, in the sections that seemed safe, in order to strengthen their forces in the sections that were being attacked. Naturally, the Germans always tried to bring up reinforcements with such quickness as to suggest that they were working with a large reserve. But there is such a thing as intelligence men, working in or behind an enemy's lines, calculating the movements of his trains, the amount of supplies and ammunition he received, and deducing from this information the exact number of his troops. As the Germans were working in Belgian and French territory, all the precautions they took against espionage could not interfere with the working of certain channels of knowledge open to the commander of the

INDIAN TROOPS WITH TRANSPORT ON THEIR WAY TO AN ADVANCED POSITION IN FLANDERS.

LORD ROBERTS IN FRANCE, WHERE HE WENT TO GREET THE INDIAN TROOPS, OF WHICH HE WAS COLONEL-IN-CHIEF.

OUR GALLANT GURKHAS MARCHING THROUGH A TOWN ON THE CONTINENT.

GERMAN OFFICERS STUDY-
ING A WAR MAP.

the Prussian Guard and other reinforcements. They captured Givenchy on December 20th, and imperilled the entire British line. The 1st Manchesters by a splendid effort recaptured the village and the old trenches in the evening. But they, in turn, were cut off from all their supports by a curtain of shrapnel fire, falling everywhere, behind and around them, from the German guns. No troops could move out to them. Yet the Manchesters held out bravely, and at last fell back, after being continuously in action for twenty hours. Meanwhile, the British commander was hurrying up reinforcements, and the Indian Army Corps, with the support of the First Army Corps, recaptured the position. Nothing had been gained, apparently, but the effect **German concentration** was seen at once on the Belgian coast.   **at La Bassee** The enormous concentration of German

forces of the highest quality at La Bassée had exposed another part of the German lines to attack. It remained to be seen if the hostile commander could also reinforce his troops on the Yser as quickly as he had strengthened the garrison of the La Bassée trenches.

On December 22nd, 1914, the Allies only held a very narrow bridge-head at the Belgian town of Nieuport by the mouth of the Yser. In order to extend and strengthen this bridge-head, a fairly strong force of Zouaves and Turcos swept out and fought their way through the dunes by the sea, and captured the inland village of St. Georges. In about twenty-four hours the German commander made the answering move of collecting a similarly strong force, and launching it in violent counter-attacks

allied armies. Moreover, General Joffre had a fine body of airmen, who kept watch upon the movements of trains and supply columns in the enemy's lines.

He knew exactly how the Germans stood, and the Germans knew that he knew; for he took occasion to prove to them the soundness of his knowledge. And this was the way he did it.

On December 18th our Indian Army Corps began the feint of a grand offensive movement by the Allies. Advancing from Givenchy, the Meerut Division swept upwards towards the outlying German trenches round the rise of La Bassée.

TEUTON SNIPERS AT WORK IN A SHELL-WRECKED BUILDING.

went into action on the left. Their gallant leading brigades dashed through the deep slush into the German position, and captured it at the bayonet point. **Heroic Indians** The men of the Meerut Division were at **and Manchesters** first equally successful on their side. But their advanced companies were soon thrown back by a heavy counter-attack by the enemy, and as they retreated at night to their own entrenchments the situation of the Lahore Division became desperate. It was not until morning broke on December 19th that the Lahore troops saw their danger. The German artillery at La Bassée put a shrapnel curtain behind them, and they were fixed in the captured trenches with their flank left in the air, owing to the retirement of the Meerut troops. They could be enfiladed on both flanks, and no reinforcements could reach them across the fire-swept zone in their rear. They could only hold on till nightfall and withdraw in the darkness.

Then the Germans counter-attacked in greater force with

Then the Lahore Division against the new French trenches. But General Foch threw in more men from his reserves, and by December 30th the French troops had still further advanced to the flank of the main German position—the Grand Dune. Thereupon the Germans fell back and ceased to counter-attack, thus giving clear evidence of the general weakness of their line.

Then, on January 1st, 1915, the French Commander-

PRUSSIAN INFANTRY BEING INSPECTED BY AN OFFICER BEFORE RETURNING
TO THE TRENCHES.
They wore cotton trouser overalls and their rifles were bandaged to prevent the sights from being filled
with sand in the trenches.

LIEUT.-GENERAL EDWIN ALFRED HERVEY ALDERSON, C.B.
Commander of the Canadian Division of the British Expeditionary Force.

KING GEORGE AND KING ALBERT, ACCOMPANIED BY THE PRINCE OF WALES AND THEIR STAFFS, ON THEIR WAY TO THE BELGIAN LINES IN FLANDERS.

in-Chief ordered a movement of advance in Alsace at the extreme southern end of the German front. Here the Chauseurs Alpins, working through the snow, sleet, and frozen slopes of the Vosges Mountains, had a happy success. They placed most of their light guns in concealed positions on their front, so as to command the valley through which they were moving. On the lower ground they came out to attack, dragging a single battery with them. When the Germans, based on Mulhouse, counter-attacked with 6,000 men something like a French rout happened. The French fled, abandoning their guns, and the Germans, elated by their victory, swept down in full force to

Alpine soldiers' clever ambush

capture the battery. The result was that two thousand of the enemy were killed, two thousand surrendered, and most of the German guns were taken, the French losses amounting to scarcely more than two hundred men. It was one of the neatest little ambushes in the war. Having broken the defending hostile force, the French advanced in earnest, and captured the approaches to Mulhouse. This was the great sectional test action. For it took the German commander four days to collect a force capable of making a strong counter-attack.

This long delay showed that he had no powerful reserves, but had to detach men by companies all along his line, some coming from such a distance from the scene of conflict that it took them four days to arrive at their new position. General von Falkenhayn, it was clear, had no large reserves or new formation on the western front. He was able to see that General Joffre was well acquainted with the fact, and was playing with him as a cat plays with a mouse.

It was then that Field-Marshal von Hindenburg was refused any more first-line troops. They were all needed badly in France and Flanders, and the Kaiser came to Laon, the headquarters of Field-Marshal von Heeringen, to hold a council of war. For the situation immediately in front of Laon, along the heights of the Aisne, was growing very serious. From the natural fortress, formed by the seamed and broken

262

plateau, most of the troops urgently needed north and south had been taken. The German commander relied upon his strong artillery power, sited on the most formidable line of heights in the western field of war, to beat back any attack. For both British and French troops had failed to carry the plateau in September, 1914, when they came to it, flushed with the victory from the Ourcq and the Marne. But in midwinter the new French army east of Soissons, which had replaced the British force when our men went to Ypres, had been supplied with the new armament of heavy howitzers, designed to keep down the fire of the German artillery. Along the whole of the front the enemy was losing the special advantage he had possessed in the matter of heavy ordnance.

French attack Soissons heights

For this reason the heights around Soissons had become more open to assault, and on January 8th, 1915, ten thousand French infantrymen crossed the Aisne by a series of pontoon bridges and attacked the hill, four hundred and thirty feet high, against which our Third Army Corps had failed the previous September. Since that date the Germans had strengthened their barbed-wire defences, and had extended their trenches. But the lines were now held so feebly that, after a terrific bombardment, the French carried the firing-line, the support-line, and the reserve-line at ten separate points, and then broke the counter-attack at the point of the bayonet. For forty-eight hours the struggle went on, the French General feeding, munitioning, and reinforcing his troops by a series of pontoons thrown over the Aisne.

On the night of January 9th two more strong German counter-attacks were repulsed, and then at dawn, after throwing the enemy back yet again, the French stormed two further lines of trenches, and captured also a copse on the plateau. A considerable body of Morocco troops, cut off two days before from the attacking French division, had managed to hide between the opposing armies. The new French advance released them, and it was their unexpected attack on the

KING GEORGE ON THE BATTLEFIELD.
During his six days' visit to the troops at the front in December, 1914, the King inspected almost every part of the British lines. He came across many mounds surmounted by wooden crosses, and in each case stopped to read the inscriptions.

enemy's flank that helped to decide the second battle. The next day was marked by an increasing violence in the German counter-attacks. General von Kluck, who was still commanding the remnant of what had once been the strongest of all German armies, was being reinforced. It appeared that a fresh army corps had been entrained to the western front to form the much-needed reserve. The Kaiser, who had a hand in the matter, sent it to reinforce Kluck's lines, and came to view the expected victory.

In the ordinary way the Kaiser would have had to suffer the disappointment which had become customary in these cases; for French aviators had observed the movement of troops round Laon, and the French general commanding the Soissons army also brought up reinforcements. But on the night of January 11th the forces of nature worked against our gallant allies. A thaw set in, and the flood from the melting snow swelled the River
Thaw causes a reverse Aisne into a fierce, broad torrent, and all the bridges except one at Venizel were swept away. Not only could the French commander send no reinforcements, but his troops fighting on the plateau, with the odds of more than four to one against them, were unable to retire.

In the darkness they got some of their guns over the Venizel bridge, while the Germans were making their grand counter-attack under cover of a very violent fire from all their guns. Two pieces of artillery had to be rendered useless, and left in the hands of the enemy, but even when the French division sent most of its artillery back over the bridge, and could not hope for reinforcements, or even for a safe retreat, it fought on with heroic bravery for two days. On January 13th the French troops made a furious counter-attack against the hill, four hundred and thirty feet high, they had lost, and their

comrades from Morocco advanced against the Hill of Crouy. In spite of the steepness of the slopes and the bogs of mud in the hollows, and the massed fire of the enemy's guns, the French captured a trench and a considerable number of prisoners. Then, having checked the enemy, they retired in good order on the night of January 13th, for the Germans had suffered so severely they were unable to press against them.

This affair was one of the most notorious in the history of the war. The German Staff proclaimed that they had won a great victory, which was compared with the Battle of Gravelotte. They claimed that they had killed five thousand French troops, had captured another five thousand two hundred men, with fourteen cannon. It followed that if they had killed five thousand Frenchmen they had wounded another fifteen to twenty thousand. So, all told, they had put out of action about thirty thousand French soldiers, in spite of the fact that there had only been a single wasted division of **Extravagant** ten thousand men fighting against them! **German claims** In matter of fact, the French lost about half their small force and two pieces of their artillery, and they remained strong enough to counter-attack at the end of the battle, and install themselves in the curve of the Aisne, covering Soissons. They repulsed a counter-attack on St. Paul on January 14th, and in so far as the aim of General von Kluck was to cut the French force in two, or hem it in on the river, it did not succeed.

For the Germans were still too weak to assume the initiative. By a violent effort they had massed forty thousand men near Soissons, and defeated the local attack of a single war-worn French division, cut off from its main army by a sudden flood, but after this small and loudly-advertised success they displayed no further activity on the Aisne. Even on the top of the plateau the French were

KING GEORGE PASSING DOWN THE BRITISH LINES AMIDST THE RESOUNDING CHEERS OF THE TROOPS.
This picture was drawn from a sketch and personal description by an eye-witness of the scene so graphically depicted. We are told that the cheers were not of the formal parade character but came from men "who could not await their strict turn to cheer." The King smiled back his acknowledgment to right and left as he passed along.

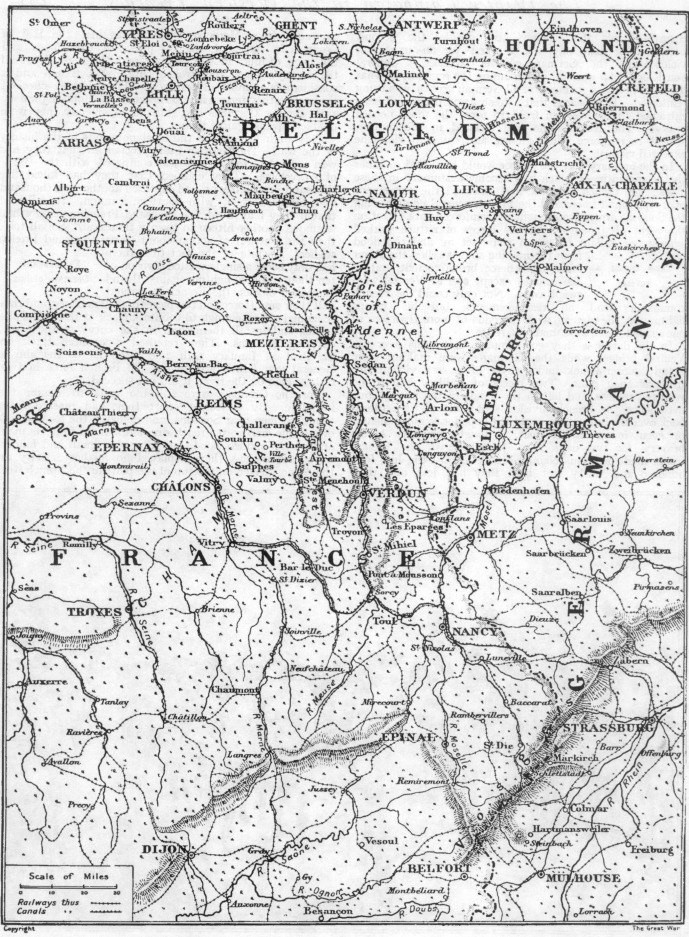

NORTH-EASTERN FRONTIERS OF FRANCE, SHOWING THE VOSGES AND THE SCENES OF
SOME OF THE FIERCEST FIGHTING IN THE WINTER CAMPAIGN.

German machine-gun section holding a barricade in Poland.

The thunder of the guns: French artillery in action.

German officers watching effect of incendiary shells on Rheims.

Field-Marshal Lord Kitchener arriving at a French railway-station.

The British War Minister with General Joffre and M. Millerand in France.

Armed canal boat on a once peaceful Flemish waterway.

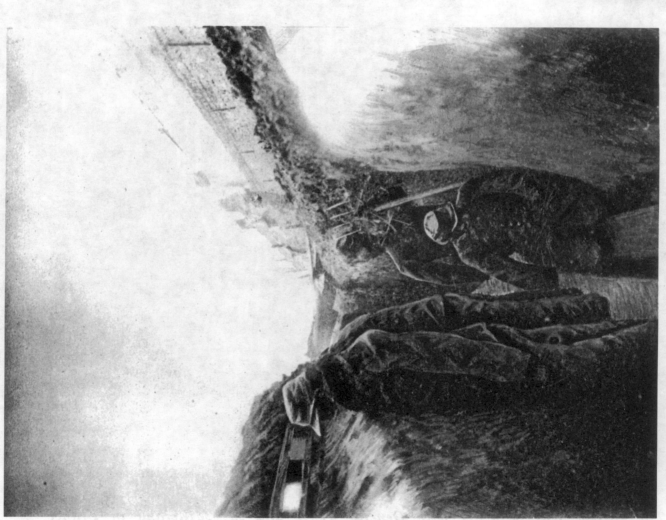

To deceive enemy airmen: Dummies in a French trench

still entrenched at the sugar factory of Troyon, won by Sir Douglas Haig's men in September; and by the river, going towards Soissons, they held on to a bridge-head at Venizel and Missy, where Sir Horace Smith-Dorrien's troops had fought.

The manner in which the Germans exaggerated their success near Soissons was significant of a weakening of their spirit. In the earlier part of the campaign their official reports of the war had been as trustworthy as could be expected in the circumstances. But both sides had minimised defeats and done all they could to sustain the confidence of their public. After the strengthening of the allied line in France and Flanders towards the beginning of 1915 the French Staff became remarkably frank in regard to all old reverses as well as new sets-back, like that which occurred near Soissons, while the German Staff took to hiding all defeats and exaggerating in an extraordinary manner every small, temporary, local success. Berlin was beflagged in celebration of tremendous victories on the Russian front when no fighting had taken place, or when the supposedly victorious German army was being surrounded and set to struggle for very life.

And later, as the spring campaign opened in the western field of war, astonishing impudent claims were made in regard to the capture of important positions such as Hartmannsweiler Hill, in Alsace, from which the Germans had really been expelled. So insistent were the false claims made by the German Staff that the French Government had at last to allow an American war correspondent to visit the summit of Hartmannsweiler Hill in order to prove to neutral nations that it was held by French troops. The same condition of affairs obtained at the British position on Hill 60, near Ypres. With steady and unabashed mendacity the German Staff maintained that its soldiers held this hill, when, as a matter of fact, our men were entrenched upon the rise, and were slaughtering the Germans in thousands on the westward slopes and in the dip of land running towards Zandvoorde.

Capture of Hartmannsweiler Hill

One cheering result of this war of words was that the French Staff drew up and published a statement of the military resources of both Germany and France at the end of January, 1915. Four million men were then known to be represented in German formations. At the outbreak of hostilities there had been nine millions of German men available for service, but of these half a million were needed for railways, administrative duties, and vital industries. Germany had lost on both fronts one million eight hundred thousand men in the first five months of the campaign, and out of these half a million had

"THERE HAVE BEEN ARTILLERY DUELS AT VARIOUS POINTS."

This sentence is repeated in nearly every official communiqué. Our photographs (from top to bottom) show respectively a French "75" sending its answer to a German challenge, one of Austria's heavy field-pieces at the moment of firing, and a Belgian gun in action. The incessant thunder of the guns led to innumerable cases of what is known as "shell shock."

AN ANGLO-GERMAN RIFLE CONTEST DURING A LULL IN THE BATTLE.

In the latter days of 1914 trench amenities became few and far between. Earlier in the campaign the contiguity of the trenches, some of which were no more than fifteen or twenty yards apart, lent itself to occasional rivalry of almost a friendly, or at least a sporting, character. The incident depicted above arose from the placing by a British soldier of an empty bottle on his trench edge as a challenge to the Teuton marksmen. When the Germans found no trap was intended they entered into the spirit of the thing, and provided marks for our men to fire at. On the occasion illustrated a German stepped boldly out of his trench, with an empty tin, upon which a bull's-eye had been roughly marked, and placing it on a branch in the snow, called upon the Britishers to fire at it.

been able to rejoin the Army after being cured. The definitive loss up to the middle of January was thus about one million three hundred thousand men, not counting the sick or the casualties in the last great battle in Poland. Therefore, Germany's available reserve in January amounted to three million two hundred thousand men. Many of them had been untrained in time of peace, and one quarter were regarded as inefficient by German military authorities, while eight hundred thousand of them were men of more than thirty-nine years of age. The French Staff concluded, somewhat optimistically, in their statement of the case, that the total available reserves of the German Empire were about two million men.

French estimate of German strength These were just sufficient to fill the gaps on both fronts up to November, 1915. It was further estimated that Germany had in January, 1915, eight hundred thousand partly-trained men from this reserve available for a new offensive movement. If Germany could be induced to create new formations with these eight hundred thousand men, and launch them in a new attack to break the allied line instead of using them in an economical way to replace the wastage of two hundred and sixty thousand men a month which was being incurred on both fronts, then the end of the war would be brought nearer.

Hence it became the aim of General Joffre to induce General von Falkenhayn to resume the offensive in France and Flanders. To this end he continued to exert an increasing pressure on the enemy's lines from the North Sea to the Swiss frontier. He threatened to break through in one of three places. Neuve Chapelle, near Lille, Perthes, near Rheims, and Eparges, between Metz and Verdun, formed the three points against which the Allies pressed. In between these foci of attack were several places of minor importance, from which railways and roads serving the German lines were imperilled. And far to the south the menace of a sweeping movement through Mulhouse to the Rhine was maintained for several months. Then there were many places of small importance in themselves, where a scarcely perceptible swaying movement went on all through the winter. The ferry town of Berry-au-Bac, on the Aisne, became world-famous through frequent mention in the official communi- **Fresh German** qués, and the Four de Paris, in the **offensive** Argonne, acquired a similar renown. Tracy au Val, below the western slopes of the heights of the Aisne, and Cuinchy, near La Bassée, on the British section, were other little points of renown in the history of the interlocked wrestle between the first-line armies of France and Germany, with Belgium and Britain intervening.

The first serious attempt by the Germans to renew their offensive was made on January 25th, 1915. Apparently the only reason it was made was that the birthday of the Kaiser was approaching, and the Duke of Würtemberg, on the Ypres front, and the Crown Prince of Bavaria, on the Lille front, wished to present their Emperor with a birthday gift of some valuable strategical positions. But the

GRAVES OF MEN OF THE 1st LOYAL NORTH LANCASHIRE REGIMENT: BRITISH PATROL HALT TO DO HONOUR TO THE DEPARTED BRAVE.

operation was not planned in a large way. The French troops holding the trenches near Zonnebeke, eastward of Ypres, were assailed at dawn by a German brigade, the leading companies of which advanced to the attack without any preliminary bombardment of the allied position. The French batteries opened fire when the Germans were hung up in the wire entanglements, and then formed a curtain of lead in front of the main force of attackers. The German reverse was as sudden as it was complete. None of the storming parties reached the French trenches. Three hundred German troops were killed round the wire entanglements, and many more were caught by the allied artillery as they retired at a break-neck run.

More serious was the attempt to penetrate through the allied line in front of Béthune, which town was a principal railway-head for the Allies' positions north of the Lys River. Béthune was more important than Ypres; for if it had been taken, the Germans would have been able to threaten the British communications with Boulogne and the French communications with Calais. Prince Rupert of Bavaria, therefore, thought that Béthune would be a handsome birthday present for his Emperor on January 27th. He began by attacking Neuve Chapelle at dawn on January 25th. This was only a feint to induce Sir John French to concentrate in the wrong direction. The grand attack was launched against the French and British trenches on the south of the canal from La Bassée to Aire. At the same time another fierce assault was made on the British position north of the canal at Givenchy.

Strategic importance of Bethune

The German guns round La Bassée massed their fire to clear a path for their infantry, but our artillery answered by shelling the enemy's gun positions; and the artillery duel ended in our favour. At eight o'clock in the morning the German infantry attacks were made against Givenchy and Cuinchy, by the canal, and against the Béthune road, south of the canal. In both places the Germans succeeded in capturing some of the allied trenches. At Givenchy they swept over our firing-line and captured the village. But as they surged forward down the street our men met them with the bayonet, and in a desperate fight at close quarters, lasting for four hours, the enemy was driven back. Practically every German who penetrated our lines was killed or captured. But the Germans were remarkably resolute. After being bayoneted out of the village they made five attacks on the north-east corner of our position, and the slaughter went on until the enemy had had enough of it and withdrew. Our casualties in this part of the struggle were fairly light, while the losses of the enemy were heavy.

Kaiser's ghastly birthday gift

Meanwhile the German attack on the other side of the canal went on all day. As the Germans came along the main Béthune road they were caught by our machine-guns, till their bodies littered the ground over which they were advancing. But with fine determination the Bavarians held together, and took a part of our trenches in the brickfields near La Bassée. Then, at one o'clock in the afternoon, our troops made a counter-attack, with the help of a section of General Maud'huy's army, and

GRIM HARVEST OF A FRENCH "75"

These Germans were convoying the transport cart against which they are seen postured by the hand of Death when they were located by the gunners of a "75." A single, well-placed shell found them, and in an instant ended for ever their part in the war.

FRENCH SOLDIERS ABOUT TO SEND A BOMB HURTLING INTO
A GERMAN TRENCH THIRTY YARDS AWAY.

FIXING A BOMB AT THE END OF A MODERN CATAPULT.

BOMB-THROWING CATAPULT USED BY THE FRENCH.

ANCIENT ROMAN INVENTION ADAPTED FOR USE IN MODERN WAR.

Three of the photographs on this page illustrate how the catapult—an engine for hurling projectiles, first used as an implement of war by the ancient Romans—was adapted for use in the Great War. The bottom view is of British troops armed with rifle-grenades, the invention of Mr. Marten-Hale. Hand-grenades, first invented in the sixteenth century, were used with deadly effect by the Japanese at Port Arthur in 1904.

THE DESPERATE FIGHTING NORTH OF ARRAS: GERMAN ATTACK REPULSED.

Official French communiqués issued in February, 1915, reported continued fighting north and north-west of Arras. On February 17th, north of Arras, our allies gained two lines of trenches and repulsed a number of violent counter-attacks such as that represented in the above spirited drawing. Numerous German officers were killed, while a mortar and several hundred bombs were captured. The fighting was especially severe near the railway line at Blangy and Roclincourt.

BRITISH PRISONERS BEING MARCHED THROUGH DOBERITZ.
Döberitz, where one of the prisoners' camps was situated, is about twenty miles from Berlin.

drove the enemy back a considerable distance in furious hand-to-hand fighting. Our original trenches, however, were so strongly held by the Germans with machine-guns that our troops had to make a fresh line close behind the one they had lost. But the Germans paid dearly for one small and unimportant gain of ground they had achieved. It was reckoned that the total cost of the attempts made by the Duke of Würtemberg and the Crown Prince of Bavaria to win a birthday gift for their Emperor by January 27th represented the best part of the bayonets of a German army corps. The two points of attack, at Zonnebeke and Givenchy-Cuinchy, were twenty-eight miles distant from each other. There was no tactical

connection between the two advancing forces and no co-ordinated effort. The local defences of both Ypres and Bethune were so strong that an attacking force of some two hundred thousand men would have been necessary to defeat the armies of Sir Douglas Haig and Sir Horace Smith-Dorrien. The attacks were just wild, spasmodic, forlorn hopes, the result of which was that the Kaiser had the ghastly birthday present of 25,000 killed or badly-wounded soldiers.

And what little ground they won was soon lost. For on the night of January 27th our men made a nocturnal attack up the Bethune road and won back some of their trenches with little loss. This brought the Germans out

FRENCH AND BRITISH OFFICERS IN GERMAN HANDS.
The officer on the extreme left of the fore rank has been identified as Colonel W. E. Gordon, of the Gordon Highlanders.

NEUVE CHAPELLE IN RUINS.

on alone towards the second barricade, sixty yards behind the first, and captured it single-handed after killing three more German soldiers and taking two others prisoners. The remarkably small losses of our attacking party were due to the skill and audacity of the heroic Irish Guardsman. His feat was the most extraordinary individual affair conducted by any infantry-man in the British Expeditionary Force.

While our men were accomplishing this success at Cuinchy, the French were equally prospering on our right flank, south of the

ANOTHER VIEW OF THE HAVOC WROUGHT BY BRITISH GUNS AT NEUVE CHAPELLE.
Neuve Chapelle, the scene of the memorable British offensive movement in the second week of March, 1915, lies at the junction of the road from La Bassée to Estaires and the road leading via Croix Blanche and Fleurbaix to Armentières. It was strongly held by the Germans, and the British victory was prepared for by the massing of three hundred and fifty guns on a front of barely two thousand yards, the terrible effect of which is graphically shown in the above photographs.

again, south of the canal, on February 1st. Advancing also before dawn, they took one of our small trenches by the canal, but as soon as the sun rose and our airmen were able to direct our guns, the victors were shelled out of their position. Then our infantry swept out in strong force, and not only drove the Germans from the trench they had captured but seized one of the German posts upon the canal embankment. Our supports then came up, and, rushing through our firing-line, pushed on to the second German post, driving out the garrison at the point of the bayonet. From this position our men were able to take the enemy on the flank.

They fought their way along the German trench southward, throwing hand-grenades in it until they had dislodged the foe from a considerable length of his line, and captured two of his machine-guns. The hero of this dashing

Michael O'Leary's dashing exploit

and important little affair was Sergeant Michael O'Leary, of the Irish Guards. He was one of the leaders of the storming party who captured the German posts. Rushing ahead of his comrades, in the face of a sweeping rain of fire, he shot some of the Germans holding the first barricade and bayoneted the others. Then he went

Béthune road. Here the Germans made three attacks. The first two were beaten back by the French artillery, but in the third attack the enemy reached the trenches of our Allies. The French, however, had only been holding their fire, so as to give the Germans no means of escaping. They opened upon them at point-blank range, brought down all the front line, caught the supports as they rose, and then shrapnelled the last line of reserves. Only three Germans got back to their own trenches.

The reason for all this activity round La Bassée, at a time when the boggy ground was unfavourable to any

SHELL-SHATTERED BUILDINGS IN THE VILLAGE OF ST. ELOI.
St. Eloi is situated where two main roads meet—the road from Ypres to Armentières and that from Ypres to Warneton. The Germans occupied St. Eloi on March 14th, 1915, but the next morning the village and the whole of the trenches except one were recaptured by our troops.

HOW THE TABLES WERE TURNED ON THE GERMANS.
Above is another photograph showing the terrible effect of the massed British gun fire at Neuve Chapelle. The Germans, who prepared an overwhelming force of artillery before the war, and were the first to employ the concentrated action of heavy guns in field warfare, cried out bitterly when the tables were turned on them.

movement, was learned from the German prisoners. From our position on the canal we had brought to bear an enfilading fire on some of the German trenches. Our machine-gun officers could not see what damage they were doing, but according to the prisoners the German losses had been so grievous that it seemed worth while to risk the lives of thousands of men to capture Cuinchy. Our artillery, sited near this position, was also doing terrible damage. In two days, said one of the prisoners, his company lost thirty men from our shell fire. On February 2nd the Germans in the enfiladed trenches broke and fled without being attacked. Many of them left their rifles and equipments behind—a clear indication of the demoralisation produced by our heavy howitzer shells. It was found out that one German company with a total strength of one hundred and sixty men had lost one hundred and thirty men in six days' work of garrisoning the trenches at Cuinchy. The losses had been entirely due to shells and bombs from our howitzers and mortars. Then on February 1st the remaining thirty men were all killed, wounded, or captured. Two neighbouring companies were reduced to twenty men each. The total German losses on this fragment of the front were four hundred and forty out of four hundred and eighty.

Slight as the incident was, it was highly significant of the general conditions under which the Germans were maintaining the great trench campaign throughout the winter; for by far the larger part of the German casualties were the result of the newly-won superiority in artillery power possessed by the Allies. Some of the German trenches round Lille had been deepened to nine feet, with a view to obtaining protection from our 9·2 in. howitzer and the heavy French rifled mortar. The Germans, according to the somewhat sanguine calculations of the French Staff, were losing men amounting to five army corps a month, in the western theatre of war. There was no need to push them back to the shorter line running from the Dutch frontier through Liège, and thence to the Belgian Ardennes to Metz. Far more damage could be done to the enemy by allowing him to retain his existing lines, which he was unable to hold in ample strength, while he was under-

Deadly British shell fire

A SHATTERED GERMAN HOUSE-FORTRESS.
All that was left of a house outside Neuve Chapelle after the British victory. Many of these houses, in positions of vantage, were occupied by the enemy, who in some cases worked as many as half a dozen machine-guns from the doors and windows. These houses had to be taken one by one after desperate fighting at close quarters.

taking an offensive movement against Russia. He was being lured by the hope of obtaining a decision in the eastern theatre of battle in time to resume the offensive in the west in overwhelming strength. Meanwhile his first-line armies were being worn down in their stationary, defensive lines.

Until the Germans stooped to the degrading savagery of employing asphyxiating gases, in extreme contravention of the customs of civilised warfare, there was no need for General Joffre to alter his plan of campaign. The Germans possessed in the coal-fields of Belgium and Northern France and the iron mines of Lorraine and other regions, the grand prize of the war. This made them equal, if not superior, to the people of the United States in their capacity for coal, iron, and steel production. Indeed, they could look forward to excelling the Americans and becoming the greatest steel producers in the world, if only they could hold the territory they had occupied. This economic advantage of their position tended to induce them

The grand prize of the war

LIEUT. L. G. HAWKER, D.S.O.
Dropped bombs on German airship shed at
Gontrode from a height of only 200 feet.

CAPTAIN F. P. NOSWORTHY, R.E.
Awarded the Military Cross for conspicuous
heroism at Neuve Chapelle.

PRIVATE EDWARD BARBER, V.C.,
Grenadier Guards, awarded the Victoria Cross
for bravery at Neuve Chapelle.

to hold on to every inch of ground they had occupied. Meanwhile their new formations were being used up in Russia, as soon as they were prepared for the field. None could be spared in the winter for any movement of importance in France and Flanders.

All these things entered into the scheme of strategy of the great Frenchman of genius who directed the armies of the western Allies. He did not want to break through the German lines in the winter. As against the sacrifice of men which the Germans were making, General Joffre sacrificed some of the principal economic interests of France and Belgium. The sufferings of the oppressed civil population of Belgians and Frenchmen behind the German lines scarcely entered into the calculation, for it was doubtful if they would not suffer more than they were doing if the tide of battle ebbed over their fields, villages, towns, and cities. The allied armies would

General Joffre's economic sacrifice have been compelled to bring their artillery to bear upon all the positions occupied by the German rearguard. Hence the anguish and misery of non-combatants in Belgium and Northern France were likely to be increased by a sweeping offensive movement of the allied armies.

The almost stationary method of French warfare appeared to be preferable from the French and Belgian point of view, especially as the British Expeditionary Force had only been augmented by a few additional army corps. Sir John French now had two main armies, one under the command of Sir Horace Smith-Dorrien at Ypres, and another under the command of Sir Douglas Haig near La Bassée. But they only held about the same length of front as the original three army corps and the 7th Division. Great Britain was not yet in a position to make a great military effort. A very considerable number of the men and company officers composing our original Expeditionary Force had been put out of action. Our comparative losses, however, were slight when contrasted with

LANCE-CORPL. W. D. FULLER, V.C.
Another Grenadier who won the V.C. at
Neuve Chapelle.

SERGEANT MICHAEL O'LEARY, V.C.,
Irish Guardsman, who killed eight Germans and
captured two at Cuinchy.

those of the French and the Russians. They were still very much slighter when contrasted with those of the Germans and Austrians. Heavily as our heroic little regular army had suffered, the vital resources of our Empire were barely touched by the terrible campaign of six months. We had, in fact, escaped lightly from the dreadful crippling effects of the greatest war ever waged on earth, and yet we had given, by means of our sea-power, no small assistance to France and Russia.

If the German Fleet had been able to blockade the French coasts, when France had lost nearly all her coal and iron mines, the result would have been deplorable. Not only would the French have been threatened by a landing of German troops in their rear, but they would have been unable to draw upon the factories of the United States for munitions of war. In the same way a German squadron might have **Influence of British** cut off Russia from **sea-power** the factories of Japan and America, and the German Fleet would have allowed Germany to develop practically all the resources of her own country and the mining regions of Belgium and France, with no competition from the manufacturers of war material in oversea nations, benevolently neutral to the Allies.

All this was prevented by British sea-power. The French Commander-in-Chief was able to look without anxiety at the temporary loss of his chief mining districts, for the French armament firms obtained from abroad all the coal, iron, and other ores they could not produce at home. By great expense of treasure General Joffre effected a great saving in the blood of his people. The underlying principle of his conduct of the war was, in fact, his magnificent economy of French lives. He never forgot that Germany had a population of 68,000,000, increasing at the rate of 800,000 every year, while France had a population of under 40,000,000, which was diminishing instead of augmenting.

STRONGLY - FORTIFIED BRITISH TRENCH AT NEUVE CHAPELLE.

General Joffre was a statesman as well as a soldier, and he fought with an eye on the future of his race. It was the profound and blank spirit of pessimism, produced in all the educated French classes by the results of the previous war with Germany, that had sapped the vital breeding power of France. The glorious renaissance of the entire French nation, foreshadowed by the resurgence of soul ensuing on the victory of the Marne, could be trusted to produce after the war an expansion of life-energy that would gradually heal the terrible gaps in French manhood. In the meantime General Joffre had to take full toll from the German nation for every French life lost. He wanted three dead Germans for every one dead Frenchman. So he continued to increase his artillery and store of shells, and keep the Germans outstretched between the North Sea and Switzerland. His aim was to kill the enemy—kill and wound him at the rate of a quarter of a million a month— instead of trying to drive him back on to a shorter and stronger line. Not until the new German formations began to appear in April, 1915, in the western field of war did the subtle, far-seeing, and sternly logical Commander-in-Chief of the Allied Armies alter his plan.

On the other hand, he had to maintain the threat of a general offensive movement, in order to continue to relieve the pressure on Russia. To this end he secretly accumulated a vast store of shells around Perthes, on the Champagne sector. At the same time he made the feint of a decisive attack against the weakest part of the German lines at St. Mihiel, between Verdun and Toul. At the beginning of the new year the French troops round Perthes were four miles from a railway in the German lines, which fed the German front and helped to link the German army in Champagne with the German army in the Argonne. The loss of this cross-country railway would have been serious for Germany, and if an attack were made in over-whelming force, with cavalry and motor-artillery ready to make a sweeping movement through the gap, the result would have been decisive. Perthes was, in fact, one of the most inviting places for the grand French offensive which General Joffre had been deceitfully threatening since the middle of December, 1914.

So, in the second week of February, 1915, a French army of a quarter of a million men was collected near Perthes, in front of a section of German trenches not more than twelve miles long. The section extended from the village of Souain to Ville-sur-Tourbe in the Argonne. The German line in this region was at first only held by two divisions of Rhinelanders. But the French wore them down early in the year by superior heavy gun fire directed by able and daring aviators. In this region French airmen, from January to March, made three observation flights for every one made by the enemy, and the fire of the French artillerymen, directed by their airmen, was also thrice as powerful. The consequence was that the German commander became alarmed at the pressure exerted upon this part of his line, for the French infantry continually made short rushes against the bombarded German trenches, which were being pushed back at the rate of a few yards a day. This part of the front rested mainly on a chalk soil, through which the rain drained rapidly, leaving the surface—a rolling waste with the rises topped by fir plantations—dry enough for military movements. The Germans brought up 80,000 more men. Some of them came from the La Bassée position, others were fresh troops originally intended for an offensive movement in the north.

French pressure near Perthes

BRITISH WOUNDED FROM NEUVE CHAPELLE: A PHOTOGRAPH TAKEN AT A FRENCH RAILWAY STATION.

It was the knowledge that the Germans were bringing up reinforcements in order to attempt to resume the offensive that led General Joffre to concentrate in great force at Perthes.

He wished to impose his will upon the enemy commander and to direct the movement of the German troops. This he did by throwing a quarter of a million men against the hostile lines in Champagne. The German troops then massed just where he required them so **The Battle of** to do. The battle lasted twenty days, **Champagne** from February 16th to March 7th. The French won scarcely a mile of ground in depth, capturing a ridge overlooking the railway line feeding and connecting the German armies. At the rate at which they progressed it would have taken them a lifetime to push the enemy over the frontier. The achievement of the long battle was not, however, the capture of the ridge overlooking the railway, for the French artillery had already been able to bombard this hostile line of communication by indirect fire from the former French line.

The sole object of the French commander, General de Langle de Cary, was to press against the enemy and force him to concentrate round Perthes. This pressure was continued, until at least 220,000 German troops were massed against the 250,000 French troops who were attacking. Then an enormous number of French howitzers and guns, brought up behind the twelve-mile front, opened fire in an extraordinary way. Over a hundred thousand shells were dropped into the packed German lines, and though the Germans in turn brought up sixty-four field batteries, twenty-two batteries of heavy guns, and an additional regiment of field artillery, the vast volume of French shell fire could not be kept down. The French artilleryman commanded the field—a thing he had not done in such overwhelming power since the days when Napoleon taught men that shell fire was a solution of the problem of trench warfare.

In the small area of ground which the French won they picked up and buried ten thousand dead Germans. There must have been several thousand more corpses in the new German lines running through the village of Tahure. The French aviators, directing the French batteries, maintained the practical command of the air all through the long action, and kept gun and howitzer fixed on the large targets presented in the movement of 220,000 hostile troops. Altogether it was reckoned by the French Staff that from 55,000 to 60,000 German soldiers were put out of action. So terrible were the German losses that the Great German Staff made the frank confession that they had lost more men against the French on the narrow front at Perthes than in the campaign of their fourteen army corps in East Prussia against the Russians. The Germans did not lose a single gun, but at least one-quarter of the finest battalions of their first-line armies in France were killed or seriously wounded. The French losses, on the other hand, were not more than ten thousand. Such was the war of attrition, as General Joffre conducted it when he was fully supplied with the armament needed in

the modern trench warfare. But the terrible wastage of the German garrison of the lines in the Perthes section was only one consequence of General Joffre's scheme of operations. He was anxious to know from what parts of the rest of the front General von Falkenhayn had drawn troops to assist in holding back the menace of a great French advance. In the last week in February it was discovered that at least six batteries of field artillery, six battalions of the Prussian Guard, and two heavy batteries of the Guard had come from Neuve Chapelle and the region north of La Bassée. It therefore followed that Sir Douglas Haig's army round Neuve Chapelle was being weakly held, and that the German demonstrations between La Bassée and Ypres were only meant to mask the enfeeblement of the enemy's forces there. So out of the French victory at Perthes there grew the even more important later British victory at Neuve Chapelle

At this time the condition of our men in the trenches was remarkably good. They had had a hard time of it through the winter in the region south of the Lys, for the Germans held the higher ground about Lille, and entrenched on ridges, hills, and slopes with a good drainage. Our troops, on the other hand, occupied the flat, water-logged plain, almost the only dry spot being at Givenchy, where there was some rising ground, over against the German stronghold of La Bassée. Our lines came through clay soil, holding the water that ran from the high German positions. It was in this shell-pitted, undrainable bog, in a land of mist, rain, and bitter winter winds, that Lord Roberts caught a chill in the second week in November, 1914, which resulted in an attack of pneumonia. He had been visiting the Indian

Elliott & Fry.

LIEUT.-GENERAL SIR JAMES WILLCOCKS, K.C.B., K.C.S.I., K.C.M.G., D.S.O.
Commanding the Indian Army Corps.

Corps round Givenchy, and the brave old master-gunner died within sound of the guns at the town of St. Omer on November 14th. The circumstances of the death of the hero of Kandahar were such as he would have chosen. For it was given to him, in his old age, to pass away on the battlefield. But our soldiers could not help regretting that his wise old kindly face would be seen no more.

It was then that King George conceived the happy idea of paying a visit of honour to our Expeditionary Force. No pinchbeck War Lord was he, trying to keep up in an era of intense military specialisation the pretence of being the chief captain of his people on the battlefield. He left to the men who had given their whole lives to apprenticeship in the art of **King George** high command the full honour of their **at the Front** positions. He was a trained sailor who could take a light cruiser into action, but claimed no more knowledge of practical warfare than that. He came to his Army on December 1st, 1914, as the civic leader of all his peoples. By his presence on the field of battle he desired to show his incomparable soldiers what their country thought of their heroic achievements from Mons to Le Cateau, from the Marne to the Aisne, and—greatest feat of all—the defence of Ypres. In days of peace he had paid visits of honour abroad to Emperors, Kings, and Presidents.

General Sir Douglas Haig, K.C.B. etc.
Commanding First Army with the Expeditionary Force.

CONSTRUCTING A BRUSHWOOD GUN-SHELTER.
How our artillerymen disguised their guns from the prying eyes of enemy airmen.

Now he travelled to the Continent to make a visit of honour to the British private soldier and the Indian private soldier. This memorable act of State began on Tuesday, December 1st, with a tour to the Indian troops and the Fourth Army Corps. Two boy gunners, neither twenty years of age, had the Victoria Cross pinned on their tunics by their King. Then the troops lining the roads close to the enemy's trenches gave a fierce, long-sustained shout that must have startled the Germans and set them wondering. The King went walking down the lines, his eyes sparkling with interest, his face radiant with happy pride in the fighting men of his Empire. He inspected their trench kit of goatskins and strawbags and decorated their luckiest heroes.

So far-stretched was the British front that the next morning, Wednesday, King George had to motor seventy miles to visit his Third Army Corps. **Greetings of loyal affection** All branches of the service greeted him with loyal affection, and, keen on practical details, he inspected their rest-homes, their baths, and the places in which they made charcoal for use in warming braziers in the trenches.

On Thursday the gallant First and Second Army Corps were visited by his Majesty. They were the veterans of the battlefield, having come into action at Mons on August 22nd, and fought for a month without a single day's rest till they entrenched on the Aisne. From the headquarters of the Second Corps King George went on to the battlefield. On his right were the factory chimneys of Lille ; on his left was the ruined Cloth Hall of Ypres, with German howitzer shells bursting in the town as he watched, and sending up their columns of black smoke. A British battery, close at hand, opened fire in turn on the enemy's trenches. The King now stood in the centre of the conflict. All through his visit the sound of the enemy's guns and the thunder of the British batteries had rung in his ears. Hostile aeroplanes, with bombs, had risen on the northern skyline, but their pilots had not approached. Far over the head of our Imperial King circled for days a guard of airmen. The British Army knew how to defend its monarch against every form of attack. It had the lordship of the air as well as an invincible front.

To find the last really historic companion picture to the

TYPICAL BRITISH SAND-BAG BARRICADE.
Constructed by men of the H.A.C. at the front.

King's visit we should have to go back five hundred years, and then turn to the plain of Agincourt, close to the upper course of the same River Lys by which our khaki-clad troops were now entrenched. There Henry of Monmouth, in the autumn of 1415, had reviewed a few thousand English men-at-arms and archers, after their victory over forces four times as numerous.

Our troops were greatly cheered by the visit of honour from their King. And they needed cheering in their soaking trenches and dug-outs, as winter wore on. In December and January, especially, they suffered very badly from a malady of the legs which was called frost-bite. It was really occasioned by a stoppage of the circulation of the blood in the feet ; **Malady of the trenches** the wet, tight puttees of the troops, the chill dampness of the trenches, and long hours of stationary trench work were among the causes of it. A system of rousing exercises behind the firing-line and a regular and frequent relief from garrison work helped to restore the health of the men and to keep them in good spirits. The

GERMAN PATROL ADVANCING
CAUTIOUSLY IN THE FOREST
OF THE ARGONNE.

GERMAN SCOUTING PARTY IN THE ARGONNE.

While one officer is seen carefully scanning a map, and another searching the landscape through his field-glasses, the horses are kept ready at hand for immediate flight.

Indian troops were the surprise of the winter campaign. It might have been expected that they would have found the cold, misty, wet climate and water-logged ground more trying to their health than was the case with British troops. But things fell out contrariwise; for there was less sickness in the ranks of the Indian soldiers throughout the long wearing winter than among their comrades from the British Isles.

In addition to the problem of the health of the much-tried troops, the position of affairs in our Expeditionary Force at the opening of the spring campaign in 1915 was not without anxiety. The character of Sir John French's Army had considerably changed. Many of the veteran regular troops were dead, crippled, or recovering from their wounds, and their place was supplied by drafts of reservists, Territorials, and units of the new national forces. Nearly all these men had to endure the rigour of an almost immobile winter campaign, living in earthworks such as the cave-men of the early Stone Age would have scorned as shelters. Had they all come fresh into the fight, their vigour of body and native stubbornness of character could have been depended

282

upon. But what would they now achieve, in their stale condition, against an enemy famous for his military skill and protected by all the defences that modern technical science could construct? Such was the question to which the British victory of Neuve Chapelle was to be a decisive answer.

Sir John French, no mean judge of the character of fighting men, had discerned in advance the sterling qualities of his new troops. He was, in fact, relying upon his knowledge, which he shared only with his officers, to produce a surprise effect. It was notorious that the German estimate of the new British troops was very low. The Germans were loud in praise of our young regular troops, saying that each private soldier who fought from Mons to Ypres was equal to a first-class non-commissioned officer. But they reckoned, when our casualties began to exceed the number of troops we had first sent out, that the character of our Army would be found to be weakened. In short, they thought that Britain had struck her hardest blow by **A surprise for** land, and that the German conscript **the enemy** soldier would henceforward meet only very inferior fighting material before him in the British lines. Neuve Chapelle was again to show the German that he was wrong.

The British commander had a surprise for the enemy, not only in the quality of his new troops, but in the tactics of battle. Like the French commander at Perthes, who had prepared the way for our advance, we were secretly arranging in the first week of March, 1915, for a sudden, disconcerting development of the Napoleonic use of artillery power. Battle tactics were developing with surprising rapidity on the western front, and the Germans, who

GERMAN ARMY CORPS MARCHING INTO GALICIA TO
RELIEVE THE HARD-PRESSED AUSTRIANS.

thought themselves safe in their deep trenches, were holding
to an antiquated idea.

The French, with their alert, inventive minds, and
the British, somewhat slower of intellect, but with a
fine constructive power of imagination, had discussed
things together and made trial experiments against
the German trenches, with the result that they had
arrived, in a month or two, at some startlingly novel
doctrines in regard to the method of attack. Perthes had
been just a preliminary essay; Neuve Chapelle was
designed to reveal fully the new development in modern
warfare.

Sir John French planned the accumulation of a huge
store of shells in front of Neuve Chapelle, and ordered
some three hundred and fifty guns and howitzers to
be hauled to sites commanding only two or three
miles of the German trenches. While this was being
done our Royal Flying Corps held the air all around
our lines, where the secret concentration
Our secret was being made. The enemy's trenches
concentration were photographed from the sky and
the photographs were measured and
studied by the artillery officers of our First Army. Then
the ordnance was laid in advance, and a few trial shots
fired under aerial observation, to make quite sure that
the target was covered.

At the same time the German system of espionage
working at our base, along our lines of communication,
and even at our front, had to be checked. Trains and
supply columns were marked for destinations at which
they did not arrive, and gigantic masses of shells were
received in unusual ways by the First Army, and
stored handy to the batteries, yet in very inconspicuous
places.

For a week the secret work of preparation went
on, our airmen chasing away every enemy machine which
attempted to reconnoitre over our lines. In other parts
of the front our artillery had to fire more than usual, to
palliate the slight weakening of our front caused by the
concentration of ordnance against Neuve Chapelle. All
this delicate, difficult, intricate preliminary labour was
brought to a promising end without the enemy getting
any warning of the coming event from his airmen or
Intelligence Department.

RUSSIAN PRISONERS OF WAR COMPELLED TO HELP IN
THE TRANSPORT OF SHELLS.

WITH THE GERMAN ARMY IN POLAND.
German soldiers returning in the evening from the trenches carrying
machine-guns on their backs.

283

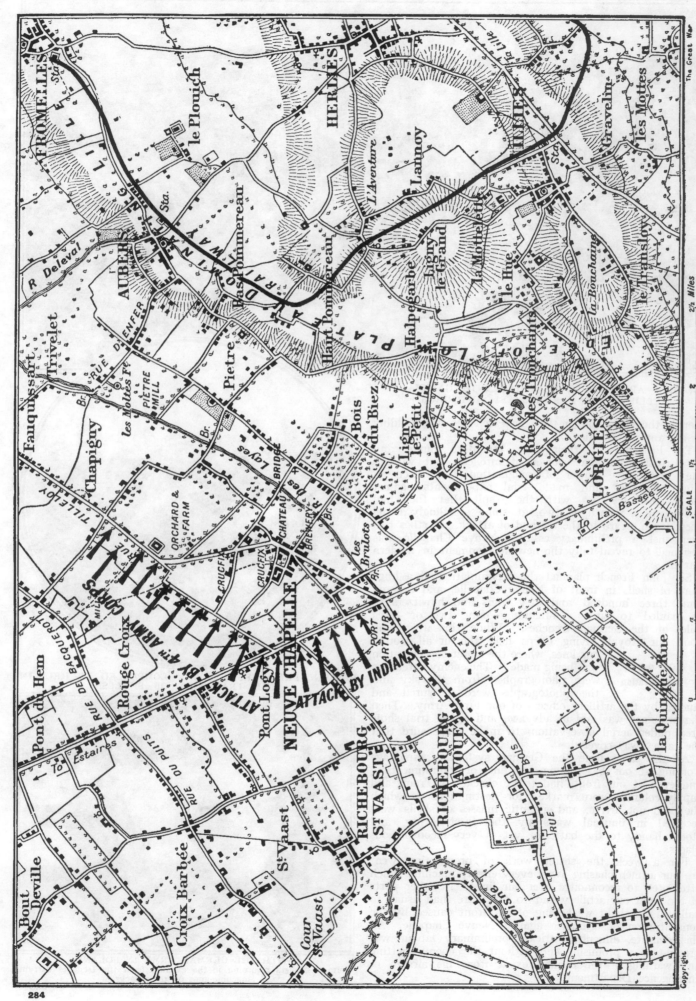

MAP OF NEUVE CHAPELLE AND AUBERS, SHOWING THE LINES OF ATTACK BY THE FOURTH ARMY CORPS AND THE INDIAN ARMY CORPS.

The Great War

Copyright

SCALE

Kilometres

Miles

FROMELLES

Sta.

le Plouich

R Deleval

Sta.

AUBERS

HERLIES

ILLIES

L'Aventure

Lannoy

Gravelin

les Mottes

le Transloy

RUE D'ENFER

Fauquissart

Trivelet

les Moles F

PIÈTRE MILL

Piètre

Hart Pommereau

Bas Pommereau

Ligny le Grand

la Motte-Petit

le Hue

la Bouchaine

Chapigny

Br.

Br.

Loyes

Bois du Biez

Ligny-le-Petit

Rue des Tronchants

LORGIES

TILLELOY

ORCHARD & FARM

CHATEAU BRIDGE

BREWERY

R.

Br.

Fau. Biez

To La Bassée

Pont du Hem

RUE DE BACQUEROT

Rouge Croix

CRUCIFIX

CRUCFIX

Les Brulots

Br.

FORT ARTHUR

RICHEBOURG ST VAAST

RICHEBOURG L'AVOUE

la Quinque Rue

BY 4th ARMY CORPS

ATTACK

Pont Logy

NEUVE CHAPELLE

ATTACK BY INDIANS

RUE DU PUITS

To Estaires

Bout Deville

Croix Barbée

Cour St Vaast

St Vaast

Bois

RUE DU BOIS

THE STORMING OF NEUVE CHAPELLE AND THE BATTLE FOR THE RIDGE.

Sir John French Prepares a Surprise for the Enemy—How Guns and Shells were Secretly Accumulated in Front of Neuve Chapelle—The New Shock Tactics in Trench Warfare—Our Airmen Attack the Enemy's Rear and Bombard His Railways—Our Artillery Gives the Germans Another Terrible Lesson in Modern Warfare—The Fourth Army and the Indian Corps Storm the Enemy's Lines—The 23rd Brigade Held Up by Barbed Wire—The Lincolns, Berkshires, and Garhwalis Capture the Village—Hitch Caused by the Destruction of Our Field Telephone—The 25th Brigade Works Through Neuve Chapelle and Releases the Middlesex and Scottish Rifles—The Checks at "Port Arthur" and Pietre Mill—Unfortunate Delay in Bringing Up the British Reserves—Neuve Chapelle Won in a Single Hour—All Further Progress Prevented by German Reinforcements—Magnificent Charge by London Territorials and Leicesters—Enthusiasm of the Indian Troops after Witnessing the Power of Our Guns—Mist Interferes with Our Further Artillery Attack Upon the German Position—Enemy Counter-attacks in Great Force, but is Beaten—The Fourth Army Corps Swings Up Against Aubers Ridge—Our Cavalry Prepares to Charge the German Guns and Open a Path to Lille—We are Defeated Just When a Grand Victory Seemed Almost to Have Been Won.

THE action of the British army in March, 1915, at Neuve Chapelle was designed to have a more magnificent scope than the action General de Langle de Cary's forces had the month previous at Perthes. The British troops were to crown, by a sudden, violent effort, the long, gradual labours of their French comrades. The French soldiers had attracted and were still holding firmly a considerable part of the German garrison of the trenches between La Bassée and Lille.
The enemy's lines in front of our First Army were seriously weakened, and the only force capable of reinforcing the menaced trench garrison was a body of Saxons and Bavarians, resting at Tourcoing after a turn in the trenches near Ypres. It was hoped that the immortal 7th Division and the 8th Division, forming the Fourth Army Corps, and the Indian Army Corps, composed of the Meerut Division and Lahore Division, would break through the German front and recapture Lille, while our First Army Corps advanced against La Bassée.

One of the reasons why this was not done was the difficult nature of the ground. Beyond our trenches, set in low-lying, flat, marshy country, was the village of Neuve Chapelle, also on the plain. But east of Neuve Chapelle,

and near the hamlets of Aubers, Illies, and Fromelles there was a large, low, horse-shoe ridge, formed by the edge of an upland running towards Lille, Roubaix, and Tourcoing, three of the most important industrial cities of France, lying just below the easternmost slopes. On the upland were the principal batteries defending the captured centres of French industry, and defended themselves by the last earthworks of German infantry at Neuve Chapelle. Our advance in October, 1914, had been arrested at Illies on the ridge, when we were trying to turn the German position at La Bassée. In short, our troops now had to move across boggy ground, through barrier after barrier of wire entanglements, over streams, past hedges, fortified houses, ditches, orchards, and woods, with hostile artillery sending a plunging fire from the horse-shoe ridge ahead.

Then, instead of employing a quarter of a million men on a narrow front, as the French commander could do with his national Army of four and a half million troops, Sir John French could only muster 48,000 bayonets for the most important offensive movement in the western field of war since the Battle of the Marne. He had no more troops to spare in order to make a more comprehensive effort.

[Lafayette.
GENERAL SIR BRUCE M. HAMILTON, K.C.B.
Commanding the Sixth Army.

BRITISH MARKSMEN BEHIND A SAND-BAG BARRICADE.
Often the shallow nature of the ground in Flanders did not allow of effective trench-digging, and our men fought from behind fortifications constructed with sand-bags and carts.

wastage of six months' struggle with fifty to fifty-two enemy army corps, our new army in March, 1915, was not remarkable in number and efficiency. It consisted of six army corps, numbering 144,000 bayonets, and arranged in two armies under Sir Douglas Haig and Sir Horace Smith-Dorrien. The men in the field were excellent—excellent in strength of character and in fighting skill—but there was still not enough of them.

In these circumstances, Sir John French improved upon the example of the commander of the great French army **Shells in the place** round Perthes, and **of lives** massed still more artillery than usual in support of his storming parties. Against a front of German trenches just over two miles in length we had four hundred guns and howitzers. We were using shells in the place of men's lives, and using them in such enormous quantities as to produce quite as overwhelming an effect

At home, new battalions of otherwise well-drilled soldiers of the new volunteer armies were still waiting for rifles and cartridges in order to begin their musketry training. The artillerymen necessary to support them in battle were either waiting for guns or for shells in order to acquire battle efficiency by actual practice. Neither in camp nor in munition factories had the work yet been carried out necessary to equip a large, national British Army. Moreover, the recruiting was not proceeding at such a rate as would justify the expectation of our putting an army of the modern Continental size into the field.

In spite of the official optimism of some of our politicians, we still seemed likely **Our Army in** to remain, as in the days of **March, 1915** Napoleon, a great sea-power with a comparatively small military force. Our Army was growing larger, it is true, but it was only growing enormous in comparison with our very small regular force. Compared with Germany's original military resources of seven and a half million men, and even with France's wonderful production of an Army of four and a half million men, after the

as the charge of dense formations of infantry in German fashion. It was really new tactics, this gigantic employment of artillery power. For the British commander

AFTER NEUVE CHAPELLE.
Three wounded Germans photographed with a British lieutenant and an interested group of British soldiers after taking part in the fateful Battle of Neuve Chapelle.

intended to use in half an hour almost as many shells as the French General at Perthes had employed in a week.

In addition, Sir John French and his Chief of Staff, Sir William Robertson, with the General of the First Army, Sir Douglas Haig, were planning to use the striking force of some of the British Flying Corps in a novel manner, as already explained in Chapter LIV., when dealing with the development of aerial power in the war. Bomb-throwing aviators in speedy machines were designated to impede the enemy's communications while his front was being attacked In particular, the railway bridge at Menin, over which reinforcements from the Duke of Würtemberg's army might be sent to the help of Prince Rupert of Bavaria's forces, was marked for bombardment. Also

COMRADES IN SUFFERING RETURNING TO THE BASE.
This photograph, taken at a French wayside station, shows the rough-and-ready conveyance of the wounded in horse-waggons to the hospital base.

FRENCH RED CROSS DOGS FOR THE FRONT.
Returning from a review in the Tuileries Gardens, Paris.

BELGIAN DOGS OF WAR.
These animals were used to draw the lighter machine-guns. Our photograph shows them being fed by Belgian artillerymen.

the Courtrai railway junction, by which German troops could come southward from neighbouring Belgian depots, was selected for attack. In the course of the battle one of our airmen, Captain G. I. Carmichael, flying at a height of only one hundred and twenty feet above Menin bridge, dropped a 100 lb. bomb, which destroyed a pier, and another aviator wrecked Courtrai railway-station. Later, the railway junction at Don was bombarded, and part of a train destroyed there, by Captain G. F. Pretyman, and Douai junction was also badly damaged. Our artillery also took part in this bombardment of **British airmen's** the enemy's lines of communication. **effective work** On March 10th the railway-station at Quesnoy, east of Armentières, was shelled just as German troops were entraining to reinforce the fighting-line. Many casualties were caused by this long-range fire, directed by a British aerial observer.

The idea was to cut the attacked German force at and around Neuve Chapelle from any considerable channel of reinforcements. In a more immediate manner, our massed artillery was partly directed at a critical moment in the action to the same end. Altogether, the planning of the battle was distinguished by a masterly boldness and originality. All the practical lessons of the Great War were digested into a sound, brilliant, classic example of modern offensive tactics.

Only by a surprise attack could a position of such strength as the Germans occupied be carried. And the opening surprise was complete. At a quarter past seven on Wednesday morning, March 10th, 1915, our artillery was lazily shelling the enemy's lines. It seemed just the customary way of disturbing the slumbers of the Bavarians ; but, in matter of fact, our artillerymen were making sure of their ranges. Then, at half-past seven, began the most terribly concentrated bombardment yet known. Pieces of every kind took part in it. The field-guns, unable to pitch their shells into the German trenches, fired low over them to smash paths through the wire entanglements for our charging infantry. The howitzers sent a plunging fire of 15 in., 9'2 in., and 6 in. high-explosive shells into the excavated earthworks in front of the doomed village. In the distance could be seen great masses of flame, smoke,

earth, and brickwork, all ascending together as the great shells burst among the hostile entrenchments and houses. The noise deafened and appalled. The shrieking of the shells in the air, their explosions, the thunder of the guns merged into a single volume of terrific sound. The discharges of the pieces were so rapid that they resembled the fire of a gigantic machine-gun. During the thirty-five minutes of the incessant bombardment our troops could show themselves freely and walk about in safety. But the fumes of the deadly lyddite were **Path of advance** blown back towards the neighbouring **opened** British trenches, and in one place the upper half of a German officer's body was cast by the explosion into our lines.

At five minutes past eight the gunners lengthened their fuses and pitched their shells clean into Neuve Chapelle village. This left open the path of advance to the bombarded hostile trenches, and signal whistles sounded along the British front. Out ran our men, their officers leading. The Indian troops advanced in a flanking movement,

287

THE KAISER INSPECTING A GROUP OF GERMAN ARMY DOCTORS.

the 25th Brigade were lucky. For the German wire entanglements in front of them had been reduced to four-inch lengths, and blown over with their supporting posts into the German trenches. This result had been achieved by very accurate fire from our field artillery, shooting just over our own trench lines, with the guns anchored on specially - prepared platforms. It was the first time in the war that the direct fire of field-cannon had been scientifically used in this novel manner. It saved the lives of thousands of our soldiers, and practically revolutionised the conditions of modern trench warfare. Combined with a plunging, heavy howitzer fire on the entrenchments, it enabled the attack in favourable circumstances to be carried out at less cost than the defence.

It was the second grand lesson in modern tactics that our "contemptible little army" had taught the Germans. First our infantry had defeated the rushing charges in dense formation, according **A lesson in modern** to the Prussian system, and had **tactics** annihilated the enemy at fifty yards by the mad minute of rapid fire. This had led to the Germans adopting the same defensive method, which they extended into the great campaign of trench warfare. But now the British artilleryman, with an inventiveness equal to that of our musketry instructors, had devised another new system for breaking down wire entanglements and blowing up trenches, which cleared the field for a surprise attack by our rapid-firing riflemen.

from Richebourg St. Vaast and the Rue de Bois, against the south side of Neuve Chapelle; the British troops swept up in rushes against the main western German position in front of the village; for the weakness of the German lines at Neuve Chapelle was that they formed a salient, jutting into the British front. The salient was attacked on two sides, just as the enemy had continually assailed our salient at Ypres.

The design was to envelop, by attacks directed both west and south of the village, the enemy force that would be driven by the dreadful artillery fire from the entrenchments into the houses. As a matter of fact, when the British and Indian troops met in Neuve Chapelle they captured or killed the Germans in the village, taking in all some two thousand prisoners. This result was largely due to the effective plan of attack arranged by Sir Douglas Haig. Against the German trenches on the north-west of the village there advanced the 23rd Brigade and the 25th Brigade, forming part of Sir Henry Rawlinson's corps. Then against the German entrenchments south of Neuve Chapelle went forward the Garhwal Brigade of Sir James Willcocks's Indian Army Corps.

Both the Garhwal Brigade and

KAISER WILHELM IN EAST PRUSSIA.

The success of the action depended mainly upon the extreme accuracy of direct fire by our light field-guns, for where the gunners had not shot away the German wire entanglements our troops were held up by these obstacles. Such was the case with our 23rd Brigade that rushed forward on the left of the 25th Brigade, but was held up by an unbroken tangle of barbed - wire in front of the first German trench. Most of the Germans left alive in the deep trenches were maddened with fright,

PRUSSIA'S WAR-LORD DECORATING OFFICERS OF THE GERMAN FLYING CORPS WITH THE IRON CROSS.

THE KING OF BAVARIA IN THE TRENCHES.
King Leopold of Bavaria visited the German trenches in Flanders and made stirring speeches of encouragement to the troops.

half-dazed by the explosions, and eager to surrender. But where the wire was still unbroken, two undaunted German officers with a machine-gun stood firm and cool, and poured a galling fire into our baulked men. The leading companies of the "Diehards" (Middlesex) and the Scottish Rifles suffered heavily. The utmost the 23rd Brigade could do was to lie down and scrape up cover under a murderous fire, and thus hold the enemy.

Meanwhile the two more fortunate brigades, better served by their artillery, swept along unimpeded, taking more prisoners than they wanted at the moment, and capturing trenches. The Lincolns and Berkshires seem to have led the British Brigade, while the Second 39th Garhwalis were the foremost troops of the Indian Brigade. With hand-grenade work and bayonets they cleared the first hostile line of all Germans who showed fight, assembled the prisoners, and then held the captured positions in preparation for the next step of the advance.

Behind the Lincolns and Berkshires were **Field telephones cut by fire** waiting the Royal Irish Rifles and the Rifle Brigade. It had been arranged that, on capturing the trenches, the leading troops should swerve to right and left, so as to let the Irishmen and the Rifle Brigade through to capture the village. In the same way the Second 39th Garhwalis had to stay in the trenches they took, and let the First 39th Garhwalis rush out and capture the dense woodland of the Bois du Biez, behind Neuve Chapelle. But at this point there was a hitch in the execution of the brilliant plan of Sir Douglas Haig. The trenches had been captured in a swift rush, much quicker than had been expected by our artillery officers. Our guns were still forming an impassable curtain of fire in front of Neuve Chapelle, to prevent any German supports in the village reinforcing the firing-line. But the firing-line had been captured, and our own gun fire prevented our men from making a surprise attack on the village. Such things always happen in war. As a matter of fact, all our field telephones had been cut by the enemy's

GERMAN CROWN PRINCE AND HIS UNCLE.
The Kaiser's eldest son in conversation with Prince Henry of Prussia during the latter's visit to the Crown Prince's Headquarters at the front.

fire, and there was no communication between our advanced infantry and the enormous number of guns and howitzers, some of which were placed miles in our rear.

No soldier ever grumbles over a mishap of this sort, for the effect of an enemy's fire in a hotly-contested action usually disarranges some of the delicate machinery of a modern army. This is one of the reasons why soldiers are conservatively distrustful of all newly-invented instruments of warfare. The new weapons may work excellently on the peaceful, undisturbed testing ground; but shell and shrapnel charges, streams of bullets from

FRENCH "75" ON A REVOLVING
PLATFORM.

machine-guns, and chance rifle shots upset all things on a battle-field. A battery suddenly changing position in a moment of extreme urgency, when only the effect of the guns can be thought of, sometimes crushes and breaks all the ground wire on a large section of the fighting-front. Thus the accident to our field telephones was nothing unusual.

In spite, moreover, of this interruption, the village of Neuve Chapelle and the roads leading north and south-west from its eastern end were captured in the morning; for at ten o'clock the Rifle Brigade raced head-long into Neuve Chapelle, where they were met by the little muscular hill-men of Nepaul, the 3rd Gurkhas. The two regiments had known each other and worked together when brigaded in India, and when they met in the captured village,

ON OUTPOST DUTY—" SOMEWHERE ON THE
CONTINENT."

smeared with the dust and blood of victory in an advance conducted from different directions, Briton and Indian hailed each other in triumphant friendship.

A wild and terrible scene

Wild and terrible was the scene around them. In the autumn of 1914 Neuve Chapelle had been a quiet, pleasant, picturesque French village, with a white, old-fashioned manor house, a mill-stream and a mill, farmhouses set in apple orchards, and a little churchyard, with a great crucifix rising by the side of the church.

But when our guns had done with it, Neuve Chapelle was more desolate than the scene of an earthquake. Only the shell of the church remained. In the churchyard, skeletons had been blown out of their coffins by the great shells, and the bones of the dead forefathers of the hamlet were scattered on the

grey-clad corpses of the barbarians of Germany. All the houses were unroofed, with their rooms blown out, and great gaps made in the walls. But two things strangely remained erect amid the ruins—the great crucifix in the churchyard and another large cross by the old white manor house. Pitted with bullet-marks, these emblems of the faith of Christendom remained above the wreck and rubble of the hamlet.

But there was little time for our troops to remain spectators of the scene. They could scarcely hear each other speak, for our massed artillery was still maintaining a curtain of shrapnel fire beyond Neuve Chapelle to keep off the German reinforcements.

Annihilating shrapnel fire

The Germans on the slopes of the distant ridge tried to work down through the wood, with the intention of forcing our men back in a hand-to-hand combat. But they could not get through the curtain of death flung out from our guns. As our prisoners afterwards reported, all attempts made by the enemy to strengthen his fighting-line were checked by the annihilating fire of our guns.

Practically, therefore, all the German troops in the village were for the time in a state of siege. Through the thick pall of shell-smoke on all sides some of them emerged from cellars and dug-outs, holding their hands above their heads, all their fighting spirit knocked out of them by our terrifying guns. Others, still gallantly lusting for battle, dodged round the shattered buildings, fired from the blown-in windows, from behind carts, and even from a barricade of tombstones. Then there were unroofed houses from which the brave survivors of machine-gun

MASKED BRITISH GUN THAT WORKED HAVOC IN ENEMY'S RANKS NEAR YPRES.

parties tried to sweep away our leading sections. But the 25th Brigade soon worked round to the left of Neuve Chapelle, and, turning the flank of the Germans entrenched behind the unbroken wire entanglements, released the heroic Middlesex Regiment and the Scottish Rifles This completed the capture of the whole of the village of Neuve Chapelle, which was accomplished by eleven o'clock in the morning

After this, however, there was considerable delay in the general British advance. The check to the left of the 23rd Brigade had kept back other forces of our 8th Division, and had compelled part of the 25th Brigade to turn and fight northward, out of its proper line of advance. All the leading infantry was much disorganised by the violent effort of fighting through the enemy's trenches, and then shooting and bayoneting a way through the buildings of the village. Also, the interruption of telephone communications between our outflung front and our distant rear still hindered **"Port Arthur" and** our guns from accurately co-operating **Pietre Mill** with our attacking infantry. Houses held by German machine-gun parties might have been quickly shattered if our guns could have been brought to bear upon them at once. As it was, our infantry often lost heavily in trying to capture such difficult positions simply by rifle-shot and bayonet. In particular, there were three fortified German posts which were difficult for unaided infantry to attack. One lay at the extreme right of the line, where a German trench defended by barbed-wire remained uninjured, with its garrison, by a group of ruined houses. This was called by our soldiers "Port Arthur." By the other end of the line was a still stronger German position at Pietre Mill. In between Pietre Mill and "Port Arthur" was a bridge over the stream Des Layes. This bridge was also fortified and held by Germans with machine-

guns. Besides these hostile strongholds, there were more German machine-guns posted in the houses along the Pietre road. So, altogether, there was much work to be done around the captured village before our two army corps could hope to advance towards the ridge leading to Lille.

The reorganisation of the leading brigades of the Fourth Corps and the re-establishment of telephonic communications between our advanced front at Neuve Chapelle and our rear took some **Fourth Corps** hours. It was half-past three in the **reorganisation** afternoon of that glorious Wednesday before Sir Henry Rawlinson's troops were able to renew their attack. And the gallant Indian warriors, under Sir James Willcocks, were in similar difficulties, and were not prepared to advance farther until about the same time.

During the interval there was carried on the vitally necessary work of forming our new line in the rear of Neuve Chapelle, making deep trenches, with parapets and shrapnel cover against the enemy's batteries on the ridge, with communicating trenches and support earthworks. Meanwhile, Sir Douglas Haig was employing all the leading

BRITISH ARMY SERVICE CONVOY ON THE ROAD.   INSET: VIEW OF THE ROAD FROM NOORDSCHOCTE TO PYPEGALE.

forces of the rest of the First British Army in keeping the enemy engaged on his front. His famous First Army Corps, that had fought from Mons to the Marne and stormed the northern heights of the Aisne in September, 1914, and then held Ypres in October against all the forces that the German Emperor could concentrate against it, was now holding the positions at Givenchy and Cuinchy

Held up by barbed wire

and the brickfields round La Bassée. Simultaneously with the attack on Neuve Chapelle the First Army Corps advanced from Givenchy on the German lines in front of La Bassée. But here our field-guns, in their preliminary bombardment, had not succeeded in destroying the German wire entanglements. The fact was that only one or two of our brigades of light artillery had at once mastered all the exceeding difficulties of their strange new task. After the battle, the most successful of the light field artillerymen at Neuve Chapelle were sent as instructors in the novel art of wire-entanglement destroying along our front. But at the first essay there were many failures, and round Givenchy

was thrown out of gear, and when at last the village was won, with various German strongholds still resisting fiercely, a new plan of action had to be thought out quickly. This, again, is usually what happens in battle. Deep-laid preparations, such as the Germans often stake everything on, are merely the work of industrious talent for war. They assume a passive enemy who fights in routine fashion. The commander of genius has a faculty for improvising rapidly new means of attack or defence to suit the continually changing situations of actual warfare.

It was in between Neuve Chapelle and Aubers that the most impregnable German machine-gun positions were situated. There was an orchard north of Neuve Chapelle from which the Germans threatened the flank of any advance on the Aubers ridge. Then further eastwards was the Pietre Mill stronghold, strengthened by a defended work and roadside houses with hostile machine-guns, that held up our 22nd Brigade. Farther to the south an entrenched German garrison at the cross-roads, six hundred yards north-west of Pietre, stayed the forward movement of the 24th Brigade. All these checks in the neighbourhood of the ridge impeded any forward movement of the 7th Division.

But about eleven o'clock in the morning, when the interval of reorganisation occurred in Neuve Chapelle, some of the troops of Sir Henry Rawlinson's renowned Division were ordered to advance towards Aubers. This was partly done to stretch out to the full the enemy's available forces, and help to weaken the resistance behind the captured village. By this time the German artillery, though greatly outnumbered by our massed guns, began to act vigorously and shell our front.

Two battalions rushed forward in long waves and disappeared in the battle smoke. Then the rest of the brigades charged. All through the day the men were magnificent. Anywhere their officers led them they went. The air was alive with shells and bullets, making a buzzing noise as in a tropical forest in midsummer. There was an open stretch swept by a terrible gun fire. The troops crossed it in rushes and gained the shelter of some houses. The advanced battalions had captured a trench beyond, and the Germans tried a counter-attack, but were repulsed. The remnant of a leading regiment passed by, sixty men going to the rear. An officer asked them where they were going. " We've stormed every —— trench and every —— village

MAP OF THE FIERCELY-CONTESTED AREA IN THE VICINITY OF NEUVE CHAPELLE.
With smaller scale plan of the country between Ypres and La Bassée.

especially the hostile tangles of barbed-wire were insufficiently cut to enable the infantrymen to make progress. All they could do was to pin the German troops in their entrenchments and prevent them from reinforcing the Neuve Chapelle front. In short, our First Army Corps only demonstrated.

Equally unsuccessful, through no fault of theirs, was the 7th Division of the Fourth Corps, operating to the left of Neuve Chapelle, against the Aubers ridge. The Immortal Division, the heroes of Ypres, had bad luck. As Sir Douglas Haig appears to have planned the action, the 7th Division was to wait until the leading brigades of the 8th Division had captured the German trenches and take Neuve Chapelle; then, as the German position at Aubers was shaken by a flanking movement, they were to advance and storm through Aubers and win the ridge running towards Fournes and Lille.

But when the 23rd Brigade was held up by unbroken wire, north-west of Neuve Chapelle, the provisional scheme fell through. The movement of the 8th Division

in this —— country," said one of the men. " All our officers are shot, and we thought it about time someone else had a go."

By half-past five in the afternoon part of the Division had, by heroic fighting, worked its way almost opposite to Aubers. There it was ordered to storm some of the outlying houses. Crawling out of their trenches, our troops advanced across the open under a heavy fire from

The attack on Aubers

the enemy's artillery. But our guns had still some ammunition to spare, and though they could not silence the opposing batteries, they did great damage to the German entrenchments. However, our advanced infantry could not make much progress, and as darkness fell they dug themselves in on the ground they won. All night they were incessantly bombarded. Then at dawn on March 11th they tried again to carry Aubers, but the enemy's shell fire from the ridge was overwhelming. The attack failed. But, in matter of fact, it was only a strong demonstration; for the situation at Neuve Chapelle, on which a success at

Speaight

General Sir Henry Macleod Leslie Rundle, Commanding the Fifth Army.

Remarkable instantaneous photograph of a small isolated Russian force surrendering to Austrians

A scene behind Austrian earthworks during a battle in the Carpathians.

Troop of Uhlans leaving cover in Champagne district to charge the French.

Field=Marshal French makes a wayside inspection of infantry on their way to the trenches.

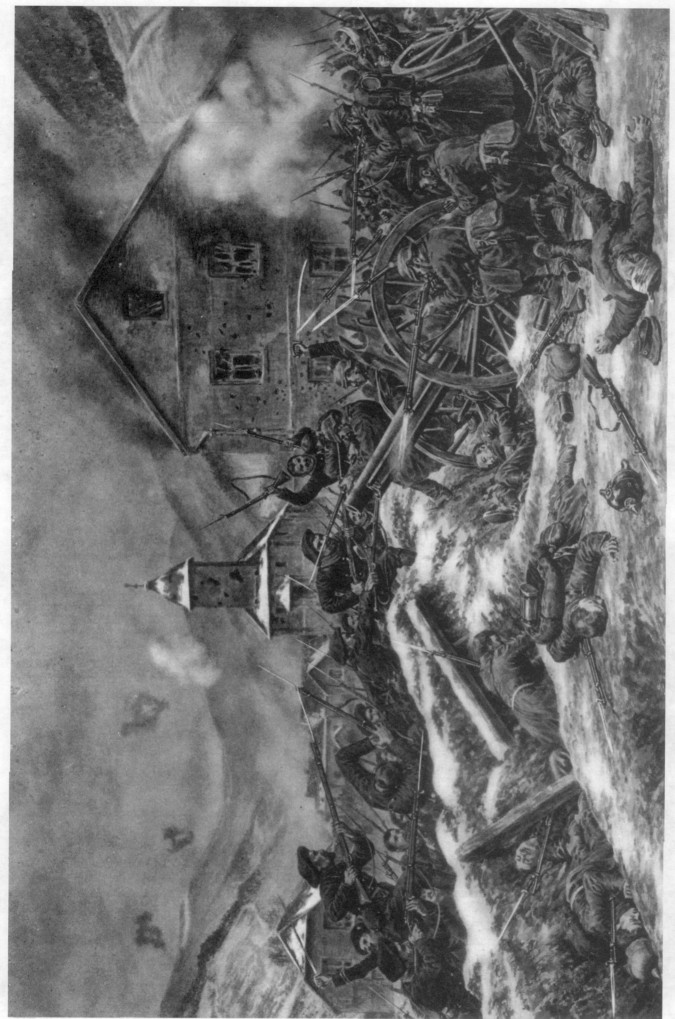

The capture of Steinbach by the French in the first week of January, 1915.

Aubers depended, had not much improved since the previous day.

It is important neither to underestimate nor to exaggerate our achievement at Neuve Chapelle. Our plan of attack there was brilliantly conceived, and executed generally with remarkable skill and noble gallantry. The slight check in regard to the breaking of telephone communications and the failure to destroy part of the hostile wire entanglements were ordinary inci-

Ground won in a single hour dents of battle. Such things, and even more of them than occurred, were allowed for in advance, for our actual success was so rapidly achieved that its quickness was a surprise to our Staff. We won more ground at Neuve Chapelle by artillery fire and infantry charges in a single hour than a quarter of a million of our French comrades at Perthes had gained in a week. And we only deployed 48,000 men to obtain this result.

But great as our success was, it might have been far greater. In the considered opinion of Sir John French, the fault that prevented the grand extension of our offensive movement rested with Sir Henry Rawlinson, commanding the Fourth Army Corps. He did not use his reserves at the critical moment. He was rather too cautious and prudent, content with sure, small gains rather than foresightful adventurous ones. He should have thrown his reserves forward into the fight on the morning of March 10th. At eleven o'clock on that morning when the village had been won, the disorder in our fighting-line, caused apparently by tactical errors, might at once have been restored if strong reserves had at once taken on the work of pushing the enemy back. For the Germans were then still reeling from the tremendous surprise attack, and their line might have been completely pierced with comparatively little loss if the entire weight of the Fourth Army Corps had been brought to bear quickly at the critical point.

A delay of four and a half hours in restarting the attack prevented us from making progress ere night fell, and interrupted the work; for by the next morning the enemy had recovered from his dismay and surprise, and by making new entrenchments and bringing up strong reinforcements he was able to check our advance. Our victory of Neuve Chapelle was won in three hours on the morning of March 10th, and won with comparatively little loss. It was afterwards that we had 1,751 men and officers taken prisoners, and 10,000 officers and men killed or wounded. Of our total losses of 12,811 men less perhaps than 2,000 were in the actual victory. "The difficulties might have been overcome at an earlier period of the day," says Sir John French in his despatch, "if the general officer commanding the Fourth Corps had been able to bring his reserve brigades more speedily into action."

By noon on Wednesday the German position by the orchard and farm in the north-east of the village was carried by the troops of the Fourth Corps. There our 21st Brigade had at first been able to form up in the open, without a shot being fired at it, owing to the enemy's resistance being paralysed by our terrific gun fire. But when the Worcesters afterwards came to the farmhouse, the Germans had recovered from their dismay. Still, they could not put up such a fight as they afterwards did at Pietre Mill. The Worcesters chased them round the orchard trees with the bayonet and captured the farmhouse, and found one remarkably fat German trying to squeeze his body up the chimney. On the other side of Neuve Chapelle, however, where the Indian Brigades were operating, "Port Arthur" still held out strongly. The First 39th Garhwalis made an heroic effort to storm it. At the sound of a whistle the men leaped from their trenches and charged across the ground. But they were raked by machine-gun fire; before they reached the barbed-wire entanglements all the officers of the leading companies were killed, with many of the men. Staggering under the terrible fire, the battalion swerved to the right, and after a wild, sharp, hand-to-hand fight they captured part of the trench. But there they were fixed by German troops occupying the other trenches. The battalion had twenty officers and three hundred and fifty men killed and wounded before the fight ended. Cut off from the rest of the army, the gallant little hillmen held on, till the 2nd

MAKING THE BEST OF IT.
An impression of the lot of the British despatch-rider in rain-soaked Flanders.

Leicesters came to them with a rush, and one of their bombing parties crept down the communication trench and pelted the Germans with hand-grenades, forcing them out into the open. About half-past five in the afternoon "Port Arthur" was stormed at the point of the bayonet. We were then in possession of all the enemy's trenches on a front of four hundred yards, having driven in to a depth of three-quarters of a mile from our own lines.

Among the regiments who greatly distinguished themselves in the second part of the attack was the Territorial Battalion of the Royal Fusiliers. The Londoners made a magnificent charge **Territorials' magnificent charge** on the last German stronghold. Yelling, they tore across the shelled field, dropping men as they went along, while some of our regular soldiers cheered them as they passed. No German machine-gun could stop them, and in a swift and violent attack with cold steel they stormed the enemy's position and rounded off the conquest of the village.

Meanwhile the delay in bringing up our reserves enabled the Germans to bring up reinforcements, and to organise a stubborn resistance along the Pietre road, and on the edge of Biez Wood by the stream of Des Layes. It is known that at the German headquarters at Lille preparations for a general retirement had commenced, so overwhelming had been the first unexpected onset of the British forces. But every German soldier that could possibly be collected was sent over the ridge to stop the gap. More machine-guns were brought down to the new German firing-line, and the Bavarian and Saxon troops resting at Tourcoing were hurried up towards Aubers and Biez Wood. On the evening of the day of victory the Gurkhas made a gallant attempt to drive through the new German lines. They stormed up the rising ground and penetrated into the wood. But the Germans had a machine-gun stronghold northward, at the bridge over the stream, and from

DESOLATE FLEMISH BATTLE AREA.
Embankment built by the German invaders in Flanders.

this position they got a blast of enfilading fire on the Indian troops, which compelled our men to retire. Sir Douglas Haig then brought up three battalions of the First Army Corps, while his guns were shelling the fortified bridge over the River Des Layes. But by this time the enemy was also reinforced in great strength, and all that the Indian Corps and the Fourth Army Corps could do was to entrench on the ground they had won, and labour with the utmost energy to make good shelters against the enemy's artillery fire.

When day broke on Thursday, March 11th, the fortunes of war were against us, as the weather was very foggy. We were relying on our artillery to break **German artillerymen's advantage** down the houses and other defended positions which the Germans were holding all along our front. But our airmen could not see clearly enough to direct the fire of our guns, and our engineers had not been able to get the quantity of material necessary to restore all our telephonic communications.

The German artillerymen on the ridge had the advantage of knowing exactly the range of all the lost entrenchments of their infantry, and having brought up new supplies of munitions in the night they opened a furious shrapnel

fire. As a matter of fact, there were few veritable trenches along the ground we had won, for the soil was so marshy that water was struck at a depth of two feet. So instead of excavating earthworks on both sides in this region, we built up barricades of sand-bags, with ordinary wire entanglements in front of them. As a general rule, the enemy's defences were superior to ours, with loopholes of bullet-proof steel and concrete work, and immense quantities of timber, making altogether comfortable and secure shelters. But round Neuve **Our sand-bag** Chapelle the German works were inferior **barricades** to ours in construction, drainage, and sanitation, and though our men set to work to alter and improve some of them, and reversed the position of the sand-bags, barricades, and wire posts, many of our defences were new constructions thrown up in the night close to the new German lines. These lines were of an extraordinary strength. For instance, on one section of the German front, two hundred and fifty yards in length, there were fifteen machine-guns. Their concentrated fire made any attack by our infantry impossible of success. Only our guns could break a path, and, unfortunately, the weather was adverse to our system of aerial fire-control.

EN ROUTE TO THE TRENCHES.
Across wooden pathways made over the marshy land in Flanders.

On the other hand, our rifle fire was remarkably good. If, as was reported, the Germans had eight machine-guns to a battalion, yet our more capacious magazine rifles helped to restore the balance of fire. After their bombardment on Thursday morning the German troops came down in close order to recapture Neuve Chapelle. Our men held their fire till the enemy was forty paces away, and then knocked the deep, dense German lines to pieces. Not only was the attack beaten back, and hundreds of prisoners taken, but both the Indian and British troops advanced in bayonet charges against their beaten foes. The Highland Light Infantry, however, had a hard struggle to maintain

PEACE AND WAR.
A ploughman tilling the soil in Northern France. Meanwhile the officer in charge of a French armoured motor-car, map in hand, is keeping a keen look-out for the enemy.

their ground. Overwhelmed by masses of Germans, they were driven out of the trenches they had taken, but they swept out again, and in a fierce struggle with bayonets and grenades they recaptured the position. Again they were driven out, yet again they returned in one more magnificent charge and captured the trenches a third time, and held them. The London Brigade, already seen at the top of their fighting on Wednesday, fought with the same tenacity and skill, and proved themselves soldiers of the first order. And grand work was done southward by our regular troops, the Irishmen especially shining by the progress they made.

Grand work by Irishmen As for the troops of the Indian Corps, fighting round Biez Wood, they were wildly happy. Our overpowering bombardment of the enemy's trenches the day before had been a revelation to them. Hitherto they had bravely and stubbornly fought the campaign, thinking that the odds in artillery power were heavy against them. They did not know what havoc our howitzers were working in the enemy's lines, but they had abundant evidence of the deadly work of the high-explosive shell and shrapnel charges blown from the German batteries on the high ground in front of them. So they had come to the conclusion that the German-log were the masters of all the world in artillery, while Indians and Britons excelled in personal courage. They themselves never faltered while they had an officer to lead them; but until Neuve Chapelle they could not help feeling despondent over our apparent inferiority in guns.

What they saw at half-past seven on Tuesday morning took them with amazement. Their trenches were close to the German lines, and they could see these lines suddenly transformed into a wall of leaping fire and thunder-blast as thousands of our high-explosive shells struck home. Then, for the first time in France, the Indian troops drank the full delight of battle in the manner of their fighting forefathers. For months they had patiently endured the enemy's gun fire, accepting it with a sort of fatalism as a thing that their generals would never be able to master. But suddenly their grim and steady desperation was changed into vehement and soaring hopefulness. They had always been ready to die, but now it seemed to them that death on the battlefield when all the odds were equal was a happy thing. It was the wounded Indian troops who smiled most in their pain, for what had depressed them was the fear that the German-log, though inferior in manly fighting, would win by their modern machines of

"THE WATCHED POT."
Preparing a meal in a British out-door kitchen on the Continent.

war. Some of the officers of British regiments had had the same dread. While recognising the personal courage of the German machine-gun officers, who in many cases were quite equal to any Briton in cool and fearless daring, they did not think that the average German soldier was as good a fighting man as the average British soldier. Nevertheless, they thought that Germany might win by reason of the remarkable ability of German Staff work, the remarkable number of the enemy's pieces of heavy artillery and machine-guns.

All through the British Army there was a feeling of personal ascendancy, dashed by a half-admiring dread of the superiority of the German machinery of war. Our new Chief of Staff, Sir William Robertson, was well aware of this doubtful feeling. He had risen from the ranks, and he knew the mind of both the British and the Indian private. He had a chief part **Sir William** in planning our tremendous opening artil- **Robertson's success** lery attack, and he designed it with the double purpose of renewing the spirit of confidence in all our troops and of destroying the enemy's entrenchments at little cost of life to us.

But if the British soldier was cheered by our unexpected display of artillery power, the Indians were excited to enthusiasm. In some places on Thursday and Friday they could not be kept in their trenches. They clambered up on to the parapets in order to use their rifles more freely and get a clear view of the enemy. In some of the captured trenches there was not standing room on the raised step, or banquette, for all the men to shoot at the same time. The troops below could not restrain their impatience. They wanted turn and turn about, and some of them pulled down the men in front and sprang up in their places.

Throughout Thursday, March 11th, the fighting continued almost as fiercely as on the previous day. Our store of shells had, of course, been much reduced, and as our war factories at home were, for want

GERMAN OFFICERS' UNDERGROUND DWELLINGS.
To increase the comfort of these quarters doors and windows were torn from houses in devastated districts. Even mats were not forgotten, and telephonic facilities were provided.

ELABORATE GERMAN CAVALRY SHELTERS.
These shelters, photographed in the western war area, were thatched with straw and carpeted with hay to protect the horses from cold and wet.

ground in and behind the wood was untouched by our gun fire, and the enemy's losses must have been very heavy.

The general situation on Thursday night was the same as on Wednesday night. We could make little further progress, and the Germans, on their part, could not drive us back.

But the Crown Prince of Bavaria, commanding the Westphalian Army Corps, the Münster Army Corps, and Bavarian troops in this little section of the front, was determined not to lose Neuve Chapelle without a still fiercer struggle than any that had yet occurred We have seen that it took the German Commander-in-Chief four days to reinforce in overwhelming strength his lines near Mulhouse. It then took him nearly two days to strengthen his line at Perthes. On the present occasion it also took him two days to bring up three army corps against our Fourth and Indian Corps. The Westphalian troops had been shattered by the storming of their lines and the defeat of their counter-attack, and the destruction by our aviators of railway points on the German line added to the difficulties of **Prince Rupert's** Rupert of Bavaria. But by Friday **counter-attack** morning, March 12th, he had collected sufficient men to attempt the reconquest of Neuve Chapelle.

On the following day a thick mist covered the plain and the ridge, and checked the fire of our artillery. Our airmen had to drop two or three hundred yards above the enemy's position in order to reconnoitre for our guns. The enemy's shells continued to break the telephone wires between our leading brigades, and the artillery officers with them directed the fire of the guns from advanced observation posts. At half-past nine in the morning, for instance, over a hundred feet of our wire was destroyed, and there was a long delay in getting it mended. At forty minutes past ten the Germans made their grand attempt to get back Neuve Chapelle. They came down in masses along the whole front round the village and to the north of it. The troops that tried to debouch from Biez Wood were blown away by our guns, some of our batteries having loaded and laid on this mark, waiting only for a signal from the observation officer to curtain the wood off with shrapnel. Elsewhere the Germans were broken by four bursts of rapid fire from our breastworks, and thrown back with heavy loss. The ease with which the Germans were repulsed was so remarkable

of foresight and organisation, inadequate to supply the needs of our fighting men, the Germans, with their superior organisation for the production of munitions, began to recover the advantage. The mist also helped the hostile batteries to escape being again mastered by our guns, and the artillery on both sides kept up a rain of shrapnel on the opposing infantry. Our gunners were principally interested in Biez Wood, in which the German troops gathered for their counter-attacks. When these attacks were beaten off, our guns opened on the wood. They searched it from end to end with rafales—or squalls of fire—to use the technical term by which the brilliant French artillerymen described the deadly method in which they handled their quick-firers. Not a patch of that they only reached our trenches at one point north-east of the village. There they were driven out and pursued with the bayonet. As the afternoon wore on the Westphalians especially began to surrender in companies. Many of the men were exhausted. They said they had had no food for days, that all their officers were killed, and whole battalions destroyed.

This condition of things induced Sir Douglas Haig to counter-attack in turn. At half-past two in the afternoon there was another overwhelming outburst by our artillery. Every British gun was brought to bear on Aubers ridge, north of Neuve Chapelle. This was the battle in which we lost most heavily. From Neuve Chapelle our men could be seen through field-glasses advancing just where the shrapnel appeared to be thickest. The 2nd Scots Guards, the 1st Grenadier Guards, the Borderers, the 2nd Gordons, and their 6th Territorial Battalion were among the troops that tried to storm the ridge. For four hours the struggle went on. Near to Neuve Chapelle there was a fierce contest round Pietre Mill, where the 6th Gordons, under Lieutenant-Colonel Maclean, fought their way up to the houses, using grenades and bayonets. The Colonel fell with a bullet in his body by a trench, and a subaltern brought some morphia to ease his agony. "Thank you," said the dying Scottish leader. "And now, my boy, your place is not here. Go about your duty!"

The Rifle Brigade made heroic attempts **Rifle Brigade's** to reach the ridge. They rushed through **heroic effort** the zone of shrapnel, and then faced the German machine-guns and rifles, and with terrific losses took a trench. There they stayed with their dead and wounded around them, the latter being unable to raise their heads owing to the devastating fire that swept the ground. More troops tried to advance towards Aubers, and reached the line by the Rifle Brigade, but could not get any farther. Aubers, wrecked by shells from our guns, was taken, but none of our men could reach the ridge just above.

At one time it looked as though Sir Henry Rawlinson, with the Fourth Army Corps and its supports, would achieve one of the grand successes of the war. Our 2nd Cavalry Division, under General Gough, came from

Estaires, along with the North Midland Division. At four o'clock on Friday afternoon the 5th Cavalry Brigade, under Sir Philip Chetwode, rode out for immediate action along the Rue Bacquerot, fronting the Aubers ridge. The cavalrymen were to charge through the gap made by the infantry, take the enemy's batteries on the high ground, and open the road for a general advance to Lille. But our infantry attack against the heights failed just when it seemed to be almost success- **Offensive operations** ful. Our troops could not win the ridge, **suspended** and as Sir John French had no reserve army corps to use up in battering a way through the German lines, he directed Sir Douglas Haig on Friday night to suspend offensive operations and hold and consolidate the ground won by the Fourth and Indian Corps. "Most of the objects for which the operations had been undertaken had been obtained, and there were reasons why I considered it inadvisable to continue the attack at that time." Thus the British Commander-in-Chief afterwards wrote in his despatches on the battle.

Our losses in the three days' fighting were very severe, especially among company officers killed or wounded while leading their men onward. A considerable number of our "missing" troops consisted of advanced companies isolated in the trenches they had captured round Aubers and then overwhelmed by the enemy's counter-attacks. The casualties on both sides were about equal.

ON THE YPRES-POELCAPELLE ROAD AFTER THE FIGHTING ON APRIL 25TH-27TH, 1915.
Inset: A striking photograph illustrating the amazing proximity of the conflicting armies. In the foreground is a French communication trench across a village road, with barrels on the parapets for protection against the fire of the enemy. It would have been fatal to cross the road except by means of the trench.

We captured Neuve Chapelle with slight losses, and punished the enemy terribly when he counter-attacked in vain endeavours to recover the village. But he in turn inflicted terrible losses on our troops when we tried to extend our victory by winning the Aubers ridge. But, seeing our gallant attempt on the ridge involved mighty issues for France—the recapture of Lille and the mining district, and the breaking of the German front, leading perhaps to a general retreat—our men did not die in vain. If there was a defect in the plan of attack on the Aubers ridge it was one that could not be avoided. We had too

The nation and the victory
few men. The operation was carried out by the left wing of the Fourth Army Corps, numbering possibly little more than ten thousand bayonets. Our Army in the field had not increased sufficiently in number by the middle of March, 1915—after seven and a half months of volunteering, drilling, rifle-making, gun-making, and ammunition manufacture—to enable our commander to strike with any force. Where Hindenburg could launch seven Divisions of Death on a narrow opposing front that he wished to break, our General could not afford to sacrifice twelve thousand men.

Even as it was, our nation seemed to be staggered by the cost of the victory of Neuve Chapelle. A predecessor of General Joffre, in the high command of the French Army—General Bonnal—had refused to look to our country for help against Germany, because of this tendency of our people to want a victory without paying the price for it. He thought a fighting alliance with Great Britain in a great Continental war would lead to a moral disaster to France, as our outcry against the unavoidable heavy losses of each important battle would undermine the temper of the French public. Happily we were made of sterner stuff than General Bonnal supposed, and, though some of our organs of public opinion complained of the casualties in the Neuve Chapelle-Aubers Battle, the people generally took the matter in the way our soldiers did. The partial achievement was of so striking a character that it was well worth the full cost. The fact that the German front had been driven in, despite a formidable system of fortifications developed for five months by the enemy, was a surprise to friend and foe. The thing that seemed to be a practical impossibility was proved to be an achieved fact.

Then, as our victory at Neuve Chapelle was connected with the previous French victory at Perthes, so from our success General Maud'huy's army round Arras built up another triumph for the allied cause. For part of the German reinforcements that held the ridge were drawn from the position of Notre Dame de Lorette, between La Bassée and Lens, and fronting General Maud'huy's troops. As soon as this was known, the French soldiers in turn bombarded and attacked the hill of Notre Dame de Lorette, and gained a footing thereon, leading to the great victory of Carency in May, 1915. All things considered, Neuve Chapelle is one of the high glories of the British and Indian Army. Sir John French's estimate of the achievement is set out in a Special Order of the Day addressed to Sir Douglas Haig and the First Army : " I am anxious to express to you personally my warmest appreciation of the skilful manner in which you have carried out your orders, and my fervent and most heartfelt appreciation of the magnificent gallantry and devoted, tenacious courage displayed by all ranks whom you have ably led to success and victory."

The effect of Neuve Chapelle on the enemy was extraordinary. He was overwhelmed by the blow struck by our artillery—the arm in which he confidently reckoned his superiority was beyond contest. So desperate indeed was the state of mind of the German General Staff that soon after the battle orders were given for a series of experiments on animals with cylinders of asphyxiating gases. Meanwhile the defences of the ridge at Lille were strengthened by concrete works and armour-plate covers. Only a quarter of a million of the new German **Germany resorts to poison** troops were allocated for an attempt at offensive action on the western front. The main new formations were sent against Russia in the hope of obtaining a rapid decision on what appeared to be the weaker side of the allied forces. The Franco-British lines were regarded as being too strong for an immediate attack. Thus again the tactical initiative was left in the hands of General Joffre, and, in a vain essay to steal it from him by an inhuman surprise Hindenburg came west to see to the employment of poisonous gases—already used against the Russians by means of bombs—while General Falkenhayn went east to beat down Russia by heavy artillery attack before she could be munitioned through the port of Archangel.

WITH THE H.A.C. IN NORTHERN FRANCE.
Trenches captured from the Germans. Note the zigzag formation.

THE KING INSPECTING

CHAPTER LIX.

TROOPS AT GLASGOW GREEN.

ORGANISING THE DEFENCE OF THE REALM : A RETROSPECT.

German and British Plans Contrasted—Individual Rights Sunk in Interest of the Commonwealth—Money Markets and the Coming Danger —Banks and the Gold Supply—Mr. Lloyd George and Lord Rothschild—The Moratorium—How the Threatened Panic was Stayed— War and Trade—Harmony Between Employers and Employed—Government and the Railways—State Insurance of British Shipping—Regulation of Food Supplies—Defence of the Realm Act—Equipment of the New Armies—A Committee of Production— Drink Factor and the Shell Supply—The King's Example—Problem of the Alien Enemy and How it was Met—German Spies —The Cases of Karl Lody and Karl Ernst—Sinking of the Lusitania—Anti-German Riots—Mr. Asquith's Statement.

T this stage of our historical record it will be well to make a brief survey of the extraordinary economic conditions resulting from the declaration of war, and to show how the British Government grappled with the stupendous task of organising the nation on a war footing. Germany had prepared as carefully for the financial and industrial struggle that was bound to follow the outbreak of war as she did for her fighting in the field. Britain left most of her preparations until war began.

The German organisers knew what was wanted. Their first need was gold. An intimation was evidently given to certain banking organisations holding large quantities of international securities to turn them into sterling, and for months before war actually came they were engaged in a steady process of selling stocks and bonds abroad, securing the gold and banking it in Germany. Raw material was also accumulated, particularly raw material required for the manufacture of explosives.

Industrial experts classified the factories and workmen. Every man had his task marked out for him. The very supply of chloroform and artificial limbs for the wounded had been arranged for. All that remained when war was declared was for the nation to fall into line and carry out its instructions.

On our side there were no corresponding plans. Our ideal had been individual freedom. Capital was free to do as it pleased; labour was free to work where it wished. Suddenly this

THE DOCKERS' BATTALION.
Lord Derby and Captain Williams, Adjutant of the Dockers' Battalion, after the inspection of the Dockers at Liverpool on April 12th, 1915.

old fundamental idea of the supremacy of personal rights had to go. The State, we realised, must now come first, and the ancient rights of the private person must for the time take second place. The factory must manufacture, not what was most profitable to the owner, but what was most useful for the Empire. The workman must labour, not where he pleased, but where his services were most required. The railways passed, almost without notice, into the hands of the Government. The financier and property owner discovered that the " sacred rights of property " had been amazingly curtailed. The Stock Exchange was closed for a time, and then only allowed to do what business the authorities approved. The newspaper was no longer able to publish what it pleased. Private correspondence became subject to censorship. During some months any citizen charged with acts detrimental to the safety of the State could be tried by courts-martial.

Let it be said at once that this curtailment of individual rights was made with the consent of the nation. Here and there objection may have been raised to some particular demand. But the nation as a whole recognised that in time of war individual rights must be sunk in the interest of the commonwealth. The story of the change covers a very interesting period in the history of the war. Up to the beginning of the first week in August the great majority of people in Great Britain did not believe there would be war. A strong party in the Cabinet was known to be opposed

BRINGING UP A "4.7," A STIRRING REMINISCENCE OF TRAINING MANŒUVRES, THE OUTCOME OF WHICH WAS SEEN IN MANY A FAR MORE STIRRING INCIDENT AT THE FRONT.

to it; newspapers like the "Daily News," the "Manchester Guardian," and the "Nation" were striving for non-intervention; organisations like the International Arbitration League declared that: "It is the clear duty of the Government to remain strictly neutral." The average man was influenced not so much by these as by his own knowledge that a European war had often before been threatened and never came. He was confident that at the last moment some way out would be found.

The first signs of the urgency of the coming danger were seen in the money markets. The stock exchanges of Europe began to face ruin. Everyone wanted to sell, none to buy. Prices fell to what a week before would **Alarm in the money** have seemed impossible figures. In **markets** London, firm after firm, including one of those best known on the Stock Exchange, were broken. On Wednesday, July 29th, seven firms were hammered. Foreign houses, particularly German and Austrian, were pouring securities on London, and selling them for whatever they would fetch. The Stock Exchange had to close its doors on Friday, July 31st, to prevent general collapse. On July 22nd the bank rate was three per cent. On July 29th it was raised to four per cent., then to eight per cent., and then, on Saturday, August 1st, to the impossible figure of ten per cent.

At the same time the banks began to guard their gold. The Bank of England took steps to protect itself, and banks generally met demands on them with banknotes in place of sterling. These notes were transferable into gold at the Bank of England on demand, and on Friday and Saturday that week London witnessed the extraordinary spectacle of a queue of people waiting outside the Bank of England to obtain gold for paper. It seemed that a great financial panic was inevitable. We were face to face with the possibility of the entire overthrow of our credit system and of a general run upon our banking institutions.

It was fortunate that the first Monday in August is a Bank Holiday. This pause gave the authorities opportunity to prepare to meet the situation. Mr. Lloyd George, the Chancellor of the Exchequer, who up to this time had

been regarded by the City of London as its worst enemy, now won confidence and gratitude by his courageous action. He called the financial kings of London into conference on that memorable first Sunday in August. He and Lord Rothschild had been open foes. They sank their enmity, and with the heads of the great banks laid common plans to meet the crisis. The Bank Holiday was extended for three days more. A moratorium proclamation was issued on Monday, August 3rd, and was subsequently extended to November 4th, with an extension for a month for bills that fell due up to that date. To meet the shortage of gold, one-pound and ten-shilling Treasury notes were put into circulation. Steps were taken to prevent people from withdrawing their deposits from banks through panic and for the purpose of hoarding.

"Nobody should be so foolish and indeed wicked as to add to the difficulties of the financial and commercial situation by selfishly drawing out unnecessary amounts of money in groundless apprehension that it is advisable to hoard it during the crisis. If a man's credit is good there is no advantage to be gained by keeping more money in hand now than at any other time." This quotation is typical of the exhortations that appeared in all the newspapers about this time.

For a few days people in Britain were faced with a very real shortage of money. The Bank Holiday had been extended from the Monday until the Friday morning. No cheques could be cashed. The banks on the previous Saturday had paid out **The threatened panic** cheques, wherever possible, in £5 notes. **stayed** Restaurants, shops, and even clubs refused to cash these notes, declaring that they were stocked up with them. The result was that many well-to-do people could not find sufficient money to pay their current minor expenses. This, however, was a very temporary trouble. During the time of the long Bank Holiday people had opportunity to think over the situation. Almost every man decided in his own mind that it would be not only a disloyal but an absurd thing to doubt our national financial stability. He would leave his money in the bank, and

GETTING A "4·7" INTO POSITION. THIS TYPE OF GUN, WHICH PROVED SO SERVICEABLE IN THE SOUTH AFRICAN WAR, HELPED TO MAKE HISTORY AGAIN IN FLANDERS.

would go on with his normal life as usual. And so when the banks reopened there was no fresh rush on them. Here and there a super-nervous individual tried to withdraw large sums. The banks had now the power to refuse to pay him, which power they used.

The threatened panic was stayed, but the financial and industrial situation in Britain during the first week in August was anything but promising. When the average merchant or manufacturer returned to his desk after the holiday he found himself face to face with very perilous prospects. His investments were not now immediately available. He could not sell them even at a ruinous sacrifice, for the Stock Exchange was closed. He could not borrow on them, for the banks were chary in making loans. Foreign payments had ceased to arrive, and debts on the Continent of Europe could not be collected. Business men who had been able a month before to command scores of thousands of pounds now found themselves hard pressed to raise enough money to pay their weekly wages bill. Debts owing by them could not, it is true, be enforced under the moratorium proclamation. But the British business man did not want to damage his own credit by pleading the moratorium.

Business was immediately curtailed. A large part of British trade had been with abroad. Most of this ceased immediately, especially so far as the Continent of Europe was concerned. Home buying dropped. The wholesaler would not lay in further supplies which he might not be able to sell; the retailer would not accept extra stocks. Thus day by day during that first week in August the manufacturers found their mail composed of little more than letters cancelling orders. To many of them it seemed that business had come to an end.

Our foreign trade relations

Articles of luxury, objets d'art, pictures, and the like became suddenly unsaleable. The West End dressmaker found that her best customers were no longer thinking of fresh stocks of costly and beautiful attire, but were absorbed in work for the sick or in preparations for the wounded. Entertaining ceased, and the army of caterers for the luxuries of the well-to-do found themselves idle. Holiday-

makers returned home as soon as war was declared, and the tens of thousands of lodging-house keepers and hotel-keepers at the seaside and in the country found their living gone. Advertising largely ceased. No new business was promoted, and old business was paralysed.

This condition of things naturally told on employment. Thousands of young women shorthand typists and general assistants were thrown out of work by the closing down of financial offices. Some factories ran on half time, and some shut altogether. Here and there patriotic business men, possessed of unusual resources, did not permit their people to suffer. "You have stood by us in good times. We will stand by you in bad," they said; and they paid wages in full and kept their staffs unbroken.

Employer and employed

Others who could not do this made often enough great sacrifices. Nothing was more remarkable at this time than the coming together of employers and employed. Factory owners kept open at heavy loss, so that there might be something doing for their people. Employers in some cases met their men and discussed the situation with them. Here and there the workers took the initiative. "We recognise that there is not enough business coming in to keep all of us employed," the workers in one large house wrote to their chief. "We know that some read-justment must be made. We should be glad if, in place of discharging part of the staff, you would allow us to keep together, to share the loss in common, and to have wages reduced all round rather than some be discharged and others kept on at full wages."

The crisis brought out in remarkable fashion the good relations existing, as a whole, between British employers and their hands. There were, of course, excep-tions. But in the vast majority of cases they faced the crisis together. Still, the industrial outlook during the month of August was black. It seemed as though Britain must inevitably face a winter of general unemployment and of deep distress. How this forecast was completely falsified will be shown later. Between Sunday, August 2nd, and Tuesday, August 4th, when the Cabinet, after long consideration, decided to support the neutrality of

305

Belgium by force of arms if necessary, a great change passed over Great Britain. Plans for home defence, which had been carefully worked out by the War Office, came into effect. Railway-stations, bridges, and water and lighting works were suddenly placed under military guard. News came up from a hundred points around the coast of the digging of trenches, the barricading of streets, and the like. At first people refused to take these measures seriously, and laughingly declared that it might be imagined the authorities thought the Germans would invade us. The note of

good-humoured banter soon changed to a more serious tone. A number of Germans suspected of espionage were suddenly arrested, and it is said that a very carefully - planned German scheme was thus crushed. A bill enabling the authorities to move or restrain the movements of undesirable aliens was passed through the Commons on the day war was announced. The navigation of aircraft of every kind, and particularly over the whole of the United Kingdom, was prohibited. Shipping was placed at the command of the authorities, who were given power to commandeer what boats they required for the service of the Government.

Two of the most important measures carried out in the first week for the nationalisation of our resources were the taking over of the railways by the State and the establishment of a Government scheme for the insurance of shipping against war risks.

The State control of railways was announced on Tuesday night, August 4th, **Government and** and it at once **the railways** came into force. Under an Act of Parliament, passed in 1871, the Government possessed power to assume supreme control over the railways of the United Kingdom, in order that the lines, locomotives, rolling-stock, and staff might be used as one complete unit in the service of the State for the movement of troops, stores, and food supplies. The Order-

in-Council, announcing that this power was to be used, stated: "It is expedient that the Government should have control over the railroads of Great Britain. . . . Although the railway facilities for other than Naval and Military purposes may for a time be somewhat restricted, the effect of the use of the powers under this Act will be to co-ordinate the demands on the railways of the civil community with those necessary to meet the special requirements of the Naval and Military Authorities. More normal conditions will in due course be restored, and it is hoped the public will recognise the necessity for the special conditions, and will in the general interest accommodate themselves to the inconvenience involved."

Unsuspected by the country at large, this step had been **War Office** fully prepared **foresight** for long before war began. For this we have to thank the War Office. A War Railway Council was in existence, under the direction of the Army, and included representatives of the Admiralty and the Board of Trade. The work of this Council was to lay down general schemes of what the railways were required to do in the way of moving troops and supplies. The actual executive administration of the lines was placed in the hands of the Railway Executive Committee, a board composed of the general managers of the railways. Behind it was an organisation, the Engineer and Railway Staff Corps, consisting of the very pick of the railway world, whose members were at once placed in high administrative transportation posts,

HOMES FOR BRITISH WAR WORKERS.
The top photograph is of houses in course of construction in the new munition-workers' town at Well Hall Station, near Woolwich. In the spring of 1915 twelve hundred dwellings were being erected where once were one hundred acres of cultivated ground. Centre: One of the houses nearer completion. At foot: General view of a street in the new town.

not only at home but on the Continent. The primary work of the Staff Corps was to assume the running of the railways in case of invasion.

The Government guaranteed that during the time of official control the receipts of the railways should equal

WOMEN AND GIRLS IN OUR MUNITION FACTORIES.
Photographs taken in a Leeds ammunition factory. Left: Machine-workers making metal cartridge-cases. Right: Cartridge-making. Centre: Inspecting cartridge-cases.

those they had recently been earning. The result of this guarantee was far-reaching. From now on it was no longer the aim of the railways to attract traffic by special means to their lines, but to meet the Government needs. All the usual railway propaganda, advertising campaigns, canvassing for passengers, and the like, were cut off in a day. Trains were held up or lines closed whenever necessary. Excursion facilities gradually lessened until, in the spring of 1915, it was announced that on account of the military requirements cheap fares and excursion rates would be cancelled altogether. The private traveller suffered to some extent, although not so much as might have been expected. But the work for the Army was done with splendid efficiency. The way in which the First Expeditionary Force was carried to the South Coast and embarked secretly, rapidly, and without a hitch, will go down in history among the greatest of railway feats.

A memorable railway feat — Still more important, if anything, than the conveyance of the Expeditionary Force southwards was the constant preparation to keep our lines day and night ready so that at any moment a defence army of, maybe, 200,000 men, drawn from many centres, could be concentrated on one spot to resist an attempt at invasion. When it is borne in mind that the railways were working very short-handed, a large number of their men being at the war, that they had lost some of their chief organisers for administrative work on the Continent, and that they were primarily from August onwards working for the Government, it will be realised that the way in which they still catered for the civilian element stands to their great credit.

The scheme for insuring British shipping against war risks was necessary if our shipping was to continue its work freely. Everyone assumed before war began that Germany would have large numbers of armed cruisers scattered over the seas, and that these would for a time, until we could hunt them down, destroy an appreciable percentage of our ships. The Germans, it turned out, were not so well prepared with their cruisers as we expected. But the fear of them alone was enough to force insurance to an impossible figure if nothing was done. A State Insurance Office was started in London, and the State announced that it was prepared to insure eighty per cent. of the risks on ships and to insure cargoes at moderate fixed rates.

The result of this State guarantee, and of the protection afforded to our shipping by the Fleet, was soon made

STAMPING PIECES OF METAL FOR CARTRIDGE-CAPS.

CANADIANS REPLENISHING THEIR WATER-CART.
A scene on the River Avon, near the camp of the Canadians on Salisbury Plain.

The Cabinet formed a Committee on Food Supplies, which met the representatives of the multiple grocery firms and of the Grocers' Federation, and it was decided to set up a maximum retail figure announced by the Government for certain staple foods, such as sugar, butter, cheese, lard, bacon, and margarine. The Government went further than this. The price of sugar had been forced up to, in some instances, as much as 7d. a pound. The State purchased an immense quantity of sugar, sufficient for the national supply for many months, and arranged its distribution through the wholesale trade at a much more reasonable price.

The problem of the anticipated winter distress and unemployment among the working classes engaged widespread attention during August and September. The Dominion of Canada sent a million bags of flour for the relief of our poor, and other dominions and provinces followed suit. The Prince of Wales's Fund was established to meet the distress—a fund that within nine months was to exceed five million pounds. The Board of Trade established a new department for the promotion of fresh industrial enterprises. This department, managed with an initiative and zeal such as are not usually looked for among officials, brought all manner of fresh enterprises to the attention of our tradesmen. The chairmakers of Luton were lacking work; a Board of Trade official showed them how to make bentwood furniture so as to capture the Austrian trade. Nottingham mills were given samples of fresh lines wanted abroad. Dundee was put in touch with new Continental buyers. The East End little master was shown how to make fasteners or bag frames, and where to sell them when made.

Fresh industrial enterprises

A WATER—NOT A GAS MAIN.
Engineers laying down a water-supply system in the North of France.

manifest. A number of merchant vessels were taken over by the Government for transport work. The others were insufficient for the work awaiting them. The great German mercantile fleets had been driven from the seas by the British Navy. France had no ships to spare. Japan, with her growing shipping, gained enormously. But the main benefit fell to the British shipowners. There came the greatest boom shipping had ever known. Rates doubled, trebled, and quadrupled in a very short time. Old ships almost derelict, which a few weeks before had been unsaleable, now fetched more than they cost when new. Shipowners who had struggled along with small fleets of tramp boats now found that every boat left to them by the Government was a little gold-mine. Sailors and officers demanded much higher wages, and got them. This represented a very small share of the gains. Many men made fortunes from their ships in the autumn and winter of 1914-15.

The steadily growing activities of the State revealed themselves in another direction. Immediately war grew probable, a number of middle-class people started hastily buying large supplies of foodstuffs against any emergency. In some cases they laid in fantastic quantities of preserved foods, more than they would consume in a year in the normal course of things. Some shopkeepers tried to meet this rush by refusing to supply anyone except their regular customers, only selling them their usual quantities. Others, including some great wholesale houses, quickly raised prices. This rise fell most heavily on small and struggling retailers in poor districts, who could not afford to keep large stocks. As a result they had to increase prices for their customers, and the poorest classes were made to pay.

Regulation of food prices

CHANNEL ISLANDERS IN WAR TIME.
Detachment of the Royal Guernsey Light Infantry (Guernsey Militia), marching off after parade. This island force has a history dating back hundreds of years.

There was much talk of a business war against Germany. While our soldiers were fighting the German armies in the field, our merchants and manufacturers were to establish British trade where German had formerly prevailed. We were to reconquer the South American market, to make an end of German manufactures in Canada, to do the business formerly done by Germany in China, and to have Australian trade once more to ourselves. This talk was very popular for a time. Then it died away, as people came to realise that we had something very much more important to do than to make fresh trade conquests. Our business was to beat Germany in the field of war. That required all our efforts, and the public mind had to be **Temporary talk of trade conquests** devoted to that. People felt that there was something a little paltry in so much talk of trade benefits at this crisis. Hence various campaigns, such as the " Business as Usual " campaign, faded out of sight as the serious purpose of the war loomed larger and larger.

When arrangements had to be made for the arming, clothing, and equipping of Lord Kitchener's New Army of a million men, it was found that it was hardly possible for the Yorkshire mills to turn out the khaki, for Sheffield to produce the guns and bayonets required, or for Birmingham to find the small arms. Every firm which catered for the soldier in any way was quickly overwhelmed with orders. Firms that had never done military work before transformed their plant. The Birmingham steel-pen maker now turned to the manufacture of buttons by the million, and cartridge - cases by the ten million. The Hawick manufacturer of fine tartans was commanded to make khaki. At first traders sought for Government work. After a time the Government came to them, with directions that they were to turn out certain amounts in a given time, and with stern intimation that if they did not they might expect to have military representatives take the control of their mills from them.

This threat was rendered possible by a remarkable measure, passed in the early days of the war, the Defence of the Realm Act.

The Defence of the Realm Act was in many ways the most extraordinary legislative measure passed by the British Parliament for many years. It specified a number of acts for which civilians could be tried by court-martial. These acts included communicating with the enemy, spreading false reports or reports likely to cause disaffection, giving assistance to the enemy or endangering the successful prosecution of the war. The person deemed by the military authorities guilty of any of these offences could be arrested and tried as if subject to military law, and as if **Defence of the Realm Act** he or she had, on active service, committed an offence under the Army Act. In other words, the military authorities could arrest any persons they pleased and, after court-martial, inflict any sentence on them short of death. In addition, the military authorities were allowed to demand the whole or part of the output of any factory or workshop dealing with military supplies, and to take possession of any factory or workshop they required. They were also allowed to take any land they needed. This, in effect, made the civil administration of the country entirely subservient to the military administration.

The Act created surprise, and while the majority of people were willing to accept it, believing that the powers under it would not be abused, a number of eminent peers, including several famous judges, among them such men as Lord Halsbury, Lord Parmoor, Lord Loreburn, and Lord Bryce, objected. Lord Halsbury declared that he saw no necessity to get rid of the fabric of personal liberty that had been built up for many generations. " I do not think that the liberty of the subject is so trifling a matter that it can be swept away in a moment because some of us are in a panic."

ROYAL GUERNSEY ARTILLERY AT PRACTICE.
An officer directing the fire of his battery from behind a mass of granite boulders.

EAST ANGLIAN COASTGUARD AWHEEL.
A picturesque photographic study of Essex Cycle Scouts riding along one of the coast roads, which they patrolled day and night on the look-out for the approach of enemy raiders by sea or air.

The Act, nevertheless, passed into law, and the military authorities, as expected, used their great powers prudently. But the feeling grew that it was not right that all the ancient limitations on the supreme authority should go, and when the House of Lords met on January 7th, 1915, Lord Parmoor introduced an amending Bill, to restore to citizens their right to be tried by ordinary courts. The Government promised, if this was withdrawn, to bring in a similar measure itself. It did so, and a new law was passed, giving any accused civilian the right to choose whether he should be tried by civil court or court-martial. It was provided, however, that in case of special emergency, such as invasion, this choice would be withdrawn. The change was welcomed in responsible circles. Even great emergency did not justify the Government, it was felt, in maintaining a law under which legitimate criticism could be suppressed. The effect of the law, even after amendment, was, however, to vest in the Government authority such as it never had before the war began.

Unemployment almost abolished

By the beginning of 1915 the industrial position in Britain was very different from what had been anticipated. The war, in place of leading to a shortage of employment, had almost abolished unemployment. The Army and Navy required vast quantities of guns, shells, and equipment. More warships had to be built, and those partly built had to be pushed on night and day to be ready in the shortest possible time. The great shipyards on the Tyne, on the Clyde, and at Belfast were almost overwhelmed. Private orders could scarcely be looked at, and small yards unsuitable for naval work were sending their men to help in the bigger warship yards. At Newcastle firms like Armstrong's were bringing down miners from the coalfields to help

to build their new sheds, and were employing armies of women to fill shells and to aid in other work. Glasgow manufacturers were conducting an active advertising campaign in many other parts of the country to attract workmen, urging them to go and help in Government work. In Birmingham, in the expressive phrase of one manufacturer: "Having secured all the good workmen, and all the poor workmen, they were now bringing in women and boys, one-armed men and one-legged men to help." Northampton had never been so prosperous before in its history. Our great manufacturing centres **Government control** were producing goods **of workshops** not alone for the British, but for the French, Russian, and Belgian Governments. In many centres they were working seven days a week, with day and night shifts.

Even this was not enough. The Government obtained further powers enabling it to acquire and control factories and workshops. It appointed a Committee of Production, with extensive powers, and mapped Great Britain out into a series of districts. The scheme was gradually evolved of allotting a certain amount of war work to each district and expecting it to produce it. The amount was sufficient to keep all available labour busy then.

Still the authorities were not satisfied. Lord Kitchener led the demand for more shells. "The output," said he, "is not only not equal to our necessities, but does not fulfil our expectations. The progress of equipping our new armies and also in supplying the necessary war material for our forces in the field has been seriously hampered by the failure to obtain sufficient labour, and by delays in production of the necessary plant." He declared with the utmost emphasis that unless the whole nation worked, not only in supplying manhood for the fighting field, but also in supplying the necessary arms, ammunition, and equipment, successful operations would be delayed.

Lord Kitchener and Mr. Lloyd George both emphasised the delay caused in factories by slack work and irregular time-keeping, due to excessive drinking among workmen. Having acquired many approved factories, and transformed them for producing war material, the Government now set about getting the utmost out of the men. Two steps were proposed to insure this—an appeal to the patriotism of the workmen themselves, and the restriction of temptations to drink. The appeal to the workmen was carried out by a series of meetings throughout the country, notably by a great meeting at Newcastle-on-Tyne on April 20th, 1915, when Mr. Asquith talked with the Tyneside men, face to face, about their share in helping the nation to carry on the war. He declared that he did not come there to accuse the men of remissness. "The miner, the shipbuilder, the engineer, the iron and textile worker, the railwayman, and the docker—everyone who contributes, whether by brain or by muscle, to maintain and increase the supply of munitions, upon which the efficiency of the fighting forces depends—is, in as true a sense as any of our gallant sailors and soldiers, a patriot and a combatant," said he. "Success in this war is a question of munitions," said Mr. Lloyd George.

The appeal to the workmen was on the whole successful. In some centres they went back to their tasks with

MEN OF THE ROYAL NAVAL DIVISION IN TRAINING AT THE CRYSTAL PALACE, SYDENHAM.

MARCH-PAST OF THE PARIS GARRISON BEFORE GENERAL GALOPIN, WHO SUCCEEDED GENERAL GALLIENI AS GOVERNOR.

renewed zeal. They agreed to the temporary suspension of many of their Trade Union regulations, and recognised that in war time even Unionism must be modified. " Shall we deliver the goods ? " asked one of the men's leaders at the close of a great gathering. The answering " Yes ! " came like a thunderclap

The campaign against drinking was not so successful. The King led the way by pledging himself and his household to personal abstinence during the war, and Lord Kitchener and numbers of our leading men followed. But when it was proposed by the Government to increase the taxation on spirits, beers, and wines to an almost prohibitive degree, such opposition was set up by many of their own supporters in the Liberal ranks, by the entire Irish Party, and by strong sections of the Opposition and the Labour group, that this proposal had to be withdrawn.

By the early summer of 1915 the civil life of Great Britain had been largely transformed. Parliament had fallen for the time to a comparatively minor place, while the administrative authority of the heads of the Government had increased enormously. Section after section of industrial life, that had formerly been under private control, was now supervised and controlled by the State.

MILL AS OBSERVATION POST.
British artillery officer on the look-out for the enemy—" somewhere in France."

War work took the main place in every industrial centre. There was a scarcity of workmen, due to the large numbers who had joined the new armies, and in some cases their places were taken by women. The civilian was no longer free to go where he pleased, should the military authorities desire to stop him. The task of leaving or entering a country was made one of great difficulty by severe passport regulations. The visitor to a strange place had to fill up a form declaring **Necessary sacrifice** his identity, hotel guests had to be **of private rights** registered in the same way as had long prevailed on the Continent. Great Britain was fighting for her life, and her people knew that, faced with this supreme issue, the rights and privileges of ordinary times must of necessity go.

The sacrifice of personal rights had been gladly made by the nation. It was a temporary sacrifice made to save honour and Empire, the safety of our women and the honour of our homes.

The Government at the outbreak of the war was called upon to decide what should be done with the very large numbers of Germans in Britain. For years Germans had come and settled here in growing hosts. German financiers were among the leaders in our banking world ; German stockbrokers formed a section of their own on the Stock Exchange ; German importers and exporters dominated branch after branch of commerce in London and in many of our great provincial cities. It was notorious that the young German clerk, speaking three languages and requiring little wage, had ousted the British from thousands of offices. Most of our great hotels were run by Germans or Austrians, while as waiters the only serious competitors of the German were Italians and Swiss. The old English waiter had almost disappeared. Germans had captured the greater part of the baking trade of London, and their food stores were scattered over the City and the West End. Many people **Enemy aliens** with German names and of German **in our midst** descent were naturalised ; very many more were not. We had German clubs and unions galore. Whole sections of Bloomsbury, Highgate, and St. Pancras were overwhelmingly Teutonic.

What was to be done with these people ? The problem was admittedly not easy. Among the German and Austrian subjects were some, like the Czechs, who hated Germanism more than ourselves, and who had fled to this country as a refuge against its tyrannous rule. There were others who had lived here for many years, had married English wives, whose sons were serving in the British Army, and who were passionately English. But these were the exceptions. The vast majority of the Germans here were, as might be expected, devoted to their Fatherland. Tens of thousands of the young men were German Army reservists, eager to return to their regiments to fight us. Among them there existed an elaborate and carefully-organised spy system, fastened on Great Britain like a leech on its victim.

The Government hesitated to employ its authority against these people. Even when it was seen that British subjects caught in Germany at the beginning of the war were to be treated in the harshest possible fashion, our authorities still held their hand. Known spies were arrested and some two hundred suspected spies were kept under watch. A few hours after war broke out the Home Secretary issued a notice allowing Germans to leave this country during the subsequent six days. Thanks to this extraordinary permission, young German reservists, amounting in numbers to a division of the Army, were enabled to return home, rejoin their colours, and fight against us. Some wholly inadequate precautions were taken. German financial undertakings were placed under special supervision, and a series of minor checks on alien enemies were instituted. Espionage was made a military offence, punishable with death. Alien enemies were not allowed to keep carrier pigeons, photographic apparatus, or arms. The houses of Germans and Austrians were raided and searched. Later on a certain number of Germans and Austrians of military age—at first nine thousand, rising afterwards to nineteen thousand —were arrested and confined in detention camps as prisoners of war. A number of Germans and Austrians attempted to change their names in order to pass as British. This was forbidden by a special Order-in-Council.

Germans and Austrians remaining in Britain were ordered to register, and to submit to certain regulations limiting their right to travel over the country. Many of them evaded these regulations in every possible way.

It soon became evident, however, that these measures were utterly insufficient to counteract the activity of German secret agents in this country. There were a certain number of outrages, particularly in Government works, unexplainable except as the deliberate work of active enemies. Some of these—as, for example, the series of fires that took place in Portsmouth Dockyard—were not allowed to be published at the time, owing to the system

BRINGING UP A TANK OF WATER FOR THE TROOPS. AN INDIAN MULE-DRIVER IS SEEN IN THE REAR.

TAKING STOCK OF SUPPLIES IN A TOWN AT THE REAR OF THE FIRING-LINE.

WITH THE MEN OF OUR ARMY SERVICE CORPS AT THE FRONT.

Unloading sacks of provender at a supply base. Never before had the men of our Army Service Corps so many varied calls upon their resourcefulness, and never before the Great War had these " universal providers " of the Army worked more splendidly or efficiently than they did under the skilled direction of the Quartermaster-General.

313

of secrecy then enforced here. Cases that came before the courts increased the public uneasiness. Thus one boarding-house keeper in Bloomsbury was shown to be the wife of a German general. Spy after spy was brought to trial, and the evidence afforded best proof of the dangers of their system. Two of the most noted cases were those of Karl Lody, a German naval lieutenant who was shot after trial at the Tower of London for espionage, and Karl Ernst, a naturalised British subject, a hairdresser in North London, who was sentenced to seven years' penal servitude for acting as distributor of letters for one of the German spy organisers. Many Germans settled on the East Coast at possible invasion points. Some of them were found in possession of wireless apparatus. It was quite evident months after the war broke out that German agents in this country were succeeding, by some means or another, in communicating valuable information to our enemies. The authorities tried to check such leakages by making it more difficult for people to leave the country and by subjecting travellers to minute search and investigation. But every official step against the Germans themselves in Britain was taken with evident reluctance, and many of the aliens who were first interned were gradually released. Attacks on this leniency met with the reply that everything was done with the approval, if not at the direction of, the military authorities.

Here and there the activity of the authorities was quickened by slight displays of public resentment against German businessmen. But until the spring of 1915 these displays were very rare. People contented themselves for a time with very generally refusing to employ German subjects. Thousands of Germans and Austrians had, in consequence, to come on to the public funds for relief. The Germans in this country did little to conciliate public opinion. Numbers of them adopted an exceedingly belli-cose attitude—rejoicing openly over German victories,

Rejoicing over German victories

boasting what would happen to England when German armies came here, and aggressively flaunting their views in a way that aroused the wonder of neutral visitors at the patience of the British people in submitting to them.

This patience was finally subjected to too great a strain. On May 7th, 1915, came the news of the sinking of the Lusitania. Some Germans in England were foolish enough to show their glee. As details were published in this country of women and children in the monster liner done to death without warning, the popular passion flared up. The butchers of Smithfield ordered German butchers away. The merchants of the Baltic Exchange told Germans there they would no longer endure their company. On the Stock Exchange men of German descent were warned to go. Starting in East London, there came a number of riots against German tradesmen, that spread widely over the country. As is nearly always the case in popular rioting, the demonstrations were taken up by mere pillagers who attacked shops generally, and who were less influenced by the desire to demonstrate against Germans than by the wish to rob and steal.

Effect of anti-German riots

The anti-German riots, deplorable as they were, had one immediate effect. The Government was stirred to action. In a speech in the House of Commons on May 14th, 1915, Mr. Asquith stated that of the alien enemies in this country there were some nineteen thousand interned, and some twenty-four thousand males and sixteen thousand women at large. He proposed that, with certain excep-tions, all adult male enemy aliens should, for their own safety and for that of the community, be segregated and interned or, if over military age, be repatriated. Women and children of suitable age were also to be repatriated, exceptions being made in special circumstances. As for the people of German birth who had become naturalised and who were, therefore, in law British subjects, they were only to be proceeded against in cases of proved necessity.

INSTANTANEOUS CAMERA RECORD OF SHRAPNEL BURSTING OVER THE BELGIAN TRENCHES IN FLANDERS.

CHAPTER LX.

THE FIGHT FOR THE DARDANELLES.

The Lesson of the German Fortification of the Belgian Coast—German Guns Drive off British Ships—Scheme for Combined Greek, French, and British Landing Force Falls Through—British Cabinet Decides to try first a Naval Bombardment—Political Considerations Underlying this Adventurous Policy—How the Germans Strengthened the Defences of the Dardanelles—Entrance Forts Destroyed by Close-range Fire—Allies' Apparent Success in the First Basin of the Dardanelles—Gallant Work by the Mine-Sweepers—The Queen Elizabeth Intervenes—Important Part Played by Naval Air Squadrons—Mishap to the Amethyst—Opening of the Grand Attack on the Turco-German Forts—Admirable Skill and Patience of German Gunners—Loss of Bouvet, Irresistible, and Ocean—Complete Failure of the Naval Operations—Fleet Waits for the Help of Mediterranean Expeditionary Force—The Great Landing Battles.

E have seen that in the third week of October, 1914, a squadron of British warships began to operate off the Belgian coast and assist the French and Belgian troops along the Yser. In spite of the valuable aid of our long-range naval guns, the German Army succeeded in bringing up heavy batteries, and, though we had 12 in. guns in our battleships, skilfully directed by observers in flying machines, our ships were at last compelled to withdraw. Our warships carried out their main work of assisting the Belgian Army to hold its positions in the inundated polders north of Fournes, but they were unable to prevent the German artillerymen from fortifying the coast and establishing a dangerous submarine base at Zeebrugge. The work which the Germans did under continual bombardment by our naval guns was of remarkable importance. It was an achievement that settled the question of the power of ships against land batteries in the conditions of modern warfare. By using part of his siege train from Antwerp, including several of the monster Krupp howitzers, the enemy was able to fortify all the coast, and lay a new minefield round Zeebrugge, despite the fact that our squadrons off the Belgian coast were heavily reinforced.

Seeing, therefore, that we had not been able to master a short stretch of coast with our naval guns, and hinder the enemy from fortifying it, it did not seem likely that any naval attack upon a strong line of forts guarding a winding, narrow waterway would be successful. But in

January, 1915, Mr. Winston Churchill, the First Lord of the Admiralty, appears to have decided for himself that the Dardanelles ought to be opened, and that they could be forced by the British Fleet. Lord Fisher, the First Sea Lord, was opposed to the scheme, as he maintained that the aid of a large army was indispensable to the bombarding squadrons. This seemed also to have been the opinion of the experienced chiefs of the French Navy. At the outset it was hoped that some part of the Greek Army would assist in the operations. A small French Expeditionary Force, composed of Senegalese troops and Zouaves, was collected in North Africa, under the command of General d'Amade. There may also have been some arrangement for detaching a small portion of our forces in Egypt to help in attacking the gates of Constantinople and the Black Sea. But all this part of the scheme fell through when the King of Greece refused to follow the advice of his Prime Minister, M. Venizelos. M. Venizelos seems only to have promised the Allies to send one division (20,000 men) to the Dardanelles, but King Constantine would not agree even to this small amount of aid being given. The effect was that practically no military help against the Fifth Turkish Army, entrenched on the Gallipoli Peninsula, could at the time be granted to the combined British and French squadrons which were preparing to attack the Dardanelles forts. In these circumstances it might have been well, from a military point of view, to postpone the attack on the Turkish straits until a decision had been obtained in the western

Lafayette.

GENERAL SIR IAN HAMILTON, G.C.B., D.S.O.
Commanding the Expeditionary Forces in the Dardanelles.

SANATORIUM ON HALKI, ONE OF THE PRINCE'S ISLANDS, FORTIFIED ON ACCOUNT OF THE WAR.

BRITISH ADMIRALTY YACHT IMOGENE OFF THERAPIA.
A photograph taken a few weeks before war was declared on Turkey.

theatre of war against the first-line armies of Germany. The danger of a purely naval expedition up the Dardanelles was well known to the naval officers at the Admiralty. It had been placed on record in 1877 by that great leader Admiral Hornby, who in that year was directed to force a way to Constantinople. He warned the authorities at home that, while it was practicable for a squadron to run past the forts—which were far weaker in those days, and were not supplemented by mines and torpedoes—the fleet would, none the less, be helpless in the Sea of Marmora. Its supply of coal, ammunition, and food would be cut off, because the enemy would be certain to mount guns on the cliffs, which for more than six miles overhang the northern shore of the Dardanelles at the point where the channel closes to little over half a mile. It is never more than two miles in width. "Guns thus placed," he said, "could not fail to stop transports and colliers," and the fleet would be exposed to terrible danger. He therefore urged the necessity of occupying the Gallipoli Peninsula with British troops before entering the Sea of Marmora. When, by a stroke of singular daring aided by good luck, he passed the Dardanelles, the Turks offered no resistance. But he had no illusions as to his position. "There seems to be an idea," he wrote from the Sea of Marmora

Admiral Hornby's warning to the First Lord of the Admiralty, "that this fleet can keep the Dardanelles open. Nothing can be more visionary. Not all the fleets in the world can keep them open for unarmoured ships. Small earthworks on the cliffs would always prevent their passage."

Still earlier, in the days of the old sailing ship, Admiral Duckworth, who with a British squadron ran past the forts and anchored before Constantinople in 1807, pronounced the operation "the most dangerous and difficult ever undertaken." It was also fruitless, as the Turks refused to be terrified, and he had to beat a speedy retreat as the only alternative to finding himself without water and food. The evidence of history was certainly not encouraging.

The advice of naval officers seems to have been overridden by Mr. Winston Churchill, the first Lord of the Admiralty, in consideration of the critical condition of the political problems of the Mediterranean. Both the British

and the French Navy had a large number of powerfully-armed warships, which were too slow to take part in the manœuvres of a general fleet action. There were battleships, such as those of the Canopus class, which were slower than the latest type of German submarines. They could not be used in the North Sea with our swift super-Dreadnoughts. Moreover, our Grand Fleet was so strong in both gun power and speed that even our newest battleship with 15 in. guns—the Queen Elizabeth—could safely be detached from it. There were also battle-cruisers, like the Inflexible, which could safely be spared from Sir John Jellicoe's command.

Altogether, we had a surplus of naval force, over and above our Grand Fleet and Mediterranean Fleet, and no **Gunpower a deciding factor** immediate use for it could be found except in the Dardanelles. A considerable portion of this surplus was composed of old and slow types that were destined for the scrap-heap at the end of the war. But their guns in most cases were very powerful, and it seemed well worth while to use them against the land forts of the Dardanelles, even at the risk of serious injury to the ships in an attempt to force a passage. As had been seen in the case of the Canopus in the action off the Falkland Islands, her low speed made her practically valueless in a running engagement. It was clear that any great battle in the North Sea would be a running fight. Any slow British battleships present

THE FAMOUS MOSQUE OF ST. SOPHIA, CONSTANTINOPLE.

PANORAMIC VIEW OF CANDILLE, THE BRITISH COLONY ON THE BOSPHORUS.

THE " TOUR BRULEE," CONSTANTINOPLE.
There is a legend that when this iron-bound
tower falls the Ottoman Power will fall with it.

THE LARGEST MOSQUE IN THE TURKISH CAPITAL.
The Egyptian obelisk (left) is on the site of the old Byzantine Hippodrome, where
executions once took place. This and other views on this page were photographed
on the eve of the war with Turkey.

THE SULTAN'S PALACE ON THE BOSPHORUS.
Part of the Imperial yacht is seen on the right of the photograph.

DIAGRAMMATIC VIEW OF THE ENTRANCE TO THE DARDANELLES, ILLUSTRATING THE WORK OF THE BRITISH FLEET IN THE EARLY DAYS OF MARCH, 1915.

would tail off during such an engagement, and be left without the protection of destroyers—a prey to enemy submarines.

There were at least three reasons for attempting to force the passage of the Dardanelles, at a foreseen loss of some of our obsolescent warships. In the first place, a stroke at the heart of the Ottoman Empire would be the best defence against Turkish operations against Egypt and on the Persian Gulf. If successful, it would check the Turco-German intrigues in Persia, Afghanistan, and the Indian border.

In the second place, an attack upon the waterway between the Mediterranean and the Black Sea would appeal to Italian **The foreseen and the unforeseen** sympathy, steady Bulgaria, and stimulate Rumania. Indeed, the mere fact that Britain and France were assailing in force the heart of Turkey would be sufficient to paralyse all German and Austrian designs in the Balkans. Then, in the third place, the success of the scheme would, by opening a warm water road for the munitioning of Russia, have a profound and practically decisive effect upon the course of the main land campaign; for Russia was sadly deficient in heavy artillery and shells. It was foreseen that her position in regard to war material would become critical by the spring of 1915. The opening of the Dardanelles would enable guns, shells, and rifles to be landed at the Black Sea ports, close to the main lines of battle.

One thing, however, was clearly not foreseen by Mr. Winston Churchill and the members of the Liberal Cabinet who supported his plan. When the attack on the Dardanelles had proceeded as far as the first severe check to the British and French bombarding fleet, no withdrawal from the situation created thereby was possible. Britain, France, and Russia were important Mohammedan Powers. They were fighting the Ottoman Caliphate, which, though a usurpation, had for centuries been recognised by Moslems as the practical directing force of their religious world. So long as the Powers of the Triple Entente conserved their military prestige, the Ottoman Sultan and the Young Turk war party using him as their marionette were unable to influence seriously the Mohammedan subjects of the Christian nations. For the Ottomans themselves were leagued with Christian Germans, Austrians, and Hungarians. There was no sound pretext for a Holy War. On the other hand, if the prestige of Britain and France were temporarily lowered in the Orient by a great Turkish victory in the Dardanelles, the consequences might be gravely felt in India, Egypt, and Northern Africa. Thus, even in the political field, the advantages won in one quarter by a serious display of activity might be fully balanced by disadvantages elsewhere, unless the naval attack on the Dardanelles by the Fleet were backed by the landing of a very large Franco-British army.

There were thus complications upon complications in the affair, and our French allies, with their passion for logic and clarity of thought, would have preferred to do one thing at a time, and settle the main struggle with the Germans before detaching a large army for action far outside the grand theatre of conflict. But our Cabinet, led in the matter by the dashing and enterprising Mr. Churchill, somewhat reluctantly consented to face serious risks in the chief field of operations for the sporting chance of winning a great Mediterranean victory by a swift, single **A serious preliminary** stroke. It is at once our failing and our **failure** strength as a nation that we lack prudence, and almost delight in hazardous enterprises. Instead of always calculating the means to an end, we engage in great risks, and rely on the standing luck of our fighting men, which, in ultimate analysis, means that we trust, in the event of preliminary failure, to win through at last by our large, general reserves of strength.

Certainly the Dardanelles campaign opened with a preliminary failure of a serious nature. As Lord Fisher had foreseen from the naval bombardment of the Belgian coast, the old saying that ships alone were useless against forts still held true under modern conditions of artillery fire. Even in the summer of 1912 the Italians had hesitated to attack with both troops and ships the Straits leading to Constantinople.

THE TURKISH PORT OF SMYRNA, WHICH WAS BOMBARDED BY A FORCE UNDER
VICE-ADMIRAL SIR RICHARD PEIRSE IN MARCH, 1915.

The Admiralty officially stated that the reduction of the Turkish defences at Smyrna were " a necessary incident in the main operation."

319

At that time the Turkish defences were weak, the forts were out-of-date, and the minefield at Dardanus was covered by batteries which mounted few guns of large calibre. Passing the minefield one reached the Narrows, where the forts of Kilid Bahr and Chanak were armed only with plunging fire batteries. So weak were the defences in 1912 that another minefield was laid in front of the Narrows to supplement the batteries. Nevertheless, the Italians were so daunted by the difficulties of that tortuous and insidious waterway that they would not risk their fleet in attempting to force the passage.

The Turks began to strengthen the defences of the Dardanelles in September, 1914, some months before they opened hostilities against the Allies. They were greatly helped by a cargo of mines brought to Constantinople in the second week in August by a German steamer that accompanied the Goeben and the Breslau in their flight from Mediterranean waters. A considerable number of powerful guns and howitzers, some of 14 in. calibre, were obtained from the Teutonic Empires. Motor-batteries, worked by German gunners, were largely used, and rails were laid on one shore at least for the employment of very heavy but mobile howitzers. In the Gallipoli Peninsula four distinct lines of trenches were dug near Krithia, and carried from this point round all the important heights which dominate the line of advance towards the Narrows. The works at Bulair, in the neck of the Peninsula, which had proved a strong defence against the Bulgarian Army in the Balkan War, were further strengthened. Forty thousand troops were entrenched on the Peninsula to prevent the forts on the European side of the Straits from being attacked in the rear by the Franco-British landing-force. Another Turkish army corps was held ready to reinforce the Gallipoli garrison if need should require. The forts on the Asiatic shore were

WITH THE AUSTRALIANS AT THE DARDANELLES.
The men were photographed as they were climbing down the side of a transport into the small boats in which they were rowed ashore.

this immense force from the Franco-Belgian front. So the fleet was ordered to try to carry the waterway by naval gun-power alone.

Chief among the bombarding warships was the Queen Elizabeth, with her eight 15 in. guns, each throwing a shell weighing 1,720 lb. to a distance of fifteen miles or more. She possessed besides twelve 6 in. guns, and a powerful anti-aircraft armament. She used only oil fuel, giving her a designed speed of 25 knots. She was 650 feet long, with a displacement of 27,500 tons. It was reckoned that one of her shrapnel shells threw out something like two thousand bullets. Her high-explosive shell, when it made a direct hit at a distance of ten miles or so, produced the most tremendous destructive effect of any missile used by man. "Black Bess," or "Lizzie," as the pride of the British Navy was called by our admiring seamen, was a potent influence on the political side of the action by the Allies It might be said that she did more harm to the Turks by the popular interest she excited in the Balkan States than by the blows she dealt to the Turkish forts.

When neutrals saw that our Grand Fleet in the North Sea was so strong that a new battleship with eight 15 in. guns could be spared from the Mediterranean, their confidence in the eventual victory of the Allies was restored. Among the other important ships was the early battle-cruiser the Inflexible, with a nominal speed of 25 knots, and eight 12 in. guns, and the two last pre-Dreadnought battleships, the Lord Nelson and the Agamemnon, with a speed of about 18·5 knots, each armed with four 12 in. guns and ten 9·2 in. guns. Then there were several older battleships, armed with four 12 in. guns and twelve 6 in. weapons apiece. Such were the Irresistible, Duncan, Cornwallis, Vengeance, Ocean, Goliath, Albion, and Canopus.

Of the same general type, but still more ancient, were the battleships Majestic and

supported by well-entrenched troops, amounting to at least another army corps. Large reinforcements were available in the interior of Asia Minor and round Smyrna. It looked as though an army of half a million British and French troops would be needed to attack from the land the forts and Turkish armies on both sides of the Dardanelles. At the time it was quite impossible to spare

Prince George. The Swiftsure and Triumph were newer ships, purchased from Chili in 1903. They mounted four 10 in. guns and fourteen 7·5 in. guns apiece. A number of cruisers, such as the Euryalus, Amethyst, Dublin, and Sapphire, with destroyer flotillas, mine-trawlers, and a seaplane-carrier, the Ark Royal, made up the British fleet. The French Navy, whose main forces were

A camp of the Australians on the Gallipoli Peninsula.

Transports and battleships in the Dardanelles.

Australians disembarked and ready to move forward in the Dardanelles operations.

The great attack on the Turkish defences of the Dar

Kum Kale Fort on fire, while one of the British landing=p

Australian troops preparing for the assault by land.

...eltering under the glacis of the immense Turkish stronghold.

The sinking of H.M.S. Irresistible during an attack on the forts at the Narrows of the Dardanelles, March 18th, 1915.

occupied in the Adriatic, detached a group of old battle-ships. These were the Suffren, with four 12 in. guns and ten 6·4 in. guns; the Bouvet, with two 12 in., two 10·8 in., and eight 5·5 in. guns; the Gaulois, with four 12 in. and ten 5·5 in. guns; and the Charlemagne, equally ancient, with four 12 in. and ten 5·5 in. guns. The top speed of the Suffren was only 16 knots, and that of the three older ships was less. The only representative of the Russian Navy was the Askold, a 1903 cruiser, with twelve 6 in. guns.

The allied fleet was at first commanded by Vice-Admiral Sackville Carden, but he retired indisposed a couple of days before the main action against the forts was undertaken, and was succeeded by Vice-Admiral de Robeck. The French squadron was commanded by Rear-Admiral Guépratte, who carried out his part of the work very gallantly from his flagship the Suffren, while not concealing his opinion that the naval attack was useless without the simultaneous co-operation of a large allied military force.

Naval leaders of importance

Vice-Admiral Peirse, with some of the ships of our East India Squadron, conducted operations against Smyrna and neighbouring points, with a view to distracting the enemy by the feint of a landing on the Asiatic coast. Another naval leader of importance in the allied attack was Captain Johnson, who directed the difficult and dangerous work of the mine-trawlers in the Dardanelles. Then Wing-Commander Samson, with some of the squadrons which had done much good work in France and Flanders, came to direct the aerial work of reconnaissance and fire control by the officers of the Royal Naval Air Service.

The German Emperor had sent one of his best naval men, Admiral Usedom, with a large number of gunnery officers and gunners, to direct the defences of the Dardanelles. A German general, Liman von Sanders, with a multitude of German officers, controlled the Turkish land forces in Gallipoli. According to a German war correspondent, the Ottoman troops were everywhere commanded by German officers in the Dardanelles operations. Deeply embedded between the hills were enormous position-guns, with ammunition chambers dug out of the earth, and filled with waggon-loads of explosives and vast quantities of shells. Close at hand were tents in which the officers had been living for months past. In the Sea of Marmora a great flotilla of boats maintained communications at night between the Gallipoli Peninsula and the Asiatic shore, thus preventing any attempt at reduction by famine in the case of the Allies getting command of the Bulair lines at the neck of the Peninsula.

For some months before the main attack opened there had been desultory firing at the entrance forts to the Dardanelles, just by way of keeping the Turks and Germans there in a state of anxiety. But the main attack was a surprise for the enemy, for they had then ceased to expect that we should attempt so daring a thing as the forcing of the greatly-strengthened defences of the Straits. On February 14th, 1915, the gunnery-lieutenants of some of our battleships set out in a destroyer to have a good look at the forts they were to attack. Four miles off the land they came under fire, but the shooting was very bad, and none of the German shells struck the reconnoitring

ADMIRAL DE ROBECK (LEFT) WITH HIS STAFF INSPECTING MARINES.
The Admiral, whose photograph is inset, succeeded Vice-Admiral Sackville Carden as Commander of the Allied Fleet in the Dardanelles.

little warship. At eight o'clock on Friday, February 19th, 1915, the historic engagement began.

The allied fleet of battleships and battle-cruisers steamed off with bands playing to their positions, and at a quarter to ten the bugles sounded " Action Stations," and everybody disappeared under cover. About ten minutes afterwards the fore turret of the leading British battleship opened fire. Its 12 in. shell fell over the forts. The next fell short, but near. Then, by these bracketing shots, the range was obtained ; the third shell got home, and a great cloud of stone and brickwork rose high in the air. For an hour the leading ships worked hard at their guns. Then, about noon, the leading ships drew back, and another squadron of big-gunned vessels took their place. At each crash of the guns great clouds of grey smoke rose from the forts, and flames appeared from a

or three of the guns, overturned by the first bombardment, seem also to have been set up again. But the entrance forts, with their nineteen guns, ranging from 6 in. to 11 in., and their smaller armament of another eleven guns less than 6 in. calibre, were not able to withstand the terrific fire brought against them. The Germans seem to have left the old entrance forts unstrengthened, except for one new earthwork and a mobile howitzer battery working behind Kum Kale.

By Monday, March 1st, both entrance forts and their magazines were destroyed, and under the shelter of our battleships the mine-sweepers began to clear away a line of mines which had **Mine-sweeping** been observed by our naval airmen. **by night** At eleven o'clock in the morning the Triumph, Ocean, and Albion entered the Straits and bombarded White Cliff Fort and Dardanus Fort, some ten miles up the Dardanelles, towards the Narrows. In the night the mine-sweepers, with remarkable daring and skill, swept within a mile and a half of Kephez Point, with land batteries and field-guns firing at them

LANDING ON THE GALLIPOLI PENINSULA.
Troops disembarking by means of a trawler.

Turkish camp on the hillside and from a large barracks in the town by the forts. The Germans and Turks attempted no reply, as the allied fleet kept beyond the range of their guns.

But the long-range bombardment had not put the hostile batteries out of action. An exciting time followed when at three o'clock in the afternoon the Vengeance, Cornwallis, and Triumph, with the Suffren, Gaulois, and Bouvet, closed in to try and finish off the first forts of the Dardanelles. Far out to sea the Inflexible and Agamemnon kept up a long-range covering bombardment with their 12 in. guns, while the ships that closed in used only their secondary armament. By nightfall the forts round Cape Helles had been very badly battered, and had ceased to reply, and on the other side of the Straits only **Operations stayed** one battery remained active. The Ger- **by bad weather** man shells had pitched close to the French and British ships, and some had passed between the masts. But the enemy's shooting was not good ; not a single hit was obtained on any unit of the fleet.

For a week afterwards the great battle between ships and forts was interrupted. There was a hurricane of wind, with short, high, hurrying seas, that made aerial reconnaissance and steady naval gunnery impossible. But the weather became quieter from February 25th, and the attacking fleet steamed up again to see if anything were left of the forts. Our naval airmen found that in the interval the enemy had prepared several new gun-positions, but no guns had been mounted in them. Two

ACTIVITY IN THE ÆGEAN SEA.
British landing-party setting out in the ship's boats.

GUN CREW OF THE FRENCH BATTLESHIP CHARLEMAGNE.
This remarkable photograph was taken during the operations in the Dardanelles. The men are seen on the hammock-protected upper deck, and are wearing anti-concussion caps to lessen the effect of the firing of the big guns.

Xeros and bombarded the forts on the Bulair line, blowing up several ammunition depots. On Thursday our battleships were able to advance about four miles into the Straits, which brought them to within two miles of the danger zone. Ten miles ahead of them was Chanak, with Kilid Bahr opposite, where the channel narrowed to a breadth of less than two miles. Here it was that forts, field-batteries, and mobile howitzers were thickly clustered on both sides of the waters leading to Nagara Point. In addition to their numerous guns of position, their field-howitzers, shore torpedoes, and electric mines fixed on the bed of the channel, the Germans and Turks had a formidable weapon of defence in the strong current flowing from the Black Sea to the Mediterranean. In the month of March the rivers of the Black Sea were in flood, and the consequence was that there was a great volume of water flowing with fierce, swift current through the Narrows. A modern torpedo, the Leon, was admirably suited to the circumstances. It consisted of a powerful floating mine which could be set in torpedo fashion to drift in a current, bobbing up and down, and with a good knowledge of the direction of the current it could be employed with deadly effect against any target in narrow waters.

The only protection used against this torpedo was an old-fashioned torpedo-net round each battleship. But by reason of its curious oscillating movement the Leon mine was likely to pass under the net and explode on the ship's hull. Moreover, if a battleship went into action with her torpedo-nets out, her speed was much reduced, and the old slow vessels, constituting the main part of the attacking fleet, wanted to get every knot possible out of their engines. It was by moving in curves in Erenkoi Bay, within the basin of the Dardanelles, that they managed to disconcert the German and Turkish gunners and escape from the shells pitched at them. Thus, for what seemed at the time good reason, no means of protection was used against the Leon torpedoes.

In the meantime the main business of destroying the modern-gunned and newly-strengthened defences of the Narrows was taken in hand. On March 6th the Queen Elizabeth opened fire from the Gulf of Xeros, throwing her huge shells over the Gallipoli Peninsula and across the Narrows on to the forts of the Asiatic coast around Chanak. The 12 in. guns of the Agamemnon and Ocean fired in the same way at a range of 21,000 yards on forts Hamidieh I. and Hamidieh III. by Chanak. These forts had each four 14 in. guns, together with eight 9·4 in., one 8·2 in., and four 5·9 in. But they were utterly helpless against the far-flung indirect fire of "Big Lizzie" and her companions, coming over the hills from the unseen Ægean Sea.

Attack on Narrows' defences

furiously as they worked along. A squadron of allied destroyers answered the hostile guns and succeeded in keeping down their fire. The next day Fort Dardanus, on the Asiatic side, and Fort Suandere, on the Gallipoli side, were bombarded by the Canopus, Swiftsure, and Cornwallis. The German Ottomans then began to fight the fleet with greater power and fury. Every available field-gun and howitzer on Achibaba, or Tree Hill, and on the southern slopes of Pasha Dagh pitched high-explosive shells against the three British battleships. And Fort Suandere worked all its guns with the utmost speed. Each ship was struck, but their armour held good, and the only casualty was one man slightly wounded. At ten minutes to five on the winter evening the forts ceased to fire, being apparently badly damaged, and after continuing the bombardment for another forty minutes the battleships withdrew.

A fog the next day prevented observations as to the effect of the bombardment, but our landing-parties found that forty of the enemy's guns had been destroyed, including six modern field-guns near Cape Helles. On Wednesday, March 3rd, the French squadron steamed into the Gulf of

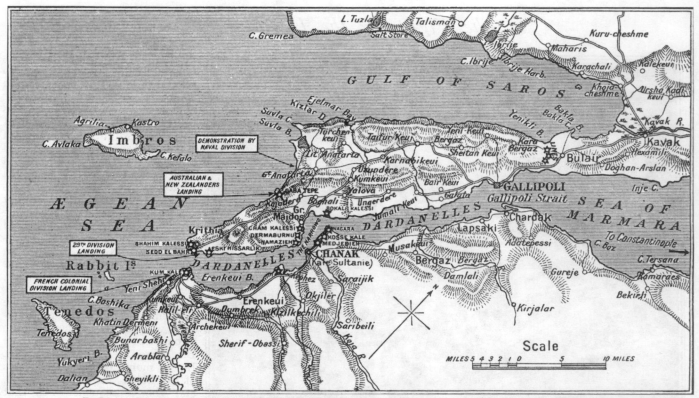

EXPLANATORY MAP OF THE OPENING OPERATIONS IN THE FIGHT FOR THE DARDANELLES.

We were then fighting the Turks and their German masters mainly with seaplanes. It was entirely the modern flying machine, carrying an officer with range-finding instruments and an instrument for wireless relegraphy, that made the bombardment of the Narrows practicable. Our naval airmen, darting about the sky, were alone able to direct the elevation and traverse of the great battleships' guns. The gunnery officers of the Queen Elizabeth could see nothing except the sandstone cliffs of the Gallipoli Peninsula and the scrub-covered heights of the Pasha Dagh beyond. Even if observation balloons had been used, at a distance of thirteen miles from the low-placed and masked forts and earthworks, no exact work of position-finding and spotting would have been possible.

In some cases officers in the fire-control stations of battleships circling within the Straits were able to watch certain of the bombarded forts and signal the results of the fire to the Queen Elizabeth and her companions in the Gulf of Xeros. But this was not practicable in the attack on the most difficult defences of the Narrows. The task of directing the guns had to be carried out by airmen, and whenever there was a fog, or even a mist, the work of the fleet was seriously interrupted. The conditions of this extraordinary naval action were the same as those governing the action of land artillery in Flanders and France. Everything depended upon the clear vision of the observing airman. He worked at his best when the clouds were high and the weather calm. When the scene of action was veiled with haze, the guns could only be **Forts blanketed** trained by means of measurements on **by mist** the map, and as the effect of their fire was then incapable of being known, they were just as likely to be wasting costly ammunition and wearing away uselessly the tubing of the great naval guns, as to be damaging the enemy.

Little progress therefore was made in the bombardment during hazy weather, and there were also continual delays owing to storms. The tail-end of winter was indeed the worst of all seasons for naval operations in and round the Dardanelles. And as it was a mild winter, the flooding of the Black Sea set up an especially strong current in the Straits in February and March, and the general moisture of the air at the opening of spring led to the hostile forts and field-batteries being blanketed by mist for a week or more at a time. The upshot was that, soon after every hostile bombardment, the Germans were able to repair much of the

328

damage done. Only the old forts at the entrance were quite destroyed, and even at Helles and Kum Kale motor-batteries and new gun-sites were prepared close to the landing places, thus making the destruction of the old entrance forts an affair of small permanent importance.

The most notable achievement of the allied fleet in the first week of March was the effect produced upon the Italian mind. The " Giornale D'Italia," a newspaper closely connected with the Government of Signor Salandra and Baron Sonnino, urged the **Alarm in** necessity for an Anglo-Italian agreement **Constantinople** with the view to the intervention of Italy on the side of the Triple Entente. Other powerful organs of Italian opinion advocated the same policy, and the Government began to act in a most vigorous way with a view to the denunciation of the treaty with Austria and Germany. In Bulgaria and Rumania there was a similar strong current of public opinion in favour of intervention on the side of the Allies, the Bulgarians especially being excited by the prospect of renewing their struggle with their old enemies the Turks. In Constantinople was a deep and widespread feeling of alarm. Even the wife of General Liman von Sanders and the wives of many German officers fled to Bucharest, and the Germans were hissed by the crowd when they appeared in the streets.

All this, however, was due more to the prestige of the British Navy and to the British reputation for tenacity than to the actual amount of progress made in forcing the Dardanelles. But on March 9th the Queen Elizabeth entered the Straits for the first time and attacked the forts in the Narrows by direct fire. In the afternoon the fog again interrupted the bombardment, but the next day it was resumed with more fury, and with so much success that German military writers began to prepare their public for the forcing of the Narrows and the bombardment of Constantinople. The town of Chanak was wrecked, and only two minefields were said to be still intact. So by the end of the second week in March the Straits had been swept for twelve miles up to Kephez Point, and only a desultory fire from the field-guns assailed the ships using this stretch of water.

A grave mishap to the British cruiser, Amethyst, however, revealed the signal dangers of the whole enterprise. While inside the Dardanelles, apparently covering the mine-sweepers, she was suddenly fired upon by a concealed Turkish battery, and suffered terrible loss in a few minutes. As the result of a dozen hits by the Turkish guns one-fifth of her crew were put out of action. No detailed account of this unhappy affair, in which her men displayed the utmost gallantry, was published by the Admiralty, and this led to the absurdest legends obtaining credence. Thus it was said that she had run through the Narrows and entered the Sea of Marmora. The nation was thus allowed to rest under a complete misconception of the tremendous difficulty of the task before its Navy. For if a single light

Mishap to the Amethyst ship could pass the Turkish batteries, it seemed to the uninstructed that it would be a simple matter for a fleet of battleships, protected by stout armour, to make the passage. Even German naval writers appeared at the time to suppose that the Amethyst had run through the Narrows, as far as Nagara Point, but this seems to have been only a modern Greek myth.

The Teutonic defenders of the Straits displayed an admirable patience and restraint in handling their big guns, allowing small targets, such as destroyers and light cruisers sent to draw their fire, to steam up without being attacked. Only the German motor-batteries, as a rule, fired on these small vessels. The allied naval commander naturally wanted to discover the positions of all the enemy's guns; and, like a chess-player sacrificing pawns with a design to get a strong line of attack on his opponent's more important pieces, Admiral de Robeck threw out his destroyers and a light cruiser or two and watched for the flashes from the great guns along the waterway. But the Germans were not to be drawn in this fashion. They suffered terribly at times from the long-range fire of the allied battleships, and if Turkish officers had been controlling the forts and earthworks the position of all the guns would quickly have been revealed. The Teutonic discipline, endurance, energy, and ingenuity with which the defence of the Dardanelles was conducted deserved high praise.

The Germans had their full reward when the first great attempt was made to approach the Narrows. This took place on Thursday, March 18th, a day of good weather and clear air, when the entire scene of operations was spread out in a bright picture at the feet of the observers on the island mountain of Tenedos. Above the low-lying hills on the Asiatic shore the view extended down to the wide first basin of the Dardanelles, with the shattered forts of Seddul Bahr by Cape Helles, and the stretch of low land at the village of Krithia, rising up to Tree Hill. Beyond Tree Hill was the valley of Suandere, from which mounted the great rocky clump of the Pasha Dagh. At the foot of the Pasha Dagh were the white walls of the village of Kilid Bahr, and it was here that the chief defences of the Straits were concentrated. They consisted of ten forts, lying opposite to the forts on the Asiatic side at Chanak. Immediately north and south of the main forts were five other batteries at the base of Pasha Dagh. On the Chanak side there were also three additional forts. Then, farther to the north, in the rocky bend of the Narrows by Nagara, there were two forts on the Gallipoli cliffs and three forts on the Asiatic promontory. As already explained, the Germans also had guns on the hillsides, some of them running on rails in and out of excavated caves, while others were moved by motor-vehicles, or hauled along on a light railway track. Below the Narrows there was a fort at Kephez Point, and another fort opposite it on the Gallipoli cliff. Still more southward there was another fort by the ravine of Suandere. This was thought to have been silenced, as for some days it had made no reply to the fire of our ships, and the forts almost opposite it at Dardanus and White Cliffs seemed to have been put out of action. But, as a matter of fact, Suandere and Kephez forts, guarding the first narrow strait, were not much damaged by the preliminary long-range bombardment. The German gunners there were only reserving their fire for the great struggle.

At a quarter to eleven o'clock on Thursday morning the Triumph and Prince George entered the basin and began to shell these two forts. Then from the entrance to the Dardanelles the Queen Elizabeth, Inflexible, Agamemnon, and Lord Nelson shelled the forts at Kilid Bahr and Chanak. Every gun and howitzer on both sides of the Straits returned the fire, when at about twenty-two

WITH OUR NAVAL MEN IN THE DARDANELLES.
A big gun and its crew with ammunition in readiness. A transport is lying off the landing-stage.

minutes past twelve Admiral Guépratte led his squadron up the Dardanelles and engaged the forts at close range. All the ten battleships engaged were hit, but they silenced every gun at Dardanus and Suandere, and put Fort J at Kilid Bahr and Fort U at Chanak out of action. A German war correspondent at Chanak said that the town looked like being reduced to a rubbish heap. Gigantic walls, that had stood all the storms of four and a half centuries and seemed to have been built for eternity, heaved under the earthquake shock of the great shells and went up in hurtling lumps **The bombardment** of earth and stone. Ship after ship **of Chanak** steamed into the bay, fired her guns, and then swerved round in an ellipse, followed by other vessels, each in turn coming into the firing-line. Shells flew in all directions towards Dardanus and the howitzer batteries by Suandere and on the forts on both sides of the Narrows.

At Chanak there was a tremendous fire caused by the great shells of the Queen Elizabeth. The camp, barracks, and buildings used by the Germans were a heap of rubbish, and though according to the German statement only one

THE SINKING BOUVET—A FEW MOMENTS BEFORE SHE DISAPPEARED.

A FEW OF THE SURVIVORS OF THE BOUVET ON BOARD A BRITISH WARSHIP.

damaged by the hostile batteries. All this, however, was less injury to the fleet than had been reckoned in the most hopeful estimate of the cost of the grand attack at close quarters. But just when things were going well the first disaster occurred. At twenty-five minutes past one all the forts ceased firing, and six more of our old battleships steamed inside the Straits to relieve the Suffren, Gaulois, Charlemagne, and Bouvet, with the Triumph and Prince George. But as the Bouvet was returning in the basin, north of Erenkoi village, she was struck by a mine. There was a column of vapour followed by a spout of dense black smoke, and in less than three minutes the old battleship sank with most of her crew, six hundred officers and men. There was only a patch of bubbling water when the Charlemagne steamed up to try to rescue the drowning sailors.

Loss of Bouvet and Irresistible

The ammunition of the Bouvet seems to have been exploded by the mine, and the internal explosion caused the ship to sink so quickly that only a few of the crew had time to jump overboard.

It seemed pretty clear that the Germans were sending Leon torpedoes down with the current, the torpedoes being adjusted to float out of sight below the surface of the water and strike the battleships at a considerable depth; for as soon as the Bouvet sank, our mine-sweepers came out under the terrible fire of the enemy's artillery and gallantly swept the channel again through the minefield at the approach of the Narrows. Nearly every night the Turks used to row out in small craft from the shore, towing mines with them, which they released in the middle of the channel so that they would drift towards the entrance to the Straits. This practice was well known, and the battleships always made a roundabout course in leaving Tenedos Roads for the Dardanelles, in order to avoid the currents along which the ordinary mines drifted.

Mine-sweeping, however, could not protect the fleet against the Leon torpedoes; for about nine minutes past four in the afternoon, as the Irresistible was steaming

gun was destroyed, most of the others were overthrown and buried in the earth, or otherwise temporarily disabled. The same condition of things seemed to obtain round Kilid Bahr when the action ceased at nightfall. Most of the batteries were upset or covered with earth or thrown out of position by great holes made beneath them. Had it been entirely a contest of gun against gun, the battleships would have dominated the Narrows sufficiently to allow landing-parties of the Royal Naval Division to complete the work of destroying the enemy's main defences. The forts on the Gallipoli side especially suffered badly from the long-range fire which the Queen Elizabeth poured into them from her position under Kum Kale. One of her shells produced a tremendous outburst of flames, rising like a volcanic eruption above the hills, and followed by a great canopy of smoke. She also exploded a powder magazine at Chanak.

Work of the Queen Elizabeth

Only two of the allied ships were seriously damaged by the enemy's shells. The battle-cruiser Inflexible was heavily hit, and her forward control position shattered by a heavy shell, and the old Gaulois was also badly

THE LAST OF THE FRENCH BATTLESHIP BOUVET.

The Bouvet was blown up by a drifting mine in the Dardanelles on March 18th, 1915, and sank so rapidly that only 64 of her crew of 621 were saved. The above photograph, obtained from another warship close by, gives a vivid impression of the vessel heeling over after striking the mine.

TRANSPORTS AT THE ENTRANCE TO THE DARDANELLES.

along in the firing-line, she also was blown up, and began to list heavily. Happily, she remained afloat for nearly an hour and three-quarters, and, in spite of the massed fire which the German guns poured upon her and upon all vessels that stood by to save her crew, our destroyers managed to save most of the officers and men. But scarcely had this been done when, at five minutes past six, the Ocean was also struck by one of the deadly missiles which M. Leon had invented. Again, with great skill and gallantry, practically the whole of the crew was safely removed under a hot fire. The work of rescue was done in a way that excited the admiration of the French sailors. The loss of life on the British ships was slight, having regard to the large scope and importance of the operations. But the loss of three old and slow battleships was a heavy price to pay for an unsuccessful attack upon all the principal fortresses of the Dardanelles. Our fleet had been badly defeated. Though the Secretary **Hidden instruments** of the Admiralty remarked at the time, **of defence** "The power of the fleet to dominate the fortresses by superiority of fire seems to be established," this appears to have been a surprisingly sanguine interpretation of a series of staggering disasters.

For unfortunately it was not a question only of the comparative strength in gun fire of the ships and the forts. The German defenders of the Dardanelles had torpedoes of a new type, in addition perhaps to ordinary torpedo-tubes firing from the shore, and electrically-controlled mines along the channel. By these hidden instruments of defence they undoubtedly transformed the artillery duel on March 18th into an important victory over the bombarding fleet. The admiral in command of the allied naval forces was unable to resume the attack upon the forts until means had been devised for protecting the ships against floating torpedoes and drifting mines. Then a large allied army had also to be employed. The check was an affair of a more serious nature than the British Government were inclined to admit at the time.

The Ottoman victory in the Dardanelles much heartened the Turks and their German masters. Moreover, it greatly lowered the traditional prestige of Britain throughout the Ottoman dominions, and in the more independent Moslem world of Southern Arabia, Persia, and Afghanistan. Even in the bazaars of Egypt some gossipers began to speculate about a possible renaissance of the lordly power of the ancient Ottomans. In characteristic British fashion we had entered upon one of the grandest adventures of empire at a time when we were hard put to it in another direction. We had converted the Turk, with his traditions of French and British invincibility, dating from the Crimean War, from a half-dispirited opponent into a confident enemy. Such was the result of amateurish interference in the gravest problems of national strategy.

TURKISH SHELL FALLING PERILOUSLY NEAR H.M.S. ALBION IN THE DARDANELLES. INSET: VILLAGE AND FORT OF KUM KALE ON FIRE DURING THE BOMBARDMENT OF MARCH 4TH, 1915.

GREEK VOLUNTEERS WITH THE FRENCH IN THE NEAR EAST.

A BURIAL SERVICE—THE DEAD HONOURED BY THE FLAG.

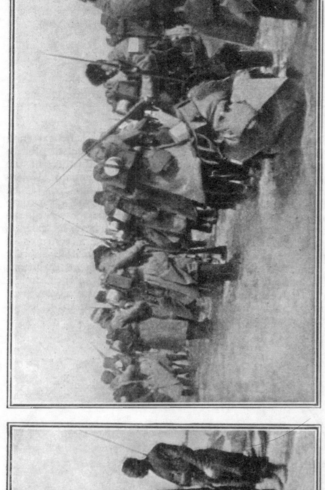

ALGERIANS SALUTING THE WOUNDED IN THE DARDANELLES.

TURKISH PRISONERS CAPTURED IN THE DARDANELLES.

The Turk, after being badly defeated by Bulgarians, Serbians, and Greeks in the recent Balkan War, had come to Gallipoli and Chanak oppressed by the legend of the invincible British and with a romantic sympathy for the gallantry and daring of the French. Without the help of the German he would certainly have crumpled up and broke out in riot in Constantinople when the allied fleet assailed him with 12 in. and 15 in. shells. But the upshot of his victory in the Dardanelles was that the Turk

Turks' self-confidence recovered fully recovered his self-confidence and became, as his fathers had done at Plevna, one of the most formidable fighting men of the world.

Equally important was the result of their victory upon the minds of the German commanders and officers who had conducted the principal work of defending the Dardanelles. They had been almost ready to accept defeat when the bombardment was proceeding vigorously. But when night fell on March 18th they became inspired to more severe efforts by a success with which they were themselves surprised. For example, the German officer in charge of the battery at Chanak had most of his guns damaged when

BREAD FOR THE TROOPS IN THE NEAR EAST.

FRENCH TROOPS ON THE MARCH AT MUDROS.

he ceased fire at half-past six on Thursday evening. But by working all night at high pressure he repaired the battery, and on Friday morning all the guns except one were again ready for battle. By the end of March even Kum Kale Fort, at the entrance to the Straits, was again active, a motor-battery having been placed in operation there by the Germans. Then across the water at Seddul Bahr field-guns were placed in earthworks to command the bay. Every night for five weeks, from March 18th to April 25th, the work of strengthening all the Gallipoli Peninsula and the Asiatic shore went on under the direction of the German officers. Our airmen could see long camel transport trains coming from the interior of Asia Minor towards the coast, and troops were concentrated from north and south to form the large Fifth Army, under the command of General Liman von Sanders.

It was in these difficult circumstances that the British nation benefited by the deeds of its fighting men of old. For though the puppet Sultan at Constantinople was proclaimed Ghazni, or victorious, by the Germans and Germanised Turks—who directed all the attitudes of the old feeble man—the ancient reputation for tenacity of Englishmen, going back to the days of Richard Cœur de Lion, served us well in all the Mediterranean countries

and in the independent Moslem States. It was not doubted that the surprising check to our imposing naval forces would quickly be retrieved. For some time the general opinion held that the allied fleet, which was reinforced by three more battleships—the French Henri IV. and the British Queen and Implacable—would again attempt to force the Dardanelles without waiting for a landing army. But stormy weather set in, and though the Black Sea Fleet of the Russian Navy tried to disconcert the enemy on March 29th by bombarding the outside forts and batteries of the Bosphorus, the attack on the Dardanelles was not resumed.

The fact was that the allied admirals had decided at a council of war that nothing more could be done without the help of a large army. The difficulties of the situation continued to increase. After the intervention policy of the Greek Prime Minister, M. Venizelos, was defeated by King Constantine, everything went wrong. As originally planned, the attack on the Straits was to have been a combined affair, in which twenty thousand Greek troops and eighty thousand French, Australian, New Zealand, British, and Indian soldiers would have taken part. It was the withdrawal of the offer of Greek aid that **The Greek offer withdrawn** led to the disastrous use of naval forces alone. For the Allies lost their arranged bases at Salonica and Mitylene, and though with the tacit consent of M. Venizelos the fleet continued to use as a base the Greek island of Lemnos, this very slight measure of assistance was also withdrawn by the new Greek Premier, M. Gounaris.

No spot remained near the scene of operations at which the allied troops could be collected, for the two neighbouring Turkish islands of Imbros and Tenedos were small and

TURKISH TORPEDO ATTACK ON THE BRITISH TRANSPORT MANITOU.

The Manitou was attacked in the Ægean Sea on April 19th, 1915, by a Turkish torpedo boat, which fired three torpedoes, all of which missed. The torpedo boat was chased, run ashore, and destroyed on the coast of Chios. Expecting the destruction of the transport (seen on the right), the troops took to the boats. Our photograph shows boats picking up men in the water, some of them from a partly submerged boat of the transport.

almost waste, with little accommodation. The bases to which the attacking force was reduced after the loss of Lemnos were Alexandria and Cyprus—both more than two days' steaming for transports going to the Dardanelles. Many more steamers had, therefore, to be engaged for the transporting, provisioning, and munitioning of the troops, with the result that the work of preparation occupied five weeks.

All this was a great gain to the Turks and Germans.

Prussian intrigues at Greek Court The Prussian intrigues at the Greek Court, leading to the sudden fall of the great Cretan fighting statesman, M. Venizelos, practically saved for a while the Ottoman Empire, and cost us many battleships and the lives of tens of thousands of men. When the Kaiser arranged for his sister to marry the Danish King of Greece, he accomplished without knowing it at the time one of the most brilliant strokes of diplomacy in history. For, as a well-known German military expert, Colonel Gaedke, stated in the first week in April, the Allies would have had a good chance of success had they launched both ships and troops against the Dardanelles early in March, according to the plan originally arranged with M. Venizelos.

As it was, when the allied army was ready to attempt to carry the Gallipoli Peninsula its task had become an almost impossible one. With five weeks' more work the German engineers had turned the hilly tongue of land into one of the most formidable fortresses in existence. From the lines of Bulair to the pom-pom battery at Cape Helles the Peninsula was about forty miles long. Its greatest breadth, just above the Narrows, was thirteen miles, but in other places southward it varied from one and a half miles to seven miles. The main attacks of the Allies were delivered against the narrow mile and a half tip, and the seven-mile mountain tract extending from the Ægean Sea to the forts round Kilid Bahr. The Turks had chiefly to defend about seventeen miles of coast, behind which were three clumps of high, broken ground, and a series of ridges and valleys. They had trenches on every cliff, arranged in lines one above the other; they had artificial caves containing machine-guns and small quick-firers; they had thousands of dug-outs, each containing a week's food and ammunition for a sniper. They had also some hundreds of miles of wire entanglements, usually concealed in the low thorny bushes that covered the hills, and line after line of entrenchments on every ridge; while the powerful German artillery was hidden in every possible way, especially by dug-out chambers in the hillsides.

Along the rampart of cliffs were only a few beaches, where landings could be made. Here the German sappers

A MAN FROM THE MANITOU ALONE ON A RAFT.

The casualties in connection with the attack on the Manitou were twenty-four drowned and twenty-seven missing. The above photograph was taken from a vessel which took part in the rescue. One of the survivors was rescued from a raft on which he was found floating alone.

PART OF THE WALLS OF SEDDUL BAHR AND OLD CANNON LYING IN THE SEA AFTER THE BOMBARDMENT.

INSIDE VIEW OF THE FORTIFICATIONS OF SEDDUL BAHR SHATTERED BY SHELLS FROM THE ALLIED FLEET.

ONE OF THE HEAVY CANNON USED IN THE DEFENCE OF SEDDUL BAHR.

THE BEGINNING OF THE FIGHT FOR THE DARDANELLES.

Remarkable camera pictures of the Turkish defences at the western entrance to the Dardanelles after the Franco-British bombardment. The lower photograph shows part of the outer walls of the fortifications. In circle: Trenches and cannon behind Seddul Bahr, with panoramic view of the Turkish fortress town.

had constructed wire entanglements beneath the shallowing sea, to hold up the troops as they left the boats and waded to the shore. In all cases these underwater obstacles were commanded by machine-guns hidden in holes in the rock or earth, and invisible to any reconnaissance from the decks or fighting-tops of the battleships. The exact number of Turkish troops with German officers garrisoning this " Gibraltar " of the Dardanelles is not known. About 100,000 men were available at the beginning of the action, but they were enormously reinforced from Adrianople and from Asia Minor, and at last a considerable part of the army opposing the Russians in the Caucasus Mountains was transported to this most vital area of conflict. Through the Bulair lines northward and across the Narrows eastward the Army of Gallipoli, as it weakened under the immense slaughter, was continually

Shells to Turkey through Bulgaria strengthened by three-quarters of the entire military forces of the Ottoman Empire. Moreover, the Germans and Austrians were able, in spite of the strain upon their cartridge and shell factories, to pour a great store of ammunition into Turkey through Bulgaria. Our attacks on the Dardanelles in March and April so used up our supplies of shells that our First Expeditionary Force between Ypres and La Bassée was for a time starved of high-explosive shells in some critical weeks of the spring campaign.

Altogether the cost to Great Britain of the attempts to force the Straits between the Mediterranean and the Black Sea was very heavy; and no small part of this cost was borne by Sir John French and his men in Flanders. A considerable number of our best troops, who would otherwise have been available in the main theatre of the war, were diverted, together with enormous stores of shells and war material, to the attack upon the Dardanelles. But it must always be remembered that our strong and tenacious action in this apparently secondary field of warfare may have brought about, in May, 1915, the intervention of Italy and the launching of her great Army on the flank of Austria-Hungary. Our naval losses also were more than compensated when the battle squadrons of Italy stripped for action and prepared to engage the Austrian Fleet. On the other hand it might be more strongly contended that Italy was moved at last more by the difficulties of the Allies than by their successes. She joined the Triple Entente after a series of grave reverses,

notably the Russian defeat in Galicia and the British defeat in the Dardanelles.

Certainly, from a military point of view, the operations in the Gallipoli Peninsula were extremely serious. Sir Ian Hamilton, one of our most distinguished generals, who had first been designated to lead our new Fourth Army in France, was now appointed Commander-in-Chief of the Mediterranean Expeditionary Force. Serving under him were General d'Amade, the conqueror of Morocco, commanding a division of Senegalese troops and Zouaves, Major-General **Sir Ian Hamilton's** Birdwood, commanding the Australian **appointment** and New Zealand contingents, and Major-General Hunter-Weston, commanding the British 29th Division. There were sixteen battalions of Australian infantry and some four battalions of New Zealand infantry, with engineers and artillery. A British naval division, an armoured-car division, and a number of naval air squadrons took part in the battles. A hundred and fifty ships were needed to transport the troops from their Egyptian base.

These set out on April 21st, but instead of making direct

SEDDUL BAHR DEFENCES.
Part of the Turkish fortifications at Seddul Bahr after the bombardment by the Allied Fleet.

for the Turkish coasts they put into the roomy Bay of Mudros, on Lemnos Island, waiting for the most favourable weather.

The spectacle in the great bay was wonderfully imposing. The ships varied in size from the Queen Elizabeth to the blue fishing smacks of the islanders. Famous liners, which have carried the British flag in every sea, were collected into a fleet of transports of the largest size ever seen, and the warships covering the entrance to the bay with their guns formed one of the mightiest naval forces.

AFTER THE BOMBARDMENT OF SEDDUL BAHR.
Seddul Bahr is situated on the north side of the entrance to the Dardanelles. Our photograph shows a mill that was struck during the naval shell fire.

CHURCH SERVICE ABOARD H.M.S. QUEEN ELIZABETH IN THE DARDANELLES.
Above are seen the huge muzzles of the warship's 15 in. guns. The photograph was taken by the official photographer to the Dardanelles Expedition.

This great fleet, composed of spare vessels of the British and French Navies, had to guard against an attack by hostile torpedo craft. The thoughts of many Frenchmen and Britons went back to the days when their forefathers set out under Richard of England and St. Louis of France on the early Crusades. Now men from lands undiscovered in the days when the Turks first rose to power were uniting with their kinsmen of the chief crusading nations of Europe in what was probably the last crusade the Christian world would ever make against the Turks.

Even in the age of St. Louis a German Emperor had been ready to conclude peace with the Saracens in order to have his hands free to ravage the fairest cities in Northern Italy. Now the infidel Hohenstaufen was **Hohenzollern and** succeeded by another Sauban tyrant, the **Hohenstaufen** Hohenzollern, who had reduced the Turks to vassalage with a view to a greater attempt to reduce the enlarged modern world into a German dominion. It was notorious that the mad dream of the Hohenzollern was based upon romantic memories of the Hohenstaufen, whose excessive lust of conquest had ruined Germany and had crippled her for six centuries. But, by forcing the Turks to league with him, the new German Emperor had shown less talent for statecraft than his mediæval model; for Turkey had at once become the pivot of a new turning movement in the politics of the Balkans and the Mediterranean countries. By putting an end to the Turkish neutrality the German intriguer had given the Allies a lever by which they might bring Italy, Rumania, and even Bulgaria, over to their side simply by undertaking the last and the greatest of the Crusades.

For three days the huge fleet of transports and warships in Mudros Bay waited for the period of calm, settled weather that was needed to make a landing. Sir Ian Hamilton was faced with a larger and more difficult task than his fellow Scotsman Sir Ra'ph Abercromby had undertaken in March, 1801, in Aboukir Bay. In one day's violent action on a flat shore, commanded only by sandhills, Abercromby had made a landing in Egypt in the face of a storm of shot and had driven back the enemy. From the fighting-tops of our ships our modern soldiers and sailors could see through their glasses the beach in Asia Minor where Abercromby had practised landing tactics for weeks with all his troops and seamen before he sailed for Egypt. Sir **Hamilton follows** Ian Hamilton followed Abercromby's **Abercromby's** example, and while the fleet waited at **example** Mudros Bay every soldier was taken from the transports and trained at embarking and disembarking from warships and troopships to the shore and from the shore to the ships. The bluejackets showed the men, heavily laden with their kits and rifles, how to climb up and down the ships' sides by means of rope ladders, how to row and steer the disembarking boats, and how to use boathooks.

By general consent the Australian, New Zealand, and Tasmanian troops were the finest body of men ever sent forth by any country to the field of battle. The average height in some of the battalions was close on six feet, and every man looked like a trained athlete. Many of the privates held better positions in civil life than their officers.

THE TOWN OF GALLIPOLI AT THE ENTRANCE TO THE SEA OF MARMORA.

This led to an intensely democratic spirit in the Australasian Army, with excellent discipline, however, and a keenness for battle which was quite extraordinary. The attack on the Suez Canal had been a disappointment to the men from the lands of the Southern Cross. They were eager for as tough a job as the regular British Army had undertaken at the Aisne, at Ypres, and at Neuve Chapelle. In the Dardanelles they obtained what they wanted. For in the new Plevna the stubborn courage and magnificent endurance of the Turks and the powerful armament and superb organising skill of the German Staff gave our Second Expeditionary Force, consisting of about a hundred and fifty thousand men, one of the most arduous and terrible combats in all the annals of warfare. To speak

these operations were dependent on the state of the capricious spring weather, and a rough sea would leave one part of our army ashore while its main force and its supplies were held off the coast. The beaches were very few in number, the rampart of steep cliff being practically continuous, especially on the side where the Australasians proposed to land. Above the cliffs were hostile gun-positions on the inland hills commanding every line of approach.

No surprise attack was possible at the end of the Peninsula. There were only six beaches there, and the 29th Division, under Major-General Hunter-Weston, made a straight rush from the boats at each landing-place, and by hard, furious, and unceasing fighting drove the Turks back and obtained a footing. The Australasians, however, were

Imposing spectacle at Enos

LIGHTHOUSE AND ROCKS, GALLIPOLI.

VILLAGE OF BULAIR FROM THE SOUTH-WEST.

quite plainly, we were faced in the Dardanelles with a task that verged on the impossible. Half a million men at least were needed to carry it through. Even with half a million men it would have been a hard, long, and costly operation. The Turks and Germans had **Accomplishing the** good reason to suppose that they could **seemingly impossible** drive every landing-party back into the sea, as in the first weeks of the battle they announced they had done. Only men of British stock, exalted to a height of heroism surpassing that of their forefathers, could have accomplished what our Second Expeditionary Force achieved. For they accomplished the seemingly impossible.

Sir Ian Hamilton had to land an army in the face of an enemy who had had full warning for two months that a landing in force would be attempted. He had to put on shore food, water, guns, horses, ammunition, and a thousand articles necessary to keep an army in the field, and to make arrangements to remove a large number of sick and wounded. All

luckier. It seems to have been originally planned that they should row to a beach by the promontory of Gaba Tepe, on the Ægean coast, some miles northwest of the point which the British were storming. In order to weaken the opposition which the Australasians would meet, our Naval Division set out in advance of them, and made great preparations to force a landing more northward near Suvla Bay. This was only a continuation of the earlier demonstrations by our fleet. Our sailors had steamed to Enos, close to the Bulgarian frontier, and made a show of clearing the way for the landing of the whole of the Expeditionary Force there. The spectacle at Enos was so imposing that the King of the Bulgarians came to watch the great landing battle. But it was only a British ruse to draw Turkish troops away from the Gallipoli Peninsula and misdirect any immediate reinforcement from the real field of conflict. The demonstration against Suvla

BRIDGE AT KAVAK DESTROYED BY FIRE OF ALLIED BATTLESHIPS IN MARCH, 1915.

Bay later was similarly intended to move the Turkish troops away from Gaba Tepe. It was successful in achieving this end, and it prepared the way for the splendidly audacious feat of the Colonial contingents.

On Friday morning, April 23rd, the stormy weather subsided, and at five o'clock in the afternoon the first transport steamed out of Mudros Bay, followed by other huge liners, all their decks yellow with khaki battalions. The bands of the fleet played them out, and the crews of the warships cheered them on to victory. The last salutation from the fleet was answered by a deafening cheer from the soldiers on the troopships. Then the Australasian division of liners, with its assistant battleships, steamed towards Gaba Tepe, which was made about one o'clock a.m. on Sunday, April 25th. It was a beautiful, calm night, with the sea lit by a brilliant crescent moon ; the soldiers rested in preparation for their tremendous exertion, and were afterwards served with a last hot meal. At twenty minutes past one the boats were lowered, and the troops fell in on deck and embarked in the boats, in complete silence and with great rapidity, without a hitch or accident of any kind.

The steam-pinnaces towed the boats towards the shore, the great battleships also steaming towards the land. By ten minutes past four the three battleships arrived two hundred and fifty yards from the coast, which was just discernible in the starry darkness, the moon having sunk. The boats, which had been towed behind the great warships, now went ahead, in snake-lines of twelve, each boat being crowded with troops so that the gunwale was almost flush with the water. The operation was timed **An historic Sabbath** so as to allow the boats to reach the beach **morn** in darkness before daybreak, so that the Turks would not be able to see the targets before the Australasians reached the land. Every eye was fixed on the grim, sombre sweep of cliff and hill just in front, which was so dark and silent that it seemed as if the enemy had been completely surprised.

But at ten minutes to five, as the leading boats approached the beach, an alarm light on the hill flashed for ten minutes. It was soon followed by a burst of rifle fire from the beach, where the Turks were entrenched. Soon a British cheer rang out and the rifle firing diminished as the dawn broke in a haze at half-past five on this historic Sabbath morn.

As some of the steam-pinnaces returned men learnt what had happened. When the Australians were about two hundred yards from shore the enemy opened fire with rifles and machine-guns. Happily, most of the bullets went high, yet many men **Australians use** were hit in the crowded boats. In grim **their bayonets** silence the others rowed with all their might till they reached the five-foot watermark. Then, without waiting for orders, the troops leaped into the sea and waded to the beach, and there, forming up roughly, they charged at the line of flame marking the first Turkish trench. The men of the landing-party had been warned not to fill their magazine rifles until daybreak, as a hot rifle fire from them would have given the enemy's batteries the target they were vainly searching for in the darkness. The Australians, therefore, used only their bayonets.

In about a minute they had taken the trench on the beach, captured a Maxim gun, and killed or dispersed all the defenders. Facing the small victorious force was a steep cliff, like the cliffs of Folkestone. It was covered

HOISTING THE "AERIAL" AT A NEW WIRELESS STATION ON THE SUEZ CANAL. IN CIRCLE: FIXING WIRELESS. APPARATUS FOR FIELD WORK. THE INDIANS WERE PARTICULARLY INTERESTED.

with thick undergrowth, and about halfway up it was another trench, from which the enemy directed a terrible fire on the beach and on the boats. Three boat-loads of men were wiped out before they could land, and the troops of the first landing-party dropped in large numbers from bullets poured on them from three sides. The Australians flung down their packs and climbed up the cliff, lifting themselves up from foothold to foothold by clutching at the shrubs. In less than a quarter of an hour most of the Turks holding the cliff trench were killed by the bayonet or put to flight. The Australians cut through the wire entanglements just before the sky whitened at daybreak and made a complete surprise attack.

A complete surprise attack

When the sun rose, and the outlines of the yellow coast and the green hills beyond became clear, it was seen that a happy mistake had been made. Instead of landing at Gaba Tepe, just north of the rocks, the boats had turned in the darkness towards Sari Bair, a great clump of sand-stone rock rising from nine hundred and fifty to nine hundred and seventy-one feet. At the intended landing-place there was a long slope from which the enemy

VIEW TAKEN BY OFFICIAL PHOTOGRAPHER OF THE INTERIOR OF THE DISMANTLED FORTRESS OF SEDDUL BAHR.

could have poured a terrible fire. But at Sari Bair there was only a forty-foot stretch of sand, where the sand-stone cliff rose almost sheer from the edge of the water at flood-tide. After the Australians had stormed the cliff in the darkness the situation of the Colonial contingent was by far the best throughout the expeditionary force. There was no slope down which hostile infantry could fire, and the bluffs, ridges, and broken ground formed good cover to the troops after they had passed the beach.

In other respects, however, affairs were extremely difficult when the sun rose. For it shone right in the eyes of the gunners on the battleships, and prevented them from supporting our infantry attacks. On the other hand, the Turkish sharpshooters, with the light behind them and the clear breadth of sea in front, could direct a deadly fusillade upon every target. Some boats, having broken away from their tows, drifted down the coast under fire. One came near the shore with only two Australians un-wounded in it. The two men jumped into the water and dashed furiously into the fight. Meanwhile, the task of the seamen running the boats from the beach to the troopships became very perilous. There were from six to eight

seamen pulling each boat. They had to row the troops to the beach under fire, return under fire for more troops, and continually repeat the process during the early part of the day, in which it was impossible to check the enemy's fire. It was here that British midshipmen, many of them boys of sixteen fresh from Dartmouth, where they had only received a few months' training, conducted themselves with an heroic coolness recalling the best traditions of the midshipmen of Nelson's days. To the older men, naturally, the extraordinary gallantry of the lads was very moving.

It is indeed said that some of our sailors were at last unable to resist the temptation to join in the fight. Taking rifles from the wounded troops, they left their boats and fought with the soldiers. One party of seven sailors attacked a band of two hundred and fifty Turks, and the Colonial troops were delighted with their helpers, and induced them to stay on with them. This was the reason why so many small boats were abandoned on the Gallipoli coast. It was not altogether in keeping with good naval discipline, but the blood of the sailors was up, and they could not resist an opportunity for joining in the fight on the slightest pretext. The admiration felt by the seamen for the soldiers was high and intense. The two Services were soldered together by that manly love of comrades which is the supreme source of the fighting spirit of heroic peoples. There were times when our men melted like women and stooped above their dead, kissed them, and then went out in white, Berserker-like fury to fall in their turn upon the foe. Heroism, like panic, is contagious. It was an epidemic of heroism that kept our men going at Gallipoli as it had kept them going at Ypres. Modern education, and particularly the general habit of daily newspaper reading, had made all men of British stock somewhat more susceptible in mind than their forefathers. But this suscepti-bility of intelligence had not weakened the old fundamental qualities of character. The Australasians, especially, were quite a new type of Britons. They were both fire and granite —volcanic lava—and the fight they put up on Sari Bair was a thing of epic quality.

The speed, violence, and drive of their first attack were unparalleled in British warfare. The ground they worked over was a confused triangle of ridges, ravines, bluffs, dales, and long slopes, stretching across the Peninsula to a point above the Narrows. The surface was either bare, crumbly, yellow sandstone, or a dense undergrowth of shrub about six feet in height. It was so broken that Turkish snipers were able to work a few yards in front of our lines without being spotted. No movement on a large scale could be regu-larly organised, for as soon as the men moved forward in open order they were lost to the view of their officers in the thick scrub. It was the most remarkable of all soldiers' battles, for the winning quality was the initiative and resource of the leading men of each section, clambering over cliffs, working their way up and down ridges, much of the work being done even without directions from the corporals.

First landing battle won

By the time the sun had fully risen the Australians had gained the first ridge of Sari Bair, and by a quarter-past nine the first landing battle was won; for the

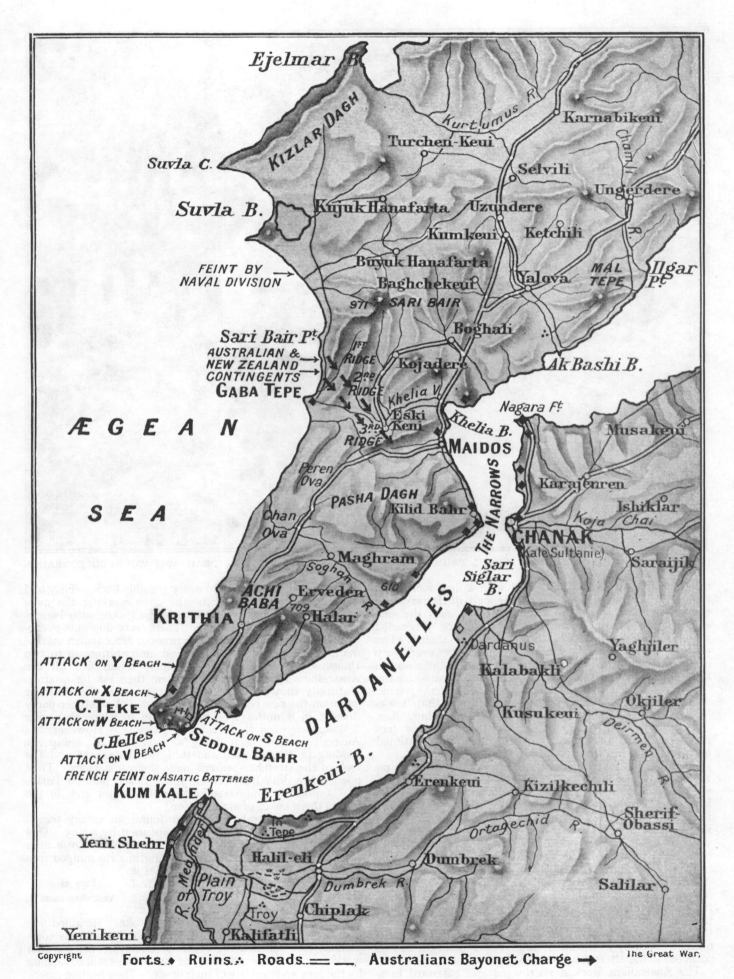

Ejelmar B.

KIZLAR DAGH

Kurtlumus R.

Karnabikeui

Turchen-Keui

Suvla C.

Selvili

Chamli R.

Suvla B.

Ungerdere

Kujuk Hanafarta   Uzundere

FEINT BY
NAVAL DIVISION →

Kumkeui   Ketchili

MAL
TEPE   Ilgar
P.

Buyuk Hanafarta

Baghchekeui   Yalova

971   SARI BAIR

Sari Bair P.

AUSTRALIAN &
NEW ZEALAND →
CONTINGENTS

GABA TEPE

1ST
RIDGE

2ND
RIDGE

Kojadere

Boghali

Ak Bashi B.

Khelia V.

Nagara Ft.

Musakeui

Æ G E A N

3RD
RIDGE

Eski
Keui

Khelia B.

MAIDOS

Karajenren

S E A

Peren
Ova

Chan
Ova

PASHA DAGH

Kilid Bahr

THE NARROWS

CHANAK
(Kale Sultanie)

Ishiklar

Koja Chai

Saraijik

Maghram

Sari
Siglar
B.

ACHI
BABA   Erveden   610

709   Halar

KRITHIA

SOGHAN R.

Dardanus

Yaghjiler

Kalabakli

ATTACK ON Y BEACH →

ATTACK ON X BEACH →

C. TEKE

ATTACK ON W BEACH →

C. Helles

ATTACK ON V BEACH →

141   ATTACK ON S BEACH

Seddul Bahr

D A R D A N E L L E S

Okjiler

Kusukeui

Deirmen R.

FRENCH FEINT ON ASIATIC BATTERIES

KUM KALE   ↓

Erenkeui B.

Erenkeui

Kizilkechili

Sherif-
Obassi

Yeni Shehr

In Tepe

Halil-eli

Dumbrek

Ortagechid R.

R. Meander

Plain
of Troy

Dumbrek R.

Salilar

Troy   Chiplak

Yenikeui   Kalifatli

Copyright   Forts ♦ Ruins ∴ Roads ══ Australians Bayonet Charge →   The Great War.

MAP OF THE DARDANELLES AND GALLIPOLI PENINSULA, SPECIALLY DRAWN TO ILLUSTRATE
THE OPERATIONS BY LAND AND WATER WHICH BEGAN IN THE SPRING OF 1915.

FRENCH SOLDIERS IN CAMP AT SEDDUL BAHR SORTING OUT THE KITS OF THEIR DEAD AND WOUNDED COMRADES.

covering force of Australians held such a firm footing on the crest that the intense fire of the enemy died away, and though sniping went on throughout the day the disembarkation of the remainder of the force proceeded without interruption save from shrapnel shells. The position of the victorious battalions was, however, very difficult. The proper thing for them to have done was to have entrenched on the conquered ridge and waited for the main force to disembark. But the ground **Surprise for German commander** was so broken and scrubby that it was hard to find a good entrenching line.

When the troops thought they had cleared a space they were still subjected to a continual and punishing fire from the snipers.

Then as the light became good the German gunners on the heights brought their artillery into action. There were first two guns at Gaba Tepe, which enfiladed the landing beach with shrapnel. But one of our cruisers moved in close to the shore and battered the sandstone rocks with high-explosive shell so that the enemy guns there were silenced. In the meantime the Australians on the crest, smitten on both flanks and worried all along their front, began to move out in search of their foes. The fact was their landing at Sari Bair had been quite a surprise for the German commander. Only a weak force had held the beach, and only a scattered body of snipers occupied the mountain, trying to hold back the Australians until the Turkish divisions, sent towards the wrong places round Suvla Bay in the north and Gaba Tepe in the south, collected in the afternoon at Sari Bair.

The Australians worked northward and eastward in a series of fierce bayonet rushes. Then, encouraged by the slight opposition they met, they went ahead in a burst of charges down the ravines and up the ridges. The

Turks and Germans played every possible trick. They had machine-guns in the scrub, the men working the guns having their hands and faces stained green, with boughs and bushes tied about them. There were dug-outs everywhere, each with its sniper, a German or Macedonian marksman, with several days' food, and ammunition up to two thousand rounds. Some of them would fire till the Australians were five yards off, and then ask for quarter. Naturally they did not get it. Others tried the stretcher game on the raw recruits from oversea. A stretcher-party dressed in a uniform of khaki came to a trench crying "Make way for the stretcher-party!" However, the Australians had been doing a good deal of newspaper reading in Egypt, and something in the accent and the look of the stretcher-bearers made them suspicious. They opened fire, killed a German and a dozen painted Turks, and found in one stretcher a machine-gun and in the others three boxes of ammunition.

When the Australians in turn found an enemy trench they did not take the trouble to capture it by a ruse. One of the first works on the heights was stormed by a man famous for his reach and great strength. He jumped into the trench and lifted the Turks out of it with his bayonet, driving the steel through their bodies, and then flinging them over his shoulder in a movement **Fury of Australian onset** that released the blade for the next stroke. He killed five men in this way, but could do no more, because his companions had finished the other Ottomans. This bayonet work went on all the morning, the Australians still advancing by the fury and rapidity of their onset. Their leading troops worked down the Khelia Valley, and by one of the most tremendous efforts in history they seem to have crossed the last and third ridge and got within a few hundred yards of

BRITISH ENCAMPMENT IN THE VICINITY OF THE DARDANELLES. VESSELS OF THE ALLIED FLEET IN THE OFFING.

ROAD-MAKING UNDER THE PROTECTION OF THE GUNS—ONE OF MR. ASHMEAD-BARTLETT'S DARDANELLES PHOTOGRAPHS.

ANOTHER VIEW OF A BRITISH BEACH ENCAMPMENT NEAR THE WESTERN ENTRANCE OF THE DARDANELLES.

TURKISH DEFENCES ON THE GALLIPOLI PENINSULA SHATTERED BY THE FIRE OF THE ALLIED FLEET.

Maidos, the key to the Narrows. In front of them, across the water, was Nagara Point. Had it been possible to make this attack in force and bring up guns and entrench on the ground won in the extraordinarily impetuous charge, the road to Constantinople would practically have been conquered in a few hours.

But the vehement covering force of Australians had gained more ground than it could hold. There were only two or three thousand troops, without food or guns, and lacking even in Maxims. Most of their work had been done with the bayonet, and in the afternoon the German commander brought his main force against them and almost outflanked them. But at the critical moment the New Zealanders came to the help of the Australians, and after retiring from the third ridge back to their early position on the first ridge, the gallant Colonial troops dug themselves in. Then the Indian troops disembarked, **Turks' horrible** and after the second rush of the Austral- **torture of wounded** asians, the combined and strengthened force of Australians, New Zealanders, and Indians again advanced to the third ridge, after repulsing some furious counter-attacks by the Turks.

As twilight fell the enemy brought up more reinforcements, and his counter-attacks were supported by a heavy bombardment of our position from hostile batteries which our naval guns could not reach. So dangerous did the pressure on our lines become that Major-General Birdwood drew the troops back to the first ridge during the night, and his Staff devoted all their energies to strengthening the position and getting some field-guns ashore to deal with the enemy's artillery. The Australians had suffered heavily in their first retreat from the point near Maidos. Nearly a fourth of their force was put out of action, and by a dreadful misfortune the wounded men of their leading companies fell into the hands of the Turks and were horribly tortured and mutilated before being put to death.

In the fighting on Sunday the Colonial contingents probably lost more men than did the enemy through the covering force advancing across the Peninsula without waiting for their supports. Whatever the losses of the Australians were, they and the New Zealanders and Indians had their full revenge when they held the ridge and prevented the Turks from driving them into the sea; for the Turks attacked in dense formations all during Sunday night and Monday morning. Our troops met them in the British way—reserved their fire, and then emptied their magazines at point-blank range into the advancing masses. A single Australian platoon, supported by

RUINS ON GALLIPOLI PENINSULA AFTER THE BOMBARDMENT.

Marines, was charged by half a battalion of Turks. They waited till the Turks were ten yards away, gave them the mad minute of rapid fire, and then leaped forward in turn and smote the remaining upright figures with hand-grenades. No Ottoman who took part in that charge escaped. All along the front on Sunday night the conflict continued with an intensity like that of Le Cateau and Ypres, for Liman von Sandars had a similar advantage in artillery power, and he used the Turks in shoulder-to-shoulder lines, advancing in human billows against the British front.

When Monday morning dawned the landing battle at Sari Bair was won, in spite of the fact that another Turkish army corps was moving up on the north-east for the grand assault which was to drive our men into the sea. The German artillerymen had brought all their guns into play and had moved up more batteries for the final bombardment. During the whole of Sunday **Landing under** night the hostile gunners had maintained **rain of shrapnel** a rain of shrapnel over the landing beach, with a view to hindering our disembarking operations and disabling our troops when they were impotent to defend themselves. Our battleships had tried to support the troops by a heavy fire from their secondary armament, but as the enemy's gun-positions at this time were not known our ships could not do much to keep down the enemy's fire.

But on Monday morning the position was reversed. The Turks could clearly be seen moving in large numbers along the heights, and the position of their supporting batteries could be spotted by their flames. Moreover, every time they had fired in the darkness of Sunday night naval fire-control officers in the fighting-tops of our battleships had been spotting the flashes and comparing notes and measurements. The Queen Elizabeth and seven other warships steamed up to take part in the grand battle. The seven older ships moved close inshore, **Turkish barbarities** each of their chief gunnery lieutenants **avenged** having a marked map of this section of the enemy's territory. "Lizzie" stood farther out to sea, so as to get a howitzer effect with her guns by pitching the shells as high as possible into the dales, where our airmen reported the enemy were gathering for shelter preparatory to the advance.

Then, as the Turkish infantry moved forward to the attack, they were punished for all that they had done to the Australian wounded. Every kind of shell carried by our warships was thrown at them, from the 15 in. shrapnel of the Queen Elizabeth to the little shell of the 12-pounders. The thunder and concussion made by the

was visible, and a similar cloud of cordite could be seen southward of Cape Tekeh, where another division of British battleships was canopying the hill of Achibaba with another continual burst of shrapnel fumes. Nearer at hand a battleship and a cruiser, close inshore at Gaba Tepe, were covering the low ground with their secondary armament and dropping shells into the Straits on the other side. Then beyond the battleships the great liners, in which the troops had been transported, lay out to sea to avoid the Turkish guns.

On land we still kept the enemy back by rifle and machine-gun fire. For two hours the Turks pressed their attack, while our naval guns inflicted terrible losses on them and our infantry smote them down in heaps before our trenches. But in spite of all the scientific instruments of slaughter employed on both sides, the great landing battle ended in a primitive way. It could be seen that the Turks were becoming demoralised by the overwhelming fire of our naval guns. The German officers found it difficult to bring them up to the attack, and had to pack them closer than ever in order to keep control over them.

Major-General Birdwood at last let **Position at Sari Bair** them advance through our shrapnel zone, **secured** gave a general order for rapid fire, and then, after the magazine rifles and machine-guns had done their work, there was a flash of steel along the trenches. The Colonial troops leaped out with the bayonet and charged the staggered, reeling Turks, who broke and fled.

They were bayoneted in the back as far as the shrapnel zone. But here our troops fell back, and, in answer to a wireless message, the eight warships turned all their guns on the fugitive enemy and pounded them with shrapnel. On Monday afternoon our position at Sari Bair was secure. The trenches were deepened so that our men could not be shaken by shrapnel fire, and though the Turks were still in overwhelming numbers in

THE BROKEN FORTRESS OF
SEDDUL BAHR.

entire armament of the great naval squadron were beyond description. The hills on which the Turks were collecting were transformed into smoking volcanoes, the common shell forming craters hung with black smoke, while the 15 in. and the 12 in. shrapnel burst in white canopies over the exploded rocks and uprooted bushes. An enemy warship tried to reply across the Peninsula, but the Triumph nearly struck her with two 10 in. shells, and she retired to a safer position, from which she was able to do no damage. Our ships were soon hidden from the troops they were protecting by vast rolling clouds of cordite. But the day was so clear that all the coast-line

CORNER OF THE FORTRESS OF SEDDUL BAHR AFTER BOMBARDMENT BY THE BIG
GUNS OF THE QUEEN ELIZABETH.

LANDING OPERATIONS IN THE DARDANELLES. REMARKABLE CAMERA-RECORD OF THE VARIED ACTIVITIES ON BEACH V, TAKEN BY THE OFFICIAL PHOTOGRAPHER FROM THE S.S. RIVER CLYDE.

comparison with the troops we had put ashore, they were too much demoralised to attempt another attack in force. Only their snipers continued to harass our lines on Monday night. Some of our field-guns were landed, with several Indian mounted batteries, and our entrenchments were firmly established on a wide front, covering the whole of the foreshore on which disembarking operations were still proceeding.

Like General von Kluck at Maubeuge, who announced to his General Staff that he had got the British army in a ring of iron, General von Sanders had been so confident of the success of his plan that he had proclaimed in advance that he had driven our Second Expeditionary Force into

Von Sanders' over-confidence

the sea. This news was published at Constantinople in the same way as Kluck's anticipation of an event which never happened was wirelessed to all the world from Berlin. The German General at Gallipoli had expected to find at Sari Bair a line thinly held by Colonial troops exhausted by their losses and labours of the previous day of landing. His aim was to force this thin line into the sea by a great concentration of infantry and an unceasing bombardment by shrapnel shells. But, as of old, thin lines held by men of British stock were not easy to break. The Australians and New Zealanders had from the first been determined to a man to die rather than give up the ground they had won at such heavy cost on Sunday, for they knew it would have been impossible to re embark the army if the ring of hills commanding the beach had been lost.

Most of the men were volunteers who had only had a few months' training, and had come under fire for the

first time in circumstances calculated to try the nerve of veteran troops. The sixteen thousand Australian infantrymen had suffered badly on Sunday, and should have been, therefore, capable of being demoralised by an attack in overwhelming numbers. But the Australians were not made that way. All they wanted to do was to avenge their dead. No man cared what happened to himself, except that he regretted when he was wounded and so prevented from killing more Turks. Not since the French Revolution have new recruits fought with such combined impetuosity, steadfastness, and long-sustained fury as the Australians and New Zealanders displayed when their foes gave them the opportunity of exacting full revenge. For every mutilated, tortured Australian soldier left in the bush in the retreat from the Narrows a hundred Turks died the next day.

Australasians' impetuous valour

On Tuesday morning, April 27th, a fresh Turkish division was brought up to Sari Bair and launched against our trenches after a heavy bombardment by the German batteries. But the result was the same as on Monday. The Turks came on time after time, and were shot down in multitudes, and by three o'clock in the afternoon all the spirit of the twelve thousand fresh hostile infantrymen was broken. The Australasians again advanced with the bayonet and won more ground, enabling them to strengthen their defences. All that the German commander then could do was to maintain a curtain of shrapnel over the beach and the neighbouring waters, in order to impede the disembarking operations. But the hail of bullets made little impression on the work on the pinnaces, boats, lighters, and tugs, and the seamen who manned

346

them ; for though the shrapnel bullets churned up the water with the spectacular effect of a hailstorm, the material damage inflicted by the intense and costly bombardment was slight. Certainly it was out of all proportion to the expense, labour, and intrigue which the Turks and Germans had been put to in collecting their store of munitions in Gallipoli. The more shells they used on " Folkestone Leas,"

Shells on "Folkestone Leas" as the stretch of foreshore and cliff was called, the less shells they would have when the final tussle opened. Nothing could budge the Colonial troops, and by all working like frenzied navvies, building roads, making concrete works, dragging guns up the cliff, constructing bomb-proof shelters, and turning their stretch of foreshore into an invisible town, they fortified their position between Sari Bair and Gaba Tepe so that they were able to reduce the garrison and send a considerable force to help the British troops at Seddul Bahr, at the end of the Peninsula.

As in Flanders, France, and Egypt, so in the Dardanelles the Indian troops proved themselves of high and splendid courage, fighting with great skill and tenacity. To their help the Australians were much indebted. But owing to the widely separated scenes in which the warriors of India continually fought—at La Bassée and Neuve Chapelle, along the Suez Canal, and at Sari Bair and the southern end of the Gallipoli Peninsula—the achievements of the Indian peoples in all the work of the war is difficult to appreciate. So it may be worth while, at this important point in their warlike task, to interrupt the main narrative and bring out the value and scope of the aid given by India to the Empire. Then in the following chapter we can continue the story of the Dardanelles operations and describe the series of magnificent feats accomplished by the 29th Division on the beaches of the southern end of Gallipoli Peninsula.

INDIAN TROOPS, JUST LANDED FROM THE DARDANELLES TRANSPORTS, ON THEIR WAY TO THE FIRING-LINE.
UPPER PHOTOGRAPH : LOADING AMMUNITION FOR USE AGAINST THE TURKS.

INDIAN MAXIM SECTION

CHAPTER LXI.

IN THE FIELD.

THE GREAT WAVE OF LOYALTY AND IMPERIAL ENTHUSIASM IN INDIA.

Bernhardi's False Prophecy—Germany's Mistake—Lord Hardinge's Splendid Work—Caste, Customs, Prejudices, and Religious Differences Placed Aside—Surendranath Banerjee's Eloquent Testimony—Loyal Attitude of Responsible Moslems—The King-Emperor's Message—India's Military Strength—Importance of the Native States—Contributions of the Ruling Princes—Their Offers of Personal Service—Arrival of the Indian Expeditionary Force at Marseilles—A Royal Greeting—Sir James Willcocks's Stirring Order of the Day—How the Indians Bore Themselves in the Field—Memorable Charge of the Bengal Lancers—German Plans to Confuse and Perplex the Indians—An Example of Prussian Audacity—Lord Roberts's Visit to His Old Comrades-in-Arms—The Indians at Neuve Chapelle—Effect on India's Future of the Services of Her Sons in Europe—A Typical List of Gifts to the Indian Government.

VISCOUNT HARDINGE OF PENSHURST, VICEROY OF INDIA SINCE 1910.

NO more confident prediction was made in Germany in the days before the Great War than that immediately Britain was fighting for her existence India would rise in revolt against her.

The Indian chiefs—Nizam and Nawab, Maharaja and Raja, Shah and Prince, Sawbwa and Rao, princes of ancient lineage and hereditary power—were one and all to seize this chance of striking off the shackles of our rule. Moslem races, fired to fanaticism by the careful preaching of a Holy War from Constantinople, were to fly to arms against Great Britain. The ancient jealousies of the hundred and one peoples who make up our vast Eastern Empire were to be rekindled, and a greater mutiny was to drive the hated British into the sea. Here a Maharaja was to lead his old troops upon us ; there the advocates of native rights were to provoke the people to rise. A witches' cauldron of hatred and strife was to be stirred, and Britain was to be robbed of the brightest jewel in her crown.

Bernhardi, the prophet of the new Germany, exultantly forecasted this. " There is another danger," he said, " which concerns England more closely, and directly threatens her vitality. This is due to the Nationalist movement in India and Egypt, to the growing power of Islam, to the agitation for independence

in the great Colonies, as well as to the supremacy of the Low German element in South Africa. In India some 70,000,000 of Mussulmans live under English rule ; but now that a pronounced revolutionary and Nationalist tendency shows itself amongst the Hindu population, the danger is imminent that Pan-Islamism will unite with the revolutionary elements of Bengal. The co-operation of these elements might create a very grave danger capable of shaking the foundation of England's high position in the world."

This was what many sober and carefully informed German leaders expected. For years they had studied India microscopically. Numbers of German officials, representatives, and secret agents —from the Crown Prince on a visit of State to the underling whose work it was to promote unrest in the bazaars—had examined and reported on India from east to west. They knew all about the secret societies plotting against Britain. Every speech railing at us was carefully noted. Every bomb-thrower's deed was marked as another nail in the coffin of our Empire.

The Germans made one great mistake. They took notice of the slight movements of unrest which came to the surface as the scum rises to the top of the great waters. But they did not realise that for every one revolutionist there were a thousand satisfied supporters of our rule, and ten thousand who were content to live

H.H. The Nizam of Hyderabad.

H.H. The Gaekwar of Baroda.

H.H. The Maharaja of Mysore.

H.H. The Maharaja of Gwalior.

Mobile mountain battery from the frontier of Afghanistan in use in France.

Detachment of Indian cavalry on the march near the Franco=Belgian frontier.

Indian infantry carrying Maxims into action under fire in France.

Indian infantry on their way to support the British at the front in Northern France.

351

H.H. The Maharaja of Kashmir.

Sir Pertab Singh, Regent of Jodhpur.

H.H. The Maharaja of Bikaner.

H.H. The Maharaja of Patiala.

their life peaceably under the British Raj, without troubling their heads with affairs of State. The native rulers, whom they pictured as shackled and fretting under the limitations of British supremacy, knew very well that never before had they or their people enjoyed such sustained abundance, such general prosperity, and such peace. Part of the unrest which the Germans observed so closely was actually due to the fact that in India there was little for the ancient warrior tribes to do. The old dominant and dominating races—the men of Hyderabad, Jaipur,

Wonderful harvests of goodwill and Gwalior—now found their fighting arms growing stiff for want of exercise. Idleness sometimes leads to mischief.

The Germans did not understand that in recent years the British Government had, by a policy of Imperial reform, done everything in its power to meet the natural native demands for increased self-government. Lord Morley had introduced schemes which now were bearing wonderful harvests of goodwill. The King-Emperor and the Queen-Empress, by their visit to India at the close of 1911, and their solemn crowning at Delhi, had made themselves real personalities to their Indian subjects, and their visible power, dignities, and goodwill appealed forcibly to the imagination of an Oriental nation. India was fortunate in having Lord Hardinge as Viceroy at this time, a statesman whose great work for India was even more appreciated by the rulers and people there than understood by people at home.

If our enemies were astonished and disconcerted at the conduct of India immediately after the outbreak of war, it may be admitted that they were not the only people to be surprised. The British did not expect that India would be so blind to her own interests as to play into the hands of Germany. But few among us had the imagination or the courage to anticipate the overwhelming wave of loyalty and Imperial enthusiasm which swept over the race. As the news travelled over the wires that the Empire was at war, the hand of India flew to its sword. Rulers of the great States summoned their armies together and hastened to offer all they had to their Emperor. From the Nizam of Hyderabad down to the chieftains on the Indian frontier ruling over a few villages the response was the same. The great princes offered money—scores of lacs of rupees ; they offered their very jewels ; they presented their soldiers, their horses, and their guns for their Emperor's service. The ruler of the ancient State of Rewa sent one question, "What orders from his Majesty for me and my troops ?" The Punjab Chiefs' Association passed a resolution expressing the determination of the Punjab aristocrats to serve Britain in war as well as in peace. Even the Grand Lama of Tibet proffered his aid. The Bengalee merchants raised big war funds. Most wonderful of all to those who know the East, the women of India broke the conventions that kept them from public life, and, from the Maharanis on their thrones to the humblest wife of Hindu, Moslem, or Parsee, they brought forward their silver and gave their personal gifts for the men at the front. India reached still greater depths of sacrifice. Men broke even the barriers of caste to serve, and as one Indian speaker truly said, " Indians have renounced every-

thing—caste, customs, prejudices, and religious differences—and laid down their lives to fight for their King."

Those Germans who believed that India would aid them had counted especially on two classes—the advocates of greater self-government and the Mohammedans. The former were represented by the Indian National Congress, a gathering in which on some occasions bitter criticisms had been heard of certain aspects of British rule. The Indian National Congress of 1914 opened in December, and for the first time in its history the Governor of the province in which it was held was present. No criticisms of Britain were heard now. Surendranath Banerjee, the famous Nationalist leader, voiced the feelings of his people when he declared : " The best prospects of India are linked up with the permanence of British rule. We desire to proclaim to the Kaiser and to the enemies of England that behind the British Army is the whole Indian people, who as one man will defend the Empire and die for it. The loyalty of India is consecrated by the blood of our fellow-countrymen who have died in Europe. If England demands it, the last pice we have and the last drop of blood

INDIAN SOLDIERS SORTING LETTERS INSIDE AN HOTEL WHICH WAS BEING USED AS A MILITARY POST-OFFICE.

that flows through us will be at the service of the Empire."

" This is not the time to deal with matters upon which we may differ," said the President of the Congress, Bhupendra Nath Basu. " We must present to the world the spectacle of a united Empire. India can put a wall of Indian soldiers in the field against which the German militarism will hurl itself vainly. India is oblivious of the past and impregnated with the future."

The attitude of the Moslems proved **Hindu and Moslem** equally disappointing to our foes. When **loyalty** Germany had succeeded in inducing Turkey to go to war with Great Britain there was a possibility that the Moslem peoples might, under the influence of religious zeal, join in a Jehad against us. The most fantastic stories were spread abroad. The German Emperor had, it was confidently reported, himself become one of the faithful, and was leading the hosts of the faithful against the infidel. Great Britain, it was rumoured, intended

INDIAN MAXIM-GUN SECTION IN FLANDERS.

BENGAL LANCERS—A PHOTOGRAPH TAKEN JUST AFTER THEIR LANDING IN FRANCE.

to make the Caliph—the religious head of the faithful—the mere subordinate of itself, to dictate his appointment, and to control him. Here and there in Central Asia, and in some parts of Africa, the more ignorant Moslem peoples rose to the bait. In India, while there was undoubtedly some danger and much uneasiness from the poorest and most ignorant sections of the Moslem races, the responsible Moslems knew Britain better and threw all the weight of their influence and authority on our side. Many of the ruling chiefs called their peoples together and urged on them that this was no religious war and that the Koran did not require them to fight for Turkey. "Turkey has made herself a tool in Germany's hands,"

Aga Khan's view of Turkey

said the great Moslem leader Aga Khan. "She has not only ruined herself, but has forfeited the position of trustee of Islam."

The Nizam of Hyderabad, the premier native ruler of India, issued a manifesto declaring that " it is the bounden duty of the Moslems of India to adhere to their old and tried loyalty to the British Government, whose cause I am convinced is right and just. I give expression to the hope," said he, " that as I, following the traditions of my ancestors, hold myself ready to devote my own person and all the resources of my State and all that I possess to the service of Great Britain, so will all the Mohammedans of India, especially my own beloved subjects, hold themselves wholeheartedly ready in the same way."

Even women leaders spoke for us and worked for us. One of the most important of them among Mohammedan rulers is her Highness the Nawab Begum of Bhopal, a progressive modern woman of the East, the only ruler in India of the female sex, who combines a strict Mohammedanism with modern methods. Among the faithful she is famous for having made a pilgrimage to the holy cities of Arabia.

354

Among westerners she is known, among other things, for the deep interest she takes in education and for her work for the higher education of the sons of the ruling chiefs. Her family is traditionally loyal. Since one great occasion, in 1778, when they stood by Colonel Goddard in days of great danger, the fidelity of the rulers of Bhopal has been proverbial. The Begum rose to the occasion. When the first whispers of disaffection among Mohammedan peoples were heard she called her officers and all her leading men together and addressed them. She told them with the utmost earnestness and conviction that Turkey was wrong, that this was no fight of Islam against Christianity, but a fight in which Great Britain was standing for world-liberty and justice. She did more than talk. She poured out the resources of her State for the Empire, and contributed men, horses, and money for the cause. She sent her heir-apparent, the Nawab Nasrulla Khan, a minor, to the front in command of the Bhopal contingent of troops. She joined forces with the

Begum of Bhopal's example

Maharaja of Gwalior in organising and raising funds among the chiefs for the Indian hospital-ship Loyalty, which was to prove so useful in the months ahead.

The Council of the All-India Moslem League, at a meeting at Lucknow, assured the Viceroy " that the participation of Turkey in the present war does not and cannot affect our loyalty in the least degree, and that the Council is confident that no Mussulman in India will swerve even a hair's-breadth from his duty to the Sovereign." Private Moslem gentlemen of influence urged all of their faith to assist the mighty British Empire, pointing out that under the rule of their Emperor they had perfect religious freedom.

The difficulty of giving, in a reasonable space, an adequate idea of the doings of the Indian peoples in the Great War lies in the vast extent of our Eastern Empire and the variety and multitude of its peoples. They are numbered by hundreds of millions. They talk among them twenty-four native languages, apart from minor dialects. They differ among themselves in the most amazing way in religion and in their manner of living. What relation is there, it may be asked, between the fierce fighting tribes of the north and the meek ryot of Bengal ? What is the link between Calcutta the Splendid and the barren marches under the shadow of the Himalayas ? How, it has often been asked, can all these diverse fabrics be woven into one vast nation ? How can a Rajput and Bengalee, Afridi and Hindu, man of Madras and man of Kashmir join in common aspiration and united nationhood ?

When war broke out the British Government had to decide whether or not it should use Indian troops against European peoples. The ruling princes of India, the soldiery, the men of the fighting north, and the very Indian students in London demanded the right to serve. They felt that, with the vast issues at stake, unless they showed themselves willing and obtained the right to take actual part in the fighting in the war, India could never hope to rise to the place she desired in the Empire. The British Government had, however, to keep other considerations in mind. Throughout India the people are taught respect for the white man. To many of them he is seen solely as an administrator, a ruler, and a judge. To bring scores of thousands of Indian troops into intimate contact with the working peoples of Europe might, it was felt, lower the white man's prestige. In the Boer War these considerations prevailed, and, greatly to the disappointment of the Indian peoples, and despite their most urgent demands, they were not employed on active service. "This," they were told, "is a white man's war." But early in the Great War the British Government decided that Indian troops were to be employed in Europe, and a message was sent from the King-Emperor to the princes and peoples of India which touched the emotions of the whole of the Far East. The King-Emperor's message, part of which has been quoted already on page 194 of Vol. II., was as follows:—

To the Princes and Peoples of My Indian Empire :

During the past few weeks the peoples of my whole Empire at home and overseas have moved with one mind and purpose to confront and overthrow an unparalleled assault upon the continuity of civilisation and the peace of mankind.

The calamitous conflict is not of my seeking. My voice has been cast throughout on the side of peace. My Ministers earnestly strove to allay the causes of strife and to appease differences with which my Empire was not concerned. Had I stood aside, when, in defiance of pledges to which my Kingdom was a party, the soil of Belgium was violated and her cities laid desolate, when the very life of the French nation was threatened with extinction, I should have sacrificed my honour and given to destruction the liberties of my Empire and mankind. I rejoice that every part of the Empire is with me in this decision.

The King-Emperor's message

Paramount regard for treaty faith and the pledged word of rulers and peoples is the common heritage of Britain and India.

Among the many incidents that have marked the unanimous uprising of the populations of my Empire in defence of its unity and integrity, nothing has moved me more than the passionate devotion to my Throne expressed both by my Indian subjects and by the Feudatory Princes and the Ruling Chiefs of India, and their prodigal offers of their lives and their resources in the cause of the Realm. Their one-voiced demand to be foremost in the conflict has touched my heart and has inspired to the highest issues the love and devotion which, as I well know, have ever linked my Indian subjects and myself. I recall to mind India's gracious message to the British nation of goodwill and fellowship which greeted my return in February, 1912, after the solemn ceremony of my Coronation Durbar at Delhi, and I find in this hour of trial a full harvest and noble fulfilment of the assurance given by you that the destinies of Great Britain and India were indissolubly linked.

The British Government had considerable forces of different kinds in India upon which it could draw. In the first case there were 75,000 British soldiers, the regular Indian garrison. It would not have been wise to deplete this garrison too much, but it was possible to take away large numbers of trained and hardened soldiers and to replace them by Territorials. Next there came the regular Indian Army, an army strong in numbers, rich in traditions, and trained to a point of high efficiency. The regular Indian Army numbered 160,000 men, including over 3,000 British officers and officials, **India's military** and it had 40,000 reserves to be drawn **resources** upon. It was largely raised from the fighting Mohammedan races, and in the years immediately before the war, starting with the time when Lord Kitchener was Commander-in-Chief, its entire organisation had been remodelled and its artillery and transport brought up to a war standard. It would be difficult in the space of a few paragraphs to give any adequate notion of the traditions that lie behind this Army, traditions which even the hour of madness of the Great Mutiny could not wholly wipe out. The Indian Army is drawn in the first place largely from the military peoples of the Punjab. High in rank among its soldiers are the Sikhs, acclaimed by many as some of the finest fighting men in the world. They are the military adventurers of the Far East. They

SIKHS ON THE MARCH IN FRANCE. THE SMALLER PHOTOGRAPH AFFORDS A GLIMPSE OF THE GURKHAS EN ROUTE FOR THE FRONT.

AN INDIAN SCOUT ON DUTY ON A WAR-WORN HIGHWAY OF FRANCE.

Sweden ! I wonder if everyone calls to mind that the Maharaja of Gwalior has more subjects than the King of Denmark ; or that the Nizam of Hyderabad governs a people twice as numerous as the people of the Netherlands and three times as numerous as the people of Ireland."

The native States are a series of semi-independent kingdoms and principalities, some of vast extent, rivalling England in size, some mere collections of hill-side huts, whose entire area can be surveyed from a neighbouring height. In all they cover about 700,000 square miles. Their princes retain, with some limitations, their ancient state and dignities. External affairs are controlled by the Indian Government. In each State there is a British Resident, a carefully selected high official who exercises a certain limited supervision and guides the ruling prince when necessary, by friendly counsel, in promoting honest administration and good government. It is not his business to interfere in any way with the ordinary affairs of State. But it is his business to be a man to whom the prince and his advisers can go in hours of real need for advice and aid. If a bad ruler arises, who wastes the resources of his State in notorious corruption and extravagance, the British Resident endeavours to restrain him, and if he fails, the ruler may even be deposed. The reigning families are encouraged to bring up

adhered to our side in the days of the Mutiny, and have done much good work for us since, and are men of fine physique, strong principles, born soldiers. The Rajputs, the fighting tribes of the Punjab, have served us well, as have the Dogras, the Pathans, the hillmen of the north, the Afridis, the Baluchi, the Jats, and the Sujars. The Brahmin regiments, charged through and through with pride of race and pride of caste, boast of their soldiery. Then come the little Gurkhas, whose reputation as hill fighters, as stealthy breakers into enemy entrenchments, as scouts, and as men who with their knives alone are more dangerous than most soldiers with magazine rifles, spread throughout the German ranks long before they reached Europe. The Garhwalis, fighting hillmen, small and lithe, are very like the Gurkhas, and yet distinct from them. The Mahrattas, drawn from the Deccan, have given us many regiments. The Mohammedan peoples of the Eastern Punjab and of Hindustan are represented both in infantry and in cavalry. From the Madras Presidency come admirable regiments of Mohammedans, Tamils, and Pariahs.

Importance of Indian Native States

In addition to the regular Indian Army there were other forces for the Crown to draw upon, the volunteers, including Anglo-Indians, numbering some 40,000 and the Imperial Service troops from the native States, numbering over 20,000, and capable of being increased to eight or ten times that total within a reasonable time.

Few people outside of India realise the great place the Indian native States hold there. "I wonder," said the Marquis of Lansdowne on one occasion, " whether everyone realises that the Maharaja of Mysore rules over a population which exceeds in numbers the whole of the population of

their young princes in the hardy, open-air fashion, and with the discipline of European royal families, rather than in the old luxury traditional for princes in the East.

The result of this British influence, wise, prudent and constantly applied, had been to create a revolution in the ways of many of the native States. The palace of the prince no longer continued to be the centre of elaborate celebration, but had become the organising headquarters of capable, strenuous, reforming rulers. Education, sanitation, and modern medicine had been introduced, and more rights for the women had been granted and secured. The prince, formerly rarely seen abroad, save in hours of state when, decked with jewels, he lolled lazily atop of his elephant, moving through his obsequious subjects, went freely among his people in his Norfolk jacket and riding-breeches. Often enough he drove his own motor-car. He was alive and alert. " Our fathers were brought up to be idle," said one of the great rulers of India recently to a European visitor.

"Enjoyment and extravagance were held up before their eyes as the most sacred duties. It is in our English schools **The lesson of " Noblesse oblige "** that we have been taught the lesson of *noblesse oblige.* Where our forebears were living riotously at the cost of their subjects, Indian princes to-day are working hard to advance the weal of their people."* Britain had given to these Indian princes, the rulers of the native States, security on their thrones, and peace for their people, and had aided them to make the most of the resources of their States. Many years ago the question arose what return in the way of military service they could make to us. The rulers of

* "A German Staff Officer in India." London, 1910.

the different States desired to maintain large armies of their own at their own cost, and in the old days they did so. There were, however, two drawbacks to this. The expense of these armies ate considerably into the State revenues, and, in the hands of doubtful princes they were always a potential danger. On the other hand, it was recognised that they were also a source of potential strength. This was proved in the Indian Mutiny, when troops from the native States helped the British splendidly. In 1885, after the Pendjeh incident, when Britain seemed at the point of war with Russia, it was decided to regularise the military system of the native princes. Regiments were raised in each State, under the control of their own rulers, known as the Imperial Service troops, whose training, equipment, and arms were similar to those of the regular Indian Army. They were supervised by an Inspector-General, and represented a force of 20,000 of as good fighting men as could be wished for. It was understood that they would be at the call of the Imperial Government when required.

From the beginning it was the ambition of the ruling princes to have their soldiers employed in the battles of the Empire. At every sign of war they were among the first to come forward with the offer of their armies, accompanied often enough by the offer of themselves. In many of the border expeditions, in Somaliland, at the relief of Chitral, and in the expedition to China the Imperial Service troops did well. All who knew India were confident that the native princes would again hasten with offers of help, and this expectation was not disappointed.

Let us go down the list of these rulers, whose names and dignities themselves give us a glimpse of the romance and splendour of India, and note what they did at this time. First come the Nizam of Hyderabad, the Gaekwar of Baroda, and the Maharaja of Mysore, the three rulers each entitled to a salute of twenty-one guns, the outward symbol of their rank.

The Nizam of Hyderabad, ruler of the largest and most important State in India, who governs a population of over thirteen million people, and who measures his domains by the scores of thousands of square miles, **Nizam of Hyderabad's princely gift** made gifts worthy of his position and State. He sent a contribution of sixty lacs of rupees (about £400,000) towards the expenses of the war, the largest individual donation received by the Government of India. He desired to make his contribution equal to that of his late father, who subscribed a similar amount to the British Government during the Russian crisis of 1885. The rulers of Hyderabad have been ever loyal, and in accepting the Nizam's gift

the Viceroy wrote that it was only one more proof, if such were needed, of the Nizam's intense patriotism and devotion to the British Raj. In addition to this, the Nizam also expressed a desire to defray the entire cost, while on active service, of the 1st Hyderabad Imperial Service Lancers and of the 20th Deccan Horse, of both of which regiments he was honorary colonel. These State troops were among the first to be accepted for active service with the Expeditionary Force, and did marked service on the Continent.

The Maharaja of Mysore made a magnificent gift of fifty lacs of rupees (£333,000) for expenditure in connection with the Indian Expeditionary Force, a gift which stands out as one of the most munificent of the princely contributions received by the Indian Government. The Maharaja also placed at the disposal of the Government his cavalry—the Mysore Imperial Service Lancers—a splendidly-equipped regiment of picked men and horses, which was soon to earn distinction on the field of battle in France.

A RUDE CHANGE FOR INDIANS: FROM THEIR NATIVE SUNSHINE TO THE FROZEN TRENCHES OF FRANCE.

The Maharaja of Mysore, his Highness Shri Sir Krishnaraja Wadiyar Bahadur—who rules, as has already been said, over a population which exceeds in numbers the whole of the population of Sweden—is a prominent example of many of the great Indian princes, who by their personal example are bringing their people to new stages of efficiency. The success and prosperity of his great State is known everywhere. Its progress owes much to his own fine leading. "It is not government, nor forms of government, that have made the great industrial nations of the world," he declared in a notable speech, "but the spirit of the people and the energy of one and all working to a common end."

THE INDIAN TURBAN IN A FRENCH RURAL SETTING.

The Maharaja of Mysore is essentially a working prince, who not only devotes his time and attention to the affairs of his State, but who has displayed throughout his reign sound sense and real business ability. He is well known as a fine horseman, a keen rider to hounds, a polo and racquet player, and a musician of taste and skill. He is deeply interested in racing, and his colours are familiar at the great race meetings of India. He is also interested in motors, and frequently drives his own cars with nerve and ability.

The Gaekwar of Baroda, his Highness Shri Sir Sayaji Rao III., has long been a familiar figure in England and America, where

Baroda a modernised East

his princely splendour, his great hospitality, and his essentially modern outlook on life have made him the object of much attention. His State is one of the richest and most fertile in India, and maintains an army of 1,500 cavalry, 3,182 infantry, and 93 artillery. He has for years been active in the introduction of reforms among his people. Believing that the mastery of the modern world will be won by the educated, he has enforced compulsory education among his subjects. Baroda under his rule represents a modernised East. In the Boer War his

Highness offered to supply the British Government with horses for mounted troops in South Africa, an offer that was gratefully accepted. Now, in addition to subscribing liberally to the leading war funds, he placed all his State troops and all his resources at the service of the King-Emperor.

There is, perhaps, no more outstanding figure in India to-day than Major-General Sir Pertab Singh, the veteran chief of the fighting Rajputs and Regent-Maharaja of Jodhpur. Sir Pertab Singh demonstrated years ago that the fire of his race burns in his veins with undiminished power. He is a great soldier and has seen much active service—in China, in the frontier campaigns, and elsewhere. Lord Roberts

The veteran Sir Pertab Singh

counted him among his closest personal friends. The Rajput chief was seventy years old when war broke out. He at once demanded that he should be allowed to serve in person with the Expeditionary Force, and before he left for the front in company with his young nephew the Maharaja of Jodhpur, who was only sixteen years old, and with four of his sons, he made a touching farewell speech in the forenoon to the great crowds that assembled to bid him farewell. "Englishmen are shedding their blood like water for the great cause," said he. "Now is the time for the Rajputs to show their gratitude

INDIAN INFANTRY TAKING MAXIM GUN FROM MULES TO CARRY IT INTO ACTION AGAINST THE GERMANS.

to the British Raj and shed their blood for the King-Emperor." As the train left, the crowd sent up a shout of "Victory to the British Emperor!"

Another great military figure in India was the Maharaja of Gwalior, who also saw active service in China and in the Chitral and Tirah campaigns. His Highness was particularly anxious to accompany the Gwalior State troops with the Indian Expeditionary Force, but, to his great regret, this was found impossible owing to reasons of State. Unable to serve in the field personally, he devoted himself to helping the cause in other ways. He provided thousands of horses for remounts, contributed handsomely

[Ernest Brooks.

H.H. THE BEGUM OF BHOPAL.

[Bourne & Shepherd.

H.H. THE MAHARAJA OF BARIA.

[Backhouse.

THE NAWAB OF SACHIN.

[B. Framji.

H.H. THE RAJA OF SITAMAU.

[Bourne & Shepherd.

H.H. THE MAHARAWAL OF DUNGARPUR.

to the Prince of Wales's Fund, sent £5,000 for the sufferers in Belgium, and planned, in co-operation with the Begum of Bhopal, the hospital-ship Loyalty for the Indian wounded. The Maharaja's best-known gift was the splendid motor-ambulance fleet, purchased at a cost of £22,000. When King George inspected this fleet of motor-cars, motor-lorries, and motor-cycles at Buckingham Palace, and accepted them in the name of the Navy and the Army,

Gift of motor-ambulance fleet he telegraphed to the Maharaja : " This is yet another proof of your unswerving loyalty to my throne and person, and of your thoughtful interest in the welfare of the Empire."

The ruler of the State of Kashmir, Major-General his Highness Maharaja Sir Partab Singh Bahadur, subscribed to the Indian Fund for the equipment of the Expeditionary Force, and spoke at a great meeting of twenty thousand persons at Srinagar in support of the fund. He worked enthusiastically at the task of stirring

Service Transport Corps, which he had raised, for service with the Indian Expeditionary Force, an offer gratefully accepted by the Imperial Government. This corps had already seen service in the Chitral and Tirah campaigns, and consisted of 1,200 ponies, 558 folding iron carts, 16 ambulance tongas, and 775 officers and men.

Another of the ruling princes who volunteered for active service at the front was the Maharaja of Bikaner, one of the most popular of the Rajput chiefs. Colonel his Highness Sir Ganga Singh Bahadur of Bikaner had long been known in India for his splendid public and military services. As far back as 1899, when, a young man in his teens, his State was threatened with ruin through the great famine of that year, he organised the resources of his people, and provided for relief in a way remarkable in one little more than a lad. Then came the British Expedition to China in 1900. The Maharaja commanded the Camel Corps from his own State, which did most valuable service both there and later on in Somaliland. In the days of peace which followed he showed ability to adjust himself to the new conditions of New Asia. He inaugurated a representative assembly for his State in order that his people might be developed along the way of constitutional government. When news came of the outbreak of war he placed himself and the entire resources of his State at the service of the Crown.

He wrote to the Viceroy and offered both his Camel Corps and the Sadul Light Infantry for immediate service, and offered to enrol and equip 25,000 of his subjects as a special emergency Imperial Service Contingent. As he reminded Lord Hardinge, his ancestors had done similar service in the Mutiny. The Maharaja's Camel Corps proved of great service in Egypt. On one occasion when patrolling to the east of the Suez Canal it came on a much larger Turkish force, attacked it and beat it off.

It is well known that the fighting Rajput chiefs took part in the war against Germany with special vehemence, because some of them had been subjected to constant insults by German officers during the Allied Expedition to Peking in 1900. The Germans had openly treated them as coolies, and flaunted their honours and dignities. The chiefs knew the Germans for what they were. Thus the Maharaja of Bikaner, in talking with an English correspondent about this time, said that even fourteen years before, when he first came into contact with German methods of warfare, he was pained and astonished to note their ruthlessness. On one occasion, after the capture of Peking, he heard a German officer gloatingly tell a group of British Staff officers that he had raided some villages that day and had killed every Boxer he could find. Asked how he identified the Boxers, he replied that he searched every man to be found, and shot anyone who had on his clothing or about his person anything coloured red, taking that to be sufficient evidence of his identity with the Revolutionist movement. Another Rajput chief, when learning that he could go on service in Flanders, muttered with stern satisfaction." Now I'll show them who's the coolie."

The young Maharaja of Patiala, a prominent member of

SOME OF THE OFFICERS OF OUR INDIAN TROOPS IN FRANCE PARTAKING OF A FRUGAL LUNCH IN CAMP.

up his people to support the Government and do everything in their power to bring the war to a speedy and successful conclusion. The troops from his State were soon to distinguish themselves across the water. The Maharaja was sixty-two years old, and his great State, covering just over 79,000 square miles, contains some of the finest and most picturesque scenery in the Empire.

The State of Jaipur ranks among the most prosperous and best governed in India, and for this its people have largely to thank the keenness, the far-sightedness, and the reforming spirit of their present Maharaja. He has spent crores of rupees in modern improvements. He has provided free education throughout Jaipur, and to-day there are 1,135 schools and colleges there. The Jaipur School of Arts is famous throughout the world. His Highness contributed in the most generous manner in men and money for the war. His personal gifts included £19,800 for the Indian Expeditionary Force, £6,600 for the Prince of Wales's Fund, £6,600 for the Imperial Indian Relief Fund, and many minor gifts. He offered the Imperial

Germany's treatment of the Indians

[*Vandyk.*

H.H. THE MAHARAJA OF JODHPUR.

[*F. Bremner.*

H.H. THE RAJA OF CHUMBA.

[*H. Moller.*

H.H. THE MAHARAJA OF SIRMOOR.

[*London Stereoscopic.*

H.H. THE THAKUR SAHIB OF MORVI.

[*C. D. Silva.*

H.H. THE MAHARAJA BAHADUR
OF CHHATARPUR.

INDIAN INFANTRY ADVANCING TO TAKE UP A POSITION AND AVAILING THEMSELVES OF ALL THE COVER THE GRASSY HILLOCKS AFFORDED.

the Imperial Cadet Corps, joined the Expeditionary Force at the outbreak of war. Besides liberally contributing to war funds in India and in England, his State troops were also accepted for service, and acquitted themselves with credit and distinction. A crack shot, a keen cricketer, and polo player, his athletic skill and sporting instincts now served him in good stead.

The Aga Khan's determined loyalty The Aga Khan, or to give him his full title, his Highness Aga Sultan Sir Mahomed Shah, Aga Khan, rules over no State, but is one of the greatest religious and social forces in India, the spiritual head of over sixty million of the Khojas community of Mohammedans there. The wonderful history of his sect and the traditions of his family read more like romance than sober fact. Although without a kingdom, the Aga Khan has great revenues, mainly derived from the free-will offerings of his people. He is an all-round sportsman and a strong supporter of the turf. At the outbreak of war he was at Zanzibar, and he at once hurried to England to offer his services to the

Imperial Government, and offered, if need be, to serve the King-Emperor as a private in any infantry regiment attached to the Indian Expeditionary Force. He showed in the most unmistakable fashion his determined loyalty, and his attitude in the most critical hours did much to reassure the wavering.

The great Indians serving with the Expeditionary Force included: Honorary Major-General H. H. Sir Pertab Singh, G.C.S.I., G.C.V.O., K.C.B., A.D.C., Maharaja-Regent of Jodhpur; Honorary Lieutenant H. H. the Maharaja of Jodhpur; Honorary Colonel H. H. Sir Ganga Singh Bahadur, G.C.S.I., G.C.I.E., A.D.C., Maharaja of Bikaner; Honorary Major H. H. Sir Madan Singh Bahadur, K.C.S.I., G.C.I.E., Maharaja-Adhiraj of Kishengarh; the Maharaja of Baria; the Nawab of Sachin; the Maharaja of Idar; the Mahajara of Bharatpur; the Raja of Rutlam; the Raja of Akalkot; the Nawab of Rampur; the Mir of Khairpur; Honorary Captain the Honourable Malik Umar Hayat Khan, C.I.E., M.V.O., Tiwana; Honorary Lieutenant Raj-Kumar Hira Singh

ANOTHER IMPRESSION OF OUR INDIAN TROOPS IN ACTION. HERE ALSO THE MEN ARE SEEN MAKING THEIR WAY WITH THE MAXIMUM OF CAUTION.

[Bourne & Shepherd.

H.H. THE MAHARAJA OF KAPURTHALA.

THE CHIEF OF KALSIA STATE
(S. Rani Shri Singh Sahib Bahadur).

[Johnston & Hoffman.

H.H. THE MAHARAJA OF JAIPUR.

[Vandyk.

H.H. THE MAHARAJA OF KOLHAPUR.

[F. Bremner.

H.H. THE MAHARAJA OF JIND.

[Bourne & Shepherd.

H.H. THE MAHARAJA OF TRAVANCORE.

of Panna ; Honorary Lieutenant Maharaja-Kumar Hitendra Narayan of Cooch Behar ; Lieutenant Malik Mumtaz Mahomed Khan, Native Indian Land Forces ; Resaldar Khwaja Mahomed Khan Bahadur, Queen Victoria's Own Corps of Guides ; Honorary Captain Shah Mirza Beg.

Imperial Service troops were also accepted from the following States, and were later serving at the front : Alwar, Bharatpur, Bikaner, Faridkot, Gwalior, Hyderabad, Indore, Jaipur, Jind, Jodhpur, Kapurthala, Kashmir, Mysore, Patiala, Rampur.

The Indian Expeditionary Force as despatched to Europe in September, 1914, consisted of 70,000 men. This was not all. Other forces were sent to Mesopotamia and elsewhere, and by the spring of 1915 India had put in the field in the several theatres of war, including the British troops sent from India, a force equivalent to nine complete infantry divisions, with artillery, and eight cavalry brigades, besides several smaller bodies of troops, aggregating more than an infantry division, in minor and outlying spheres. She had placed at the disposal of the Empire for service out of India, so Mr. Asquith stated in a notable speech at the Mansion House, London, twenty-eight regiments of cavalry, British Indian, and Imperial, and one hundred and twenty-four regiments of infantry, British, Indian, and Imperial. The Prime Minister declared : " When we look at the actual achievements of the force so spontaneously despatched, so liberally provided for, so magnificently equipped, the battlefields of France and Flanders bear tribute to their bravery." Lord Hardinge, in a speech dealing with the despatch of troops, was able to point with justifiable pride to what had been done, and to declare significantly : " We are not at the end of our military resources."

The voyage of the Expeditionary Force to Europe was carefully planned. It was well known that the Germans intended, if they could, to destroy some of the transports with their raiding cruisers, or to torpedo them en route. The ships, however, were guarded the whole way across by the allied fleets, and the first divisions arrived without loss in Marseilles in the later part of September, to be quickly followed by others. The dark-skinned troops, as they landed and marched through the streets of the rock-bound southern French port, had a remarkable reception. The people of France could not do enough for them They cheered and shouted, broke into their ranks, and heaped gifts on

The voyage to Europe

them. " The troops, who literally leaped ashore," said Mr. Douglas Crawford, writing at the time from Marseilles, " were fighting men to the last ounce, hard and fit, and ready, had the word of command been given and had the thing been practicable, to march straight from the quay to the fighting-line. Not a few of the Sikhs, lithe, black-bearded giants, were deeply concerned to know if I thought the war would be over before they could get to grips with the common enemy, and it was a burden off their minds when I assured them there was absolutely no likelihood of anything of the kind coming to pass. Never has the port of Marseilles, used as it is to cosmopolitan crowds and the multi-coloured habiliments of Africa, witnessed a scene so kaleidoscopic as that presented to-day by the defiling of thousands of soldiers down seemingly numberless gangways and along quays lit up by brilliant sunshine."

The reception at Marseilles

The new-comers when they arrived at Marseilles found messages waiting for them from the King-Emperor. There was one to the British troops expressing the King's implicit confidence in them : " Duty is your watchword, and I know your duty will be nobly done." The message to the Indian troops was in Urdu, and when translated into English read as follows :

I look to all my Indian soldiers to uphold the Izzat of the British Raj against an aggressive and relentless enemy. I know with what readiness my brave and loyal Indian soldiers are prepared to fulfil this sacred trust on the field of battle shoulder to shoulder with their comrades from all parts of the Empire. Rest assured that you will always be in my thoughts and prayers. I bid you to go forward and add fresh lustre to the glorious achievements and noble traditions of courage and chivalry of my Indian Army, whose honour and fame are in your hands.

Lieutenant-General Sir James Willcocks, who commanded the Indian Army Corps, issued a stirring Order of the Day to his troops on October 10th, as they were moving up to the front :—

Soldiers of the Indian Army Corps:
We have all read with pride the gracious message of his Majesty the King-Emperor to his troops from India. On the eve of going into the field to join our British comrades, who have covered themselves with glory in this great war, it is our firm resolve to prove ourselves worthy of the honour which has been conferred on us as representatives of the Army of India. In a few days we shall be fighting as has never been our good fortune to fight before, and against enemies who have a long history. But is their history as long as yours ? You are the descendants of men who have been mighty rulers and great warriors for many centuries. You will never forget this. You will recall the glories of your race.

INDIANS IN ENGLAND : STALWART SONS OF OUR EASTERN EMPIRE GUARDING THE ROUTE AT THE ADMIRALTY ARCH WHEN PARLIAMENT WAS OPENED BY THE KING.

WOUNDED INDIANS RECUPERATING IN CAIRO. FROM THE ROOF OF THE HOSPITAL IN THE CITADEL THEY COULD OBTAIN FINE VIEWS OF THE TOWN AND SURROUNDING COUNTRY.

Hindu and Mohammedan will be fighting side by side with British soldiers and our gallant French allies. You will be helping to make history. You will be the first Indian soldiers of the King-Emperor who have the honour of showing in Europe that the sons of India have lost none of their ancient martial instincts, and are worthy of the confidence reposed in them. In battle you will remember that your religions enjoin on you that to give your life doing your duty is your highest reward. The eyes of your co-religionists and your fellow-countrymen are on you. From the Himalayan Mountains, the banks of the Ganges and Indus, and the plains of Hindustan, they are eagerly waiting for the news of how their brethren conduct themselves when they meet the foe. From mosques and temples their prayers are ascending to the God of all, and you will answer their hopes by the proofs of your valour. You will fight for your King-Emperor and your faith, so that history will record the doings of India's sons, and your children will proudly tell of the deeds of their fathers.

The Expeditionary Force arrived in Europe fully equipped for war. Great care had been taken to study the caste requirements of the troops, to provide the special foods demanded by them, and to meet their particular needs in other ways. The medical arrangements were all complete, with field ambulances, base hospitals, and ample provision for conveying the wounded from the front, including the hospital-ship Loyalty, to which previous reference has been made. A special Indian Soldiers' Fund, under the patronage of Lord Roberts, was opened, and some scores of thousands of pounds were quickly raised to supplement the clothing and comforts already provided by the Government, and to help the men in ways that could hardly be attempted officially.

At the beginning, far-fetched notions were entertained both in Germany and among the Allies as to the fighting capacity of the Indians. They were supposed to possess powers of dash and endurance unequalled by Europeans. The Gurkhas were credited with a marvellous capacity for penetrating the trenches of the enemy without being seen, and the keen knives of these hillmen were said to be more formidable than a rifle in European hands. Similar claims were made for other branches of the Army. Those intimately acquainted with the Indian peoples knew that those who held extravagant ideas of what the Indians could do were bound to be disappointed. That the Indians would do well was taken for granted. But the Indian in Europe was obviously fighting under disadvantages in a climate very different from his own—damp, not dry—among winter conditions that were bound to test his physique to the uttermost, amid methods of war such as he had never experienced before. The Indian's idea of war is to fight in person, to risk your physical strength and skill in arms against the physical strength and skill in arms of your foe, to stand up man to man in a direct, fierce, overwhelming, personal struggle. What he was asked to do now was something very different. It was to engage in a long, dreary trench war; to live day after day, week after week, in sodden, soaking, freezing holes in the ground; to lie still for a week at a time under the heavy fire of the enemy's artillery; to fight a foe whom often enough he never saw. It says much for our Eastern troops that they worthily maintained the honour of their country under these conditions.

The Lahore Division arrived in the concentration area

AN INDIAN BUGLER.

in the rear of the Second British Army Corps on October 19th and 20th. It was quickly followed by others. When the Meerut Division arrived at the corps' headquarters the Indian Army Corps then took over the line previously held by the Second Corps, enabling some of the British troops to be drawn back into reserve. Two and a half brigades of British infantry and a large part of the artillery of the Second Corps remained to assist the Indian Corps in the defence of this line, until the Ferozepore Brigade, which had been supporting the cavalry farther north, joined the remainder of the Indians, thus enabling two and a half battalions of the British brigades to retire. At the beginning of November the Secunderabad Cavalry Brigade and the Jodhpur Lancers came.

The Indian troops at once found themselves plunged into the heart of the fighting. The Germans were resolutely

INDIAN TROOPS IN ENGLAND.
Before going to the front many Indian units underwent preparatory training in England to fit them for the new and strange conditions of warfare.

endeavouring to push on, determined to clear the road to Calais. No sacrifice was to be too great, no slaughter too heavy to accomplish their aim. They were backed with very heavy artillery. Their troops advanced to the assault time after time, and they displayed, it may be generally admitted, a reckless daring which nothing but the coolness and determination of the numerically weak British troops could have foiled.

The Indians had fought in wars up to now in which artillery had played but little part. Here they found themselves in a war

Trial of Indian nerves

where artillery was the dominating factor. They soon got to know the Minenwerfer—the trench mortar of the Germans—which, with a range of some five hundred to six hundred yards, throws a bomb loaded with high explosive weighing up to two hundred pounds. The Indians hated the trenches, with the cold, the wet, and the mud. But they were soon to find that even the deepest trenches were only a partial protection from the

enemies' weapons. They were in a strange land, dependent on their British officers and interpreters for intercourse with the white people around. Everything was strange and bizarre to them, and it would not have been surprising if, amid this novel and terrible maelstrom of death into which they had plunged, their nerves should temporarily have failed.

Nothing of the kind, however, happened. The Indian Cavalry took over some ground previously held by the First French Cavalry Corps and did excellent service. Time after time the Indians stood up against the most constant bombardments and the heaviest advances. Sir John French was able to say of them in a general review of the situation : " Since their arrival in this

Sir John French's tribute

country and their occupation of the line allotted to them I have been much impressed by the initiative and resource displayed by the Indian troops. Some of the ruses they have employed to deceive the enemy have been attended with the best results, and have doubtless kept superior forces in front of them at bay. The Corps of the Indian Sappers and Miners have long enjoyed a high reputation for skill and resource. Without going into detail I can confidently assert that throughout their work in this campaign they have fully justified that reputation. The General Officer commanding the Indian Army Corps describes the conduct and bearing of these troops in strange and new surroundings to have been highly satisfactory, and I am enabled from my own observations to fully corroborate his statement.''

The story is told of how at one point the Germans had been pressing the British lines heavily for three weeks until our men were almost worn out. They kept up a ceaseless artillery fire, and every now and then they would attempt to charge. The soldiers held the line without flinching, although they were scarcely able to move from sheer fatigue.

INDIAN STRETCHER-BEARERS REMOVING WOUNDED AT A HOSPITAL BASE.
The Indian Red Cross work on the Continent was the subject of general commendation.

At last there came a moment when it seemed that the Germans had a chance of success. The ceaseless artillery fire had been heavier than ever and had cost us dearly. Fresh German infantry came up, and as nightfall approached they started to advance on our wearied lines. One British soldier who was there relates what happened : " Just when they were half-way towards our trenches the Bengal Lancers, who had arrived the day before and were anxious to get into it, were brought up. Splendid fellows they

IN AN INDIAN RED CROSS CAMP
AFTER NEUVE CHAPELLE.
British officers and orderlies taking the roll of
the injured and inspecting preparations for
their care and treatment.

WOUNDED INDIANS ROUND A CAMP-FIRE.
They took the fortune of war with the utmost cheerfulness and found considerable solace in
the cigarette.

looked as they passed us on their fine chargers, and we broke into cheers. They smiled back grimly, with their eyes glancing ahead and their fingers nervously feeling their lance shafts. At the word of command they swept forward, only making a slight detour to get out of our line of fire, and then they swept into the Germans from the left like a whirlwind. The enemy was completely taken aback. The Turcos they knew, but these men with their flashing eyes, dark skins, and white, gleaming teeth, not to mention their terribly keen-edged lances, they could not understand. The Lancers did not give them much time to arrive at an understanding. With

Bengal Lancers' great charge

a shrill yell they rode right through the German infantry, thrusting right and left with their terrible lances, and bringing a man down every time. The Germans broke, and ran for their lives, pursued by the Lancers for about a mile. When they came back from their charge they were cheered wildly all along our line, but they did not think much of what they had done."

The Germans, backed by their admirable system of secret service, laid many plans for confusing and perplexing the Indians. German spies, dressed in Indian uniforms, would go up and give wrong instructions at critical moments. Here is a typical incident told by the "Observer" attached by the Government to the Indian Army Corps:

"The audacity of the enemy cannot be better illustrated than by a well-authenticated statement of what took place last night in a trench held by a Gurkha regiment. A figure silhouetted in the moonlight and wearing a complete Gurkha uniform approached the end of the trench and delivered the message: 'The Gurkhas are to move farther up the trench; another Gurkha contingent is advancing in support.' Puzzled by this announcement, the officer in charge replied, 'Who are you? Where do you come from?' To which the only answer was: 'You are to move up to make room for other Gurkhas.' The English was good, but something—or many small things—excited

the officer's suspicions. 'Answer, and answer quickly,' he said. 'If you are a Gurkha, by which boat did you cross?' The question was, in the circumstances, no easy one to answer, and the German (for such he was) turned at once and fled. But he had not gone five yards before he fell riddled by bullets. If the officer had been deceived, the trench, of course, would have swarmed with Germans almost before the Gurkhas had made room for them."

One of the most remarkable and touching incidents in the early campaign of the Indian troops—an incident which will be remembered generations hence throughout the East—was the farewell visit of Lord Roberts to his old soldiers at the front. Lord Roberts was determined, despite his years and despite the pleadings of his friends, to go to Flanders and do what he could to cheer some of his comrades there. He reached Boulogne on November 11th, and first visited the Indian wounded on the hospital-ship. The stricken Indian **Lord Roberts and** soldiers strove as he entered the wards **the wounded** to rise up from their beds and greet him. The veteran Commander-in-Chief went from one to the other, with a word of comfort and good cheer for each, unable to conceal his own emotion as he gazed on their battered and stricken forms. From Boulogne he moved on to the headquarters of the Indian Corps, where he was received with great state. He spoke to the Indian regiments in their own tongues, and marched through the ranks of the men drawn up in his honour, his very presence an inspiration to them all. Great Indian commanders who had served under him were there. Men who had fought in the ranks under him time after time in great battles gazed up at the slight figure of the veteran Field-Marshal again.

He had planned to cheer up the wounded in more than one hospital, and to inspect the troops in many lines. But in the course of his tour he was seized with a chill, taken with congestion of the lungs and pleurisy, and was unable to rally. He died at the front after a few hours' illness, amidst the armies for whom he had lived and worked and fought so long. Some people in England **Effect of Lord** spoke of his end as a tragedy. It must **Roberts' visit** ever be a tragedy for his country to lose so great, disinterested, and simple a leader of men. But for Lord Roberts himself surely there could have been no tragedy in such an end, but rather the worthy culmination of a long life dedicated to the single purpose of loyalty and devotion to monarch and Empire. From end to end of the Indian Army the story of how Roberts Bahadur had come again among them and had died among them, served as a fresh inspiration and a fresh stimulus.

There came days in the fierce October - November struggle around Neuve Chapelle when it seemed that our men must be overwhelmed. Then it was that the Indians stood their ground firmly, doggedly, unflinchingly. Day after day they fought without ceasing, enduring losses rarely equalled up to that time. Their casualties in officers were particularly heavy, and their loss was severely felt. The European officer who leads Indian troops is a picked man, who has lived for years among them, who speaks their own tongue, and who knows them intimately. Some companies, it was said, lost

SIKHS IN CAMP IN FRANCE.
An interval for reading.

every officer in their first engagement. One particular section was reported to have had sixty per cent. of its effectives killed, wounded, or missing. The Anglo-Indian officer could not well be replaced without long delay. The language difficulty alone made it of little use for an officer without special qualifications to attempt to fill his post.

On Wednesday, October 28th, there was a closely contested battle around Neuve Chapelle, in which the Indians played a large part. Two days previously the Germans, advancing in the evening, had attacked this village and captured part of it. A terrific hand-to-hand combat of the most murderous description followed. All day on Tuesday our men tried again and again to push the enemy back. Then on the Wednesday morning some of the Indian regiments—the 47th Sikhs and the 20th and 21st Companies of the 3rd Sappers and Miners—made a big counter-attack, driving the Germans out of the greater part of the place with the bayonet. As the Germans fled into the fields beyond, the Indians attempted to pursue them. They at once came under the fire of concentrated machine-guns, and could go no farther.

Five days later the Germans attacked a **Colonel Norie's** portion of the line to the west of Neuve **excellent leadership** Chapelle with great determination. They pierced our line, and for the moment things threatened to be very serious. The situation was saved by the excellent leadership displayed by Colonel Norie, of the 2nd Gurkha Rifles. From October 25th until the end of the first week in November the Indians were practically continuously engaged in the great fight which brought about the holding up of the German winter campaign.

All India was thrilled by the news that in the fighting one Indian soldier, the first of his race, had earned the

AN INDIAN BAKERY.
Native cooks baking chupatties (unleavened cakes) at the front.

"LIGHT REFRESHMENT."
Milking one of the thousands of goats provided for our Indian troops in the field.

Victoria Cross. Khudadad, an infantryman of the 129th Duke of Connaught's Own Baluchis, was in the fighting at Hollebeke, on October 31st. The British officer in charge of his detachment was wounded and helpless, and other guns had been put out of action by a shell. Khudadad, although badly wounded himself, continued working his machine-gun until the other five men of his detachment had been killed. The bestowal of the highest military decoration on this soldier touched the heart of India. Now, indeed, her people felt, India was really sharing danger and honour with Great Britain.

The Indian Cavalry Corps chafed at first at the little use that could be made of them. This fighting gave little or no opportunity for horsemanship. Their commander strongly urged that his men should be allowed to share the work of the trenches. As a result, various units of the Indian Cavalry took their regular turn in trench fighting.

After the great stand of Neuve Chapelle there followed the dreariest time of all, a time infinitely more trying to the Indians than the fiercest battles—the winter trench war. The wet, the cold, and the dreary mud, often up to one's middle, tested the Indian physique to the utmost. "This is not war," they said one to another. As the winter grew more and more severe, it became a question whether it was wise or not to keep them longer at the front during the worst of the weather. Then came fighting at Givenchy, where the Indians suffered very heavy loss. It was thought that the time had now come to give some of the Indian regiments a temporary rest. They were transferred for a time to the South of France, and the Indian line was shortened.

This, however, was only temporary. In the great British advance on Neuve Chapelle on March 10th the Indians once more played a distinguished and prominent part, sharing the honours of the day with the Fourth Army Corps, the attack on the whole German position being entrusted to the Indian Corps on the right and the 4th Army Corps at the centre and left. Following a powerful artillery bombardment of the German position, which wrought terrific destruction, the 23rd and 25th Brigades of the 5th Division stormed the German lines, and simultaneously the Garhwal Brigade of the Meerut Division, which was occupying a position to the south of Neuve Chapelle, rushed forward. Apart from the British attack elsewhere, which it is not necessary to describe here, the Garhwal Brigade, together with the 25th **Garhwal Brigade's** Brigade, carried the German entrench-**brilliant advance** ments and pushed right on into Neuve Chapelle itself. Owing to the delay in bringing up reserves and other causes, our advance was not carried as far as it should have been, but for this the Indians were not to blame. The Indian Corps and the British troops dug themselves in that night. Next morning they attempted a further attack, but it was soon seen that this would be impossible without a renewed heavy artillery bombardment. Weather conditions made this now impossible. The Fourth Corps and the Indians tried again and again, despite the heaviest slaughter, to capture the positions fronting them. The effort was vain. The Germans had recovered from their surprise. Backed by reinforcements, they now had every point well covered

with machine-guns, and every attempt to make further progress was repulsed. All that could be done was to hold and consolidate the ground the Fourth Corps and the Indians had gained so brilliantly and at such heavy cost.

A vivid account of the scene after the first advance on the village of Neuve **Vivid story of** Chapelle was given by Mr. Valentine Wil-**Neuve Chapelle** liams, the famous war correspondent :

" It is now half-past eight, the hour when folks in England are comfortably sitting down to their breakfast, when trim maids are bringing tea to the bedsides. Neuve Chapelle is ours, but the German resistance is not broken. Only a few hundred yards from where Riflemen and Gurkhas are fraternising in the first flush of victory, Britons are traversing the last stern stage of a soldier's career in the field—the path of death. . . . . .

"We are with the First 39th Garhwalis, a tough regiment that showed its worth in Burma and in the Tirah campaign. Whistles blow, the men leave their trenches. Instantly they are withered by a fearful blast of fire. The German trench is untouched. So is the barbed-wire, two hundred yards of it. The Garhwalis never waver. All the officers of the leading companies

STRANGE, EXOTIC SCENE ON THE BORDERS OF THE NEW FOREST.
Some of the Indian actors who took part in an entertainment given by the Indian Art and Dramatic Society at Barton-on-Sea, New Milton, on the borders of the New Forest, to the Indian troops at the convalescent hospital there.

are killed, right ahead of their men. The battalion staggers under the blast of fire, loses its direction, swings to the right, and captures, after fierce in-fighting with bayonet and knife, a section of trench there, only to be cut off in the upshot by the Germans in the intact trench. . . .

" Five of the Garhwalis' officers are dead now, killed in the first line after prodigies of bravery. In this fight the battalion is to lose twenty officers and three hundred and fifty men killed and wounded. The Germans have started to shell the Garhwalis' trenches. But the men, though without officers, are steady. These stout little hillmen have seen their officers fall, fearlessly exposing themselves. They remember that, and it keeps them firm."

From now on the Indians shared to the full the summer campaign of the British.

What is to be the effect on India itself of the active share of the Indian troops in the European campaign? It would be idle to deny that from end to end of India there has arisen the expectation that this may be the start of a new era in Indian Government.

THE TRANSPORT RIVER CLYDE AS "THE NEW HORSE OF TROY."

One of the most thrilling stories of the war is that of the transport River Clyde landing British troops on Gallipoli by running ashore, and, under cover of darkness, pouring out her great cargo of men from doors cut in her sides. Photograph taken after the historic landing battle.

THE RIVER CLYDE AFTER THE TERRIBLE LANDING BATTLE AT SEDDUL BAHR.

This photograph shows exactly how the troops contained within "the new Horse of Troy" were got ashore by means of lighters and gangways.

CHAPTER LXII.

THE TERRIBLE LANDING BATTLES ROUND SEDDUL BAHR.

How the Senegalese and Zouaves Stormed Kum Kale—Turkish Entrenchment in Asia Minor Carried—The Five Battle Beaches of the Glorious 29th Division—Lack of High-Explosive Shells for Bombarding Turkish Trenches—How the Implacable by Bold and Skilful Handling Swept the Turks from Cape Tekeh Beach—The Heroic Struggle Round Cape Helles—British Troops Held Up by Wire Entanglements on the Shore—The Death-Trap from which Our Men Fought their Way Out—Success of the Landing-Party in Morto Bay—The Problem of the Impregnable Beach of Seddul Bahr—Extraordinary Ruse of the British Sailors—The New Horse of Troy Advances into the Bay and Rests by a Reef Opposite a Sandbank—The Tragedy of the Sandbank and the First Landing-Party of Fusiliers—Two Thousand British Troops Imprisoned in a Transport Smitten all Day Long by the Fire of the Enemy—Night Falls and the Fusilier Brigade Leaves the New Horse of Troy—Furious Hand-to-Hand Conflict in the Old Castle of Seddul Bahr—How the Dublin Fusiliers with the Munsters and Hants Carried the Hill Above the Beach—Major Doughty-Wylie and Major Grimshaw Lead the Irish Bayonets—Lieut. Bastard's Single-Handed Attack on a Turkish Machine-Gun Fort—The Turkish Army Counter-Attacks in Dense Formation and is Half Destroyed—General British Advance Towards Krithia—Insecure Position of Franco-British Army on Gallipoli Peninsula—Turks Begin the Torpedo Campaign against our Fleet.

O F all the tasks ever set any army, there had been none so desperately difficult as that which faced our troops on Sunday morning, April 25th, 1915, at the southern end of the Gallipoli Peninsula. Even the landing operations by the Australian and New Zealand Army Corps at Sari Bair were easier than those of the 29th Division round Seddul Bahr and Cape Helles. All the beaches there, and especially the wide, open, shallow stretch of Morto Bay, were dominated by mobile German batteries firing from the other side of the Strait behind Kum Kale. It was a vital necessity to master the fire of the enemy on the Asiatic shore, in order to enable the 29th Division to land and establish itself. So, by arrangement with Sir Ian Hamilton, the French Colonial Division, under General d'Amade, steamed in its transports to Kum Kale, protected by three French battleships. The French General selected as his landing-ground the most historic battlefield in the world—the far-famed windy plain of Troy, stretching below the hill on which Troy stood, to the mouth of the Meander, or Simois River. The landing was made west of the river by the mouth of the Meander, where the French

A DISTINGUISHED GROUP AT CAIRO.
Right to left : Lieut.-General Sir John Maxwell (Commander of the Forces in Egypt), Harvey Pasha (Chief of Cairo Police), Prince Alexander of Battenberg, and (in front) the Sultan of Egypt.

transports poured the Marines and Senegalese troops into small boats early on Sunday morning, April 25th, when the landing conflicts were raging on the other side of the Strait. The boats were towed by trawlers and torpedo craft to the mouth of the river at half-past nine in the morning, under a fire of shells and bullets from the ruined citadel of Kum Kale. Some distant German batteries at In Tepe were also trained on the French Marines and coloured troops. Every man in one boat was put out of action by a shell bursting in it.

A French captain was the first to wade ashore, and though wounded he charged the fort, followed by his men from Senegal. The place where the French troops had to win a foothold was only a few yards in extent, forming a ledge, under the grim, overhanging, black mass of the citadel of Kum Kale. In this holed, shattered, and dismantled entrance fortress, bombarded into ruins by the fleet two months previously, the Germans had placed machine-guns and riflemen sheltered beneath the old thick walls. There was also a machine-gun on a neighbouring windmill, while the mobile German batteries operated behind the next village of Yeni Shehr. All the defences were well and cleverly organised, but

371

INDIAN BAGGAGE WAGGON PROCEEDING TO THE POINT OF EMBARKATION FOR THE DARDANELLES.
In the foreground is a native with some of the goats provided to supply the troops with milk.

the battleships still retained their advantage over this narrow line of hilly land between the river and the Asia Minor coast.

As the French captain and his Senegalese troops scaled the breach in the walls of the fortress the machine-gun on the windmill opened fire. But a shell from a French battleship knocked the gun and all its crew from the top of the mill into atoms, and the French troops pushed on with heroic determination through a storm of shrapnel and machine-gun fire, and bayoneted the Turks out of the old courts and then advanced on the village. In the French division were Zouaves who had come from Nieuport and the Yser. In the judgment of these veterans the hurricane of shell and machine-gun fire that swept them at Kum Kale was the most terrible thing they had encountered in the war. It showed again that the German organisers of the defences of the Dardanelles were

Heroism triumphs over machinery fully justified in thinking that they could prevent any opponent landing upon Ottoman soil.

But heroism triumphed over all the machinery of slaughter. House by house the covering force of some 3,500 men fought their way onward. In one place some five hundred Turks surrendered, but, seeing how few were their captors, they shot down two of the French officers and ran away. Then, strongly reinforced, they returned and recaptured part of the village together with a French machine-gun. But the French, in violent and unceasing hand-to-hand fighting, with no artillery to help them and no trenches as cover against the continual rain of shrapnel, fought and held nearly a mile of ground. They recaptured the machine-gun and again drove the enemy back. They found it safer to keep in hand-to-hand conflict with their foes, getting so well mixed up that the hostile guns could not play on the fighting front without killing more of their own men than French troops.

The main effort of the enemy was made on Sunday night, when a fresh division was pushed up to support the attack. Four times in succession did the German officers lead the

Turks against the houses and bits of broken wall held by the French. But each time a dense, charging multitude, coming up in wave after wave, was broken by infantry fire and machine-gun fire and then routed at the point of the bayonet. On Monday morning the French could see hundreds of corpses on every hundred yards' depth beyond their front. They had shattered brigade after brigade by fire directed by the searchlights. The Turks had at last retired in the darkness and entrenched between the coast and the river in front of Yeni Shehr.

Meanwhile our magnificent Allies had landed in the night a battery of their deadly light field-guns—the "75's." These were trained on the Turkish trench. Then the French battleships and an auxiliary cruiser opened a flanking fire on the trench, while the field battery swept the hostile position with a frontal fire. The affair was all over in a few minutes. Most of the Turks bolted inland, only to be slain in a shrapnel zone formed by the battleships' guns. The remaining five hundred men saw that they could not escape and, throwing down their weapons, they came towards the French, waving handkerchiefs and white flags. The resistance at Kum Kale was thus completely broken during the critical period in the landing of British troops two miles across the Straits, where reinforcements had been got ashore at Seddul Bahr, and our troops were holding the first line of hills that saddled the Peninsula.

Kum Kale resistance broken

Having thus accomplished with splendid heroism its preliminary work at Kum Kale, the French covering force re-embarked with no attempt at attack by the Turkish infantry. Only the distant batteries inflicted some losses by shrapnel fire, but the guns of the French battleships took full revenge; for the Turks were caught by high-explosive shells in the village of Yeni Shehr, and not a house was left standing. Every building in the country round about holding snipers and machine-gun parties, was blown up by the "75's" or the naval guns, and though the Turco-German Staff at Constantinople claimed that the French division had been driven back into the sea, not a single Turkish infantryman or a single German gun occupied the land around Kum Kale when the French returned to their boats on Monday night.

This part of the operations was excellently planned and executed; for if the German batteries had been able to fire from behind Kum Kale the task of our 29th Division would have been quite impossible. Even as it was the landing battles round the southern end of the Peninsula of Gallipoli were long, terrible, and arduous. They rank with the attack on the Aisne plateau, the defence of Ypres, and the conflicts on the crests of the Carpathians. We have seen that the Australians escaped their worst landing

Long and terrible landing battles difficulties by a surprise embarkation on a part of the coast where even they had not expected to land. But the 29th Division could make no surprise attack.

The cliffs at Cape Tekeh, Cape Helles, Seddul Bahr, and De Totts Battery, at the eastern point of Morto Bay, rose from fifty to a hundred feet. Above the cliffs was an open plateau, rising in places not far from the sea's edge to 138 feet, 141 feet, and 256 feet. Two miles inland the hills began sloping up to the dominating ridge of Achibaba, or Tree Hill, 730 feet above sea level. Then, hill over hill, the ground ran to the rocky, broken clump of Pasha Dagh, at the Narrows. The Germans had everywhere the finest possible field for direct gun fire, innumerable ravines and hollows, in which to shelter their howitzers, and milelong slopes like the glacis of a mighty fortress, down which their entrenched infantry could shoot with their machineguns helping them, and preparing for their charges.

In many places at the end of the Peninsula there was no foreshore, and jagged rocks made a landing impossible. But five beaches were selected for the operations. On the Ægean shore was a gap where a stream, flowing north of the village of Krithia, broke down the high cliff. This was known as Beach Y. South of it, and north of Cape Tekeh, was Beach X. Then just south of the promontory of Tekeh was Beach W. Full south, between Cape Helles and Seddul Bahr, was Beach V. Then in Morto Bay, between Seddul Bahr and De Totts Battery, was our fifth and last landing-place, known as Beach S.

The plan of attack was different from that at Sari Bair. No surprise in the darkness was possible, as the beaches were defended by underwater wire entanglements and by the main forces of the Fifth Turkish Army entrenched on the high ground and flanking all the **Underwater wire entanglements** beaches. The defending troops were supported by light field-guns and 6 in. howitzer batteries in formidable numbers, working with marked ranges, and completely swept the whole field of fire. Our troops were transferred just before dawn to tow-boats, some of which were towed by the battleships and others by steamtrawlers and pinnaces. The trawlers were to cast off the boats on nearing the beach, leaving the soldiers to row ashore with the help of a few seamen. It was hoped that a terrific bombardment of the enemy's positions by every gun in the battleships, including the Queen Elizabeth, would master the enemy's fire.

But as the ships, apparently, used shrapnel shell chiefly, against which the German engineers had skilfully made

RESTING UNDER THE SHADOW OF SHATTERED TURKISH DEFENCE WORKS.
Photograph taken after the huge fortifications had been reduced and our men were firmly established where they landed.

deep trenches, the extraordinary volume and fury of our naval bombardment did not in most cases have an effect commensurate with the tremendous effort made. What was needed was high-explosive shell in immense quantities. Only high-explosive shell could smash up the enemy's earthworks. But as is well known, shell of this kind was sadly lacking in our munition stores at home. Sir John French in Flanders could not get all the high-explosive shells he needed, and even at Neuve Chapelle the French artillery had to come to our aid. At the Dardanelles, where the enemy was magnificently entrenched for a long siege warfare, the lack of high-

Lack of high-explosive shell

explosive shell seems to have been the principal factor of failure in the military operations.

These operations had been suddenly designed and ordered, allowing no time for the efficient preparation and organisation of our instruments of attack. Fleet and army had to get to work with all possible speed, and make use of such means as were available. Shrapnel was plentiful, as it had been found of little use in trench warfare; the Navy had a fair supply of common shell, but high-explosive shell was very rare. This was the principal reason why the landing battles cost us so many lives and why, after the landing, the progress of our troops was so very slow. From beginning to end we were fighting against a superbly entrenched enemy without the proper means of destroying his entrenchments.

In ultimate analysis this condition of affairs was due to the fact that our military authorities before the war broke out were unable to get as good a fuse for high-explosive shell as the Germans possessed. Either through a total failure of the scientific intellect of our Empire, or through the neglect by the Government to put the problem of the high-explosive shell into the hands of men of science capable of solving it, our shell remained inferior to both the French and the German shell. The fuse

Implacable captain's bold tactics

was so delicate that when this type of projectile was first introduced shells were known to explode if jolted over a rough road.

The only real success in the preliminary bombardment was obtained round Beach X, north of Cape Tekeh. It was due to the bold tactics of the captain of the Implacable. At dawn the covering ship, the Swiftsure, started a fierce and continual fire against the cliffs—using, of course,

AUSTRALIANS AND BLUEJACKETS ON BOARD A WARSHIP IN THE DARDANELLES.
In circle: Turkish torpedo-boat driven ashore on the coast of Chios, after its attack on the British transport Manitou.

WATER DISTRIBUTION TO THE TURKISH PRISONERS AT SEDDUL BAHR.

shrapnel. But at eight minutes to six the Implacable, also employing shrapnel for her 12 in. and 6 in. guns, closed for action. Instead, however, of remaining in deep water, the captain navigated his ship within five hundred yards of the shore, till there were only six fathoms of water to float the old battleship that displaced 15,000 tons. With her four 12 in. and her twelve 6 in. guns she smote the cliffs at point-blank range, so that the shrapnel smashed into the enemy's trenches and machine-gun chambers in the sandstone with a battering effect. Not a Turk was able to show his head above the bluff of shrub-grown rock, and our

The enemy again surprised

troops were towed into the beach and there they landed without any opposition, climbed up the cliff and entrenched. When they advanced inland they were badly worried by a Turkish battery at the village of Krithia. But again the gunnery lieutenants of the Implacable came to their aid, and when the position of the battery was signalled to the battleship the guns were knocked out of action. Had the other naval bombardments of the enemy's positions by the seashore been as rapidly successful as the affair on Beach X, remarkable progress might have been made.

The landing on Beach Y, northward nearer Krithia, also went well. The embarkation at this point was a greater surprise to the enemy than the operations round the end of the Peninsula. Only three light cruisers, the Dublin, Amethyst, and Sapphire, helped with their guns—the Dublin having eight 6 in., and the two older warships twelve 4 in. pieces each. But the light draught of these unarmoured cruisers enabled them to get close to the shore, and with their small guns they bombarded the high cliff so that a covering force of two battalions and one company landed with scarcely any resistance from the Turks and obtained a firm footing on the heights.

Far more difficult was the disembarkation on the next beach southward, known as Beach W. It consisted of a bay with a wide stretch of sand running like the mouth of a funnel into an inland valley, dominated on one side by the hills extending to Cape Tekeh, and commanded on the other side by the cliffs ending in Cape Helles. The natural defensive strength of the position was extraordinary, for the covering force had to land on a shelterless stretch of sand, with the enemy holding in front of them a crescent of broken, rising ground, pouring down a flanking fire on both sides and a frontal fire from the centre. The

GENERALS IN CONSULTATION.
General d'Amade talking with a British military attaché and General Gouraud conversing with Colonel Descains at the military headquarters in the Dardanelles.

German engineers had much improved the natural advantages of the ground. There were wire entanglements in profusion, and a great system of shrapnel-proof trenches.

In vain did the battleships bombard the Turkish defences with all their armament for three-quarters of an hour. The guns were not able to destroy even the lines of barbed-wire on the foreshore. The boats that made for the beach were confronted by a hedge of undamaged wire entanglements, and the crowded troops were exposed to a murderous cross-fire from pom-poms, machine-guns, and entrenched riflemen. In the centre of the bay every brave man who waded **Murderous defences** ashore and heroically dashed forward to **of Beach W** cut the wire was shot down. Meanwhile, another beach party, consisting of Engineers and Royal Naval Division men, made for the shelter of Cape Tekeh in the second line of tow-boats. Here another landing-party had got into difficulties, and after rowing through a heavy fire the men climbed the cliff, holding on to the extreme edge of it with desperate courage.

Hearing the shouts of these men the party in the second tows came to their assistance, scrambling up the cliff rifles in hand. The two parties then advanced and captured a Turkish trench in a furious bayonet charge, and thus checked the enfilading fire which was still being poured on the foreshore. About the same time the cliffs on the other side of the bay were carried by our men, and both our landing-parties on the horns of the crescent displayed such marksmanship that the Turks were afraid to leave their trenches and charge them. At ten o'clock another regiment was landed. The reinforced covering column then worked up the valley and cleared the enemy from their central position. Only then was it possible to cut the barbed-wire entanglements, remove our wounded from the beach, and begin disembarking ammunition and stores. For we then held the crests commanding the terrible death-trap of Beach W. The men there were in somewhat the same position as the Australians and New Zealanders between Sari Bair and Gaba Tepe. Snipers and distant hostile batteries rained rifle and shrapnel bullets over the disembarking operations; but the holes

AT THE GATES OF THE DARDANELLES.
British torpedo-boat destroyer on patrol duty opposite Seddul Bahr after this place had been reduced by the fire of the Franco-British battleships.

in the cliffs from which the German machine-guns had been firing were in our possession.

All round the southern part of the coast, however, the troops were not able to advance. They were most successful when they merely entrenched on the cliffs they had won and covered the principal work of disembarkation. At Beach Y the men tried to work inland, and thus clear all the southern plateau from the opposing Turks. But our troops were outflanked and punished so heavily that all the force at Beach Y re-embarked on Monday morning. This was the only landing failure the British had in the Peninsula.

The troops at the next landing-place, Beach X, also moved forward on Sunday morning, according to the co-ordinated plan of attack arranged by the General. They were checked, after fighting their way inland for a thousand yards. At this point the landing-force on their right at Beach W had been timed to meet them. But, as we have seen, Beach W had proved to be a death-trap, and the men there had enough to do to win a footing. The consequence was that the right flank of the troops advancing from Beach X was exposed, and the men retired towards the cliff, where a desperate **Desperate Sunday** battle went on all Sunday night. It **night battle** ended, however, in a British victory, and on Monday morning the troops north of Cape Tekeh again advanced.

On the other side of the end of the Peninsula, at Beach S, by Morto Bay and De Totts Battery, the landing was effected with few losses and a fine dash. For though the enemy had a trench along the shore, the British battleship at this point was more successful than the ships that fired at the wire entanglements on the death-trap beach. The Turkish position was well battered by the naval guns, and then carried at the point of the bayonet by a landing-party of seven hundred men.

The enemy howitzers then swept the lost beach

with shrapnel, but our troops were in a fairly safe position in the circumstances, as they were swarming up the cliff and also working round the shoulder of a hill on the left. They reached the old battery on the top by ten o'clock in the morning, and in the afternoon they had made a line of trenches on the plateau, from which they were able to hold the 2,000 Turks in front of them. They formed the right wing of the force that was trying to get astride of the **The worst** Peninsula, occupying the position it **landing-place** was intended that the French troops should work from when the demonstration against Kum Kale was completed. On Tuesday morning the Zouaves, Senegalese, and some Paris regiments took over the trenches by De Totts Battery, leaving our successful little landing-force free to strengthen the British line on the left.

Between De Totts Battery and the death-trap of Beach W was the worst of all the landing-places. This was Beach V, lying under the old castle of Seddul Bahr, and extending towards the high cliff that rose sharply from the foreshore round Cape Helles. The beach was only a few hundred yards wide, and the strong current of the Dardanelles swept round it with great power, making any landing by row-boats a disastrous affair. The lie of the ground was similar to that of Beach W, with a smaller sandy foreshore,

TURKISH SHELL EXPLODING IN THE SEA.
Falling wide of its mark, the missile only sent up a fountain of steaming foam.

fronted by a broken valley and enfiladed from the heights on either hand. On the left, at Seddul Bahr, was the modern entrance fort to the Dardanelles. Its two great guns had been dismantled by our fleet, but the bomb-proof chambers were intact, and the German engineers had constructed a system of trenches and barbed-wire entanglements extending round the valley and connecting with the solid masses of masonry of the old ruined castle. The ruins still afforded excellent cover to sharpshooters and Maxim-gun parties, and the broken walls of the village of Seddul Bahr had also been skilfully worked into the enemy's new system of earthwork defences. Behind the village was a hill one hundred and forty-one

H.M.S. Majestic, which was torpedoed on May 27th, 1915, leaving Mudros Bay.

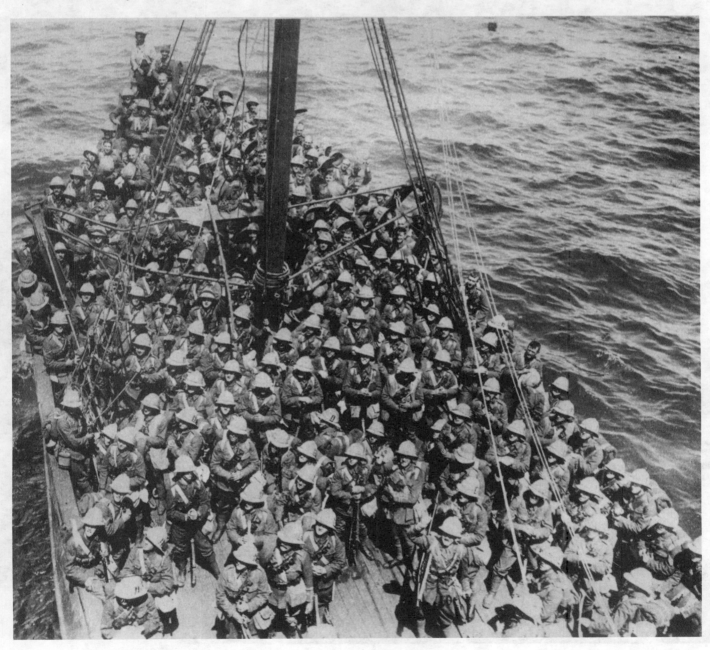

British troops going ashore at the Dardanelles from the transport Nile.

Carrying stores to the Australian camp on the Gallipoli Peninsula.

Tending wounded Australians who landed on Gallipoli Peninsula under heavy fire.

378

Men of the Australian Light Horse who fought so gallantly on the Gallipoli Peninsula.

Australians hauling the first gun to be landed by the Allies in the Dardanelles.

Ruins of Seddul Bahr with foreshore where the troops landed in May, 1915.

Major-General Birdwood, C.B., in command of the Australian troops.

feet high, now famous as Doughty-Wylie's Hill. On this commanding position the enemy had constructed a maze of trenches and barbed-wire hedges from which the beach was dominated at point-blank range. As in the case of Beach W, the foreshore and valley were also trenched and set with barbed-wire. Farther inland were the heavy howitzer batteries of this terrible fortress, which even in the ordinary way would have been one of the most formidable positions that any troops had ever been called upon to take. But instead of coming overland against the stronghold and entrenching against the enemy's fire and working forward by saps, our troops had to attack without any cover from the sea, advancing in little boats against an adverse current of the great Strait.

INTERIOR OF THE TURKISH BATTERY AT CAPE HELLES.
Heavy cannon on a turn-table guarding the entrance to the Dardanelles.

It was proposed that the River Clyde should run herself ashore on Seddul Bahr beach, as high up as possible. But the current swung her out of her course, and she went too far eastward close to a reef of rocks. The water above the reef was too deep for the men to wade through, but the steam-hopper also beached herself alongside, forming a gangway. Under a tornado of fire from the enemy, a lighter was also got into position, and the most difficult of all the landings began. While the River Clyde was grounding, a covering party in eight tows also reached the shore. But fifty yards from the water's edge was a barbed-wire obstruction spanning the beach. It was undamaged by **Tragedy of the** our naval guns, and the enemy waited **sandbank** till our covering party was held up on the wire, and then played on them with three machine-guns. All our men would have perished entirely but for the fact that there was near the sea a sandbank about five feet high. Under the lee of this shelter the survivors dug themselves in. All the while the River Clyde was rattling under the tempest of pom-pom shells, machine-gun fire, and shrapnel. One of the gangways was destroyed as soon as it was let down, and though our Maxims from the bridge and casemates answered the enemy's fire, they could not beat it down.

THE LIGHTHOUSE AT SEDDUL BAHR.
Part of the old fortifications is shown, with obsolete cannon and stacks of ammunition.

Only the ingenuity of Admiral de Robeck and his Staff made the landing attack practicable. Two miles across the Strait was the town of Troy, which the ancient Greeks had captured after a long siege by means of the ruse of the wooden horse. Very likely memories of Homer inspired our fighting seamen with the idea which they had been reducing to practice during the weeks of preparation. They took a large collier, the River **Admiral de Robeck's** Clyde, cut great doors in her steel sides, **ingenuity** and filled her with 2,000 troops on Saturday night, April 24th. Her bridge was turned into a fort by means of steel plates, and casemates were built in her bows and lower bridge, from which twelve machine-guns were worked by the Maxim section of the Naval Division. A string of lighters, towed by a steam-hopper, moved by the side of the new Horse of Troy, the lighters being intended to form a sort of pontoon bridge from the ship to the shore if need required.

It was death to venture outside. But at the word of command, part of the Fusilier Brigade, under General Napier, dashed out and tried to reach the foreshore. The short-range fire of the Turkish machine-guns swept them off the planks as they ran, mowed them down in the barges, knocked them over in the water, and took a ghastly toll of those who reached the beach and rushed for cover to the sandbank. Of those who fell into the water during the race down the gangway and across the barges, many were drowned. Wounded and weighed down by their packs and full cartridge-belts, many an heroic Fusilier perished in quite shallow water. Yet there was no hanging back. General Napier, who was hit by three bullets early in the conflict, lived just long enough to send his men a message. He said he would like to kiss the whole Fusilier Brigade.

There were the Dublin Fusiliers, who had three companies wiped out; the Lancashires, who went with the first tows and suffered terribly, and the Munsters, some of whose platoons also reached the sandbank. It was wonderful to see how the men conducted that race with death to the shore. The Lancashires got caught in an underwater entanglement, and were there swept by machine-guns. The survivors struggled out of the water into a minefield, and those who extricated themselves from this new peril were again enfiladed by machine-guns. Only fifteen men were left alive in the platoon that reached the beach. But with an undauntedness glorious alike to the annals of their regiments and their country, they held on gamely, and tried to rush a Turkish trench. It was an impossible feat. The Turks poured a shower of bullets at them and then charged with the bayonet. Somebody in H.M.S. Majestic was watching the Lancashires. Two shells from the battleship's guns struck the trench as the Turks were rising to the charge, and the survivors of the fifteen Fusiliers thereby accomplished the apparently impossible. For, rushing on the staggered enemy, they shot or bayoneted those that did not flee, and captured the trench.

Miracles of courage were performed by the men under the sandbank, who went out and brought to shelter their wounded comrades struggling in the

Miracles of courage performed

water. Some of the rescuers also got the wounded men into the boats and away to the ships. Often the rescuers were killed and the wounded men shot a second time. The grandest figure in the scene of horror and heroism was a seaman from the River Clyde. Calmly smoking a pipe, he went about the beach amid a hurricane of bullets, getting the wounded into safety, and working all the time with an amazing unconcernedness. Meanwhile a party of the Fusiliers, who had landed in tow-boats, scaled the cliff to the village of Seddul Bahr and carried on a close-range rifle fight with the Turkish infantry in the streets and ruined buildings. But our men were too few in number and too much exposed in position to force their way into the town. They had at last to give up the unequal combat and scrambled down the cliff to the shelter on the beach.

By the afternoon there were about two hundred men under the sandbank. Digging holes in the sand, they crawled under cover, and there they had to remain until nightfall. It had been seen that any further attempt at

a landing would mean the entire destruction of the Fusilier Brigade and the 2nd Battalion of the Hampshires working with them. So the new Horse of Troy—the River Clyde—remained all day by the beach with 2,000 men inside her. Meanwhile the situation had been greatly improved by the success of the landing on Beach W, under Cape Helles. A battalion of infantry there began to climb up the steep slopes of the crest. So quickly did they move that the sailors watching from the battleship could hardly realise that the troops were meeting fierce resistance and losing heavily at every step. But there was no stopping to count the cost. The troops swarmed out on the crest of Cape Helles and entrenched there, and in the afternoon a couple of guns were landed. It was hoped that the men holding Cape Helles would be able to work round towards Seddul Bahr and facilitate the operations of the Fusilier Brigade by clearing the high ground round the sandbank.

The German engineers had foreseen everything. They had reckoned on losing Cape Helles, while holding up our landing-party at Seddul Bahr. Round the plateau eastward of Cape Helles lighthouse was a barrier. It consisted of meshes of wire, the barbs **German science** only an inch apart, supported on iron **and foresight** posts. This barrier was ten yards in width. It ran from Cape Helles to Seddul Bahr Fort. Behind it was a series of trenches, zigzagging in a rough circle, forming a redoubt held by a strong body of German infantrymen, who were able to fire in any direction in order to prevent any force which might force a landing at Cape Helles from giving any help to the landing-party in difficulties at Seddul Bahr. It was precisely this situation which had arisen, all of which goes to show what science and foresight the Germans employed in fortifying the Gallipoli Peninsula.

Yet, supported by the fire of our warships, the troops at Cape Helles worked up to the very edge of the barbed-wire by the end of Sunday afternoon. Then, as nonchalantly as if they were clipping a hedgerow at home, they began to cut a path through the jungle of barbs, while enduring a furious fire from the redoubt. And when some of our infantry tried to dash through in daylight the Turkish fire

ARRIVAL AT CAIRO OF RED CROSS TRAIN WITH WOUNDED FROM THE DARDANELLES.

BRITISH TROOPS WITH THEIR RIFLES IN READINESS AS THE TRANSPORT STEAMS SHOREWARD AT THE WESTERN ENTRANCE TO THE DARDANELLES.

GUNNER IN BRITISH BATTLESHIP IN THE DARDANELLES TAKES A HURRIED MEAL WHILE WAITING ORDERS BY TELEPHONE.

was too hot for an advance on so small a front as had been made through the wire barrier. Not till night fell were the men able to work forward and get some command over the Turks holding up the landing on Seddul Bahr beach.

In the darkness of Sunday night the two thousand troops in the River Clyde at last managed to get ashore without a single further casualty. The operation was conducted with such silent skill that the enemy did not perceive until it was too late that anything was happening. Then they opened a raging rifle fire on the ship, and maintained it until close upon dawn. But the ship was empty, and while it was serving as a decoy target the troops, having got ashore with all the ammunition, food, and water they needed, began to push up under the shelter of the cliffs below the castle.

Ship used as decoy

At eleven o'clock at night the Turks became seriously alarmed, and swept the entire beach with a violent fusillade. But our men were lying down under cover and suffered little loss. Again they went forward in the darkness, and worked their way into part of the ruined castle and the shattered fort. Our centre also advanced, and won a firm hold on the shore ; and when day broke on Monday, April 26th, an attempt was made to close round the enemy from the castle cliff on one side and the central beach. The attack, however, was held up by machine-guns from one of the towers of the castle, and our men had again to take cover until the Cornwallis battered the towers down with her guns. Then, by hard fighting through the ruined village behind the castle, the British troops worked out in the open country, only to be again held up by the principal work of defence of the German engineers—the Doughty-Wylie Hill.

This green mound, one hundred and forty-one feet above sea-level, had been converted into a system of earthworks and wire entanglements, from which the German machine-gun officers, pom-pom crews, and Turkish infantry swept the beach in front, Cape Helles on their right and Seddul Bahr on their left. The condition of our wasted and weary troops, who had been fighting all night and morning and losing heavily, was very serious. The loss in officers during the landing had been disastrous, and though all the men they had got through unwounded were desperately eager to close with the enemy, there was in many cases nobody left to lead them.

A critical situation

It was in these circumstances that Colonel Doughty-Wylie came ashore and began to talk to the men. He was a Staff officer, and he had no business to be where he was. But the situation was critical, and it was because

383

GHEZIREH PALACE HOTEL, CAIRO.
Converted into a Red Cross hospital where Australians and New Zealanders, wounded in the Dardanelles, were attended to.

THE WORLD'S LARGEST HOTEL AS A HOSPITAL.
Heliopolis Grand Hotel, Cairo, used as a hospital for Australasian wounded. It contained 800 rooms, with saloons annexed to each.

SIDE VIEW OF GHEZIREH PALACE HOTEL.

them all thrown back by a sweeping fire from the machine-gun. While the men took cover Lieutenant Bastard ran forward to the opening through which the machine-gun was playing, thrust in his revolver, and emptied all its chambers. He must have killed or wounded some of the gunners, for the fire was at once reduced. The young lieutenant escaped at the time by a miracle, but afterwards, while passing a loophole in the fort, he got a bullet through his cheek.

The glorious 29th Division

The speed and dash with which the Irishmen took the fortified hill were, according to the soldiers themselves, the grand feature of the most remarkable landing battle in military history. One of the Worcesters afterwards said that he did not mind being wounded when he saw what the Irish Fusiliers did. But the fact was every regiment of the 29th Division distinguished itself by its dauntless skill and invincible tenacity. In addition to the first battalions of the Dublin, Munster, Lancashire, and Inniskilling Fusiliers, and the second battalion of the Royal Fusiliers, the landing battles at the southern end of the Gallipoli Peninsula were fought by the 1st Essex Regiment, the 2nd Hants, and 1st Scottish Borderers, 2nd South Wales Borderers, 1st Border Regiment, 4th Worcesters, and 5th Territorial Battalion of the Royal Scots. Magnificent work was also done by the Chatham, Deal, Portsmouth, and Plymouth Marine Light Infantry, and the Drake, Hood, Nelson, Howe, and Anson Battalions of the Naval Division.

It was at noon on Monday, April 26th, that the Turks fled from their last defences on the hill, enabling Beach V to be cleared. This prepared the way for a further advance inland, enabling our line to be stretched right across the southern end of the Peninsula. When General Liman von Sanders came down in great force on April 28th to make the grand attack which was to push our troops back into the sea, we in turn had constructed a system of trenches from the Ægean coast to the Dardanelles shore. Against our trenches the packed lines of Turks fell in thousands, for our veteran troops of the 29th Division were the flower of our little regular Army. Among them were officers and men who had fought from Mons to the Marne, and from the Aisne to Ypres. The Turkish infantry of the line shot poorly and could not attack in extended order. The enemy's machine-gun parties were both brave and skilful, and their sharpshooters, mostly Moslem Macedonian refugees, were also courageous and marksmanlike. But the Turkish infantry could not attack in a scientific manner. The men bunched together too much, and heavy though our losses had been in the landing battle, we gave the enemy more than we had received when he made his first attempts to drive back and drown us in the sea.

In a sustained effort on the night of Wednesday, April

he knew the men had lost their officers that he assumed command. Carrying only a small cane, he walked about in the tempest of fire, talked to the men, cheered and rallied them, and formed them up for the charge. At his orders they fixed their bayonets, and, leading them with his cane, he took them up the fortress hill, and fell dead in front of them. The Fusiliers passed over his body, cut through the barbed-wire, bayoneted the Turks, and captured the height. And in honour of the man who led them they called it Colonel Doughty-Wylie's Hill.

Doughty-Wylie's heroic death

The Dublin Fusiliers, with the Munsters on their left and the Hants on their right, made the great charge. Major Grimshaw, of the Dublin Fusiliers, was as heroic as Colonel Doughty-Wylie, and fell like him on the field of battle. A younger hero of the Dublins was Lieutenant Bastard. He led his men against the fort, only to have

WOUNDED TURKISH PRISONERS, WITH NURSES, WALKING IN THE GROUNDS OF THE NEW RED CRESCENT HOSPITAL OPENED AT CAIRO UNDER THE PATRONAGE OF THE SULTAN OF EGYPT.

FIRST BATCH OF GERMAN AND TURKISH PRISONERS FROM THE DARDANELLES ARRIVING AT CAIRO UNDER AUSTRALIAN ESCORT.

28th, the Turks pressed forward in close-order formation on our thinly-held line, intending, after the manner of the Germans, to smash their way through by sheer weight of numbers. But they were everywhere repulsed. Long lines of their dead lying in front of our trenches marked the high-water mark of their onslaughts. They also attacked the French in dense masses on the same night, but they withered under the rapid fire of the Lebels, and were routed by a fierce counter-attack at the point of the bayonet. Again on the following Saturday the Turks concentrated against the French front, while making only a spasmodic effort on our lines. Some of the Senegalese troops on Saturday gave way after their officers had fallen. But the Zouaves went forward in a grand bayonet charge and recaptured the ground.

CARRYING AUSTRALIAN WOUNDED FROM CAMP HOSPITAL TO TRANSPORT.

On the left is a remarkable photograph, also from the Dardanelles, showing how the wounded were raised on board ship by means of cranes.

The Peninsula had to be reduced by slow and laborious siege-work against the most skilful military engineers in the world. It was impossible to dispute the excellence of the leadership of the German officers. Brutal and overbearing they may have been, but they held the Turks together in a superb way, and by their tenacity in attack got all that was best out of the fatalistic temperament of the Ottoman peasantry. Indeed, they got more out of the Turk than Osman had done at Plevna, and gave us in the Gallipoli Peninsula the most difficult feat our Army had ever to accomplish.

Our soldiers and sailors worked as well as they fought. By the beaches piers were built out into deep water so that the largest lighters could come alongside. Roads were cut along the cliffs, and a system of lighting devised to allow the work to go on in darkness as well as in daylight. At night the southern end of the Peninsula, formerly so barren and deserted, had the appearance of being one of the world's greatest seaports. The multitude of

The first stage of the great battle ended in the middle of May with the Turks entrenched across the slopes of Achibaba, and the allied troops holding the ground south of Krithia village. The campaign had become a matter of trench warfare, and the winning of the Peninsula was a question of how many men we could afford to lose in order to capture each trench and each hundred yards of ground. Nothing could be done without large reinforcements and an enormous supply of ammunition. For our Mediterranean Expeditionary Force was only starting on its labours after its series of heroic contests for the landing beaches.

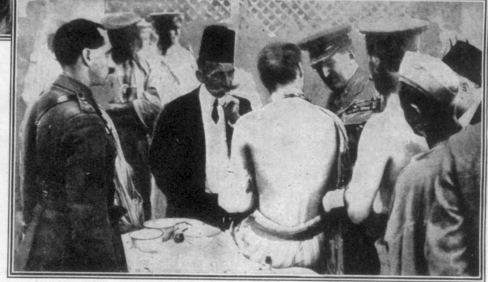

THE SULTAN OF EGYPT AND LIEUT.-GENERAL SIR JOHN MAXWELL TALKING TO A DARDANELLES PATIENT IN THE HOSPITAL AT HELIOPOLIS, CAIRO.

ONE OF THE 15 IN. GUNS OF H.M.S. QUEEN ELIZABETH.
Each of these guns is capable of sending a shell weighing about a ton a distance of twenty-four miles.

lights ashore made the coast look as though several towns had sprung up, and out to sea, like an enormous mass of ocean commerce, were a hundred great transports, and a mighty fleet of warships lay packed outside the still-bolted path to Constantinople.

The position of our fleet remained insecure. In the middle of April one of our new submarines, the E15, entered the Dardanelles at night to make a reconnaissance of the minefield at the end of the first basin. But it was caught by a strong current and carried towards Kephez Point, where it grounded, most of the crew being captured by the Turks. A day or two afterwards a Turkish torpedo-boat, officered by Germans, slipped out of the Dardanelles and made a torpedo attack on the West Hartlepool steamer the Manitou, which was full of British troops. Though three torpedoes were fired at the transport all of them missed, but twenty-four men were drowned, owing to one boat capsizing in the water, and another boat being lost through the breaking of a davit. In addition to the men drowned twenty-seven were reported missing. The hostile torpedo-boat, a small craft of ninety-seven tons, was chased by the Minerva and some British destroyers and destroyed on the coast of Chios. The crew of thirty-four men, including seven Germans from the Goeben, were made prisoners.

This was a poor beginning of the torpedo campaign

PRINCE SAID HALIM PASHA.
The Turkish Grand Vizier.

DSCHEWAT PASHA.
In charge of Dardanelles Defences.

against our immense fleet of battleships and transports. But the German seamen who conducted it were to improve with practice, and to introduce by means of a flotilla of submarines a new and powerful factor antagonistic to the success of our naval and military operations against the Dardanelles. All things considered, the situation round the Gallipoli Peninsula in the middle of May was one of great anxiety.

In regard to the control of the operations of our united Services by brilliant and daring politicians, it is usual to refer to the exploits of the elder Pitt, as related by ordinary historians. According to the works of these men Pitt, though a mere politician, was the most masterly leader of our naval and military forces we ever possessed. But we must point out that our leading military historian, Mr. Fortescue, after studying very closely the operations conducted by Pitt, came to the conclusion that this famous politician, with the advantage of having only two effete and badly governed countries to act against, not infrequently wrought more mischief than good when he interfered. Pitt's example was certainly misleading to the inexpert modern politicians, who, at a time when we were opposed by the mightiest military empire in the world, acted as amateur strategists and dictated plans of campaign with the best intentions but without the knowledge and experience required.

BRITISH WARSHIP ATTACKING THE OUTER FORTS OF THE DARDANELLES.

GERMAN SUBMARINE THAT SUNK THE FALABA.

THE PIRATE CRAFT SEEN FROM DECK OF THE FALABA.

PASSENGERS WAITING TO BE TAKEN OFF THE VESSEL.

TWO OF THE FALABA'S BOATS "TURNED TURTLE."

PASSENGERS CLINGING TO FALABA'S UPTURNED BOAT.

CHAPTER LXIII.

DEVELOPMENT OF THE SUBMARINE WARFARE TO THE SINKING OF THE LUSITANIA.

By Percival A. Hislam, author of "The North Sea Problem," "The Navy of To-Day," etc.

British Submarines in the Mediterranean—Perilous Exploit of the B11—The First Naval V.C. in the War—Hostile Underwater Craft in the Channel—Loss of the Formidable—Captain Loxley's Heroic Message—German Mines on British Trade Routes—Sinking of the Viknor—The Clan McNaughton Mystery—French Naval Watch on the Strait of Otranto—Austria's Initial Essay in Submarine Warfare—The Léon Gambetta Torpedoed—Disregard of the Rights of Neutrals—A Ten Months' Record of Losses—Why the Enemy's Boats Concentrated on Merchantmen—The German "Blockade"—Delight of the German Press—Blood-Lust and the Falaba—The War Against North Sea Fishermen—Captain J. W. Bell of the Thordis Retaliates—Attack on the Transport Wayfarer—Blockade of German Ports Declared by Great Britain—The U28 and U29 Sent to the Bottom—Treatment of Submarine Prisoners—Aircraft Aid in Submarine Attacks—The Most Horrible Crime in Civilised Warfare—German Jubilation over the Torpedoed Lusitania.

ALTHOUGH the watch of British submarines on the German coast, which had begun a few hours after the declaration of war, was maintained with undiminished zeal, the increased precautions taken by the Germans after the sinking of the Hela and the S116 proved sufficient for many months to save the enemy's fleet from further loss. The impossibility of putting to sea without serious risk of meeting superior British forces would alone have sufficed to reduce the surface-keeping ships of the enemy to a state of impotence. The submarines, however, besides adding to the firmness of our grip on the enemy, were able to do some extremely useful work as scouts, penetrating hostile anchorages and returning with information of vital importance to the commander-in-chief.

But although our submarine flotillas in home waters had little opportunity for proving their fighting worth, the turn of events at the eastern end of the Mediterranean enabled them to show the world that the coming of new weapons had not detracted from the old-time skill and daring of the British seaman. In the late autumn a combined British and French fleet, under the command of Vice-Admiral Sackville H. Carden, had carried out a brief bombardment of the Turkish forts at the entrance to the Dardanelles, more to test the

nature of the defences than for any other reason, and the ships then withdrew, leaving only a patrol to blockade the Strait, while plans for the grand assault were matured.

Among the vessels left behind to maintain the blockade were the submarines of the B class, which had been stationed in the Mediterranean for a few years before the outbreak of war, and in the early morning of December 13th, 1914, the B11, commanded by Lieutenant-Commander Holbrook, set out on the perilous task of reconnoitring the interior of the Strait. The B11 belonged to one of our earliest classes of submarines. She was launched in 1906, and had a displacement of only three hundred and sixteen tons, while her best speed when submerged was only eight knots, allowing a margin of no more than three or four knots over the powerful current that runs through the Dardanelles from the Sea of Marmora into the Ægean. With this little craft, manned by a crew of two officers and fourteen men, Lieutenant-Commander Holbrook set out to perform one of the most difficult pieces of submarine navigation ever attempted.

It was three o'clock in the morning when the B11 left her parent ship, and in view of the perilous nature of the enterprise everyone left letters behind to be sent to those dearest to him if the vessel never returned. As the entrance to the Strait was approached the vessel submerged, in order that she might not be seen from

THE U36 CROSSING THE BOWS OF THE DUTCH STEAMER BATAVIER V.

the look-out stations ashore. Once within the Dardanelles progress was difficult. The current was strong and treacherous, but the B11 battled bravely against it, and slowly won her way ahead. The channel was known to have been liberally mined by the Turks, and it was necessary to proceed at a considerable depth below the surface. The greater part of the journey was made at a depth of sixty feet, the vessel rising occasionally so that a swift glimpse of her whereabouts and surroundings might be obtained through the periscope.

Under five rows of mines The B11 had been under way nearly nine hours when, having successfully passed under five rows of mines, she came to the surface within striking distance of a Turkish battleship that had been stationed on the inner side of the field to prevent its being swept or countermined. As soon as Lieutenant-Commander Holbrook sighted the ship he took his boat down to a depth of forty feet while the torpedo was made ready for firing, and then slowly brought his vessel up until she was no more than fifteen feet from the surface and a clear view of the Turkish vessel could be obtained. Almost at the moment of the torpedo's

ARMED GERMAN SUBMARINE TENDER WAITING TO CAPTURE THE DUTCH STEAMER ZAANSTROOM.

discharge the submarine was sighted, and instantly guns began to blaze away at her from the shore and the ships in the vicinity. But the Whitehead had been truly aimed, and as the B11 dived again a tremendous explosion was heard as the weapon reached its mark.

The B11 had performed more than she set out to do; but she had a very narrow escape from disaster herself, for as she dived to escape the enemy's fire she struck the bottom in thirty feet of water. It was an anxious moment for all on board. Other submarines that attempted later to emulate the feat of the B11 were brought to disaster in just this way. But the crew had full confidence in their commander, and he justified it. For some distance the submarine crept along the bottom, scraping the shingle as she went, and then, happily, she found herself in deep water again, and was able to get down to sixty feet. Then Lieutenant-Commander Holbrook made a " porpoise " leap to the surface, and had the satisfaction of seeing the battleship settling fast by the stern; but he also saw that several of the enemy's torpedo-boats and destroyers were scouring the Strait for a sign of his craft, and he promptly went down again, and did not reascend to the surface until he had got well clear of the Strait nine and a half hours later. To keep a vessel of the B class submerged for this length of time was in itself no mean feat.

The torpedoed battleship proved to be the Messudiyeh, which had been launched on the Thames in 1874, and reconstructed and fitted with new armour and guns in 1901. One hundred of those on board were killed, including several German officers; and an extraordinary touch of comedy was added to the incident by the official Turkish announcement that " the old battleship Messudiyeh sank at her anchorage as the result of a leak." It was a leak, in all truth; but it was caused by the explosion of two hundred pounds of British gun-cotton. " For most conspicuous bravery " displayed in this exploit Lieutenant-Commander Holbrook was awarded the Victoria Cross. This was the first announcement of a naval V.C. in the war; but in April it was stated that Commander H. P. Ritchie had been awarded the coveted decoration for gallantry at Dar-es-Salaam in November, so that the distinction of priority belongs to this officer. Lieutenant Sydney T. Winn, second-in-command of the B11, received the Distinguished Service Order, and the fourteen petty-officers and men who were on board were all granted the Distinguished Service Medal.

The following day the B9 entered the Strait, but she had not proceeded far before her periscope was seen from the shore, and no fewer than eight observation mines were exploded round her. Providentially she escaped injury, and she got away safely after diving to eighty-five feet. A month later the French submarine Saphir endeavoured to get through. Entering the Dardanelles on January 15th, 1915, she got as far as Nagara when, in diving to avoid mines, she struck the bottom and was compelled to come to the surface in a disabled condition. The shore batteries at once opened fire, and in a few moments the vessel was sinking. Many of her crew were killed, but ten were picked up by the Turks; the commander gallantly refused to be saved and went down with his ship. The Saphir was a vessel of three hundred and eighty-six tons, launched in 1908, and carried an armament of six torpedo-tubes.

In home waters the New Year was ushered in with disaster. Hostile submarines had occasionally been seen in the Channel, and towards the end of November two British merchantmen, the Malachite and Primo, had been sunk by these vessels in the neighbourhood of Havre. Our warships, however, had become more accustomed to the tactics of submarines, and although the patrols were maintained in undiminished force, no successful attack was made on them from November 11th, when the old gunboat Niger was sunk off Deal, down to the end of the year. Then the spell of immunity was suddenly broken. Among the ships engaged in the patrol of the Channel was a squadron of obsolescent battleships under the command of Vice-Admiral Sir Lewis Bayly, who cruised more or less regularly between Devonport and the mouth of the Thames. The activity **Old ships on patrol work** of the enemy's submarines in the North Sea had already shown how unwise it was to employ old and big ships of low speed upon patrol work, and it is obvious that adherence to anything like a settled programme would enable the enemy to lay his plans some time in advance and place himself in a favourable position for delivering an attack.

On the night of December 31st, 1914, the squadron was

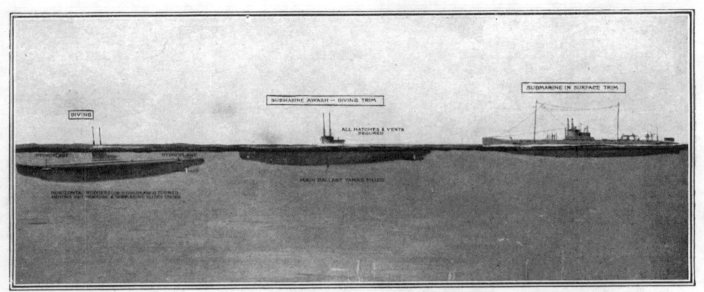

First Stage—From surface trim to diving.

Second Stage—Discharging a torpedo while submerged.

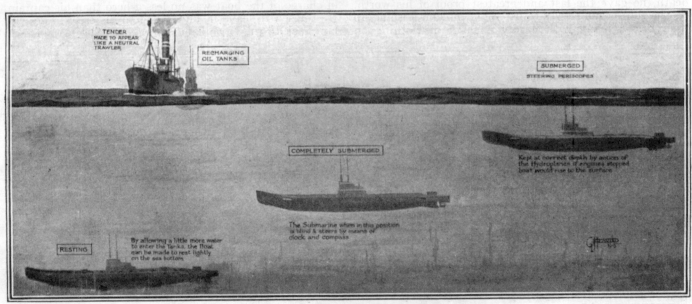

Third Stage—Submerged after sinking its prey.

HOW THE GERMAN SUBMARINE WENT ABOUT ITS DEADLY WORK.

GERMAN PILOT APPROACHING THE ZAANSTROOM.

THE CAPTURE OF THE ZAANSTROOM.
On the left the U36; in centre, the Zaanstroom; on right, the armed tender to U36.

steaming slowly down the Channel through a heavy sea, the end of the line of battleships being brought up by the Formidable, under the command of Captain Arthur Noel Loxley. There were no destroyers in company, although the experiences of our ships when bombarding the Germans on the Belgian coast had conclusively proved that vessels of this type offered the best possible protection against submarine attack; and the great ships went leisurely on their way at a speed of seven or eight knots. Officers and men had welcomed the coming of the New Year, and everything had settled down again to order and watchfulness, when suddenly at about half-past two in the morning a torpedo struck the Formidable on the starboard side just abaft the fore magazines. Had the vessel been hit a few feet nearer the

Loss of the Formidable

bows she would probably have been blown to atoms almost instantly. As it was, she remained afloat long enough to adorn our naval history with one of the most noble episodes of which it can boast.

It was realised from the first that the ship was doomed. Captain Loxley had won his way to the hearts of his men, and was loved as few officers have been since Nelson, and now in a heavy gale and a torrent of rain, facing certain death, he gave the last and greatest proof of his worth. As the ship began slowly to list the men came rushing up from below, many with hardly a shred of clothing on

them. Captain Loxley was on the bridge, his little terrier Bruce by his side, and for three hours he remained there, giving orders and encouraging the men by his wonderful coolness, until the great ship slowly turned over and took him to the bottom. His first words to the men as they assembled on the sloping, sea-swept decks were: "Steady, men! No panic! Keep cool and be British. There's tons of life in the old ship yet." The men needed no reminder of their duty. Boats were hoisted out, many of them to be smashed against the ship's side, while some that got safely away were swamped and sunk by the heavy seas.

The noise of the exploding torpedo was heard in one of the other ships, and immediately she came to stand by and give what assistance she could. But Captain Loxley would not have it. The **Captain Loxley's** Formidable had been attacked by a sub- **heroic message** marine, and he knew that if another vessel came to his aid she would probably share her fate. Instantly, therefore, he gave the order for the signal to be sent: "Keep off. Submarines about." The sending of that signal made his own end doubly certain, but it probably saved the lives of many hundreds of men in the ship coming to his aid. "That," said the Earl of Crewe in the House of Lords, "was a very gallant act, and worthy of the highest traditions of the British Navy."

Under the orders of Commander C. F. Ballard and Lieutenant H. D. Simonds, some of the boats got safely away. After some time the light cruiser Topaze endeavoured to get near the sinking ship to pick up survivors, but the heavy seas made it impossible. She did manage, however, to throw a line into a cutter containing thirty-five men, who were hauled safely on board. The coxswain in charge of the boat was no less a hero than his captain. He refused to leave it, and called to his crew to go with him back to the Formidable and get another load of men.

BRITISH DESTROYERS ON PATROL DUTY OFF THE COAST OF FRANCE.

THE DESTROYER DESTROYED—CREW OF THE SINKING GERMAN SUBMARINE U8 SIGNALLING OFF DOVER TO BRITISH WARSHIPS FOR ASSISTANCE, MARCH 5TH, 1915.

To do so would have been impossible, but nothing would make the man abandon his intention until an officer dropped into the boat and literally forced him out of it.

Captain Loxley remained at his post to the end. Those who were saved from the disaster stated that as they left the ship the men on board were calmly smoking, awaiting the inevitable end, and singing the song which had swelled through the ship in such different circumstances only a few hours before—" Auld Lang Syne." The captain himself never left the bridge, but remained there, a type of the British sea spirit to the last, a cigarette between his lips and his faithful dog by his side. He spoke a few words of praise to Lieutenant Simonds for the manner in which that officer had attended to the boats ; and the last words he was heard to utter were : " Good-bye, lads. Every man for himself, and God help you all ! "

Captain Loxley's last words

The men who had succeeded in getting into the boats still had a fearful battle for life before them, and many died of exposure before they reached the shore or help came to them. One of the most heroic of the many gallant deeds done that wild winter's morning was accomplished by William Pillar, skipper of the Brixham trawler Providence. The little vessel was running for shelter to Brixham before a heavy gale, and had to heave-to owing to the violence of the wind. Suddenly the crew caught sight of an open boat driving through the mountainous seas, hidden some-

times for minutes together in the trough of the waves. Captain Pillar swung the Providence clear. The crew, with almost superhuman efforts, took another reef in the mainsail and set the storm-jib, for until that had been done it would have been disastrous to attempt a rescue. The warship's cutter was seen to be drifting to leeward, and the captain decided to jib (take the wind on the opposite quarter)—a perilous manœuvre in such weather, since the mast was liable to give way.

Four times did the gallant smacksmen seek to get a rope to the cutter, and at last success attended their efforts. The boat was hauled as close alongside as the seas permitted, and one by one the exhausted sailors leaped on board the trawler. Seventy-one men owed their lives to the magnificent seamanship of Captain Pillar and the splendid courage of his crew of three, and the story of the rescue thrilled the country as greatly as the heroism displayed by everyone on board the lost battleship. Captain Pillar and his men were decorated by the King with the medal for gallantry in saving life at sea, and gifts of money were made to them by the Admiralty.

Brixham trawler's gallant skipper

In the sinking of the Formidable there were lost, besides Captain Loxley, thirty - three officers and five hundred and thirteen men. The ship was of 15,000 tons, and had been completed at Portsmouth in 1901 at a cost of £1,022,745. She was armed with four 12 in. and twelve 6 in. guns.

A DEED OF HEROISM IN THE DARDANELLES.
Lieutenant Brooke Webb and some of the men who destroyed the E15 on the night of April 18th, 1915, when the submarine ran aground and was in danger of falling into the hands of the Turks.

APPROXIMATE VIEW OF THE CAVERNOUS HOLE THROUGH WHICH THE SEA RUSHED WHEN THE LUSITANIA WAS TORPEDOED BY THE GERMAN SUBMARINE U21 OFF THE IRISH COAST ON MAY 7TH, 1915.

The circumstances attending her loss were the subject of much comment. Lord Charles Beresford, in particular, complained that battleships should not have been sent to cruise at slow speed in waters where hostile submarines were known to be without an escort of fast torpedo craft. This was the first occasion on which a ship was attacked and destroyed by a submarine during the hours of darkness, and the exploit was one which reflected much credit on the efficiency and skill with which the attacking vessel was handled.

During the few weeks following this calamity we sustained some heavy losses among the vessels that had been taken over by the Admiralty from the mercantile marine at the outbreak of war and commissioned for various naval duties. In the early morning of January 16th, 1915, the Char, a small vessel engaged in examining the cargoes of suspected ships sent into the Downs, collided with the steamer Erivan and went to the bottom with all on board—three officers of the Naval Reserve and eleven men. Much more serious was the loss of the armed merchantman Viknor, which before the war was a well-known pleasure steamer called the Viking. Towards the end of October it became known through the sinking of merchantmen that the Germans, probably by means of ships flying neutral flags, had succeeded in laying large numbers of mines on the trade routes that lead to England round the north coast of Ireland. All possible precautions were taken to protect our ships from these weapons, but on January 26th the Admiralty announced that the Viknor, which had been engaged on patrol work in these waters, had not been heard of for some days, and it therefore had to be assumed that she had been lost with every officer and man on board. The cause of her loss was uncertain, but as some bodies and wreckage were washed ashore on the north coast of Ireland it was presumed that during the bad weather the vessel either foundered or—being carried out of her course—struck one of the enemy's mines in the waters where the Germans were known to have laid them. Questions were raised as to whether the mounting of guns on her upper deck might have affected her seaworthiness and increased her liability to founder, but nothing could be proved on that point. Commander E. O. Ballantyne, twenty-one other officers, and about two hundred men were lost with the ship.

A month later, on February 25th, the Admiralty announced the loss of another armed merchantman—the Clan McNaughton—with twenty officers and two hundred and sixty men. The cause of her disappearance was never discovered. She was last heard of on February 3rd, and the discovery of wreckage belonging to her led to the conclusion that she, too, had probably foundered in a gale. Commander Robert Jeffreys was the officer in command. In our last great naval war we lost about three times as many ships by wreck as we did in action with the enemy.

On March 11th another large auxiliary cruiser was lost, but the victim in this case—the Bayano—was torpedoed by a hostile submarine. The cruiser was patrolling off the south-western coast of Scotland when, at about five o'clock in the morning, a violent explosion occurred near her bows. This was quickly followed by a second—German submarines usually fire two torpedoes in quick succession when attacking a large ship—and such was the effect of the weapons that the Bayano rapidly settled down by the head and went to the bottom in less than four

Loss of the Bayano

minutes, leaving such of the crew as were able to get on deck to save themselves if they could by clinging to the floating wreckage. There was no time to launch the boats, but two of the three rafts were cut adrift, and on these a number of men were saved. No one on board the cruiser saw any sign of a submarine, but one or two of the vessels that hurried up in response to the brief wireless call for help were chased away by an enemy craft. Subsequently, however, the survivors were picked up, but there were only twenty-six out of a total crew of two hundred and forty. The captain, Commander Henry C. Carr, and eleven men of the Newfoundland Naval Reserve were among the lost.

It was not only the British Fleet that was exposed to the attack of hostile submarines. In the Mediterranean the gallant Navy of our French Ally was charged with a duty very similar to that of the Grand Fleet, for while the latter had to prevent German warships from getting on to the Atlantic trade routes, and from interfering with the transports that were constantly crossing and recrossing the Channel, the French forces in the Mediterranean had to exercise a similar control over the Austrian Fleet in the Adriatic. Using Malta as his base, the French commander-in-chief, Admiral Boué de Lapeyrère, maintained a close watch over the Strait of Otranto—a task that became increasingly imperative as the Allies began to concentrate their forces for the opening of the Dardanelles. This guard could not be maintained without exposing the French ships to the risk of torpedo attack, but it hardly needs saying that the risks were cheerfully accepted in the common cause.

At the beginning of the war Austria had seven submarines in service, and seven in various stages of construction. From time to time reports were published of the arrival of new vessels at Pola, sent in sections overland from Germany to be put together in the Austrian dockyard. It was not until the war had been in progress nearly five months, however, that the enemy's underwater craft made any attempt on the French Fleet. On December 21st submarine U12, command by Lieutenant Egon Lerch, reached the southern end of the Adriatic, and there, after lying in wait for some time, she succeeded in stalking the French Dreadnought Jean Bart. She fired two torpedoes, one of which missed its mark by a hundred yards, but the other struck the 23,000-ton battleship in the bows and tore a huge rent in her side. Fortunately, however, the Jean Bart was solidly built in accordance with the latest ideas of naval architecture. Her bulkheads and watertight doors stood out against the strain, and she was able to make her way into port, some hundreds of miles distant, under her own steam and without further

mishap. One of the ship's officers, in writing of the incident to a French newspaper, told a little story which affords an admirable illustration of the spirit of the French Navy. "What I shall remember all my life," he said, "is the sight of my master carpenter. He was on the forward deck when the explosion took place, and for a moment was completely stupefied. Quickly recovering himself, his thought was only of the outlet valves, and he rushed below to open them. He was not so quick as the water, though, and when I went below myself I perceived my master carpenter swimming about in the hold in the middle of the wine barrels. The work took him an hour, but he accomplished it."

Master carpenter's heroism

The Austrian version of the affair was not without its amusing side. The enemy declared that it was the Dreadnought Courbet that was torpedoed, and that she sank after colliding with the Jean Bart. As a matter of fact, the Courbet was nowhere near the scene, while the Jean Bart was repaired and had rejoined the fleet in less than two months.

Three days after this incident the French submarine

RESCUE WORK AFTER THE DISAPPEARANCE OF THE LUSITANIA.
It was announced in June, 1915, that the Kaiser had conferred on Captain-Lieutenant Hersing, commander of the U21, the Order "Pour le Mérite," in recognition of his "gallant act" in torpedoing the Lusitania. The same submarine sank the Pathfinder in September, 1914.

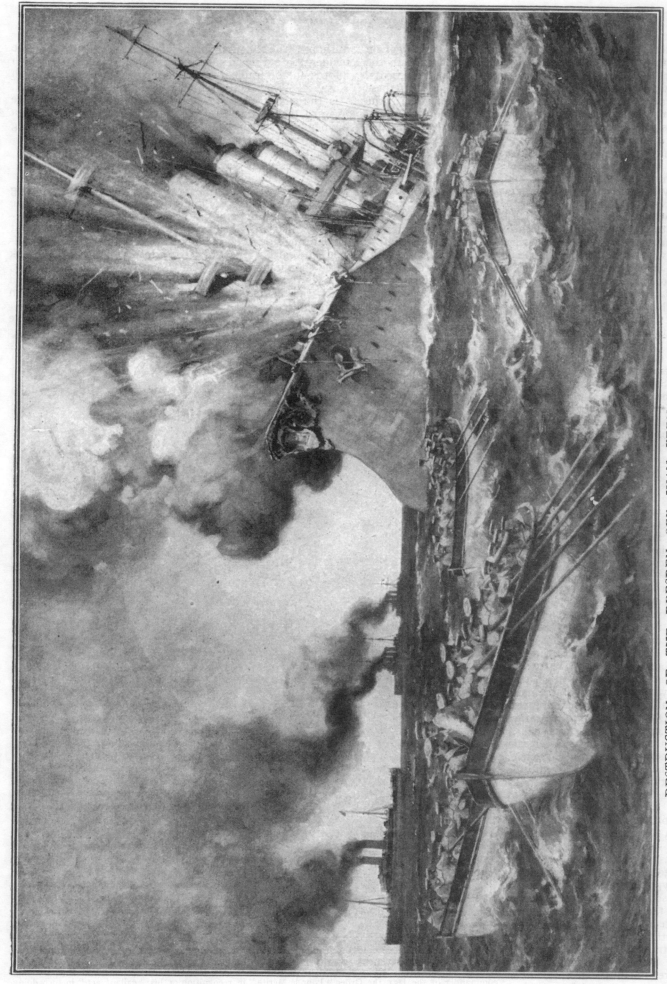

DESTRUCTION OF THE DRESDEN OFF JUAN FERNANDEZ ON MARCH 14TH, 1915.

The Dresden was the last of the regular German cruisers on the high seas, and to the loss of these vessels is attributed in large degree Germany's indiscriminate war on peaceful trading ships, unarmed men, and defenceless women.

Curie, a small but modern vessel of three hundred and ninety tons, carrying seven torpedo-tubes, made a plucky attempt to enter the harbour at Pola with the object of attacking the Austrian ships within. She safely passed the outer defences, and was creeping slowly along towards the inner harbour, when she was suddenly fouled by a heavy steel net rigged across the entrance. In extricating herself from this obstruction the submarine rose to the surface, and the Austrians, having been warned by the movements of the buoys supporting the net, immediately opened a heavy fire, which rapidly smashed in the sides of the submarine and sent her to the bottom. All the crew were picked up, with the exception of the commander, who chose to go down with his ship.

The second Austrian submarine attack on the French Fleet was, unfortunately, much more successful than the first. On the night of April 26th-27th the armoured cruiser Léon Gambetta, flying the flag of Rear-Admiral Sénès, was steaming slowly across the mouth of the Adriatic, en route to Malta. Without any warning of impending attack, a terrific explosion occurred amidships, in the neighbourhood of the engine-room. The dynamos were wrecked, and the whole vessel plunged into darkness, while the wireless apparatus was destroyed, so that it was impossible for the ship to send for help. Those who had not been killed or injured by the explosion rushed on deck, but there was no sign of panic. Orders were given for the guns to be manned in case a glimpse might be caught of the enemy. Down below the engineers worked frantically to get the dynamos going again, but all to no purpose. A few minutes after the first explosion, when the ship was already heeling dangerously, a second torpedo struck her, and she began to settle down rapidly. One or two boats full of men got away, and one or two were swamped as the 12,000-ton ship disappeared beneath the waves. The men in one of the boats, seeing her gallant commander on the bridge, called to him to jump, so that they might pick him up. With a farewell wave of the hand, he answered :

Last of the Leon Gambetta " No. Think of your own lives. My destiny is here. I die with my ship. Vive la France ! "

All the officers of the doomed ship gathered on the bridge, and not one of them was saved. The noise of the explosions was fortunately heard at the lighthouse on Cape Santa Maria di Leuca, and a flotilla of Italian torpedo craft was immediately sent out to search for survivors. It was a most gallant action on the part of the nation that was shortly to join hands with the Allies in the most chivalrous war since the Crusades, for the boats might

SOMEWHERE AMID THE NORTHERN MISTS.
British naval officer's impression of the quarter-deck of one of the ships of the Grand Fleet at night after a snowfall.

easily have been mistaken for French vessels, and fired upon or torpedoed by the Austrians. They searched the sea for hours, but were only able to pick up one hundred and thirty-seven survivors out of a crew of some seven hundred and twenty. All the bodies that could be recovered were taken ashore and given reverent burial.

The Léon Gambetta was a serviceable armoured cruiser of 12,000 tons, completed in 1905, and armed with four 7·6 in. and sixteen 6·5 in. guns. Her successful assailant was the U5, a submarine of two hundred and sixty-nine tons submerged displacement, carrying two torpedo-tubes, and commanded by Lieutenant Georg Ritter von Trapp. The French fleet of armoured cruisers was so strong in comparison with that of Austria that the sacrifice of the Gambetta was by no means a shattering blow for our Ally; and, although the loss of nearly six hundred brave men is no light matter even for the greatest of sea Powers, the manner in which they faced death will always remain an inspiration for France, and so, perhaps, prove

THE LOSS OF THE FRENCH CRUISER LÉON GAMBETTA, TORPEDOED IN THE STRAIT OF OTRANTO, APRIL 26-27TH, 1915. Her gallant commander's last words were : " I die with my ship. Vive la France !" Our illustration is from the painting by Paul Lévéré. As the vessel went down all her officers were at their posts.

of even greater value than the ship and her mortal crew.

To the British mind the idea of carrying on warfare by means of submarines, mines, and similar methods has always been repugnant, but by the custom of nations the use of these weapons has come to be regarded as legitimate and proper, so long as they conform to the laws relating to the general conduct of war. The use of submarines is a legalised form of warfare ; but a submarine has no more right than a battleship or a cruiser to disregard the rights of neutrals, wantonly to attack and destroy the lives of non-combatants, or even to sink a merchant ship without taking the proper steps to ascertain its real enemy character. For the first few month Germany conducted the war at sea in a manner which, in comparison with the behaviour of her armies in Belgium and France, was almost honourable ; but as the pressure of the sea-power of the Allies began to make itself more and more strongly felt, so our enemies fell rapidly away from their earlier standards, until at last their submarine flotillas became little better than a horde of savages, scattering death and destruction among men, women, and children, reckless of the flag under which they sailed, careless of international agreements to which the seal of Germany had been set, and subject in not the remotest degree to the elementary dictates of common humanity.

The genesis of this indiscriminate war waged upon peaceful trading ships, unarmed men, and defenceless women is to be traced to two main sources, and the principal of these was undoubtedly the utter failure of those deeply-laid schemes which Germany had prepared for the embarrassment and destruction of our oversea trade. The Dresden, the last of the regular German cruisers on the high seas, was destroyed on March 14th off the island of Juan Fernandez. The Kronprinz Wilhelm, the last of the auxiliary cruisers specially commissioned for the annihilation of our commerce, sought refuge in an American port in April, and in due course was interned for the remainder of the war. From the opening of hostilities down to the inglorious exit of the Kronprinz Wilhelm, a period of nearly nine months, German cruisers succeeded in capturing or destroying a total of only fifty-four British merchantmen out of a total of over twenty thousand. Every regular cruiser engaged in this work was sent to the bottom ; and two of the armed merchantmen had been sunk, others captured, and the remainder interned in neutral ports. The definite and complete collapse of a campaign of which so much was expected drove the enemy to the adoption of other means for achieving the same end.

Another point which weighed heavily with him was the dwindling success of his submarines when used for their legitimate purpose of attacking warships. In the first few weeks of the war these vessels cost us many good ships and hundreds of valuable lives ; but the Fleet rapidly adapted itself to the new conditions. In the first five months of the war enemy submarines destroyed eight of our warships in home waters, their total tonnage being 67,700. In the second five months the record fell to two ships of 6,333 tons, and only one of these— the old destroyer Recruit, of 385 tons—was a regular warship. Therefore, besides having learned by costly experience that his surface-keeping ships were useless for attacking our commerce, the enemy also came to realise that his submarines were becoming less and less valuable for attacking our warships. The result was that the submarines were

Genesis of indiscriminate war

PIRATE SUBMARINE U12, RAMMED BY THE BRITISH DESTROYER ARIEL AND FIRED ON BY H.M.S. ATTACK, MARCH 10TH, 1915.
Out of the submarine's crew of twenty-eight the number saved was ten.

diverted from the vain hunt for our battleships and cruisers and concentrated upon the merchantmen using our ports.

It has been seen already that the submarines first began their attacks upon our merchantmen in October, when the Glitra was sunk in the North Sea, after ample opportunity had been given to her crew to save themselves. But in December Admiral von Tirpitz gave a very plain hint at a new development that was in contemplation. Early in November the British Admiralty, ascertaining that the German Government had been strewing mines on the high seas by employing apparently innocent trading ships flying neutral colours, declared the whole of the North Sea a "military area," warning merchant ships of all nations that they must only use certain routes, from which they would deviate at their peril, either from mines or from patrolling British warships. The object was to increase the strictness of the examination service, so that no German minelayer in disguise might be able to get out.

The dependence which Germany had placed upon the abuse of neutral flags was shown by the execration with which this announcement was received. For some reason or another, however, neutral Powers declined to see that the measure would ruin them, obstinately as the German tried to convince them of the fact. The climax of these arguments was reached when Von Tirpitz addressed the United States through an interviewer in the following terms : " America did not raise her voice in protest, and has done nothing, or very little, against the closing by Great Britain of the North Sea against neutral shipping. What would America say if Germany should declare a submarine war against all enemy trading vessels ? " Incidentally, Great Britain had not " closed the North Sea."

German "blockade" declared A few weeks later a definite declaration of policy was made. " Just as Britain has designated the area between Scotland and Norway as an area of war," ran the official German memorandum, " so Germany now declares all the waters surrounding Great Britain and Ireland, including the entire English Channel, as an area of war. For this purpose, beginning from February 18th, 1915, it will endeavour to destroy every enemy merchant ship that is found in this area of war, without its always being possible to avert the peril that this threatens to persons and cargoes. Neutrals are therefore warned against further entrusting

crews and passengers and wares to such ships. Their attention is also called to the fact that it is advisable for their ships to avoid entering this area, for even though the German naval forces have instructions to avoid violence to neutral ships in so far as they are recognisable, in view of the misuse of neutral flags ordered by the British Government and the contingencies of naval warfare, their becoming victims of an attack directed against enemy ships cannot always be averted."

Thus did Germany declare indiscriminate war upon merchant ships of whatever nationality that might be found by their submarines in the waters surrounding the British Isles. The reference to the "misuse of neutral flags" by this country was based upon the fact that on one occasion when approaching Liverpool **"Misuse of neutral flags"** and passing through waters where hostile submarines were known to be lurking, the Cunard liner Lusitania had flown the American flag ; but this, as the Admiralty pointed out, had always been regarded as a legitimate *ruse de guerre* so long as the ship flying the neutral flag committed no act of war until she had hoisted her own colours.

The organised "submarine blockade" was not due to start until February 18th, but it really began at the end of January, although, of course, numerous merchantmen had been sunk before then. On the 31st of that month half a dozen British merchantmen were attacked, in most cases without the least warning being given to the crews so that they might have an opportunity of saving their lives, even if not their personal belongings. Some were torpedoed in the neighbourhood of Liverpool and some in the Channel, and among the latter was the steamship Tokomaru, which was bringing from New Zealand 97,000 carcases of mutton, the proceeds of a fund raised in that Dominion for the relief of Belgian people who had been driven from their homes by the Germans and deprived of their means of livelihood. No warning was given in this case, but the vessel took an hour and a half to sink, and the crew were saved by French torpedo-boats.

The submarine in the Irish Sea, the U21, behaved with comparative decency towards its victims, giving the crews time to leave before sending the ships to the bottom. But the vessels in the Channel were either commanded by men of a different stamp or they were acting under a different set of orders. The latter seems the more probable explanation, in view of an official statement issued by the German Admiralty at this time, which ran : " England is about to ship to France a large number of troops and a great quantity of war material. We shall act against these transports with all the military means at our disposal." Whatever the instructions issued to the enemy's submarines in the Channel, they were interpreted in the most barbarous spirit. In the afternoon of February 1st a deliberate attempt was made to sink the British hospital-ship Asturias. This vessel, carrying a full hospital staff of doctors and nurses, was making for Havre in order to embark wounded British soldiers and bring them across to England. In accordance with the Hague Conventions, to which Germany had subscribed, she was painted white, with a broad band of green running from stem to stern, and huge red crosses painted in prominent positions on her sides. According to the sworn statement of the master of the ship, it was broad daylight when, at about five o'clock in the afternoon, the conning-tower of a German submarine was sighted at a distance of about five hundred yards, and immediately afterwards the track of a torpedo was seen making directly towards the ship. The master immediately altered his course, and rang down to the engine-room for full speed, with the result that the torpedo missed its aim and passed close under the stern ; but it was not Germany's fault that her list of crimes at sea was not swollen by the sinking of a ship whose character she was pledged by her own word and by every impulse of humanity to respect. It is true that some weeks later a sort of official apology was issued, but it perverted the facts to such an extent as to amount to no more than an attempt to justify the crime.

Dastardly attack on hospital-ship

The apparent success of the war upon unarmed merchantmen gave rise to wild shrieks of delight in the German Press, where it was freely advocated that all ships entering the " war area " should be sunk on sight, without regard to their nationality or to the safety of whatever passengers they might be carrying. But the German Navy seems to have required little encouragement in this direction, as the incidents already described conclusively prove, though many officers in command of submarines seem to have been unable to descend to the depths of inhumanity and callous murder demanded of them by their Government and their countrymen. The majority, however, had no qualms about it, and those who made the slightest effort to save the lives of men, women, and children

came to be looked upon in this country as the Prussian equivalent of a gentleman.

There was great confidence in Germany in the moral effect of the " submarine blockade." It was firmly believed that, with this menace facing them, British ship-owners would refuse to risk their ships at sea, and that officers and men would decline to place their lives in jeopardy. The enemy made no allowance for the fact that the British merchant seaman comes of fighting stock, and is not frightened merely because he is told he ought to be. The enemy received his first lesson in this direction a week before the official opening of the " blockade." On February 10th the steamer Laertes, bound for Amsterdam, was intercepted in the North Sea by a German submarine, and peremptorily ordered to stop, and the skipper of the submarine must have been more than a little surprised when, instead of doing so, the Laertes clapped on extra speed and proceeded to steer an erratic course in order to avoid the torpedoes that the Germans were expected to fire. The Laertes hoisted the Dutch flag, and the submarine had no means of knowing she was not Dutch. But a torpedo was fired, and the Laertes dodged it ; and then the submarine uncovered a gun and opened fire on the ship. Even this did not impress the steamer. She kept on her way at full speed, and soon had the pleasure of seeing the submarine drop astern and give up the chase. It was Germany's first taste of the spirit of the British merchant service, and the Admiralty were so delighted with the example which Captain William H. Propert, of the Laertes, had set to his brother officers in the mercantile marine, that they awarded him the Distinguished Service Cross, and gave him a commission as a lieutenant in the Royal Naval Reserve.

Plucky example of the Laertes

The inauguration of the blockade was accompanied by no diminution of British shipping or in the volume of traffic dealt with at our ports. Ships were torpedoed and crews were wantonly murdered. On February 19th the Cardiff steamer Cambank was attacked without warning off Anglesey, and three men were killed by the explosion, while a fourth was drowned. On the same day the campaign against neutral shipping was opened by the torpedoing off Folkestone of the Belridge, a Norwegian ship carrying oil from New Orleans to Amsterdam, and having therefore nothing whatever to do with

LIEUT.-COMMANDER HOLBROOK, V.C., AND CREW OF THE B11, PHOTOGRAPHED ON BOARD THE SUBMARINE'S PARENT SHIP, AFTER SINKING THE TURKISH BATTLESHIP MESSUDIYEH IN THE DARDANELLES, DECEMBER 13TH, 1914.

THE MARCH OF THE MILLIONS: RUSSIAN TROOPS ON THE WAY TO CRACOW.

RUSSIAN INFANTRY FORMING UP OUTSIDE A VILLAGE IN READINESS FOR AN ADVANCE.

NEW RUSSIAN TROOPS EN ROUTE TO THE WARSAW BATTLE-LINE.

MACHINE-GUN IN ACTION IN AUSTRIAN TRENCH.

this country or even with a British port. Fortunately, the vessel did not sink, and was towed into the Thames, where pieces of a German torpedo were found on board.

It is not necessary to give a detailed account of the " warfare " conducted by German ships against merchant-men. In a few instances the officers of the enemy ships showed some little consideration for the crews of the vessels they attacked, giving them ample time to take to their boats and even, in some cases, towing the boats towards the shore. When the Delmira was sunk off the French coast on March 25th the submarine U32 came up alongside the boats and asked the officers if they would like a bottle of wine—an offer, needless to say, that was refused. In the great majority of cases, however, the conduct of the Germans was marked by a callous brutality, and a mad blood-recklessness that was in every way worthy of the doings of their countrymen ashore. German submarines killed their first woman victim on March 15th, when the Fingal was torpedoed without warning off the Northumberland coast. **Germans' mad** Of her crew of twenty-seven, six **blood-recklessness** men and the stewardess were murdered.

It was at the end of the same month that the character of the German submarine service was revealed in its naked iniquity. On March 27th the steamship Aguila was intercepted in the Irish Sea by the U28 and ordered to stop. Instead of doing so the vessel put on her best speed in an endeavour to escape ; but the submarine proved the faster, and when at last the Aguila was overhauled and came to a standstill the exasperated Germans gave the passengers and crew only four minutes to take to the boats. Almost before it was possible to begin to get the boats out the submarine opened fire on them. Three of the engine-room staff were killed by shells as they were scrambling into the boats and many of the seamen were wounded. A heavy sea was running, and in the confusion caused by the enemy's fire one of the boats was capsized, adding two women victims to the record of German infamy. On the very same day, however, this exhibition of blood-lust was eclipsed. The steamer Falaba, outward bound from Liverpool, and carrying nearly two hundred passengers— men, women, and children—was stopped at the mouth o:

WITH THE FORCES OF THE EMPEROR FRANZ JOSEF IN EAST GALICIA.
The troops are seen trying to save a village which has been set on fire by shell. In circle: Austrian troops firing from behind a stone barricade.

OPEN-AIR BANQUET GIVEN TO TROOPS AND REFUGEES BY RUSSIAN OFFICERS TO CELEBRATE A VICTORY OVER THE GERMAN INVADERS.

the St. George's Channel by the U36. In spite of the large number of people on board, the submarine gave them only ten minutes to get into the boats and away. It was, of course, absolutely impossible to do this in anything like the time, and the expiration of the ten minutes found many of the passengers still on board, while others were in boats that still lay alongside the ship, waiting for passengers to jump into them. The submarine was only a short distance away, with numbers of her officers and men on her decks. They watched the frantic efforts of the people on the Falaba to save their lives; they could hear the agonised cries of women and children as they ran about in search of safety; they could see the decks still crowded, and the loaded boats in the water close by; and with all these things happening within less than two hundred yards they slewed the submarine round and drove a torpedo into the ship.

The scene that followed can be imagined. Many were killed by the explosion. Boats were shattered and their occupants thrown into the water, while the liner rapidly took a heavy list that precipitated the others into the sea. The submarine came slowly on, a score of men on her decks. By reaching out their hands they could have pulled a few children—or even, perhaps, a woman or two—on board. They did nothing of the sort. On the contrary, those who were fortunate enough to survive the massacre agree almost unanimously that the officers and men on the submarine laughed and jeered as their vessel forged its way slowly among their drowning victims. One hundred and twenty-one lives—innocent lives—were destroyed. The German Navy had another victory to inscribe on its banners.

The Falaba horror

Our gallant fishermen in the North Sea were selected as special targets for these murderous attacks. Some were fired upon with guns, which killed or wounded members of their crews. On April 18th a German submarine tor-

pedoed the trawler Vanilla without warning, and when another fishing vessel came along to pick up the crew, the submarine turned her guns upon the would-be rescuers and forced them to let their comrades drown. Instances of the same thing could be multiplied, and it is satisfactory to know that a full and complete record of these atrocities is kept by the Admiralty. Refugee ships, hospital ships, passenger ships, fishing-boats—all came alike to these Germans who disgraced the name of seamen; but there were not many things in their record much worse than the sinking of the Harpalyce. This ship was engaged in bringing relief from the United States for the stricken and impoverished people of Belgium. She flew a large flag to indicate her business. Along her sides, in letters visible at a distance of eight miles, were painted the words, "Commission for Belgian Relief." Above and beyond all this, she carried a safe conduct issued by the German Minister at The Hague, which was intended, or pretended, to save her from all interference at the hands of German warships. Yet on April 10th this ship was deliberately torpedoed in the North Sea by a German submarine and sent to the bottom, three of her crew being killed. It was another instance of the value attached by a German to his pledged word.

Belgian relief ship sunk

Many were the occasions when a threatened British ship refused to be cowed by these murderous pirates. The feat of Captain Propert, of the Laertes, has been already recorded. It was repeated under even more difficult circumstances by Captain John Green, of the steamer Vosges. On March 27th this ship was attacked by a submarine. The captain at once ordered all the firemen below, and called for volunteers from among his passengers to assist them. The submarine chased and opened fire from straight astern. The first round was blank, but the next hit the ship in the after part. All this time the vessel was going at top speed, and altering her course as necessary

IN GALICIA : HELPING A WOUNDED RUSSIAN INTO AN AMBULANCE.

out suddenly sighted a submarine, and Captain Bell immediately ordered all hands on deck in case of emergency. In a few minutes the track of a torpedo was seen making towards the vessel; but the stopping of her machinery upset the enemy's calculations, and the weapon passed clear. Something then appeared to go wrong with the submarine's engines, for she drifted towards the Thordis, and the latter was steered so as to bring her bows on to the vessel. A heavy wave came and lifted the steamer on its crest, and when she descended there was a tremendous crash as she fell on to the hull of the submarine. Large quantities of oil appeared on the surface, and the submarine was not seen again. An expert investigation by naval officers convinced **Enemy attacks on** them, by the condition of the hull of the **transports** steamer, that she had actually sent the vessel to the bottom. Many rewards of money had been offered for this effective sort of work, and the officers and men shared a total of £1,160, while Captain Bell was made a lieutenant in the Naval Reserve, and was awarded the Distinguished Service Cross.

In view of the fact that the German declarations relating to attacks on merchant shipping had laid special stress on the assumption that we were about to ship large numbers of men and quantities of material to France, their failure to attack our transports with any success was most remarkable. Many thousands of journeys had been made across the Channel by ships loaded with men, munitions, and stores, presenting a perfectly legitimate target for German attack. In the first ten months of the war only one vessel was even hit. This was the liner Wayfarer, torpedoed one hundred miles off the Scilly Isles on April 11th. She was towed into Queenstown, where a hole forty feet long and several feet wide was found in her side. No detailed statement of the in-

to keep the submarine well astern. The chase continued for an hour and a half, during which time the Vosges was repeatedly hit and the engine-room badly pierced by shrapnel. The chief engineer was killed near the stokehold while he was exhorting the firemen and volunteers to further efforts. Several of the crew were injured, and a lady passenger received a slight wound in the foot. At last the submarine sheered off; but the steamer was in a sinking condition, and it was fortunate that she met a patrol-boat, to which every-one was transferred, for she went down two hours after the chase was ended. All the crew were rewarded, and Captain Green received the Distinguished Service Cross and a commission in the Naval Reserve.

WOUNDED AUSTRIAN HELPED BY FRIEND AND FOE.

cident was issued, but on May 28th the following Army Order was published :

"The Secretary of State for War desires to place on record his warm appreciation of the gallant conduct and devotion to duty displayed by Major R. A. Richardson,

Equally plucky was the behaviour of the steam-tug Homer. On April 8th this little vessel was towing the French sailing-ship General de Sonis up the Channel, when, off the Isle of Wight, a German **Merchantman** submarine appeared and called **sinks a** upon them to surrender. Captain **submarine** Gibson, of the Homer, paid no attention, but, awaiting his opportunity, slipped the tow-rope and steered straight for the submarine under a shower of bullets from the enemy's machine-gun. The Homer missed the submarine's stern by no more than a yard and then steered for the Owers Lightship, pursued by the enemy, who fired a torpedo that missed its mark. The tug got safely into port with seven bullet holes in her and the General de Sonis arrived later under sail.

The first merchantman which actually sank a submarine was the Thordis, a vessel of less than eight hundred tons, commanded by Captain J. W. Bell. The incident occurred on February 28th, when the ship was off Beachy Head. The look-

RUSSIAN RED CROSS WORKERS LENDING SUCCOUR TO WOUNDED PRUSSIAN PRISONERS.

The sinking of the German submarine U8 off Dover, March 5th, 1915.

Germany's "grand coup" in crime: The sinking of the Lusitania and th

of over 1,200 non-combatants off the Old Head of Kinsale, May 7th, 1915.

With the Russian Army—Communion Service before battle.

and the officers, non-commissioned officers, and men of the 1st Warwickshire Yeomanry on the occasion of a torpedo attack on the transport Wayfarer on April 11th, 1915. Through the prompt action of Major Richardson, and the marked efficiency of the officers and men under his command, only five lives were lost out of a total of one hundred and eighty-nine men, and all the horses, seven hundred and sixty-three in number, were brought safely to shore. The Secretary of State for War is proud of the behaviour of the troops, and regards it as a good example of the advantages of subordination and strict discipline. He cannot close this order without expressing his admiration of the coolness and courage of Captain David Cownie and the officers and crew of the Wayfarer.''

Premier and "submarine blockade"

Although the details are meagre, the incident must be placed on record as the first instance of a submarine—or any other—attack on a British transport, vessels of which class must have travelled many hundreds of thousands of miles in the first ten months of the war.

It was not until March 1st that the British Government announced any special retaliatory measures against the "submarine blockade." Hitherto, although the enemy's shipping had been wiped off the seas, commerce was still carried on with German ports by neutrals, provided that they were not carrying contraband. On March 1st, in the House of Commons, Mr. Asquith reviewed the policy and behaviour of German submarines, and added :

" Germany is adopting these methods against peaceful shipping and non-combatant crews with the avowed object of preventing commodities of all kinds, including food for the civil population, from reaching or leaving the British Isles or Northern France. Her opponents are therefore driven to frame retaliatory measures in order, in their turn, to prevent commodities of any kind from reaching or leaving the German Empire. These measures will, however, be enforced by the British and French Governments without risk to neutral ships or to neutral or non-combatant lives, and with strict observance of the dictates of humanity. The British and French Governments will therefore hold themselves free to detain and take into port ships carrying goods of presumed enemy destination, ownership, or origin."

In short, the British Government at last declared a blockade of German ports—a measure which, in the opinion of many, should have been taken much earlier in the war.

In the meantime the British Navy had not been idle in dealing with the menace of the submarine. A very large number of vessels—torpedo craft, cruisers, and specially commissioned auxiliaries—were kept in all the waters known to be infested by these craft; but the submarine, unfortunately, is in the position of being able to make fairly certain that the ground is clear before coming to the surface. If, when the periscope was raised a few feet above the water, a hostile warship were discovered, the submarine could, without the least difficulty, descend again to await a more favourable opportunity. A large, slow-moving warship might be attacked, as several were in the early days of the war ; but when a submarine sights a fast vessel, such as a destroyer, her safest plan is to get out of sight as quickly as possible. It must be remembered, too, that the submarine was a new weapon, calling for new means of defence or counter-attack, and it was necessary that the Admiralty should take every care not to give the slightest hint to the enemy as to the means that had been devised for dealing with these craft. In most cases, therefore, the authorities contented themselves with announcing the bare fact of the destruction of a hostile submarine, without giving any details, and there were other cases in which even that information was not given, but held back until its publication could not be of the slightest use to the enemy. It is therefore advisable to give only those details which the Admiralty saw fit to make public at the time.

The first enemy submarine to be accounted for by our Fleet after the institution of the "submarine blockade" was the U8, which was sighted off Dover on March 5th by a flotilla of British destroyers. Captain C. D. Johnson, commanding the flotilla, immediately made such dispositions that when the submarine came to the surface again one or more destroyers were bound to be in the vicinity. Success attended his efforts. When the U8 rose again she was promptly attacked by the destroyers

AUSTRIAN GENERAL STAFF'S INSTRUCTIONS BEING SIGNALLED TO THE VARIOUS COMMANDERS DURING THE FIERCE FIGHTING IN POLAND.

Ghurka and Maori, and damaged so that she quickly sank. The whole of her crew were taken prisoners, and in connection with them the Admiralty issued the following announcement : " The Board do not feel justified in extending honourable treatment to the twenty-nine officers and men rescued from the submarine U8. This vessel has been operating in the Strait of Dover and the English Channel during the last few weeks, and there is strong probability that she has been guilty of attacking and sinking unarmed merchantmen, and firing torpedoes at ships carrying non-combatants, neutrals, and women. There is, of course, great difficulty in bringing home particular crimes to any individual German submarine, and it may be that

Admiralty and the crew of U8

the evidence necessary to establish a conviction will not be obtained until after the conclusion of peace. In the meantime, persons against whom such charges are pending must be the subject of special restriction, cannot be accorded the distinctions of their rank or be allowed to mingle with other prisoners of war." This was a perfectly correct attitude to take up. Indeed, the ends of justice would have been no more than served if those submarine murderers

THE TSAR GREETING HIS OFFICERS IN THE FIELD.

TSAR'S BROTHER AT THE FRONT.
The above picture was obtained on the Upper San River south of Przemysl. The figure in the foreground is the Grand Duke Michael Alexandrovitch the Tsar's only brother. He has had a very distinguished career in the Russian Army.

had been treated as pirates were in the old days, and strung up on gibbets in prominent places *pour encourager les autres.* Unfortunately, however, Germany was in a position to retaliate, and it was promptly announced that if any distinction were drawn against the crews of submarines reprisals would be exacted upon an equal number of British prisoners in the hands of Germany. This was, in fact, done. Twenty-nine British Army officers, prisoners in Germany, including near relatives of Sir Edward Grey and Sir Edward Goschen, were placed in solitary confinement in isolated fortresses, and allowed only the usual

rations of a private soldier. The British Government shrank from carrying the policy of reprisals to sterner lengths; and the irony of the situation lay in the fact that the submarine prisoners were, in fact, treated in exactly the same way as the others, but were kept in different quarters. Even this small degree of discrimination was abandoned after a few weeks, much to the general satisfaction.

Another enemy submarine, the U12, was destroyed on March 10th off the Firth of Forth. The first intimation of her whereabouts was given by two trawlers, and a hunt was immediately organised. The submarine discharged two torpedoes at the destroyer Attack, and as she came to the surface to see the result, was discovered by the destroyer Ariel (Lieut.-Commander J. V. Creagh), which proceeded to charge full speed at the vessel. The submarine dived, but she was too slow in sinking. The Ariel, keeping dead on her course, sped over the spot where the **Destruction of U12 and U29** submarine had disappeared, and as she did so she struck the periscope and bent it completely over in such a way that it prevented the hood of the conning-tower from being raised. The loss of the periscope blinded the submarine. She came to the surface again, and the Ariel and other destroyers immediately opened fire on her, maintaining it until the crew came out of the hatches with their hands raised in token of surrender. Eighteen of the crew of twenty-eight were drowned.

The next success was recorded by the Admiralty on March 26th in the following brief statement: "The Admiralty have good reason to believe that the German submarine U29 has been sunk with all hands." This achievement, the method of which was not announced, was one of the greatest so far attained, for the lost boat was commanded by Commander Otto Weddigen, who, when in command of the U9, had sunk the Aboukir, Hogue, Cressy, and Hawke. The loss of this capable officer caused much regret in Germany, where it was even proposed that his memory should be immortalised by always using the word "Weddigen" instead of torpedo The French Ministry of Marine issued statements on February 24th, March 5th, and March 31st, claiming the destruction of German submarines, but in no case was the number given of the vessel alleged to have been sunk. Further, many other merchant ships besides the Thordis undoubtedly struck submerged bodies of one sort or another, but in such cases, where no prisoners were taken and no relics recovered, it was naturally a matter of very great difficulty to be certain of the destruction of the vessel.

Aircraft, both seaplanes and dirigibles, took part in these attacks on merchant shipping, but with no success. Many bombs were wasted in attempts to destroy British vessels, but an American steamer, the Cushing, was struck on the taffrail, while the Norwegian ship Diana was assailed

Aircraft attacks on shipping

by an aeroplane from which hundreds of eight-inch steel darts were dropped on to the decks. Many of the crew would undoubtedly have been killed or injured had they not taken refuge below when the aircraft came in sight. Submarines joined with a will in these attacks on neutrals. The Dutch steamer Medea was sunk in the Channel by the U28 on March 25th, after she had been stopped and her papers examined, so that the Germans could have been in no doubt as to what they were doing. At about the same time the Italian steamer Luigi Paradi was sunk, to be followed early in April by the Swedish vessel Folke. The most glaring example of this wild policy of indiscriminate destruction occurred on April 14th. The Dutch steamer Katwyk, carrying a cargo of grain from Baltimore for Rotterdam consigned to the Dutch Government, came to anchor in the evening a few miles from the Noordhinder Lightship. The necessary lights were placed in position, and the Dutch flags fore and aft were illuminated by special electric lights. The name of the ship and of her port—Rotterdam—were painted in huge letters along the side. Without the slightest warning this vessel, carrying the property of the Dutch Government, was torpedoed by a submarine and sent to the bottom, the crew fortunately being able to save themselves. The German Admiralty at first insisted that it must have been a British vessel that fired the torpedo, but later they admitted it to have been one of their own craft. Norwegian, Danish, and Greek vessels were treated in the same way, and the Germans did not even hesitate to insult the American flag. The aerial attack on the Cushing has been recorded. On May 1st the United States steamer Gulflight, carrying a cargo of oil, was torpedoed off the Scilly Isles. She did not sink, but the captain died of heart failure, while

two men were thrown overboard and drowned. Other neutral Powers appeared to be indifferent to the damage inflicted upon their citizens by this peculiar method of making war, but the case of the Gulflight gave rise to serious diplomatic tension between the American and German Governments.

There has now to be recorded the most horrible and outrageous crime in the history of civilised warfare.

Driven to desperation by her impotence to affect our position seriously, Germany planned a grand coup. She advertised her intentions extensively in America. On May 1st, 1915, the giant Cunard liner Lusitania was due to leave New York for England, and the same morning the following announcement, issued from the "Imperial German Embassy, Washington," appeared in a number of American newspapers :

Travellers intending to embark for an Atlantic voyage are reminded that a state of war exists between Germany and her Allies and Great Britain and her Allies ; that the zone of war includes the waters adjacent to the British Isles ; that, in accordance with the formal notice given by the Imperial German Government, vessels flying the flag of Great Britain or any of her Allies are liable to destruction in those waters ; and that travellers sailing in the war zone in ships of Great Britain or her Allies do so at their own risk.

To emphasise the warning, most of the prominent Americans who had booked a passage by the Lusitania received a telegram on the morning of the vessel's departure in these terms : "Have it on definite authority Lusitania is to be torpedoed. You had better cancel passage

Evidence of premeditated crime

IN THE ADVANCED GERMAN TRENCHES BEHIND MLAWA. THE SMALLER PICTURE SHOWS GERMAN SNIPERS ON THE ROOF OF A FARMHOUSE IN POLAND.

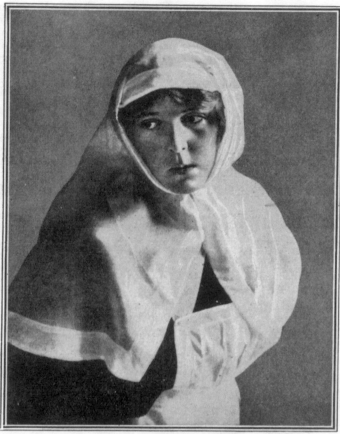

BRITISH AMBASSADOR'S DAUGHTER AS NURSE.
Miss Meriel Buchanan, only child of the British Ambassador at Petrograd. She took a deep interest in the work of the British Hospital in the Russian capital.

immediately"; and the message was signed either "John Smith" or "George Jones." Hardly anyone paid serious attention to these things.

And so the Lusitania set out on what was to prove her last voyage. Her commander, Captain W. T. Turner, when interviewed in America before the sailing, expressed his belief that the warnings were merely "bluff," and that in any case the speed of his ship would enable him to avoid a possible assailant. As the unhappy event proved, however, when the critical moment came the Lusitania was not using that high turn of speed in which her commander had placed such confidence.

The normal course of the Lusitania lay across the Atlantic to the south-western point of Ireland, whence she would steam along the south of that island, and so up the Irish Sea to Liverpool. During the week of her last crossing there was a remarkable outburst of submarine activity in these waters, and particularly in those between Dingle Bay on the west and Queenstown. The collier Fulgent was sunk off the north of Valencia Island on April 30th; on May 5th the sailing ship Earl of Lathom was sunk off the Fastnet, while another British vessel narrowly avoided a torpedo thereabouts on the same day.

The Lusitania's Other submarines were reported as having **voyage of doom** been sighted in the mouth of the Shannon, and in Dunmanus Bay, so that all the evidence pointed to a large concentration of these craft having been made off the south-west coast of Ireland for some particular purpose.

The Lusitania crossed the Atlantic at a speed of twenty-one knots—considerably below the rate she was capable of. As she got into the British seas the vessel reduced speed to about eighteen knots, so that she might arrive off the Mersey at such a time as to be able to proceed straight in without waiting for the tide. It has been remarked that in view of the known presence of submarines in the waters through which the ship would pass, it would have been

better to direct her to take a more circuitous route at her full pace rather than to reduce her speed. At a speed of eighteen knots she steamed along the south of Ireland on a lovely spring day, only a few miles off the coast, not even taking the trouble to steer a zigzag course. Such assurance did the Admiralty feel in her capacity to elude the hostile submarines that no attempt was made to provide an escort for her.

It was well past mid-day, and many of the passengers were down below at lunch. Everything seemed to promise well for a happy ending to the voyage. The look-outs had been doubled, and Captain Turner was pacing the bridge anxious, no doubt, but confident.

Suddenly from the other end of the **Tragedy of misplaced** bridge there came the cry, "There's a **confidence** torpedo!" Captain Turner rushed across, but it was too late to do anything to save the ship. Almost as soon as he had seen the track caused by the ejection of compressed air from the weapon, the torpedo struck the Lusitania on the starboard side between the third and fourth funnels.

Instantly the great ship began to heel, but never at any time was there the slightest disorder among the passengers or crew. The vessel was so huge that many on board did not for a moment imagine that the dull boom they heard was the explosion of a torpedo against her hull, and those who did know what had happened were confident that a vessel of such a size would not succumb. Every available boat was ordered to be launched at once. Lifebelts were served out, and as the ship listed more and more, confidence gave way to despair. The boats on the port side could not be lowered—they simply dropped against the side of the ship; and many of those on the starboard side had to be attended to by the passengers themselves. The tragedy was over, so far as the ship was concerned, in eighteen minutes. She was struck by the torpedo just before 2.15 p.m. on May 7th, 1915. She gave a final lurch and disappeared just after 2.30.

There was no ship in the vicinity at the time.

FRENCH VOLUNTEER WITH THE RUSSIAN FORCES.
M. Gabriel Elchain, a volunteer in a Siberian regiment, receiving a gift from a member of a deputation from the municipality of Petrograd.

AUSTRIAN OFFICERS WATCHING EFFECT OF ARTILLERY FIRE IN THE CARPATHIANS.

THE AUSTRIAN ARCHDUKE FRANCIS SALVATOR IN CONVERSATION WITH A GERMAN OFFICER.

But fortunately there were watchers ashore who in the far distance had seen the disaster, and with all possible despatch a swarm of vessels was sent out from Queenstown. But this was locking the stable door after the horse had been stolen, and the rescuers arrived only to save those who had been fortunate enough to get into the boats, or to find some other sure means of keeping afloat.

There had been 2,016 people on board the Lusitania, and over 1,200 had been murdered in cold blood, including score upon score of women and children, and people of all nationalities. The whole world rose in execration of Germany at this unparalleled crime. That it had been premeditated there was ample proof; and because a warning had been issued that wholesale murder was intended there was no palliation of the heinous offence. Out of two hundred and eighteen American citizens on board only seventy-nine were saved.

World's horror at Lusitania crime The depraved German mind found it possible to justify and rejoice over this act of barbarity. They asserted that the Lusitania was armed and carried ammunition. Collector Malone, of the Customs service of the port of New York, asserted positively that there were no guns, either mounted or unmounted, on board. There was not an ounce of explosive on board.

THE ARCHDUKE CHARLES FRANCIS JOSEPH, HEIR TO THE AUSTRIAN THRONE, PHOTOGRAPHED IN A RAILWAY CARRIAGE WHILE ON A TOUR OF INSPECTION.

Great as Germany's crimes had been before, nothing could have set the feeling of the world against her so strongly as this fiendish and useless massacre. American opinion especially was strongly roused because of the number and prominence of the United States citizens who were lost. Germany had, in short, deliberately challenged another enemy to enter the field against her. From the military point of view that was the only result of the sinking of the Lusitania. One of the victims was a member of large firm of manufacturers in Connecticut which had previously refused on moral grounds to manufacture munitions for the Allies. The murder of a partner changed their attitude, and the firm promptly laid down the plant required for turning out shells.

There was a wide impression that, in view of all the circumstances, the Admiralty should have taken some special measures for the protection of the Lusitania. The official reply to that suggestion was that **British Admiralty's lame excuse** even two destroyers could not be spared from their other duties, and as the decision of the Admiralty must be paramount in war, that reason had to be accepted. But it carried no conviction to those who remembered that the cost of the Navy had always been regarded as, in part, an insurance premium for the protection of the mercantile marine. This was, in fact, one of the gravest mistakes of the war

413

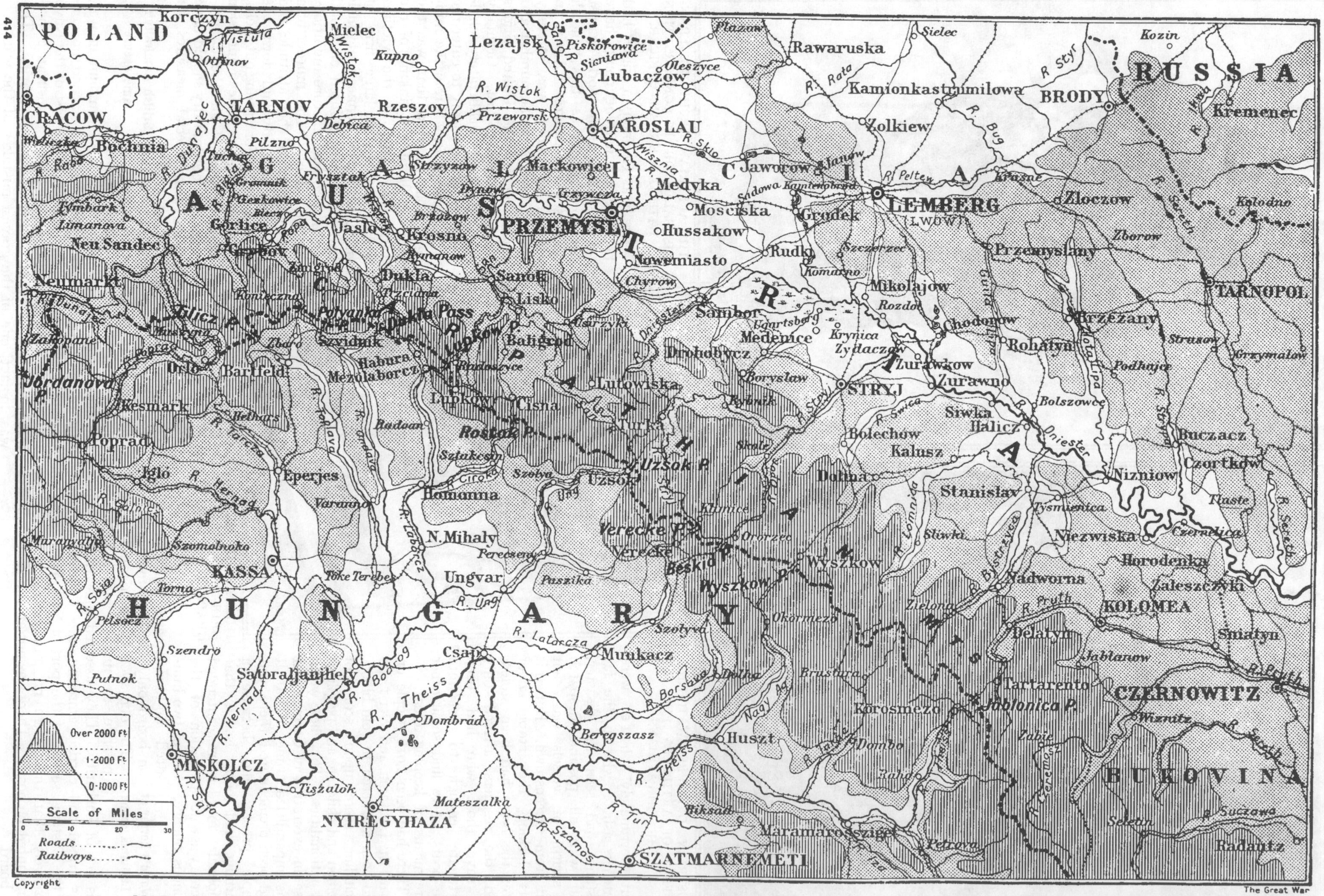

MAP OF THE REGION OF PRZEMYSL AND THE BATTLES OF THE MOUNTAINS AND RIVERS OF GALICIA.

The Great War

Copyright

Scale of Miles

Over 2000 Ft.
1–2000 Ft.
0–1000 Ft.

Roads
Railways

CHAPTER LXIV.

PRZEMYSL & THE BATTLES OF THE MOUNTAINS & RIVERS.

Russians Rely on the Spring Floods to Defend their Northern Front—Surprise Attack on Seaport of Memel—Failure of Both German and Austrian Flank Attacks—Russians Strike at Hungary Over the Carpathian Passes—Russians' Disadvantages in Munitions and Equipment—Fierce Mountain Conflicts in Hungary and Galicia—Terrible Sufferings of Austrian and Hungarian Troops in Winter Battles on the Snow-covered Heights—Przemysl Blocks the Railway Communications of Southern Russian Army—Lacking Siege-Guns, the Russians Resolve to Starve Out Garrison—Extraordinary Condition of Affairs at Przemysl—Kusmanek has More Troops than He Can Feed—Tries to Save Food by Sending His Soldiers Out to Die in Sorties—Austrian and German Relieving Armies Fight their Way Towards the Beleaguered Fortress—Furious Battles Upon the Crests and Slopes of the Mountains—Complete Failure of the Austro-German Relieving Armies—Surrender of Przemysl.

T the beginning of March, 1915, the victory which the Russians had gained at Prasnysch had a definite effect on all the operations along the whole East Prussian frontier. The German commanders, Eichhorn and Bülow, strove in vain to retrieve their defeat by making another concentration at Willenberg and striking again at Warsaw through the frontier town of Chorzele. With its central thrust and flanking movement, the battle extended in the first week in March from Suwalki to Plock. The Russian general, owing to the magnificent tenacity of his advanced troops, had been able to throw forward from Kovno a force at least equal to the combined armies of Eichhorn and Bülow. For a week the Russians held the enemy all along the line, and then slowly drove forward in fierce and incessant conflicts, in which both sides employed in a daring fashion, amid the thawing river-marshes, squadrons of armoured motor-cars with quick-firers and machine-guns. The Russians especially used the modern war-chariots round Prasnysch in the old way, sending them in front of the infantry in a charge against the German trenches. The cars and their crews were sacrificed to break the German line, where they fought to the death with a view to producing such disorder in the hostile front as would allow the Russian infantry to follow in their wake and smash through.

Having suffered from the success of this new form of attack on their entrenchments, the Germans attempted on

GENERAL ARTAMONOV, THE RUSSIAN COMMANDANT AND MILITARY GOVERNOR OF PRZEMYSL, AT LUNCH WITH HIS STAFF.

March 9th to use their armoured motor-cars in the same manner. Every available squadron of them was collected in the neighbourhood of the fortress of Osoviec. There the position was very intricate. The armoured cars formed the advanced force of a column which was engaged in trying to outflank the Russian column that in turn was attempting to outflank the German line in front of Osoviec. But our Allies were prepared for the onrush of the hostile war-chariots. They countered the charge by a furious sweeping fire from the screened batteries of their field-guns, and in spite of the swerving, zigzagging manœuvres of the car-drivers, the Russian gunners got home on the leading cars, and smashed them up before they could operate against the infantry.

The Russian commander, however, did not pursue on the East Prussian frontier the advantages he had won, for he had no desire to get the Russian Army again entangled in the Masurian Lakes district. All he fought for was to gain time so as to allow the forces of Nature to co-operate in the defensive tactics which the Grand Duke Nicholas had imposed upon the Warsaw-Petrograd line of communication. For though the weather in the second week of March continued to be surprisingly cold, remaining at freezing-point in the shade, the great thaw was likely to occur as soon as the wind changed. The released water, owing to the unusual delay in the arrival of the warm spring wind, would flood the Niemen, Bobr, Narew, and the other frontier rivers and streams. Consequently,

RUINS AT PRZEMYSL WHEN SURRENDERED BY THE
AUSTRIANS.

franc-tireur practice on the part of their own people was a revelation of the qualities of the modern German mind. For they proclaimed that if Memel were burnt down, according to the Teutonic law in such cases, they would burn down towns and villages in Poland by way of reprisal. The Russians, however, acted in the ordinary civilised manner. Having defeated the civilian force opposed to them, they did not dream of taking vengeance upon the more peaceful part of the population. They held Memel until the Germans weakened their frontier force by bringing up a fresh army against them; then, having accomplished their object of distracting the enemy and insulting the pride

some hundreds of miles of swamp would protect the Russian frontier in a most effectual manner. There would only be a few causeways to defend, and forts and earthworks with batteries already commanded these lines of invasion. Hindenburg's attempt to work around and behind Warsaw before the thaw took place had been defeated, and so far as the Russians were concerned this was an end to the matter. Instead of engaging in any further adventure in East Prussia, they wanted to use their new Kovno army to reinforce their lines on the Bzura, Pilica, and Nida Rivers.

Russian attack on Memel

But before doing this a single brigade of the Kovno army undertook one surprising adventure. On March 17th it worked round the northern stretches of the Niemen River and surprised another small German force near Tauroggen. Having captured two guns and motor-lorries full of ammunition, the Russians employed this welcome addition to their slight artillery power in an attack upon the German seaport of Memel. Making a long night-march by one of these feats of physical endurance that distinguish the Russian peasant, the attacking force surprised the city and tried to carry it in a bayonet charge. But the German Landsturm troops were assisted in the house-to-house fighting by most of the German population. From the German point of view it was a fine patriotic thing for German non-combatants to fight for their homes. Francs-tireurs were only criminals when they were Belgians, Frenchmen, Russians, Serbians, and Italians. The Germans massacred the population of a village if a single person there used any means of defence, and they burned down towns if a shot were fired, even by a militiaman. But these extraordinary rules of warfare only applied to the lesser breeds who lack the light of "kultur." There was a higher law for German villagers and townsmen, as was seen at Memel.

The Russians, however, were not to be denied. They used the captured German guns and German ammunition against the barricades, which were being defended by two regiments of Landsturm and a large number of civilian inhabitants. The shells broke down the resistance of the Germans, and the remnant of the garrison and population fled to the sandy peninsula that protects the harbour, and there German warships steamed up and covered them with their guns. The position which the German authorities took up in regard to this flagrant example of

CUPOLA OF TOWER, FORT NO. 11, PRZEMYSL, DESTROYED
BY THE AUSTRIANS BEFORE SURRENDER.

of the Prussian aristocracy by the occupation of an important Prussian seaport, they withdrew fighting over the frontier into Courland. So deeply were the Prussians vexed by this unimportant little raid that they gathered a strong force and tried to conquer Courland. And for this they were able to spare men in both the eastern and western theatres of war, where great battles were raging.

The battle in the Carpathians

On the eastern front, after the victory of Prasnysch, Hungary became the danger-area in the Teutonic Empires. From the point of view of the German Commander-in-Chief, the indecisive operations north of Warsaw remained useful only as long as they detained there a large Russian force. After Prasnysch Hindenburg had to submit to the will of the Grand Duke Nicholas and agree to the Carpathians being the critical field of battle. The German attempt on the left flank had failed by the Niemen and Narew; the Austrian attempt on the right flank in the Bukovina had also been checked. All along the central river front—along the Bzura, Pilica, Nida, Vistula, and Dunajec—the Austro-German forces were for the time completely exhausted by their enormous losses, and on both sides of this section of the fighting-line a condition of stationary trench warfare obtained.

This left the Russian commander free to choose his own point of attack and concentrate all available troops there. There was, however, one very important factor that interfered with his free choice of the scene of his offensive movement. He had fewer guns and howitzers of the heavy class than the enemy possessed. What was worse, his store of large, high-explosive shells was almost exhausted, and even his field-artillery had to be exceedingly economical in the use of ammunition. In these circumstances he could not take the proper line of attack and drive in on Cracow and the industrial

OUTWORKS OF A FORT AT PRZEMYSL, HIT BY AN AUSTRIAN 42 CM. MORTAR.

RUSSIAN 18·5 CM. GUN IN FORT NO. 10, PRZEMYSL, AFTER BOMBARDMENT BY AUSTRIAN ARTILLERY.

region of Silesia. The mighty agricultural population of the Russian Empire, stretching almost across two continents, was baffled by the culminating achievements of all the slow and involved forces of urban civilisation. For the second time in history "the little street-bred people" of the city were more powerful than the men who led open-air lives in field and forest.

Strength of the "street-bred people"

For thousands of years the saddle had been master of the plough. Loose congregations of semi-nomad tribes of horse-rearers and cattle-breeders had been the practical lords of the world. Never had the more settled and more peaceful farming races been able to resist the charging squadrons of wild horsemen from the steppes. Every era in the early agricultural stage of civilisation was broken by the irruption of the barbaric horsemen. They overturned every ancient empire. Then came the rise of the little inventive city States, which managed, by the elaboration of new instruments of slaughter and novel tactics, to check the larger forces of the sturdier barbarians. But with the invention of gunpowder the advantages which the cities enjoyed were spread more equally among the peasantry of Europe. The free cities fell under the power of kings,

largely because the king was able to arm the serf and yeoman with weapons equal to those employed by city dwellers.

This condition of things obtained down to our day. The sturdy and more enduring countryman could outmarch, and therefore outmanœuvre, the more intelligent, but less strongly-built townsman. The Germans depended almost entirely upon their peasantry for their first-line troops, and one of the chief reasons why their Government checked free trade in agricultural produce was to enable the peasantry to flourish at the expense of the urban industrial population.

German fear of the moujik

France was still regarded with respect because, owing to the fertility of her soil, she was principally a nation of small-holding peasants, likely to prove good marchers and steady fighters on the field of battle. But the Germans feared most of all the Russian moujik, because of his famous powers of physical endurance. Great Britain was supposed to have lost the chief source of her ancient valour by reason of her system of free trade, which had oppressed, impoverished, and depopulated the countryside for the sake of obtaining cheap food for the less vigorous stocks in all the industrial centres.

This was the German idea of the matter, and owing to Germany's success in the Danish, Austrian, and French wars it was generally agreed that the correctness of this idea was established by German military successes. All that the British people hoped was that their public health system had mitigated some of the principal disasters of their general movement towards urbanisation. We trusted that with the French people we should be able to hold out until the vast agricultural population of Russia began to press with irresistible force against Germany. But to everybody's surprise it was discovered, when the war had lasted for four months or less, that the working man of the urban class, when perfectly organised and disciplined, held the fate of the world in his hands. So tremendous had been the development of modern applied science that the factory dominated the battlefield. It was one of the greatest revolutions in class values in history. The cities were supreme over farm and cattle range. For the cities produced, in continually increasing volumes of production, the terrible machinery of slaughter, without which the civilised intelligent peasant infantryman was as helpless as the Zulu armed only with spear and assegai.

This extraordinary change in the conditions of modern warfare told most heavily against the soldiery of Russia, for the activities of the Russians were almost entirely agricultural. General Sukhomlinoff, the Russian Chief of Staff, displayed great energy in mobilising all available factories in the Empire. But, unfortunately, the only industrial region of much importance in Russia was that extending from Lodz to the frontier of Silesia, and it was in the possession of the enemy. Most **Russia's lack of** of the Russian seaports were closed by **munitions** ice, and though some ammunition was obtained through Port Arthur it was not sufficient for the needs of the Russian armies. The result was that our heroic allies had to rely on the bayonet and the shrapnel-proof trench. Millions of Russian peasants were ready to take the field, but were held back by a lack of rifles and artillery.

In these circumstances the Grand Duke Nicholas, on recovering the initiative, selected as his region of attack the high-wooded sandstone heights of the Eastern Carpathians. Here, in a mean altitude rising from 3,250 feet near the sources of the tributaries of the Dunajec to 5,000 feet south of the sources of the San, one of the greatest

Tyrolean regiments, but the Russians, moving on snow-shoes in superior numbers, ambushed and slaughtered the brave and splendid Tyroleans. Austria had no more troops of the same class to supply their place, and in both the Carpathian field of war and the later area of mountain conflict in the Alps the early disasters to the Tyrolean troops had bitter and serious consequences.

We have seen in a previous chapter the tactics employed by the Russian commander General Brussiloff in the first phase of the Battle of the Carpathians. His subordinate general officer, General Dimitrieff, was entrenched along the Dunajec and Biala Rivers, where he resisted for months all Austro-German attacks from the direction of Cracow and the Neumarkt Pass. With his left wing near Gorlice, Dimitrieff helped also to fight back all attempts made to relieve Przemysl from the south-west. The main forces of the Russian southern army held the Dukla Pass, some fifty miles south-west of Przemysl, and were fighting their way towards the next important break in the mountain ridge—the Lupkow Pass. Some forty miles south-west of Lupkow is another important mountain road and mountain railway—the Uzsok Pass—which was being held by the enemy, and attacked by the Russians. Then another twenty miles farther south-west was the Tuchla Pass, controlling the road from the town of Munkacz, on the Hungarian plain, to the town of Stry, on the Carpathian foothills below Lemberg, in Western Galicia.

TRANSMITTING ORDERS BY TELEPHONE FROM THE RUSSIAN HEADQUARTERS STAFF TO THE FIRING-LINE.

The main lines of the situation remained unchanged for months. The Russians tried to work down from the Dukla Pass; the Austro-Germans tried to work up from the Tuchla Pass. Between these two passes stretched 180 miles of mountain ridge, with a breadth of about fifteen to twenty miles, the altitude running from 2,000 feet on the lower northern scarps, to 5,000 feet on the central summit. Some of the heights were over 6,000 feet, and at times men on either side would try to get a machine-gun near the summit of one of these treeless, breezy mountain-tops. There was another field of conflict farther south, where the Austrians advanced through the passes leading towards Stanislav and Kolomea. Then more southward still, with the altitude of the Carpathians rising higher as they trended to the Rumanian frontier, were the forested heights of the Bukovina.

battles in the annals of the human race was fought. It began in midwinter when the mountains were covered with snow, and the wind in the high passes was so chill that the water in the bottles carried by the troops froze as they walked. Immense stretches of pine forest covered the slopes, walls, and peaks of yellow rock. The consequence was that there was seldom a clear field of fire for the enemy's superior artillery. The vast mountain forests, breast-deep in snow and cloaked often with low-hanging clouds, gave back to the Russian infantryman his natural advantage over his opponent.

For one thing the terrible climate suited him. He was accustomed to bear a greater rigour of Arctic cold than any other European. The Austrians of the plains were killed or crippled in hundreds of thousands by the severity of the winter mountain weather. The Bavarians showed more powers of endurance, yet they also suffered from frost-bitten feet, while the Russian troops lost no men whatever from this cause. The only men in the Teutonic Empire who could fight in the snow on the Carpathian heights with anything like the resisting powers of the Russians were the Tyrolean sharpshooters. Good men they were, and greatly enduring, but there were too few of them. Austria weakened her southern mountain defences against Italy by denuding the Tyrol of the

The position of the Russians was excellent at Dukla. The mountains in this region were low and bare, and the passes were broad, well-made roads, rising by easy gradients from the plain. The high ground was also lacking in breadth. All this made the maintenance of Russian communications an easy matter. The enemy, on the other hand, had worked southward over higher mountains and across a far broader **Rival positions at** stretch of broken highland country, **Dukla** where the forests were more extensive, the population scantier, and the roads fewer and steeper. The maintenance of Austro-German communications was therefore difficult. At the extreme end of the hostile front in the Bukovina the breadth of mountainous land was enormous—some three hundred miles.

At the other end of the Carpathian battle-line, round Dukla, the Russians had only nine or ten miles of falling mountain slopes in front of them before they reached the Hungarian river-valley. There were ten of these river-valleys running south from the Carpathian heights, and the

HURKO FORT, PRZEMYSL, AFTER THE AUSTRIANS HAD SURRENDERED TO THE RUSSIANS.

RUINED DEFENCES OF PRZEMYSL, AS FOUND BY OUR RUSSIAN ALLIES, AND LEFT BY THEM FOR THE AUSTRO-GERMANS.

passes extending from the river valleys formed the means of operations from Dukla to Kolomea. But all the ten river valleys converged quickly in the Hungarian plain, where the mountain streams flowed into the Theiss River. The Russians had only to work round the Ondava valley, from which the Dukla Pass ran; then, on a front of twenty miles or so, they would get astride the branching lines of communication, which were feeding the Austro-German front of one hundred and fifty miles in Galicia and the Carpathian rampart.

How Brussiloff saved Calais

In other words, by advancing southward from the Dukla Pass the Russians could turn completely the enemy's front and attack him in the rear, after cutting off all his supplies.

This was the reason why General Brussiloff held on only to the Dukla region, and slowly pushed forward there against a desperately stubborn resistance. On all the rest of the front he was content to hold back the Austrians and Germans. He occupied at Dukla the decisive position, and by continually pressing forward he compelled the hostile commanders to mass against him for the defence of the Austrian communications. So hard pressed were the Austrians that three Bavarian army corps, under the command of General von Linsingen, were sent to the Carpathians to assist them. The Bavarians held the Lupkow, Uzsok, and Tuchla Passes. But they were not strong enough for their task. More German aid had to be sent, until the German forces under von Linsingen amounted to half a million men. Great was the tax upon the military strength of Germany. The Germans had to stand entirely on the defensive in France and Flanders, and also in Poland, when half a million of their best troops were urgently required in the Carpathians for the defence of Hungary. But unless this large measure of help had been given, the Hungarians would have been compelled to make terms with the Triple Entente, with the result that the Austrians would also have followed the same course. Bavaria in particular was drained of men of military age for the sake of Hungary. The German aid was not willingly given; it was the consequence of some very outspoken statements of the Hungarian position made by Count Tisza.

As we shall afterwards see, the pressure which General Brussiloff exerted against Hungary from his commanding position on the Dukla Pass saved Calais from falling into the hands of the Germans in May, 1915. General Brussiloff in the spring of that year was able to do what neither General Joffre nor Lord Kitchener in combination could effect. He was able to force General von Falkenhayn to employ, on a given stretch of front in Galicia, all the new and tremendous machinery of war which Germany had been building up for nine months.

The Russians had won the Dukla Pass at Christmas, 1914, but for eight weeks afterwards they could do little more than hold on to their new position and strengthen it. All along the eastern front our heroic allies were still outnumbered by the German, Austrian, and Hungarian forces controlled by Field-Marshal von Hindenburg. It was not until the end of March, 1915, that the Kitchener of Russia, General Sukhomlinoff, was able to place at the

disposal of the Grand Duke Nicholas the new army which at last gave the Russian Commander-in-Chief a full equality in infantry force with that of the enemy. It was the arrival of a considerable supply of rifles, cartridges, and light quick-firing guns in March and April, 1915, that enabled the Russians at last to put into the field forces nearly equal in number to those of their foes.

Until this was done General Brussiloff remained on the defensive without losing the initiative. The Austrians and Germans had continually to attack him on the front he chose, by reason of the two advantages he possessed. He held at Dukla the gate into Hungary, and he also encircled at Przemysl a fortress of the importance of Metz, with a garrison of 150,000 German and Austrian troops. Therefore, the tasks he set the enemy were to drive him from the Dukla Pass and to relieve Przemysl.

The Bavarian army tried to carry out both these extremely important undertakings by advancing from the Lupkow and Uzsok Passes to the upper reaches of the San River. For months unending furious battles went on along the San and its tributary streams, by the towns of Baligrod and Lutoviska. The aim of the enemy was to reach the Sanok-Sambor railway, which was only about ten miles north of Baligrod. Then, less than forty miles north of the railway, was Przemysl. At almost any time, two days' hard marching would have brought Linsingen's army to the beleaguered fortress city of Galicia. So his nights and days were spent in massing his troops for attack after attack on the lines held by the Russian southern army on the outlying heights and foothills of the Lupkow-Uzsok section of the Carpathian battle-front.

PLAN OF THE DEFENCES OF PRZEMYSL.

At the same time the Austrian Arab commander, Böhm Ermolli, with equal incessancy, tried to drive through towards Lemberg from the Tuchla and Jabloniska Passes. The operations of the Austrian Arab general, however were only of secondary importance. Except when he managed to threaten one of Brussiloff's lines of railway communication by an advance against Stanislav, Böhm Ermolli succeeded only in amusing himself, without endangering the Russian conquest of Eastern Galicia.

His Austrian and Hungarian troops had the most difficult country to work in, and they weakened fearfully in the bitter winter weather. Tens of thousands of them were killed by their own army contractors. Their winter uniforms, supposed to be made from thick wool material costing thirteen shillings a yard, were really fashioned out of thin, light, summer dress material for women, worth at the most half-a-crown a yard. The Government had given the full price, and the army contractors,

Killed by army contractors

after paying bribes to the officers entrusted with the duty of examining the quality of the uniforms, made a fortune. They did not enjoy their enormous profits for many months, being, in fact, shot or sentenced to penal servitude, together with the officers whom they had bribed. But this tardy act of justice did not save the troops from death by exposure. In less than two weeks' fighting and marching through the snow and brambled undergrowth of the mountain forests the clothes of the men were worn to rags.

TWENTIETH-CENTURY "CAVALRY" SCOUTS—A MOTOR RECONNOITRING PARTY.

They had to sleep in the open air with the temperature far below freezing-point, and in the first week of March, when warm spring weather was expected, there was another deadly cold snap, in which the temperature fell again below freezing-point even in the plains. On the northern slopes of the mountains, 3,000 to 6,000 feet above sea-level, where the battle continually raged, the last ounce of endurance was worn out of the Austrian soldiers. More than 100,000 of the troops were put out of action by frost-bite. Then another 120,000 men in the Carpathian battles were stricken with pneumonia or consumption. Of the cases of frost-bite, 50,000 recovered, but of the pneumonia and consumption casualties only 20,400 were, after hospital treatment, made fit enough to resume fighting. In order to fill the gaps in the fighting-line the Dual Monarchy, in the spring of 1915, had practically to resort to a general levy of the people. All men up to the age of fifty were called out for military service, except in the case of persons engaged in armament work and vital food industries.

Never had the tottering structure of the Austrian monarchy been so terribly tested. At the beginning of the war the available resources of Austria-Hungary were excellent. A thorough and honest system of organisation and administration would have enabled the Hapsburg Empire to crush rapidly and easily the attacks of the peasantry of Russia. The Austrian Army was large; the Austrian system of railways excellent, permitting the rapid movement of troops; and the Skoda armament works at Pilsen and Trieste surpassed those of Krupp in the production of very heavy and yet mobile howitzers. But the Austrian nobility was a vain,

GENERAL HUBERT, AUSTRIAN CHIEF OF STAFF IN PRZEMYSL.

empty, self-complacent, and miserably inefficient class, with no constructive intelligence and no gift for leadership. The merchant class, largely composed of able but avaricious aliens, was eager to make money out of the necessities and misfortunes of the nation. The number of scandals concerning army contracts was enormous, not only in regard to the supply of ladies' summer dress material to the army fighting in winter in the Carpathians, but in regard to army stores of almost every kind. The aristocratic Austrian officer had ever been remarkable for being in need of money, and as inspector of army stores he let what patriotism he possessed rest in a cheerful faith in the heroism of the working classes, while he worked with the contractors in as profitable a manner as possible.

The Hungarian magnates, many of them men of great wealth and strength of character, proved themselves on the whole an efficient fighting aristocracy. There were army scandals in Budapest as well as in Vienna. For in Budapest the manufacturers and merchants showed as much conscience in their dealings with their Gentile fellow-countrymen as their fellow-traders in Vienna. Nevertheless, the Hungarian territorial troops were usually well enough clothed and well enough armed to show their inborn qualities of spirit. They fought remarkably well, and became, indeed, the supreme fighting force of the Dual Monarchy. The only Austro-Germans who could compare with them were the Tyrolese troops. The Tyroleans were too small in number, however, and their best regiments were entirely destroyed by the spring of 1915 in mountain conflicts with the Russians. The Hungarian soldiers also were not very numerous. For the total Magyar population

SENTENCED TO DEATH—RUTHENIAN SPIES UNDER AUSTRIAN GUARD IN GALICIA AWAITING THEIR TURN FOR EXECUTION.

of both sexes and all ages was at the beginning of the war only about ten million. So it was upon the Teutonic, Bohemian, Russian. Polish, Rumanian, Italian, Croatian, Serbian, and Mohammedan mixture of races—the most extraordinary in the world—that the main task of defending the Hapsburg Empire fell. As there was no common bond of veritable patriotism in this medley of peoples, the officers and army contractors often combined to diminish their means of warlike strength by every possible kind of malpractice. There were several large mutinies, ending in the shooting of thousands of the soldiers, and the general disruption and corruption were so great that it needed only a Russian descent into the Hungarian plain for the Empire of the Hapsburgs to fall into inter-militant fragments.

There was a time when it seemed that the fortress of Przemysl would decide the fate of the mosaic Empire it was built to defend. The Austrian stronghold on the San River had been remodelled and strengthened by a

famous Swiss engineer after the affair of Agadir in 1911, when the Teutonic Empires decided to open hostilities in three years, and bent all their energies in the interval to the work of preparing for the tremendous struggle. When the new fortifications of Przemysl were completed in 1913 the experts of the German Great Staff examined the fortress very carefully, and congratulated the Austrian Staff upon the strength of the new works. In the considered judgment of the German authorities, Przemysl had been transformed into a strong place superior to Thorn, and at least equal to Metz. That was as much as to say that it was the finest modern fortress in Central Europe. It consisted of nine main works, arranged in a circle around the town.

Przemysl, the Austrian Metz

In these main works were guns of enormous size, mounted in armoured towers, operated by electricity, and automatically disappearing after the gun had discharged its shot. Each of these works was placed on one of the foothills of the Carpathians, at an altitude of 1,000 to 1,350 feet above sea-level. The distance between the main works ran from 2,000 yards to 10,000 yards, there being marshes and other natural obstacles in the wider spaces to help in the defence. In the gaps between the main works there were nine smaller forts, with armour-plate cupolas, quick-firing guns, armoured machine-guns, and motor-batteries. Further, in the course of the siege, a considerable number of temporary works were erected all along the twenty-five-mile ring. There was also a girdle of closed trenches, wire entanglements, and land mines, the last-named being worked from the forts by means of electric current. The railway running from the Russian frontier to Lemberg and Cracow was bent round so as to pass through Przemysl.

PLAYING A RUSSIAN REGIMENT TO THE TRENCHES.

RUSSIAN CAVALRY CROSSING A RIVER SOMEWHERE ALONG THE EASTERN BATTLE-FRONT.

So as long as the fortress garden-city of the Carpathians held out, an invading army fed from Kieff would lack the use of the main railway when operating in Eastern Galicia. This is what occurred when the armies of Generals Brussiloff and Dimitrieff advanced in September, 1914, from Lemberg towards Cracow. Their railway communications were cut by Przemysl, and all through the autumn, winter, and early spring General Dimitrieff in particular had to rely entirely upon the small branch railway bending up and down by Ravaruska. The Russian forces at the Dukla Pass were also hindered by the control over the Galician railway system exercised by the enemy at Przemysl. The Russians could not maintain their offensive movement over the Dukla Pass against Hungary by a long, strong, persistent culminating effort until the trunk railway was in their hands. In other words, the Russians could not feed and munition an overwhelmingly numerous army in the Battle of the Carpathians until they had captured Przemysl.

But, as we have seen, the Russian War Minister, General Sukhomlinoff, could not arm his new armies for the winter campaign. So the fall of Przemysl was not an urgent necessity in the Russian plan. There had been an occasion when its swift capture would have been a great benefit to the Russian forces. This was in September, 1914, when General Dimitrieff, advancing with amazing speed from Lemberg, hoped to take Cracow by surprise and capture it. Przemysl stood in his way. He massed his artillery against two of the forts, shattered them in a fierce, swift hurricane of shell, and then launched an army corps at the gap. But the main works of defence held good, and the leading Russian brigades were felled in thousands with such rapidity that the attempt to rush Przemysl

The railway factor in Galicia

by a quick, violent, storming attack came abruptly to an end. Then in the middle of October, 1914, Field-Marshal von Hindenburg's advance against Warsaw and Ivangorod compelled the Russian Commander-in-Chief to alter his entire front; for the Germans and Austrians were superior in number to the Russians and were able to choose their points of attack and to force the Russians to concentrate in answer to their movements. The troops investing Przemysl had to be drawn off to strengthen the fighting front.

But when Hindenburg was thrown violently back, and his right wing, composed of Austrian and Hungarian troops under General Dankl, was severely handled and almost broken on the Upper Vistula and the Lower San, the situation in Przemysl became curious. General Kusmanek, the commander of the fortress, did not at first know whether the strength of his position had been augmented or decreased. His proper garrison numbered

THE POISONERS' WAR—A LESSON IN THE USE OF A RESPIRATOR.

about eighty thousand troops. But after the smashing blow delivered by General Dimitrieff against the Austro-German force, seventy thousand more fugitives—German, Austrian, and Hungarian soldiers—retired into the fortress to avoid capture. The result was that Kusmanek had on November 12th, 1914, when the second siege began, double the number of troops that had originally been assigned to the defence of the stronghold. In itself this was a matter of congratulation, for the ring of forts measured twenty-five miles round. The proper garrison for a system of trenches of this extent, reckoning on the Continental estimate of two men to a yard, was eighty-eight thousand men. That left no reserve of the original

KITCHEN IN WAR PRISONERS' CAMP AT KÖNIGSBRÜCK, NEAR DRESDEN.

garrison to fill the gaps caused by casualties and sickness, and to provide for the sorties in great strength which would be required when the Russian front was pressed by the grand relieving army of Austrians and Germans. Thus, from a purely military point of view, General Kusmanek could look with pleasure on the enormous increase of his forces.

Unhappily for him, the economic situation was not so favourable. The store of food in Przemysl had been measured only by the requirements of the original garrison. Since the fall of Lemberg streams of civilian and military fugitives had passed into the city, with somewhat the effect of a locust swarm. By the middle of November, 1914, the year's food supplies had so diminished that even **Przemysl's diminished** the original garrison would not have **food supplies** been able to live on the stores for more than eight months. The enormous addition of seventy thousand more soldiers reduced the period for which the fortress could hold out, without further supplies, to five months.

Yet, on the whole, General Kusmanek does not seem to have been discontented with the position of affairs. He reckoned on being able to use the larger part of the

fugitive troops in strong and vehement sorties before they brought his stock of provisions down to danger point. His superfluous troops were so numerous that it was likely they could battle their way through the investing force near the road to the Lupkow Pass, at a time when the main Russian southern army near Lupkow was straining every nerve to meet the **Kusmanek's hopeful** attacks of the relieving army from **calculations** Hungary. If only the troops making the sortie could break through the line of investment they would take Brussiloff's men in the rear at the moment when the relieving forces were pressing on the Russian front. The result of this would be something more important than the relief of Przemysl. The Russian forces round the Dukla Pass would be cut off, together with a considerable portion of Dimitrieff's army fronting Cracow, in Western Galicia. All the land between Cracow and Przemysl would be cleared of Russians, and there would be an admirable opportunity, after the Russian front was broken, of turning and encircling the entire Russian forces in Galicia. In short, what was contemplated, as the result of an overwhelming sortie from Przemysl, was the complete destruction of the southern Russian army under General Brussiloff.

Brussiloff had no siege-artillery, and even his available force of field-guns was not large. No idea

FRENCH AND RUSSIAN PRISONERS PEELING POTATOES IN A DETENTION CAMP.
These two pictures are from German sources, and purposely exaggerate the provisioning of the camps.

of a bombardment duel with the great pieces of ordnance at Przemysl could be entertained. The Russian commander could profit only by the enormous number of troops in the fortress and revert to the old-fashioned method of reduction by famine. Only five divisions of Russian troops of the third class, old reservists more than forty years of age, were detached for the siege operations. They were placed under the command of General Selivanov, a veteran of seventy years, who had served in all the Russian wars since the Turkish war of 1877. His forces at first were much inferior to the Przemysl garrison, there being

WAR TIME IN AUSTRIA'S SERBIAN PROVINCES—A GERMAN ARTIST'S IMPRESSION OF A STONE QUARRY WHERE MEN OF THE HERZEGOVINIAN LANDSTURM WERE AT WORK.

about 100,000 Russians to 170,000 Germans, Austrians, and Hungarians. General Selivanov's field-guns were largely the outworn artillery of the southern army, the tubes having lost their exact rifling by constant use since the beginning of the previous August. When new field-artillery arrived for the army in Galicia General Brussiloff, instead of sending the old guns back to Kieff to be re-rifled, gave them to General Selivanov.

The old general kept his batteries well out of range of the great new guns of Przemysl, and entrenched on a wide circle of hills at a long distance **Russian and Austrian** from the girdle of forts. His sole object **chivalry** was to stop anybody from getting in or out of the beleaguered fortress-city. He made no attack, but simply waited until General Kusmanek attempted a sortie. Then, as the enemy troops advanced beyond the shelter of their great guns of position, they were shot down close to the wire entanglements in front of the Russian trenches.

No serious attempt was made to break the ring of investment until December 10th. General Kusmanek was then informed by wireless that a relieving army was advancing from the Carpathians and steadily gaining ground towards Limanova. Thereupon the garrison of Przemysl began to make sorties in great force. Although they helped the relieving army to gain a little more ground, they did not succeed themselves in breaking through Selivanov's circle of defences, for the besieging commander was reinforced at some expense to the Russian fighting-line on the Carpathian front, and all that Kusmanek achieved was to reduce considerably the amount of mouths he had to feed. The siege then went on in a quiet, leisurely manner for a month. The situation at Christmas was quite friendly and peaceful. By means of their airmen the Russians distributed thousands of Christmas-cards over the invested fortress. "We wish a happy and a peaceful Christmas to the heroic defenders of Przemysl. Let peace reign on earth, and happiness in the hearts of men." Thus ran one of the cards of greeting. On January 12th, the Russian Christmas, the garrison returned this act of Christian chivalry. Not a shot was fired, and the Austrian outposts came forward to the Russian advanced guard and gave

them Christmas-trees. But in the middle of January Kusmanek began to grow seriously alarmed at the rapid diminution of his food supply. More of the garrison was sacrificed in vain attempts at a successful sortie, while the Russian sappers began to drive their trenches closer to the ring of forts. The decisive struggle took place in the middle of February, when the southern Russian army was swinging round from its position on the Dukla Pass and winning ground towards Lupkow. Instead of the relieving army in the Carpathians helping the garrison of Przemysl, the garrison troops had to fling themselves out in fierce night attacks, less with a view to breaking through than with the design to compel Selivanov to ask for more reinforcements.

The old Russian general had a difficult task. As his lines ran in a much larger circle than the ring of forts he was investing, he needed many more troops than the men he was wearing down. As the power of making attacks really rested with the beleaguered Austrians, they could mass at night and break forth for an advance in any direction they chose. The Russian commander could not concentrate in advance against them, but had to leave the defence of the assailed section of trenches in the hands of the ordinary number of men there. The only consequence of the repeated attempts to break through the investing line, conducted by the valiant Hungarian General Tamassy, was that General Selivanov was compelled to use the proper number of men in garrisoning his trenches —two to a yard—which, on a circular **Fall of outer** front of fifty miles required an army of **fortifications** 176,000 troops. These were infantry-men, and the total Russian besieging forces may at last have amounted to 200,000 men.

Even this was not very much more than the number of foes against whom they were operating. And these foes had an overwhelming superiority in heavy artillery. But with undaunted courage the Russians sapped forward, building their trenches by special devices, perfected since the outbreak of hostilities, which gave some protection to the troops against even the heaviest projectiles. The outer forts and field fortifications soon fell into the hands of the Russians, who mined and counter-mined, completing each piece of their mole-like work by a night attack with bayonets and hand-grenades.

But though they were able to push their trenches so near as to bring in view the churches and roofs of Przemysl, they remained incapable of capturing one of the main forts. The Austrians asserted that from November 12th, 1914, to March 1st, 1915, merely three shells fell in the city. Having only short-range artillery, all that the Russian commander could do with it was to cover every path and road by which the enemy could make sorties. He relied almost entirely on shrapnel, which he employed against the hostile troops as they came into the open. Every night the Russian searchlights on the distant hills swept all the country in a regular, constant manner, seeking for signs of a sortie, and telegraphing to the gunners the range and direction of any advancing body of hostile troops.

In the second week of March the situation of the defenders became desperate. For some time they had been subsisting on short rations, but these had given out suddenly ; for it was found that a large store of tinned meat had been either supplied in an old, rotten condition by some fraudulent army contractor, or else had gone wrong

Brussiloff, knowing the position of affairs in Przemysl, had foreseen all the attacks of the relieving armies. Indeed, one of the chief reasons why only three shells fell in the beleaguered city during the siege of five months was that the Austrian movements had been long foreseen. The shells had been saved with a design to employ them in shattering the supreme attack by the relieving armies.

To General Brussiloff the condition of Przemysl was a matter of only secondary importance. His main object was to defeat all the forces that Germany, Austria, and Hungary could bring against him across the Carpathian Mountains. The Hungarian plain, sown with winter wheat, sufficient to nourish the Central Empires for months, was the grand objective of the southern Russian army. Przemysl was only valuable as a means of luring the hostile relieving armies into a difficult position during the winter months, when the Russian War Minister could not arm the million or more new Russian troops waiting for equipment. **Brussiloff's grand objective**

General Brussiloff was offered a powerful park of heavy siege-guns in January, 1915, but he said he could do without it, if it could be used with effect elsewhere. The park was, in fact, employed along the opposite flank of the great

SPOILS OF WAR—RIFLES AND MUNITIONS CAPTURED BY AUSTRIANS IN THE CARPATHIAN CAMPAIGN.

Russian battle-front, and the Siege of Przemysl went on with extraordinary quietness except for the sorties of the famishing garrison. When, however, in March, 1915, the offensive movement of the German and Austrian relieving armies culminated in an attack upon Brussiloff's Carpathian front, there was no need to prolong any further the agony of the beleaguered fortress town. By then the siege had served its main purpose, and had dragged the forces of Austria-Hungary beyond the limit of their strength. To complete his grand design Brussiloff needed at once the 200,000 men detained around Przemysl. So General Selivanov was at last ordered to close in upon the doomed city and carry it, if need be, by storm.

On Sunday, March 14th, the veteran general opened the attack, for which all the means had been available since the previous January. The operations were

through being kept too long by the military authorities. The preserved meat was quite putrescent ; it was impossible to use it in any way, and there was nothing left for the garrison to eat.

General Kusmanek informed the Austro-German armies along the Carpathians of the situation by wireless messages, with the result that everything possible was done to relieve the falling fortress. The battles upon the crest and slopes of the mountains raged with terrific fury. Large German reinforcements arrived for General von Linsingen, and every man that Austria-Hungary could at once put into the field was railed up through the Latorcza valley to strengthen General Böhm Ermolli. In a magnificent spirit of heroism the Germans, Austrians, and Hungarians fought their way through the snow, ascending and descending the frozen rampart of rock, and deploying around the upper vast reaches of the San River. Holding again the Lupkow Pass, the Austrians swept out towards Baligrod, and at the same time advanced from the Uzsok Pass northward. By a tremendous effort and an enormous sacrifice of men the Teutons and Hungarians almost touched the railway thirty miles south of Przemysl. Unfortunately for them, General **Attacks of relieving armies**

started in the north by the village of Malkovice, along the railway line from Jaroslav. Heavy howitzers were brought up by the railway, and the bombardment of the strong main fort dominating the highway to the north was begun. At the same time the smaller works on this northern section were assailed, and the hostile batteries were so well mastered that on Tuesday, March 16th, the Russian infantry carried the heights and entrenched themselves within rifle-shot of the forts. The Austrians tried to recover some of the ground by using an armoured train along the railway. The train came along at night with a large body of troops in the hinder carriages, but the Russian searchlight men spotted it and directed the guns on it, and the armoured train was swiftly and completely wrecked by shell fire.

The Russians advanced in open formation, by crawling in short rushes, and drove the defenders from the miles of trenches along the high-road and railway. The ground was covered with snow, making it easy for searchlights on both sides to light up advancing or retreating troops, who then came under a tempest of shrapnel. Happily, there was a birch wood, with a stretch of thick, short undergrowth, along the line the Russians were taking, and it served them as cover from observation till they were close on the railway.

AUSTRIAN HOWITZER BATTERY IN ACTION.

we should fall into the power of the enemy like a helpless crowd. Hero - soldiers, we must break through, and we shall ! "

This impassioned and moving appeal appears to have been made to all the infantry and cavalry forces of the garrison. But such was the feeling of utter dispiritment, due perhaps partly to want of sufficient food, that only 20,000 men answered it. These were mainly Hungarians, comprising the 23rd Honved Division, part of the 23rd Landwehr Brigade, and the 4th Regiment of Hussars. Led by the brave Hungarian General Tamassy, this fighting remnant of the garrison marched out beyond the forts

All through the night the screech of shells and hum of bullets were terrible, and in the blue light of the bursting bombs and in the lanes of flame from the searchlights, with a fort exploding on the skyline, the scene was a sort of ghastly modern Doomsday. The soldiers' faces in the blue radiance had a strange and eerie appearance.

The great forts tried to retrieve the defeat on the northern section by a continual bombardment of the closing-in lines of Russian trenches. Twenty thousand rounds of big-gun ammunition were fired daily on March 15th and March 16th. But the Russians were too deeply entrenched to be shattered by even this terrific fire. They continued to advance from the south as well as from the north, **Kusmanek's eloquent** occupying the village of Krasiczyn south-**proclamation** westward. It was against the southern Russian trenches that most of the great shells were flung on March 17th, preparatory to the final sortie of the garrison. General Kusmanek served out the last rations, and issued a proclamation to the troops :

"Soldiers, half a year has passed while we children of almost all the nationalities of our beloved country have incessantly stood shoulder to shoulder against the enemy. Thanks to God's help and your bravery, I have succeeded, despite the enemy's attacks, despite cold and privations, in defending the fortress against the enemy. You have already done much to win the acknowledgments of the Commander-in-Chief, the gratitude of the country, and even the respect of the enemy.

"Yonder in our beloved country, thousands and thousands of hearts are beating for us. Millions are waiting with held breath for news of us.

"Heroes, I am about to make my last demand of you. The honour of our Army and country requires it. I am going to lead you out, a steel wedge, to break through the iron ring of the foe, and then, with unflagging efforts, move farther and farther till we rejoin our Army, which, at the price of stubborn battles, has already approached quite near to us. We are on the eve of a big fight, for the enemy will not willingly allow the booty to slip through his fingers. But, remember, gallant defenders of Przemysl, each one of you must be possessed by the single idea, 'Forward, ever forward!' All that stands in our way must be crushed.

"Soldiers, we have distributed our last stores ; and the honour of our country, and of every one of us, forbids that after such a hard-fought, glorious, and victorious struggle

AUSTRIAN ARTILLERY IN THE CARPATHIANS.

at five o'clock on Friday morning, March 19th. They advanced in an easterly direction in a determined manner, but were unable after nine hours' fighting to reach the Russian trenches. Eight thousand of them were killed, and nearly four thousand were taken prisoners.

At the same time as the Przemysl garrison made its last vain essay to break through, a furious battle was opened all round Przemysl by the relieving armies. The attack raged especially west and east of Gorlice. The Austro-Hungarians used 12 in. howitzer fire under cover of which twenty battalions flung themselves against the Russian trenches, but they were held up on the wire entanglements, and there shot down by machine-guns and magazine rifles. Another attack was **Quarter not asked** delivered by a Honved brigade against the **nor given** height held by our allies near Ciezkovice.

Only a Russian battalion held the position at first, and their line was taken, but they counter-attacked, with two battalions hurrying to their aid, and beat the enemy back by noon. An hour afterwards the entire 39th Honved Division swept out in a great charge. Despite their heavy losses, the Hungarians got through the wire entanglements and took the height. But the Russians were reinforced, and drove them back. Three times the position was lost and won, but at four o'clock in the afternoon the remnant of Russians made a fourth counter-attack. Such was the frenzy of battle on both sides that neither asked nor gave quarter; and after slaughtering all their foes the Russians recovered their trenches. The swaying battle-line extended from Gorlice in Western Galicia, across the Carpathians, to Svidnik in Hungary, then back over the Carpathians near the Lupkow Pass, to Baligrod and Lutoviska; thence over the Dniester and along the Stry River. In no place did the relieving armies break through. All their vigorous and costly attacks were intended solely to withdraw attention from Przemysl, and to provide favourable conditions for the final sortie of the garrison.

But, as we have seen, the larger part of the troops in Przemysl were much too enfeebled to attempt to break out. After the Hungarian division was repulsed, no course was left to General Kusmanek but to prepare for the act of surrender.

Meanwhile the Russians pressed the attack relentlessly on Friday night and Saturday against the east and north front. But across the sound of the guns there suddenly came a series of still more thunderous explosions. Shocks

RUSSIAN ARMOURED MOTOR-CAR IN USE ON THE GALICIAN FRONT.

like earthquakes were felt. The Austrians were blowing up the great forts, motor-batteries, magazines, bridges, and everything likely to be useful to the victors. One of the smaller forts with quick-firing guns was captured by the Russians in time to save it from entire destruction. But all the main works of defence were so thoroughly dynamited that Przemysl lost all its importance as a place of strength. The famous 12 in. Skoda howitzers were exploded into fragments. Then every soldier was ordered to destroy his rifle. It was a pitiful sight to see them do it. Many kissed the rifle first, and wept while hammering it to bits.

This had to be done, as there was no time to gather the rifles and destroy them in one pile. **The main forts dynamited** Then, as the Russian shells began to fall on the aeroplane sheds, four Austrian airmen made their last voyage from the fortress in the two last machines left intact. The scene below them was indescribably terrible. From the exploding ammunition stores smoke and flame shot up in clouds, the military buildings and warehouses were on fire, and the flying machines were in danger of being overturned by the force of the explosions. Then on Monday morning, March 22nd, 1915, General Kusmanek,

who had opened negotiations for surrender on Saturday, gave up the fortress.

It was not the first time that Przemysl had been taken by a Russian force. It had been first captured by the Russian Duke Oleg in the year 907. It was afterwards lost, but again besieged and retaken in 1031 by the Grand Duke Jaroslav. Under the successors of this prince of the House of Moscow the whole of Galicia became an important Russian Duchy, peopled almost entirely by Russians. But when Russia weakened under the attacks of the Mongols, their neighbours, the Poles, became the leaders of the Slav world, and the Polish King Casimir, after a long struggle, got possession of Przemysl, and **Fruit of a hundred victories** subdued all the Russians in Galicia. Then at the time of the division of Poland, the Russians were compelled to allow their old Duchy of Galicia to fall into the hands of a still more alien race than the Poles—the Austrians.

The recovery of the "Gibraltar" of Galicia was thus a matter of great rejoicing among the Russians. It marked the beginning of the last stage of the slow, painful development of the great Slav race. At the time when the Mongols were overwhelming China, destroying Mohammedan culture, sweeping down towards India, and finally menacing the entire destruction of European civilisation, Russia had been the breakwater of the white races. The breakwater had been submerged by the Mongolian flood, but before going under it had sufficiently broken the force of the barbaric hordes to enable Poland, Silesia, and Hungary to drive out the invaders. Then, after remaining vassals for two centuries to the Mongolian power, the Russians, under the leadership of their princes of the House of Moscow, conquered their conquerors, and by winning all the Mongolian land of Siberia, established a great empire without thinking to do so; for all they first set out to achieve was to break the Mongolian power so as to render impossible another great invasion from the east. Meanwhile the old Russian Duchy of Galicia, in which the native Russians, under first Polish and then Austrian and Hungarian tyranny, had sunk into the condition of half-savage peasants living in extreme poverty in mud huts, excited the attention of the free Russian races.' For, in spite of centuries of persecution, most of the Russians of Galicia still held to the Russian form of religion. Their religion, their language, and their folk-lore were indeed the only elements of national culture remaining to the lost and oppressed Galicians, who by the irony of historic memories of their former wealth were still known as "Red-Gold" Russians.

All this goes to explain the general enthusiasm excited in the people of all the Russias by the news of the recapture of Przemysl. To them it was something more important than a victory. It was the long-desired fruit of a hundred victories, beginning with the uprising against the Mongols, and concluding with the recent defeat of the first-line armies of Austria and Hungary. Before the Poles captured Galicia from their weakened fellow-Slavs, the town of the Carpathian foothills had been known by its original Russian name of Peremysl—the Polish form of Przemysl was a later growth. To the Russians it was a mournful memory of ancient national disasters. So, as in the case of Lemberg, one of their first acts was to restore to the Russian city its old Russian name.

From a military point of view the fall of Przemysl, which gave the Russians control over the trunk railway of Galicia, and thus strengthened their hold on the recovered duchy, was an event of high importance; for the Austrians then lost about one quarter of the territory of the Dual Monarchy, with a population of eight million. As Galicia had contributed to the Austro-Hungarian Army about one-fifth of its recruits, the effect of the loss was increased. Moreover, Galicia was a province of enormous natural wealth. It was the only centre of oil production in the Teutonic Empire; its coal reserves were calculated at twenty-five thousand million tons, and its great salt-

THE LONELY SHRINE—GERMAN ARTILLERYMEN GREET THEIR AUSTRIAN ALLIES BESIDE A WAYSIDE SYMBOL OF THE PRINCE OF PEACE.

WITH THE AUSTRIANS IN THE SNOW-COVERED CARPATHIANS—GUNNER ABOUT TO FIRE ONE OF THE HEAVY HOWITZERS WHICH PROVED SO EFFECTIVE IN SIEGE OPERATIONS.

mines, almost within reach of Dimitrieff's army, were the salt-treasury of Europe.

The last matter did not seem of much importance on March 22nd, 1915. The question whether the Germans and Austrians would lack an abundance of salt did not seem to have much bearing upon the course of the war. But common salt is properly known as sodium chloride. It can easily be resolved into its elements of sodium and chlorine. Chlorine can be obtained in vast quantities from the Galician salt-mines in the form of a greenish-yellow gas, which eats the lungs out of the men that breathe it, leaving their dead, agonised bodies purple from lack of oxygen. This was why the fall of Przemysl was a matter of extreme ·concern to the German and Austrian General Staffs.

The fall of the fortress released General Selivanov's army, together with a large part of the army of General Dimitrieff, which had assisted in the final operations. General Dimitrieff was holding the Dunajec at Tarnov, and the great salt-mines were only about forty miles distant from his front. By the fall of Przemysl his railway communications through Lemberg to Kieff were much strengthened. His army could now be fed with a stream of munitions that would be calculated to carry him quickly towards the salt-mines at Wieliczka. Indeed, he had reached these mines in his first fierce swoop towards Cracow during the previous autumn. As we now know, the secret new plan of campaign with poison gases, drawn up by the German Staff and approved by the Austrian Staff, was based upon the resources of the Galician salt-mines. The Russians, trusting to the signature of the German plenipotentiary appended to the Hague Convention forbidding the use of asphyxiating gases in civilised warfare, did not guess at the time how menacing was their position from the German point of view. Had only the diabolical German scheme been suspected, it could have been at once countered by using the quarter of a million troops set free by the fall of Przemysl to reinforce the Dunajec line for an immediate advance

Salt-mines and poison gas to the next river, the Raba, where from the surrounding heights the salt-mines could have been bombarded and captured. As we shall see, it was partly the fear that the Russians should get information of what was going on and attempt to capture the salt resources of the Teutons, that determined the future course of the campaign in both the eastern and western theatres of war. The guilty are always suspicious, and though the Allies do not seem clearly to have foreknown what the Germans intended doing, the Germans were apprehensive of being attacked before they had fully prepared their new, ghastly, scientifically-savage instrument of torture and destruction.

Although the Russian Secret Service is often regarded as superior to the similar Intelligence system of the Germans, no foreknowledge was obtained of the vital importance of the Galician salt-mines. So far as could be seen, their capture would only interfere with the enemy's cookery and means of preserving meat, and the Russian Commander-in-Chief thought that a descent on the Hungarian plain, though a far slower and more difficult operation than the short advance on the salt-mines, promised results of more importance; for the condition of affairs in Przemysl when the Russians entered the fallen city was significant of a spirit of general disintegration in the Austro-Hungarian Army. The captured garrison consisted of 131,000 men and nearly 4,000 officers.

Fallen fortress's ghastly contrasts

Very few of the officers cared anything about the hardships endured by their men, or made any attempt to relieve their condition. Up to the last they had their three meals a day, with fresh meat, wines, and every luxury, while their own orderlies begged for a slice of bread. The private soldiers were seen to fall in the street from lack of nourishment. Yet the officers, until the day before the surrender, retained a large store of oats to feed their 2,000 private thoroughbred riding-horses. The horses were at last killed to prevent them from falling into the hands of the Russians; and when the conquerors entered the town, they found the Austrian and Hungarian soldiers, half-crazed for want of food, gouging into the bodies of the slaughtered thoroughbreds, their faces and hands smeared red with blood as they devoured the raw and dripping flesh. Some of the Cossacks, who are by no means men of a sentimental or delicate disposition, wept like women when they beheld the shocking spectacle of starving men gorging themselves on raw meat with the fury of starving wolves.

It was because the Austrian officers in Przemysl conducted themselves in this manner that most of their men had refused to march out and fight in answer to the appeal of General Kusmanek. Kusmanek, a Bohemian by race, was distinguished from the Austrian officers. A carrier pigeon was cooked for his last meal, but instead of eating it, he gave it to a wounded soldier. His great defect was, in fact, his general kindness of heart. He should have sent half of his garrison, at least, in December, to fight their way out, or to be killed or captured. He should have despatched all the fugitive troops that had taken shelter in the fortress, and turned the guns on them if they tried to return. Przemysl might then have held out for a year, as the probability would have been against the Russians capturing it. But as General Kusmanek was in constant communication with the Archdukes and Court favourites forming the high command of the Austrian forces, it is likely that this course was ordered by his superior officers.

WAR DOGS OF THE RUSSIAN ISMAILLOVSKY REGIMENT.

CHAPTER LXV.

PRZEMYSL AND THE ADVANCE OF THE GREAT GERMAN PHALANX.

Capture of Lupkow Pass and Menace to Hungary—Disgrace and Dismissal of Hindenburg and Rise of Mackensen—Falkenhayn Creates the Grand Phalanx to Capture Calais—Position of Hungary Compels him to Swing the Phalanx against the Southern Russian Army—Tremendous Hurricane Fire against the Short Russian Front in Western Galicia—Radko Dimitrieff Stands Up against the Withering Blast—Holding the Austrian Archduke on the Dunajec, he Withdraws the Remnant of his Men from the Biala River—Mackensen's Phalanx Tries to Advance Through the Gap and Get to the Rear of the Southern Russian Army—Magnificent and Decisive Stand Made by Dimitrieff against Terrible Odds—General Ivanoff Sweeps into the Battlefield with Strong Reinforcements—Mackensen Defeated by Superior Strategy on the Wisloka—General Brussiloff's Victories in Bukovina and South of Lemberg—Battles of Jaroslav and Sieniawa—The Army of the Austrian Archduke Defeated in Poland and Northern Galicia—Russians Win a Week's Breathing Space owing to the Slow Movement of the Grand Phalanx—Why the German Commander Could only Move his Enormous Fighting Force at the Rate of Three Miles a Day—Russian Front in Peril at the Salient of Przemysl—Having Removed all their Stores, the Russian Troops Retire from the Town.

AFTER the fall of Przemysl. it was known, both from the reports of prisoners and from information received from Russian Intelligence officers, that the general condition of Austrian troops along the Carpathian battle-line was deplorable. For the Austrian officers were more careful in looking after their own interests than in tending to the well-being of the soldiers under their command. We have given in the previous chapter some of the extraordinary figures concerning the sickness prevailing in the Austrian Army. It was fairly evident to General Brussiloff that the military forces of the Dual Monarchy were approaching a condition of extreme weakness. Only by the help of half a million German troops did they still hold the rampart of the Carpathians. The Russian design was, therefore, to press the enemy most strongly at his weakest point, and while holding the main German eastern armies from the Niemen to the Lower Vistula, to advance over the Carpathians into Hungary.

The advance began the day after the fall of Przemysl. Half of the 200,000 troops released by the success of the

GENERAL ARTAMONOV.

The Russian Governor of Przemysl photographed in his quarters during the Russian occupation. Note the portrait of the Emperor of Austria untouched. Had the situation been reversed, it is certain a portrait of the Tsar would have been defaced by the Austro-Germans.

siege operations were sent southward towards the Dukla and Lupkow Passes. There they strengthened the front of the Russian southern army, and the reinforced troops began steadily to push both the Austrians and the Germans over the crests of the mountains. In the neighbourhood of the Dukla the three road passes of Polyanka, the Dukla, and the Jaliska were won by the Russians, and they descended the Hungarian slopes towards Bartfeld, Svidnik, and the valley of the Laborcz River. Then in the higher and more densely-wooded heights between the Lupkow and the Uzsok Passes our Allies conquered, in the first week of April, 1915, the towering forested ridge of the Polonina Mountains and approached Rostok Pass. From this point they progressed by fierce and incessant forest fighting through the high snows to the Smolink Hills, situated beyond the main Carpathian ridge, on the Hungarian decline. The only reverse the Russians met with was around the railway-station of Mesolaborcz, in Hungary, where one of their divisions was trapped in a valley and badly cut up.

But this was only a small, temporary check in a great and steadily-successful advance by something like three-

IN A RUSSIAN TRENCH—AWAITING THE ORDER FOR A
BAYONET CHARGE.

quarters of a million men of the southern army. Every
day the Russians took from 2,000 to 7,000 prisoners, with
a few mountain guns and a dozen machine-guns. This
was the regular result of the steady process of attrition
by which all the hostile forces were being worn down and
forced back in disorder into the Hungarian plain. In the
second week in April the enemy's powers of resistance
suddenly weakened in a general manner, and the Russians
were able to advance twenty miles in
twenty-four hours between the Dukla and
Uzsok Passes. About this time a heavy
snowstorm raged on the great heights,
and the more robust Russian peasants advanced through it
on a ninety-mile front, over pathless steeps, with six feet of
drifted snow in places. By sheer superiority of physique
they pushed back, in the frozen tempest, the less enduring
Teutons and Magyars, and fought their way to the upper
waters of the Uzsok River. The German regiments sent
to relieve the Austrian army had to renew their front

**Fighting on
Carpathian Heights**

line four times. Then they, too, fell back towards the
lower slopes on the Hungarian side, where the snow was
melting in the warmer climate.

In one month's fighting on the Carpathian heights the
Russians captured 40,000 men and 4,000 officers, twenty
guns, and an immense number of machine-guns. The
Austrians had four distinct armies deployed along the
mountain range from Bartfeld to the Rumanian frontier.
Assisting them were ten German army corps. Then
another Austrian army, operating from Cracow, faced
General Dimitrieff along the Dunajec River. Every available man from the Dual Monarchy was thus massed against
the southern Russian army which General Brussiloff was
pushing over the Carpathians into the Hungarian wheat-
plain. So fierce and relentless was the pressure exercised
from Galicia against Hungary that the German General
Staff had to stand on the defensive in France, Flanders,
and Poland in order to collect the army corps needed
to save Hungary. At the beginning of the third week
in April it was reckoned that the opposing forces on the
Carpathians numbered 3,000,000 men.

The main points in the conflict were the Homonna
Railway, ascending the Lupkow Pass, and the Munkacs
Railway, crossing near the Tuchla Pass. On the Homonna
line the Russians by mid-April were twenty miles into
Hungary. On the Munkacs line the Germans were still
trying to advance towards Stry. But they were in
danger of having their lines of communication cut by
a sharp Russian advance into the valley of the Theiss.
On April 18th the weather changed at last and brought
the Russians for a time to a standstill. For the warm spring
rain washed the snow from the Carpathian
peaks, with the result that the mountain   **Capture of Lupkow**
torrents were turned into turbulent   **Pass**
floods and the lower valleys into lakes,
while in many places land which had been hard and frozen
was transformed into impassable swamps. Being mainly
on the southern slope of the mountains, with a web of
railways close behind them, the Austrians and Germans
tried to profit by the spring floods, and brought up heavy
artillery—8 in., 11 in., and 12 in. howitzers—into the Carpathian region. Then, in the last week of April, they
delivered a great massed attack against the heights held
by the Russians upon the Homonna and Munkacs lines.
But the Russians beat them down by machine-gun and rifle
fire and hand-grenades.

The Lupkow Pass was captured and an advance was
made from the Hungarian side against the Uzsok Pass.
This threatened to cut off the German force defending
the pass, and when this was done there would be a
gap of seventy miles in the Carpathian defences—quite
a large enough door for Brussiloff to flood the Hungarian plain with a large force of troops. Such was the
position in the last week in April, 1915. On Field-Marshal
von Hindenburg, who was responsible for the disastrous
situation, fell the disgrace of the disaster. He had completely failed. In his bull-like rushes against Ivangorod
and Warsaw, Grodno and Prasnysch, he had wasted army
corps after army corps. Possessing, in a railway system
designed by the elder Moltke, the finest instrument of
invasion in the world, he had done little more than turn
it into a huge platform for military acrobatics that wasted
men by the hundred thousand without producing a single
definite important gain.

A council of war was held on the eastern front, at which
the Emperor William decided to dismiss Hindenburg from
his high command. The decision was not made public,
by reason of the extraordinary popular faith in the victor
of Tannenberg. But for all that the act of dismissal
was carried out. Hindenburg retired for a time at least
from the Army, and devoted himself once more to the
pleasures of the punch-bowl and a country life. His
appearance at Ypres was merely a pretence. He was not
in command there, but was sent, for the sake of his false

Last moments of H.M.S. Majestic, torpedoed off Gallipoli May 27th, 1915.

A trench in Flanders—where British soldiers fought and died.

German shrapnel bursting behind a hastily-built French barricade.

French engineers constructing a reserve trench behind the firing-lines.

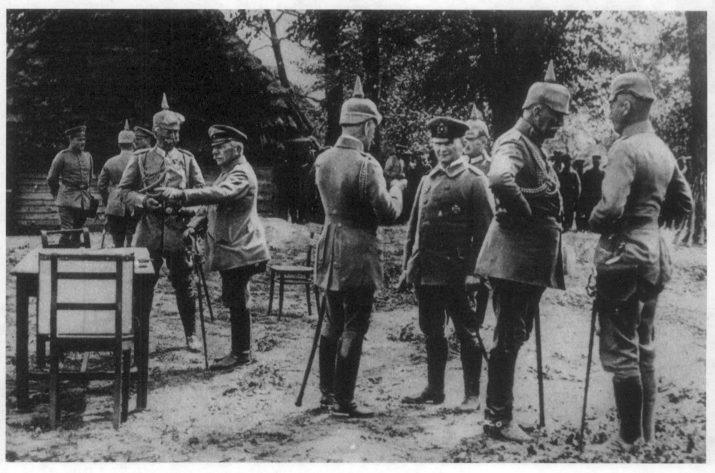

Kaiser (left) and General von Emmich at German headquarters in France.

reputation as a conqueror, to hearten the troops of the Duke of Würtemberg and the Crown Prince of Bavaria.

The former Minister for War, General von Falkenhayn, who had succeeded the younger Moltke as Chief of Staff, took over the enormous task of directing operations on both the eastern and the western fronts. General von Mackensen, who had become the favourite general of the Kaiser by reason of the skill and fury in attack he had shown in the battles round Lodz, was appointed to lead the main German forces in Galicia. General von Linsingen, commanding the German troops on the

Mackensen succeeds Munkacs-Stry line, was further reinforced **Hindenburg** and given larger powers of command.

The Austrian Archduke Friedrich, nominally in chief command over the Austro-Hungarian forces, was placed under the control of Mackensen; the Archduke Ferdinand, commanding the army along the Dunajec, was also subordinated to Mackensen, and all the other Austrian and Hungarian commands were also strictly subjected to German leadership.

What especially angered General von Falkenhayn was the lack of strategical insight displayed by Field-Marshal von Hindenburg and Hindenburg's Chief of Staff, General von Ludendorff. After their failure along the Bzura and Pilica front, and along the East Prussian borders, they had responded too blindly to the offensive movement made by the Russians in the Carpathian region. All they had done, when General Brussiloff pressed over the Dukla Pass and menaced the Lupkow Pass, was to concentrate against the advancing Russian lines. In the opinion of General von Falkenhayn, the Russian pressure should have been countered by a sudden and sharp flank attack from Cracow against the Dunajec and Biala river lines. To this purpose the formidable German reinforcements should have been used, instead of being wasted in indecisive mountain conflicts on the Russian positions in the Carpathians.

The correctness of this view was generally admitted at the Austro-German council of war, and the Kaiser entrusted Falkenhayn with the task of remedying Hindenburg's and Ludendorff's mistakes. Ever since Falkenhayn's failure on the western front to break through at Ypres and capture Calais, he had been preparing to make good this plan of his in the spring of 1915. All through the winter and early spring the German artillerymen in France and Flanders had been ordered to observe a strict economy in the use of high-explosive shells. This was the explanation of the momentary allied ascendancy in artillery power, remarked by both the French and British commanders at the close of 1914. Germany was quite as formidable in heavy armament as she had been, and it was calculated that in the manufacture of munitions she was still seventy-five per cent. more efficient than Britain and France combined. In all German and Austrian armament factories the work had been kept going day and night by three eight-hour shifts in the early months of the war. But after the defeat at Ypres the supply of munitions was increased, by engrossing every power-lathe formerly used for ordinary work, and setting the armament mechanics and labourers on a general twelve-hour shift, the men working in weekly turns of twelve hours' day work and twelve hours' night work.

The fierce winter battle on the Bzura, Pilica, and Nieder

Rivers, and the operations of the German army of half a million men north of Warsaw along the Bobr, Narew, and Niemen Rivers, necessitated the use of a vast number of high-explosive shells. In all their battles against the Russians the Germans used their superior artillery power in a wasteful manner. This waste was partly balanced by the economy observed upon the western front, and with the extreme speeding up of all the gun-making work and munition factories, General Falkenhayn had his new war machine ready for operations by the middle of April, 1915. Krupp and Skoda and other gunmakers had provided him with two thousand new heavy pieces of ordnance, and three millions of large, heavy, high-explosive shells. There were also 2,000 new or fairly unworn pieces of field-artillery, and for these also there were thousands of truckloads of high-explosive shell ready. At the same time the manufacture of machine-guns had gone on at high speed, enabling the ordinary fire-power of the infantry to be enormously increased.

It was Falkenhayn's original intention to use this new war-machine to break the Franco-British front, either at the western end near Calais, where he made his first

FIELD-TELEPHONE STATION NEAR THE AUSTRIAN HEADQUARTERS IN GALICIA.

attempt, or at the eastern end near Metz, where the nephew of the elder Moltke had proposed to attack before he was superseded as Chief of Staff by Falkenhayn. But with Hindenburg's complete failure in both strategy and tactics, in the eastern theatre of war, Falkenhayn's scheme for a decisive spring campaign in the west had to be postponed. So successful was the southern Russian army under General Brussiloff that by the middle of April it was in a position to advance into the Hungarian plain and cut the communications of all the German and Austrian troops on the **Falkenhayn's Western** Carpathian front. By his extraordinary **scheme postponed** success, combined with the general lack of munitions of war in Russia, General Brussiloff drew on his men the crushing blow intended originally for the French and British troops.

The position of the southern Russian army was very curious. It was advancing in great force all along the Carpathians on a front of more than one hundred and fifty miles; but on its right flank, looking towards Cracow, there was a lateral position of about seventy miles, held only by a small entrenched army of 160,000 men, under the Bulgarian commander, General Dimitrieff. By selecting for attack two places on this short lateral front, the

IN PRZEMYSL AFTER THE
FALL.

existence of all the Russian
armies in Galicia and Hungary
could be menaced. The
Austro - German means of
communication round Cracow
were excellent. There were
two lines of railways running
from Cracow to Dimitrieff's
positions at Tarnov, near the
Dunajec River, and at Gorlice,
on the Ropa stream. Then,
midway between Cracow and
Tarnov, the two railways
were connected by a cross-
country line, enabling troops
to be manœuvred in trains from south to north or
north to south. In the south, on the Lower Dunajec,
was the railway junction of Neu Sandez, from which
another railway ran into Northern
Hungary. There were thus three railways, by means of which the thousands
of heavy howitzers and the millions of
high-explosive shells could be transported for action
against the narrow lateral Russian front in Western
Galicia.

**Hurricane fire
against Dimitrieff**

Towards the end of April General
Dimitrieff observed the concentration
of enemy forces against his line.
He was far from suspecting that the
greatest military machine known in history was being brought against his comparatively small forces. He asked for
reinforcements, and General Ivanoff, on
the Nida front north of him, and
General Brussiloff, on the Carpathian
front south of him, sent what men and
guns they could spare.
But when the blow fell on the
night of April 30th, 1915, the force
of it was beyond anything that man
had experienced.

In estimates published before the
war, the entire artillery power of Germany was placed at 4,000 guns and
howitzers. This was a larger number
of pieces of ordnance than either France
or Russia was credited with possessing.
Our Army, for instance, only had seven
hundred guns. About seven hundred

guns was the number used by General
Dimitrieff to defend his lines along the
Dunajec and the Biala Rivers until the fall
of Przemysl enabled him to increase his
artillery. When reinforced, he had about
250,000 troops between the Lower Vistula
and the Carpathian heights, but a good
many of them lacked their artillery corps,
as there was still a serious shortage of
munitions. Massed against them were
more than a million Germans, Austrians,
and Hungarians, with their artillery corps
of about 2,000 guns, behind which was
Falkenhayn's enormous new siege train
of 2,000 heavy pieces, including some
howitzers of 17 in. calibre.

The front was far too short for the
deployment of the enemy forces. Both
the guns and the
troops were arranged
in a step for-
mation, or
echelon system. Yet the
echelons were so close
together that there was a
practically solid line of
front from the point where
the Dunajec flowed into the
Vistula to the point where
the Biala valley merged
into the Carpathian heights.
The Austrian army of the
Archduke Ferdinand ad-
vanced on the night of
April 30th against the
Dunajec front. Mackensen,
with part of his troops and
1,000 pieces of siege-artillery
in addition to his ordinary
artillery corps, attacked
south of Tarnov, between that town and Gorlice.

**Falkenhayn's enor-
mous siege-train**

The Archduke was unfortunate, as Austrian Archdukes
sometimes are on the field of battle. Some of his forces
advanced in the darkness down the Vistula at the junction
point between General Ivanoff's army in Poland and
General Dimitrieff's army in Western Galicia. He was
given German troops for this important operation, and
they managed to entrench by the river, forming themselves
into a spear-head driven between the two Russian armies.

AUSTRIAN OFFICERS LEAVING PRZEMYSL.

DEPARTURE OF THE AUSTRIAN GARRISON FROM
PRZEMYSL.

On paper their position appeared to constitute a formidable menace to their opponents, but the Russian infantry attacked them on the night of May 2nd and annihilated them with the bayonet. Elsewhere along the high banks of the Lower Dunajec the Austrian army was unable to advance. The gunners used hundreds of thousands of shells against the Russian positions, but they did not succeed in putting the Russian light field-artillery out of action. The result was that every attempt made by the Archduke to throw pontoon bridges over the stream by day or night was defeated by our Allies' shrapnel fire.

Only at one point, between the outflow into the Vistula and Tarnov, did the Austrians succeed in **2,000 men for a** crossing the river. At **bridge-head** the town of Oftinov there had been a ferry in peace time, but the river flowed between two very high artificial banks, and the Russian artillery was so well hidden that even the hurricane fire from the enemy's howitzers could not find it, though hundreds of Austrian and German airmen were searching for the Russian guns and directing the fire of their own pieces. But the German engineers had been working for some weeks round the ferry. They had driven several large tunnels through the bank on their side, leaving only a wall of earth on the river frontage. In the tunnels ran pontoons, fitted with wheels, and filled with men. In the night the wall of earth was blown up, and twenty pontoons were wheeled out and floated across the river under cover of a terrific bombardment. It was an exceedingly ingenious plan of attack, yet the troops, who floated across the river in the darkness, did not succeed as well as they expected. For, though the Russians were surprised, they sank nine

RUSSIAN PROVISION COLUMN ENTERING PRZEMYSL.

FIXING A RUSSIAN NOTICE OUTSIDE A PUBLIC BUILDING IN PRZEMYSL.

of the pontoons and killed or wounded most of the men in the remaining eleven bridge-boats. At a loss of two thousand men a bridge-head was won on the opposite side of the Dunajec on the morning of May 1st. But the Archduke's army could get no farther than the bridge-head. All the Lower Dunajec was firmly held by the Russians for a full week, from April 30th to May 6th. It was only at 10 a.m. on May 6th that Tarnov was reoccupied by the Austrians, and until four o'clock in the afternoon of the same day the Russians held some of the commanding heights on the east bank of the Lower Dunajec. Considering **Archduke Ferdinand's failure** the overwhelming power of artillery and men possessed by the Archduke Ferdinand, and the extraordinary skill of his engineers, the surprise attack on the Russian positions on the Lower Dunajec was a ridiculous failure. With everything in his favour, he took six to seven days to win two or three hundred yards of water and land. In the meantime General Ivanoff, commanding the Russian army in Central Poland, was able to march hundreds of thousands of men across the Vistula to the help of General Dimitrieff's small army. Even the Caucasian corps, formerly on the Bzura front near Warsaw, was able to march into Western Galicia before the Archduke Ferdinand brought his army across the Dunajec. The Austrian command and the Austrian troops were absolutely incompetent. Their incompetency, joined with the heroic intrepidity and fighting skill of Dimitrieff and his men, saved the Russian Empire from a vast and decisive disaster. Along the Biala, above Tarnov, the enemy started with an advantage in the lie of the land, for in many places the banks were higher on the western side of the river than on the eastern side. It was along the Biala, with his centre at Ciezkovice, that General von

RUSSIAN DETACHMENT PASSING THROUGH A STREET IN PRZEMYSL.

Mackensen attacked. His front extended only about twenty-five miles, from Tuchov to Gorlice. He had at least half a million men, including all the remnants of the Prussian Guard and the best Bavarian and Saxon troops from the French and Flemish front. His crack troops numbered 150,000, and the rest of his men were mainly drawn from the First German Reserve. He had 1,500 heavy guns, including most of the available 17 in. howitzers. Opposed to him were two army corps of General Dimitrieff's army, reduced by the wastage of war to 60,000 men. There was thus somewhat less than one Russian to every yard of front, and as there were three lines of Russian trenches the trench garrisons amounted to about one man to four yards. Mackensen began the attack with what the Germans called a hurricane fire. For four hours every gun and howitzer was worked as fast as human hands could work it, and 700,000 high-explosive shells were pitched into the Russian trenches—more than

SLOVAK OUTPOSTS IN SOME OLD RUINS IN THE CARPATHIANS.

ten shells to each Russian soldier. The quantity of projectiles used by Mackensen on this narrow front in four hours was double the amount usually regarded as necessary for a six months' siege of a great and well-provisioned fortress.

Falkenhayn had been inspired by the British artillery achievement at Neuve Chapelle. The plan, execution of which he had entrusted to Mackensen, merely consisted in a grandiose, but quite unoriginal, imitation of the new tactics of rapid, heavy artillery fire invented by Sir John French, Sir William Robertson, and General Foch. There was no escape from the 17 in. Skoda shells, or Pilseners, as the Russians named them. Each shell weighed 2,800 pounds ; in its flight it rose nearly five miles in the air, and it penetrated twenty feet into soft ground before it exploded. Every living thing within one hundred and fifty yards of the explosion was killed. and many persons farther off

were also slain. The main damage was not done by the metal fragments, but by the enormous pressure of the exploding gas. The gas got into the body cavities, and in its further process of expansion tore the flesh apart. Men who happened to be close by entirely disappeared ; not the slightest remains of their clothes or of their flesh could be found. Their rifles melted like metal struck by lightning. Scores of men at a distance who escaped metal fragments, stones, and showers of earth, were killed, lacerated, or blinded by the pressure of **Awful effect of** gas. The gas also broke in the partitions **Skoda shells** and bomb-proof roofs of shelters, and as the force of the explosion travelled everywhere along the air, no winding of the trenches was a defence against the terrible pressure.

At Ciezkovice on May 1st the Russians managed for a time to hold their ground even under the hurricane of shells. They remained silent and motionless until the German infantry advanced to occupy the wrecked trenches ; then they opened fire at six hundred paces and repulsed them. But more southward, at Gorlice, there was no battle. The famous naphtha town was battered into a heap of ruins, only one wall with a tower standing in the midst of unimaginable devastation. The immense oil-tanks were set on fire at the first attack, and for days the flames shot up into the clouds, making the place look in the distance like a gigantic torch. The Russians who survived the first inferno of shell fire beat back the advancing infantry and retired in the night north-eastward to Biecz.

Then, on the fourteen-mile front from Tuchov-Biecz, Mackensen, by means of long-range fire from his heavy artillery and a bombardment at shorter range by his field guns, delivered another attack on May 2nd. But between Tuchov and Biecz there are three streams and the Branka Mountain, with a peak 1,600 feet high. The peak dominates a considerable stretch of the lower course of the Biala. General Dimitrieff made full use of this advantage in the lie of the land, and though he had only light field-artillery firing shrapnel he held the enemy up for another three days. It was not until May 5th that the Grand Phalanx, as Mackensen's enormously-gunned army was called, succeeded in blowing a path through the Russians' three lines of defences east of the Biala. In other words, General Dimitrieff, by a magnificent six days' resistance on his southern front and flank, gave the southern Russian army, operating in Hungary from the Zboro, Dukla, and Lupkow Passes, full time to withdraw in good order away from the mountains and back to the San. Only the 48th Russian Division, under General Korniloff, was cut off by the enemy while retiring from the Dukla Pass on May 6th. Korniloff's troops were surrounded on all sides, but their commander skilfully massed them in the direction of the **Dimitrieff's** San Valley, and by a violent attacking **magnificent stand** movement through the densely-wooded foothills the division shot and bayoneted its way out of the German ring of flame and steel and rejoined its parent corps on Friday, May 7th.

With this brilliant exception, there was no disaster to the Russian movement of withdrawal, for though a gap was forced between the two army corps holding the Biala line, and the right flank of one corps was crushed by the hurricane shell fire, the brigades which lost most heavily retired undemoralised. Some regiments had only three hundred men left, but still remained full of fight, and practically all the hostile infantry attacks, led on this front by the Prussian Guard, were defeated ; for the two corps held out so stubbornly that the famous Caucasian corps arrived in time, after an all-night march, and went forthwith into battle and closed the gap. Every time the Germans advanced beyond the cover of their guns the Russian infantry moved out and counter-attacked. The Russian losses were heavy, and many of the regiments were reduced to half or a quarter of their number. But the men had

REMARKABLE FLANK VIEW OF THREE ADVANCED RUSSIAN TRENCHES ON THE EASTERN FRONT.

WHERE THE GROUND BRISTLED WITH BAYONETS.

A noticeable feature of the top photograph is the shallow pit dug between the foremost trenches for the officer. In the lower view a Russian officer is seen scanning the enemy's position through binoculars while the men, with bayonets fixed, are waiting for the word to charge. In oval: A Russian howitzer battery.

AUSTRIAN FIELD-GUN BATTERY IN THE CARPATHIANS.

ARCHDUKE CHARLES FRANCIS JOSEPH INSPECTING TROOPS IN POLAND.

the scheme of General von Falkenhayn. Falkenhayn had not massed a million men, with four thousand guns, against the short Dunajec and Biala line merely with a view to pushing back the four Russian army corps there and recapturing Przemysl; for the front on which he worked was so narrow that he could not employ his men along it. Only five German army corps went into action on the Biala front against the two Russian army corps holding the position, and along the Dunajec the Archduke Ferdinand used only about three Austrians to one Russian. The main Austro-German force was waiting in the rear of the fighting-line until the time came for it to perform its special duties. What was intended was to blow a hole about thirty to forty miles wide in the Russian front. Then through this hole all Mackensen's troops, with only their light field-artillery, were to **Falkenhayn's** dash against Lemberg and get in the **grandiose project** rear of General Brussiloff's forces. Mackensen's task, in short, was to envelop entirely the southern Russian army, against which Linsingen and Böhm Ermolli were still pressing on the south.

In addition to this grand operation, another great encircling movement was intended against the central Russian army, under General Ivanoff, entrenched along the Pilica and Nida Rivers, and linking with Dimitrieff's forces near the junction of the Vistula and the Dunajec. For while one half of the Grand Phalanx swung through the gap to the rear of Brussiloff's army in the south, the other half of the Phalanx, according to Falkenhayn's plan, was to move through the gap and turn northward across the Vistula and get in the rear of Ivanoff's army, cutting its communications with Ivangorod. It will be seen that the scheme was of a grandiose nature, and the power employed in its attempted execution was of incomparable magnitude. Had it prospered, Russian armies amounting to two million men would have been destroyed. The Russians, besides, would have lost the greater part of their artillery, leaving the Empire permanently crippled. The army in front of Warsaw would have been left in the air and compelled hastily to retreat, dragging with it all the Russian forces guarding the Warsaw-Petrograd Railway.

scarcely any bullet-wounds—it was entirely shell fire that had pounded them out of the trenches. For this reason the Russians remained in wonderfully good spirits. All they desired was to catch the German infantry away from the big guns and show that, man for man, they could outfight the enemy.

"Wait until it gets dark, little brothers!" the Russian privates would say, looking towards the Germans, and intending the message for them. And when darkness fell on the battlefield and the squadrons of hostile aeroplanes were unable to direct the fire of the big guns, the Russian soldier got to work in the woods on the flank of the enemy's foremost columns. Then the enemy began to keep up an intense bombardment all night. Under cover of this fire, his troops went forward, but as soon as the guns had exhausted their temporary stock of shells the Russians turned back at dawn and recaptured their trenches by a furious charge, retreating when the German gunners got a fresh supply of ammunition and resumed the hurricane fire. The Third Army lost **Third Russian** about fifty guns, most of them being **Army's tenacity** destroyed by heavy shells. A few of the batteries were deliberately sacrificed in covering the retreat of the infantry, and according to the accounts of a Hungarian novelist, who was an eye-witness of the scene, the Russian gunners of the rearguard fought on, amid an overpowering tempest of fire, until they had used all their shells.

The result of the extraordinary tenacity of the Third Russian Army was magnificent. It completely defeated

The Germans and Austrians would then have been able to conduct the summer campaign into the heart of Russia, if need be; or, as they hoped to do, they could have then held the enfeebled Russians back with part of their forces while they swung the victorious Grand Phalanx across Central Europe and launched it against its original target in France or Flanders.

As soon as the magnitude of the force employed by Mackensen was revealed, every intelligent man could see how enormous was the scope of Falkenhayn's plan. For this reason the entire civilised world looked with feverish anxiety to the conflict in Western Galicia. But for a time the situation was saved by the marvellous endurance of the diminishing troops of the Third Russian Army and the heroic skill of their commander, General Dimitrieff. It may be doubted if there can be found in military history any man to compare with Radko Dimitrieff. Neither the retreat of Sir John Moore to Corunna nor that of Sir John French to the Marne was as difficult as the operation conducted by the great Bulgarian. Indeed, **A great Bulgarian** the greatest of all retreats in modern **soldier** times—the retreat of the Russians under Barclay du Tolly and Kutusoff before the Grand Army of Napoleon—was not so magnificent an achievement as that which Radko Dimitrieff accomplished.

At the beginning of May he gave ground at Gorlice in the south, but hung on the upper course of the Dunajec with desperate tenacity. By this means he kept in connection with General Ivanoff's army and obtained reinforcements from it; and when the town of Tarnov fell, the two linked Russian armies withdrew down the Vistula towards the next great tributary, the Wistoka. At the

same time, by a more sudden retirement from Gorlice towards Jaslo, Dimitrieff removed from the zone of high-explosive shell fire on his southern flank, while keeping in close touch with General Brussiloff's forces round the Dukla Pass. Then when the three Russian armies—Ivanoff's, Dimitrieff's, and Brussiloff's—were closely linked together, the direction of all the combined operations was taken over by the oldest of the three commanders—the veteran General Ivanoff. Behind him was the Grand Duke Nicholas and the Russian Staff, who decided the national lines of strategy; but the great retreat was chiefly fought by Ivanoff, with Dimitrieff and Brussiloff assisting him. By May 7th the position of the Russians was secure; for though they were compelled to continue to give ground, the cohesion of their forces, instead of being weakened by the blow from the German battering-ram, was strengthened. Before the blow fell, General Dimitrieff, trusting to his formidable system of trenches to maintain his defensive action, had lent a division of his two southern army corps for operations on the Carpathians. Mackensen knew of this position of affairs from his spies, and launched the Grand Phalanx against the weakened place in Dimitrieff's front. And when, after a week's furious and incessant fighting, Dimitrieff's front remained unbroken, the position in regard to infantry power was improved. Reinforcements were poured into Galicia, and a considerable new army was collected in the Lublin province. Munitions were railed eastward from Kieff to Lemberg, and brought westward from Ivangorod and sent down to Jaroslav. Brussiloff shortened his line, enabling him to lend men, and Ivanoff withdrew from the Nida, in Poland, and

Mackensen outmanœuvred

CHEERS FOR THEIR BRITISH ALLIES.
With their rifles at the salute the men of the famous Fongorijski Regiment are giving "Three cheers for King George!"

STRIKING CAMERA-PICTURE OF A FULL-DRESS PARADE OF RUSSIAN TROOPS—SOMEWHERE ON THE EASTERN BATTLE-FRONT.

abandoned Kielce, with its copper-mines, and established a new line running from the Pilica and over the Lysa Gora heights through Opatov to Sandomierz, close to the junction of the Vistula and the San Rivers. This considerable shortening of his line enabled him also to throw large bodies of men and guns into the Galician battles.

What, however, the Russian commander could not do was to extemporise an artillery power equal to that of the enemy. A thousand heavy guns of position are not made in a day or a month, and three million high-explosive shells from 6 in. to 17 in. in diameter cannot be manufactured on the spur of the moment. The port of Archangel was closed to ordinary traffic in May to enable the British and French Governments to pour into Russia every gun and shell, rifle and cartridge that could be spared. The operations of our First Expeditionary Force were interrupted, and our large reinforcements were to some extent delayed by the necessity to loyally help our great Ally when, in the midst of great difficulties, she was fighting with heroic efficacy the common battle of civilisation; for Russia was withstanding the blow that might have been aimed at France, Britain, and Belgium, and the Western Allies naturally did all they could to pour warlike stores and weapons in a continual stream through Archangel. At the same time the Siberian Railway was working at high pressure, connecting the Galician battlefield with the armament factories of Japan and America. With all this outside help Russia could not, in a few weeks, get anything like the artillery power of her enemies; but she did equip a fresh army and get some hundreds of howitzers of a lighter model, which were the most useful of all in battles of manœuvres on the open field.

The Grand Phalanx which Falkenhayn had built up had one very serious defect. It was the hugest battering-ram mortal man had ever constructed. The difficulty was that it would only act in battering-ram fashion. Placed in position, with a solid definite obstacle to work against, it could quickly smash that obstacle into fragments. But when the obstacle withdrew at a speed of twenty miles a day, the battering-ram could not at once pursue it and immediately get to work again. Mackensen's extraordinary number of heavy artillery, and his store of millions of high-explosive shells, some weighing more than a ton each, could only be moved along a railway by means of hundreds of trains. The Russians thoroughly destroyed all railway lines as they retreated, and badly damaged every metalled roadway. The consequence was that the battering-ram could only move forward at the speed which the Germans and Austrians were able to rebuild the railway. The speed varied from three miles to five miles a day at the most. Something like four miles a day was therefore the average rate of progress of Mackensen's army and its enormous siege train.

The German Commander-in-Chief had sacrificed mobility to power. Basing his plan entirely on the conditions of the trench warfare system obtaining throughout the western front, and extending over the larger section of the eastern front, he had constructed a war-machine that could break through any trench system and shatter any fortress, but which could not pursue an enemy. As a matter of fact, both the Germans and the Austrians were too eager to pursue. On each occasion when the Russian lines withdrew from the zone of heavy shell fire the attacking infantry advanced in an attempt to transform the retreat into a rout. The Russians waited for them with light field-guns, machine-guns, and infantry concealed in woods and ditches from the eyes of reconnoitring hostile airmen. It was then that our Allies got in time after time a damaging counter-blow.

This was also the explanation of the extraordinary and continual conflict of statement in the Russian and Austro-German official reports on the Galician struggle.

Outside help for Russia

Defect of the grand phalanx

RUSSIAN OFFICERS AS PRISONERS OF WAR.
A captured Cossack general walks at the head of this sad procession in the town of Augustowo.

through on the Russian front on the Biala River. On Sunday, May 9th, Mackensen's army was further reinforced from Cracow. It crossed the Wislok at Krosno, and the troops deployed in dense lines along the high range of hills running from Stryschov on the Wislok to Brozov on the tributary stream of the Stobnica. It was only a sixteen-mile front, ending about thirty miles west of Przemysl. Covered only by their light field-artillery, the German troops, with the battered Prussian Guards still at their head, manœuvred in a brilliant and impetuous manner under the most brilliant of German commanders, and making a frontal attack against the Russian centre, broke it by pressure of massed numbers. It was a well-fought, well-managed victory in the old, orthodox Prussian manner. Mackensen sacrificed his men in tens of thousands at the decisive point until they had advanced so close that neither the Russian bayonet nor the Russian shrapnel could master its final charge of the surviving locked and roaring ranks of Germans

This time no orderly retreat was possible. Mackensen had repeated his achievement at the Piontek marshes, north of Lodz. He had clean broken through the Russian front. No orderly retirement was possible for our Allies. But as General Russky at Lodz had changed Mackensen's triumph into a disaster, so now General Ivanoff, with heavier odds against him, turned a defeat into a glorious feat of arms. He gave way in his centre, making no attempt

Ivanoff's swift counter-manœuvre

The Austrians and Germans made premature claims to victories on all the chief points of attack along the Wisloka, Wislok, and San Rivers. Mackensen, for instance, claimed to have captured Rymano on Wednesday, May 5th, and to have forced the passage of the Wislok. But two days afterwards he again claimed to have captured Rymano. The town of Debica, on the Lower Wisloka, was also apparently won twice by the army of the Archduke Ferdinand. In both cases the explanation was that the Russians withdrew from a hurricane of shell fire, only to return and slaughter the German and Austrian infantry when it advanced too confidently to occupy the position. At Debica railway-station the Russians used armoured motor-cars with terrible effect against a hostile division that tried to move quicker than the battering-ram behind it.

There was, however, one occasion when Mackensen's army almost succeeded in retrieving its failure to break

PRUSSIAN CAVALRY ON THE MARCH.
This very striking photograph was taken in the evening twilight near Prasnysch.

to retrieve the position there, but sent all his reserve troops in a long, swift march southward towards Krosno. By means of their magnificent marching powers the Russians rounded the enemy's flank, and in a series of furious charges worked round still farther and menaced his rear. First a German division gave way, then an army corps, enabling the Russians in front also to advance southward to take part in the surprise turning movement. By Sunday evening Mackensen was losing on his right flank double what he was winning on his advanced centre. In fact, his whole line was in process of crumbling up, the Russians having got a hook round it. He had to draw back his victorious troops and send them to his rear, and check the Russian flanking movement. The Russian commander was not able to press his advantage, through lack of a decisive number of men on the Przemysl front. But he completely stopped Mackensen's advance and was able to retreat to the San River in a tranquil manner.

One of the reasons why the Russian counter-stroke was not fully driven home at Krosno was that a large part of the new reinforcements was operating in the Bukovina. Here, on the same Sunday evening as Mackensen in Galicia received his first severe check, a battle was raging on a forty-mile front from Obertyn to

RUSSIAN ORDERLIES ATTACHED TO THE CAUCASIAN NATIVE DIVISION.

Czernovitz. A large Austrian army, under the Archduke Eugene, was trying to work up to the Dniester, and then, in co-operation with the German army moving towards Stry, envelop Lemberg from the east, and cut the Russian communications with Kieff. In conjunction with the severe pressure that the armies of the Archduke Ferdinand and Mackensen were exercising on the east, and the army of Linsingen and the army of Böhm Ermolli were exercising from the south, the enemy's flanking movement in the Bukovina was a very serious matter. But General Brussiloff had good railway communications with Russia at Tarnopol, north of the Dniester. That is to say, he could get reinforcements and munitions quickly, and his local commander-in-chief, General Ivanoff, agreed that the Bukovina front was the best suited for a counter-blow.

Russian victory at Czernovitz

So on May 9th the Russians offered battle round Czernovitz, and advanced in impetuous attack for two days, throwing the enemy back with heavy losses. Some 5,000 prisoners were taken and six guns, and the advanced enemy forces holding the bridge-head on the Dniester at the railway town of Zalestchiki were routed. At the same time a strong attack was made upon the hostile forces working up from the Carpathian Mountains. More

than 5,000 bodies were found in front of the Russians on the mountain slopes of the Javornik range. In five days 20,000 prisoners were taken between the Dniester and the Pruth Rivers, and the Russians captured the town of Nadvorna, and cut the railway between Bukovina and Austria. This for the time being put an end to the Austrian attempt at a flanking movement from the Bukovina. A new commander, General Pflanzer, replaced the Archduke Eugene, the latter going to the Italian front.

The Austrians still lacked driving power. All the chief work in the struggle for Galicia was done by German troops under Mackensen or Linsingen. Linsingen's fighting army was the chief force in the south. It worked with Pflanzer's Austrian army in the Bukovina on its left, and on its right was Böhm Ermolli's Austrian army, working through the Uzsok Pass towards Sambor, and General von Marwitz's Austro-German army, advancing through the Dukla and Lupkow Passes, and linking with Mackensen's Grand Phalanx. Of all these four southern armies Linsingen's was the chief striking force. It was composed largely of Bavarian troops, and operated along the Munkacs-Stry railway, with a direct aim against

German advance on Lemberg.

Lemberg. More than half a million men were employed by Linsingen, with a large amount of light field-artillery, including many 6 in. howitzers. Some 12 in. pieces of ordnance were also brought up over the mountain range as the railway was rebuilt. But the difficulties of communication were so great that the heavy artillery power of this second great German army remained very much inferior to that of Mackensen's force.

The result was that Linsingen, having to meet Brussiloff on fairly equal terms, was continually defeated in his advance against Lemberg. Indeed, Linsingen was only able to advance when Brussiloff resolved to shorten his line with a view to assisting the Third Russian Army.

As General Ivanoff viewed the situation, the entire success of Falkenhayn's scheme depended on the progress made by Linsingen. Mackensen and his mighty Phalanx, crawling forward at a speed of four miles a day, had failed to break the Russian front and encircle the southern Russian army. The movement of the Phalanx was therefore no longer a menace, but merely a new development of the war of attrition. The vast and cumbrous moving siege train could be left to exhaust itself in continual frontal attacks, with the Russians giving way very slowly as they wore down the enemy. If necessary, this kind of Russian retreat could be carried on for months, at the rate of four miles a day, without Mackensen getting farther into Russian territory than the Austrian Archduke Friedrich had done in August, 1914, before he was completely overthrown and routed.

But the position of Linsingen's army was different. It was making a flank attack against the Russians at the same time as the Phalanx was making a frontal attack. If the flank attack succeeded, the consequence would be an overwhelming disaster to all the Russian forces in Galicia. So both General Ivanoff and the Grand Duke Nicholas devoted special attention to the struggle between Linsingen and Brussiloff. Brussiloff completely retired from the Carpathian front in the middle of May, and took his stand in the valley of the Dniester from Drohobycz

RAILWAY BRIDGE OVER THE WIER.
The destruction of the Wier Bridge the day before the Austrian surrender caused delay in sending food to the garrison of Przemysl.

through Stry to Bolechov. He had a good main road just behind his front, and a railway line running to his centre. It was a position similar to that he had held in the winter of 1914 all along the Carpathian front, having a network of railways behind him, while the enemy's lines of communication ran over the mountain rampart. It took Linsingen four days to get all his men, guns, and munitions across the heights and arranged in battle order on the foothills above the Galician plain. He began his grand attack on May 19th, and the struggle went on day and night. The Russians never stirred from their trenches, but shot down the enemy's massed formations as they neared the wire entanglements. The battle went on incessantly for two weeks, Linsingen bringing his heavy artillery into action with massed fire effects on May 25th.

Meanwhile the Russian right wing, which had been partly outflanked, drew back a little at Slonsko, but the strength of the Russian front was not changed. Dense columns every day descended the slope of the Carpathians to reinforce Linsingen, a movement from East Prussia being stopped by the German Staff in order to use the men in the southern Galician battle. But at the same time the Russian Staff was also pouring troops through Tarnopol and Lemberg to the assistance of Brussiloff. The battle-front was only forty miles long, and the German commander packed his men together in deep lines, in the old-fashioned Napoleonic fashion, which took no account of the development of the power of the modern rifle, machine-gun, and quick-firer using shrapnel shell. For instance, against the narrow Russian trenches in front of the petroleum town of Stry, sixty thousand Germans advanced on May 29th. Fully a third of them were slaughtered, but the rest forced back the Russians and took the town.

Brussiloff's victorious right wing

Theoretically, they had broken the Russian front. But the Russian commander had had good time to prepare a counter-stroke. He knew that Linsingen's right wing was composed of Austrian troops quite exhausted by the hard fighting. So, as the remnant of the three German divisions entered Stry, he retired on his centre, having already massed his reserves on his left wing. There he struck at the Austrian troops, captured all their positions, and then dealt the familiar counter-stroke against the rear of Linsingen's victorious centre. The affair was a repetition of the similar outflanking and rear attack against Mackensen at Krosno during the first week in May. But Brussiloff's general position was stronger than that of Radko Dimitrieff, for Brussiloff was not fighting for a retreat and to prevent a rout. His forces were at the time as strong as those of Linsingen. He had seen the enemy's blow at his centre coming, and had deliberately given way there with a view to bringing about the annihilation of Linsingen's army. For two days his victorious right wing continued to curl round the enemy's rear in desperate hand-to-hand fighting over the Carpathian foothills towards the Stry-Munkacs railway line, by which Linsingen's men were fed and munitioned.

AUSTRIAN PRISONERS EN ROUTE FOR LEMBERG.
This photograph, taken just after the fall of Przemysl, shows the prisoners halting for a hasty meal.

AUSTRIAN PRISONERS AT LEMBERG.
Permission was given by the Russian authorities for their captives to be visited by relatives and friends.

Linsingen's left wing was allowed to advance about twenty miles northward to the town of Mikolajov, on the Dniester, which in turn was barely twenty miles from Lemberg. In short, Linsingen's left wing was only a day's march from the railway centre of Galicia. There he would be far in the rear of the Russian armies facing the forces of Mackensen and the Archduke Ferdinand on the San River. The lure was very enticing, and it lay more-over in the line of the weakest resistance. Linsingen was, of course, well aware of his danger, but he thought that he could prevent Brussiloff from getting in his rear in the south.

For two days the result of this most interesting manœuvre hung in the balance. Brussiloff had the situation well in hand, and was eager to pursue his advantage, and envelop his too adventurous opponent. But the Grand Duke Nicholas and the Russian Staff, and also General Ivanoff, were doubtful. There was no question but that Brussiloff could bring off his great stroke, but the problem was whether this large and yet only local success would be purchased at too heavy a cost to the general Russian position in Galicia; for the Russian line on the San, north and south of Przemysl, was in danger. The Phalanx had crawled up again to the Russian front, and another retirement had become neces-sary. Help was again needed from Brussiloff to strengthen the Third Army, and Brussiloff was therefore ordered to give over all his operations and entrench along the Dniester River.

The Russian position on the Dniester was very strong. In the western reaches above Sambor and Drohobycz there was a twenty-mile stretch of wide river-swamps, fed by the melting snows of the Carpathians, and forming for the time an impassable defence. Then, in the more eastward reaches, there were open cultivated spaces with intervals of dense woodland along the northern bank. The Russian general strongly entrenched along the open spaces, and placed most of his guns there. In the forests he left only advance-guards with machine-guns to defend the crossings. On nearing the river, Linsingen made a general reconnaissance in force on a front of forty miles. He was beaten back at all the towns and open spaces, but won a bridge-head at last near Zuravno, where the northern

The position on the Dniester bank of the river was thickly wooded. Here the army of Count Bothmer, which constituted the main striking force of Linsingen's command, crossed the Dniester on the night of June 6th, after having lost some ten thousand men two days before in a fruitless attempt on the Russian bridge-head near the junction of the Stry and Dniester.

Having at last got across the Dniester by Zuravno, Count Bothmer advanced through the forest for two days, winning a stretch of ground on the northern bank some fourteen miles long and ten miles broad. But around this wooded tract the Russians closed in on the night of June 8th, and then in a long, violent hand-to-hand struggle of a thousand conflicts screened from each other by the trees, the Germans were pushed back over and into the river. It was a soldiers' battle with the bayonet, similar to that which had occurred in the forests near Ivangorod in October, 1914. All the Russians' stores of ammunition were running low, cartridges as well as shells; but by getting the

enemy into a deep forest, where none of his guns was of much use, General Brussiloff, in spite of the heavy material odds against him, won on June 9th a decisive victory on the important flank position along the Dniester. The Russian Staff calculated that, in the month's fighting between the Carpathians and the river, Linsingen's army lost, on a front of forty miles, 150,000 men. Twenty-five guns, more than a hundred machine-guns, and forty thousand prisoners were taken, and serious symptoms of demoralisation were perceptible in Linsingen's force.   **Recapture of Przemysl**

Meanwhile General von Mackensen, with the Grand Phalanx and its supporting armies, continued to make progress in the direction of Przemysl. In frontal attack after frontal attack Mackensen battered his way forward, losing men by the hundred thousand, and yet increasing his infantry forces as his siege train crawled along; for the German Staff, directed by General von Falkenhayn, fed the Phalanx with every available soldier in the two Central Empires. Mackensen's great siege train slowly moved along the railway, from Gorlice to Jaslo, and thence northward to Rzeszoff towards Jaroslav. He attacked Jaroslav on Friday, May 14th, meeting only a single Russian division, en-trenched for a rearguard action on the hills west of the town. For two days the division held back the Germans, while the main Russian forces crossed the river and entrenched along the eastern bank.

Then, on Monday, May 17th, the real battle began. The Prussian Guard Corps, with the Tenth Army Corps and the Forty-first Reserve Corps and a composite Corps, advanced across the fords of the San, between Jaroslav and the town of Sieniawa. Their forward movement was heralded by a tempest of heavy shells from the enor-

A SNAPSHOT IN VIENNA.
These waggon-loads of bedding were for the use of the Austrian Army immediately after mobilisation.

mous German batteries. But such was the skill of General Ivanoff in choosing his ground and directing the counter-attack that Mackensen only won from one to three miles' depth of ground east of the river. Then, entrenching some of his reserve troops along the foothold won along the east bank of the San, the German commander put the larger part of his siege train on the railway, and travelled back to Sanok in the south, and thence towards Przemysl.

For the Russian General Staff the solely vital problem was to keep the Russian lines intact for as long and wearing a fighting retreat as the German Staff cared to impose upon the Russian armies. But in the last anxious days of May it seemed to some of Russia's western allies as if the obstinate attempt at a long defence of the perilous salient at Przemysl might give Mackensen the opportunity for the grand stroke of breaking through the Russian forces. It was almost with a feeling of relief that military circles in Britain and France heard that the enemy had recaptured Przemysl on Tuesday, June 1st. The delay in retiring was then revealed. The Russians had filled the city full of military stores. To prevent these stores from falling into the hands of the Austrians and Germans, a small, heroic rearguard manned the entrenchments while the war material was being rapidly removed by the double-track railway to Lemberg and the broad highway running due east. What the Austrians recovered was nothing but the empty shell of what had been their mightiest stronghold.

END OF VOLUME 3.

THE GREAT WAR

VOLUME 4

Frontispiece Vol. IV. THE GREAT WAR.   From the Painting by C.M.Sheldon.

"The Smile of Victory."

THE GREAT WAR

THE STANDARD HISTORY
OF THE ALL-EUROPE CONFLICT

EDITED BY

H. W. WILSON

Author of "With the Flag to Pretoria"
"Japan's Fight for Freedom" etc.

and

J. A. HAMMERTON

Editor "Harmsworth History of the World"

PROFUSELY ILLUSTRATED

VOLUME 4

LONDON
THE AMALGAMATED PRESS LIMITED
1915

CONTENTS OF VOLUME 4

SPECIAL PHOTOGRAVURE PLATES

THE GREAT WAR

THE STANDARD HISTORY OF THE ALL-EUROPE CONFLICT

VOLUME 4

CHAPTER LXVI.

THE BRITISH OFFENSIVE AND THE SECOND BATTLE OF YPRES.

The Superiority of German Staff Work—The Difficulties of Sir John French and his Staff—The Germans Profit by the Lesson of Neuve Chapelle—No Important Forward Movement Possible on the British Front—Gauging our Weakness, the Germans Resume their Attack on Ypres—Violent Conflict at St. Eloi—British Counter-Attack Succeeds—Opening of Battle for Hill 60—Heroic Defence by the East Surreys—French Division North of Ypres Broken by Sudden Gas Attack—Extreme Peril of the Unsupported Canadian Division—Fifty Thousand Germans Attack Eight Thousand Canadians—Magnificent Stand Made by Our Overwhelmed and Enveloped Colonial Troops—How the Canadian Scottish and the 10th Canadian Battalion Recovered the Guns—The Left Wing of the Canadian Division is Involved—Heroic Frontal Attack by Combined British and Canadian Forces Saves Ypres—Heroic Part Played by British Territorials and Yeomanry in the Desperate Struggle—The Miners of Durham Hold the Gravenstafel Ridge—Shell-Trap Farm and the Monmouth Territorials—A London Shopman, with Six Men, Holds the German Army at Bay—A Soldier's Account of a Soldiers' Battle.

S we have seen in the previous chapter, the chief of the combined German and Austrian Staffs, General von Falkenhayn, took steps to anticipate the grand attack which the Allies in the west intended to make in the spring of 1915. But the urgent necessity of driving back the Russian armies that had invaded Hungary, owing to Hindenburg's failure in strategy, brought about a reversal of Falkenhayn's plan. In the long ordeal of battle it had been proved that the plan of campaign drawn up by the former conqueror of France and Austria — Moltke — and developed and put into execution in August, 1914, by his nephew, was based on a wrong view of the general position.

The younger Moltke and his generals had proceeded on the assumption that France was the weaker and Russia the stronger of their enemies. They had therefore attacked the weaker nation in overwhelming force, while practically standing on the defensive against the stronger nation, until by their victory in the west

they could concentrate all their principal armies against the foe they most feared—Russia. At least six-sevenths of the entire military strength of Germany was used against France in the first phase of the war. With perhaps two exceptions, all the twenty-five and a half German army corps of the first line were employed on the western front, with most of the thirty army corps of the first reserve. Hindenburg won the victory of Tannenberg in East Prussia in August, 1914, mainly with Landwehr and Landsturm troops, and part of the garrisons of Königsberg and Thorn. All the best German troops, numbering over two and a half millions, were then in Belgium and France.

Falkenhayn was a man of a trenchant and able character. He came to the opinion that the elder Moltke, with all his followers, had been disastrously wrong, and when he got into his hands the entire control of all the military forces of Germany and Austria-Hungary — which happened after the dismissal of Hindenburg—he completely reversed the Moltkean plan of campaign on a double front. Recognising that France was the stronger enemy, he adopted for the

ON THE ROOF OF AN OFFICERS' BOMB-PROOF SHELTER.

A   1

time a purely defensive position against her, and used all other available forces for an offensive campaign against the relatively weaker armies of Russia. It was a bold and novel plan, which had been advocated by Bernhardi, and undoubtedly it was sound. Had it been adopted in August, 1914, the probabilities of a decisive German success, first against Russia and then against France, would have been greatly increased. For Russia certainly began the war with a comparatively small force of men and guns, and if Germany and Austria had combined both their first-line armies and a large part of their reserve troops against her, she would have been badly defeated. Kieff and Odessa would have been lost, and in all probability St. Petersburg—or Petrograd, as we must now call it.

A STREET IN SHELL-SHATTERED ARRAS.

The Germans would have had little to fear in a defensive campaign against France. This is proved by the course of events on the western front in the spring of 1915. The excellence of organisation of the German Staff work in this defensive campaign was incomparable. It showed that nations like the Japanese, the Chilians, and the Turks were not mistaken when they regarded the War Academy in Berlin as the best centre of military knowledge in the world.

Since the days of Frederick the Great our country has followed the lead of the Prussians in many military matters, and the tradition then established was maintained by our War Office down to the outbreak of the present hostilities. The reorganisation of our Army after the **The German lead in organisation** Boer War was partly guided by the German model. If Mr. Brodrick did little more than introduce the German style of cap, his successors made some attempt to develop—though timidly and half-heartedly—the German system of organisation in England. We remained, however, far behind our masters in the foresightful preparation of the weapons and instruments of war, and in the intellectual quality and organising genius of our Staff work. These lessons we had to learn, along with the French, by costly experience of actual war.

The German Staff gave us our first lesson in trench

warfare on the Aisne. We used open trenches and few heavy howitzers, few machine-guns, and fewer high-explosive shells. In spite of these disadvantages, our men, by their superior courage and superior personal skill, stormed the plateau by the river. But the German Staff was equal to the occasion. It at once introduced, on a vast general scale, the system of barbed-wire entanglements, shrapnel-proof trenches, and an extraordinary number of machine-gun redoubts.

The French Staff at once reorganised its work on the German model, and took immediate steps to increase its heavy artillery, to speed up the manu-facture of shells, and to double the **Activity of the** number of machine-guns used by every **French Staff** battalion. By February, 1915, the French nation, within the limits of its crippled industrial strength, was well on the way to profit by all that it had learned on the battle-field from the German Staff.

Our country was not so alert and active, not so generally intelligent and generally well organised. This was partly due to the fact that our people inclined to look upon the war as an adventure which did not require their entire energies. But in a more direct way it was occasioned by a gap between our War Office and the Commander-in-Chief in the field and his Staff. In France the Commander-in-Chief in the field was, for most practical purposes, in the position of a dictator. Parliament was his servant, for the mind and soul and energies of every Frenchman were bent upon the task of defeating and expelling the invader, and deputies, senators, and all the members of the Government were anxious only to know what they could do to assist General Joffre and his Staff. This intense and universal spirit of co-operation endowed General Joffre with the unexpressed but real powers of a dictatorship.

The position of Sir John French and his Staff was entirely different. They alone knew by actual experi-ence what was needed in all the changing and developing conditions in modern scientific warfare into which mighty nations threw their entire forces. But

THE TOTTERING TOWERS OF THE CHURCH AT MONT ST. ELOI.

between Sir John French and the eager, patriotic British people stood the War Office, manned by men who were apt to think—for, as Mr. Lloyd George has said, the professional mind is very conservative—that the lessons of the South African War were the last word in military science. Then, again, between the British

A GERMAN SHELL BURSTING OVER THE SHATTERED
TOWN OF YPRES.

Lille or by General Foch north of Arras. Therefore, on both these sections of the front concrete systems of entrenchments were constructed with steel loopholes and perfect cover against rifle, machine-gun, and shrapnel fire. Tens of thousands of newly-trained machine-gun parties with new machine-guns were brought to the Franco-British front to hold the first line of trenches. Most of the infantry were withdrawn into concrete shelters in the last line, connected by telephone with the advanced observation posts, from which every movement of the opposing forces was watched. The support trenches were linked to the front by means of tunnels, which the Germans said "resembled the Englishman's 'Tubes' in London." The idea was, **Concrete trenches** of course, to mitigate the consequences of **and machine-guns** sudden bombardments like that which had opened the Battle of Neuve Chapelle, and at the same time to maintain along the front an annihilating fire-power against any sudden infantry attacks. The new German system was admirably conceived and perfectly executed. As a British officer said, when we made our first capture of a small section of the newly-modelled German trenches : "Our men are better men than the Germans, but the German Staff work has us completely beaten."

To speak quite frankly, in the warlike operations on the Continent of Europe, Great Britain remained almost impotent at the time when France and Russia had the right to expect that our enormous resources of human force and industrial power would mature into the decisive factor in the Great War. At the opening of hostilities our politicians had talked much about organising at once the entire energies of our country in the cause of civilisation. After nine and more months of battles on land, in which Belgium and France, Serbia and Russia, wavered between

people and the War Office there interposed Parliament, containing men with a certain gift for persuasive oratory or a certain amount of wealth and degree of rank, but without a first-hand knowledge of science, and quite devoid of any power of appreciating and solving modern military problems. There were also in our country some large bodies of persons of a very unwarlike temper—descendants of the stocks that had been half frightened and half scornful of the use of the sword ever since the days of the Armada. They were very anxious for the maintenance of the principle of voluntary enlistment—which in ancient practice meant the use of the press-gang—because, for three hundred years, men of their way of thinking had escaped from the duty of defending their country by land and sea, while growing increasingly prosperous through the blood shed by the more spirited and patriotic members of our noble and working classes.

Sir John French, therefore, remained at the mercy of the authorities at home. If they thought that shrapnel was more useful against concrete and armour-**Home judgment** plated trenches than high-explosive shell, **and ammunition** or that a generous allowance of machine-guns to a battalion was a useless luxury, their judgment in the matter obtained. Even at Neuve Chapelle, in the middle of March, 1915, the British artillery was mainly restricted to the use of shrapnel shell, and the high-explosive projectiles were supplied by the gunners of General Foch's armies who assisted in the battle.

After Neuve Chapelle the German commanders along the British front—Prince Rupert of Bavaria and the Duke of Würtemberg—took effectual steps to prevent the repetition of the British success. The German Staff at the opening of the war had provided their armies with steam trench-making machines. To these machines were added, along the German front in the spring of 1915, concrete-making machines. The German Staff feared most of all a grand offensive movement by Sir John French around

STEEPLE OF ASYLUM CHAPEL, YPRES, THROWN DOWN
THROUGH THE ROOF BY A GERMAN SHELL.

GENERAL FOCH (LEFT) WATCHING THE DEVELOPMENT OF FRENCH OFFENSIVE MOVEMENT NORTH OF ARRAS.

national disaster and national salvation, our unattacked, rich, busy, highly-industrialised free country still played almost as small a part as crippled and manacled Belgium in the land operations in the vast and world-shaking struggle. The various fronts held by the Allies measured about 1,656 miles. The Russians held a front of 850 miles, the French held a front of 540 miles, the Serbians and Montenegrins defended 218 miles ; the British front was 30 miles long, and the Belgian lines about 18 miles long. This was apparently the utmost we could do in the decisive theatre of war at a time when, according to an extraordinary statement made by Mr. Lloyd George, we had thirty-six divisions of troops ready for battle. Thirty-six divisions are eighteen army corps ; in eighteen army corps there are nearly three-quarters of a million of infantrymen, supported by an artillery corps of more than 2,000 light and heavy field-guns. With 500 heavy howitzers, including our converted 9·2 in. naval gun, and 500 heavy pieces of artillery from the Creusot and other French works, and twenty million high-explosive shells, we might have had, in the late spring of 1915, a tremendous battering-ram at least equal in power to the Grand Phalanx with which Mackensen was endangering the entire military position of Russia. As, however, it appeared from Mr. Lloyd George's speeches that we were producing in a month, after three-quarters of a year's organisation of our industries on a war basis, less high-explosive shell than German and Austrian factories were turning out in a day, our long and loudly announced grand advance in the spring of 1915 did not take place.

Our failure in shell supply

What stores of war material we prepared for the liberation of Belgium were partly diverted to the operations in the Dardanelles. These operations were designed mainly with a view to opening a short, direct, and convenient route for supplying Russia with munitions of war to enable her to maintain the pressure against Hungary. Owing to the superiority of German Staff work in the Gallipoli Peninsula and the lack of high-explosive shells for our naval bombardment of the Turkish position, the forcing of the Dardanelles was not achieved in time to help Russia. She not only lost her footing on the Hungarian plain, but was deprived of the magnificent railway system in Galicia, and thrown back entirely upon her own meagre, inadequate railways, where her position became for the time difficult. So difficult was it that the port of Archangel was closed to ordinary traffic for some time in the spring to enable the French and British military authorities to pour into Russia all the war material they could possibly spare. Our proposed great offensive movement was not a matter of vital necessity at the moment, but to prevent the breaking of the Russian front and the destruction of one or more of the Russian armies was almost a matter of life and death. For this reason among others our main army serving in France and Flanders did not receive the heavy reinforcements that were expected to reach it in the spring.

Why our Army was held back

During all the late spring and early summer the British Expeditionary Force, by reason of its weakness in armament, had to remain on the defensive, no important forward movement being possible. The utmost Sir John French's men achieved, through a lack of high-explosive shell and of additional heavy artillery, was to make some heroic bayonet and grenade attacks on the first and second lines of German trenches. But most of these local operations were in the nature either of counter-attacks or of diversions, intended to pin the Germans to their positions and prevent the movement of hostile troops. All the important offensive operations on an important scale after the affair at Neuve Chapelle were conducted by the French, who possessed large and unfailing supplies of high-explosive shells of all calibres, including the biggest.

The situation on the western front was then practically stationary. In the great battles beginning at Charleroi and Mons in August and ending at Ypres in November, 1914, the German Staff had two and a half million troops in France and Flanders, and then increased their number to three million and more. When this force of such unparalleled magnitude was greatly reduced by casualties, strong drafts and new formations brought it up again at the beginning of the winter of 1914 to two and a half million men. But when Hindenburg opened his second campaign against Warsaw, the losses on the Bzura were so heavy that about half a million troops were taken from France and Flanders. This left fifty army corps on the western front, composed in all of two million men, of whom one million two hundred thousand were infantry. Then, when the Grand Phalanx was formed under Mackensen, twenty-four battalions of the Prussian Guard, eighteen battalions of the Eighteenth Army Corps, sixteen battalions of the 56th Division, nine battalions of the 16th Bavarian Division, and nine battalions of the 119th Division were taken, mainly from the British and Belgian front, to form the spear-head of the Phalanx. In all about three army corps were removed from the western front. The French, British, and Belgian troops were then faced by 1,128,000 German infantrymen only, holding a front of five hundred and eighty-eight miles. A considerable stretch of this front was the mountainous land of the Vosges, which could be defended with comparatively small forces, armed with a large number of machine-guns and artillery.

But there remained at least some four hundred miles of front in country of an ordinary character, where on the Continental system of reckoning, the trenches required a garrison of two men to a yard. There were needed, therefore, 1,408,000 infantrymen to garrison a fairly level front, and at least another 300,000 infantrymen to hold

At the first attempt a German 150 mm. shell burst well in front of the concealed French battery, far wide of the mark.

The second shell burst much closer to the battery and more to the right. This photograph was taken some seconds after the explosion.

The third shell, though at fault, burst closer to its mark than either of the previous two.

At the fourth attempt the German gunners sent their huge projectile **very** near to the French position.

The fifth and sixth shells fell behind the concealed battery, between it and a blockhouse eighty yards to the rear.

The sixth shell fell only fifteen yards from the blockhouse from **which** these instantaneous photographs were obtained.

FAILURE OF GERMAN GUNNERS TO LOCATE A CONCEALED FRENCH BATTERY.

THE AWFUL EFFECT OF A FRENCH MINE EXPLOSION UNDER A GERMAN TRENCH.
French Staff-officers watching the explosion of a great mine under a German trench.   Effect of the explosion is shown on opposite page.

the mountainous, or very hilly regions. So, altogether, at a low estimate, the Germans required over a million and a half of infantry. This was the number they had possessed in France and Flanders early in the winter of 1914. In the spring of 1915 they were about 400,000 infantrymen short on the western front. They were this amount short for defensive purposes. For a strong and sweeping offensive movement they were nearly a million men short.

The French Army, on the other hand, had sixty-two and a half army corps on the front, according to a statement published by the French Staff, which **The offensive left to Joffre** enabled it to put a million and a half infantry into the trenches. France also had another million and a half men in her depots. Belgium, in spite of her calamities, had three army corps in the field, while Britain increased her original small force of two army corps and a division to something more than a quarter of a million men. We had, indeed, a million men ready in regard to drill and training, but for reasons already mentioned their equipment was incomplete. The general result was that the French Commander-in-Chief had to do what he could in the way of an offensive movement with his own men and munitions, leaving the British force to stand, like the Belgian force, on the defensive.

In these circumstances General Joffre spent some months in improving his position. As we have seen in the study of the French actions at Perthes, in Champagne, and at Soissons, on the Aisne, the German commander countered every attack by rearranging his troops and massing them as quickly as possible at the point of danger. This he did by means of the lateral railway lines running in the rear of all his front. These lateral railway lines became the object of a series of systematised attacks by General Joffre.

He intended to get his heavy guns and howitzers, at important intervals along the front, in such a series of positions that they could at the decisive moment rake the German system of lateral railways, and thus prevent the transport of troops, artillery, and munitions from point to point. This was all done by way of preparation for the launching of the grand allied attack that would clear France, and perhaps Belgium, of the invaders. General Joffre wished to win beforehand so many points of vantage against the enemy's lateral lines of communication that he would be able to check all considerable attempts at concentration while he was making his great thrust forward. None of his preparatory operations revealed what point he had selected for the attempt to break the German front.

He advanced against at least ten sections of the German lines. In particular he attacked round Lille, towards Lens, towards St. Quentin, towards La Fère, over the plain of Champagne, through the Argonne, towards Metz, towards Saarburg, towards Colmar, and towards Mulhouse. Everywhere his immediate object was to get gun-positions dominating the roads and railways used by the Germans. But it was difficult for the German Staff to divine whether the French commander was not at any given place of attack opening a path for an advance in large force. There was an incessant pushing **German Staff** movement by General Joffre, and wher- **getting nervous** ever the Germans staggered more French forces were at once brought up. The enemy had therefore to counter-attack in a very strong and determined manner in order to save himself. In Alsace a small local victory won by an advanced French battalion brought an entire German army corps to the assault of the lost hill position. This showed how nervous the German Staff was getting. The British Expeditionary Force came in for many blows by reason of its defensive attitude. Whenever the French Army won a striking local success over the Germans, and then violently defeated a counter-attack, the German Staff seems to have ordered the Duke of Würtemberg or the Crown Prince of Bavaria to strike out at the British

6

WEEKS HAD BEEN SPENT IN SAPPING TO REACH THIS GERMAN POSITION.
The French in possession of the mined position. Artillery officers contemplating the result of their work.

front. It was not always cool, sound, strategical calculation, but often a rankling passion to avenge the Neuve Chapelle defeat that inspired the movements against the British lines.

Immediately after the Battle of Neuve Chapelle an attempt was made to return the sudden blow by rushing part of the line held by our Second Army, under General Sir Horace Smith-Dorrien. As a point of attack the enemy chose the village of St. Eloi, at the important junction of two main roads running from Ypres to Armentières and Warneton. Our lines enclosed the village eastward, and included a large mound on the southeast of it. The hostile sappers had run a mine under the mound, and after a hurricane fire of heavy shells on our eastern trenches the Germans exploded the mine, and then launched an infantry attack. Our riflemen and gunners brought the enemy down in large numbers, but the Prussian system of close-packed formations proved successful.

Our first line of trenches was carried, and though our infantry still offered a determined resistance, they were enfiladed, and compelled to retreat as evening fell. The hostile force then drove on, took our support trenches and the mined mounds, and occupied the village. At half-past two on the morning of Monday, March 15th, our 82nd Brigade attacked in the darkness, and at the bayonet-point captured part of the trenches in the village. It was here that the Canadian troops had their first deadly tussle with the Germans, for Princess Patricia's battalion marched from its billets, joined the 4th Rifle Brigade, and attacked the mound with great vigour and fighting skill. At the same time two Irish battalions—the 2nd Royal Irish Fusiliers and the 1st Leinsters—with the 2nd Duke of Cornwall's Light Infantry and the 4th Rifle Brigade, distinguished themselves in the heroic counterattack. In the first rush our troops were only partly successful, but just before dawn the men of the 82nd

The fighting at St. Eloi

Brigade and the "Stonewall" 80th Brigade stormed all the barricades the Germans had built across the streets, mastering the terrible fire of the enemy's machine-guns, and recaptured all their trenches eastward and westward of the village.

The fighting in the darkness, lighted only by searchlights and by the blaze of shells, was extremely fierce. But except for the mound, which was mined and bombarded into shapeless ruin, all our lost ground was recovered by Monday morning. The German commander was at the end of his resources, for he only sent out two hundred men to make a last assault. A few may have got back by crawling; the rest were heaped up before our trenches.

Assault on Hill 60

It afterwards appeared that our artillery, judging their target by a sort of divination, placed their shells right on the German supports and broke them up. This was the reason why our counter-attacks were so successful.

A month then passed without the enemy attempting to retaliate. This was a sign of weakness on his part, and Sir H. Smith-Dorrien looked for a point of attack. There was a small hill about two miles north-east of St. Eloi, known as Hill 60 (so called because its height—60 metres or 200 feet—enabled it to be distinguished on the map). It was not much of a position in itself, but it screened the German batteries firing on Ypres from the neighbouring ridge westward at Zandvoord. The Bedfords had driven their trenches close to Hill 60, and their sappers tunnelled below the ground and constructed three large mines under the low rise. As a matter of fact, the German sappers were also busily engaged in mining under the Bedfords' trench, but our men heard them at work, and laboured with exceeding energy to outrace them. The race in destruction was won on the evening of Saturday, April 17th, when our mines exploded, blowing three large craters in the hill. Nearly all the one hundred and fifty German troops manning the hill

7

SECTION OF GERMAN BARBED-WIRE ENTANGLEMENTS RUSHED BY THE BRITISH.
The passage was forced under heavy gun fire, indicated by the pall of smoke in the background.

trench perished, and the Bedfords leaped up, charged, and captured a quarter of a mile of the enemy's broken line.

So suddenly was the assault carried out that our men met with scarcely any resistance. They occupied the craters, building up defences of sand-bags, and though the German guns and howitzers bombarded them all the night they did not suffer much damage. The real fight opened at seven o'clock on Sunday morning, April 18th, when a strong German infantry force advanced in close formation against the hill. Our guns caught them; but they were Saxons and brave fighters, and they pressed on up the hill slope for a bayonet charge. But by this time the Bedfords had been reinforced by the West Kents, and the West Kents are one of the finest fighting regiments in the world; they may have equals in the Worcesters and others, but they have no superiors. In addition, we had about thirty motor machine-guns, which were brought to the hilltop. The machine-guns took the enemy in front,

while our shrapnel fire raked his flank. Twice the Germans tried to charge up the hill. Our men sang songs as the foe charged, and killed him first in hundreds and then in thousands.

All day Sunday the German commander continued to hurl his troops against our trenches. As the hill formed a salient, the German corps commander was able to attack it from three sides, and bring a cross-fire to bear on our hastily-made defences. All day our men held out without reinforcements, waiting until the enemy collected for the charge, and then meeting him with magazine-rifle fire and with the sweeping stream of bullets from the machine-guns. But by continuing the pressure at all costs, the hostile commander managed to capture the southern edge of the hill at about six o'clock in the evening. The British brigadier-general opposing him had, however, full control of the situation, and sent up a battalion of Highlanders and the Duke of Wellington's Regiment to strengthen the weary Bedfords and West Kents. The Highlanders, tall, sinewy men, went to **The rival claims** work with the bayonet and hand-grenade, **to Hill 60** and greatly helped to sweep the Germans from their last foothold. Night fell with our troops firmly entrenched in the conquered position.

Meanwhile the German commander, writing his nightly reports to headquarters, anticipated events by saying that he had recaptured the hill. So the next day the neutral world was astonished to hear from Sir John French that Hill 60 was in his possession, and to learn from the Duke of Würtemberg that he also possessed Hill 60. Thus it came about that a little local affair, on an unimportant mound, became one of the most famous conflicts in the Great War. For some months there had been an increasing disagreement between the daily official reports published by the German and French Staffs. The neutral public did not know what to think of the matter, and by tacit, spontaneous agreement in Europe and America, Hill 60 was made a test case.

This was extremely awkward for Duke Albrecht of Würtemberg and his too-confident subordinate general. All they could do in the circumstances was to turn their statement into a prophecy by the recapture of the lost

IN A BRITISH TRENCH AT YPRES.
The photograph was taken a few moments before the order was given to charge the enemy's lines.

mound of earth. But, naturally, Sir John French acquired a deep and personal interest in the now world-famous hill of conflicting reports. Large reserves of British troops were moved towards the position ; our artillery there was reinforced, and our rough sand-bag defences were improved by the engineers. All Sunday night the German guns thundered against the little hill. The intense, hysterical rage of the Germans at being caught in a misstatement, and then baffled by force of arms, caused them to cast off the last shreds of civilisation. One more scrap of paper was torn up —the Convention signed at The Hague on July 29th, 1899, by which the German Government, with all other civilised Powers, undertook not to employ projectiles whose only object was to diffuse asphyxiating and noxious gases. Our men on Hill 60 were smitten on three sides by projectiles filled with compressed poisonous gases. The East Surrey Regiment, who held the mound at the latter part of the long fight, suffered terribly. Their faces and arms turned a shiny, grey-black colour, and they

Germans use poisoned gas groaned as they struggled for breath, the membrane of their throats thickened, and their lungs were eaten up by the chlorine fumes. Death in many cases was very slow in coming ; the horrible, ghastly torture lasted from one to three days.

But in spite of the fumes our men fought on. Private Dwyer, of the East Surreys, holding a position on the crest, was especially remarkable for his heroic fighting skill. In between the bursts of artillery fire, hostile storming parties with hand-grenades tried to bomb their way through our trenches. But they were beaten back in violent and bitter hand-to-hand fights in the labyrinth of winding approaches surrounding the trenches. The battle went on till Wednesday morning, April 21st, when the enemy was again driven over the edge of the hill. By this time the Germans had brought their field-guns within close range of our position ; but our airmen and gunners made the adventurous hostile infantry pay for its daring, and by Wednesday evening the German guns had had enough of it and withdrew.

Some of our officers and men on Hill 60 had stood against the German guns and the Prussian Guard at Ypres the previous November, and they said that the little hill battle was by far the more terrible ordeal. The ground

BELGIAN VISCOUNT (LEFT) AND A COMPANION IN THE BELGIAN TRENCHES.
They are wearing captured German helmets.

our troops held was only about two hundred yards long and two hundred yards broad. Hundreds of guns were massed against it, and for four and a half days the mound was buried in tons of metal and high-explosive, and wreathed in clouds of poison gas. Yet our men did not give way, though the shell fire destroyed whole sections in an instant, and so filled the trenches with dead bodies that reinforcements could only reach the front line by climbing over their dead comrades. In spite of the infernal destruction, the wonderful British soldier remained not only cool but cheerful. What cheered him was the fact that he did not need to be told that the Germans perished by the thousand—he could see it.

Still the Germans would not accept defeat. They waited until the wind blew at about four miles an hour from their trenches, and then, on the morning of May 5th, they completely blotted out Hill 60 in a high, greenish-yellow fog of poison gas. The East Surreys, who had

TRAGIC SCENE IN A VILLAGE IN FLANDERS, WHERE A GERMAN SHELL HAD BURST NEAR A BRITISH TRANSPORT WAGGON.
The four horses were killed instantly. Their driver was thrown from his seat and seriously injured. A comrade is seen about to assist him.

B

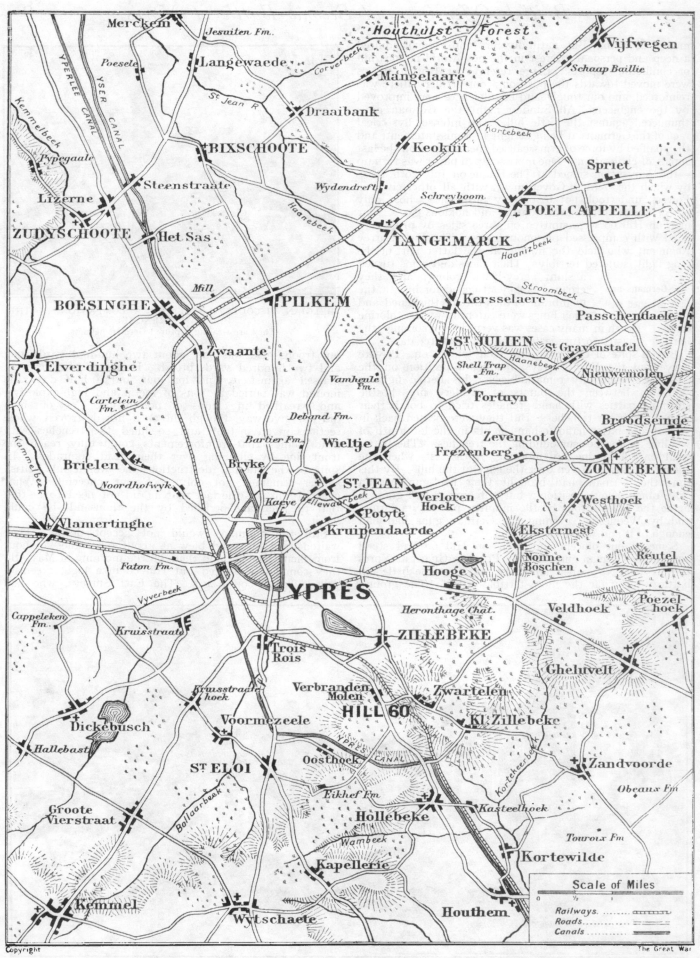

Scale of Miles

Railways ......
Roads ......
Canals ......

MAP SHOWING THE PLACES MENTIONED IN OUR HISTORICAL NARRATIVE OF THE BRITISH
OFFENSIVE AND THE SECOND BATTLE OF YPRES.

FIELD KITCHEN OF THE FRENCH ARMY IN THE
VICINITY OF NEUVILLE ST. VAAST.

beaten the enemy back on May 1st, now had to
retire to escape complete asphyxiation. But when
the gas-cloud passed they charged back up the
hill, where the enemy in turn had placed a great
number of machine-guns. Helped by a heavy shell
fire from our guns, the East Surreys reached some
of their lost trenches in the first rush, and then
fought on indomitably. In the end, neither side
held Hill 60. There was no hill to hold. It was
blown up and scattered by tens of thousands of
high-explosive shells. But we held the trenches
close by, and formed them into the base of our
salient round Ypres.

In the meantime the entire salient of Ypres
had become the scene of a long and most
desperate battle—one of the most desperate
battles in the whole war. Our delay in resuming

Desperate battle round Ypres

the offensive after Neuve Chapelle was
an undisguised revelation of weakness,
and the German Staff decided therefore
to attack. Reinforcements amounting to
about 150,000 men were sent through Belgium, in addition
to the troops sent to replace the larger part of the Prussian
Guard and other first-line soldiers moved to the eastern
front to form the Grand Phalanx. In the matter of men,
however, the odds were not against our Second Army, as
we had fairly large reserves. Falkenhayn, who directed
the operations, was not relying on infantry power. In
this respect he had a severe lesson at Ypres the previous
autumn, and he profited by it. In spite of the material
needed to build up the 4,000-gun battering-ram against
Russia, the German Commander-in-Chief had such enormous
resources that he was still able to overwhelm us with
artillery fire. He brought up the great Krupp naval
guns, and the 17 in. howitzers and 11 in. howitzers which
had been used along the Belgian coast in repelling Admiral
Hood's battleships and monitors.

This new siege train was placed in position against Ypres,
and provisioned with an extraordinary amount of shells.
But even this was not enough to ensure absolute success.
So about the end of March a new weapon of destruction

BARRICADE OF ELECTRIFIED WIRE IN FRONT OF A FRENCH
TRENCH.

was brought to the front. All along the German lines
round Ypres—northward, southward, and eastward—gas-
cylinders were placed on March 30th, 1915. Each steel
cylinder was about fifty-three inches long, and was filled
with various kinds of gases—chlorine and formaline being
most widely employed. The cylinders were stored in bomb-
proof casemates, in the proportion of one to every six and
a half feet of the front. The officers directing the gas
operations then waited until the wind was in an easterly
or north-easterly direction. They had a long time to
wait as the south-westerly spring breezes were blowing.

They patiently whiled away the time by putting their
troops through the respirator drill, and our men afterwards
noted that among the German respirators
taken were some marked with the date **German respirators**
1911. Apparently the German Staff had **dated 1911**
contemplated employing poisonous gas
at the time of the Agadir crisis. In this case, as in others,
they had only agreed to Germany signing the Hague Convention against the use of asphyxiating gases with the
object of preventing other countries from preparing in
advance any form of defence against the weapon they
intended to use. They were especially apprehensive of
the use of gas by our country, which, by some, was

11

supposed to be the feature of the famous war plan prepared by Admiral Cochrane, son of the scientific Lord Dundonald. They believed in getting their blow in first, and used the humanitarian machinery of The Hague in order to disarm us, while they were secretly arming themselves. This was one more instance of the scheme of universal slaughter prepared in every detail by the German military class.

For more than three weeks the Germans vainly waited for a steady, favouring wind. It never came, and on Thursday, April 22nd, after they had been killing dogs by the hundred in asphyxiating experiments, they resolved to profit by a south-easterly wind blowing towards the French part of the front, north of Ypres. Here a French Colonial division of Zouaves and Turcos held the line stretching from Dixmude to Langemarck. Behind them was the Yser Canal, and in front of them a tract of wooded

IN THE FRENCH LINES—OFFICIAL PHOTOGRAPH OF A COMMUNICATION TRENCH.
Although the Germans were unexcelled in the art of trench-making, the French proved not less thorough in their construction.

country held by part of the Duke of Würtemberg's army. At Langemarck the allied line was continued by the men of the Canadian Division under General Alderson. Behind the Canadians was the village of St. Julien, and on their right was Zonnebeke and the Roulers road, from which our lines swerved round south-west to Hill 60. The German general calculated that, if the French Colonial Division was broken north of Ypres, the line of the Canadians could be turned and Ypres captured in a sudden, driving, overwhelming sweep. The German soldiers appear to have been instructed in this plan, for their battle-cry was : " Forward and into Ypres ! "

The gas-cylinders were opened about five o'clock on Thursday afternoon. The gas had been pumped in under great pressure, so that when the cylinders were opened it

spurted out with great force, and did not float upon the wind until it was about a hundred yards from the German trenches. There, losing its impetus, it gathered into a low-lying cloud of greenish colour, which turned yellow as it streamed up to a height of about two hundred feet. The ghastly fog-bank drifted slowly down the wind, remaining thick on the ground owing to the density of the gases, and pouring into the French trenches and surprising all the troops there.

First their eyes began to smart under the influence of the formaline vapour, then the deadly chlorine acted on the membrane of their throats, and so thickened it that they began to choke. Last, and worst of all, **Ghastly effects of the chlorine** the chlorine entered the delicate fabric of the lungs and ate it away with a horrible, torturing, burning effect, leaving the stricken, helpless victims outstretched in the trenches, fighting in vain for air, and perishing in the most cruel of agonies. The luckiest men were those who quickly fell half suffocated, and got into the thickest poison-fumes, for they had a fairly quick death. Those who were able to drag themselves away, with their throats nearly closed, their lungs half burnt out, and their eyes protruding from their blackened faces, had sometimes to endure a week's torture before they won the peace of the grave.

There was no defence against the gas. The unprepared Frenchmen and Algerians either died, or fell back towards the Yser Canal, half blind, and suffering greatly. Then behind the gas-cloud came the German troops. Their advanced outposts wore gas-proof helmets, while the main force of infantry was provided with respirator masks. They brought up machine-guns and occupied the low ridges north of Ypres, and forced a passage across the canal by Steenstraete and Het Sas villages, and constructed fortified bridge-heads on the western bank. More than a thousand bodies of half-choked, but still living men were picked up by the enemy, and proudly numbered among their prisoners. Thirty guns were captured, including four 4·7 in. British guns which had been lent by the Canadian Division to strengthen the lines held by their French comrades.

The position of the Canadian Division was then one of extreme peril. They were holding a line of about 5,000 yards, with two brigades in the trenches and a third brigade in reserve. The 3rd Brigade had joined on with the French line a little south of the hamlet of Poelcappelle. The 2nd Brigade continued the British line southward towards Zonnebeke. When the French retired, the 3rd Brigade was left jutting out into the void, and the Germans began to assail it in the rear as well as in the front. Brigadier-General Turner showed a magnificent grasp of the situation. He extended his men in open order in a south-westward direction, while still holding on to Poelcappelle. Brigadier-General Curry, commanding the 2nd Brigade, also extended his men quickly towards Poelcappelle. The result was that the two Canadian Brigades were drawn out into a very thin line, which formed a sort of **Peril of Canadian Division** broad, blunt wedge covering the northern approaches to Ypres from Zonnebeke to the Yser Canal.

Against the Canadians were at least two German army corps, supported by innumerable machine-guns and heavy artillery. Reckoning infantry forces alone, there were 50,000 Germans against 8,000 Canadians, and when the attack opened there still was a gap on the left of the Canadians' thin and hastily re-formed line. There was no time to bring up the reserve brigade from its billets and hurry British reinforcements with guns to the northern side of

Elliott & Fry.

Admiral Sir Henry Bradwardine Jackson, K.C.B.,
Appointed First Sea Lord, May 27th, 1915.

Field=Marshal Sir Evelyn Wood, V.C., inspecting the Inns of Court Offi

Remarkable photograph of a British attacking party taking cover in a ne

...ining Corps, which gave so many able young officers to the New Armies.

...red German trench, the broken wire entanglements being seen on the left.

A French "75" trained on the Germans at 2,800 yards. Only the muzzle is visible.

Serving a French heavy gun in position in the St. Aubin region.

Ypres. The result of the unexpected gas attack had been obtained so quickly that the German forces had swung against the Canadians long before any help could arrive.

The Canadians were raw troops, most of whom had been neither trained nor disciplined at the outbreak of hostilities. Their officers were mainly men of the professional classes—young lawyers, college professors, estate agents, and business men. There was just a sprinkling of veterans of the Paardeburg days. The divisional commander, General Alderson, was a brilliant man of **How Ypres was** war, who had won fame by his masterly **saved** handling of the regiment that never lost a trench—the West Kent. He had some first-rate British Staff officers, but as a whole his division was formed of troops of the third class, according to the Continental way of estimating soldiers. They were neither regulars of the first line nor reservists of the second line, but quite a new formation, trained since the war began. As a matter of theory, therefore, they should have done badly. For they were in such a position of extreme and overwhelming danger that, had they been first-line troops like the French soldiers retiring on their left, they might have been excused for giving ground. Their situation was hopeless and agonising ; for if they gave ground, with the odds at more than five to one against them, Ypres was lost.

To the eternal glory of Canada, they rose to the tragic occasion, these eight thousand overwhelmed men, and saved the British Army from a terrible disaster. All through the evening and night of Thursday they held their ground, with the apex of their newly-formed line running in the direction of St. Julien. The enemy did not at first show much daring. He was too cautious at the opening of the conflict in seeking for the path of least resistance. With quick and cool resourcefulness the amateur forces of Canada met the veteran first-line troops of Germany and fought them off, taking the fiercest assault at the apex above St. Julien instead of at the gap near the canal.

Time was thus gained for the 1st Brigade to arrive, together with British reinforcements. Then about midnight the Canadians, under the direction of their skilled and resolute commander, General Alderson, made the stroke that really saved Ypres. In front of the Canadian Scottish of the 3rd Brigade and the 10th Battalion of the 3rd Brigade was a wood containing the four lost guns that had been lent to the French. The trees could be seen in the light of the misty moon about five hundred yards away. The wood was occupied by 7,000 German troops, who had built forts defended by machine-gun parties with sand-bags. No enemy was visible as Colonel Leckie led the Canadian Scottish forward and Colonel **Canadians' heroic** Russell Boyle led out his 10th Batta- **advance** lion. But when the leading companies were in the hollow, about two hundred yards from the mass of trees, the line of hostile machine-guns squirted upon them a continuous sheet of bullets.

Yet the four charging lines never wavered. When one man fell another took his place. The survivors of the two battalions burst over the low ridge and through the hedge where the Germans were entrenched, and then entered the shadowy wood. Here it was wild hand-to-hand fighting in clumps and batches amid the brushwood, the Canadians having only their rifles against the machine-gun forts forming the German support line. The brushwood fighting suited the Canadian temperament in the white-hot stage. Yelling, rushing, stabbing, firing, they got the Germans on the rush, turned them into a demoralised mob, broke into their last trench, and chased them

through the wood. Two more Canadian battalions were waiting outside as a reserve, to be flung into the fight at the critical moment. But there was no critical moment. The 2,000 charging troops swiftly routed more than three times the number of enemies and, leaving a broad trail of dead and wounded foes behind them, swept out from among the trees and went at the double another five hundred yards into the German lines. There, however, they were brought under a cross-fire, and in a stubborn fight they retired and entrenched round the wood they had captured. In the wood they recovered their 4·7 in. guns, or at least the wreck of them, as the pieces had been blown up by the enemy.

All through the night the battle continued, the enemy's shrapnel fire sweeping the wood as a tropical storm sweeps the leaves in the forest. At six o'clock on Friday morning the left wing of the Canadian Division by the wood became

ON THE ALERT IN A FRENCH FIRST-LINE TRENCH.

terribly involved. The German commander tried both to break it and to outflank it. This movement General Alderson answered by another forward leap. Two Canadian battalions of the 1st Brigade, with 4,000 British troops, advanced against the German position. Guns and Maxims played on the thin khaki lines as they moved forward in quick rushes. The 4th Canadian Battalion came under an annihilating fire, but as it wavered, its commanding officer, Lieut.-Colonel Burchill, came forward with a light cane and rallied his men, only to fall dead at their feet. That should again have dismayed them ; instead, it only maddened them. With a scream of anger, the entire battalion surged forward, and in a direct frontal attack, carried out in clear daylight, the German trench was stormed at the bayonet point. This trench was the most important point in the enemy's movement of advance, for it represented the apex in the breach made in the Allies' original line. The position

LT.-COL. RUSSELL LAMBERT BOYLE.
10th Alberta Battalion (killed).

BRIG.-GENERAL M. S. MERCER.
Commanding the First Canadian Brigade.

LT.-COL. C. B. LECKIE.
Commanding the Canadian Scottish.

was not only captured by the Canadians and the British, but was held by the victorious troops for four days under a continual bombardment. The men never budged, and when they were at last relieved by fresh troops the line was still held as they had won it.

Meanwhile, Brigadier-General Turner with the 3rd Brigade held the left flank of the new salient north of St. Julien. Twice on Thursday the Germans attacked through a fog of poison gas, but the brigade held the wood all the Thursday night. Then on Friday morning the brigade was again suffocated by a cloud of deadly fumes. The gas was especially thick over the trenches held **Highlanders' fight** by the 48th Highlanders. They could **to the death** not live in it, so they gave ground and let the gas blow away; then the heroic survivors charged back through a terrible cannonade and rifle fire and recovered their trenches. Their commander, Colonel Curry, was a magnificent leader. Directed by him, the battalion held on with the bayonet when their ammunition ran short, and at a loss of six hundred and ninety-one officers and men out of a total strength of eight hundred and ninety-six, the 48th Canadian Highlanders fought both the masses of Germans round St. Julien, with a handful of Buffs, Turcos, and Zouaves holding the east of the village.

One Highlander company with its medley of Allies fought to the death in the village. Not one man got away. At last the situation became dramatically critical. The Dublin Fusiliers were coming up at the double to reinforce the overpowered Canadians. Could the Highlanders hold out? They did! When the Dublins were still a quarter of a mile away, the fight in the Canadian second line— the first line had been lost—was over. Ypres was saved. Among the wounded officers of the Canadian Highlanders was a lineal descendant of Colonel McKay, who climbed the Heights of Abraham at Quebec with General Wolfe. Buried by a heavy

BRIG.-GEN. R. E. W. TURNER,
V.C., D.S.O.
Commanding the Third Canadian Brigade.

18

howitzer shell, he crawled to a dressing station with a bad wound in his head. He was adjutant to the regiment, and though half unconscious he gripped all the time some regimental papers with which he had been dealing when the " coal-box " fell.

Equal in heroism to the 48th Canadian Highlanders were their comrades of the same brigade, the Royal Highlanders of Montreal. One of the Royal Highlanders' officers, Captain McCuaig, fell seriously wounded in a hastily-made trench, and, refusing to move, continued to direct his men. At last the situation became desperate. A considerable force of German troops swung past the unsupported left of the **How Captain McCuaig** brigade, and slipping into the wood of **died** St. Julien, attacked the Canadians from the rear. The Montreal Highlanders then received peremptory orders to retire. The men wanted to carry their maimed captain with them. But he would not let them do so, knowing that the burden of his body would slacken their speed of movement and add to the risk of all their lives. All he asked for was two more loaded revolvers in addition to that which he was holding in his right hand. Then he ordered his men to draw back as quickly as they could, and with his three revolvers he waited, his smitten body racked with pain, to strike down the first line of the oncoming Germans, and thus win more time for his men to retreat. The end of this very gallant man reminds one of the conduct of Captain Oates, in the South Pole Expedition. The British race does breed great-hearted gentlemen.

On Friday afternoon, April 23rd, seven battalions of British troops arrived and strengthened the Canadian line. At the same time the Zouaves and the Belgian Carabiniers attacked the Germans from the west along the Yser Canal and recaptured the village of Lizerne. But this gain was outbalanced by the advance of the heavy German artillery along

CAPT. McCUAIG.
Montreal Royal Highlanders (killed).

THE ONCOMING FOE—OUR MEN AWAITING THE ORDER TO CHARGE.

An extraordinarily vivid photograph of a rare incident. For once the Germans came out to charge a British trench, and our men are seen awaiting the order from their officer to meet the foe in the open.

"PARDON, KAMERAD!" DEMORALISED GERMAN SOLDIERS IN THE ACT OF SURRENDERING EN MASSE INTO THE HANDS OF THE VICTORIOUS FRENCH.

the northern section of the Ypres front. The Canadian salient, with its ill-made, shallow trenches, was fearfully battered by heavy shells; and though each attempt made by the hostile infantry to carry our trenches under cover of the bombardment was defeated, the pressure of the two massed German army corps became overpowering. For the Germans only fought rearguard actions against the French and Belgians along the Yser Canal, while swinging their main forces against the Canadians and British troops. Ypres was their objective. All Germany was feverishly anxious for news of the capture of Ypres.

Our men fell back upon St. Julien, and then, with the 3rd Canadian Brigade still fighting on a double front, the brigade uncovered St. Julien and retired towards Ypres. For several hours after the brigade had retired, the sound of rifle firing still came from St. Julien village. There the Canadian rearguard, every man of whom deserved the Victoria Cross, fought a long and

Superb example of British courage hopeless battle against annihilating odds, and perished to save their comrades.

With the retirement of the Canadian left, the Canadian centre held, and the 2nd Brigade under Brigadier-General Curry had to repeat the manœuvre of the 3rd Brigade. The Brigadier-General extended his line and flung his left flank southward, and fought on until Sunday afternoon. By this time his field fortifications had been wiped out by the high-explosive shells of the enemy's heavy artillery. But the men held on until they were relieved on Sunday by British troops.

In the meantime a remarkable achievement had been performed by the British Brigade during the retirement of the Canadians from St. Julien. General Alderson was in personal command of the reinforcements, and under his directions the left wing of the Canadian Division broke connection with the Canadian centre, leaving a gap in our lines a little below St. Julien. Through this gap poured the British soldiers. They were going to their death, most of them, in a break-neck assault upon the advancing victorious German front. As they passed the heroes of Canada, the veterans of the British Army gave a great, deep-throated cheer of admiration for the wonderful recruits from the land of the maple leaf who had saved Ypres.

Then the British Brigade went on to death and victory. The Germans swept it, front and flank, with machine-gun fire and sprayed it for a thousand yards with shrapnel. Our men went down like waves breaking on a beach.

But though wave after wave fell spent and broken, the tide of British courage moved onward. All the artillery of two German army corps could not arrest its movement. Neither could the German infantry. Our troops went over the enemy trenches with the bayonet, drove in the German front, and completely stopped the German advance all along the line. It was this magnificent tiger-leap of the British reinforcements that rounded off the superb defence of the Canadians and saved our position. By Sunday evening our lines ran from Fortuin, south of St. Julien, towards Passchendaele in a north-easterly direction. British troops garrisoned the rough trenches, with the shrunken 2nd Canadian Brigade in reserve. But the enemy still continued to press the attack on Ypres in a furious manner, by artillery bombardments varied by advances of massed infantry. On Monday morning, April 26th, Brigadier-General Curry again led his tired and battered men, reduced to a quarter of their original strength, into the firing-line.

All that day they held the apex of the British position north of Ypres, and they did not retire to their billets until the following Wednesday. This concluded the deathless feat of arms of the Canadian Division, by which it won the right to stand side by side with the immortal 7th Division of the regular British Army, by whose magnificent tenacity Ypres was in the first instance saved from German attack. What is particularly remarkable about the feat of arms of the Canadians is that it was the achievement of one of our new formations. The men were scarcely of the military standing of our Territorial troops. They occupied the same position as the civilians in the armies that Lord Kitchener had formed since the outbreak of hostilities. Yet they equalled the finest performances of the best regular troops—the performances of the Iron Division of France and the Immortal **A deathless feat of arms** Division of Britain. Great was their deed, but greater was its significance. The German Staff must, when they learnt of it, have begun to reflect seriously upon the probable qualities of our new national armies.

In the new Battle of Ypres the heroism of the Canadian troops was well matched by that of the British Territorials and Yeomanry. Splendid work was done by the Durham miners, forming the 8th Durham Light Infantry, under Lieutenant-Colonel Turnbull. These unseasoned troops, unused to trench work, were called upon in the middle of the night of April 24th to relieve the Winnipeg Rifles on the Gravenstafel ridge, north of Zonnebeke. The enemy were only three hundred yards away, and the miners were heavily bombarded with gas shells, and then attacked by a German force at least twice their own strength. Yet they held on for seven hours before they fell back in good order. Then, during their retirement, they were enveloped by the Germans, but they hacked their way out with bayonet and bullet, and displayed a stubborn courage all through the action against overwhelming numbers. Other Territorial troops of the Durhams held the line around Zonnebeke and Frezenberg on Monday, April 26th, and fought with great tenacity.

Story of Shell-Trap Farm For all the people of the North of England the ground between the canal at Ypres and Gravenstafel and Zonnebeke was hallowed in the spring of 1915. There were the Northumberland Territorials, forming part of the great counter-attacking brigade, in leading which General Riddell fell. They assaulted the village of St. Julien in the afternoon of April 26th in order to save our left wing near the canal. There was no time to reconnoitre the position, and all that the men could do was to storm along until they were stopped. This soon happened, because the enemy had put up wire entanglements and directed his guns on the barrier. But the Northumberlands got into the enemy's trenches in isolated parties, and under a terrific bombardment they held their position until the evening. The York and Lancaster Regiment also distinguished itself, when reinforcing the Rifle Brigade, by helping to shatter the German advance. The Northumberland Fusiliers, less than 1,000 men, faced a great German column, which formed the main strength of the enemy's attack, fought it with machine-gun fire and a minute of mad rifle fire, and completely broke it up. When the head of the column was blown away, the rest of the German troops broke from the line and fled to cover.

Shell-Trap Farm was one of the pivots of the battlefield, and was held by North of England men. The farm was a group of old Flemish buildings in the north-eastern part of the Ypres salient, near Fortuin. It won its new name from the extraordinary number of shells which the Germans dropped into it, until they knocked it into shapeless piles of bricks and pitted the ground, which they carpeted with fragments of metal. Then the attacking infantry tried to win the ruins as a shelter for their machine-gun parties. The result was a series of most desperate hand-to-hand conflicts. First a company of the 2nd Essex charged through the enemy's terrible artillery fire and captured the farm, bayoneting every man there. But in the night the Germans recaptured the position. At dawn, however, two platoons of the 1st East Lancashires went out with the bayonet and killed or routed the Germans. They were bombarded all day, about ten shells being sent for every Englishman holding the trench, and the next night the German infantry once more stormed and carried the farm. But the South Lancashires then swept like a whirlwind through the shelters and dug-outs and cleared them of Germans.

Shell-Trap Farm then became one of the most important posts on our line. It remained the everlasting target of the German howitzers in the Forest of Houthulst, and in the wood in front of Roulers. But many weeks passed before the German infantrymen attempted again to storm it. The moat round the farm was choked with dead bodies, English as well as German, but, as our soldiers could see with their own eyes, the enemy's losses had been something like ten times as heavy as ours.

In the first place, the farm seems to have been held by a patrol of the Monmouth Territorials. **How the Monmouths held on** They were cut off by shell fire, and a shell came through the roof and killed all the officers and non-commissioned officers in the building. One man then swam the moat and went to headquarters to report the condition of affairs. The Brigadier-General sent a message saying he hoped the "Terriers" would stick. The messenger got back to the farm through the curtain of shell fire, and soon afterwards a bandolier was flung over the moat to a waiting despatch-rider. In it was a scrap of paper on which was written "Of course we'll stick." And the little shattered Territorial patrol hung on to Shell-Trap Farm and beat back the enemy until our artillery

WONDERFUL CAMERA-RECORD OF A THRILLING MOMENT AT BOIS LE PRÊTRE.
On the left a grenade is being fired from a section of the advanced French trenches into the German lines. On the right the troops are on the point of leaving the trenches for a bayonet charge.

HOW THE NORTHUMBERLAND FUSILIERS MET AN ATTACK ON THEIR FIRST-LINE TRENCHES AT YPRES.

The trenches of "The Fighting Fifth" were distant only about a hundred yards from those of the enemy. In the early hours of morning the Germans attacked in force. They were met, however, with steady and continuous rifle fire, while the machine-gun seen on the left of the picture did some excellent work. It was, said an eye-witness, pretty hot work for a few minutes. But our men could not miss the masses of the advancing foe, and then our artillery began to play on the attacking force and on their communication trenches in the rear.

BRITISH RESPIRATOR PARADE AND INSPECTION.
An addition to our soldiers' daily routine, made necessary by the poisoned-gas campaign of the enemy.

"AFTERNOON TEA."
British wounded, on their way to the base hospital, are afforded a welcome relief at a small French railway station where tea was prepared for them by Red Cross men.

began to register hits on the spot. The few survivors then left the shell-trap, and the Germans took their place, only to be blown up by our guns, and then poked out by the bayonets of the 2nd Essex.

The men of Lancashire and Essex were again engaged side by side at the end of April. They were holding at night a line which was suddenly enveloped in a great cloud of poison gas. The wind carried the fumes most densely against the Lancashire Fusiliers. Most of the men, being without respirators, retired to let the gas pass before they charged and recovered the trenches. But there was no need for a charge, for one of the Lancashire Fusiliers, John Lynn, jumped on the parapet with a machine-gun and poured a stream of bullets towards the German trenches. He worked by guesswork, being at first unable to see through the poison-cloud. Then, as it thinned out, he caught the oncoming German line and shattered it, and with his throat half choked and his lungs badly burned, he remained crouching on the parapet. wait-

Lancashire Fusilier's brave deed ing for the next charge. The second time the Germans made only a half-hearted attempt to capture our trenches, and the single-handed heroic soldier smote them once more before they regain d their own lines. Private Lynn died the next day from asphyxiation, being awarded in death the V.C.

The 7th Argyll and Sutherlands had a happy adventure in one of the gas-clouds. Their brigadier ordered them to rush through the gas and retake a trench from which our men had been driven by the fumes. The Scotsmen went at the double through the green wall of death, recaptured the trench, and then began to see what had

happened to them. Not a man was hurt. Yet the brigadier, who afterwards went through the thinnest point of the gas-belt in order to reach his men, suffered very badly. In spite of his sufferings, however, he refused to go back for medical treatment. Maybe the long-headed, canny Scotsmen held their breath while they were racing through the fog of death. But even this must have wanted some doing, and the feat of the Territorial Highlanders was one of the most remarkable things in the war.

In addition to the continual clouds of poison gas, the troops defending Ypres had to withstand for nearly three weeks an artillery fire of extraordinary violence. The Germans had brought up from the coast more powerful parks of big howitzers and large-calibre guns than they had used in October and November of the previous year. Our entrenched infantry had to endure a deadly enfilading fire from pieces of ordnance of all sizes—from the 17 in.

GENERAL JOFFRE PRESENTING DECORATIONS TO FRENCH OFFICERS AFTER THE BATTLE OF ARRAS.

Dicke Bertha to the Minenwerfer, that threw out a sausage-shaped cylinder of high-explosive. On one small field through which our lines ran nine hundred shells of large calibre fell in two hours. It may be doubted whether the Russians on the Dunajec between Gorlice and Tarnow received more shells per man than our troops did in the last week of April and the first eight days of May. Had the German guns been able to place their shells exactly on our trenches, our entire defending force between Zonnebeke and the canal north of Ypres would have been annihilated by high-explosives.

During the critical days following the break and retreat of the French Division our men were fighting on three fronts. They had the enemy in their rear as well as on their left flank and before their eastern firing-line. They had hostile machine-guns at the back of them, hostile heavy batteries and surging waves of attacking infantry north of them, and the weight and metal of the principal forces of the Duke of Würtemberg directly in front of their old trenches. Terrific as had been the violence of the German attack in the first Battle of Ypres, it was surpassed in horror by the mechanical and chemical means of destruction employed by the enemy in the second battle for the shattered Flemish mediæval city. All our men could do was to sit tight and endure, day after day, the stifling gases and the terrible shells. They crouched hard against the sides of the trenches, or sheltered in the dug-outs, and there they were frequently called to dig their comrades from under masses of earth and overturned sand-bags.

Germans fear their own gas

Had the German infantryman possessed the pluck and dash displayed by his countrymen in the first battle, he might have won Ypres. But apparently he was frightened by his own poison fumes. He had been told so much about their deadliness that he was afraid to advance until the green fog had entirely disappeared. Then, when he did advance, his reception at the hands of our infuriated troops took the heart out of him. The Englishman is a very patient creature, with an extraordinary capacity for long-suffering. As the Belgian chronicler Froissart said in the days of Edward III., " The English-man suffers very patiently for a very long time. But," added Froissart, "in the end he pays back terribly." It was so at Ypres. When our men went Berserker, the silent, frigid fury of their onset was like nothing else seen on this bloodstained planet. They lived only in hope of an infantry attack by the enemy. The men of one battalion, holding the extreme right of the northern face of the salient, actually leaped from their trenches and cheered the Germans when they saw the flash of enemy bayonets. " Give us a chance to get at you ! Oh, God, give us a chance to get at you ! " they shouted. The Germans did not get at that battalion. Most of them were piled up dead or disabled within fifty yards of our trenches ; the rest fled.

Froissart's verdict verified

Not a single German infantry attack was pressed home. The men could be seen forming up on the Gravenstafel ridge in double battalions or in brigades, and then advancing under cover of a furious bombardment from their massed guns. Over the riddled fields they came, in solid masses of a green-grey colour, until our men could see the tense, anxious faces. But every time great gaps would suddenly be blown out of the advancing host, as our artillery caught them in the open with shrapnel. Before the gaps could close up our storm of rifle fire and the stream of bullets from our machine-guns would widen the gaps and break off all the edges of the surging grey masses.

For the first time in the war a large number of the German

24

infantry showed signs of abject terror. There are cowards in every army, and the first-line battalions of Germany were not free from them. But in the summer, autumn, and winter of 1914 and the early spring of 1915 the general reputation of the German troops in the western theatre of war was good. They fought skilfully, and when in difficulty they stood their punishment like men. But in the second Battle of Ypres the German infantry went to pieces. They showed no driving power, and lost all their best opportunities when there were large gaps in our line. They relied for their victory entirely upon their guns and chemicals, and when they found that our angry men, far from being annihilated, were waiting to get at grips with them, they either became mad or helpless with terror.

The fiendish cruelty of cowards

The madmen among them went to the extreme limit of cruelty. After bayoneting our asphyxiated and helpless troops, left behind in the continual retreats from the poison clouds, they took several of our wounded, both Canadians and British, and crucified them by means of spikes on the doors of Flemish farm buildings. According to the evidence taken on oath by the Mayor of Exeter, an extinguished fire was found beneath the feet of one of our dead, crucified soldiers. It was the Würtembergers under Duke Albrecht of Würtemberg who did this thing. On the other hand, many of the Würtemberg troops became sentimental and pious in their terror. One middle-aged German ran blindly in the charge made by his battalion, and when the charge was shattered by our rapid rifle fire the man continued to plunge forward until he nearly

reached the trench held by the North Somerset Yeomanry. Then he knelt down and said his prayers. The Somersets just waited until he had finished praying.

Our cavalry played a fine part in the later fighting on the Ypres salient. The North Somerset Yeomanry and the Leicestershire Yeomanry suffered heavily, and while the former were partly forced back the Somerset men managed to stick to their position. About the same time the 3rd Dragoon Guards were buried in the ruins of their blown-out trenches, and the wood in which the 1st Royals were lodged was set on fire. The position was restored on May 15th by a splendid charge of the 10th Hussars. The Germans at the time held a position by the two farms at Verloren-Hoek, between Zonnebeke and Ypres. First of all our aeroplanes circled over the Germans and reported the result of the first ranging shots of our artillery. Then the target was found, and our batteries worked at high pressure for a time, and as their limbers were nearing depletion three British armoured motor-cars came down the road from Ypres, swung round Frezenberg, and opened on the German trenches at point-blank range with quick-firing guns. After all this preparation the 10th Hussars made their great charge. One of our airmen, watching them from the skies, said that they came forward in the steady and regular manner of a parade movement. With them were the Leicestershire Yeomanry and a squadron of the Royal Horse Guards. In a swift, violent dash the cavalrymen took the trenches and destroyed or routed the hostile garrison at Verloren-Hoek. But no sooner had the German infantry been defeated than their heavy guns

10th Hussars' great charge

REPRESENTATIVE GROUP OF OUR INDIAN SOLDIERS IN A NATIVE MULE WAGGON. A QUAINT PHOTOGRAPH TAKEN IN A FRENCH VILLAGE.

bombarded the lost position, with the result that our men were blown out of the recovered line.

The second Battle of Ypres was a contest of flesh and blood against a gigantic machine. Whenever men met men our soldiers won. But when our front was hidden in a gas-cloud or the smoke of a great curtain of exploding German shells our troops had to retire, and then return and win back their position by a hand-to-hand contest. Yet both the Canadians and British Territorials were men fresh from home, flung suddenly into the most nerve-shattering conflict without, for the most part, having seen a shot fired in battle. They had to endure one of the most violent artillery bombardments, complicated by the horrible devilry of the poison-gas clouds. The breaking of the French line occurred in so unexpected a manner that there was no time for Staff preparations. Ypres had to be saved

EVENTIDE ON THE BATTLEFIELD.
With a French burial party. So many a hero—friend or foe—passed to his last resting-place.

with a wild rush by every man available to fill the gap and strengthen our thin and enveloped line.

The Territorials were led by amateur officers like the Canadians—by men who had spent their lives mainly in business offices. Nobly did they play their part, but owing to the suddenness of the first overwhelming surprise of the gas attack against the French Division, Sir Horace Smith-Dorrien and his Staff had to leave the event largely in the hands of their men. It was a soldiers' battle. Leaders like General Alderson planned and executed the counter-strokes, but the continual victories were won by the personal fighting quality of the private soldier. He was not defeated, because he would not admit defeat. Everything was against him—position, guns, numbers, superiority of machine-guns, gas-attack equipment, and the means of defence against gas attacks. The Germans had every possible advantage, but our men won through because they were one of the finest fighting stocks in the world, though perhaps they did not know it. The virtue of the race rose triumphant above imminent disaster, and

A soldiers' battle

it was the virtue of a peaceful commercial race, stamped both by Napoleon and by the modern Germans as a race of shopkeepers. Undoubtedly, we did keep shop, and grew prosperous thereby ; but when the time came for our business men, miners, and mechanics to handle a rifle, there was not much difference between them and the most famous of their fighting forefathers. And if any difference were there, the balance of merit resided with the modern Briton. In the second Battle of Ypres some of our troops held their trenches without relief for twenty-one days. Some of the men at Crecy, Agincourt, or Waterloo would have flinched from such a superhuman ordeal.

In the trenches for twenty-one days

A German Staff officer went so far as to remark to a foreign war correspondent visiting the German lines that our Territorial battalions were even better fighters than our regular troops. The praise was excessive, and reminded one of the old Roman proverb of being beware of the enemy when he comes bearing gifts. Our superbly-trained soldiers of the regular Army could not be placed second even to our heroic Territorials. Both of them had special qualities. The regular was the supreme master of his profession ; the Territorial, lacking the perfect training of his comrade, had a higher degree of cultivated intellectual power, and a noble kind of courage, born of imaginative fear quelled by an ecstasy of will-power. A highly-educated man is likely to go into his first battle in a state of tense apprehension, but when his native strength of character tells on his imagination he is apt to fight in a white heat of heroism. Thus did our Territorial troops and the Canadians, who resembled them in training and station of life.

Prominent among the tens of thousands of heroes of the second Battle of Ypres was Lance-Sergeant Belcher, of the London Rifle Brigade, a Territorial battalion. He was a characteristic representative of our nation of shopkeepers, being a young business man in one of the large furniture firms of London. The London Rifle Brigade did fine work all through the long, wearing fight. They first held a trench near Shell-Trap Farm, and with their left resting on the hamlet of Fortuin they endured a terrific bombardment, losing one hundred and seventeen men from shell fire in a single day. Yet when the German infantry attacked in the darkness they wiped out the assailers.

At last there were only two hundred and seventy-eight men left out of the Territorial battalion, and ninety-one of these fell during the day in the fierce attack made upon the trenches held by our cavalry on the road running from the hamlet of Wieltje up towards St. Julien village. Lance-Sergeant Belcher was in charge of an advanced breast-work south of this road on the morning of May 12th. The sand-bags were blown in by the hostile guns, and the violent and continuous bombardment went on until Belcher was left with only eight of his men and two Hussars. This little band elected to hold on by the road after the troops near them had been withdrawn. Except for them, the road was clear for the Germans to break through our front by Wieltje and make a flank attack on our Fourth Division.

Four of Lance-Sergeant Belcher's men were knocked out, and the trench was blown to bits. Yet all during the day the sergeant and his remaining troops—seven men in all—held the German army at bay, for every time the enemy collected for an attack Belcher ordered rapid fire. The Germans were only from one hundred and fifty to two

Fit Again.

To the Rest Camp.

In the Rest Camp—The Hay Cart.

The Sick Lines—Probing for Shrapnel.

Back to the Base. .

MORE SKETCHES OF EQUINE LIFE FROM AN OFFICER AT THE FRONT.

These delightful pencil sketches, illustrating phases of equine activity at the front, were sent to THE GREAT WAR by the well-known animal artist, on active service as an officer, to whom we and our readers are indebted for the sketches on page 365 of our second volume. They are reproduced untouched.

hundred yards away. But by maintaining a bold and also a skilful front, and by using so quick and deadly a fire that the breastwork seemed fully manned, the amazing London Territorial completely daunted the advancing German column, held the Wieltje road in the most critical phase of the battle, and saved a British division from a disastrous flank attack. This achievement ranks with that of the Worcesters at Gheluvelt in the first Battle of Ypres.

Seven men save a division But the Worcesters were a battalion when they saved the British line. Belcher and his men were only seven riflemen.

Similar in method and scope to the achievement of Lance-Sergeant Belcher, though perhaps not quite so important as the saving of an entire division, was the deed of Captain Railston, of the 1st Rifle Brigade. His trenches were almost blotted out by shell fire; traverse after traverse was destroyed, and the men fell in great numbers. A retreat was suggested, but Captain Railston would not think of it. He carried on so well that, though he was twice buried and wounded by heavy shell fire, he held the Germans off all day. Only three men and the captain were left, but by running up and down the trench and firing rapidly when a hostile advance was attempted, the four defenders held the position until two companies of another regiment arrived to support them. Captain Easton, of the 4th East Yorks Territorials, also held out with desperate and resourceful tenacity. He was hit three times, but he continued to move up and down the line, directing and cheering his men, who drove the enemy back with magnificent courage under a murderous bombardment.

Then in the desperate conflict of May 8th, when the Germans tried to break our line at Frezenberg, fine gallantry and fighting skill were displayed by Sergeant H. Crook, Corporal E. Smith, and Pte. W. J. Tookey, all of the 1st Yorkshire Light Infantry. The sergeant handled a desperate position with such coolness and ability that it was largely due to his efforts that our line remained unbroken. Corporal Smith undertook to carry a message for reinforcements under a terrific shell fire. The trench was full of dead and wounded; he could not work along it, but crawled outside to carry out his task. Private Tookey also took a message under heavy fire. When he crawled back to a wood, he found it occupied by the enemy, and waited until darkness fell; then he moved out and reported to his commanding officer. Captain Henry Mallison was in charge of the Yorkshiremen at Frezenberg, and directed the fire that drove back every infantry attack delivered by the enemy. All day the British trenches were raked and shattered by a severe and accurate bombardment, but not until night, with both flanks turned and no relief in sight, did Captain Mallison and his men retire fighting to their second line, a thousand yards in the rear.

Another hero of the Ypres battle was Sergeant W. Cooke, of the 2nd Dublin Fusiliers. Hidden on the roof of a farmhouse, he was sniping the enemy in a very effective manner when a gas-cloud swept over the ground. The green flood was only seven feet high, and the sergeant escaped it, but on coming down, when the air seemed to have cleared, the remnant of the poison fumes made him feel dizzy So back he climbed to his place on the roof.

There he saw a German lieutenant with ten men crawling down a trench towards our lines. With deadly rapid fire the Irish sergeant picked off the ten enemy privates. Then leaping from the farmhouse roof, he ran to the end of the trench, and levelling his rifle at the officer, took him prisoner.

But the stories of individual heroism in the fiercest of all struggles for Ypres are too numerous for the purpose of an historian. Officers and men won military honour by the hundred. Even the main actions of all the battalions cannot be related. But in addition to the regiments already mentioned, the 3rd and 8th Middlesex, 1st Highland Light Infantry, the 2nd Seaforths, the Welsh Regiment, and the 2nd East Kents added to their glory. On the fatal night of April 22nd it was Colonel Geddes of the Buffs, with a detachment of five battalions, who occupied the gap in our line. The Pathans, Sikhs, and Gurkhas arrived after a long night march from the south, and went furiously into action on Monday, April 26th. But the enemy had won so strong a position from Pilken to Gravenstafel that our reinforcements could not do more than save Ypres.

LANCE-SERGEANT D. BELCHER, V.C.
London Rifle Brigade.

The breaking of the French line on our left gave the Germans a sweeping field of fire over our lines of communication. Ypres itself was the most dangerous spot on the battlefield, and the entire civil population fled, leaving the street littered with dead and wounded, the rubble of fallen houses, and shattered vehicles. The shells poured on all our rear at Vlamertinghe, where our men were billeted, on our base at Poperinghe, the bombardment of the Hazebrouck railway line being terrific. This mighty curtain of shell fire was employed by the enemy to prevent reinforcements coming up while they were making a grand effort to break through to Calais. Sir John French at last decided to shorten the Ypres salient, and on the night of May 3rd our troops withdrew from Zonnebeke and Zevencot towards Wieltje and Frezenberg. The enemy then tried to cut through our shortened salient by a driving attack on its southern base, which was the famous Hill 60. But after a desperate struggle this movement was defeated. Then on May 8th the hostile massed guns poured out a tornado of high-explosive shells on our entrenchments left of Zonnebeke. Every yard of ground seemed to be churned and pulverised, and our new trenches were pounded into ruins. But when the German infantry advanced to drive us out of Ypres they were slaughtered in a ghastly way.

The Ypres salient shortened At one point of our lines they had to advance over a thousand yards of open ground. Battalion after battalion of them melted away under our fire. At other points they reached our trenches, only to be driven off with bayonets. All along the curving front they were repulsed. But our lines—which had a front of nearly sixteen miles and a depth of more than five and a half miles before the French Division was asphyxiated on our left—were reduced in the first week in May to a shallow, blunt curve, with a depth of only three miles and a front of only eight miles. Our position, therefore, was much more exposed to the concentrated fire of the German artillery from three sides.

In the second week in May the German bombardment of our Ypres position was resumed with fury, the German infantry attacking from the north-east and south-west.

Presented with "THE GREAT WAR." Part 49.

Photo. Boute.

Her Majesty, Elizabeth, Queen of the Belgians.

WHERE THE BRITISH AND BELGIAN LINES MET ON THE BATTLE-FRONT IN FLANDERS.
Allied infantrymen fighting side by side in the trenches as they fought in the memorable retreat from Antwerp. On the right of the photograph a Belgian officer is seen directing the fire of his own men against the ruthless ravagers of their country.

Here trenches were lost and recovered, and lost again, and again recaptured. The chief attacks came from the wooded tract south of the Menin road. The Germans came on always in close formation, until it was reckoned that 150,000 of them had been vainly sacrificed in the second Battle of Ypres. The town was worth nothing to us. It was a weakness, and not a source of strength. On pure strategic considerations we should have retired over the canal, and have made this water and the Douve River the moats guarding our first and second lines. But Sir John French would not retire from Ypres because moral motives were at the time of more importance than sound, scientific dispositions. The entire German public wanted Ypres. All that happened in the eastern theatre of war interested them less than Ypres. So, by the most desperate feat of endurance in history, our troops held on to Ypres against overwhelming odds, while using their main strength and striking at the enemy in another direction.

We have refrained until now from introducing into this history any direct, first-hand descriptions of fighting by our men; for one man's picture of his section of a modern front is usually too fragmentary a thing for the general purpose. Yet in the wild, confused, and desperate conflicts that marked the second phase of the struggle for Ypres, the adventures of many a single soldier of our Second Army had an uncommon representative character, especially when he was marched from point to point in rapid manœuvres, each ending in a violent contest. We shall, therefore, conclude this chapter in the epic of Ypres with a hitherto - unpublished description of the large share of fighting that fell to a private in the Queen Victoria's Rifles. It is calculated to bring home to the reader, in a way no general account can do, the prolonged intensity of effort which was required of each individual in this great soldiers' battle :

At 7 p.m. on Saturday night, April 17th, 1915, while on rest at "Canvas Town" (the hut encampment near Vlamertinghe), a terrific bombardment commences. We know this is the beginning of a big attack at Ypres, and that Hill 60, on which the R.E.'s have been working for weeks preparing mines, is to be blown up. The bombardment continues all night, but does not disturb my sleep. At 7 a.m. the next morning (Sunday, 18th) we are awakened by the shouting of " stand to " orders. Battalion sports had been arranged, and the enjoyment to which we had been looking forward is knocked on the head. We hastily get our breakfast. Orders are made and cancelled, but we finally move off at 9.15 a.m. and march to Ypres. Here we are put in a temporary billet, in a remaining undamaged portion of a fine old convent.

We " stand by," and I disport myself on the lawn outside smoking and chatting, but not for long. Very soon comes the order for my platoon and another to " fall in " in clean fatigue, and we march a short distance to what is known as the Lille Gate. Here we collect barbed-wire entanglements, and proceed in the direction of the firing-line. All is well till we pass Brigade Headquarters and get on to the railway track. Then shrapnel begins to fly about in a very discomforting fashion, but we practically take no notice. Slightly wounded men, chiefly K.O.S.B.'s from last night's attack, pass us continually, and serious cases come by on stretchers. An R.A.M.C. stretcher-bearer is hit in the head by a shrapnel bullet. One of our fellows takes his place. We reach the railway cutting, close to the dressing station, and leave our entanglements ; then return to Brigade Headquarters and make several more journeys with ammunition, rifle, and hand-grenades. A shell catches the roof of a barn adjoining Headquarters, and it is soon in flames. There are several casualties. We make our final journey, and this time we carry the goods through a long communication trench. It is a tedious job, for wounded men are continually passing us on their way to the dressing station. We reach the front-line trench. Two companies following us are to make a charge at 6 p.m. There is no time for us to get out in safety, and our officer decides it is better to take our chance in the trench. The whistle blows at 6 p.m., and the fine Yorkshire lads are over the parapet.

A terrific bombardment follows. The air is thick with fumes from asphyxiating gas, and our eyes smart terribly. We are practically useless, but do what little we can handing along ammunition, bandaging and helping the wounded. I have to close my eyes as a man is brought along—his brains are hanging out of his head. When news comes that the attack has been successful and the bombardment ceases, we file along the communication trench into the railway

THE FIRST TERRITORIAL V.C.
Second-Lieutenant Geoffrey Harold Woolley, of the Queen Victoria's Rifles. At Hill 60, on the night of April 20-21st, 1915, he picked up a hand-grenade which had been thrown into the trench, and before the fuse had burned to the charge threw it out, thereby saving many lives.

BEHIND THE FIRING-
LINE AT YPRES.
Ambulances waiting to convey wounded out of the
danger zone.

GALLANT RED CROSS WORK UNDER FIRE.
A French Red Cross doctor, after tending a wounded soldier in a communication trench near Moncel, is conducting his patient to a place of
safety. A dead comrade is seen lying in the foreground.

THE HUNS' VENGEANCE ON BRICK AND STONE.
Baulked twice by the British in their effort to take Ypres, the Germans
made every prominent building in the beautiful old-world city a target
for their big guns, with the result that only shaking ruins of the historic
Cathedral were left, all the exquisite stained glass being shattered.

cutting, and eventually arrive safely
back at our billet at 9 p.m. Our
casualties in the two platoons total
four wounded only—surprisingly small
considering. We have some hot stew,
having had nothing to eat since our
hurried breakfast before leaving our
huts; then we turn in, and I am soon
sound asleep.

At 7 a.m. the next morning (Monday,
19th), we are hurriedly paraded (the
whole battalion), and are marched in the
direction of the railway once more, but
this time across fields, and not by the
road as yesterday. We are halted when
we arrive at the embankment, and take
possession of a dug-out—about a mile
from Hill 60. Adjoining the embankment is a large pond, and I take the
opportunity of having a wash. The
day passes uneventfully. Beyond us
motor-ambulances pass continually
bearing the wounded from the dressing
station to hospital. About mid-day
the Germans begin shelling Ypres with
their renowned "Jack Johnsons." It
is fortunate we shifted, I am thinking.
At dusk a party goes back to fetch
rations and the post. I light a candle
in my dug-out, and read the letters I
have received, after which I try to
snatch a few hours' sleep, but cold
keeps me awake.

The next day (20th) is spent in a similar fashion till seven p.m.,
when orders come along to get ready to march away. We go across
fields, and very shortly come under disconcerting shell and rifle
fire, entailing a number of casualties, finally reaching some more
dug-outs in a wood on the left of the railway cutting. Shelling
continues. My friend Devereux and I secure a dug-out between us,
and start work improving it with our entrenching tools as far as is
possible. About 11 p.m., 13th and 14th platoons are called out.
We leave our packs and haversacks in the dug-out, and our
captain leads us once more to the cutting. He is wounded just
before we gain the communication trench, and the platoon officer,
Mr. Summerhayes, takes his place. We are all unaware what is in
store for us. A roughly-made communication trench from the
original fire trench to the summit of Hill 60 is traversed.

We are soon busy firing. Dawn (21st) gradually appears, and
the enemy begins bombarding with hand-grenades. One by one I
see my pals fall. Maisey and Pearson a little
way on my right are lying—never to move   **"Pals fall one by
again. Mr. Woolley * takes command after   one"**
Major Lees and Mr. Summerhayes have been
killed, and the remaining officer of the Bedfords in sight. What a roar and tumult! Maxim guns are
hammering away, shrapnel bursting above us, and blinding
flashes follow the explosion of hand-grenades. My rifle becomes
too hot to hold, and I throw it aside for another. A bomb
explodes a few yards away on my left among the Bedfords. What
happens to them I don't know. I feel no longer a human being.
Simply mechanically I continue firing. A glance to the rear—
Corporal Peabody is attending a wounded man. Mr. Woolley
appears at the mouth of the communication trench and encourages
us by saying reinforcements are coming up. A blinding flash, and
something hits me full in the face—a feeling as though someone has
smacked the bristle side of a stiff brush in my face. My hand
instinctively goes up—no, there is no blood. Only fine particles
of earth have reached me, but Devereux and Wickens are both
wounded from the same explosion, and grope their way to the rear.

The Devons begin to arrive, and as they come up, we make our
way to the rear—crawling on hands and knees along the low, badly-
damaged communication trench into the original fire trench, and
from there to the communication trench leading on to the railway
cutting. Passing the Northumberland Fusiliers on our way, we
reach another communication trench, leading from the railway to
the support dug-outs, which are in what was once a wood. But few
trees are left—mostly short stumps, for the tops have been blown off.
Here we are gathered into some sort of order, and go across a couple
of fields to some more dug-outs.

Till now my nerves have stood me well; but as I recall the fearful
sights I have witnessed, and realise the majority of my pals are
gone, I give way and break down, sobbing like a child on its mother's
knee. Presently I pull myself together and have a little food. It
is about 11 a.m. (Wednesday, April 21st). I obtain permission to
return to the wood to secure my pack. With some difficulty I locate
the position of the dug-out Devereux and myself had occupied the
previous night, but I happen to spot the packs. The dug-out had
been transformed to a shell hole, and it was lucky for us both we
weren't in it at the time; my haversack is missing.

Night falls, and tired out, cramped though my position is, I sleep
soundly till late the next morning (Thursday, April 22nd.) About

* Sec.-Lieut. G. H. Woolley, awarded Victoria Cross, May 22nd, 1915.

mid-day we receive orders to be ready to move. We work our way back across the fields, keeping well under cover of hedges till we reach Zillebeke, turning off from there to the left and once more regaining the railway. A few minutes' halt, and we proceed along the embankment to the Lille road into Ypres. A mile the other side of Ypres a halt is made, and the battalion is formed up once more. Food is eaten. Presently we again fall in, and General Smith-Dorrien makes a speech congratulating the regiment on the part it had played, after which we proceed to a new hut encampment about a mile farther back, arriving there about 4 p.m. Most of the fellows, being very fatigued, dropped down in their places in the huts to sleep ; the more energetic went in search of water for washing, others to surrounding farms for coffee and eggs ; I was among the last.

Presently French transports come hurrying from the direction of the firing-line. No notice was taken at first, but the stream seems never ending. All manner of rumours fly around. I return to the camp. Everywhere troops are asking questions, yet all is marvellously orderly. Soon comes the order to " stand to." We are paraded, magazines are charged, and all ready to march off. Official news comes that the enemy has broken through the first line of the French, but the Canadians are holding the second line. We are marched across a couple of fields, and begin digging a trench. We are on this for a couple of hours or so, and then return to our huts, being told to be ready to move at a moment's notice. Two hours' sleep is snatched, and we are on the move again, and go along the railway track in the direction of Vlamertinghe. We bivouac in a field. Our field kitchens supply hot tea, and rations are issued.

Dawn breaks (Friday, April 23rd), and we take cover from aeroplane sight, lining the hedges. About 10 a.m. the brigade starts on the move. Our battalion brings up the rear. We pass Vlamertinghe and proceed towards Elverdinghe. No one knows where we are bound for, yet we are all under the impression we are going to a permanent encampment for a rest. We reach a farm and rest in a field.

Another meal is made, and about 4 p.m. the brigade is on the move again. We pass a village, and after about a three-mile march we reach the Yser Canal and cross a pontoon bridge. Our battalion is spread out in extended order on the far side of the embankment. We are in reserve to an attack. The attack is successful, and we are told certain trenches are taken. We remain on the embankment all night, and about mid-day the following day (Saturday, April 24th), orders arrive to be ready to move. We tramp across fields, recently ploughed and sown, passing the village of St. Jean on our right. Everywhere troops are on the move. An enemy aeroplane has seen what is happening, and soon shells begin to drop—not a few here and there, but a perfect hailstorm of metal. Troops are moving up everywhere. Order is kept marvellously considering. We stumble along as quickly as we can. I don't know who is leading us, or where we are making for. The air is thick with smoke, and breathing becomes difficult. Presently we reach a partly-built rampart, and are told to spread ourselves out as much as possible, and dig ourselves in behind it. Operations are soon begun. Higher up a shell has burst among our men ; another bursts within a few yards of the spot where I am working. I have just time to fall flat—surely that can't have missed me ?—yes, I am quite all right, though Chalmers has got a nasty piece in his thigh.

We are only digging a few minutes when orders come to advance towards a farm building. Making our way in our own time we reach a pile of mangel-wurzels—I stay behind this for a breather. Half-right from this, about two hundred yards away, is a trench, and it is there we are to make for. Having recovered my breath, I make a dash. The enemy have evidently spotted us, and a machine-gun is soon busy. Gad, I never heard so many bullets whistle past me before ! I reach a sort of " don't care " mood, and plod across to the trench as best I can, for I am absolutely whacked. I reach it in safety, and flop down on some straw in the bottom, thoroughly exhausted.

The trench is held by Canadians, but they are very few, and my company links up with them. Apparently this was originally a support trench, but owing to the enemy having been successful in taking some trenches of ours in front of a wood, this position is now a front-line one. We arrive just after the Germans had made an attack on some other trenches, and had been repulsed, and as they retreat across an open space, between a farm building and the wood, we are able to pepper them well from our position. The range

" A hailstorm of metal "

RESPIRATORS IN THE TRENCHES.

Photograph taken under fire of Belgians working a machine-gun and wearing respirators as protection against German poison-gas.

FRENCH MACHINE-GUN AND CREW IN A TWIG-LINED TRENCH.
First in the field with the mitrailleuse in 1870, the French quickly showed their efficiency in machine-gun warfare in their second great struggle against the German foe.

THREE HIGHLANDERS WHO DEFEATED FIFTY HUNS.
Attacked at La Bassée by fifty Germans while escorting a convoy, these gallant Scots put a period to the fighting days of no less than seventeen of the foe, and the other Huns fled for dear life.

hundred yards from the spot where I am. They are sending over some very heavy stuff. My pals must be having a pretty hot time up that end. The farm buildings are used as a headquarters by the Canadians. The range is soon found, and smoke issuing from the buildings shows us a fire has occurred. Soon ammunition begins to cackle off, and this goes on for some hours. A lot of stores, etc., must have been lost. The bombardment lasts about three-quarters of an hour, during which time I count ninety shells that have been sent over. News come along that one of the shells dropped on the parapet of the trench farther up on the right, and Corporal Beard and Rifleman Monker had been injured. Dusk comes on, and being anxious to fill my bottle, I volunteer to get some water from the pump at the farm. I take another fellow with me, and we pick our way through the ruin to the pump, and begin filling the bottles. There are a lot of other fellows (Canadians) also on the same search; others are in search of whatever they can find in the way of spare rations, etc.

Suddenly another shell comes over, bursting beyond the buildings. Fellows scuttle away like rats; my pal and I make hasty tracks for our trench again. Having reached it in safety I sit down and laugh, for it is really most amusing to see everyone suddenly dart away in all directions, dropping the tins of jam which they had been confiscating. The rest of the night passes peacefully, and we are able to continue the work of fortifying our trench. Roberts, unluckily, gets a stray bullet in his arm. But it is a nice, clean wound.

Devastated village homes

The grey dawn (April 26th) begins to appear, and with it a heavy mist. About 4 a.m. our adjutant appears, and tells us to hurry and get ready to be relieved. It is most essential to get away before the mist rises, for it is now almost broad daylight. We file out and are led across fields, reaching the village of St. Jean, through which we pass. What havoc and devastation has been done! A few days ago people were living here, and now, roofless houses, shattered walls, shell-holes dotting the cobbled road. Furniture is lying in the streets, the smouldering remains of a motor-ambulance stands on the side of the road; dead men and horses are lying everywhere, and not always whole bodies, alas! We leave the road, and go across country once more; at last, striking the canal, we move along the banks. This embankment is now a mass of dug-outs, for it has been heavily shelled since we were last there. All had seemed so undisturbed before, and I plucked cowslips which grew among the grass. We rest a few minutes when we have crossed the pontoon bridge, and then continue our march back to the farm near Elverdinghe. We are all played out by this time, and many

"PROTECTION AGAINST ENGLISH GAS BOMBS."

A German paper published the above illustration with the description quoted. The gentle Hun is represented as wearing "a face mask and oxygen apparatus for rendering aid to the asphyxiated." The fact that Germany introduced poison gas, and that the British at this time had made no use of it whatever, was ignored.

was eight hundred yards, but I think we accounted for a few —anyhow, not many reached the wood. This is the first occasion on which I have had a real target—and didn't I enjoy it, too!

As darkness came, we began to get busy improving the trench. There was a plentiful supply of good turf to be dug behind the trench, and very soon we began to make ourselves a fairly safe shelter. Rain, however, began to fall, and this did not cheer our spirits. Dawn arrives (Sunday, April 25th). About 7 a.m. heavy rifle fire opens from the wood, which is half-left from our position, and presently we observe the cause—a kilted regiment is advancing to attack. The bark of a dog sounds above the rifle fire, and, sure to behold, there is the figure of a big black dog running ahead of the Scotties. What a fine sight—yet what a terrible sight!—for an enormous lot of the poor chaps are falling. The distance is far too much to cover (about eight hundred yards), and in broad daylight, too. Very soon the attack is given up, and those who are left make their way back. Things quieten down a bit. I snatch an hour or two's well-needed sleep.

About 2 p.m. the enemy start shelling some farm buildings about fifteen yards in the rear of our trench, but about one

TRAPPED VICTIMS OF THE TEUTONS' POISON GAS.
The two photographs given above show French soldiers suffering from the initial effects of the poison gas introduced by Germany into "civilised" warfare.

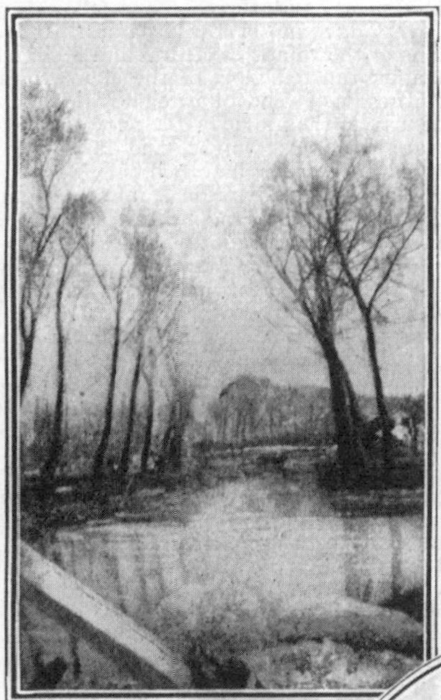

SCENE OF THE FIERCE FIGHTING NEAR ARRAS.
The river was here the dividing line between the French and German forces, which were separated by about two hundred yards.

have had to fall out on the way. Now for a wash and a shave, for I have had neither for seven days. A pond close by, though not very clean, is very welcome, and after a good scrub down I feel a new man. The rest of the day is spent in lounging about and feeding. There is plenty to eat, for beyond our own parcels, those of our killed and wounded pals are split up amongst us, and these are not inconsiderable in number.

We remain at this farm resting till Thursday, April 29th, getting three full nights' sleep. On this day we receive orders to parade at 6 p.m. for the trenches again. We are going to reinforce another regiment.

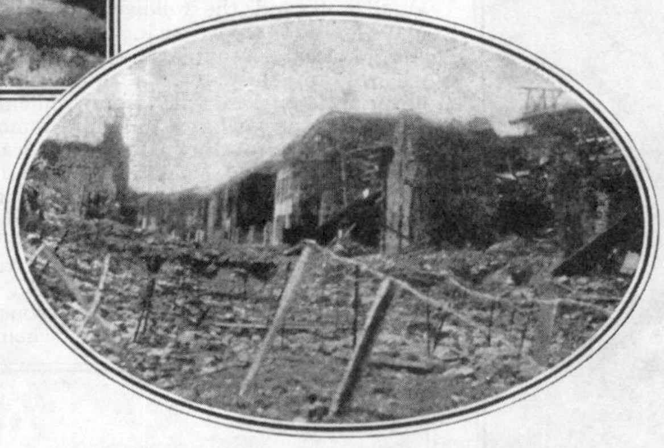

A STREET IN BATTLE-SCARRED CARENCY.
In and around this village, north of Arras, the French won a great victory in May, 1915. Remnants of German wire entanglements are to be seen in the foreground.

Once more the pontoon bridge is crossed, and we occupy a newly-made trench adjoining the French. It is only for twenty-four hours, and we are relieved the following night. What a mixture of troops there is at this part of the line! French, British, Canadians, Indians, Turcos, Zouaves, and Moroccans! I shouldn't think the enemy could break through again in a hurry. We reach our barn once more soon after midnight, but have very few hours of sleep, for we know we have to be on the move again at daybreak. At 4 a.m. (Saturday, May 1st), we sleepily "fall in," and go across fields to some woods, and are told we shall bivouac here for a bit. We are all soon busy fixing up shelters of sorts, with the aid of branches and our waterproof sheets. We rest undisturbed at night.

The following morning (Sunday, May 2nd) our chaplain arrives, and delivers a short service. It is an impressive sight to see us formed in a square, and hear us singing hymns, our voices echoing through the woods. The weather is glorious. I could enjoy living here like this for months, if the weather kept fine. Just after we had our tea, the ominous cry of "Orderly sergeants at the double" rings through the wood. We march some miles across the fields; presently we are halted and told to lie down with our equipment on. The brigade is apparently in reserve in case it's needed, as the enemy has been attacking during the day. We lie in this field and shiver for several hours; the night has turned very cold. We are not allowed to smoke, as no lights must be shown. Soon after midnight we learn "the situation is well in hand, and the battalion may return to the woods."

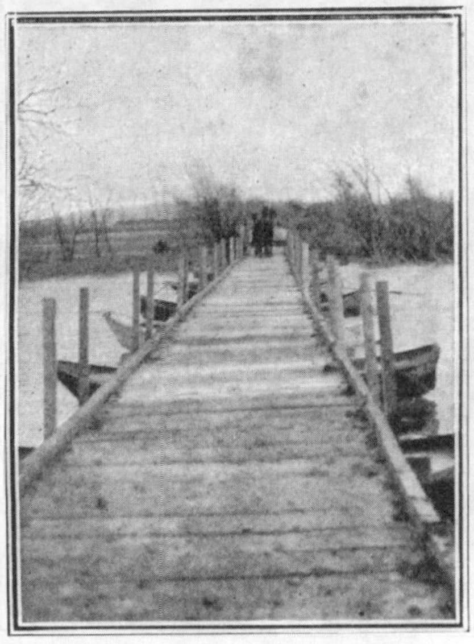

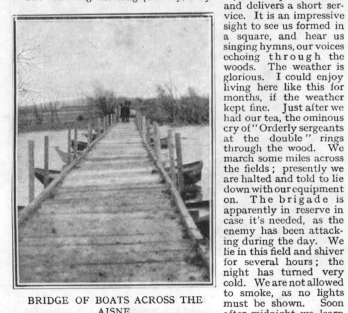

BRIDGE OF BOATS ACROSS THE AISNE.
The engineers of all the allied armies had extensive practice in building, rebuilding, and destroying bridges.

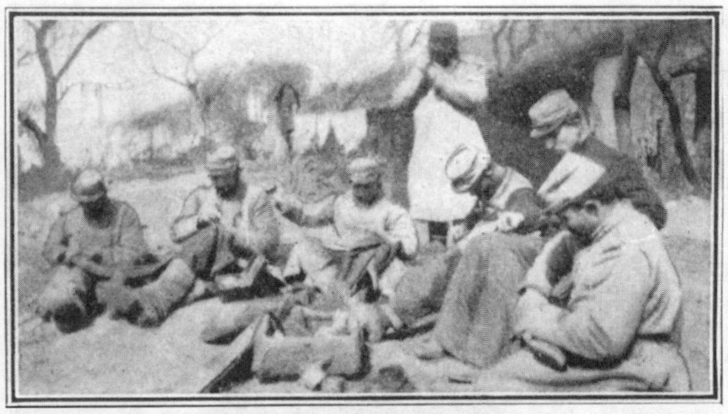

AN INTERVAL FOR REFITTING.
Some of our gallant French allies in an interval between the fighting have sat down to a little tailoring and shoe-making. As shown in the view, their linen has been attended to likewise.

We march back by road, via Vlamertinghe. The enemy seems to have made a mess of the town since last I saw it. We reach the woods just before daybreak (Monday, May 3rd), and re-erect our shelters. During the afternoon we have orders to shift to another part of the woods. No sooner have we settled down than the order comes to march up once more and "fall in." Another march across fields—the same old game—"stand by" in case needed. We dig ourselves in and are allowed to sleep. I dig a fairly comfortable and safe hole for myself into which I crawl, and am soon sound asleep, only to wake shortly, feeling rain falling on me, and an uncomfortable wet feeling underneath me. I get up, and find I have been lying in a pool of water. Feeling cold and miserable, I take a little run up and down to get the blood moving in my body. As daylight begins to show itself, the cheerful news comes that we are to proceed back to a hut encampment for a rest.

A long tiring march via Vlamertinghe, Oudendhem, and we reach some huts at a village. Tired out though I am I cannot resist the bubbling stream I espy a few hundred yards in the distance, and laden with my washing equipment and a clean set of underclothes, I make ahead for it, and am soon enjoying a good swim. A run round the field in the sun, and I quickly dress. The afternoon I spend lying in a field writing letters. After tea I "turn in," and get a good twelve hours' sound sleep.

Rumours about Hill 60

Soon after breakfast the following morning (Tuesday, May 4th) rumours fly about to the effect that Hill 60 had been lost. At 10 a.m. we have a rifle inspection, after which there was to be a parade for pay. This is cancelled, and orders are suddenly flung at us to draw rations for twenty-four hours, and proceed to march away. At 1 p.m. we move off in the direction of Ypres once more; the other regiments in our brigade are ahead of us. We march across country, and about 4 p.m. rest in a field. Our cookers supply us with stew and tea, then we are on the move again, and the sinking of the sun sees us in a reserve trench about one and a half miles behind the firing-line. We only stay here about an hour, for we move higher up and occupy the dug-outs on the railway embankment, where we remain all night, and during the next day (Wednesday, May 5th). At dusk we move up to the support dug-outs in the Larch Wood, on the left of the railway cutting behind Hill 60, but not single-handed. In addition to our full marching order we have to carry ammunition, rations, etc.

Another fellow and

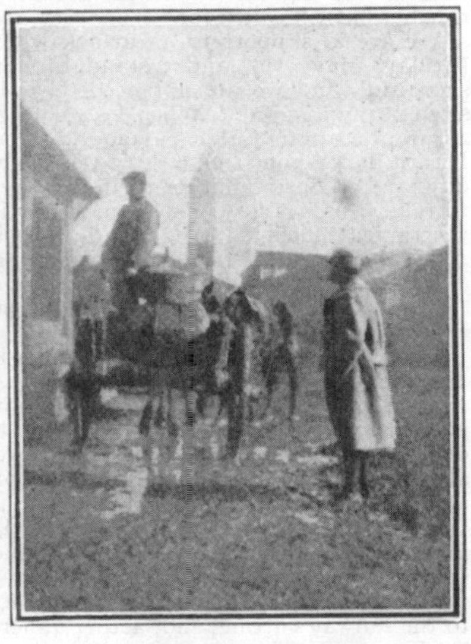

A PRIVILEGED SPOT.
This little town was one of the few that could boast of a belfry unharmed by gun fire. A French soldier is seen here on fatigue duty as water-carrier.

LIEUTENANT-GENERAL SIR HERBERT PLUMER, K.C.B.
Appointed in January, 1915, to the command of the Fifth Army Corps, Lieutenant-General Sir Herbert Charles Onslow Plumer, K.C.B., was specially mentioned by Sir John French, in the despatch of June 15th, for his " fine defence of Ypres throughout the arduous and difficult operations during the latter part of April and the month of May."

myself share the weight of a box of ammunition. Gad, what hot going ! Sweat pours off me, and soaks through all my clothes, overcoat included. I don't know how, but by sheer grit we at last " get there." One's power of endurance is unknown until really tested. Having " delivered the goods," we are told off to remain in the dug-out till called for.

We are in support to an attack which commences about 3 a.m. (Friday, May 7th), and " stand to " in readiness. The attack is successful, and we are not needed, and I snatch an hour or two's sleep in my dug-out. When I awake I am shocked to hear that our adjutant, Captain Culme Seymour, has been killed. The colonel, too, I learn, has " gone sick." We remain where we are throughout the day, and at dusk, another regiment having come up during the day to relieve us, we go back in small parties across the fields, skirting the ruined Zillebeke village, and alongside the reservoir, eventually reaching some dug-outs. They are known as **Ypres in** the artillery dug-outs, having been made for the R.F.A. We strip ourselves of our kit, and **flames** at 9 p.m. parade with rifles and bandolier, and are taken across to Brigade Headquarters. Here we are given bundles of fifty sand-bags.

Another journey across the fields to the Larch Wood. It is easier going this time without our heavy kit to carry. We return to our dug-outs and sleep till morning (Saturday, May 8th). We are not allowed to light fires, but by the aid of rifle rags, pieces of candles, and other kinds of fat I brew some tea and have breakfast. During the day we bask in the sun, sleep, read, or write letters. At night my company is paraded again with rifle and bandolier. We draw spades at headquarters.

To-night we are on a digging fatigue, and tramp across the fields to the railway cutting and, acting under an R.E. officer, we are soon working repairing a communication trench which has been badly damaged by shell fire. We get back just before dawn (Sunday, May 9th).

During the day the enemy continues to search for a battery of guns. Some of their shells come uncomfortably close to us, and one

actually drops on our embankment, and three of our fellows are wounded. Ypres is shelled every day, and is now in flames. It is a lovely sight at night—portions of the ruined cathedral and a church steeple stand silhouetted against the red glow of the sky. Night falls—another fatigue to the firing-line. The following day (Monday, May 10th) passes in the same way as the previous day or two. Only a certain number of men are required to-night, and it is " D " company's turn to " stand by," so we are undisturbed.

The next night (Tuesday, May 11th) we are on a ration fatigue. Our guide is a man from the South Lancs, and he takes us along the railway. This is, of course, the shortest route, but we know the Germans have it pretty well marked. We start off with a few shrapnel bursting over on our right. We rest for a few minutes by the embankment. Hardly have we sat down than I hear the " plunk " of a bullet, followed by an exclamation of pain by poor little Jameson, who is lying just in front of me—he has got it in the thigh. Two men remain behind with him and we proceed, the rest reaching the cutting in safety. On the return journey two more fellows are hit. We rest till dusk the following evening (Wednesday, May 12th) when the brigade is relieved.

Another long tiring march to a village, where we rest for three-quarters of an hour and have some hot tea ; then proceed to a hut encampment. We arrive there about 6 a.m., and after a little breakfast I am soon fast asleep. **Invalided to** A draft of one hundred and forty men arrives. The next day (Friday, May 14th) I don't feel **the coast** at all well, and the following day (Saturday, May 15th) I report sick, and am sent to hospital—13th Field Ambulance at Reninghelst—where I remain till Monday, May 17th, when I am shifted in a motor-ambulance to Boeschepe. This hospital is little or no improvement on the last, but my case nominates me for base, and I am removed on a stretcher to a bone-shaking old horse-drawn Red Cross waggon.

A long ride and I arrive at Bailleul, and am placed in a clearing hospital, where I remain till next morning. Another ride in a motor-ambulance to the Bailleul Station, and thence to the ambulance train —six hours' journey, and evening finds me being placed in a nice soft bed in a pleasant room overlooking the sea at No. 14 General Hospital, Wimereux, near Boulogne. And now here I sit, gazing with longing eyes across the glorious blue sea in the direction of dear old England. When, ah ! when, shall I see it again ?

A FRENCH AERIAL " TORPEDO " ABOUT TO BE FIRED.
One of the new weapons employed in a war remarkable in history for the employment of machinery against men. The above view is of a French trench from which an aerial " torpedo " is about to be fired, while a second projectile is being held in readiness for the next shot.

PICTURESQUE WAR-TIME SCENE IN NORTHERN FRANCE.

French engineers conducting a cavalry regiment over a river. Some of the horses were conveyed across the water in pontoons, while others swam across. The engineers were equipped with swimming jackets for the work in hand.

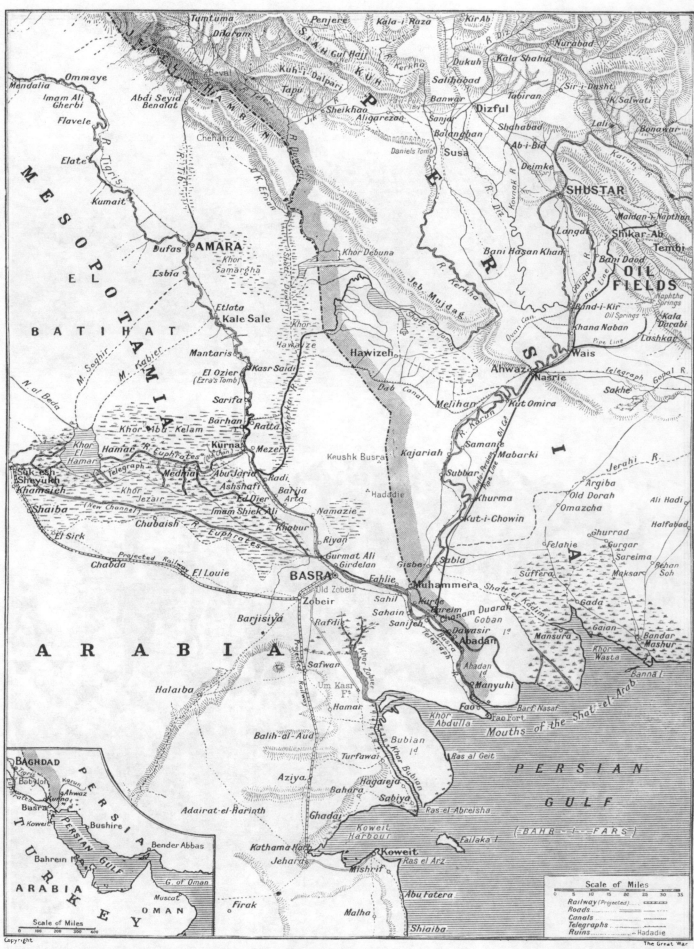

MESOPOTAMIA—THE STORIED LAND "BETWEEN THE RIVERS" WHERE GERMANY PLOTTED
AND TURKEY PAID THE PRICE.

Specially-drawn map of the region of the Persian Gulf, showing the valleys of the Euphrates and Tigris, the mouths of the Shat-el-Arab, the oil-
fields, and the areas of the fighting between British-Indian and Turkish troops from November, 1914, to June, 1915.

CHAPTER LXVII.

THE FIGHTING AROUND THE PERSIAN GULF.

Turkey, under German Influence, Jeopardises her Asiatic Possessions as well as Constantinople—The Storied Land around the Euphrates and the Tigris—British Interests in the Persian Gulf—German Traders and the Native Chiefs—The Bagdad Railway Scheme—Our Reply to the Turkish Challenge—The Expeditionary Force from India—A Night Attack by the Enemy—Operations on the Shat-el-Arab—General Barrett enters Basra—Turks Driven Across the Tigris near Kurna—British Occupation of Mezera—Seizure of Kurna—German and Turkish Stories of British Defeat—The Withdrawal from before Ghadir—Further Reinforcements from India, under Lieut.-Gen. Sir J. E. Nixon—The Battle of the Tamarisk Woods, near Shaiba—Flight of the Enemy—Turkish Leader's Reported Suicide—British Occupation of Nakaila—Sandstorms and Floods Delay the Pursuit—Fighting by Land and River—Surrender of Amara.

WHEN Turkey, flattered, cajoled, and perhaps threatened by the Kaiser's emissaries, threw down the gage of battle to Great Britain and her Allies in November, 1914, she jeopardised not only Constantinople, but also her Asiatic possessions which, since the end of the Balkan War, had formed the greater part of the decaying Ottoman Empire. "He that hath command of the sea," said Francis Bacon three hundred years ago, "is at great liberty"—and this liberty permitted Great Britain to choose the time and place of her attack.

Stretching across Asia Minor from the shores of the Mediterranean Sea, the Sultan's possessions bend southward until they touch the head of the Persian Gulf. Here, in the narrow strip of land between Persia on the one side and the Arabian desert on the other, the Rivers Euphrates and Tigris flow towards the Gulf, their waters making this region one of the most fertile in the world. At Basra, about sixty miles from the sea, they unite, and make their way together under the name of the Shat-el-Arab.

The land around the Euphrates and the Tigris is one of the oldest and most famous homes of civilisation. According to some authorities, the Garden of Eden was here, and here certainly is the site of the once mighty city of Babylon. Secular as well as sacred history is full of memories of this fertile region, and so, too, are romance and legend. Bagdad was the scene of the

wondrous adventures of Haroun al-Raschid, as narrated in the "Arabian Nights," and though these are mythical, the Sultan himself really existed, living in great magnificence amid his city's "shrines of fretted gold." Basra, a city nearer the sea, is also associated with the "Arabian Nights" and with the life of Sindbad the Sailor. To the Tigris valley belongs the great historical exploit known as the Retreat of the Ten Thousand, for it was by this route that Xenophon led the lost army of the Greeks until they saw the sea in the distance, greeting it with rapturous cries of welcome, for, like ourselves, they belonged to a sea-girt land. The influence of the Greeks is seen in the fact that the district between the Tigris and the Euphrates is called Mesopotamia, the word meaning "between the rivers."

In the seventeenth century, about a hundred years after the great Turkish Sultan, Sulyman the Magnificent, had conquered Bagdad, the land between that city and the coast became part of the Ottoman Empire, then just at the height of its power, and in spite of frequent disorder and rebellion it remained so until our own days. But even before this Englishmen had visited the Persian Gulf. Far off in the reign of Elizabeth our traders made their way thither by sea, and since that time our interest in the lands bordering it has been maintained and increased.

The increasing interest of Britain in the Gulf is largely owing to its nearness to India. At Bundar Abbas, a place at its mouth, the East India Company had a station early

[Elliot & Fry.

LIEUT.-GEN. SIR ARTHUR ARNOLD BARRETT, K.C.B., K.C.V.O.
Commander of the British-Indian Expeditionary Force in the Persian Gulf.

BRIGADIER-GENERAL WALTER S.
DELAMAIN, C.B.
Commander of the Poona Brigade.

[Elliott & Fry.

in the seventeenth century, and for nearly two hundred years there was here constant fighting between this company and its Dutch and Portuguese rivals. The companies and their wars passed away, but Britain and her Indian Empire remained, and to strengthen this much was done in the nineteenth century to extend our influence along the shores of the Gulf. It was surveyed and buoyed by ships of our Navy, which also performed the more difficult task of hunting down the pirates and acting as the policeman of this inland sea. Political residents were sent to various places along the coast, but, except Bahrein Island, no territory was taken. Britain's mission there, as elsewhere, was to keep the peace, this being done to allow the Arab and Persian tribesmen to live undisturbed in their own way.

Two years ago, or thereabouts, Great Britain added to her interests and responsibilities in this region. At the head of the Gulf very valuable oil-fields were discovered, and these were soon opened and worked by the Anglo-Persian Oil Company. In 1913, when oil began to be extensively used as fuel for the Navy, it was announced that our Admiralty had secured a controlling interest in these oil-fields, and evidently they were intended to furnish a great proportion of the oil required by our ships.

Great Britain and Turkey were for long the two Powers most concerned in this region, but late in the nineteenth century a third appeared there, and this was Germany. German traders, prominent among whom was the firm of Wonckhaus, took up their abode here, obtained concessions from native chiefs, and, as in Africa, used fair means and foul to extend the influence of the Vaterland.

A word or two about Wonckhaus & Co. may not be out of place here, as the career of this firm shows the careful and persevering way in which the Germans went to work to obtain a foothold. Presumably they were agents for a Hamburg firm, and they began by dealing in shells and pearls, and making the acquaintance of the native population around the Gulf. At first they were at a small place called Lingah, but in 1901 they transferred their headquarters to Bahrein, opening branches a little later at Basra and Bundar Abbas. They appeared to have plenty of money, but, as far as one could see, they did not make very much out of their trading enterprises. The next step was to ask the Sultan of Bahrein for a monopoly of the pearl fisheries of the Gulf—which incidentally did not belong to him—and when Great Britain stopped this, an attempt was made to secure the island of Halul, in the centre of the Gulf. This, too, failed owing to British action.

On another island in the Gulf is Abu Musa. There some Arabs had secured a concession for working the deposits of red oxide, and in 1906 this was taken over by the indefatigable Wonckhaus. The Sheikh of Shargah, who had granted the concession, objected to the transfer, and appealed to Great Britain, the result being that the employees of Wonckhaus were forcibly removed from the island. Now came the time for which the German Government had been waiting, and, we think we may say, preparing. A protest

The firm of Wonckhaus

was lodged, but the case was obviously weak, and soon it was abandoned. An attempt, following somewhat similar lines, to secure a concession for carrying out irrigation works in the valley of the Karun also failed. Wonckhaus & Co., however, were undismayed, and in the same year, when the Hamburg-Amerika Line began to run a line of steamers to the chief ports on the Gulf, they appeared publicly as the agents of that famous house.

Germany's great scheme for bringing this district under her authority was the construction of a railway—the Bagdad Railway—which should connect the Mediterranean Sea with the Persian Gulf. To this the Turkish Government had assented, and a German company, behind which was the Deutsche Bank, had been formed to carry out the work. Great Britain, however, was not unaware of this project, nor yet of Germany's other intrigues in this neighbourhood, and something had been done to thwart them. The question of the railway was being discussed by the representatives of the two countries when the Great War broke out.

Bagdad Railway intrigue

It did not require a genius to point out the advisability of sending a British force into the Persian Gulf in November, 1914. By doing so we were answering promptly the Turkish challenge, giving a fresh proof of the omnipotence of our sea-power, and taking the offensive, which counts for so much in war. But these were, after all, only minor considerations. The major ones were that we were protecting our material interests in the Gulf and in the oil-fields and were striking a blow at Germany, without whose support Turkey would be a negligible quantity.

The force detailed for this expedition was provided by India, and consisted of a division of infantry and certain

THE BURDEN AND HEAT OF THE DAY.
British troops entrenched in the vicinity of the Persian Gulf. The condition of the weather at the time is indicated by the fact that the men were wearing sun-helmets.

Indian cavalry on the march on the flooded Shaiba road.

After the fight at Shaiba—Turkish prisoners escorted by Gurkhas.

Advance of the gallant Dorsets near Basra.   Of the eighteen miles of their route, nine miles were under water.

CAMERA-PICTURES OF THE CAMPAIGN IN THE PERSIAN GULF.

A TROPHY OF VICTORY.
British-Indian troops with a gun taken from the Turks in the Persian Gulf campaign.

VIEW ON THE SHAT-EL-ARAB, NEAR BASRA.
Basra was occupied by the British on November 23rd, 1914.

auxiliary troops—pioneers, sappers and miners, and light cavalry. The division was commanded by Lieutenant-General Sir Arthur Barrett, and consisted of three brigades, each of which contained one battalion of British troops, the remainder being native regiments. The British battalions were the 2nd Dorsets in the Poona Brigade, the 1st Oxfordshire Light Infantry in the Ahmednagar Brigade, and the 2nd Norfolks in the Belgaum Brigade.

The grass had not grown under the feet of Sir Arthur Barrett, and when war was declared by Turkey the Poona Brigade under Brigadier-General Delamain was at Bahrein, while the remainder of the division was ready to sail from Bombay. On November 7th General Delamain left Bahrein for the fort of Fao, which stands at the mouth of the Shat-el-Arab. With him were H.M.S. Odin, an armed launch, and some Marines with a Maxim gun from H.M.S. Ocean. For an hour the guns of the Odin bombarded the fort, and then, the Turkish fire having been silenced, the soldiers and Marines were landed. Fao was then occupied, and without loss of life a base for further operations was secured.

Fao Fort occupied Leaving the Marines at Fao, General Delamain's brigade was taken up the Shat-el-Arab, and was disembarked at Sanijeh, about thirty miles from the sea, where the men prepared an entrenched camp and waited for the arrival of their comrades from India before advancing to Basra.

Meanwhile, General Delamain's task was to clear the Turks and their Arab auxiliaries from the neighbourhood, and thus to facilitate the coming advance. On November 9th the enemy attacked the camp at night, but was re-

pulsed, and on the 11th two Indian battalions drove him from a village which he occupied. On the 15th there was a fight in which the Anglo-Indians were not quite so successful, as they retired without driving the Turks entirely from the neighbourhood of Sahain. However, supported by the gunboats on the river, they shelled the enemy out of his trenches, suffering on their part some thirty-five casualties.

Two days previously the brigades from Bombay had reached the mouth of the Shat-el-Arab. Crossing the bar they steamed up the river on the 14th, passing Abadan, the headquarters of the Anglo-Persian Oil Company, where the refinery, with its extensive tanks and buildings, **Turkish defeat near Sahil** looks very out of place in the barren surroundings. At Sanijeh, where the Poona Brigade was, they disembarked, a difficult feat owing to the banks of the river, which are here about eight or ten feet high, being very muddy and slippery.

While the troops were resting in the camp at Sanijeh, news reached General Barrett that a Turkish army was advancing from Basra against him, and so on the 17th he ordered the Anglo-Indians to move forward to meet it. They found Sahain deserted, and the fight took place near Sahil, a few miles farther up the Shat-el-Arab. The Turks were entrenched among date groves, and between them and our men was a bare plain, which, in addition to its lack of cover, recent rain had turned into a quagmire. In spite of these disadvantages our men advanced steadily, as soon as the artillery, both from the batteries and from the gunboats, had prepared the way for them. With an English regiment at either end of the line, the Turkish position was carried in about three hours; the Turks fled in disorder before the final charge with the bayonet could be delivered. They were pursued for about a mile, but the state of the ground made it impossible for this pursuit to be effective, while, according to one report, a mirage hid them from the eyes of our men.

The Turkish force engaged in this battle was estimated at 4,500 men, and its losses were stated to have been over 1,500. Many wounded, eight guns, and much ammunition fell into our hands. The Anglo-Indian troops had three hundred and fifty-three casualties, thirty-eight officers and men being killed. Of these one hundred and thirty were sustained by the Dorsets, which battalion had the place of honour in the attack on the Turkish trenches. On

General Joffre with Sir John French and Sir Douglas Haig at the Front.

Under Two Flags: March-past of British Cyclist Section before Sir John French, S

Regiment of Chasseurs Alpins marching past General Joffr

[Photo: S. d'A.

las Haig, General Joffre, the late General Gough, and Allied Staff officers in France.

[Photo: S. d'A.

cinematograph) after a distribution of decorations in Alsace.

British Army officers in front of their billets in the Ypres salient.

Mr. Asquith and Sir John French with Allied Staff officers at the Front.

TYPICAL SCENE FROM THE FIGHTING NEAR
THE PERSIAN GULF.
Indian troops firing from a sand-bag protected trench in
Mesopotamia.

the same day a storm sank many of our boats, with
heavy loss of rations and kits.

A day or two after this engagement word was
brought to the British camp that the Turks had
evacuated Basra, and that the Arabs had begun
to plunder the place, in which were a few British
residents. Accordingly, on the 21st, General
Barrett asked for two battalions to make a dash
to the city, and the two selected were the 2nd
Norfolks and the 110th Mahrattas. These were
crowded on board two paddle-steamers, the Medijeh
and the Blosse Lynch, their embarkation being very
difficult owing to the mud and

General Barrett rising tide. The rest of the division
enters Basra was ordered to march across the
desert to the same objective.

To impede an advance up the river the Turks had sunk
some steamers therein, and at the same place had stationed
a battery of guns. These were silenced, the other obstacles
were also overcome, and on the 22nd the two battalions and
General Barrett entered Basra—to find that the custom-
house had just been set on fire. No opposition was offered
to their entrance, and soon the British flag was flying over
the German Consulate. During the night the remainder
of the force, having accomplished a march of thirty miles,
encamped just outside Basra.

The formal occupation of Basra took place on the afternoon of the 23rd. The Union Jack having been hoisted, a
proclamation was read aloud in Arabic, and a salute was
fired by the warships in the river. On the 24th the
military governor, Major Brownlow, took up his residence
at the German Consulate, the Consul and some other
Germans being taken off to India. Basra, which now
came into British hands, is the centre of the date trade,
and a port through which some £2,000,000 of goods pass
every year. From it the Hamburg-Amerika Line had been
running steamers, and it was intended to be the terminus
of the Bagdad Railway.

During the remainder of the month a camp was prepared outside Basra, and preparations were made for
dealing with further Turkish attacks, which would doubtless be delivered from the great military station of Bagdad.
Attention was also paid to Kurna, a town on the right bank
of the Tigris, where, so our scouts discovered, a Turkish
force was collecting. To ascertain its strength, Lieut.-Colonel
Frazer was sent out on December 3rd, with some Indian
troops, a detachment of the Norfolks, some artillery, and

BASRA, FROM THE SHAT-EL-ARAB.
H.M.S. Espiègle in the foreground.

other units, his small force being supported by gunboats
and armed launches. The enemy was encountered on
the left bank of the Tigris, nearly opposite Kurna, and
there the troops were landed, while the warships went
ahead and shelled the town. Leaving seventy prisoners
and two guns in our hands, the Turks were promptly
driven across the river, but this was all our men could do.
Kurna was evidently strongly defended, and although
Colonel Frazer's column reached the bank of the river
opposite the town, it was not prepared to force its way
across in the face of a heavy fire. Accordingly it was withdrawn to its original camp below Kurna, which was hastily
entrenched, while word was sent to Basra that further
assistance was necessary. In this engagement the assistance of the warships was very valuable. The Espiègle
and the Lawrence silenced some of the enemy's guns, but
the latter vessel and also the armed launch Miner were
damaged by shells.

On the 6th, Brigadier-General C. I. Fry arrived with the
7th Rajputs and the rest of the Norfolks, and the attack
was renewed. Mezera, a town on the
left bank of the Tigris, was occupied, **Mezera and**
and for the second time the Turks were **Kurna taken**
driven across the river to Kurna ; but,
for the second time our men were compelled to retire after
reaching the river bank.

Another plan was then tried. To the north of the town
some sappers swam across the Tigris, and having got a
steel hawser across, constructed a flying bridge. Across
this the 104th Rifles and the 110th Mahrattas marched,
and as soon as they were entrenched, Kurna was practically

Indian cavalry advancing under difficulties near Basra. They are riding through floods from six inches to three feet in depth.

A moving and picturesque spectacle. Arrival of an Anglo-Indian convoy at Shaiba. Pack mules about to be unloaded. Artillery in the background.

OUR LOYAL INDIANS CONQUERING NEW TERRITORIES IN THE EAST FOR THEIR KING-EMPEROR.

A BRITISH POSITION "SOMEWHERE IN MESO-
POTAMIA."
The photographs on this page give a vivid impression of
two meteorological aspects of the Persian Gulf campaign. In
the above picture is seen an entrenched and gun-protected
position " somewhere in Mesopotamia." It had the advantage
of being dry.

AN UNEXPECTED INUNDATION.
In February and March the Tigris and the Euphrates usually overflow their banks
and flood the surrounding country, with results such as that shown above. Our
men were hard put to it to rescue their kits from the rising waters.

enveloped. The Turkish leaders realised this, and
on the 8th they offered to surrender. General Fry
told them that the surrender must be unconditional,
and on this intimation the town and garrison were
given up to the British, who subsequently occupied
the place. In it were 1,100 soldiers and nine guns.
Our losses in these operations were about one
hundred and sixty killed and wounded. Entrenched
camps were established at Kurna and Mezera, and
the whole district between those places and the sea
was securely held by the British.

For some weeks after the British seizure of
Kurna neither side undertook any offensive operations. The Anglo-Indian force was
Enemy reports of engaged in strengthening its position,
British defeat General Fry's measures including the
despatch of a garrison to Ahwaz, a town
well inside the Persian frontier on the Karun River, and
important because the pipe line from the oil-fields passes
near it.

On January 21st, 1915, a brigade, supported by three
gunboats on the river, was sent out from Mezera in
order to ascertain the strength and disposition of
the Turkish force which was gathering in the neighbourhood, and which, during the previous two or three days,
had been harassing our patrols and outposts. After a
northward march of about six miles, the enemy's outposts
were sighted on a range of sandhills, behind which was the
Ratta Canal. An artillery duel began, in which the
enemy's aim was very bad. Our men then advanced, drove
the Turks across the canal, and themselves approached
within six hundred yards of it, from where they were
able to shell the Turkish dhows and camp. About noon,
having fulfilled their mission, they received orders to retire,
and returned unmolested to Mezera. Their total casualties
were about fifty, and the loss of the Turks was estimated
at four hundred or thereabouts. The report brought back
to General Barrett was that the enemy had about 5,000
men and six guns.

This withdrawal of our troops was hailed with delight
in Germany and Turkey, and was transformed into a great
British defeat, as the following statement issued in
Constantinople on the 23rd shows : " On the 21st instant

an English force, under cover of three gunboats, took the
offensive against our troops near Kurna, but they were
driven back with heavy loss."

In February and March the Tigris and the Euphrates
usually overflow their banks and flood the surrounding
country, and for the time being this put a stop to the
fighting. In Persia, however, there was an engagement
on March 3rd, in which the British forces lost heavily.
Near Ahwaz a few Turkish regiments were gathering around
them a body of discontented tribesmen from Persia and
Arabia, and to discover the strength of this force, a British
contingent was sent out from the town. At Ghadir the
Turks and their allies were located, but unfortunately they
were much stronger than we had believed possible, and in
the face of some 12,000 foes, our men had no option but
to retire without undue delay.

The withdrawal was safely effected, but not without
difficulty. The Turks made determined efforts to cut off
the retreat, and several times hand-to-
hand fighting took place. However, **Severe hand-to-hand**
Ahwaz was reached at last, and as the **fighting**
enemy did not return to the attack, it
was assumed that he had lost heavily. His casualties
were estimated at six hundred killed and many wounded.
The losses of the Anglo-Indian force were nearly two
hundred. The 7th Rajputs had four of their white officers
killed and their colonel severely wounded.

On the same day (March 3rd) a body of cavalry made a
reconnaissance towards Nakaila, a place about twenty-
five miles north-west of Basra. While returning to camp

EN ROUTE TO THE PERSIAN GULF.
Scene on board a transport conveying part of the British-Indian Expeditionary Force which so greatly distinguished itself in the fighting against the Turks in the neighbourhood of the Persian Gulf.

with these went Lieut.-General Sir J. E. Nixon, K.C.B., who on his arrival took over the command of the whole force. Nothing was said officially about its composition and numbers; but, speaking in the House of Lords on March 16th, Lord Crewe described it as "a considerable army," and we shall probably be not far wrong if we estimate the number of soldiers then in this theatre of war at 30,000 or 40,000.

The Turks also received considerable reinforcements, probably from Bagdad, and on April 11th they attacked three of our positions. Kurna, Ahwaz, and Shaiba, one of the forts protecting Basra, were the three; but one only was seriously assaulted On the 11th, and also on the 12th, Kurna was bombarded at long range, but no infantry attack followed, and the

they were followed by 1,500 enemy horsemen; but these were skilfully drawn on to a position where infantry with machine-guns and field-artillery were concealed. These opened fire upon them, and having suffered heavily they fled back to Nakaila. Unfortunately, in this little affair four British officers were killed and two were wounded severely.

In anticipation of the end of the flood season, the authorities in India sent further reinforcements to Ahwaz and Kurna, and

AT THE MOUTH OF THE SHAT-EL-ARAB.
British officers in a transport on their way to the battle-front in Asia Minor.

only damage done was the destruction of part of the bridge across the Tigris Our guns, both those on shore and those in H.M.S. Odin, however, appear to have inflicted a good deal of loss upon parties of the enemy who were seen in boats. Similarly, at the same time, Ahwaz was bombarded; but here again no damage was done, and although large bodies of hostile cavalry appeared on the horizon nearly all round the British position, they made no offensive movement.

On Shaiba the attack was more determined, but was equally ineffective. **German officers lead the Turks** After a certain amount of artillery fire, the Turkish infantry, led by some German officers, advanced in extended order towards the south, south-west, and west of our lines. For three hours in the morning they came steadily on, and then they began to dig themselves in. In the afternoon the attack from the south was renewed, but this made no further progress. During the night of the 12th the Turks kept up a desultory fire, and early on the following morning our cavalry found that a

MAJOR-GENERAL C. V. F. TOWNSHEND, C.B.
With Colonel Sir Percy Cox he commanded the forces which captured Amara.

party of them had occupied some rising ground about a mile to the north of our position. These men were easily dislodged by an Anglo-Indian attack, and the enemy next approached from the west and was driven back with equal ease. When our men ceased their pursuit they had captured eighteen officers, three hundred men, and two guns. Many of the prisoners were in a starving and hopeless condition, and some had marched the whole of the five hundred miles from Bagdad.

The prisoners reported that the attacking force was composed of about 10,000 regular infantry, 1,000 regular cavalry, and perhaps 12,000 irregular **The battle near** levies of Kurds and Arabs. They had **Shaiba** assembled at Nakaila and were commanded by Suliman Askeri and Ali Bey. In addition to the direct attacks, armed parties of them were sailing about on the flood water between Basra and Shaiba, with the object of interrupting the British communications.

The time had now come for a British offensive, for although the Turkish attacks had been repulsed, the enemy, strong and undaunted, was still entrenched near Basra, and

[*Elliott & Fry.*

COLONEL SIR PERCY COX, K.C.I.E.
Chief British Resident in the Persian Gulf. He shared the command with Major-General Townshend in the capture of Amara.

the heat and glare were terrific, and although the enemy could not be seen, a constant and accurate rifle fire came from his trenches. Nevertheless, our men struggled on, and about 4.30 the Dorsets and the 117th Mahrattas led the way into the trenches, a great charge made by the whole line driving out the enemy at the point of the bayonet. According to one account, the Turks hastened their flight because they mistook an advancing line of hospital carts for fresh batteries coming into action. In this battle the British

BRIG.-GEN. C. I. FRY AND STAFF OF 18TH BRIGADE.
The 18th Brigade captured Kurna and the Turkish garrison, including the Vali of Basra, over 30 officers and 1,100 men.

on the 14th there was an engagement which really deserves the title of a battle. The whole Anglo-Indian force moved out from its camp near Basra towards Zobeir, a few miles to the south. Very soon the Turks were driven from an advanced position about two and a half miles away, and then our men found themselves in front of their main lines.

This main position was in the shape of a crescent with tamarisk woods behind it and on either flank. In the wood and in well-concealed trenches before it were some 15,000 Turkish soldiers, with six big guns. Towards them the the Anglo-Indian troops advanced steadily for five hours, from 11.30 in the morning until 4.30 in the afternoon. The plain was absolutely bare,

BETWEEN THE BATTLES IN ASIA MINOR.
Officers attached to the British-Indian Expeditionary Force enjoying a rest and smoke in the desert.

casualties were about seven hundred, and the list contained the names of seventeen British officers killed, these including Lieut.-Colonel H. L. Rosher, of the Dorsets, Lieut.-Colonel T. A. Britten, of the 110th Mahrattas, and Major G. C. M. Wheeler, of the 7th Lancers. The victory, however, was worth the heavy price paid for it, for the Turks were thoroughly routed; they fled in great disorder to Nakaila, and report said that their leader, Suliman Askeri, committed suicide.

The action was followed by a vigorous pursuit. By river and by road the Turks sought safety in flight. Twelve boats full of fugitives were either taken or sunk, and the total losses of the enemy were about 2,500, of whom over seven hundred were prisoners in our hands. The booty taken included large quantities of tents, equipment, stores, and ammunition, as well as several machine-guns. The neighbourhood of Basra was entirely cleared of the enemy, who soon continued his retreat beyond Nakaila, which was occupied by our cavalry on the 17th, and it was ascertained that there were no Turks nearer than Rattava, which is fifty miles from the city.

This victory near Shaiba was decisive, and the month of May was mainly occupied in clearing the country **Turks vacate** of the remnants of the enemy. **Persian soil** Only near Ahwaz and Kurna were the Turks at all troublesome. In the former locality they were found to be in some strength on the Kharkhed, and thither our troops marched against them. Unfortunately, however, the march was delayed by severe sand-storms and by a rapid rise of the river, and before the enemy's camp was reached, the Turks had fallen back to Amara, thus vacating Persian soil. The British column, therefore, which was led by General Gorringe, was occupied in punishing the tribes which had assisted the enemy. Of these one or two offered some resistance, but this was soon beaten down, and their strongholds, with some of their other property, were destroyed. Others asked for terms and surrendered a number of rifles.

The Turks near Kurna were dealt with on May 31st, soldiers and sailors both taking part in the enterprise. Starting at 1.30 a.m., our men, partly by wading and partly in boats, succeeded in turning the enemy's position, while his guns were soon silenced by our artillery and naval guns. By noon the heights had been seized and the Turks were in flight, leaving behind them three guns and about two hundred and fifty prisoners.

KURNA AFTER ITS CAPTURE.
Effects of the British bombardment on a custom-house by the Tigris.

WAITING FOR THE TURKS.
Indian artillery in readiness somewhere on the Persian Gulf battle-front.

CAPTURED TURKISH FIELD-GUN.
A considerable number of the enemy's guns fell into the hands of the British during the advance up the Shat-el-Arab.

TURKISH PRISONERS IN SHAIBA FORT.
The British victory near Shaiba in April, 1915, was costly but decisive, and many hundreds of prisoners were taken.

As the force from Ahwaz had done, the Turks from Kurna retreated to Amara. This is an important town on the Tigris about sixty miles from Kurna, and it was the next object of our attentions. A flotilla consisting of the Comet and some launches, carrying General Townshend and Sir Percy Cox, the chief British Resident on the Gulf, reached the place on June 3rd, and at once the Governor surrendered it, the garrison of one thousand men becoming prisoners of war.

In and around Amara the British captured about eighty officers and 2,000 men, seven field and six naval guns, twelve large steel barges and four river steamers, and a quantity of rifles and ammunition. This ended a successful campaign. The Turkish forces in Mesopotamia had been defeated and partly destroyed, and the whole of the country between Amara and the sea was in British hands.

HIDDEN FROM THE ENEMY.
British gun protected by sand-bags and cleverly concealed by an earthwork. The photograph was taken in the vicinity of Kurna.

The delta of the Shat-el-Arab was protected by the garrison firmly planted at Kurna and Mezera, on either side of the Tigris, and the mouths of the river were guarded by British warships.

PICTURESQUE VIEW OF THE 10TH MULE CORPS ON PARADE AT BASRA.
In the arid wastes of Asia Minor no less than in the hilly regions of the North-West frontier of India the mule proved a most serviceable aid to our gallant troops.

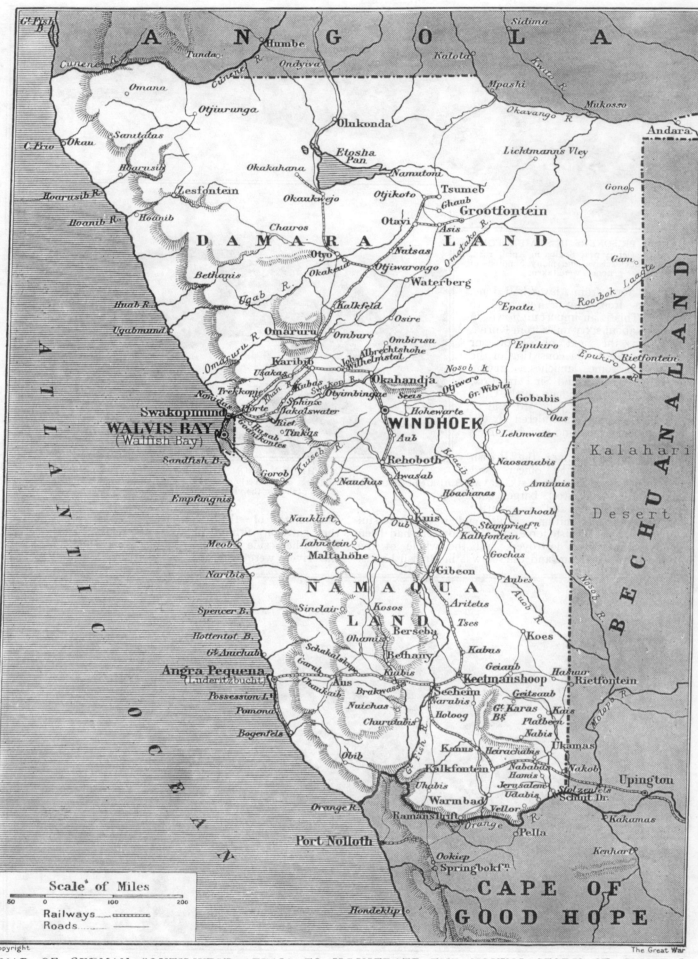

MAP OF GERMAN SOUTH-WEST AFRICA TO ILLUSTRATE THE MOVING STORY OF GENERAL
BOTHA'S BRILLIANT CAMPAIGN AGAINST THE GERMANS.

CHAPTER LXVIII.

BOTHA'S VICTORIOUS CAMPAIGN IN GERMAN SOUTH-WEST AFRICA.

With the Aid of Brilliant Lieutenants South Africa's Soldier-Premier Outgenerals, Outmanœuvres, and Outwits the Enemy How Germany Prepared for a Place in the South African Sun—Her Hopes of a Boer Rebellion—General Botha, having Quelled the Malcontents Stirred Up by Beyers, Christian De Wet, and Maritz, Takes the Field with the Northern Army—General Smuts and the Southern Command—A Circle of Steel Drawn Round the Foe—Germans Poison the Wells with Cattle Dip—The Movements Conducted by Sir Duncan Mackenzie, Colonel Van de Venter, and Colonel Berrange—Death of Sir George Farrar—Surrender of Windhoek " by Telephone "—General Botha's Historic Entry into the Capital—The War against Nature and against Man—Triumphant Conclusion of the Campaign.

B Y the end of the nineteenth century Africa, like the rest of the world, had been explored and divided up, and in this division Germany secured a share—or, rather, we should say, several shares. One of these was a big stretch of land on the west coast, north of the Orange River, which divides it from the Cape of Good Hope. In April, 1884, the German Government announced that Herr Lüderitz, a Bremen merchant who had taken possession of certain points on this coast, was under the Kaiser's protection. Since then this territory has been known as German South-West Africa. The northern part, however, is sometimes called by its older name of Damaraland, and the southern part Namaqualand.

This colony contains 320,000 square miles, and is therefore just about the size of Germany and Italy together. On the west it has a sea coast of about eight hundred miles ; on the north it is bordered by the Portuguese colony of Angola ; and on the east by Bechuanaland, a British protectorate. Its southern frontier, the shortest of all, is the Cape of Good Hope. It has a population of about 100,000 natives, mainly Bushmen and Hottentots, and about 15,000 German settlers. A large part of the colony is mere desert, but much of it is suitable for farming, and in this the Germans have made

their homes and introduced their cattle. South-West Africa is fairly rich in minerals, especially diamonds. In 1906 extensive diamond mines were discovered near Lüderitz Bay, and these have put a good deal of money into German pockets. Copper is also found in the country, but as far as is known at present little or no gold is there.

On the coast there are two ports—Swakopmund about the centre, and Lüderitz Bay, called also by its older Portuguese name of Angra Pequena, in the south. Near Swakopmund the British have a little settlement called Walfish Bay. The capital of the colony is Windhoek, a town in the interior about two hundred miles from Swakopmund. On this possession the Germans have spent a good deal of money, chiefly in building railways and in developing their two ports. The main lines of railway form three sides of a square of which the sea coast is the fourth. Starting from Swakopmund, a line runs east to Windhoek, and then turns south, and makes for Keetmanshoop, completing the round by reaching the coast again at Lüderitz Bay. In addition to these main lines there are two others. One runs south from Seeheim to Warmbad, a place only a few miles from the British frontier, and the other serves the extreme north of the colony. We do not know what was in the minds of the Germans when they laid these lines over

GENERAL BOTHA AND STAFF ON THE SOUTH-WEST AFRICAN VELDT.
It is noticeable that General Botha and his officers are levelling their glasses in different directions. The success of the campaign was the more remarkable because the South African Premier was known to be suffering from ill-health at its commencement.

AN INTERESTING VIEW OF A ROUGH-AND-READY TROOP TRAIN IN GERMAN SOUTH-WEST AFRICA.
Officers and men alike belonging to General Botha's victorious forces contented themselves with the inconveniences of this form of travel.

some hundreds of miles of inhospitable desert, but perhaps they, too, like Cecil Rhodes, dreamed of " Empire to the northward."

When the Great War began, the Germans in South-West Africa were ready with their plans. In 1904 they began a war with a native race—the Hereros—whom they extirpated with fiendish cruelty after nearly three years of fighting. At the close of the war a number of disbanded soldiers had settled on the land. These formed a very useful reserve, and with the 3,500 regular troops in the colony and a number of volunteers, the **German hopes of** Governor may possibly have had some- **Boer rebellion** thing like 10,000 men at his disposal. This force was well furnished with artillery, and included a camel corps some five hundred strong. Ammunition and military stores of all kinds were also plentiful.

The Governor, Dr. Seitz, and his associates, realised probably quite as well as we did ourselves that they would get no help whatever from Europe, but they had high hopes that a successful rebellion of the Boers in British South Africa would be of material assistance to them. Accordingly, early in August, 1914, their two ports—Swakopmund and Lüderitz Bay—were abandoned and all works of naval importance were destroyed ; and their garrisons, with their stores, retired to Windhoek. The Germans then bent all their energies towards assisting the Boer rebels, and the story of this failure has been told already in Chapter LII.

The question of South-West Africa did not escape the attention of the Imperial Government, and soon after the outbreak of the war there was some correspondence on the subject between the Colonial Secretary, Mr. Lewis Harcourt, and General Botha. Mr. Harcourt said that the authorities in London attached a good deal of importance to the conquest of this German colony, and asked the South African people to undertake the work, and so to perform " a great and urgent Imperial service." Botha's

task was not an easy one, for there was a certain difference of opinion about the desirability of an offensive campaign against Germany, but after due consideration he and his colleagues decided to accept the invitation " in the interests of South Africa as well as of the Empire." Towards the cost of the work the Imperial Government offered a loan of £7,000,000.

Owing to the rebellion, it was some months before Botha was able to give his mind and the resources of his country to this task, but he never lost sight of it, and as soon as the back of the Boer revolt had been broken, preparations were made for an invasion of German South-West Africa. As early as September 18th, 1914, Lüderitz Bay had been seized by our sailors ; a little later the valuable diamond mines passed into our possession, and on Christmas Day a body of South African troops reoccupied Walfish Bay, which had been temporarily in the possession of the Germans. On December 31st the Union Government announced that they proposed to commandeer men for the coming campaign, and not to depend wholly on volunteers ; for, as their communiqué said : " In view of the danger of invasion, it will be necessary to employ much larger forces than at first intended, in order to destroy the enemy and rebel forces, so that they may **Swakopmund sown** never again menace the peace of South **with mines** Africa." Further proof of the ubiquity of the Navy was given on January 14th, 1915, when Swakopmund was occupied. It was found absolutely deserted, but undamaged. The Germans, however, had sown the place with mines, and before these had been discovered and removed two troopers of the Imperial Light Horse had been blown to bits.

The two German ports were now in Botha's hands, but there were other entrances into South-West Africa, and these, too, had to be secured. The Orange is crossed at two main drifts—Schuit Drift and Raman's Drift—and the latter of these had been seized by our men during the

GENERAL AND MRS. BOTHA AT A RAILWAY STATION IN GERMAN SOUTH-WEST AFRICA.
Mrs. Botha made a long special railway journey to bid her husband " God speed " in his advance into the enemy's country.

rebellion, when there was a good deal of fighting along the line of the river. Early in January, 1915, an attack was made on Schuit Drift. This was seized, and the enemy driven across the river.

At the beginning of February the four principal gates into the German colony were held by the Union forces, the climatic conditions were becoming more favourable, the rebels had been crushed, and Botha could press forward with his plan of invasion. This was well conceived, well planned, and well executed, and as it was furthermore justified by its complete success it deserves to be studied by all those interested in military operations. It cannot, of course, be compared with the gigantic movements in Europe, but within its own limited sphere it was a model campaign.

The plan proposed was an enveloping advance on Windhoek from the coast and from the south, the railways to be taken on the way. For this purpose the Union forces were divided into two armies, called the northern and the southern. The former, which was commanded by Botha himself, was to assemble at Swakopmund, and to march along the railway line to the German capital. The southern army, under General Smuts, was entrusted with a more complicated task. For the first part of this it was divided into three columns. One under Sir Duncan Mackenzie was to advance inland from Lüderitz Bay, while another, under Colonel Van de Venter, was to move across the Orange and along the railway leading from Warmbad. The third column, under Colonel Berrange, was to start from Kimberley, and after crossing the Kalahari Desert, was to clear the enemy from the south-eastern section of the colony. In the neighbourhood of Keetmanshoop the three were to unite, and Smuts was to lead them northwards to join Botha.

A circle of steel

While this circle of steel was being drawn around the Germans they made one effort to break through. At Kakamas, on the Orange, a British garrison stationed there to protect Schuit Drift was suddenly and violently attacked by about six hundred Germans on February 5th. At eight o'clock in the morning big guns and Maxims opened fire upon the station, but the defenders were ready, and in a short time the assailants were beaten off. They lost nine men killed, twenty-two wounded, and fifteen taken prisoners, while on the Union side the casualties were one killed and two wounded. On hearing of the engagement, Colonel Van de Venter marched out from Upington to cut off their retreat, but the Germans were too quick for him.

German effort to break through

Since its occupation by the British, Swakopmund had been a very busy place. Men and stores were landed there in considerable quantities, and a railway line, protected by blockhouses and sea walls, was built along the few miles of coast which separate the port from Walfish Bay. Early in February General Botha left Cape Town to take over the direction of operations, and on his way he called at Lüderitz Bay, near where Sir Duncan Mackenzie's men had been encamped for some time past, engaged in making preparations for their campaign. Proceeding to their bivouacs, which were about forty miles inland, the Premier reviewed them and told them he hoped they would soon get the order to move forward.

On the following day, February 12th, Botha reached Swakopmund, and on the 22nd his army moved out, a heavy fall of rain having made its task easier. On the 23rd Nonidas and Goanikontes, two stations on the line to Windhoek, were occupied without serious fighting, although some resistance had been expected, as the Germans were in some strength at the former place, and with their outposts and patrols there had been several skirmishes. Nearly a month was then spent in preparing an advanced base, and in finding out something about the strength and disposition of the enemy.

On March 19th Botha was ready for another advance.

In accordance with his orders, two brigades of mounted men left Husab, he himself accompanying the first, which was commanded by Colonel Brits. Its object was to attack Riet, an important place south of the railway, which commands the high road to Windhoek, where the enemy was known to be in strength; and to complete its work, the Bloemhof commando was ordered to move round its flank, to seize the dominating height of Schwarze Kopje, and to cut off the enemy's retreat.

At daybreak on the 20th the brigade came in front of the German position, which was a very strong one. Its right rested on the Swakop and its left on the foothills of the Langer Heinrichberg, while its guns, skilfully placed, commanded both the main road and the river. A frontal attack was necessary, and our men advanced without flinching, their progress being splendidly assisted by the guns of the Transvaal Horse Artillery. At length they reached the German lines, and in the evening the enemy was driven out in disorder. For some reason or other the Bloemhof commando failed to reach its allotted place, and so the retreat was unhindered. During the engagement a party of snipers under Captain Lemmer did good work in preventing the Germans from destroying the water-holes.

Meanwhile, the second mounted brigade was carrying out its part of the programme, which was to seize an important section of the line running to Windhoek. For this purpose it was divided into two columns. One under Colonel Celliers cut the line between Jakalswater and Sphinx, and seized a train full of supplies; and then, having thus hampered the movement of any reinforcements from the direction of Windhoek, attacked Jakalswater itself. There, however, the German position was a very strong one, and the assault on it failed; but it served the secondary purpose of preventing the enemy from sending assistance to other parts of the field. Forty-three prisoners were taken by the Germans.

Clearing the railway system

The second division of this brigade, led by Colonel Alberts, marched against Pforte, another station on the line, where the enemy, with two big guns and two Maxims, was found strongly posted. He was soon surrounded, however, and while our men charged up to one of the big guns, our battery killed the gunners of the other. The Germans then surrendered unconditionally; two hundred and ten prisoners were made, and the spoil included the four guns and a large quantity of ammunition. The enemy lost twenty killed, three of them being officers.

For the next five or six weeks after these operations Botha was busy clearing the railway system of the enemy. Two main lines run from Swakopmund, the northern to Grootfontein, Tsumeb, and the north of the colony, and the southern to Windhoek. The main line of advance for the Union force was along the second of these; but to prevent any attack on its flank it was necessary also to hold the other. For fifty miles this was secured, and to guard it the Kimberley regiment, under Colonel Skinner, was stationed at Trekkopje, then our railhead.

GENERAL SMUTS CONGRATULATES THE IMPERIAL LIGHT HORSE ON THEIR SUCCESS IN GERMAN SOUTH-WEST AFRICA.
The above photographs represent an interesting event at the close of the campaign in German South-West Africa—a review at Johannesburg of the 2nd Imperial Light Horse by General Smuts. In the top view the General is accompanied on his right by Lieut.-Colonel Davies, the C.O. of the Light Horse, and on his left by Major Hawkins, the Camp Commandant. When the lower photograph was taken General Smuts was addressing the men before they disbanded.

SOME GALLANT SOLDIER SONS OF THE EMPIRE—OFFICERS OF THE RAND LIGHT INFANTRY.
Reading from left to right. Back row: Lieutenants B. H. L. Dougherty, H. W. Kelly, D. H. Stewart, J. O. Henrey, Captain H. R. Lawrence, Lieutenant G. A. Leyds. Second row: Captain W. Wilson, Lieutenants D. A. Pirie, L. D. Durham, W. G. Preston, J. L. Shenton, G. H. Metcalfe, J. P. E. Douglas. Front row: Captains G. H. Langdale, S. M. Page, P. H. Franks, T. P. Atkins, Major W. J. Thompson, Lieutenant-Colonel J. M. Fairweather, D.S.O., Major W. A. Abbott, Captains C. G. Durham, W. Richards, A. C. Pedersen.

On April 26th some seven hundred Germans with twelve guns attacked this encampment, and a hard fight, lasting about four hours, took place. The object of the enemy was, after peppering our lines with shell and shrapnel, to get round the two ends of our trenches and enfilade them. But the plan miscarried, although the Germans got within about one hundred and fifty yards of their objective. Some armoured cars belonging to the Naval Air Service forced them into a position whence our guns and rifles could reach them easily, and they retired, leaving twenty-five killed and wounded behind them. The Union force had three officers and eight men killed and about forty wounded.

We must now return to the doings of the southern army, and first of all to those of the column commanded by Sir Duncan Mackenzie. He cleared out the Germans and took some stores from one or two places in the neighbourhood of Lüderitz Bay, and then without difficulty seized a substantial stretch of the railway line. On February 22nd his advanced guard was at Garub, a station seventy miles inland, which was occupied without opposition, and from there some scouts pushed out and fought a skirmish with the retiring Germans, who were mounted men covering a troop train. The leader of our scouts was wounded, and leaving him and one of their comrades in the hands of the enemy, our men were forced to retire.

At Garub, Mackenzie had the worst part of his march

THE SOLDIER-PREMIER'S "SPECIAL SALOON."
A snapshot of General Botha leaving his "special saloon" (a horse-box) on one of the trains used by him in the operations in German South-West Africa.

behind him. He had crossed the desert which fringes the sea coast, and was approaching the hills and the fertile land beyond. At Garub there was a plentiful supply of water, and henceforward his anxieties on this score, although not removed, were considerably lightened. While here, the British camp was attacked by a hostile aeroplane, which dropped shells and hand-grenades near our guns.

Fifteen miles beyond Garub is the important station of Aus, the principal resting-place for the caravans journeying from north to south, and in searching the mountainous country between the two places our men had a stiff task. Sand was plentiful, but food and water were less so, and the enemy had filled up the bore-holes and poisoned some of the wells. Towards the end of March loud explosions were heard from the direction of Aus, caused, doubtless, by the destruction of the railway line by the Germans, and it seemed as if they were preparing to evacuate the place. This was the more surprising because, owing to its situation among the hills, Aus could be made into a strong defensive position, and the enemy had done a good deal to fortify it.

Mines had been laid, trenches dug, and the passes through the hills fortified, but when the time came everything was abandoned without a struggle.

This was partly due, no doubt, to the strength and skill of the advancing force. On the night of March 30th a body of our mounted infantry marched silently out, and in the morning

THE GUNS THAT SPOKE FOR UNION—ONE OF GENERAL BOTHA'S BATTERIES IN ACTION IN GERMAN SOUTH-WEST AFRICA.

was in possession of two of the important passes giving access to Aus. Once there they threatened the flank and the retreat of the Germans, and the whole position was at once vacated.

On the following day our men entered the place. Several mines were exploded, but without any serious casualties. One of the mines was composed of thirty pom-pom shells and a hundred sticks of blasting gelatine. The buildings in the town were found undamaged, but they had been stripped of everything useful, and the bridges and culverts had been destroyed. In a short time, however, these and also the railway line had been repaired, and a further move was possible.

With Col. Van de Venter's column We must now turn to the movements of the force led by Colonel Van de Venter, the most important section of Smuts's army.

Safely across the Orange at Schuit Drift, Van de Venter and his column soon came into touch with the foe. Sweeping over a wide district in the south-east of the colony they occupied a group of stations, including Ukamas, Nabas, Jerusalem, Velloor, and Heirachabis, and before the end of March they had seized two or three German camps, containing a large quantity of supplies, horses, and live-stock. One of these was at Platbeen, about fifty miles north of Ukamas, and another was at Geitsaub. At both there were skirmishes, and at

the cost of one man killed and two wounded our force made twenty-eight prisoners and killed six of the enemy. On April 30th Van de Venter reached the railway at Warmbad, its terminus, twenty-five miles from the frontier, and occupied it without opposition. From there he pushed along the line so rapidly that two days later his men entered Kanus, a station sixty-five miles to the north.

At this time Van de Venter's headquarters were at Kalkfontein, a station twenty-five miles north of Warmbad, and here on April 11th he was joined by General Smuts. The task immediately before them was that of driving the enemy from the slopes of the Karras Mountains, on

A 4·7 IN THE DESERT.
These weapons had to be most carefully covered so that the desert sand could not get into and choke the working parts.

which he had one or two advantageous positions. The plan adopted was to advance in three columns. Van de Venter himself marched near the railway and to the west of the mountains, while a second detachment moved to the east of them; somewhat in the rear and acting as a reserve was a third column, which took the road through the hills. The manœuvre was completely successful. Threatened on all sides, the enemy withdrew without putting up the semblance of a fight, and the region was entirely in our hands. On April 18th a mounted brigade under Colonel Villiers occupied Seeheim, the place where the line from

ONE OF THE MACHINE-GUNS USED AGAINST THE GERMAN AVIATORS.
This machine-gun, used as an anti-aircraft weapon, was familiar to the Union troops as "The Skinny Liz." It did most serviceable work in checking the activities of the Teuton aviators.

AFTER THE SURRENDER OF WINDHOEK—HOW THE GERMAN PRISONERS WERE CONVEYED TO THE COAST.

Warmbad joins the railway from Lüderitz Bay. According to one account, the Germans hurriedly evacuated this junction because they mistook a party of scouts for our main body. They did not even have time to destroy the bridge which here crosses the Great Fish River.

By this time Van de Venter's column was in touch with Colonel Berrange's force, which, it will be remembered, had set out from Kimberley. British Bechuanaland was crossed without hindrance, the only difficulties encountered arising from the nature of the country, and in March the enemy was first sighted near the border. At Hasuur, fifteen miles north-west of Rietfontein, on April 1st, Berrange captured an entrenched position with slight

ARMOURED CARS AT WINDHOEK.
The armoured car, which proved invaluable in the pursuit of Christian de Wet, was eminently useful also in scouting and patrol work.

loss, and from then he fought his way steadily westward to the neighbourhood of Keetmanshoop.

Keetmanshoop was now surrounded, and its occupation, either peaceably or otherwise, was only a question of days. This town, the business capital of German Namaqualand, is the eastern terminus of the railway line, and is nearly two hundred miles from the coast. On April 19th the Germans quietly vacated it, having first rendered the telegraph and telephone wires useless, and on the 20th it was occupied by our men. A day or two later General Smuts travelled along the railway from Keetmanshoop to Aus, thus show-

ing how completely the line was in the hands of the Union forces.

Before Smuts could concentrate his whole force it was necessary for Sir Duncan Mackenzie's column, which was left at Aus, to join the others, and this was done in May. From Aus there was no need for Sir Duncan to keep to the railway line, for it was already cleared of the enemy; and so, with his mounted men, he struck out to the north-east. The towns of Bethany and Berseba—with their names redolent of the piety of their Boer founders—were occupied without hindrance, and the railway line was reached on April 24th at Aritetis, a station seventy miles north of Keetmanshoop. Once on the railway line Mackenzie began to act in conjunction with Van de Venter against the enemy retreating from Seeheim and Keetmanshoop. On the 22nd part of Van de Venter's pursuing force had come up with the Germans at Kabus, twenty miles to the north, where an indecisive engagement had taken place. The enemy, about six hundred strong, with three or four guns, withstood our attack and continued his retreat, although he left most of his wounded in our hands. The Union force, however, lost twenty-two men taken prisoners.

The fight at Kabus

Mackenzie now joined in this chase. He learned that the Germans who had

APPLIED SCIENCE IN THE AFRICAN SAND WASTES.
A motor-mounted searchlight and heliograph used in General Botha's brilliant campaign. The searchlight was fitted at the rear, and the operator's quarters were in the centre of the car.

UNDER THE SHADOW OF TABLE MOUNTAIN.
1st South African Mounted Rifles at Cape Town. The photograph was taken just before their embarkation for the front. Their rifles had cloth covers to protect them from the desert sand. The S.A.M.R. constituted South Africa's "first line of defence."

HOW GENERAL BOTHA KEPT IN TOUCH WITH THE ENEMY'S MOVEMENTS.
A wireless outfit used in General Botha's campaign, photographed with the men who worked it.

fought at Kabus were taking train at Gibeon, a station forty miles to the north of Keetmanshoop, and at once he decided upon his method of attack. His whole force having approached within two miles of Gibeon, a small party was despatched to destroy the railway to the north of that place, and one brigade, the 9th, was sent forward to engage the enemy. The 9th Brigade was unequal to the task before it, and having suffered severe loss and left seventy prisoners in the hands of the enemy, it fell back upon the main body. This skirmish took place during the night of April 27th, and on the following morning Mackenzie attacked the Germans with his whole force.

The Battle of Gibeon was soon over. The enemy was driven from the field and pursued for **Mackenzie's success at Gibeon** about twenty miles, and only the rocky and difficult nature of the ground prevented the destruction of the whole force. As it was, our seventy prisoners were rescued and seven officers and two hundred men were captured, as well as both the enemy's field-guns and several Maxims. In addition, the cutting of the railway line delivered into our hands a train, a number of transport waggons, and a quantity of live-stock. The British losses were three officers and twenty men killed, and eight officers and forty-seven men wounded. Among the killed was Major J. H. Watt, of the Natal Light Horse.

The success of Mackenzie's march, first across the coastal desert, and then over the one hundred and twenty miles of arid country which lie between Bethany and Gibeon, was due very largely to the exertions of his quartermaster-

general, Sir George Farrar, and it was, therefore, a great loss to the Union forces when Sir George was killed in a railway accident near Gibeon on May 18th. It was the end of a full and adventurous career. He had been sentenced to death for his share in the Jameson Raid, had fought against the Boers in the war of 1899-1902, and until the last was the controlling spirit of a great mining organisation.

It is now time to inquire again how Botha was faring in the north. After the fighting around Jakalswater on March 20th the northern army halted for a while, and it was not until May 1st that Kubas, a place thirty miles nearer Windhoek, was occupied by Colonel Brits. It was hastily evacuated by the Germans, and around it miles of entrenchments were found, and over a hundred contact mines were discovered and removed. A further advance took our men to Otyimbingue, which is only sixty miles from the capital, and a skirmish there resulted in the capture of twenty-eight enemy soldiers.

On May 5th the important railway junction of Karibib was reached and occupied, whence a march of twenty **Windhoek's surrender by telephone** miles took the army to Johann Albrechtshöhe, and a further ten to Wilhelmstal.

Windhoek was now almost in sight, as the van of the army under General Myburgh was rapidly approaching it, and on May 10th General Botha, who was then at Karibib, was informed by telephone that the place was prepared to surrender. With a small escort he set out at once in his motor-car, and on reaching the capital on the following day he was met by the Burgomaster, with whom the terms of capitulation were arranged. On the 12th a detachment of the Union forces under Myburgh formally entered the town, and at noon there was an interesting and historic ceremony. Escorted by a long and imposing array of mounted burghers, the soldier-Premier took up his station before the courthouse, from the steps of which a proclamation was read in English, Dutch, and German. This placed certain districts of South-West Africa under martial law, promised protection to those who obeyed its provisions, and expressed regret at the intention of the Germans to continue a hopeless struggle. The Union Jack was then hoisted, and the troops presented arms. In an address to his men Botha thanked them for their services in carrying out an enterprise " of the utmost importance to the Empire and the Union, as it means practically the complete possession of German South-West Africa."

Before the arrival of the British the German troops had withdrawn to Grootfontein, which, it was stated, was now their capital. However, some 3,000 Europeans remained in Windhoek, and with them were 12,000 natives, who thus passed under British rule. The wireless station, a valuable high-power one, situated about a mile from the town, was found intact, and with its capture Germany had lost all those she possessed outside Europe. On the railway a great quantity of rolling-stock was seized, and the government of the capital and the surrounding district was entrusted to Colonel Mentz.

Something still remained to be done before the German field force was destroyed, but the major **Endurance under** operations were over, and these had been **natural difficulties** carried out with a maximum of skill and a minimum of loss. To Botha himself the very highest praise is due, but something should be put down to the ability of his subordinates, and still more to the endurance of his men. Their chief enemy, indeed, was not the German, but the desert, waterless and sandy. Water was always scarce, often very scarce, and as an instance of this we may quote from a divisional order, which said: " It has been observed that water is being used for washing purposes. This practice must cease immediately."

The dust-storms and heat were very trying. As one soldier said: " Every day we have awful dust-storms lasting for hours, and the shade temperature always over a hundred degrees." Sometimes tents were blown to ribbons, and the sand came along at times like sleet. As a proof of the violence of these storms we are told that two hundred Cape boys were employed day and night shovelling the sand off forty miles of railway, and although they made a clear passage for the train in the morning, when it returned in the evening there was as much as four feet of sand over the rails. But this was not the worst evil caused by the sand. " A good many men," we are told, " have to be operated on to remove sand from their salivary glands under their tongues. When they eat, the saliva, trying to force its way through, causes a good deal of pain and swelling." Truly, as this correspondent

STRIKING CAMERA-PICTURE FROM GERMANY'S LOST COLONY: THE PRIDE THAT WENT BEFORE THE FALL.
Before evacuating Warmbad and the southern part of their colony the German forces in South-West Africa rounded up the natives and cleared them all up to Windhoek along with the European children. They thought that the Union troops would never get to Windhoek. The smaller view shows some officers of a German battalion preparing to leave Warmbad.

VIEW OF THE KOLMANSHOP DIAMOND MINE, GERMAN
SOUTH-WEST AFRICA.
One of the richest diamond mines in the world.

says : " Fighting men is a joke to fighting Nature "—at
least in South Africa.

A further hardship, which happily only happened once
or twice, was due to lack of provisions. Now and again,
especially in the final spurt, the troops got too far in front
of the transport waggons, and after the capture of Windhoek
they were for some days on half and then quarter rations.

But the difficulties attributable to Nature were increased
by the action of the Germans. In filling up the bore-holes
with sand the enemy was but following a Scripture pre-
cedent, for in the Bible (2 Kings iii. 19) we read how Elisha
ordered the Kings of Judah and Israel to stop all the wells of

**Germans poison
the wells**

water of the Moabites ; but what shall
we say about their action in poisoning the
wells, and thus violating one of the oldest
and most respected of the laws of war ?

We have already stated that near Aus Sir Duncan
Mackenzie found the wells of drinking water had been
poisoned, the only extenuating circumstance being that
warning notices had been affixed to them. At Swakopmund,
in January, the British on seizing the town discovered that
six wells had been poisoned by means of arsenical cattle
dip. On his arrival Botha took up the matter, and on
February 23rd he wrote to Lieutenant-Colonel Francke,
the German commander, drawing his attention to the fact
that such an act was contrary to Article No. 23 (a) of The
Hague Convention, and informing him that, if the practice
was persisted in, he would hold the officers concerned
responsible and he would be reluctantly compelled to employ
such measures of reprisal as might seem advisable.

In reply, Francke defended the action of his men, who had
orders " not to allow any water supplies to fall into the

SWAKOPMUND—A GERMAN PORT NO LONGER.
Swakopmund, one of the two important ports in German South-West
Africa, was occupied by the British on January 14th, 1915. Our
photograph shows the Union Jack flying over the Custom-House.

hands of the enemy in a form which allows such supplies
to be used either by man or beast." He added that to
prevent " injury to the health of the enemy," instructions
had been given to mark with warning notices the wells
which had been so treated. Botha answered that this
reply was unsatisfactory, and repeated his former threat.

However, all his difficulties were at length overcome,
and these cannot be summarised
better than in the words of Mr.
Asquith. Speaking at the Guildhall on May 19th, a week after
the capture of Windhoek, the
Prime Minister said : " Their undertaking has been no slight one.
A force of about 30,000 men,
rather over half of whom are
mounted men, with guns, horses,
medical stores, mules, and transports, have been conveyed oversea
five hundred and seven hundred
miles, in addition to the large
land force which has been operating on the German Union frontier. All supplies, every pound of provisions for the men, much of the
water for their consumption, every
ton of forage for horses and mules,
have had to be brought from
Cape Town. All the railway
material for rapid construction
had also to be brought from Cape
Town, and all these men, horses,

IN THE HANDS OF THE ENEMY.
Men of the 1st South African Mounted Rifles, taken prisoners at Sandfontein, marching through Windhoek,
with wounded in waggon at rear. They were afterwards liberated by the victorious Union forces.

guns, supplies, and materials had to be landed at two ports, Lüderitz and Walfish, at which appliances for disembarkation for such operations had not been constructed."

The campaign had been so successful that there was no need for General Smuts to keep his whole force in the field, and in May a portion of it was sent back and disbanded. In thanking these men for their services, Smuts mentioned that the country had been subdued in much shorter time than had been anticipated, and that the casualties had been comparatively few.

The business of dealing with the Germans still in arms, who had all been herded into the inhospitable north of the country, was left to General Botha's army. One column marched along the railway towards Grootfontein, while others swept the country to the south-east of it. A few days after the occupation of the capital, Colonel Mentz came up with a party of the enemy at Seeis thirty-seven miles to the east, and there, without loss to himself, he took one hundred and fifty-two prisoners, some waggons full of provisions, guns, and ammunition. About the same time General Manie Botha had a skirmish with the enemy about fifteen miles from Wilhelmstal, and a mounted brigade had one somewhat farther to the east. Meanwhile, on the railway line General Botha occupied the station of Omaruru, about eighty miles from Windhoek, where he took some prisoners, and a day or two later he was in possession of Kalkfeld, forty miles farther north. This place had been entrenched and prepared for resistance, but as a result of our flanking movements it was abandoned.

In the inhospitable north

Still the Germans declined to give battle, and Botha's mobile column swept victoriously on. On June 26th Otjiwarongo, a station on the railway, and Okandyande, a town eight miles to the south, were occupied, while wide encircling movements gave us possession of the whole of the district around Waterberg. At Okandyande two hundred and fifty interned civilians were liberated.

Fifty miles, or thereabouts, beyond Otjiwarongo the railway line forks, one branch going to Grootfontein and the other to Tsumeb. Near the junction stands Otavi, near which place are extensive deposits of copper, and as soon as the Union forces were securely planted at Okaputu and Omarasa, two intermediate stations, they made a dash for it. At 6.30 on the evening of June 30th General Manie Botha, with the 5th Brigade, left Okaputu, and at dawn on the following morning his scouts came into touch with the enemy. Later in the day a general action developed near Osib, and although the nature of the ground gave certain advantages to the defenders, and the attacking force had covered forty-two miles in sixteen hours, yet Manie Botha's skill and promptitude and his men's courage and endurance prevailed, and before nightfall Otavi was occupied. At Otavifontein—to give the town its full name—there is a good supply of water, and so arid is the neighbourhood that the possession of this practically means the possession of the surrounding country.

General Lukin's great march

From Omarasa, five miles south of Okaputu, another mounted brigade—the 6th—led by General Lukin, had set out at the same time as the 5th, and between the two came General Botha with the Headquarters Staff. Unlike Manie Botha, Lukin did not have to fight, but the excellent condition of his men was proved by this march of forty-eight miles in twenty hours without appreciable pause. The casualties among the Union forces in this operation were four killed and seven wounded. They took twenty-seven German prisoners and a machine-gun.

GENERAL BOTHA'S COLUMN AWAITING THE ORDER TO ENTER WINDHOEK.
With part of the northern army of the Union General Botha entered Windhoek, the capital of German South-West Africa, at noon on May 12th, 1915. He was met outside the town by the Burgomaster, having covered the final stage of the march by motor-car. When he entered Windhoek he was escorted by a motor-column and an impressive cavalcade of mounted burghers.

OVERSEAS CELTS WHO TOOK PART IN GENERAL BOTHA'S VICTORIOUS CAMPAIGN.
The 2nd Battalion of the Transvaal Scottish " at ease " outside Pretoria railway station before entraining for German South-West Africa. General Botha's forces included also a number of " Transvaal Irish."

A single day's rest was all that Manie Botha's men needed after their strenuous march and their running fight through a country covered with bush, and while they were taking this a regiment of mounted rifles was sent to seize the pass through the hills at Eisenberg. This having been done, the main body was soon on the move again towards Grootfontein.

This fight near Otavi was the last real stand made by the Germans. Brave as they unquestionably were, they never showed themselves unwilling, either at Kiao-Chau or elsewhere, to surrender when further resistance was useless. Supplies were failing, for Botha's generalship had deprived them of one advantage after another. They had been driven into the wildest and most inhospitable parts of the country; they were losing, one after the other, the places where food could be stored and water found; and, moreover, they were in a district where the natives—with good reason, if half the stories told are true—were fiercely hostile to them. Above all, Botha's columns were closing round them, and this they knew full well. They could die fighting, as James IV. and his spearmen did at Flodden, or they could surrender. They chose the latter alternative, and during the first days of July were making preparations for it.

Away to the west of the line to Tsumeb two columns were sweeping through the country. At Asis General Myburgh had left the railway, and at **Preparations for** Chaub, sixteen miles south of Tsumeb, **the surrender** he had met a body of Germans. What followed can scarcely be called a fight, for with only one man killed Myburgh took eighty-six prisoners, and on July 8th marched right into Tsumeb, where five or six hundred more surrendered. He also captured some field-guns, and released a number of his comrades who were in the hands of the retreating Germans.

Moving in a still bigger arc was Colonel Brits. On June 30th he left Otyisasu, five miles west of Otjiwarongo, and passing through Otyo and Okakeua, he reached the German port of Namutoni. There he took one hundred

64

and fifty German prisoners, seized their supplies and, like Myburgh, liberated a batch of our men. It was then officially stated that all the Union prisoners in German hands had been released.

By this time Dr. Seitz, the German governor, was in communication with General Botha about a surrender. Botha presented his terms in the form of an ultimatum, and while they were being **General Botha's** considered his men stood to arms ready, **ultimatum** if need be, for a final battle. This, however, was not to be. On the stroke of time the terms were accepted, and at two o'clock on the morning of July 9th, at a spot described as Kilometre 500 on the railway between Otavi and Khorab, the conditions of the capitulation were agreed to and signed by Botha, Seitz, and Col. Francke, the commander of the enemy's troops. All the Germans surrendered unconditionally. It is a tribute to civilisation that in that distant part of the world Botha was able to " ring up " Myburgh on the telephone, and to inform him of the surrender.

The terms of surrender provided that the officers should be released upon parole, and that the men should be interned in the country. The two paragraphs dealing with this question may be quoted in full.

The active troops of the said forces of the said Protectorate surrendered shall in the case of officers retain their arms and may give their parole, being allowed to live each under that parole at such places as he may select. If for any reason the Government of the Union of South Africa is unable to meet the wish of any officer as regards his choice of abode, the officer concerned will choose some place in respect of which no difficulty exists.

In the case of other ranks of the active troops of the said forces of the said Protectorate, such other ranks shall be interned under proper guard in such place in the Protectorate as the Union Government may decide upon. Each non-commissioned officer and man of the other ranks last referred to shall be allowed to retain his rifle, but no ammunition. One officer shall be permitted to be interned with the other ranks of the artillery, one with the other ranks of the remainder of the active troops, and one with the other ranks of the police.

These conditions referred only to the regular troops

and to the police. Reservists were allowed, upon surrendering their arms and signing a form of parole, to return to their homes and their civil occupations. Civil officials were allowed to retain their homes, but not, of course, their positions. Government property and all warlike stores became the property of the Union of South Africa.

The work of attending to the details of the surrender was entrusted to Brigadier-General H. T. Lukin, and a revised estimate of the number of prisoners gave it as 204 officers and 3,293 of other ranks (of these rather less than half were regulars) ; 37 field-guns and 22 machine-guns were given up at this time. The formal surrender took place at Otavi, where the prisoners

The campaign's victorious conclusion began to arrive on July 11th. Several of them were wearing a cross, not of iron, but of black cloth edged with white cord, this being apparently the nearest approach they could get to the decoration so dear to the Kaiser's heart. They stated that their provisions were almost at an end.

Two brigades, one mounted and one infantry, remained with General Lukin to look after the prisoners, but as regards the others, arrangements were made for their return to the Union where, it is hardly necessary to say, the victorious conclusion of the campaign was hailed with great rejoicing.

The whole operations had been carried out with singularly little loss of life. The final figures are not available, but on June 14th, when the heaviest of the fighting was over, the Union Government issued some particulars about the casualties suffered by its forces. Altogether, both in the rebellion and the campaign in South-West Africa, these numbered 1,612. The dead amounted to 406, of whom 97 were killed in action by the Germans and 98 by the rebels, 58 died of wounds, and 153 from disease, accident, or misadventure ; 606 were taken prisoners by the enemy, but, as we have seen, these were released by us.

The losses of the enemy can only be estimated very roughly. The rebels lost 190 killed and between 300 and 350 wounded. Of the Germans, 103 are known to have been killed and 195 wounded ; but these figures are certainly well within the mark. Before the surrender, 890 Germans were prisoners in South Africa. Thus, with the 700 or 800 taken by General Myburgh, and the 3,497 officers and men who surrendered on July 9th, we have accounted for nearly 6,000 of the enemy, or rather more than half the total number who were thought to have taken the field under Colonel Francke. The estimate of 10,000 may have been excessive, but not, we think, greatly so. A good number doubtless returned to their homes at various stages of the campaign ; the killed were certainly in excess of 103, and many must have died from disease and hardship.

At the cost of some 2,000 casualties — less than many a single day's loss suffered by our armies in Flanders — General Botha had captured a territory over 300,000 square miles in extent, and had brought 15,000 white folk and 100,000 natives under the rule of King George. It is an undeveloped land, but a rich one. Already it has produced diamonds and copper

to the value of £7,000,000, and in it about 33,000,000 acres are used for pasturage. Its foreign trade amounted to nearly £4,000,000 a year, and under British rule this is capable of great expansion. Before the surrender the damage done to the 1,400 miles of railway had been made good, and a regular service of trains was running. Moreover, the line from Upington in Cape Colony was, in June, extended to Kalkfontein, thus linking up the Union system with the German one.

And what shall we say more? Just this, that General Botha and his men deserved the praise showered upon them by the King and his subjects all over the world. On July 13th, in moving that the thanks of the House of Commons be given to Generals Botha and Smuts and the forces under their command, Mr. Asquith said :

I ask the House at this, the earliest opportunity, to testify to the admiration and gratitude of the whole Empire, first to the illustrious General, who is also Prime Minister of the Union, and who has rendered such inestimable service to the Empire, which he entered by adoption, and of which he has become one of the most honoured and cherished sons, and to his dauntless and much enduring troops, whether of Burgher or British birth, who fought like brethren, side by side, in the cause which is equally dear to all of us—the broadening of the bounds of human liberty.

While the chief glory of this astonishing success belongs to General Botha, the British race will not forget his great lieutenant, General Jan Christiaan Smuts, Minister of Finance before the war and Minister of Defence during it. What Stonewall Jackson was to Lee that was General Smuts to Botha. The two were a perfect combination, and they worked with an energy, decision, courage, and loyalty that placed the Empire in their permanent debt. General Smuts in his earlier life had attracted the prophetic eye of Cecil Rhodes, who foretold that he would be one of the greatest of South Africans. He fought brilliantly in the Boer War, proving himself almost as redoubtable an opponent as General Botha. He loyally accepted the settlement at the Peace of Vereeniging ; and in the critical hours of 1914, when it **South Africa's "Stonewall Jackson"** seemed to many that the Boers were wavering, he reminded them with speeches and messages of burning eloquence that the cause at stake was the cause of their kinsfolk, since among them were thousands with Flemish blood in their veins.

To his men General Botha himself paid a well-earned tribute. "The main feature of the last operations," said he, "has been the incessant marching by day and night over great distances, at great speed, without water." And he continued : "The marches performed by one and all deserve to rank highly as military achievements." No wonder that Lord Kitchener telegraphed : "We shall warmly welcome you and the South Africans who can come over to join us."

Lord Kitchener's hope seemed likely to be realised, for the Imperial Government accepted the offer of the Union Government to provide some batteries of heavy artillery and a contingent of men to serve in Europe. Meanwhile, whatever may be the future of South-West Africa, its speedy and economical conquest will remain as a monument to the genius of the great Boer General and the endurance and heroism of his men.

SOUTH AFRICAN MOUNTED RIFLES BEHIND BARRICADES OF STONE AND SCRUB.

H

FRENCH SOLDIERS IN ACTION WITH A MACHINE-GUN IN AN ANGLE OF A TRENCH AT NEUVILLE ST. VAAST.

The trench shown had been captured from the Germans; and the above vivid record of the way in which it was turned to advantage by our gallant allies is the work of one of the official French photographers.

ROYAL ENGINEERS LAYING | CHAPTER LXIX. | A FIELD TELEGRAPH.

THE BATTLES OF HOOGE, ROUGES BANCS, AND FESTUBERT.

Poisoned Streams at Ypres and the German System of Atrocities—Blowing a Poison Path through our Trenches at Hooge—Magnificent Recovery of Sir Herbert Plumer's Men—Attempted Advance of our First Army at Aubers Ridge—Our Shrapnel Fire Fails to Destroy the Enemy's Entrenchments—Heroic Charge by the Kensington Territorials—The Black Watch Fails for Lack of Support —Lacking Shells, the British Army Works Forward with Bombs and Bayonets—Great Night Attack by 7th Division and 2nd Division—Check to Indian Army Corps and Magnificent Rush Forward by British Troops—Driving Two Wedges into the German Salient near Festubert—7th Division and 2nd Division Link Hands and Cut Off the Germans—Canadian Division and Highland Division Carry On the Advance—The Achievement of the Welsh Fusiliers with Captain Rockwell and Sergeant-Major Barter— How the Cameron Territorials Tricked the Enemy—Splendid Gallantry of the Scots Guards and the Queen's—The Modern Grenadier and his Terrible Skill in Trench-Clearing—Grand Charge by the Canadian Scottish—The Second Canadian Brigade and the Awful Struggle for the "Bexhill" Redoubt—Why the Battle of Festubert Came to an End.

THERE seems to be little doubt that the gas attacks on Ypres, which began on April 22nd, 1915, as already described, seriously interfered with the plans made by Sir John French for a great forward movement in the spring. The loss of fifty guns by the French division north of the town exposed our defending troops under Lieutenant-General Sir Herbert Plumer to a sweeping, overwhelming fire from the strengthened German batteries. Large bodies of troops, such as the Lahore Division, had to be moved rapidly from their position near Neuve Chapelle—from which Sir John French had originally intended to strike towards Lille— and make a night-march to the north of Ypres and there help the French, Belgians, and Canadian Divisions. All through the month of May Ypres remained a position of great weakness in our lines, and our defence of the shattered city needed such sustained and desperate efforts that the British Army was only able to play a comparatively small part in the offensive operations against the German front.

All the time Sir Douglas Haig drove in against the German lines southward, the German commander weakened the force of the British attack by a furious assault northward against Sir Herbert Plumer's position. It is thus impossible to

deny that the enemy obtained an important advantage by his barbarous use of poisonous gases. For though he did not thereby win Ypres, he seriously checked any forward movement by our right wing in the direction of Lille. In the latter part of May the Germans seemed still confident that they would capture Ypres by means of their gas attacks. Every time the wind changed from a western or south-westerly direction to north or north-east the clouds of green death were sent against our lines. Sometimes the barbarians were slain by their own foul weapon. South of Pilkem some of the men of the 240th Reserve Regiment were suffocated by their own gas, through a cylinder in their trenches being blown up by a French shell. Soon afterwards a direct hit, obtained by our artillery on a German trench south of Ypres, produced an extraordinary column of thick fumes, which immediately descended on the German lines, thus showing that it was formed of something much heavier than the smoke of a high-explosive shell.

It was in this section of the battlefield that the Germans resorted to the last but one of all possible methods of warfare of pure savagery. Some of our men were suddenly stricken by a new disease. It looked at first as though they were suffering from jaundice; but they also had the dropped wrist, which is a symptom of poisoning. Our doctors in the hospital asked

A POST OF PERIL.
General Michelet inspecting an advanced post of the French Army near Ypres.

for a sample of the water from the stream coming from a position held by the Bavarians. When the water was analysed it was found to contain arsenic. Only one thing then remained for the Germans to do in order to rival fully the Aztecs of ancient Mexico and the head-hunters of the Solomon Islands. They had begun by killing our wounded and then torturing our men whom they had taken prisoners. They had afterwards spread cholera germs brought from Galicia among the Belgian troops on the Yser. Then in many of the German prison-camps in which our men were confined there had been a sudden and general outburst of deadly diseases, which looked as though German bacteriological science was being employed in so secret and subtle a manner that we should be able to find no cause for making reprisals upon German prisoners of war in our hands. The diseases in question could, in a natural way, only be conveyed by means of vermin, and having regard to our national habits of cleanliness, it was extremely unlikely that if our men were allowed to keep themselves clean they would, when at ease in German

Horrors of Teuton savagery

A BY-WAY AMID THE RUINS OF MONT ST. ELOI.
A view taken by one of the official French photographers.

camps, willingly endure the constant irritation of insect pests.

The Germans also weakened our men whom they had taken prisoners by a process of slow starvation, which tended to reduce them to such a condition that the contagious diseases introduced into the German prison camps would have a quicker and more deadly effect. It was while this subtle and modernised reversion to the most savage treatment of prisoners of war was occurring that the horrible poison gas was employed by the Germans on a general scale. As we have seen, it was accompanied by the new attempt to terrorise our soldiers by letting them see their wounded hanging crucified against barn-doors. Not long after this our men also saw, from the trenches to which they had retired after an unsuccessful charge, the enemy spraying burning liquid on the wounded men we had left behind during our retirement. Compared with all these things the poisoning of a stream south of Ypres was a small affair. General Botha's men had already suffered from this barbarism, and it was only to be expected that the Germans would employ it also on the European field of war. But the poisoning of streams was very significant in that it practically exhausted the armoury of savageries which the enemy had developed. They

had done everything that the most degraded creatures in human shape could do, with the sole exception that they had refrained from cannibalism. Only in this regard could the head-hunters of the South Seas and the savages of the Amazon claim any superiority over them in respect to rigorous methods of terrorising their foes.

Naturally our men were far from being terrorised. Our regular Army had fought against savages of every kind for some hundreds of years. And while sentimental members of the Radical and Irish wings in our Parliament, such as Mr. King, of North Somerset, were protesting in advance against our Army using asphyxiating gases against the Germans, our troops in the trenches refused to surrender, and preferred to die rather than fall into the clutches of fiends. "Their mistrust of us was such," wrote a German Catholic priest, "that, seeing the situation was hopeless, the English Rifle Brigade tried to commit suicide." Almost every single man of them had to be put out of action with hand-grenades, according to the priest. This statement coming from a German source, confirmed the report of our own men concerning what they saw done to their wounded. The fighting Briton does not choose death merely by reason of hearsay information. Our men had seen things with their own eyes — things the enemy had deliberately planned they should see—that was why our wounded tried to kill themselves. Yet in this same month of May a captured German soldier wrote home: "I hope the English prisoners in Germany are treated as well as I am. To-day I learned football."

As a matter of fact, we did not take many prisoners. This was due to two causes. In the first place, Germans shot their own men down when they tried to surrender in large bodies; and in the second place, most of the fighting was of a desperate hand-to-hand nature, with bayonet and grenade, in which men battled in great fury to the death. This kind of fighting suited our troops, especially as their natural courage had been exalted to a height at which they ceased to care much whether they lived or died. It was the gas attacks that changed the mood of our men, and made each of them eager to die with a large group of dead Germans around him. They were haunted by the purple-black, agonised features of their smitten comrades, and they fought as fought the Highlanders in the relieving army in the Indian Mutiny, when each man carried a relic of the dead women and men he was vowed to revenge. The fury of the British onsets appeared to have resounded through Germany, for on some prisoners were found letters from relatives and friends at home commiserating them on

Fury of the British onsets

their sad fate in having been sent against British troops. There were, besides, clear and definite pieces of evidence of a feeling of fear among the German soldiers themselves; for in the last week in May the Germans broke our line at Ypres, broke it very badly, but lost their advantage because their absolute lack of courage prevented them from advancing through the large gap in our lines.

The attack began before dawn on Monday morning, May 24th. First of all a violent bombardment with gas shells was opened at 2.45 a.m. against our lines, running from Wieltje, north-east of Ypres, to Hooge, on the Menin road. Near this stretch of trenches, about two and three-

[Lafayette.

General the Right Honourable Louis Botha, P.C.

Historic scene outside the capital of German South-West Africa. General

rranging with the Burgomaster for the surrender of the town of Windhoek.

General the Hon. Jan Christiaan Smuts, South African Minister of Defence.

quarter miles long, the Germans had placed an extraordinary number of gas-cylinders. These they opened before day-break, and their supply of available gas was so great that it continued to pour over our lines for some hours. Then behind the green clouds came the usual infantry attack. It was launched in tremendous force under cover of a terrible artillery fire, at a time when the enemy hoped to catch most of our men asleep and choke them by the gas before they could use their respirators. As a matter of fact, many of our troops were only awakened from their dug-outs by the torture of the fumes they had inhaled, and though our lines held on the north, the gas poisoners carried our trenches at Wieltje and round Bellewaarde Lake, south of the Menin road. Meanwhile, the great German siege train, with most of the Duke of Würtemberg's artillery, maintained a hurricane fire over almost every yard of ground immediately in front of Ypres, in Ypres itself, and behind Ypres. Our front was broken, reinforcements were shut off by a barrage of shrapnel and high-explosive shell, and nearly all our men in the firing-line were suffering more or less from gas. The 2nd Royal Irish and the 9th Argyll and Sutherland were badly poisoned, and driven out of a farm, which the enemy took and fortified. All our troops of the Fifth Army Corps and the cavalry force under General de Lisle, had a bitter fight to maintain their ground. Yet the German infantry hesitated to advance; only the German machine-gun officers displayed any pluck or dash. Sir Herbert Plumer organised counter-attacks, and by noon our infantry were again established on their old line north of the Roulers railway. And by the evening our original position on the south of the Menin road was cleared of Germans, though our line there had to be drawn back somewhat. The hostile machine-gun parties kept us out of Wieltje; but, on the other hand, the entire advance in great force made by the Germans was stopped. An attack made in the night by our troops on the lost farm did not succeed, but the next day Sir Herbert Plumer's men succeeded in consolidating their positions, their line passing through Wieltje toward Hooge, where the cavalry divisions proceeded slowly to advance eastwards.

The work done by our Second Army round Ypres, from the middle to the end of May, was of an unparalleled kind. It cannot be fully described at the present time, as a complete description of this series of nightmare battles might reveal too much. "Tell thou never thy foe that thy foot acheth," said Hendynge, one of our very old and quite forgotten writers. But there can be no harm now in saying that the artillery with which Sir Herbert Plumer and his single army corps held Ypres in the most critical days of May was insignificant. In comparison with the German ordnance the batteries on our front were too light and too few in number, so that they were of small service.

We had to hold the Germans back with bullet, bayonet, and a comparatively small number of machine-guns. The only way of escaping from German shell and German shrapnel was to close in a hand-to-hand conflict with the German infantry and get so mixed up with them that the German artillerymen had to lift their fire all along the line, and devote their attention to keeping off any possible reinforcements. The hand-to-hand conflicts were a relief to our troops, enabling them for a time to escape from the devastating German shell fire. It was largely because the German infantry did not feel that a scrap with the bayonet was a holiday from death that it did not put any drive into its attack. The result was that the German guns were beaten at Ypres because the German infantrymen could not even do the work of clearing up the fragments of our lines smashed by their gunners.

The Duke of Würtemberg must have been a very angry man at the end of May, but his anger could not have been

When the Germans hesitated

Why the German guns were beaten

more than a ripple of feeling when compared with the indignation of the Crown Prince of Bavaria. One of the reasons why we had scarcely any heavy guns at Ypres was that the batteries were being used round La Bassée in capturing the trenches held by the Bavarians. The German Staff was well aware of this condition of things. This was, indeed, the explanation of the continual and most furious assault on our Ypres front. The action of Sir John French was the most adventurous piece of strategy in the war. His confidence in his men had something really sublime about it. Having tested the Territorial troops during the first gas attack on our Ypres line, he apparently thought that they were fit to stand against anything. So he left them with little else than their rifles and their respirators, to hold out against the greatest mass of German artillery on the western front and against

TYPICAL EXAMPLE OF GERMAN "KULTUR."
Interior of the tower of the beautiful library at Ypres after its wanton destruction by the emissaries of Prussia's "higher civilisation."

the most complete system of German gas attacks, and removed their artillery southward for the grand offensive movement against the ridges that defended Lille.

The attack on the Lille ridges began on Sunday, May 9th, by a general advance of our First Army between La Bassée and Armentières. The fighting extended from the village of Bois Grenier to that of Festubert, the principal attack being delivered against the German position at Rouges Bancs, near Fromelles and the Aubers ridge, where we had been held up in the Battle of Neuve Chapelle. At the same time that our First Army, under Sir Douglas Haig, swung up against the low plateau in front of Lille, a great French force, under the direction of General Foch, made a fierce onslaught upon the German lines between La Bassée and Arras. It was a combined Franco-British offensive movement, undertaken partly with a view to relieving the

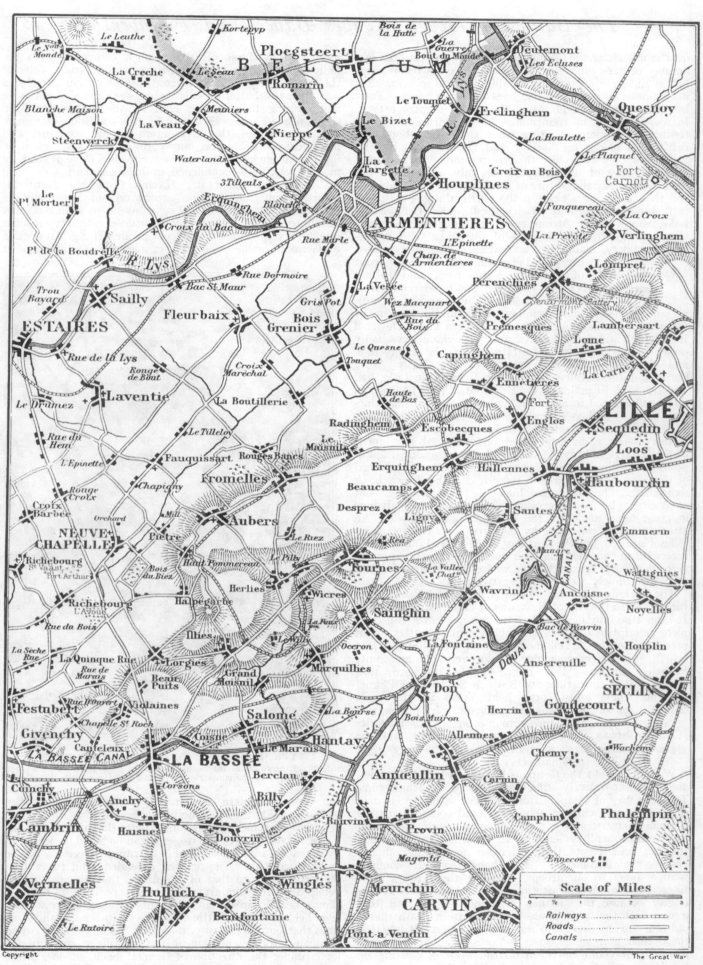

MAP OF THE BATTLE FRONT BETWEEN ARMENTIERES AND LA BASSÉE.

Showing the fortified horse-shoe ridge which formed so formidable a barrier to the British attack on the German entrenchments before Lille.

74

pressure upon Ypres, and partly with a view to reconquering Lille and its rich coal-mining regions and breaking the German front. It was also designed to help the Russian armies retreating in Galicia.

Both the British and the French artillery tried to smash in the German trenches by an overpowering bombardment. But while the French gunners were fairly successful by reason of their enormous supply of high-explosive shells, which they used for weeks at the rate of a hundred thousand shells a day, our massed guns and howitzers, employing mainly shrapnel, made no practicable breach in the enemy's fortified lines. Yet our bombardment, which started about half-past five on Sunday morning, was on a larger scale than at Neuve Chapelle. In a sudden thunderclap of sound thousands of guns massed along the front and broke out with a roar of fire. The German lines were veiled in drifting clouds and puffs of white, black, green, and yellow smoke. Then the German batteries replied, and guessing that an attack was intended and that every trench and barricade on our front was crowded with troops, the German gunners sent thousands of shells crashing along our parapets. Our men were prepared for this counter-blast, and were waiting for it in covered positions. The German infantry, on the other hand, being taken by surprise, had hurriedly to reinforce their firing-line for the coming battle. So extreme was the haste that large numbers of the opposing forces, being unable to get to the front quickly enough by their communication trenches, came into the open and advanced at the double. Then it was that shrapnel did more damage than high-explosive shell, and the Germans suffered very badly before they reached cover.

For three-quarters of an hour our guns pounded the German line, and part of the front parapet of sand-bags was crumbled up in patches. But when our guns lifted their fire and made a shrapnel curtain round the enemy's support trenches, the damage done to the enemy's barricades and wire entanglements was seen to be but slight.

For the Germans had changed their weapons of defence. Instead of ordinary barbed-wire, such as our field-guns had swept away at Neuve Chapelle, they had specially manufactured barbed cables from 1½ in. to 2 in. in diameter, which could not be severed with ordinary cutters, and which resisted shrapnel fire. To make these cable entanglements more difficult of reduction by artillery, the Germans had thrown up banks, looking like trench parapets, behind which extended the entanglement area protecting the real trench. All that our men could do **Barbed cable** when faced by an unbroken and uncut- **entanglements** table barbed cable defence of this kind, was to cast their overcoats upon the barbed edge, and then try to clamber over it while the German machine-guns were playing upon them.

There was only a narrow space, less than two hundred yards wide, between the British and the German trenches. In many places the sand-bag barricades, built man-high on the marshy lowland soil, were close enough for the opposing troops to talk to each other. Very narrow was the long strip of No Man's Land running between the khaki-coloured sand-bags on the British side and the piebald, black-and-white sand-bags on the German side. Over both the khaki and the mottled line of breastworks

roared and screamed the tempest of death, and for a while no infantryman could peer above the parapet and live. But our massed guns lifted their fire on the hostile batteries as well as on the hostile entrenched infantry; and with a cheer the troops of our 8th Division rose from their covered position, and tore in a charging line against the black-and-white breastworks.

In front of them was a horse-shoe ridge, forming the last obstacle between them and the plains which led to Lille. At Rouges Bancs the ridge sweeps away in a north-easterly direction, and by the **Heroic advance by** hamlet there lies a small wood, similar **Territorials** to that which had proved a stumbling-block at Neuve Chapelle. But happily the wood was quietly captured by our Indian troops, the Pathans and Gurkhas, before the bombardment opened, and the way seemed clear for a great infantry advance. The 1st Gloucesters, the 2nd Sussex, the Northamptons, and the Kensington Battalion of the London Regiment were among those that led the assault. Behind the assaulting line were the Sussex Territorials, 2nd King's Royal Rifles, 1st North

THE PIPES THAT CHEER.
Scottish Rifles returning tired and worn from the trenches, but kept going by the bagpipes' cheery skirl.

Lancashires, and the Liverpool Regiment Territorials. To meet our onslaught the Germans brought up great masses of men whom they had been concentrating in Lille, but in spite of these our men, in fifteen and a half hours of desperate fighting, stormed the first line of German trenches and even got on the slope of the ridge. After that, however, they could not advance farther. From their unbroken fortified lines the Germans brought to bear such an extraordinary number of machine-guns that nothing but some hundreds of thousands of high-explosive shell could have blown a clear path for our infantry.

In the famous triangle west of La Bassée, where our First Army Corps and Indian Divisions tried to advance, the German commander used an admirable stratagem. He left his first two lines empty of men and material during our bombardment, and waited in great strength for our infantry advance in his concreted and armour-plated third line.

At the same time he transformed the famous brickfield by La Bassée into a terrible machine-gun fortress, from which a sweeping deadly fire was poured on our troops. Heavy were our losses in this section when, after nearly carrying the enemy's position, our men drew back to their own trenches, the Bedfords and the High-

NEW WEAPON FOR FIRING PROJECTILES USED BY THE GERMANS IN TRENCH WARFARE IN FRANCE.

landers having especially distinguished themselves by the fury of their charge. Had reinforcements been at hand at this point at the critical moment, we might have won an important victory; as it was, things remained after the battle in about the same condition as before. Our First Army was repulsed both south round La Bassée and north below Bois Grenier. But in the centre the Kensington Territorial Battalion (the 13th London) won one of the highest honours of the war, for they were the only battalion that succeeded in doing its task that day. The moment the British artillery ceased, the Kensingtons were over their parapet, and, charging right through, they captured at the point of the bayonet the first, second, and third lines of German trenches on the front. Some of them swept directly onward up the ridge, while one company turned to the right, another company to the left, and bombed and bayoneted the Germans out of their trenches for two hundred yards or so

In the meantime the two regular battalions on either side of the Kensingtons should also have advanced over the German trenches and connected with **The Kensingtons'** the gallant Territorials. But both the **terrible ordeal** regulars were held up by machine-guns and wire entanglements, and they never got through. All the Kensingtons could then do was to try to hold on to what they had gained. The German counter-attacks steadily increased in violence, yet the West Londoners went on bombing expeditions on their left wing, where they held the enemy at bay for hours, until he brought up trench mortars. All the time their right wing was floating in the air, and the Germans were trying to envelop and crush it, while their artillery massed its fire all day long against the little London wedge driven into the defences at Lille.

At a quarter-past eleven on Sunday morning the Kensingtons in the front trench were cheered by a message from their brigadier, saying that reinforcements were coming. But when the reinforcing battalion advanced it was caught by the enemy's guns. The Germans then massed in great strength against both flanks of the Kensingtons, and our men got the order to retire. Their retreat was a terrible business, for they had to fight their way through the German lines again in order to regain their own position. The afternoon and evening were hours of nightmare horror to the men fighting their way back,

waist-deep in mud and foul, crawling water in the German communication trenches, cut off by an enemy they could not see, and isolated from the rest of the Fourth British Army Corps. The hottest time was the final scramble back to the British trench in the evening, across a hundred yards of bare, flat ground, swept by German machine-guns and rifle fire. It was eight o'clock on Sunday night before the last of the heroic Kensingtons reached their own parapets.

The battalion, which had won a name at Neuve Chapelle, was now reduced to a shadow. Before the remnant was withdrawn from the front to act as guards on the line of communication, General Sir Henry Rawlinson rode out to address the small band of West Londoners. He told them that though their last attack could not be supported, it had not only relieved the **General Rawlinson's** pressure on Ypres, but had directly helped **fine tribute** General Foch's army to advance between La Bassée and Arras. "By your splendid attack and dogged endurance," said the commander of the Fourth British Army Corps, "you and your fallen comrades have won imperishable glory for the 13th London Battalion. It was a feat of arms surpassed by no battalion in this great war."

In the part of the line in which the Sussex and Northamptons tried to advance our troops never reached the German lines. They were held up from forty to eighty yards in front of the black-and-white barricade, and there mowed down by shrapnel, machine-gun, and rifle fire. Many brave things were done; our men were splendid but helpless; no one could get on or get back, and when the order to retire was given it was very difficult to carry it out. In the afternoon another attack was delivered by the Black Watch and the 1st Cameronians, some of the

CLOSE VIEW OF ONE OF THE LARGER AERIAL "TORPEDOES" USED IN THE FRENCH TRENCHES.

ABANDONED BARRICADES AT THE ENTRANCE TO A WAR-STRICKEN VILLAGE IN NORTHERN FRANCE.
Fighting of the fiercest character took place here before the enemy were driven out, leaving their hurriedly constructed stone barricades behind them.

ANOTHER GERMAN BARRICADE CAPTURED BY THE FRENCH AFTER DESPERATE FIGHTING.
A vivid official photograph of a hotly-contested corner of Neuville St. Vaast.

slightly wounded men of the first British assaulting line joining in the Scottish charge after lying out under fire for twelve hours. But the gallant Scotsmen were repulsed with as heavy losses as the Sussex and Northamptons. And the few that, by a tremendous effort, got into the first German trench were killed. Men fell in clumps and clusters, the dead lying crumpled where they fell, the wounded hobbling or crawling back to shelter from the shells or bullets. Right to the foot of

Called back through enemy's fire the German parapet the attack was pushed, but there it stayed and died. The Scotsmen carried a flag with them; it could be seen fluttering and swaying through the clouds of smoke and dust.

The plan had been for the Scotsmen to gain a footing in the first German trench, and then bomb their way along while reinforcements were sent them. But when at terrible cost they had taken a small section of the enemy's first line, they had to be called back through the enemy's

NOVEL GERMAN TRENCH IN NORTHERN FRANCE.
Trench cut through a ruined farm to facilitate the observation officer's movements in connection with gun fire-control.

deadly curtain of fire. The chief reason was that our artillery had been overpowered and could not keep down the German batteries and thus maintain a clear space where our infantry could push up against the hostile barricades. Some of our guns seem to have run right out of the high-explosive shell needed to smash the German machine-gun forts. In both the sections of the line—that held by the Kensingtons and that which was won late in

the afternoon by the Black Watch—there were nests of German machine-guns, requiring only a few well-placed 6 in. high-explosive shells from our side in order to shatter them.

But there were no such shells at hand, and any infantry reinforcements had to be sent across the zone swept by a tempest of bullets from the German machine-guns. In these circumstances Sir Douglas Haig, in what must have been the saddest moment of his life, gave the order for his entire line to withdraw to its own trenches. The retire-

WITH THE HUN IN HIS HOUR OF EASE.
Somewhere in Flanders the German soldiers adapted a communication trench to the purposes of a skittle-alley.

ment was a dreadful business—one of the most pitiful scenes in the war. Our men swarmed out of the German breastworks and doubled back towards their own trenches. Some of them ran fast, some walked slowly and reluctantly, here and there carrying or supporting a wounded man; and on them all fell the scourging bullets from the victorious German line, with showers of bombs bursting in blasts of destruction. Our men were undoubtedly angry and exceedingly sore over the whole affair. As they put it, they had got their foot inside the door, but no help was sent to enable them to force it open. But it was soon known at home that the lack of high-explosive shell had been one of the principal causes of our defeat. The men who died around the ridges of Lille did not die entirely in vain, for the whole nation suddenly became aware of our disastrous shortage of lyddite shells, with the result that the Government was reconstructed on a national basis, and the most persuasive of our statesmen was appointed Minister of Munitions, and entrusted with the task of organising every available shop and **Our disastrous** factory possessing a lathe into a shell- **shortage of shells** making plant.

Meanwhile, the position of Sir John French seemed to have become extremely difficult and perilous. For the enemy knew at last that he was lacking in high-explosive shell. The German armies at Ypres and around Lille were officially informed that the British troops could do nothing against them, and that, at Ypres in particular, the British artillery had been so weakened that the German infantry was in a position to gain anything it liked. But the British Commander-in-Chief had a subtle mind as well as a vehement and passionate will. He apparently encouraged the British war-correspondents attached to his headquarters to reveal completely the woeful position of his ordnance. Then by night he quietly moved a large number of heavy pieces back to Ypres and drew largely on his available stock of shells, while the House of Commons was rocking in blank dismay at the public revelations concerning the position of our artillery at the front. The rearrangement of our guns, after the failure of our assault on the Lille ridges, was conducted with as extreme a secrecy as the earlier concentration of forces at Neuve Chapelle. The consequence was that when, in the last days of May, the Duke of Würtemberg's army advanced on Ypres in a mood of excessive and careless optimism it was received by such a tremendous hurricane of both high-explosive and shrapnel shells that it lost all further power of attack. New German formations had to be sent in large numbers through Belgium in order to restore to the German forces round Ypres the strength to enable their commander to contemplate the possibility of attempting another forward movement.

The rearrangement of our guns, while greatly assisting our much-tried and greatly enduring troops on the north of our line, had the very serious disadvantage of weakening our powers of attack round the Lille plateau. Yet from the point of view of General Joffre and his chief executant, General Foch, the prospect of the campaign in the west depended upon maintaining the striking force of our First Army between La Bassée and Bois Grenier. At any cost in life we had to increase at once, and go on increasing, our pressure against the left wing of the German army under the Crown Prince of Bavaria, which was covering Lille. For General Foch was trying slowly to smash his way through the German fortifications between Lille and Arras, and unless we also advanced on the north of Lille, and thus compelled Prince Rupert to keep a large number of men, guns, and shells for use against us, he would be able to counter the French attack by massing all his principal forces in a mighty defensive movement.

Rearrangement of our guns

It was one of those occasions that test the qualities both of mind and character in a commander Sir John French was not found wanting, and with his Chief of Staff, Sir William Robertson, and the commander of his First Army, Sir Douglas Haig, he invented a way out of the difficulty. His men had been unable to make progress even when the British artillery was concentrated, at some risk to Ypres, against the Aubers ridge. So as guns were for the time of little use, the British commander went back to the most primitive weapon of war—the spear—in its modern form of a long knife attached to the end of a rifle. In plain words, a bayonet attack was intended. It seemed an impossible thing, having regard to the enormous strength of the enemy's defences. But it was just because it was impossible that it was likely to succeed.

Bayonet attack near Festubert

For it possessed the grand winning element of an utter surprise. The point selected for an attack was a salient of the German lines by Festubert, which formed a bulge between Neuve Chapelle and La Bassée. Viewed from the British trenches, the German position seemed to be a stretch of bare, flat fields, dotted with ruined cottages, farm buildings, and orchards. In reality it was a network of pitfalls. Hidden in the coarse, high grass were ditches, filled with mud and slimy water, and in some places the ground was hardly more than a morass. The German batteries, placed on the high ground westward, had all the ranges marked, and by means of telescopic sights could sweep every yard of the ground. But if only our men could quickly get into the German trenches, from seventy to three hundred yards distant, the hostile batteries would for the time lose most of their advantages.

The front selected for the first attack ran from the neighbourhood of Festubert on the right to Richebourg l'Avoué on the left, and many very awkward obstacles had to be overcome before the first German trenches were reached. The attack was planned for May 12th, and the famous 7th Division was moved south to support it. The weather on the chosen day was misty and dull, interfering with our aerial observers. So the operation was postponed to May 15th, the Canadian Division being in the meantime also moved south to support the proposed

BUREAU OF THE GENERAL STAFF OF THE 11th FRENCH DIVISION.
The French official photographers missed little of human interest in their pictorial record of the war. In the above view of one of the temporary divisional headquarters, evidently a room in a commandeered hotel, the eye is arrested by the notice on the wall on the extreme right: Défense de chanter " (Singing is prohibited).

VICTORS AND VANQUISHED—WONDERFUL CAMERA-PICTURE OF A MINE-SHATTERED GERMAN TRENCH.
Following the explosion of a carefully laid mine, which shattered the enemy trench out of all semblance of its original form, our men charged the position, which was found filled with the dead and dying foe. British soldiers, some of whom fell wounded by the side of the enemy, stood on guard while awaiting the order for a further advance.

advance of the First British Army Corps. There was no moon on the night of Saturday, May 15th, and the sky was sombre, but not pitch dark. The position in front of our lines was held by the 7th Westphalian Army Corps, which had suffered badly at Neuve Chapelle, and had filled its gaps largely with weedy and ill-grown youths, many of whom were under twenty years of age. The Westphalian had been a famous corps, but its new recruits were of a poor type and badly weakened it.

The Indian Corps began the attack, leaving their trenches at half-past eleven at night, advancing from Richebourg l'Avoué in a south-westerly direction. The enemy, however, was ready for an attack. The moment our **Enemy's first line broken** men left the trenches the sky was lighted up with innumerable flares, shedding a clear white light over a very large area. Through this deadly radiance the German machine-guns and automatic rifles fired with terrible effect. Many of the Indians were shot as they clambered over their own parapets, and their advance was checked. Their comrades, the British troops of the 2nd Division, were more fortunate. By a magnificent rush they broke into the enemy's first line and cleared the Germans out with bayonet and hand-grenade and got into their second line in some of the most furious fighting in the war; for the British troops attacked with great bitterness as well as fierce determination. They were not only eager to avenge their asphyxiated comrades at Ypres, but they had also debts of their own to pay, as the German soldiers in this part of the front were notorious for the ghastly inhumanity with which they had been killing our wounded men. Before daybreak the 2nd Division had won a firm footing in the enemy's lines.

All the battalions forming our right wing, with the
80

exception of the Territorial troops, had gone through the first Battle of Ypres in October, 1914, where they suffered grievous losses. All of them had had to be constantly renewed by drafts, and their officers were mostly fresh young men, who by reason of their lack of experience should have weakened our famous First Army Corps, which had been Sir Douglas Haig's original command. But the new subalterns proved admirable. They were keen, popular, and competent, and in the novel conditions of warfare, which every man had to learn from the beginning, the young officer with six months' service and a fair share of intelligence picked up the business almost as quickly as a veteran, while retaining the additional advantages of youth and its glorious optimism.

The rapidity with which our renewed and rejuvenated First Army Corps widened the foothold it had won on Saturday night was remarkable. The Indian troops, after their failure on the left, threw their flank back to connect with our original line. But our centre and our right bombed and bayoneted their way through the German barricades, and com- **Great night** pletely cleared out the Germans in **surprise attack** masterly hand-to-hand fighting; and then joining hands stormed the German second line, penetrating six hundred yards through the hostile salient along a front of eight hundred yards.

All this was only a preliminary step in our plan of operations. About three o'clock on Sunday morning, when the German commander was absorbed in the task of massing men for a counter-attack to recover his two lines of lost trenches, the glorious 7th Division went into action and broke into another side of the German wedge at Festubert. This was the great night surprise-attack with the bayonet. The German entrenchments north of Festubert were of a most formidable character. Hundreds of thousands of high-explosive shells would have been needed to level them to the ground, and even then the bank-protected barbed cable entanglements might still have held up our troops in daylight, and enabled the German machine-guns to smite them down. But in the darkness our men, moving forward in a swift wave, twelve hundred yards long, got over the entanglements by covering them with overcoats or blankets, knocked the Germans out of the front trench with hand-grenades, leaped over the sand-bags to finish the work with the bayonet, and then clambered out on the other side. They took the second German line in the same manner, and also the third line, and then rushed one supporting point after another until they had broken twelve hundred yards behind the German front in the direction of the Rue du Marais, running towards the village of Lorgies, just at the foot of the first ridge of the Lille plateau.

Many of the German prisoners were captured as they were sitting round fires in their bomb-proof shelters. One German non-commissioned officer said that the attack **Formidable wedges** by the 7th Division had only come a **in German lines** quarter of an hour before it was expected. As it was, our newly-won positions formed on Sunday morning, May 16th, a couple of formidable wedges driven into the German lines, with a distance of only a thousand yards between them. But small though the intervening space was, it was very strongly held and fortified. It included two lines of breastworks constructed so as to give a field of fire in both directions.

and there was a series of redoubts, consisting of strongly-fortified farm buildings, all linked together by shrapnel-proof trenches. The hostile breastworks were armed with machine-guns protected by steel shields, which could only be destroyed by high-explosive shell. Having no shells of this sort handy, our men tried to advance towards Festubert by bombing their way with hand-grenades. Another forty yards was gained in this manner, but this success was followed by a check. At half-past ten on Monday morning our troops made a determined effort to cut off the Germans in the space between our two wedges by pressing across their communications northwards from La Quinque Rue. The

BULLET-PROOF AMBULANCE STRETCHER USED FOR RESCUE WORK IN THE TRENCHES—THE INVENTION OF COL. CANTLIE, R.A.M.C.

THE FIENDS BEHIND THE POISON FUMES—GERMAN TROOPS FIRING THROUGH THEIR GAS-CLOUDS.
Photograph taken in the German lines in Northern France, showing the Kaiser's troops, after they had liberated their poisonous gas-fumes, firing through the vapour at the men who might have been overcome by its asphyxiating power.

THE POISONERS AT WORK—GERMAN GAS-BOMBS BURSTING.

HEAVY FRENCH GUN IN THE ARGONNE FOREST.

operation could not be carried out, as by this time the Germans had been strongly reinforced, and their machine-guns, automatic rifles, and heavy batteries swept away our assaulting line.

Yet the British soldier did not lose heart. Small bombing parties continued to work along the German trenches in spite of the terrific fire, making progress at various points during Sunday afternoon, and capturing two hundred prisoners. At the same time our artillery had a fine field for shrapnel work all along the rear of the enemy's lines, where German troops were collecting to reinforce their front. For example, forty motor-'buses filled with troops, and accompanied by a large body of infantry, were seen by our airmen on the road from La **The German** Bassée to the village of Violaines, just **counter-attack** south of Festubert. Our guns massed their fire on this large and easy target, and after heavy losses the German infantry broke and fled to cover. Our batteries also made good practice on the enemy's gun positions on the westward ridges, and when night fell on Sunday our general position was very encouraging.

In the night the German counter-attack was directed against our advanced position north of Festubert, where our troops had penetrated through the entire series of hostile entrenchments, and had built a rough barricade of sand-bags behind the German lines. We lost this end of our northern wedge, but our position there was so much

82

exposed that the loss of it did not matter; for at daybreak on Monday morning, May 17th, Sir Douglas Haig closed in with all his force upon the half-encircled Germans. Every available gun and howitzer was brought to bear on the two lines of black-and-white breastworks and on the fortified posts and farm buildings. The Germans were already surrounded on three sides, and our artillery got a smashing cross-fire effect, similar to that which the Germans had obtained on our salient at Ypres.

Round Festubert the British infantry did not wait on their guns and then hesitate, but closed with the enemy. The 7th Division pushed on towards the Rue d'Ouvert, and the 2nd Division more **Our engineers'** slowly forced its way towards the Rue **perilous work** de Marais and Violaines. Our hand-grenade parties worked forward with furious skill under the cover of their artillery, and the two British wedges lengthened out and joined together before noon, cutting off all the Germans in between, closing on them with the bayonet, and taking some three hundred prisoners. The two assaulting divisions then joined hands and turned eastward, and worked all the afternoon against the machine-gun posts and network of entrenchments, and clusters of fortified buildings between La Quinque Rue and Rue de Bois. A fierce conflict raged especially round Cour de l'Avoué Farm, where the enemy had a series of very strong works. Among the German troops holding this position was a battalion of Saxons who had been hurried down from the north that morning and flung in to reinforce the battered and hard-pressed garrison.

In spite of machine-guns and bullet-proof defences our troops worked around the farm, while our engineers looked after their telephonic communications with our distant batteries. This was the most important task in the whole of the operations; for, as at Neuve Chapelle, the wire was continually getting broken just when our infantry needed the guns to knock out the machine-gun posts. Our engineers had to work out in the open in the shell-swept zone of fire, patching up the wires in order to keep the telephones in working order. Splendidly did they work round the fortress-farm on Monday afternoon, with the result that at the critical moment our infantry held their hand while our massed batteries poured a smashing fire into all the farm buildings. There were then about seven hundred Saxons holding the position. They had already been badly handled by our bombing parties, and when our guns got to work from the rear, they gave up the fight and came out in a mass to surrender. But as they made no definite signal, our troops raked them with rifle fire.

The survivors, still some hundreds strong, threw down their weapons and held up their hands, and one of them waved a white rag tied to a stick. Meanwhile our guns continued firing, and before the observing gunnery officer could decide whether the offer to surrender was genuine, or whether it was another German trick for getting a good opportunity for a counter-charge, the affair was brought to a ghastly conclusion from an unexpected quarter. North of the farm was a large body of Prussian infantry; farther east were some Prussian batteries in telephonic communication with the Prussian troops. As soon as the Prussian commander saw what the Saxons were doing, he ordered his men to open rapid fire from the flank. And as they enfiladed the Saxons, the Prussian batteries eastward shelled the surrendering mass of

Saxons butchered by Prussians men. Under the combined fire of German guns and German rifles the Saxon battalion was completely annihilated before it could get to shelter. In all the terrible scenes of the war there has been no stranger spectacle than these grey masses of Teutonic soldiers, standing out in the open, weaponless, with their hands raised, amid their dead and wounded, and there being butchered by their own countrymen before the amazed eyes of the British infantry.

While these events were occurring on our northern wing on Monday, good progress was at last being made in the south along the German trenches below Festubert. The hand-grenade and the bayonet continued to prove the best weapons of the British infantryman. All our troops had, in fact, become British grenadiers, in the original meaning of that name, and in spite of the extraordinary develop-

ment of the power and range of modern artillery, they went back to the ancient method of warfare—the hand-bomb. Except that their manual missile was filled with high explosive in place of the charge of gunpowder used by the old grenadiers, our successes were won in a way that Uncle Toby and Corporal Trim in "Tristram Shandy" would have appreciated and admired. The fighting south of Festubert was purely a soldiers' battle, composed of a winding string of isolated and desperate hand-to-hand combats. The German trenches were narrower than ours,

FRENCH COLONIAL TROOPS CONSTRUCTING BOMB-PROOF SHELTERS IN A FOREST CLOSE TO THE FIGHTING AREA.
The smaller view is taken from a German paper. It purports to represent "Hand-grenades left behind by the British," and of a nature so dangerous that the Kaiser's troops were ordered not to touch them, but to leave them to be exploded by being shot at.

being constructed so as to give more defence against shrapnel fire. But when the garrison was attacked by storming bomb-parties, and outflanked and enfiladed, there was no room for it to escape. The only alternative was death or surrender. And by reason of the rapidity of our attacks, due to a wholesome dread of the German machine-guns, the only warning the enemy often received was a shower of grenades, instantly followed by bayonet work.

Trenches heaped with dead In some places the trenches suddenly captured by our bombing-party were almost too horrible to enter, being heaped with bodies, some blown to pieces by our preliminary artillery bombardment, others shattered by our deadly grenades. On the extreme right of our general line of attack, the Germans were pressed back in such large numbers along their communication trenches that they presented a target to our machine-guns near the base

of the German salient at Givenchy. By mid-day on Monday our First Army captured altogether two miles of the enemy's front. All during the afternoon and evening our men continued to work forward, in their close and deadly method of fighting, and by nightfall they held a continuous line along the whole of the original German firing-trenches, from the south of Festubert along La Quinque Rue, east of Richebourg l'Avoué. In many places our troops were in possession of the entire system of German entrenchments, with its three lines of shrapnel-proof breastworks and machine-gun posts. Our two attacking forces had been connected up, and the enemy only held a few supporting points and fortified posts in the rear of their original lines.

Our army was in fine fettle. Yet our men seemed to have small personal cause for joy. They were all wet through, and most of them were covered completely with slime; for in the night attacks it had been impossible to avoid falling into the deep, watery ditches that intersected the ground in all directions. There had been little time for sleep, and little opportunity for anything like a meal. Yet after fighting continuously for more than forty-eight hours, under a heavy shell fire, and against a well-entrenched enemy with magnificent weapons, our First Army was exceedingly happy.

The only discontented men were the brigades which had been held in reserve, **The mood of our men** and had had nothing to do. It was said that one of these brigades, having been held back after an order to advance, found only one way of working off its feelings. Every man spent the rest of the day in sharpening his bayonet. Principally, it was the enemy's use of asphyxiating gases that produced this mood in our men, but the torpedoing of the Lusitania had also something to do with it. Then there were certain small local incidents which did not tend to fill our men with the pure milk of humanitarianism. For example, on Monday afternoon some sixty khaki-clad figures ran towards one of our trenches, one man among them saying, "Don't shoot—we are Grenadier Guards."

RED CROSS WORK UNDER FIRE—AN INTERESTING OFFICIAL FRENCH PHOTOGRAPH TAKEN IN ALSACE-LORRAINE.
In circle: A similar record of French ambulance work in another section of the five-hundred-mile French line.

A TIME-HONOURED CUSTOM OBSERVED IN FRANCE: TAKING THE COLOURS INTO ACTION.
Spirited camera-picture of French soldiers of the 206th Regiment of the Line setting out for an advanced post with their beloved symbol of liberty—the Tricolour.

When, however, an officer worked towards them the supposed Grenadiers fired at him. They were all Germans dressed in uniforms taken from our dead. Happily the officer was not hit, and his men emptied their rifles and charged with the bayonet ; and though some of the Germans tried to run away, all were killed.

We expected a great counter-attack on Monday night, but the Germans had thrown so many men into the last battle that they had no fresh troops available for a night assault. Our troops consolidated the position they had won, and next morning, Tuesday, May 18th, our centre advanced against the large, three-cornered space stretching 1,200 yards north of La Quinque Rue. The cross-roads by the little hamlet of La Quinque Rue were captured, and an advance of three hundred yards was made south - eastward of the hamlet, the German hold being restricted to two fortified farms on the cross-country road near its junction with the highway running from La Bassée past Neuve Chapelle to Estaires.

This completed the work of the 7th Division and the 2nd Division in the Battle of Festubert. After a continual fight of four days and four nights, waged in fierce and bitter hand-to-hand combats, the comparatively small force of 24,000 infantrymen was reduced in number and greatly fatigued. So it was withdrawn from the line to rest on May 19th, the 7th Division, the heroes of the first Battle of Ypres, being

BELGIAN HEADQUARTERS STAFF IN CONSULTATION IN THE YSER VICINITY.

relieved by the Canadian Division, the heroes of the second Battle of Ypres, while the 51st Highland Division relieved the 2nd Division, the victors of the Aisne. Before relating the achievements of the Canadians and Highlanders at Festubert, we must give some detailed account of the deeds of the men of the 2nd and 7th Divisions, who broke off the German salient, and prepared the way for the further advance.

The hero of Festubert was Company Sergt.-Major Frederick Barter, attached to the 1st Royal Welsh Fusiliers. This battalion, composed of North Wales miners and Birmingham men, had fought in the Battle of Ypres, coming out without an officer and with only thirty-five men. Brought up to full strength, it went into the advanced line on Saturday night, May 15th, with orders to charge the enemy's trenches as soon as our bombardment ceased. Our gun fire was very heavy, yet it did not destroy the German parapets. Still, when our guns lifted—that is to say, when they sent their fire over the trenches and on the German rear to prevent reinforcements rushing up—the wire entanglements of the enemy were wrecked.

The Welsh Fusiliers had to cross a hundred and fifty yards of ground between their trenches and the enemy's position. Shells from the German howitzers began to fall thickly behind the waiting battalion, and when they put up their six-foot scaling ladders, and dropped over their parapets, with an

FRENCH "75" AGAINST GERMAN
AIRCRAFT.
French official photograph, taken "somewhere
in Alsace." The gun, concealed from the aerial
foe, had just fired at a Taube. The officer
and some of the crew are seen following through
their glasses the flight of the shell.

BRITISH DECORATION FOR A FRENCH OFFICER.
An officer of the Fourth French Army Corps coming up to receive a decoration from Prince
Arthur of Connaught. General de Langle Cary is on the left of the photograph.

by our gallant sappers in preparation
for the charge. There was naturally
some bunching round the bridges, and
our second line caught up the first,
many men jumping into the ditch and
swimming across the water. The
German barricade, in spite of all difficulties, was reached in less than three
minutes, and the Fusiliers rushed into
two breaches made by our gun fire,
and cleared the trench with the
bayonet. Though enfiladed by German
machine-guns, Captain Rockwell and
his men then pushed onward, while
the distant German howitzers concentrated on them a heavy fire of high-
explosive shell. The Fusiliers had only
one machine-gun remaining from those they had brought
with them in their charge. Sergeant Butler, who handled
the Maxim, was badly wounded, but he stuck to his work,
and helped to clear the trench for nearly
six hundred yards. So quickly did the   **Welsh Fusiliers'**
Fusiliers work that they met on the   **rapid advance**
way about thirty-five men of the Scots
Guards who joined them, and made prisoners of a number
of Polish miners from Westphalia, who were very glad that
they could get out of the fighting.

Such, indeed, was the rapidity of the Welsh Fusiliers'
advance that they came under the fire of their own guns,
and had to lie under cover for an hour while the British
artillery bombarded the second-line trenches in which the
enemy was still holding out. Then, as the shelling ceased,
a German officer with two men rushed down the

eight-foot jump into the zone of fire, their position
was terrible. From the unbroken breastwork the
Germans smote them down with a machine-gun
fusillade and automatic rifle fire as they leaped. Their
commanding officer, Lieut.-Colonel Gabbett, fell dead, with
five bullets in his body, the moment he left the trench. An
instant later the second in command, Major Dixon, was
shot through both legs close to his own trench. But the
Welsh miners and Birmingham men, though thinning at
every step, never faltered. Led by Captain Rockwell, the
first line pressed on with the second line close behind it.

In the ordinary way the men could have done the
hundred and fifty yards' spurt in twenty seconds or less. But
instead of having a run across country, they had to get
over a broad, deep ditch, about a hundred feet from
their breastworks, by means of narrow bridges placed

communication trench with a machine-gun. This was a handy reinforcement, for the gun came in very usefully when the three men had been killed. Six hundred yards from the captured German position was an orchard, and the Fusiliers worked towards this by bombing their way along the German communication trench. Here it was that Sergeant-Major Barter distinguished himself. He called for volunteers, and with the eight men who responded

Sergeant-Major Barter's heroism he bombed the German trench for five hundred yards, capturing on the way three German officers and a hundred and two men.

In this part of their position the Germans had laid mines at intervals of twenty yards. But the experienced sergeant-major happened to find one of the leads. He cut it and searched for more, and found ten other wires, connected with dynamite mines, all of which he rendered useless. The bombing party got to the end of the orchard, 1,200 yards from the point at which the Fusiliers had set out. By the orchard were half a dozen ruined cottages, held by the German machine-gun parties, and though there were only four bomb-throwers left, they cleared the first cottage beyond the trench, but could not storm the second building, thirty yards away on the other side of the road. It was packed with German infantry in addition to several machine-gun sections. There were now only about fifty of our men left. They established a post in the first cottage, and dug a ditch running at an angle from the long German communication trench, in order to stop the terrible enfilading fire which the men in the cottages were pouring on them. All through Sunday, Captain Rockwell

and his gallant little band, forming the end of the larger wedge which we had driven into the German salient, held on to the first cottage in the communication trench by the orchard. In the course of the day Captain Rockwell sent seven orderlies back with messages for reinforcements, but only one of them got through. The German artillery maintained a curtain of fire between the position won by the Fusiliers and the British lines, and hostile machine-guns swept all the open country across which the advance had been made.

Many deeds of kindly valour were done by the ambulance men and other attendants on the wounded. Lance-Corporal Welsh, a man of great strength, began the work of rescue as soon as our attack opened. Seven men, including Major Dixon, were carried by him through the heavy fire. All the stretcher-bearers of the battalion worked for twenty-four hours without rest, and among the surgeons, Lieutenant Kelsey Fry, R.A.M.C., was remarkable for his heroism.

PROGRESS OF "LA REVANCHE": ADVANCED FRENCH POST IN "THE LOST PROVINCES."

At the eastern extremity of their long battle-front our allies made slow but steady progress over the borders of Alsace-Lorraine. The above official photograph shows one of their outposts on the alert behind a barricade disguised by foliage and flowers. In the smaller view are some of our own men as they appeared just after the awful fighting in the vicinity of Festubert.

After carrying Lieutenant Gladstone out of action on his back, he worked for hours between the trenches, dressing the wounded, until he was struck by shrapnel. Meanwhile Captain Rockwell and his handful of men withdrew from the cottage and orchard on Sunday night, and then held on to the German communication trench for two days, until the weakened battalion was relieved by fresh troops. The relieving force then pushed back into the orchard and stormed the other cottages, and **Gallantry of the Warwicks** prolonged their position so that the two British wedges met and cut off all the German troops on the western side.

Two companies of the Warwicks went through the Welsh Fusiliers and gained a position that was choked with German dead and wounded. All the Warwicks were Birmingham men, and they won great glory for their famous city. The battalion stood a heavy bombardment with high-explosive shell for seventy-two hours. What saved them was the marshy state of the ground after a tempest of rain

The German shells sank too deep into the mud to do much damage, and many of them failed to explode.

THE THRILLING MOMENT BEFORE THE CHARGE.
Striking photograph of a French trench taken as its occupants were leaving it for a bayonet charge on the enemy's position, which had just been shelled.

Those that went off made little ponds round the dug-outs of the Warwicks, and as the explosions were cushioned by the soft and sodden fenland, the shell-blasts were less deadly than usual. A shell-blast is the sudden expansion of air produced by the exploding gas of the shell. It is more deadly than the fragments of steel that fly around when the high-explosive is detonated. Lieut.-Colonel A. Brook, commanding the 8th Territorial Battalion of the Royal Scots, was killed by a shell-blast while sitting in a German bomb-proof shelter which had been captured by his men.

The Scottish Territorials were on the left of the attacking line, and through shelled in a dreadful manner they held on to the position they had won, and gave not an inch of ground before the German attack. Another first-rate Scottish Territorial regiment was the 4th Camerons. Formed at Inverness, it was composed of the flower of Highland country life—deer-stalkers and shepherds, men of Skye and the Outer Islands, tall and sinewy, rugged Gaels, most of them speaking their ancient tongue. They advanced on Monday evening, May 17th, with orders to take five hundred yards of the German breastworks, at the

end of which were ruined houses, which the Germans had converted into machine-gun posts. The ground over which the Highlanders had to advance looked level and easy: but it was cut up by deep and broad dykes, into which the water from the Lille ridges drained. The Camerons surged forward with the old Highland ardour, and when they reached the ditches certain fine athletes made a long jump and got across dry-footed. Others were delayed by having to swim the water. The jumpers went straight for the German trench, and their front line suffered heavily. But the next line came up in time to kill all the Germans remaining in the trench, most of the enemy having fled when the leaping "kilties" drew near.

The detachment found the fortified houses too strongly held, and sent a message to headquarters for machine-guns and bombs. Meanwhile the Germans counter-attacked with trench mortars and hand-grenades on both flanks, and the front of the Territorials was squeezed until their position became untenable. In fact, their capture was apparently inevitable ; for they could not leave the protection of the trench, as the open ground in their rear was swept with such a torrent of fire that it was death to venture in it. Only two deer-stalkers with an officer managed to crawl away in the darkness of Monday night and report the situation to headquarters. But the Highland shepherd is a man of much ingenuity. He found a way out of the death-trap. The German trench was covered with flooring, and on pulling up the boards one of the Camerons discovered that some deep ditches traversed their position. The detachment jumped into the water and mud, and floundered back to safety ; but Lieut.-Colonel Fraser was killed while covering their retreat. He held the trench until all his men got away, and was then struck by a bullet when about to make his dive into the secret escape dyke.

The most heroic of all the Scottish regiments were the Scots Guards, under Sir Frederick Fitz-Wygram. They had shared with the West Kents the honour of having never lost a trench ; but when they charged towards the orchard, which the Welsh Fusiliers were attacking, one of their companies pushed ahead with such speed that it was cut off in the position it won.

It was thought on Sunday night that the Scots Guards had surrendered ; but two days afterwards the progress of the British advance brought them to the spot where the Scotsmen had been enveloped. There were eighty of them with two officers, all lying dead on the field of honour. Around them was a ring of dead Germans numbering nearly two hundred. The Scots Guards still held the great honour of never having lost a trench. To the men who saw it there was no sadness in this high scene of Scottish valour. It was a sublime and inspiring thing. The troops took fire from it, and went into the fight steeled to any deed of desperation. As already mentioned, **A scene of Scottish valour** a party of the Scots Guards fell in with the Welsh Fusiliers in the enemy's firing-line and enabled the North Wales miners and Birmingham men to stab and bomb their way to the orchard.

The men of London, who filled the ranks of the West Surreys—the Queen's—also displayed a fine gallantry. In bombarding the German position in front of them our guns had not cut the wire entanglements The consequence was that the two leading companies of the Queen's were held up by the obstruction and shattered by machine-gun fire and heavy howitzer shells. B and C Companies

French engineers preparing a mine destined to work death and destruction in the enemy's trenches a short distance away.

Picturesque view of a strongly organised French trench over the Alsace border-line. While most of the men were on the qui vive and their officer was dictating to an orderly, two soldiers were calmly angling in the adjacent stream with a view to securing some variety in the regulation diet.

CONTRASTING ASPECTS OF LIFE IN THE FRENCH TRENCHES.

dropped down, and sent back word to our guns to open fire again on the German parapets, and when the position had been further shelled for fifteen minutes the remnant of the battalion charged once more and captured the German firing-line and communication trench, making an advance of a thousand yards. One man of the Queen's, Private Harvey, was badly wounded in his right arm in the attack on the communication trenches; but when volunteers were called for to form a bombing party he came forward.

"Luckily I'm left-handed," he said, "so my right arm won't trouble me." He joined in the hand-grenade attack upon the

LOOKING LIKE MEMBERS OF THE VEHMGERICHT.
French soldiers wearing the special masks provided by the military authorities as protection against the German poisonous gases.

TYPE OF SMALL GRENADE.
The French soldier in this photograph is holding a small German grenade. Though insignificant in appearance, this weapon, which was fired from a rifle, was composed of quite a number of parts and filled with explosive of a most destructive character.

fortified houses at the end of the orchard, and threw his bombs as coolly and as skilfully as any of his comrades. But his bandaged arm, bound in a sling formed from part of his shirt, made him a conspicuous target for the German snipers in the farm buildings, and he was shot dead. Another remarkable private of the Queen's was Williamson. The adjutant of the South Staffordshires saw him bringing wounded men across the open ground, swept by the enemy's machine-guns. The man looked quite fagged out, and as he staggered under his human

burden the adjutant told him to get under cover and rest for awhile. "No, sir, my place is in the firing-line," said Private Williamson, "and I must get back." And across the zone of death he went into the position captured by his battalion. It was a shallow affair this German communication trench—not much more than a line of hurdles without a solid breastwork of sand-bags, and only high enough to make a target for the German batteries. On Sunday evening the Queen's had to fall back to the first line of German trenches, which had been reversed and made into a new British line. They held out for three days, never losing touch with their brigade headquarters, and maintaining a position from which the next British attack was launched across the hostile salient.

The King's Liverpool Regiment, which took up the attack on Monday on the other side of the salient, carried out a fine piece of work. The troops worked their way with the bayonet towards the farm of Cour d'Avoué, and, under Lieutenants Hutchinson and Fulton, one of their bomb parties went up a German communication **Fine work by the Liverpools** trench, capturing on the way more prisoners than they could easily manage—some two hundred in all. Another two hundred they drove into the open field, indirectly bringing about the dreadful scene already depicted, in which the Prussians turned their rifles and guns on the Saxon garrison of the farm.

Our bomb-throwers were the chief authors of the victory of Festubert. The hand-bomb or grenade which they used was one of the novelties of modern warfare. It was designed to clear the labyrinth of galleries and underground refuges in which the Germans sheltered when their position was being gained. Much more than simple bravery was required of the bomb-thrower. He needed all the skill and quick sense of judging distances of a cricketer, who is both a good cover-point and a good long-stop. He had to hit the wicket from any distance, and hit it quickly, and there can be little doubt that practice in fielding on the cricket-pitch helped to make our soldiers superb and deadly grenadiers of the modern sort. The general opinion after the Battle of Festubert was that the Germans had become more afraid of our hand-grenades than they had of our bayonets. In the attack made by the Liverpool bombing party the Germans actually shrieked with terror as they fled along the trench. An entire company surrendered to a single khaki figure standing with uplifted hand with one grenade in it.

The Germans seemed to have had so lively an imagination that it undermined their nerves. Each man felt the bomb exploding on his face; whereas, in fact, it would only have put a few of them out of action, even if they had been caught in a bunch. Our men carried five or six grenades each, so that when the fighting was fierce one of the party had frequently to go back to get a fresh supply of bombs. These he had usually to bring across the zone of fire, and the less he thought about what would happen if his bombs were exploded while he was carrying them, the less wear and tear there was on his nerves. As a matter of fact, the stolid temper of the British character was a chief source of our fighting strength. Even the new troops soon ceased to forecast in imagination the effect of a howitzer shell on their persons. There were so many messengers of death continually flying around that the message lost all the edge and vehemence it would have possessed in the ordinary ways of civilian life. Our men fell back on the stock of

Our iron-nerved bomb-throwers instinct they had inherited from their forefathers, and became as stolid and as iron-nerved as Wellington's troops, while showing a finer quality of nature.

In the second phase of the Battle of Festubert Lieut.-General Alderson played a chief part. This officer had first distinguished himself as colonel of the West Kents, and had then been appointed commander of the Canadian Division, by the handling of which he saved Ypres in the first gas attack. When his Division withdrew from the battle-front it was exhausted but not shattered, despite its terrible and heroic labours; and, brought up to strength by reinforcements from the Canadian base in England, it moved south, and again entered the firing-line on May 17th. Lieut.-General Alderson was then promoted to the well-merited position of an Army Corps commander, being given temporarily, in **Lieut.-General** addition to the Canadian Division, **Alderson's promotion** the command of the 51st Highland Division and the artillery of the 2nd and 7th Divisions.

To the Canadians fell the task of continuing the progress made by the 7th Division by attacking an orchard near La Quinque Rue. This was done by two companies of the Canadian Scottish under Lieut.-Colonel Leckie and two companies of the 14th Royal Montreal Regiment under Lieut.-Colonel Meighan. In their first night attack, on May 19th, only the flanking company of the Canadian Scottish fought its way to its allotted position. The other company failed to maintain the right direction in the nocturnal advance over unknown ground. In the charge some five hundred yards had been gained, and the Colonial troops dug themselves in, under very heavy shell fire, and connected with the Wiltshire Regiment on their right and the Coldstream Guards on their left.

The advance had been checked mainly because there had been no opportunity of reconnoitring the ground. But a reconnaissance was made on May 20th by patrols under Major Leckie, brother of the commanding officer

ALMOST BUT NOT QUITE BRITISH—BELGIAN SOLDIERS IN THEIR NEW KHAKI UNIFORMS.

ONE OF THE FIELD-KITCHENS PRESENTED BY THE CITY
OF MANCHESTER FOR USE BY THE BELGIAN ARMY.

Colonial troops executed a very neat variation in modern tactics. The Canadian artillery, by arrangement, opened a heavy fire on the German front, while the Canadian infantry rigged up their trench ladders and fixed bayonets, with rather more than the usual bustle preliminary to another advance. The Germans fled from their two front lines of breastworks to escape the shells, and then, as our guns lifted and began to sweep their third line, they crowded back into their firing trenches, partly to avoid the changing direction of the bombardment, but mainly to repulse the expected attack of the Canadian infantry. As soon as it was seen that the front line of breastworks was crowded with Germans, the guns shortened range, and, working at the highest possible speed, swept with the intense blast of their fire the packed first line of the enemy. The Canadian infantry, mean- **Storming the** while, was resting under cover ; not a man **" Bexhill " redoubt** had moved. The official German wireless the next day announced that a desperate attack by British troops had been repulsed with fearful losses, but the truth came out in a voice, with a German-American accent, that cried the next evening to the Canadians : " Say, Sam Slick, no more dirty tricks to-night ! "

While the 3rd Brigade was carrying out the operations in the Quinque Rue orchard, their comrades of the 2nd Brigade were held up a mile to the south by a German redoubt to which the name of " Bexhill " was given. Here the losses of the Canadians were very heavy. First the 10th Canadian Battalion was checked in its attempted advance, by reason of the nature of the ground and the ineffectiveness of our artillery fire. Our shrapnel shell had had no effect upon the thick wire entanglements. So our guns again kept on firing until night fell, and then, lighted by the enemy's flares and star-shells, the survivors of the gallant 10th Canadian Battalion, with the hand-grenade company of the 1st Canadian Brigade, tried once more to storm the " Bexhill " redoubt. Two companies of the 10th Battalion took part in the night attack. The

of the Canadian Scottish, and after a couple of very brilliant skirmishes it was discovered that the orchard was defended by a very large force of Germans, and that its capture would be a difficult task. Nevertheless, it was resolved to carry out the attack by daylight, the ground being so full of obstacles that the men had, at any cost, to be able to see their way.

In the afternoon our artillery opened up a searching, smashing fire on the tract of fruit trees, the bombardment increasing in intensity until the moment came for the wave of infantry to roll forward. The two Canadian companies dropped out of their trenches and charged forward with gallant steadiness, while the enemy directed a torrent of machine-gun and rifle fire and shrapnel upon them. The ordeal culminated just at the **Adroit Canadian** edge of the orchard, for there the charg- **tactics** ing Canadians found themselves faced with a deep, broad ditch, full of water, on the other side of which was a wire entanglement. In the men jumped, neck-deep, and made for a gap in the wire which had previously been discovered by the reconnoitring party. There were not many Germans in the orchard, and three platoons of Canadians cleared out the hostile machine-gun parties which had been left to defend the firing-line.

In accordance with their usual custom the Germans had withdrawn to their support trench when our artillery fire grew hot, and they intended to let their machine-gun parties hold up our advancing infantry in the thick of the trees, while they launched a flank counter-attack along an abandoned trench running in a south-westerly direction. But this scheme was completely frustrated by an unexpected movement on the part of the Canadians. They only sent a small force into the orchard to clear it, while one company occupied the trench in which the flank attack was to be expected. There they beat off the enemy, while the three platoons in a magnificent rush fought double the number of Germans out of the orchard.

Having consolidated their new position the enterprising

IN A WELL-PROTECTED CORNER OF THE FRENCH
FIRING-LINE.

company on the left of the advancing line met with fearful opposition, being practically annihilated by the enemy's machine-guns.

But the right wing, although also raked by the fire from the redoubt, reached the enemy's trench-line, running south from the fortified position, and bombed the Germans out of the position for four hundred paces, and then erected a barricade to hold what it had won. But at daybreak on May 22nd the hostile howitzer batteries on the western ridges furiously bombarded the captured trench. All day long the great high-explosive shells pitched in and around the captured breastwork and smashed it to the ground. The troops in the southern end of the trench suffered heavy losses. The Canadians would not lose

Heavy losses of Canadians what they had won, being inspired by the words that General Alderson had spoken to them when he took over the command of their division. He had said that he came from a regiment, the West Kent, whose boast it was that they had never lost a trench, and the shattered and desperate Canadian troops at "Bexhill" redoubt were determined that they also would not let go. So they built another barricade out of the black-and-white sand-bags scattered by the German shells, and held on to what remained of the trench.

Then in the night the position was taken over by a detachment of British troops, and a detachment of the 1st Canadian Brigade, King Edward's Horse, and Strathcona's Horse, after several German infantry attacks had been beaten back. At daybreak on May 24th two companies of the 5th Battalion and a company of the British Columbia Regiment stormed ahead, with the German machine-guns playing on them; and in two stubborn charges, in which all the troops displayed a majestic courage, the "Bexhill" redoubt was at last captured at eleven minutes to six on the evening of May 24th. The Canadian artillery then surrounded the captured fortress with a shrapnel curtain, while the victorious 5th Battalion, under Major

FRENCH OFFICERS WATCHING THE ENEMY THROUGH A PERISCOPE.
Special interest attaches to the screened loopholes. So expert became the Germans in snap-shooting through the firing apertures along the French trenches that our allies made cloth screens for the loopholes, which were withdrawn only when signs of an advance on the part of the enemy were noted through the periscope.

Edgar, dug itself in. It had cost the Brigade fifty-five officers and nine hundred and eighty men to make this important advance with which the Battle of Festubert concluded. On the day that the Canadians captured "Bexhill," the 2nd London Territorials did a fine piece of work in winning more of the enemy's trenches and making good the ground gained to the east and north.

By this time the enemy had been driven from a strongly-entrenched and fortified position along a front of four miles, for an average depth of six hundred yards. The Germans had suffered very heavy losses, the smallest items of their loss being the ten machine-guns and seven hundred and eighty-five prisoners captured by us. As we have seen, much of the fighting consisted of very fierce hand-to-hand conflicts with bayonet and hand grenades, and the losing side, after each **Sacrificial** British advance, sacrificed men by **counter-attacks** the thousand in vain counter-attacks.

In spite of our comparative lack of high-explosive shell, the damage done by our artillery and by the French guns lent us by General D'Urbal, commanding the Tenth French Army, was very considerable. The hostile infantry was caught in masses as it bunched for an attack or as it fell back on its third lines. On the other hand, our losses in all the operations between Bois Grenier and La Bassée, from May 9th to May 25th, were also very heavy. The German positions along the ridges were too strong to be carried by our army with its existing equipment.

Quite as serious as our lack of millions of lyddite shells was our comparative deficiency in machine-guns. The German machine-gun, built on the same model as our Maxim, had proved to be one of the chief surprises of the war. The German Staff had displayed something like genius in its organisation of machine-gun fire. Only our

INTERESTING PHOTOGRAPH OF A GERMAN HILL TRENCH.
The view illustrates how a trench crosses a hill. The trench shown was protected half-way by a high and massive traverse.

L

Admiralty, in its best creative periods, was worthy to compare with the Great German Staff in completely thinking out the possibilities of a new weapon, applying it to new tactics, and adjusting all the other forces of wa to harmonise with it. The German machine-guns helped their own infantry as field batteries would do, breaking a path for them, especially in the case of a counter-attack, covering their retreat or temporary withdrawal, and reinforcing their fire-power, if there was nothing else to do.

The French and British armies, on the other hand, confused the fire-power of machine-guns with the fire-power of the rifles of the infantry. They allowed at the start two machine-guns to every battalion, while the Germans, with an actual average of ten machine-guns to a battalion, could on occasion mass seventy machine-guns to help the manœuvres of a single battalion.

It was largely due to the way in which the Germans handled their machine-guns as a distinct arm that they won the great and almost decisive victory of Charleroi in August, 1914. It was commonly thought at that time that the enormous number of these weapons was the source of the German superiority in fire-power. Apparently it was only discovered gradually that there was a new system of tactics underlying the enemy's use of his mechanical streams of bullets; and at the end of the Battle of Festubert it was plainly evident that the new German machine-gun tactics constituted the most important of all instruments in the German system of defences. Under it our offensive movement had completely broken down. In spite of the progress made by our First Army in the fenland round La Bassée, the main German entrenchments on the Lille ridges, beyond the marshy ground, remained impregnable. Except for the fact that we had detained large forces all around our front, from Ypres to La Bassée, our terribly costly operations throughout the spring campaign had completely failed of effect. The amount of ground we had won near Festubert was more than out-balanced by the ground we lost in front of Ypres. The German machine-gun had defeated us, **Victory by** mainly because we lacked the lyddite shell **machine-guns** which was required in enormous quantities to shatter every hostile machine-gun redoubt. The Germans employed machine-guns to cover every retirement, being quite unconcerned about their loss so long as they carried out the operation. But we could not afford a prodigal expenditure of human life when the enemy was chiefly risking only a small part of his gigantic machinery of war. So the Battle of Festubert came to an end simply because the British commander decided that the price he was asked to pay for each hundred yards of progress was too heavy.

At the same time there was another important considera-tion that went to the making of Sir John French's decision. Originally the combined Franco-British advance between Armentières and Arras was planned with a view to helping the Russian Army. We have seen that twenty-four battalions of the Prussian Guard, with some other units, were removed from the western front to the eastern field of war to form the spear-head of Mackensen's Phalanx in Galicia. All through the month of May, 1915, this Phalanx drove against the southern Russian army, and continually threatened to divide and envelop the Russian forces. The German Staff then had something like three-quarters of a million recruits who were nearing the completion of their training. Had most of these new forces been thrown into the Galician and Polish battlefields, they would have added very greatly to the dangers menacing the armies of our eastern ally. It was therefore a matter of vital urgency for France and Britain to prevent as many new German troops as possible from reinforcing the attacks against the retreating Russian front. At the same time as the Russians had failed to firmly hold the Austro-German forces, the long-designed Franco-British offensive movement in the west lost its immediate importance. In fact, it became for the time almost impossible, owing to the sudden, unexpected, and general weakening of the Russian advance into Hungary. The entrance of Italy into the war had also produced a revolution in the strategy of General Joffre. The Italian Commander-in-Chief, General Cadorna, proposed a slow, cautious, and steady pressure against all the German and Austrian lines in the west and south. In his view there should be no marked, vehement, and decisive forward movement until the enemy was firmly held on all sides, and especially until the Russians sufficiently recovered to resume their pressure along the thousand miles of eastern front. Owing, it is said, largely to the sound and comprehensive ideas of the Italian Staff, this closely co-ordinated system of movements by all the confederate nations attacking the two Central Germanic Empires was adopted by the Quadruple League, and studied in detail by the connected Staffs of France, Italy, Britain, and Russia. It was further proposed that a kind of consulting and connecting Central Staff of French, Italian, British, and Russian officers should be formed with the object of harmonising all movements from east, west, and south against the Austro-German armies. In the meantime the British Expeditionary Force in France and Flanders resumed a defensive attitude, having done at least a very fair share of the work of attracting large new German forces against its lines, and thus helping its distant comrades in Russia to recover their power of initiative.

A revolution in strategy

RED CROSS DOCTORS WHO HAD TO WORK LYING DOWN.
Two Belgian Red Cross doctors, having crawled out of their trench to succour a wounded soldier under fire, were compelled to render first-aid lying down. They then fastened a rope round their patient, and by this means drew him back to safety.

Flight
Sub-Lieut.
R.A.J.
WARNEFORD
V.C.

Presented with "THE GREAT WAR" PART 57.

ITALIAN ARTILLERY IN ACTION · **CHAPTER LXX.** · ON AUSTRO-ITALIAN FRONTIER.

ITALY'S ENTRY INTO THE WAR.

By Charles Tower, Special Correspondent in Italy.

The Political and Ethnological Reasons for Italian Intervention—Austrian Breaches of the Triple Alliance—The German Hand in the Austrian Glove—Italy Regarded by Germany and Austria as a Negligible Quantity—How Germany Set to Work to Remedy a Diplomatic Blunder—A Tense and Enthralling Drama of Intrigue with the World for Audience—Prince von Bülow's Mission to Rome—The Erzberger Plot—Giolitti: A Latter-Day Marius—Salandra the Sphinx—Baron Sonnino, Salandra's " Chief of Staff "—War the Only Salt to Detach the Financial Leeches of Germany—How Italy's Early Neutrality Helped the Allies— Plot and Counterplot and the Rival Demonstrations of the Neutralists and Interventionists—Italian Denunciation of the Triple Alliance—The Vespers of War—The Answer of the Women of Italy to the Germans who Maligned Them—The Call to Arms and the Opening Phases of the Campaign in the Trentino and Towards Trieste.

ON Monday, May 24th, 1915, as midnight finished striking, Italian mountain-troops, the famous Alpini, moved out in little companies to cross the Austrian frontiers. Italy had joined the Allies.

The history of the intervention of Italy in the Great War was to outward appearance one of dramatic surprises ; actually, it is a record of infinitely careful preparation by statesmen who never wavered from their determination, and who struck not when " all was over except the shouting," but when all things were ready.

Apart from the growing popular exasperation against the German methods of warfare, which culminated with the murder of the Lusitania passengers, there were two principal reasons, political and geographical, which had from the outset determined the two Italian statesmen—Signor Salandra, the Premier, and Baron Sonnino, the Foreign Minister—to take the course which they held to be dictated alike by humanity and interest. The geographical consideration may be readily understood by anyone who will study a large-scale map of the Italian frontiers as they existed before the war.

Whatever other changes the gradual unification of Italy, during the first seventy years of the 19th century, may have

SIGNOR SALANDRA.
President of the Council and Minister of the Interior in Italy.

produced, it did not deprive Austria of the possession of the Trentino, or Lower Tyrol, and of the country on both sides of the Isonzo valley with the peninsula of Istria. The latter, which like the Trentino was inhabited principally by Italians, contains the important harbours of Pola and Trieste. The latter was an almost exclusively Italian town. A third harbour, Fiume, in Croatia, is also Italian by history and race. The frontiers imposed upon Italy had not only left in Austrian possession these large tracts of country inhabited chiefly by a population Italian both in birth and sentiment (the " Irredenti," or unredeemed Italians), they had also rendered the task of defending Northern Italy against possible Austrian aggression extremely difficult.

To understand this it is necessary once more to consult a good map. The Trentino, it will be seen, runs down like a wedge into Italy. Its frontiers were formed by a series of mountain chains cut only by narrow and difficult passes, except where the two lines of railway run to Trent, along the Val Lagarina just east of Lake Garda, and through the Val Sugana farther east. The Austrian frontier formed a mountain wall, with a series of high points or peaks to serve as watch-towers.

Farther east, in the country above Venice, the Austrian frontier was formed by the line

HEAVY BUT MOBILE GUNS USED BY THE ITALIANS AGAINST THE AUSTRIANS.
Something in the nature of " the biter bit " was the case of Austria when Italy entered the Great War. Austria found not only that the Italians were provided with heavy pieces of ordnance, but that these great weapons were adapted for use in the precipitous mountain passes which form the boundaries of the two countries.

from interference or observation behind the mountain ramparts. In addition, the Austrian possession of the Trentino compelled Italy to defend the long outer circuit of that province with all the advantages on the Austrian side.

Italy's primary military desire was to remedy this intolerable handicap, just as her primary ethnological desire was to reunite with the mother country the intensely patriotic Italians living in the Trentino and in Istria.

There was, however, a second consideration which virtually compelled Italian intervention.

Under the terms of the Triple Alliance which bound Italy to Austria and Germany, it had been agreed that in the event of Austria obtaining specific advantages by alteration of the division of territories amongst the Balkan States, Italy should receive corresponding compensation. It was further laid down that Austria should not undertake any action calculated to make such alteration without consulting Italy as her partner in the Alliance. Once already, before the Great War, Italy had not received the compensation to which she considered herself entitled. When Austria permanently annexed the two nominally Turkish provinces of Herzegovina and Bosnia, Italy considered that an alteration such as was indicated in the terms of the Triple Alliance had taken place. But compensation was not given, on the ground that though these two provinces were nominally under Turkish suzerainty, they had in fact been administered by Austria, and thus the alteration was only one in name and not in fact. At the time, Italy was not in a position to make any effective protest, because the other European Powers were either unwilling or unable to make this aggressive Austrian action a *casus belli*.

But a much graver breach of the terms of her alliance

of the Carnic Alps, another rocky wall very abrupt on the Italian side, but much more accessible towards Austria. Here, too, there were at intervals high mountain watchtowers, which afterwards became the scene of long struggles. One of the most famous was the Freikofel.

The eastern frontier of Italy towards Klagenfurt, Lubiana, and Trieste was formed by the Julian Alps, except at the delta of the Isonzo valley, where the country was fairly open as far as the ridge of hills commanding the towns of Gorizia, Gradisca, and Monfalcone.

Speaking generally, then, the geographical frontiers of Italy had been so fixed that while her own concentration of troops could be overlooked from the Austrian watchtowers, and any attempt by her to attack Austria must apparently break at once against the impenetrable mountain wall, Austrian troops, on the contrary, could be assembled and concentrated for attack by any chosen route secure

with Italy was perpetrated by Austria in July, 1914. When Austria delivered to Serbia the ultimatum which meant war—a war whose results, if localised, could only have meant the **Austria's breach of** disappearance of Serbia as a free and **faith** sovereign State from the map of Europe— she did not take the trouble to acquaint her ally Italy with her intentions. This, however, she was bound to do under the terms of the alliance.

It is fairly evident that both Austria and Germany regarded Italy then as a negligible quantity. They knew that her arsenals and her treasury were depleted, and that the credits voted by Parliament had not sufficed to replenish them—had, indeed, hardly more than paid off the balance due for military requisites during Italy's African campaign.

The Italian statesmen were quite alive to this factor.

King Victor Emmanuel III. of Italy.

Trained mountaineers as well as soldiers—Italy's famous Alpine troops forcing a frontier pass in the Carnic Alps.

On the way to Monte Nero: The Italians, by great daring, placed guns in position on the mountain (seen on the left).

General Count Luigi Cadorna, Italian Commander=in=Chief.

Those who saw clearest knew that the Austrian and German Governments would never have dared to treat Italy so if she had been in a military and financial position to make good her claims to consideration at once. The contemptuous insult rankled, but the Italian statesmen possessed their souls in patience until they were ready to avenge the insult with the sword.

It may be admitted that the German Government soon perceived that a diplomatic blunder had been committed. The establishment of the Salandra-Sonnino Cabinet in place of the German-ophil Giolitti " tyranny," as it was called, opened the eyes of the German Foreign Office to the fact that Italy was not disposed to leave herself any longer without the armour necessary to make her voice heard. As they had done in other neutral countries, so in Italy, German and Austrian agents began to stir up difficulties for the Salandra Cabinet, to mobilise all the forces which for one reason or another were opposed to any Italian intervention in the war. There began a long campaign of intrigue in Italy, supported with lavish bribery by German agents, and only ended when, all things being at last ready, the Salandra Cabinet was able to demand of the country and the King a free hand to take such action as Italian interests required.

Perhaps in no country affected by the war was the drama of intrigue, the one great human drama of the combat of honesty of purpose and cleanness of hands against corruption and lies, played with such a wonderful setting and, it may be added, to so rapt an audience. It was drama, tense and enthralling, and as drama the history of it should be related. It was a theme such as a Shakespeare might have prayed for. Up to the end the audience, which was the whole civilised world, except perhaps a few diplomats, was kept in suspense by Salandra the Sphinx. It will be simplest, perhaps, to try to enumerate the principal *dramatis personæ*, and then to describe the setting.

Salandra the Sphinx   The head of the Italian Government was Signor Salandra, a man of whose personal characteristics so little was known that even his friends believed him mainly a party politician. He became Premier, as most people had supposed, as a stop-gap when the great Italian dictator, Signor Giolitti, laid down the reins of power he had held so long. Salandra's was a Conservative Government. As such it could not actually command a majority, but, on condition of its becoming a war government, it received the support in the country of the " Radical-Interventionists," that is, of that large section of liberal opinion which believed that Italy was bound by all her traditions as well as by all the dictates

ITALIAN TROOPS OVER THE FRONTIER.

An Italian artist's impression of an incident in the occupation of Ala, in the Adige Valley, Trentino, on May 27th, 1915. To the people of the Peninsula, Lower Tyrol (Trentino) and Trieste were as Alsace and Lorraine to the French, territories that belonged by ancient right to the mother country.

of humanity and prudence to aid in crushing the German tyranny. Thus it came about that the two most important newspapers in Italy, the Conservative " Corriere della Sera " and the Radical " Secolo," were united in support of a Conservative Government.

It will be clear to readers who remember the creation of the National Cabinet in Britain that Signor Salandra's Cabinet had become also a National Italian Cabinet. But there were difficulties, and the chief of these difficulties was the man who was called the Italian dictator, Signor Giolitti. It is necessary for an understanding of this final war of Italian unification that one should understand something of the position and character of the latter-day Marius. His position had for years been unique. At once the ablest politician in Italy, and one of the most skilful wire-pullers, he had for years dictated Italian policy, just as he had filled Italian posts, prefectures, governorships, and commands with devoted adherents. His " capital

THE DUKE OF THE ABRUZZI.
In command of the Italian Navy.

national policy which could give a clear lead in the circumstances which prevailed in Europe after August, 1914. He was not, as has sometimes been assumed, an enemy of Great Britain; on the contrary, he was, in many ways, an ardent admirer of this country. His ideal for Italy was a naval agreement with Britain as the strongest sea Power, and at

Where Signor Giolitti failed

the same time a close military attachment to Germany as the most important land force. His fault lay in a failure to see that he could not thus keep a foot in each camp; he was not prepared to take and keep a line when at last the great division became inevitable.

In addition it must be admitted that, like others of his party, he was obsessed by an insane jealousy and suspicion of France, a suspicion which had previously led Italy to suffer a grave neglect of Italian military preparations in the east, while piling up protective armament westwards. It is perhaps also true that Giolitti was not by nature a fighter. The colonial campaign which Italy undertook under his dictatorship in 1911-12, the Turkish war for the conquest of Tripoli, was not well prepared. On the part of Giolitti it may have been half-hearted, a concession to supposed popular sentiment, or an appeal to the "expansionist" vote, rather than the deliberate outcome of statesmanlike decision.

It was asserted that he dared not take the people into his confidence either as to the real cost of that war or as to the depletion of Italian resources afterwards. He refused to accept the responsibility of asking the large credits required for repairing the breaches in Italian armaments, and it is quite conceivable that he intended Salandra to act simply as a *premier-fainéant* who should bear the responsibility of replenishing the arsenals and then, when Giolitti gave the word, should retire again into obscurity.

city," so to speak, was Turin, where, in reality all the wires controlling his puppets were centred. His party organisation was wonderfully complete, and even after physical weariness had compelled him to drop for a time the reins of power, the Italian Parliament still contained a majority of his supporters.

It is perhaps doubtful whether Signor Giolitti had any inter-

GABRIELE D'ANNUNZIO.
Italian poet, and official chronicler of the war.

Unfortunately for his plans, Signor Salandra and his brilliant coadjutor Baron Sonnino—the latter, by the way, has English blood in his veins—refused to allow themselves to be treated as men of straw. Having accepted responsibility for Italian fortunes in this gravest hour of European history, they determined to choose the line they deemed best, and to stick to it. As we shall see later, when Giolitti tried to resume his old position as dictator, he found that the reins of power had slipped for ever from his grasp. There had arisen a king in Egypt to whom Giovanni Giolitti was unknown.

The story of Italian intervention contains a number of other Italian names now famous; but it may well be that great influence was exercised by some whose names are hardly mentioned now in connection with the dramatic events of 1915. All over Italy, and especially in Lombardy, men who saw clearly what the end must be were at work to teach, explain, and warn. Senator Albertini, of the family controlling the "Corriere Della Sera," may have exercised in Lombardy far more influence than is suspected. The Socialist deputy, Leonida Bissolati; the brilliant historian, Guglielmo Ferrero, of Turin; Eugenio Chieva, the Milanese deputy, should each have a place among the *dramatis personæ*; and there are many others.

As we have seen, Signor Salandra's Cabinet set to work at once to restore the breaches in Italy's defensive armaments. **Italy's new Cabinet** The host of German spies **at work** very soon reported to the German War Office that the Italian preparations appeared to be of a thoroughly practical character, and their reports were presently backed by communications from Germany's diplomatic representatives at the Italian Court and at the Vatican. The *premier-fainéant* turned out to be a man of singular taciturnity, while his chief of staff, Baron Sonnino, began to display a painful interest in diplomatic conversations. Germany discovered to her surprise that her despised onlooker had some cards, and was minded to take a hand in the game. We say Germany because almost up to the end it does not appear that the Austrian Government, under its octogenarian monarch, succeeded in ridding itself of its blinkers. Or if, indeed, there were Austrian statesmen who realised the

THE DUC D'AOSTA.
Cousin of King Victor Emmanuel III.

GENERAL VITTORIA ZUPELLI.
Italian Minister of War.

VICE-ADMIRAL LEONE VIALE.
Italian Minister of Marine.

ITALY'S SOLDIER-MOUNTAINEERS—THE FAMOUS ALPINI—IN THEIR ELEMENT.

The top view shows a detachment of the Alpini entrenched behind barricades of snow in the Julian Alps. As is the case with their fellow Latins, the French, they take their colours into action. In the lower photograph we have a vivid camera-record of these rugged warriors on the march through one of the mountain passes on the Austro-Italian frontier. Inset : Machine-gun section of the Alpini in action.

HOW VENICE GUARDED HER ART
TREASURES.
The Doges' Palace, with its magnificent arches
strengthened by solid pillars of brickwork against
the effects of explosives.

danger, it would seem that the traditional jealousy of Italy which had always inspired the House of Hapsburg rendered void any effort to agree with the enemy while they were in the way with him.

It will be remembered that Austria had omitted to consult Italy before presenting her German-made ultimatum to Serbia. In consequence there could be no doubt that Italy was at least relieved of all responsibilities under the Triple Alliance, and almost immediately she declared her neutrality.

Indignation in Berlin There was considerable indignation in Berlin where, a few days earlier, demonstrators before the Italian Embassy had acclaimed the Italian ally, and subsequently there was ill-treatment, official and unofficial, of Italian workmen employed on railway construction and in mines in Western Germany. Actually, however, the Italian declaration of neutrality had already done the Allies one invaluable service—it had released for the struggle against the invading Germans a considerable number of French troops which must otherwise have been retained on the Italian frontier.

" I will never forgive you," the Kaiser is said to have telegraphed to the King of Italy, and although the message is doubtless apocryphal, it probably expresses well enough the common feeling in Germany. But from refusal to aid the Germanic Powers to active intervention against them was a long step. While, as we have seen, the Salandra Cabinet was steadily completing the Italian armour, unostentatiously

calling up various classes of the reserves (many men being called by letters delivered by hand instead of through the post), piling up ammunition, and preparing down to the last detail the equipment necessary for the difficult mountain warfare, German agents were busy all over the country in mobilising every kind of assistance against the Interventionists, as the war party was called.

One of the earliest steps taken by Germany was to purchase a number of newspapers all over the country. Some of the principal Neutralist papers, such as the "Stampa" ("Press") of Turin, which was Giolitti's organ, were not indeed in the pay of the German agents, but others undoubtedly were. The methods of the German newspaper agents may be illustrated by **German newspaper** an incident which **intrigue** occurred in Milan. One of the editors of a certain Berlin newspaper agency, which at one time was inspired by the German Foreign Office, arrived in Milan in the autumn with his wife, and proceeded to call upon the proprietors of some of the smaller Lombardy papers with a view to discovering how far they could be utilised for German purposes. He finally discovered an unimportant publication in dire financial straits, and after some beating about the bush, announced that he was empowered to offer a handsome subsidy if the paper would adopt a prominently Neutralist and pro-German attitude.

SAND-BAGGED AGAINST BOMBS.
Court and steps of the Palace of the Doges, Venice, protected by sand-bags against the Austro-German Huns. The smaller photograph shows the work of protecting the statue of Bartolommeo Colleoni, a captain of the Venetian Republic (1475), pronounced by Ruskin the finest equestrian statue in the world.

THE OLD ROME AND THE NEW: MODERN MOTOR-TRANSPORT WAGGON PASSING THE ANCIENT COLOSSEUM.
A symbolical camera-picture, taken when Italy took her place in the Great War, by a photographer with a gift of imagination and a sense of historic contrast.

The proprietor considered the proposition for a little while and finally said : " Well, we will promise in return for your subsidy to print articles favourable to Germany, but once a week you must let us have a smack at Austria ! "

In Rome, Naples, Turin, and other large cities German agents began to attempt a similar campaign of corruption ; but their most effective work was a great deal more insidious. Just as was done in America, and probably even in England, German agents set to **Secret campaign in** work to stir up opposition to a war **the cities** policy among the labouring classes, not neglecting the women. Their arguments, founded always upon individual self-interest, were sufficiently specious. Italy, they argued, could obtain, as the reward of abstention from fighting, any territorial compensations she might fairly consider her due. Even within the limits of her neutrality she could do good business with the belligerents. She could " capture trade," refill her treasuries, and, in fact, fulfil generally the purposes of her existence. But if she went to war she must inevitably sacrifice a number of lives, she must incur a burden of debt which would express itself to the labouring man in the form of new and lasting taxation ; she would demand military service of numbers of men hitherto exempt ; business would be at a standstill, and since ultimately Germany would in any case win, the position of Italy after the war would indeed be terrible.

To the Socialist leaders the German agents offered an even more telling argument. " Now," they argued, " you have got a powerful organisation capable even of seizing the reins of power in a capitalistic city like Milan. You have your men well in hand and, since after the war labour will have a predominant voice, if you maintain your organisation now you will be able afterwards practically to dictate your terms. But if Italy goes to war, your position will collapse like a house of cards. Military authority in war time swamps all civil power and privilege. Your organisation can never be so influential or so absolute as that entrusted to the military ' tyranny,' and furthermore the seeds of individual liberty, the rebellion against oppressive class legislation and capitalistic domination, will be killed. Your adherents will be imbued with the military spirit—those of them that are left alive—and your own influence over them will have vanished for many a long year."

For the women they had yet another line of argument. " Remember Tripoli," they said. " Remember the killed, the maimed, the sick. See what is happening elsewhere, and consider that this is no African campaign. The Austrian armies will invade Italy. Venice will be destroyed ; Milan wrecked by Zeppelins. And when all is done, even if you win, who is to earn bread for you and your children when your sons and **Hoisting the disaster** husbands lie rotting among the Alpine **bogey** snows ? If war were necessary, you, as Italian women, could not complain. But war is not only not necessary, in your case it would be a gross breach of faith as well as a colossal folly."

There was yet another class of the Italian community to whom the German agents were able to make a very special appeal—namely, the rich merchants of Lombardy. For many years Italian banks and commercial houses had been more and more infested with Germans. Germany had sent her most skilful bankers, her most enterprising

105

YOUNG ITALY RESPONDING TO THE CALL TO ARMS.
Mobilisation of Italian infantry.

commercial agents to show the Italians how to do brilliant business. They were welcomed for their methods, and presently obtained such a hold that it was no longer possible for Italy to rid herself of them without the wrench of war. They were as leeches, but unlike leeches they never dropped off from satiety. War was the only salt that could detach them. When the hour foreseen of German business states-manship arrived this great force of German influence was brought to bear upon Italian merchant feeling. Their prosperity, they were warned, would be shaken. Their Germanised banks would fail, and bankruptcy would rear its ugly head even in Lombardy, the parent of the banking system of the world. There is no doubt that the long struggle of the Neutralists was greatly aided up to the very last by the doubts and fears instilled by the German agents into the Italian merchant class.

But the whole German campaign did not reach its maximum tension until the arrival in Rome of the German Imperial Agent-General, Prince von Bülow, concerning whom and his activities it is necessary to speak at some length. Before he became **Prince von Bulow's** German Foreign Secretary, and then **mission** Chancellor of the German Empire, Prince von Bülow (then only " Count ") had been German Ambassador in Rome. He had married a Sicilian lady, the daughter of Donna Minghetti, and after his fall from power had been accustomed to spend a considerable portion of each year in Rome and on his wife's Sicilian estates. He possessed a suave personality, and was a bland, somewhat indolent courtier, but an excellent host with charming manners and a certain smooth bonhomie which, while it delighted the Italians, was not always understood by the gruff Prussians of the Bismarckian school. He very rarely employed bluster, and was perhaps fonder of genial bluff. Yet he was certainly more successful as a diplomat than the Chancellor, Von Bethmann-Hollweg, who succeeded him. And when it finally became clear that some accomplished wire-puller must be sent to Rome to direct the German intrigues in Italy, the choice naturally fell upon Donna Laura Minghetti's popular son-in-law. " At last," said

ANOTHER MOBILISATION SCENE IN AN ITALIAN TOWN.
Inset in circle is a stirring photograph of Italian cavalry on the move.　The horsemanship of the Italian cavalry is superb.

ITALIAN FIELD ARTILLERY AT THE GALLOP.
The gun team is seen advancing over rough ground to a new position. Early reports from the Italian front gave glowing accounts of the work of the Italian artillery.

some of the Berlin papers, when Prince von Bülow took train for Rome, "we have *one* diplomat in the service."

Very soon after his arrival Prince von Bülow made his house the centre for all the Neutralist intrigues in and out of Parliament. Supper-parties, dinners, luncheons succeeded each other. The doors were constantly open to admit one or other of the Giolittan senators or deputies. Among the most prominent of them was Cirmeni, the "Rome correspondent" of the "Stampa," who was the most prominent of the Neutralist Press men, and certainly the best Press agent Prince von Bülow possessed. The German campaign throughout Italy was now pressed, not only with energy, but with a huge expenditure of money in all directions, and simultaneously Prince von Bülow himself began to open overtures with Baron Sonnino in order to discover what territorial concessions the existing Italian Government considered necessary. In the meantime, of course, schemes were evolved for a restoration of the Giolitti tyranny if the Salandra Cabinet proved unmanageable.

Austria as German puppet It is easy to understand that, even though Prince von Bülow was in reality the Agent-General for the Central Empires, certain diplomatic limitations had to be retained. Italy had no open cause of quarrel with her ally Germany, except in so far as she was bound to disapprove of the more brutal features of the German invasion of Belgium and Northern France. She was not negotiating with Germany for any concessions, nor was it nominally Germany which had evaded, to say the least of it, the terms of the Triple Alliance. Yet the Italian Government was not in the least in the dark as to the true authorship of the Serbian ultimatum or of the European War; nor could it disguise from itself the fact that circumstances being as they were, Germany could and did, to a certain extent, dictate Austrian policy during the war. As the event proved, the obedience of Austria to German dictates could, however, be strained beyond its limit. It followed, nevertheless, that while Prince von Bülow was not charged with any mandate to make concessions on behalf of Austria, and thus had no more than the character of an intermediary, he was actually the person with whom the Italian Government had to negotiate.

At the same time it was not long before his other less

KING VICTOR EMMANUEL'S CAVALRY CROSSING A RIVER ON INFLATED BAGS.

THE PASSAGE OF THE ISONZO RIVER.
There was heavy fighting for possession of the heights commanding the banks of the Isonzo in the early stages of the Italian advance towards Trieste.

ITALIAN CAVALRY PATROL MAKING A HALT FOR REFRESHMENTS: A PICTURESQUE SOUVENIR BY AN ITALIAN PHOTOGRAPHER AT THE FRONT.

official activities became manifest. The German Embassy became the rendezvous at all hours for the Neutralist journalists of the Cirmeni type, for the senators and other worthies who perceived that the star of their patron Giolitti was threatened with eclipse, and—by the back door—for the host of "agents," naturalised and unnaturalised, which infested the cities of Italy.

Under the ægis of the prince the Neutralist campaign began to take the form of demonstrations in the principal towns. Counter-demonstrations were, of course, organised by the Interventionists, and finally the two parties began here and there to clash. Knives and revolvers, sticks and stones came into play, until finally, for the preservation of order, the authorities **Plot and** were obliged now and again to call upon **counterplot** the troops. Some scenes illustrative of this stage in the drama will be described presently. But it is necessary first to sketch the course of plot and counterplot up to the last weeks which preceded the Italian appeal to the sword.

The primary object of the Italian Government was, of course, to gain time until the military preparations were completed. The objects of Prince von Bülow were two: First, if possible, to make the Italian Government define the terms, territorial and otherwise, which it considered the minimum acceptable ; and secondly, by dribbling out concessions, bit by bit, to convey the impression that every reasonable demand was being granted, and that Italy could gain, without firing a shot, at least as much as she could hope to gain by successful war. If the prince could force the Italian Government to show its hand early, his agents and abettors, Cirmeni and others, could appeal publicly against a Government which, while pretending to act solely in the best interest of Italy, really showed itself determined to fight in any case by making impossible demands. In fact this accusation was actually brought against Salandra and Sonnino at the last, but it was countered in the splendid speech wherein the Premier showed that the concessions offered were little more than visionary.

The Giolittans also were cunningly preparing for a coup. They knew, of course, that with infinite patience the Salandra Cabinet was making good the deficiencies in arms and ammunition which the Giolitti Cabinet had left. Their idea was to effect a coup d'état at the last moment, to take over the situation carefully prepared by the Salandra Cabinet, and assume subsequently the credit for any victory, diplomatic or in the field, which Salandra's preparations enabled Italy to achieve.

Meanwhile the Garibaldians—that is the remnant of those who had fought for Italian freedom with the national hero in 1865 and those who formed their adherents now— were conducting a vigorous campaign throughout Italy for the freedom of the Italian districts still under Austrian rule. They also were preparing a theatrical coup when the time was ripe. And, lastly, there was a strong but much less obvious movement **Garibaldians' new** in Northern Italy which had for its object **fight for freedom** the democratisation of public control, the prevention of another Giolitti tyranny, the diminution particularly of Jesuit influence, and the introduction of democratic institutions such as they saw in England. This party realised very early that an eventual triumph of Germany must mean a victory for oligarchic government and the defeat at any rate for a long time of really free institutions. They were prepared to go to any length to prevent the Prussianising of Italy as a result of the war. Their main objective was to combat Germany through a war with Austria.

For many weeks Baron Sonnino held his hand. He refused to be drawn by Prince von Bülow, and continued to insist that since Austria had by her actions broken the terms of the Triple Alliance it was for her to state what reparation she was prepared to make. Prince von of the intrigue carried on by Germany in Rome—namely, the so-called "Vatican Plot." Yet it cannot be omitted altogether, and may therefore be touched upon lightly as follows:

Among the coadjutors of Prince von Bülow in Rome was a certain Herr Erzberger, the leader in the German Reichstag of the powerful Catholic Centre party, next to the Socialists the most numerous and on the whole the most influential of the bourgeois parties. He was sent to Rome to encourage the resistance of the Roman Catholic Church to an Italian war with Austria. There was a clear political reason for this resistance. Austria was the last remaining Great Power (since Spain could no longer claim the title) where the Roman Catholic clergy and the Roman Church possessed a dominant voice in the affairs of State. The influence of the Pontificate was supported in turn by Austria which, since the disestablishment of the Church in France, had become the "eldest daughter."

The Erzberger conspiracy

So far as Germany was concerned the Church of Rome was most influential in the south and west, and here also

DISMOUNTING "THE HORSES OF ST. MARK."
These famous pieces of bronze, whose movements had already become historic, were once again taken from their position on the basilica of St. Mark. at Venice, and deposited in a place of greater safety.

"VENICE PRESERVED."
A further view of the methods adopted by the Venetians to protect the Palace of the Doges from enemy explosives.

Bülow's suave diplomacy was not able to get round this obstacle, and while secretly encouraging the Giolittans he was obliged openly to press upon his Government the necessity for Austrian concessions. Meantime the Neutralist Press at his inspiration continued to report far-reaching Austrian offers and to urge that with a little good-will every point which Italy could legitimately demand might readily be obtained.

It may suffice to enumerate some of the points on which the Italian requirements and the unwilling Austrian concessions most obviously collided.

Austria desired that the cession of the Trentino and rectification of the frontier at other points should be conceded after the war as a reward for Italian neutrality. Italy demanded that all territorial concessions should come into force at once as reparation for the Austrian breach of agreement. Italy demanded that the Italian districts of Istria should be surrendered absolutely; Austria offered only to make Trieste a "free city" under Austrian suzerainty. Italy demanded not only that concessions should be immediate, but also that Germany, as the obviously predominant partner, should give guarantees for the effective maintenance of the concessions after the war.

Italy demands guarantees

There is no doubt that even those concessions which Austria did eventually bring herself to make were extracted from her very unwillingly and under German pressure. There is also no doubt that after the war, if it had turned out successfully, Austria would have begun an intrigue at once for the restoration of the old frontiers. One is reluctant at this stage to write of one feature

were the strongholds of the political Centre party whose fortunes were bound up with Catholic influence. It was neither unnatural nor unintelligible that Roman Catholic Germany and Austria should endeavour to range on their side the influence of Italian Catholics and also through the Pontificate to appeal to Catholics in neutral countries.

What additions the Austrian and German delegates to the Vatican may have promised to the international power and prestige of the Papacy it is perhaps unnecessary to inquire. The grave factor in the situation was that Herr Erzberger personally and through his emissaries endeavoured to set on foot a secret agitation against the war—that is against the King's advisers—through the medium of the Roman Catholic clergy.

It is clear that traps were laid for the Pontiff himself. He was induced to grant an audience to a German-American journalist who subsequently used the conversation for the

MAP OF THE KINGDOM OF ITALY, INCLUDING SICILY AND SARDINIA

Specially drawn to illustrate the national ideals Italy hoped to realise by joining the Allies. Beyond the boundary line of the north and on the Eastern shore of the Adriatic will be seen the Trentino, Istria, and Dalmatia, territory mainly inhabited by Italians but under Austrian dominion, which it was Italy's fervent desire to embody in Greater Italy.

passed here and there along the road a company of men or youths in civilian clothes marching with head up, chest out, and with an unmistakably military swing. If he had inquired who these were he would have learned that they were just men doing some voluntary training in case—well in case they should be needed. Sometimes, when they got away from town or village out among the long rows of mulberry trees they broke into song—the hymn of Garibaldi, the Mameli hymn, or the song, "Trieste of my heart." These "training walks" were at once a preparation and an advertisement, and the Socialists inspired by the German intriguers took pronounced objection to them. They in turn organised certain bands of youths and workmen, armed them with stones and cudgels, and proceeded to waylay the companies from behind ditches or garden-palings. Once or twice the attack was sufficiently unexpected to break up the companies and scatter them, while their assailants jeered; but presently the companies themselves took to carrying stout cudgels, and then the assailants became the assailed and were put to flight. These were the first collisions, and they took place as a rule far enough from the city to prevent their being reported in detail.

Coming nearer to the city by the royal road which leads from Monza through the suburb of Greco to the Venice Gate the Milanese citizen would find the usually busy thoroughfare deserted, the tram service suspended, and most of the shops with their iron shutters down. There was a "general strike" proclaimed by the Socialists, either as a protest against some injury to a workman or on "general principles." But the quiet of the Monza road gave way, when the traveller had passed the city gate, to the turmoil of a mob thronging past the cathedral

purpose of affecting the sympathies of Roman Catholics in the United States and in other neutral countries.

The Austrian clergy in the frontier districts endeavoured to stir up racial antagonism between Slavs and Italians, and they were not innocent, after the outbreak of war, of devices for delaying the Italian advance, for which the recognised punishment on discovery is a blank wall and a file of riflemen. The misuse of the tenets of religion for the support of treacherous intrigue is always an unpleasant subject to discuss, and it is perhaps unnecessary for our present purposes to follow it further.

We may now turn to a description of some of the dramatic incidents which preceded the Italian declaration of war.

On a Saturday, almost any Saturday, in April a Milanese citizen, returning by road from Pavia in the south, or from Varese at the foot of the Alps in the north, might have

to the Piazza del Duomo, the great square in front of the cathedral, which was the scene of most of the mass meetings during the weeks preceding the war

Mass meetings in Milan

Here, if it was a "Neutralist Saturday," large crowds would be gathered round some Neutralist orator, and hence would start one of the processions which towards evening paraded the city demonstrating against one or other of the Interventionist papers, and sometimes cheering outside the German Consulate. The Neutralist processions were never very big, but they were well organised, and amongst the leaders were almost always some of those "hyphenated" Italians who had abandoned their German citizenship but not their German sympathies.

A day later the Piazza del Duomo would be filled by a much bigger crowd carrying the red, white, and green

WITH THE 81st ITALIAN REGIMENT, ONE OF THE FIRST TO
CROSS THE ISONZO.

TYPICAL ITALIAN INFANTRY, FAMOUS FOR THEIR STAYING POWER, IN ACTION. IN CENTRE: AN ITALIAN LIGHT FIELD-GUN.

Italian flag entwined with the colours of Trieste or with the symbol of Garibaldi's "honourable red shirt." From the Piazza the Interventionist procession would pass singing down every one of the main arteries of the city, and it was during one of these processions that the most serious disturbance took place.

At first the Neutralists and Interventionists held their meetings on the same day, and collisions were not infrequent. But after a time the Carabinieri (armed police) were instructed to end these simultaneous demonstrations, and they began to clear off ruthlessly whichever party was manifestly merely trying to break up the other's assembly.

After a few weeks, accordingly, the assemblies took place on succeeding days; but as the support of the Interventionists increased and the Neutralists obviously lost ground, they resorted to other tactics. Little gangs would wait in side streets until the Interventionists began to disperse, and would then attack small parties, tearing the Trieste or Garibaldi favours from men's coats or ladies' dresses, and sometimes handling their victims very roughly as well. Finally, on Thursday evening, May 13th, matters reached a climax. A big procession of **Matters reach a climax** Interventionists had been arranged for four o'clock in the afternoon. Towards evening a part of the procession left the Piazza del Duomo and moved down the Corso towards the Venice Gate. As they passed the gateway, and began to bear to the left past the public gardens, a gang of Neutralists, who had concealed themselves among some artificial rockwork, opened fire upon the leading files with revolvers. The second shot hit a young doctor in the face, passing out through his cheek; but most of the shots went high, and

those who were injured were mostly hurt in the sudden swerve of the leading files of the procession and the rush to get back to the gate.

At three o'clock next morning a formal council of war was held by the organisers of the Interventionist demonstrations. After a good deal of angry discussion it was decided that another **A hint to** even more imposing demonstration **the "Germans"** should be held on the following day, and there was a significant hint that the "Germans" should not this time find them without means of defence.

There can be little doubt that the fight at the Porta Venezia would have led to grave scenes in the streets of Milan if the political situation had not suddenly taken a turn which held even the most enthusiastic demonstrator in suspense.

Naturally there was no doubt felt that while a small proportion of the Neutralist leaders were genuinely convinced that Italy ought not to go to war, the violent Neutralist demonstrations, on the contrary, were both inspired and assisted by German intriguers, whose main desire was to make it appear that feeling against the war was so strong that something resembling civil war must result if the Government finally rejected the Austrian proposals. This manœuvre had two consequences. In the first place, the Interventionist leaders determined to make it clear that no Government could look for any real support even in quelling disorders which did not take account of the strong war sentiment in Northern Italy; and in the second place the consciousness of German intrigues began to express itself in anti-German demonstrations, which after the war took a regrettable turn.

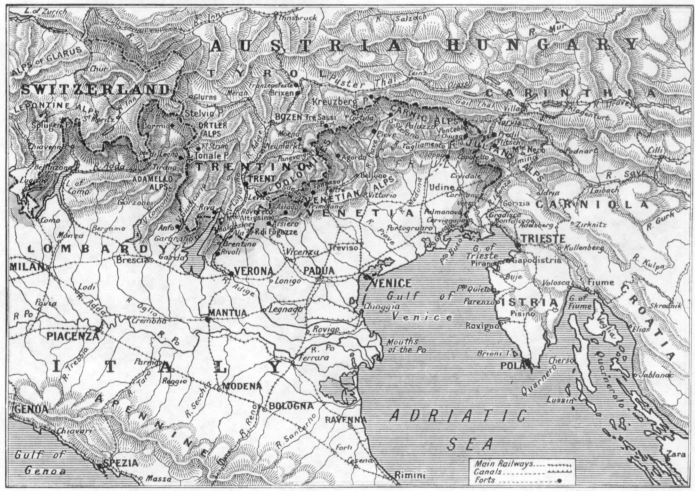

MAP OF THE ITALO-AUSTRIAN WAR AREA, INDICATING BOUNDARIES, THE PRINCIPAL MOUNTAIN PASSES, FORTS, AND COMMUNICATIONS.

ITALY'S RESPONSE TO AUSTRIA'S BREACH OF FAITH.
One of the big guns adapted by Italian artillerists for use in mountain warfare in action against the Austrian foe. In size and shape this enormous weapon is similar to the French 155 mm. cannon.

Even before the war Germans in Milan received a severe warning of the temper of the mob. The Siemens-Schuckert works, the great Berlin factory of electrical and other machinery, had a Milan branch occupying large premises on the Viale Venezia, a street running along the lines of the vanished city walls. The walls themselves are replaced by a high embankment, planted with an avenue of trees enclosing the fine public gardens. A small crowd of demonstrators, marching along the Viale Venezia, had assembled outside the Siemens-Schuckert establishment, and was denouncing the numerous atrocities committed by the Germans in Belgium and elsewhere. Some young German employees, left in charge of the establishment, apparently believed that an attack on the place and on themselves was immediately contemplated. Opening a window near the roof, they produced revolvers and began to fire on the mob. It is possible that they were only employing blank cartridge, but the mob was infuriated by the foolish action of the Germans, and very soon an attack (which had certainly not been originally contemplated) was made on the establishment. Crowbars were fetched from some neighbouring works, and in a few minutes the iron shutters on the ground floor were forced open. Then the huge doors gave way under repeated assaults by men wielding a wooden ram, and the foremost of the crowd forced their way into the house. It would undoubtedly have gone hard with the Germans in the place had not some Carabinieri come up just at this moment. They cleared off the crowd, and entering the establishment

KING VICTOR EMMANUEL AT THE FRONT.
On the entry of Italy into the war her King immediately put himself at the head of his troops in the field.

succeeded in removing the Germans to safe quarters. But the temper of the crowd from that time became much less gentle, and when the final crisis came it would have taken very little to provoke serious bloodshed.

In the meantime the "Garibaldi" movement had produced a crisis to which we must now turn our attention. Early in the war the Garibaldians had set on foot a movement to recognise in some practical way the aid given by France to Italy during her own War of Independence. This movement ultimately resulted in the enrolment in France of a special corps of Garibaldi volunteers who fought with the French troops in Alsace. The corps suffered severely in one of the German assaults, and one of the members of the Garibaldi family fell at the head of the volunteers. The news of this engagement had a wide-spread effect in Italy, and undoubtedly helped largely to popularise a movement for celebrating in some special form the fifty-fifth anniversary of the sailing of the one thousand Garibaldian volunteers for Marsala in 1860. This anniversary fell on May 5th, and it was decided to celebrate it by holding a great meeting on the scene of Garibaldi's embarkation with his thousand volunteers just below Genoa, at the Quarto dei Mille. A memorial statue was prepared, and was to be unveiled on the scene of the embarkation, while a great patriotic demonstration was to be addressed by Gabriele D'Annunzio, the Italian poet and playwright, who had come to be recognised as the spokesman of the Irredentist and Interventionist movement. There is no doubt that as the arrangements for the great demonstration took shape, the leaders of the movement believed that it might carry the Italian Government " off its feet," and that it would provide King and Cabinet with a fitting oppor-tunity for declaring their policy. Both the Premier, Signor Salandra, and the Foreign Secretary, Baron Sonnino, an-

Garibaldian celebration cancelled

nounced their intention of being present, and finally it was announced that the King him-self would witness the unveiling of the statue. An immense concourse of people from all parts of Italy was expected, and the State railways made arrangements for running a number of special trains to Genoa. The day was awaited with intense anxiety.

Everybody took it for granted that now at last Italy would declare herself, and it seemed that there could be no question on which side her decision would fall. But two days before the ceremony the whole official programme was suddenly cancelled. It was announced from Rome in the morning that the Premier would not attend the meeting. Then a second communiqué declared that, owing to the gravity of the international situation, Baron Sonnino would not leave Rome, and that none of the Cabinet would absent themselves from the capital. Finally, towards noon, it was further officially announced that the King would not be present. At first it was supposed that the German and Austrian Ambassadors had declared that they would be obliged to regard the presence of the King and Ministers at the ceremony as indicating an end of the negotiations, and that this notification had compelled the Ministry to decide what steps they would take in view of this unwarrantable interference. Later

ITALIAN LEADERS AT THE FRONT.
Generals Di Mayo and Besozzi inspecting an aviation camp.

it was rumoured that Gabriele D'Annunzio had declined to make certain modifications in his pro-jected speech, and that the King, if he listened to them, could hardly pre-serve the ordinary diplo-matic formulas preceding the outbreak of war. Actually, no doubt, two things combined to deter-mine King and Ministers upon the course they adopted. The Austrian negotiations had reached a point at which the Italian Government could not do other than announce that the Triple Alliance was no longer binding. We have already seen that the terms of the alliance had been broken by Austria. At the beginning of May Italy finally made it clear that the concessions she demanded were no longer to be regarded as consideration for a maintenance of the alliance, but

GENERAL CONRAD VON HOETZENDORF.
Chief of the Austro-Hungarian Head-quarters Staff.

The Triple Alliance denounced

as the alternative to Italy's joining the Allies. The Triple Alliance was denounced by Italy on May 4th—that is, the day before the Garibaldian ceremony.

Three factors had thus combined to prepare Italian public opinion for intervention. There was the desire to " realise national aspirations "—there is no better expres-sion for the Irredentist and Garibaldian movement—and there was the growing sense of the hopelessness of any decent civilised life after the war unless Germany were crushed—a factor which Germany certainly underestimated —and, finally, there was the increasing exasperation as the plots of German and " Germanising " agents in Italy became clearer. The appalling stories of brutality to Italians within Austria's borders helped to fan the flame of Irredentist zeal, the sinking of the Lusitania and the use of poisonous gases broke the back of pro-German opposition even amongst the Germanised merchant class,

GRANDSONS OF GARIBALDI IN THE NEW FIGHT FOR FREEDOM.
Left to right : Ezio (seated), Beppino, Menotti, Sante, Riciotti. They were enrolled in the 51st Infantry Regiment, known as the Alpini Brigade.

and the attempts at wholesale bribery of Press and public officials brought public feeling to boiling-point.

After May 4th there was not really any question as to what the Salandra Cabinet would and must do. There was only a question whether it itself could carry its measures into effect without an appeal to the country. In the "great twenty days" Germany played her last card—Giolitti.

She had already succeeded in persuading a small section of Italian Colonial troops in Tripoli to revolt, but the story of the rebellion and the casualty list failed of their expected result. They merely stiffened Italian feeling, particularly since the "Agenzia della Stampa" was able to state on May 6th that the Government had proof of German complicity in the outbreak. The "Secolo" of Milan expressed the general feeling when it wrote on May 6th: " If Austria or Turkey *or any other country* has relied upon our reputation for impressionability and has believed that a military check in Africa might be sufficient to weaken our purpose, that calculation is undoubtedly erroneous. Where others have sought means of demoralising us they may chance to find the spark which will light the conflagration they have feared and we have awaited."

Germany's last card

There is, perhaps, little doubt now that Salandra's Ministry would have precipitated events in the first week in May had not the Russian retirement begun in the north, and had not the Italian Minister for War become cognisant of a shortage of munitions on the part of the Allies. It must always be remembered to Italy's credit that instead of "flying to the succour of the victors," she came to the aid of the Allies when their star seemed for the time to pale. It may be (and the records of the Italian General Staff will no doubt show it later) that some revision of plans was necessitated by the situation.

Baron Sonnino's demands

On May 11th one of the Italian deputies, Signor Canefa, specified in a Genoese paper the demands—in addition to immediate territorial concessions—which Baron Sonnino had presented to Austria and Germany. They were the immediate evacuation of Belgium and guarantees for the respecting of the integrity of Serbian territory.

On May 10th German and Austrian Consulates throughout Italy began to advise their nationals to quit Italy, and an hour or two after the issue of the warnings by express letter the Consulates were besieged by people asking for passports. The exodus which began then continued for about ten days, when the majority of Germans and Austrians who could get away had taken refuge in Switzerland.

THE ANTI-GERMAN DEMONSTRATIONS IN MILAN.

Demonstrations in the principal cities assumed serious proportions in the weeks immediately preceding Italy's entry into the war, and the Carabinieri were frequently called out to quell disorder, especially in Milan. The above photograph shows the destruction by fire of enemy property in front of the Palazzo Settentrionale, at Milan, by a populace enraged by the treatment of their countrymen in Austria and Germany.

From the 11th to the 14th the Interventionist demonstrations reached their maximum of violence. One or two German shops, some Austrian cafés, and so forth, were broken open and the contents destroyed in Milan, Venice, and elsewhere.

May 11th saw demonstrations throughout the country no longer of a "Garibaldian" character, but of violent indignation at the sinking of the Lusitania, and the Union Jack began to appear combined in one flag with the French, Russian, and Italian colours. On the evening of the 14th occurred the treacherous attack with revolvers upon the Interventionists issuing from the Porta Venezia,

Signor Salandra and Baron Sonnino had expounded to him the situation as it had developed, he professed himself dissatisfied and refused to advise the King to continue to support the Salandra Ministry. Signor Salandra had no alternative. On May 14th he and his whole Ministry resigned.

Constitutionally the King was bound to attempt a compromise. Giolitti himself would not, or, as is more probable, dared not attempt to form a Ministry. Alternatives were tried without success, and meantime Italy, north and south, came nigh to civil war. Grim and determined men met in midnight conclaves to decide upon their course of action, and they decided that proof must be given at once that the country was in no mood to tolerate the intrigues of the German agents.

The colours of Trieste and the Trentino, even the banner of the House of Savoy, disappeared from men's caps. Printing presses worked all through the night of the 14th and the day of the 15th to turn out millions of little white cards bearing the inscription, "Death to Giolitti!" and huge red-white-and-green posters bearing the yet more significant warning "War or Republic!" In Rome a furious mob stormed the Parliament house and threw up barricades in the streets; and in Milan, Turin, and Genoa men prepared for fighting in the streets.

WITH THE ITALIAN NAVY.
Italian destroyer discharging a torpedo.

and on the same day Giolitti, who had gone to Rome to take the measure of the situation, struck his last blow.

Gathering all the weight of his authority, all the influence of his years of dictatorship in and out of Parliament, he forced his supporters to a declaration that they would not support the Salandra Government in its existing form. This meant that when Signor Salandra should ask the House of Parliament (Chamber of Deputies) for a ratification of the measures already taken, and for the various votes necessary to give the Government a free hand for the prosecution of the war, he would meet, if Giolitti could make good his threats, an adverse majority.

It is doubtful, to say the least of it, whether Giolitti at this stage believed that war could be avoided. It is possible, as has already been suggested, that he would have preferred to fight the last " Italian War of Unity " himself; it is certain that when matters came to the point he found his power in the country shattered, his reputation, owing to the intrigues of Prince von Bülow, soiled, and his authority so blunted that he dared not take up again the reins of Government. Even after

ABOARD AN ITALIAN DESTROYER.
A torpedo crew at work.

Let us go once more to the Piazza del Duomo, in Milan. It is afternoon. The sun is already low in the west, and the beautiful old brickwork of the Palace of Merchants is a red blaze of splendour. An immense crowd packs every corner of the square. Men are aloft on ladders along the colonnade of the Galleria; they have climbed on to the electric-light standards; they pack the windows and roofs of the four-storied houses and shops round the square, and still they are fighting their way in from the side streets.

FIRING THROUGH THE MIST ON THE MOUNTAIN SIDE.
Italian infantry in action on the northern frontier.

THE CAPTURE OF MONTE NERO.
Italian troops advancing to the assault. The smaller view shows an Italian artillery column taking a brief rest near the battle-front.

In the middle a great papier-mâché figure of Giolitti is lifted aloft on a pole, and angry men begin to harangue the crowd.

Now the doors of the cathedral are opened, and the congregation gathered to listen to Benediction swarm out from the cool, dim aisles into the roar and fury of the square. Suddenly the crowd begins to sway westwards. From both sides of the cathedral rows of grey-coated figures preceding the cocked hats of the Carabinieri (armed now with rifles) move in steady line towards the centre of the square; and, as they move, the crowd is pushed, shouting and struggling, towards the western approaches. Steadily the pressure is increased. The square is emptying, and as the last of the worshippers leave the cathedral the grey line of troops reaches the western side of the Piazza. But the work the crowd was appointed to do is done. Upon every pillar of the Colonnade, upon the tramway standards, upon the hoarding by the side of the cathedral, from the windows of the houses, and round the base of the statue of Victor Emmanuel II. flame out the placards, " O Guerra o Republica ! " " War or Republic ! Choose ! "

And before night the message of Lombardy is flashed to Rome.

It is impossible in short space to hope to give any impression of the fury of the crowds which throughout Italy demanded the return of the Salandra Ministry. But there is no doubt that any **The peril of** alternative statesman who might have **civil war** attempted in other circumstances to try to form a Cabinet must have recognised the warning that his first task would be to quell a civil war. And very wisely one and all refused to face a situation which called now for the one Ministry that the people would tolerate.

Once more, and for the last time, we stand by the tomb of San Carlo in front of the high altar in the cathedral. For the last time the sun strikes through the wonderful " jewel-window " and throws coloured lights upon the

PICTURESQUE VIEW OF BERSAGLIERI CYCLISTS ON THE MARCH.
Inset is a striking camera portrait of an officer of Bersaglieri.

INVENTOR OF WIRELESS TELEGRAPHY AS SUB-LIEUTENANT.
Commendatore Marconi, who entered the Italian Army as a Sub-Lieutenant of Engineers, leaving his commander's headquarters after having taken the oath.

pavement. The voice of the beloved Cardinal, Archbishop Ferrara, delivers the message of the Gospel of humility from the great marble pulpit. There is a movement at the back of the cathedral, a stir of men moving excitedly towards the door, and presently, even as the Cardinal leaves the pulpit, someone whispers in men's ears " Salandra is recalled ! "

Out once more into the blazing sunshine of the Piazza— out amongst the crowd sweeping again from every street into the great square, while from a thousand throats rises the long, sibilant cry, " Salandra—Sonnino ! "

A white sheet, wet from the " Secolo " presses, is thrust into our hands. It contains three words—

" SALANDRA IS RECALLED ! "
Once more the loud cry " Salandra—Sonnino ! " is raised, and swiftly as it assembled the crowd begins to disperse.

From the distance a silver trumpet calls. It is the call to arms !

Any account of the entry of Italy into the war would be misleading which did not take account of the part played therein by the women of Italy. The record must not merely include the great work undertaken by **The call to** ladies in connection with the volunteer **arms** nursing institutions, or in the preparation of bandages, or even in the care of the many refugees from Trieste and Trentino. These things have their parallels in every other country involved in the war, though Italy managed to invest them in some cases with a curiously characteristic charm. When war was declared one might pass down a dull street towards the Porta Venezia and looking through a " restored " Renaissance gateway catch sight of a garden scene which might have rejoiced Boccaccio. Under the wide-spreading trees of an ancient

walled garden, or about the fountain of a pillared cortile, would be seen a pretty woman with the glorious Venetian colouring, surrounded by her friends, and sometimes her servants, sitting engaged upon some handiwork. And one or the other would be telling a story. But the handiwork would be the making of masks against gas-poisoning, and the stories would be of the departure of friends and relatives for the front. Elsewhere, within the red-brick walls of a convent close, the nuns would be at work while one of them read from the life of Pius IX. or perhaps the story of Pius X. and the Curé of Ars.

And every group was a picture. But these things are accidents of stage-setting and southern colouring. It is accident, for instance, that the Great War will be connected for ever in some **Attitude of Italian** memories with the sound of a guitar **women** at midnight following a day of riot ; in others, with the song of a Neapolitan boatman ; and in others with a sudden swirl of printed news-sheets broadcasted over the packed seats of the great arena.

But the attitude of Italian women to this war was not accident. German spies in high quarters had urged that the women would rebel ; that they would throw themselves in front of the troop-trains, as legend says they did once before. The reality proved how little these Germans knew of the " woman-country beloved of earth's male lands."

" Have ye not heard . . . " what the Queen-Mother replied to the violent message from Berlin ? The Kaiser had telegraphed to Queen Margherita begging her to use her influence with her son, King Victor, in favour of Italian neutrality. She replied, " The House of Savoy reign one at a time."

FROM SILENCED AUSTRIAN HOWITZERS.
The pieces of exploded Austrian shell shown above, weighing just a hundredweight, were picked up by Italians somewhere along the frontier after a battery of Austrian howitzers had been silenced.

When the women—mothers, sisters, and wives—marched with their men through the streets to the station, men rarely or never heard the exhortation, "Take care of yourself"; it was always "Get yourself honour." In the women of Italy there was something of the Roman yet.

There is recorded the letter of a Venetian marchioness to her friend in Milan, all of whose sons had gone to the war. It begins and ends with the old Roman appeal to strength of heart and mind as well as of sinew. "Sia Forte!—Vale. Be strong. Think of your sons with love . . . but also with courage. You must be strong. It matters nothing if you suffer. Sia Forte."

It was the answer of the women of Italy to the Germans who maligned them.

As twelve finished striking on the night of May 24th little companies of the Alpini, Italy's famous mountaineers, set out from San Giorgio and Palmanova and Cividale on the eastern frontier; from Paluzza and San Stefano and Pieve in the north; from Agordo, Feltre, and Asiago; from Brentino and Malcesine towards and on Lake Garda; from Gargnano on the western shore of the lake, and from other points all along the mountain frontier up to the Stelvio Pass. They moved silently in single file; for silence is of the essence of Alpine fighting—silence and surprise.

After an hour or two of march they would be halted above a rocky spur where a deep trench was driven right and left. Then an officer would address them. "You can see for yourselves," he said, "what were our frontiers. You go forward to make new ones." There was an attempt at a cheer, suppressed instantly by the N.C.O.s, and then began the long, steep climb in Indian file, up narrow mountain-tracks with an overhanging rock on one side and a drop to a torrent on the other, through patches of snow knee-deep and hardly crisped by the night frost, or under the sudden violence of a terrific storm of sleet and rain which broke along the Trentino frontiers before dawn. So they climbed steadily, but even as dawn broke they hurled themselves **Austria's** forward upon a shelter-trench excavated **mountain shield** in the autumn of 1914 upon the rocky plateau. It was empty. Some cooking utensils lay about, and in one place (on the Monte Altissimo) a mess of pottage was still warm in a pot over the ashes of a fire behind a spur of rock.

As the sun rose, lighting up the snow-peaks, the first Austrian guns from the rock-fortresses beyond crashed out their deadly salute!

At the beginning we saw that the Austro-Italian frontiers had been fixed so that they provided Austria with a convenient mountain shield for her assembly of troops and with mountain outposts whence her sentries might observe Italian movements of concentration below. Whether because the Italian declaration of war found her unprepared, or because—as is more probable—her first line of mountain defences was never intended to be more than an advanced guard, Austria practically did not defend certain of the heights which she had fortified in the autumn. Monte Altissimo, between Lake Garda and Ala in the railway valley (Val Lagarina) leading to Rovereto, was captured without a blow being struck. Similarly the troops in the east met with little real resistance until they reached the Isonzo, and, as we have seen, the conquest of the outlying Austrian positions was necessary in order to clear the Italian **Watch-towers** flanks. The Italians were able to reach **taken by assault** Cervignano, Verso, and Cormons on the roads towards the great circuit of Austrian fortifications —Gorizia, Gradisca, Monfalcone—which are really the advanced works of Trieste, with very little fighting except against armed police and treacherous franc-tireurs.

Similarly, towards the Trentino, they occupied Cortina d'Ampezzo and Ala, and places on the main roads into the Trentino between these two without very severe fighting. And again, while the Austrians held their winter fortifications on the Stelvio and Tonale Passes in the west they abandoned their first line between the Val Giudicaria and Lake Garda.

It is probable—though this has not been clearly demonstrated—that even beyond the Isonzo valley the Austrians had not expected to do more than delay the Italian advance upon the fortified system called collectively Tolmino, and after the Italian troops had descended to the river at Caporetto orders were given for an immediate advance upon Tolmino.

But on the night of May 25th a terrific storm burst throughout the Alpine region. The weather broke up completely, and for nearly a week (May 25th to 31st) progress was almost impossible. This delay enabled the Austrians to bring up fresh supplies of men and guns and provisions, and resulted in Tolmino holding out for two months longer than either side had expected.

Between the Trentino and the Isonzo front runs, as was already explained at the outset, the mountain wall of the Carnic Alps. Here the Austrians held their first line, and it was only after stiff fighting—though, from the nature of the ground, with small bodies of men—that the Italians were able to take some of the Austrian watch-towers by assault, and some, as in the case of the Freikofel, by surprise.

In general, it may be said that it was not until the beginning of June that the Italians really began their long struggle to breach the second and strongest line of Austria's mountain ramparts and fortified strongholds.

IN THE ISONZO REGION: BRINGING UP RELIEF SECTIONS FROM THE BASE.

CHAPTER LXXI.

THE MARVELLOUS WORK OF THE RED CROSS.

How the Nation was Confronted by a Medical Problem of Appalling and almost Overwhelming Magnitude—" The Best Army Medical Service in the World " and its Thousands of Self-sacrificing Voluntary Workers at Home and in the Overseas Dominions—Rise and Equipment of the Hospital City—The Fleets of Motor-Ambulances and the New Hospital Trains—Organisation of the Casualty Clearing Houses, Hospitals, and Convalescent Homes—Tracing the Wounded and Missing—Work of the British Red Cross Society and the Order of St. John of Jerusalem—Noble Women and Brave Men—Heroic Services in the Field—Splendid Story of the Munro Ambulance at Dixmude—British Aid to Serbia.

T HE work of the Red Cross in war is three-fold—to prevent disease, to treat the wounded, and to heal the sick.

Twenty years ago the one business of the doctors with a fighting army was to treat the wounded. It was long before it was realised that for every soldier killed by shell or bullet three or four were incapacitated by preventable illness. Even as recently as the Boer War typhoid, not bullets, was the real scourge of our Army.

War creates disease. This has been shown in every big war in the history of the world ; it was shown in the Great War. Old diseases, supposed to have been almost swept out of existence, revived. Spotted fever, a complaint mainly found among young soldiers, appeared in the autumn of 1914 in various parts of England. Filth diseases arose in various Continental countries, diseases directly caused by the sheer inability of the soldiers to change their clothing for long periods at a time or to keep themselves clean. Typhus swept over Serbia, claiming its victims wholesale. Tetanus (lock-jaw) complicated the early surgical work at the front to a serious degree, and necessitated wide-spread special precautions against it. It was supposed to be due to infection from the highly cultivated Belgian soil. In the winter months frost-bite, previously almost unknown to British doctors, attacked num-bers of men in the trenches. Then the presence of large armies over a very narrow area of ground for nearly a year at a time brought its own menace. Many

Elliott & Fry.

SURGEON-GENERAL SIR ARTHUR SLOGGETT.
Of the admirable work of Sir Arthur Sloggett and all branches of the medical services in the field under his direction Sir John French repeatedly expressed his warm appreciation.

scores of thousands of bodies of the victims of war lay in the fields and trenches and in the choked canals of Flanders and Northern France. It was not always possible even to bury them. Decaying bodies mean contagion and give rise to epidemics.

Add to this the new problems of surgery, caused by the complicated and often poisoned wounds from bombs and from high-explosive shells. The tortures of the poisoned victims of German asphyxiating gas lent a horror hitherto unknown to war. Our Army doctors had to care not only for the great armies at the front, but for over two million new troops at home. Our medical and surgical resources, taxed as never before for our own needs, were further largely drawn upon for the relief of some of our Allies, more particularly for Belgium and Serbia. Obviously the medical problem suddenly created by the Great War was one of ap-palling and almost overwhelming magnitude.

The British Army Medical Service was at the outset, for its size, among the finest and most efficient known. One of the greatest medical authorities of our time, Sir Frederick Treves, made opportunity in the early days of 1915 to bear his testimony to the magnificent way in which it did its work. " It is, I believe," he said, " the best Army Medical Service in the world. When the story comes to be told, it will be found that its work is not merely admirable, it is marvellous."

But the British Army Medical Service was maintained on the basis of having to deal with a few thousand wounded men. Care-ful preparations had been made for expansion in time of war, but no one anticipated hostilities with hundreds of thousands of sick and wounded requiring treatment within a few months. The service was ill-equipped with ambulances. Doctors had suddenly to be drawn from every part. Trained workers, nurses, and ambulance men had to be found by the ten thousand ; hospitals had to be constructed to hold vast armies of patients ; hospital cities had to be planned ; great fleets of cars were required to convey the wounded from the front ; and a vast supply of material had to be quickly produced, from iodine for the antiseptic treatment of wounds to artificial limbs, in quantities undreamt of before.

The necessary work was accomplished by the co-operation of all possible forces. The chief of these —the responsible directing organi-

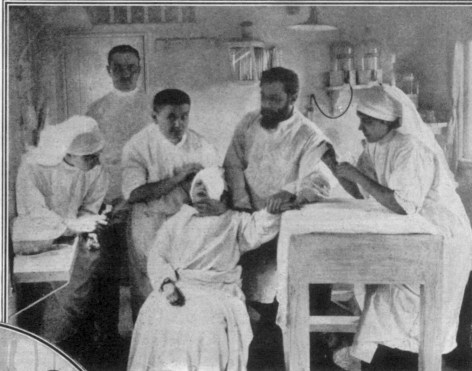

A WONDERFUL RUSSIAN MILITARY TRAIN.
Scene in the operating theatre on one of the Russian military trains. This train, in addition to being equipped for rendering every form of medical aid to wounded soldiers, had also bathing accommodation for the troops in the field.

BELGIAN PRIEST CONDUCTING EXHAUSTED SOLDIERS TO AN AMBULANCE.
A striking incident during the terrible fighting around Ypres.

sation—was the Army Medical Department. This department sought and welcomed the assistance of the numerous volunteer organisations, most of them under the direction of the British Red Cross Society and the Order of St. John of Jerusalem in England. Vast stations for the wounded sprang up as though by magic. During the rapid movements in the early days of the war when, it seemed for a time, that the German army would take possession of the whole of Northern France, our medical base had to be moved from place to place. Then Boulogne, the great pleasure city on the Strait of Dover, **Vast stations** was made the British Continental base, **for wounded** and Etaples close by was transformed into a hospital city, planned to receive 50,000 wounded.

The Order of St. John provided in a few months 13,500 experienced ambulance and hospital workers. The Empire was scoured for fully-trained nurses, and in addition to these, hosts of women assistants were enrolled in Voluntary Aid Detachments. These V.A.D.'s, as they were known, were most of them accustomed, before the war began, to lives of leisure, ease, and plenty. They threw themselves into their unpaid mission with an enthusiasm and good-will that were the admiration of all who saw them. They became the assistants of the trained nurses, and counted nothing menial or unworthy in their work—from scrubbing floors to helping to dress hideous wounds. Without their aid the task of the nurses would have been almost impossible.

Motor-ambulance cars were especially needed to carry the sick from the front to the hospital bases. In a few months over one thousand motor-ambulances were at work. Numerous hospital trains, some of them fitted with every convenience that could aid the lot of the wounded —from an operating theatre to an X-ray installation— were put on the rails in France. Hospital ships, painted a dazzling white and **Floating palaces** marked with immense red crosses to **for the sick** protect them from attack by enemy submarines or destroyers, moved across the waters, floating palaces for the sick.

The work of a general in war is not to see after the wounded, but to defeat the enemy. If any great commander were to pause in his operations in order that the wounded might have better attention, or were to hold the advance of the supply of ammunition for guns at the front to make a way clear for the passage of the wounded to the base, he would be regarded as unfit for his command. War is a hard business. The wounded soldier is, from the point of view of the fighting commander, an encumbrance to be taken away as quickly as possible. This may sound harsh and unfeeling. But a little reflection will show that it is the only course possible. Hence it was that, when the British armies were fighting in Flanders, the first requirement in the medical treatment of the men was to get them away from the front immediately, and to leave the front clear for the real operations of war. Fortunately, the elaborate system of railways, the nearness of the fighting-line to the sea coast, and the growing supply of motor-cars made this possible to a very unusual degree.

When the First Expeditionary Force came in active contact with the Germans around Mons no one anticipated the terrible slaughter that occurred, the rapid retreats, and the armies of wounded demanding immediate attention. There was then no adequate force of motor-ambulances at the front. Had there been, large numbers of our wounded who fell into the hands of the enemy would have been saved.

Very much had been done to improve our medical service since the days of the Boer War. The progress, particularly in personnel, was enormous; but the tragic events of the great retreat revealed for the first time the full magnitude of the medical problem before the nation, and then the more elaborate equipments that we know to-day were quickly brought into being.

Medical organisation at work

Let us see how the medical organisation worked. Start at the beginning, with the soldier in the field. Every soldier carried with him a simple first-aid equipment for hastily bandaging any wounds.

In the heat of the battle the wounded had often enough to wait for some time where they fell. On some occasions wounded British and Germans fell in the same trench, and the men who an hour or two before had been seeking one another's lives, now, as they lay broken and bleeding, sought to afford one another aid.

An interesting picture of such a scene was given by a young French cavalry officer as he lay dying in a trench. He had strength enough before he passed away to write a message to his wife describing the end:

There are two other men lying near me, and I do not think there is much hope for them, either. One is an officer of a Scottish regiment, and the other a private in the Uhlans. They were struck down after me, and when I came to myself I found them bending over me, rendering first-aid. The Britisher was pouring water down my throat from his flask, while the German was endeavouring to stanch my wound with an antiseptic preparation served out to their troops by the medical corps. The Highlander had one of his legs shattered, and the German had several pieces of shrapnel buried in his side.

In spite of their own sufferings, they were trying to help me; and when I was fully conscious again the German gave us a morphia injection, and took one himself. His medical corps had also provided him with the injection and the needle, together with printed instructions for their use. After the injection, feeling wonderfully at ease, we spoke of the lives we had lived before the war. We all spoke English, and we talked of the women we had left at home. Both the German and the Britisher had been married only a year. . . . I wondered—and I suppose the others did—why we had fought each other at all.

French officer's dying words

I looked at the Highlander, who was falling to sleep exhausted, and in spite of his drawn face and mud-stained uniform, he looked the embodiment of freedom. Then I thought of the Tricolour of France and all that France had done for liberty. Then I watched the German, who had ceased

AGONY FOR WHICH THERE MIGHT BE SOME AMELIORATION BUT SELDOM A CURE.
Two pathetic camera-records of Russian soldiers tortured by German poison gas. The larger view is of a Russian field hospital just after the sufferers had been brought in from the trenches. In the smaller photograph Russian nurses are seen offering soothing drinks to the victims of Germany's diabolic form of warfare.

to speak. He had taken a prayer-book from his knapsack, and was trying to read a service for soldiers wounded in battle. And . . . while I watched him I realised what we were fighting for. . . . He was dying in vain, while the Britisher and myself, by our deaths, would probably contribute something toward the cause of civilisation and peace.

Often enough the wounded at the front were helped as they lay by doctors who advanced under fire and treated on the spot those who could not be moved. Many a doctor lost his life in this way, and many a doctor earned undying glory. There are few more splendid records than those of the eager young medicos who put regulations on one side and went where danger was greatest. They were unarmed, for the British Red Cross worker must not carry weapons. They knew that if the Germans came up suddenly and caught them their lot at the

Doctors earn undying glory

OUR WAR MINISTER CHATTING TO AN INDIAN HERO.
Lord Kitchener is seen conversing with Subadar Mir Dast, of the 55th Coke's Rifles, who won the V.C. in Flanders. With the War Secretary is Colonel J. N. Macleod, commandant of the hospital for wounded Indian soldiers at Brighton.

best would be long imprisonment, and at the worst might be torturing death. The Germans largely ignored the regulations of the Geneva Convention, providing for the protection of doctors and Red Cross workers. Doctors left behind in retirements were often enough treated as ordinary prisoners of war, and sent to Germany for long periods of confinement before they were exchanged. Hospitals floating the Red Cross were on innumerable occasions subjected to the heaviest fire. Doctors were shot and stabbed on the field when on their work of mercy. There is too much evidence that often this was not accidentally but purposely done, possibly to wreak individual spite against the hated English. Cases were reported at different times where Germans used the Red Cross as protection when bringing concealed weapons—machine-guns and the like—to the front.

Among the known cases of doctors who won the Victoria

Cross a few may be mentioned. Captain H. S. Ranken was attending to the wounded on the battlefield at Haut-vesnes on September 19th and September 20th, 1914, when he was severely wounded himself, his thigh and leg being shattered. He hastily attended to his wounds, trying to stem the flow of blood, and then turned again to the others struck down around him, treating them until he could do no more. Then, and not till then, he let himself be carried to the rear. The delay and the efforts he had made after receiving his wounds proved fatal. He died shortly afterwards.

Lieutenant A. M. Leake earned the Victoria Cross in 1902 in the South African War. Early in the Great War he was given the further extraordinary honour of a clasp for bravery. In the fighting around Zonnebeke while exposed to constant fire he rescued a large number of wounded who were lying close to the enemy's trenches. Lieutenant Leake's exploit aroused widespread interest. Men recalled his previous doings. He earned his Victoria Cross while tending the wounded under heavy fire from forty Boers at one hundred yards' range at Vlakfontein. He was then shot three times, but refused water to relieve his own thirst until six or eight wounded comrades had some.

Another V.C. hero was Captain F. A. C. Scrimger, of Montreal, one of the Canadian Contingent. Captain Scrimger was in charge of an advanced dressing station outside Ypres on April 22nd, the day when the Germans made their great attack and employed asphyxiating gas for the first time. The dressing station was some old farm buildings. Suddenly these became the target for the German artillery. Shell after shell came crashing around. Captain Scrimger carefully directed the removal of the wounded. One officer was lying severely wounded in a stable. The doctor picked him up and carried him under fire as far as possible. At last it was impossible to go farther, so Captain Scrimger remained by him, exposed to the full fury of the battle, until help could be obtained. Then the captain turned to other cases, and during the anxious days when the Canadians by their grand and stubborn stand held back the Germans north-east of Ypres, he made himself prominent even in that army of heroes by his day and night devotion to his duty among the wounded at the front.

Sometimes the wounded man lay waiting on the field until he recovered consciousness, and then rolled or stumbled or dragged himself to the rear, or until he found someone to help him along. Often enough he was picked up by the ambulance workers, or by one of the army chaplains, men whose heroism won universal admiration. These ambulance men and padres exposed themselves freely. It was their business to carry the wounded back to the regimental aid station, where the waiting doctor gave quick first-aid treatment. This post was possibly in a barn or in a dug-out, and was usually exposed to the enemy's fire. The Red Cross, unfortunately, was in many cases worse than no protection; German gunners, time after time, seemed to seek it out as a target for their shells.

Heroic ambulance men

There was no time at the first-aid post, particularly when a big fight was on, to give more than the most necessary immediate treatment, quick bandaging, and the administration of a restorative, or possibly an opiate. Then the patient was sent on as soon as possible, by motor-ambulance or in any way possible, to the nearest dressing station. The motor-ambulance men in the front line of the armies had a task as dangerous and as exacting as the most adventurous heart could desire. Time after time, more particularly in the early days, it was their lot to clear the wounded out of villages during retreats, when the enemy's advancing guards were almost on them. Many of them showed a daring scarcely possible to exaggerate in taking their cars into the front fighting-lines.

Lieut.-General Sir Henry S. Rawlinson, K.C.B., commanding the Fourth Army Corps.

German trenches on Braunkopf Hill, Alsace, bombarded by the French

The Braunkopf, stormed and taken by the French, June 20th, 1915.

German trenches on the Braunkopf under fire just before the assault.

Victorious French gunners firing German machine-gun from a captured trench.

With a British battery at the front: The tense moment when an order arrives by field telephone from the observation officer.

It was their business first to get the wounded down to the nearest dressing station, and often when the task seemed impossible they accomplished it.

The cold official records of the military decorations bestowed for distinguished conduct tell of many deeds of heroism among the doctors and men of the Royal Army Medical Department. One of the first was Private T. Giles, who was given the Distinguished Conduct Medal for his action on October 26th, 1914, when time after time he carried the wounded over fire-swept ground from the collecting station to the ambulance-waggon.

A few days afterwards Captain James Steward Dunne won a Companionship of the Distinguished Service Order for his gallantry at Messines. He established a dressing station just behind the trenches, and went repeatedly into the trenches to attend to wounded men who could not be moved. Captain Patrick Sampson earned the same decoration for his frequent and conspicuous gallantry while on medical work.

On November 12th two privates in the medical service were given the Distinguished Conduct Medal. One of these, Private N. Freshwater, won it by gallantry in leading a party of stretcher-bearers in daylight under heavy rifle fire over a quarter of a mile to bring back wounded. The other, Private J. Kendrick, was in charge of a small house near the front, with two wounded British soldiers and five very badly wounded Germans under his charge. It was impossible to remove them. Heavy fighting was proceeding all round. The man stood by his charges. He gave all his own rations and his water to the wounded men, and then he went out into the open, in the heart of the fighting, and reached the nearest outpost, under fire, endeavouring to procure some more water for them.

Sergeant A. E. Joseph received the medal for his work around Veldhoek. He went out in the woods night after night where the fighting was heaviest and gathered up the wounded who had fallen there.

The list of December 17th, 1914, contained the names of five members of the medical service who had won the medal by their gallantry in tending the wounded under circumstances of exceptional danger. One of these, Private A. Burns, remained in an evacuated dressing station tending dangerously wounded men under continuous fire for forty-eight hours. The position was subsequently recaptured and the men were saved.

On January 18th, 1915, nine men attached to the medical service were decorated. Of these, Sergeant F. Woodward was in a room at Kemmel attending to the wounded when a shell burst and he was stunned by the concussion. When he recovered consciousness he resumed the care of his patients. Private W. J. **Gallant deeds under fire** Matthews collected the wounded under heavy shell fire until he himself was severely wounded.

In February Captain F. M. Loughnan won the Military Cross for assisting to rescue the wounded while exposed to heavy shell fire. In the following month Lieutenant Eric C. Lang was decorated for his bravery in rushing forward in full view of the enemy, picking up an officer whom he had seen fall badly wounded and bringing him in. Dr. Campbell Greenlees, temporary lieutenant, was

made a Companion of the Distinguished Service Order for his services in attending to the wounded under very heavy fire at Neuve Chapelle. He had twice previously, before this, been brought to notice for similar acts of gallantry. Another doctor, Lieutenant J. G. Priestly, gained the Military Cross at Neuve Chapelle for his continual attendance on the wounded with great gallantry, while he himself was badly wounded.

In the list for March 29th the **In a shelled** name of Lieutenant T. W. Clarke **dressing-station** was given for the Military Cross. He was at Neuve Eglise on March 5th, with the 14th Field Ambulance dressing station, when the station was destroyed by shell fire. One officer and five men were killed, and nineteen wounded. Lieutenant Clarke was among the wounded, having been struck by the first shell, but he continued to attend on the others until he collapsed.

At Neuve Chapelle in March Lieutenant A. C. Hincks earned the Military Cross for his conspicuous gallantry and devotion in collecting wounded while under fire.

WITH THE R.A.M.C. IN THE NEAR EAST.
Stretcher-party carrying wounded from the firing-line in Gallipoli.

One act of Lieutenant Hincks stood out specially. On the night of March 13th and 14th, while he was attending to a wounded man, a shell struck the ambulance-waggon, killing the man and rendering Lieutenant Hincks unconscious. On recovering he at once proceeded to collect the wounded under fire and continued to do so throughout the night.

Dr. J. M. Gillespie, a temporary lieutenant in the Army Medical Corps, won the Military Cross at Ypres on May 24th and 25th by dressing the wounded in the open under fire. On the night of May 25th he heard that there were some British wounded close to the German trenches near Bellegarde Farm. He crept up and searched for them right under the German lines. He had as his colleague Temporary-Lieutenant J. H. McNicholl, who saved the lives of many men by attending to them under heavy rifle and shell fire, and who went with Dr. Gillespie in the perilous journey in the woods. "He has shown the greatest courage in attending to the wounded in action," said the official report.

A writer in "The Times" gave a picture of the work of danger of the men of the convoys when sent to collect the wounded from the first-aid posts:

"GIVE UNTO THY SERVANTS THAT PEACE WHICH THE WORLD CANNOT GIVE."
Wounded soldiers from Gallipoli and their nurses attending a church service in No. 2 General Hospital, Cairo.

WAITING FOR THE HOSPITAL TRAIN.
Mrs. Goodchild, who worked voluntarily as chauffeur, with her own motor-ambulance in Cairo.

OUTSIDE THE RAILWAY STATION AT CAIRO.
Wounded British and Colonial soldiers, after reaching Cairo from the Dardanelles, completed their painful journey to the hospitals in Red Cross motor-cars.

In this convoy work there is a considerable element of danger, particularly when, as sometimes happens in great pressure, the ambulances are sent to collect the wounded at the first-aid posts.

Yet it is the ambition of every man serving at the base to go out with a convoy, and the men who have had the good fortune to go have shown admirable pluck under trying conditions.

Once the first-aid post was an old cottage just behind the trenches. Shells and bullets were falling all around it, and to reach it the convoy has to rush a very dangerous piece of open ground. Under the shelter of the cottage walls they were able to load up the ambulances in comparative safety. As an ambulance left this shelter a shell burst in front of it, but a moment later the car emerged unharmed from a cloud of smoke and dust.

The clearing of the field hospitals is scarcely less dangerous. The convoy is often working along a road which is daily under fire, and the hospitals have to be frequently evacuated while the shells are falling perilously near. . . . The sections have at times to work at night where no lights are allowed, and great care and skill are required to avoid serious accidents. It is much to the credit of the drivers that very few casualties have occurred, although occasion- **Clearing the field hospitals** ally cars have had to be pulled out of ditches or shell holes under fire. At the present moment a section of one of the convoys is stationed in a town which is being continually bombarded, both by shell and aeroplane bomb. The men are billeted in a house without a single window, and only a few days ago a shell fell in the yard of the house and made a hole big enough to bury a horse in. In another town, quite recently, a bomb was dropped in the midst of three ambulances which had been drawn up outside the convoy headquarters. Fortunately the drivers had entered the building to obtain new brassards, but the cars were brought into Boulogne riddled with shrapnel bullets.

At the dressing station the men received more thorough treatment than was possible at the advanced post. The patient had his wound dressed and stitched, and was injected with anti-tetanic serum to prevent lock-jaw, the most dreaded plague of the wounded in the early days. Then he was moved still farther back, where he was given food and drink; and then he was passed on by motor-ambulance to the casualty clearing station.

This station was often enough at a rail-head, or in an old railway station waiting-room. There were Army Nursing Sisters here as well as doctors. The nurses had sought in vain the privilege of going nearer the front. To stand at one of these stations for a few hours, as the writer of this chapter has done, and to see the wounded brought in during the progress of a heavy fight, in almost

THE MERRY HEART THAT "GOES ALL THE DAY."
A happy camera impression of a ward at Lunar Park Hospital, Cairo. In spite of their pain our men displayed the traditional British "grit."

constant procession, was to witness one of the saddest sights of war. The men had their wounds bound up, and possibly had been operated upon already. Many of them were under the influence of morphia, or so worn out by the shock or fatigue of their wounds that they could scarcely open their eyes. In the height of a great engagement some of the busiest of these stations handled as many as a thousand men a day.

The casualty clearing station was supposed to be nothing but a clearing-house from which the patients were rapidly transferred by hospital train or by motor-ambulance to the base or to England. A certain proportion of the cases, however, were always so badly wounded that it was impossible to send them farther, so they had to rest for a time here. The others went on, some to Boulogne, some to Etaples, and many straight on to England. All were most carefully watched by doctors and nurses in the train and in the boats all the way. Frequently a man wounded in Belgium on the morning of one day would on the afternoon of the following day be landed from a hospital

ship at Dover, and from there would be carefully conveyed by special train to one or other of the establishments waiting to receive him all over the country.

Marvels of organisation

Sometimes even this record was beaten. There was one case of a Highlander, wounded during an attack at the front in the early hours of the morning, who was treated on the spot, hurried to the casualty clearing station hospital, taken down to the base, put on board ship, washed, dressed, reclothed in hospital kit, made comfortable, given a good meal, landed in England early in the afternoon, and put to bed in an English hospital, smiling and happy despite his wound, twelve hours after he was struck by the fragment of shell in the trenches.

The work of distributing the wounded in England was centralised and arranged with the utmost exactitude. It demanded and received the greatest care, so that no possible accommodation was allowed to go to waste, and no excess of patients was allowed to be sent to any one point.

In the summer of 1915 the most adequate idea of the scope and character of the Red Cross work could perhaps be best obtained at Boulogne. Most English people who

ANOTHER VIEW OUTSIDE CAIRO RAILWAY STATION.
Some of our men from the Gallipoli cockpit were able to finish their journey to hospital on foot.

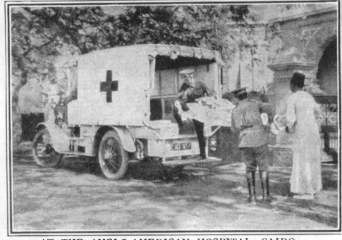

AT THE ANGLO-AMERICAN HOSPITAL, CAIRO.
A critical case from the Dardanelles. The sufferer is being gently lifted from an ambulance at the gates of the Anglo-American Hospital, Cairo, which was reserved for wounded officers.

IN A HOSPITAL KITCHEN.
The above photograph was taken in one of the hospitals in France while dinner was being prepared for the patients.

WOMEN CHAUFFEURS ON RED CROSS SERVICE.
"Les chauffeuses" proved careful as well as expert motorists in France, and released many men for active service in the trenches.

the railway was cleared, partitioned, and in an incredibly short time was in complete working order and full of patients. Armies of nurses and doctors came over— Territorial nurses, Dominion nurses, Red Cross nurses, and nurses attached to private organisations. All day long ambulances rushed through the streets. The most prominent ships in the harbour were the big, white-painted Red Cross steamers for the wounded.

Some of the greatest and most famous surgeons and physicians in England abandoned their practices and settled in the district, under Government orders, going as consultants and as chief operating surgeons from hospital to hospital. Research departments were opened, under the direction of word-famous patholo-
gists, in order that the immense **Our duty in days** material available might not go to **to come** waste.

The real tragedy of the place could perhaps best be felt by the visitor to the great Casino hospital. The vast chambers there held line after line of beds, as close together as they could well be placed. The lofty halls, the gaily painted walls, and the air of luxury, ease, and reckless enjoyment which still clung oddly about the place, seemed strangely out of keeping with the work going on. From the great broad windows the patients gazed out on to the sea, with the shores of England little more than an hour's journey away. The visitor could not fail to be impressed by the signs of good, kindly management everywhere. At the Casino, as in almost every hospital great or small where our wounded went, doctors and nurses did everything that kindness, sympathy, and admiration could devise to make them comfortable, to keep them happy, and make them well. Those who lost their dear ones in the Army hospitals during the war at least have the consolation of knowing that in their last days they had the best their country could give them. Red tape, officialism, and formalism were as largely as possible swept on one side.

Here were lads and men, drawn from every part, companions in common suffering. The lad from Sutherland-shire, never, alas! to raise his head from his pillow again, summoned a sudden smile as the visitor talked to him, not of battlefields, but of his old home on the Highland hills. The young London clerk, three months ago keeping office hours in Lombard Street, gazed ruefully at his bandaged

have travelled on the Continent know Boulogne as it was, with its gay Casino on the sea front, its numerous hotels given up in summer time to pleasure seekers, its picturesque fisher folk, and its delightful surroundings. Boulogne strove with Ostend and Scheveningen in the old days for the right to be regarded as the premier pleasure resort of the north. In the early weeks of the war it seemed as though Boulogne would fall into German hands. When, however, the advancing Franco-British armies reoccupied the line of Flanders to the sea, Boulogne quickly developed as a hospital centre. In the great days of October and November, 1914, when the culminating German attack in the direction of Calais was made and failed, Boulogne was for the moment almost overwhelmed with the numbers of wounded poured into it. Tens of thousands fell along the front. Hospital trains, as full as they **Boulogne Casino as** could be, and motor-ambulances packed **a hospital** with wounded, brought their burdens here, three and four thousand men a day.

Then it was that the medical and Red Cross authorities showed their skill in organisation. The big Casino was taken over, and the halls that had rung with the cries of the croupiers and of the players of petits chevaux now were filled with long lines of beds for the wounded. Hotels, one of them scarce completed and not yet open for visitors, were also taken over. In addition to those in Boulogne itself, numerous other establishments were opened at Wimereux, Tréport, Le Touquet, Abbéville, and other surrounding resorts. One monster warehouse close to

OLD-WORLD FRENCH ABBEY AS ARMY HOSPITAL.
The above beautiful camera-picture was taken in the grand courtyard of the Abbaye de Royaumont, Oise, where many of the wounded were nursed back to health and strength.

SIR JOHN FRENCH'S SISTER AS HOSPITAL NURSE.
Mrs. Harley (sister of the British Commander-in-Chief in France) conversing with wounded French soldiers in the garden of the Abbaye de Royaumont, which was converted into a military hospital under the personal charge of Mrs. Harley and a number of society ladies who gave their services voluntarily. Inset is a view of an operating theatre which suggests a striking contrast to the surgical methods of an older time.

ROYALTY AND THE RED CROSS.
Queen Elena arriving at Florence on a Rome Red Cross "special" to inspect the hospitals for Italian wounded.

arm, and wondered if the doctors were merely trying to comfort him when they told him he would soon be all right again. From the corner, where the screens were drawn around a bed, came sounds of groaning. " The poor fellow is quite unconscious," the doctor murmured. " We have done all we can. It will soon be all over." Here were many who would soon be well—for the great majority of the wounded recover. Some would recover only to go into the world maimed for life. Standing in that great ward, the moans of the dying seemed to mingle with echoes of the old cries of the croupiers that had so often sounded there: " Faites vos jeux, messieurs !— faites vos jeux !" For some here, at least, the game had been played.

It would have been well if all Englishmen and Englishwomen remaining at home could have seen wards such as these. They would then have been enabled to realise, as perhaps never before, the solemn duty of our nation in the years to come to care for those men who gave their best for their country, their health, their limbs, and their full power of providing for themselves.

In times of peace comparatively little is heard of the great voluntary organisations whose business it is to keep the machinery always going for dealing with the wounded when war breaks out. Best known of these is the Red Cross Society, taking its name from the familiar symbol— the reversal of the colours of the Swiss national flag— denoting everywhere throughout the Christian world work for the sick and wounded.

Up to 1905 two organisations, covering to some extent the same field, were in this country—the National Aid Society and the Red Cross Council. The first was founded **Vital need of** by Lord Wantage, himself a gallant **voluntary aid** and famous soldier, who had won his Victoria Cross in the Crimean War, and who knew, from life in the field, the sufferings of the wounded and sick in a campaign, and the need to help them.

Lord Wantage's idea has been the note of the Red Cross work since. It was well expressed in Lady Wantage's " Memoir " of her husband :

What he (Lord Wantage) saw and experienced during that campaign (the Crimean War) impressed itself deeply on his mind ; he realised that, however well organised an Army Medical Service may be, it never has been, and never will be, able to cope adequately with the sudden emergencies of war on a large scale, and he held that voluntary organisations, unimpeded by official restrictions, are alone capable of giving auxiliary relief and of providing extra comforts and luxuries with the requisite promptitude and rapidity. He felt, moreover, that the British people would always insist on taking a personal share in alleviating the sufferings of their soldiers, and that some recognised and authorised channel through which public generosity could flow was a matter of paramount importance.

The National Aid Society did magnificent work in the twenty-five years of its life, raising and spending half a million of money. In 1898 the Central British Red Cross Council was formed by the authorities representing the War Office, the Admiralty, and various voluntary bodies. Experience in the Boer War showed that the dual organisa-

tion was capable of great improvement, and in 1905, on the direct suggestion of Queen Alexandra and of the late King Edward, the two were joined together as the British Red Cross Society, a body wholly voluntary, and in times of peace wholly independent of the War Office and the Admiralty.

This organisation was formally reorganised by our own Government under the Geneva Convention as being responsible for this work. One part of its activities in times of peace was to organise Voluntary Aid Detachments, to train men as stretcher-bearers and as male nurses, and to instruct women in first-aid and in the elements of nursing. It also drew **A famous** up schemes for dealing with contin- **foundation** gencies that might arise. For example, it elaborated a plan, in conjunction with the Territorial organisations, for medical services in case of the invasion of this country.

Working independently of the Red Cross Society was another body, the Order of St. John of Jerusalem, more generally known as the St. John's Ambulance Brigade. This order claims descent from a famous foundation which arose in the earliest days of the twelfth century, with the object of giving shelter and assistance to pilgrims to the Holy Land, who were at that time suffering under the heel of the Turk.

Its task to-day is very different. From its home at St. John's Gate, in Clerkenwell, it organised ambulance brigades which are a familiar feature in most parts of England. It had, in the days before the war, some 30,000 members who had secured their certificates in first-aid, who worked under discipline, and many of whom had been given a certain amount of training each year in War Office

ITALIAN HEIR-APPARENT HELPING THE RED CROSS CAUSE.
The Prince of Piedmont, the only son of the King of Italy, selling postcards in the Quirinal at Rome for the benefit of the Italian Red Cross. He is seen attended by a guard of Boy Scouts.

German officers under special electrical treatment.

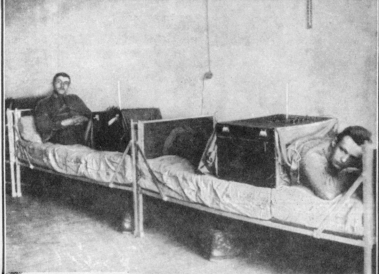

Strange electrical apparatus in use in a German military hospital.

Scene in a German hospital gymnasium.
PRUSSIAN DEVICES FOR RESTORING MUSCULAR STRENGTH TO THE WOUNDED BY MEANS OF ELECTRICITY.

King to the humble private citizen, picked out some of the choicest of their treasures and sent them for the sale.

The King sent a superb wheel-lock sporting rifle, dated 1646. The Queen gave a handsome tortoise-shell fan with eagles' feathers and set with her monogram in diamonds. One peer sent a genuine Strad. A famous millionaire sent a splendid Elizabethan tiger-ware jug. One giver sent the seal of Mary Queen of Scots, another a Highland pistol once used by Prince Charlie. Still another gave five pages of Dickens's original manuscript of the "Pickwick Papers." There were great pictures, rare autographs, splendid prints—in all, a veritable museum. A very large sum was realised. By the latter part of February "The Times" was able to announce that the amount subscribed had passed a million pounds, and by midsummer the total had exceeded a million and a half, a larger sum, it is believed, than was ever raised in public charitable subscription before. The nearest approach to it was the Mansion House Transvaal War Fund, which reached a final total of £1,131,860.

As a result of "The Times" undertaking the collection of the necessary money, the leaders of the Red Cross movement were set free to give their whole attention to the essential work of providing for those stricken in the war. In too many cases the leaders of great charities are mainly absorbed, of

and Admiralty hospitals on the understanding that they should offer themselves should war break out.

At the start of the war the authorities appealed to the St. John's Ambulance Brigade for volunteers. There was an immediate response. The Ambulance volunteers enabled the members of the Royal Army Medical Corps to be released from home work and to go out with the Expeditionary Force. In addition, some six hundred and fifty St. John's Ambulance men were mobilised and sent out with the force. The services of these St. John's Ambulance workers and of other voluntary workers secured by the Order of St. John were of unquestioned value.

It became evident at the beginning of the war that these voluntary bodies would have to expand their activities to a degree undreamed of before, and would further have to raise money on a previously unknown scale. A joint War Committee was formed of the British Red Cross and the Order of St. John, and the task of raising the money was undertaken, at the request of Lord Rothschild, the President of the Joint Committee, by "The Times."

A magnificent donation of £20,000 from Mr. William Waldorf Astor practically started the fund. Public organisations at home and in the Dominions helped liberally, and all manner of schemes for raising the funds were devised. Thus there was a great sale at Christie's, lasting many days, of works of art and of curios. People of every rank, from the necessity, in raising money to do their work, rather than in the work itself. This was avoided here.

The first great task that fell to the Red Cross was the sudden improvisation of a fleet of motor-transports. Old horse-ambulances were still being used. Their slowness, jolting, and inadequacy were responsible for much needless suffering among the wounded. If it were possible, wounded men were taken down from the front in the motor-waggons which had brought up stores. These motor-waggons were almost springless, accentuating every jolt in the road, particularly on the pave roads of Northern France. They were trying enough for hardy and able-bodied men to travel in, but hideous for the wounded.

Money was asked for motor-ambulances. Within three weeks funds were raised to purchase over five hundred.

BRITISH GIFT TO THE FRENCH ARMY.
Mr. Walter Gibbons, chairman of the ambulance committee of the Automobile Association, presented to President Poincaré and the French Army Council thirty-one fully equipped motor-ambulances. Our photo shows the French President inspecting the cars at the Invalides, in Paris. Sir Francis Bertie, British Ambassador, is in the foreground and Mr. Gibbons just behind.

Motor manufacturers went to work day and night, and by the end of January, 1915, over a thousand motor-ambulances and other motor-vehicles were at work. An army of trained drivers had been enlisted to handle them, and over 100,000 patients had been carried in them.

Then the societies established a number of hospitals of their own. In France six were opened immediately around Boulogne, and three in or near Calais. The voluntary hospitals offered by British donors to the French and Belgian Governments were inspected and supervised.

Red Cross hospitals in England The Red Cross established several hospitals in England itself. The largest of these was the King George's Hospital in Stamford Street, London.

This great establishment, the new building of H.M. Stationery Office nearing completion, was taken over by the Red Cross, and its extensive floor space, covering nine acres, was turned into a vast home for the wounded, at a cost of £100,000. It provided 1,650 beds. Its roof-garden, covering an acre and a quarter, soon became a prominent landmark in London. Next to King George's Hospital came another vast Red Cross hospital at Netley.

The British Red Cross had 2,300 Voluntary Aid Detachments, with a membership exceeding 67,000. With the aid of these some six hundred auxiliary hospitals were equipped, and rest stations were formed for attending to

the wounded on the way to hospital. Convalescent homes were established. One department of the Red Cross which constituted a romance—often enough, alas! a very painful romance—was for tracing the wounded and missing. Its agents travelled throughout the battle-stricken regions of Northern France, searching everywhere for news which could relieve the anxiety of those at home.

Another great department of the Red Cross work was the provision of supplies for the hospitals at the front. Immense stores were wanted that could **Tracing wounded and missing** not possibly be had from the Government, from X-ray outfits to tooth-brushes. The societies provided them. Garments and comforts for the wounded were sent out by the hundred thousand, not only to our own armies on the Continent, but to wounded in almost every centre of the war.

It may be asked why it is necessary for voluntary societies to do work such as this. The care of the wounded soldier is the business of the Government. Why not leave it to it? The question was answered by Sir Frederick Treves in a speech which is well worth quoting here:

The answer to the question is a very easy one. There is no Army Medical Service in the world that can be maintained in times of peace on a war standard. It would be ridiculous to have, let us say, five hundred

OUTSIDE THE HOTEL DES INVALIDES, PARIS.
British motor-ambulances, referred to above, lined up outside the Hotel des Invalides for the presidential inspection. It is worth recalling that the famous building shown in this picture was founded by Louis XIV. as an asylum for old soldiers, and placed on a sound footing by Napoleon, whose ornate tomb is under the dome of the Church of St. Louis, on the southern side of the hotel.

WOUNDED SOLDIERS IN BLENHEIM'S PLEASANT SHADE.
The famous Duke of Marlborough's historic seat near Woodstock was placed at the disposal of the Red Cross authorities for the benefit of the wounded. The pleasure gardens are some twelve miles in circumference.

FISHING IN THE LAKE AT BLENHEIM PARK.
Some of the convalescent soldier-guests of the Duke of Marlborough found health-giving recreation in the practice of the Waltonian art from the banks of the lake at Blenheim.

well-trained Army doctors in regular pay where only five are required for service in times of peace. It would be preposterous to lay in an enormous store of perishable material when a war might not take place for twenty or thirty years. It is a problem that every country has had to face.

When war breaks out, and this war came upon us so suddenly, the Army Medical Service has need for immediate help. It must appeal to the civil population and to the civil medical profession. There is no other means of obtaining the immediate need that the Service requires.

For example, the moment war broke the demand came upon us for doctors; send ten doctors, send twenty, send fifty, and they went off in batches as fast as we could supply them. The War Office at the same time was enrolling civilian surgeons. But please remember that the War Office methods must be slow—they must be slow if they are to be efficient. You cannot take in a host of men without going through the elaborate system that the War Office insists upon—inquiry and knowledge of character, qualifications, state of health, past experience, the terms of a commission, and matters of that sort, all of which occupy time.

With regard to civilian surgeons and physicians, the British Red Cross Society is in close touch with them, and we can and did send out as many as twenty surgeons at a few hours' notice.

Wonders of Red Cross methods

The same thing also applies to stores. I need not say that in a great business like the Army Medical Service there must be a certain series of forms to be gone through in order to draw stores—order, economy, and efficiency demand such formalities. We can supply stores without any formalities. Those who wonder what the Red Cross Society has done should see our store at Boulogne. It is an astounding sight. It is packed up to the ceiling with medical stores and the endless articles required for the sick and wounded, ready at any moment, day and night. There is always a staff there, always a motor-lorry outside, and the moment the order comes it can be executed on the spot.

I give you what is the most trivial example that I can think of. When the cold weather set in there was a sudden demand for hot-water bottles for men in stretchers and in the trains coming down to the hospital at the base. As a matter of business to get these hot-water bottles through the War Office would take time—examining samples and prices, entering into contracts, and other processes must take time.

Sir Alfred Keogh got that telegram at, let us say, nine o'clock; it came to us about ten o'clock, before twelve those hot-water bottles were on the way to France. It is a curious illustration of Red Cross methods how we came to have some two hundred hot-water bottles in our possession. In the month of September a lady had the forethought to see that—hot

as the weather was then—hot-water bottles would be needed in the winter, and that the best time to beg them was when it was hot and when people would say: "Don't, for Heaven's sake, talk of hot-water bottles now!" She ultimately accumulated in this way two hundred hot-water bottles, and they were sent to France immediately the demand arose.

I dare say you know the French soldier has a little ampoule of iodine in a glass, which you can break with the fingers and rub the iodine over a wound. Well, our men had not got this item in first-aid, but a gentleman came into my office and said, "Is there anything you want?" I said, "Yes, we want iodine ampoules." He gave me £1,000. I was able to order 133,000 ampoules, which were sent out as soon as they could be completed.

Non-essentials that matter

The War Office provides what is essential. Now, from the point of view of a sick man himself, it is the non-essentials that matter. What is essential is a bare, whitewashed room like a monk's cell, one bed, one chair, and one table. In sickness it is the non-essentials that add so much to a man's comfort. Let us quote some of the most trivial: A bright bed-cover—an important item, because of all things made by the hands of man there is nothing that expresses a deeper sense of melancholy than the brown Army blanket—soft pillows, bed-rests, things to write with, people to write, books to read, and then that great collection of really good things known by the name of medical comforts. Their value I cannot express. Then in the matter of clothing think how—to a sick man—a nice soft night-shirt compares with the night-shirt that bears the stamp, and, I must add, the metallic crease of the Army Service Corps laundry. It is the small matter which often makes all the difference

A PLUCKY FIRST-AID WORKER.

Miss Hutchinson, head chauffeur of the First Aid Nursing Yeomanry, with her motor-kitchen. She did excellent work at Ypres. The plucky little lady, who had given up her respirator to a Canadian, suffered slightly from the German poison gas.

between the comfort of a sick man and his merely enduring his trouble.

The British Red Cross did not stand alone. Allied organisations from the Dominions did their share splendidly. The Australasian societies liberally subscribed to the British funds, and looked well after their own men. The Australasians opened a hospital at Wimereux, staffed and maintained by Australasians, and their contingent was accompanied by an ample and adequate medical and nursing organisation, which aroused great admiration.

In Canada the work of the Red Cross was taken up at the very beginning with immense enthusiasm. When the Canadian Contingent arrived in England, the ships that bore the troops carried, not merely a full medical and nursing staff, but every kind of medical comfort likely to be required.

Overseas Red Cross work

About the same time as the contingent reached Plymouth, Colonel Hodgetts, the Chief Commissioner of the Canadian Red Cross, arrived in London and established himself in an office in Cockspur Street. This office became a centre through which a constant stream of gifts poured into the United Kingdom and into France. Large donations of money were given by the Canadians to the British Red Cross. Many motor-ambulances were purchased. Comforts of all kinds, foodstuffs and supplies, were gathered and distributed with the most lavish hand. These gifts were by no means confined to the Canadian troops. In addition to the large gifts of money, a number of motor-ambulances were presented to the British Red Cross. A coach was provided for a hospital train which Princess Christian was procuring, and a Canadian Ward was built in a hospital which the St. John Ambulance Society was constructing at the front. The Canadian Red Cross came to England to help us, and it did so. It did great and much-needed work. In addition to the establishment at Le Touquet, the Canadian Red Cross made itself responsible for the construction, maintenance and administration of a great hospital at Cliveden, Mr. and Mrs. Waldorf Astor's well known Thames-side estate. Mr. Astor offered the Canadians the use of Taplow Lodge, Cliveden, and the grounds around it, and undertook **The great hospital** sweeping structural alterations and ad- **at Cliveden** ditions to make the place suitable.

Early in 1915 the Duchess of Connaught's Canadian Red Cross Hospital, as the new establishment was called, was opened with one hundred and eight beds. It was complete in every detail. The main building was a transformed tennis-court, which made as cheerful looking hospital as could be devised. Its white walls, and its roof of green painted glass, its floors covered with green linoleum, and its abundant flowers, combined to produce a very pleasant effect. The lofty roof and the fresh country air largely robbed the place of the familiar hospital atmosphere of iodoform and antiseptics. The operating theatre was one that the finest London hospitals might well have

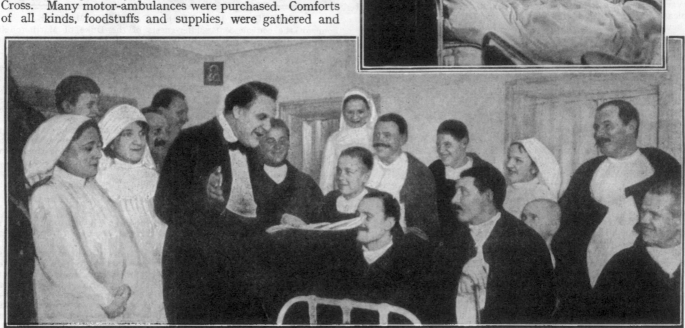

INDUCING THE WOUNDED TO FORGET THEIR PAIN.

The above photograph was taken in the hospital at Moscow, founded by M. Shaliapine, the famous Russian operatic singer, for the benefit of the wounded in the Great War, and shows the great artist in the act of entertaining his appreciative and grateful guests. Inset is a view of the interior of a German hospital where a conjurer was amusing the wounded by tricks with cards.

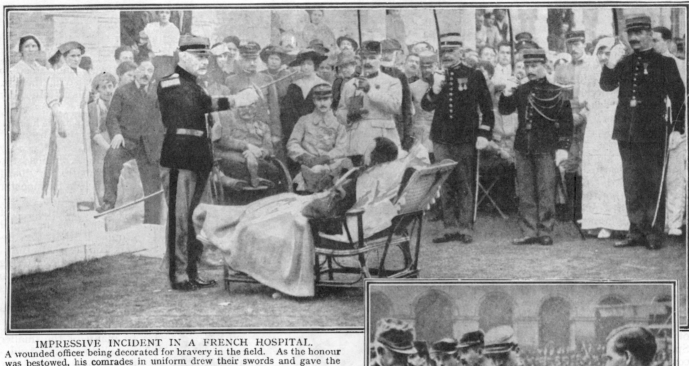

IMPRESSIVE INCIDENT IN A FRENCH HOSPITAL.
A wounded officer being decorated for bravery in the field. As the honour was bestowed, his comrades in uniform drew their swords and gave the military salute.

envied, on account of its size, light, and perfect aseptic conditions. The accommodation was surprisingly excellent when it was remembered that it was created in a short time, out of what had been an adjunct to a big country house.

Cliveden hospital was placed under the charge of Colonel C. R. Gorrell, an Ottawa physician. Colonel Gorrell proved himself a born organiser, one who recognised that successsful hospital administration is largely a matter of attention to detail. The place showed at every turn the results of his minutely careful administration.

Cliveden hospital, although nominally Canadian, and although wholly staffed by Canadian doctors and Canadian nurses and orderlies, received Canadian or British wounded indifferently. Thus, in the first batch of men to arrive there were ninety-nine soldiers of British regiments to one Canadian. When it became evident that more hospital accommodation would be necessary, large wards were built in the grounds of Cliveden, holding a further five hundred patients. The second Canadian hospital was established at Beachborough Park, at Shorncliffe, the home of Sir Arthur and Lady Markham, by the Canadian War Contingents Association.

Splendid gift to Canadians

This association was formed by the Canadian community in England to attend to the comfort of the Dominion troops in Europe. It did a great deal of good work in many directions, and among other things it established and maintained a hospital of its own. The south-east portion of Kent was chosen as the most suitable site, the nearest possible point to the front. Then some members of the Committee searched around for a house. They cast envious eyes on Beachborough Park, the home of Sir Arthur and Lady Markham near Shorncliffe, a fine country house, with beautiful gardens and lawns, and with sloping hills guarding it from the cold winds.

Sir Arthur and Lady Markham, hearing of their search, promptly offered their house as a gift. They had already tendered it to the War Office as a military hospital, but the War Office authorities were doubtful if they would require it. Lady Markham had already taken very prominent work in the medical side of the war, serving in Belgium in the early days, and organising different funds at home. She not only gave the house to the Canadians but gave her personal services. She remained at Beachborough Park—when it became the Canadian Queen's Military Hospital—as working head of its domestic, as apart from its purely medical and surgical side. Sir William Osler, the Regius Professor of Medicine at Oxford, and Mr. Donald Armour, the eminent surgeon of Harley

THE KISS OF HONOUR.
The above photograph was taken in the Court of Honour of the Hotel des Invalides on the occasion of a presentation of medals to wounded heroes by General Cousin. One of the recipients of the Military Medal had to be carried in a bath-chair. Having pinned the coveted decoration on his breast the General saluted him, after French custom, with a kiss.

Street, both of them Canadians, became respectively Physician-in-Chief and Surgeon-in-Chief.

Beachborough Park opened in October, 1914, with close on fifty beds. Its first consignment of patients was over fifty Belgians fresh from the front, with wounds that had received little or nothing beyond first-aid. Some of the men had lain four or five days in the field before being brought in. The staff toiled over them for thirty-six hours, two nights and a day, without rest. When the Canadian troops reached the front, Beachborough Park became, as it continued from then on, a reflection of the great battles in which the Dominion troops took part. The establishment was so successful that after a few months it was determined to enlarge it, and wards were built in the grounds, enlarging the accommodation

Belgians at Beachborough Park

to about one hundred and fifty patients. It would be impossible to detail all the places that were opened in England for the accommodation of the wounded. The Royal Army Medical Department took over numerous old buildings, schools, factories and the like, and in addition built temporary hospitals in parks and gardens on a wholesale scale. It absorbed race-tracks and transformed lunatic asylums; voluntary hospitals all over the country opened their doors to the wounded, the London Hospital alone placing three hundred beds at the disposal of the authorities. A number of private houses and nursing homes, particularly in London, were turned into special hospitals for doctors. Among the best known of these were the hospital at 27, Grosvenor Square, and Queen Alexandra's Hospital for officers at Highgate. Special sections of the community provided hospitals The American community established and maintained a fine hospital at Paignton, Devon, in one of the most beautiful country houses of Southern England.

Special hospitals were established for the Indian troops, the most famous of these being the Lady Hardinge Hospital in Brockenhurst Park. A number of famous houses were turned into hospitals,

Famous houses as hospitals notably Highbury, Mr. Chamberlain's old home outside Birmingham, and the library buildings of Blenheim Palace.

In numbers of suburbs and country places local committees took over and adapted mission-halls and schoolrooms, running them largely with the co-operation of local

voluntary workers, under doctors and trained nurses. Some of the Army medical authorities were understood to look on these smaller hospitals with only partial favour. They believed that the greatest economy was obtained by massing numbers of wounded together in large special buildings. Doubtless this was in some ways true; but the voluntary hospitals in the suburbs of London and in the country gave an atmosphere of friendship **Escaping the hospital atmosphere** and sympathy very hard to maintain in monster institutions.

The advantage of treating men in small groups is that they escape the hospital atmosphere. The scattering of the men helped to bring the war home, as it could be brought home in no other way, to the people of Britain. In many of the smaller establishments regulations about visitors, for example, which had to be strictly interpreted in large establishments could be read more leniently. People of all classes were allowed to go and see the soldiers when they were well enough to be seen, even if they were not friends or relatives. Many people learned from the wounded among them the real import and seriousness of the war, and had their patriotism and determination stimulated and strengthened.

There was another advantage. Returned soldiers, broken in body, found good friends able to help them in days to come. The old dislike and suspicion of the soldier, which undoubtedly existed among certain classes of British people in the days before the war, was utterly broken down.

A STREET SCENE IN BELGRADE.
Stretcher-bearers and ambulance workers carrying a wounded soldier through the streets of the Serbian capital.

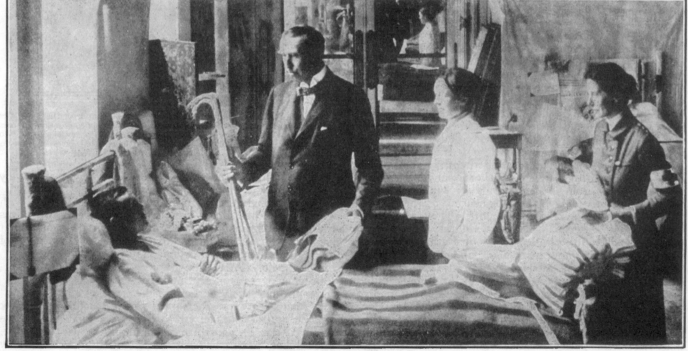

GIFTS TO THE WOUNDED FROM QUEEN MARY.
A special envoy from Queen Mary presenting garments and walking-sticks to British soldiers in Claridge's Hospital, Paris.

THE EAST REPAYING HER DEBT TO WESTERN MEDICAL SCIENCE : STRIKING PHOTOGRAPH OF A WARD IN THE HOSPITAL OF THE JAPANESE RED CROSS MISSION IN PARIS.

The Japanese Red Cross Mission did some wonderful work in the care of the wounded, and its capable staff was most highly spoken of by all the patients.

Wounded Thomas Atkins became, as he ought to be, the hero to his own people, who now had opportunity to show their appreciation of him. A great wave of goodwill to the wounded soldiers swept over the country. People whose interests had rarely before extended outside their own family circle opened their homes to them. They would ask them to tea, take rows of seats in the theatres for them lend their motor-cars or take them in their cars for drives, and tend to their personal comfort.

The claims of the Belgian people made a special appeal to the British nation, and numerous parties of surgeons and nurses went out more or less independently to help the wounded during the early fighting. The best known of these was Dr. Hector Munro, and his experiences may be taken as a notable example of others.

Dr. Munro, at the beginning of the war, abandoned for a time his practice in London and volunteered for service in Belgium. His first experiences showed him the great need of motor-ambulances for the Belgian Army, and returning to London on September 22nd, 1914, he issued an appeal which was to have widespread results.

He stated that he proposed to raise a small ambulance corps, with two surgeons, a staff of twenty helpers, and four cars. " I have just returned from Belgium, where I visited Ostend, Bruges, Ghent, and Antwerp, to inquire as to the need for Red Cross work there. The difficulty is to get the wounded from ten to thirty miles around Ghent into the town. There are admirable hospitals round Ghent. One large hotel has been converted by the Belgian Red Cross into Hôpital Militaire No. 2, and is splendidly manned with surgeons, doctors, and nurses. But it is impossible to get the wounded in there quickly enough. There are about 2,000 Uhlans wandering in the district, and there are occasional small skirmishes, ending in one or two men being killed and a dozen or so wounded. The wounded crawl away into cottages, or lie about in the open fields, where they remain unattended. Last Sunday there were 3,000 wounded to take into the town of Antwerp."

His party was quickly organised. Miss May Sinclair, the

CONVALESCENTS IN KIMONOS.
Convalescent patients at the Japanese Hospital in Paris wore kimonos which were made by the nurses in their spare time.

well-known novelist, acted as his secretary. Lady Dorothie Feilding, daughter of Lord Denbigh, acted as his chief of staff, and a group of men and women volunteers were enlisted. Unlike most doctors, Dr. Munro did not seek for professional nurses, but enlisted the aid of a number of eager women who had received some training in first-aid and were keen to serve.

The ambulance corps was first stationed at Ghent, and after a few days of waiting it quickly found itself in the thick of service. It soon won a high reputation for the daring of its members in penetrating into the firing-line, bringing their light cars up as near to the front as possible, and rescuing men from where danger was greatest. Their conduct during the great battle of the sea-coast in October, 1914, attracted wide notice.

The Belgian Army was at this point holding the line from Nieuport to the sea, and found itself called upon to meet the tremendous attack of an overwhelming German force. The Germans centred their attack upon Dixmude, paving the way by a terrific artillery fire. Time after time they came on to the attack. Time after time the Belgians drove them back. But the fire of the heavy German guns wrought great havoc, and the houses in the town were soon packed with many wounded. Then it became evident that Dixmude could not be much longer held. The Belgian medical authorities declared that it was no use trying to get the wounded away, as cars could not pass through the inferno of fire and hope to return. Dr. Munro and a small group of assistants, including Lady Dorothie Feilding, Miss Chisholm—a girl of eighteen —and a son of the Belgian Prime Minister, determined to make the attempt. They had two motor-ambulances and four light cars. The two ambulances were driven by British chauffeurs, who were going under fire for the first time. The party made straight for the heart of Dixmude.

The venture seemed madness. Mr. Ashmead-Bartlett, the war correspondent, who made one of the party, described the scene :

There was not an inch that was not being swept by shells. There was not a house, as far as I could see, which had escaped destruction. The whole scene was so terrible, so exciting,

PRINCESS HENRY OF PLESS AS A GERMAN NURSE.
Princess Henry of Pless with wounded Germans at a hospital near Berlin. The daughter of Colonel and Mrs. Cornwallis-West, and sister-in-law to the Duke of Westminster, her husband Prince Henry was a Lieut.-Colonel a la suite of Prussian cavalry, and formerly secretary to the German Embassy in London. The princess took a deep interest in Red Cross work.

and passed in such a dream that it has left only a series of pictures in my mind.

Suddenly, behind a low row of houses, we came across a mass of French gathered together for shelter, very excited, but well under the control of their officers. There was a cart, in which they were piling ammunition-boxes. I remember the officer calling : "Pas si vite, pas si vite !" Then someone ran up and said : "Il-y-a les blessés la-bas !" Dr. Munro took the first motor and rushed down a side street to get them. He told me afterwards that he had not gone a hundred yards when there was a deafening crash and a whole chimney fell ten yards away, blocking his passage and forcing him to return. However, he found three other wounded in a house, and piled them in the car, whereupon the chauffeur rushed out of Dixmude and never stopped for four miles. Meanwhile we were left with the two unwieldly motor-ambulances. An officer of Marines explained to De Broqueville that there were many wounded in the Town Hall. To get there we had to turn the cars round. There is nothing more unpleasant than having to turn cars under such circumstances. However, the two chauffeurs never turned a hair, although one of them afterwards confided to me he was scared to death. Every time a shell came crashing amongst the roofs we thought our end had come. So did the Marines, who crowded closer together, as men always do under such circumstances. It was only a short way to the Town Hall, which occupies one side of an open square, which was an inferno in itself. The shells were bursting all over it, and, in addition, it seemed to catch every stray bullet fired by the

Germans at the trenches, only a short distance away. The Hotel de Ville was a sad sight. The top part had been completely riddled with shells, and smashed to bits ; just behind it was what looked to me like a very fine old church, blazing furiously and threatening every minute to set fire to the Town Hall. On the top of the steps of the Hotel de Ville lay a dead Marine, who had been struck by a bullet just as he was apparently running in there for cover. A French surgeon greeted us on the steps, and told De Broqueville he must get his wounded out of the cellar otherwise they would most likely be burnt to death. He was quite calm, and directed our party where to go. Inside the Town Hall was a scene of horror and chaos. It was piled with loaves of bread, bicycles, and dead soldiers. I had never seen so many bicycles I suppose some cyclist troop had left them here on their way to the trenches. We rushed down to the cellars and dragged up the wounded, who were all lying-down cases, and had to be placed on stretchers, which seemed, under the circumstances, to take an endless time. All the while the shells were crashing overhead and the bullets whistling through the square.*

* "The Daily Telegraph," October, 1914.

As Mr. Ashmead-Bartlett well said : "The splendid courage shown by the English ladies is one of the wonders of this war of wonders. It makes one proud to know one belongs to the same race. But those who go and play a man's part on the battle-field share the glory of those who work all night and all day attending to the wounded under conditions which allow of a minimum of repose and comfort. All are heroines of that type which only emergency brings forth."

English heroines
at Dixmude

The story of the work of the Munro Ambulance at Dixmude attracted widespread attention, and much public support, and by December the volunteer corps had thirteen cars. It was engaged all along the line of the Belgian retreat. Eventually it settled down at Furnes, making its headquarters there, and its work extending along the line of thirty miles from Nieuport to Ypres. One of the members of the corps was wounded in the leg at Nieuport, and received the Legion of Honour. Another was poisoned from the fumes of a shell that burst near to him, and was ill for some weeks.

Soup-kitchens were established for feeding starving and exhausted men, and warm woollen underclothes and gloves were supplied for Belgian troops in the trenches. Mr. Ramsay Macdonald, M.P., worked for a time with the party.

Mrs. Knocker, Mrs. Gleason, and Miss Chisholm—three members of the party—established themselves at Pervyse

ARCHDUCHESS ZITA CHATTING WITH AUSTRIAN WOUNDED.
The Archduchess Zita, wife of the heir to the Austrian throne, is seen visiting wounded Austrian soldiers on the roof-garden of one of the hospitals in Vienna. She was accompanied by the Archduke Karl-Stephen, and the archducal party was shown round the hospital by Dr. Spitzy, the chief medical officer.

CROSS AND CRESCENT: TURKISH PRISONERS HAVING THEIR WOUNDS DRESSED BY THEIR BRITISH CAPTORS AFTER A BATTLE IN GALLIPOLI.

This place was right on the line of the German fire. It had been fiercely cannonaded for some time, and most of the village was completely wrecked. The ladies worked in the cellar of a house, where they collected the wounded and sick for first-aid. After some time, yielding to the urgent representations of the Belgian authorities, they left their cellar and moved towards the centre of the village. Ten minutes after they had moved a shell came crashing on to the house in which they had lived unharmed for two months. Mrs. Knocker was a skilled motor-driver, and the story is told that, before going to Belgium, she drove to London and offered her services as a despatch-rider to the War Office. This was promptly declined, on the ground that women motor-cyclists were unsuitable. On her way back to her home at Salisbury, Mrs. Knocker came across three male motor-cyclists carrying Government despatches, who were standing by their broken-down machines, unable to repair them or to get on. Mrs. Knocker executed the repairs and started them off.

King Albert conferred the Order of Leopold upon Lady Dorothie Feilding, Miss Marie Chisholm, Mrs. Knocker, and Mrs. Gleason, an American lady, for their work.

Early in the war it became evident that the French Army medical authorities would be greatly aided by some outside help. In France, where almost every able-bodied man was called to the front, it was not **American helpers in France** possible to draw to the same extent on volunteers from the country itself, as could be done here. Consequently, volunteers were obtained from England and America, and a number of ambulance units got to work. One of the most notable of these was the Anglo-American Volunteer Motor-Ambulance Corps, organised by Mr. Richard Norton and placed under the command of Colonel Barry. It was formally attached to one of the northern divisions of the French Army, and it did services which, in the opinion of the French authorities themselves, it would be difficult to overestimate.

The majority of the workers in this convoy were well-to-do young Americans, who could drive, and who in some cases provided their own cars. They largely maintained themselves. This volunteer corps was representative of the great American philanthropic activity in aiding the sick, feeding the hungry, and checking disease all along the different fronts.

Nowhere was the need of Red Cross work greater than in Serbia. This country, poor and devastated by previous wars, found itself, when it had driven the Austrian armies out of its borders, in a most pitiable state. There were thousands of sick and thousands of wounded waiting attention. Great numbers of Austrian prisoners had been taken, an epidemic of typhus started among them, and among the refugees, **Serbia's pitiable plight** and spread over the country with amazing virulence.

There were no Serbian trained nurses, although a certain number of Serbian ladies had begun to learn the elements of training, and there were few doctors left. Famine threatened the country. The ha'penny roll in some parts fetched a shilling. British doctors who had come to the country to help did their utmost. They were swallowed up in the magnitude of the task before them.

The sick died all over the country, in many cases with none to attend them. Wounded men, carried for days on bullock-waggons from the front—journeys every moment of which must have been exquisite agony—found no doctors to attend to them when they arrived at their stations. The country seemed to reach the very depth of possible misery.

When the cry of Serbia went out to the world, expeditions were quickly organised in Britain. The Serbian Relief Fund made renewed efforts, and was able to initiate and support many activities. Hospital parties were formed. Mrs. St. Clair Stobart, who had already done great work in Belgium and in Northern France, took a large party of doctors and trained nurses to Krajeuvitch. American doctors and philanthropists helped also.

The Red Cross parties that arrived at the front paid heavy toll among their members in deaths from typhus and typhoid as the price of their aid. But the typhus was stamped out and the worst was overcome.

A POIGNANT PICTURE FROM THE FRONT—FRENCH SOLDIERS RENDERING THE LAST HONOURS TO THE FALLEN BRAVE.

In the above deeply moving war tableau, retained for us by the camera from its original scene in the immense plain of the Woevre, a priest is shown blessing the graves of the gallant men who had recently fallen in defence of their beloved country. As the unarmed troops in the foreground were about to place their humble floral tributes on the newly-turned earth, a regiment marching in the rear on its way to the front line presented arms in honour of the dead, whose fate they went forward to face unshrinkingly and with undaunted courage.

144

THE NEW CATHEDRAL AND

CHAPTER LXXII.

THE ROYAL PALACE, BERLIN.

GERMANY DURING THE FIRST YEAR OF THE WAR.

By Frederic William Wile, late Berlin Correspondent of "The Daily Mail," author of "The Men Around the Kaiser," etc.

Revelation of Germany's " Potato-bread Spirit "—The Factors which Enabled the Teutonic Empire to Prove Herself Self-contained and Self-supporting During the First Year of the Great War—Examples of the " Furor Teutonicus "—How the German Government Manufactured " Public Opinion " by Means of a Bridled Press—A Campaign of Lies and a Deluded People —The Formal Systematisation of all Germany's Non-Military Assets—The Socialist Danger—Frantic Finance—The Food Supply and the Doctrine of National Thrift—" I am Proud to Thirst and Hunger for the Fatherland "—" Germany Expects Every Acre to do its Duty "—The Raw Materials for Industry—How Women Helped in the War—General Survey of the Position in July, 1915.

O the world at large, unacquainted through personal knowledge with the mania and genius of the Teuton for organisation, Germany in war time proved to be no inconsiderable revelation. When we have spoken of the enemy's " preparedness," most of us meant his military preparations. Few took into account what Mr. Lloyd George so aptly called " the German potato-bread spirit "—the readiness and ability of the nation at large to adapt itself to war conditions in the most infinitesimal department of its life.

The name is legion of persons in England who confidently expected such economic dislocations in Germany at the outbreak of war, to be followed by early " collapse," that internal domoralisation would prove as valuable a force in bringing the Kaiser to his knees as the allied legions storming at his frontiers. Those who conjured up such a vision had miscalculated. That the Germans proved to be practically self-contained and self-supporting in respect of every vital resource of war—during the first year of Armageddon, at any rate—

KAISERIN AS PHOTOGRAPHER.
The Kaiser and Field-Marshal von Hindenburg photographed by the Kaiserin. The War Lord as seen in this picture bore manifest signs of the strain of war. The proceeds of the sale of the photograph in Germany were devoted to the service of the German Red Cross.

stands out as a fact no less remarkable or significant than their military successes.

The Germans demonstrated that wars are carried on under modern conditions by those " behind the front " as well as by the heroes who bare their breasts to the foe in the firing-line ; that business methods are as essential to victory as military science. " Silver bullets " and bread-tickets are not things over which the war historian is accustomed to wax eloquent, but hard-beset Germany showed that they are as essential to the successful conduct of mighty campaigns as machine-guns and high explosives.

In husbanding and administering the sinews of war which are not strictly military in character, impartial observers must reluctantly admit that much-derided German organisation achieved triumphs unapproached by anything which took place in Great Britain. German mobilisation and administration of internal resources for war-making—such as credit, food supply, and raw materials —will, without question, remain a model of its kind for all time. Certain features of it, modified to suit British temperament and conditions, were adopted in this

Room set apart at Friedberg camp for the accommodation of six officer-prisoners.

Music-room provided for the recreation of officer-prisoners at Friedberg. Inset: The officers' canteen.

Room of a senior prisoner Staff officer at Friedberg, simply but sufficiently furnished.

Mess-room in the officers' quarters of the prisoners-of-war camp at Friedberg, Germany.

HOW OFFICER-PRISONERS FARED AT FRIEDBERG: AS SEEN THROUGH A GERMAN CAMERA.

country. It will not be surprising if others are borrowed as time goes on. Britons were not competing with the Hun in the field of inhumane warfare—though that might have had its uses—but they need not have been ashamed of following closely the developments of the system which enabled Germany, after a year of hideously exhausting world-war, to present at its end almost as invulnerable a front as she did at the beginning.

Germany remained strong and formidable primarily because the whole nation went at war. It was clear that she would not be broken till the spirit of all her 70,000,000 men, women, and children was smashed.

Why Germany remained strong

Lest the impression be created that the writer believes that Germany's success in keeping the wolf from the door at the start denoted her capacity to do so perpetually, let it be said at once that no notion could be more fatuous. Signs of the approach of collapse existed in plenty. The financial situation became particularly foreboding. No amount of scientific organisation could obliterate or banish obvious indications. It was both foolish and idle to predict when that prostration, the shadow of which could be dimly seen, would be felt. The only safe prophecy was that the break-up was likely to be gradual rather than precipitate, though the final stages might be rapid. Enough occurred, in any circumstances, to cause the Allies to dismiss from their minds any encouragement they might once have derived from the hope of a Germany either divided against herself or unable to conduct war behind an almost hermetical blockade by both land and sea.

Such considerations were the monopoly of hide-the-truth and sham-victory patriots. Face-the-facts men and women would have none of them. They belonged to the " Russian steam-roller " aggregation of yearnings unfulfilled. After the Allies had blasted their way to the German frontiers, and killed off twice the 2,000,000 odd fighting men already put out of action, the time would have come to visualise " Germany's collapse " as a thing of imminent probability. At the time of writing, it was little more substantial than a cheering mirage. Victory had to be built on more solid foundations.

The great masses of the German people, who were no more initiated into the secrets of their diabolical war party than were the peoples of foreign countries, were as effectually stunned by the suddenness and wantonness of the war as those against whom the "Furor Teutonicus" was about to be launched. Certainly, as I recall July in Berlin in 1914, I think back upon a Germany filled with uncertainty and anxiety as to what the thunder-clouds in Eastern Europe, which gathered after the assassination of the Austrian Archduke at Serajevo, might precipitate.

Germany was so universally immersed in her peaceful pursuits and midsummer pleasures that the man in the street, at least, scouted war as something almost too absurd for serious contemplation. Germany was happy, prosperous, he soliloquised. " The world knew her strength ; who would dare attack her ? " he asked himself.

We know now that the pacific Germany of July became the war-thirsty, England-hating Germany of August ; that a war party which a few weeks before numbered an infinitesimal, but noisy and all-dominating, minority of perhaps 1,000,000 Germans, soon developed into a war party which engulfed the Fatherland from the Baltic to the Vosges. But it was a deluded Germany, a cruelly-deceived and befooled Germany, which had now come to be. It was made mad for war by a lying presentation of facts and hypnotised into misconceptions which even time has not swept away. Out of them grew the barbaric hate of England, which was not only the most amazing aspect of the war's commencement, but has remained its most portentous phenomenon.

Befooled but mad for war

Myself a victim of Prussian war-lust gone mad, within half an hour of the declaration of hostilities between Britain and Germany on the night of August 4th— when I was dragged from my lodgings by three sabre-brandishing policemen on a grotesque charge of espionage— I had no idea that the simultaneous assault on the British Embassy building was anything more than a passing manifestation of fury. I had long been a believer in " the phlegmatic German." I knew that his country was the home of the most shocking crimes in modern history ; that the murder instinct was almost a cult. But I did not hold the nation capable of mass-hatred, blind, unreasoning and ferocious, even against the England whom it had always envied and feared.

The war, however, was not many weeks old when Germany adopted a new National Anthem—the "Hymn of Hate" against England. It was the ballad of vengeance

HIS EXCELLENCY JAMES WATSON GERARD.
United States Ambassador at Berlin.

and malice which the descendants of Goethe and Wagner presently elevated to the level of Holy Writ.

This mediæval chant of malevolence unalloyed was the composition of a minor German poet named Ernst Lissauer. A private in the ranks of the Prussian Army, it gave him both national and international fame, and it was not long before the Iron Cross was bestowed upon him for his classic enrichment of Culture's literature. The English translation, a very vivid piece of verse, is stronger, if possible, than the German original. It is the work of an American woman, Barbara Henderson, who contributed it to the columns of the "New York Times." It was my privilege to make the first publication of the poem in England in "The Daily Mail." It was given in pages 307-308 of the second volume of THE GREAT WAR.

Lissauer's vitriolic ballad spread throughout the length and breadth of the German land like wildfire. No mendacious leading article in the newspapers, though there had been no lack of effort in that direction, had so satisfactorily interpreted German popular hatred of England. It was sung and recited, day and night, in hundreds of cafés, cabarets, music-halls, and theatres, and was even introduced as a feature of the entertainment at private social functions. Delivered before huge audiences in the glittering all-night coffee-houses or beer-halls of Berlin, Hamburg, and Munich, the "Hassgesang gegen England" aroused demoniacal outbursts of mingled fury and enthusiasm. People clenched their fists, shook them aggressively in space, hissed, stamped,

NEW GERMAN MAN-KILLING DEVICE.
Examples of the "revolver-cannon" captured from the Germans by the French. The barrels were rotated by means of a handle as seen on the near gun, to the left of the photograph.

and applauded when the singer or recitationist would rasp out, with all the scorn and ferocity of which human expression is capable the final "England!" with which each stanza closes.

For many weeks "Deutschland, Deutschland über Alles," the battle-hymn of the Fatherland, sank to the level of a second-rate ditty. The "Hassgesang" was the only sentiment deemed thoroughly symbolic of German love of country.

While Lissauer's hate hymn was at the zenith of its glory, some genius whose name, unfortunately, will be lost to posterity, **"Gott strafe England!"** invented "Gott strafe England!" (God punish England!) as the most patriotic form of greeting which one German could exchange with another. Friends meeting in the suburban trains or trams on their way to business no longer exclaimed "Guten Morgen!" They shook hands solemnly and sighed: "Gott strafe England!" When they parted at night, it was not "Guten Abend!" but "Gott strafe England!" Then they began stamping it—with a rubber stamp which was sold by the thousand for that purpose—on their letters to correspondents at home and abroad.

Postcards by the million blossomed forth, with the national motto, "Gott strafe England!" Scarf-pins for men made their appearance in the windows of cheap-jewellery shops, inscribed "Gott strafe England!" The legend was reproduced in a score of different designs on cuff-links, brooches, and even wedding-rings, while hardly a schoolchild was without a badge or button emblazoned with the Fatherland's new prayer. Handkerchiefs were embroidered with it, pocket-knives had it enamelled on their handles, and many a packet to some loved one in the trenches went forth with a pair of black-white-red (the Imperial colours) braces imprinted: "Gott strafe England!" On a medal, which decorated thousands of German breasts, was engraved: "Give us this day our daily bread; England would take it from us; God punish her!" Crown Prince Rupprecht of Bavaria placed the Royal approval on the sentiment in the notorious battle-order to his army, to "annihilate the British arch-foe in front of us" at any and all cost. **Prince Rupprecht's notorious order**

Germany's hate of England was due, of course, to the complete frustration of her plans for a short, sharp, and decisive war by the intervention of the British

"SHOOTING STARS."
German officer making a demonstration with a special pistol used for firing luminous balls.

Army and Navy. The masses furthermore were led to believe that the whole war was "instigated" by England for the purpose of crushing the dangerous and despised German commercial rival. Wholesome respect for the British Fleet had always existed in the Teutonic breast, even in Von Tirpitz's, but there was never anything but withering scorn for the "contemptible little British Army." When it was realised, as it was before the war was six weeks' old, that Britannia had thrown into the balance of Armageddon both by land and sea a weight so ponderous as to imply for Germany the whole difference between victory and defeat, the Fatherland's long pent-up animosity to England burst forth in a rage which was to know no quenching. The country's fury had an earlier cause than the realisation of German impotence against an alliance which included Great Britain. There was fury with the German Imperial Government for deceiving the nation into a belief that Britain either could not or would not take part in a Continental war.

Government newspaper organs throughout the month of July, when Germany was crouching for the attack so stealthily that no responsible statesman or journal in Britain could be made to seriously believe in the imminence of her assault, had been magnifying

Germany's attempted "bargain" the danger of "civil war" in Ireland and "grave domestic strife" in England due to Suffragette activities. Prince Lichnowsky, German Ambassador in London, was reporting to the Berlin Foreign Office—truly enough—that there was a vigorous anti-war party in Mr. Asquith's Cabinet. When the fateful August 4th came, up to which hour the German people had been kept in profound ignorance of their Government's base attempt to bargain for Britain's non-participation, their disappointment was both natural and violent.

It was to such emotions at first, at any rate, that they gave

and delayed the German General Staff's carefully-laid plans—how fatally, impending events on the Marne were soon to prove—but the 60,000,000 or 62,000,000 million Germans who were not already in uniform had work to do no less vital to the success of the campaign than the fighting men.

The story of how civilian Germany was mobilised and organised for war is the story of the Fatherland's life and times during the first year of the war. It lacks the glamour and the glory of the battlefield, but the field-marshals of German finance, shipping, commerce, science.

THE WAGES OF THE WOUNDED.
Wounded German soldiers drawing their paper money at the army pay-office in Berlin.

trade, industry and agriculture will claim, when the history of the Kaiser's great adventure is written, a place no less immortal than his Hindenburgs and Mackensens.

The Hun legions had no sooner violated Belgian territory and invaded France than the organisation of the purely civilian and domestic departments of the German war scheme was begun. Indeed, it was begun, in the sense of having been broadly thought out, long before William II.'s thunderbolts were actually launched. In one or two important respects—finance, for instance —"mobilisation" had preceded the war itself by many months;

THE POLYGLOT PRUSSIAN.
At numerous foreign language schools in Berlin taken over by the Government thousands of German soldiers received instruction. Our photograph shows a typical military class studying Russian.

vent—hatred of "the treacherous cousin." Some day even the Germans will know the truth, and many of them, no doubt, will be ashamed of the satanic depths to which they sank during the war in the exuberance of their Anglophobism.

Their early malevolence spent, Germans pulled themselves together for war pure and simple. The mobilisation of the Kaiser's long-prepared and perfectly-equipped military machine had proceeded with that faultlessness which two generations of making ready insured. Belgium was invaded—resisting, it was true, but crumbling steadily before cruelly superior force. Her resistance disarranged

for one of the most brazen advance preparations of Germany for this war, com-**Forging the** pleted for all the world to see, which it did **Teuton thunderbolts** not measure in its full dread meaning, was the "finance mobilisation" of the German Imperial Bank. Another preparation for Armageddon, so blatant and palpable as to make men wonder now how any sane politician anywhere in the world could have been taken unawares by Germany's war when it did come, was the 1913 Army Bill. This provided for strengthening the military establishment at a cost of £50,000,000, raising the "peace footing" of the Army to 900,000 officers and men, and

s

increasing the permanent " war chest " from £6,000,000 to £18,000,000. The German Government proclaimed that all these measures were " steps to insure the preservation of peace." One's mind might fairly have reeled, in presence of them, at what Germany would call steps of preparation for war.

The formal mobilisation of all her non-military assets did not set in, however, till after the Kaiser's troops were pounding at Liège and plunging toward the Marne. No asset, material or moral, was left out of account. All were doomed to " organisation." For the purpose of dealing with them in detail, it will be well to tabulate

THE INGENUITY OF THE HUN.
Railway truck converted into a running telephone exchange. The picture was taken in Russian Poland.

them, more or less in the chronological sequence in which each subject was dealt with :

1. Public opinion.
2. The Socialist danger.
3. Finance.
4. Food supply and thrift.
5. Raw materials for industry.

Life in Germany during the first year of the war revolved, broadly speaking, round the efforts of the Government to regulate these cardinal things. That Germany in the second year of war was still a terrible
"Public opinion" foe in being was due to the extraordinary
in Germany success with which Government and people had co-operated in the task which had been officially described as the nation's noblest and gravest duty—to " hold out."

In the Anglo-Saxon or French sense, there is no such thing as " public opinion " in Germany. The Germans are a ruled, not a ruling race. Dr. Theodore Barth, a distinguished German Liberal politician, used to describe " representative Government " in his country—exemplified

by the Reichstag " debating society " and the so-called Prussian " Parliament "—as " a lie." Practically voiceless in peace, it was a moral certainty that German public opinion on the eve of a Government-willed war and during war would be completely mute.

Certainly, during ten days, between July 25th and August 4th, 1914, when Germany and Britain were parleying over questions which meant peace or war in Europe, or at least Anglo-German peace or war, the Kaiser's people were kept utterly in the dark. Not until three o'clock on the afternoon of August 4th, when the 　**Fanning the** German Chancellor confessed in the 　**flames of hate** Reichstag that, because " necessity knows no law," German troops were at that moment already violating Belgian territory, had the Fatherland even the remotest inkling of the tremendous forces which German aggression had set in irrevocable motion. German public opinion, as far as it was reflected by its Press, had thus been effectually muzzled and gagged in the earliest hours of the war. The deception of the country continued from that moment. It was to grow, indeed, in respect of thoroughness and ruthlessness as the war proceeded. At first there was only suppression of unpalatable facts, both political and military. The White Paper issued by the German Government on August 3rd confined itself to that insidious form of untruth which consists of omission. Under military and police censorship the newspapers were also required to commit falsehood by omission. Then positive untruth followed—wholesale, continuous, and under direct Government control and " inspiration."

Thus were the first flames of German hatred fanned with stories of wells in Alsace-Lorraine poisoned by French military surgeons. Thus was the populace stirred into murderous fury by fantastic stories of " swarms of spies," with consequent attacks—in nearly every case without a glimmer of reason—on hapless British, French, and Russian subjects still " guests " on German soil. Thus was frenzied patriotism engendered on the eve of the declaration of war by tales about the " unlawful invasion " of Germany by French aeroplanes and the " treacherous crossing of our eastern frontier by Russian patrols." This at the behest of a Government which had kept its people and the world in sublime ignorance of its own criminal stroke against Belgium !

Public opinion in Germany was not misled and muzzled in simple consequence of the necessities of a war censorship. People in Britain have themselves had experience of the censorship, and from the glass-house they have inhabited during the war are in no position to throw stones at the German enemy. But in respect of systematic, organised feeding of the country with lies about conditions at home and abroad, nothing, happily, occurred in Britain during the first year of the war to compare, even feebly, with the mendacity of which the befooled German people were the victims.

On occasions innumerable the British censorship was ludicrously stupid. It treated this nation of grown-ups like babes in arms. It compelled the country, for the most part, to wage war in the dark, but it did not make of deception a positive virtue, or deliberately stuff untruth, day in and day out, down the Empire's throat.

The German General Staff expected to win the war without mobilising the Fatherland's liars. It planned as we know, to capture Paris in " a few weeks," to turn about and crush Russia before the Tsar's armies were in battle motion, and then to deal with Britain. Liège and other events having supervened, explanations became urgently necessary if that priceless asset, public confidence, was not to be forfeited, so the liar brigades were called up for active service. They took the field gleefully in mass formations. Presently every printing-press in the Fatherland proceeded to belch forth what turned out to be an inexhaustible supply of malevolent and prevaricatory ammunition. The abrupt stoppage of the onrush to Paris

British prisoners at work under guard recovering waste land for agricultural purposes.

At the provision waggon. Distribution of food to British prisoners of war in Germany.

The first stage. A convoy of British soldiers taken captive by Germans during the fighting in Flanders. In circle: Industrial spade-work.

CAMERA-PICTURES OF THE EVERYDAY LIFE OF BRITISH PRISONERS OF WAR IN GERMANY.

was " explained." The Crown Prince and Von Kluck had executed nothing but a tactical and strategic " withdrawal " from the lines they had once occupied almost within sight of the coveted prize. Cholera, too (so the German troops were told) was raging in Paris, and German commanders could not reconcile their " duty " to their men with pushing forward the self-checked, " irresistible advance." Operations in Belgium " were taking a normal course." The General Staff's plans had experienced " local disarrangement," but the main objective was being achieved " entirely on the projected lines."

The liar legion now turned its attention to the atrocities with which the German army in Belgium was horrifying the civilised world. To begin with (averred the legion) there had been " no atrocities." They were the figments of Belgium's disordered imagination and the inventions of Germany's enemies. A University of Berlin professor disposed of the atrocities question to the complete satisfaction of all Germans by " diagnosing " them in his laboratory of psychology in Unter den Linden as " mass hypnotism," induced in the Belgian national mind by the natural and

GERMAN SOLDIERS BEING INOCULATED AGAINST THE CHOLERA SCOURGE.
The successful use of inoculation against infectious disease was one of the many remarkable scientific phenomena of the Great War. Probably the mortality due to cholera among the Austrian troops made the Germans specially active in taking all possible precautionary measures against this terrible scourge.

inevitable terrors of invasion. The Belgian men, women, and children who had supplied gruesome details of " atrocities " had been " hypnotised " into liars. The only " atrocities " which had really occurred were those inflicted by the cruel and brutal Belgians themselves upon Germany's heroic soldiery, at whom, in the guise of guerrilla warrior-defenders of their territory and liberty, the invaded populace had had the effrontery to " snipe."

It was the Belgians, not the Kaiser's culture-bearing hordes, who hacked off hands, ears, and **The Kaiser and** feet, gouged out eyes, burnt, pillaged, and **" poor Belgium "** raped. If German soldiers had resorted to excesses, they had only " retaliated," and done so " with a heavy heart." Civilian Belgians had suffered only " self-inflicted " indignities and hardships (explained the erudite Berlin professor of psychology). They had no right, morally or legally, to deny the invader the hospitality of their country. The destruction of Louvain and Aerschot was an act of poetic retribution, not vandalism. And the Kaiser's heart "bled for poor Belgium."

This, and more, Germany was told, and this Germany

implicitly, blindly believed. The result was the production of a state of national callousness in the country, which will remain for ever a blot on the German name. It engendered a stereotyped condition of mind toward " frightfulness," as a legitimate method of warfare, that was destined to make the average German look upon submarine murder (like the Lusitania **Lies about the** massacre) and asphyxiating gas not **Grand Fleet** only with utter indifference, but as weapons put in the Fatherland's hand by Providence itself for the overthrow of Germany's unholy foes.

Lies of every conceivable sort about Germany's enemies henceforth became the Government's favourite means of regulating public opinion about the war. England became the special target of the German Official Press Bureau's campaign. The truth about every solitary incident associated with the British name was systematically distorted. The British Fleet's first important naval loss—the sinking of the Aboukir, Cressy, and Hogue by submarine U9—was described as having " set every knee in Britain quaking." London was depicted as " panic-stricken," and Sir John Jellicoe's armada was said to be " skulking in craven fear in impregnably - fortified harbours," while the officers and men aboard them were trembling neurotics.

That was to prove the keynote of German comment on the British Navy throughout the war. As submarine warfare grew and was eventually succeeded by acknowledged piracy, lies about the Grand Fleet increased in magnitude and ingenuity. Sublimely oblivious of the fact that Von Tirpitz's " High Sea Fleet " had degenerated, thanks to wholesome respect for Jellicoe, into a " High Canal Fleet," the Press of Germany was instructed to delude the people into believing that the Kaiser's ships had effectually " bottled up " Britain's Navy. The Germans were only waiting outside Britain's mined waters for " a chance " to smash the cowardly foe. The Germans continued to believe this myth, because they were not permitted to know the truth.

Sir John French's army was now making its presence increasingly felt. That " contemptible little " force had not been captured on the Marne ; not only that, but it was proving an ineradicable thorn in the German side in Flanders during the German's frenzied attacks round Ypres and the Yser Canal in the October fighting. The Official German Lie Bureau thereupon gave the cue for misleading the country about the British Army. It was an aggregation of " incompetent mercenaries," who had been given long legs, as the comic Press proceeded to illustrate, merely for the purpose of " running away " from German heroes. German troops disliked meeting British troops, because the latter were " cowards " and did not test the real mettle of the Kaiser's soldiers. The British were waging the war as a " sport." They did not take it seriously like the Germans. They were not a " worthy antagonist." They surrendered on the slightest provocation. These particular lies were destined to be short-lived. As more and more Germans came in contact with the " island mercenaries," cold steel and deadly aim from British rifles enforced a respect which increased by leaps and bounds as the war went on. After a while

From a painting by John S. Sargent, R.A.

General Sir Ian Hamilton, commanding the Expeditionary Forces in the Dardanelles.

French engineers convoying war horses across a river in Northern France.

The handsome creatures, having enjoyed their dip, gallop along the opposite bank.

A sporting chance : British soldiers "making a dash for it" across an opening in a long sand=bagged communication trench in France.

156
P.

nobody in Germany considered Sir John French's "little army" contemptible.

Lies about British recruiting followed the tarradiddles about British cowardice in the field. Although Germans knew perfectly well that heroic and extraordinary measures to raise an army were unavoidable in a democratic, non-military nation, they proceeded, for their own purposes, to distort and exaggerate the measures to which Lord Kitchener resorted. They pictured England as sordid, indifferent, unpatriotic, and decadent ; predicted ignominious failure for the recruiting scheme ; told absurd falsehoods about "the heavy cash inducements" necessary to coax Britons to come to their country's defence ; described Ireland as in a state of open revolt against recruiting propaganda, and said Germany need give herself no anxiety over "the imaginary millions" which Kitchener would never raise except "on paper."

Fables about the conditions in British oversea Dominions were also widely diffused. India was "on the verge of revolution"; Egypt was in a condition of "internal unrest which would tie up a huge British army in that region" for the duration of the war ; South Africa would follow the gallant lead of De Wet and throw off the conqueror's yoke ; Australia, Canada, and New Zealand, preoccupied in material self-development, had only indifferent interest in the Motherland's fate. The "handful" of "amateur soldiers" they might eventually send to Europe would only be so many more easy victims for the invincible German military Juggernaut. England had already organised "a menagerie of all the wild races of the earth" against cultured Germany. A few thousand Indians, "Australian kangaroos," New Zealand bushmen, South African rangers, and Canadian plainsmen, more, or less, need cause Germans no concern.

Lies about British economic conditions also became merrily common in Germany. London ceased, very early in the war, to be "the metropolis of the financial universe." The sovereign of England had been compelled to yield pride of place to the German mark as the world's chief medium of exchange. British industry, no matter who won the war, was lamed for ever. The 1915 War Loan, following its "failed" predecessor of 1914, had only been "pulled through" by offering the public "unprecedentedly attractive" terms. Mr. McKenna's scheme was "beneath the dignity of a Finance Minister." It was characterised by methods "with which we are familiar only in the case of bankrupt companies which it is desired to reorganise or liquidate." Mr. Lloyd George's plans to organise the industrial forces of Britain were belittled as "Utopian and doomed to fiasco." On such predigested baby-food were the German people brought up after August 4th, 1914.

Spoon-feeding the German people

The Government-controlled Press policy in Germany throughout had one great, general, definite purpose : To explain away the failure to end the war by the scheduled time and to buoy up national hope with the idea that "victory," though deferred, was "certain." Every pretext which could conceivably serve this end was gleefully seized upon. Germans were made to think that the "truth"

was visible only in their own Press, that everything published in enemy countries was false. Some day the scales will fall from eyes which suffered from the grossest case of official astigmatism in all history.

At the last general elections in Germany the Social Democratic party polled 4,250,000 votes, which was far and away the largest number recorded by any political organisation in the Fatherland's history. It represented about one-third of the entire voting strength of the Empire, and resulted in the election to the Imperial Parliament (Reichstag) of 111 deputies out of a Chamber of 397 members. Although the German governmental system withheld from Parliament any real power except the ability to block votes for supply—and whenever that happened the Kaiser-created "Government" dissolved Parliament and repeated the process until a pliable assembly was secured—the world in general, doubtless, expected that the Social Democrats would, when the emergency arose, act as a strong deterrent to war. They were the one avowing party of peace and pacifism in Germany. They

Attitude of the Social Democrats

WHERE THE GERMANS BURROWED UNDER THE SWISS FRONTIER.
A stoutly-constructed German trench which, according to the Germans themselves, was carried underground into Swiss territory. The flag bearing the Geneva Cross and the formidable wire entanglements marked the Swiss frontier. The trench terminated in a subterranean burrow, and this, for storage or mining or other reason, extended for more than one hundred yards beyond and beneath the neutral border-line.

had repeatedly opposed army and navy legislation, and were persistent and consistent antagonists of militarism and all its works. Their one promise to the Government and the nation to shoulder arms was conditional upon a war of defence pure and simple. Herr Bebel, the adored autocrat of German Socialism, publicly declared more than once that if the Fatherland's territory were ever invaded by the foe, he and all his comrades would unhesitatingly do their duty as Germans and patriots. What they would do in the case of a war of aggression, deliberately provoked by Germany, they also left in no doubt. They made it plainly understood that patriotism of that sort had no claim on their loyalty, and that a general strike, paralysing Militarism's power to make war, would almost certainly be declared.

Having sedulously induced the country to believe that the storm-clouds which followed Serajevo were about to break in upon an innocent and pacific Germany, it was manifest that the German Government would delude the powerful Social Democratic party by similarly specious

PRINCE HENRY OF PRUSSIA LEAVING FOR THE
FRONT.
Prince Henry, of "mailed fist" memory, had a tremendous send-off
when he motored through the German capital on his way to the front.
He is seen driving his car, while his chauffeur had charge of a favourite dog.

GERMANY'S ARMED AMBULANCE MEN.
Squad of German Red Cross men leaving Berlin. The rifles they carried
offered a somewhat startling if typical contrast to the brassards on their
arms. Berliners bestowed on them flowers and other farewell gifts.

The parliamentary group, in solemn council assembled,
voted by practically unanimous ballot to rally round the
flag with the rest of the nation. Herr Haase, Bebel's
nominal successor, stood up in his place in the House
on the fateful afternoon of August 4th and, amid platitu-
dinous and apologetic protestations of Social Democracy's
"constitutional abhorrence" of war, militarism, and aggression, pledged his party's 111 votes to the measures for which
the Kaiser's Government needed parliamentary sanction.
Ten minutes later Haase's cohorts were
on their feet cheering with the rest of a **"United Germany"**
war-mad Reichstag the Chancellor's **in the field**
sentiment, shrieked in tones of defiant
passion, that a united Germany, "Ja das ganze Volk"
(yea, the entire people), was now in the field. Dr. Frank,
a brilliant young Baden lawyer, widely looked upon as
the future Socialist chieftain, enlisted as a volunteer in
the Army, and fell in the earliest weeks of the war.

Throughout the autumn and winter of 1914 German
Social Democrats remained nominally loyal to the war.
The "Vorwärts" and other party organs gave intermittent
indications of shamefacedness at the completeness with
which the "Red" doctrinaires had in one brief afternoon
belied half a century of principles, but nothing savouring
of real recantation was apparent. The military censorship,
which had an iron grip of the Press, watched Socialist
journals with special vigilance; but apart from minor
transgressions like veiled hints at "food price usury,"
brutality to soldiers in the trenches, and suggestions that
eventual terms of peace ought not to include annexation
of conquered territory, Socialist papers were well behaved.
They were confiscated and suppressed on, perhaps, half
a dozen occasions, but for altogether innocuous offences like

persuasion. On August 1st, 2nd, 3rd, 1914, the Imperial
Chancellor was absorbed in delicate negotiations with the
leaders of the various Reichstag parties anticipatory of
the famous war-session of the House on August 4th. It
was of the utmost political importance for Germany's
purposes that a picture of unalloyed harmony should be
presented to the world. The Socialist
Reichstag's famous leaders demanded, in accordance with
war-session their party tenets, evidence that the
hostilities for which the Government re-
quired £265,000,000 of emergency war credits and £75,000,000
of loans authorised were of a "defensive" character.

The "proofs" were furnished. The "sword had been
forced into the Emperor's hand" by Russia and France.
Germany found herself in "a state of necessity which knows
no law." The Fatherland was in imminent "peril."
Invasion was at its door—all its doors. Socialism wilted.

158

those just mentioned. Of a return to first principles in respect of war as an abhorrent and unrighteous thing, German Social Democracy gave no sign. Meantime, millions of Socialist artisans were in the field, and tens of thousands of them bleeding for the Kaiser.

In the spring of 1915 the first semblance of a rift in the lute manifested itself. The same Herr Haase, who had proclaimed his party's sup-

A rift in the lute port of the initial war credits in August, 1914, proclaimed himself a bitter opponent of further credits. Of the same opinion were two other Socialist leaders, Herr Bernstein and Herr Kautsky. It came to light that roundly 25 per cent. of their fellow-members of the parliamentary group shared their views; that the resolution to vote the third war credit of £500,000,000 on March 20th was only approved by a vote of 77 to 23; that a proposal to vote £250,000,000 instead of £500,000,000 was defeated by only 64 to 34. A schism, unmistakable though not of direct and immediate moment, was evidently at hand.

In a speech at Frankfort - on - the - Main, on April 28th, Herr Haase made statements which indicated plainly that the Social Democratic party, or a large section of it, now realised it had been shamefully duped by the German Government, and even cheated in respect of certain promises

GUNNERY EXERCISE.

GERMAN TRAINING "SHIP" SET UP IN THE MIDDLE OF A FIELD.

made in return for the party's war-credit support. "We desire no general strike," said Haase. "Everyone should do his duty as a citizen, but that does not impose the obligation to vote unlimited war credits. That would be equivalent to declaring the bankruptcy of all the principles for which we have hitherto stood."

On June 19th Herren Haase, Bernstein, and Kautsky published in the Leipzig party paper a manifesto entitled, "The Need of the Hour," fulminating against further support of war credits by the Socialist

WITH THE GERMAN "WARSPITE" LADS IN TRAINING—AT RIFLE PRACTICE.

In view of the difficulties presented by the British Fleet, the training of Germany's future sailors was carried out on land, somewhere in the vicinity of Kiel or Cuxhaven, where a fully-rigged "ship" was set up in an open field. Restricted as the lads were in their preparation for a sailor's life, their elders under the command of Von Tirpitz had scarcely more favourable opportunities for service. owing to the same cause.

IRON RINGS FOR GOLD.
German civilians giving up gold rings to a Government official. In exchange they received iron rings inscribed: "For our country."

organisation on the ground that the original war credits supported previously were for "a defensive war," while the King of Bavaria had just blurted out that the war was a war of conquest. Other Socialists, like the ultra-Radical Liebknecht, went further and shrieked, amid pandemonium in the Prussian Diet, that "the masses demand peace." Haase, Bernstein, Kautsky, Liebknecht, Braun, and party comrades who shared their views obviously constituted a German stop-the-war group. But in reality they meant, for the time at least, no more than Mr. Ramsay Macdonald, M.P., or the British Stop-the-War Committee meant in this country.

A few days after the Haase-Bernstein-Kautsky manifesto and the peace demonstration in the Prussian Diet, the "Vorwärts" was suppressed by the military authorities for "treasonable" peace clamour and denunciation of the Royalties who were talking out of school and unblushingly acknowledging that Germany's "defensive war" was a war of aggression.

All these episodes meant, without doubt, that Socialist sentiment towards the war was in a state of ferment: that it was no longer in that condition of blind unanimity which evoked the Imperial Chancellor's enthusiasm in August, 1914. But the Allies would have **Mobilisation of German finance** been guilty of absurd self-deception if they had concluded that German Socialism had already become an effective aid in the problem of crushing the common enemy. It was still securely under the boot-heel of the military dictatorship enthroned in Berlin.

One of the conspicuous preparations of Germany for war, which Europe resolutely declined to measure at its real magnitude, was the policy of the German Imperial Bank, inaugurated as early as the spring of 1913, which was officially described as "Finance Mobilisation." The Government institution proclaimed the urgent necessity of making the Fatherland impregnable against the sudden emergency of war—language made familiar by Admiral von Tirpitz and the Minister for War when they periodically asked the Reichstag for fresh battleships and battalions—by accumulating well in advance a huge gold reserve. At that time—June 1st, 1913—the Reichsbank held, roundly, £55,000,000 of gold. The authorities proceeded forthwith to augment it to unprecedented proportions. Germany's favourable trade balance enabled her to import profitably gold from abroad, and by dint of such measures and the inculcation of "gold-saving habits" at home, the Imperial Bank found itself in possession, in August, 1914, of a "record" reserve of £65,000,000. During the war gold was "called up" by resorting to unheard-of and even grotesque practices—such as

THE SELF-SACRIFICE OF THE GERMAN PEOPLE.
Gold and silver plate and jewellery given to the German Government, exhibited so that art dealers might buy them for gold. A typical incident at one of the receiving bureaux is represented in the circular view.

granting half-holidays to schools which collected a certain minimum of gold money, for which the bank would exchange paper or silver. Newspapers organised gold-collecting bureaux, and daily preached the necessity of paying gold into the Reichsbank as a prime defensive necessity of

"A prime defensive the realm. Gold dis-
necessity" appeared, before the war was a week old, as if by magic, and nothing but paper, nickel, and silver money was in circulation in Germany. Notes for even as low a denomination as one mark (1s.) and two marks (2s.) were issued. To hoard a gold coin came to be a treasonable misdemeanour, and the patriot who would pay in even a single 10-mark (10s.) piece and accept paper or silver in return, was entitled to consider that he was "doing his bit" for the war. By July 1st, 1915, the Reichsbank claimed to be in possession of a gold reserve of nearly £120,000,000—nearly double the amount in hand when the war began.

As the gold reserve rose,

RUSSIAN GUNS IN BERLIN.
These pieces of captured Russian ordnance were displayed outside the Royal Palace at Berlin with the object of convincing the populace of the all-conquering powers of the German arms.

IN A BERLIN STREET.
German soldiers examining a quick-firing gun captured on the Russian front.

ENTHUSIASM IN THE GERMAN CAPITAL.
To promote public confidence in Germany special parades were organised of guns captured from the Allies. The above photograph is of a crowd which congregated in one of the principal thoroughfares of the German capital to witness one of these processions.

Germany's system of frenzied war finance set in. A German banker friend, a privy councillor, admitted in private that "we have had our engraved blocks for the stamping of paper currency ready for years. All we shall have to do is to reel it off the presses in the desired quantities." That is exactly what Germany did for a year. The country was full of money, paper money, engraved promises to pay—some time.

Outside Germany, and doubtless inside it as well, it was quite impossible to guess even approximately at the sum total of German fiat money in circulation. One may only be certain that it was incalculably in excess of the £120,000,000 gold reserve supposedly on hand in the Imperial Bank for its redemption. The German Government finance system, as was publicly admitted by the leading commercial organ, "Frankfurter Zeitung," rested not on any tangible security, but on confidence. The German Government told the people that their vanquished foes would pay the piper; that gold indemnities of dazzling magnitude were to be brought back to Berlin by the victorious armies which had **Dreams of dazzling** subjugated London, Paris, and Petrograd, **magnitude** and that if Germans would only content themselves meantime with the Government's paper pledges, these would be redeemed in due course, at the rate of 100 pfennigs to the mark (or at their full nominal value).

The German Government at the outset financed the war by loan, and evidently intended to continue the process, as the Chancellor of the Exchequer in Berlin, Dr. Helfferich, announced, as long as might be necessary. German war loans were 5½ per cent. issues, and aggregated to July, 1915, £725,000,000. Already Germany was saddled with an annual interest charge of £39,875,000. There were intimations from Berlin of another war loan of £400,000,000, with additional interest burdens of £22,000,000. It was only the Socialist newspapers which had the temerity to conjure up for the country's contemplation the financial nightmare that would oppress the Fatherland in perpetuity if the

DINNER-TIME AT SPANDAU.
German soldiers drawing their rations.

GIFTS FOR DEPARTING TROOPERS.
Red Cross nurse distributing gifts to men of the German Landsturm before they left for the front.

With that unfailing adherence to specialisation characteristic of the Teuton, he laid down the principle early in the war that each branch of economic life should look after and regulate its own particular necessities. Thus the farmers, with the help of their great national Agriculturists' League, which was at once both a political party and a co-operative association, were early in the field with a " War Credit " Bank. Partially subsidised by State funds, this bank extended cash credits at low interest and on easy terms to needy farmers and landowners, and vastly facilitated the production of the great crop Germany gathered in the summer of 1915. The two great industrial combines of the country—the Manufacturers' Union and the Central Association of German Industry—also formed war credit banks for the benefit of their members. For the accommodation of the general public throughout the country the Berlin War Credit Bank was organised, the capital being furnished by the great banks and leading business corporations, while the Imperial Bank placed at its disposal a continuing discount credit of £10,000,000. The War Credit Bank's dividend could not, by the articles of agreement, exceed 4 per cent., and surplus profits were to be bestowed upon the dependents of fallen soldiers.

One of the real limits of Germany's endurance was the risk of collapse in her finance and credit system as herein outlined. Up to the middle

fortunes of war, " after all," ran against it. The German Government made much of the ease with which the nation had thus far met all war-loan demands. There were boastful tales of vast over-subscriptions, and flamboyant proclamations of the country's abilities to meet any fresh demands that might be imposed upon it in the days yet to come. The German savings-banks, thanks to the cultivated virtue of national thrift, contained in July, 1914, upwards of £1,000,000,000 of deposits, while the German national wealth was estimated in 1913 at between £18,800,000,000 and £19,850,000,000, and to be increasing annually by from £550,000,000 to £600,000,000. It was pointed out that the effective blockade of Germany by land and sea had resulted in so complete a stoppage of imports that she was " saving " by compulsion the £500,000,000 or £600,000,000 which she had been accustomed to spend abroad every year for imported goods. Germany, of course, was by the same token prevented from prosecuting her rich export trade,

Germany's lost foreign trade worth, according to the statistics for 1913, £495,600,000 a year; but she had an enormous home market to depend upon, and swollen domestic orders compensated to no inconsiderable degree the loss of her foreign trade.

The measures hitherto discussed concern merely the financing of the war itself. For the financing of the hardly less vital requirements of German internal commerce and trade, prompt and far-reaching arrangements were made.

of July, 1915, all had gone well. But her bankers knew that the system was fictitious and unstable, and contained the seeds of self-destruction. If Germany were to win, all would be well. If she lost, she would be confronted by the most utter ruin and bankruptcy in the **Playing for great stakes** history of nations. She was playing for great stakes, for with the result of the war her entire economic existence was wrapped up. The recklessness with which her soldiers were sacrificed is the measure of Germany's extremities.

In hardly any other direction did German organisation in war time accomplish such successful results as in respect of the food supply and national thrift. That after a year of war the enemy was still removed from danger of collapse by starvation was due to his prompt, thoroughgoing and efficient measures for conserving breadstuffs, meat, and fodder, and drilling the country, frugal by inherited tradition, in the arts and necessities of war economy. In the early days of the war grave anxiety prevailed as to bread supply. In Berlin, in August, 1914, there were panic-stricken purchases of flour and other cereals by citizens lest the stoppage of supplies from abroad and the enormous requirements of the Army should bring famine upon the civilian population.

Germany was reaping when war broke out a somewhat more than average harvest, but serious doubts were entertained as to whether the yield, in the extraordinary conditions of war, would tide the country over until the next crop. Prices rose from week to week, and uneasiness became so acute with the dawn of 1915 that on January 25th the Imperial Government instituted a practical State monopoly in breadstuffs by commandeering the remaining grain supply, in order to put a peremptory stop to "bread usury" on the part of speculating farmers and millers. The monopoly was enforced by means of two separate agencies—a semi-official "War Grain Company," which was clothed with arbitrary, confiscatory, price-regulating, and policing powers over grain stores, and by the establishment of bread rations, whereby the public could obtain bread only on exhibition of "bread cards." The daily allowance per person was at first fixed at 225 grammes (nearly 8 ounces). Later on the allotment was decreased to 200 grammes (about 6¾ ounces). Local communities were furnished with breadstuffs by the War Grain Company on the population basis, and charged with the duty of distributing it to the people, so-and-so much per capita, children receiving less than adults. Discretion was given to the authorities to increase the ration in accordance with peculiarly local requirements. Miners in Silesia, for example, were allotted, owing to the exacting nature of their occupation, a heavier bread allowance than a clerk or merchant in the same district.

The bread-card system

The bread-card system was relentlessly enforced. People eating in cafés or restaurants or elsewhere outside the domestic establishment were served with bread only on presentation of cards. Exceptions were made only in the case of strangers; but if these remained in a place for any

length of time they, too, had to provide themselves with bread-cards like regular residents. The "help yourself" bread-basket, an old-time feature of German restaurant life, disappeared. Bakers, of course, played an important role in the ration system. They received an allotment of flour corresponding to their sales for a given week, their supplies for the succeeding week being reckoned on that basis.

Mapped out at the inception with typical Teuton thoroughness, the breadstuffs situation was so taken in hand that the Imperial authorities were shortly able to announce with confidence that, by practising Spartan economy and adhering strictly to the ration regulations, Germany's supplies would easily last over "the critical months" between the spring and autumn of 1915. The 200-gramme daily ration was based on a census of breadstuffs stocks taken in March. A later census, in May, having determined that the surplus at the end of the harvest year would amount to nearly 700,000 tons, or about half as much again as had been expected, it was decided that local authorities might, in special cases, increase the 200-gramme ration to 220 grammes.

Mr. Lloyd George's epigram

Besides taking over the breadstuffs supply and regulating distribution of bread on the ration system, the German authorities resorted to drastic action to prevent reckless use of the diminishing supply of wheaten flour. Arbitrary laws were passed requiring bakers and householders to mix a large, fixed percentage of rye with wheaten flour; excesses were made a misdemeanour punishable by fine and imprisonment. The most rigid provision was a decree requiring bread and rolls, and even pastry, to be baked from a mixture of rye and wheaten flour and potato meal.

It was the country's prompt and loyal adaptation of its habits to "potato flour" and "potato bread" that caused Mr. Lloyd George to coin his celebrated epigram that "England had more to fear from Germany's potato-

THE RAID ON THE GERMAN KITCHENS FOR MUNITIONS OF WAR.
Quite early in the war there was a shortage of copper in Germany, and all spare articles of this metal in domestic use were requisitioned by the Government. The above picture shows children bringing in old cooking vessels, chandeliers, etc., to one of the collecting depots in Berlin.

bread spirit' than from Hindenburg's strategy." It was not easy for the people with the biggest appetite in the world to accustom themselves to potato-bread and potato-rolls with the morning, noon, and afternoon coffee, which took the place of the tea of the English. But "War Bread" ("Kriegsbrot," or "K-brot," as it came to be called) soon became popular. The Kaiser and the Crown Prince caused it to be known that "War Bread" was being served exclusively at their messes at the front, and the baker who sold or the citizen who ate the old-time wheaten loaf or pastry was looked upon as a traitor.

Meantime the State took the question of the potato and meat supply vigorously in hand. Germans are tremendous potato eaters, and the available stores were vanishing at even a faster rate than breadstuffs, owing to

LEARNING TO WRITE WITH THEIR LEFT HANDS.
An example of Teuton thoroughness. As Germany's maimed soldiers became convalescent, schools were opened at which they received instruction from lady teachers in the art of writing with the left hand.

the necessity of using potatoes as fodder for pigs, Russian fodder imports being no longer available. Shortly after the War Grain Company was formed, an Imperial Potato Distribution Bureau was organised in Berlin, and went to work on the basis of a national census of stocks on hand. Prices were arbitrarily fixed, confiscations legalised, and retail dealers instructed to peddle out their supplies on a fixed per capita scale. It was eventually determined that there were more potatoes on hand than at first calculated, and, while State control of them was not relinquished, regulations for distribution and prices were gradually relaxed. But prompt State intervention served the purpose of guaranteeing that the German potato supply, as in the case of breadstuffs, would last until the 1915 harvest.

German potato supply assured   Germany was much worse off for meat than for breadstuffs or potatoes. Economists as late as June, 1915, were predicting that only a miracle could stave off disastrous conditions in respect of this commodity. Government action, taken as far back as January, compelling local communities of more than 5,000 inhabitants to

purchase and store preserved and smoked meats to the extent of 15s. per head of the population, had apparently not made the meat situation secure. No fresh meat was reaching the market. That already slaughtered had been pickled, and was being doled out on some more or less rigid ration system to butchers and consumers under municipal control. The supply was far below the demand, and prices were correspondingly high.   **Ten food commandments**

Realising that no organisation of food supply, however scientific, could be effective without popular co-operation, the German Government was sleepless in its inculcation of thrift among the people. The German is frugal by nature and habit. He is intensely patriotic besides, so that appeals to abjure extravagance and live exclusively the simple life did not fall on deaf ears. Early in the war the Burgomaster of the famous Westphalian industrial city of Dortmund gave expression to the national spirit when, at the end of a "thrift meeting" in the Town Hall, he suggested that every true German should adopt the motto: "I am proud to thirst and hunger for the Fatherland."

The following "ten food commandments" epitomise the "potato-bread spirit" which enabled Germany to "hold out." They were displayed, in varying forms, in many public places—in railway carriages, in stations, in shops, restaurants, and even kitchens of private houses:

THE CARE OF THE CHILDREN.
How the children of Berlin were looked after while their parents were away at the front. An American who returned from Germany in August, 1915, stated that "nearly every woman in Berlin was a widow and every child an orphan."

GERMANY IS STANDING AGAINST A WORLD OF ENEMIES WHO WOULD DESTROY HER.

I.—They will not succeed in defeating our glorious troops, but they wish to starve us out like a besieged fortress. They will also fail in that because we have enough breadstuffs in the country to nourish our population until the next harvest, but nothing must be wasted.

II.—Breadstuffs must not be used as fodder.

III.—Therefore, be economical with bread in order that the hopes of our foes may be confounded.

IV.—Respect the daily bread, then thou wilt have it always, may the war last ever so long.

HIGH-EXPLOSIVE SHELLS: THE DECIDING FACTOR IN THE FIRST YEAR OF THE WAR.
Germany's supply of high-explosive shells appeared to be inexhaustible. The above photograph shows how they were transported from factory to base in wicker baskets.

V.—Teach these maxims also to thy children.

VI.—Do not despise even a single piece of bread because it is no longer fresh.

VII.—Do not cut off a slice more than thou needest to eat. Think always of our soldiers in the field who, often in some far-off, exposed position, would rejoice to have the bread which thou wastest.

VIII.—Eat war bread. It is recognisable by the letter K. It satisfies and nourishes as thoroughly as any other kind. If all eat it, we do not need to be anxious as to whether we shall always have bread.

IX.—Whoever first peels potatoes before cooking them wastes much. Therefore, cook potatoes with the jackets on. Thou savest thereby.

X.—Leavings of potatoes, meat, vegetables, etc., which thou canst not use, throw not away, but collect them as fodder for cattle. Such leavings will gladly be called for by the farmers.

The British Board of Trade stated that the most marked rises in food in Berlin in May, 1915, compared with the month previous, were in the prices of veal, **Food prices in** mutton, pork, beef, bacon, and lentils. **Germany and England** There were slight falls in the prices of potatoes, rye bread, and rye flour. These changes brought the general level of food prices in Berlin in May to about 65 per cent. above those for July, 1914, and about 69 per cent. above those of May, 1914. The general increase in British retail food prices from the beginning of the war to a parallel date may be estimated at 35 per cent. for the cities and at 30 per cent. for small towns and villages.

No sketch of Germany's war-time food regulations, of course, would be complete without reference to the extraordinary preparations undertaken for a record-breaking 1915 harvest. Long-continuing drought in the months of May and June probably caused a considerably smaller yield than was at first counted upon, but the harvest in any event cannot but have been an extremely large one, thanks to the super-intensive methods of cultivation resorted to. Land in comparatively arid Germany is always exploited to a degree unusual in more fruitful territory, but in 1915 fields never planted before in their existence were ploughed and sown. Even town-lots were utilised for agricultural purposes.

The decree went forth from Imperial headquarters that in war "Germany expected every acre to do its duty." The whole Empire, therefore, was converted into a vast field, and had **"Every acre to** not drought supervened, it is probable **do its duty"** that the crop would have provided a surplus for exportation. At any rate, the unprecedented measures adopted in respect of planting yielded crops which promised to tide the Germans over still another autumn, winter, and spring of war. The whines that rigorous British naval policy threatened civilian Germany with "starvation" were political cries pure and simple, designed to deceive, and to extort the sympathy of neutral countries. The Fatherland at no time during the war had ever really been menaced by the spectre of starvation. It had not only the broad acres of uninvaded Germany and Austria-Hungary to draw upon, but fertile conquered territory in France, Belgium, and Russia, and the problem of agricultural labour was solved by the

WAR BREAD FOR GERMAN SAILORS.
Voluntary helpers at a Berlin depot packing bread for the Navy into bags specially designed to keep the contents fresh for many days.

RETURNING WHENCE THEY CAME.
Germans who had been taken prisoners on the battlefields of Flanders marching through London to the railway-station, for transference back to the Fatherland in exchange for our men who were arriving back from the prison camps in Germany.

presence on German soil of 1,750,000 prisoners of war. War, like all business in Germany, was carried on by experts. It was therefore strictly in accordance with preconceived realisation of what war means that its purely business side was promptly linked up with the military and naval establishments. Not many days had

Conserving supplies of raw materials gone by after August, 1914, when a "War Raw Materials Division" was added to the Ministry of War, and in charge of it the Government placed one of the keenest young business men in the country, Dr. Walther Rathenau, son of the founder and head of the famous Allgemeine Electricitäts Gesellschaft (General Electrical Company). It was Rathenau's primary task to conserve all existing supplies of raw materials essential

to the prosecution of war—copper, cotton, brass, steel, iron, coal, petroleum, etc.—and arrange for their replenishment on the largest scale possible.

As to munitions, German industry in Krupp's vast establishment was already "organised" on a prodigious scale, but the Government immediately began impressing into munition-manufacturing service countless establishments which, customarily dependent on export trade, were now free to turn their plants into arms, armament, and ammunition works, and to produce exclusively the multifarious impedimenta of war.

The great German chemical industry, also dependent to a large extent on foreign markets,

EN ROUTE TO THE FATHERLAND.
Another view of German prisoners leaving England for their own country. One of the men belonged to the sunken Mainz.

at once became a powerful adjunct of the German war-establishment. The asphyxiating gas with which the Kaiser's armies tried to suffocate their way to Calais was one of the diabolical achievements of German chemists in war time; but their talents were turned, no doubt, to more legitimate tasks as well—such as the discovery of a process for extracting nitrate from the air when imported nitrate was no longer obtainable.

Petroleum supplies, cut short by stoppage of traffic with the United States, gave the Germans less concern when their armies had reconquered the Galician oilfields than earlier in the war.

WHAT EAST LONDON SAW OF THE HUN.
The exchange of war prisoners gave Londoners in the vicinity of Stratford railway-station, where our German prisoners were entrained on their way back to the Fatherland, an opportunity of studying types of the men who at the bidding of the Kaiser carried fire and sword through peaceful Belgian cities and the once pleasant land of Northern France.

Rubber, of which enormous quantities were used in this motor war, was notoriously short in Germany. One of the first war measures taken was the commandeering of all the rubber in private possession for the uses of the Army motor-transport department.

With the closing of Italy as a source of supply, copper no longer reached Germany from outside sources, but in addition to vast accumulated stocks in the country and valuable stores found in the captured industrial districts of France, Russia, and Belgium, there was the incalculable quantity "buried" in every great manufacturing community like Germany and which, in a pinch, could be

HOME AGAIN FROM GERMAN PRISON CAMPS.
The Germans made numbers of our Royal Army Medical Corps prisoners. After great delay these were released, and at the same time an exchange of disabled prisoners of war was agreed to. Above and in circle are photographs taken at St. Pancras as the returned Red Cross men were driving away from the railway-station at the end of their long journey home.

all shadow of possibility the enemy's power to replenish her cotton reserves. The action of the German military authorities in restricting the use of cotton for purely commercial purposes was sufficiently eloquent. Such supplies of raw cotton as were still on hand were obviously to be devoted henceforth exclusively to the production of ammunition. In pursuance of its policy **A "War Cotton Committee"** of associating practical business men with the conduct of the war, the German Government appointed a "War Cotton Committee," headed by the president of a leading cotton spinners' federation. It was the duty of the Committee to ameliorate as far as possible the dislocation

utilised for war purposes. There was the copper already used for telephone, telegraph, and cable purposes, roofs, buildings, bells, and a host of other objects.

Cotton was the raw-stuff causing Germany the greatest anxiety. In ordinary times she imported £20,000,000 worth per annum from the United States. As the British Government declined to declare cotton contraband of war, Germany contrived by means of importation direct and through adjacent neutral countries to secure immense quantities, even during the existence of the British blockade. As Sir William Ramsay repeatedly pointed out, cotton was indispensably necessary for the continued production of German explosives, and it seemed incomprehensible, in the circumstances, why the British Government hesitated to take action which would annihilate beyond

THE KINDLY DUTCH AND OUR RETURNING PRISONERS.
A young Dutch lady distributing gifts to returning British prisoners of war just before they went on board ship for the cross-Channel passage to England.

in the textile trades which the Army's cotton requirements necessitated.

The war organisation of German industry made heavy drafts on the services of women. It was estimated that 500,000 of them were at work in situations hitherto held by men who were serving with the colours. Women played a particularly important rôle in the munitions industry. In all branches of industrial life they took men's places with eminent satisfaction to all concerned. On the tramway lines, as conductors, women were at work almost from the hour of mobilisation. Probably in no trade or calling of any kind were they any longer unfamiliar figures.

Soldiers, after all is said and done, win war. At any rate the number of men a nation can continue to put in the field represents along with the money question the real limit of her endurance. It is difficult to calculate how many fighting men Germany had under arms after a year of war. Six or seven millions would probably not be an overestimate. Her losses in killed, wounded, and missing were hideously heavy—not less than 3,000,000 up to July 15th, 1915.

Germany after a year of war

The German armies now in being (said a writer in "The Times" of July 5th, 1915) consist of the trained manhood of the country between the ages of twenty and thirty-nine, of some portions of the trained men between the ages of thirty-nine and forty-five, of an uncertain number of men of military age untrained before the war, and of a very large number (anything between 1,000,000 and 2,000,000) of volunteers —men over or under military age, and men of military age who enlisted, although they had not been called upon. The country still contains very large reserves of able-bodied men of fighting age. Many of the available sources of supply have not been tapped at all, and no question has yet arisen of raising the age for compulsory service above forty-five, as was done in Austria-Hungary early in 1915.

An asset of moral worth purely, but of enormous importance, was the universal confidence that Germany was waging a winning fight. What thoughts inspired the German man in the street when he contemplated the military and naval situation at the end of the first year of Armageddon? He knew, first of all, that his own country and that of his Teutonic ally Austria-Hungary were practically cleared of the invader; that Germanic hosts held practically all of Belgium, including the capital and Antwerp; that the combined military strength of Great Britain and France had not been able to dislodge Germany from either

GERMANY FROM WITHIN.
Senior schoolboys, who had been formed into a corps of " Boy Recruits," arriving at Döberitz for a course of training.

A MEMORABLE INCIDENT IN 1914.
Removing the Imperial Insignia from the doorway of the German Embassy in London after the declaration of war.

Belgium or 15,000 square miles of occupied French territory; that Russian Poland, or the bulk of it, had been conquered by the legions of the two Kaisers, and that important sections of the Russian Baltic provinces were in German hands; that the German military establishment, barring heavy losses in personnel which could easily be made up by waiting levies, was practically intact and as strongly-equipped, generally speaking, as when war began; that the German battle fleet was still a fleet in being, and relatively stronger in gunpower and fighting effectiveness than it was in August, 1914; that German submarine warfare had made the danger of a surprise or sudden offensive against the Kaiser's fleet or coasts by Britain's superior Navy almost a matter of impossibility, so long as the German Armada refused to give battle in the open; that many hundreds of thousands of tons of both British warcraft and merchant shipping had been sent to the bottom by German torpedoes and mines; that, thanks to German organisation, leadership, and equipment, even the Turks were able to offer desperate resistance to the allied forces of Britain and France, and impose on the British Army heavier losses in a four months' campaign than Britain suffered during the entire Boer War.

A spirit of confidence

These are iron facts, which Germans pondered over and from which they derived comfort and sustained confidence. They knew that their merchant marine had been obliterated from the oceans; they knew that Hamburg and Bremen were as cities of the dead; they knew that their oversea prides—German South-West Africa and Kiao-Chau—were in the enemy's hands; that the most of their colonial empire had ceased to exist as German territory. At the same time they realised what perhaps they wished they had realised years before, that Germany isolated in Central Europe was very potent as a purely self-contained nation, and they believed that time was fighting at least as effectually for them as for their foes. They were convinced they could not be dislodged from the military positions they occupied. They believed the war had already been won by them, and that while future events might bring about changes here or there, the objectives already achieved would remain firmly in the Kaiser's hands. There was work ahead for the Allies, for Britain in particular, if the Germans were to be wakened from their complacent dreams.

CHAPTER LXXIII.

THE STRATEGY OF GENERAL JOFFRE AND THE WAR OF ATTRITION ALONG THE FRENCH FRONT.

The Superbly Inventive French Mind Works Out a Grand Design—General Pau's Organising Tour through Eastern Europe and Italy—Germany and Austria Find the Weak Link and General von Falkenhayn Succeeds in Postponing the General Offensive Movement of the Western Allies—Defection of Rumania—Weakness of the Southern Russian Armies—Italy's Noble Conduct—Result of General Joffre's Strategy—Testing the Enemy's Line in the West—Renewal of the French Invasion of their Lost Provinces—Heroism of the Chasseurs Alpins in the Snow-covered Forested Heights of the Vosges—Hartmannsweilerkopf—Advance along the Fecht to Metzeral—Mining and Counter-mining—Preparing the Way for the Great Advance through Lorraine—The German Wedge from Metz—French Mastery of the Woevre—Les Eparges—Army of Toul Pierces the Forest of Apremont—Aerial Torpedoes—French Tactics at Ailly Wood—The Man behind the German Crown Prince—Why the Gateway of St. Mihiel was Allowed to Remain Open.

WE have now arrived at a point at which we can connect all the incidents and events of the spring campaign which have been related in the chapters dealing with the movements of the Russian and British armies. It will be recollected that there was a general expectation of a very important offensive movement by the Allies, and that this movement was expected to occur in May, 1915. All the operations of British, French, and Belgian troops, from February to April, were undertaken with a view to preparing the way for the destruction of the German armies occupying Belgium and Northern France. This destruction did not take place at the arranged date, and no real attempt indeed was made to destroy the enemy. For this reason the history of the events along the French lines, about to be related, is likely to make a disconcerting impression, because it details a chain of circumstances which promised to lead to a magnificent conclusion, but ended apparently in nothing.

It is, therefore, only fair to the reader to explain in

GENERAL PAU.

One of the most distinguished soldiers in the French Army, he was entrusted in the early part of 1915 with an important mission to Eastern Europe and Italy to arrange a great general offensive in the West. He lost his right hand at Wörth in 1870.

advance on what hopes the grand success of the spring campaign had been founded, and on what grounds the decisive forward movement was postponed. After the Battles of Champagne and Neuve Chapelle and the Russian victories in the Carpathian Mountains in February, 1915, the French Staff decided that Germany and Austria might be defeated well within a year if only all the operations of the attacking nations were closely and punctually co-ordinated. With this view General Pau, the right-hand man of General Joffre, set out from France on a tour through Eastern Europe, through Russia and the Balkans to Italy. Naturally, a man of his ability could not be spared from the French Staff at the most critical period of the history of France merely in order to undertake political and diplomatic work. The fact was that he left his country, charged with a military task even more important than that which his chief, General Joffre, was performing. His work was to organise a general European campaign against the Germanic Empires, to harmonise the military efforts of Britain, France, and Belgium with those of Russia and Serbia, and then work into the general plan of attack the expected movements of the armies of Italy and Rumania.

At this time the southern Russian army was attempting to force its way down the southern slopes of the Carpathian Mountains and thus to reach the wheat-plain of Hungary. In the western theatre of war both the French troops and the British troops had dented the enemy's lines and manifested a marked superiority in fighting power. The common, unenlightened opinion was that the Franco-British troops had only to make one great effort in order to break the hostile front at the point selected by General Joffre. It is possible that this could have been effected at the time by the sacrifice of some hundred thousand men. But the French Commander-in-Chief and his Staff do not seem to have desired to push the enemy back to the shorter line. They intended to accomplish a larger result than this, and possibly to destroy most of the German forces occupying Belgium and Northern France. This was the reason why General Pau made his tour through Eastern Europe and Italy.

He had a grand design. On a given day in May some seven nations were to throw every available man and gun against Germany and Austria-Hungary—the Russians on the east, the Rumanians on the south-east, the Serbians on the eastern south, the Italians on the western south, and the French, British, and Belgians on the western front. With Russia advancing down the Carpathians, Rumania striking across the Bukovina to Tran-sylvania, Serbia invading Southern Hungary and Bosnia, and linking with the uprush of the Italians along **A masterpiece of the French mind** the Alps and towards Trieste and Fiume, the fate of Austria-Hungary seemed in prospect to be very disastrous. And as all the attacks were timed to occur on the same day as the Franco-British offensive was launched against the German lines at three or more places between Switzerland and the North Sea, the general pressure of all the co-ordinated attacks would, it was estimated, be tremendous. There would be no further oppor-tunity for Germany to reinforce one front at the expense of another. She would have at once to throw all her reserves of troops into an in-creasing succession of danger-points, until the enormous, general, and unintermittent strain along

GENERAL JOFFRE AT THE FRONT—SURVEYING TRENCHES THAT HAD BEEN CAPTURED FROM THE ENEMY.
Inset is an interesting photograph of General Maud'huy taken in July, 1915, during the visit of Generals Joffre, Maud'huy, and Foch to the reconquered territory in Alsace.

AMONG "THE BLUE ALSATIAN MOUNTAINS."
A fine camera-picture of a review by General Joffre in Alsace. Standing behind the General were a number of officers and Red Cross workers who had been decorated for bravery.

a front of something like two thousand miles became impossible to resist, and breakage after breakage took place, ending in a general disaster all along the line.

Such was the scheme of operations, marked by a stern logic and economic employment of great forces surpassing the efforts of Carnot and his great disciple Napoleon. It was a masterpiece of the French mind in the greatest hour of the French nation—a greater hour than even that of Valmy, when the explosion of force in the young French Republic first shook all the thrones of Europe. France had learned much since Valmy, and since Wattignies, Marengo, and Austerlitz. She had first invented the new method of warfare by a nation in arms, and had taught almost every man in Europe to become a soldier, and to wage national wars instead of dynastic or cabinet wars. Of all the pupils of France, Prussia had learned the

An old lesson recalled

lesson best, and had so improved upon it as to defeat her instructor by the armed power of an entire nation, when France in 1870 had forgotten her own teaching and had fallen back upon a professional army.

Recalled to the terrible lessons of her own revolutionary wars, France had, under her third republican system of government, recovered by a sort of instinct of race the genius she had possessed and developed under the Committee of Public Safety. Her national army was at a deadlock in its long wrestle with the national army of the more populous empire. Her immediate ally, Great Britain, was still unready to accept the national system of warfare, mainly because the British people had escaped by their insular position from the dreadful lesson in war that Napoleon had wished to teach them. Britain was still in the intermediate stage between a professional and a national army, and, like revolutionary France and the Northern States of America in the early period of their struggles for life, was trying to muddle through by means of a voluntary levy in mass. The British people had, moreover, muddled the business of arming their new volunteer forces, and after nine months of war could not throw much more than half a million men into the chief battlefield, where the great decision alone could be obtained.

GENERAL JOFFRE ADDRESSING THE MAYORS OF ALSATIAN TOWNSHIPS REOCCUPIED BY THE FRENCH.

"AFTER FORTY-FOUR YEARS OF SORROWFUL WAITING."
One of the first messages written by General Joffre after the outbreak of the Great War was addressed to the "Children of Alsace." When he visited the reconquered territory in July, 1915, he met with an enthusiastic reception. Our photograph forms a notable souvenir of the welcome that was accorded him.

M. MILLERAND, FRENCH MINISTER OF WAR, AND GENERAL BALFOURIER, ONE OF THE ARMY CORPS COMMANDERS, AT CARENCY.
The French War Minister, accompanied by M. Albert Thomas, Minister of Munitions, visited Arras and Carency in the summer of 1915. They were received by General d'Urbal, commander of the Arras army, and spent some time with the sectional commanders.

It was in these circumstances that the superbly inventive French mind worked out, in a new manner, the solution to the problem which Napoleon had set Europe a hundred years before. Under Napoleon the novel French weapon of a national army, intended only for defence, had been transformed into an aggressive instrument of universal dominion. Europe, after many disasters, had countered this extraordinary form of attack by a very rough-and-ready and loose-jointed system of Continental warfare. The nation in arms was overthrown at last by a continent in arms, but the achievement was scarcely more scientific in execution than the massing of tribal hordes for the common purpose of defending their individual existences.

The intention of General Pau and his fellow-workers on the French Staff was to organise and **Germany finds the** co-ordinate the new Continental counter-**weak link** attack against the national armies of the Germanic Empires. No loosely-jointed attacks by modern armed hordes would prevail against the remarkably well-organised methods of the masterly German Staff.

German military science was unquestionable, and it could only be completely answered by a display of military science of the same quality, but on a larger scale and with a wider scope. Happily the Italian Commander-in-Chief, General Cadorna, and his Staff were, as we have already seen in a previous chapter, also anxious that all the movements of the allied armies should be closely and punctually harmonised into a Continental system of strategy in order to increase to the uttermost the advantages possessed by the seven combined nations. By the middle of April the main outline of the general offensive movement had been settled, and most of the important details worked out by the various Staffs in consultation with General Pau and other connecting Staff officers. But Germany and Austria-Hungary were well aware of what was intended, and by finding the weak link in the Russian

advance into Hungary and striking at it, by that remarkable concentration of force known as the Grand Phalanx, General von Falkenhayn succeeded in postponing for at least a considerable period the great general offensive which General Pau had arranged.

The first immediate effect of the swift, terrible German counter-stroke was the defection of Rumania. The powerful land-owning classes of Rumania took a businesslike view of the situation, and decided that, with the Russian army in full retreat from Galicia, and still in danger of overwhelming disaster, it would be extremely unwise to carry out their part of the general plan. The Bulgarian Government also, which had at **Rumanian and Bulgarian defection** first been inclined to fall in more or less with the scheme of the seven friendly nations, turned once more towards Vienna and Berlin and, without straining its position of neutrality, favoured the Germanic cause and listened to proposals from Turkey for a rearrangement of territory.

In Italy also the well-planned intrigues of Prince Bülow and the Austrian Ambassador seemed at first to have produced an extraordinary change of views in the mind of Signor Giolitti, and this man, who was practically dictator in the modern Parliamentary system of Italy, completely lost all the courage he had displayed when he revealed, some months previously, that the Germanic Empires had resolved upon a European war in 1913.

Under the far-reaching influence of Signor Giolitti there was for a time as distinct a movement of hesitation in Italy as there was in Rumania. Only a quite unexpected and overwhelming resurgence of popular

ONE OF THE GUNS THAT SPOKE FOR "LA REVANCHE."
Photograph of a concealed "75," taken by the French photographic service somewhere in Alsace when the Tricolour was once again floating over part of the old French province.

THINKING OF "HOME, SWEET HOME."
British soldiers, after months spent at the front, packing up their kits at
St. Omer railway-station, preparatory to entraining for England on leave.

WITH THE BRITISH TROOPS IN THE NORTH OF FRANCE—ROYAL ENGINEERS HAULING AMMUNITION WAGGONS
OVER ROUGH GROUND.
In circle: Stacking barbed-wire for use against the Huns.

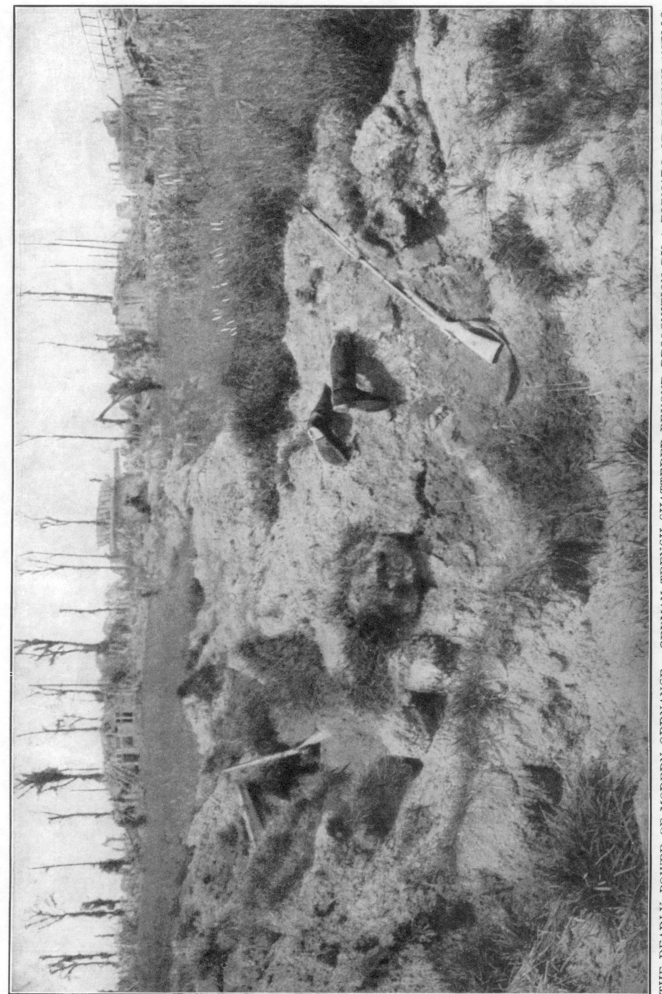

THE DEADLY POWER OF MODERN ORDNANCE: GERMAN TRENCH SHATTERED BEYOND RECOGNITION BY A TORNADO OF BRITISH SHELLS.

The track of the trench as it was originally may be indicated roughly if a semicircular line is drawn downwards from the butt of one of the rifles to that of the other. On the left of this remarkable camera-record of the havoc of modern war may be seen the entrance to a dug-out, while on the right is a German buried under the debris. The German positions are shown in the distance.

feeling in Italy swept away the parliamentary power of Signor Giolitti and brought the country heroically into the terrible struggle at a time when the prospects of the Allies were extremely un-favourable.

But noble as was the conduct of the Italian nation, it did not alter the general strategical position. The weakness of the southern Russian armies influenced every section of the battle-front, and totally checked the execution of the plan proposed by General Pau. The plan was, in fact, still-born, and the prospect of overthrowing the Germanic Empires was postponed until such time as Russia was able to recover her power of initiative.

In particular, all along the western front the French, British, and Belgian armies merely continued that process of attrition which had been going on since the beginning of winter. Here and there a local offensive movement was undertaken, generally with success, but no determined effort was made to break the enemy's front. General Joffre resigned himself to a more restricted, but still very useful, scheme of operations. The German Staff was preparing a very large mass of new

General Joffre's immediate task troops composed of recruits of the classes of 1915-16, of Ersatz reserves, Landsturm, and of men rejected for service on account of physical disabilities, but called to the colours by reason of the urgency of the situation. These troops were well equipped and well armed, but most of them had done no military service, and had had little more than three months' training. The intention of the German Staff was to throw something like three-quarters of a million of these men against the Russians, to form an enormous reinforcement of the already large German and Austrian armies. It was thought that the very strongly constructed lines of entrenchment in France and Flanders would enable the German armies there to hold out, without serious trouble against the French and British attacks until a decision had been obtained in the eastern theatre of war.

General Joffre's immediate task, therefore, was to convince the German Staff as quickly as possible that a very large number of the new recruits were urgently required along the western front. In spite of all the terrible difficulties in their way, the western Allies had to show themselves ready to undertake the genuine grand offensive movement if Germany persisted in throwing all her available new forces against the Russians. There thus remained all through the

SEQUEL TO A DUEL IN THE AIR.
Tragic end of one of the Von Bülows, an observation officer of the Prussian Guard, whose bomb-carrying Aviatik was brought down by a French air-man at Braine, near Soissons.

"EVEN AS MEN WRECKED UPON A SAND, THAT LOOK TO BE WASHED OFF THE NEXT TIDE."
A grim record from the battle-scarred land of France. The above photograph was taken after a charge by French infantry. In circle: French sanitary officers inspecting a captured German trench lined with German dead.

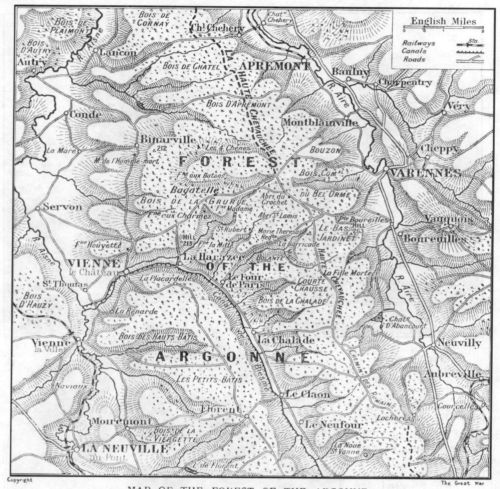

MAP OF THE FOREST OF THE ARGONNE.
The army of the German Crown Prince, half shattered in the forest fighting in the Argonne, proved powerless to drive down and complete the German " buckle " round Verdun.

spring campaign a possibility, which at times increased to a probability, that the French, British, and Belgian armies would be called upon to sacrifice even a quarter of a million men or more in order to break and rout the enemy forces in front of them. The decision rested with the German Commander-in-Chief. All he had to do in order to bring about the result was to allow his lines to weaken under the assaults made upon them by French and British troops ; for the French commander was always well prepared to throw a very large army behind his ordinary assaulting lines if his continual movement of attack was not checked.

There was no attempt at concealment of the object of General Joffre's assault. Indeed, no veil of secrecy was possible. In every case, both sides put the matter to the ordeal of main force. The French army in great strength, with a very large supply of high-explosive shells, bombarded and stormed some important German position. From this position it continued to advance until it met a stronger German army. There then ensued a very fierce series of counter-attacks by the Germans, in which they seldom

The ordeal of main force

recovered their lost position, but always succeeded at last in preventing the breakage of their lines. The French general then attacked in the same manner a hundred miles or more away and took another German position, with the result that the enemy had again to strongly reinforce his wasted and beaten troops.

All this could not be done merely by shifting the German troops from one part of the western front to another. As explained in a previous chapter dealing with the French system of campaign, General Joffre possessed such a mastery of numbers over the enemy that he completely

checked by a series of finely timed attacks the trick of concentrating troops against his assaults. All concentrations, except occasionally for small local purposes, became inadequate to the tasks that were set the Germans by General Joffre. Only by large and continual reinforcements was the German General Staff able to prevent the great reconnaissances in force made by the Allies from being transformed into the most desperate and savage attempt known to history to obtain a grand decision. Here the personal character of General Joffre and his chief men, such as General Foch, Sir John French, General de Castelnau, General Dubail, and other allied army commanders, told heavily on the calculations of the German Staff.

The Germans knew the temper of soul of the captains of France and Britain. They knew that if an opening were given for the great blow, that blow would be delivered with extreme fury, remarkable skill, and heroic driving power. Therefore General Joffre obtained the result at which he aimed. The new German formations were not launched *en masse* against the Russians. They were fairly equally distributed between both the western and eastern fronts of war. In spite of all the rumours that came from Holland during the summer of 1915, there was no transport of troops either way from the western or eastern theatres of conflict. But both fronts were very strongly strengthened, Austrian and Hungarian levies largely taking on the eastern front the place of many of the new German troops, railed into France after having originally been destined for the Russian seat of war. Italy profited by this result of General Joffre's strategy, and Serbia also. Austro-Hun- **How Italy and** garian troops first intended to reinforce the **Serbia profited** Austrian and Serbian fronts had in large numbers to be sent to Russia to supply the place of the new German formations drawn off to France and Flanders.

Therefore, though the present chapter is lacking in events of an apparently decisive character, it must be borne in mind that each French attack was of an extraordinary interest at the time when it developed into a local success. It was never known in advance whether the German Staff was at last ready to take the risk of weakening its lines in the west in order to win a definite victory over the Russian forces in the east. It was only when the mighty German counter-attack was delivered that each affair lapsed into one of the commonplace but useful battles of position in the war of attrition.

The Battles of Champagne and Neuve Chapelle were conflicts of this stagnant but wearing sort. About the time when the British troops were making themselves masters of Neuve Chapelle village the French troops were testing the German line. General Joffre, as a rule, made a double attack along the German front at very widely separated points during the spring of 1915. It was his chief method of preventing the enemy from countering his assault by shifting troops. Sometimes the French Commander-in-Chief would start three fierce battles simultaneously along the German front, with a space of more than four hundred miles between his northern and southern points of attack.

His favourite scene of diversion was the high pine-wooded ridge of the Vosges between Münster and Thann, with a more southerly point of advance towards Altkirch. In this long stretch of difficult mountain country fighting went on continuously between the warlike mountaineers of France and a mixed mass of German troops, supported by large siege-guns. Many years before the war a brilliant school of French military writers had worked out a plan for countering the German advance into France by a movement on the right wing, beginning in Alsace and continuing through Lorraine. Such a movement had been attempted in the first month of the war, but had been severely checked by the great battle in Lorraine which the French called the Battle of Morhange and the Germans the Battle of Metz. The French there lost very heavily and were thrown back by the army of Metz and the Bavarian troops. But after General Foch had saved the situation, when commanding only a division, and had then, as commander of an army corps, played the chief part in helping General de Castelnau to check the Bavarians on the hills round Nancy, the French invasion of Alsace-Lorraine had been resumed. The army based on Belfort, and, composed mainly of mountain troops from the French Vosges and the Pyrenees, held the Col de la Schlucht in

Invasion of Alsace-Lorraine

the High Vosges, near Münster, and the country north of Thann as far as the last high green ramparts of rock near Hartmannsweilerkopf and the hills between Belfort and Mulhouse.

The German army defending the Rhine valley, between the wall of the Vosges and the wall of the Black Forest, was constantly hard put to it to maintain its positions, for the advance of the French mountaineers continued all through the spring and early summer of 1915. The

AN OPEN-AIR CONCERT BEHIND THE FIRING-LINE IN FRANCE.
The series of concerts given by Miss Lena Ashwell's Concert Party in 1915 gave infinite pleasure both behind the firing-line and in the hospitals in France. The above photograph shows an appreciative audience of French and British soldiers. In circle: A concert in the rain. An officer is seen assisting to protect the pianist from the downpour.

x

ST. CRISPIN'S DAY IN FRANCE.
Not only on October 25th, but at frequent intervals, was the memory of St. Crispin and his brother Crispinian honoured in the French lines. Inspections of footgear were frequent, and boots found the worse for wear were quickly replaced. To this was largely attributed the splendid marching qualities of the French infantry.

FRENCH ARTIST IN AN INDIAN CAMP IN FLANDERS.
The French Government, in addition to organising a photographic war service, appointed an artist, M. Jonas, to collect pictorial "documents" of the progress of the war. In the above picture this well-known artist is seen in a camp in Flanders painting some typical representatives of our Indian Expeditionary Force.

slopes. So a fresh brigade or division, and at times even a fresh army corps of the enemy's best men, had to be railed in haste down to Alsace, and there used up against the victorious mountain troops of France.

The Chasseurs Alpins of France resembled the Bersaglieri of Italy. They were the finest flower of French manhood, severely trained and severely tested for their powers of physical endurance. They marched much quicker than an ordinary first-line soldier, and marched much longer ; and though the Bersaglieri regiments, with their record of six miles an hour, with complete fighting kit and ammunition, were unsurpassed for strength of body, the Chasseurs Alpins—the French Alpine light infantry—were equal to their new brothers-in-arms as fighters. They were as slim as the Boers, with a talent for improvising novel ruses, which made their remarkable tenacity in both attack and defence a thing of edge as well as of weight.

They were the heroes of the great Argonne battles in which the Crown Prince's army had been crippled ; they had suddenly **Heroes of the Argonne**
appeared on the extreme western wing between Hazebrouck and Lille in the autumn of 1914, during the race to the sea, but their main scene of operations was the sombre pine-forests of the Vosges Mountains, rising like a great fortress wall above the plain of the Rhine between Basle and Strassburg. It was to capture this high, broad, water-seamed rampart of rocks that they had been trained from early manhood to fight and endure, and though their

Germans brought up many 12 in. Austrian howitzers and one or two 17 in. Krupp howitzers ; but though this unusually heavy artillery impeded the French advance, it did not block it. This was due to the fact that the quality of the German infantry in Alsace was not entirely good. There were considerable bodies of men of the Landsturm, who acted as relieving regiments to the first-line forces ; and, by a method which angered and puzzled the German Staff, the young and vigorous Alpine troops of France divined when the opposing trenches were held by the middle-aged, half-trained Landsturm regiments. The consequence was that the positions held by the Landsturm were usually stormed and captured, and the German first-line troops had then to be hurried up from their billets to make a counter-attack under such disadvantages that they were generally shattered as they charged up the

COURTESY TO THE CONQUERED.
German prisoners of war being conducted through French trenches to the rear of the firing-line and so protected from their own artillery fire.

FRENCH WIRE-CUTTING AUTOMOBILE.
Type of French motor-car on war service fitted with strong steel shield for cutting its way through the barbed-wire entanglements used so liberally by the Germans across roads the Allies were expected to travel over.

numbers were small in comparison with the stretch of country in which they operated, they carried out their work in a very effective way.

All through the winter they remained on the defensive, occupying a line of mountains from the neighbourhood of the town of St. Dié to the neighbourhood of St. Amarin. In spite of the difficulty of victualling the troops holding the snowed and frozen crests, the positions were maintained through the winter against the attacks of the Germans wintering for the most part in the valleys, where they could easily be fed and supplied. The much-enduring Frenchmen, being in possession of dominating points, would not retire from them simply to get more shelter and better food and quicker supplies of ammunition. The Germans in the valleys had greater facilities for concentrating for attack and bringing up heavy artillery. The French troops were often far removed from their base, and isolated in small forces on the snow-covered, forested heights.

As we have seen in a previous chapter, the mountain of Hartmannsweilerkopf, rising nearly 4,000 feet above sea-level, north of the town of Thann, was occupied by the French, and then lost through the troops being cut off on the icy slopes. But it was recovered by a magnificent charge and fortified in the early spring after a series of fierce conflicts which made it famous throughout the world. The last battle for the summit of Hartmannsweilerkopf took place on April 27th, after it had been occupied for a single day by the Prussian Guard, who used asphyxiating gases. Naturally, the Prussian Guard did not come hundreds of miles from La Bassée, with their

Hartmanns-weilerkopf

poison apparatus, on a task of small importance. Yet the mountain they were ordered urgently to recapture does not at first glance appear to be the key to any position. Several neighbouring heights, such as Molkerain and the main mass of the Ballon of Guebweiler, overtop it. But the famous lower height rises at the end of a valley overlooking the plain of Alsace and the Rhine, with the Black Forest directly in front of it. It was an observation station of dominating power, and as the French Army had placed its heavy artillery on the next and higher peak of Molkerain, the guns could be directed by means of telephone from the observation mountain at any target in the Rhine valley. Such was the reason for the incessant conflict for the possession of the summit of Hartmannsweilerkopf, the principal battles occurring on January 19th, March 26th, April 26th, and April 27th, 1915. After the last victory the French batteries commanded the railway

TRENCH TOWARDS THE SUMMIT OF HARTMANNSWEILERKOPF.

This spur of the Vosges, near Steinbach, in Alsace, was the scene of most sanguinary fighting between the French and the Germans. The Germans had converted the summit into a fortress. It was taken by the French on March 27th, 1915, recaptured by the enemy about a month later, and then retaken by our allies.

field-guns and siege-pieces, working in the rear of the marked ranges. Hosts of men laboured at the fortifications from dawn to dusk; the forests were also fortified, barbed-wire being stretched from tree to tree, and wolf-pits dug, as Bruce did in preparation for the Battle of Bannockburn, with ranges of spikes and land-mines along every possible way of approach. In some places preparations were made for setting the pine-woods on fire by means of petrol and incendiary bombs.

But the French artillery triumphed over all difficulties. The light 3 in. gun, firing twenty rounds a minute, proved a superb weapon in mountain warfare. It blew away the wire entanglements, destroyed the trenches and machine-gun redoubts; and then, while the heavy artillery in the French rear shut Metzeral off westward by a curtain of shrapnel, the mountain troops charged down northward on Metzeral, while their comrades advanced on the other side by the hamlet of Altenhof. The German trenches on the slopes were carried and the enemy retired into the village houses, which had been strongly fortified. But the French general did not waste his infantry in attempting to carry the village by storm. The light French guns were again brought into action close to the battle-line; and when night fell Metzeral smoked in the darkness like a gigantic torch. The French guns had set the village on fire, and as the survivors of the garrison troops fled, again the guns smote them. Then lengthening their range the French gunners caught also the German reinforcements vainly hurrying up to enable a counterattack to be organised. The Germans drew back some five hundred yards, leaving the burning village in the hands of the French army.

from Colmar to Mulhouse, and were ready to advance when General Joffre gave the order. In the meantime, in order to keep the Germans in Alsace from growing venturesome, another line of attack against Colmar was slowly cleared by continual fighting along the valley of the Fecht, where the village of Metzeral was captured by a storming attack on June 22nd, 1915. The French troops had then before them scarcely four leagues of the wooded, difficult river valley to conquer, in order to come to the plain of Alsace at Turkheim, where in ancient days the great French commander Turenne, from whom Marlborough learned his trade of war, had won Alsace by a great victory.

The German commander employed every possible means of checking the advance along the Fecht to Metzeral. The broken ground, as a Swiss observer remarked, had been divided into small fields, by hedges of barbed-wire and mazes of concrete and armoured trenches, with machine-gun redoubts—all strengthened by a large number of

The attack along the Fecht was directed from Gerardmer over the neck in the mountains known as the Col de la Schlucht. But it could not proceed at most much farther than Münster until another movement more to the north got under way. This second movement was based on the town of St. Dié, interesting to Americans as the baptismal place where the new continent of the western world first received the name of America. A few miles to the north of St. Dié is a line of hills with some scattered hamlets known as the Ban de Sapt. On this line the Bavarians had entrenched after their victory at Morhange in August, 1914. The French Commander-in-Chief, therefore, had first to clear the Ban de Sapt before resuming the sweeping movement through Lorraine in conjunction with the movement through Alsace. From this fortified position on French territory the enemy was able to threaten a flanking attack against any French force working up into

Menace of the Ban de Sapt

Famous French leaders: General Joffre, General d'Urbal (left), and General Foch (right).

The French Commander-in-Chief conversing with the Mayor of an Alsatian town.

General Joffre and General de Maud'huy surveying the reconquered region of Alsace.

An Alsatian welcome to the French Generalissimo and General de Maud'huy.

General Joffre decorating soldiers of the French Moroccan Division.

183

A winged messenger of death: Firing a French aerial torpedo=shell.

Lorraine. The French army based on Nancy was operating still more northward close to the frontier and about five miles from the German town of Château Salins. It was making steady progress in spite of the enemy's fortifications and violent counter-attacks.

Meanwhile the Ban de Sapt, connecting with the high rampart of the Vosges, in front of Strassburg, remained a menace. But the French sappers towards the end of April began to win the mastery over the enemy. The first affair of importance took place at the village of La Fontenelle on the summit of a height 1,900 feet above sea-level. Here the French troops had, by months of work, constructed a strong system of entrenchments protected by advanced posts. The Germans laid siege to the height, and at the end of March their saps were driven to within twenty yards of the French advanced posts. During the siege the German infantry made several attempts to carry the position by storm, but were repulsed with great losses. But when the enemy saps appproached all infantry assaults ceased.

The youngest French recruit could guess what the next stroke would be. The German sappers had sunk shafts, and begun to drive a mine under the summit. Our allies counter-mined and blew up one mine, and had a fierce struggle with hand-grenades and melinite bombs in one of their advanced works. The struggle was of a curious and terrible kind. The ground was swept by machine-gun and artillery fire on either side and no man could cross it and live. So the fighting took place underground in a maze of deep, narrow trenches and tunnels. After the struggle had gone on for three days, the French engineers brought it suddenly to a conclusion. They buried some hundredweights of high-explosive

AN ANCIENT WEAPON ADAPTED TO MODERN WARFARE.
" L'Arbalète Lance-Grenade," an adaptation of the old cross-bow for hurling explosives, used most effectively by the French in trench warfare. Known familiarly as " The Grasshopper," this weapon threw a deadly bomb a distance of from twenty to eighty metres.

in their front trench, and constructed new traverses by which the garrison troops could retire. When the conflict was at its fiercest the French gave way and fled, and the victorious Germans crowded into the captured position crying : " Surrender, Frenchmen ! Surrender ! "

French engineers' master-stroke The French maintained a strong resistance, to give the enemy a full opportunity of increasing the number of his attacking troops. Then the great mine of cheddite (a powerful high-explosive) was exploded, and when the fumes had lifted, the French went back to their position and put it in order, while their guns kept the enemy off by a barrage of shrapnel. Every German had been destroyed. The following night the French garrison could hear the German officers trying to get their men to renew the attack. But louder than the officers' orders came the answer of the terrified troops : " Nein ! Nein ! " Soon afterwards the French at last began to advance. It was their first movement of advance

in this region since the August battle on the Grande Couronné de Nancy. They went forward slowly, as they had in turn to fight against a powerful system of defence works ; but slow though their progress was it was continual, and what was even more important, it was effected at comparatively little cost of life ; for the French engineers were masters of their science ; they had learned many lessons from the enemy, and had improved upon them by means of that quick power of intelligence which is the mark of the French mind.

While the Ban de Sapt was thus being cleared for a further advance over the Vosges towards Strassburg by the army based on Epinal, the army based on Toul and Nancy performed a double work. By hard forest fighting in the woods around the Grande Couronné de Nancy and in villages such as Reillon, near the French edge of the frontier going towards Saarburg, it prepared the way for the old and much studied plan of a grand advance through

WOUNDED FRENCH SOLDIERS ARRIVING AT A FIRST-LINE FIELD HOSPITAL.
The men received first-aid at an advanced dressing station, whence they were removed by motor-ambulance to the field hospitals. After treatment in these they were drafted first to the casualty clearing stations and then to the base hospitals and depots for wounded.

bourhood of Calais. The breaking of the eastern line of fortresses would, at any time in the campaign, have brought the Germans round the eastern flank of the Franco-British armies, and compelled those armies to withdraw in furious haste south of Paris. The continual storming attacks along the road to Calais were of lesser importance in the large strategical problem of the war when compared with the plan of operations which the Crown Prince could not carry out. This plan of operations had been carefully designed by Moltke and the German Staff long before the outbreak of hostilities, and the results of its breakdown were very disastrous when General Sarrail, with the Verdun army, and General

A STREET IN MARŒUIL BOMBARDED BY THE GERMANS.
The village of Marœuil, between Arras and Carency, was one of the bases from which the attacks on Neuville St. Vaast and The " Labyrinth " were pushed, and it was subjected to a very violent bombardment by the Germans.

Lorraine. But at the same time the army of Toul co-operated with the army of Verdun in dealing with the situation created by the partially successful advance of the German forces from Metz. As has already been related in the description of the Battle of the Marne, the army of Metz, under Field-Marshal von Heeringen, made in September, 1914, a very strong and determined assault against the line of forts running along the Meuse, and connecting Verdun with Toul. The object was to drive a wedge between Verdun and

The attack on Verdun   Toul from the east, while the army of the German Crown Prince drove another wedge eastward from the Forest of the Argonne. When the two wedges met Verdun would be completely encircled, and it was hoped would quickly be captured. This design remained half completed for many months. The army of Metz carried out its part of the work, and all through the winter, spring, and summer maintained at St. Mihiel, on the Heights of the Meuse, the wedge it had driven into the French system of frontier defences.

But the army of the Crown Prince, half shattered in the forest fighting in the Argonne, was powerless to tighten and complete the German loop round Verdun. The Crown Prince had been given command of the greatest striking force of his country, with the object of exalting the prestige of the future Kaiser by the most decisive victory in the war; for by breaking through the French fortified line at Verdun and Toul, and completing the encirclement of Verdun, the Crown Prince would have struck an even heavier blow than the western German wing was vainly attempting to deal in the neigh-

Gouraud—the lion of the Argonne—with a single army corps of mountain troops, threw back the Crown Prince's forces, while General de Langle de Cary's army was hammering eastward at the German positions in the Argonne Forest during the advance from the Marne.

When the retreating Germans in the middle of September, 1914, made a firm stand along the Aisne and the Suippes Rivers all that remained of the main German plan of attack was the wedge driven through the Heights of the Meuse by the army of Metz. But **Castelnau's advance** this wedge was soon reduced in size; **northward** for while the army of Verdun under General Sarrail was throwing all its force against the Crown Prince's army, part of the army of Toul, under General de Castelnau, advanced northward towards Pont à Mousson, a French frontier town close to Metz, and tried hard to cut across the German salient and recover all the French territory up to the frontier between Metz and Verdun. The immediate result obtained towards the end of September, 1914, was that the army of Metz was strongly enclosed north and south and partly driven back.

Only a small French force, however, seems to have been employed for this purpose, and General Joffre was quite content with the comparatively small advance it made. For ten months or more the French Commander-in-Chief allowed the wedge driven from Metz to remain in the most dangerous part of his line. Even when the French and British forces outnumbered at last the Germans by nearly nine to five, the broad hostile spear-point at St. Mihiel was only slightly reduced in breadth by a little pressure against both its edges. There appear to have been two reasons for the extraordinary complaisance of the great French strategist. One reason was of a geographical nature ; the other

FRENCH FIELD POST STARTING FOR THE FRONT.
An incident at Hermaville, the General Headquarters of the French army operating in the Arras region. The field post, described as one of the lesser triumphs of the war, is seen as it was leaving for the front.

SERVING OUT SOUP TO FRENCH OUTPOSTS.
The soup was served hot from a two-horsed field kitchen, and the photograph supplies interesting evidence of the excellent commissariat arrangements of our allies. The village and its cemetery, the gateway of which is seen in the background, had evidently suffered from gun fire.

occupied by the French forces rose on an average from three hundred to three hundred and fifty feet above the plain of the Woevre. The distance between the high position held by the Verdun army at Bois Haut near Les Eparges and the high position held by the Toul army at the Bois le Prêtre, on the opposite side of the wedge, was only about twenty miles. With the new powerful heavy siege-guns from the Creusot foundries, both French armies at Bois Haut (High Wood) and Bois le Prêtre (Priest's Wood) could command every acre of the German salient running down to the Meuse at St. Mihiel. Howitzer fire could be directed

was of a more subtle, psychological kind. In regard to the geographical position, we must look at the map of the country between Metz and Verdun. Between the two cities extends a clay plateau, seamed with water-courses, and dappled with shining patches of water, forming ponds and lakes of considerable size. There are also many patches of woodland amid the moist and fertile farm-lands of the Woevre, as the flattish upland between the Meuse and the Moselle is called. Westward, above the sunken course of the Meuse, is a line of hills, mostly bare, known as the Heights of the Meuse. On these hills was constructed the chain of smaller isolated fortresses which connected Verdun with Toul. Then, running in a north-easterly direction along the highway from Commercy, through Pont à Mousson, were more hills, the most important of which, in the circumstances of the war, was the wooded height known as the Bois le Prêtre. The German wedge rested chiefly on the lower marshy ground between the Heights of the Meuse and the hills connecting with the Bois le Prêtre. The heights

The German wedge from Metz

by aeroplane observers in the modern way against the railway line by which the Germans brought up artillery, ammunition, and general supplies from Metz. The railway ran from Metz to Thiaucourt, a town about five miles north-east of the Bois le Prêtre. But beyond Thiaucourt the line swerved away from the Heights of the Meuse and ran through the French trenches. It was therefore useful to the enemy only as far as Thiaucourt ; but from this point they rapidly built a light railway along the old Roman road running to St. Mihiel. The distance of the new German railway, with all its windings, was less than twenty-five miles, and as the materials were stored in advance at Metz, the work was carried out quickly. By means of the new railway connection a large number of very heavy howitzers were brought up to the heights around St. Mihiel, and the entire plain of the Woevre was transformed with remarkable speed into a gigantic fortress of earthworks, wire entanglements, machine-gun redoubts, and artillery pits, garrisoned by the larger part of the army of Metz. The

Transformation of the Woevre

GENERAL DUBAIL ON A VISIT TO THE FRENCH HEADQUARTERS IN ALSACE.
With General de Castelnau, General Dubail (seen facing the camera) saved Nancy in August, 1914, after the retreat of the French army which had penetrated between Metz and Strassburg.   On the right of our picture is a "Minenwerfer" (or trench-mortar) captured from the Germans.

Woevre thus became a grand extension of the entrenched camp of Metz.   It was both the barbican of the Lorraine fortress and the gate by which half a million or more German soldiers could be sent forward to hew their way towards Central France.

The French commander made no attempt whatever to alter the situation.   Under his orders the Verdun army on the north and the Toul army on the south of the wedge merely kept the enemy occupied by continual but local struggles for the hills above the plain.   The fighting in the Bois le Prêtre went on for many months ; and there was also a steady pressure through the Forest of Apremont, and its continuation northward—the Wood of Ailly—the latter being about a mile and a half from the fort of the Roman Camp, which defended St. Mihiel.   Between Apremont and the Bois le Prêtre was a line of hills, some of which were four hundred and fifty feet above the plateau.   These hills were held by the Germans.   The French put little or no pressure against them, for it was unscientific and expensive to attempt to advance all along the line, when there was a couple of key-positions from which the vast and formidable fortress system of the Germans could be commanded.

Both sides knew what these two keys were.   The first was the Bois le Prêtre with a lower wooded hill in front of it—the Forest des Venchères, immediately overlooking Thiaucourt.   The second key, and the more important, was the hill of Les Eparges, lying immediately in front of Bois Haut, and overlooking the hamlet of Combres.   For all practical purpose Les Eparges was the winning position in the long, slow, terrible wrestle for the Woevre between the army of Verdun and the army of Metz.

A long, slow, terrible wrestle   The two fortress towns were really besieging each other, and each attacking the hostile works at the point where they met in the Woevre.   The two cities were only thirty miles apart, and as their ring of main forts extended far into the intervening country they could have bombarded each other with 12 in. guns had it been worth while to waste expensive ammunition.   Instead of doing so, they extended their field fortifications until there was only a hundred yards or less between the advanced trenches.

The garrison of Metz, after its victory at Morhange in August, 1914, was the first to extend its range of action ; and in September, 1914, it bombarded one of the isolated forts on the Heights of the Meuse, Fort Troyon; and after very narrowly failing to take it, used its 12 in. howitzers

against the more southernly isolated fort on the Roman Camp near St. Mihiel, and there forced the passage of the Meuse, and occupied the village of Chauvoncourt on its further bank.   This constituted the famous gateway through which a grand German attack might at any time be launched against the rear of the entire Franco-British-Belgian front.   The gateway, however, was blocked from the outside, for the time being, by the French army in the Forest of the Argonne ; **Attack on Les Eparges** for the high, wooded ridges of the famous forest, which for centuries have been one of France's great barriers against invaders, dominated completely the German positions around St. Mihiel.   Holding the enemy at this point, the French commander began in the early spring of 1915 to make himself master of the Woevre by a movement in a more important direction.

We have in a previous chapter seen that the French offensive movement opened in February, 1915, with an extraordinary bombardment and rush of infantry in Champagne, where the Germans lost 40,000 men out of a defending force of 200,000 troops.   While the Battle of Champagne was at its height the French Staff gave an order for the Verdun army to attack the hill of Les Eparges.   The first assault was made on February 17th by means of a mine explosion, after which the first German line was captured without a struggle.   The enemy, however, counter-attacked, and there followed a terrible hand-to-hand struggle, lasting about seventy hours, in which the attacking French regiment was at last pressed into a part of the captured trenches and swept by heavy fire from the German guns.   The position was untenable, and nothing remained but to retire or die fighting.   But the Frenchmen, in electing to take the latter course, found another solution to the problem.   In their last desperate charge, in which they left the first German trench and tore farther up the hill, they completely shattered the 8th Bavarian Regiment in front of them, and extended their footing on the height so that they were able to break down all the enemy's farther counter-attacks.   The fighting on Ash Wednesday on Les Eparges had such results that it caused a feeling of terror throughout Bavaria.   A letter was afterwards found on a prisoner—a baker in a little German town.   His wife wrote to him that : " All the town is full of the news that 4,000 of our men have been slaughtered near Verdun."   Another Bavarian woman wrote to her husband : " The doctor tells us that the 8th Regiment was completely wiped out."

GERMAN SHELL BURSTING BETWEEN ADVANCING FRENCH TROOPS.

In the Great War cavalry made charges on foot as well as took their turn in the trenches. Above is a remarkable camera-record of a German shell bursting between two lines of French Dragoons and killing two of them while the men were charging on foot with bayonets fixed—"somewhere in France."

A SHATTERED HOMESTEAD IN ALSACE—ALL THAT WAS LEFT OF THE MAYOR'S HOUSE AT ASPACH LE HAUT AFTER THE FRENCH HAD DRIVEN OUT THE ENEMY.

This was so ; and the 4th Bavarian Regiment was sent forward to occupy the long ridge. But the general commanding the Woevre operations did not feel satisfied that his key-position was safe with the French holding his first line. He brought up 5,000 engineers, who worked on shifts, day and night for a month, strengthening the fortifications. They drove a tunnel from the village of Combres through the mountain of clay to the German defences near the summit. In the tunnel they built a light railway line, by which supplies and reinforcements could be hauled up by steam-power quickly,

A tunnel through a mountain without interference from the French batteries. To provide against a heavy shell bombardment of the defence works, the troops were sheltered in large, underground chambers, eighteen feet below the surface. All the machine-guns in Metz were brought up, with many mine-throwers of large calibre, and the artillery was strengthened by sixteen additional batteries of heavy howitzers placed in concealed sites in the neighbouring plain. Aerial torpedoes of terrible power were also forwarded by the new railway, and the garrison of 4,000 infantrymen and 5,000 engineers was given the support of an entire division of infantry. The German general saw his officers, and told them that Les Eparges must be held at any cost, even at the cost of a hundred thousand men.

Meanwhile the army of Verdun made no further movement of importance until the First British Army, by the shock of its surprise attack at Neuve Chapelle, caused the entire German line to tremble. In order to concentrate round Lille, the German Commander-in-Chief reduced the garrison of his trenches at every possible point. In particular, a considerable number of men were moved from the army of Metz. This was the opportunity for which General Sarrail had been waiting ; and on March 19th three French battalions charged up Les Eparges ridge and broke the 4th Bavarian Regiment.

190

The main work was done by the great new Creusot howitzers which moved by means of a light railway all round the entrenched camp of Verdun. They were massed against the ridge, and their terrible shells penetrated into the eighteen-feet-deep caverns, and by their blast put out all the lamps, while the falling earth closed the passages. Most of the men in the shelters were captured by the charging French infantry. The new first line of German trenches was occupied without a struggle by reason of the deadly effectiveness of the French siege-artillery. But from their second line the German troops violently counter-attacked, and in a fiercer struggle than that of February, they fought day and night until March 21st, by which time the French troops had advanced 380 yards along the ridge, which had a total length of about 1,580 yards, and a height of about 1,135 feet above sea-level.

On March 27th a single battalion of Chasseurs charged from the conquered trenches towards the summit, and though the colonel and all the company captains were wounded, the desired result was obtained, and a new point of vantage rushed for the final attack on the summit. In the previous fighting the Germans had tried to hold their front trenches by means of a few machine-guns, the main body of troops retiring into the underground shelters when the bombardment **French Chasseurs'** opened, and returning by tunnels when **great charge** the infantry attack was expected. But after the success of the Chasseurs, the front German trenches had to be held continually in force to guard against another surprise assault by infantry, using only bomb and bayonet, and unheralded by heavy artillery fire. It will be remembered that Sir John French at Festubert, at a later date, omitted the preliminary bombardment, with a view to taking the Germans by surprise when they were trying to defend their front trenches in too economical a manner. No doubt the French Staff had communicated to Sir John French full details of the Les Eparges surprise attack.

By this time at Les Eparges the attacking and defending forces were so closely approached that the Germans began to lose heart. The supporting division replaced the two shattered Bavarian regiments, and in the rainy evening of April 5th, when the clay soil was a slide of mud in which men sank up to their thighs, the decisive attack was made. Two French regiments advanced through the curtain of rain towards the western side of the summit. A single aerial torpedo launched by the Germans caused enormous loss to one of the assaulting lines, but in the thick weather and twilight air most of the French troops escaped the fire of the defenders and entered the German trenches. Night fell on a furious hand-to-hand struggle, that went on all through the darkness. But when dawn broke a large, fresh body of enemy troops fell upon the victorious but worn-out French battalions and compelled them to retire. Yet again, as soon as night fell, the French infantry charged forward into the trench on the east of the summit, and also climbed up some way on the west. It was still raining, and they fought on all the night, and when dawn again broke they had won another five hundred yards.

Once more the German commander sent **Fighting in rain and darkness** up fresh forces through the tunnel; but fresh French forces also arrived, and the Frenchmen, wet through, muddied all over, and often dropping their mud-clogged rifles and using their bayonets as knives—knives being handier than fixed bayonets in a narrow trench—stabbed and bombed their way forward. All the enemy's counter-attacks were repulsed, and at five o'clock in the morning of April 7th the struggle suddenly ended.

The German commander was trying to carry out his plan of holding Les Eparges at any cost. He sent out his last supports by the tunnel from Combres village, but as the troops debouched from the other side of the tunnel, the French howitzers caught them in a torrent of shrapnel fire. Every man was **A torrent of** swept away before he could reach the **shrapnel fire** trenches held by the French infantry. The German commander, meanwhile, was rapidly collecting an army corps from the Woevre, with a view to pushing it up the hill. Large bodies of troops massed in Combres village; but it was now daylight, and French aerial observation officers, in communication with heavy French batteries concealed in the village of St. Remy, a mile and a half south-east of Combres, directed the howitzers against the gathering masses at the foot of Les Eparges. The larger part of the enemy's reinforcements was broken up by the French guns before it could form for attack. Those that escaped the French artillery were beaten back by the French infantry, and so heavy were the enemy's losses that all the rest of the day and all the following day he attempted no further counter-attack.

All the while the rain continued, making the movement of French reinforcements through the muddy clay very difficult. It was not until the morning of April 8th that two fresh battalions of infantry and a fresh battalion of Chasseurs arrived on the ridge. They at once went into

THE RAILWAY-STATION AT ASPACH LE HAUT, ALSACE, PART OF THE TERRITORY REOCCUPIED BY THE FRENCH.

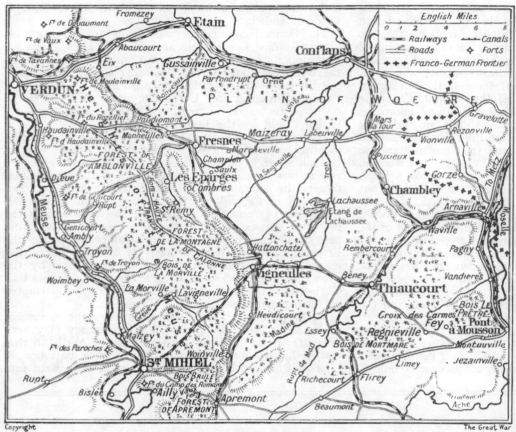

MAP OF THE HEIGHTS OF THE MEUSE AND THE PLAIN OF THE WOEVRE.
On the Heights of the Meuse were constructed a chain of smaller isolated fortresses which connected Verdun with Toul. The German "wedge" from Metz rested chiefly on the lower marshy ground between the Heights of the Meuse and the hills connecting with the Bois le Pretre.

action, and in an hour's bayonet fighting they captured the summit.

The enemy held only a little triangle of ground at the eastern extremity of the ridge, but the key to the position was in the hands of the French, and all counter-attacks were swept away by shell fire and machine-gun fire, without bayonet or bomb work. The French general conducting the operations then relieved all his fatigued, happy, and triumphant troops, and sent out sappers to put the trenches in order, and to reconstruct and enlarge the system of communicating earthworks. The fresh regiments brought to Les Eparges advanced in the everlasting rain in the afternoon of April 9th to complete the victory. It had been arranged that the heavy French artillery should produce something like an earthquake in the fragment of defences still left in the enemy's hands. But at the critical moment a blanket of mist fell upon the height, making the aerial control of the guns impossible. So the French infantry had to carry out the work at more expense, but with magnificent bravery. They went forward in a furious charge in the evening, followed by hand-to-hand fighting in the darkness. Rain and fog made searchlights, star-shells, and other modern means of illuminating the battlefield practically useless; and at ten o'clock at night the French infantrymen had felled every German on every yard of the long height, and Les Eparges was

How Les Eparges was won

completely won. Two counter-attacks were beaten off with ease on the nights of April 11th and 12th, the French artillery being used in such a way as to make every attempted attack on the ridge on the part of the Germans only a laborious form of suicide.

But the German commander was not defeated. He was a man whom it was absolutely impossible to defeat. Having sworn that he would hold Les Eparges, he found a remarkable way of fulfilling his word. He withdrew his troops from Combres village in the ravine, and entrenched

them upon the lower neighbouring hill. This hill had hitherto been known as Combres Hill, but the ingenious German commander rebaptised it by the name of Les Eparges. So, according to the official published reports of the German Staff, Les Eparges was still occupied by their army of Metz.

While the attack upon the original Les Eparges was being conducted by the army of Verdun, the army of Toul profited by the severe strain which its comrades in the north were imposing upon the common foe. For many months part of the Toul forces had been fighting from the south against St. Mihiel and Thiaucourt. By the Heights of the Meuse they had withstood all the winter the shock of the enemy in the Forest of Apremont. Their lines in places were only two miles from the forts defending St. Mihiel, and the commander of Metz exerted all his strength to end the battle in this region which had begun in September, 1914. The largest siege-guns in Metz were brought down by the light railway, with millions of hand-grenades, hundreds of thousands of bombs, and thousands of the huge aerial torpedoes which had been invented by a Scandinavian officer.

The French were at first at a disadvantage, owing to their lack of heavy field-artillery, but the Creusot and other gun factories, by a magnificent effort of endurance and skill on the part of their workmen and designers, armed the French forces with huge howitzers in the winter of 1914. The result was that the army of Toul, which

The advance to Ailly Wood

was still the most important army in France, as it guarded the flank of all the Franco-British-Belgian line, was put on a level of equipment with the enemy. By the spring of 1915 the positions along the eastern frontier fortresses were reversed. Instead of the Germans trying to invest or break the great French entrenched camps, the French began to press strongly against the German fortifications protecting Lorraine. The army of Toul shelled, bombed, and mined its way through the Forest of Apremont, in which every tree was either broken by shell fire or blown to brushlike stumps of wood by aerial torpedoes and grenades.

Towards the end of March the French trenches had been driven through the Forest of Apremont towards the bare height crowning Ailly Wood. The advance was conducted by sapping until the French engineers issued from the northwest of the Forest of Apremont and dug their way along a ravine leading to a steep height in Ailly Wood known as "the fortress." Here the Germans had constructed a very strong system of armoured earthworks, forming the outer defence to St. Mihiel, lying less than two miles northward. Against this fortress the army of Toul massed their machinery of slaughter in the first days of April. By this time they also possessed aerial torpedoes, consisting of large, cigar-shaped tubes of metal, filled with high-explosive and steadied in their flight by a propeller. The aerial torpedoes were ejected from a kind of mortar, by means of a small charge of powder, and when they were

Chasseurs-à-Pied, a " crack " French Light Infantry Corps, after clearing the sand bags of the first-line enemy trench, are seen charging the second-line trench on the Heights of the Meuse to the east of the Argonne Forest.

Chasseurs-à-Pied in a German trench they had gallantly stormed and captured. They were photographed in the act of clambering over the parapet in order to charge again and capture the trench beyond.

FRENCH LIGHT INFANTRY IN ACTION ON THE HEIGHTS OF THE MEUSE.

SILENT WITNESSES TO A BIG ARTILLERY ACTION—EMPTY SHELL-CASES OF THE FAMOUS FRENCH "75's."

thrown into the air the propeller and rudder kept them on the mark. The French used many of these new missiles, and the three German lines on the hill were destroyed, together with the accessory defences. All the garrison perished, many being thrown up into the air, with trees and sand-bags, when the terrible land torpedoes struck home. At the same time the French gunners, acting as observers at a distance of only three hundred and sixty feet from the German lines, directed the new heavy siege ordnance against the enemy's machine-gun redoubts. Then, after some hours of this ghastly, mechanical slaughter, the labours of the French engineers were completed. They had driven three mines into the hill, and at noon on April 5th the mines were exploded, and before the fumes were blown away the French infantry advanced in three waves against the shattered fortress.

The troops were ordered not to enter the German trenches for any purpose, but merely to clear them out. They used the ordinary hand-grenades, and also little boxes of high-explosive which they called colanders, and threw in the manner of the classic discobolus. Avoiding the German trenches, which had probably been mined by the enemy in case he lost them, the French infantry swept round and took their foes in the rear of the hill by means of two flank movements, which completely swept the ground, and then united behind the fort. The entire German force on the hill was either blown up by torpedoes or heavy shells, or slain in the infantry rush by hand-bomb or bayonet. Only on the right of the hill were two French companies held up by machine-guns, after capturing three lines of trenches. In the evening the enemy tried to obliterate his lost positions by the massed fire of his heavy guns, but the French artillery had been concentrated round Ailly Wood in superior force and, directed by observers in aeroplanes, it poured so tremendous a fire on the German batteries that these were silenced. At six o'clock in the April evening the German infantry attempted a counter-attack. But it broke and retreated, being caught by a hurricane fire of shrapnel from both the light French field-guns and the Creusot heavy howitzers.

Genius of the French gunner

This engagement at Ailly Wood was a masterly example of modern French artillery tactics. It showed on a small scale, and at a point of great strategic importance, the genius of the French gunner, who, by the perfection of his Staff work and the excellence of his material, ranks—as he did in the days of Napoleon—above the artillerymen of every other nation. Our own gunners were very good, their marksmanship being exceedingly effective, but the French Staff work excelled even that of the German Staff, and was, therefore, superior to ours. The incomparably lucid and logical power of the French intellect was as admirably displayed in its Staff work in the reorganised French armies of 1915 as it was in the works of Pascal, Descartes, and Taine. There was a kind of mathematical rigour in modern French military work which produced a feeling of terror in the minds of the German Staff. To take a small unimportant point, there was no interruption in the work of mechanical slaughter by the French guns by reason of the destruction of telephonic communication between the observers and the batteries. Possibly the French used a dozen wires from each observation post in order to guard against the destructive effect of the enemy's shells. However this may be, the affair in Ailly Wood was a work of slaughter conducted with terrible and unfailing rigour, which produced great losses among the enemy at a cost of only a couple of hundred casualties to our allies. The action showed that it is sometimes possible to carry an intricate and very strongly fortified position at very little cost of life, provided that all the modern scientific instruments of destruction are lavishly employed in a well-prepared and well-designed manner.

Corpse-strewn German trenches

On April 6th, after the hill fort was captured, the general directing the attack launched his troops on the left of the enemy's position into a maze of German trenches. But as the German commander strongly reinforced his front, the French troops retired through the deep cuttings, and the work was resumed by the heavy French howitzers and the aerial torpedo section. Once more they blew up three lines of hostile trenches, leaving to their infantry only the work of occupying the blasted and corpse-strewn lines. The entire garrison of the works was annihilated; a few prisoners were taken—all wounded. No unwounded German escaped. The enemy then had no fresh force to continue the action, and two days elapsed before he could collect sufficient troops to make a counter-attack. Then all the German artillery in the region of St. Mihiel massed its fire on Ailly Wood, and under cover of this tempest of destruction the re-formed German infantry made eight distinct, separate attempts to recover the position by storm.

But the French engineers had not wasted time in the two days' interval allowed them. Not a single piece of

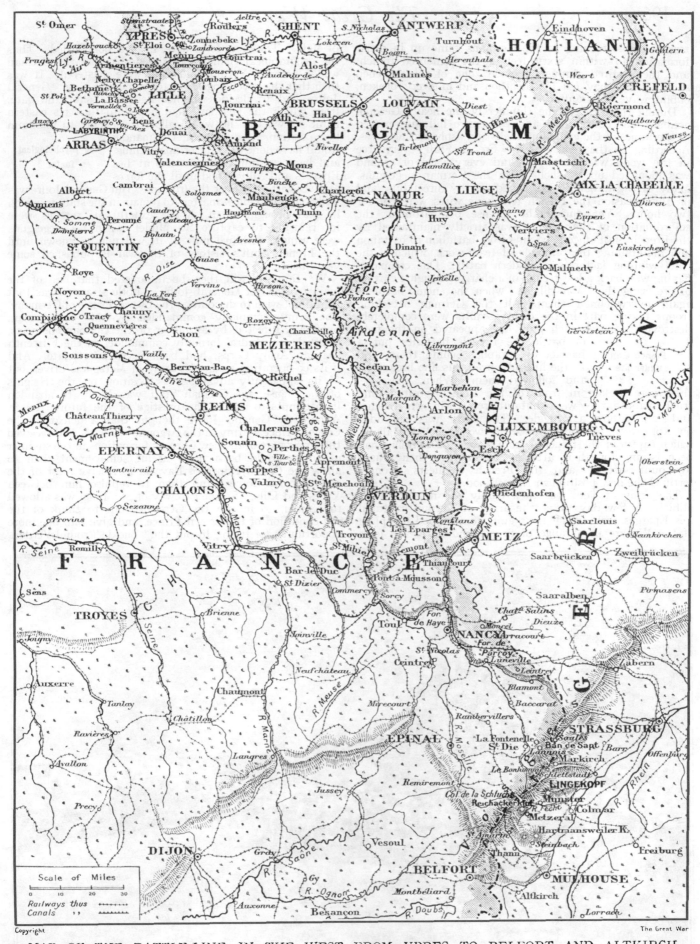

MAP OF THE BATTLE-LINE IN THE WEST FROM YPRES TO BELFORT AND ALTKIRCH.

This map has been carefully drawn to indicate the scenes of the fierce fighting along the eastern frontier of France, and to illustrate the German attacks on Verdun and the French advance in Alsace-Lorraine.

trench was lost; and, as the Germans came up in dense formation to within sixty feet of the armoured trench, and then retired through a wide zone of thick French shrapnel fire, they fell by the thousand in every broken, ebbing wave of assault.

During the struggle the thunder of the heavy German artillery was continuous, and the entire hill disappeared in the fumes of the exploding shells and asphyxiating gases. According to the report of the French Staff, every tree in the wood was destroyed, and every yard of ground was ploughed up by shells from the German siege-guns. Many of the trenches were wiped out by direct hits, and on this occasion the French telephone wires were cut for two hours. Yet during the intense bombardment the co-ordination of the defence was strictly maintained by the French Staff officers, passing from battalion to battalion and maintaining the principle of team-work, which is the chief winning factor in a modern battle. One company, having won back a lost trench in a charge through a curtain of fire, sang the "Marseillaise" when the enemy batteries again overwhelmed them. All the German attacking troops taking part in the eight assaults were completely destroyed; for as each grey line appeared on the field of battle the French batteries put a **French elan** barrage of shrapnel behind them, and **under fire** as the line advanced this line broadened and followed them. When, therefore, they were broken in front of the French position and tried to retire, they were shut out from their own trenches and slain without a struggle. The battle was concluded on April 10th by the advance of two French battalions, which captured the trenches from which the Germans had been issuing for their attack. The enemy then ceased to counter-attack, and the French engineers strongly fortified the new position in Ailly Wood.

The army of Toul was then barely one mile from St. Mihiel. A few days later the army of Verdun captured Les Eparges, from which their guns commanded the plain of the Woevre in a range of fire extending to the forts of Metz. The Metz forts were, in fact, bombarded. Thus the geographical elements in the problem of the German wedge between Verdun and Toul were mastered. It was then that the psychological factor came into play. General Joffre had to decide whether he would shut the gate, from which the Germans had hoped to turn his eastern flank, or whether he would allow the enemy to maintain his position. A German commander would have done the safe, ordinary thing, **The psychological** and have continued the battles at Les **factor** Eparges and Ailly Wood until the forces at Metz withdrew over the frontier. But General Joffre was well content to allow matters to remain in the state to which he had brought them. What exactly his reasons were for refusing to capture St. Mihiel, when his siege-guns were almost within a mile of it, will not be known until the French Staff's history of the war is published some years hence.

We think it will then be discovered that one of the main reasons for General Joffre's subtle strategy was that he did not wish to discourage the Crown Prince of Germany. The army, nominally commanded by this young man, but really directed by an officer of the German engineers, General von Mudra, formerly commander of the Fifteenth German Army Corps, had been very unfortunate. And if its co-operating wing, the army of Metz, was driven out of its apparently advantageous position on the Heights of the Meuse, the German Staff was likely to abandon its attempts to restore the prestige of the future Kaiser. Apparently General Joffre thought that a defeat of the Crown Prince's army in the Argonne—when it had received the larger part of the new German formations in the summer of 1915—would be a more useful achievement than to allow the Crown Prince of Bavaria to receive most of the new German forces, and then to repulse him between Ypres and Lille. So the gateway of St. Mihiel was allowed to remain, to induce the German Staff to think of the sad condition of the Crown Prince, and give him one more opportunity for trying to put the "buckle" round Verdun.

"POUR LA PATRIE!" FRENCH TROOPS, THEIR HAVERSACKS WELL SUPPLIED WITH NECESSARIES, ABOUT TO ENTRAIN FOR THE FIRING-LINE.
A picturesque episode at a small countryside railway-station in the South of France.

HOUSES OF PARLIAMENT

CHAPTER LXXIV

FROM THE EMBANKMENT.

THE "SILVER BULLETS": A DRAMATIC STORY OF WORLD-WIDE FINANCE.

By A. W. Holland.

The Aftermath of an Era of Extravagance—How the Great War Found us Financially Unprepared—The Drain of British Gold to Germany—Great Britain on the Horns of a Dilemma—Neutrality or a Big War Indemnity to Germany—Fall of our National Credit—The Government and the Crisis—How the Financial Panic was Stayed—The British Navy and Overseas Commerce—Developments in the American Exchange—The Bank of England and Foreign Bills—Russia's Heroic Course—Meeting the Cost of Armageddon : £3,000,000 a Day—Looking to the Future—An Unprecedented Object Lesson in the Forgotten Virtue of Economy.

LORD ROSEBERY'S position as phrase-maker to the British Empire appears to have been taken by Mr. Lloyd George, whose reference to "silver bullets" attracted a good deal of attention. We do not know whether the Chancellor of the Exchequer, as Mr. George was then, had in mind the old superstition that a silver bullet will kill a witch when an ordinary leaden one is powerless to do so, or whether he had been reading Robert Herrick's lines :

Fight thou with shafts of silver, and o'ercome,
When no force else can get the masterdom ;

but we do know that he was referring to the important part played by finance in carrying on and conducting war, and that he used the phrase "silver bullets" as a synonym for money.

It is quite easy to exaggerate the importance of finance in war, and nearly as easy to underestimate it. Money alone, though it be poured out like water, is powerless to secure victory, or Crœsus and not Alexander would have been lord of the ancient world, and Rothschild, not Napoleon, dictator of the modern one. Without skilful generals and brave soldiers it can do nothing, but with them it may well be the deciding factor in a great struggle, for it can buy for them the arms and equipment they need. The

THE MINISTER OF MUNITIONS.
In May, 1915, on the reconstruction of the Cabinet, Mr. Lloyd George undertook the formation and temporary direction of a new department called the Ministry of Munitions. In our photograph Mr. Lloyd George is seen accompanied by Mr. J. Howard Whitehouse, M.P.

present war has shown us, even if we did not know it before, that no nation has a monopoly of courage, that each can easily find thousands of men willing to go to almost certain death ; and so, with the human factor equal or nearly so, it is fair to assume that victory will fall to the nation, or group of nations, whose finances can stand the greatest strain—that is, the one which can arm the greatest number of men. In other words, money makes the big battalions possible, and the big battalions mean victory.

Fortunately for Great Britain and her Allies, the British Navy was ready for war in that fateful last week of July, 1914, but in other directions we were not equally prepared. Our Army, although, as far as it went, one of the best in the world, was much too small to stem the German rush into France, and to-day we know to our cost that a force ten times its size would have been none too big for the task which our heroes strove so gallantly to perform between Mons and the Marne. We realise now that we ought to have strained every nerve to make Great Britain a great military as well as a great naval Power.

It was in our financial arrangements that we were least prepared of all, and that in spite of our traditions. When France was striving to dominate Europe it was British ships and British gold which turned the scales in favour of the smaller nations. During the Seven Years' War

Z   **197**

THE KING'S VISIT TO BIRMINGHAM MUNITION FACTORIES.

During a tour in the Midlands in July, 1915, his Majesty visited the works of Messrs. Kynochs, Ltd., the Birmingham Small Arms Company's factories at Small Heath, and the waggon works at Saltley. He manifested deep interest in all he saw, and spoke in warm terms of the zeal and cheerfulness with which the hands at the various factories were working, not only to maintain but to increase the output of munitions of war, so that the end in view—victory for the Allies—might be achieved.

the elder Pitt found the money for Frederick the Great to continue the fight against France, and during the Napoleonic Wars his son followed the same policy, for all the coalitions against Bonaparte were rendered possible by financial support from Britain. Against those twin bulwarks—the valour of our seamen and the gold of our traders—the genius of Napoleon spent itself in vain. But in years of peace and plenty we had forgotten all this. We had entered upon an era of extravagance, which is the worst possible preparation for war, and we took up arms with an enormous handicap upon us.

After the South African War our national expenditure had increased by leaps and bounds. In the financial year 1898-99 it was £117,000,000; but in 1913-14, the last year before the war, it had grown to nearly £200,000,000, while for 1914-15 it was estimated at £206,000,000. This, however, is only part of the story. Following the example of Parliament, local authorities all over the country spent money with the utmost freedom, and a cynical person might be pardoned for thinking that they were vying with each other in a laudable endeavour to bring the country to bankruptcy, or, at least, to see how much it could really stand. Moreover, although they put about fabulous and misleading stories of our wealth, the most optimistic of our amateur financiers had not the hardihood to declare that our income was growing at the same rate as our expenditure.

An era of extravagance

From time to time a few voices were raised against this orgy of extravagance, and prophecies about its consequences were uttered. In measured language bankers and financiers, men who knew what they were talking about, pointed out that this heavy expenditure, although doubtless desirable from some points of view, was gravely weakening our resources in the event of war, but their protests were ignored or derided, just as were those of Earl Roberts when he drew attention to our unpreparedness for war from the purely military point of view. It was clear that economy was looked upon rather as a vice than as a virtue, and that the age of thrift in national affairs was over. The very worst day's work ever done in the recent history of this country was when an influential group of politicians began to look upon taxation as something desirable in itself, something other than a necessary evil. Those responsible for the management of our finances apparently never gave a moment's thought to the possibility of war; they spent our money right royally, evidently believing that the age of perpetual peace

had come, and that we had no need to trouble about financial reserves or anything of the kind. Truly, as the old proverb says, " There are none so blind as those who will not see."

The extravagance of the past ten years had weakened our financial resources, and made it more difficult for us to raise the money required for carrying on the war than would have been the case if economy and preparedness had been our national watchwords.

During twelve years of peace and great trade prosperity taxation was greatly increased, whereas a policy of prudent finance would have taken this opportunity of reducing it. Before the war broke out the income-tax, called rightly the sheet-anchor of our national finances, had been increased to the high figure of 1s. 3d. in the pound. In addition to this, there was a super-tax, graduated in a somewhat complicated fashion, which made the tax on big incomes just over 2s. 6d. in the pound. Before the Boer War the tax stood at 8d. in the pound, and there was no super-tax. Verily, people asked, if these things were done in the green tree, what would be done in the dry? With an income-tax of 2s. 6d. in the pound they knew.

Before the Boer War the untouched reserve of income was 19s. 4d. in the pound, and the untouched reserve of capital varied from 92 per cent. upwards. That is, a Chancellor of the Exchequer could say, referring of course only to the payers of direct taxes: " I am taking 8d. in the pound of each man's income, and a certain percentage, not exceeding 8, of each man's capital when he dies; therefore, if a great war breaks out, I shall have 19s. 4d. in every pound of income, and 92 per cent. or more of all capital on which to draw." He was like a man who has deposited securities worth £2,000 with his bankers, and has only drawn against them to the extent of £100 or less.

Our finances in 1914

How different was the position when the Great War broke out. Instead of 19s. 4d. in the pound, the Chancellor had only 18s. 9d. on which to draw, and in many cases much less than this. Of the big incomes, those which could contribute the most in times of emergency like then he had less than 17s. 6d. in the pound left. As regards capital the position was even worse. From 92 per cent. and upwards the reserve had been reduced to 80 per cent. and upwards. The plain fact is that such taxation leaves much less money in the pockets of the taxpayers, and that, therefore, they are less able to pay heavy taxes when these are most necessary. This war has taught us a good deal, and it should teach us a lesson which we had quite

SIR C. A. PARSONS, K.C.B.
Central Committee of Inventions Board.

DR. G. T. BEILBY, F.R.S.
Central Committee of Inventions Board.

forgotten—i.e., the wise financier is the man who allows money to fructify in the pockets of the people, who takes from them as little as he can possibly do with, not as much as he can possibly spend.

There is another and perhaps a more serious result of this extravagance. It greatly weakened our credit, and credit is the life-blood of a nation just as it is of a business. A good business man will sacrifice anything rather than let his credit suffer, and the decline of the credit of a country is a very serious matter to the people of that country. Many pointed triumphantly to the fact that German credit or French credit had fallen as much, or nearly as much, as British credit, but this argument only appeals to the frivolous. To maintain the high standard of British credit ought to have been our statesmen's constant and dearest aim, but here, too, they were found wanting.

In speaking of our national credit, we are referring to something which touches every one of us, and **The burden on** not merely the people **posterity** who buy stocks and shares, as many ignorant persons profess to believe. The higher a nation's credit, the more cheaply it can borrow money, and when we needed such big sums for carrying on the war, it was of the utmost importance that we should be able to borrow cheaply. But unfortunately we could not do this. Careless and ignorant politicians had seriously weakened our credit, and the consequence is that we and our children and our grandchildren must pay millions a year more than we need have done if reasonable provision had been made for the possibility of war. Here is a burden so big that no possible scheme of taxation can throw it wholly on the rich. Of it we must all take a share, and so help to pay the heavy price of incompetence. The only redeeming feature is that it may perhaps be a lesson to us in the future.

At the time of the Boer War this country could borrow as much money as it wanted at 3 per cent. or thereabouts, but thereafter its credit had steadily declined. In 1902 every £100 of Consols was selling at about 95, but from then until the end of 1905 the price fell steadily to about 85. Then, in October, 1905, came a slight spurt, but afterwards the fall was renewed, and it proved continuous.

The seriousness of the fall in the price of Consols, that is in the price of British credit, between 1902 and 1914 has not been fully realised. As we have said, the period was one of peace and prosperity. Trade was good, the revenue was rising, and the National Debt was being paid off. By all the laws of political economy, British credit ought to have risen steadily, and yet it fell almost without a break during these twelve years, and outside a small circle no one seemed to care. Before July, 1915, this steady fall had taken Consols first below 80 and then below 70, and no one knew where it would stop. Evidently investors, both at home and abroad, thought less and less of the credit **Consols and** of Great Britain. After **national credit** all, said many, this only concerns the holders of Consols, and they, like other people, must take the rough with the smooth. They forgot that the price of Consols regulated the prices of all other British securities, not excepting house property, and that in these the working classes, through their trade unions, their insurance societies, their savings banks, their building societies and the like, had a very big interest. They forgot that a fall of this kind, if it continued beyond a certain point, would render most of these societies insolvent, and they had a warning of what to expect when, in 1911, the Birkbeck Bank failed for this reason. Finally, they forgot—and this is our most important point —that the price of Consols fixed roughly the rate which the Government had to pay if at any time it was necessary for it to borrow money. However, the time was coming when this

EARL ST. ALDWYN.
Chairman of Committee of Advice on New Financial Issues.

THE RT. HON. REGINALD McKENNA.
Appointed Chancellor of the Exchequer in May, 1915.

THE RT. HON. HERBERT SAMUEL.
Appointed Postmaster-General in May, 1915.

INTERCESSION DAY IN LONDON: IMPRESSIVE DRUM-HEAD SERVICE AT ST. PAUL'S CATHEDRAL.

Sunday, July 25th, 1915, was observed in London as a day of intercession on behalf of the King, the nation, and the land and sea forces of the Empire. More than 3,000 Territorial troops attended a service conducted on the steps of St. Paul's Cathedral by the Bishop of London, and a great congregation of the general public filled one half of the circle of the Churchyard, and spread in mass down Ludgate Hill. Before the Bishop's sermon (based on Matt. xvi. 26: "For what is a man profited, if he shall gain the whole world, and lose his own soul?"), the troops, led by their bands, joined in singing the hymn "O God, our help in ages past." "We summon then the soul of England," pleaded Dr. Ingram in his closing words, "to arise in all its grandeur and strength at this crisis of the day of God. Come from the four winds, thou Breath of the Spirit, and breathe upon this great people that hope and faith and love may once again revive, and the world be saved again by the 'Soul of a People.'"

ANNIVERSARY OF THE OUTBREAK OF WAR.

On August 4th, 1915, the King and Queen, with Queen Alexandra, and the leaders of the nation attended a special intercessory service at St. Paul's Cathedral, when the Archbishop of Canterbury preached from 1 Cor. xvi. 13. Our photograph shows the King and Queen on their way to the Cathedral.

specious argument would be disproved, when the state of British credit would be a matter of vital importance to every Briton. It came on August 4th, 1914.

In 1896 investors were quite willing to lend money to the British Government if they were provided with interest at the rate of £2 10s. a year for every £100 lent. At the time of the Boer War they wanted 3 per cent., but when the Great War broke out they asked nearly 4 per cent., and the Government had either to pay this or go without the money, which of course they could not do. **Why investors got** But why, someone may perhaps ask, were **bigger interest** investors able to get bigger interest for the same amount of money? The reason is simple. It is because the price of Consols had fallen. For £68, or perhaps less, an investor in July, 1914, could buy £100 of Consols, and so could get £2 10s. a year for every £68 which he invested, or something like £3 14s. for every £100. This being so he would not, obviously, lend his money for a mere 3 per cent., when he could buy the very highest kind of security to bring him in over 3½ per cent. If, in these circumstances, the Government had asked for money at 3 per cent. they would have got none, and so when they wanted it they had to make sure of getting it by offering a higher rate of interest. There is no mystery about this matter. The price of money—that is, the rate at which it can be borrowed—is, like the price of everything else, regulated by the simple law of supply and demand. Thus it came about that the first borrowings for the present war were at the rate of just under 4 per cent., and later, when an enormous sum was needed, it was necessary to offer 4½ per cent. and other advantages.

Let us suppose that the Great War had broken out in 1896 or thereabouts. At first the Government would have been able to borrow very large sums quite easily at 3 per cent., or probably a shade less; but as the war proceeded they would, as is always the case, have been obliged to pay more. Roughly speaking, we may say that during the twenty years or so before 1914 British credit had fallen by about one-third. In 1915 we had to pay from 4 to 4½ per cent. for money, whereas in 1896 we had only to pay 3 or 3½ per cent., 1 per cent. less. In 1915 the British people were beginning to pay for this decline in our national credit. For every £100,000,000 which our Government borrowed it had to pay £1,000,000 a year more than it would have done if it had been borrowing in 1896. This represents interest at the rate of 1 per cent., and the calcula- **A costly** tion is a simple one. If the war costs **lesson** £1,000,000,000 we must pay an extra £10,000,000 a year for it; if, as is more likely, it costs £2,000,000,000, we must pay an extra £20,000,000 a year, and so on. Such is the price of financial unpreparedness for war, of being governed by men who refuse to look disagreeable facts in the face. For years and years —we know not how many—our people must go on paying something between £10,000,000 and £20,000,000 a year more than they need have done if their rulers had practised the stern virtue of economy. However, the milk is spilled. All we can do is to take to heart the costly lesson—for of nations as of men it is true that whatsoever they sow that shall they also reap.

We are, of course, aware that other causes—among them the widening of the area of investments and the increased

THE BISHOP OF LONDON AND THE WOUNDED.

Before conducting the drum-head service at St. Paul's Cathedral on July 25th, 1915, the Bishop of London visited the Church of St. Martin-in-the-Field, and spoke a few words to some wounded soldiers who were waiting there, together with an escort of the London Rifle Brigade, of which Dr. Ingram is chaplain.

GUARDING THE NARROW SEAS FROM THE GERMAN SUBMARINE MENACE.

Vivid pictorial impression of an exciting incident during coast patrol work. The suspicious-looking object towards which the destroyer is seen making at full speed looked very like the eye of a periscope, but proved on closer investigation to be nothing more deadly than a fragment of wreckage.

output of gold—contributed to the fall in the price of securities. But, as far as this country is concerned, the chief cause, we are sure, was extravagance, both national and local, and this brought upon us the first of the two great financial handicaps with which we entered upon the Great War.

The same financial unpreparedness, the same reluctance to face unpleasant possibilities, was with us to the very end.

Our forfeit to Germany

Our politicians sincerely wanted peace, of that there is no doubt whatever; but they made the fatal mistake of thinking that good intentions were enough. The result was that in July, 1914, Germany, prepared for war in every conceivable way, caught this country at a great disadvantage financially. Though we did not know it at the time, we were really on the horns of a dilemma. We had either to remain neutral in the coming struggle, or to forfeit a large sum of money to Germany. For our honour and safety we chose the latter alternative, and Germany secured what may be not unfairly described as a war indemnity from this country.

Let us examine carefully what happened in the last week of July, 1914. The London Stock Exchange is the biggest market for securities in the world, and, thanks to the telegraph, every day stocks and shares from all parts of the world are sold there. Its prices, which are affected by reports and rumours from every quarter of the globe— earthquakes in Japan, railway accidents in America, rainstorms in Africa, and drought in Australia—are known everywhere in a few seconds, and the " House," as it is called, has been aptly likened to a barometer. It is a barometer which shows at a glance the financial conditions in every country of the world.

Heavy selling of stocks on German account—though

the fact was not then known—began early in July and continued through the first half of the month. The hint had been given by the German military authorities to their bankers to prepare for war. They prepared by unloading as far as possible their obligations upon the British people, handing over to us securities, and taking for those securities gold. On Friday, July 24th, there was a certain amount of anxiety and nervousness on the Stock Exchange, and in financial circles generally, on account of the international situation, and on the following day this feeling was still more pronounced. There was a good deal of selling, especially selling of foreign securities, and prices fell heavily in every department. Hopes were entertained that the Sunday's rest might give the depression time to pass away, as it had often done before ; but, unfortunately, this was not to be. Monday and Tuesday were worse than Friday and Saturday had been, and on Wednesday it was certain that the crisis was no ordinary one.

The business of the Stock Exchange is conducted on an elaborate system of credit, and every fortnight or thereabouts accounts are made up. Stockbrokers buy stocks and shares for which they cannot pay, in the hope that before the day of settlement arrives they will be **Failures on the Stock Exchange** able to sell them at a profit. If, however, they cannot do this, they can quite easily borrow money on the stocks they have bought, and so get over the difficulty in that way.

This system works well enough in normal times. When prices are falling, falling without a break, the banks and financial houses are naturally very reluctant to lend ; and this was the case in July, as the next settling day, which was Wednesday the 29th came near. Many stockbrokers had on their hands stocks which they could not sell at anything like the prices they had given for them a few days before, and on the security of which it was very difficult to borrow, and so it is not surprising that they looked forward to Wednesday with alarm. As an instance of the seriousness of the fall, it may be mentioned that the ordinary shares of the Canadian Pacific Railway fell 22½ points in a few days.

When Wednesday came the fall in prices continued, selling orders came from every part of the world, and in the midst of the general uneasiness it was announced that seven firms had failed ; in the phraseology of stockbrokers they were " hammered." The only bright spot was that the number of failures was so few; many more were expected. Many stockbrokers, however, were hanging, like Mohammed's coffin, between the heaven of solvency and the earth of insolvency.

On Thursday the selling continued, the uneasiness became more marked, and more failures seemed likely. There had been international crises before, plenty of them, and panics and failures on the Stock Exchange, but never a day like Thursday the 30th. A known danger can be met and dealt with, but an unknown danger is a much more terrible thing. All over the Stock

The dread of the unknown Exchange was the dread of the unknown, and all awaited Friday morning with the gravest anxiety, for clearly this state of affairs could not continue without a big catastrophe.

As soon as the Stock Exchange was opened, it was seen that the position was worse and not better, and it was evident that something had to be done. Accordingly before twelve o'clock the authorities closed the Stock Exchange until further notice, and the smaller exchanges in other parts of the country followed this example. The settlements were indefinitely postponed, and so many were saved from ruin ; the business of buying and selling shares was stopped, and prices could not fall any further.

Never before in the history of the " House " had such a step been necessary.

In addition to the Stock Exchange, the money market was violently disturbed during these anxious days. There was a demand for gold, and to protect its reserve the Bank of England raised its rate on Thursday, July 30th, from 3 to 4 per cent. This was not very surprising, but on the Friday the position was so serious, the demand for gold was so insistent, that the Bank Rate was doubled at one stroke. It was made 8 per cent., a clear sign that there was something wrong. **Bank Rate at 10 per cent.** This meant that banks and financial institutions which wanted to borrow money from the Bank of England had to pay 8 per cent. for it or do without it. It meant, too, that every other borrower had to pay more, for just as the price of Government securities regulates the prices of other securities, so the Bank Rate regulates the rate at which practically all money is lent.

Still the demand for gold continued. People were willing to pay 8 per cent., or perhaps it would be more correct to say they were obliged to pay it, for they had unexpected liabilities to meet, and as the stock of gold in the Bank was diminishing, the Rate was raised on Saturday to 10 per cent. It had not been as high as this since 1866, the year in which Overend and Gurney, the well-known bankers, failed. To use the expressive American phrase, " money was talking."

This big demand for gold was closely connected with the state of the foreign exchanges. Each country has a rate of exchange with every other country with which it does business, this being the rate at which the debts of one country are set off against the debts of the other. Let us take a simple illustration, that of the exchange between England and France. Every day a good deal of business is done between the two countries, and each owes the other money for all sorts of things. Now France pays her debts

KEEPING WATCH AND WARD—BRITISH DESTROYER "TALKING" TO MINE-SWEEPERS.
Two branches of the silent but highly efficient work of our Navy are illustrated here. On the left we see the deck of a destroyer on guard duty, and on the horizon can be discerned two mine-sweepers with which she is communicating, vessels engaged in highly perilous but necessary work, of the value of which the general public, safe at home, can have had but a very imperfect idea.

in francs and England pays her debts in sovereigns, and the rate at which these are exchanged for each other is called the rate of exchange. Usually it is about twenty-five francs twenty centimes for the sovereign, but it falls and rises according to circumstances.

The rate of exchange varies a little from day to day, according to the nature of the business done. If England owes France more than France owes England, we say that the French exchange is falling, because Frenchmen, not having so much to pay, are not giving quite so much for a sovereign as they were doing, and vice **Fall in foreign** versa. Thus at the rate of exchange the **exchanges** debts of one side cancel the debts of the other without any money changing hands, but sometimes there is a big balance remaining, and one side or the other must send actual gold to make this up. In practice it is found that England sends gold to France when the exchange is as low as 25 francs 12½ centimes for the sovereign and France sends gold to England when it is as high as 25 francs 32½ centimes. With other countries the principle is exactly the same. When one country owes another large amounts we find that the exchange is going against it, and it must send out gold to pay its debts.

LORD KITCHENER'S CALL FOR MORE RECRUITS.
"It would be difficult to exaggerate the value of the response that has been made to my previous appeals," declared Lord Kitchener at the Guildhall on July 9th, 1915, "but I am here to-day to make another demand on the manhood of the country to come forward in its defence." Our photograph shows the War Secretary, with the Lord Mayor, at the Guildhall balcony, responding to the tremendous cheering of the assembly outside.

The last week of July saw violent fluctuations in the foreign exchanges. As regards France the exchange fell below 25 francs for the sovereign and other falls were equally severe. The curious fact was that nearly all the exchanges—the American one being a conspicuous exception—were going against England; were reaching and sometimes passing the point at which gold could be withdrawn from London, the so-called gold-point. The result was the enormous demand for British gold which so disturbed the money market.

Let us recapitulate. In the last week of July there was a financial panic, which was marked by the heavy selling of securities and the constant demand for gold in London. The two were closely connected, and—this is of the greatest importance—*both came from abroad.* Foreigners were selling securities in London, and so England's debt to them grew bigger and bigger. This drove down the foreign

exchanges until several of them reached the point at which gold must be exported. It was exported, and then the Bank of England took steps to protect its stock by raising the Bank Rate to 10 per cent.

About July 14th German banks and financiers began to sell securities in large quantities, and on the 18th, so Sir Edward H. Holden told the shareholders of the London, City and Midland Bank, the Dresdner Bank caused a great commotion by selling its securities and advising its clients to sell their securities. The selling mania spread, and as the foreign stock exchanges could not, or would not, do the business, the securities found their way to London and produced the panic of July 30th and 31st.

In this way the Germans got gold for their securities, but they did something else. About July 24th and 25th the German banks in London withdrew all the gold they could lay their hands on. They called in loans, and their refusal to find the usual funds for the stockbrokers was one of the minor causes of the trouble on the Stock Exchange on July 29th. They pledged German securities with British banks, and so got the power to take still more gold from this country. Between July 22nd and July 29th the reserve of gold in the Bank of England fell from £40,164,000 to £38,131,000, and on July 30th a further £1,200,000 was taken for abroad. This was in addition to the gold, an unknown amount, which was withdrawn from banks other than the Bank of England.

This was one part of the plot to get as much gold from England as possible, but there was another, and here we must refer to bills of exchange.

By means of bills of exchange foreign trade is mainly carried on. An English merchant, let us say, having sold goods in Germany, does not receive for them a cheque, but a bill. To use technical language he " draws on " the man who owes him for the goods, and by signing the bill the latter promises to pay him in three or six months or some other stated period. The seller " accepts " the bill himself, or perhaps hands it over for " acceptance " to someone to whom he is indebted. This means that the " acceptor " makes himself responsible for the bill, in case the person on whom it is drawn fails to find the money at the proper time.

Our merchant has now got his bill, but it is not yet due for payment, and perhaps he wants money before it is. If so, he goes to a bank or to a financial house which deals in bills of exchange, and there he can, if the security is thought good, discount the bill—that is, get money for it ; this varies according to the rate of the exchange and the rate of interest at the time, but it is always something less than the face value of the bill. Then at the end of the time the discounting house collects the money from the German firm. Many of these bills, we may add, are as good as bank-notes ; for instance, any with the name of Rothschild on them would be, and they can be passed from one person to another just as notes can.

In London many of the houses which accepted and discounted bills of exchange were German, or at least were controlled by Germans. This gave the enemy, as he was soon to become, an enormous advantage.

In July these and other houses held a **Enemy's enormous** large number of bills of exchange, **advantage** representing money due from German buyers to British manufacturers, and there was a great and somewhat sudden desire to get rid of them. As fast as possible the bills were sold to English firms, and wherever they were able the sellers took gold for them.

This raid on British gold was the chief, but it was not the only feature of this financial campaign. During the earlier part of 1914 German merchants had ordered unusually large quantities of goods from this country, woollen goods from Yorkshire being bought on an exceptionally big scale, and most of these were paid for in the customary way by bills of exchange.

At the end of July the position was this. The German

THEIR OLD WORK IN A NEW GUISE.
Right and left: Durham miners who had enlisted in the New Army
preparing a practice sap.

YORKSHIRE RECRUITS GETTING READY FOR ACTIVE SERVICE AT THE FRONT.
Men of a Yorkshire service battalion in training. Trench-digging and sapping.

financiers had got the gold and the German merchants had got the goods, while the British financiers had got the paper money—stocks and shares, bills of exchange, and the like. In ordinary times this would not have mattered. The stocks and shares could have been sold in the ordinary way, the bills of exchange collected as soon as they fell due, and gold sent from Germany to meet the debts. But on July 31st it did matter. *If war broke out between Great Britain and Germany, all this paper money, all these bills of exchange, would be worthless,* for no one can collect debts in an enemy country. Our financiers were not unlike men who had parted with their gold in exchange for tickets in a lottery.

In these ways the German financiers got the better of us, and we may now ask the question—why did they act thus? There is only one possible reply. On or about July 16th they knew that a European war was **Counting on British** certain, and they made use of their **neutrality** knowledge to put their own country in an advantageous position. On the 14th the Kaiser had promised his absolute support to Austria against Serbia, and on the 14th or 15th his son, the Crown Prince, told some Berlin bankers to act cautiously. Forewarned is forearmed. While others were doubting, the Germans were preparing for a grim and mighty struggle in which guns and ships, men and money were all to play their part.

In these critical days the German financiers devoted their chief attention to this country. They knew France and Russia would fight, no doubt they wanted them to do so; but with us it was quite otherwise. It is now practically certain that the Germans counted on British neutrality, and they took very astute measures to make that neutrality a business proposition. They had so managed matters that we stood to lose a great deal of money if we entered the war. They could say to our politicians

Submarine crew enjoying the relaxation of a little fishing at sea: A crab being hauled in.

—we know they did say to them —"Think what you will lose if you go to war. You had far better remain neutral." Our neutrality was indeed advocated by a prominent German in a letter which appeared in the "Westminster Gazette" on August 3rd. To this base argument we refused to listen, and as all the world knows, we took up arms on August 4th to defend the neutrality of Belgium. Even then, although somewhat disappointed, the German financiers had a card in reserve. They were able to make us pay a big price for our intervention, in addition, of course, to the ordinary expenses of a great war.

No one can say exactly how much the Germans got from us in July, 1914, but it must have been a very considerable **A neglected** sum, and this **danger** we are justified in calling a war indemnity. There is a story told of how two men went into partnership. When this began, A provided the money and B the experience; but when it came to an end, A had the experience and B the money. Without unduly straining the meaning, A may well stand for Great Britain and B for Germany.

This skilful plot, or manœuvre, was assisted by the supineness of our Government, and also by the presence of a number of Germans, both naturalised and unnaturalised, in responsible positions in the City of London, a

Diver removing an obstruction from a propeller. Above: A submersible going full speed ahead.
INCIDENTS IN LIFE ABOARD A BRITISH SUBMARINE.

danger to which attention had been called, with the usual negative result, in the past. We do not accuse all, or indeed any large part, of these gentlemen of treachery, but it is surely not uncharitable to believe that they were reluctant to think any ill of their fellow-countrymen, and were, therefore, not on their guard against their machinations. The serious fact is that they were in positions of authority at a critical time. Englishmen, we like to think, have not often cause to be ashamed of their country, but never, since the days of Hengist, has there been such good reason for whole-hearted shame as there was when, in the House of Commons in August, 1914, Mr. McKenna stated that the recent naturalisation of a German financier, Baron Schröder, was necessary for the financial stability of the City of London.

For our failure to divine and counter the German plot of July, 1914, the Government must take much of the blame. Did they know what was going on, or did the bankers and the diplomatists, in whom they trusted, fail to warn them? Possibly the diplomatists were, as usual, above taking notice of these common business matters, and the bankers—or at least the German section of them—asserted that everything was quite all right. We do not know. We know that the Government did nothing, and we feel tolerably certain that they put too much faith in the words of their German friends.

Reason for national shame

But what, some may ask, could the Government have done? They could have prevented the withdrawal of gold and the pledging of German securities. They could have intimated quietly that any loss suffered by our merchants would be made good out of the property in the British Empire owned by Germans—

a property which has been valued at as much as £300,000,000—and they could have done other things. All they needed was to ask the advice of a British banker and to act on it at once. The only drawback is that strong measures at that critical time would have required more backbone than any British politician has possessed since Lord Palmerston.

But they did nothing, although at the eleventh hour the Committee of the Stock Exchange and the Directors of the Bank of England saved the situation —or what was left of it. So it came about that we started our war with two serious financial handicaps—impaired credit, the consequence of an era of extravagance, and enormous debts owing to us, which for the time being were lost.

At the eleventh hour

Before war began on Tuesday, August 4th, our financial system, the pride of Englishmen everywhere, had for the moment ceased to exist. Like the Cheshire cat in " Alice," our credit had vanished and only its grin remained. Credit

GERMAN TORPEDO-BOATS AT BATTLE PRACTICE IN THE NORTH SEA.
The smaller view is of a German torpedo discovered floating on the surface. This sinister wanderer was taken in charge by a British destroyer and towed to a place of safety.

had vanished ! Let us try and realise what these few words mean.

By means of credit, it is not too much to say, 99 per cent. of our business is transacted ; but credit can only be used in a highly civilised society, in a country which has good laws and a good government, wherein people trust each other. It means that instead of paying for the goods we buy, we promise to pay for them—for cheques, banknotes, postal orders, drafts, bills of exchange, and other forms of paper money are nothing more than **What financial** promises to pay. The great majority of **panic means** us no longer give one article in payment for another, as our ancestors did in the days of barter ; we no longer give gold and silver as our great-grandparents did ; we give pieces of paper which are nothing more than promises to pay. In themselves these are worthless ; people accept them because they believe that those who promise to pay—whether it is the Bank of England, Messrs. Rich & Co., or John Jones, tailor—can pay and will pay.

If this belief is destroyed or weakened, credit is destroyed or weakened. Then people will no longer take pieces of paper in payment of their debts ; they want gold, something which has a value in itself. Something of this kind happens in times of wars and tumults. People become suspicious and distrustful, and consequently they prefer gold to paper money. Hence we have a big demand for gold at the banks, especially the Bank of England, such as there was in the last week of July, 1914, and if this reaches any great size, it develops into a panic. A financial panic means a demand for gold, the reason being that credit has been wholly or partially destroyed. Paper money is suspected, because people wonder if the promise to pay will be carried out.

On Monday, August 3rd, credit had vanished. Everybody wanted gold for his or her paper money, and the amount of gold in the country was not sufficient to pay us sixpence in the pound all round. The disappearance of credit meant that even the richest firms were bankrupt. Doubtless they had a large amount of paper money in their coffers, but this was valueless ; doubtless they owned plenty of stocks and shares, but these they could not sell. The plain fact remained that, like the bankrupt, they had not enough gold to pay their debts, and people were reluctant to take anything else.

On the Friday and Saturday private persons had withdrawn large sums in gold from the banks, and they were preparing to withdraw more, while many took their notes to the Bank of England and exchanged them for gold. If this had continued it is obvious what would have followed. It would have been a case of first come first served ; the gold would soon have been exhausted, and then national bankruptcy would have come upon us. In the past, financial panics had been met by suspending the Bank Acts, the Acts which compel the Bank of England to give gold for notes, but this course was not taken in the crisis of 1914.

Fortunately, Monday, August 3rd, was a Bank Holiday, and this accident helped matters considerably. It prevented, for the time being at least, a run on the banks, and it gave the authorities an extra day in which to do something to deal with the crisis. Parliament was sitting, and so Ministers could introduce any legislation which they thought necessary.

The first question tackled was that of bills of exchange. Towards the end of the previous week the foreign exchanges had ceased to work, and consequently no payments from abroad were reaching London. On Tuesday business would be resumed as usual, a number of bills of exchange would fall due, and in any case these had to be met. Many of them were in the hands of the Bank of England and other banks, and they would ask the acceptors for payment, whether or not they received it from their foreign clients who had bought the goods and given the bills. Under existing conditions, with nothing arriving in London, the accepting houses were faced with ruin.

On Monday, therefore, to relieve them from this serious predicament, an Act called the Postponement of Payments Act was passed through Parliament, the whole business being carried out in a few hours. This gave the Government the power to issue a Royal Proclamation postponing any kind of payment, and the same evening they acted on it. Before midnight a proclamation had been issued postponing the payment of all bills of exchange for one month, or until September 4th and later. For one month the accepting houses could not be compelled to meet the bills due, although, of course, they could do so if they wished.

The same day other urgency measures became law. The Bank Holiday was extended for three more days, and so the banks would remain closed until Friday morning, and it was stated that as soon as possible, in order to conserve our stock of gold, the Government would issue notes for £1 and 10s., and that these would be legal tender. This meant that a man could not refuse to take them in payment of a debt, as he can a cheque or a large amount of silver, although he could change them into gold at the Bank of England. At the same time postal orders were made legal tender.

On August 4th, the day war was declared, another Royal Proclamation ordered a general moratorium for a month, one applying not only to bills of exchange but to debts of other kinds. By it the payment of all debts of over £5 was postponed for a month. People could pay them if they liked, and many did like, **Passing of the** but they could not be compelled to do so. **crisis** The courts would take no notice of a man who applied for a writ or a summons for debt unless the amount was under £5. Rent was not included in this moratorium, but a new Act of Parliament made it difficult for landlords to distrain on tenants for arrears.

In various ways people were urged to leave their money in the banks and to go about their business of buying and

LORD KITCHENER'S CONFERENCE WITH GENERAL JOFFRE.
A souvenir of Lord Kitchener's visit to the French front in August, 1915. The War Secretary spent two days with the French Generalissimo, and the occasion called forth some interesting recollections of his early service with the French Army in 1870. Our photograph shows the British War Minister with M. Millerand, General Joffre, General Foch, and General Dubail returning from the trenches.

Right Honourable Arthur James Balfour, First Lord of the Admiralty.

British battery at its deadly work on a sand=ridge in Gallipoli.

Charge by the Royal Naval Division on the Gallipoli Peninsula.

Rear=Admiral Stuart Nicholson, M.V.O., in the trenches near Cape Helles.

Lord Montgomery, of the Headquarters Staff, in Gallipoli.

View of a Turkish town on the Dardanelles as seen from a French aeroplane.

The same town from another direction showing the Turkish forts guarding the bay.

selling, paying and receiving, as usual. The appeals had a good effect, the excitement died down, and on the Friday, when the banks were opened, everything passed off smoothly. There was no run on them ; money was paid in and paid out almost as usual, and a very serious crisis was over. On the previous day, the 6th, the Bank Rate had been reduced from 10 to 6 per cent., and on the following day, the 8th, to 5 per cent., quite a moderate rate for a time of war. On Thursday, Friday, and Saturday in the previous week over £10,000,000 in gold had been withdrawn from the Bank of England, but on the same three days of the week under consideration over £6,000,000 in gold was received. This showed clearly that public confidence, the foundation of our credit system, was returning rapidly.

So far so good ; but we were by no means out of the wood. The moratorium could not last for ever, and some day or other the bills of exchange and other debts must be paid. The measures taken in the first week in August were only temporary ones, designed to serve the very useful purpose of giving time for consideration ; but that was all. We had merely postponed the day of reckoning.

How the banks were protected

From September 4th the moratorium was extended for a month, and from October 4th for another. From November 4th there was a partial renewal, but on December 4th it really came to an end. For some time before that date, however, little notice had been taken of it, and its disappearance was hardly felt. By that time business was going on as usual and debts were being paid in the ordinary way.

We must now say something about the steps taken to bring about this desirable result, and it will be best to divide those who were affected by the breakdown of our credit system into classes. First come the banks. The big joint-stock banks, about a dozen in all, held about £600,000,000 of money belonging to the public, and if all this was withdrawn they were ruined, while in no possible case could they pay it all out in gold ; there was not enough, or anything like enough, in the country. Much of the money they had lent to stockbrokers and tradesmen, who had given them stocks, shares, and other property as security for it ; but with the stock exchanges closed these could not be sold, or only sold with great difficulty and at considerable loss.

The banks were saved primarily by the good sense of the people, who realised that there was no cause for alarm, and that their money was as safe in the banks as in their own pockets. Moreover, if they wished to withdraw unreasonable amounts, the banks could protect themselves by the moratorium and refuse to pay ; and this was not without its effect. The result was that their deposits were not depleted to any great extent. However, in case of need, the Government gave the banks a further measure of protection. They offered to advance to them Treasury notes up to 20 per cent. of their deposits ;

Position of the stockbrokers

but the banks only took up about £13,000,000 of these, whereas they had the right to take up ten times that amount. This transaction was described as follows by Sir Edward H. Holden, Bart. :

These notes were issued to the English, Scotch, and Irish banks, and the Savings Banks—in other words the Government placed on deposit with the bankers a certain amount of these notes which were put into circulation. By the end of September the banks had repaid the amount received from the Government with the exception of about one million sterling ; by the end of October practically the whole amount was repaid. These Treasury notes were issued in the first instance without a gold basis, but the Government undertook to pay them in gold if required.

The last sentence explains the real nature of the assistance.

Next come the stockbrokers, and their position has already been explained. The moratorium and the closing of the Stock Exchange protected them, but only for a time. When the moratorium ended they expected the

banks to call in loans, and as their securities were practically unsaleable they would be unable to repay the money, and would therefore be ruined. It was estimated that in August the stockbrokers owed the banks something like £70,000,000 or £80,000,000.

Between the Government and the banks an arrangement was made for the protection of the stockbrokers. The Government offered to advance money to the banks up to sixty per cent. of the value of the securities which they held from the brokers, on condition that these were not offered for sale until six months after the conclusion of the war. At the same time many of the stockbrokers managed, in various ways, to reduce the amount which they owed to the banks, and before the end of the year their special difficulty had been overcome.

All through the autumn of 1914 the Stock Exchange remained closed, although some business was done by

"THE ALLEY-WAYS OF DEATH AND GLORY."
A street trench well barricaded, ruin in the background, but stout hearts and cheery faces to the fore.

stockbrokers " in the street." This meant that stocks and shares could be sold, but not as freely as before ; prices were not known in an instant, but were a matter of bargain and arrangement. This was not entirely satisfactory, and soon there was some talk about reopening the " House." At length the Government and the Stock Exchange authorities agreed upon a scheme, and the reopening took place on January 4th, 1915. The Stock Exchange had been closed for just over five months.

The London Stock Exchange was only opened, however, under very serious restrictions. The system, by which a man sells shares which he has not got and which he could not pay for if he had, was suspended ; every purchase had to be " taken up " and paid for at once. In a word speculative buying and selling, the mainstay of Stock

Observers, from a coign of vantage in a tree top, wiring instructions to the guns.

Exchange business—the Hamlet of the piece—was forbidden.

Another restriction was the introduction of minimum prices for Consols and other leading securities. To prevent our credit being further injured by another fall in prices, it had been decided in the previous September that Consols should not be sold below a certain price, and when the Stock Exchange was reopened this principle—an unsound one— was extended. The minimum price of 68½ was fixed for 2½ per cent. Consols, and other minimum prices in much the same proportion.

It cannot be said that this experiment was very successful.

Stock Exchange at work again Prices are like water, sooner or later they will find their proper level. Artificial restrictions can hamper business, but they cannot raise values. If Consols are not worth 68½ in relation to other things, no legislation on earth can make them so. As a matter of fact, there was a good deal of buying and selling at prices below the fixed minima, and, surreptitiously perhaps, these soon found their right level. In this way the London Stock Exchange got to work again after a fashion, and the smaller exchanges in other parts of the country

followed its example. Stockbrokers had been saved from wholesale bankruptcy, for that certainly would have been their fate if nothing had been done for their protection.

As for the acceptors and holders of bills of exchange, they were protected for one month by the Royal Proclamation of August 3rd, but their position would not be satisfactory until the foreign exchanges were working again, and they could obtain remittances from abroad.

As regards allied and neutral countries, the difficulty was soon over, and for compassing this desirable end the British Navy must have its meed of praise. As soon as it was seen that our command of **The Navy and** the sea was assured, foreigners began to **overseas trade** ship goods as usual to this country, and it was these goods which really paid their debts to us. They were the real exchange; the pieces of paper were but symbols, worthless without the goods themselves. Remittances then began to reach London, and before September 4th, 1914, the accepting houses found themselves in a position to meet many of their bills.

With regard to one neutral, the United States, there was a special difficulty. In August, as is usual at that time of the year, there was a big balance owing to this country which, unless the unexpected happened, would be discharged by exporting the cotton crop. But owing to the breakdown of the exchange, and still more to the paralysis of the shipping industry, merchants did not for a few days send any cotton across the Atlantic, and so the £90,000,000 or so remained unpaid. However, the American bankers came quickly to the rescue, and shipping soon resumed its normal activities. To right the exchange, £20,000,000 in gold was sent from New York to Ottawa, where it was held on account of the Bank of England, and this difficulty was overcome. American bills of exchange were

An instruction class in progress.   In circle: Cyclist tapping the wires and sending information to headquarters.

BRITAIN'S NEW ARMY IN TRAINING: LESSONS IN FIELD TELEGRAPHY.

REHEARSING FOR THE GRIM DRAMA OF WAR.
Getting out of the "enemy trench." A phase of the training in trench warfare undergone by men of the New Army at Aldershot.

LEARNING TO BAYONET ENTRENCHED GERMANS.
The grenade-throwers having prepared the way, the infantry charged with the bayonet, the "enemy" being represented by sand-bags.

MEMBERS OF THE NATIONAL GUARD GETTING FIT FOR HOME DEFENCE
The City of London National Guard Volunteer Corps learning the art of trench-digging in some waste ground near the site of the old G.P.O., under the direction of their commandant, Colonel G. T. B. Cobbett, who is seen on the extreme right of the picture.

met as usual, and in a while the balance against the States disappeared.

While speaking of the American exchange we may mention its later developments. As the war proceeded, we bought more and more goods from the States, not only foodstuffs, but arms and ammunition in great quantities, and at the same time we were unable to send there the customary amount of manufactured goods. To illustrate this point we may mention that, in the first three months of 1915, the total exports of the United States were £177,000,000, against £116,000,000 in the corresponding period of 1914. On the other hand the imports fell from £101,000,000 to £84,500,000. The result of this was that a great trade balance was soon piled up against us, and the American exchange fell away to such a point that we had to export gold. Steps were taken, however, to stop this fall by British sales of American securities. These were bought by Americans, and the price paid for them was set off against the debt we owed the States. Nevertheless, the balance against us continued to grow, and in the

The American exchange

summer of 1915 the state of the American exchange was again a source of anxiety to our bankers and financiers.

There still remained, however, the German and Austrian bills of exchange, of which, unfortunately, our accepting houses held a large number, and the most difficult part of the business was to know what to do with them. It was quite certain that as long as the war lasted they would not be met in the ordinary way.

On August 13th it was announced that the Bank of England would discount—that is advance money on—approved bills of exchange, and would, moreover, allow an acceptor, if necessary, to postpone meeting the bill when it fell due. This arrangement only applied to bills accepted before August 4th, and the Government undertook to make good any loss which the Bank might sustain in this connection.

Facilitating fresh business

This was but half the problem. Something had to be done to deal with the bills which would begin to fall due on September 4th, and on that very day the Government scheme was announced. It authorised the Bank of England and the joint-stock banks to find the money to meet the bills, charging interest on the money advanced at 2 per cent. above Bank Rate. The acceptors on their part had to undertake to collect, as soon as possible, the money from their clients and pay it over to the Bank, and within twelve months of the conclusion of the war they must repay everything. Any loss incurred would fall upon the nation, for the Government took this step " in order to facilitate fresh business and the movement of produce and merchandise from and to all parts of the world." This arrangement worked very

MODERN MEN-IN-ARMOUR : REVIVAL OF MEDIÆVAL MEANS OF DEFENCE.
British and French soldiers wearing helmets of specially hardened steel, fashioned to protect the head and eyes against shrapnel and shell splinters while fighting in the trenches. The smaller view is of French infantry wearing the new " calottes métallique," and taking temporary cover behind a hedge. As the war progressed there were advocates of a return to the practice of wearing breastplates and using shields.

AN INCIDENT OF THE FRENCH NATIONAL FETE DAY, JULY 14TH, 1915—WOUNDED HEROES ARRIVING AT A CELEBRATION CENTRE.

well, and did a good deal to restore normal business conditions in the money market.

As for the merchants and manufacturers, the ordinary traders of the country, they were unable, owing to the general suspension of credit, to obtain much of the money owing to them; but, on the other hand, they were protected by the moratorium, and for the time being they could not be sued for the money they owed.

This trouble, however, soon righted itself, as we have already explained, but some of them had a further difficulty, for they had sold goods to Germany and Austria-Hungary, and for these they would get nothing; at least, until the conclusion of the war.

The Government came to their rescue just as it had aided the holders of bills of exchange. It arranged that the banks should advance to such of their customers as were in difficulties owing to the non-arrival of remittances from abroad 50 per cent. of such debts as were approved by them. The trader would be responsible for the repayment of this loan, but if any loss resulted from it the State would bear 75 per cent. of it and the bank concerned the remaining 25 per cent. Some advantage was taken of this scheme, especially in Yorkshire, and it helped business to right itself.

Big difficulties surmounted Before the end of 1914 our financial system had been restored. The big difficulties had been surmounted, and the machinery was working, not perhaps as smoothly as usual, but still it was working. The exchanges were operating, and debts, both home and foreign, were being paid. The gold in the Bank of England had steadily mounted up until it reached something like £70,000,000, a result partly due to the extended use of paper money, of which over £34,000,000 had been issued in £1 and 10s. notes. True there was not yet a free market in stocks

and shares, and the balance of trade was being severely disturbed, while no debts could be collected from German and Austrian traders. Difficulties lay ahead, but by saving us from wholesale bankruptcy the Government had done something to atone for its inaction during the critical days before the war.

In 1915 fresh difficulties arose about the French and the Russian Exchanges, but these were soon set right. As regards France the conditions of the war after the first German advance compelled that country to buy largely in Great Britain, and the effect of these purchases was soon reflected in the Paris **Russia's heroic** Exchange, which rose somewhat. In July, **course** therefore, some London financiers agreed to steady it by taking over French bills to the extent of about £5,000,000.

This meant that for some time, at least, France had no need to trouble about meeting these bills, and thus the transaction eased the situation.

Russia, too, soon owed this country a good deal of money for goods purchased here, and in the ordinary way would have met this by heavy shipments of wheat. But with Archangel frozen up and the Dardanelles closed this was impossible, and so Russia stood in much the same relation towards Great Britain as Great Britain towards the United States. Russia took the heroic course of paying her debts in gold, and £8,000,000 was shipped to London, but this was not enough. As in the case of France our financiers came to the rescue. They raised £10,000,000 on behalf of Russia by means of Treasury bills, this being practically a loan which relieved our ally of part of her obligations until the situation should take a more favourable turn.

Of more immediate interest to the general taxpayer was the actual financing of the Great War, and this big problem was anxiously considered by those responsible

CANADA'S ENTHUSIASTIC RESPONSE TO THE CALL OF THE MOTHERLAND.

Wonderful camera-record of the scene at Victoria, British Columbia, as one of the troopships laden with volunteers for the front was about to leave the docks on its long voyage to Europe.

MR. J. PIERPONT MORGAN.
Head of the American financial firm acting as British war agents in the United States. He was fired at and wounded by a German-American fanatic on July 3rd, 1915. His assailant committed suicide.

for our finances, and indeed by all men of business in the land. During the summer of 1915 the cost of carrying on operations by land and sea was £3,000,000 a day, and there was a prospect that it might rise to £4,000,000 a day and possibly more.

It may be well here to draw attention to the fact that this country made war on a much more expensive scale than did any other of the combatants. For £3,000,000 we did not get anything like the same amount of men and material as France, Germany, and Russia did, and this makes comparisons difficult if not impossible. For this there are several reasons. Our Army was a voluntary and not a conscript one, and this made it much more expensive. We paid separation allowances on a much more generous scale, and our workers received higher wages, which meant of course that it cost us much more

Meeting the cost of the war to provide the food, clothing, and arms for our men, the ammunition for our guns, and the fodder for our horses. On the other hand, apart from the damage done by German battle-cruisers on our East Coast, no part of our land had been ravaged by the invader. France, Russia, and Austria, to say nothing of Belgium, had suffered enormous loss in this way, and even Germany, successful though she had been in keeping the fighting outside her own country, had a good deal of property in East Prussia destroyed.

The cost of the war could only be met by borrowing on an enormous scale, and for this everyone was prepared. We anticipated a startling increase in our National Debt, which before the war amounted to £651,000,000. A certain proportion of the expense of the war could be met from taxation, and figures were quoted showing the amount raised in this way for our past wars, but in any case the few extra millions which could be obtained in this way would be only a drop in the ocean. Taxation was already at a very high level, and this made borrowing more necessary.

The first step towards financing the war was taken on Wednesday, August 5th, 1914, when Mr. Asquith asked the House of Commons for a vote of credit for £100,000,000. This proceeding, however, had nothing to do with finding the money, it merely authorised the Government to spend it. The spending began at the rate of about £1,000,000

a day, and, for the time being, this was provided by issuing Treasury bills. This meant simply that the Government borrowed the money for a fixed period, three or six months, from bankers and financiers. It was a temporary expedient. In November the House of Commons sanctioned a further vote of credit for £225,000,000.

On November 17th the country was given some idea of the financial position. Before the war, in May, 1914, the Chancellor of the Exchequer had presented his Budget for the year, showing that he expected to spend some £206,000,000 during the twelve months, and increasing the income-tax and death duties to make the revenue up to that amount. At this time, however, there was no thought of war, and so when this came he had to present a fresh balance-sheet. The dislocation of trade which was caused by the war, and the losses suffered by so many people, would certainly have the effect of reducing the revenue, **A fresh balance-sheet** while on the other side he had to add the cost of the war to the ordinary expenditure, which was already heavy enough. The cost of the war between August 4th, when it began, and March 31st, when the financial year ended—a period of eight months—he estimated at £328,443,000, and in addition he thought he should lose £11,128,000 of the revenue on which he had reckoned. Consequently, he had to find an extra sum of £339,571,000.

A certain sum was raised by taxation. As from December 1st, 1914, the income-tax was doubled. This meant that for the year under consideration—April 1st, 1914, to March 31st, 1915—everyone would pay one-third more, and the demand notes were made out on those lines. The yield was expected to be £12,500,000 for the current year and £44,750,000 in a full year. In these figures the super-tax, which is really part of the income-tax, and which was also doubled, is included.

Other increased taxes were the duties on beer and tea. On beer an extra 17s. 3d. was charged on every barrel, this working out at a halfpenny on the half-pint, and on tea the duty was raised from 5d. to 8d. a pound. In these ways an extra £3,000,000 was raised for the expenses of the current year.

The sum of £15,500,000 was all that could be raised by fresh taxation, and so in one way or another £324,000,000

THE LATE LORD ROTHSCHILD.
Lord Rothschild, who died on March 31st, 1915, aged seventy-four, was in frequent consultation with Mr. Lloyd George and the Treasury officials, and helped greatly to preserve British financial stability in the critical days of August, 1914. He lent also his great support to the cause of the Red Cross.

LIEUT.-COLONEL LORD DERBY.
Commander of the King's (Liverpool Regiment) 1st Dockers' Battalion. The battalion, consisting of three hundred and fifty men, was inaugurated at Liverpool on April 12th, 1915.

An inspection parade. Types of the sturdy men from Britain's oldest colony.

Section of ammunition column. Each waggon is drawn by four mules.

Serving out rifles to the men in the ranks. In centre: Getting used to foreign service kit.

Signalling staff of the Newfoundlanders training in England.

NEWFOUNDLANDERS FOR THE FRONT: SOME OF THE VOLUNTEERS FROM BRITAIN'S OLDEST COLONY.

Newfoundland sent a fine body of men to assist the Mother Country. They went into training in one of the home counties, where the King inspected them and spoke highly of their soldierly qualities.

had to be borrowed; £2,750,000 was taken from the money —the sinking fund—which is devoted to the repayment of the National Debt, for it was obviously rather silly to be paying off debt with one hand and borrowing more with the other; it was robbing Peter to pay Paul with a vengeance. The balance, it was decided, should be raised by a loan—by an appeal to the public.

Much thought was spent on the form which this loan should take. Borrowing, even for Governments, is not always an easy matter. The rate of interest must be fixed, and this was a difficult and anxious proceeding. If too little was offered the money would not be obtained; but, on the other hand, it would be wasteful to give more than was really necessary. The object of our financiers was to find the golden mean.

It was decided that the new loan should be for £350,000,000, and that the rate of interest should be 3½ per cent. For £100 of it investors were only asked to pay £95, so that actually the interest worked out at more than 3½ per cent. The usual advertisements were issued in the newspapers; the banks, insurance com-

The First War Loan panies, and other financial institutions were asked to help, and when the subscription lists were closed the amount required had been obtained. A moment's reflection will show that the loan did not bring in £350,000,000 in cash, but 3,500,000 times £95, or £332,500,000. With this sum the Government could pay off the existing Treasury bills and carry on the war, they hoped, until the end of March. On March 1st the House of Commons

authorised the Government to spend another £250,000,000, and with the end of the financial year people looked forward anxiously to the coming of another Budget statement.

This was made on May 4th by Mr. Lloyd George. Dealing with the year which had just ended, the Chancellor said that the revenue had produced about £6,000,000 more than he anticipated, for it had reached £226,694,000. Unfortunately, the expenditure has also exceeded his estimate, having amounted to £560,474,000. Con-

Piling Ossa upon Pelion sequently, the amount added to our National Debt during the year was £333,780,000, or practically the amount raised by the loan in November. This had been spent, and more borrowing was inevitable.

Big as were the figures of the year 1914-15, those for the year 1915-16 were bigger still. In truth, they were staggering; nothing like them had been known in our history. The cost of the war, said Mr. George, had now grown to £2,100,000 a day, and although he did not

GENERAL BOTHA'S TRIUMPHANT RETURN TO CAPE TOWN.
General Botha had a most enthusiastic welcome on his return to Cape Town, on July 22nd, 1915, from his successful campaign in German South-West Africa. Above he is seen acknowledging the salute of the naval guard of honour. Mrs. Botha is standing to the right of her husband. At foot: Contingent of Union forces with native drivers, passing through Budde ley Street, Cape Town, on their way to the City Hall.

then propose any additional taxation,* he hinted broadly that if the war continued something more must be obtained in this way.

When would the war end? The uncertainty on this point made it difficult for the Chancellor to present his estimates for the coming year, and so he took the unusual course of presenting two. In one he assumed that the war would be over by the end of September, in the other that it would last a full year more—that is, to March 31st, 1916.

In either case the revenue would not be seriously affected, and this Mr. George estimated at £270,332,000, of which £103,000,000 was to be drawn from the payers of income-tax. This was **Expenditure £3,000,000 a day** £43,698,000 more than was raised by taxation in the previous year. The difficulty was with the expenditure. If the war ended by September this would, the Chancellor thought, amount to £786,678,000, but if it continued through the financial year it would reach £1,132,654,000. If the war ended in September we had to borrow £516,346,000, if it continued until March we had to borrow £862,322,000.

With that Mr. George sat down, and the question of financing the war was given a rest until June. On June 15th, 1915, Mr. Asquith asked for another vote of credit for £250,000,000, and in his speech he made some remarks on the financial position. He showed that the daily expenditure on the war had grown to £2,660,000, half a million more than Mr. George's estimate, and he added that "as our financial obligations to our Allies would not grow lighter, the total expenditure would be not much under £3,000,000 a day, and possibly might be more." He said that on June 14th the Government had £56,000,000 in hand, a sum which would carry on the war until the end of the month.

About the details of this expenditure we know very little, but something can be gleaned from Mr. Asquith's figures. During April, May, and June, 1915, the Army was

---

* The extra taxes on beer and spirits proposed by Mr. George were quickly abandoned, so they need not be considered here.

costing rather more than £1,600,000 a day, the Navy just about £500,000 a day, and about £500,000 a day was being spent in other ways.

A loan of great magnitude was clearly impending, and the way for this had been cleared in January. It was then stated that, without the previous consent of the Treasury, no appeals for public money would be allowed, and to grant or withhold the necessary permission a small committee under Viscount, afterwards Earl, St. Aldwyn, was set up. This was, undoubtedly, a serious encroachment on individual rights, and in some sense a blow at business enterprise, but it was warranted by the special needs of the case. The Government would require for the purpose of the war every penny which the public could lend.

Particulars of the new loan were announced before the end of June, and these revealed several novel and interesting features. In the first place no definite sum was asked for. The Treasury had power to borrow up to £900,000,000, but it was stated that they would be satisfied with £600,000,000 or thereabouts. The interest payable was 4½ per cent., a liberal rate even bearing in mind the decline in our credit, but not too much, as events proved, to secure the sum desired. As usual the money could be paid all at once or in instalments between July 10th and October 26th, and the first half year's dividend was due on December 1st, 1915.

The question of keeping up the price of the new stock had evidently been carefully considered, and this was important. With the experiences of the past few years before them, with their **The Second War Loan** capital dwindling steadily away, as had been the case with the holders of Consols and all other high-class securities, investors, it was known, would be very reluctant to face this risk again. They had been once bitten and were now twice shy.

To get over the difficulty the Government undertook to repay the loan at par, to give back £100 for £100, and to do this between 1925 and 1945. As early as 1925 they have the right to repay, and in any case they must

IN RURAL FRANCE: RUSTIC GUARD AT A BOMBARDED VILLAGE LISTENING TO A NOTICE BEING READ OUT BY THE MAYOR.

Horses swimming across a stream guided by
soldiers on a raft.

BRITISH YEOMANRY IN TRAINING.
Interesting sidelights on the training of a squadron of yeomanry in crossing rivers, and landing
horses, guns, and equipment. Rafts were made with barrels and poles, while the horses swam
over, either towed from rafts or guided by soldiers swimming with them in the water. The
photograph immediately above shows the men loading a raft with rifles and equipment.

repay in 1945. With this guarantee
it was hoped that the price of the
stock would not fall much.

The same aim, the maintenance of
the country's credit, dictated the conversion proposals which were associated
with the loan. Holders of Consols and
of the 3½ per cent. War Loan issued
in November, 1914, were to be allowed
to convert their holdings into the
new loan. If the investor held the
3½ per cent. War Loan he must pay
another £5 for every £100, and it then
became a 4½ per cent. stock, but this
was allowed only on the condition that
he doubled his holding. It was a
bait to get more money out of him.
Similarly, Consols were to be exchanged
at the price of 66⅔ for every £100 of
the 2½ per cent. stock. Every £75
invested in Consols could be changed into £50 of the new
loan, but here again only on the condition that another
£50 was taken up. This had to be done before October
30th, 1915, and it was expected that £250,000,000 of
Consols would be exchanged.

The really novel features of the loan were two. First,
the investor was assured that if in future the Government
found it necessary to borrow money at more than 4½ per
cent. the money now invested would also receive a higher
rate of interest—5, or whatever the new rate per cent.
might be. This again was done to reassure investors,
especially those who thought that by waiting they would
get still more interest on their money.

The second and more important of the novel features
of the loan was the appeal to the working classes. In
every possible way—by Press and pamphlet, by politician,
employers, and labour leaders—they were urged to put
their savings, actual and prospective, into it, and for their
special benefit bonds for £5 and £25 were on sale at all
the post-offices, a discount of 8d. being allowed on every
£5 invested in this way. But this was not all. Vouchers
for 5s. and for multiples of 5s. were also sold, and on
these interest at the rate of 5 per cent. was reckoned.
In addition to the accumulated interest
the investor would receive a bonus of 1s.   **Chances for small**
on every £5 when he exchanged his   **investors**
vouchers for bonds. When the vouchers
reached £5, they could be exchanged for a bond, on
which interest could be paid half-yearly in the usual way.
The money invested in buying vouchers could be withdrawn in cash through the Post Office Savings Bank, a
proviso which doubtless removed the dislike which many
felt at locking up their money, and the bonds of £5 and
£25 could be sold through the Post Office at a small cost.
The amount which one person might obtain in this way
was limited to £200.

To give the small investors a good chance, the Government did not at first put a limit of time to their applications
as they did to those who wanted bigger amounts. As
regards the applications for the bonds of £5 and £25, they
reserved to themselves the right to close the lists at any
time, and in July they stated that the scheme would be
modified from the end of the month. This modification,

WITH THE VOLUNTEER RESERVES IN ESSEX.
Men of the 11th Battalion Essex National Volunteer Reserve engaged in
field operations. A "gassed" volunteer receiving treatment in the
trenches.

223

however, was not serious. The bonds could no longer be purchased through the Savings Banks, but could be bought at any money-order office until November 30th, 1915. Between December 1st and 15th the interest and bonus on these had to be collected, and the certificates exchanged for regular scrip of the War Loan. As before, no individual could obtain more than £200 of stock in this way.

As regards the vouchers for 5s. and multiples of 5s., it was stated that these would remain on sale until December 15th, and that between December 1st and 15th they must be exchanged for certificates of £5 and multiples of £5. It was also indicated that those who had vouchers totalling less than a complete £5 would be allowed further time in which to purchase the balance, and it was hinted that this method of investing in the War Loan might be continued after December 15th. Alternatively, purchasers of these fractions of £5 might have the money refunded to them by the Post Office. Arrangements were made for the sale of vouchers through the trade unions, friendly societies, and in factories and workshops, and for five months this machinery was to remain at work.

This "great national appeal to every class for a great national purpose," was a great success. On July 13th, 1915, Mr. McKenna announced the figures. Through the Bank of England 550,000 persons had applied for £570,000,000. This, of course, included all the big subscriptions, such as £21,000,000 each from Lloyd's and the London, City and Midland Banks, and enormous sums from the Prudential and other insurance corporations. Business men, however, all over the country, hastened to put their surplus funds into the loan, and among the earliest of **A world** these was the Amalgamated Press, Ltd., **record** with £25,000. This sum of £570,000,000 did not include converted securities. It represented "new money," and established a record as being "far and away beyond any amount ever subscribed in the world's history."

As regards the small subscriptions, the list was still open and the money was still pouring in when Mr. McKenna spoke. He said, however, that up to the previous Saturday (July 10th), 547,000 persons had applied for £15,000,000 of the loan, but a week later Mr. Herbert Samuel stated that this figure had risen to £24,000,000 and did not include those who had applied for the 5s. vouchers.

This excellent result was largely due to the co-operation and loyalty of employers. Many of these—big and little firms alike—agreed to assist their employees to buy vouchers or bonds. This assistance took various forms, but the most usual was for the employer to advance the money for the purchase and for the employee to repay it by weekly or other instalments. The Post Office was empowered to make special arrangements in these cases, allowing the employer to pay for the loan by instalments, extending in some cases to as much as two years. A Parliamentary War Savings Committee was formed to encourage such schemes as these, and it was stated that its appeals met with a remarkable response. The people, so long merely recipients, took some part in finding the "silver bullets" so necessary for the successful prosecution of the Great War.

It was impossible for us, as Mr. Lloyd George said, to conduct this war on limited liability principles, and we had already lent £10,000,000 to Belgium, and a smaller sum to Serbia. In February, **Looking to the** 1915, the Finance Ministers of the three **future** Powers of the Entente met in Paris and agreed to unite their resources, and in June a similar arrangement was made with Italy. This did not mean, we were told, a joint loan, but it might mean a still more serious demand on the financial resources of this country.

Our financial arrangements also provided for assistance to the Colonies, and in February £30,000,000 had been set aside for this purpose. This was a wise and economical precaution, and as the money will be repaid, not a serious liability, for it prevented the Colonies from making their own demands on the money market.

With the end of the war not in sight, prophecy, as George Eliot has reminded us, is the most gratuitous form of human error. We know, however, enough to say that we shall be fortunate if we finish it for £2,000,000,000, the interest on which will mean an annual charge of £90,000,000. The cost of war pensions will be hardly less than another £20,000,000 a year, and a similar sum at least, should be provided for the repayment of the debt. There is an extra £130,000,000 a year to be found, even supposing that the Army and Navy cost us no more than they did before the war, and that the revenue is maintained. Taxation at the high level of 1915 would not meet this.

We hope to come through the ordeal, but it will have been the ordeal of fire, and one of its results will be to alter entirely our ideas of taxation and expenditure. If it turns us back to the simple and forgotten virtue of economy we shall not have passed through it in vain.

LORD KITCHENER'S VISIT TO THE FRENCH FRONT.
In August, 1915, Lord Kitchener visited the Allied Armies at the front and had long interviews with General Joffre and M. Millerand. Our photograph shows the British War Minister and party on their way to review the French troops.

CHAPTER LXXV.

THE FRENCH ADVANCE TOWARDS LENS AND THE BATTLE OF "THE LABYRINTH."

The Western Allies have to Relieve the Pressure on Russia—General Foch Undertakes the Difficult Operation—Attack Directed against the Weakest Part of German Front—First British Army Co-operates with Tenth French Army—Complexity and Subtlety of the General Plan—Battle of Notre Dame de Lorette—Hill Stormed by a Single Movement—Terrible Struggle in the Darkness over the Ruined Chapel—Capture of the White Way—How the French Gunners Won Carency Village—Subterranean Battles in Cellars and Tunnels—Ablain Enveloped from North and South—Captain Sievert's Diary of the Battle—Terrible Sufferings of the Enemy Troops—Fine Achievement by the Foreign Legion at the White Works—More Mole Warfare Thirty-three Feet below Neuville—Foch's Army is Checked by "The Labyrinth"—Extraordinary System of Defences Constructed by the Germans—Three Weeks' Struggle in the Underground Maze—Victory of the French Army—French Soldier Proves a Finer Fighter than the Boche.

AT the time when we wrote the account of the Russian retreat from the Dunajec and Carpathian line, it was not advisable to state the chief reason of the disaster to our allies. The enemy was no doubt well acquainted with the temporary cause of the weakness of Russia, but it was thought best for all friendly historians of the war to refrain from discussing the matter. Russia had put most of her eggs in a single basket. More than half her fighting armies throughout the campaign had been supplied with smokeless powder and high-explosive shells from one great munition factory at Ochta, which is nearer to Petrograd than Woolwich is to London. Among the leading workers were men of German stock and brilliant talent, drawn from the German population of the Western Russian provinces. German Secret Service agents appear to have won over some of these men, and the result was that, at the critical hour in the history of Russia, all the works at Ochta were blown up by a series of tremendous explosions in the nitrating tanks, detonating

THE FRENCH WAR MINISTER AT CARENCY.
M. Millerand chatting with General Alby (one of the French corps commanders) and General de Castelnau (commander of the Second French Army) at Carency.

the materials used for shell-filling. Petrograd shook as in an earthquake. Thousands of the trained workmen were killed, and nearly all the munition plant was destroyed. If Woolwich were entirely wiped out in a similar way by German agents, our country would not be crippled; for we have not centralised our manufactures of explosives. Russia was quite crippled. Most of her guns were put out of action, because they lacked both shells and charges, and even the supply of smokeless powder for the infantry seems to have run perilously short. Great siege-guns were being produced at the Putilof works, capable of coping with the largest pieces of ordnance made by Skoda and Krupp; but after the destruction of Ochta there was so extreme a dearth of ammunition that nothing could be done against the heavy artillery used by General von Mackensen.

Russia had therefore to fight for time, while her principal Allies came to her assistance by the circuitous Archangel route. In particular Britain and France had to give up all thought of a great spring offensive, to husband their stocks of

TOTTERING BRICKS AND ABAN-
DONED BARRICADES.
The village of Villers au Bois, near
Carency, after the Germans had been
driven back.

have been simultaneously assailed
by very large massed bodies of
allied troops, each backed by an
overpowering concentration of
light and heavy artillery. But
this would have been too expensive a series of operations for
what was really only a demonstration in great force. It would
have been expensive in shells,
especially at a time when Russia
was almost broken for want of
shells.

General Foch, therefore, could
only select one comparatively
small section of front. He chose
the small lateral line between
Lille and Arras, as being, in the
eyes of the German commander,
the chief danger-point on the

A RESTAURANT NO MORE.
All that was left of the refreshment-room facing the railway-station after the French victory at Carency.

ammunition, and pour as much
shell and smokeless powder into
Russia as they could safely spare.
The German whose designs were
carried out in the destruction of
the Ochta works certainly deserved
the gratitude of his country, for it
was by far the greatest stroke in
the war. Besides directly crippling
Russia, it checked the striking
power of France and quite defeated
the intentions of Lord Kitchener
and Sir John French. As our
two armies were holding only a
small section of the line, it was
more convenient to the general
interests of the Allies that we
should, instead of employing
our increased

Supplying Russia forces, postpone the entry into action
with munitions of our national armies, and bend our
chief energies to the task of supplying
Russia with the munitions which had suddenly become
to her a matter of life or death.

Meanwhile the German lines in France and Flanders
had to be very seriously menaced. There were two
reasons for this. The Germans had to be prevented from
weakening their western front to reinforce the troops
under General Mackensen and General Linsingen. They
had also to be convinced that they needed another half-
million men in order to keep their lines in the west from
breaking. The only way in which the German commander
in France could be compelled to keep every man he had
there, and call urgently for a large part of the newly-trained
troops in Germany, was by the Allies severely pressing him.
Therefore, a part of the great offensive movement by the
Allies had to be undertaken, and pushed with much strength
and much tenacity until the desired results were obtained.

General Joffre selected General Foch for this difficult
and delicate operation. Had the grand offensive really
been intended, it would not have consisted of a single
assault against one sector of the German front. Two,
three, or four widely-separated lines of advance would

German front. It was so situated that if a French army
suddenly broke through, it could get on the main railway
lines of communication some days before the German
armies along the Aisne could withdraw with their guns.
Moreover, immediately behind the German entrenchments
north of Arras were the richest coal-mines in France, and
the principal industrial region. The mines and industrial
plant were quite as useful to the Germans as they would
be to the French. So both strategically and economically
the threat of a strong French advance on the Arras front
was likely to make a very disturbing impression upon the
Great German Staff. For this reason it was undertaken.

The movement began on the morning
of Sunday, May 9th, 1915, by a concerted   **The advance**
action between the Tenth French Army,   **on Arras**
under General Foch, with General d'Urbal
and General Maud'huy, and the First British Army, under
Sir Douglas Haig. We have already related at length
the events of the series of attacks made by the First British
Army between Armentières and La Bassée in the second,
third, and fourth weeks in May. Our men's part in the
affair was only of secondary importance, owing to their
lack of high-explosive shells. In effect, they merely
demonstrated vigorously against the left wing of the army,

commanded by Prince Rupert of Bavaria. They forced this commander. by fiercely attacking his salient at Festubert, to concentrate strongly against them with both guns and men, when he was in dire need of more men and guns on his left wing, that covered Lens, Douai, and his main railway communications. We have already seen that Prince Rupert tried to relieve the British pressure against him by getting the Duke of Würtemberg to strike at Ypres. Our Second Army at Ypres had to fight against desperate odds, in order to allow the main strength of the Allies to be thrown against the German positions in

DESTROYED BY GERMAN ARTILLERY.
The Farm d'Attiche, Carency, which was in the front of the battle-line and was destroyed by the German guns. Occupied by French troops, the position was defended by a network of trenches, as shown in the photograph.

SHATTERED BY SHOT AND SHELL.
A corner of Carency after its occupation by the French. The buildings were blown or shaken into fragments and the trees shorn of bark and foliage by the bombardment.

fundamental virtue of military obedience. The only man who can know everything in an army is the commander-in-chief. At times even his army generals, to say nothing of more subordinate officers, must work at the tasks assigned to them, inspired only by blind faith in the leadership of their chief. It may, for instance, be doubted whether Sir Herbert Plumer fully knew why he had to fight against terrible odds, at a time when his nation, which is one of the great industrial Powers of the world. had had nine months in which to organise and increase its military resources. Certainly some of Sir Herbert Plumer's officers, ignorant

front of Lens. Our men at Ypres wondered why they had not more heavy guns, and especially why they had not more shells.

It could not be explained to them at the time, but the fact was that, by one of the most loyal and far-reaching schemes of military co-operation, Sir Herbert Plumer's troops at Ypres were fighting in May, 1915, both against Mackensen's Grand Phalanx in Galicia and against the Crown Prince of Bavaria's system of defences round Lens. It was the heroic powers of endurance of our half-asphyxiated, outgunned, and outnumbered men at Ypres that largely helped to repair the disaster at Ochta. Some of the shells that they needed so badly were being despatched in haste to Archangel, and some of their own guns that should have defended them were being used to put pressure upon Prince Rupert of Bavaria and compel him to insist upon hundreds of thousands of new German troops, already designated for the Russian front, being sent exactly to that section of the battle-line in France where General Foch wished them to be fixed.

An Ypres problem explained

All this complexity and subtlety of plan, in the minds of the high command of the western Allies, serves to bring out in the strongest possible light the old, everlasting,

" Theirs but to do and die ! "

of the remote disaster which had entirely changed the general situation of the Allies, fought on amid their breaking lines, with something like despair for their country. Nevertheless, they stood to the task set them, and by their stoic courage achieved it. "Theirs but to do and die!"—to die without knowing why one is dying, when it seems as if one's death is due to a mistake on the part of the leaders of the nation. This faithfulness to death is that which constitutes, in the hours of extreme ordeal, the grand saving virtue of a people.

The French troops, after their magnificent recovery at the Battles of the Marne and the Grande Couronne de Nancy, never again had to fight in such despair as overtook our soldiers in the middle of the spring campaign. When the effects of the disasters of Morhange and Charleroi were repaired, the Frenchman lived in such an atmosphere of transcendent faith in the virtue of his people that nothing could trouble him. To General Joffre, his commander, and to M. Millerand, his Minister of War, he gave a confidence that fully equalled that which his forefathers placed in Napoleon after Austerlitz and Jena. The consequence was that the fighting power of the French soldier was increased twofold or threefold. He felt so absolutely sure of final victory that he was ready to die in battle before it was attained, knowing that by his death he would contribute to the salvation of his country. He knew that whatever happened to him, his life would not be wasted. It would be for ever one sound, solid building-stone in the new foundations of rejuvenated France.

This feeling was common. One French soldier, hearing of his wife's death, seemed strangely glad. A comrade asked him what was the matter. "My wife is dead," said he, "and my sister has adopted my little boy. Nothing whatever now attaches me to life, and if only I can make the Germans pay a good price for me before I go, I shall be quite happy." Not even the soldiers of the first Napoleon surpassed in courage the soldiers of Joffre. Frenchmen themselves remarked that the soul of Jeanne d'Arc seemed to have become incarnate in the four and a half million men arrayed for the salvation of France.

ANOTHER VIEW OF THE RUINED FARM D'ATTICHE, CARENCY.

The famous jest of the brilliant caricaturist Forain, showing the soldiers talking among themselves and saying, " Pourvu que les civils tiennent ! "—" Provided the civilians do not falter ! "—became one of the spiritual forces in the war. It did more to rally and invigorate French public opinion outside the trenches and the barracks than a series of most eloquent speeches by politicians could have done.

Stoic gravity of the French   The only element of weakness in the situation was the general expectation that the grand offensive movement in the spring would produce such results that no winter campaign would be necessary. The retreat of the Russians, therefore, was a grave disappointment, and the postponement of the action of the new large British armies increased the silent, stoic gravity of the French mind. Yet nothing could diminish the confidence of our allies in the ultimate victorious issue of the great struggle, and when General Foch prepared for the great demonstration at Lens he found as fine a body of troops under his command as a commander could wish for.

As the spear-point of his attack he employed Zouave and Chasseur regiments. Their superb qualities had been revealed by severe battle tests, but General Foch, a man of daring temperament, brigaded with these veteran troops large bodies of the youngest recruits in the French armies. Some of them were lads who in the ordinary course of events would not have been due to begin training until 1916; most of them were boys of the 1915 class, who had been rapidly trained since the outbreak of hostilities. According to ordinary military standards of judgment, **Foch's superb** these youngsters should have been the **spear-point** weakest element in the French forces. But General Foch knew his countrymen, and placed the boys with his very best troops, confident that the ecstasy of their patriotism, the vehemence of their youth, and the fine practical training they had received would make them as splendid a cutting edge in battle as were the older and more experienced men.

The task set the Tenth French Army was one of terrible difficulty. In the previous autumn campaign the Germans had occupied two ranges of hills in front of Lens. Where the hills sloped into the plain, north of Arras, they had constructed a gigantic fortification known as the Labyrinth. Along the outer rampart of hills beginning northward in a high spur, crowned by the little chapel of Notre Dame de Lorette, three or more lines of earthworks extended westward to the village of Ablain, and then swerved south-eastward to Carency. From Carency the German line ran to the hamlet of La Targette, four miles north of Arras, and then continued eastward through the village of Neuville St. Vaast, where they linked up with the Labyrinth. All this system of works, with its underground passages, armoured forts, and light artillery pits, was covered by the far-flung fire of hundreds of siege - howitzers, heavy field artillery, and naval guns, sited on and behind the second line of hills to the east running through the village of Vimy, below which, still farther eastward, extended the plain of the great French coal-fields.

In a bird's-eye view, such as the French airmen enjoyed in their continual voyages of reconnaissance, the German line formed a wedge of hills, the point of the wedge being Ablain. General Foch used three great striking forces against the point of the wedge. The first force struck out at the hill of Notre Dame de Lorette, the second force struck at Ablain, and the third force at Carency. At the same time an advance was made from the north against Lens, the scene of conflict being the village of Loos, and another advance was made southward against the town, the battlefield being La Targette and Neuville St. Vaast. In addition to all these movements a severe and persistent pressure was maintained along the entire front of the armies commanded by the Crown Prince of Bavaria from Armentières to Arras. Prince Rupert was never allowed to weaken one part of his front to strengthen another part. He had to leave his men in the positions in which they found themselves, until reinforcements arrived from the sweepings of the German army of occupation in Belgium, or from the depots in Germany. All the hostile front, from

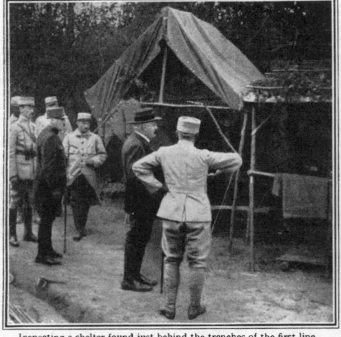

Inspecting a shelter found just behind the trenches of the first line.

The French War Minister passing through the first-line trenches.

On the field of battle. M. Millerand having the details of the battle explained to him.

M. Millerand interested in the booty captured by the French at Carency: Machine-guns, cannon, rifles, etc. In front of the Minister is General Fayolle. Above: The French War Minister in the trenches with General de Castelnau and staff.

AFTER THE FRENCH VICTORY AT CARENCY: M. MILLERAND'S VISIT TO THE BATTLEFIELD.

FRENCH GRENADE-THROWERS IN ACTION IN THE CALONNE TRENCH.
The fighting on June 26th, 1915, at the Calonne trench was exceedingly violent, and developed into hand-to-hand conflicts. The Germans employed burning liquids, and under cover of clouds of smoke reached their old first line. They were repulsed with heavy losses.

garrison retired into underground caverns, thirty-three feet below the surface, while a couple of officers remained with periscopes behind the visible parapets, waiting for the bombardment to cease, and watching for the advance of the French infantry.

The redoubts were also connected, by underground telephone wires, with batteries of field-guns, some of which at Ablain swept the hill on the south, while others at Souchez were able to get a flanking shrapnel fire on any hostile force advancing up the eastern slopes. There was also an enormous concentration of heavy German artillery north-east of the hill, at Angres and Lievin, which would cover every part of the height by means of direct or indirect fire.

A division of Baden troops garrisoned the Lorette height, and the divisional general was promised reinforcements in two days. Against him came a single French division of both old and young troops, each man of it being well aware that he was going to his death, and being sternly joyful about it. The French commander waited until the attack on the Aubers ridge by the First British Army occupied the entire attention of the Prince of Bavaria. Then at ten o'clock in the morning the French gunners lengthened their range, and under cover of their fire all the first French line clambered over their parapets and charged. The French field-guns had done their work well. All the enemy's wire entanglements were destroyed. Moreover, the heavier shells had broken down all the trenches, and the three German lines were captured in a single movement of advance by the first French line. The men bombed their way into the remaining machine-gun redoubts, until they were held up by the series of rear-posts behind the enemy's centre high on the slope of the hill.

The victorious troops spent the night in rebuilding the German lines they had captured, while the sky was lighted by a continuous bombardment of the position by the enemy's distant heavy batteries. In the morning of May 10th the first French line was about to leap out again and try to capture the crowning entrenchments round the chapel, when an order came from General Foch for the men to lie down and get as much cover as they could. A reconnoitring French airman had seen a grand German counter-attack preparing round the sugar factory at Souchez. As the great column advanced, the heavy German guns deluged the hill with high-explosive shell, which would have swept away the French infantry had it been exposed. But owing to the quickness of eye of the airman, it was the counter-attacking column that got caught in the open by the French guns. As it withdrew under a torrent of shrapnel, the French infantrymen made

Switzerland to the North Sea, was kept taut by the allied armies, while Foch's men drove in the great fortified hilly salient near Lens.

At each point of attack the battle opened at the same hour and in the same manner. On the morning of May 9th some thousands of French guns poured a hurricane of high-explosive shell into the German trenches. The artillery fire was especially concentrated on the Lorette spur ; for as this rose some two hundred feet above most of the other hills, it was the main key to the general position. The Germans here had six lines of trenches, strengthened by concrete, and barred by two or three zones of barbed-wire. At every hundred yards the trenches were flanked by machine-gun redoubts. One of these redoubts, north-east of the chapel, was surrounded by a wolf-pit, lightly covered with turf, with bayonets stuck at the bottom, to catch those who fell in. During the bombardment the

On the Lorette spur

their charge and captured another line of trenches. Some of the younger troops attacking the hill from the south exceeded their orders.

Seized with the lust of battle they took the trench, but instead of occupying it they turned aside into a ravine running towards Ablain, and killed or captured the German company which formed the garrison. The young adventurers ought to have been then cut off by the enemy's counter-attack, but this expected hostile movement did not take place. The column had fallen back on Souchez in such a condition that it could not move out again. On the other hand, no progress could be made against the flat hill-top round the chapel. The fortress there was so well supported by the German guns at Angres that each assaulting line was swept back. It was seen that more ground would have to be cleared round the dominating height before the decisive assault could be made. In the night the advanced line of troops was reinforced, and the next day the enemy was driven back from the southern buttresses. Then in a fierce night attack, in which the French advanced by rushes from one shell-hole to another shell-hole, the spur commanding Ablain was won.

By this time the attacking division had been sadly reduced in numbers, but the men fought on in scattered bodies, crouching in the large pits in the hill-side made by the great high-explosive shells. In the communication trenches the conflict went on continuously with hand-grenades and bayonets. But the bayonets were found to be too long and awkward for use in the narrow trenches, and the Frenchmen found the knife was handier. Happily, their Army Ordnance Corps was equal to the occasion, and the Tenth Army discarded its rifles and bayonets and did most of its work with automatic pistols and hand-grenades. The rifles were brought up for use with machine-guns, when the enemy's trenches had been entirely captured and rebuilt and garrisoned against the counter-attack. And even then the pistol and knife were kept at hand for trench fighting.

In spite of the sweeping fire from the Angres batteries, the advanced troops on Lorette Hill were well fed by their heroic cooks, and supplied with cigarettes; and when the reinforcements arrived the final attack was made in darkness on the night of May 12th. The French troops crept out of their holes and sheltered from the enemy's distant guns by snuggling against the breastwork of the hill-top. Three inches above their heads were the barrels of the German machine-guns, but as these opened fire on the advancing lines of the French supporting companies, the advanced troops pulled down the German sand-bags and, getting their bodies half over the breastwork, shot

A CASE OF EMERGENCY IN THE TRENCHES.
French officer, suddenly overcome, apparently by long kneeling in the trenches, being massaged by his orderly under fire.

down the German machine-gun officers. While this extraordinary combat was proceeding, the line of supports won a respite from the stream of bullets, and reached the barricade in turn and clambered over. Then in the interior of the fortress, in black darkness lighted only by passing shells, there was a long and terrible hand-to-hand fight. The French bore the Germans back across the levelled walls of the **Terrible hand-to-hand** chapel, over all sorts of cellars, bomb- **fighting** proof shelters, and shell-holes, and when day broke the battle-line was about five hundred feet east of the ruins, and the enemy was clinging on to the last spur.

But as daylight broadened the French advance was entirely checked; for the German gunners became aware of the situation, and swept all the lost ground on the hill with such a tempest of fire that the victorious troops had to dig out shelters and make communication trenches as best they could, in order to survive. The position the Frenchmen occupied had an outline in the shape of a

REMARKABLE CAMERA-PICTURE OF A BRILLIANT CHARGE BY A REGIMENT OF FRENCH ZOUAVES.

Section of Zouaves charging German trenches on the plateau of Touvent, in the region between the Oise and the Aisne. The men, "their bayonets flashing in the sun," to quote the official record, dashed forward over nearly two hundred yards of the enemy's trenches, the whole line advancing, as it were, with one movement. The enemy was overwhelmed, and had very heavy losses in men and guns.

spoon. The works round the chapel were the ladle from which the handle extended in the form of communication trenches. The Germans had laid great dynamite mines under the fortress, but happily the electric leads had been exposed by the ploughing shells during the French bombardment. The French troops were able to discover and cut the leads, but though they managed to escape being blown up their condition was terrible.

First the German infantry counter-attacked from three sides, and when these attacks were driven off, every German gun and how- **Five days of** itzer in a semicircle **slaughter** of twelve miles worked at high pressure for five days and five nights. Many Frenchmen died; not only was the original attacking force wiped out by the huge high-explosive shells, but successive reinforcements were blown to bits, buried, suffocated, or mangled.

At intervals the German infantry, occupying a position on the slopes known as the White Way, stormed up to see if all power of resistance had been destroyed. But there were always Frenchmen round the vanished chapel waiting to receive them. Meanwhile the French sappers channelled and tunnelled the hill amid the falling shells, and by May 17th all the conquered positions were linked together, and the work of munitioning and victualling the troops was facilitated. For four more days the refortification of the height continued, and then on May 21st the German trenches on the White Way spur were attacked from three sides.

The northerly attack was a fine piece of combined artillery and infantry work. The infantry charged while their guns were still working furiously, and then stopped a few yards from the zone of fire and signalled, by means of a flag, to their gunners to lengthen the range just another few yards. Some of the men were hurt by their own shells, but so close was the infantry charge to the supporting shell fire that the trenches were carried in a fraction of a minute with scarcely any loss.

At the same time the **French victory** southern attack, also **of Lorette** following very closely upon the French zone of shell fire, cut the communications of the garrison troops in the White Way, while the middle attack drove into the central German trench. All the survivors of the garrison not only surrendered but flung down their arms and ran with uplifted hands towards the French position, in order to escape from the fire of their own artillery. This concluded the French victory of Lorette, in which, after a struggle of thirteen days, one of the most important positions on the German front was captured at a loss of at least a division of enemy troops.

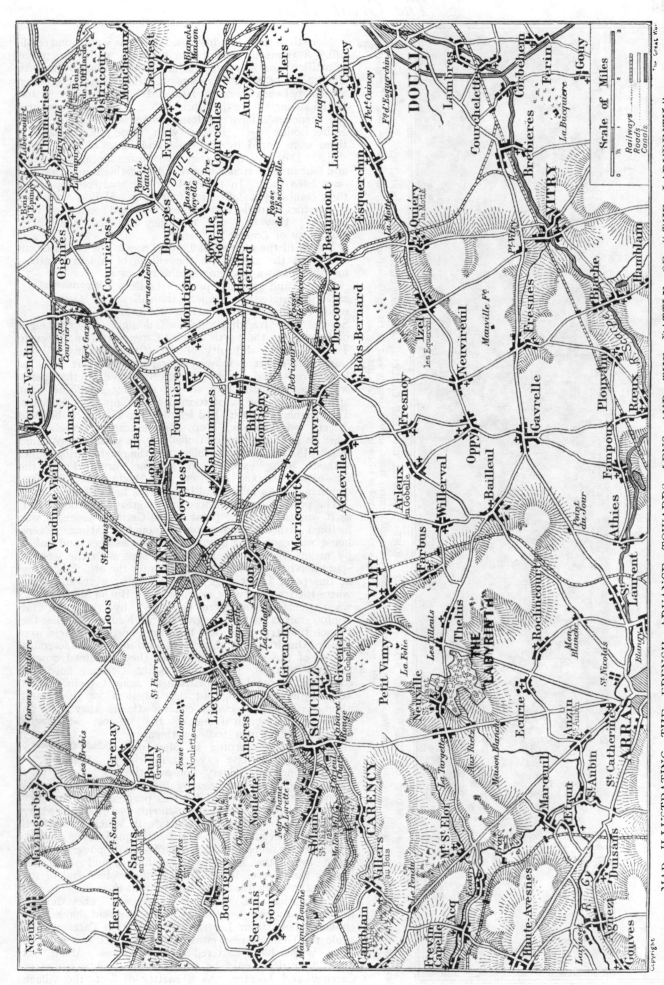

MAP ILLUSTRATING THE FRENCH ADVANCE TOWARDS LENS AND THE BATTLE OF "THE LABYRINTH."

The advance on the Arras front began on the morning of May 9th, 1915, by a concerted action between the First British Army, under Sir Douglas Haig. The movement ended in a decisive victory in "The the Tenth French Army, under General Foch, with General d'Urbal and General Maud'huy, and the Labyrinth," an intricate system of underground defences constructed by the Germans, on June 19th.

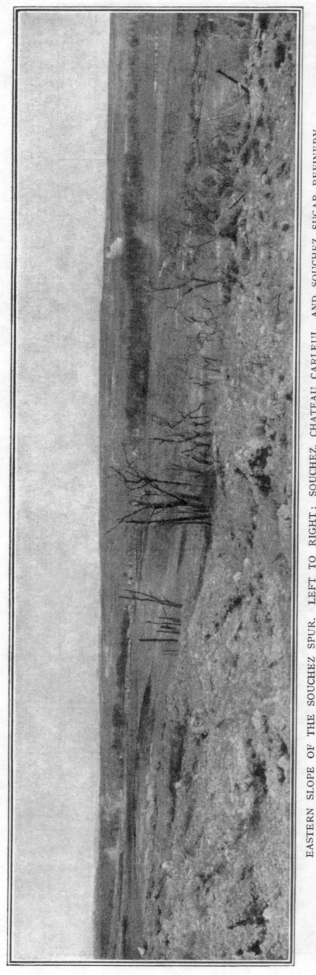

EASTERN SLOPE OF THE SOUCHEZ SPUR. LEFT TO RIGHT: SOUCHEZ, CHATEAU CARLEUL, AND SOUCHEZ SUGAR REFINERY.

Scene of some of the most awful fighting in the Great War. The sugar factory was taken and retaken many times, and the struggle went on for months without decisive result on either side. The moats of the Chateau Carleul, filled with water, served as a base for the enemy's defences.

More than three hundred dead Germans were found on the hill. A thousand were taken prisoners, and a few pieces of artillery and scores of machine-guns and bomb-throwers. Thousands of other Germans were killed in the counter-attack between Lorette Hill and Souchez. The victors of the struggle were dreadful to look at as they came from the trenches. Their uniforms were torn to rags, their entire bodies were covered with blood; and many of them were dazed by the blast and fumes of the German shells. Day and night they had been slipping with hand and foot in their trenches over indescribable things that had once been men. In some places the shattered bodies of their comrades and foes lay four deep. Hollow-eyed were the victors, and their jaws often trembled; but they were content; they had won, and they had kept, the Hill of Our Lady of Loretto.

Not until the fortress of Lorette was in the hands of our allies was the capture of the village of Ablain possible; for Ablain was a low-lying, double row of peasants' and working people's houses, extending more than a mile, in the valley road running from Souchez towards Servin. The straggling village was dominated by the height of Lorette on the north and by Carency Hill on the south. To add to the difficulty of the attacking army, all the slopes on either side were covered with fruit trees or forest trees, and under this screen of foliage the enemy was able to manœuvre troops, machine-guns, and light artillery, and the reinforcements sent up from Souchez. The German engineers had left nothing to chance, but had driven long, narrow, deep communication trenches to Souchez and Givenchy en Gohelle, down which troops could pass to the firing-line at Ablain and the neighbouring points without being exposed to shrapnel fire. From the fan-shaped sloping position at Ablain the Germans commanded the main road from Arras to Bethune.

Importance of Ablain

The position was therefore one of great importance and, as it was the extreme point of the German wedge, it was fortified with an extraordinary amount of labour. Every house was connected by underground passages, and linked by means of deep communication saps with the wooded spurs north and south. All the winter the attacking army at this point had rested in the low-lying westward plain, where the trenches were very watery. But in March, 1915, when the Germans were weakened by the need for reinforcements in Champagne and at Neuve Chapelle, the French infantry of the line had, by a surprise attack, won some of the drier ground together with some of the foremost houses of the village. And there they remained quietly for two months, while the distant German howitzers conducted a regular bombardment against them. Their sappers, however, dug out deep shelters for them, and after beating back several counter-attacks, they lived on fairly peaceably, in spite of the interest which the German artillerymen took in them.

But on the morning of May 9th their gunners at last gave them the help they needed. Every house in the long village was destroyed by high-explosive shell, some 20,000 rounds being used for this purpose. At the same time the enemy's wire entanglements were shattered by the new weapon of trench warfare in which the French Army had specialised. It was a little quick-firing cannon, made on the revolver principle. Its small, powerful shells swept away the barbed-wire obstacles, and while the heavier guns were still playing on the eastern end of the village, the French infantry leaped from their trenches and took a considerable number of the houses. They did not however advance very far, as they would have been enfiladed both from Lorette Hill and from Carency Hill, while the German siege-guns at Vimy, directly in front of them, would have battered them to pieces. Ablain did not fall until it could be encircled by the conquerors of Carency and Lorette. As a matter of fact, the village

Village destroyed by shell

Boring operations in an underground mine—" somewhere in France."

French sappers at work underground : The making of a half-gallery.

In a control station : Engineer officers in charge of mining operations.

Commencement of a mine : Gallery entrance at the bottom of a firing-trench.

MINE WARFARE: METHOD OF AVOIDING "STALEMATE" BETWEEN RIVAL TRENCHES.

By force of circumstances, trench warfare led to mine warfare, which was adopted with a view to making a breach in the enemy's lines and abruptly destroying his flanking dispositions at the moment of attack.

was won on May 12th by the French guns. Using incendiary shells they set on fire every ruined cottage in which the Germans were sheltering, and left the infantry the task of collecting the spoil and the day's prisoners and occupying the conquered ground.

Ablain was only an episode between the grand event of Lorette and the grand event of Carency. The capture of Carency was a very arduous affair. The village lay in a hollow, which was dominated by a wooded hill. The houses formed five groups, one in the centre, and the other four admirably placed for defence on the north, west, south, and east. Each group of walled buildings had been transformed by the enemy's sappers into a modern fortress. The shattered brickwork was merely used as bullet-proof shelters for machine-guns. A single man watched with a periscope for a movement by the French troops. The garrison of machine-gun men, grenade-throwers, and sharpshooters lived far underground at a depth no howitzer shell could penetrate. Tunnels and deep, narrow saps enabled the garrison to be relieved for a furlough at Lens or Lille, and kept well supplied with food and ammunition.

conducted by means of mine shafts and mining saps; but in spite of the underground struggles which occurred, no damage whatever was done to the enemy's position. On the contrary, this position was continually strengthened, especially after the success of the British hurricane bombardment attack at Neuve Chapelle. Neuve Chapelle was the dearest local victory in the Great War. It so alarmed the German Commander-in-Chief that he reorganised entirely his system of defences, at a cost of many millions of pounds, and the labour of tens of thousands of men, he constructed a modern "Gibral-tar" all along his front. We taught the German that he had made a mistake, but we did not ask a sufficient price for our lesson. So he was able to set his lines thoroughly in order before we and our allies seriously attempted to break through.

A modern "Gibraltar"

General Foch, however, with his subordinate commanders, Generals d'Urbal and Maud'huy, was fairly well aware of the enormous improvement in the German defence works. Every yard of the line had been photographed by French airmen, and the combined films had been studied by the French Staff and measured to scale with the utmost exactitude by the French gunners. Some millions of shells had then been accumulated by the French batteries. These batteries were strengthened by a collection of heavy howitzers from other sections of the front, some of our gunners coming to Carency to increase the tempest of high-explosive shell. According to the German official report, one of our Indian divisions was also attached to the Tenth French Army, and took part in the battle in the northern section of the line of advance from Vermelles towards Loos.

DIED ON THE FIELD OF HONOUR.
French soldiers conveying the bodies of two officers to their last resting-place.

On the hill above them were light field-guns, tubes for firing aerial torpedoes, and hundreds of machine-guns. Other guns were hidden in the surrounding orchards, and also many useful field-howitzers, all the batteries being connected with observation stations on the hill-top. Then in front of this formidable and almost invisible system of fortifications were four lines of trenches, strongly garrisoned by troops, who moved in and out through tunnels.

Mine warfare at Carency
The French were in as sorry a position before Carency as they were before Ablain. They were in the Artois plain, and the water from the hills drained into their trenches, where they often stood with the mud up to their middles. They had tried to win a footing on the high ground on December 18th, 1914, but as they advanced against the village from the north and west, they were stopped by machine-gun fire, and though they charged again on December 27th they were again mowed down and forced to retire. For some months afterwards the fighting was

Our gunners were full of admiration for French artillery tactics. According to our men, the French artillerymen were more cold-blooded, scientific, and effective than our artillery generals allowed our battery officers to be. It will be remembered that at Neuve Chapelle some of our war correspondents complained that our infantry had, on one occasion, suffered from our shell fire. The uninformed popular opinion of this country thought that the accidental slaughter of Britons by British guns was a fearful sign of incompetence. What the German practice in the matter is remains uncertain, but the French practice is to clear the way for an infantry charge by a narrow and intense zone of shell fire extending from a point only a few yards ahead of the assaulting line.

Sometimes a hundred or fewer Frenchmen were killed and wounded by their own guns. But the sufferings of the infantry in this respect were more than repaid by the devastating clearance made immediately in front of them by the extraordinarily close fire of their artillery. Our artillery were so afraid of hurting their own countrymen that they did not maintain the shell fire to the very last instant of the infantry shock. The result is that we saved a score of men from our own guns, and then lost five thousand men in the German lines, because the interval between our bombardment and our infantry attack enabled the enemy to recover. The tactics of the French gunners seemed cruel, for they killed more of their own men than

General Sir Bruce M. Hamilton, K.C.B., commanding the Sixth Army.

Watching effect of British gun fire from a sand=bagged ruin near the German lines.

Relief party advancing along "Regent Street," in Ploegsteert Wood, near Ypres.

R.A.M.C. orderlies giving first=aid to the wounded after a successful advance.

An interlude in the Ypres salient : British officers at " afternoon tea."

After the French victory at Carency: Shattered German trench on Hill 125, with ruins of the village in the background.

we did, but for every French life they wasted they saved a thousand French lives during the struggle in the German trenches.

It may also be worth while to point out in this connection that the French gunners still wanted their infantry to wear very bright red trousers. They regarded the khaki of the British soldier and the field-grey uniform of the German soldier as enormous mistakes. It was a fierce old French artillery general who stoutly stood out for **Was khaki a** the retention of the old-fashioned uniform **mistake?** of the French infantryman, and there can be little doubt that a year's experience of modern Continental European warfare demonstrated the far-sighted wisdom of his views. Invisible colours are useful for mere sharpshooters. Wellington dressed his sharpshooters in green during the Peninsular War to enable them to creep over grass and among trees without being seen ; but he kept the British infantry of the line in the brightest red, and it looks as though there would be fewer British casualties to-day if our soldiers were dressed in red.

For when the infantry charges, wave after wave in close or extended order, they usually meet with no opposition. As a matter of course, they have behind them a great and over-powering mass of artillery, which is shattering the enemy's trenches and turning it into a line of volcanic flames and deadly lyddite fumes. It is very rare that even the bravest of hostile machine-gun officers will stand up and work his gun when the opposing artillery is fully at work. Often our men were able to leave their trenches and charge the enemy without being shot at, while their massed guns were working. It did not matter if they were clad in khaki or in bright red. The arch of hell fire over their heads protected them. But when at last the infantry charged, the colour of their clothes became a matter of the highest importance to their own gunners. If the colour was khaki, the gunners soon lost sight of them, and had to leave them a large zone to fight in, and rely on telephone messages and signals for the further direction of their fire. But if the charging infantry had a bright uniform, as the French troops had, their artillery-men, working light field-guns fairly close to the line of combat, could see with their own eyes the position of their own infantry, and then place their shells twenty yards or so in front of them during the entire movement of advance.

This is what happened in the Battle of Carency. The overwhelming preliminary bombardment was conducted in the usual manner for a space of three hours on the morning of May 9th. The new trench cannon broke down the wire entanglements and the parapets of the German entrenchments, while the heavy howitzer shells crashed into the fortified houses and into the concrete underground caverns. Then, when the lines of Chasseurs swept out with fixed bayonets, the lighter French guns maintained a line of fire close in front of them, and the trenches were carried and the village entered by one violent movement—in one bound, as the French themselves said. The attack was made mainly from the south and the east, across a ravine near the road running from Carency

to Souchez. At only one point on the right, where the enemy was sheltered from gun fire in a hollow, was there any resistance. This spot in the fortifications was, however, almost encircled the following day by another French advance across the Souchez road. The hostile island was then conquered, and in a series of house-to-house attacks the Chasseurs and the young French troops hacked their way into the village. The struggle went on underground through the passages connecting the houses and in the shelter caverns where the garrison used to rest. The French suffered badly while trying to advance over ground, against the loopholed buildings from which machine-guns were trained on them. It was impossible to carry the village by storm, even when the French field batteries were brought up close to it.

The place was a warren ; the defenders went underground when the French artillery opened fire, and by means of subterranean telephone wires they brought their heavy batteries to bear on anything they could not reach with their own machine-guns. The French infantry had to ferret them out with hand-bomb and knife, with little

THE CAMERA IN RUINED CARENCY.
Striking photograph, taken through a hole in a wall, of a street in Carency after the village was retaken by the French.

help from their own artillery. While this ghastly mole warfare was going on, the Saxon, Baden, and Bavarian troops holding Carency were able to communicate in almost absolute security with Souchez and Ablain by means of deep, narrow communication trenches. But on Tuesday, May 11th, the French regiments entrenched on the Souchez road fought their way into Carency Wood, east of the village, and after a terrible fight, in which they held off counter-attack after counter-attack launched from the direction of Souchez, they cap- **Battle for the** tured the main communication trenches. **quarry**

The Germans in Carency then had only the route to Ablain open to them. General Foch tried to enclose this by a sudden double attack eastward and westward. But the French troops attacking from the east, over the position that they had conquered in Carency Wood, were surprised by a large and formidable fortification. On a wooded hill there was a great quarry hidden amid the trees, which had been excavated out of the chalk hill to a

THE SCENE OF TWENTY-TWO DAYS' FIERCE AND INCESSANT CONFLICT.—

Only a single division was used by General Foch from May 9th to June 1st, 1915, in capturing Carency, Ablain, the works round Malon Hill, and the sugar refinery at Souchez, and he only lost about one thousand men killed and two thousand slightly wounded. The success of these operations against the most formidable system of defence works ever used in open field warfare, was due to the remarkable artillery power of our allies.

depth of two hundred and sixty feet, and strengthened by casemates and bomb-proof caverns. Another regiment was sent up to reinforce the attacking troops, and the battle for the quarry opened with a surprise success on the part of the French. Two hundred and fifty German troops came out into the open on the wooded hill, with the intention of making a stand behind the wire entanglements which they had laid between the trees. But instead of charging, the French colonel sent a message along his field telephone, and the light French guns, in a sharp, intense, massed shrapnel fire, completely wiped out the hostile troops who had ventured above ground. Then the attack on the quarry opened, and went on for seventy-six hours of incessant fighting. The French lost heavily in covering the open ground leading to the subterranean fortress, but no losses could daunt the men. The more terribly they suffered, the stronger grew their will to conquer. The western wave of attack slowly mounted the hill on one side, preceded by a rain of high-explosive shell from the distant French batteries. At the same time the eastern line of attack swept into the forest, and at half-past five on Thursday, May 13th, a line of waving hand-kerchiefs rose about thirty yards away from the advanced French trench. The French never stirred. Their comrades had often been trapped by the enemy's trick of offering to surrender. But the Germans this time were in earnest. Rising up, their hands lifted above their heads, they came out of the fortress along the communication sap, crying " Kamerad! Kamerad!" There were more than a thousand of them, and one of their officers said to the victorious French general: " Your shooting was mathematical. Your infantry came on so quickly that they could not be withstood."

As the prisoners filed westward in the gathering darkness a series of fires broke out in the valley northward.

Victory at Carency and Ablain

It was Ablain burning, Heralded by the fire of their guns, the victorious French troops swept down the northern slopes of the hill, and using the communication saps made by the Germans, they swung against the eastern end of Ablain, and after a grim hand-to-hand struggle that lasted all night they crowned the victory of Carency and Lorette by capturing the enemy's central position at Ablain and another thousand prisoners.

The extraordinary thing about the Battle of Carency and Ablain was the economy of force that General Foch employed. Only a single division was used from May 9th to June 1st in capturing Carency, Ablain, the works around Malon Mill, and the sugar refinery at Souchez. In twenty-two days' fierce and incessant conflict, in which ground was continually being won, the division only lost 3,200 men. Of these, 2,000 were but slightly wounded, so that the ultimate loss amounted to scarcely more than 1,000 men out of 20,000. The division picked up 2,600 German corpses, and made altogether 3,100 prisoners. And all this was achieved against the most formidable system of defence works ever used in open field warfare. When the Crown Prince of Bavaria at last obtained the new formations he needed in order to stop the French advance, he launched eleven divisions—nearly a quarter of a million men—against the sugar factory at Souchez and the other positions won by the French troops. Yet, in spite of its enormous numbers, the fresh German army could not recover the lost ground. Though the enemy fell in tens of thousands, his lost hills of Artois were never recovered by him.

French and German losses

Certainly the French lost heavily in other parts of the battlefield. There were, for instance, as unsuccessful attempts at an advance north of Notre Dame de Lorette as our troops had made at Fromelles. But in the long and wearing attacks on the main German position, General

242

—ABLAIN, ST. NAZAIRE, AND CARENCY SEEN FROM THE SOUCHEZ SPUR.

In one battle round Souchez in June, for example, they used 300,000 high-explosive shells in twelve hours on a small section of the German front. The artillery, it is noteworthy, did not support the infantry; the main work was done by the guns. The infantry—relying chiefly on knives, pistols, and grenades, in hand-to-hand conflicts with the foe—" cleaned-up " afterwards.

Foch, after the first violent movement, endeavoured to maintain a slow but continual progress at a comparatively small loss of men.

The chief reason for the remarkable ascendancy of our comrades-in-arms was their artillery power. In one battle round Souchez in June they used 300,000 high-explosive shells in twelve hours on a small section of the German front. The French Army had entirely reversed its tactics. The artillery did not support the infantry; the artillery did the main work, and the infantry merely cleaned up after it. The rifle was almost **Captain Sievert's** an obsolete weapon, and so was the **diary** bayonet; for the French guns enabled the advancing infantry to get so close to the enemy that infantry action was, as we have seen, a sharp hand-to-hand affair with knives, pistols, and grenades.

From the diary of Captain Sievert, a German officer who fell in the battle, we have a very illuminating account of the French advance from the enemy point of view. On May 9th the captain was ordered to hold out on the Carency-Ablain line. But in the preliminary bombardment his battalion suffered terribly. Only one experienced officer was left — himself — together with two reserve officers and two hundred and seventy-two non-commissioned officers and men. The battalion therefore lost more than two-thirds of its effectives in the opening hours of the battle.

" I again ask," he wrote, " that the battalion be relieved. I again ask (he underlines it) for reinforcements. It is absolutely necessary that I receive the large number of hand-grenades that I have already demanded. We lack illuminating pistols. The troops did not bring any with them."

On May 11th the captain writes that he has received nothing, and that it is impossible for him to make an attack:

" 3.30 a.m.—I have informed the regimental Staff that it is im-possible for me to execute the nocturnal operation in combination with the 2nd Battalion of the 11th Regiment and the 13th Battalion of Light Infantry. For owing to lack of indispensable material the success of the operation cannot be assured. I asked for a large number of hand-grenades, but have received only one hundred and twenty for use on both sectors. The unanimous opinion is that success is entirely improbable. The enemy has an abundance of grenades, and by means of them he stops our movement, and even makes us retreat slightly at certain points. Besides, the French artillery is firing to-day without interruption, and inflicting losses on us."

At last, on the evening of May 11th, the battalion is relieved, and it rests until May 19th. Then, as it again enters into action, the woes of the diary-writer increase. First of all the German Staff work is bad. Wrong orders are given, and the sectors of action are confused. The battalion wanders about, groping for its position, marching and counter-marching under the fire of the French guns.

" 3.30 a.m.—I ask what sector we are to capture. Answer: ' That on the right ! '—which is to say the one we know already. I ask if the battalion should at once continue its march through Souchez as far as the ravine. Affirmative answer. I set out with Boger at a quarter-past eight. We follow the brook. The path is not to be commended. Artillery fire above our heads, and also all round about. We reach Souchez streaming with sweat. Indescribable scene. A frightful heap of ruins. The street is littered with shell fragments. The Staff of the 11th Reserve Regiment of Infantry is in a cellar. Souchez is completely destroyed by shell fire. They have mistaken the south for the north. It isn't on the northern slope but on the southern slope below Lorette Hill that we have to relieve—or rather reinforce—a battalion. Therefore we have not to go through the ravine at Souchez. They gave me only very superficial information about the sector we are to relieve. To all our questions the only answer is : ' I do not know. There is no connection between the various points.' I ask for information about war material (sand-bags, ammunition, hand-grenades). I am told that all the necessary material is on the spot. Nothing precise can be told about anything."

Faulty German Staff work

The battalion ends by getting to Ablain. But there they find a dreadful state of things.

EXAMPLE OF THE "FUROR TEUTONICUS": SAVAGE WORK OF THE HUNS IN A ONCE PROSPEROUS CORNER OF BELGIUM IN 1915.

The range of wrecked buildings seen in the above wonderful panoramic view formed what was once a prosperous flour mill at Lizerne, near Steenstraate, not far from Ypres. Scarcely a stick or stone was left standing by German shot and shell. The photograph was taken in the presence of the King of the Belgians, and Professor Bastin, the well-known artist, was commissioned to reproduce the scene on canvas.

SEEN FROM A CAPTURED GERMAN TRENCH.

Remarkable photograph taken by a Belgian officer from a captured German trench in Flanders.

WRECKED BY FRIEND AND FOE.

A section of the battle-area in Northern France reconquered by the French.

" I set out with the adjutant, guided by a man. Rain and mud. The road from Souchez to Ablain is impracticable and exposed to an incessant shell fire. Like Souchez, Ablain is only a heap of rubble. Only a quarter of the spire remains of the church. Our guide doesn't know the way. We search for it ourselves; sweating, groping about, slipping at every step, we reach the battalion at last. Officers present: Captain Winkler, the surgeon, several company commanders, and myself.

" The spirit of the men is very low. Heavy losses. Desperate situation. The surgeon still has seventy bad cases in the shelter. The ambulance men are gone. Still, we ought to get the wounded away, sending soldiers to carry them. Winkler refuses. I insist, and manage to prevail. Yet I doubt if it can be successfully done. Suddenly a shell bursts at the entrance. Winkler thinks he is struck, but it is only the shell-blast. But a drummer of the 111th Battalion is stretched dead at the door. The light fades. It becomes as black as a cellar. This occurs three more times.

" When we were in Souchez ravine we did not think there could be anything worse than that. Now we know we were wrong. Not only are we exposed to the enemy's fire front and flank, but they are shooting us in the back. No connection with the forces on the right. The French have cut through there There is a gap of six hundred yards between **Ablain worse than Souchez** the neighbouring battalion. And to think we have been put into this furnace after having fought for twelve days in Souchez ravine! Otherwise, there is nothing to write about. Same shell fire as usual. They are pitching huge bombs at us; it is terrible. We can't discover the position of their bomb-throwers. We cannot venture outside, for we are visible on all sides."

The Staff orders arrive in a confused way, and are only executed after much discussions. The victualling is bad, and the connections irregular.

" The companies have been led towards (illegible word). A different decision has been taken in regard to the third company, without informing me of the change of plan. The seventh company has gone to Souchez ravine, and then returned to Souchez. There the order came for the men to mount at once on the heights, but they were taken off to stop a gap at another point. The seventh company of the 11th Reserve Regiment must therefore stay on here without food. The troops must be content with their reserve rations.

" The situation is frightful. I asked to be relieved. No reply. At seven in the evening I at last learn that we are attached to the 157th Regiment of Infantry, and connected with Givenchy. There is no question of relieving us. To-night, at eleven o'clock, we are about to make another attack on Lorette Hill. If only we can succeed in chasing those dogs from the height! Since the afternoon of May 17th I have eaten only a large slice of bread and butter brought from Lens. To-night they brought us food, but all cold. Impossible to light a fire.

" The seventh company should be relieved to-day. The relief should be furnished by the 3rd Battalion of the 157th. They send us a section of six groups. I cannot consent to one hundred and twenty men being replaced by forty-eight men. Row on the telephone with the commander of the 3rd Battalion. I refuse to let the company go. By this stand of mine, I get out of them the third company of the 111th Regiment, and then I give way. But the effectives occupying this position are truly weak. We cannot stand out against anything **A row on the telephone** like an energetic attack. We have grown apathetic in this mouse-trap. I have asked the battalion to hold out to the last man. Though the three companies are now united, the assistant surgeon has not come."

On May 18th the position of affairs becomes desperate. The battalion can do no more, and the men see they are being killed for nothing.

" For five days the French have naturally had the time to establish themselves solidly. It has become still more difficult to attack them. I have, in spite of myself, the impression that our high command is being induced to abandon the position. At the same time many other points must be given up—ours, for instance. It seems to me that prestige (a matter of self-love) is the motive. We must recapture the hill of Notre Dame de Lorette.

" 19th May, 7.15 p.m.—Last night, at ten o'clock, I sent a message to Souchez regarding the situation, with sketches showing the shell-fire effects. I asked for a decision about the seventh company, which is without food and which has been two days

FRONTIER DEATH-POSTS IN THE DEBATABLE LAND NEAR CARENCY.
Barbed-wire entanglements, partly demolished, on land near Carency, which was captured and recaptured several times in the summer of 1915.
In oval: Another corner of Carency, showing the awful havoc wrought by the guns.

FRENCH ENGINEERS AT WORK IN THE ARGONNE.
Official French photographs showing a small communication railway in course of construction in the Argonne.

"All to-day the battalion is exposed to the enemy's gun fire coming from all directions. Again my battalion has been three days and three nights in the trenches without being relieved. The units that held this critical position before us were relieved at the end of two or three days.

"I again demand that they take the trouble to relieve my absolutely worn-out men. Need of illuminating shells. I have asked for them several times, but have never received any. The trenches are badly made, and scarcely capable of being defended. The active co-operation of real sappers is indispensable."

longer in its trenches than any other company. I have also asked for the positions of the other two companies, which have been used at another front without informing me of it. The messenger reached Souchez at half-past eleven, and found nobody there. The battalion cannot learn under whose orders it is placed, and where its new commander is. At last, in the afternoon, we are told that we are now under the orders of the Staff of the 157th Regiment.

"The enemy continues to fortify his position on the south-eastern slope. He has built important works there. Victualling is a matter of grave difficulties. It takes two and a half to three hours to reach the travelling kitchens. The road is under shell fire. My men are absolutely exhausted. I demand that my battalion be relieved."

On May 20th, at three o'clock in the morning, Captain Sievert sends another appeal. His men break away at every fall of a shell. It is necessary to threaten them with courts-martial to keep them in the position.

German troops demoralised

"The company commanders are united in complaining of the complete exhaustion and demoralisation of their men. We have great trouble in getting them to stick in the trenches. They run away at each shell. We are compelled to push them back from the rear. Even the example given by the company officers is almost without effect. This state of things is the result of the excessive efforts demanded from the men from May 2nd to May 13th, and of physical and moral overwork, interrupted only by a few days' rest.

246

But no reinforcements arrive. At ten o'clock at night Captain Sievert is in despair. Here are the last entries in his diary, containing the reports he addressed to his original regiment, the 111th, and to the 157th Regiment, to which he had been attached :

"May 20th, 10 p.m.—To the 111th Regiment and to the 157th Regiment.

"The bombardment to-day has completely destroyed the remains of our trenches. The men have been without cover for three days. You can't call them positions. The men are stretched out beneath the eyes of the enemy. Impossible to hold the place with my weak effectives. I demand an officer be sent here from the high command to take account of the position. Of all that I have asked for—illuminating shells, sand-bags, etc.—nothing has arrived. We are left to drift. Once more I demand, instantly, that the fourth company of the 111th be placed at my disposal. The enemy's artillery fire is dreadful, especially the heavy howitzer shell that can be heard slowly coming. Everybody is anxious, and wondering where they are going to strike. The parapet trembles, the iron fragments and clods of earth fall on us. How much longer are we to remain in this mouse-trap ? I think my nerves are worn out. The bombardment has attained the utmost violence. Indescribable."

Captain Sievert in despair

Here ends the diary of Captain Sievert. It shows what superhuman efforts were imposed upon the hostile forces even before Italy entered the struggle. It indicates also the effect of the gradual but incessant movement of the

A GERMAN TRENCH IN ARRAS.
On right : Interior of a French trench in the Argonne.

DREAMING OF THE BLACK FOREST?
Picturesque view of a German position on a mountain-side in the Vosges, between which and the corresponding range of the Black Forest on the other side of the Rhine there is a remarkable similarity.

Tenth French Army. In the captain's notes there is hardly any reference to the action of the French infantry. The German battalion is slowly worn down by gun fire, and then the exhausted survivors are suddenly annihilated by the long prepared infantry charge. The French general was lavish of time, but very economical in regard to the lives of his men.

The heaviest French losses seem to have occurred in the first movement of advance on May 9th. The Foreign Legion had a terrible struggle in the system of German works lying between Carency and Neuville St. Vaast, and known, from the outlines made by the trenches in the chalk, as the White Works. For three hours the artillery smote the position, and then at 10 a.m. on May 10th—the same minute as the entire first French line charged—the Foreign Legion swept out. All the wire obstacles were cut; the first German trench was full of corpses, stacked one on the other. The garrisons of the second, third, fourth, and fifth lines **Foreign Legion's** retreated, under shrapnel fire from the **great charge** French guns. But the legionaries reached them with the bayonet, and after an advance of an hour and a half they penetrated nearly three miles into the German front.

But the enemy then made a stand on a line of high ground, and the legion had to pass over four hundred yards of open fields to reach the slope. Onwards they ran under a hell-fire fusillade. The leading lines withered away, the scanty survivors taking cover in old shell-holes full of water. There they remained until nightfall, with German machine-guns firing in front of them and French machine-guns shooting over their heads. Companies of two hundred and fifty men were reduced to fifty men—few officers surviving. The general directing the legion was wounded, and the colonel. Three out of every four commandants were killed. But the legion was proud of itself. It had done its duty. It had taken all the five German lines in a single charge, and driven its front three miles nearer the enemy's line of retirement. The legion, **Famous fortress** 4,000 strong at the start, had taken 2,000 **of the Labyrinth** prisoners, six guns, and a large number of machine-guns, and killed at least 2,000 Germans.

A few miles south-east of the White Works was the main German position. It consisted of a series of trenches west of the hamlet of La Targette, the houses of the hamlet, a system of works behind La Targette at the village of Neuville St. Vaast, and then, behind Neuville, the famous underground fortress of the Labyrinth. Yet a single French division was set the task of breaking through this unparalleled organisation of defences. But backing the division was a mass of French batteries that exceeded in power and weight of missiles the guns opposed to them. As in the more northerly sectors of the battle-line, the preliminary bombardment on the morning of May 9th

GRIM WORK IN "GOD'S ACRE": FRENCH ALPINE INFANTRY HOLDING THE CEMETERY AT SOUCHEZ.
The cemetery at Souchez was, like the sugar refinery not far away, taken and retaken during the fighting north of Arras. Above: General Fayolle and officers of his Staff. General Fayolle commanded the attack at Carency.

PRIZE DISTRIBUTION AT THE FRONT
During a brief spell of rest a French machine-gun section organised a sports meeting, which took place on the anniversary of the outbreak of war. Our photograph was taken just before the prize distribution.

was fearful in intensity. The German barbed cables, as thick as a man's finger, were completely destroyed, and when the French infantry rushed across the fields, stretching for a hundred and fifty yards between the hostile fronts the German troops did not shoot; for the French guns still bombarded the ground a few yards away from the van of their infantry.

Only the enemy machine-gun officers, firing from concrete redoubts, attempted to stay the advance; but some of the French troops encircled the machine-gun forts and hand-bombed the small garrisons, while the main charging force tore into La Targette, and fought in the orchards and streets. Their light guns followed them, the horses trotting, and smashed by close-range fire the fortified houses and other machine-gun redoubts. At half-past eleven in the morning—ninety minutes after the first line charged—the troops in the sector were fighting in the first houses of Neuville.

At the same time the centre of the French division, working from the Bethune road and through the hamlet of Biez, reached the first line of enemy **In Neuville churchyard** works on the southern outskirts of Neuville. Here the attacking troops drove northward towards the churchyard, where the Germans had constructed a system of defence behind the tombstones. Twice during the day the French regiment took the churchyard, and twice they lost it; but close to it they held five lines of trenches captured in the furious struggle.

So far, the plan of attack was working out more rapidly than had been expected. Neuville, like Ablain, was being surrounded on three sides. But the right wing of the assailing division could not get forward. As it charged northward from Ecurie, with the object of penetrating behind Neuville, it was completely held up by the Labyrinth. The flanking outworks of this extraordinary invisible fortress poured a devastating fire into the French right wing. Yet with glorious stubbornness the charging lines, though thinning at every yard, went on and flooded into the southern end of the Labyrinth.

Barely could the victors save themselves from annihilation by building up sand-bag barricades in the German saps and tunnels, and digging for the electric wires connected with the mines which the enemy sappers had prepared against the day of defeat. Though the French right wing escaped complete destruction, its losses were

THE USE OF THE HAND-GRENADE.
Mannequin used by French soldiers in grenade-throwing practice.

IN DEADLY EARNEST.
French infantryman throwing hand-grenade into a German trench.

heavy, and it could make no farther advance. As soon as the full strength of the Labyrinth was perceived, General Foch altered his plan. Keeping only his footing in the subterranean stronghold, he swung heavily against Neuville the following day—Monday, May 10th—and began the systematic conquest of the village.

Neuville was a curious village. The Germans lived some thirty-three feet below the street. The cellars of the houses were strengthened by a topping of cement a yard thick, and underneath the strengthened cellars was a subterranean town, the caverns being connected by large, main tunnel thoroughfares with narrower side

A subterranean town

galleries. The garrison troops circulated like moles during the battle, coming up in the most unexpected places. There was one tunnel in particular that ran under the French lines, and in the rear of the attacking troops a hidden German officer studied the French preparations through a periscope, and telephoned fire directions to German batteries miles away eastward at Thelus and Vimy. There were indeed German guns and howitzers on three sides of Neuville, and they maintained a furious fire on the French soldiers. But in the long Battle of Neuville, lasting from May 9th to May 13th, neither the German nor the French guns were predominant; for it was a battle of cave-men, going on often at a depth to which no ordinary shell ever penetrated. What was needed was a new concrete-piercing shell with a delayed fuse action. The new submarine warfare was paralleled by just as novel a subterranean warfare.

The Germans were armed with knives and bombs; the French had also pistols. Each group of houses was attacked through the cellars, and every evening there was never a recoil on the part of the French to be registered. Slowly, but continuously, they progressed in the most terrible sort of fighting in which men ever engaged. By their inventiveness, their grim audacity, and deadly tenacity the regiments won forward. Drawn largely from the eastern frontiers, the Meurthe and Moselle region, where the German beast had left the mark of its lust and cruelty, the men of Lorraine had been shaped under fire,

THE SOLACE OF FAITH: WITH GERMAN PROTESTANTS AND FRENCH ROMAN CATHOLICS IN NORTHERN FRANCE.
Lutheran pastor preaching to German soldiers from a rustic pulpit in a secluded dell near Soissons. Below: A celebration of the Mass. French soldier approaching the improvised altar at which a priest is officiating.

DISMOUNTED CAVALRY DEFENDING A TRENCH.
In front of the trench are barbed-wire entanglements. The enemy had taken up a position in the shelter of the woods in the distance.

and they were burning with a passion of vengeance—vengeance for their murdered and tortured kinsfolk and their irretrievably ruined homes.

By Saturday night, May 15th, they held all the mass of the village, with the exception of its northern corner, and their progress in the interior of the subterranean defence works was accompanied and consolidated by their progress outside Neuville. On May 11th the churchyard was again captured by a splendid charge through a cross-fire of hostile machine-guns. The men who fell were avenged that night, when the Germans made a violent counter-attack. They were allowed to advance within thirty yards of the new French position, and then they were shot down by rapid fire and bayoneted in a sudden, leaping charge made by the defenders. None of the attackers escaped except a hundred men and four officers, who were taken prisoners. There were no more attacks on the churchyard, which was developed into the radiating centre of the French operations, by which the village was slowly conquered. Seven guns, thirty Maxims, 2,040 prisoners, and two cows kept in the caverns for milking, were some of the spoils.

There remained the Labyrinth, the maze of blockhouses, shelters, saps, caverned chambers, and armoured concrete defences and tunnels, on which the German engineers had exhausted all their science. It was built around two sunken country lanes, from which spread, for a mile and a half on either side, works of every kind, amply furnished with machine-guns and bomb-throwers. Naturally it was the weakest point in the entire German front; so the enemy engineers had for months used all their skill and increasing experience to supply Nature's defects by art and make their weakest point their strongest.

General Foch's difficulties

The French attack on May 9th barely bit into this tremendous novel fortress. On the following days the situation was not improved, and every attack, either from north or south, was exposed to a flanking fire. General Foch was then faced by the problem of either losing men or losing time. If he wished to break through the enemy's front and recover Lens, and perhaps Lille, he had to act quickly, before the Crown Prince of Bavaria obtained reinforcements in men and artillery. On the other hand, if he merely wished to put pressure on the hostile commander and continue to wear the German front thin by

FRENCH ARTILLERY IN ACTION.
A photograph taken in the Vosges. The men are lowering shells down an improvised slide for use by a heavy gun below.

RETURNING FROM A DAY IN THE FIELDS.
Thousands of French soldiers in the intervals of the fighting were drafted into the fields to assist in gathering in the crops.

251

a process of attrition, there was no need to send men to their death by the tens of thousand.

General Foch used only four thousand men in the Labyrinth, but he allowed them to take their own time. His main intention was to help Russia and attract the new German formations to France and Flanders instead of allowing them all to proceed to the eastern theatre of war. General Foch, the Lorrainer, was a man somewhat of the stamp of Sir John French, the Irishman. By temperament he was impulsively daring—a Hotspur— but by training he was cautious, being, like the British commander, a bookworm in regard to the story of the literature of war. So when he made a plan, he first built a solid, practicable design, well adjusted to the forces he employed. But he topped the scientific scheme with just the possibility of a great, decisive, happy stroke, depending largely for its execution on the condition in which he found the enemy.

A cautious Hotspur

The strength and extent of the Labyrinth made the superstructure of General Foch's design valueless. So he confined himself to carrying out, at as small a cost as possible, the solid part of the operations. The approaches

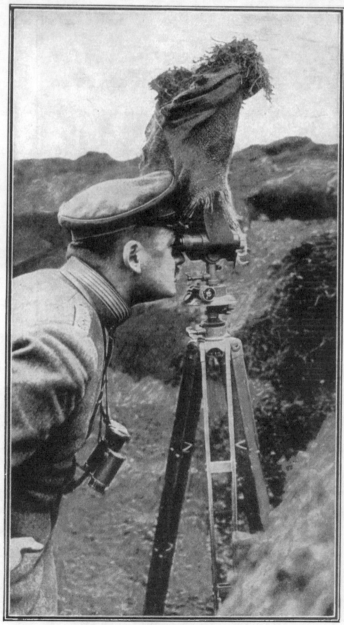

IN A GERMAN TRENCH.
Novel protection for a periscope field-glass.

to the Labyrinth were dominated by numerous German batteries, including 11 in. and 12 in. howitzers, placed at Givenchy en Gohelle, at La Folie, Thelus, Farbus, and at Beaurains, south of Arras. There were thus cross-fire effects from the north, east, and south. The French had a powerful artillery, but it was entirely concentrated on the east and south-east.

The ordnance on either side was practically impregnable. It could only bombard the hostile infantry So while the French guns smote the German soldiers and the German guns smote the French soldiers, the opposing infantrymen smote each other. The attack opened on May 30th after the first German lines had been destroyed by bomb-throwers. Three French regiments charged—one on the north, one on the west, one on the south. On the north and the west the charging lines won to their goal, but the regiment on the south was again held up. Then the German batteries hammered at the lost German position, but the Frenchmen stood their ground, and in the night there was a furious attack and counter-attack, in which our allies lost and won again the position. Then from the front trenches the mole warfare began, down Kluck Passage, Eulenburg Passage, the Festival Hall and other cavernous ways. The ghastly fighting with knives and shattering hand-bombs never stopped night or day. Bare-headed, in shirts with upturned sleeves, the human moles fought, with petards for blowing up sand-bag barricades, bomb-throwers, aerial torpedoes, knife and pistol.

The French were more daring. They adventured more above ground, on exploring expeditions and leaping raids ahead of the barricaded saps where the combat was raging. One French lieutenant, on June 1st, climbed over the barricade in the central hollow road and, finding it feebly held, returned with sixty men and took by surprise the unprepared garrison of two hundred and fifty men resting in the deep-dug chambers, and made them all prisoners. The chief French losses occurred among the reserve troops. The regiment that was doing the fighting was always too close to the German soldiers for the German batteries to risk a shell at them.

Meanwhile the French sappers drove a parallel, in the ancient way, towards the Eulenburg Passage, one of the principal lines of the Labyrinth. A field of scarlet poppies stretched between the parallel and Eulenburg Passage, and on June 16th the French infantry charged through the poppies suddenly and leaped into the enemy's line. There followed a struggle in Eulenburg Passage lasting three days, and the end of it completed the French victory. An entire German regiment of 4,000 men, the 161st, perished. A Bavarian regiment was also shattered, and a thousand prisoners taken. The French had only 2,000 men put out of action, many of whom were only slightly injured.

The general results of the series of battles on the Arras front were more important than the similar series of battles on the La Bassée sector. The Tenth French Army, by reason of its superior supply of high-explosive shell, did more damage to the armies of the Crown Prince of Bavaria than did our First Army. It threw the enemy off the line of heights he occupied; it captured the most important underground system of defences that the Germans had constructed in any field of war; and it attracted against its newly-won position eleven new divisions, which it proceeded to wear down without giving ground. To the French soldier the concluding struggle in the Labyrinth was an inspiring affair. He at last recognised that he was, without any shadow of doubt, a better all-round fighter than the German soldier. His artillery was more skilfully handled, his shell supplies were equal to those of the enemy, and his personal prowess was much superior to that of the experienced first-line veteran troops of Germany. The Frenchman was slow to come to this conclusion—he remembered 1870; but the conclusion was forced upon him—by himself.

Completing the French victory

CHAPTER LXXVI.

THE FALL OF LEMBERG AND THE RUSSIAN RETREAT
FROM GALICIA.

Serious Position of the Russians after the Battle of the San—The Great German Trust Magnates Enter Into the War—How They Organised at Once All their Resources in War Industries—Intrigues with the Pro-German Party in Russia—Failure of Russian Bureaucracy and Triumph of the Duma—Hindenburg Comes to the Help of Falkenhayn—Tremendous German and Austrian Losses—New and Grandiose Scheme of Attack Prepared by Hindenburg—The Problem of the Polish Quadrilateral of Fortresses—Russia Left without Help from Her Allies—Austrian Repulse at Moskisca—German Victory at Lubaczov—Marvellous Feat of Russian Cavalry—German Line Broken and Advance Held Up—Wonderful Skill of General Ivanoff in Conducting the Great Retreat—Mackensen Rescues the Austrian Armies on Either Side of Him and Turns Lemberg from the North—Russian Armoured Train Checks the Enemy's Advance—Fierce Flanking Battles along the Dniester Front—Linsingen's Army is Shattered and Pflanzer's Force is Partly Ambushed in the Deep, Winding River Channel—Failure of Mackensen's Main Plan—He Turns Northward Towards Cholm, and the Russians Make a Stand East of Lemberg—The Terrible Crime of Ravaruska.

AFTER the fall of Przemysl in the first days of June, 1915, the extraordinary strength of the attacking German forces became clearly apparent The Russian commander, General Ivanoff, at first thought that the breaking of the lines of the Third Army at Gorlice might have been prevented. For it appeared, on inquiry, that Radko Dimitrieff, the leader of the Third Army, had been so over-confident of holding the enemy that he had not adopted the usual and proper precautionary measure of constructing fortified lines upon which to retire behind his position. When, therefore, his front was suddenly broken, no further means of resistance were available, and part of the Third Army was shattered. This very grave disaster was adjudged the result of negligence on the part of the famous Bulgarian general, and he was afterwards relieved of his command. But General Ivanoff still hoped to retrieve the situation by bringing part of the central Russian army across the Upper Vistula, and making a stand along the line of the San River.

But, as the fall of Jaroslav and Przemysl revealed, the position of affairs was far more

GENERAL POLIVANOFF.
A brilliant strategist. He succeeded General Sukhomlinoff as Russian Minister of War.

serious than had been expected. The provision of additional entrenched lines and the closer co-operation of the Russian forces did not solve the difficulties, for these difficulties were of a peculiar nature. Military experience, military skill, and even military genius could not overcome them. There was needed a profound and far-reaching revolution in Russia in order to stay the advance of the Germanic forces.

The Russian Staff, including the Russian Minister of War, General Sukhomlinoff, had been mistaken about the character of the struggle, even as had been the French Staff and the British Staff.

All the allied military leaders thought that they were still contending against a similar body of military leaders, composing the German Staff. This was the capital source of the error. In so far as the German Staff represented the mind of the German aristocracy and the German bureaucracy, its organising powers in the war were exhausted by the autumn of 1914. It was then that the critical battle for Calais came to an end, owing to a lack of munitions in the German armies. The mistake in regard to the character of the war was common to all the Staffs. Germany, it is true, displayed somewhat more

PICTURESQUE VIEW OF MITAU, THE CAPITAL OF THE BALTIC PROVINCE OF COURLAND, SHOWING THE SCHLOSS.
Courland (or Kurland) was partly Germanised in mediæval times. Towards the close of the eighteenth century it was incorporated with Russia. It derives its name from that of the old Kurs, a Lettish people.

foresight in the main matter than did her opponents, but the military men of every contending country miscalculated what provision of war materials would be needed to win a decisive victory on land.

But to the great advantage of Germany, her Staff first clearly appreciated the chief problem in modern warfare between highly industrialised nations, and called at once in the autumn of 1914 for the help of the men they needed. In this manner Germany won a start of nearly six months in the veritable preparation for the critical period of the terrible struggle; for more by luck than by prevision she found, ready made to her hand, the new instrument required. This instrument consisted of the gigantic German trust system of production which, modelled first upon the American trust system, soon surpassed it in range, closeness of control, general efficiency, and concentrated power. Three hundred men dominated the industries of the country, and of these three hundred men about a score, like Ballin, Stinnes, Thyssen, Rathenau, Funke, Haniel, and Kirdorf, formed an inner oligarchy.

Kaiser and Trust magnates

Linked with the German money trust, connected with the Government, and in many cases in close personal touch with the Kaiser, the German trust magnates controlled all the industrial activities of the Empire. They were chiefly responsible for bringing about the war, as a quick means of gaining a world-wide dominion in commerce, and saving themselves from a very great crisis in over-production, which the lack of financial staying power would have rendered most dangerous to Germany. Far from being of a pacific nature, as captains of industry should be, according to the doctrines of the Manchester school, they were more bellicose than the Prussian country squires.

They were inspired by the warlike policy of promoting trade which their ancestors, the German merchants of the old Hansa towns, had practised with success for centuries till broken by England in the days of Queen Elizabeth. The modern German trust magnates provided the Social Democratic movement with traitor leaders, who voted at once for war when the time came for deeds and not words. Kaiser Wilhelm II. had long since recognised that the leaders of the German trusts and cartel systems were the real governors of his Empire, and he entered into league with them, just as German Emperors of old entered into league with the Hansa merchant princes.

The industrial oligarchy of Germany undertook, in the

THE MARKET-PLACE IN MITAU.

autumn of 1914, the work of bringing all the manufacturing energies of the German and Austrian Empires to bear upon the battlefield. No long, difficult, and defective process of organisation was needed, as was afterwards the case in France, Britain, and Russia. The German trust system immediately amalgamated with the military system, and worked smoothly and rapidly, like an enormous machine, for war purposes. Hundreds of men of science, forming the research departments of the various syndicates and companies, ceased for the time trying to defeat foreign manufacturers

HARBOUR OF LIBAU, OCCUPIED BY THE GERMANS ON MAY 7TH, 1915.

GENERAL VIEW OF LEMBERG FROM A HEIGHT NEAR
THE TOWN.

Lemberg, the Capital of Galicia, situated in a beautiful and romantic
district, was captured by the Russians on September 3rd, 1914, and
retaken by the Austrians on June 22nd, 1915.

by the discovery of fresh improvements in articles
of commerce, and studied how to facilitate the work
of slaughter. In recent years Germany had begun to
surpass both America and Britain in the production of
power lathes. Her extraordinary output of lathes, combined with her intense organisation of production, enabled
her at once to increase in an extraordinary manner the
number of shells and guns manufactured.

She had also begun to lead the way in Europe in concrete
work. The main streets in cities like Düsseldorf were
being rebuilt with magnificent and well-designed façades
of armoured concrete just before the war. Men and
materials were conveyed to the front to make impregnable
defences for the Army. Even the German asphalt paving
syndicates found important warlike work. Rapidly they
transformed the muddy, unmetalled roads of Poland into
firm causeways, along which guns, ammunition, provision
trains, and troops could move at a great speed.

The leaders of German industry, in fact, solved at once
the problem of the invasion of Russia, which had defeated Napoleon, puzzled Moltke, and
frightened the modern German Staff. By
energetically increasing the production of
motor-vehicles, while road making and
railway building went on, the difficulty about communications was entirely overcome. It was on the
Russian troops, tramping in an unending downpour of rain
through a land of mud in the summer of 1915, that the chief
strain fell. The Germanic armies had good roads behind them
for supplies, and also for movements of manœuvre.

The problem of communications

At the time when the German trust magnates threw
all their magnificent forces into the war, Russia was
fighting with little more than her crippled Government
ordnance works at her back. A considerable
number of Russian factories were managed by
German technical experts, who were ready to
check any production of war material. The workshops, factories and foundries controlled by the
Russians themselves were neglected by the military
authorities and depleted of workmen by the mobilisation. Moreover, the total production of the Russian
works was small in comparison with that of
Germany. Some of the Russian captains of
industry advocated that the German managers
and German technical advisers, who were hindering the manufacture of war material, should be
dismissed and replaced by British, or even by
American, factory managers. But unfortunately,
the large, harm-working German element concerned
in the direction of Russian industries was at
first supported by the reactionary party in the
Russian Government. Some of the reactionaries

GERMAN LANDSTURM MARCHING ALONG THE PRINCIPAL
STREET IN LODZ.

RUSSIAN GUNS TAKEN BY THE ENEMY.

A GERMAN FORAGE STORE IN POLAND.

THE GRAND DUCHESS TATIANA.

were not averse from seeing their country defeated, so long as the democracies of France and Britain were still more deeply involved in disaster.

They hoped that, after a sharp trial of strength in which Russia's weakness would be evident, the Tsar would be induced to make peace with the Kaiser, and then league with him against the democracies of Western Europe. But all this web of intrigue, treachery, bureaucratic indolence, and negligence was suddenly broken by the blow intended to support the Pro-German party and the reactionaries. As the Third Russian Army began its long retreat and the Russian public learnt that the series of reverses was due to a lack of munitions and equipment, there was an abrupt, unforeseen resurgence of mind, soul, and character among the educated townspeople of the Empire, similar to that which had taken place in Italy when Prince Bülow and Signor Giolitti seemed about to triumph. The Russian municipalities started to agitate ; they pointed out that the bureaucracy had failed to provide means to defend the Empire, and that only a popular assembly, in close touch with the industries of the country, could organise **General Sukhomlinoff** quickly the production of warlike **superseded** material. In the meantime a central committee of soldiers and business men began to quicken the production of high-explosive shell.

There were riots in Moscow and other cities—not against the Government, but against the German element in Russian trade and industry. So fierce was the temper of patriotism that not only was the professed German party, once headed by Count de Witte, overthrown, but the far more loyal leaders of reactionary bureaucratism were deprived of power. General Sukhomlinoff, the Russian War Minister and reorganiser of the Army, fell, because of his political views. He was replaced by General

Polivanoff, a brilliant strategist, who favoured parliamentary institutions. Several other powerful Ministers were succeeded by men willing to work with the Duma. The extraordinary change made in the British Cabinet, when Mr. Lloyd George abandoned the control of the Treasury in order to speed-up the production of munitions, had a considerable effect upon the Russian mind. The Russian manufacturers—as loosely organised as British manufacturers—felt that they could produce the best and quickest results by following **Triumph of the** the example of their western Allies. **Duma** They felt also that an alert parliamentary control would help them more than their slow, routine, bureaucratic management of affairs, for a bureaucracy seldom produces men of any business capacity.

This large, quiet revolution in the promotion of national efficiency and in the intensification of patriotism did not immediately produce any marked improvement in the conduct of the war. It was necessary to recall tens of thousands of miners and workmen from the Army, in order to get full supplies of coal and iron, and relight many foundries that had been closed down on mobilisation. Power lathes, crucibles, and presses had to be imported, and new factories for high-explosives and smokeless powder established. Some persons estimated that it would take fully six months before the industrial energies of Russia were developed to a proper degree of productiveness. Meanwhile the Russian Commander-in-Chief had to fight for time against a splendidly equipped opponent,

THE TSARITZA.
The photographs on this page are of the Russian Empress and her daughters as Red Cross nurses.

who was willing to sacrifice half his army for a rapid decision.

The Grand Duke Nicholas seems to have been opposed by the Kaiser in person, for it was the feverish anxiety of Wilhelm II. that inspired and directed the plans of attack made by the German Staff. So long as things went well in

THE GRAND DUCHESS OLGA.

THE TSAR, WITH MEMBERS OF HIS SUITE, ON A TOUR OF INSPECTION AT THE FRONT.

Tsar Nicholas II. left Petrograd for the front on the twentieth anniversary of his accession. He did much to inspire his troops. "France," he declared to M. Jean Cruppi, in August, 1915, "can count upon my unshakable will to fight on until definite victory is achieved."

Galicia with the Grand Phalanx, under Field-Marshal von Mackensen, the German Commander-in-Chief, General von Falkenhayn, continued to be free from interference from the popular favourite, Field-Marshal von Hindenburg. We have seen that in April, 1915, Hindenburg was practically dismissed from the command of the armies on the eastern front, because his violent, bull-like rushes around Warsaw had cost hundreds of thousands of lives, and yet had not saved Hungary from invasion. But the new favourite of the Kaiser, Field-Marshal von Mackensen, with the help of Falkenhayn's new strategic plan and an enormous equipment of heavy artillery, did not succeed in the manner expected. It is reckoned that the Grand Phalanx and its connecting German and Austrian forces lost half a million men in the Galician battles.

Important as Mackensen's advances were from a political point of view, they were even more of a **Von Mackensen's** drain on the human resources of the Ger-
costly failures manic Empires than Hindenburg's driving attacks. Moreover, with everything possible in his favour—the opportunity of surprise, overwhelming forces at the critical point, thousands of pieces of heavy ordnance, and practically inexhaustible supplies of shells—Mackensen had not accomplished the task set him. He had not divided the Russian forces and enveloped the southern army; he had used up half a million men to put out of action an equal number of Russian troops. Unless the enemy could shatter one of the Russian army groups at comparatively little cost to himself, or unless he could penetrate sufficiently into the interior of the country to cripple its manufacture of munitions or its naval forces, there was little to be gained by a long, continual struggle in which the losses on both sides were equal

As a matter of fact, the German and Austrian casualties in the eastern theatre of war at last rose in three months—May, June, July, 1915—to one million men. Russia suffered just as badly, but she had a larger population on which to draw. Therefore, though the numerical losses were about equal, the comparative losses, in regard to the remaining resources of recruitment, told heavily against the German, Austrian, and Hungarian peoples. By
the end of July, Austria-Hungary was   **Recall of**
calling out men of fifty years of age to go   **Von Hindenburg**
on active service; and Germany, as was
known from a letter found on a dead German officer on the western front, was calling out men of the age of forty-seven.

The Russian commander, therefore, could look forward to exhausting the enemy by a slow fighting retreat, in which all attempts of the Germans to obtain and force a decisive battle would be eluded. The Kaiser was well acquainted with the situation. For both political and military purposes it was urgent for him to win a rapid decision against the Russian forces in the field. The German party in Russia were anxiously awaiting such a decision in order to use the event to bring pressure to bear upon the Tsar and his advisers. The victory over the democracies of Europe, which would lead to the even more important result in German domestic politics of fettering the German labouring and peasant classes for generations to come, depended upon winning a victory over the Russians before their industries were re-established for warlike purposes.

In his need the Kaiser turned to the man he had sent away—Hindenburg—and a few days after the battle on the San around Przemysl it was reported that Prince Henry of Prussia and the popular old Field-Marshal had

257

GERMANY'S HUGE WAR MACHINE.
The completeness of the huge German war machine is exemplified in the thoroughness of its searchlight service, of which we give two photographic illustrations, one of a section on the march, the other of a lamp being tested for use against aircraft. A full searchlight equipment was attached to each German army corps. The Brobdingnagian lamps were fitted on specially-built carriages, and a searchlight section on the road had the appearance of part of an artillery train.

advanced from the frontiers of Eastern Prussia on the one hand and along the Vistula on the other, gripping all Russian Poland in an enormous pair of pincers.

The Russians first proposed to crack the pincers by placing four great s t r o n g h o l d s—Grodno, Novo Georgievsk, Ivangorod and Brest Litovsk—in the region of conflict where all the invading forces would most strongly co-operate. This fortress scheme—known as the Polish quadrilateral—was, however, abandoned after the experience gained at Port Arthur during the Manchurian war. Though a space of one hundred miles was left on the longer side of the fortressed region, for large armies to manœuvre in it while pivoting on the siege-guns in the strongholds, the new Russian school of strategists were averse from the plan. They put no faith in fortresses. They held it would be best to surrender Poland to the invader without a struggle, and meet him in a battle of manœuvres on the open field near the important railway-head of Brest Litovsk. This decision was arrived at in 1910. It much alarmed the French Staff. The French Chief of Staff thought that the value of the alliance with Russia would **Problems of Polish** be seriously diminished if when war **quadrilateral** with Germany occurred the Russian Army stood on the defensive far away from its frontier, and thus allowed the Germans to mass their forces for a long period against the French armies.

There certainly was some solid ground for this objection. If Russia retired beyond the Polish quadrilateral without offering battle, leaving the Germans the easy task of fortifying and holding the Vistula line until France was beaten, the position of both Allies would in turn become extremely perilous. The extraordinary plan of opening the campaign by a great retreat was a skilful countermove against the system of railways of invasion with which Moltke had surrounded the Russian frontier. But it was only valid in a war between Germany and Russia alone. In a struggle between Germany and Austria on the one part, and France and Russia on the other part, Russia was bound, in the common interest, to show from the beginning more activity, and strive at once for a decision. The upshot was that the scheme of an advance round Bessarabia into Galicia was prepared against the Austrians, and the Polish system of fortresses was retained as a means of delaying any encircling movement by the Germans from East Prussia and Silesia.

But after the enemy had forced the passage of the San River in June, 1915, the Russian Staff reverted to its former plan for a single-handed struggle with Germany. By then Russia had faithfully done all she could to help France. It was France that was hemmed in by the enemy along a fortified line, and Russia was left to face a mighty,

gone to Libau, the important captured Russian seaport on the Baltic coast, to examine the position there and plan a combined naval and military campaign on the remote northern edge of the eastern battle-front.

Falkenhayn, with but partial success, had tried to retrieve the errors of Hindenburg. Hindenburg was entrusted with the task of remedying the lack of success in Falkenhayn's plan. This he proposed to do by repeating on a larger scale the movement towards Prasnysch and the Narew front, on the north-east of Warsaw, and combining it with an extension of his former attacks on the still more northerly Niemen line, between Kovno and Grodno. At the same time, in his discussions at Libau with Prince Henry of Prussia, the admiral of the German Baltic Fleet, Hindenburg designed an extraordinary prolongation of the German forces towards Riga, on the road to Petrograd, and the Riga assault by land was to be completed by action taken in the gulf with a strong German naval force.

Altogether, it was the most grandiose scheme of attack ever undertaken. The German and Austrian forces brought into action approached in number three **Grandiose scheme** million men. In its main outlines the **of attack** campaign was based upon the plan made by the older Moltke for a war between Germany and Russia. The principal difference resided in the fact that Mackensen's group of armies, operating near Lemberg, were in a much better position than would have been a German force advancing from Silesia. Mackensen could strike directly up at Brest Litovsk, the chief entrenched camp in Russia, cutting the Ivangorod railway on his way, and thus facilitating the progress of the next advancing armies marching directly on Ivangorod and Warsaw.

The Russian Staff had for many years been aware of this tremendous scheme of attack, in which the forces of invasion victorious host of Germans and Austrians, who were together much superior in numbers and gun-power to the first-line German armies that would have invaded Russia in a war without allies on either side. All thought of any stand in any fortress system was abandoned. Even the eventual loss of the important railway-head of Brest Litovsk was sadly contem- **Russia's critical isolation** plated as a possibility. The Russian public looked anxiously at the news from the Franco-British front, hoping that the enemy's lines there would suddenly be broken by a terrific assault, the success of which would completely relieve the pressure on their hard-pressed armies.

But the Russian Staff indulged in no such hopes after the news arrived of the indecisive results of the battles of Carency and Festubert. In regard to munitions, the French and British forces still remained inferior in productive power to Germany. They were not so badly off as Russia, but they were not in a position to undertake to provide four thousand guns on a narrow front with a stream of three millions of shells, such as Mackensen had employed. They could not yet equal the German achievement in artillery power. Even when using 300,000 shells in one day on a comparatively small section of the enemy's lines, they had not been able to produce the irresistible shattering effect like that at Gorlice. Therefore the Russian Staff,

appreciating the situation, looked for little immediate assistance from the west.

On the other hand, the Dardanelles operations might have had an important bearing upon the solution of Russia's difficulties. Had someone in high command not muddled, early in 1915, the original design for a military surprise attack on Gallipoli in combination with a naval bombardment, Russia might have been assisted greatly by a new Balkan League, and a quick, direct line for sea-borne supplies from her Allies. As it was, the temporary failure of our subsequent attempts to capture the defences of the Dardanelles only tended to make Greece and Bulgaria doubtful of the outcome of the Great War. For some months our costly siege warfare in Gallipoli helped to lighten the pressure of the Turks against the Caucasian armies of Russia; but owing to the slow progress we had made by June, 1915, the Russian Staff could not then place much hope in any **The siege warfare in Gallipoli** rapid, decisive victory in the Dardanelles. They had, indeed, thought of coming to our help there by landing an army in front of Constantinople. But this army had to be diverted into Galicia, when the Third Army fell back half shattered from the Dunajec line.

So neither from the south nor from the west was there any immediate prospect of Russia receiving assistance.

PART OF THE GREAT BATTLEFIELD IN POLAND, WHERE THE RUSSIAN TROOPS WERE DRIVEN BACK BY GENERAL VON MACKENSEN'S GRAND PHALANX.

The ground was almost denuded of trees by the shell fire of the opposing forces. Transport of heavy guns in this section of the eastern battle area was beset with extraordinary difficulties, but the Germans transformed the muddy, unmetalled roads of Poland into firm causeways, along which guns, ammunition, provision trains, and troops were able to move at a speed which surprised the Russian Staff.

She had, like France after the disaster of Charleroi, to dree her own weird, and seek by a fighting retreat to exhaust her victorious enemy. Between April 28th and June 1st, 1915, the Russian forces in Galicia had been diminished by about a quarter of a million casualties. The heaviest losses occurred among Dimitrieff's troops in the first days of May; but in the battles on the San, at the close of the month, General Ivanoff, despite the hurricane fire of the enemy's heavy artillery, greatly reduced the forces of Mackensen's Phalanx. This remarkable result was accomplished by skilful tactics and brilliant Staff work, backed by the cool, steady fighting power of the Russian infantryman. He retired from his entrenchments during the bombardment, and then returned to meet the infantry attack, and shot the Germans down by his own broken wire entanglements.

The battles along the San River

In the battles along the San River the German and Austrian infantry was patently beaten, and if General Ivanoff had only had half the number of shells used by the

MEMBERS OF THE GERMAN STAFF OBSERVING A CRITICAL ACTION IN THE FIGHTING ON THE RUSSIAN FRONT.

enemy, he would have won a decisive victory. As it was, he reckoned that he put out of action along the entire Galician front the extraordinary number of six hundred thousand hostile troops, his own losses amounting only to about half those of the enemy. Even if the German losses were overestimated, the severe shaking which the enemy received had the important result of maintaining the spirit of the southern Russian army, despite the depressing features which cannot be avoided in a long and difficult retreat. The Russian soldier felt what the British soldier had felt when he was being driven from Mons to the Marne. Far from being demoralised, he was certain that he could defeat the German soldier as soon as his gunners were able to meet the enemy gunners with something like an equality of weapons. In the meantime, however, the ordeal was dreadful, for Mackensen received continual reinforcements, which enabled him to retain half a million men on a narrow front in a formation recalling that of the Macedonian Phalanx.

After the fall of Przemysl the position of the enemy

forces was as follows: The army of the Archduke Joseph Ferdinand was held along the Lower San as far as Sieniava. Mackensen's army was advancing east of Jaroslav along the railway towards Ravaruska. Böhm Ermolli's army —mainly Austro-Hungarian—was fighting on the road to Lemberg, at the town of Mosciska. An army under Count Bothmer was working near the Dniester marshes. Beyond these marshes in the south, a group of armies under General Linsingen—mainly German in composition—had forced the passage of the Dniester at Zuravno, and was trying to advance on Lemberg and take on the flank General Ivanoff's main forces. Then in the Bukovina the army of General Pflanzer was fighting on the Pruth River, and trying to connect with Linsingen's right wing and take part in a grand flanking movement, which aimed at enveloping the southern Russian army.

On paper, the flanking movement along the Dniester was the most dangerous of all the operations against the Russians. Bothmer, Linsingen, and Pflanzer seemed about to win Lemberg by a quick, direct march from the south, that would leave the Archduke, Mackensen, and Böhm Ermolli little or nothing to do. But, as a matter of fact, both Linsingen and Pflanzer were more in danger of being annihilated than their opponents; for General Brussiloff, still commanding on the Dniester front under the direction of General Ivanoff, had been strongly reinforced from Kieff and Odessa. He really held his immediate enemies in his hand, and if only the advance of Mackensen's Phalanx could have been arrested, Brussiloff would have swept back to the Carpathian barrier.

There was a similar state of affairs in the northern section of the Galician battlefield. The Austrian army holding the western bank of the Lower San was at the mercy of Ivanoff's strong right wing. At the beginning of June the Archduke's front was broken at Rudnik, where an Austrian division was shattered, losing four thousand prisoners and a number of guns and Maxims. The Archduke's army was driven back for a day's march in the angle between the San and the Vistula Rivers, and German reserves had to be hurried up into the river angle to prevent an immediate disaster. The Austrian army of Böhm Ermolli also got into serious difficulties in trying to advance in the first week in June along the road from Przemysl to Lemberg. Its advance was stopped at the town of Mosciska, where a furious battle raged for a week.

On the other hand, Mackensen's Phalanx, kept up to full strength by constant drafts and supplied with millions of high-explosive shells, continued to move forward and succour the Austrian armies on either side of it. A large number of Mackensen's heavy howitzers were hauled by motor traction towards the River Lubaczovka, in the direction of the town of Ravaruska. In other words, the Grand Phalanx turned away from the Lemberg road and struck out in a north-easterly direction, leading towards Brest Litovsk. Its path lay on the flank of the victorious Russian army holding the Lower San. This army had therefore to retire northward to the river line of the Tanev stream, and as it retired the Austrian Archduke's forces

Mackensen rescues Austrian armies

RUSSIAN CAVALRY ON THE MARCH IN GALICIA.

Russia's cavalry performed many notable exploits during the rearguard fighting in Galicia. After the German success at Lubaczov, in June, 1915, General Polodchenko's cavalry charged the victorious German infantry, sabred them, put them to flight, and then galloped deep into the German rear.

COMPANY OF RUSSIAN LANCERS HALTING FOR A REST NEAR A WOOD ON THE POLISH FRONT.
IN CIRCLE: RUSSIAN OFFICERS STUDYING PLANS—"SOMEWHERE IN POLAND."

A PICTURE FULL OF LIFE AND MOVEMENT. PHOTOGRAPH TAKEN IN THE RUSSIAN LINES AS A NUMBER OF CANNON CAPTURED FROM THE ENEMY WERE BEING BROUGHT IN

were able to recover from their defeat and follow it cautiously.

In Vienna this movement was acclaimed as a great victory for the Archduke Joseph Ferdinand. The Royal commander had been so continually unfortunate that any progress of his army was made the very most of in Vienna, where both the princes of the reigning House and the entire Austrian aristocracy had shown themselves to be so inefficient in war that the entire foundations of the national life of Austria-Hungary were badly shaken. As a matter of fact, Mackensen had done all the work and had rescued the Austrian army from another disaster. So the Prussian party in the southern Empire was able to justly claim that even the advance of the Archduke's army was only another argument in favour of allowing the Hohenzollern to become the masters of the Hapsburg territories.

Mackensen also had to help the Austro-Hungarian forces under the Arab general Böhm Ermolli, for when Böhm Ermolli tried on the evening of June 4th to **Battle of the Lubaczovka** storm the Russian position at Moskisca by mass attacks of infantry he suffered such terrible losses that his troops could not be induced to go forward again. Like the troops of the Archduke Joseph Ferdinand, they had to wait until Mackensen turned the flank of the Russian position for them. This the German Field-Marshal did in one of the most violent conflicts of the war—the Battle of the Lubaczovka. The Lubaczovka is a tributary of the San, flowing down from the range of hills between Ravaruska and Lemberg. It is crossed near Jaroslav by a highway that runs in a north-easterly direction into the Lublin province of Russia; it is also crossed by a railway running to Ravaruska and the Russian frontier. Mackensen sent his heavy artillery along both the high road and the railway, and General Ivanoff concentrated against him along the river front and offered battle; for everything was going so well for the Russians in the first week of June on all other sectors of the Galician field of war that the Russian commander felt that it was worth while again testing the strength of the Grand Phalanx.

The struggle lasted more than a week. Mackensen having at least half a million men arranged in echelon formation, brought them up group after group, and flung them against the Russian river front. Each assault was prepared by the fire of thousands of guns, that hurled asphyxiating bombs as well as high-explosive shell and shrapnel on the Russian trenches. The Russian troops showed extraordinary endurance and extraordinary heroism, but they were gradually worn down by the succession of fresh forces brought against them. They had no rest day or night for more than a week, while the units of the Phalanx had each some days of respite from fighting after they had delivered their attack and been withdrawn into reserve. Sheer physical exhaustion at last incapacitated the Russian infantry, **Ninety-six hours'** and it looked as though Mackensen **exhausting struggle** would win, after six weeks' effort, the opportunity of striking a decisive blow at the Russian army. He had collected fifteen German army corps between the Lubaczovka and the Visznia Rivers, where his men outnumbered the Russians by more than three to one, in addition to possessing an artillery superiority of more than six to one. But the German commander had the same fault that had been observed in Kluck, Bülow and the Duke of Würtemberg in their combined advance through Northern France—he used his men like machines.

Instead of husbanding their physical powers until the critical moment, he drove them forward all the time, wringing on all occasions the last ounce of energy out of them. When they were at last drawn back into reserve, they wanted a full week or more to recover. He showed none of the arts of the good jockey, who rides his horse in its natural stride during the earlier part of the race, and only whips and spurs it when the winning-

MAP ILLUSTRATING THE RUSSIAN RETREAT FROM GALICIA IN THE SUMMER OF 1915.

RUSSIAN MACHINE - GUN IN ACTION.
A camera-record made by a journalist under fire. The gun was in operation in a Russian first-line trench in Po'and.

killed and wounded, but the force of their unexpected blow was such that it entirely checked the advance of the mighty German army; for Mackensen made no further attack that day on the exhausted Russian infantry, and the Russian commander was able to withdraw, with his front unbroken, towards the hills near Ravaruska.

The occasions on which cavalry has charged unbroken infantry since the introduction of breech-loading rifles are very few. They could almost be counted on the fingers of one hand. And when it is remembered that Mackensen's artillery corps amounted to 2,500 guns, to which had been added the great battering-ram of the mighty siege train of newly-built Austrian and German howitzers, the escape of the Russian cavalry brigade seems marvellous, and its success superhuman. Nothing but absolute desperation could have led General Polodchenko to attempt the stroke. And the incident throws a terrible light on the straits to which the Russian forces had been reduced in their six weeks' struggle against the Phalanx. Even when the exhausted infantry was saved as by a miracle from annihilation, the task with which General Ivanoff was faced was one of extreme difficulty. Yet he was practically victorious at every point except one. For while he had been fighting on the river between Jaroslav and Ravaruska, his southern armies had been completely victorious along the Dniester, and, as we have already seen, his northern army could at any time check the advance of the Archduke Joseph Ferdinand's forces. But as there was one weak link in the Russian chain, a further retirement was necessary.

The Archduke had to be allowed more opportunities for advancing, for it was necessary to weaken the Russian army opposed to him, by drawing off reinforcements to strengthen the Ravaruska front, and give the exhausted infantry there time to rest and recover. The forces opposed to Böhm Ermolli had also to be weakened for **Strengthening the Ravaruska front** the same purpose of strengthening the Ravaruska position. And the Austrian army under Count Bothmer, which had just suffered a serious reverse at the town of Mikolaieff, about twenty-two miles due south of Lemberg, was also allowed a freer path when it turned to co-operate with Böhm Ermolli's forces at Komarno. But this process of weakening the stronger parts of the Russian front was balanced by a judicious choice of ground for the next battle. In between Przemysl and Lemberg was the famous lake line of Grodek, formed by a river running from north to south and flowing into the marshes of the Dniester. On a miniature scale the ground resembles that of the Masurian Lakes, and as the weather was very rainy the watery stretches and green swamps over which only four tracks ran, two of these being railway lines, needed but

post comes into sight. Mackensen whipped and spurred his men forward from the beginning to the end of the struggle. The result was that, when he threw the last of his fresh troops into the battlefield on Sunday morning, June 13th, 1915, the rest of his immense force was as outworn as was the Russian infantry. His fresh troops broke through the Russian lines west of the town of Lubaczov, and began a rapid advance in a northerly direction. The Russian infantry was entirely exhausted. It had been fighting for ninety-six hours without relief, and, like our First Army Corps in the neighbourhood of Le Cateau, the men had not enough strength left to march.

But at this moment—one of the most critical moments in Russian history—General Polodchenko rode out with three regiments of cavalry—the Don Cossacks, **Russian cavalry's great feat** the Kinburn Dragoons, and the Chernigov Hussars. These cavalrymen charged the unbroken lines of victorious German infantry, sabred them, and put them to flight, and then galloped deep into the German rear, shook the enemy reserves, and captured five machine-guns. This extraordinary cavalry charge against unbroken infantry ranks among the greatest military exploits. The losses of the Dragoons, Hussars, and Cossacks only amounted to two hundred

Major-General Sir Sam Hughes, Canadian Minister of Militia.

Lord Kitchener watching effect of French shell fire near German lines.

British War Minister, M. Millerand, and General Joffre in advanced French trench.

Lord Kitchener meets General Baratier, who was with Col. Marchand at Fashoda in 1898.

British War Minister, M. Millerand, and General Joffre in North=Eastern France.

Storming of the farm-house and castle of the Count von Schieminski, near Jaroslav, by the Prussian Guard on May 16th, 1915.

few men for their defence. Then, about ten miles north of Grodek, the approaches to Lemberg were protected by entrenched hills that extended to Ravaruska. It was the firm stretch of fairly level ground round the town of Janov, north of the lake system and south of the hill country, which formed the weak point in the new Russian position. This stretch of open country had been seamed with trenches and hedged with wire entanglements, and the fresh troops brought from other parts of the front were massed there. Janov was also connected by railway with the Russian depot city of Rovno, and armoured trains with quick-firing guns were prepared for action.

But though the new Russian lines were marked by many unusual features of natural strength, General Ivanoff no longer thought of attempting to make any decisive stand against the march of the Phalanx. He did not intend to risk his armies in a battle for Lemberg. Lemberg was a city of both military and political importance. From the military point of view, it was highly valuable as a great railway centre, from which a web of railway lines radiated in all directions. From a political point of view, the loss of the capital of Galicia would be a severe blow to the prestige of Russia, would check the action of the Rumanians, and strengthen the German intrigues in Bulgaria and Greece. Lemberg certainly was worth fighting for, and if Ivanoff had had the guns he would have fought for it. But after the trial of strength with the Phalanx on the San and at Lubaczov, the Russian commander resolved that every apparent stand he made should be only a rearguard action on an important scale.

Though his army continued to fight with great fierceness, their fighting was only the smaller part of the work of the troops. Their most laborious task was that of making new field fortifications, step by step, every few miles beyond their front. In the end they seamed with trenches the vast stretch of country between the Vistula on the west, the Dniester on the south, and the Bug and its tributaries on the east and north-east. At every three to five miles the ground was broken by battle-lines, which, like the successive ripples of sand in a large shallow bay, showed where each wave of the slowly-advancing flood of invasion was temporarily checked. General Ivanoff, by means of his extraordinary series of defensive operations, reduced the campaign intended to break him into a war of attrition. At every three or five miles of his retreat he engaged the enemy forces, and fought them until Mackensen brought his siege artillery into action.

Ivanoff's masterly defensive

To the general public the spectacle of a retreat is a spectacle of disaster, for the common tendency of unenlightened opinion is to look on war as a game for points—geographical points. But from the military point

WITH THE ENEMY IN RUSSIAN POLAND.
Men of the Austrian Landsturm (reserves) in the trenches.

of view the clash of great national armies tends at times to resemble naval strategy. So long as a fleet is intact and able to keep the sea, it does not matter over what vast distances it conducts its manœuvres of concentration, provided the concentration is effective. An army in being resembles a fleet in being, in the old and full sense of the term. So long as it retains its fighting cohesion and its power of manœuvring, the forces opposed to it must win a decision or fail of effect. Certainly there are some high advantages in conducting a forward driving movement, but at the end of a long campaign of this sort one thing counts, and one thing only—the fighting cohesion of the opposing forces, and the power of manœuvring which is derivable from their cohesion. A long and difficult retreat is the greatest of all tests of the genius of a commander and of the organising and co-operating qualities of all the Staff officers of his army. For this reason, the story of a successful retreat is the most illuminating and interesting of military histories. It has all the romance of a continual desperate fight against heavy odds, and this romance is enhanced by a display of science on the part of the general and endurance on the part of the troops which may in the end turn the retreat into a great military triumph.

Naval and military strategy

By reason of the German tendency to overweeningness, it was probable that they would despise the retreating Russians, even as they had despised the retreating French and British armies in the great drive towards Paris. Whenever a German Army general or a German divisional general imagined that he had exhausted his opponent, he had a tendency to become so over-confident that he would launch what he thought was a decisive infantry assault without proper artillery preparation. Kluck left hardly any guns to meet our army on the Marne, because he thought that he had demoralised our troops. The German and Austrian generals on the eastern front had a similar bias towards rapid action at any cost, at the hour in which they calculated a decision could be obtained. General Ivanoff and his subordinate commanders always watched for these moves of over-confidence in their opponents. It was indeed at these times that the Russians got the opportunity of more than balancing their losses from gun fire, by a succession of swift, punishing counter-strokes. In the battle for Lemberg, General Ivanoff only stayed long enough on his line of lakes and hills to take toll of the enemy's forces. His defensive positions enabled him to punish very severely the Austrian army under Böhm Ermolli, which was fighting directly west of Lemberg. There was especially a furious battle near Komarno, where an Austrian advance force tried to get through the Grodek lakes.

Furious battle near Komarno It was beaten back by the Russian artillery about June 18th, and for the next three days there was a fierce struggle between the Austrian troops and the Russian forces holding the lakes. The Austrian attacks were broken, in spite of the terrific bombardment that heralded every infantry advance. The Austrians were repulsed on the river, the Russian infantry there being unexpectedly assisted by an excellent supply of both light and heavy shells railed down from Kieff. According to a German prisoner, the Austrian army lost nearly half its effectives in trying to penetrate through Grodek, and through Dornfield, fourteen miles south of Lemberg. But on Tuesday, June 22nd, 1915, Böhm Ermolli's shattered forces were able to march in triumph into Lemberg without a struggle.

It was Mackensen's Phalanx which again came to the help of the beaten Austrians. Mackensen had made a great turning movement in the region of Zolkiev, some seventeen miles north of Lemberg. He first attacked the Russian positions in the open country round **Ermolli's entry into Lemberg** Janov, and forced the Russians there across the hills and across the Ravaruska railway to Zolkiev. At the same time his left wing, which had been resting on the former battlefield of Lubaczov, tried to swing farther northward in a wheeling movement round and above Ravaruska. This wing movement was defeated in a series of terrible contests that ended in the Germans being flung back towards Lubaczov. But Mackensen's centre was so strong that it was impossible to arrest its advance except by a pitched battle. This, as we have already seen, General Ivanoff was determined to avoid. So he slowly gave ground on the hill line between Ravaruska and Lemberg, and withdrawing his troops from the city, he allowed the Austrian army to benefit by the pressure that Mackensen was exerting upon him in the north.

Sufficient resistance, however, was maintained against all the enemy forces to enable Lemberg to be completely cleared of all war material. The stores were sent by railway into Russia, or conveyed by long strings of carts behind the retreating armies. The main body of the troops about Lemberg withdrew towards the river line of the Bug, while strong rearguards held up the enemy in the regions of Ravaruska, Zolkiev, and Bobrka. Böhm Ermolli, emboldened by the ease with which he had taken Lemberg, tried to follow up the retreating Russians along the railway lines. But the Russians violently counter-attacked his

GENERAL VIEW OF THE RUINS OF THE TOWN OF JOZEFOV, ON THE VISTULA.
Jozefov is situated in Russian territory between Kielce and Krasnik, a little to the north of the Galician frontier. Our picture shows Austrian captors driving cattle through the ruins.

A BLAZE WHICH LASTED FOR EIGHTEEN DAYS.

As in 1812 so in 1915, the Russians when compelled to retreat destroyed everything likely, if left, to prove of value to the foe. Above is a remarkable view of oil-wells in Galicia which were set alight by our allies and blazed for eighteen days, sending up pillars of smoke and flame, visible as far away as Bucharest, the capital of Rumania.

SOLDIERS OF THE TSAR.
Group of Russian soldiers, with towels and clean linen, awaiting their turn for a bath in the special Red Cross train which followed the Russian Army in the field, and was provided with bath-rooms, laundry, operating-rooms, etc.

A TYPICAL MUSCOVITE.

forces in the region south-east of Lemberg, and there broke another of his divisions which was trying to connect with the German armies on the Dniester under Bothmer and Linsingen.

On the same date the Grand Phalanx of Mackensen was also attacked between Zolkiev and Ravaruska. Around Ravaruska the Russians brought an armoured train into action in an unexpected manner, and broke a German division with the help of its quick-firing guns, making two thousand Germans prisoners, and capturing thirteen of their machine-guns. This series of **Armoured train** magnificent rearguard actions checked **in action** the enemy's advance and enabled the southern Russian army, which had been holding the Dniester line, to avoid being outflanked.

After the fall of Lemberg most of the weight of the enemy's attacks fell upon the forces under General Brussiloff. All through the war Brussiloff had never been defeated. It was he who had done most of the work in capturing Lemberg in September, 1914, and it was his troops that had stormed the rampart of the Carpathians and invaded the Hungarian plain. Even when he had

272

been compelled to retire from the mountain line to the Dniester front, he had trapped Linsingen's army and had put at least half of its effectives out of action. His last great victory at Zuravno had been achieved just after the loss of Przemysl by Ivanoff's troops at the beginning of June. All the next week he fought back the armies of Bothmer, Linsingen, and Pflanzer along the Dniester, from Zuravno to Nizniov, and along the Pruth River through Bukovina to the Russian frontier. There was a string of battles along a front of **Fighting along** something like a hundred and fifty miles, **the Dniester** following the looping, intricate course of the Dniester and its southern tributary streams. In many places the main river flowed in a large volume of water between high bluffs, making long winding turns, with only a narrow neck of high land between the eastern and western channels. The Russian troops entrenched with artillery across the neck of each bend. The enemy threw his forces over the river in the unoccupied part of the loop, with the result that this detached force broke against the Russian position, and was thrown back in deadly disorder to the river.

It would be tedious to give the names of all the riverside villages at which the enemy vainly attempted to penetrate the southern Russian front. There were battles in forests, battles on the edge of the marshland, battles on the river cliffs, and at the towns where the railway lines from Hungary crossed the stream. All the battles ended in the same way—few of the enemy troops that crossed the river returned to their main armies, for Brussiloff had behind him the Tarnopol system of railways, and he was able quickly to manœuvre his troops and his artillery and reply to every move of the enemy. By the middle of June the German army under Linsingen was exhausted, in spite of the fact that it had received a continual stream of reinforcements by the Stry railway, and the assistance of several divisions from Bothmer's forces.

The task of forcing the Dniester was then given to Pflanzer's army, which had been operating in the Bukovina. It advanced from the town of Kolomea over the hills to the hilly bend of the Dniester at Nizniov, where a railway line crossed the river. On the night of June 13th the Tyrolese rifles were annihilated by a Russian cavalry charge across the railway bridge. The next day Pflanzer brought up his heavy artillery and made an infantry attack under an arch of shell fire, and after a struggle of three days he captured Nizniov at a terrible cost of life. Then, in a violent effort, he pushed the Russians back from the river and captured some of the villages near the confluence of that famous northern tributary stream of the Dniester, the Zlota Lipa.

Tyrolese rifles annihilated

It was along the Zlota Lipa that Brussiloff had won his first important victory in the first Galician campaign in August, 1914. It was also along the Zlota Lipa that General Ivanoff had ordered the southern Russian army to make its final definite stand when the main Russian forces in Galicia had retired northward to the line of the Bug River. It was unfortunate for General Pflanzer that he had used all the main strength of his army in capturing a position which General Brussiloff needed, for the southern Russian army had not put out its strength in defending the bridge-head. It had acted against the Austrians under Pflanzer as it had acted against the Germans under Linsingen. It had allowed the enemy to capture the position with extraordinary loss of life, while firing from cover at the charging masses of infantry and pouring shrapnel at them, and then giving ground before the pressure became severe on its own front. Meanwhile, fresh field fortifications were being constructed across the river for the decisive stand of the Russian army, and trainloads of shells were being brought from Tarnopol for the principal battle.

General Brussiloff always contrived to make his decisive attacks when the enemy troops faced him with their backs to the river, and with only a few pontoon bridges behind them when they retreated. It was a simple device which he had repeatedly practised throughout the Dniester combats. He placed a few heavy howitzers of long range in a position to command the pontoon bridges of the enemy, and then waited for them to cross the river in great force before delivering his counter-stroke. It was by these annihilating tactics that he had wrecked Linsingen's army so completely that Linsingen's name disappeared at last from both the German and the Austrian daily communiqués. Pflanzer crossed the Dniester at Nizniov in great force on June 19th, but his troops were hemmed in between the

Linsingen's army shattered

THE FORTUNE OF WAR: AN EPISODE IN GALICIA.

Meeting between Russian prisoners proceeding under escort to the German rear and German Reserves on their way to the trenches. The German Reserves were wearing putties.

PATROL OF AUSTRIAN CAVALRY RECONNOITRING: A PICTURESQUE STUDY FROM THE SOUTH-EASTERN FRONT.
In order to save their horses in traversing this undulating country, the men are leading them downhill. The picture suggests poignant contrasts between the summer calm of nature and the storms of war.

deep windings of the river, and there bombarded furiously and swept by machine-gun and rifle fire for four days and nights. A remnant of some three thousand Austrians surrendered on June 22nd. On the same day Linsingen's army, which had also thrown large forces across the Dniester, higher up the stream near Zuravno, again met with an overwhelming disaster. The German troops were driven back to the river and forced into the water, where some managed to swim to the islands in the middle of the stream. Those who remained on the northern bank were captured.

This double blow at Linsingen and Pflanzer had an important effect upon the end of the Galician campaign. It entirely defeated the military aim of Mackensen. When he drove his Phalanx in a turning movement north of Lemberg, he confidently expected that Böhm Ermolli's troops would shake the retiring forces directly in front of them and throw them into confusion. Then it was designed that Bothmer's army should drive in from the south-east, while Linsingen and Pflanzer were engaging Brussiloff's army and driving it back from the Dniester front. As planned, the operations promised to achieve Mackensen's and Falkenhayn's long-considered plan for enveloping and destroying the southern Russian army. But owing to the strength of this army and to the genius of its commander, it shattered the forces brought against it, and became the pivot on which all the other Russian forces swung in their long movement of retirement.

The deep-sunken waters of the Zlota Lipa, running up to the range of hills east of Lemberg, close to the sources of the Bug River, were chosen as the final **The retreat on Halicz** line of the Russian retreat in Galicia. The line left the Tarnopol railway and the Brody railway in Russian hands, giving rapid means of transit to Odessa and Kieff. But instead of withdrawing with all speed to this river line, General Brussiloff continued to harry the German and Austrian forces in front of him. Having thrown Linsingen over the Dniester, he swung away from the scene of his victory at

Zuravno and joined in the attack on the central Austrian army at Bobrka, south-east of Lemberg. Here the battle raged until June 27th, when, after the enemy had been severely handled, a rearguard held the position until the main southern Russian forces were entrenched on the Gnila Lipa, a river a hard day's march eastward. It ran into the Dniester, and at its confluence was the town of Halicz, one of the famous battle-scenes in the first Galician campaign. During the retreat on Halicz, Linsingen made a final attempt to snatch a decisive victory, and sought with all his remaining troops and a large reinforcement from Germany to break across the Dniester and take the

WITH THE TROOPS OF FRANCIS JOSEPH: TRENCH VIEW IN ONE OF THE CARPATHIAN PASSES.
Above: Prisoners in the hands of the Austrians.

THE WAR IN THE GALICIAN OIL-FIELD AREA: A SCENE AT BORYSLAV.

Boryslav, in Galicia, is a great centre of the Austro-Hungarian petroleum industry. The naphtha mines here were fired by the Russians to prevent them from being of service to the oncoming foe. Our photograph gives a vivid impression of the conflagration, which served as a formidable screen between the retiring Russian forces and the enemy.

Russian army on the flank. In desperate fury, surpassing even his former attacks on the Stry, he launched division after division across the river. The men came on in close-packed columns in the old-fashioned Napoleonic manner, but the columns were wiped out with shrapnel and machine-gun fire by the Russian rearguard. The **Cossack advance from Chotin** fiercest drives failed at a hundred paces from the defending trenches, and in their counter-attacks the Russians took large numbers of prisoners. Böhm Ermolli's army and Bothmer's army co-operated with Linsingen's forces in trying for a week to break through the rearguard of the southern Russian army. But by the night of July 3rd Brussiloff had effected a strong and orderly retirement from the Gnila Lipa to the Zlota Lipa, where a system of magnificent field fortifications enabled his army to hold out with ease for many months.

A victory by the extreme left wing of the southern Russian army helped to strengthen the general position. In the middle of June the Cossack forces operating in Bukovina retired to the frontier as a precautionary measure. But when General Ivanoff's troops were secure and there was no danger of the Russian line breaking, the Cossacks advanced from the region of Chotin, and delivered a succession of fierce actions south of the Dniester, and their driving force carried them in the last week of June within fifteen miles of Czernovitz. All

FEEDING GERMAN SOLDIERS IN PRZEMYSL.

GERMAN ARTILLERY GOING INTO ACTION NEAR GORLICE.

General von Pflanzer's troops in this region were badly shaken. More than a month elapsed before they were sufficiently strengthened by reinforcements to attack again the Dniester line. The attack occurred about July 18th on a river-town just to the north of Bukovina, but it failed completely.

In the main field of struggle, from the Stry to the Zlota Lipa, General Brussiloff's army had conducted a fighting retreat for six weeks. In the course of this retreat it had taken 53,000 prisoners and had practically destroyed Linsingen's army. Having regard to the damage done to the enemy, it was one of the most extraordinary retreats in history. The explanation was that Brussiloff's forces were full of fight, and capable of standing their ground against the three hostile armies operating on their front. When they were obliged to retire through the weakness of another part of the Russian line, they went back by forced marches to carefully chosen positions of great natural strength. At each of these positions they made a stand **Brussiloff's historic retreat** for several days, compelling the hostile infantry to advance across the open ground and attack them, while they themselves remained under cover with excellent artillery at their back. In each case the enemy paid the maximum price for the advance he made. When he had

AUSTRIAN ARMOURED TRAIN USED IN THE CARPATHIAN CAMPAIGN.

been severely handled, a small rearguard was left to make another feint at a strong defence, while the main force stole away in the darkness at night to maintain the connection with the other retiring armies, and to take up another deadly line of natural defences.

It is not usual for a retreating army to take large numbers of prisoners; but all the forces under the control of General Ivanoff did so, for the Austrian troops which were used in all the attacking forces, and even brigaded in the Grand Phalanx under Mackensen's personal command, were dispirited. Even the recapture of Lemberg did not renew their confidence. As an Austrian officer explained : " The Germans have taken over our country, and are sole masters over all of us. They put us in the forefront, sacrificing us by thousands, while they keep close to their artillery. They simply use us to tire out the Russian defence, in order to facilitate their own attacks. We are doomed to die in any case, if not from the Russian bullet and bayonet, then from the Germans behind us. That is why we are indifferent to victory, and only too glad to be taken prisoners." The Austrians also complained that they had to live in a half-starved manner on **Austrians** inferior food, while the Germans in Galicia **"doomed to die"** insisted on being provided from Austria and Hungary with most liberal provisions. The discontent of the Austrian soldiers deepened when the news came of the outbreak of the war with Italy. Eleven companies of Tyrolese sharpshooters came out of their trenches on the Dniester front and offered themselves as prisoners. They may have been Italians of the Trentino region, disgusted at having to battle for the Germans and

Austrians. By this defection of the Tyrolese the Russians won nearly eight miles of the enemy's defences, which greatly assisted them at a critical moment in the retreat.

In all, some two hundred miles of ground were lost from May 1st to July 3rd between the Dunajec and Gnila Lipa. The Russians continued to hold the country twenty-five miles east of Lemberg. Their lines ran from the Rumanian frontier along the Dniester as far as Nizniov. Thence they extended northward to Sokal, and continued along the marshy banks of the Bug to- **Germans shoot** wards Cholm, Lublin, and Brest Litovsk. General Ivanoff threw only a weak force **5,000 prisoners** along the river swamps, for the ground there was so bad that the enemy could not make any progress over it. Owing to the incessant rains there were difficulties even in maintaining communications with the Headquarter's Staff. General Ivanoff's chief forces withdrew from Ravaruska along a new Russian railway running to Cholm. The railway is not marked on any map, as it was built in the autumn of 1914, after the Russian conquest of Galicia. This new railway was of inestimable value to the Russian commander; for, after the battle north of Lemberg, Mackensen swung his Phalanx up northward towards Cholm, instead of endeavouring to complete the entire reconquest of Galicia.

His German troops had suffered severe losses round Ravaruska, and in a frenzy of baffled anger they committed near that town the most shocking crime in modern military history. During the fighting they captured five thousand Russians, shot them all, and buried them in a huge, common grave. The Russian General Staff published

INTERIOR OF A TEXTILE FACTORY IN GALICIA WRECKED BY THE RUSSIANS TO PREVENT IT FROM BEING OF ANY USE TO MACKENSEN'S AND HINDENBURG'S GREAT ARMIES.

THE WORK OF MACKENSEN'S GRAND PHALANX: GERMAN OFFICERS CONTEMPLATING THE RUIN WROUGHT BY THEIR ADVANCE AGAINST THE RUSSIANS IN GALICIA.

RUSSIAN PRISONERS ENGAGED IN CONSTRUCTIONAL WORK FOR THEIR AUSTRIAN CAPTORS. THE TWO GUARDS SEEN IN THE BACKGROUND SEEM TO HAVE LOOKED UPON THEIR OWN TASK AS A LIGHT ONE.

a statement concerning this crime against humanity, based on statements made by soldiers belonging to the Sixth Austrian Army Corps. A multitude of five thousand prisoners cannot be murdered by wrathful privates of the line. A general's orders must have directed the deed, and as General Mackensen was in command the responsibility rested upon him. It was one of the chief things that the Russian people laid up in their memory for consideration on the settlement of the war. In other places on the fighting-line, single Russian soldiers falling into the hands of the Germans had been tortured and shockingly mutilated with a view to compelling them to reveal the position of their country's forces. This systematic resort to mediæval means of extracting information from prisoners seemed at the time to mark the limit of German barbarism. But the murder of a body of five thousand men proved that no limit could be set to the process of decivilisation in a people that still boasted of its morality and its culture.

After the fall of Lemberg the army of Mackensen remained for some time inactive near Ravaruska, after **Occupation of** having been repulsed by the Russian force **Tomaszov** co-operating with an armoured train on June 25th. It was one of the usual halts of the Phalanx, necessitated by its immense expenditure of ammunition and the difficulty of obtaining sufficient shell for its thousands of guns. But towards the end of June the Phalanx, with fresh stores of shell, crossed the Russian frontier and began to advance between the River Wieprz and the River Bug. The town of Tomaszov was occupied on June 29th after a conflict with General Ivanoff's rearguard. This advance of the Germans enabled them to threaten a rear attack westward on the Russian forces opposing the Archduke Joseph Ferdinand's army, along the Tanev River. The Russians therefore withdrew from their Tanev front towards Lublin.

This retirement of the western wing of General Ivanoff's army had a marked effect upon the armies of General Alexieff, which were defending Warsaw and Ivangorod in the great bend of the Vistula. Alexieff and Ivanoff had the broad, swift waters of the Vistula between them, and they had to keep strong forces in line across the river, to prevent the enemy on **The third battle** either bank from breaking through. No **for Warsaw** overlapping was possible. As Ivanoff's force retired under pressure from Mackensen's Phalanx, Alexieff's force had also to withdraw, to prevent the troops of the Archduke from crossing the river and getting on his rear.

Thus the decisive influence of Mackensen's movement began to extend in an enormous manner. From a position only a few miles north of the boundary of Eastern Galicia, it was able to shake the Russian line near Warsaw and, in particular, to compel the retreat of the Russian army on the Pilica, nearly two hundred miles east of the point at which he was striking. Such was the beginning of the third battle for Warsaw, which was to prove more successful than all the furious direct rushes that Hindenburg had made upon the ancient capital of Poland. Mackensen was undoubtedly an abler strategist than the older German commander, under whom he had risen to distinction. His plan of attack was well made and carried out in a strong manner. But it had the defect of needing so enormous a train of heavy artillery that its movement of advance was extremely slow. It had taken him exactly two months to advance from Gorlice across Western Galicia to Tomaszov, the distance between the two towns in a straight line being under one hundred and twenty miles. It was not much more than an average of two miles a day. It was still a long, long way to Moscow by the Mackensen-Falkenhayn method, and Hindenburg and Prince Henry of Prussia hoped to find a quicker path to Petrograd.

GERMAN PIONEERS REPAIRING THE BRIDGE BETWEEN THE OLD CITY OF WARSAW AND PRAGA SUBURB.

THE GIGANTIC ATTEMPT TO ENVELOP THE RUSSIAN ARMIES.

German Plan for Annexing Baltic Provinces—Cavalry Raid into Courland and Capture of Libau—Petrograd Army Makes a Counter-Attack—Prince Henry of Prussia Tries to Take Riga from the Sea—Terrible Hand-to-Hand Struggle on the Dubissa—Another German Squadron Defeated near Gulf of Riga—Germans Make a More Violent Attempt by Land—Russky again Successfully Counter-Attacks—Great Naval Battle in the Gulf of Riga—Success of British Submarines—Migration of Letts and Lithuanians—Hindenburg's Grandiose Plan to Capture Central Russian Armies—Austrian Archduke Defeated at Krasnik—Hindenburg Batters at the Russian Flank—The Doom of Warsaw—The Most Dramatic Situation in History—Hindenburg and Mackensen, with Two Million Men, Try to "Sedan" the Russian Armies—Hindenburg is Defeated on the Narew Front—Mackensen Comes to his Help by Breaking the Russian Railway Line—Woyrsch Cuts the Russian Front between Warsaw and Ivangorod—Extraordinary Migration of the Polish Nation—Fall of Warsaw and Ivangorod—Kaiser Wilhelm Offers Terms to Russia—Sublime Spirit of the Russian People—Why the Kaiser had to Continue to Advance after he Won the Vistula—Wonderful Spread of the Democratic Movement in Russia.

ON April 30th, 1915, when Mackensen was making his first attempt to break and envelop the Russian armies on the Carpathian front, an important movement occurred at a point some four hundred miles distant from the extreme left wing of the Teutonic forces. A German army corps, screened by all the available cavalry of the Central Empires, made a great raid across Lithuania into Courland. In the first week in May the raiders penetrated a hundred and twenty miles into Russian territory and menaced Riga. They won a victory over the small Russian forces of defence near the town of Shavli, lying midway on the railway running from Tilsit to Riga. A German cruiser squadron, based on Dantzic, co-operated in the flat Baltic coast with the wing of the German land forces. By means of a combined naval and military attack, the valuable commercial port of Libau was captured by the enemy on May 8th. The next day the German squadron appeared at the port of Windau, which lies more to the north, and soon afterward reconnoitring destroyers adventured into the Gulf of Riga.

At first the general opinion of the Russians was that the enemy intended merely a diversion and a plundering expedition. The

ADMIRAL GREGORÓVITCH.
Russian Minister of Marine. To his energy and initiative was largely due the renaissance of the Russian Navy after the Russo-Japanese War.

German advance over the Niemen seemed to have been made in reply to the Russian dash on Memel, described in a previous chapter. Even when the pressure of the hostile forces became heavy, the movement was thought to be only an attempt to capture forage and grain stores, and attract to the Baltic provinces some of the fresh Russian troops needed on the Galician battlefields. This, however, was a mistaken view. The German Staff proposed to conquer the country, partly for a strategical purpose and partly in the hope of being able to occupy it permanently. The German people seriously considered that their work of annexation in the west, accomplished in 1870 by the seizure of Alsace and Lorraine, needed to be rounded off in the north-east—in Lithuania, Courland, and Livonia—before the complete unity of the German Empire was achieved. This had for years been popularly regarded in Germany as one of the main objects in a war with Russia, and the modern German school of political historians had forged beforehand all the evidence for the right of annexation.

There was nothing in common between the people of the Baltic provinces and the Teutonic race. The people were Lithuanians and Letts, using a language of their own, which was the most ancient of all Indo-European forms of

GOADED INTO SACRIFICE BY THE IRON WHIP OF THE PRUSSIAN HIERARCHY.

Austrian Generals taking observations from a trench in Poland. Whatever may have been Austria's part in precipitating the world-war, her armies, as hostilities progressed, moved more and more at the dictation of her ally. An Austrian officer declared: "The Germans have taken over our country and are sole masters over all of us. They put us in the forefront, sacrificing us by thousands, while they keep close to their artillery."

HAPPY ENOUGH FOR THE TIME BEING.
Austrian officer's sleeping quarters in the field.

speech—more ancient than the Sanscrit of the Hindus. They were, however, related to the real Prussians who form the large serf element in modern Prussia. Like their Prussian kinsmen, they had been conquered in the thirteenth century by bands of German knights, who converted them to Christianity and reduced them to a state of serfdom. From these conquering knights were descended the German nobles of the Baltic provinces **German influence in** of Russia. These nobles had fought for **Baltic provinces** seven centuries for their own hand, accepting any strong master—Bohemian king, Polish king, Swedish king, or Russian Tsar—so long as they were allowed to hold the native peasantry in utter serfdom. They had been well content with Russian rule until the Tsar took measures to raise all the peasants of the Empire from a state of serfdom. The German nobles of the Baltic provinces then became the leaders and inspirers of all reactionary movements in Russia. They

282

fought against every current of liberalising force, and played the principal part in Prussianising the Russian system of bureaucratic government. They wanted to retain over their own peasants the same power as the Prussian squire **Sowing the** retained over the people his forefathers **seeds of reaction** had enslaved.

When Russia generally began to turn to democratic France and democratic Britain for inspiration in the art of reforming her institutions, the German military settlers in the Baltic provinces appear to have considered that, in the last resort, they would stand to gain by the German conquest of their country. Some of these men had displayed remarkable skill in war during the Manchurian campaign. Thereby they won important commands at the beginning of the present war; but in spite of their former achievements against the Japanese, they failed in an extraordinary way when they were placed at the head of Russian armies to fight the Austrian and the German. Soon after the outbreak of the war the Austrians won an easy victory in the Lublin Province against a Russian force commanded by a German baron. But when this same Russian force was placed under a Russian commander, it enveloped and shattered two hosts of invaders. Another German baron of the Baltic provinces, General Rennenkampf, was more subtly unfortunate. The Russian commanders who acted with him were defeated, but Rennenkampf himself did not patently fail until he was entrusted with the task of completing the encirclement of Mackensen's force near Lodz, when he invalidated a superb manœuvre on the part of General Russky by not marching his troops to the battlefield at the appointed time.

We do not, of course, intend to imply that there was no loyalty to Russia in the German military caste of the Baltic provinces, for after the removal of Rennenkampf, other distinguished German barons were entrusted with important duties by the Grand Duke and the Tsar. But there can be little doubt that a considerable part of the German element in Russia had been prepared, in the three years previous to the outbreak of hostilities, to work for the weakening of the Russian Empire and the annexation of the ancient dominions of the Brethren of the Sword and the Teutonic Order. When the German Staff had at last, as it thought, stretched the Russian power of resistance to breaking-point in Galicia, and then broken it, the campaign for the conquest of the Baltic provinces was developed with swift and striking force.

The loss of Libau

It is difficult to say whether anything more was intended at first than the occupation of the country as far as Riga, for the forces used at the beginning of May were too small to threaten a great turning movement between Kovno and Riga against the railway communications between Warsaw and Petrograd. Throughout the critical period of the struggle between Warsaw and Brest Litovsk, the German army between Kovno and Riga, though strongly reinforced, struck no blow eastward of decisive importance. This, however, may have been due more to the skilful counter-movements made by the Russian army in the Baltic provinces than to a lack of grandiose unity of plan in all the manœuvres of the Austro-German forces between Riga on the Baltic and Chotin near the Rumanian frontier.

The loss of Libau on May 8th was a serious blow, for the port was a large centre of trade and manufacture, and was usually free from ice throughout the year. The Government had constructed on the narrow sandy peninsula an extensive system of moles and breakwaters for sheltering the Russian war fleet; and though the naval fortifications had been dismantled in recent years owing to the Russian Baltic Fleet being unprepared to hold the inland sea, the great harbour was a useful advanced base for the German warships, which had been operating from Dantzic. Libau became a menace to Riga. But on the day on which the former port fell, a Russian army advanced from Mitau, near Riga, and speedily forced back the invaders. The Germans had constructed a fortified position south of Mitau, but a rapid flanking movement compelled them to hurriedly retreat and leave a large amount of war material in the hands of the Russians. Then on a broad front the Russians closed round the German land forces between Riga and Kovno. A regiment of the ubiquitous Prussian Guard, brought from the British front to co-operate with a division of Bavarian cavalry, was advancing against the railway to Petrograd. The Germans had enveloped part of the Russian line of defence, the Bavarian horsemen having reached the rear of the Russian troops. But before the invaders could achieve their victory, they were suddenly taken in flank by a hard-riding Cossack force. The Bavarians were broken and scattered, and in their disorderly flight they dragged the Prussian Guard along with them for some twenty miles.

Invaders forced to retreat

GENERAL VON PUCHALLO, ONE OF THE AUSTRIAN COMMANDERS, AND HIS STAFF. A PHOTOGRAPH TAKEN IN A RUSSIAN TOWN.
During the fighting retreat of the Russian forces in Galicia the Austrian commanders did not appear to have distinguished themselves. The German Field-Marshal von Mackensen had to rescue Austrian armies on either side of him.

THE PRUSSIAN INVASION OF
COURLAND.
German troops massed on the quay at the
seaport of Libau.

So Below had to wait until the training of the German reserves was sufficiently completed to enable his army to be trebled in number. Meanwhile he tried to relieve the general pressure on his front by concentrating a force and launching it swiftly across the Dubissa to the north-east of Kovno. But his troops were again thrown back over the river on May 23rd. In turn the Russian general massed against the German line near Shavli and broke it on May 28th, capturing nine guns and large stores. The town in which the Germans were lodged was set on fire and after being burned out of their position, the invaders were caught by a force of mounted Cossacks and sabred as they ran. By the end of the month of May it was clear

General von Below, the hostile commander, tried to counteract this check to his main raiding force by massing against the Russian centre at Shavli. But instead of retreating at this point, the Russians joined battle on May 10th and drove the Germans out of the town. Next day the enemy returned with still larger forces and tried to recapture Shavli; for this was the most important road and railway centre in the Lithuanian province, and possession of it was vital to the German plan of campaign. Five times during the night the German infantrymen tried to storm the Russian lines, but on each occasion they were shattered. Despairing of carrying the city by

ADVANCE OF THE ENEMY INTO RUSSIA.
Blown-up forts on the east front of Libau abandoned by the Russians in May, 1915.

**The struggle
around Shavli**

a frontal attack, Below sent out at dawn a strong outflanking column. But the column was ambushed, losing five of its guns and many prisoners. Then on May 14th came a shrewd Russian stroke, which cleared the greater part of the province of the invaders. In a series of fierce fights over the flat country, densely wooded and full of lakes and marshes, the German forces were thrown back over the Windau and Dubissa Rivers. Their trenches on the Dubissa were carried at the point of the bayonet, some thousands of prisoners being taken, among them being Saxon and Bavarian infantry regiments from the French front. Apparently it had been the intention of the German Staff to draw a large number of veteran troops from France and Flanders in order to achieve the conquest of Courland and menace Petrograd. But the furious attacks delivered by French and British troops around Lille and Lens, and in particular the progress which General Foch made around Carency all through May and June, entirely upset this plan. Far from being able to let any troops go, the Crown Prince of Bavaria had to ask for an additional quarter of a million men in order to make a stand at Souchez.

that the land attack on Riga had for the moment failed. Yet it was then that the first of the extraordinary attempts to transport troops into the Gulf of Riga north of the city was undertaken. In the morning of June 3rd a German destroyer flotilla, scouting in advance of its cruiser squadron, tried to enter the gulf. But the Russians had one old, useful battleship in the wide shallow bay, together with a destroyer and submarine force. The Russian warships were attacked by enemy seaplanes, but all the aerial bombs missed their targets, and the airmen were driven off by anti-aircraft guns. There then followed one of those obscure engage-　**Riga and Windau** ments about which the Russian Admiralty　　**attacked** gave scarcely any particulars, and about which the enemy remained quite silent. Some of the German ships were led into a mine-field, and also attacked by submarines. According to the official Russian statement, three German ships were either sunk or put out of action, but the names of the vessels were not given.

The attempt to force the passage through the Gulf of Riga lasted from June 3rd to June 6th, and it was apparently during this attack that a small, old-fashioned Russian submarine had a stroke of luck. It had been lying for weeks in the narrow sea-way near the entrance to the gulf, watching for something to happen. It rested on the bottom of the deep passage, where it had to rise at least three times a day to get air, being one of the little petrol-engine boats that only stayed for a few hours under water. But at last as it lifted its periscope it saw two modern German battleships close at hand making the passage. The Russian lieutenant fired two torpedoes into the leading ship, and certainly exploded something, but he could not discern what had happened, for his single periscope was shattered just as the second torpedo was released. He dived for safety, and when forced at last to rise he found no enemy in sight, and managed to reach his own

COURIERS OF " KULTUR."
German cavalry entering the conquered town of Shavli, in Courland.

SHAVLI FROM THE RAILWAY.
The railway-station was set on fire by the Russians before their retirement.

port. Again on June 28th a German naval force, consisting of an old battleship of the Siegfried type, with four light cruisers and a vanguard of destroyers, made an attack on the Baltic coast at Windau. The town was only defended by a company or two of territorial troops, as the Russian general kept the line of his army some seventy miles west of the coast for reasons of strategy. He could not risk having part of his forces cut off in a corner, so he concentrated on the inland rivers, between Riga and Kovno. Windau remained an apparently undefended coast-town like Libau. But when a landing-party of German Marines dashed into Windau, after the port had been bombarded,

Terrible fighting on the Dubissa

a flotilla of Russian destroyers steamed up and opened fire. The German admiral was alarmed, though not so much at the destroyers as at the thought that there would be a strong Russian naval force behind the sea-scouts. He put his ships about abruptly, and went southward; and the landing-party had to undergo a severe shelling before it regained the ships.

Meanwhile the land battle continued to rage with extreme fury along the River Dubissa, a tributary stream which flows into the Niemen west of Kovno. At the little

Lithuanian town of Rossieny the stream shallows for half a mile, so that it can be crossed on foot. Here General von Below's troops, increased at the beginning of June to three army corps (130,000), stubbornly tried to break the Russian front in another long, desperate struggle. By the pressure of close masses they bore the Russians back over the stream. The Russian commander threw more of his men into the fight, and after spraying the enemy with shrapnel, delivered a bayonet attack.

The enemy was driven over the river, and every man who fell, even slightly wounded, was drowned, as, though the stream was shallow, its current was too strong for an injured man to contend against it. Then it was the turn of the Russians to retire, as the German commander brought new forces into the field. Five times that dreadful

A causeway of dead men

day did the Dubissa change hands. The effect of the struggle was ghastly; the river was dammed with bodies; the dead men formed at last a causeway over the waters; and in the evening the Russian gun-teams galloped across this human bridge and achieved the hard-fought victory by pouring shells on the Germans.

At the end of the first week of June the hostile army commander, General von Below, was again reinforced, his forces being increased to nine divisions (150,000 men). But, though he did not know it at the time, he was contending against one of the best minds in Russia—General Russky, the man who broke the Austro-Hungarian first-line armies, and afterwards trapped Mackensen near Lodz. Russky had been compelled to give up the command of the armies in the bend of the Vistula owing to a very serious illness. But in the spring of 1915 he recovered sufficient health to take over the control of the Petrograd army.

It was first thought that he would not have to lead his new troops into active service for several months, by which time his health would be quite re-established. But the menace to Riga and Livonia, with the indirect threat at Petrograd itself, brought Russky in person into the new battlefield. His chief object seems to have been to economise his forces. He did not want to launch all the Petrograd army into Courland, and win a cheap victory there, while the Germans and Austrians were massing in a more critical direction farther south for a decisive blow at Ivanoff's or Alexeieff's armies. Russky had to stand ready to reinforce other parts of the front in case of need. So he only put into Courland sufficient troops to hold the line running from Kovno to Riga. But at the same time he guarded against any surprise attack on this line by maintaining a more forward first position along the Dubissa and Windau Rivers. Only as the pressure of the enemy definitely increased against his forces there did he throw more men into the field.

Fighting went on continuously along the river-line until July 13th without any important change of position occurring. Then Below was again reinforced, so that his

THE CHART OF DESTINY.
Officers of the Russian Headquarters Staff studying a large-scale map of the eastern war area. The Great War made the following of the late Lord Salisbury's advice, "Study large maps," a matter of grim necessity.

command became one of the strongest army groups on the eastern front. Nearly 400,000 men seem at last to have been put under his orders. As already explained, Hindenburg and Prince Henry of Prussia met at Libau on June 19th, and there planned a combined military and naval scheme of operations. The idea seems to have been to advance through Riga on to Petrograd, and then, by the capture of the Russian capital, to drive the Russian Fleet to accept battle in the Baltic against a superior German naval force. But the new naval opera-
German design against Petrograd tions, directed by Prince Henry as admiral of the German Baltic squadron, did not open happily. On July 2nd a detachment of German ships went steaming towards the Riga Gulf in a dense fog. It was caught by a more powerful Russian cruiser squadron. The German ships consisted of a cruiser of the Augsburg type, the light cruiser Albatross, fitted up for mine-laying, and three destroyers. They were seen off the Swedish island of Gothland at 7.35 a.m., at a distance of twenty-three leagues from the coast.

The main opening into the Gulf of Riga lies opposite the northern part of Gothland, so the German design was evident. But in spite of the fog, which greatly hampered the fire of the Russian gunners, the engagement was fiercely maintained for half an hour. The cruiser of the Augsburg class then fled southward, profiting by her speed and the thick mist, and the Russian ships massed their guns upon the Albatross. The three German torpedo-boats emitted clouds of **British submarine's brilliant feat** smoke in order to screen the light cruiser from the Russian gunners. But the Russians maintained a destructive fire, and at nine o'clock in the morning the Albatross lowered her flag and steamed toward the coast. The Russians at once ceased firing at their sinking enemy, and the crippled ship was beached six leagues from Ostergarn Lighthouse.

Thus ended the second naval attempt upon Riga, the defeat of the advanced force of light cruisers and destroyers being seriously aggravated by the brilliant feat of a British submarine officer, Commander Max K. Horton, who on July 2nd torpedoed and sank the valuable pre-Dreadnought battleship Pommern. The Pommern, with her four 11 in. guns, her sixteen 6·7 in. guns, six torpedo-tubes, and crew of seven hundred and twenty-nine men, was part of the main German naval force detached for the Riga Gulf operations. She was sunk by the British submarine a day after the Russian cruisers defeated the German light cruiser force scouting in advance of the German battleships. The loss of a good battleship of the 1905 class and a light cruiser seems to have been a serious check to Prince Henry of Prussia's part in the Baltic campaign.

The Schlesien, a capital ship of the same class as the Pommern, also had some casualties on July 2nd. So it looked as though the second German battle squadron, of which the Pommern and Schlesien formed part, was engaged in the abortive attempt on Riga Gulf.

Hindenburg tried to remedy the naval disaster by a sudden and very violent attempt to capture Riga with a land attack. General von Below's army was strengthened by another hundred thousand or more men, and on July 14th he massed upon the extreme north end of his line at the town of Goldingen, and thrust the Russians back from the Windau River in a fortnight of terrible incessant fighting. The port of Windau was captured by the Germans, and the northern Russian wing in Courland was pressed back to the town of Tukum, and then to Schlock, almost within cannon-shot of the outskirts of Riga.

The southern wing of Russky's forces had to withdraw from Shavli and the line of the Dubissa River in order to keep in touch with their comrades around Riga. Using another river, the Muhs, as a protection for their uncovered flank, the heroic defenders of Shavli retired fighting, and linked up with their forces on the north, which held the River Aa, and with their forces on the south which connected with Kovno. Russky's line then stretched for two hundred and fifty miles from a point a little west of Riga to a point a little west of Kovno.

The German newspapers at the beginning of August, 1915, confidently predicted that Riga would be captured

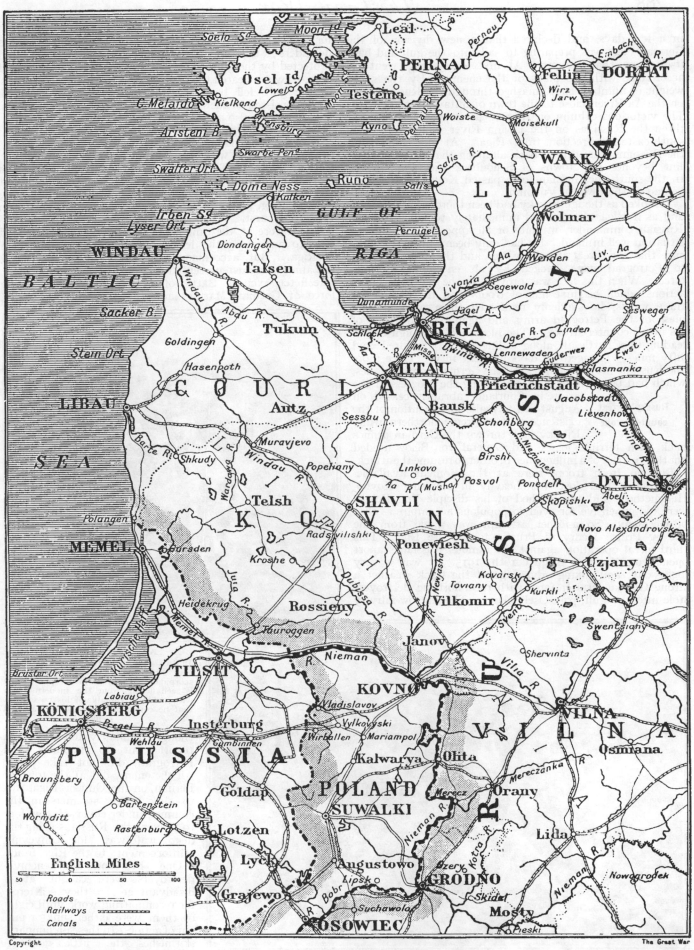

MAP OF THE CAMPAIGN IN COURLAND, KOVNO, AND THE GULF OF RIGA, ILLUSTRATING THE
GERMAN ATTACK ON THE ROAD TO PETROGRAD.

287

in a few days, and declared that a new division of the German Fleet was preparing to sail into the gulf and base itself upon that seaport. At first everything went in accordance with the plans of the enemy. By the sheer weight of numbers they smashed through the Russian lines on the Aa River, close to the town of Mitau, south of Riga. The victorious column on August 3rd captured Mitau and threw the Russians on the Dwina River, which runs in a south-easterly direction from Riga. At the same time the Russians were driven back all along the centre of their line beyond the towns of Schönberg and Ponewiesch. In the south the German force passed Kovno, and settled behind at the town of Vilkomir.

It looked as though Russky had been thoroughly defeated, and as if Riga was doomed immediately to fall. But the Russian commander, in spite of all appearances, had the situation well in hand. He had only been waiting to make sure that the direct threat to Riga and the indirect threat to Petrograd were backed by an enormous German force. When this fact was proved by the hard rearguard actions which his first line of troops had to conduct for three weeks, he suddenly reinforced them with a large mass of the Petrograd army, and again launched one of his great counter-strokes. The blow fell on August 7th, leading to a battle all along a line of two hundred and fifty miles. It raged for days in great fury. Once more the Russians won a victory, and the German communiqués, which had been full of news concerning the progress of the army in Courland, abruptly ceased on

Russky's great counter-stroke

August 8th to make any mention of the existence of its extreme northern wing. Russky had thrown the German armies back with terrible losses, and General von Below needed another quarter of a million men in order to resume the attack.

But no fresh troops were at the moment available. Hindenburg had lost too heavily in storming Kovno. His method, and the method of his disciple Von Below, were too expensive for even so populous an empire as that of Germany. So another attempt was made from the sea by Prince Henry of Prussia to capture Riga. This third naval operation against the famous Russian seaport opened on Monday, August 16th, 1915. It was a very foggy day, and taking advantage of the thick weather a strong German cruiser force with reconnoitring destroyers stole into the gulf, past Osel Island. The narrow fairway

for large ships had been sown with contact mines by the defenders; but under cover of the milky mist, and protected by the guns of their cruisers, a German flotilla of mine-trawlers cleared the passage, and the Russian warships in the gulf fell back without revealing their strength. They consisted in fact mainly of destroyers and gunboats. But there was also an old battleship, the Slava, with four 12 in. guns and twelve 6 in. guns, which had been secretly placed in the gulf to deal with any venturesome German cruisers. The retirement of the Russian forces was carried out mainly with a view to concealing the presence of the Slava until the decisive moment. Meanwhile, a running fight went on in the broad misty waters from August 16th to August 21st.

The third naval attack on Riga

There were at the time rumours that the Germans had tried to land along the deep-water channel running north of Riga. But, according to the commandant of Reval, the affair was misrepresented by some of our newspapers. The fierce, exciting Battle of Pernau, between a strong force of German Marines and the Russian local levies,

A POLISH FUGITIVE.
If Russia chastised the Poles with whips, the Prussians chastised them with scorpions. The Pole in our photograph is seen fleeing from the modern Huns with the most valuable of his possessions that he could collect in the time allowed to him.

though brilliantly described in a report sent to London from Petrograd, did not take place. All the enemy did at the town of Pernau, on the Gulf of Riga, was to sink three steamers in the channel, under cover of the fog, to prevent the Russians using the deep waterway for conveying reinforcements to the Riga front.

One by one the enemy's destroyers were caught at a disadvantage, as they scattered for reconnoitring work, until eight of them were either sunk or put out of action. In these preliminary skirmishes the little gunboat Sivoutch (or Sea Lion) nobly distinguished herself. She was a vessel of nine hundred and sixty

WOUNDED RUSSIANS ON THEIR WAY FROM WARSAW.
The Polish capital fell into the hands of the Germans in August, 1915, after two earlier, but ineffectual, attempts had been made to capture it.

tons, with a speed of only twelve knots and a crew of one hundred and forty-eight men. Her captain, Commander Cherkasoff, had won renown at Port Arthur, and he made the action in the Gulf of Riga one of the glories of Russian history by the heroism of himself and his men. The little Sea Lion was pursuing an enemy destroyer in the mist when she came within sight of a German cruiser, which was escorting the hostile torpedo craft. The cruiser closed with her to a distance of four hundred yards, and her shells set the little boat on fire fore and aft. But the men of the Sea Lion continued to work their guns. Having sunk one of the enemy's torpedo craft, the Sea Lion still answered shot for shot, when her deck-plates were red

FORESTALLING THE MARAUDING FOE.
Before abandoning Warsaw the Russians stripped the city of all that was likely to prove of military value to the enemy. Bells were taken from the belfries, and metal—especially copper—accessories from the factories, to be railed in advance on the line of retreat.

"THE ARTILLERY OF THE CHURCH."
" Bells," said the German Emperor, Joseph II., " are the artillery of the Church." His successor, Kaiser Wilhelm II., would have turned the bells of Warsaw into munitions of oppression. The Russians forestalled him by removing them—in the cause of liberty.

hot, and at last the crew went down to death all standing. Meanwhile, two of the German cruisers either got too close to the Slava or to a new mine-field, the Russian General Naval Staff refraining from any precise information on the matter ; for, as future naval attacks by German squadrons on the Riga region were anticipated, the composition of all the defending Russian forces continued to be kept as far as possible secret. It may have been the **German losses off Riga** loss of the two cruisers, the eight destroyers, and an armed liner which decided the German admiral to withdraw from the gulf on August 21st ; or the retreat may have been due to an even greater disaster to the vessels placed under the command of Prince Henry of Prussia.

The Prince had apparently been apprehensive that the forces he had sent into the gulf might be suddenly assailed in the rear by a flying squadron of powerful battle units steaming from the Russian naval base in the Gulf of Finland. With a view to guarding against a surprise attack of this

sort, some of the finest German Dreadnoughts were temporarily detached from the High Sea Fleet at Cuxhaven, and brought up the Baltic as a watching force. But watching them in turn was a British submarine flotilla, and one of our skilful submarine officers, by the most brilliant stroke in underwater warfare in the first year of the war, was said by the Russians to have torpedoed the German battle-cruiser the Moltke. She was one of the ships that had taken part in the raid on our East Coast, and in the running battle-cruiser action in which the Blücher was sunk. The reported loss of the Moltke, which had not up to the date of writing been confirmed by the British Admiralty, brought to a definite end the third attempt **Fate of the** of the enemy to reach Riga and start the **Moltke** advance on Petrograd by a successful naval operation. Both on land and by sea the schemes hatched by Hindenburg and Prince Henry of Prussia at Libau in the third week of June had failed in a very disastrous manner. Petrograd was, for at least some time to come, secure against the bull-like attacks of the old Field-Marshal and the timid, amateurish essays in naval warfare made by the brother of the Kaiser. Meanwhile the land campaign in the Baltic provinces was resumed with increased fury, and the people fled as the Germans extended their lines of attack.

It was a strange country which the Letts and Lithuanians left behind them when General von Below's armies began to advance. It was a land of burning farms, flaming meadows, and fiery forests. As it was known that the enemy badly needed forage, even the grass was destroyed. Light chaff was sprinkled over the pastures, and oil was poured on the chaff and set alight. By their own confession, the German troops were dismayed at the widespread fires lighting the nocturnal sky. It stirred in them memories of the fate of Napoleon's Grand Army, which had set out from Kovno in the summer of 1812 and perished in the wilderness which the retreating Russians made behind them.

In the towns all the manufacturing plant was conveyed by railway into the heart of Russia, and all manufacturing materials were removed. Even the church-bells were transported to Moscow, and the horses, cattle, sheep, and goats moved in vast droves along the roads left open by the Russian army for the migrating nations of the Baltic provinces. Many of the rearguard actions **and local** counter-strokes were undertaken with a view to gaining more time for the terrible task of dispeopling and laying waste the country which the Russian commander was surrendering to the enemy. Through Riga the people streamed to the railway-stations at the rate of ten thousand a day. They were mainly workmen, with their families, from the manufacturing towns of Courland and Lithuania. Valuable men they were to Russia, not only for the immediate production of munitions, but for the general reorganisation of Russian industries. Hundreds of railway trains were specially provided for them, many of them being transported as far as the Ural Mountains, where the larger part of the mineral wealth of Russia was being mined. Everything possible in the circumstances was done to prevent the fugitives from passing under the control of German taskmasters. Yet so immense was the pressure of the emigrants at the railway that they had

Great exodus from Courland

at times to wait days to get a ticket, and when at last the ticket had been bought, more days passed before a seat was found on a train. Each train that brought fresh battalions of the Petrograd army to the Courland battle-field returned to the capital packed with fugitives. Happily, the troops under General Russky had the situation well in hand, and by fighting fiercely for time they enabled the organisers of the great migration of the people to prevent any disaster occurring. Then the kindly, charitable Russian peasantry along the routes to Central Russia helped the wandering streams of farming folk to feed their animals and themselves. Food was abundant in Russia, for the great export crop of 1914 had been retained owing to the closing of the Dardanelles. When the people and all the farming stock had been removed throughout a deep zone behind the fighting-line, little but the empty farms, the railways, and telegraph lines remained to serve the troops. And as the soldiers began to prepare merely for rearguard actions, the Board of Evacuation, with its centre at Moscow, entered upon its last task. Hundreds of special goods trains were brought up and loaded with the cranes and heavy materials. Each group of goods was marked with its new destination. Then, as the rearguard action opened, other trains went to the working end of their lines, carrying gangs of labourers, and took up the rails, packed them in the trucks with the sleepers, and ploughed up

An empty land for the foe

THE ATTACK BY AUSTRIAN TROOPS ON THE CHOLM-LUBLIN LINE.
Some of the men were so exhausted after forced marching and constant fighting that they threw themselves on the ground and lay there helpless at different stages of their arduous advance. The Austrian centre was eventually broken by the Russians on July 9th, 1915, when they lost 15,000 men and dozens of machine-guns. Above: One of the celebrated Skoda guns in action.

THE WAR AGAINST INFECTION.
Apparatus for disinfecting clothing in use by the Austrian forces in Galicia. Typhoid and cholera were reported to be very prevalent.

the permanent way with dynamite and special machines of destruction. At the same time a staff of electricians removed for transportation all the material of the telegraph lines. So when the rearguard at last fell back, nothing but bare earth and burning buildings was left to the enemy. It is said that not a single railway carriage was captured by the Germans.

Very pathetic was the appeal which the Lettish refugees addressed to the Russian people. After describing the situation in Poland, occupied by the enemy and covered with ruins, the appeal ran : " Long files of fugitives are crossing the neighbouring provinces, knocking at the door of their more fortunate inhabitants, and **Refugees' pathetic** relying on their hospitality. Help us ! **appeal** We are strangers to you in language, and most Letts hold to another form of Christianity than yours. Our names will sound in your ears like the names of foreigners—and yet we are your countrymen. For more than seven hundred years we have held back the German thrust towards the east, and if the Baltic provinces are not now German land, this is due to us. We are your advance guard. Help us ! Do not be slow in showing that Russian hospitality which is known throughout the world and the charity of the compassionate Russian heart. We are a hard-working people, who can be useful to you by the knowledge we possess and the talents we have."

It is doubtful whether General von Below's raid into Courland was originally planned by Hindenburg. For, as we have seen, it began in May, when, according to a telegram of congratulation sent by the Kaiser to his Chief of Staff, Falkenhayn was in supreme control in the eastern theatre as well as in the western field of conflict. Hindenburg, however, was definitely restored to power by the middle of June, when it could be seen that Mackensen, with a million men, had lost all

opportunity of encircling or breaking the southern Russian armies. Hindenburg seems to have retained Falkenhayn's scheme for the conquest of the Baltic provinces as a means of diverting the attention of the Grand Duke Nicholas, and masking his own main preparations. These were simple, straightforward, but enormous. The German Marshal collected about a million men, and arranged them in three mighty armies from Kovno to Mlava. The forces around Kovno were under the command of Eichhorn, who had been fighting in the Niemen River region for many months. Connecting with his southern wing were two great armies near Prasnysch, under General von Scholtz and General von Gallwitz. Scholtz and Gallwitz were further reinforced by an army under General von Beseler, the conqueror of Antwerp, who was again provided with a siege train of many 11, 12, 17, and 20 in. howitzers. He was to shatter and storm the great Russian entrenched camp of Novo Georgievsk on the Vistula River, while the armies of Gallwitz and Scholtz burst through the Russian lines on the Narew **Hindenburg's** and Bobr Rivers, and got in the rear **ambitious project** of the Russian army defending Warsaw.

This in itself would have been no mean achievement, but the scope of the scheme did not content Hindenburg. He intended not only to destroy the central Russian army under General Alexeieff, but to deal at the same time a tremendous flank blow against the left wing of General Ivanoff's forces, between Ivangorod and Brest Litovsk. In order to accomplish this, it was necessary to allow time for the group of armies under Mackensen to progress into line at Cholm and Lublin. And the central Austro-German forces, operating in the great bend of the Vistula in the direction of Warsaw and Ivangorod, had also to be allowed time to fight their way closer to the central Russian armies.

The general position, therefore, remained for some weeks very deceptive in appearance. Nothing occurred to show that Warsaw was in immediate danger. Hindenburg, with a million men under his orders, remained quietly at his base in the East Prussian railway town of Allenstein, and forbade his corps and army commanders to exercise any marked pressure on the Russian forces entrenched around Prasnysch. Then his neighbour, Prince Leopold of Bavaria, commanding the Austro-German forces on the

AN ATTACK UNDER A SMOKE CLOUD.
Russian counter-attack under a veil of smoke caused by firing a wood in the face of the advancing Prussians.

Rawka River in front of Warsaw, remained also very quiet, after a vain attempt to throw the Russian army back by means of a poison-gas cloud. On the right of the Bavarian Prince was the remnant of the first-line Austro-Hungarian army, which General Dankl had led across the Russian frontier in August, 1914. Dankl had gone to the Italian front, and his twice-shattered army had been strengthened by fresh troops, stiffened with a large German element, and placed under the command of General von Woyrsch. Woyrsch operated between the Pilica River and the Upper Vistula, but he was firmly held in front of Radom by General Alexeieff's troops. He made progress only when Alexeieff had to swing down along the stream, in order to maintain connection with Ivanoff's forces between the Vistula and the Bug.

Ivanoff was still opposed by the Austrian army under the Archduke Joseph Ferdinand and the Grand Phalanx

THE MONEY-CHANGERS: AN UNCONVENTIONAL INCIDENT IN THE RUSSIAN WAR AREA.
German soldiers exchanging their money with Russian prisoners of war.

motionless, and in stupendous strength, to leap unexpectedly upon their northern flank, the position of the Russian armies in Poland was one of horrible peril.

Moltke's feat in shepherding the French army into the trap of Sedan was a small affair compared with that which Hindenburg was devising, in collaboration with his old rival Falkenhayn. They had taken a plan formed by General von der Goltz, and worked it out in terms of big gun transport. All that scientific calculation and prevision could do had been done. The result seemed as certain as human effort could make it. Having regard to the impressionable character of Kaiser Wilhelm II., it is not to be wondered that he swelled with vain glory before the event, and began to make speeches about the war ending in a series of great German victories by October, 1915.

Planning a new Sedan

There was, however, one change in the circumstances of warfare since the days of Sedan. The reconnoitring aeroplane made great strokes of surprise, that needed long preparation, somewhat difficult to conceal. The Grand Duke Nicholas learned enough to make him suspicious, and he sought for some means of delaying the immense movement of envelopment. He selected the weakest link in the chain that was being dragged around him. This weak link was the Austrian army at Krasnik, under the Archduke Joseph Ferdinand. Its artillery was more powerful than the Russian, but the Austrian guns were too far from their railway-station in Galicia, and as there was only one firm road by which ammunition could be brought up, the opposing Russian army, with the railway behind it at Lublin, was able to get a quicker supply of shells.

The Lublin army seems to have been the Third Russian Army, formerly commanded by Radko Dimitrieff. Its original four army corps had been half shattered on the Dunajec, but its record was still a fine one. Its original 96,000 bayonets had taken more than 300,000 prisoners since entering into action in Galicia in August, 1914. Most of the survivors were now sent back into Central Russia to rest, and into the cadres was poured new material composed of the best fighting men available in Russia; a new general was appointed—a man unknown in Western Europe, but with a high reputation among his own countrymen. The Eighth Russian Army had retired alongside the Third, and had also been severely handled. It also was reorganised from the best fighting material in Russia, for the design was that it should hold up Mackensen's forces at Cholm, while the Third Army struck at the Archduke.

The battle began on July 2nd. With about a third of a million men, the Archduke deployed on a front of ten miles at Krasnik, and tried to break the Russians in a series of fierce night attacks. But his men were held up on the Wysnica, a tributary of the Vistula that runs through Krasnik. The battle continued for some days, with extreme fury, along the river and a brook flowing into it. After some heavy losses the Austrians managed, on July 4th, to push the Russians back and occupy the town of Bychava,

under Mackensen. And, as in the Galician campaign, it was the slowly-moving, gigantic force of Mackensen's Phalanx which controlled the situation. On July 1st Mackensen occupied the Polish town of Zamosc, through which a firm road ran northward to the railway-station of Cholm. The Archduke Joseph Ferdinand occupied the Polish town of Krasnik, through which a highway ran to the railway-station of Lublin. Between the army of the Archduke and the army of Mackensen there ran the River Wieprz, with marshland on either side of it soaked with the extraordinary rainfall of the previous month. The position is worth examining on a map. It will there be seen that Krasnik is barely twenty-five miles south of Lublin, and that Zamosc is about the same distance from the railway running to Cholm. As the Cholm and Lublin railway connected Ivangorod and Warsaw with the great Russian depot city of Kieff, all the Russian armies in Poland were menaced by the enemy forces at Krasnik and Zamosc. And with Hindenburg waiting, silent,

Peril of the Russian armies

The Emperor of Russia with the Grand Duke Nicholas at the front.

In British trenches: Under shell fire on the battlefield of Neuve Chapelle.

Lieut.=Colonel Birchall's death while leading the 4th Canadians at Ypres.

The Manchester Regiment captures the village of Givenchy.

With the R.H.A. in Flanders: Rushing a gun to the firing=line.

On the line of the Russian retreat: A halt for refreshments by the roadside in Poland.

at the foot of a hill six hundred and fifty feet above sea-level, known as Hill 218. The Archduke joyfully claimed that he had broken through the Russian front on either side of Krasnik. But the battle had not ended; it was only beginning. The Austrians had been merely contending with a well-posted rearguard, and after they had expended much of their strength in advancing over **The Austrian centre** the river, the main Russian force came **broken** into action. It drove at the Archduke's flank on the Vistula, and Woyrsch's troops had to be flung across the stream to reinforce the Austrian army. At the same time the Russians attacked the Archduke's right wing above Turobin, and Mackensen had to hurry a large part of his forces across the difficult ground on the Wieprz River. Then the Russian troops attacked the Austrian centre, lying across the road to Lublin, and in a fierce, persistent, driving movement, lasting till Friday, July 9th, they broke the Austrian centre, captured some 15,000 men and some dozens of machine-guns.

The Austrians withdrew to the high ground around Krasnik, leaving in front of them a strong force on Hill 218, which dominated the country. The Russians made several attempts to carry the height, but the Austro-German machine-gun parties, helped by their artillery fire, countered all the attacks. In turn, the Austrians swept down upon the hill, and tried to carry the village at the foot. But they were repulsed. By this time the two armies were fully entrenched against each other, and, as in a week's incessant fighting the Austrian army lost in prisoners alone 22,464 men and two hundred and ninety-seven officers, its total casualties were very heavy. They seem to have amounted to about one-third of the Archduke's entire forces.

In so far as the Lublin army had aimed at breaking and routing the forces of the Archduke Joseph Ferdinand, and then getting on the flank of Mackensen's Phalanx, the great Russian counter-attack had failed. But in so far as it had been designed to check the enemy's advance, it had succeeded. The Austrian army of invasion was weakened in a very serious manner, and instead of being able to co-operate in a forward movement with Mackensen's force, it had to be saved from destruction by the German Marshal. This aggravated the weight of fighting thrown on Mackensen's men, and though they stubbornly crawled onward, along the causeway leading to Cholm, they had to pay a terrible price for every mile they won. Mackensen's enormous battering-ram of heavy artillery had to have a railway built for it from Ravaruska along the line where the temporary Russian light railway had been destroyed.

There was only a single firm road running through the muddy Polish fields, and this causeway had been damaged as much as possible by the retreating Russians. As is known from German and Austrian soldiers' letters, the advance towards Cholm, after the extraordinary rainfall of the previous June, was a terribly exhausting struggle against Polish mud. Men and horses were severely strained with the labour of movement, and the Russians inflicted severe punishment on the weary German advance forces in a series of flank conflicts along the eastern tributaries of the Wieprz. Mackensen could do nothing without

thousands of guns behind him to command the battlefield, for his infantry had had much of its pugnacity knocked out of it. On July 16th he tried to get into line with the Austrian forces at Krasnik by carrying by storm the Russian entrenchments east of the town of Tarnagora, along the Wolika River. But his men fell in heaps in front of the water-course, without effecting any advance. Again, on July 17th, Mackensen tried to break across the river by massed infantry attacks, supported only by machine-guns and light field artillery. But the German troops were shattered at every point between the Bug and the Wieprz, and in the evening of that day the victorious Russian rearguard charged with the bayonet and cleared a large river-side forest of the enemy.

The German Field-Marshal succeeded after a fortnight's delay in getting his great howitzers dragged up to the battle-front, and there accumulating a great store of shells. By a hurricane fire he destroyed the Russian trenches on either side of the highway to Cholm at dawn on July 18th, and captured the town of Krasnostav on the Wieprz River. This was a decisive success, for Krasnostav was only seven and a half miles from the railway running

HOW THE GERMANS CONQUERED THE POLISH MARSHES.
Owing to the swampy nature of the ground in their line of advance in Poland, the Germans had to construct this special railway for the passage of Mackensen's enormous "battering ram." Apart from its military significance, the achievement throws an interesting light on Teutonic engineering skill.

through Cholm and Lublin, and connecting Kieff with Ivangorod and Warsaw. In ordinary circumstances it was only an easy half-day's march for Mackensen's troops from Krasnostav to the railway. General Ivanoff's armies, of course, were able to make the short journey a matter of considerable difficulty to the invading force, but there were other circumstances which entirely changed the situation, and made the Lublin and Cholm battlefield for the time a scene of secondary importance.

For Hindenburg had shown his hand. Either by design or from over-anxiety, the German Commander-in-Chief had tried to redeem the check to the Archduke Joseph's forces at Krasnik by a fierce swoop from Prasnysch. The closing-in movement had begun on **Capture** July 11th, the day when the Russian army **of Prasnysch** at Lublin completed its great counter-offensive. Hindenburg should have waited until Mackensen retrieved the local situation between the Vistula and the Bug by bringing up his heavy artillery and blasting a path to Krasnostav. But either the old German Field-Marshal, crouched for his great spring north-east of Warsaw, was

TRANSFERRING GUNS ON TO RAILWAY TRUCKS AT A SPECIALLY CONSTRUCTED SIDING.

WITH THE RUSSIAN FORCES IN POLAND.

over-anxious to make his long-prepared leap, or the German Staff was put off its balance by the apparent demoralisation of the Archduke's army, and stampeded into immediate action. However this may be, the vast strategical plan of envelopment was somewhat prematurely revealed by an exceedingly violent bombardment of all the Russian positions from Osoviec on the Bobr River to the trenches along the Wkra stream. The positions extended for nearly a hundred and forty miles north and north-east of Warsaw, with Prasnysch and Lomza as the central sector of the winding river-line.

Hindenburg opened his tornado of fire at night on July 11th, thus boldly revealing the position of his guns in the darkness by the flames they emitted, and challenging the Russian batteries to show themselves by their gun flashes. Naturally the Russian gunners attempted no reply, for each of their pieces would have been overwhelmed by the massed fire of the more numerous enemy batteries. Only the little fort of Osoviec, which commanded a road over the marshes where the Germans had only room to bring up a few guns, maintained an artillery duel. For three nights the artillery of Hindenburg's three armies swept the Russian positions with high-explosive shell. Then, on July 14th, the German infantry advanced under the arching fire of their ordnance, and captured Prasnysch, about fifty-five miles north of Warsaw. The Russian forces holding the famous village, round which they had gained so many victories, did not resist the German advance, for an attempt to do so would have meant destruction.

They fell back towards the Narew River, out of reach of the German artillery, which on part of the front seems to have included, from the start of the action, the great siege **Beseler's colossal** train under General von **siege train** Beseler. The combined artillery power of Beseler's, Gallwitz's, and Scholtz's armies could only be met by bringing into action the fortress guns of Novo Georgievsk and the heavy position artillery behind the bridge-heads along the Narew River. In the meantime the movement of the German infantry forces was continually checked, whenever these forces attacked without the help of the heavy howitzers, and great losses were inflicted upon the too confident enemy in the river marshes north of Lomza and Ostrolenka, and also south of Prasnysch. But on July 19th, which was the day when Mackensen drove forward towards the railway which connects Warsaw with Southern Russia, Hindenburg also brought up his thousands of heavy pieces of artillery and his million men towards the Narew front, menacing the north-eastern railway communications of the Polish capital.

Warsaw was then clearly doomed, together with Novo Georgievsk and Ivangorod, and the fortress bridge-heads along the Narew River. There was no question of saving Warsaw. The problem was to save the central Russian army under General Alexeieff. The position of this army constituted a vast salient. The base of the salient stretched

LIEUT.-GENERAL PAUL KNEUSSL.
He led the Bavarians against Przemysl and received the Order Pour le Mérite from the Kaiser and that of the Iron Crown from the Emperor Francis Joseph.

from Lomza on the Narew to a point near Lublin on the Vistula, the distance between the two points being about one hundred and thirty miles. From the base-line stretching from Lomza to Lublin the Russian salient extended forward nearly a hundred miles to the famous battle-line along the Bzura River. Could Alexcieff withdraw his forces from the Bzura River and from the Upper Vistula, and entrench them strongly near Brest Litovsk before Hindenburg and Mackensen were able to smash through his right rear flank and his left rear flank, and surround, capture, or annihilate the principal Russian army? Such was the terrible problem.

It was the most dramatic situation in history. The Russian forces holding the great salient were very numerous—many hundreds of thousands—but against them were armies of two million men, with an artillery power of unparalleled magnitude. The guns of the great German fortresses in the east had been placed on special carriages, and moved first by train and then by motor traction along the new asphalted roads which Hindenburg's armies made as they advanced. Two huge Austro-German siege trains battered in either side of the salient, and the lighter pieces of ordnance could be reckoned by tens of thousands. The work of feeding the guns with shells and charges was enormous, the common estimated production of a quarter of a million shells a day being under

A terrible problem

the mark. For the continued expenditure of shell by Mackensen's Phalanx on the right wing, which amounted to some millions a week, was eclipsed by the hurricane of fire which Hindenburg at the same time maintained on the Narew and Bobr front. In the great manœuvre of envelopment, Hindenburg's forces formed the marching wing, and the success of the scheme depended upon the rapidity with which they moved. Their expenditure of shell was staggering, and the sustained volume of fire which wrecked the Russian trenches was an incomparable tribute to the organising power of the great German industrial trusts. The number of power-lathes working in Germany and Austria for the army

GENERAL VON BESELER.
The conqueror of Antwerp. His success in taking Novo Georgievsk was recognised by a special visit from the Kaiser.

was calculated to stagger our Ministry of Munitions and our strangely-minded trade unionists.

The main work fell on Hindenburg's armies, owing to the fact that Mackensen could not drive forward quickly enough. After weakening his Phalanx to help the Archduke, Mackensen was firmly held for some weeks by the Russian Army at Cholm. But in the circumstances the delay in his advance to the railway line did not matter. It

GENERAL VON SCHEFFER BOYADEL, WITH HIS STAFF, BEFORE ONE OF THE FORTS OF THE POLISH CAPITAL.
General Boyadel was one of the leaders of Prince Leopold of Bavaria's army of occupation.

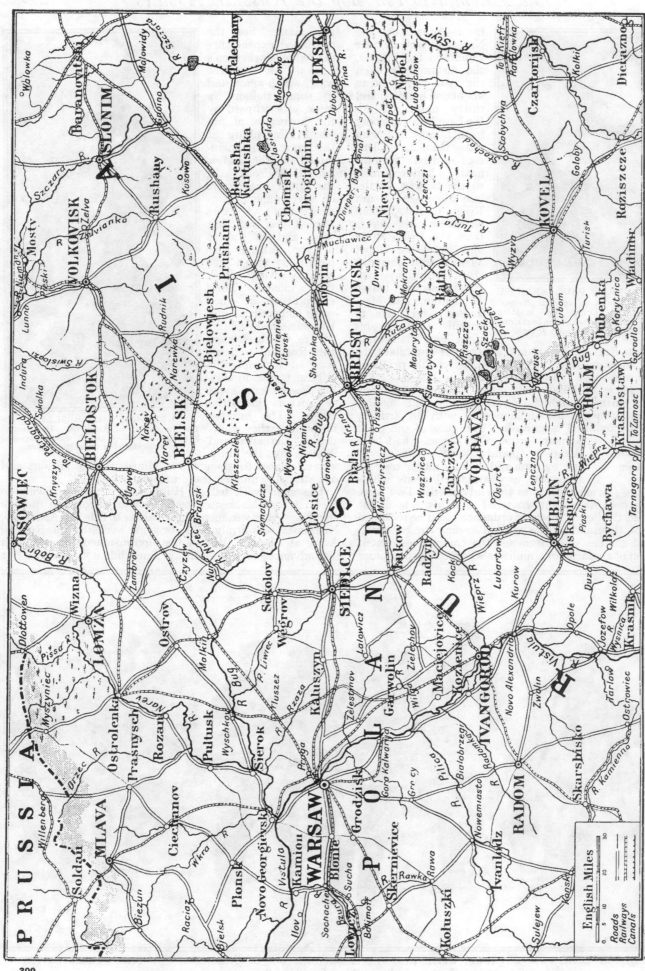

THE LAND OF THE DISMAL SWAMP WHICH FACED THE GERMAN INVADERS AFTER THE CAPTURE OF WARSAW AND BREST LITOVSK.

This map has been specially drawn to illustrate the area East of Warsaw covered by the great Russian retreat, and Alexeieff's masterly counter to the titanic Austro-German attack. The Pripet marshes are clearly indicated, together with the principal railways, roads, rivers and canals.

The Great War

Copyright

may have been subtly designed with a view to lulling the central Russian army into a feeling of false security, and inducing the Grand Duke Nicholas to risk holding on to the Warsaw front until Hindenburg's great hammer-stroke fell with terrific force on the rear flank, when Mackensen was suddenly to strike with all his power on the other flank.

The Grand Duke Nicholas, however, was not deceived. The success of his Lublin and Cholm armies did not mislead him in his general strategy, for he gave **The doomed capital** the historic order for the abandonment **of Poland** of Warsaw on July 18th. It was on this day that the remarkable strength of Hindenburg's armies was clearly revealed in a mighty swoop down from Prasnysch to the Narew River. So close did the Germans come to the Russian river defences immediately above Warsaw that the guns of the Vistula fortress of Novo Georgievsk had to be brought into action to repulse the leading German columns. Under the skilful direction of General Alexeieff, all the Russian forces in the centre swiftly concentrated round the doomed capital of Poland. The famous river lines along the Rawka were abandoned in the night, the guns being removed closer to Warsaw, to the Blonie lines, and the troops retiring under the protection of a strong rearguard, which in turn escaped to the new lines.

On this sector of the front, where Mackensen and Hindenburg had acted together the previous winter and vainly sacrificed hundreds of thousands of men in an attempt to break through to Warsaw, the enemy forces were now commanded by Prince Leopold of Bavaria—brother of the King of Bavaria. The new German commander did not display any initiative, and the Russian retirement was carried out without a hitch. General von Woyrsch, acting in the neighbouring sector between the Pilica and the Upper Vistula, with Ivangorod as his objective, showed more driving power and grasp of the situation than the Bavarian Prince. Knowing that the Russian forces in front of him were certain to be preparing to retire, Woyrsch made a fierce attack on Radom along two roads which converged on this town. Unhappily for him, the Russian commander had divined the attack and the way it would be made. He sent out two strong forces west and north-west of Radom, and the attackers were met by counter-attackers and violently thrown back. The army defending Ivangorod then fell back on its lines close to the Vistula and the bridge across the great river. Ivangorod was no longer a fortress, its works of brick being too old to withstand the heavy shells of modern siege-howitzers. The old-fashioned 6 in. guns had been removed and placed in pits behind the trenches in which the infantry worked. There were field-guns on some of the river islands and behind the wire entanglements in the riverside forests where the Russian infantrymen broke Hindenburg's first attack on the Vistula line in the autumn of 1914. The Russian heavy artillery was sited across the river, thus making a retirement from Ivangorod a quick and easy operation for the troops. As a matter of fact, they had no difficulty at any time in holding back Woyrsch's forces. Only Mackensen's and Hindenburg's distant enveloping movements put them in danger. It was the Ivangorod army and the Warsaw army that the

German Field-Marshals hoped to capture by their great flanking operations. General Alexeieff answered these flanking operations by withdrawing the menaced troops towards the Vistula and giving them shorter lines to hold, so that a considerable part of their forces could be at once sent through Warsaw and Ivangorod to reinforce the critical Narew front. In this way, the great Warsaw retreat was begun by a direct and strong movement of concentration against Hindenburg's group of armies.

Very great powers of judgment were needed in this intricate rearrangement of forces under the guns of the enemy. The German Commander-in-Chief had large reserves, kept on or about the railways in his rear. It was his object to mask the direction in which he intended to launch his reserve force and make his decisive stroke, while deceiving his opponent if possible by feints of new concentrations. This the strategical Prussian railway system enabled him to do. But General Alexeieff, by remarkable foresight, penetrated the enemy's plan with such success that, after he had extracted his forces from the German noose and withdrawn them along the railway

THE INDISPENSABLE ENGINEER—GERMAN SOLDIERS ENGAGED IN WELL-SINKING OPERATIONS IN RUSSIAN POLAND.
It was a Napoleonic axiom that an army advances on its stomach. The above photograph emphasises part of the vital work that has to be carried out behind the fighting-line where the normal drinking-water supply is scanty.

to Petrograd, the Tsar claimed him as the best Russian strategist and, taking him from his army command, made him Chief of Staff to all the Russian forces.

All the while this rearrangement of the Russian forces was taking place in the salient, Hindenburg was drawing in on the bridge-heads of the Narew River. At the same time, his northern armies fiercely attacked all along the line from Riga to Kovno and thence down the Niemen and the Bobr streams. Far in the south-east an Austro-Hungarian army, under General Kirchbach, operating on the frontier of Galicia, made a **Woyrsch's sudden** violent effort near Sokal, on the Bug, **blow** and forced the passage of the river, threatening to divide the force under General Ivanoff. In the centre General von Woyrsch, with the Landwehr of Silesia and the infantry of Transylvania, closed down on Ivangorod, while Mackensen, with the German Phalanx and the Austrian troops, still nominally commanded by the Archduke Joseph Ferdinand, suddenly brought all his reserves into action and, with his guns again supplied with millions of shells, struck with terrific force at the Ivangorod-Lublin-Cholm-Kieff railway. It was on Friday, July 23rd, 1915, that the great blow fell in the direction foreseen by General Alexeieff. For a thousand miles the Russian troops were kept at a tension by the attacking forces, each group of which advanced to the assault with the heightened energy of men who know that a great victory is within their reach. Between the Vistula and the Bug, Mackensen was washing the Russian trenches away by a tornado of shell fire. In the bend of the Vistula, Woyrsch had broken the connection between the army of Warsaw and the army of Ivangorod by capturing a river position between the two cities at Kozienice. All the Russian forces between the mouth of the Pilica and Kozienice were forced across the Vistula. Prince Leopold of Bavaria was able to close in on Warsaw from the west and south and approach within sixteen miles of the city. And while all the forces of Russia were thus apparently extended to breaking point, Hindenburg made what he thought at the time was the grand, decisive stroke.

Under his direction the army of General von Gallwitz, which for days had been bombarding all the bridge-heads of the Narew River, advanced in dense **"The grand,** masses and stormed the redoubts at the **decisive stroke"** crossing-places of Rozan and Pultusk.

The losses of the attacking infantry were dreadful, for the Russian commander had placed his heavy guns south of the river, in such sites as brought a cross-fire to bear upon any forces approaching the bridge-heads. These concealed guns had as long a range as anything made by Krupp and Skoda, and the only reason why they had avoided an artillery duel was the scarcity of high-explosive shell. But there was a useful amount of shrapnel, and when the entire German army was deployed in the open field, the long-silent heavy Russian batteries got to work. Hindenburg had to use up the **Alexeieff defeats** larger part of his reserve in order to force **Hindenburg's design** the river, and when this success had been achieved at enormous cost, it was found to be fruitless.

For, far from being broken, the Russian forces on the Narew were in tremendous strength. So strong were they indeed that, in spite of the fact that they had barely a quarter of the amount of shell which the Germans possessed, they entirely defeated Hindenburg's design. This design was to make a rapid, sweeping movement across the Narew to the Lower Bug, in the rear of Warsaw, and on Sunday, July 25th, the Berlin communiqué announced to an alarmed and half-stunned world that Hindenburg's troops were approaching the Bug from Pultusk. It was by this sort of sensational anticipatory announcement of the successes at which he aimed that Hindenburg of old had so delighted the civilian population of his country as to eclipse in popularity the Kaiser and all other generals. He sent a telegram to Sven Hedin, the Swedish Press agent of German barbarism, bidding him hasten if he wished to see the victorious entry of the conquerors of Warsaw. The Kaiser and the Kaiserin came by express train to Hindenburg's headquarters on the East Prussian frontier, in order to make a Royal progress into the Polish

NEGOTIATING AN AWKWARD BIT OF GROUND: RUSSIAN HORSE ARTILLERY CROSSING A STREAM AND TAKING THE OPPOSITE BANK.
A picturesque camera-picture from the Polish front. The splendid quality and condition of the horses are specially noticeable.

SALVAGE WORK BY THE HUNS AT A BLAZING GRANARY IN BREST LITOVSK.
When the Germans entered Brest Litovsk on August 25th, 1915, they found the citadel on fire. By putting the soldiers to salve what was left, they were able to secure as plunder a few hundred bags of grain. The above remarkable photograph shows the salvage work in progress.

capital, and a dispute arose between Vienna and Berlin concerning the problem of dividing the gains in Courland and Russian Poland between the Hohenzollern and Hapsburg Empires.

But while the two Teutonic races were opening their great quarrel over the sharing of the skin of the bear, the bear was far from being slain.

The Russian commander had been holding the Narew line merely with a thin line of troops; his chief forces were concealed in the forests extending from the south side of the river. All the actions at the crossings were merely rearguard actions, fought to gain time for the new concentration of troops. Despite the fact that the evacuation of Warsaw was rapidly proceeding, and that all manufacturing plant and materials and workmen were being moved into Central Russia, General Alexeieff seems to have been half inclined to stand and offer battle, for he was in a position of great advantage. His men were now little inferior in numbers to those of Hindenburg, and the overpowering hostile artillery was not able to work well; for as the region between the Narew and the Bug was marshy and thickly wooded, the movement of heavy guns was a slow and arduous business, and the field of fire was restricted. It was a country for hand-to-hand fighting, in which the Russian bayonet would be one of the master weapons.

Gallwitz's forces formed a salient between Novo Georgievsk and the Forest of Rozan, leaving him open to a combined attack on both flanks. This attack was delivered with extreme fury on July 26th, and though

Russians recross the Narew

Hindenburg threw into the field his last reserves from the direction of Sierok, the Germans were forced back to the Narew in disorder at several points. The Russians then closed on Sierok, which lies at the confluence of the Bug and Vistula, and recrossed the Narew, and a long, fluctuating, murderous conflict went on day and night on both sides of the river until July 30th. The German offensive movement then stopped, Hindenburg having no more infantry at hand to attempt further to force a decision. He tried to mask his weakness by bringing up siege-guns to the Narew front, and occupied the interval of artillery practice in accumulating asphyxiating gas apparatus on the northerly forest line.

All this clearly indicated what had happened—Hindenburg's gigantic stroke had failed. His men had been out-fought; even his enormous trains of artillery had been reduced to practical impotence in the battles of manœuvres in the open field. In trying to get a smashing rear flank thrust against Alexeieff's forces, he had advanced with such over-confidence, after breaking through the Russian covering troops on the Narew, that his principal army—Gallwitz's—had been caught on the flank instead and terribly mauled.

Hindenburg's men out-fought

So far as Hindenburg was concerned, Warsaw, with its protecting fortress of Novo Georgievsk, and its connecting northern entrenched camp at Grodno, might have stood firm throughout the campaign, with the Petrograd railway in the rear supplying the fighting-line. The German army under Below was held firmly in Courland. Eichhorn was vainly wasting men by tens of thousands in trying to

303

approach Kovno. Gallwitz's troops were nearly exhausted. Scholtz's army had come into action on his right, without bettering the situation, and Novo Georgievsk was encircled by a Russian army which prevented Beseler from getting his siege-guns within range of the steel-domed and concrete-walled forts.

But the failure of Hindenburg was redeemed by the success of Mackensen. On July 29th the famous Phalanx reached the railway track between Lublin and Cholm, thus turning by a flank attack all the Russian lines along the Vistula. Ivangorod, which had been munitioned and fed by the lost railway, had to be abandoned, and on its abandonment the armies of Prince Leopold, Woyrsch, the Archduke Joseph Ferdinand, and Mackensen's great force could link up and sweep forward in a vast enveloping movement on the east of Warsaw.

For more than two weeks the Russian armies, based on Lublin and Cholm, had stubbornly stood out against the victors of the Dunajec and other Galician battle-fields. All that men could do, the wing of the old southern Russian forces had done. What had defeated them at last was the road-making plant of the German Phalanx. As the roads were made, the tremendous train of heavy howitzers came closer to the vital railway line. We have seen that the lighter gunned and more mobile Russian army holding Lublin first tried to assail Mackensen's western flank by breaking through the Austrian army at Krasnik. When this desperate plan failed, the Cholm army essayed an equally hard task, and advanced directly against Mackensen's eastern flank, some thirty miles south of Cholm, at Grubies-zov. Mackensen's main artillery force was then slowly crawling towards the railway line, so that the quicker-moving Russian force was able to strike behind it.

These, it may be remarked, were the usual Russian tactics in cases where the enemy was chained to a slow, cumbersome mass of extraordinarily heavy ordnance. They gave way on the sector in which the hurricane fire of large shells made their trenches untenable, but as they gave way they massed and struck out in a side attack on a sector **Russian tactics** where the enemy had to meet them on **against big guns** more equal terms in the matter of artillery power. Unless the German commander concentrated his guns on a narrow front, in order to obtain a sudden, wrecking shell fire, by which his infantry could profit, he made but little progress; for the Russians always answered his ordinary attacks by counter-attacks. He was compelled, by the difficulty of getting hard roads for his great howitzers, and by the need for massing his artillery fire so as to obtain

decisive effects, to keep his large pieces of ordnance close together. So in the other sectors of the battle-line the Russian commander had less heavy odds against him. It was then the German machine-guns, arranged behind wire defences so as to bring a cross-fire to bear, which were the chief source of trouble. On some notable occasions, where the lie of the land favoured the enterprise, the Russians surmounted the difficulty caused by hostile machine-gun fire by launching a **Use of the** squadron of armoured motor-cars in **armoured car** front of the charging lines of their infantry. And where no armoured cars were immediately available, the Russian sharpshooters worked forward and, with well-planned help from their field-guns, broke into the enemy's field redoubts.

We may now remark, since it is fairly notorious, that in the flood-time of Russian successes on the Carpathian front, in the first months of 1915, the defects of temperament of the Russian upper class were at times very apparent. The officers of some battalions took their men into action merely with the ambition of making a great name for the battalion. They recked little of the general operations of the brigade, division, or army corps in which their men formed just a single unit of force. There was, in short, little sense of team work. In one case, it was reported, even neighbouring Russian armies failed to co-operate harmoniously at a critical moment. It is said that the Grand Duke Nicholas published an Army order in March, 1915, concerning the lack of combination of effort between regiments, brigades, and divisions.

There was a kind of Byronism, derived immediately from Puschkin, the Russian disciple of Byron, and remotely inherited from the extremely independent character of all the old Slav nobility, which seemed to survive in the officer class. It can be seen in Tolstoy's early life and writings, and it remained an element of romanticism in the terrible period of scientific warfare.

But in the great retreat this defect in certain of the fighting aristocracy of Russia was removed. Stern, capable, masterly men, such as Russky, Ivanoff, Alexeieff, and Evert, the splendid commander of the Sixth Army, maintained a firm system of Staff control, leading to a deep, patriotic sense of the high value of team work. The officers themselves were also individually trained by long, grim, actual experience of the difficulties and the achievements of co-operative efforts. The feeling that the very life of Russia was in peril put an end to all longing for personal distinction. The men had, from the beginning of the tremendous struggle, been inspired by the spirit of pure self-sacrifice, and the more self-conscious educated class felt in the days of disaster the wonderfully contagious

PRINCE LEOPOLD OF BAVARIA.
Brother of the King of Bavaria. He was in supreme command of the army to which was entrusted the final assault on Warsaw.

quality of the simple-minded peasant's faith in his country. The upshot was that, partly by the skilful direction of the leading commanders and partly by a sort of act of conversion in the hearts of the subordinate officers, the Russian forces approached the clockwork efficiency in intricate combined movements which marked the Austro-German armies. This was, indeed, the most striking feature of the later phase of the eastern campaign. The Russian armies, with their large proportion of illiterate peasantry, and their once notorious easy-going methods, proved almost a match for the best drilled and most highly organised military Power of modern times in the supreme end of all organisation—finely combined efforts.

Ivanoff's struggle against Mackensen and Alexeieff's struggle against Hindenburg formed a remarkable example of this nobly patriotic team work. The two commanders seem to have shared the service of a common reserve force that moved between the Narew front and the Lublin-Cholm line. If Ivanoff could have fought Mackensen to a definite standstill before the German Field-Marshal advanced within striking distance of the railway linking Ivangorod to Kieff, Hindenburg would, in all probability, have been defeated, together with Prince Leopold of Bavaria and General von Woyrsch.

For the Russian fortress guns on this section of the front were useful weapons when the enemy had been **Nobly patriotic** lured within their range, and the Germans **team work** were so confident of success that they could be exasperated by local defeats into undertaking very perilous projects. Hindenburg especially was a human bull, to whom any check to his time-table of prearranged victories acted like a banderillo's dart. He would send his men out to die by the hundred thousand, as was seen before in front of Warsaw, and afterwards in front of Kovno, rather than alter the direction of his rush attack.

But Mackensen, unfortunately for the Russians, was a man of more supple mind and improvising genius His quality of determination was as remarkable as that of the older German Field-Marshal and, at need, he sacrificed the manhood of his nation with the same ghastly cold-bloodedness. But it must be said of this descendant of some Jacobite Scotsman that, though touched by the modern German mob passion for **Mackensen's greatest** the "kolossal" at any cost, he retained **achievement** somewhat of the old cautiousness of his race. His expenditure of the human resources of Germany was terrific. Misled, like all other German high commanders, by the example of Napoleon as interpreted by Clausewitz, he used up men as if they were the automata of warfare, as easily and as quickly manufactured as shells. But though he purchased his results too dearly, he ever managed, after his failure on the Bzura front in the winter of 1914, to achieve some result.

And the greatest of all his achievements was the breaking of the Lublin-Cholm line towards the end of July, 1915. After he suddenly turned northward at Ravaruska in the middle of June, his progress was uncommonly slow. His average pace was only about a mile and a half a day. But though he was still faced by the armies he had broken on the Dunajec, the quality and temper of those armies had changed, and he had lost the advantage of surprise in his further conflicts with them. They had been thoroughly reorganised and placed under one of the ablest of Russian strategists, who was well informed of the smashing artillery power and great infantry force which Mackensen wielded. Yet the Russian commander considered he might fight the German to a standstill. He nearly succeeded in getting on his flank at Krasnik, and then at Grubieszov Mackensen was again held up by a thrust towards his rear. He countered it by making a strong attempt to envelop the hostile forces, which were in a dangerously advanced position, at Grubieszov, on July 22nd. A German division was destroyed in trying to

THE ENTRY OF THE HUNS INTO WARSAW: PRINCE LEOPOLD OF BAVARIA AND STAFF OUTSIDE THE ALEXANDER-NEVSKY CATHEDRAL REVIEWING THE TROOPS AS THEY ENTERED THE CITY.
In small panel: Prince Leopold of Bavaria's entry into Warsaw.

break through the Russian line of entrenched hills north of Grubieszov, and reach the railway at a point near the Bug. But this division did not die in vain. It was thrown away, with tens of thousands of other troops, in a fierce but misleading demonstration, and on July 29th, when the Cholm army had massed eastward near the Bug after the victory, Mackensen's main force worked westward up the Wieprz River, from its old advanced base of Krasnostav, and in a conflict of extreme violence broke the Russian line between Cholm and Lublin, on the evening of July 29th, and reached the railway at the village station of Biskupice.

Prince Leopold enters Warsaw

The battle was waged on both sides of the Wieprz stream on a front of seventeen miles, and it was won by shell fire from thousands of pieces, many of the largest calibre. Deep as the Russian trenches had been built in places, they were wrecked by high explosives, and the sand-bag breastworks in the river marshes were more easily destroyed. In this way wide gaps were blown in the line of defence, and under the continuing stream of shells the Austrian army corps under General von Arz, which formed part of the German Phalanx, stormed into the Russian lines and held them. The hand-to-hand fighting that followed was of furiously desperate character, for the Russians would not accept a machine-made defeat, but charged in frenzy against their visible human foes. Their counter-attacks, though at first successful, were at last shattered by the fire of guns and machine-guns well concealed, and when night fell the railway was definitely lost.

The Ivangorod garrison then had to prepare to retire, and as the troops holding this section of the Vistula weakened, General von Woyrsch, who had secured a favourable position on the river between Ivangorod and Warsaw, threw two pontoon bridges over it and advanced to cut off Warsaw on Saturday, July 31st. He was beaten back to his bridge-head at Maciejovice, but as the Russian line continued to weaken, owing to the pressure of Mackensen's forces eastward, General von Woyrsch poured his army over the river again, and on Sunday afternoon, August 1st, he had four divisions across the water. The Russian troops in the neighbourhood were forced back a considerable distance towards Garwolin, and this new irruption into our allies' lines definitely concluded the Russian stand on the Warsaw front. The Polish capital, from which everything useful was removed, except food and private property belonging to the townsmen who chose to remain, was entered by Prince Leopold of Bavaria on the morning of August 5th, 1915. A Russian rearguard held the last lines until the bridges were blown up. Then the defending troops nonchalantly marched through the lost city, having left the attacking forces a long task to restore the means of crossing the Vistula and getting guns and ammunition over to make a pursuit.

Neither the Bavarian Prince nor Marshal Hindenburg, who was acting with him, had any direct, immediate influence in bringing about the fall of Warsaw. It was Mackensen's new menace to the Brest Litovsk line, combined with the advance in the same direction by Woyrsch, largely brought about by Mackensen's manœuvre, that decided the fate of Warsaw and its neighbouring positions of Ivangorod and Novo Georgievsk.

The migration of the people from the country north and south of Warsaw, and from Warsaw itself, was a slow, enormous movement. Several million persons preceded the armies in the great retreat into Central Russia. They were mainly Lithuanians, Poles, and Jews, the proportion of Russians being very small. The Poles fled because of their well-founded terror of the Teutonic soldiers, whose deeds in Russian Poland had eclipsed all the atrocities in Belgium and France. Warsaw was emptied of material. Both factories and churches were stripped, one of the principal relics removed being the heart of the great Polish composer Chopin, which was taken to Moscow. Along the roads to Moscow, a thousand miles away, moved all the carriages, carts, and horses, the vehicles being filled with household treasures. Thousands of trucks were accumulated in the sidings, and sent full of human freight and materials on a three days' journey to Moscow by way of Vilna. The direct route through Brest Litovsk was occupied with military business, troop trains and munition trains shuttling to and fro in answer to the pressure exerted by Mackensen and Hindenburg. The wealthy people in Warsaw, who stayed to near the end, when all motor-cars had vanished, were glad of **An empty shell for** standing room in the cattle trucks. But **the victors** the gigantic evacuation was managed with great organising power, considering the circumstances, and when Prince Leopold's cavalry entered the city, there was nothing but an empty shell for the conquerors. The great noose had been drawn tight at last, but there was nothing of importance, in a military point of view, within it.

"We don't want peace," said one of the weary Russian soldiers on the outskirts of the lost city. "When we have plenty of shells we shall take Warsaw back again. We can never leave it in the hands of the Germans."

The spirit of Napoleon had risen from its tomb under the dome in Paris to inspire those old opponents of his who had become the allies of a rejuvenated France. The tradition of the retreat of a thousand miles against the Grand Army of the greatest of captains was a priceless source of moral and spiritual strength to the Russian people in the days of their dreadful trial. Every Russian peasant was confident that the Hohenzollern Emperor would advance into disaster, even as the greater Emperor had done. To a Russian a retreat had nothing of the gloomy

AFTER WARSAW: THE ATTACK ON THE GREAT RUSSIAN ENTRENCHMENTS AT NOVO GEORGIEVSK.
Austrian troops advancing. It will be noticed that the officer is calling to his men and not leading them.

ONE OF THE SHATTERED BRIDGES ACROSS THE VISTULA AT WARSAW.

significance it has for a Frenchman or a Briton. He regarded it with stoic hopefulness, as the most costly but most decisive means of attaining complete victory.

It was the high and peculiar strength of Russia that the natural faculty for recoiling a long distance for a spring, which was derived from the extent and character of the country, was enhanced by historic memories of the most marvellous retirement in history. They imbued the will-power of this extraordinary people with the quality of invincibility in the very hour of defeat. In Russia when night was darkest, dawn was nearest. Such was the moral force of a tradition

Moral force of Russian tradition prevailing among a nation of peasants, largely illiterate, but strong in faith. After the war materialists will again be found blindly contending that only material things, resolvable into chemical or electrical formula, have a veritable being, and that thought, emotion, and ecstasy of the soul are but phantasmal shadows cast by the transient combination of the atoms of the grey matter of the brain. Yet it was entirely that strange, spiritual thing, faith—faith without any immediate, personal experience substantiating it—which upheld the Russian and made him terrible to his victors in the day of their victory.

Kaiser Wilhelm II. did not ride in triumph into Warsaw. Instead, he is said to have sent, through a group of financiers, an offer of a separate peace with the Tsar, on extraordinary terms, marked by an apparent generosity that dishonoured the peace-seeker and displayed his dread of the Empire he had invaded. He offered, it was reported, Constantinople and the Dardanelles, belonging to one of his allies; and Galicia, the territory of his other allies, to the ruler whom he had seemingly defeated, and against whom he had originally engineered the war that shook the world. At his suggestion his principal Press agent, Sven Hedin, supposed to be raging with

hate for everything Russian, broke out into loud praise of Russian heroism and Russian endurance, and the docile German newspapers for a while executed variations on the same theme.

The tradition of the end of Napoleon's Grand Army weighed on the very impressionable mind of the Hohenzollern, and his extraordinary offer was also influenced by the way in which Bismarck handled Austria after the victory at Königratz. Germany and Austria had already begun to quarrel over Russian Poland, especially over the appointment of the ruler of the new kingdom and the extent of the German and Austrian territories to be restored to it. All these matters of anxiety were further aggravated **The Kaiser's extraordinary offer**

WATCHING THE AUSTRO-GERMAN ENTRY INTO WARSAW.
Standing on one of the broken bridges, with German soldiers among them, part of the resident population are seen watching the entry of the enemy troops into the city.

by a lively apprehension of the strong movement towards free government which was spreading through Russia and

THE BAVARIAN FLAG IN WARSAW.
The Bavarian colours, with the flags of Germany and Austria, floating over one of the captured forts by way of compliment to Prince Leopold.

attracting the favouring interest of Tsar Nicholas. If Russia, as a result of the war, discredited the bureaucratic system, how could the same system, reduced to a far more efficient machinery of tyranny, be maintained in Germany? It looked as though the Kaiser, for the first time in his life, began seriously to appreciate—from the point of view of German domestic politics—the subtle skill of Bismarck's ancient policy of keeping on friendly terms with Russia, even at the expense of Austria's good will.

The old bureaucratic illiberal Russia, which was being so swiftly transformed into a fiery but patriotic and self-organising democracy, had been the Hohenzollern's chief rampart against the German Social Democratic movement. Since Peter the Great violently moulded the national life of Russia upon the model of Prussia, Russia had aided her neighbour in many ways. She first saved Prussia from entire destruction after Jena, and afterwards she became the hidden mainstay of the Prussian system of government. Then, while professing to regard her as a menacing, expansive, despotic Power, the German military caste used her as a bugbear to reduce the German middle classes and working classes into a state of subjection.

Treated as a friendly neighbouring Empire, with a common interest in the maintenance of Imperial bureaucracy and in the repression of popular clamour for free government, she had even as late as 1906 helped to augment the prestige of the Prussian system. A free Russia would, soon after the war, create by the force of example and suggestion a free Germany. So the Kaiser, for the sake of his own despotic power, was moved to offer terms of peace. They were rejected. It then became his main object to crush Russia before the leaders of the Duma and the manufacturing classes could develop their production of munitions. He wished to prove to the Tsar that parliamentary institutions would produce no more efficiency in the production of munitions than the bureaucratic system of government had done. Instead of entrenching on the Vistula and transferring a million men and thousands of guns with their stream of shells to the western front, the War Lord continued the advance into Russia, for reasons of German domestic politics. This strange, unexpected liberalising Russia, where the Council of Empire was being invaded by leaders of the revered Duma, was his chief enemy. It threatened most harm to him and all that he stood for. For if the Social Democrats were faced by freed Russians, a revolution in Germany was likely to follow defeat.

The Kaiser's chief enemy

INTERESTING EXAMPLE OF MILITARY BRIDGE BUILDING BY THE AUSTRIAN ENGINEERS—THE "AUGUSTA-BRUCKE" ACROSS THE VISTULA.
In the smaller picture is seen apparatus originally intended for the preparation of hydrogen and adapted by the Austrians for the manufacture of poison gas. To the left is an Austrian captive balloon.

CHAPTER LXXVIII.

THE WAR AND THE WORKER: A YEAR'S SURVEY.

The Difference Between Ancient and Modern Wars—Nations in Arms—The Connection Between War and Poverty—The Great War a Prosperous Time for the Worker—Measures to Deal with the Anticipated Distress—Employment and Wages in 1914—The Prices of Food and their Regulation—Absence of Strikes—Employment in 1915—Big Increases of Wages—The Price of Coal Regulated—Prosperity Helped by Separation Allowances—A Serious Shortage of Labour—An Industrial Revolution—Expenditure on Luxuries Curtailed—Volunteer Labour—Mr. Lloyd George and the Lure of Drink.

I N this chapter we shall consider the condition of the people during the war. We propose to confine ourselves to the first year of warfare—*i.e.*, to the year which ended on August 3rd, 1915—and we must, of necessity, deal with the question in a very broad and general way. In the Middle Ages and later, wars were waged by small armies of professional soldiers, while the mass of the people knew little, and cared less, about their exploits. Wars, even those which were marked by decisive victories, such as Bannockburn and Agincourt, were in no real sense national. The soldier just took up and cleaned or sharpened his bow, or sword, or pike, or musket, and was ready for the fray; he did not need an army of workmen at home to keep him supplied with arms and ammunition. His food he took as required, and a transport and commissariat service did not exist.

To-day all this is changed. In modern warfare the whole people take part in some way or another, and in a literal sense the combatants are nations in arms. Those who are not in the firing-line are probably making ammunition or guns, or clothing, or are providing or carrying food for those who are, and their efforts are as important as are those of the men who serve the guns or rush the trenches. It is said, and no doubt it is roughly true, that every soldier in the field needs two men at home to keep him equipped and efficient.

[Elliott & Fry.
SIR JOSEPH J. THOMSON, O.M., F.R.S.
A member of the Central Committee of Inventions Board.
He was awarded the Nobel Prize for Physics in 1906.

For this reason it has come about that the condition of the people at home must be considered by those responsible for the conduct of a modern war almost as much as that of the soldiers at the front. If the workers are impoverished, discontented, or diseased, the fighting power of the nation will be seriously weakened. The wars of to-day are well described by the phrase "a nation in arms," and, consequently, an authoritative narrative of the Great War must make mention of many subjects which have rightly no place in the histories of earlier struggles—for instance, those of Clarendon and Napier. When, in 1066, Duke William crossed over to conquer England, the condition of the people in Normandy mattered nothing to him, and had no bearing on the issue of his struggle with Harold; in 1915, the condition of the people of this country mattered a great deal to Lord Kitchener and Sir John French.

For a period of seventy years or so—let us say after the repeal of the Corn Laws in 1846—we were told that war must be avoided because it invariably brings with it distress and destitution. This was laid down as a law to which there was no exception, and most people who had no specialistic knowledge believed it implicitly. We know now that this is not so, that war and prosperity may well go together, and the year 1914-15 —at least, as far as this country is concerned—is a case in point. Once again, in August, 1914, it was seen that the pacifists were completely wrong. They foretold want and misery, little

"MR. ATKINS" IN THE HOP FIELDS.
In England, as in France, troops not needed at the front helped in the harvest fields. Above is a view of some of our men in khaki hoeing between the bines in a Kentish hop garden.

many of us have heard our grandparents speak.

During the first year of the Great War prosperity and not adversity was the lot of the worker, and this is the outstanding fact in any discussion on the condition of the people. In this connection, we must not forget the work done by our Navy. By controlling the seas of the world, our ships not only preserved our shores from the footsteps of the foeman; they also enabled us to draw supplies of food from all parts of the world. Without this "sure shield," the plight of our workers would have been pitiable indeed, and incidentally this chapter would have told a very different tale.

work and low wages; and, instead, we had plenty of both.

The war which they had in mind, the war which brings with it distress and destitution, is the one which is waged in one's own land and neighbourhood, and this shows the soundness of the German theory that the best place wherein to conduct war is the enemy's country. When hostile soldiers are marching through the land, treading down crops, commandeering food, sacking towns, and killing non-combatants without mercy —for, like the tribesmen in Kipling's ballad,

" They will feed their horse on the standing crop,
　　Their men on the garnered grain "—

it is certain that extreme misery and privation, if not actual famine, will follow. It is the experience of this kind of warfare which was partly responsible for the idea which prevailed in August, 1914.

Where pacifists were wrong Further, pacifists confused the time of war with the time after war. The end of a war always brings with it confusion and dislocation of trade, and this has been the parent of poverty and misery. At such a time men are discharged from the Army in large numbers, while concurrently the orders for stores, ammunition, and clothing for the troops cease. A sudden transition of this kind must cause poverty and distress; but, strictly speaking, this is not due to war, but to the cessation of war. It is neither war nor peace, but sudden change, which is bad for trade.

Our own tradition about the terrible evils of war has been handed down to us from the time of the Napoleonic Wars, but it should be remembered that the misery and distress which afflicted this country were far greater after 1815 than they were before it. It was then that wages fell, unemployment increased, and bankruptcies were general, that riots and disorders broke out, and that Great Britain was filled with that unrest about which

A WELCOME CHANGE FROM "FORM FOURS."
Those of our soldiers in training who were given a turn at hop-picking found the occupation a congenial change from the parade ground.

When war was declared in August, 1914, our Government shared the prevailing idea about its ill effects on industry. At once a committee was appointed to advise on the measures necessary to deal with any distress which might arise, and on August 11th Mr. J. A. Pease, then President of the Board of Education, wrote to " The Times " explaining the scheme agreed upon, and saying : " It is feared that many workers will be thrown out of employment by the dislocation of industry caused by the war." In the cities and towns local committees were formed to assist the Central Committee in this matter; and, under the auspices of the Prince of Wales, a fund was opened which in a few months amounted to over £4,000,000. To meet the special care of women a committee was formed at the instance of the Queen, and for them workshops were opened in London. In addition, schemes for the training of women and girls, and for experiments in the creation of new industries were inaugurated.

Other measures were taken to deal with an avalanche of unemployment. A Bill, the **Plans for relieving distress** Housing Act (No. 2), was passed through Parliament, the object of which was to provide £4,000,000 for building houses, and the Development Fund and the Road Board took steps to put fresh schemes in hand. Local authorities were urged to press on public works of all kinds, and in other ways efforts were made to provide plenty of employment. At the same time, in order to alleviate the lot of those who were deprived of their livelihood, laws were passed protecting them to some extent from their creditors and making it

"Business as usual"

more difficult for landlords to distrain upon them for arrears of rent. A little later the Government promised to assist the trade unions in case they were called upon to pay out exceptional sums to their unemployed members.

In the first few anxious days of August a certain number of workpeople were dismissed, others had their wages or salaries reduced, and many more were warned to prepare for the worst; but, contrary to expectations, there was no great increase in unemployment, and it was not necessary to put into execution the many schemes prepared by the Local Government Board for dealing with distress. This fortunate state of affairs was due largely to the restoration of credit and public confidence, on which our industrial system rests, and this has already been described in Chapter LXXIV. of this history. It was aided by the enlistment of many workers and by the orders which the

regular and remunerative employment. There are several ways of testing the state of employment in this country, and although no one of them is perfect, yet all are useful and in the main correct. One is to take the case of 1,000,000 trade unionists and find out what percentage of them are unemployed at any given time. At the end of August the percentage was 7·1 as compared with 2·8 at the end of July, and 2 per cent. at the end of August, 1913. This showed a rise in unemployment, but not a very serious one in the circumstances; and, as the "Board of Trade Labour Gazette" said, it was "a figure which has frequently been exceeded in periods of bad trade, and which is much lower than that recorded during the national coal strike of 1912, when the percentage rose to 11·3." The decline in employment was general in all industries, except in shipbuilding, which benefited by increased activity on Government work, and unemployment was especially high in the cotton industry.

Another test of the condition of the people is found in the number of paupers at any given time. At the end of August the rate of pauperism in thirty-five selected urban districts was 188 per 10,000.

Pauperism and unemployment

At the end of July it was 184, and at the end of August, 1913, it was 183; so here the increase was slight. A third source of information are the figures issued every month about the work of the Labour Exchanges. On August 14th 194,580 persons had their names on the registers of these exchanges, compared with 112,622 on July 17th, 1914, and 89,049 on August 15th, 1913.

Again in certain trades, or groups of trades, those in which insurance against unemployment is compulsory, exact figures are available from time to time about the condition of the workers therein. In five big industries—building, shipbuilding, engineering, construction of vehicles, and saw-milling — 180,233 persons claimed unemployment benefit in the four weeks ending August 28th; during the

A HARVESTER IN KHAKI.
A novel scene on one of the pleasant English uplands. One of the men of the new army lending a hand with an oat-cutting machine—and probably thinking of the grim harvest his comrades were helping to reap in Flanders.

Government began to place for arms, food, and clothing for the troops.

The popular cry of "Business as usual" echoed from the platform and the Press did its part in preventing unemployment. People were urged to keep as far as possible to their usual mode of life, to dismiss no servants, to curtail no orders, to abstain from no reasonable luxury. By acting in this way, they were told, they would reduce the distress inevitable in a time of war to a minimum, and there is no doubt but that this was serviceable advice for the time being.

The parent of prosperity is

HAY-MAKING IN FRANCE.
In France much of the work in the fields was done by women; but as many soldiers as could be spared for the purpose helped to gather in the harvest. Above is a picturesque view of French soldiers at work on the hay crop.

five weeks ending July 31st, 1914, the number was 103,730, and during the five weeks ending August 29th, 1913, it was 78,229. The average amount paid out was £11,772 per week in August, 1914, compared with £8,793 a week in July, 1914, and £7,276 a week in August, 1913.

A good time for workers These facts all point to the same conclusion. There was an increase in unemployment and poverty just after the outbreak of the war, but it was nothing like so serious as we had been led to believe it would be. Moreover, from about the end of August or the middle of September, there was an improvement, until we soon reached a time when there was practically no unemployment and very little distress among the working classes.

At the end of September the percentage of unemployed among the million trade unionists had fallen from 7·1 to 5·9, and at the end of October to 4·4. At the end of the year it was only 2·5, not far from the lowest rate on record. The other tests, or at least two of them, showed the same result. On September 11th there were 207,429

DEVELOPMENT OF DEFENSIVE WARFARE: PERISCOPE ATTACHMENT FOR RIFLES.
This attachment allowed our men in the trenches to take deliberate aim without being exposed to the fire of the enemy's snipers.

names on the registers of the Labour Exchanges, but on October 16th there were only 157,248, and on December 11th only 109,208, or somewhat less than on July 17th, and nearly half the number registered on August 14th.

As regards unemployment benefit in the five trades, this was claimed by 133,692 persons during the four weeks ending September 25th, and by 124,730 during the five weeks ending October 30th. By the end of December the total had fallen to 55,610, a most significant indication of the state of trade. In September the amount of money paid out was £19,734 a week, but this was reduced to £14,190 a week during October, and to £7,780 a week during December. For pauperism the figure rose in September to 195 per 10,000, but then it fell to 191 in October, to 190 in November, and finally rose to 191 in December, when it was slightly higher than it had been at the end of August. However, it must be remembered that August is a summer month and December a winter one.

The Board of Trade in a short report summed up the position as regards employment in these words:

The outbreak of war at the beginning of August caused an immediate great decline in employment in practically all industries except shipbuilding, but especially in the cotton trade, and in the tinplate, furnishing, and jewellery trades; the percentage of trade union members unemployed rose from 2·8 per cent. at the end of July to 7·1 per cent. at the end of August, and there was also a large amount of short time. In the succeeding months of the year, however, unemployment rapidly improved, and at the close of the year the percentage of trade union members unemployed was actually lower than at the end of 1913. Some industries were still very inactive, especially the cotton trade, though even the depressed trades generally showed a considerable improvement as compared with August. Other trades, however, were enjoying an unprecedented degree of activity; this was specially the case in trades largely engaged on Government work, notably the woollen trade, the leather, saddlery, and the heavy boot trades, the hosiery and wholesale clothing trades, the engineering, shipbuilding, and many branches of the metal trades. These trades were, as a rule, working the maximum possible hours, many factories having double shifts, working day and night, and working on Sundays as well as weekdays.

A similar state of affairs was disclosed by a special report on the state of employment in October, which was issued by the Board of Trade in December. This report was based on returns received from over 20,000 industrial firms, employing altogether over 4,000,000 workpeople, or about 43 per cent. of the whole industrial population—so it should be reliable. It stated that soon after the outbreak of war it "became apparent that the restriction of ordinary industrial activities would be much less serious than had at first been feared, owing largely to the continuance of our foreign trade." The total reduction shown in the number of male workpeople employed as between July and October was 10·7 per cent., or almost precisely equal to the percentage of workmen who were shown by the figures to have joined the military and naval forces. As regards women, the total reduction in the number employed was 6·2 per cent., and as this contraction was not counterbalanced by enlistments, there was a net displacement of labour. Among both men and women, however, there was a good deal of short time in October, this being especially the case in the cotton trade; but in this respect a steady improvement made itself felt before the end of the year.

"The two fundamental needs of the population," says Professor Ashley, "are adequate remuneration for their labour and regularity in their employment." After the first shock of the new conditions caused by the war was over, regularity of employment was secured for the workers. But what about adequate remuneration for their labours?

Here again there was little or nothing about which to complain. Labour got **Tendency of wages in 1914** gradually scarcer, and consequently able to command higher wages, and this was the tendency of events in the months between the outbreak of the war and the end of the year. Exact figures about wages are not possible to obtain, but the Board of Trade returns showed that while from January to July the tendency of wages was downwards, from August to December it was upwards. The official statement said that "from August to the end of the year, four months of increase and one of

Lord Kitchener looking well pleased with the Artillery passing before him at an Aldershot review.

Detachment of infantry, part of the new army in training, marching past the King on the review ground at Aldershot.

More guns for the front : Splendid display of the new artillery under review by King George at Aldershot.

WITH THE NEW ARMY IN TRAINING AT BRITAIN'S GREATEST MILITARY CAMP IN 1915.

BRIGADIER-GENERAL R. E. W. TURNER, V.C., C.B., D.S.O.
Commanding the 2nd Canadian Division. The photograph was taken at
a review of the Canadian troops at Shorncliffe.

shipped from Atlantic or Canadian ports under existing contracts.

In every emergency, however grave, there will always be unpatriotic and greedy people, and so it was in August, 1914. Aided by the panic which led some householders to buy huge stores of provisions, merchants and shopkeepers put up prices, and to check this proceeding, the Government decided to fix maximum prices for certain articles. These were put in force on August 7th, and referred to sugar, butter, margarine, lard, bacon, and cheese; 1s. 6d. a pound was fixed as the maximum price for the first quality of butter, 10d. a pound for margarine, 8d. a pound for lard; and 9½d. a pound for Colonial cheese. For granulated sugar the price was at first 4½d. a pound, but on the 11th it was reduced to 3¾d.; for **Government and** loaf sugar it was at first 5d., but was **the increase** lowered to 4¼d. on the 11th. The price of bacon, at first fixed at 1s. 4d. and 1s. 6d. a pound, was also reduced a few days later. This was the retail price, and maximum prices were also fixed for meat, the following statement being made on August 25th: " For prime parts the advance compared with a month ago need not exceed 1d. per pound. For the coarser parts, the demand continues to be relatively greater than for prime joints, and the committee consider that an advance, compared with a month ago, of 1½d. to 2d. per pound on the average may reasonably be charged for these parts. The prices of pork and veal show no advance at present."

The general trend of food prices was upwards, and at this no one need be surprised. Many, however, were surprised that the rise was so slight, for we had entered upon a struggle about which Mr. Asquith truly said " no man can foresee the end." In September the experts of the Board of Trade, surveying the critical days of August, said that " retail prices of food began to move upward on

decrease, produced a net increase of £6,433 a week." This meant something like £325,000 a year more in wages.

Wages, however, are not really pounds, shillings, and pence; they are food and clothing, shelter and warmth, and the real question is how much of these can the working man—or rather, we should say, the working woman—buy with the money which is given her. Wages and the cost of living are two parts of the same subject. For instance, if all wages were doubled, but if at the same time the prices of food and other necessaries were trebled, people would be worse off than they are now, although we could prove that there had been a big increase in wages. Whereas, if wages were reduced by one-third and prices by one-half, people would be better off, although wages had been reduced considerably. The wages of one country, or even the wages of one district, cannot
The problem of properly be compared with those of
food prices another, unless a good deal of attention is paid to the cost of living in each.

The condition of the people centres round this question of prices, and prices, as we all know, are regulated by the relation between supply and demand. The main thing is to have a plentiful supply of food in the country, and, if this is provided, the cost of living cannot become unduly high. On the outbreak of war there was some justifiable anxiety on this score, and a committee of the Cabinet was appointed to look into the question. A statement was issued to the effect that the supply of wheat in the country together with the crops then being harvested was sufficient for four months' ordinary consumption. Further, the Government encouraged shippers to carry on their business as usual by guaranteeing war risks on wheat and flour

THE LORD-PROVOST OF EDINBURGH AT AN INSPECTION.
Lord-Provost Inches inspecting the heavy battery of the Lowland (City of Edinburgh) Royal Garrison Artillery.

Saturday, August 1st; but it was not until after the Bank Holiday (August 3rd) that any sharp general rise occurred. By August 8th prices had risen, on average, by 15 or 16 per cent. After that date, however, there was a fall in the price of most articles until, on September 12th, food prices, on the whole, were approximately 10 per cent. above the level of July."

The next movement was a rise, "a slight upward movement" taking place between September 12th and October 1st.

The law of supply and demand There were appreciable increases in the prices of sugar, eggs, and fish, and although the price of potatoes continued to fall, the general net increase over July prices at October 1st averaged about 12 per cent. During October there was practically no change in food prices, but during November there was an advance on average of between 2 and 3 per cent. The gradual increase continued, the result being that at the end of the year prices were about 18 per cent. above the level of July. The articles which showed the greatest advance were sugar, eggs, and fish. British meat did not increase much in price, but imported meat was much dearer than before the war. Obviously many people were economising by buying foreign instead of British meat, and so the law of supply and demand was at work on the prices of each.

The general prosperity was aided by the absence of strikes and labour troubles. In July there were many of these strikes and rumours of strikes everywhere, but at the outbreak of war all were composed as if by magic. As we were officially told: "Up to the end of July, labour disputes were nearly as numerous as in the corresponding period of 1913; but, on the outbreak of war, most of the outstanding disputes were brought to a close, and the disputes since then have been few and generally unimportant." To prove this, we may say that during the seven

ONE OF THE "RESCUE BRIGADE."
Qualified first-aid men were formed into a "rescue brigade" at Woolwich Arsenal, and were supplied with gas masks for use in cases of necessity.

months of peace there were 836 disputes, affecting 423,000 workpeople, while during the five months of war there were only 137 disputes affecting 23,000 workpeople.

In the general dislocation of trade which took place in August, women suffered probably more than men, and in this there is nothing at all surprising, for in their case enlistment could not take off the surplus workers. In October, however, employment among women showed considerable improvement. Army contracts created a demand for women machinists and others in the men's clothing trades, in the boot and shoe trade, and others of the kind. On the other hand, dressmakers in the most highly skilled branches had very little work, and in some cases the number of servants was reduced.

At the end of the year 1914 we may take stock of the position of the working classes. Employment was good—very good—which means that practically everybody could find work. Wages were rising, not very much it is true, but still they were rising. **Wages and prices in 1915** On the other side of the account must be set the very serious fact that the retail prices of food had risen during the war by nearly 20 per cent., or something like 4s. in the £. This was bad enough, but if anyone had prophesied that nothing more than this would happen during the course of the most tremendous war in all history, he would have been voted an optimist of the most foolish and impracticable kind.

These conditions continued during the seven months of 1915 about which we are writing. The rate of unemployment among trade unionists fell steadily from the low figure of December. At the end of February it was 1·6 per cent., at the end of April 1·2 per cent., at the end of June

THE "HORSE DENTIST."
The teeth of the horse as well as those of the soldier require skilled supervision. The above picture shows a "horse dentist" at work—"somewhere in France."

Youthful munitioner turning bombs on a lathe.

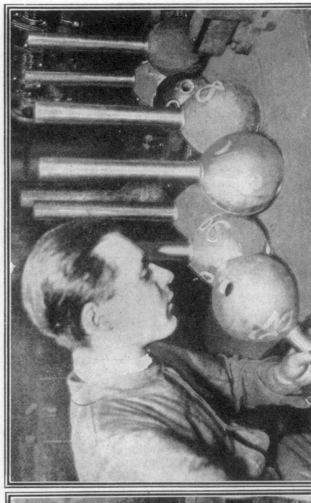

Finished bombs being tested before filling.

A batch of bomb castings ready for turning.

Measuring and cutting bombs.

YOUNG ENGLAND AT MUNITION WORK: BOYS AT A TRAINING SCHOOL ENGAGED IN BOMB-MAKING.

1 per cent., and at the end of July, after a year of war, only ·9 per cent., by far the lowest on record. The returns from the Labour Exchanges told the same tale. On February 12th the number of names on their registers was 100,616, from which it fell to 95,245 on April 26th, and to 92,025 on June 11th. On July 16th there was a rise to 99,773. To appreciate these figures properly, they should be compared with those of 1914, the previous year. On February 13th, 1914, the number on the registers was 145,297, on April 17th it was 106,472, on June 12th it was 110,853, and on July 17th it was 112,622.

As may be expected, much less money was paid out to the unemployed in the five insured trades. During the five weeks ending January 29th, 73,395 persons claimed benefit, and received on the average £8,250 a week, but during the four weeks ending March 26th these figures had been more than halved, for only 32,916 persons claimed, receiving £3,146 a week. During April and May there were further falls, and during the four weeks ending June 25th only 22,867 persons claimed, the sum paid out being only £1,378 a week. For July the weekly average was almost exactly the same as for June. It is not surprising to find that the rate of pauperism in the thirty-five selected

Wages increase : £3,000,000 a year

urban districts fell from 189 per 10,000 in January to 181 per 10,000 in April, then to 172 in June, and 169 in July. In June, 1914, it was 186, and in July, 1914, it was 184.

But these figures are as nothing compared with the extraordinary increase in wages which took place in 1915. It began in February, when increases of £17,889 a week, or something like £900,000 a year, were recorded by the Board of Trade, and there were certainly many others about which the Board heard nothing. Most of the increases took the form of bonuses, usually for the duration of the war, to meet the rise in the cost of living, and the industries mostly affected by them were the engineering, linen and jute, and dock labour groups. This movement continued, and by the end of April the increases in wages amounted to the large sum of £133,537 a week, or nearly £3,000,000 a year. Moreover, this figure was exclusive of increased earnings due to overtime, and also of changes

affecting agricultural labourers, seamen, railway servants, police, and Government employees, and, we were told, "it is known, however, that considerable bodies of workpeople in these occupations have received bonuses or increases since the beginning of the year."

"By far the largest ever recorded in a single month." This sentence refers to the increase of wages during May, which amounted to no less than £188,485 a week, most of it being in the coal-mining industry. It brought the total increase in wages during **Agricultural** the year to nearly £350,000 a week, or **labourers benefit** something like 3s. 6d. each to the workpeople concerned. In June the increases recorded were comparatively small, being only £20,000 a week, and in July only £8,000. However, for the seven months a total of £394,000 a week was reported, quite a satisfactory amount to set against the increased cost of living. While referring to this question of increased wages, it is pleasant to be able to say that the agricultural labourer—the worst paid man in the community—shared in this movement. In 1914 the weekly cash wages of 242,000 agricultural labourers

GERMAN PRISONERS AT WORK IN ENGLAND: FROM THE SANDBAGGED TRENCHES OF FLANDERS TO THE SANDPITS OF DORSET.
On returning from their labours each day the German prisoners who worked in the Dorset sandpits were given refreshments by an old lady as they passed through the wood in which she lived. The circular view shows the men at the refreshment hut.

HIGHLAND OFFICERS IN TRAINING.
A scene at firing-butts somewhere north of the Tweed.

GRENADIERS AT SNIPING PRACTICE.
Squad of Grenadier Guards on Wimbledon Common being instructed in sniping tactics.

little unemployment, except in a few luxury trades, while in a number of industries, notably coal-mining, engineering, shipbuilding, agriculture, and transport, the demand for labour greatly exceeds the supply.

Partly owing to this great improvement in employment, and partly to the rise in the cost of living, nearly two and a half million workpeople have had since August last increases in rates of wages or war bonuses, amounting to over £400,000 per week, or over 3s. per head of those benefiting. These figures are exclusive of increases which have been granted to agricultural labourers, seamen, railway servants, police, and Government employees. They also exclude increased earnings owing to overtime."

were increased by £19,337 a week, an amount equal to the accumulated net increase of the ten years 1903-14. The majority of the increases took place in the autumn—*i.e.*, after the outbreak of war—and ,the upward movement continued in 1915. In Scotland, we were told, wages in May, 1915, compared with a year before, showed a rise in every county.

The Board of Trade review In August, a year having then elapsed since the outbreak of hostilities, the situation was reviewed in the "Board of Trade Labour Gazette." This said that the disquieting conditions of August were of short duration, and by the end of September a distinct improvement had been manifested. By the end of November employment was at about the same level as that prevailing just before the war, and since November the demand for labour had steadily increased. For months past the industries engaged in supplying the requirements of the allied forces had been working at the highest pressure. The review continued :

Owing to the large number of enlistments the number of males available has greatly decreased. To meet this shortage of labour there has been a considerable transference from trades adversely affected by the war to other industries which were rendered abnormally active ; in addition, there has been, wherever possible, a growing movement in the direction of substituting female for male labour. The net result is that at the present time there is very

318

As regards the cost of living, the increase noted in the later months of 1914 continued in 1915. In January there was an advance of between 3 and 4 per cent., the most important feature being the continued upward movement in the prices of flour and bread, and in February there was a somewhat smaller increase, the chief rise taking place in the same two articles. This continued, and the upward movement of retail prices of food reported for April was accentuated in May, but this time a different article was mainly responsible for it ; this increase was owing chiefly to the sharp rise in the price of meat. A small but steady rise in retail prices was reported in June and July.

On July 30th, practically a year after the outbreak of war, retail prices of food **A year's advances** had risen by 34 per cent., the increase **in food prices** having been a fairly steady one since the fluctuations of August, 1914. For beef and mutton, prices had advanced by 40 per cent. and more, and for fish by over 60 per cent. Bread, in July, was nearly 40 per cent. dearer than a year before, and flour 45 per cent. dearer, although both were cheaper than they had been in April and May. The price of sugar had risen during the war period by 68 per cent., and thus the heaviest advance took place in an article the supply of which was taken over by the Government.

THE PRICE OF VICTORY: A GRIM CAMERA-RECORD FROM THE ARGONNE.

The above wonderful, if painful, photograph shows soldiers of our French ally removing their dead and wounded comrades from the trenches in an interval between the terrible fighting in the Argonne. The men had a grim task to perform, but carried it through with reverence for those who had fallen never to fight again, and with an equally marked solicitude for the wounded.

AN EARLY STAGE IN THE MANUFACTURE OF A SHRAPNEL SHELL-CASE.
Scene at a munition factory. A red-hot bar is being cut by what is called a "hot saw." The operation is arduous and dangerous, the men having to work in intense heat and amid showers of sparks, for protection against which they wear special spectacles and breathing-tubes.

colliery proprietor, the middleman, and the working miner protested loudly and frequently that nothing whatever in the nature of excessive profits or wages was coming their way. Neither these assertions, however, nor even the figures which were presented to prove them, altered the fact that the householder was paying 10s. or so a ton more for his coal than he had previously done, and although he could not say for certain who received this, it left his pocket, and he felt tolerably sure that it was not lost by the wayside, but that it reached someone else in some form or other.

On February 25th a committee was appointed to inquire into the causes of the rise in the retail price of coal sold for domestic use, especially to the poorer classes of consumers in London and other centres, and this committee issued a report on April 1st. In this reference was made to the reduction in the output of coal due to the enlistment of miners, the lack of shipping, and other causes, and these striking sentences occurred :

"The total rise in the cost of production and distribution has been at most 3s. per ton, whereas the price to the consumer has risen above normal winter prices by an amount varying, according to the quality of the coal, from 7s. to 11s. per ton. The net result," says the report, "is that the sums recently paid and now being paid for coal by London consumers include a large surplus above ordinary profits, after making full allowance for the increased cost of production and distribution."

The report adds that the system of fixing prices which prevails in London "gives coal-owners and merchants a common interest in high prices," and is indefensible. The recommendations made for reducing the price of coal were that reserves in or near London should be accumulated, that exports to neutral countries should be restricted, that more shipping should be made available, and finally that "if prices do not shortly return to a reasonable level, the Government should consider a scheme for assuming control of the output of the collieries during the continuance of the war."

As a consequence of the agitation and of this report, a Bill was introduced into Parliament in July, and with one or two alterations this became law in August. It provided that at the pit's mouth the price of coal should be not more than 4s. a ton in excess of the price paid for similar qualities during the year which ended on June 30th, 1914. It **The price of coal regulated** did not say anything about the profits of the middlemen, but the coal merchants of London gave a voluntary undertaking that these would be limited. Owing to the many varieties of coal, the authorities thought that it would be impossible to fix maximum retail prices, and so the Bill represented the best they could do in the circumstances

Considerable, but still less serious, were the rises in the prices of tea and potatoes. Tea rose by 20 per cent., but this included the additional duty of 3d. a pound, and potatoes by 25 per cent. The retail price of butter increased by 19 per cent., and of milk by 11 per cent. These few facts about our principal articles of food will give us some idea of the general rise, but perhaps the clearest and best idea will be obtained by remembering that a year of war resulted in retail prices rising on the average by one-third. Bearing this in mind, perhaps, after all, the rise of 3s. a week in the wages of the worker was not such an extraordinary boon.

Before the end of 1914 the Government had abandoned its scheme of fixing maximum prices for food, although the Board of Trade continued to keep a watchful eye on the price of meat; but with regard to one article of almost equal importance to the worker—coal—there was a general feeling that something of this kind should be done. During the winter of 1914-15 the price of coal rose enormously in spite of the fact that the

Rear-Admiral Charles Lionel Vaughan-Lee, appointed Director of Air Services, September, 1915.

"Nosing" shells in one of the great factories of Vickers, Ltd.

Back from Flanders to the factory: Skilled men from the trenches making munitions.

Women at work that men might fight: Busy scene in one of the munitions workshops in the summer of 1915.

A practical test of its efficacy or otherwise would come in the winter of 1915-16.

Ample employment, good wages, but on the other hand high prices for food and other necessaries describe the condition of the worker during the first year of the Great War. This was not an ideal state of affairs, but it was much more like national prosperity than national adversity, and so we are justified in referring to the period as a prosperous one.

This prosperity was due mainly to the shortage of labour and to the enormous expenditure on the war. More than £3,000,000 a day was being spent by our Government, nearly all of it in this country, in addition to large sums by France and Russia, and most of this eventually took the form of wages.

The prosperity among the working classes was helped by the increase in the separation allowances, the result being that many married women were better off than they had ever been before. As one good woman is reported to have said : " Thirty bob a week, and my husband away ; why, it's paradise ! " The increase in the separation allowances, which came into force on March 1st, 1915, was due primarily to the will of the people that, cost what it might, the dependents of the men who had crossed the sea to fight their battles should be provided for by the State. This feeling was wholly honourable ; for often in the past this country had suffered disgrace by allowing the wives and children of heroes to pass their days in penury and want. During the year under review sad cases—far too many of them—due often to the incompetence or carelessness of well-paid officials, came to light, but these became fewer as public opinion made itself felt more and more. We realised, as we had never done before, that our soldiers and their dependents had the first claim, not indeed upon our charity, but upon the wealth and resources of the whole nation, and some of us were daring enough to think that they should be paid even if Cabinet Ministers and civil servants went short. Only one grave

Providing for soldiers' dependents abuse remained—that the widows of officers who had perished in the nation's service were left with the most miserable pittances, and even these pittances they could not claim as a right.

The committee appointed to consider the question of separation allowances recommended that the wife of a soldier should receive 12s. 6d. a week, with an additional sum for each child—5s. for the first, 3s. 6d. for the second, and 2s. for each succeeding one. Of this sum of 12s. 6d. the soldier provided 3s. 6d. from his pay. To the wife of a sailor 6s. a week was recommended, with extra amounts for each child, but this was conditional upon the sailor making her an allowance of 5s. a week. The suggestions of the committee were accepted by Parliament and, as

EFFECT OF A SUCCESSFUL FRENCH MINING OPERATION.
View of the interior of a strong German position which, after being mined by the French, was carried by a brilliant bayonet assault, occupied, and then consolidated.

already stated, they came into force on March 1st, 1915, before which date smaller sums had been paid.

It will be seen that in the aggregate these allowances amounted to a large sum. We were told, in July, 1915, that there were about 850,000 married men in the Army, so we cannot be far wrong if we assume that their wives were receiving something like £1,000,000 a week. This sum must not be overlooked in considering the question before us, for together with higher wages, it accounted for the prosperity enjoyed in working-class districts, a prosperity in which the drapers, butchers, and other shopkeepers shared. One heard many stories of clothing bought on an unusual scale by the poor, of a bigger demand for the better joints of meat, of purchases of furniture and articles of this kind by those who rarely, if ever, had indulged in such extravagances before, of longer trips to the seaside, and of other evidences of prosperity. It is a matter for whole-hearted congratulation that at last fortune came to these humble folk, and even if they did not lay out every penny to the best advantage, none envied them their prosperity; on the contrary, all hoped that it would endure.

We have hinted several times already at the growing shortage of labour, and in the spring of 1915 an unprecedented state of affairs arose. The lack of workers became so serious that the nation had, of necessity, to revise its ideas and to adopt itself quickly to entirely different and novel conditions. "Business as usual," a hitherto excellent motto, became suddenly a most injurious one, the exact reverse of what was wanted.

The shortage of labour did not come all at once. As far back as September, 1914, we were officially told that there was some shortage of agricultural labourers, owing to the number of men joining the Army, and month by month this became more pronounced. In November "some shortage of labour" was reported in connection with industry generally, and so it was in December and in the first two months of 1915.

In March and April the shortage became really serious.

As regards the position in April we were told that there was a general shortage of male labour, which was especially marked in engineering, coal-mining, and agriculture. In the clothing trades there was some scarcity of female labour. Farm labour was scarce in almost every district in Great Britain ; in some districts extra labourers were unobtainable. In May a scarcity of male labour was reported by nearly all trades, and this shortage was now extending to female and boy labour in many occupations. Those who distrust official statements such as these may be referred to the advertisement columns of the daily papers about this time. There, under the heading of "situations vacant," they will find pages and pages of requests for labour of almost every kind. Further proof, if such be required, can be obtained from one's own experience.

A national awakening

This shortage coincided with a national awakening about the war. In the spring of 1915 it was generally recognised that this country would have to do much more than it had done ; would have to take a bigger share in the struggle if the Allies were to emerge victorious therefrom. Not only must Great Britain send more men to the seat of war, but, more urgent still, she must turn herself into one great arsenal, and produce guns and munitions of all kinds on an enormous scale. Nothing less than this would avail. Then came the Munitions Act, the opening of Government factories throughout the land, and the necessity of obtaining a great deal of labour to man them.

DEMONIACAL PHASE OF THE MACHINE-MADE WAR : FRENCH SOLDIERS OPERATING A CAPTURED GERMAN "FLAMMENWERFER," OR FLAME-PROJECTOR.

Above is a closer view of the dense black smoke-clouds emitted by a "flammenwerfer." At Hooge in July, 1915, British troops suffered from this inhuman projection of the German scientific mind.

The problem, although big, was fairly simple. The labour force was strictly limited in number, and consequently it must be organised and put to the best possible use. The necessary industries—agriculture, coal-mining, munitions, and transport being perhaps the chief—must be provided with men and the unnecessary ones must go to the wall. The output of luxuries must be curtailed in order that the men engaged thereon might be transferred to more useful spheres, and in general everything must be made subservient to the great work of prosecuting the war to a successful conclusion.

The changed position and the special needs of the hour were well expressed in a circular issued by the Local Government Board on March 11th: " In view of the needs of recruiting and of the demand for labour for the manufacture of war materials and for the production and transport of the necessary supplies for the population, the Committee of Imperial Defence emphasise the importance of releasing male labour of high physical quality, as far as possible from other occupations, and of substituting, where necessary, men of more advanced years or, where the conditions allow, women workers."

This industrial revolution, for it was nothing less, took place in May, June, and July, 1915, the last three months of the period under review, but its results were only just becoming apparent when the war entered upon its second year.

As in August, 1914, the national duty at this crisis was the text of innumerable speeches, sermons, and articles, but the advice given was of a very different kind. Instead of retaining in their personal service all the labour they possibly could, people were urged to do with as little as possible. They were asked to release gardeners, gamekeepers, chauffeurs, and others for more useful duties, and not to order or use articles such as motor-cars for their own pleasure or convenience. Economy in food and **A new principle in public life** dress was advocated, primarily because it would help to relieve the strain on the labour market. An entirely new principle —economy in men—was introduced into public life. Whereas in the past the patriot had been the man who gave as much employment as possible, under the changed conditions, of 1915, he was the man who gave the least.

These exhortations were not without their effect. Expenditure on luxuries was decidedly curtailed ; there was much less travelling and far fewer persons were engaged in ministering to the pleasures of others. The closing of M. Worth's London branch was a sign that economies were being made at the expense of the dressmaker, and the returns of the fashionable drapers told the same story. Ladies were seen carrying home their own purchases, shops were closed at an earlier hour to enable fewer assistants to do the work, and in a thousand ways labour-saving was the order of the day.

To get more work of the necessary kind done, large calls were made upon the army of unemployed women. In shops, banks, warehouses, and offices thousands of women took places hitherto filled by men. Women were seen issuing and punching tickets at the railway-stations, carrying round letters, and even driving vans and motors. Police-women came into existence, and by the substitution of female for

male labour probably some hundreds of thousands of men were released either for fighting or for making munitions.

Men were also provided for the fighting-line or the factory by the employment of volunteer labour in various directions. Many men, generally those who were too old for active service, were able and willing to give a few hours a week to the public service. Early in the war some of them were employed as special constables, thus enabling many policemen to join or rejoin the Army, and later, bands of workers were organised to labour during their spare time in the munition factories. Similarly volunteers were collected for work in the harvest-field, and special arrangements were made by which soldiers were allowed to assist the farmers.

To economise labour to the greatest extent possible was the nation's need, and consequently instructions were issued with a view of preventing men engaged in the vital industries—agriculture, coal-mining, munitions, and the like—from en- **Lloyd George and** listing. This protected from further deple- **the drink lure** tion the limited number of skilled workers, an indispensable asset, and something was done to get more work out of them. In March, 1915, Mr. Lloyd George told the representatives of the trade unions that for the period of the war all their rules and regulations restricting output should be suspended, and something of the kind was accepted in the Munitions Act, which also empowered the authorities to punish men who stayed away from work without proper cause.

This problem—workmen absenting themselves from their work—was responsible for a certain reduction of output, and it was attributed largely to the lure of drink. Mr. Lloyd George was understood to favour very drastic measures to prevent this, but they were not accepted by his colleagues, and were condemned by the Nationalists and Labour Party. On March 29th he said that " nothing but root-and-branch methods will be of the slightest avail in dealing with this evil," and spoke somewhat rhetorically of our three enemies—" Germany, Austria, and drink "— drink being the greatest.

Something, however, was done. Under the Defence of the Realm Act a Board was set up, and to this was entrusted the duty of controlling the sale of intoxicating liquor in the munitions, transport, and camp areas. By proclamation it could prohibit wholly or in part the sale of drink in any area, and in July restrictions were applied to certain important districts in England. In these it was expedient, for the purpose of the successful prosecution of the war, that the sale and supply of intoxicating liquor should be controlled by the State. In Scotland two large areas were proclaimed. Therein the hours during which intoxicating liquor might be sold were restricted to four and a half days a week. These various measures were, in general, successful in increasing the output of munitions and providing more soldiers for the front, while at the same time the necessary industries were kept going. More work was obtained from the workers, and in many cases men worked to the limit of human endurance ; women entered gaily upon their novel duties, and children were exempted from attendance at school in order to work in the fields, a move which was carefully watched by the authorities and by Parliament.

BRITISH OFFICERS IN THE MAKING.
Members of the Inns of Court Officers Training Corps receiving instruction in the use of a device for teaching accurate rifle-shooting.

BRITISH CHARGE AT HOOGE: WHERE TRENCHES LOST THROUGH GERMAN "LIQUID FIRE" WERE RECAPTURED.

For several months in the summer of 1915, following a severe gas attack launched by the Germans on May 24th, very heavy fighting took place around the village and chateau of Hooge. On July 19th the British blew up a mine west of the chateau and then gained 150 yards of trenches. The Germans replied on July 30th by a heavy bombardment of our line and by an attack with "flame-projectors." This caused a temporary abandonment of some of our trenches, but was punished severely by a counter-attack, in which the Liverpool Scottish and other regiments fought with splendid dash and courage. Says an eye-witness of the British charge above depicted: "One thing was made clear on this day, and that is, that in the point of endurance and courage the German is absolutely no match for the Britisher."

CHAPTER LXXIX.

THE BATTLE OF RUE D'OUVERT AND STONY MOUNTAIN AND THE STRUGGLE ROUND HOOGE.

How the First British Army Helped the Tenth French Army—The Double Thrust Against the Bavarian Crown Prince—The Romance of Plug Street—Successes of Our Mining Parties—Duck's Bill and the Destruction of the Bomb Depots—The Great Bombardment of the La Bassée Triangle—The Heroism of the Ontario Regiment—Lumberjack as a Machine-Gun Base—Private Smith's Adventures in the Death Zone—Stony Mountain Fort Holds Up Our Advance—Germans Have the Advantage of Position and Profit by It—British and Canadian Troops Retire to their Own Lines—The Great Gas Cloud at Ypres—Magnificent Achievement of the 3rd Dragoon Guards—Flame-Projector Attack by the Germans—The Battle for Hooge and the Victory of the Crater.

FTER our First Army captured the salient at Festubert in May, 1915, the British forces made no further serious attempt to break the enemy's lines. For it was reckoned at the time that the German gunners were often able to fire four shells to our one. Moreover, the new concrete defences of the enemy had proved to be of exceeding strength. The German system of works extended for miles behind their first line of sand-bags, and on the old battlefield at Messines, where the London Scottish first went into action, there was an immense field fortress, quite equal in strength to the famous Labyrinth, which had checked the French rush towards Lens.

All that our two armies could do, while Mr. Lloyd George was speeding up the supplies of munitions, was to hold the Germans on their front, and prevent them from massing against the Tenth French Army, which was continuing the struggle for the approaches to Lens. Naturally our men could not keep the Germans occupied by remaining quiet themselves. Both the First Army, under Sir Douglas Haig, and the Second Army, under Sir Herbert Plumer, had to maintain a severe pressure against the German lines. That is to say, we had to attack, sometimes at any cost and without any hope of victory, in order to facilitate the progress of the French forces on our left. The most important

THE REVIVAL OF ARMOUR.
British soldier wearing a steel helmet for protection against shrapnel.

operation of this collaborative kind was that which took place along the La Bassée Canal east of Festubert on June 15th. The Tenth French Army was then making its great effort against the Bavarian army, in an action of desperate fierceness about Souchez and round the north-eastern end of the Labyrinth. General Foch had used something like four million shells in blasting his way into the German wedge north of Arras, and he still had sufficient ammunition in hand to throw three hundred thousand shells at Souchez in a single day. The strain he thus placed upon the army of the Crown Prince of Bavaria was enormous. The prince clamoured for reinforcements, and broke out into a very serious personal quarrel with the Crown Prince of Prussia, whom he accused of deflecting into the Argonne section of conflict large new German forces that were vitally required for the protection of Lens and Lille.

As we have already seen, in the chapter relating the deeds of the Tenth French Army, the Crown Prince of Bavaria succeeded at last in getting the reinforcements he wanted, and the German Staff detached eleven divisions from the reserves destined for the Russian front, and sent them to Souchez to stay the French advance. Our First British Army took an important part in inducing the German Staff to reinforce the Lille defences with nearly a quarter of a million more men, for while the French were penetrating the enemy's position

329

near Angres and Souchez, our troops made a sudden drive into the defences of the Westphalian Army Corps at La Bassée.

The action began with a feint at a forward movement by our Second Army in the Ypres section. Some of our cavalry, in an action that will later be described in detail, carried the manor-house of Hooge at the point of the bayonet in the first week of June. While the fighting continued in this northerly sector, the inhabitants of "Plug Street" aroused the Germans in front of them by a mine explosion, followed by a charge that ended in the capture of part of the German trenches. "Plug Street" was the soldiers' name for the Forest of Ploegsteert, stretching south of Messines and north-west of Lille, and forming in peace-time the shooting preserves of a rich brewer of Armentières. His last pheasants were shot by British troops for their Christmas dinner, by which time the forest

to break through to Calais the previous autumn. The defeated enemy raised his trenches only four hundred feet from the eastern boundary of the wood. When the ground dried in the late spring, our sappers drove a shaft beneath the zone of death and made a great dynamite mine under the German defences. This sort of work was going on all along the front. Both sides had men listening in advance saps for sounds of subterranean activity, and when mining operations were discovered, a counter-shaft was driven forward with fierce rapidity, and either a counter-mine was exploded, blowing up the enemy sappers, or the hostile tunnel was rushed suddenly from the counter-shaft, and a hand-to-hand conflict was waged in the dark, narrow underground passage.

Battles of the "cave-men"

Mining was certainly one of the revived forms of ancient warfare, in which our engineers won and held the mastery, for we had far more mining successes than the enemy. We first wiped the Germans out of Hill 60 by a mine, and we repeated this success at "Plug Street" and at La Bassée. The Germans in return drove five mines at our lines in the second week in June, but the explosions did not occur close enough to our defences to damage them. At "Plug Street," on the other hand, on June 6th, the German trenches were transformed into a great crater, from which our bombing parties worked along the enemy's front. From a similar crater at Hooge the work of keeping the Duke of Würtemberg's army occupied also proceeded, and at other points held by our Second Army the necessary pressure was maintained in the middle of June.

FRENCH SOLDIERS, WEARING ANTI-POISON GAS MASKS AND RESPIRATORS, AWAITING A THREATENED ATTACK UNDER COVER OF A GAS-CLOUD.

But all this was only a demonstration, and the real attack was delivered by the First Army. A mine was driven towards the German trenches between Rue d'Ouvert and Rue du Bois, near the La Bassée Canal ; but, unfortunately, there was water below the German position near the canal, and our sappers therefore could not tunnel right under the hostile trench. When they tried to do so, they were washed out. So they kept out the water with sand-bags and clay, and stacked against the enemy's trench an extraordinary amount

was dotted with graves, littered with shell-smashed trees, and transformed into a hidden city of cave-men. It was made famous by British and American war correspondents, who found it the most interesting sight on the British front, for under the surface of the ground there was a circle of caves with the signpost, "Piccadilly Circus," from which a Regent Street ran, with a Leicester Square close by. In June there was also a fragrant Kensington Gardens in "Plug Street," composed of wild flowers, which the soldiers had transplanted from the forest nooks. All the singing-birds fled, and only the bullets from the neighbouring German trenches sang amid the trees, after missing the top of our breastworks rising just beyond the edge of the wood.

Flowers and dynamite

There had been little fighting in "Plug Street" since the Germans were bayoneted out of it during their attempts

of dynamite to make sure that the German line would be blown up.

This, however, was one of the causes of the subsequent failure of our infantry attack ; for at Duck's Bill, as the position was called, there was a salient in our line, and the opposing trenches were extremely close to each other. To guard against accidents, our troops were withdrawn just before the mine was exploded, on the evening of June 16th. But so large and powerful was the mass of dynamite that it not only destroyed the German position, but buried one of our own magazines of hand-grenades, and killed several of our bomb-throwers. Then, about the same time, another depot of bombs close at hand was blown up by a German howitzer shell. The result was that our attacking troops found themselves perilously short of hand-grenades in the critical period of the battle. The troops consisted of a British division, supported by a Canadian brigade, and

An anti-poison gas mask of the more "fashionable" type.

A Highlander wearing a mask which makes him resemble the Sphinx.

French artillerymen masked while bombarding the enemy's lines.

A weird—but effective—form of anti-gas mask adopted by the French.

SOME EXAMPLES OF ANTI-POISON GAS MASKS WORN BY ALLIED TROOPS IN THE FIRING-LINE.

"NEMO ME IMPUNE LACESSIT": SCOTTISH RELIEFS EN ROUTE TO THE TRENCHES.

Sturdy Scots, light of foot and light of heart, on their way to the trenches to convince the Huns ahead that any estimate of Scotia's fighting power based on the cartoons of German "comic" papers was likely to be a very misleading one. For many months after the outbreak of war no German comic paper was regarded as complete if it did not contain a more or less gross insult to the wearers of the glengarry and the kilt.

among them were the 1st Canadian Ontario Regiment, commanded by Lieutenant-Colonel Hill, and the 2nd and 4th Canadian Battalions, the 3rd Canadian Toronto Regiment, and the East Yorkshires. The Ontario Regiment formed the spear-head of the advance. The Ontario men had to make a frontal attack on a fortified place in the enemy's lines known as Stony Mountain. A hundred and fifty ·yards to the south was another fortified place, known as Dorchester, and this also the regiment had to seize in order to secure the right flank of the British division.

Stony Mountain was the key to the entire position, for it dominated, with its machine-guns and its northern earthworks, the ground over which the British division was about to advance. It would, however, have been useless to begin by merely attacking the hostile fort by one Canadian regiment, for this would have given the enemy full means of concentrating against the single unit of the assault. So the British division on the left also swept out to the frontal attack on the enemy's lines north of Stony Mountain, at the moment when the Ontario regiment leapt down from its breastworks.

Our artillery had been working for days in preparation for the infantry advance. In sunlight and darkness the heavy guns and the howitzers had hurled their huge high-explosive shell on forts and buildings, while the lighter field-guns knocked down the wire entanglements and burst the shrapnel in clouds over the German communication trenches, fire trenches, and billets. Among the chief targets of our guns were the famous brickfields near La Bassée, extending in front of the shapeless ruins of Cuinchy village. The brick-stacks, behind which German machine-gun parties operated, appeared to belie the new opinions regarding the superiority of the mobile heavy howitzer over the fixed, old-fashioned forts, for the great brick-stacks—square, fortlike blocks of burnt clay, caked into solid masses—were wonderfully resistant. Shells that would shatter a strongly-built house scarcely made a dent in the red masses. Our soldiers could see a shell crash full

Shell-proof brick-stacks

upon a brick-stack, and watch the blaze of the explosion and the huge cloud of smoke, turning from black to dusky red by the flying brickdust, and feel the ground rock and quiver hundreds of yards behind our own forward trenches. Yet when the red billows of fume and dust rolled away, and the spectators expected to see the brick-stack scattered and strewn about the ground, it still emerged four-square and solid, undamaged except for a notch on its top or a shallow cavity on its face.

Nests of German machine-guns

But though the stacks still stood, the heavy shells dropping upon and behind them scattered the broken bricks and the splinters on the defending force, and shook their nerves and injured their bodies. Then, north of the brickfield, there were farms and other buildings, half ruined as a rule by previous bombardments, but still showing walls that were likely to be nests of German machine-guns.

Especially was this the case with all the houses behind the enemy's lines, for it was one of the main principles of the German defence system to hold the fire trench lightly with a small force, and rely upon a close chain of strongly-fortified machine-gun forts in the rear of the trenches to check any partially successful hostile infantry advance. Every building, therefore, immediately behind the German lines had been transformed into a fortress, with concreted underground chambers and telephonic communications with headquarters.

Our howitzers and heavy guns pounded day and night at all these *points d'appui* in the enemy's system of fortification, and at the same time the ordinary trenches and deep communicating ways were hammered with lyddite shells. Naturally, the German batteries did not rest idly under this incessant cannonade. They answered shot for shot, sometimes sending, indeed, three or four shells to our one, showing that the vast expenditure of ammunition by Mackensen's Phalanx on the Russian front and the terrific counter-bombardments against General Foch's army between Arras and Lens had not produced a shortage of shell in Germany. Our forward trenches were flailed by the answering gun fire, and the villages behind our front were severely shelled. Yet, as our troops were the attacking force, they retained many advantages. They could be brought up in comparative safety and installed in well-covered dug-outs, where they might eat and sleep without anxiety, knowing that due warning would be given of the intended assault.

The enemy, on the other hand, knew from the continual and violent bombardment that an attack was being prepared, but at what time and at what place it would be made there was no indication. Some of the troops had to be kept standing to arms; the others were frequently roused and kept in suspense by artfully contrived bursts of heavier fire from our artillery, machine-guns, and rifles. For the best part of a week this preliminary work went on. In the night flares blazed over the zone between the opposing fronts, and a ceaseless rain of shell, shrapnel, and bullets prevented the enemy from profiting by the interval of darkness to repair his gapped earthworks, and replace his uptorn barriers of wire.

Throughout the day of June 15th our cannonade increased in intensity; then, as the sun was wearing low, at six o'clock in the evening, the German gunners knew that their turn had at last come, for the outbreak of shell fire from our lines rose in a crescendo of

The heroes of Canada

fury that could mean only one thing. The 18-pounders secretly conveyed to our fire trenches joined in the nerve-racking tumult, and smote at short range the nearest German machine-gun redoubts and the remaining lengths of wire entanglement. The great mine near Stony Mountain was exploded, and as the German guns poured a shrieking stream of shrapnel over our first line and support trenches, in the hope of breaking down the coming attack, the British division leaped over their sand-bags, and, with the heroes of Canada on their right, passed through their own wire defences and charged across the open ground towards the hostile breastwork, which showed through the rolling smoke by the sparkle and spitting jets of fire that came from it.

The German shrapnel descended in clamorous squalls, and the waves of khaki were in places broken by the bursting fans of shot and by the clattering streams of bullets from the machine-gun posts. But, though the attack was held up in some parts, the charging lines drove over the German parapets in other spots, and the victorious troops, bombing and stabbing their way along the trenches, kept down the rifle and machine-gun fire, and enabled other companies of their comrades to race more safely across the intervening zone and strengthen the forces fighting in the enemy's line. In less than an hour the

North Lancashire valour

German fire trenches for the length of a mile were captured by our men, and some of our troops were working down the communicating ditches into the second line of the enemy's works.

Our gains stretched from Rue d'Ouvert to Rue du Bois; the Territorial battalion of the North Lancashires were among those who distinguished themselves by their valour. Meanwhile, the Canadian troops, to whom had been entrusted one of the hardest tasks, were assailing Stony Mountain and Dorchester redoubts on the southern sector.

The leading company of the Ontario Regiment rushed forward through the smoke and dust of the mine explosion only to meet a deadly fire from the machine-guns in the German forts. But the drive of the Ontarians was irresistible, and in a single charge they captured the Dorchester redoubt and the connecting trench. The decisive position of Stony Mountain, however, remained impregnable. Every infantryman who tried to reach it was shot down. Then a bombing party, under Lieutenant Gordon, sprang forward and valiantly essayed to get within throwing distance of the fortress. But the bombers were also shot down, Lieutenant Gordon himself falling wounded in the German fire trench, where he was killed by the enemy, with two of his men—the survivors of the bomb attack.

The second and third companies of the Ontarians swept out, suffering heavily from the fire from Stony Mountain as they crossed the open ground. Both companies broke into the enemy's second line, and at once began to enlarge their footing by sending out bombing parties on either side. At the same time the captured first German

ANIMATED SCENE IN A FRENCH VILLAGE: BRITISH SOLDIERS LEAVING THEIR BILLETS AND LINING UP TO AWAIT THE COMING OF THE MOTOR-BUSES THAT WERE TO TAKE THEM TO THE TRENCHES.

REALISTIC CAMERA-RECORD OF A SHELL BURSTING OVER A TRENCH.
This photograph, which was taken but thirty yards away from the explosion, gives a wonderfully graphic idea of a shell bursting over a trench. Of the three men who were caught, one threw himself down in an effort to avoid the flying splinters. The others were knocked over, perhaps never to rise again.

First of all he was buried in our mine explosion, with which the attack opened. He was sitting in the trench singing the " Old Folks at Home " when the combination of an earthquake and tornado occurred. He managed to dig himself out, but could not find his rifle ; so he festooned himself with bombs from the dead and wounded men about him, and crawled over the zone of fire to his comrades fighting in the German lines. Five times he went forward with bombs, and though his uniform was torn with shot, his person was uninjured. He was almost the only source of supply ; for other men who had tried to do the same thing were killed. As the bombs ran short, one Canadian thrower, weeping with rage, leaped on the parapet, though already wounded, and hurled bricks and stones at the Germans until they slew him.

The 3rd Canadian Battalion was sent forward to help the hard-pressed Ontario Regiment, but as a further supply of bombs was not immediately available, the reinforcement of men did not change the situation. Three non-commissioned officers, Sergeant Krantz, Sergeant Newell, and Sergeant-Major Cuddy, succeeded in fetching up a few hand-grenades after other volunteers had been put out of action ; but the new supply was still terribly insufficient, and when another

line was set in order by rebuilding the parapet on the front facing the enemy. When a machine-gun had been brought into the new position, an advance was made down the trench in the direction of Stony Mountain. The machine-gun crew led the way, and their stream of bullets was reinforced by volleys of grenades from a bombing party immediately behind them.

A magnificent gun-crew The gunners were magnificent. They had been reduced to two men, Lieutenant Campbell and Private Vincent, and among other things they had lost, through the man carrying it being killed, the base of their machine-gun. But Private Vincent, an Ontario lumberjack, was a genius at makeshifts. He offered his broad back as a machine-gun base, and the Maxim was employed in this extraordinary way, until the German bombers got into the trench and wounded Lieutenant Campbell. But even with the enemy upon him, the lumberjack would not lose his gun. It was too hot to handle, but by abandoning the tripod, Vincent managed to drag it to safety, while his lieutenant crawled out of the German trench and was carried away in a dying condition.

It was at this time that the succession of accidents to the magazines of bombs began to tell against the fine, heroic effort of the men of Ontario ; for, as night fell, the Germans massed bombing parties down every communication trench, while their machine-guns and riflemen swept with a continual fierce fire their lost lines and the open space leading to our lines. Volunteer after volunteer went back to get bombs for the Canadians, but they were shot either going or coming. Exceptionally lucky was Private Smith, a minister's son, of Southampton, Ontario.

band of volunteers was shot down, the expeditions for bombs failed with them. The Ontario Regiment had lost nearly all its officers, and at half-past nine at night a strong accumulation of hostile forces compelled the Canadians to evacuate all the ground they had won. The retirement was carried out deliberately, but the enemy used an abundance of bombs and kept up a heavy machine-gun and rifle fire, and the men of Ontario and their comrades suffered heavily. Out of twenty-three officers who went into action only three returned unhurt.

Owing to the strength of the German position at Stony Mountain, and the extraordinary number of machine-gun posts along the line northward, the British division had also been unable to advance. The Canadians had held on, hoping that the attacking force on their left would clear the way for them. But Stony Mountain stood between the British and the Canadians, and the waves of assault first broke against it, and then, as the German army massed around the fort for the counter-attack, receded for the length of a mile across the open space. **Hand-to-hand struggle at night**

The British-Canadian forward line was gradually forced back in a bitter hand-to-hand nocturnal struggle. The fighting front was like a great firework display. Verey pistol lights—" very lights " our men usually called them —magnesium flares, and star-shells illumined the battlefield with blinding bursts of white radiance. The hand-grenades winked and sparkled in bright orange-red patches. Down the breastworks were the jetting flames of machine-guns and rifles, and overhead the screaming shells flowered in deadly splendour upon the sombre midsummer night sky.

In the changing splashes of light and shifting breadths of shadow it was impossible to follow the fortunes of the fight. But on one particular portion of the front the din suddenly swelled into an overwhelming volume of sound. The Germans were concentrating howitzers, guns, Maxims, rifles, and hand-bombs on a small section of their lost first line, and they won it back. Some of our troops said that their trench was suddenly wiped out by a rain of bombs, leaving only a handful of men to meet the German rush. Other Territorials maintained that the position could have been held. Naturally, in a confused, nocturnal conflict of this kind, the opinion of the individual fighter is apt to be mistaken ; but it seems to be well founded that the line was held to the limit of endurance, and overborne at last by the Germans, owing mainly to their ampler supply of hand-grenades.

In turn, this superiority in the quantity of hand-grenades was due largely to the advantages under which the Germans fought. Their bombing parties could be continually fed with grenades through their safe, deep, communicating trenches. The British and Canadian bomb supplies, on the other hand, had to be brought across the open zone of fire between the two fronts ; and as the artillery on both sides was furiously active, the German gunners and machine-gun crews had much the easier task in stopping our bomb supplies. It is these technical conditions of a struggle which, owing to the precision, range, and power of modern weapons, make for victory more than the most heroic personal bravery often does. The destruction of two of our bomb depots in our fire trench was another contributing factor in the failure to check the enemy's counter-attack.

The enemy bomb supplies

The difference in the positions of the counter-attacking Germans and the hard-pressed British and Canadian forces was clearly appreciated at last by the enemy ; for, having pushed our troops out of their own lines, the Germans tried to follow up by a victory the check they had delivered. Flushed with a success due to local conditions, they clambered over their recovered parapets and attempted in turn to storm our first line. Thereby the advantage of position fell to us. Our troops had then behind them a network of familiar lines, with communicating trenches, along which supplies and reserves could proceed, secure from any missiles except a chance heavy high-explosive shell or a very luckily-placed shrapnel burst. It was the turn of the foe to face artillery, machine-gun, and rifle fire in the open ground, with our observation officers directing the guns on him by telephone messages. Our heavy pieces began again to pound the enemy's first lines with lyddite, while our light guns swept the zone between the opposing fronts with storms of shrapnel. All the German attacks failed with heavy losses, and as dawn came the movements against our line ceased.

Over-confidence well punished

When the morning mist cleared away, the gunners on both sides resumed the cannonade, each aiming at the trenches of the hostile infantry. Our fire in the afternoon (June 16th) unexpectedly rose into a tremendous volume, for Sir Douglas Haig apparently was not yet willing to submit to a check. He had sent out at Rue d'Ouvert another charging line, including the Irish Liverpools and the Territorials, and selecting a smaller sector for their attack, rushed the German lines through a tempest of shells. But the footing they won was only a precarious one, and the German gunners knocked their own lost trench to pieces

A CRATER IN FLANDERS: EXAMPLE OF THE DEVASTATING FORCE OF A HIGH-POWER SHELL.
The fighting area of Flanders was scarred with huge craters such as that shown above, the effect of shells fired from heavy German guns and known as "Jack Johnsons" and "Black Marias." When our photograph was taken the cavity had been filled with rain-water.

by heavy shells and made the position untenable. Again, on June 18th, the 2nd Gordon Highlanders and other Scottish battalions charged at the Rue d'Ouvert position, only to be driven back to their own lines.

There seemed nothing that made for any definite success in all these three furious assaults on June 15th, 16th, and 18th. But though our suffering divisions and their comrades from Canada may not fully have known it at the time, each man of them was a collaborator in victory. They helped to win the French successes at Angres, Souchez, and the Labyrinth, which were announced just when our First Army became again quiescent in its own lines.

Our thrust at Rue d'Ouvert, north of La Bassée, weakened the resistance of the army of the Crown Prince of Bavaria to the thrust simultaneously delivered by the French troops near Angres, south of La Bassée. Between the two thrusting forces of the First British Army and the Tenth French Army, Prince Rupert was reduced to partial impotence. He had to give way either north or south of La Bassée, and as in his judgment it was more important to hold back the British army, which was already periously close to Lille, he threw his reserves against us, while yielding ground to our French comrades. Thus our local check—it cannot be called a defeat—was fully compensated, from the general standpoint of the Allies, by the victory of the French troops against the common foe.

It had been fairly clear since the action at Rouges Bancs on May 9th that our forces were incapable of breaking the German front with the guns and shells we then possessed. General Foch also had more gradually come to the conclusion that the Tenth French Army, which had quite as large a number of shells as Mackensen's Phalanx used in breaking through the lines of the Third Russian Army on the Dunajec, could not equal this achievement on the Lens front against the army of the Bavarian

Battlefield and workshop

Crown Prince. The German defences were too strongly constructed, too skilfully organised, and backed by too powerful an artillery to be broken by one sudden, brief, violent blow. Heavy pieces of siege ordnance were needed by the thousand, and melinite shells by tens of millions, in order to carry out completely the scheme of attack first foreshadowed in the spring of 1915 at Les Eparges and Neuve Chapelle. A decisive victory of liberation for Belgium and North-Eastern France was clearly seen to be a problem of speeding up the manufacture of an enormous number of gigantic howitzers and huge high-explosive shells. In factories only were great modern victories organised. The battlefield was merely an annex to the workshop and the chemical works.

The next important action on the British front, after the Battle of Rue d'Ouvert, was indicative of the progress of German chemistry rather than of the warlike qualities of the later formations of German troops. The affair occurred round the ruined manor-house of Hooge, lying about three miles east of Ypres, on the road to Menin. Hooge had been the headquarters of Sir John French and Sir Douglas Haig in the first Battle of Ypres, and it was from the manor-house that Sir John had watched our line break at Gheluvelt, opening the path to Calais to the Germans, which had, however, been closed again by the glorious heroism of the Worcesters. In the spring of 1915 Hooge

Hooge and the Ypres defences

again became the critical point in the Ypres defences, for after the great chemical experiment with poison gas in April, the Germans had been able to advance to the manor-house, using the Menin road for a strong, persistent movement, which continually threatened to capture at last the rubbish-heap which had been Ypres.

The Duke of Würtemberg, commanding the attacking forces, had apparently become convinced, after his poison-gas victory in April, that chemical methods of making war were the most successful. His crescent of lines about Ypres, running from a point near Pilkem in the north to a point near Hill 60 in the south, remained for months a field of chemical experiments. The grass was turned a ghastly yellow by the bleaching effects of the chlorine gas, while, as some compensation, the trenches were rendered more sanitary by the destruction of insect pests in the rolling, greenish torture fumes. Hurricane fire with poison-gas shells was a great specialty of the Würtemberg command; but the duke used both the cloud and the asphyxiating bombardment so frequently that our soldiers were compelled to perfect themselves in respirator drill, in spite of their natural British tendency to a happy-go-lucky attitude in regard to the means of defeating the scientific Hun.

When our forward trenches were organised for gas attacks, with a respirator handy for every man, and with officers watching day and night for the familiar crawling, green mist, the German commander lost for the time all power to advance. His troops were very fiercely handled, after being caught twice unawares behind a gas cloud by our grimly masked and quite unasphyxiated Second Army; for when it came to a hand-to-hand struggle between the German, who was still half afraid of being stifled by his own gas, and the scientifically protected Briton who was mad with anger by reason of the memories of his gas-tortured comrades, there was not much chance of escape for the German. Our men, besides, had the advantage of surprise.

WITH THE FRENCH ARMY: WOUNDED SOLDIER BEING HELPED BY HIS COMRADES BEHIND THE FIRING-LINE.

WAR "SERVICE" OF LONDON MOTOR-'BUSES: BRITISH SOLDIERS EN ROUTE TO THE LINES.

The effect of the asphyxiating shell was harder to dodge than the large, slow, creeping, greenish cloud, for the men were often surprised by the gun-propelled burst of poison fumes before they could put on their respirators. Hill 60 was at last lost in the first week in May by a bombardment of poison shells, swiftly followed by an attack on three sides of the wedge-like mound by German bombing parties. Our troops had to retire to a support trench just below the hill, leaving the German artillery officers the advantage of occupying the jagged crest on the mound as an observation station, from which the German batteries behind the Zandvoord ridge were directed by telephone.

Germans retake Hill 60

Sir Herbert Plumer, it was apparent, decided that Hill 60, which he had first won very cheaply by the easy method of mining through the loose earth of the mound, was not worth recovering yet again by a stubborn effort. It seemed to him that the manor-house and hamlet of Hooge was a more important point of resistance for the army of defence. So from the first week in May to the middle of August Hooge became the principal arena of the contending force. There was no decisive character in the contest. When the British army lost Hooge it did not think of retreating ; neither did the German army prepare to withdraw for a mile or so when its foremost troops were thrown out of the village.

The affair was mainly a trial of strength, and the British commander in particular only planned an attack on Hooge when he wished to prevent his opponent from sending reinforcements to other sections of the front, especially to the army of the Crown Prince of Bavaria.

Sometimes Sir Herbert Plumer received an order from General Headquarters to keep the enemy in front of him fully extended, and could not use Hooge for this purpose, because Hooge was in our possession. In these cases, an attack was made at Pilkem, which was another sector where a series of small gains of grounds were won, with tactical advantage that made the hostile commander eager to counterattack in order to recover the position.

It would be idle, therefore, to pretend that the action at Hooge was of any great importance. In a Continental history of the war both the affairs at Rue d'Ouvert and the contest at Hooge would be mentioned in a couple of lines or a short paragraph. But to us there is a peculiar historic importance in these small local battles,

WAITING FOR "JACK JOHNSONS."
Entrance to a British officers' dug-out in the trenches.

in that they marked the entry into the field of conflict of our national armies. Our splendid professional troops had almost completed their great work of holding the road to Calais until the Territorials had completed their training and the new formations were ready for the fray. As summer came on, Sir John French began to test more severely the fresh troops, who gathered in increasing numbers in our lines.

Like the region round Festubert, Hooge was one of the highly interesting scenes of the gradual change of character in our expanding forces. The finest veterans of the Regular Army fought beside Kitchener's men and the Territorials, and taught the new troops the value of team-work, and handed down to them the noble traditions of the British profession of arms. We shall be able to see the commanding officer playing first for safety in a time of crisis, by using the old first-line battalions as a spear-head, and then we shall watch him acquire more confidence in the new formations, when they have been blooded under his eyes, and launch them at last out to attack in full security that they will carry on. At Hooge in particular there was a continual change of garrison. On May 8th, 1915, the most famous of the new Canadian regiments, Princess Patricia's hard-bitten fighting men, held the chateau and the village. They were succeeded by the 9th Lancers, the 15th Hussars, and the 2nd Camerons, who recovered the position by a splendid charge which has already been described. The cavalry held the lines amid the ruins until May 24th, when the Duke of Würtemberg tried his last and greatest experiment with poison gas.

Poison-gas cloud five miles long

It was a brilliant spring day, with the heat tempered by a light breeze that veered round in the morning towards the north. The enemy had placed an enormous number of gas cylinders opposite our front from Hooge to St. Julien, and during a violent bombardment with gas shells the poisonous cylinders were opened, and a gigantic cloud was sent along the wind against our lines. The cloud was five miles long and forty feet high in places ; and it continued to pour over our trenches from three to seven o'clock in the May morning. Then behind the cloud three columns of German infantry swept out to attack, under cover of a heavy fire from all their guns. Our line was broken at Hooge and north of Wieltje. But on the greater part of the front our troops held their ground, and a series of counter-attacks enabled us to recover most of our fire trenches. At Hooge, however, the headquarters of the 9th Lancers had been badly gassed, and though Captain Reynolds and Lieutenant Maclaine of Lochbuie—the latter leading a squadron of the 15th Hussars—helped to save the general situation, we lost the chateau and other useful buildings.

The 3rd Dragoon Guards were given the task of avenging the poisoned Lancers and Hussars and recovering the position. The Dragoons took over our second line
Gallantry of the of trenches on May 29th, their position
3rd Dragoons lying south of the Menin road, at some distance from the heap of jumbled brickwork representing what had been the picturesque Flemish manor-house. The German gunners apparently were aware of what was intended, for the next day they began a fierce and intense bombardment of our trenches, which they pounded for hours with high-explosive shell, while the German infantry swept the parapets with machine-gun fire and rifle volleys. But though their trenches were blown in, the Dragoons held on until night fell ; and then, instead of retiring under the continued bombardment, one company charged at the manor-house just before dawn on May 31st, and with Lieutenant Katanakis leading them, the men bayoneted the Germans out of the ruins and the

stables. The Germans then turned every available gun on Hooge, completely battered the village into a rubbish-heap, and knocked what remained of the brickwork of the manor-house into rubble. Lieutenant Katanakis had to withdraw from the manor-house, but he held on close by with his men, and occupied the position again in the evening. All the next day the German gunners furiously continued their work of destruction ; but only one small body of hostile infantry tried to reach the ruins where our men had dug themselves in.

The Germans were killed at fifty yards from our position, and then the angry German commander put out all his power to break the gallant Dragoons. All day long on June 2nd our dug-outs, trenches, and lines of communication around Hooge were swept by a hurricane of fire from the massed German howitzers and guns ; at times the shells came over at the rate of twenty to the minute. Under cover of this storm of death a force of Germans, dressed in khaki uniforms taken from our dead, charged from the Bellewaarde Lake. They were allowed to reach the manor-house, but there one of our batteries opened on them. They tried to escape into the open, only to be caught by our concealed machine-guns. Back they went into the ruins, and out at the other side. But we had machine-guns there also, and after circling round the trap three times the Germans perished. Only about five of them managed to crawl away, and each of them in all probability was wounded. In the afternoon other attacks were made, but none got within eighty yards of our trenches. The action was one of the finest achievements of the war ; and the 3rd Dragoon Guards, on being relieved the next day, were **The enemy caught** commended by a special order for **in a trap** their magnificent courage and tenacity.

Among the relieving troops were some of our finest regular infantry, including the 1st Northumberland Fusiliers, the 1st Wiltshires, the 1st Lincolnshires, the 3rd Worcesters, with the Royal Fusiliers, the Royal Scots Fusiliers, and a fine body of Territorials—the Liverpool

THE RALLY OF INDIA TO THE CALL OF THE BRITISH RAJ: REGIMENT OF INDIAN CAVALRY ON THE MARCH IN NORTHERN FRANCE.
Above : Another view of the British motor-'bus service to the Front : A string of omnibuses carrying soldiers to man the trenches in Flanders.

BATTERY OF TRENCH MORTARS.
Interesting view taken on the French front.

Scottish. The number and quality of the men indicated that something was afoot. On June 16th our artillery was, in turn, concentrated round Hooge, and after a long and heavy bombardment our troops leaped out and stormed a thousand yards of the enemy's fire trenches round the manor-house, and penetrated at points into the German second line. The work was done with the bayonet and the bomb; and it was our bombing parties that were mainly responsible for the great success. For instance, three men of the Liverpool Scottish—Corporal Smith, Corporal Bartlett, and Private Short—attacked a trench held by thirty Germans with a machine-gun. They killed all the occupants, captured the gun, and used it in repelling a counter-attack. The German artillery then tried to recover the lost position by smashing it up with high-explosive shell, so that their infantry could safely come out to pick up the fragments. For twenty-four hours the great shells came tumbling into the earthworks, but though our men had to retire from the second German line, they hung on to the thousand yards of fire trench, and beat back the German infantry. It was a notable example of the quality of British troops in a position calling for doggedness and tenacity.

Three heroic Liverpool Scots

After a prolonged effort the German commander apparently resigned himself to defeat, and the fighting round Ypres shifted to Pilkem, where our troops in the first week of July captured two hundred yards of trench, fourscore prisoners, and three trench mortars. But on July 20th Hooge again became the chief centre of interest, as our engineers exploded a great mine to the west of the manor-house, forming a crater some fifty feet deep and a hundred and fifty feet wide, in which our men established themselves. The Germans tried to capture the crater the following day by a bomb attack, but the bombing parties were shot down. Again, on July 24th, our men shattered another charge by a bombing party. It was then that the Duke of Würtemberg brought his last chemical device into play—the flame-projector. The weapon consisted of a portable tank, filled with inflammable coal-tar material, which was pumped through a nozzle, at the end of which was a lighting device. By means of the pump the flame-jet could be thrown for a distance

A FRENCH HERCULES.
Well-known French boxer providing his comrades with a display of physical strength.

of about forty yards. A large number of these horrible instruments were brought into the forward German trenches on July 30th. Then the German artillery resumed its hurricane fire, using flame shells filled with the coal-tar preparation, as well as high-explosive shell. When the bombardment was most intense the strange, unexpected, unanswerable torrents of flame from the projectors swept our line. Our burning, tortured troops were helpless against such a form of attack. All they could do was to get out of range of the flame-jets, and in this way we lost our trenches by the crater and the chateau and the village.

The German flame-projector

339

THE SWELLING KHAKI LINE : FRENCH PEASANT WOMEN WATCHING THE EVER-INCREASING STREAM OF BRITISH TROOPS MOVING TOWARDS THE SCENE OF CONFLICT.

The village lines were, however, recovered in a counter-attack by our infuriated troops, and night fell with the enemy holding only about five hundred yards of our trenches.

No British soldier was likely to rest under even a small success won by the enemy by means of so horrible a weapon as the flame-projector. It was, moreover, necessary to prove to the German infantryman, who already admired, in spite of himself, the superior courage of the British soldier, that flame-projectors were as useless as gas-cylinders in the decisive phase of the struggle. But the task before our troops was a very difficult one. It was no question of leaping out of our trenches and hurling ourselves over some fifty yards of ground into the enemy's lines. We had retired so far in the flame attack that our troops had now to charge over open ground for more than five hundred yards, going uphill most of the way, before they could come to grips with an enemy who knew by the preliminary bombardment what was coming. There was ample space for the Germans to wipe out our advancing lines by shrapnel and machine-gun fire, if ordinary tactics had been employed in the final action at Hooge. Happily some of our guns had gone south to Carency at the end of May to co-operate in the artillery preparations for the Souchez attack. Our gunners had been extremely pleased to find that the French gunners used absolutely rigorous tactics in supporting their infantry advances. Instead of ceasing fire when their infantry closed on the enemy trench, the French gunners continued to place their shells a few yards in front of their own men. The result was that a few Frenchmen were killed by French shells in some cases.

Rigorous artillery tactics

But this accidental loss of life was repaid a hundredfold when the infantry got to work in the German lines. We had lost men at Neuve Chapelle from our own shells, and some of our gunners had, as already explained, taken to leaving a wider interval between our line of shell fire and our moving line of advancing infantry. But any interval was likely to be disastrous at Hooge, and before the action it was carefully explained to the infantry that, by keeping our artillery fire extremely close against the charging line, thousands of lives would be saved at the cost of a few accidents. The men not only grasped the point, but courageously welcomed a closer use of shell fire, and on the morning of August 9th the bombardment opened. It was close on dawn when our massed guns broke out into one of those indescribable, long-throated roars of thunder that tell both friend and foe an infantry attack impends. Sir Herbert Plumer had spent a week in concentrating so extraordinary a number of howitzers and guns that the German batteries were completely overpowered. And as the enemy possessed, in addition to his artillery corps, a large part of the siege train used at Antwerp, which had recently been strengthened by big naval guns and gigantic howitzers removed from the Belgian coast to the ridges around Ypres, it will be seen that our concentration of artillery must indeed have been enormous in order to outclass the enemy's ordnance.

German batteries overpowered

As a matter of fact, the ridge at Hooge, being barely three miles from Ypres, had to be retaken by us, otherwise Ypres itself was in danger of being lost. The German commander therefore expected to be attacked, and bent all his energies to the work of preparing a definite repulse to our forces. But our preparations, despite all the talk about German efficiency in warlike organisation, were of a brutally overwhelming character. On this occasion it was the British war-machine that knocked the enemy off his feet, without giving him a chance of maintaining a man-to-man struggle. After three-quarters of an hour of intense bombardment our troops advanced under our own shell fire in a deliberate and heroic act of self-sacrifice.

for which they were rewarded when they reached the German trenches. The barbed-wire was completely blown to pieces and the parapet was breached in many places. Scarcely had our last shell exploded, amid the ruins of the manor-house and in the crater formed by our great mine, when our bombing parties clambered through the gaps in the sand-bags. They surprised the Germans as these were still sheltering in their dug-outs waiting for the bombardment to cease. At the same time our machine-guns were rushed up to the edge of the crater, so that when the Germans gave over fighting and tried to escape

opened upon us with heavy shells and continued firing for the rest of the day, the ridge was sufficiently protected to enable it to be held. Only one small bit of trench on the low ground had to be left undefended. On all the high ground our grip only tightened under the enemy's fire.

The men would not give up the position they had won, even when the order came to do so. It may be, as they always maintained, that the enemy's fire was so heavy that the messenger was killed. The most extra- **British confidence restored** ordinary case was that of Lance-Corporal Smith and his twenty-four men. He occupied the Hooge stables when it was thought for a day that the buildings were empty. It was not until the corporal sent down for more bombs that the colonel of the relieving regiment guessed there was anyone waiting for him in the stables. Hooge was one of the most helpful episodes in the tremendous story of Ypres. It fully restored the confidence of our gunners and the confidence of our infantry in their backing of artillery.

French's "contemptible little army" was at last getting on a level of both men and equipment with the forces opposed to it. Indeed, in regard both to troops

USEFUL ON SEA OR LAND.
Naval gun on a mounting designed for use on an armoured motor-car.

they were enfiladed by streams of bullets. As a matter of fact, the Germans had little stomach for the fight, so badly had they been shaken by our shell fire, and about a hundred of them gave themselves up in the crater. The sharpest fight of all was in the trenches near the stables, where some three hundred figures in field-grey were bayoneted before their lines were captured. In other places our angry men, anxious to take vengeance upon the foe who used poison gas and flame-projectors, chased the Germans about with the bayonet, crying, with imploring voices: "Stand, and give us the chance of a fight!"

In all, some three thousand Germans were killed, owing to

Three thousand Germans killed

THE DEFENCE OF PARIS AGAINST ENEMY AIRCRAFT.
Anti-aircraft gun and its crew. A view taken on high ground on the outskirts of the French capital.

the fact that our attack had taken place at the moment when the enemy had been in the act of changing the units in the trenches. We thus caught two trench-garrison forces between our shell fire and our hand-bombs. Then, before the German batteries could resort to their usual method of trying to destroy their lost position, a large body of our engineers came up with reinforcements, each man carrying either ammunition or sand-bags, shovels or wire. We had nearly six hours in which to consolidate our position, so that when at half-past nine in the morning the Germans

and guns, the British Expeditionary Force began, in the summer of 1915, to grow so formidable that only the magnificent defences of the Germans protected them from defeat. The enemy had about two million men on the western front, which was half a million less than the forces with which he had made his gigantic movement of invasion in the summer of 1914. The German Staff, having all their strength extended against Russia, tried to supply the place of the missing troops in the west by augmenting the machine-guns and the heavy howitzers there, and by using asphyxiating shells in increasing quantities. But the Allies also strenuously increased their howitzer batteries and their accumulations of shells.

BELGIUM'S HERO KING IN KHAKI: KING ALBERT VISITING THE FRENCH FORCES.

In August, 1915, as a return visit to that paid earlier by President Poincaré to the Belgian Army, King Albert spent two days with the French Army. On the occasion of the presentation of colours to new regiments, the French President referred in glowing terms to his Royal guest. "The French Army," he said, "is appreciative and proud of the honour paid to it by the noble sovereign who has given the world an example of inflexible uprightness, and in whom soldierly valour and civic courage are allied. He offers you here the living image of the virtue which those colours ought always to keep constantly before your eyes." Our photograph shows King Albert, with whom are General Joffre and M. Millerand (French Minister of War), about to decorate some French officers. The group includes a number of foreign attachés who witnessed the memorable ceremony. On returning to Flanders King Albert sent the following message to President Poincaré: "The spirit and morale of your brave soldiers filled me with admiration."

CHAPTER LXXX.

THE INCOMPARABLE ACHIEVEMENT OF THE BELGIAN ARMY.

32,000 Belgian Infantrymen left out of 110,000—The Belgian Artillery Worn Out by Constant Use—Belgians Win at last With Odds of Five to One Against Them—The Secret Strategy of the Belgian Staff—Six Weeks' Struggle to Unite With French and British Forces—Ghent and not Antwerp the Critical Point in the First Belgian Campaign—The Real Danger to Belgium was the Advance of the Crown Prince of Bavaria on Lille—King Albert Appeals to Lord Kitchener for Help—Our 7th Division Arrives Too Late at Ghent—Magnificent Rear-Guard Action by the British Troops—How the Victory on the Yser Tempered the Belgian People to the Resilience of Steel—Extraordinary Energy of Reconstruction Displayed by King Albert—The Belgian Army Intervenes in the Second Battle of Ypres—The Secret of the Chateau of Vicogne.

LATE in the summer of 1915 the General Staff of the Belgian Army at last published a mass of detailed information, from which, for the first time, the achievement of Belgium could clearly be appreciated. The mere figures given by the Belgian Staff were gloriously eloquent. Their Army had originally consisted of 93,000 infantrymen, with 102 machine-guns, and 324 field-guns, mainly of 3 in. calibre. By the middle of September, 1914, 18,500 volunteers had received sufficient training of a very hasty kind to enable them to be thrown into the fighting-line. They brought the total number of Belgian bayonets up to about 110,000. Towards the close of the Battle of the Yser there remained only 32,000 Belgian infantrymen, with about a hundred 3 in. guns, for which there was scarcely any ammunition. The other guns were not lost, but their rifling was worn out by incessant firing. Even the remaining hundred guns that were still in action were only capable at the most of firing from half a dozen to a dozen shells each. Moreover, the larger part of the survivors of the Belgian infantrymen at the time had fought and slept in the river trenches for two weeks or more without any kind of relief, and exposed to an incessant bombardment of high-explosive shell from three hundred and fifty German guns and howitzers, strengthened by a large part of the German siege train from Antwerp, composed of

AT AN OLD FRENCH CHATEAU.
The King of the Belgians and the French President leaving a chateau at which déjeuner was served, on the occasion of King Albert's visit to the French lines in August, 1915.

8, 11, and 12 in. howitzers. The opposing German forces numbered 150,000 men, so that they had the odds of almost five to one against the Belgians. Yet the enemy was beaten—beaten in so decisive a manner that, with the help of a reinforcement of French troops, the Belgian Army on the Yser won a year's time in which to reorganise and increase its strength.

It may be doubted whether, from a military point of view, there is anything in the history of the Great War to compare with the deeds of the little Belgian Army; for even the Serbian troops, whose successes in saving their country from repeated invasion were marked by extraordinary heroism, were much more numerous, more experienced in war, and more favoured by the mountainous nature of their country. Belgium had only six divisions of infantry, and one division of cavalry, the latter consisting of 2,500 horsemen and 450 cyclists. The troops, moreover, were arranged without regard to strategy on a purely neutral system; for, with exquisite care for his nation's honour, King Albert placed one division near the coast to repel any British violation of his territory; there were two divisions near Namur, to check any French attempt at invasion; and holding two divisions in reserve near Antwerp, the King sent only his third division towards Liège to withstand the German attack. It may have been quixotic in the circumstances to have adopted so honourably neutral

AN UNOFFICIAL VISITOR.
This photograph of an English Red
Cross worker visiting the Belgian
trenches affords a happy relief from
the customary camera-records of that
area.

an attitude of defence. On
the other hand, the idealism
which inspired King Albert
was based largely upon the
consideration of the future
position of his country at the
end of the war. Belgium
had to show herself ready to
defend her neutrality at
every point, without any
regard to alliances that might
be formed in the course of
the conflict. As her state of
neutrality had been guaranteed by many of the Great
Powers, she had to wait for
a blow to be struck at her
by one of her guarantors,
before calling on any other guarantor to assist in her defence.

Thus it came about that, when a host of three hundred
thousand Germans advanced on Liège on August 4th, 1914,
there was only a single Belgian division ready to oppose
them. The Belgian force consisted of the 3rd Division,
composed of 18,500 infantrymen and 500 cavalrymen, with
60 field-guns and 24 machine-guns. Against this single
division there came seven German army
corps with two cavalry divisions. Yet this
enormous mass of first-line troops, operating with heavy artillery, had officially to
acknowledge a loss of 42,712 men in the struggle in which
it at last broke the lines of the Belgian division holding
the open spaces between the Liège forts. As a matter of
fact, the 3rd Division, as is now made clear by the Staff
reports, only fought for two days on a front of about
thirty miles along the Meuse between the Dutch frontier
and Liège. The battle opened on August 4th, and on
August 6th the 3rd Division withdrew westward, reaching
the line of the River Gette on August 8th. The Belgian
Staff, as it afterwards clearly explained, founded its
strategy entirely upon the following principles :

1. If the Belgian Army has before it only, equal enemy
forces :

(a) The enemy must be attacked at the most favourable

**Strategy of the
Belgian Staff**

moment when his positions are too much extended, or when
he is temporarily weakened.

2. When the Army is faced by very superior hostile
forces :

(b) It must maintain itself in as forward a position as
possible, on good defensive sites, barring the road to the
invader in such a way as to protect the larger part of the
country.

(c) When thus placed as an advanced guard for the
French and British forces, the Belgian Army must wait
on its positions, so that its union with these forces can be
brought about.

(d) If this union cannot be made at the time when the
enemy masses arrive, the Belgian
Army must not be exposed to certain
destruction, leading necessarily to the
total loss of territory.

**Plans to avoid
envelopment**

(e) Therefore, the Belgian Army, when alone, must avoid
a pitched battle with the enemy masses, and escape from
any enveloping movement.

(f) The Belgian Army, therefore, must always manœuvre
so as to hold open a line of retreat, allowing its ultimate
union with the French and
British forces, in view of a
common action with the
upholders of the treaty of
neutrality.

This statement illumines
all the Belgian campaign.
From the beginning to the
end of the desperate, lonely
struggle of the Belgians
with the German hosts,
their main object was to
unite for common action
with the French and British
armies. As a Belgian officer
rather sadly remarked, after
watching the first Battle of
Ypres : " If only the English
had been able to join us at
Liège, we should have kept
the Germans out perma-
nently. They could never
have broken our lines." But

BELGIAN BATTERY "AT HOME."
Belgian artillery officers entertaining British Red Cross visitors. In circle.
A large cannon ready to be unshipped for service on the Belgian front.

Saluting the colours presented to new French regiments.
King Albert is seen with President Poincaré on his left.

President Poincaré presenting the new colours. In circle:
Reception of King Albert by President Poincaré.

The King of the Belgians addressing the French officers upon whom he was about to bestow decorations.

MORE SOUVENIRS OF THE MEMORABLE VISIT OF KING ALBERT TO THE FRENCH FORCES.

BELGIUM'S SHATTERED FANES.
All that was left by German shell fire of the church at Zuydschoote. A fragile wooden cross in the little churchyard survived the hurricane of fire.

the second phase of the Belgian campaign that ended with the fall of Antwerp. But there are some points on which the report of the Belgian Staff throws an interesting light. The German commander on August 21st installed before Antwerp an army of observation, formed of two army corps of reserves, linked with three divisions based on Liège. The result was that there was at last an equality of force between the Belgian Army and its immediate enemy. The Belgians, therefore, made a fierce sortie to enable them to keep open their line of retreat to

the front from the Dutch border to the turn of the Meuse at Liège needed a trench garrison of at least 60,000 men, with large forces behind them in reserve, to stop the gaps. It would have been national suicide for Belgium alone to have attempted to hold her frontier. As soon as it was seen that the invasion was being undertaken by the largest army ever put into the field—an army that swiftly increased to nearly two million men—the overpowered, tiny Belgian force retreated towards its base at Antwerp, fighting only rear-guard actions, in the hope of winning time for a union with the French and British forces.

France, however, had been temporarily paralysed by the vast German turning movement through the Belgian plain. In spite of the construction of a series of strategical railways leading from the Rhine depots to the Belgian frontier, the French Staff seems to have doubted if full use could be made of these, and had concentrated during mobilisation its main forces around Nancy. Precious time was thus lost before the chief masses of the French troops could be swung up towards Belgium. And while the Belgian Army was hopefully holding the river line of the Gette, with the forces against it increasing to half a million, the French armies could not link on strongly with them. So on August 18th a retreat on Antwerp was necessary; for the Belgian Army, composed at the time of only two army corps, found itself in immediate contact with eleven German army corps belonging to the armies of General von Kluck and General von Bülow. The much-desired common action in union with the French and British forces was impossible to realise; and if the Belgians had attempted a pitched battle they would have been cut off from Antwerp and shattered. Therefore, the Belgian Army withdrew into its entrenched camp at Antwerp on August 20th, after resisting the enemy's cavalry and light troops for fifteen days, without having its own fighting strength seriously weakened. Owing entirely to the action of the Belgians, the invading host of Germans did not cross the French frontier until August 24th, which was the twenty-third day of mobilisation in France. Such was the really important result won by the action of the Belgian Army in the first phase of the campaign.

We have already described at length the incidents of

Effect of the Belgian resistance

IN WAR-SWEPT RHEIMS.
Official French photograph of the Rue St. Symphonei, Rheims, showing in the background the famous cathedral, the ruthless bombardment of which by the Teuton artillerists must remain for ever a blot on the German name.

the west. Then, when the Battle of the Marne opened on September 7th, 1914, the High German Commander resolved to risk everything in order to strengthen his field armies. He diverted three divisions of the army of observation from Antwerp into France, and supplied their place in Belgium by a division of Marines and two brigades of Landwehr. But the Belgians countered this move by advancing in four divisions against the right wing of the Germans and capturing Aerschot and penetrating into Louvain. The movement alarmed the hostile commander. He marched back one of his divisions to Louvain, and arrested the Ninth German Army Corps

The capture of Aerschot

of Reserve for two days between France and Belgium, at the moment when Kluck and Bülow's shattered armies were calling for reinforcements and withdrawing their last rear-guards over the Aisne River.

Altogether the Belgians prevented on the three critical days, September 11th, 12th, and 13th, the 6th Division of the Third German Army Corps of Reserve, and the whole of the Ninth German Army Corps of Reserve from fighting against Sir John French's forces and General Maunoury's troops. Thus, to a considerable extent the success on the Aisne of our First Army Corps, under Sir Douglas Haig, was conditioned by the superb and forceful sortie of the Belgian Army. And it was directly for this reason that the German Commander-in-Chief on September 14th ordered all preparations to be made for the reduction of Antwerp by heavy howitzer fire from the great siege train which had been held in reserve for use

A superb and forceful sortie

AN UNDAMAGED SHRINE.
Despite the ruin wrought all round, this shrine, attached to the tower of the church at Reninghe, escaped unharmed.

against Paris. When the siege opened, the Belgian Staff still aimed at establishing that union with the allied forces which governed all its strategy, and which yet was so distressingly delayed. The British and French public at the time, having their attention entirely concentrated upon the gigantic wrestle between the two main opposing masses, could hardly appreciate the extremely anxious position of the small isolated Belgian force

in Antwerp. After Liège, Namur, and Maubeuge, the Belgian commander and his Staff were well aware that the Antwerp forts would fall in a few days. But they held on to the doomed city in the hope that the French and British forces would at last be able to make the much-desired union, and establish a line of trenches protecting the Belgian coast, and Bruges, Ghent, and Antwerp from the invaders.

Contrary to the common opinion, the Belgian commander at the end of September, 1914, had little hope of holding on to Antwerp with his troops alone. His supreme aim was to preserve the means of uniting his army to the French and British forces; and with this view he threw out his troops towards Ghent in order to keep open his line of retreat. At all costs Ghent had to be strongly defended, and as the Belgian Army could not extend in sufficient strength from Antwerp westward, King Albert on October 4th, 1914, sent an urgent appeal to Lord Kitchener for a strong British force to land on the coast and march on Ghent; for the position of the Belgian troops had suddenly become extremely perilous. The German army besieging Antwerp was only of third-rate importance.

Urgent appeal to Lord Kitchener

The most important thing was that the main German armies in France were rapidly extending their left wing and threatening to reach the North Sea, and thus cut the line of retreat for the Belgian troops. Towards the beginning of October the Germans had reached Lille, and at this city they were only thirty-seven and a half miles distant from Nieuport. The Belgian Army, on the other hand, was nearly ninety miles from Nieuport. At the same time a large new German army, formed of newly-trained recruits, and consisting of the units of new formations—the Twenty-second, Twenty-third, Twenty-sixth, and Twenty-seventh Army Corps of Reserve—was advancing into Belgium under the Duke of Würtemberg. This large force, which increased to one hundred and forty battalions, with more than five hundred guns, was designed to occupy the country between Lille and the sea, and make a great sweeping movement past Calais, which would throw back the Franco-British line.

The Belgian Staff came to the conclusion that the best place in which to meet this fresh German attack was the line of the Terneuzen Canal running from the Dutch frontier through Ghent, and continued southward towards

A VILLAGE IN FLANDERS BROKEN BY THE HUNS.
The little village of Zuydschoote, to the north of Ypres, after bombardment by the Germans.

Lille by the upper course of the Scheldt River. Ghent, and not Antwerp, in the first week of October, was the critical point for the long-delayed union of the forces of Belgium, France, and Britain.

Unhappily, neither France nor Britain was yet in a position to co-operate with the foresightful military advisers of King Albert. Our country could only send one division of infantry and another of cavalry towards Ghent; and the cavalry was delayed in its advance by the necessity for pushing back the German forces which were already extending towards the sea.

France, pressed almost to breaking point around Arras, could only send the very small force of 5,000 Marines to co-operate with our single infantry division round Ghent. Both the French and British Staffs were at the time apprehensive of the Germans breaking through on the Arras line and cutting off all the forces—Belgian, British, and French—north of that line.

On the morning of October 9th the bulk of the Belgian

ZOUAVE KEEPING WATCH IN A BELGIAN TRENCH BY MEANS OF A PERISCOPE.
The periscope had been swathed in canvas as a safeguard against splintering by an enemy's shot.

Army was arrayed behind the canal running from Ghent to Terneuzen; and a few miles in its rear was another canal—the Schipdonck Canal—which connected southward with the Lys River. The Belgian Staff wished to make a stand on one or the other of these lines, and thus save from invasion a notable part of Flanders and the valuable naval bases on the coast. To do this it was necessary to effect at once the union with the Franco-British forces.

German advance on Ghent   But the nearest French force of importance was fighting between Arras and Lille, fifty miles and more away, and Sir John French's army was only beginning to arrive at St. Omer, nearly seventy miles distant from Ghent. Meanwhile, the besieging German army at Antwerp was rapidly extending westward, and uniting with the large new German army under the command of the Duke of Würtemberg.

The German attack on Ghent had begun on the night of October 6th, when the advanced guards of three regiments of Bavarian cavalry, and a regiment of infantry, with several batteries, opened action at the village of Nazareth,

seven and a half miles south-west of Ghent. Four battalions of half-trained Belgian volunteers, with a few Civil Guards and a few French Territorials, held off the Bavarians. Then, on October 8th, a brigade of Breton Marines, under Admiral Ronarc'h, arrived on the scene of battle with a brigade of Belgian troops, and the Germans were pushed back over the Escaut towards Melle. Then at last, on October 9th, the famous 7th Division of the British Army, under General Capper, arrived at Ghent, and the Bavarians withdrew towards Alost.

But it was too late to hold either the Terneuzen or the Schipdonck Canal lines; and on the day on which the British division reached Ghent, King Albert decided to establish his Army in the region of the Yser River. **Cost of the loss of Zeebrugge**
The coast was lost, with the important submarine base of Zeebrugge, which was to cost the British Fleet and the British merchant marine many fine vessels; and the Zeppelin menace to London was also augmented by the loss of Flanders. These advantages the German Staff won by the rapidity with which it organised and armed the four new army corps that formed the bulk of the forces under the Duke of Würtemberg. The men had received only two months' training and they were afterwards slaughtered in dreadful masses along the Yser and on the north of Ypres. But by the rapidity with which they had been thrown into the field they certainly won a large stretch of territory, which proved of the highest importance from both a military and a naval point of view.

Our country would have retained a very great advantage if only we had been able at the beginning of October, 1914—two months after the outbreak of hostilities —to have thrown six divisions into Flanders instead of one; for by saving Western Flanders we should have saved our ships from under-water torpedo attacks, directed from a base quite close to our shore.

As it was, the French and the British Staffs despaired of being able to carry out the Belgian plan of entrenching on the canal line at Ghent. General Capper and Admiral Ronarc'h were ordered to retire from Ghent at seven o'clock in the evening of October 10th. But the order could not be carried out; for by a somewhat curious coincidence, which may have been due to the efficacy of the German system of espionage, the German army began a furious attack around Ghent at the moment when the French Marines and British troops were about to retire. The French Marines counter-attacked towards Melle, and threw back the assailants. But the next day, when the Belgians had withdrawn on Bruges, and the French Marines had set out on their southward march, our solitary 7th Division was again assailed round Ghent by the powerful new German army. The battle began at ten o'clock at night on October 11th, and after our troops had thrown back much superior forces of hostile cavalry and infantry, the Germans, as midnight drew on, brought up an overpowering number of guns, and tried to blast aside the small British force which was rear-guarding the Belgian Army.

No despatch has yet been published, after a lapse of twelve months, concerning the operations of the British

Lieut.-General Sir Herbert C. O. Plumer, K.C.B.

The pibroch in Northern France: Scottish regiment returning from the trenches.

Staff cars under fire: Thrilling escape from a German "shell hole."

After a forced march: Troops arriving at their billets at break of day.

Armoured cars of our Naval Air Squadron assisting hard-pressed British lines at Ypres.

351

Blazing farm buildings in Flanders set alight by German shell fire.

division round Ghent. But from French and Belgian sources we learnt that the conduct of the Immortal Seventh during their fighting retreat towards Ypres was one of the most inspiring episodes in our military history. " Their methodical retreat," it is stated in the official account of the campaign of the Belgian Army, " was conducted by the British troops, under the fire of the enemy's artillery and infantry attacks, with the regularity of a parade movement." Meanwhile, under the protection of the screen of Belgian cavalry, engaging in rear-guard actions near the Dutch frontier, while our 7th Division held up the enemy's main forces around Ghent, the Belgian infantry was transported by train towards Nieuport, Thourout, and Dixmude. In spite of the perils of the situation, and the technical difficulties of transport along single-line railways, the Belgian forces on October 12th reached their long-sought goal.

Junction effected at the Yser

After more than ten weeks' fighting, the junction with the Franco-British armies was made at the Yser. The Belgians were much reduced in number and sadly fatigued. The 111,000 trained infantrymen and volunteers had lost more than half their strength, and were represented by 48,000 bayonets. Nearly all the field-guns were still intact; but the single-line railways from Selzaete to Bruges, and from Bruges to Thourout, had barely sufficed to carry the men and guns along the main line of retreat. The huge stores of shells and charges accumulated in Antwerp seem to have been destroyed as they could not be removed. So when the Belgian batteries were established along the Yser, recourse was had to French charges. These proved unsuitable to the Belgian guns, and owing to the wear on the rifling and the increasing lack of shells, most of the Belgian guns became for the time unusable.

Yet the fact that the little outworn army had at last won, on the edge of its native land, the long-desired union with the French and British forces, filled the men and their leaders with heroic confidence. This was finely expressed in a proclamation which King Albert made to his troops when they reached the Yser line.

"Soldiers,—It is now more than two months that you have been fighting for the most just of causes—for your homes and for your national independence. You have held back the invading hosts, have undergone three sieges, conducted several sorties, and effected without losses a long retreat down a narrow corridor. Hitherto you have been isolated in the immense struggle. But now you find yourselves by the side of the valiant French and British Armies. It behoves you, by the tenacity and the bravery of which you have given so many proofs, to sustain the reputation of our arms. It is a matter of our national honour. Soldiers, face the future with confidence, and struggle on courageously. In the position in which I shall now set you, look only at what is in front of you, and treat as a traitor to our country anyone who shall think of retreating when no order has been given. The moment has come when, with the help of our powerful Allies, we must drive from the soil of our beloved Motherland the enemy who has invaded it, in scorn of his engagements and of the sacred rights of a free people.—ALBERT.

These words clearly indicated to the outworn, half-shattered Belgian Army that its hour of extreme ordeal had arrived. No further retreat was possible. Yet, on October 15th, when the defence of the Yser line was

organised, the French front solidly extended only as far as La Bassée. Between La Bassée and Dunkirk the Belgians at the time were supported only by two divisions of French Territorials—middle-aged men with but little military training—one brigade of French Marines, and the 7th Infantry Division, with the 3rd Cavalry Division, of the British Army. Sir John French's men were still engaged in moving from the Aisne to Flanders. While awaiting the arrival of our three army corps, King Albert arrayed his troops on a long and very thin line from the seashore at Nieuport to the village of Zuydschoote, six miles north of Ypres. There were thus only 53,000 men, including the brigade of French Marines attached to the Belgian Army, holding some thirty miles of winding front, in a flat, marshy country, where the enemy had a clear field for artillery fire, and where by reason of the watery nature of the soil the trenches of the defending troops could not be dug deep enough to protect them from shrapnel. The proper number of troops for a system of trenches on a thirty-mile front is—at the rate of two to a yard—about a hundred thousand. But the Belgians could only hold the line with one man to the yard, even on difficult river salients, where the enemy was able to attack from three sides at once, in dense masses of infantry, under cover of the fire of hundreds of guns.

The situation, when the Duke of Würtemberg brought up a hundred and fifty thousand men and began to drive

WITH THE BELGIAN ARMY.
A machine-gun in position in the second line.

in the Belgian outposts on October 17th, was more than critical; it was a nightmare. General Joffre asked the Belgian Staff if their troops could hold out just for two days. But in the event this period of desperate resistance was much exceeded; for the first French reinforcements, consisting of a single division, the 42nd, did not reach the Belgian front until October 23rd. The next day the Ninth French Army Corps arrived, but had to help the British army at Ypres, as our men there were weakening. Then, when the Sixteenth French Army Corps arrived in Flanders on October 31st, they were also needed at Ypres.

Instead of resisting forty-eight hours, as General Joffre demanded, many of the Belgian troops had to bide for twelve days and twelve nights in a shallow trench, under a hurricane of shells of all sizes, mitigated only by squalls of machine-gun fire. We have already described the chief incidents in the fearful struggle along the Yser, but the figures used by the Belgian Staff were more eloquent than any description in words. The Belgian losses on the Yser were 18,000 men. They fell mostly upon the 48,000 infantrymen. Thus three men out of every eight entrenched along the river and the network of dykes behind it were put out of action. And terrible as was the

Twelve days' fearful struggle

THE WARFARE UNDERGROUND.
French sappers carrying away earth dug from a mine gallery leading to
the German trenches.

It was the long and intense German pressure on Arras which prevented the union of the Franco-British forces with the Belgian Army at either Antwerp or Ghent. But despite all these military considerations, the stand made by the Belgian Army in front of Furnes was an achievement of sublime personal prowess, to which there is no parallel in modern history. We must go back to the defence of Leyden, which led to the establishment of the national independence of the Dutch, in order to find anything to match the exploits of the remnant of Belgium's troops.

In the last small nook of their Motherland these scanty survivors of one of the smallest armies in the world withstood and defeated the fully-deployed power of the greatest military empire of ancient or modern times, which employed hundreds of pieces of artillery of a power hitherto unknown in warfare. Even in point of date our defence **Feat unparalleled in modern history** of Ypres was secondary to the defence of the Yser : for it was after the Duke of Würtemberg failed, in the presence of the Kaiser, to break the Belgian front that he moved a large part of his men and guns against the British force, which would then have been broken but for the arrival of a French army corps. It is not surprising that Britain and France threw back the Germans. France was, after all, one of the great military Powers of the world, and had already gained a resounding victory over her foes. Britain also was a powerful fighting machine, which, besides holding the seas, started the war with some 800,000 troops, including a small professional Army of extraordinarily fine quality, officered by men who had already proved themselves in a long and difficult war. But Belgium had maintained in peace time a very small force, that was scarcely

proportion of dead and wounded to the living survivors, when the struggle ended in a decisive victory for the defending forces on October 30th there was something that made still more for demoralisation among the Belgians. This was utter exhaustion of both mind and body. The troops did not come fresh into the fight ; they were weary and dispirited by the terrific bombardment they had endured at Antwerp and by the hasty retreat they had been forced to make from a city they had regarded as impregnable. And scarcely had they entrenched along the Yser when the German siege-guns again began to pound them, while the artillery corps of another large army fearfully increased the volume of shell fire. To all this was added the nerve-shaking horror of the knowledge that the light batteries of their own guns were all **Glorious stand before Furnes** rapidly wearing out of action. Who could now blame the Belgians had they at last broken on the Yser and let the Würtemberg army advance on Calais and turn first the British and then the French lines ? But they did not break. Superhuman as was the task set them they held out, and a single division of French troops with the guns of the British squadron firing over the coast was sufficient reinforcement to enable them to win one of the most decisive victories in the history of civilisation.

Both Britons and Frenchmen should be ready eagerly to admit that the Battle of Ypres was a fine thing, and the Battle of Arras a fine thing, but that the Battle of the Yser was much finer. The French held at Arras the most important gate to Calais, for if the Arras line had been broken, both the Belgian and the British lines would have been cut. From a strategical point of view neither Ypres nor the Yser was as vital a region of defence as the Arras.

SAPPERS ENJOYING A WELCOME REST.
The arduous character of the work accomplished by French sappers may be gauged by this remarkable photograph showing the rocky nature of the soil through which the passage had been hewn.

more than a militia. She was caught just when she was beginning a far-reaching scheme of reorganisation, when everything was upset and nothing was progressing. She lacked entirely heavy field-artillery, and the number of her machine-guns was quite inadequate. Each German battalion, by reason of its Maxim equipment, could produce double the fire power of a Belgian battalion, and the German heavy artillery corps clean outranged and overweighted the light Belgian field-guns. Everything was against Belgium, and the decisive Belgian victory on the Yser is an immortal example of the triumph of spiritual forces over a highly intellectualised organisation of all the means of material strength.

The results of the Belgian victory were very important. A pulse of fierce and desperate patriotism shook the souls of millions of apparently conquered people, from Ostend to Liège and the Ardennes. Shackled though

Results of the Belgian victory they were under the foot of the invader, who had burnt their villages, massacred

women, children, and old men, and destroyed some of the finest of their ancient monuments, the thrill of indomitable hope spread to them from the Yser. As they were losing all hope in God or man, a whisper of voices ran through the country, and the spirit of the oppressed population was suddenly tempered to the resilience of steel. There is a story that a merchant of Ghent was sitting at the beginning of November, 1914, in his favourite café, which was then crowded with German officers. The Fleming sat by himself, neglecting all the advances for a friendly talk made by the domineering conquerors. One German officer grew angry at the isolated attitude of the Fleming. He brought a chair to the table, placed his mug of beer down, and said, " Come, you must drink

SAPPER versus SAPPER.
French sapper listening for the approach of German sappers and in readiness to destroy their design by a counter-explosion.

with me. It is useless to repine at the fortunes of war. We have annexed Belgium, and you and I are fellow-countrymen."

" I am glad to hear it," said the Fleming; " for now that we are fellow-countrymen, we can talk with each other freely, can't we ? What do you think of the hiding we received last month on the Yser ? It was pretty bad for us, wasn't it ? "

The German officer took his beer away, and the Fleming resumed his ironic solitary position as an interested student of the manners of his conquerors. About a million and a half Belgians in the occupied territories refused to work for the invaders. Many of them would have been starved into insurrection, and then shot down in multitudes, but for the good offices of Mr. **German garrison's** Hoover, the noble American organiser of **harsh oppression** the Belgian Relief Fund, who organised a magnificent system for feeding the desperate yet invincible irreconcilables. The German garrison troops erected wire entanglements all along the Dutch frontier with armed posts at short intervals, in order to prevent the oppressed population from escaping into Holland. The German Governor of Belgium, General von Bissing, was especially anxious to keep every Belgian of military age under his strict and harsh dominion. But by many strange and adventurous ways the young fighting men of the almost conquered nation slipped out through Holland, and swelled the force gathered behind Furnes under the command of their King. The romantic fact that there were still a few square miles of free Belgium exercised strongly and deeply the imagination of the people. Tens of thousands of oldish artisans also evaded the German lines of imprisonment, and quite an important system of war industries, run entirely by Belgian intelligence and Belgian labour,

PREPARING A MINE.
Another view of the perilous and exhausting work of the sapper. The men are shown beginning work on a mine channel destined, should fortune serve, to be the means of reaching and blowing up a German trench.

began to strengthen the increasing army. The training camps spread far into France, until it was reckoned that there were a quarter of a million young Flemings and Walloons holding the lines behind the flooded river, or drilling and exercising under the command of King Albert.

The outworn guns were retubed, hundreds of new light cannon and heavy pieces were provided, new gun-sections and airmen were trained to co-operate in target practice, and the old scheme first formulated by King **Reconstruction** Leopold for the organisation of a Belgian **and development** Army of 350,000 men, which in the ordinary course would not have been realised until 1918, was carried out in a remarkable way late in the summer of 1915 by a King without a kingdom, a Government without a people, and a commander without any national financial resources. Of course, Great Britain and France were at hand to provide monetary help and maintain the national credit of the Belgian nation. But the outcome of all the assistance generously offered would have been insignificant in comparison with the results actually obtained if King Albert and his men had not risen to the occasion. The

FOR BURNING THE CLOTHES OF ENEMY DEAD.
An open-air destructor used for burning the clothes of enemy dead and thereby limiting the risk of disease spreading among the troops.

energy of reconstruction and development displayed in the tiny fragment of free Belgium was as extraordinary as the effort of heroism by which the line of dunes and patch of marshland around Furnes had been held.

Owing to the smallness of the territory, the Belgian Government was compelled to scatter. The chiefs of the administration went into exile, while the Royal commander, moving amid his troops with a soul more indomitable than that with which Wilhelm the Second travelled about his vast empire, guarded the barrier of the Yser. The legislative power being suspended, the administrative function continued to be exercised. Many of the Ministers, with their staffs, were installed at Sainte Adresse. Others divided their work and had offices part in Belgium and part in France. The Minister of Railways, whose employees continued to remain on strike in the territory occupied by the invader, had little to do. The Minister of the Colonies worked from London, the Ministry of Agriculture remained in Brussels.

In virtue of international agreements, the Belgian functionaries in the occupied territories were to be paid for carrying on their necessary labours out of the taxes collected from the people. This was done in Brussels,

where the Germans were watched by the representatives of neutral Powers, but in the small towns the officers of the State had often to support themselves as best they could. Nevertheless, the maintenance of justice, the civil courts, and the municipal and parish business went on in the invaded kingdom. With the noble aim of remedying the financial difficulties caused in the Belgian communes by the requisition of the conquerors and by the diminution of revenues, many well-to-do refugees forwarded their rates and taxes through the curious little parish of Baarle-Duc, that forms an enclave in Dutch territory.

Meanwhile the Belgian Government, cut off from its sources of national revenue, and driven from Brussels to Antwerp, from Antwerp to Ostend, and from Ostend to Furnes and Dunkirk, set to work to retrieve the position. Borrowing from Britain and France, it lost not a day in getting to work. Its task was heavy and manifold. On the little morsel of free land it was necessary to raise up a new army, the six old divisions which opened the campaign having almost ended by perishing on the banks of the Yser. Most of the machine-guns had been broken up or buried by the huge German shells, and the field-guns, as we have seen, had been worn out. It was necessary, therefore, to provide a new artillery for the new armies, and especially to create a heavier and more powerful arm that could silence the great German siege-howitzers and naval guns.

There was also urgent need to organise the revictualling services. Winter was, at the time, approaching, and the men were fighting in marshlands below the level of the sea, in the midst of an immense inundation. The rigour of the winter campaign, in trenches half filled with freezing swamp water, was alone sufficient to destroy the remaining Belgian troops if great care were not taken of them. They were all wearing summer clothing.

Their cotton rags had to be replaced by warm, woollen underclothing, and thick cloth uniforms, and their outworn shoes by heavily nailed waterproof boots. They needed a huge mass of new war material — hand-grenades and bombs, bullet-proof shields for trench firing-holes, periscopes, telescopic rifle sights, machine-gun belts, and aerial torpedoes. Then for the wounded were needed new medical corps, and the creation of national ambulances.

There was also a troublesome problem in connection with the civil population of free Belgium. It is said that when our troops, under Sir John French, began to make their famous converging movements through the lovely emerald prairies that stretched around Ypres, the British Staff began to settle the dispute between militarism and agriculture in a very practical way. **Militarism v.** Each farmer was asked what price he put **agriculture** on his buildings and lands. Usually he put the price very high, and he was well satisfied, in the circumstances, with the German guns thundering close by, to take half the money he had demanded. The Belgian General Staff wished to follow the same course of buying out the farmers of the Furnes commune. But when the Belgian officers made the attempt, there arrived such piteous supplications at the little villa sheltering the most unhappy of monarchs, that King Albert, who, with Queen Elizabeth at his side, had witnessed on the road from Antwerp to Furnes the agony of the fugitives of Belgium,

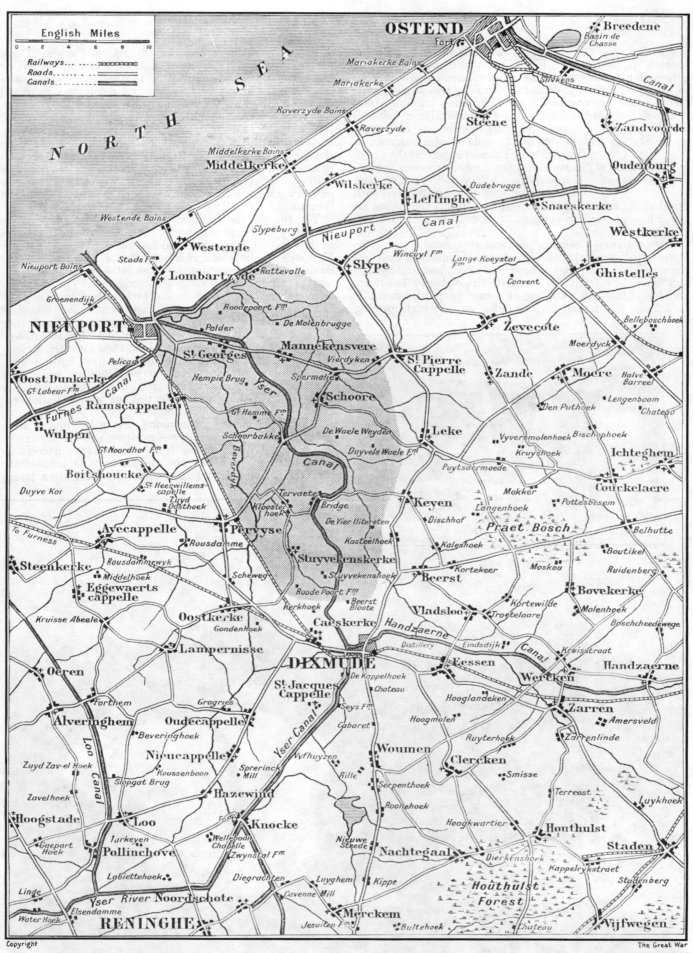

MAP SHOWING THE POSITIONS DEFENDED BY THE BELGIAN ARMY AFTER ITS JUNCTION
WITH THE BRITISH AND FRENCH FORCES AT THE YSER.

The shaded ground to the north of Dixmude indicates the area covered by the inundations.

declared firmly that he would not allow the last of his subjects to be removed from their homes. Then, on the little patch of unconquered territory, already well peopled in times of peace, a multitude of refugees was added to the great military element. In the low, damp buildings, surrounded by meadows, soaked by innumerable dykes and waterways, a large new population slept on the straw of the stables and in the musty cellars, where infants in hundreds died almost as soon as they were **Piteous plight of** born. A grave pestilence was feared, **the refugees** especially as cholera of a peculiar kind —cholera born of germs introduced with murderous intent by the Germans from the fields of pestilence in Galicia—began to appear in the Belgian trenches.

The situation became extremely critical. At this moment of peril the enemy airmen completed their reconnaissances of all that remained of unconquered Belgium, and from the distant German batteries of heavy howitzers and long-range guns a storm of bombs swept the country. It fell on the farms, on the mills, on the carts passing

down the farm tracks, on the villages, on Furnes. There were many wounded women, children, and non-combatant men. But the Teutonic essay at terrorising the civil population of the last two unconquered communes increased instead of diminished the military strength of free Belgium. Certainly the cruel bombardment produced a panic among the peasantry. There ensued another migration of the far-travelled fugitives, some of whom had come by stages from the Liège district. The country as far as the French frontier was almost emptied of ordinary life, and the little realm of liberty between Furnes and Ypres became a military camp over which incessantly played the guns of Germany.

Yet though the fugitives fled still farther, the native peasantry of Furnes-Ambacht remained till death, rooted in their soil. Quiet, placid, old-fashioned Flemings, dwelling in a rich agricultural **Stolid heroism of** land which simply continued to exist with- **the peasantry** out any industrial activities or sudden changes, they preferred to die rather than leave. They constructed dug-outs beneath their farms, and furnished their caves with the ruins of their furniture. There they slept at night, and at daytime, when the German artillery fire was not intense, they went about their ordinary agricultural work around their shell-battered farms. All of them were oldish men, often with married daughters and grand-daughters living with them; for all men of military age were either in the trenches, or training at Havre or some other Belgian camp in France.

The answer made by the young men of Belgium to King Albert's call to the Colours was glorious. From the remote villages of Wallonia, and from the equally inaccessible homesteads of Flanders, the Belgian lads stole over the frontiers, risking their lives many times and often facing

FRENCH ARTILLERY OFFICER OBSERVING THE GERMAN LINES.
Above : Belgian officers' quarters in Flanders. A " bomb-proof " erected under cover of a shell-broken farmstead.

FRENCH SCHOOL OF EXPERIMENTAL ANTI-GAS WARFARE.
In 1915, after the German introduction of poisonous gases as a means of warfare, the French established a regular course of anti-gas training. Our photograph shows soldiers furnished with protective masks descending to an underground chamber filled with poison-gas.

greater dangers than they would have to meet in the trenches.

It would be inadvisable at the time of writing to hint at the great adventures of multitudes of boyish recruits, for the German authorities were still eagerly seeking for clues to the means of escape from the system of national imprisonment which they were trying to enforce. After the war there will be many strange, exciting tales to tell of the manner in which King Albert's men came through great and manifold dangers to arm in France for the recovery of their heroic, suffering country.

The rally to the Colours

But while there was being built up on the southern bank of the Yser the youngest and most ardent of armies, work of reorganisation of equal importance was being carried out in another direction. The Belgian Government perceived as quickly as the French Government that in this factory-made war the military industrial activities of a people made for victory even more than the courage and skill of the troops in the field. In order to throw as small a burden as possible upon her labouring Allies, tiny free Belgium quickly created a great war plant of remarkable character out of material partly brought from England and partly saved from its own resources. Old factories were transformed into arsenals for the arming of the gunners and infantrymen; powder-works were set up, and in one foundry, organised with great rapidity and practical genius, the outworn Belgian field-guns, which had already sent forth each three thousand shells, were so splendidly repaired as to be able to shoot another three thousand times at the enemy.

The Belgian Government fashioned the cadres of its new camps of instruction, installed provisioning bases,

THE RETURN FROM THE GAS CHAMBER.
Army doctor examining a man on his return from the poison-gas chamber. The rubber bag in front of the masked soldier contained oxygen which the wearer was able to turn on by means of a tap.

sent buying commissions to the principal centres of production in allied and neutral States, built huge magazines for stores for half a million men, food, clothing, war and medical material.

Then, in order to connect the depots and the magazines of bread, petrol, hay, ammunition, and equipment with the field bases along the front, the Belgian Staff built a private network of railways out of the old material of their national lines, with their old national railwaymen to work the traffic. A little bit of France had to be taken over to connect the intense activity of the Furnes region with some of the large neighbouring Channel ports, and farther to the south Havre tended to

Belgium's amazing renaissance

IN A CAPTURED GERMAN TRENCH.
French soldiers, wearing shrapnel-proof helmets, in a German trench near Arras a few minutes after its capture. The parapet of the trench bears striking testimony to the effects of the preceding bombardment.

Yser could have been drained by raising the sluices when it was ebb-tide in the North Sea. It was only the flood-tide that produced the inundation, and to maintain the great lake-like stretch of water between the invading and defending forces it was necessary to keep the dyke gates down when the tide ran out from Nieuport beach.

The first task of the Belgian Commander - in - Chief was to strengthen his lines round Nieuport, so as to make sure of forestalling any surprise concentration of enemy force for an attack on the key position. After the Germans had definitely been defeated, the Belgian troops and their French reinforcements began to advance slowly upward near the coast. On November 3rd, 1914, the Belgian patrols reached Lombaertzyde, and the next day the 7th Regiment of the Line carried the town. But their artillery was too weak to enable them to hold on, and they drew back at night to their bridge-head of Nieuport. On November 8th the Belgian trenches were thrown out within two hundred yards of Lombaertzyde, and in the middle of December parts of the 2nd and 4th Division, with a French force under General de Mitry, took the town and extended to the sea on the left and the village of St. Georges on the right.

At the same time the other Belgian divisions fought their way forward, under a continual bombardment of hostile artillery, along the narrow tongues of dry land stretching across the flooded river. Islanded farms, converted by the Germans into machine-gun forts, were captured, and at the end of the year the enemy possessed on the left bank of the Yser only some listening posts and observation stations lost in the inundated plain.

In January, 1915, the French Moroccan troops and the Belgians began to enlarge the northern bridge-head by the Yser at Nieuport and attack the intricate German redoubt known as the Great Dune. The enemy answered this movement by a splendid engineering effort, and dug drainage canals from the region of inundation to the coast, by which much of the sea-water was carried off. To prevent the tide being admitted again down the Beverdyk, the mightiest of German pieces of artillery, the huge 17 in. howitzers, were brought up against Nieuport with a view to shattering the sluice-gates south of the ruined town. At the same time another army corps was sent towards the Yser front to help in forcing the Belgian lines across the increasing breadth of drying ground.

At first there was only a continual succession of advanced post engagements, in which parties of thirty or forty men fiercely pressed against each other over the narrow passages, with the artillery on **The new army** either side playing on the hostile trenches **begins to move** and machine-gun forts. But the Belgians were gathering strength, and took to opening their dyke gates to assist the drying winds of spring and the efforts of the German engineers. And when at the beginning of March, 1915, paths of advance began to appear in the waste of waters, it was the Belgians who unexpectedly worked themselves forward at Dixmude and the bend

become for the time a Belgian city, in the same way as Dieppe and Rouen acquired a transient British character. France, with the best grace in the world, shrunk a little to make more room for the marvellous and sublime remnant of a small European State which showed such incomparable powers of recovery. Belgium, reduced to the two arrondissements of Furnes and Ypres, was but one-ninth the size of her proper territory. The sixty-two remaining parishes were for the most part only churches that

"The Motherland had lost their towers, roofless walls, and **in sand-bags"** cavern block-houses. When a newspaper seller went the round of the camp, crying the name of his paper, "The Motherland," the troops lustily used at first to reply, "Yes, in sand-bags!" It seemed to them there was just enough of their native soil left to build breastworks out of it along the last strip of dyked, marshy pastures.

But the jesting vein of the Belgian soldier was but a veil to his deep feelings, like the humour of the Briton when he is in trouble, and the ironic shafts of wit with which the Frenchman laughs at fate. Deep waters move silently, and there were no hymns of hate sung in the Belgian trenches. But when the heavy batteries arrived, and the retubed field-guns came again fully into action, both the veteran and the fresh infantryman began to show, in fierce little skirmishes along the flooded river line, what a furnace of passion burnt in their hearts. The Belgian forces had their most important position between Nieuport and Nieuport Bains, for it was by this seaside town that the sluice-gates of the Beverdyk were worked to control the flooding of the polders with sea-water. Had the enemy at any time reached the sluice-gates he would have been master of the situation, for the region of the

Lighting the fuse of a battery of trench-mortars. French infantry "bombardiers" about to fire these new weapons under the watchful eye of their captain.

Two of the trench-mortars fired ; two about to be fired. The projectiles were launched from cases of unexploded German shells adapted for the purpose by the readily inventive mind of our French allies.

DEVELOPMENT OF TRENCH WARFARE: A NOVEL "BATTERY" IN ACTION.

of the Yser, and won more bridge-heads on the northern bank of the river. Then in the middle of March the watch-dogs of the Yser gained a fine strategical advantage by a fierce leap upon Oudstuyvenskerke, on the Schoorbakke road, and from this point they were able to drive the enemy back until they conquered a position which made impossible any German movement against the Dixmude bridge-head.

There was no violent dramatic onset in great force by the Belgian Army. Neither the state of the ground nor the tremendous artillery power of the enemy allowed any attempt of a decisive sort to break through the Germans' extreme northern wing. But there was throughout the spring and summer of 1915 a steady, well-designed pressure upon the hostile lines, which the opposing commander vainly tried to check by increasing the **Enemy's lost points of vantage** number of his heavy howitzers and naval guns. The fine military qualities of the Belgian troops and the scientific methods of their leaders were subtly displayed in Joffre-like strokes at all points of tactical importance, the seizure of which compelled the enemy to make continual costly efforts to regain the lost places of vantage.

Meanwhile the war of positions enabled the brigadier-generals to induct their new formations into the practical business of modern warfare, so that each body of fresh troops completed, at comparatively little self-sacrifice, their training under the fire of the hugest pieces of ordnance in existence, and learnt to face the nerve-racking bombardment with cool heads and steady hands. They were blooded to war in their little strip of free country in a way in which no other recruits could be so confidently employed. At first they had only to hold the old cobbled roads that stood above the flood, and with these communications guarded by trench after **The Belgian sniper's** trench, with a sweeping gun fire behind **opportunity** them, no surprises by the dispirited Germans were practicable. The Germans, it is true, did not remain wholly upon the defensive. They came out on rafts with machine-guns, and ingeniously attempted therewith to get enfilading streams of fire upon the Belgians' positions. But the Belgian sniper then got his great opportunity, and picked off the machine-gun crews with a few rapid shots.

When at last the water turned into mud, and the ground separating many of the Belgian and German trenches became firm enough to bear a rush of men, the defenders of the Yser manifested an aggressiveness which must have sadly disappointed the hostile commander. His laboriously constructed drainage canals turned to the profit of his daring opponents. A new German army was needed on the river line to enable him to recover the initiative, but as this army did not appear, the Belgians continued to maintain an ascendancy.

TO THE ETERNAL GLORY OF FRANCE AND TO THE HEROES WHO FELL IN HER DEFENCE.
Monument erected at Barcy to the heroes of the army of Paris who fell on the battlefield of l'Ourcq in September, 1914. Soldiers arranging wreaths sent by the French Government and the municipal authorities for the dedication ceremony.

PICTURESQUE VILLAGE CONSTRUCTED BY FRENCH ARTILLERYMEN ON THE AISNE.

Many of the artillerymen quartered in the Department of the Aisne were natives of the marshy district known as the Landes, in part of the old south-west province of Gascony. They brought with them to Northern France the methods of house construction characteristic of their native district.

Towards the end of April, 1915, when Hindenburg came to the western theatre of war, and the first great gas attack was launched, the inundation of the Yser region was still sufficient to daunt the Germans from using their new troops on the Nieuport-Dixmude line. Nevertheless, the Belgians played a gallant and important part in the second Battle of Ypres. They held a stretch of the Ypres Canal south of Dixmude, joining with the French division, which in turn connected with the Canadian division. When the Zouaves and the African troops were driven back by the cloud of poison gas, the Belgians came down from the north to their help, while the Canadians and British troops assisted in holding the line southward of the great unexpected break.

Steenstraate and Hetsas struggle It was the Belgian gunners who bombarded the poisoners out of Lizerne on April 27th, and the Belgian infantry charged with the Zouaves in the counter-attack by which the important village was recovered. Six German guns were captured, and the Belgians and their comrades swept forward towards Hetsas and threw the enemy out of his first line of trenches.

The conflict along the canal between Hetsas and Steenstraate raged as long and as furiously as the struggle in front of Ypres. From the point of view of the German commander, a successful advance across the allied line to the north of Ypres would have been an even more decisive achievement than a direct drive into Ypres. If the Belgians and French had given way, the positions of the Second British Army would have been turned. But there was no giving way. For three weeks hand-to-hand fighting went on between Steenstraate and Hetsas, while the Germans tried to draw off the Belgian gunners and infantrymen from the defence of Ypres by furiously attacking the edge of the Belgian line at Nieuport. But the Belgians were more numerous and better armed than in the days when they first held all the Yser line from the sea to Ypres. They held on to Nieuport with one army corps, advanced on Dixmude with another, and splendidly helped the Zouaves in carrying the German bridge-heads on the western bank of the canal above Ypres. The bridge-heads were defended by machine-gun forts, with powerful artillery sweeping the approaches, but redoubt after redoubt fell in the middle of May, and the allied line was made secure.

At one point between Dixmude and Ypres the Germans brought all their weight to bear on the Belgians. The Teutonic artillery swept the opposing trenches with shells filled with poison gas, and after the green fumes had apparently done their work, the masked German infantry came forward to bayonet the suffocating men and capture their guns. But the Belgians laid with their faces to the earth, getting draughts of inspirable air from the ground, while the heavy fumes from the exploding shells were impelled above them. They met the Germans **Germans met at close range** at close range with machine-gun fire and annihilated all the leading companies.

When, however, the canal line was won and firmly held, the Belgian troops, working on the left of the French division, could make but little further progress eastward; for opposite them was the Forest of Houthulst, from which a park of concealed hostile batteries, including many powerful pieces, kept up a severe cannonade. So a deadlock was established at this point; but the tenacity of the Belgians, who dug themselves into trenches with bomb-proof chambers, enabled both the French and British soldiers to swing forward farther south and rout the Germans from their trenches at Pilkem. Altogether the Belgians assisted greatly in enabling both the French and the British to recover from the loss of ground in the first great poison-gas attack.

After this brilliant affair, the Belgian Army resumed its comparatively quiet work of holding its Yser defences, and increasing its numbers and its war machinery. Desultory fighting of course continued all along the front, where the German forces were kept employed by a series of little engagements in which they never gained any advantage. There were favourite spots for testing the strength and ingenuity of both armies, and as the brick-stacks of La Bassée figured continually in the British reports, so the Chateau de Vicogne regularly occurred in

Keen-eyed Belgian scout's discovery the Belgian communiqués. The chateau was an ancient, picturesque manor-house used as a farmhouse, and lying on the road to Stuyvenskerke; the Germans occupied it, and the Belgians attacked it since November, 1914. The garrison was severely cut up by a furious bombardment of the Belgian guns, but in spite of this early success, the attacking parties could not win the chateau, though they fought for it for many months. The Germans left only a few observers in the ruined manor-house, but placed machine-guns in every window and on the roof. There was little but these machines of slaughter exposed to the Belgian gun fire, but whenever the Belgian infantry advanced to the assault they found the guns manned, and were beaten back. Night attacks and attacks in sea mists were as fruitless as sudden charges made in daylight. But after nearly ten months of repulses, an adventurous and keen-eyed Belgian

scout discovered the secret of the chateau. There were electric wires running from the ruins to the principal German lines, and the observer in the manor-house rang a number of bells for reinforcements when he saw an attack was impending. When the wires were at last cut, toward the end of August, 1915, the Chateau de Vicogne was captured with great ease.

FIELD-MARSHAL SIR JOHN FRENCH VISITING THE BRITISH WOUNDED.
The British Commander-in-Chief walking along the gangway on to a British hospital ship to inspect the wounded. In the smaller photograph Sir John French is seen on board a hospital train.

CHAPTER LXXXI.

"FOR VALOUR": HEROES OF THE VICTORIA CROSS IN THE FIRST YEAR OF THE WAR.

The History of the Victoria Cross—Its Value—V.C.'s Won During the Great War—Naval V.C.'s—Submarines at Work—Rhodes-Moorhouse and Warneford—Military V.C.'s Classified—Doctors as V.C.'s—V.C.'s Won at Mons—Acts of Gallantry in the Retreat—The Artillery at Nery—Heroes on the Aisne—The Eleven V.C.'s of Ypres—The First Indian V.C.—The Indians at Festubert—O'Leary's Feat—The Battle of Neuve Chapelle—The East Surreys on "Hill 60"—Canadian V.C.'s—Warner and Lynn Face the Poison Gas—V.C.'s Won at Fromelles—Mariner's Gallant Deed—The Londoners at Givenchy—V.C.'s Won in Gallipoli—Our Attitude to our Heroes.

"There is an honour, likewise, which may be ranked among the greatest, which happeneth rarely; that is, of such that sacrifice themselves to death or danger for the good of their country."—BACON.

S is fitting in services which have behind them a long and terrible renown, there are many honours open to the men of the British Navy and Army; but among these honours one stands out conspicuously as the most coveted distinction which soldiers and sailors, officers and men alike, can win. Needless to say, we refer to the Victoria Cross.

The Victoria Cross has not the value which comes with years—the kind of value, for instance, which makes the Order of the Garter so coveted a distinction—for it was only instituted in January, 1856, during the progress of the Crimean War. It is given, as the simple words inscribed on it say, "For Valour," which must be shown by some signal act of heroism or devotion in the presence of the enemy. It is intended to reward, not ordinary courage, but the merit of conspicuous bravery, and the man who wins it has passed the supreme and final test to which heroes are subjected.

The value of the cross is increased by the fact that it is not given at all freely or indiscriminately. From 1856 to the outbreak of the Great War, a period of fifty-eight years, less than five hundred and fifty men received it, and during that time our soldiers were fighting in every quarter of the world; for, more than any other service, our Army is entitled to claim the Latin line which asks the rhetorical question on which lands has our blood not been shed.

MICHAEL O'LEARY AT HOME.
Characteristic photograph of the gallant Irish Guardsman taken near his home in Co. Cork when he was in the Old Country on leave.

and which Mr. Fortescue has aptly chosen as the motto for his "History of the British Army." There was first the Crimean War, then the Indian Mutiny, with its deeds of incredible heroism, and then fighting in China, Abyssinia, Canada, and Ashanti. In 1879 there were wars against the Zulus and the Afghans, in 1881 against the Boers, and in 1882 there was the first of our several campaigns in Egypt. Add to these the endless struggles on the Indian frontier, the advances into tropical Africa, the expeditions into Burma, and finally the Boer War of 1899-1902. A long list of fights, thousands of brave deeds done, and yet less than five hundred and fifty Victoria Crosses awarded. No wonder that we think a great deal of a V.C., for although many have deserved it and have not received it, yet it is certain that those few who have won it have given ample proofs of their valour, and that no words can properly describe their deeds of daring. Rightly we recognise that the honour bestowed upon them is among the greatest given to mortal men; for, as Bacon says in the words at the head of this chapter, they sacrifice themselves to death, or danger for the good of their country. They are in spirit kinsmen of the three hundred Spartans who fell at Thermopylæ, and of the Swiss who died at Morgarten.

The cross itself is a bronze Maltese one, an inch and a half across. In the centre is the Royal crest, the lion and the crown, and below it a scroll on which are the words, "For Valour." It is suspended from a bronze bar, on the back of which is engraved the name, rank, and corps of the recipient. The ribbon is red for the Army and blue for the Navy. Money can add nothing to an honour of this kind, but every non-commissioned holder of the cross is entitled to a pension of £10 a year.

As we have already said, the cross, unlike some other distinctions—the Distinguished Service Order, for instance —can be won by soldiers and sailors, officers and privates alike. The official words are that it is open to every grade and rank of all branches of his Majesty's forces, British and Colonial." Until 1911, Indian soldiers

HOW CORPORAL ANGUS, V.C., CAME HOME FROM THE WAR.

Corporal Angus, 8th Highland Light Infantry, walking to his home at Carluke. Lord Newlands is on his right, and on his left is Lieut. Martin, in saving whose life at Givenchy Angus (then a lance-corporal) received no fewer than forty wounds.

were not eligible for it, as they had their own Order of Merit; but since then they have been on an equality with their brothers-in-arms in this respect.

During the first year of the Great War, the period between August 4th, 1914, and August 4th, 1915, the Victoria Cross was given to eighty-two officers and men. It is not easy to say how many men were fighting at one time or other during the twelve months, but as our casualties for the year were something like 400,000, it cannot have been much less than 1,500,000. If so, it was gained by about one man in every 18,000 or 20,000. Really a few more crosses were won during the year, but as they were not announced until after August 4th, 1915, they do not

come within the scope of this chapter. Moreover, they do not affect the broad conclusion that extraordinary gallantry and devotion are necessary to win the honour, and that it is bestowed most sparingly.

It may be well, first of all, to examine the list of the eighty-two recipients of the cross in some detail. In the first place we should say that seventy-six went to the Army, four to the Navy, and two to the Royal Flying Corps, although many of us are inclined to agree with the private's remark that every one of our airmen deserved one. However, this may also be said about a great number of soldiers and sailors, and we may be quite sure that the eighty-two names under consideration are by no means the only ones who earned the Victoria Cross for valour " in the presence of the enemy " during the first year of the Great War.

The Navy is the senior Service, so we will first of all deal with the four naval officers who won the V.C. The first was Commander H. P. Ritchie, of H.M.S. Goliath, who was a member of the naval force which was operating off the coast of German East Africa in the autumn of 1914. In August Dar-es-Salaam, the German capital, had been bombarded, and later it was again visited by British warships. In November a landing-party was sent ashore for the purpose of searching the place and demolishing certain buildings, a dangerous operation, in view of the fact that Germans were lurking about. Commander Ritchie led this party, and while superintending the work of his men he was severely wounded, not once but several times. However, he kept to his duties, " inspiring all by his example," until in about twenty minutes he received his eighth wound and became unconscious. On April 10th, 1915, he was awarded the V.C.

The landing at Dar-es-Salaam

LIEUT. (AFTERWARDS CAPTAIN) J. H. S. DIMMER, V.C., 2ND KING'S ROYAL RIFLE CORPS.
At Klein Zillebeke Lieut. Dimmer served his machine-gun until he had been shot five times—three times by shrapnel and twice by bullets. He continued at his post till his gun was destroyed.

LANCE-CORPL. W. ANGUS,
8th Highland Light Infantry.
Severely wounded at Givenchy.

PTE. ABRAHAM ACTON,
2nd Border Regt. Displayed great
gallantry at Rouges Bancs.

PTE. EDWARD BARBER,
1st Grenadier Guards. Won his
V.C. at Neuve Chapelle.

CO.-SERGT.-MAJ. F. BARTER.
Royal Welsh Fusiliers. A leading
figure at Festubert.

LCE.-SERGT. W. BELCHER,
L.R.B. Heroically defended an
important position near St. Julien.

DRUMMER S. J. BENT,
1st East Lancashire Regt. Saved
a position near Le Gheir.

LIEUT.-COM. E. C. BOYLE,
R.N. Sank two Turkish gunboats
and transport near Gallipoli.

LIEUT. W. L. BRODIE,
2nd Highland Light Infantry.
Headed a charge near Becelaere.

PTE. W. BUCKINGHAM,
2nd Leicesters. Rescued and
aided wounded under heavy fire
at Neuve Chapelle.

SERGT.-MAJOR H. DANIELS,
2nd Rifle Brigade. A Neuve
Chapelle hero. Afterwards promoted to a lieutenancy.

DARWAN SING NEGI,
Naik, 1st 39th Garhwal Rifles.
Displayed great gallantry under
fire near Festubert.

JEMADAR MIR DAST,
I.O.M., 57th Wilde's Rifles.
Exhibited great bravery in
the fighting around Ypres.

L.-CPL. F. W. DOBSON, V.C.,   LIEUT. M. J. DEASE, V.C.,   DRIVER J. H. C. DRAIN, V.C.,   L.-CPL. E. DWYER, V.C.,   LIEUT. F. A. DE PASS, V.C.
2nd Coldstream Guards.   4th Royal Fusiliers. A hero   37th Batt. R.F.A. Saved   1st East Surrey. Displayed   34th Poona Horse. Died
Won V.C. at Chavanne.   of Mons. Died of wounds.   guns at Le Cateau.   great gallantry at Hill 60.   nobly near Festubert.

The other three naval V.C.'s were all won by the commanders of submarines in the Dardanelles and the Sea of Marmora. On December 13th, 1914, before the land attack on the Turkish positions was undertaken, Lieutenant N. D. Holbrook, in command of the B11, entered the Dardanelles, and notwithstanding the very difficult current, dived his vessel under five rows of mines and torpedoed the Turkish battleship Messudiyeh. More difficult still, he brought back his boat in safety, although he was attacked by gun fire and torpedo-boats, which compelled him on one occasion to remain submerged for nine hours. To such a man nothing is impossible.

Holbrook's feat was a pioneer one, and it found emulators after our army had landed in Gallipoli. On April 27th, Lieutenant-Commander E. C. Boyle, in charge of the E14, took his submarine beneath the Turkish mine-fields in the Dardanelles and entered the Sea of Marmora. There, or in the Strait, he sank two Turkish gunboats and one large military transport, in spite of the difficulties arising from strong currents, and "of the continual neighbourhood of hostile patrols, and of the hourly danger of attack from the enemy."

The third of these naval heroes was Lieutenant-Commander Martin E. Nasmith, who, a little later, took a submarine into the Sea of Marmora. Like Boyle's, his bag was a big one, for he destroyed one large Turkish gunboat, two transports, one ammunition ship, and three storeships, in addition to driving one storeship ashore. He did this "in the face of great danger," and, moreover, after he had safely passed the most difficult part of his homeward journey, he returned again to torpedo a transport.

Our submarines in Turkish waters

The valour of these three sailors and the men under their command undoubtedly struck terror into the hearts of the people of Constantinople, and helped Sir Ian Hamilton's army by hindering supplies and reinforcements from reaching the Turks; and incidentally they showed what our seamen could and would do if the Germans were ever hazardous enough to attempt the invasion of this country. Only give our sailors a chance, and they would win as many V.C.'s as our soldiers have done.

A mournful interest belongs to the two airmen who won the Victoria Cross during the year, for both Rhodes-Moorhouse and Warneford are dead. Both were

GALLANT EFFORT TO SAVE LIFE UNDER FIRE.
Rifleman Matthews, 1st Rifle Brigade, with another man went out under fire to bring in a wounded comrade, whom three others had to leave, the enemy's fire being so hot. Matthews and his chum, when they reached their man, found he was dead. Matthews was then hit, and with his companion escaped with difficulty into the adjacent wood.

L.-CPL. D. FINLAY, V.C., L.-CPL. W. FULLER, V.C., L.-CPL. W. D. FULLER, V.C., PTE. S. F. GODLEY, V.C., CAPT. F. O. GRENFELL, V.C.,
2nd Black Watch. A hero 2nd Welsh Regt. Rescued 1st Grenadier Guards. A 4th Royal Fusiliers. Won 9th Lancers. Helped to
of Rue du Bois. wounded officer at Chivy. hero of Neuve Chapelle. the V.C. at Mons. save guns near Doubon.

heroes of no ordinary kind, and both names are worthy to be placed beside those of the great Britons of the past—Sidney and Drake, Havelock and Outram, Gordon and Roberts.

On April 26th, 1915, Second-Lieut. W. B. Rhodes-Moorhouse flew to Courtrai and dropped bombs on the railway line there. In this there was nothing very exceptional, for other airmen had done the same ; but on the return journey he was mortally wounded. In spite of his wounds he flew to his destination, thirty-five miles away, made a perfect landing, drew up and handed in his report, and then on the next day died in hospital. "Eye-Witness," in describing this deed, implied clearly that if he had thought more of himself and less of saving his machine and finishing his work, he might have descended earlier and saved his life. On May 22nd the Victoria Cross was bestowed upon him—or rather upon his memory.

The second airman was Flight-Sub. Lieut. R. A. J. Warneford, who, on June 7th, 1915, performed the unparalleled feat of destroying single-handed one of Germany's raiding Zeppelins. It appears that Warneford was flying along when he sighted the monster, somewhere on the coast of Flanders, possibly returning from its heroic task of throwing bombs upon unprotected women and children. He pursued it to Ghent, and having risen above it he dropped his bombs, and, moreover, dropped them accurately. A violent explosion followed and the Zeppelin was quickly blazing from end to end. The concussion was so great that Warneford's aeroplane was overturned and the engine stopped, but he managed to right it and dropped down to earth to take stock of the position. Although he was in the enemy's country, he flew away unobserved in about a quarter of an hour and reached his base safely.

This was a wonderful feat, the most wonderful deed of bravery and skill accomplished in the first year of the war. The nerve required to drop bombs accurately at a height of 6,000 feet and to

Zeppelin wrecked in mid-air

recover from the shock of the explosion is as wonderful as the courage which inspired one man in a tiny monoplane to attack a gigantic airship, and the skill which enabled him to avoid its fire, and finally to send it, one huge cinder, hurtling to the ground, By telegram the King congratulated Warneford and

HOW LANCE-CORPORAL HOLMES WON THE V.C.

At Le Cateau Lance-Corporal Holmes, of the 2nd Yorkshire Light Infantry, carried a wounded man out of the trenches under heavy fire. To do this he had to divest himself of his equipment. Later, the gallant corporal assisted to drive a gun out of action by taking the place of a driver who had been wounded.

369

the Victoria Cross, and these seventy-six are, after all, the staple of our story. The six naval and flying men were all officers, but among the military ones, non-commissioned officers and men were in the majority, and almost every rank was represented. Of the seventy-six soldiers, twenty-six were officers and fifty non-commissioned officers and men. Among the officers the list is headed by a lieutenant-colonel—the heroic Doughty-Wylie. Two majors—Alexander, of the Artillery, and Yate, of the Yorkshire Light Infantry— are on this roll of honour, and so are **Seventy-six** nine captains. Ten lieutenants, three **soldier V.C.'s** second-lieutenants, and one jemadar complete the twenty-six. In addition to the jemadar, two of the lieutenants belonged to the Indian Army.

Among the fifty non-commissioned officers and men, three were sergeant-majors, two sergeants, six corporals, eleven lance-corporals, one colour-sergeant, and seventeen privates. The remaining ten consisted of a lance-sergeant, a bombardier, a bandsman, two drivers in the Artillery, two drummers—Kenny and Bent—and three Indian soldiers—a naik, a rifleman, and a sepoy.

The seventy-six may be divided in several ways, but perhaps the most interesting is to apportion them among the various corps and regiments. As one would expect, the largest number belonged to the infantry of the Line, the officers and men upon whom the brunt of the fighting falls. Thirty-eight out of the seventy-six, or exactly

SERGEANT J. RIPLEY AND SERGEANT-MAJOR F. BARTER, AFTER BEING DECORATED BY THE KING.
Sergeant Ripley, V.C., of the 1st Black Watch, was a corporal when he won the V.C. for conspicuous gallantry when leading a section at Rue du Bois, where he was badly wounded. Sergeant-Major Frederick Barter, V.C., 1st Royal Welsh Fusiliers, gallantly led a party of volunteers against a German position near Festubert, when three enemy officers and over one hundred men were captured.

bestowed upon him the V.C., while General Joffre recommended him for the Cross of the Legion of Honour. On June 11th the former distinction was announced in the "London Gazette," but six days later Warneford—the only living airman wearing the V.C.—was killed while on a practice flight in Paris. His body was brought to England and thousands, who a few weeks before had never heard the hero's name, paid their respects to it on its journey to the tomb.

A special place even among brave men belongs to the five who gained the Victoria Cross under the new conditions of modern warfare—in the air and in the sea. In a strange and unknown element, amid **Britons equal to** a loneliness quite as terrible as that of **new warfare** which Coleridge speaks in "The Ancient Mariner," in charge of vessels filled with all the new and awful mechanism of death, they went gaily forward, with the simple object of doing their duty to their country. They discharged their tasks, and more than that, they proved that Britons were equal to the demands of the new warfare, demands which tax brain and body, nerve and muscle, as they were never taxed before.

We must now turn to the deeds of the soldiers who won

CONGRATULATING THE FIRST V.C. OF THE WAR.
Lance-Corporal Charles Alfred Jarvis, 57th Field Company, Royal Engineers, won his V.C. at Jemappes on August 23rd, 1914, in working for one and a half hours under heavy fire in full view of the enemy, and in successfully firing charges for the demolition of a bridge. He had a great reception on the occasion of his homecoming at Chelmsford in July, 1915.

one-half, were in this class, and with the five Guardsmen, they made a total of forty-three for the Regular infantry. Of the remainder eight belonged to the Artillery, five to the Engineers, and two—Grenfell, of the 9th Lancers, and Garforth, of the 15th Hussars—to the cavalry. Eighteen remain to be accounted for, and of these six belonged to the Indian Army, three to the Canadian, and one to the Australian contingent. The Canadians were Scrimger, Hall, and Fisher, and the Australian was Jacka. The remaining eight were two members of Sir Ian Hamilton's

Staff—Doughty-Wylie and Walford—two members of the medical corps, and last, but by no means the least noteworthy, four members of the Territorial Force. Of these three—Woolley, Belcher, and Keyworth—belonged to the London Regiment, a fine record for a young unit.

Of the infantry, the Highland Light Infantry holds the proud record of having won three Victoria Crosses during the first year of the Great War, the three recipients being Lieut. Brodie and Private George Wilson, of the 2nd Battalion, and Lance-Corporal W. Angus, of the 8th, a Territorial one.

Several famous regiments can claim two Victoria Crosses during the period. Among these are the Gordon Highlanders—Lieut. Brooke and Drummer Kenny, both of the 2nd Battalion, and the Black Watch—Ripley, of the 1st Battalion, and Finlay, of the 2nd. The Royal Fusiliers—Lieut. Dease and Private Godley, of the 4th Battalion—and the East Surreys—Lieut. Roupell and Lance-Corporal Dwyer, of the 1st Battalion—belonging to the metropolitan area, and the King's Royal Rifle Corps — Dimmer and Mariner, both of the 2nd Battalion—and the Rifle Brigade — Daniels and Noble, both of the 2nd Battalion—belonging to the South of England, show that the Scottish regiments have no monopoly of these honours. Other parts of the country are represented in the list by the Manchesters—Leach and Hogan, of the 2nd Battalion—the Sherwood Foresters—Rivers and Upton, of the 1st Battalion—the Yorkshire Light Infantry—Yate and Holmes, of the 2nd Battalion—and the Border Regiment—Acton and Smith, of the 2nd Battalion.

Sixteen other regiments had each one of our V.C.'s in their ranks. These included the Welsh Regiment, the Royal Welsh Fusiliers, the Royal Irish Fusiliers, the Cameron **Famous regiments'** Highlanders, the Cameronians, **new laurels** and the Royal Scots. The remaining ten are English: Lancashire Fusiliers and East Lancashires, Leicesters and Lincolns, Hampshires and Bedfords, Liverpools and South Staffordshires, Yorkshires and Duke of Cornwall's Light Infantry. Of the five Guardsmen who won the cross two—Barber and Fuller—belonged to the Grenadiers, and one each to the Coldstreams (Dobson), the Scots (Mackenzie), and the Irish Guards (O'Leary).

Of the eight artillerymen who won the cross three—Alexander, Bradbury, and Reynolds—were commissioned officers, and five were not. The famous L Battery of the Royal Horse Artillery had three of these heroes in its ranks—Captain Bradbury, Nelson, and Dorrell, and the remaining five belonged to the Royal Field Artillery—Captain Reynolds, Luke, and Drain to the 37th Battery, Major Alexander to the 119th, and Bombardier Harlock to the 113th. The five Engineers were all officers, save one—Lance-Corporal Jarvis. The four officers were Captains Theodore Wright and W. H. Johnston, and Lieutenants Philip Neave and C. G. Martin, D.S.O.

Among the heroes of the field of battle our doctors occupy no mean place, and during the year two members of the Royal Army Medical Corps, commonly known by its initials as the R.A.M.C., won the V.C., these being Captain H. S.

Ranken and Lieut. A. M. Leake. The latter deserves a very special mention, for he won the Victoria Cross on two occasions. During the Boer War, on February 8th, 1902, Lieut. Leake was shot while assisting a wounded officer, an action which was rewarded by the V.C., so when he won it again in 1914 he was granted a clasp to it. This honour was unique, at least during the first year of the Great War. In addition to these two, one of the three Canadian V.C.'s—Captain F. A. C. Scrimger—was a medical man, so this service should rightly count three. Of the seventy-six Victoria Crosses won by soldiers, seventy-two were gained in Flanders and the remaining four in Gallipoli.

"The British forces were engaged all day on Sunday and after dark with the enemy in the neighbourhood of Mons." This short but deeply interesting **Four V.C.'s won in** message, issued on the after- **a day** noon of Monday, August 24th, 1914, showed that the British Army, after an absence of a hundred years, was again fighting over the scenes of many of its former glories, and it was not long before officers and men began to show their traditional valour. On the very first day of actual fighting four Victoria Crosses were won.

On that August Sunday afternoon the Germans were advancing in great force against the

AN AUSTRALIAN V.C. WHO ACCOUNTED FOR SEVEN TURKS.
On May 19–20th, 1915, at a point known as Courtney's Post, on the Gallipoli Peninsula, a British trench was violently attacked by the Turks. When his four comrades had been killed or wounded, Lance-Corporal Albert Jacka, 14th Australian Infantry, found himself attacked by seven sturdy Ottomans. Jacka, defending himself single-handed, disposed of five of his assailants by rifle fire and two with the bayonet. Inset is a portrait of the heroic Australian, a native of Wedderburn (Victoria).

GALLANT YOUNG HIGHLANDER'S HEROIC DEATH NEAR HOOGE.
During a difficult and thrilling charge near the famous Hooge Chateau a party of bombers led by Lieut. T. Barrie Erskine, 4th Argyll and Sutherland Highlanders (attached to the 1st Gordons), came to a dug-out in which some Germans were barricaded and refused to surrender. Despite a fierce cross-fire, Lieut. Erskine seized a pick, and started to hew a way into the dug-out. In doing this he was mortally wounded. The gallant young officer, who had already received the Military Cross, was recommended for the D.S.O., and gazetted to a captaincy.

somewhat to the west of Mons, the 4th Battalion of the Royal Fusiliers was posted, its duty, or part of it, being to hold the approaches to one of the bridges which cross the canal. At that spot were some machine-guns in charge of Lieut. M. J. Dease, who, although badly wounded two or three times, continued to direct their fire. He did this until all his men had been shot, and later he himself died from his injuries. Dease was assisted by Private S. F. Godley, who stuck to his work for two hours after he had been wounded, and in November the V.C. was awarded to the two. On this same day a fifth cross was partly won.

At Harmignies, Corporal C. E. Garforth, of the 15th Hussars, volunteered to cut some wire under fire, and in this way he enabled his squadron to escape. His deed was noted, and so was the fact that a little later, at Dammartin, he carried a wounded man out of action. Finally, on September 3rd, Garforth saved the life of a sergeant, whose horse had been shot, by his coolness in opening fire on the enemy and so giving his comrade a chance to escape. For these gallant acts the King gave him the Victoria Cross on November 17th, the day on which the first awards for valour during the Great War were made.

On Monday the 24th the British Army was retreating from Mons, and high courage was more than ever necessary. Near Andregnies the 9th Lancers were ordered to charge the advancing German infantry, in order to assist the 5th Division, which was hard pressed by the enemy. The Lancers rode on, only to find themselves held up by barbed-wire and a target for the German guns. They lost heavily, and the remnant of the regiment found shelter under a railway embankment, Captain F. O. Grenfell being the senior officer left, and he somewhat severely wounded. In the same refuge were some gunners belonging to 119th Field Battery, which had been put out of the action and abandoned. Grenfell determined to save the guns, and called upon the Lancers and the gunners to assist him, and after having at the greatest risk discovered for them a way into safety, he and his men rushed out. Under heavy fire they pushed the guns into safety, for the horses had all been shot, and for this act of daring Grenfell received the V.C. Some months later, on May 24th, 1915, he was **Capt. Grenfell saves** killed, while his Lancers were doing **the guns** duty as dismounted men in the trenches.

This same 119th Field Battery, which was commanded by Major E. W. Alexander, had already distinguished itself on the 24th. It was stationed near Elonges, and although attacked by an enormous force of Germans, the guns were saved, being pulled out of danger

canal which runs from Mons to Condé, and along which our troops were stationed. To prevent them from crossing, our engineers were ordered to blow up the bridges, and while preparing one of these for destruction, Captain Theodore Wright was wounded in the head. However, he stuck to his task, and after the **Engineers hold up** first fuse had failed to act, he prepared **the enemy** another, which was instrumental in bringing down the bridge. Hard by, at Jemappes, Lance-Corporal C. A. Jarvis was working at a similar task. For an hour and a half, in full view of the enemy and under heavy fire, he continued to prepare charges, and at last he was rewarded by seeing the bridge shattered. On November 17th the Victoria Cross was awarded to these two engineers, but by that time Wright was dead, killed while adding to his laurels. At Vailly, on September 14th, he assisted a brigade of cavalry to cross the Aisne by a pontoon bridge, and was there mortally wounded while helping some wounded men into shelter.

To return to the fighting at Mons. About St. Ghislain,

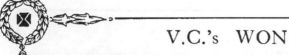

BOM. E. G. HARLOCK, (later Sergt.), 113th Batt. R.F.A. With Lieut. Leach recovered trench near Festubert.

LIEUT. N. D. HOLBROOK, R.N. Commander submarine B11. Torpedoed the Messudiyeh in the Dardanelles.

LCE.-CPL. F. W. HOLMES, 2nd Yorks Light Infantry. Won the V.C. for gallantry at Le Cateau.

LCE.-CPL. L. J. KEYWORTH, 24th London Regt. Displayed great heroism in fierce encounter at Givenchy.

DRUMMER W. KENNY, 2nd Gordon Highlanders. Saved guns and effected rescues of wounded near Ypres.

SEPOY KHUDADAD, 129th Baluchis. Won the V.C. for great bravery in action at Hollebeke.

LIEUT. A. M. LEAKE, R.A.M.C. Awarded clasp to his V.C. for his heroism near Zonnebeke.

2ND-LIEUT. J. LEACH, 2nd Manchesters. With Sergt. Hogan recovered a trench near Festubert.

DRIVER F. LUKE, 37th Batt. R.F.A. With Driver Drain saved guns at Le Cateau.

PTE. JOHN LYNN, 2nd Lancashire Fusiliers. Gave his life for his comrades near Ypres.

PTE. W. MARINER, 2nd K.R.R.C. Single-handed, silenced enemy gun near Cambrin.

PTE. HENRY MAY, 1st Scottish Rifles. Won his V.C. near La Boutillerie.

BRITISH OFFICER GIVES HIS LIFE TO SAVE THAT OF A WOUNDED ENEMY.

Above is depicted one of the bravest deeds of the war. The act of self-sacrificing heroism belongs to the autumn of 1914. Some Germans attacked a British trench, and were repulsed with heavy loss. Retiring, they took with them all but one of their wounded, whom they overlooked. A comrade came into the open to rescue him, but fell under a score of British bullets. The British officer gave the order to cease fire. Then he himself advanced to the rescue of the wounded German, but was struck by several German bullets. Then the German officer ordered his men to cease fire. The British officer carried the wounded man to the German trenches, where he saluted and handed him over to his friends. Saluting in turn, the German officer sprang from his trench, took off his own Iron Cross and pinned it on the breast of his brave enemy. The British officer gained his own lines, but died from his wounds ere he could receive the Victoria Cross for which he was recommended.

by hand by the major and three of his men. The work of this battery greatly assisted the retirement of the 5th Division, enabling it to be carried out without serious loss. Major Alexander, who had handled his battery against overwhelming odds with conspicuous success, somewhat later rescued a wounded man under heavy fire. He was given the V.C. on February 18th, but before that date he had been made a lieutenant-colonel.

The 25th passed away, and then came the 26th, which Sir John French described as " the most critical day of all," the day of Le Cateau and Landrecies. At 3.30 in the afternoon, to avoid complete annihilation, the Second Army Corps, under Sir Horace Smith-Dorrien, commenced to retreat, after having fought a fierce rearguard action at Le Cateau in order to enable the First Corps to get safely away. This movement was covered by the artillery, which held up the German advance as long as possible. On one occasion the enemy got to within a hundred yards of two guns of the 37th Field Battery, but at enormous risk Captain Douglas Reynolds, aided by two volunteers— Drivers J. H. C. Drain and F. Luke—rushed up with two teams of horses and, although under heavy fire, managed to drag one gun away. In November the **Captain Reynolds'** three were awarded the V.C. It should **acts of gallantry** be added that on September 9th, at Pisseloup, Captain Reynolds performed another act of gallantry. There our men were advancing, although a hostile battery was keeping some of them back. Reynolds discovered its position by creeping up near to it, and then turned his guns on the battery and silenced it. Six days later this officer was severely wounded.

Of the two Divisions, the 3rd and the 5th, which composed Smith-Dorrien's corps, the 5th was the last to leave its position, and among its units was the 2nd Battalion of the Yorkshire Light Infantry. Two companies of this battalion remained in the hastily-dug trenches at Le Cateau on the

26th, when practically everyone else had got away, and at length all the officers, save one, had been killed or wounded, all the ammunition expended, and only nineteen men were left. The single unwounded officer was Major C. A. L. Yate, and forming up the nineteen survivors he led them against the enemy. It was a supreme act of gallantry, but perfectly hopeless. Yate **Heroism at** was severely wounded and was taken **Le Cateau** prisoner by the Germans. Happily, it was stated later that he had not died of his wounds, as was at first reported. During this battle Lance-Corporal F. W. Holmes, of the same regiment, carried a wounded man out of the trenches under heavy fire, and later assisted to drive a gun out of action by taking the place of a wounded driver. Like Major Yate, he received the V.C. on November 25th.

After the 26th the first fury of the German attack had spent itself, but there was a good deal of hard fighting before the French and the British turned upon their pursuers and drove them back from the gates of Paris. On September 1st, for instance, when the L Battery of the Royal Horse Artillery was resting at Nery, it was surprised by a big hostile force, and before the guns could be brought into action three of them had been destroyed. However, the other three opened fire upon the superior batteries of the enemy, but soon two of them had been silenced, and only forty men of the two hundred attached to the battery remained. Under Captain E. K. Bradbury the gunners continued to serve the one sound gun, and when he had been wounded, Sergeant-Major G. T. Dorrell and Sergeant D. Nelson kept up the fire until all the ammunition was gone, although only six hundred yards away the Germans were pouring in a concentrated fire from guns and machine-guns. In the nick of time a body of British cavalry and infantry arrived on the scene, and the battery, or what remained of it, was saved. Captain Bradbury, who died of his wounds,

AN ECHO FROM NEUVE CHAPELLE: BRITISH OFFICER'S PRIDE IN HIS REGIMENT.

The moving incident which our artist has chosen for the subject of the above picture belongs to the thrilling story of Neuve Chapelle. It throws a ray of light on one out of hundreds of instances of British heroism and endurance during the battle referred to, and we should have been in ignorance of it but for a line or two of reference in a soldier's letter home. The soldier tells how one of his officers, though mortally wounded, refused to be taken from the field. " Prop me up," he said, " that I may see my regiment go forward."

was given the V.C. on November 25th, for his "gallantry and ability in organising the defence of L Battery against heavy odds," and the two non-commissioned officers received the same honour on the 17th, and were also promoted to commissioned rank. Like Captain Bradbury, Sergeant Nelson was severely wounded, but happily he recovered, although he had stuck to the guns after having been ordered to retire into safety.

On September 13th the Allies, having won the Battle of the Marne, began the crossing of the Aisne in pursuit of **Two brigades saved** the retiring Germans. At Missy two **by one man** British brigades, the 11th and the 15th, had got across the river, though their position was very precarious, and but for the exertions of one man they would have been compelled to retire. This man was Captain W. H. Johnston, R.E., who worked with his own hands two rafts across the river, taking back thereon the wounded, and returning with ammunition for the harassed brigades. He did this throughout the whole day, and was deservedly awarded the Victoria Cross on November 25th. Some time later Captain Johnston was killed.

NON-COMMISSIONED OFFICERS AND MEN OF THE KING'S LIVERPOOL REGIMENT IN THE TRENCHES AFTER THE ADVANCE AT FESTUBERT, JUNE, 1915.

This Battle of the Aisne extended over a wide front, and on the 14th three more Victoria Crosses were won. On the right of the British line, forming part of the 1st Division, was the 2nd Battalion of the Welsh Regiment, and one of its captains, Mark Haggard, took a prominent part in leading the men forward. At length he fell mortally wounded, and seeing this, Private William Fuller rushed forward for about a hundred yards, and under a heavy fire carried Haggard into safety. Fuller, by then a lance-corporal, received the V.C. on November 23rd.

Not far from the Welsh Regiment, in the same 1st Division, were the Cameron Highlanders, and a similar service was performed for an officer of this battalion by Private Ross Tollerton. The bravery and devotion of this soldier were, as the official announcement said, "most conspicuous." While carrying the wounded officer into safety, Tollerton himself was wounded in the head and hand, but nevertheless he returned to the firing-line and remained with the battalion until it retired. But this was not all. He then returned to where the wounded officer was lying, and stayed beside him for three days until the two were rescued. The name of Ross Tollerton is not perhaps so well known to the general public as are the

names of several other winners of the V.C., but there is hardly one who earned the honour more daringly or more fully. Some months later, on April 19th, Tollerton received the V.C.

At Verneuil, a little to the left of the Welsh Regiment, the line was held by the 2nd Battalion of the Highland Light Infantry, and in its ranks was a certain Private George Wilson. With a comrade Wilson crept forward to silence a hostile machine-gun, and after the comrade had been killed he went on alone. He reached the gun, shot the officer and the six men who were working it, and then captured it. He received the V.C. on December 5th.

On the 15th this engagement on the Aisne continued, and near Vendresse the 113th Field Battery was shelling the Germans, and was being heavily shelled in return. One of its bombardiers, E. G. Harlock, being injured, went away and had his wound dressed, and then returned to lay his gun. A second time the same thing happened, and a second time the bombardier went back from the dressing station to his work. He was made a sergeant, and received the V.C. on November 25th.

The Battle of the Aisne went on for four weeks, and after the first encounters the combatants betook themselves to trenches. At Hautvesnes, on September 19th, Captain H. S. Ranken, of the R.A.M.C., showed conspicuous courage in attending to the wounded when under rifle and shrapnel fire, and on the following day his leg and thigh were shattered while at work. Even after this severe injury he kept to his task, but the strain was too much for him, and another V.C. hero died of his wounds without knowing of the honour conferred upon him by the King on November 17th.

The last V.C. earned during the Battle of the Aisne fell to Lance-Corporal F. W. Dobson, of the 2nd Battalion Coldstream Guards. At Chavanne, on September 28th, Dobson distinguished himself by his "conspicuous gallantry" in bringing into cover on two occasions, under heavy fire, wounded men who were lying exposed in the open. He received the V.C. on December 9th.

At length the Battle of the Aisne came to an end, and the British army took up its position on the Yser, where it remained throughout the winter. On October 22nd the first Battle of Ypres was raging, and the Germans were making their great effort to hack their way through to Calais. Near La Boutillerie there was sharp fighting, and the Cameronians, also called the Scottish Rifles, were suffering severely. Private **Drummer saves** Henry May volunteered to go forward **machine-guns** and save a wounded man; he made an attempt, but the heavy fire killed the injured soldier before his rescuer could reach him. Later in the day May carried a wounded officer into safety, traversing with his burden three hundred yards under very severe fire. On April 19th the V.C. was conferred upon him.

The next day, October 23rd, William Kenny, a drummer in the 2nd Battalion of the Gordon Highlanders, won his V.C. He was not a fighting man, so he was employed to carry urgent messages, and on numerous occasions he took these "under very dangerous circumstances over fire-swept ground." But this was not enough for the heroic drummer. Twice he saved the battalion's machine-guns by carrying them out of action, and no less than five times, "under

Lce.=Corpl. Tombs saves four comrades.

Drummer Bent's gallantry under fire

Private Lynn's "most conspicuous bravery.

Lieut. Smyth's terrible journey with bombs.

Lieut. Leach and Sergeant Hogan recapturing a trench from the Germans.

How Sergeant O'Leary "practically captured the enemy's position by himself."

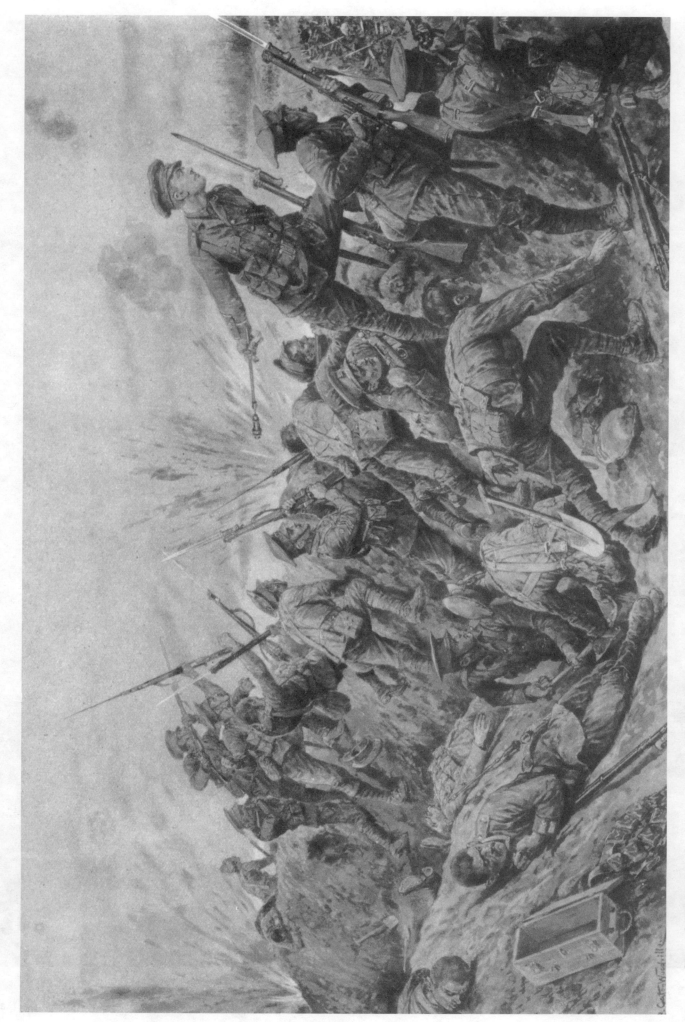

The first V.C. ever won by a Territorial: Second-Lieut. G. H. Woolley's heroic defence of "Hill 60" with a handful of men.

heavy fire in the most fearless manner," did he rescue wounded men. When super-V.C.'s are awarded to supermen, Drummer Kenny should figure in the list.

During this same Battle of Ypres the Germans, on October 29th, made a specially severe attack on Sir Douglas Haig's corps at Gheluvelt, and this was momentarily successful, some of our trenches being lost. However, Lieut. J. A. O. Brooke, an officer of the 2nd Gordons, kept cool and fearless, and under heavy fire, both from rifles and machine-guns, led two attacks on the German position, regaining one of the lost trenches "at a very critical moment." The gallant officer was killed, but a fine memorial to him remains in the announcement which conferred upon him the Victoria Cross. "By his marked coolness and promptitude on this occasion," it says, "Lieut. Brooke prevented the enemy from breaking through our line, at a time when a general counter-attack could not have been organised." The two Gordons, lieutenant and drummer, one alive and the other dead, were among those who received the V.C. on February 18th.

Away on the British right there was, on this same October day, heavy fighting around Festubert, where the Second Corps was stationed. Here, as a Ypres, a strong German attack was successful in capturing some trenches held by the 5th Division, and two attempts made by our men to recover them failed. Thereupon an officer, Second-Lieut. James Leach, and a sergeant, John Hogan, of the 2nd Battalion of the Manchester Regiment, voluntarily decided in the afternoon to make an effort to recover their lost trench. Working steadily from traverse to traverse, at length they reached it, and once there they killed eight of its German defenders, wounded two, and took sixteen prisoners. Thus the trench again became British property, and on December 22nd Leach and Hogan received the V.C.

Towards the end of October the Indian Army Corps took its place in the line of battle, and on the 31st the V.C. was won by one of its members—a sepoy called Khudadad, of the 129th Duke of Connaught's Own Baluchis. The Baluchis were at Hollebeke, and the sepoy was one of the men who were working the battalion's two machine-guns. One of these was put out of action by a shell, and the British officer in charge of the detachment was wounded, but Khudadad, although wounded himself, worked away at his gun until the five men with him had all been killed.

First Indian V.C. in the war

The first award of the V.C. to an Indian soldier for valour during the Great War was granted to Khudadad on December 7th.

Near Hollebeke is Le Gheir, where the East Lancashires were making a desperate stand against the innumerable hordes of Germans who came day after day to the attack, and there Drummer Kenny found a rival. On the night of November 1st, perhaps the most critical time in this critical battle, a certain detachment of the East Lancashires lost all its officers. Realising the situation, Drummer Spencer John Bent took command and, as we were told, "with great presence of mind and coolness succeeded in holding the position." But, like Kenny, Bent was not satisfied with one act of heroism. Previously, on October 22nd and 24th, he had distinguished himself by bringing up ammunition under a heavy shell and rifle fire, and later,

on November 3rd, he carried into cover some wounded men who were lying exposed in the open. Drums may not be necessary in a modern army, but no army can have too many drummers like Bent and Kenny. Bent's V.C. was dated December 9th, 1914.

It was at the same time and in the same neighbourhood that Lieutenant A. M. Leake, of the R.A.M.C., won the V.C. for the second time. Here we may be allowed to quote the official words. He won it for "most conspicuous bravery and devotion to duty throughout the campaign, especially during the period October 29th to November 8th, 1914, near Zonnebeke, **Double honours for** in rescuing, while exposed to constant **R.A.M.C. captain** fire, a large number of the wounded who were lying close to the enemy's trenches." As the cross could not be given twice to the same man, Lieutenant Leake was granted a clasp to it on February 18th, 1915.

We have not yet done with the Battle of Ypres. On November 7th it was still raging, and on that day, at Zillebeke, the 1st Battalion of the South Staffordshires did splendid service in capturing a German trench. The attack, or at least one attack, was led by Captain J. F.

ONE OF MAJOR RICHARDSON'S WAR DOGS: USED FOR SENTRY WORK IN A FRONT-LINE TRENCH IN FLANDERS.

Vallentin, who was shot down, and on rising to continue on his forward way was immediately killed. But his gallantry was not thrown away, because "the capture of the enemy's trenches, which followed, was in a great measure due to the confidence which the men had in their captain, arising from his many previous acts of great bravery and ability." On February 18th Vallentin's memory was honoured by the grant of the V.C.

On November 11th the German Emperor made a supreme effort to break the British line. The Prussian Guard, the corps d'élite of his Army, was ordered up and sent forward to perform a feat which its comrades had failed to do. In one or two places it succeeded, but, as a whole, the attack was a failure, and this was due, among others, to Lieutenant W. L. Brodie, of the 2nd Battalion of the Highland Light Infantry. Heading a charge, Brodie and his men bayoneted several of the enemy who had occupied a portion of our trenches and recovered some lost ground. A dangerous situation was relieved, and, as a result of Brodie's promptitude, eighty of the enemy were killed and fifty-one taken prisoners. The two V.C.'s in this fine battalion—Brodie and George Wilson—were fitting comrades.

A COMPANY OF "GOUMIERS" (FRENCH AFRICAN CAVALRY), WATERING THEIR HORSES AT A RUNNING STREAM.

Among many tragic scenes, campaigning sometimes presents, by way of a relief, picturesque impressions which might have been composed at leisure by a great artist to please the eye. Witness the scene above. The atmosphere of peace and repose is curiously imbued with a feeling of force and strength. These proud African horsemen, watering their steeds, saturated in sweat, belonged to a squadron of "Goumiers," as the men belonging to the French native African cavalry are popularly known, who had just returned from a long and costly reconnaissance.

[*From a painting by G. Hillyard Swinstead, R.I.*]

LIEUT. CYRIL GORDON MARTIN, V.C., D.S.O.
Lieut. Martin, 56th Field Coy., R.E., at Le Cateau on August 26th, 1914, held with his section a post from which the infantry had been driven, and remained there under fierce fire until relieved. He was wounded, and won the D.S.O. He won his V.C. at Spanbroek Molen, on March 12th, 1915, when in command of a grenade-throwing party of six rank and file. Although wounded early in the action, he led his party into the enemy's trenches and held back the German reinforcements for nearly two and a half hours, until the evacuation of the trench was ordered.

In the neighbourhood of Ypres the Germans continued their assault, although not perhaps with the fury of the one on the 11th. On the 12th they attacked our position at Klein Zillebeke, where Lieutenant J. H. S. Dimmer, of the 2nd Battalion King's Royal Rifle Corps, was working a machine-gun. Although he was hit no less than five times, Dimmer stuck to his post until his gun was destroyed. Very quickly, **A valorous** on November 19th, he was **Rifleman** awarded the V.C., the last of the eleven earned during the great Battle of Ypres. A finer eleven never fought or played upon any field.

During the trench warfare which followed the first Battle of Ypres the V.C. was won by a bandsman, T. E. Rendle, of the 1st Battalion of the Duke of Cornwall's Light Infantry. Serving, as bandsmen usually do on the field of battle, as a stretcher-bearer, Rendle, on November 20th, showed conspicuous bravery near Wulverghem in attending to the wounded under very heavy shell and rifle fire. In addition, he rescued some men from trenches in which they had been buried by the fire from the German heavy howitzers having

blown the parapet upon them. Rendle was awarded the cross on January 11th.

On November 23rd the Germans made a determined attack upon some trenches near Festubert held by the Indian corps. A counter-attack was organised during the night of the 23rd, and in this the 39th Garhwal Riflemen, from the northern hills, took a leading part. They cleared the enemy from some of our trenches, and in this work a naik, Darwan Sing Negi, was prominent. Although wounded in two places in the head, and also in the arm, he was one of the first to push **The Indians at** round each successive traverse, **Festubert** and he did this in the face of severe fire from bombs and rifles at the closest range. On December 7th, the same day as the sepoy Khudadad, he was awarded the V.C.

On the 24th the Indians and the Germans continued their struggle for the trenches, and Lieutenant F. A. de Pass, of the 34th (Prince Albert Victor's Own) Poona Horse, entered a German sap and, in spite of the enemy's bombs, managed to destroy a traverse. He then rescued, under heavy fire, a wounded man who was lying exposed in the open, and still later on the same day he made a second attempt to take the sap, which had been recaptured by the Germans.

MAJOR C. A. L. YATE, V.C., IN THE HANDS OF THE ENEMY.
He commanded one of the two companies of the 2nd Yorkshire Light Infantry that remained to the end in the trenches at Le Cateau on August 26th, 1914, and, when all other officers were killed or wounded, and the ammunition was exhausted, led his nineteen survivors against the enemy in a charge in which he was severely wounded. He was picked up by the enemy. Happily, it was stated later that he had not died of his wounds, as was at first reported.

PTE. J. MACKENZIE,
2nd Scots Guards. Won V.C. at
Rouges Bancs. Killed.

2ND-LT. G. R. DALLAS MOOR,
3rd Hants. Saved dangerous
situation on Gallipoli.

2ND-LT. RHODES-MOORHOUSE,
Special reserve R.F.C. Fatally
wounded near Courtrai.

LIEUT.-COM. M. E. NASMITH,
R.N. Torpedoed Turkish ships in
Sea of Marmora.

LIEUT. P. NEAME,
R.E. Displayed conspicuous
bravery near Neuve Chapelle.

While engaged in this deed he was killed, and his name appeared in the "London Gazette" of February 18th among the recipients of the Victoria Cross.

On December 14th the 2nd Battalion of the Royal Scots assisted some French troops in attacking a German position, and was successful in getting on to the edge of a hill called Petit Bois. Here Private Henry H. Robson of this regiment showed "most conspicuous bravery" in leaving his trench under a very heavy fire and rescuing a wounded non-commissioned officer. Subsequently he tried to save another wounded man, persevering in his attempts until two wounds had rendered him helpless.

Five days later, on December 19th, there was more fierce fighting in the neighbourhood of Neuve Chapelle and Festubert. Near the former place Lieutenant Philip Neame, of the Royal Engineers, was helping to rescue the wounded men. **Gallant rescues** He managed to keep back the enemy, **at Neuve Chapelle** who were firing their rifles and throwing bombs, until he had carried into safety all the wounded men who could be moved.

Not far away, at Rouges Bancs, Private J. Mackenzie, of the 2nd Battalion of the Scots Guards, was doing similar work. On one occasion a party of stretcher-bearers attempted in vain to reach a wounded man. Seeing this, Mackenzie went forward under a heavy fire and carried him back from the very front of the German trenches. A second time on that same day he attempted to perform a like act of gallantry, but on this occasion he was unfortunately killed. The names of Robson, Neame, and

SERGT. D. NELSON,
L Batt. R.H.A. (later 2nd-Lieut.).
A hero of Nery.

ACTING-CORPL. C. R. NOBLE,
2nd Rifle Brigade. Died of wounds
at Neuve Chapelle.

CAPT. H. S. RANKEN,
R.A.M.C. Died of wounds received
at Hautvesnes.

BANDSMAN T. E. RENDLE,
1st Duke of Cornwall's L.I.
Distinguished at Wulverghem.

COM. H. P. RITCHIE,
R.N. Won his V.C. at Dar-es-Salaam, East Africa.

PTE. J. RIVERS,
1st Sherwood Foresters. Another hero of **Neuve Chapelle**.

PTE. H. H. ROBSON,
2nd Royal Scots. Effected gallant rescue near Kemmel.

CAPT. F. A. C. SCRIMGER,
Canadian A. M.S. Rendered gallant services near Ypres.

Mackenzie were among those upon whom the V.C. was bestowed on February 18th.

At Rouges Bancs, two days later (December 21st), there were other gallant rescues, and the V.C. was won by two privates—Abraham Acton and James Smith—of the 2nd Battalion of the Border Regiment. First of all, the two went voluntarily from their trench and rescued a wounded man who had been lying exposed near the German trenches for three whole days, and later they went **Michael O'Leary's great feat** out a second time and brought another wounded man into safety. The pair were under fire for an hour, but both returned safely. Their honour was dated February 18th, 1915.

The first V.C. won during 1915 was gained by Lance-Corporal Michael O'Leary, of the Irish Guards, for one of the most remarkable feats performed during the whole war. It was at Cuinchy, on February 1st, when O'Leary was one of a party moving forward to storm the German barricades. When near the enemy he rushed to the front and himself killed five Germans who were holding the first barricade, and then went forward to the second one, which

was about sixty yards distant. There he killed three of the enemy and took two others prisoners. This is what the official announcement said on February 18th : " Lance-Corporal O'Leary thus practically captured the enemy's position by himself, and prevented the rest of the attacking party from being fired upon." A volume could add nothing to this simple statement of fact. In September O'Leary was given a commission in the Northumberland Fusiliers.

One of the big battles of the Great War was fought

LIEUT. J. G. SMYTH,
15th Ludhiana Sikhs. Brought up bombs **under fire at Festubert**.

PTE. R. TOLLERTON,
1st Cameron Highlanders. Won his V.C. at the Aisne.

CAPT. J. F. VALLENTIN,
1st South Staffs. Killed while leading at Zillebeke.

CAPT. G. N. WALFORD,
R.A. One of the heroes of Seddul Bahr.

SUB-LIEUT. WARNEFORD,
R.N.A.S. Destroyed a Zeppelin in mid-air.

AN EPISODE IN THE CAMPAIGN ON GALLIPOLI.
Daring British officer attacking a Gallipoli fort single-handed. Shooting down some of the gunners with his revolver, he caused the Turkish fire to slacken sufficiently for the Dublins to rush in and capture the stronghold.

leading man by throwing a bomb. After this the remainder, some fifty in number, finding it impossible to escape, surrendered to him.

Barber performed a similar feat in another part of the field. He ran quickly in front of the company to which he belonged and threw his bombs upon the enemy so successfully that "a very great number" of them lost no time in surrendering to him. When the rest of the party came up to Barber they found him quite alone and unsupported with the Germans surrendering all around him. If a novelist had depicted these two scenes, we should have admired his imagination, but not his knowledge of life. However, truth is still stranger than fiction. Barber and Fuller were honoured together on April 19th.

The throwing of bombs was a feature of this battle at Neuve Chapelle, and Private Jacob Rivers, of the 1st Battalion of the Sherwood Foresters, was one who used them to some purpose on March 12th. On the flank of an advanced company of his battalion, a large number of the enemy were massed, and seeing this, Rivers, on his own initiative, crept to within a few yards of them and hurled bombs on them. This action compelled them to retire, and consequently relieved the situation. A second time on the same day Rivers went out to perform the feat, and a second time he forced the enemy to withdraw, but on this occasion he was himself killed.

On the same day Corporal William Anderson, of the 2nd Battalion the Yorkshire Regiment, prevented "by his prompt and determined action" what might otherwise have become a serious situation. He did this by leading three men with bombs against a large party of the enemy who had entered our trenches. First throwing his own bombs, Anderson then seized and hurled those in the possession of his three companions who had all been wounded. He followed up **Doughty deeds** this attack by firing his rifle with the **with bombs** utmost rapidity at the invading Germans, who, although he was quite alone, did not wait to dispute with him. On May 22nd his name appeared in the "London Gazette" as a recipient of the V.C.

Something similar was the exploit by which Lieutenant Cyril G. Martin, D.S.O., of the Royal Engineers, won his V.C. He was in command of six men who formed a party for throwing bombs, and early in the action he had been wounded. In spite of this, however, he led his little detachment into the German trenches and remained there, holding back the enemy's reinforcements, until he was ordered to abandon the captured trench. He had been in it for two and a half hours. Martin was one of the band honoured on April 19th.

On the afternoon of March 12th the 2nd Battalion of the

at Neuve Chapelle on March 10th, 11th, and 12th, 1915, and there nine Victoria Crosses were gained. The first was won by an Indian, Rifleman Gobar Sing Negi, like his namesake, a soldier in the ranks of the 39th Garhwal Rifles. During the attack on the German position which opened the battle on the 10th, Negi was one of a party which, armed with bayonets and bombs, entered the enemy's main trench. He was the first man to go round each traverse, and was instrumental in driving back the Germans until they were forced to surrender. During the battle he was unfortunately killed, but on April 28th he received a posthumous V.C.

Grenadiers rival So much for the 10th, but the fight-
heroes of Dumas ing on the 12th was fiercer still, and nowhere more so than around Pietre Mill, where were the 1st Battalion of the Grenadier Guards. There Lance-Corporal W. D. Fuller and Private Edward Barber of that regiment showed "most conspicuous bravery." In one place Fuller, seeing a party of the enemy trying to escape along a communication trench, ran towards them and, although quite alone, killed the

Rifle Brigade was sent forward against some German trenches. Unflinchingly they advanced until they found themselves stopped by wire entanglements and shot down by machine-guns. At this moment two volunteers, Sergeant-Major Harry Daniels and Corporal Cecil R. Noble, rushed forward and cut the wire, thus allowing the battalion to make further progress. Both were wounded while engaged in this hazardous occupation, and later Noble died of his wounds. The following September Sergeant-Major Daniels received a commission.

The ninth of the crosses won at Neuve Chapelle was gained by Private William Buckingham, of the 2nd Battalion Leicestershire Regiment. The words in which the award was made on April 28th are few but fine. "For conspicuous acts of bravery and devotion to duty in rescuing and rendering aid to the wounded while exposed to heavy fire, especially at Neuve Chapelle on March 10th and 12th, 1915." April 28th was also the date on which Daniels and Noble received this coveted distinction.

The chief incidents on the western front during April were the fight for "Hill 60" and the first use of asphyxiating gases by the Germans against the Canadian lines. Before these events, however, Private Robert Morrow, of the 1st Battalion Royal Irish Fusiliers, won the Victoria Cross for "most conspicuous bravery." Near Messines on April 12th he rescued and carried to comparative safety several men who had been buried under the debris of trenches wrecked by shell fire. He did this, we were told when the award was made on May 22nd, "on his own initiative and under very heavy fire."

On "Hill 60" three Victoria Crosses were won, two of them by members of the 1st Battalion of the East Surreys. In a front trench on the hill, Lieutenant G. R. P. Roupell was in command of a company which was

V.C.'s won on "Hill 60" under severe fire during the whole day (April 20th). He was wounded in several places, but he remained at his post, and led forward his men to beat back a strong German attack. This success gave the company a brief respite, so Roupell went away and had his wounds hurriedly dressed, but insisted on returning to the front where he and his company were again under heavy fire. As evening drew on the men became fewer and fewer, and the possibility of being driven out became greater, so the lieutenant went back to the battalion headquarters to explain the position, and then brought up reinforcements, "passing backwards and forwards over ground swept by heavy fire." With the assistance of these new men he held the position during the night, and in the morning his company was replaced by another. His heroic deed was thus praised in the "Gazette" of June 23rd: "This young officer was one of the few survivors of his company, and showed a magnificent

A POST OF DANGER IN THE FIRE CONTROL.
British artillery observation officer watching the effect of shell fire and telephoning results to the battery commander. It would be difficult to exaggerate the importance of this perilous work, which is taken up, usually at a moment's notice, in some ruined building, as shown in our picture, just in the rear of the infantry firing-line.

example of courage, devotion, and tenacity, which undoubtedly inspired his men to hold out to the end."

During the same encounter one of the East Surrey trenches was heavily attacked by bomb-throwers. In this predicament Lance-Corporal Edward Dwyer climbed out on to the parapet, and although met with a hail of bombs at close quarters, managed to drive away the attackers by the effective use of his own weapons of the same kind. This deed alone was sufficient to win for him the V.C., but earlier in the same day **First Territorial V.C.** Dwyer had displayed great gallantry in leaving his trench under heavy shell fire in order to bandage his wounded comrades. In September he received a commission in the Northumberland Fusiliers.

The third V.C. won on "Hill 60" was a memorable one, for it was the first ever won by a Territorial. The recipient was Second-Lieutenant G. H. Woolley, of the 9th Battalion of the London Regiment, the one better known as Queen Victoria's Rifles. During the night of the 20th Woolley was the only officer on a certain part of the hill, and of those under him very few were left. Nevertheless, he and they resisted all attacks made on their trench, the lieutenant throwing bombs and encouraging his men through the darkness of that terrible night until they were relieved. During all this time a regular hail of bombs, shells, and shot from machine-guns fell upon the trench and its defenders. Woolley and Dwyer received the V.C. on May 22nd.

It was three days later, on the 23rd, that the Canadians were attacked near Ypres, and here they won three V.C.'s. Near St. Julien a battery was retreating and was in danger of capture when Lance-Corporal Frederick Fisher, realising the gravity of the situation, hurried forward with his machine-gun and under heavy fire made it possible for the battery to get safely away. In doing this he lost four of his men, but having obtained four more he went again into the firing-line to perform another action of great gallantry. This was to take his machine-gun forward in order to cover the advance of a supporting force, but in doing so the brave lance-corporal was killed.

Three gallant Canadians

On the following day, the 24th, a wounded man was lying about fifteen yards from a trench in the neighbourhood of Ypres. He was heard calling aloud for help, and a Canadian colour-sergeant, Frederick William Hall, tried, with the help of two comrades, to reach him. The enemy, however, was pouring in a heavy enfilading fire, and the attempt failed, the two assistants being wounded. Undeterred, however, Hall tried a second time to rescue the wounded man, and was in the very act of lifting him up when he himself fell mortally wounded in the head. In very truth he gave his life for another.

During this heavy fighting, a Canadian doctor, Captain Francis A. C. Scrimger, the medical officer attached to the 14th Battalion of the Royal Montreal Regiment, was conspicuous in rendering services to the wounded, as between April 22nd and 25th, so we were told, he "displayed continuously day and night the greatest devotion to his duty among the wounded at the front." But this was not all. On the afternoon of the 25th he was in charge of an advanced dressing station in some farm buildings near Ypres.

The buildings were being heavily shelled, and it was necessary to remove the wounded therefrom. This was directed by Captain Scrimger, who himself carried a severely wounded officer out of a stable. After a time, unable to reach a place of safety, he found it impossible to carry the officer any farther, so he remained with him, both being under fire, until help arrived. The three Canadians were awarded the V.C. on June 23rd, but Scrimger alone was alive to wear it.

During this same spell of fighting around Ypres the V.C. was won by an Indian native officer, Jemadar Mir Dast, who was attached to the 57th Wilde's Rifles, and who had already earned the Indian Order of Merit. On April 26th he led his platoon with great gallantry during a German attack, and afterwards, when all the British officers had been put out of action, he collected various parties of the regiment and kept them together under his command until they were ordered to retire. Later in the day the jemadar displayed remarkable courage in helping to carry eight British and Indian officers into safety, while exposed to very heavy fire. Truly our Indian soldiers have justified their tardy admission to places on our highest scroll of fame.

The knowledge that the Germans were using poisonous gases only spurred our men, if possible, to greater heroism, and at the beginning of May two V.C.'s were won by Englishmen in the face of this new and barbarous weapon of war. On the 1st a trench near "Hill 60" had just been vacated by our men as a consequence of a gas attack, when Private Edward Warner, of the 1st Battalion of the Bedfordshires, entered it alone in order to prevent the enemy from seizing it. Reinforcements were sent forward to help him, but owing to the gas they could not reach the trench, so Warner himself came out to them, and under his guidance they managed to reach it. By this time the hero was completely exhausted, and shortly afterwards he died from the effects of gas poisoning. However, his bravery had saved the trench, for it was held until the German attack ceased.

On the next day Private John Lynn, of the 2nd Battalion of the Lancashire Fusiliers, won for himself an immortal name for "most conspicuous bravery" near Ypres. When the Germans were advancing behind their waves of poisonous gas, Lynn, although almost overcome by the awful fumes, worked his machine-gun with very great effect against them. At length he was unable to see them, owing to the nearing clouds of gas, so he moved his gun to a higher place on the parapet, and poured a still more effective fire upon them. This heroic action eventually checked the enemy's advance, and, as we were officially told, "the great courage displayed by this soldier had a fine effect on his comrades in the very trying circumstances." Lynn's superhuman courage cost him his life, for on the next day he died from the effects of gas poisoning. Over his tomb Napier's immortal words should be inscribed: "No man died that night with more glory—yet many died and there was much glory." On June 29th the memories of Warner and Lynn—fitting companions in death—were honoured by the grant of the Victoria Cross.

Lancashire Fusilier's self-sacrifice

On May 9th the British forces delivered a successful

PTE. G. WILSON, V.C.
2nd Highland Light Infantry. Captured a hostile machine-gun near Verneuil.

COL. DOUGHTY-WYLIE, V.C.
C.M.G., C.B. Killed with Capt. Walford in attack at Seddul Bahr.

CAPT. T. WRIGHT. V.C.
R.E. Displayed conspicuous gallantry at Mons and Vailly.

A GLIMPSE OF THE ENEMY'S POSITION THROUGH A LOOPHOLE.
Striking photograph, taken through a loophole in a British trench, showing German position a few yards distant. The enemy's earthworks, sand-bags, and wire entanglements can be seen plainly, while buildings wrecked by artillery fire are observable in the background.

attack on the German position near Fromelles, and on that day four Victoria Crosses were won. A prominent place in the assault was assigned to a regiment which has a record second to none in the British Army—the famous Black Watch, or Royal Highlanders. The Black Watch attacked the enemy near Rue du Bois, and there Corporal John Ripley was leading a section on the right of a platoon. Of the whole battalion he was the first man to mount the German parapet, and, standing there exposed to fire, he pointed out to the others the ways through the gaps made by our artillery in the wire entanglements. This done, Ripley led his section through a breach in the parapet to the second line of trenches, and having reached his objective he set to work to make the position secure. Aided by a few men, seven or eight, he blocked up both flanks, arranged a good position for firing, and continued to defend the captured trench until all his men had fallen and he himself had been badly wounded in the head.

About the same time Lance-Corporal David Finlay of the same regiment was leading forward a bombing party of twelve men, and he did this with the greatest gallantry until ten of them had fallen. Then **Heroes of** Finlay showed the stuff of which he was **the Black Watch** made. He ordered the two survivors to crawl back into safety, but he himself went forward to the assistance of a wounded man, and carried him for a hundred yards under heavy fire, eventually placing him under cover. He did this, it is hardly necessary to say, quite regardless of his own personal safety.

Near Rouges Bancs the 2nd Battalion of the Lincolnshire Regiment was playing a part in this attack, and there Corporal Charles Sharpe was—unknowingly, of course—emulating Ripley. Being in charge of a party sent forward

to capture a portion of a German trench, he was the first to reach it. Once there he threw his bombs with great determination and effect, and in a short time he had cleared all the Germans from a trench fifty yards long. In the end all his men had fallen, but four others came forward to assist Sharpe, and the five made another successful attack on the enemy, using their bombs with such vigour that they captured this time a trench, not fifty, but two hundred and fifty yards long.

In the same neighbourhood, near **Trench taken** Rouges Bancs, was the 1st Battalion of the **by five men** Sherwood Foresters, and there Corporal James Upton of that regiment spent the day in attending to the wounded. As the official account says: "During the whole of this day Corporal Upton displayed the greatest courage in rescuing the wounded while exposed to very heavy rifle and artillery fire, going close to the enemy's parapet regardless of his own personal safety." One man was killed by a shell while in his arms. Moreover, when Upton was not actually engaged in this hazardous duty, he was at work bandaging and dressing the serious cases in front of our parapet, and doing this when exposed to the enemy's fire. Ripley, Finlay, Sharpe, and Upton were among the ten heroes who received the V.C. on June 29th.

The next V.C. was earned by a Territorial, like Woolley, a member of the London Regiment, but not in the same battalion, for Lance-Sergeant Douglas W. Belcher belonged to the 5th—the London Rifle Brigade. On the morning of May 13th Belcher was in charge of an advanced breast-work near St. Julien. This was bombarded fiercely and continuously by the Germans, and was frequently blown in. Near by some troops had been withdrawn owing to the

BRITISH CAVALRY EXERCISING ON THE SEA-SWEPT SAND-
DUNES OF FLANDERS.

PRINCE ALEXANDER OF TECK WATCHING ANTI AIR-CRAFT
GUN IN THE BELGIAN LINES.

STURDY SONS OF THE MAPLE LEAF FILLING SAND-BAGS FOR THE TRENCHES
DURING A LULL IN THE FIGHTING.

heavy fire, but Belcher and a few men decided that they
would remain and hold the position. This they did,
Belcher's "skill and great gallantry" being the soul of
the defence, for whenever he saw the enemy, who were
only about two hundred yards away, collecting for an
attack, he opened a rapid fire upon him. This was a
very valuable piece of work for it is practically certain
that the bold front shown by Belcher "prevented the
enemy breaking through on the Wieltje road, and averted
an attack on the flank of one of our divisions."

On May 15th the British had a success near Festubert,
and on the 16th several battalions, among them the 1st
Royal Welsh Fusiliers, were holding
some captured trenches and portions of **Welsh Fusiliers'**
trenches. In one of these portions **great capture**
was Sergeant-Major Frederick Barter,
of the Fusiliers, and he called for volunteers from among
his company to enable him to extend our line. Eight
men responded, and under Barter's lead they attacked
the German position with bombs, and captured three
German officers and one hundred and two men, as well
as five hundred yards of their
trenches. After this feat Barter
found and cut eleven of the
enemy's mine leads, situated
about twenty yards from each
other. Like several others, this
non-commissioned officer may be
said to have earned the V.C.
twice.

Two days later a lieutenant
in the Indian Army won the
V.C. near the same place. Some
bombs were badly needed at a
spot within twenty yards of the
German position, and two parties
attempted to carry them thither,
but failed. Whereupon Lieutenant John G. Smyth, of the
15th Ludhiana Sikhs, with a
bombing party of ten men,
volunteered for this duty. The
ground over which they had to
go was "exceptionally dangerous,"
and on the way eight of the ten
were either killed or wounded.
However, Smyth and the
remaining two struggled on,

exposed to the fire of howitzers, machine-guns, and rifles, and at length, having swum a stream, they brought ninety-six bombs to those who needed them. Smyth and Barter were both awarded the V.C. on June 29th.

On May 22nd there occurred the gallant deed by which Private William Mariner, of the 2nd Battalion the King's Royal Rifle Corps, won the Victoria Cross. A German machine-gun had been damaging our parapets and hindering our working parties, and Mariner decided to put an end to the annoyance. Accordingly at night, while a violent thunderstorm was raging, he crept out of his trench, through the German wire entanglements, and at length reached the emplacement of the gun. He then climbed on to the top of the German parapet, and threw a bomb under the roof of the gun emplacement. Some groaning and running away followed, while Mariner waited in silence.

Perilous work in a thunderstorm

About fifteen minutes later some of the Germans returned, and were greeted with another bomb, thrown into the other side of the emplacement, for Mariner had climbed over there and had thrown the bomb with his left hand. While the Germans fired into the darkness, Mariner lay quite still; but at length, after an hour had elapsed, the excitement died down, and he was able to crawl back to his trench, having been out alone on this work for an hour and a half. As showing his total indifference to danger, Mariner had requested a sergeant to open fire on the enemy's trenches as soon as ever he had thrown his bombs. On June 23rd Mariner received the V.C.

Mariner's feat deserves to rank with those of O'Leary and George Wilson as one of the outstanding deeds of the Great War, and so does the next on our list. On the night of May 25th the 24th Battalion of the London Regiment, the Queen's, made a successful attack on the German position at Givenchy, and there one of its lance-corporals, Leonard James Keyworth, won for that regiment, and for the Territorial Force in general, a third Victoria Cross. It was in this wise. After the assault, seventy-five men of the battalion attempted to follow up their success by a bomb attack, and a very fierce encounter took place between them and the Germans, who were only a few yards away. The nature of the fight is shown by the fact that fifty-eight of the seventy-five Londoners were either killed or wounded. Now for a simple statement of fact : " During this very fierce encounter Lance-Corporal Keyworth stood fully exposed for two hours on the top of the enemy's parapet, and threw about a hundred and fifty bombs among the Germans, who were only a few yards away." The words " for two hours " and " fully exposed " tell their own story. On July 3rd the V.C. was awarded to Keyworth.

Two more Victoria Crosses complete the seventy-two won in Flanders, and both these were gained for saving life. On June 12th, 1915, Lance-Corporal William Angus, of the 8th Battalion of the Highland Light Infantry, one composed of Territorials from Lanarkshire, was, like Keyworth, at Givenchy. Seeing a wounded officer lying within a few yards of the enemy's position, he voluntarily left his trench and rescued him in spite of very heavy fire from bombs and rifles. He had no chance whatever,

Fourth V.C. for Territorials

FRENCH CAVALRY AT WORK IN THE CHAMPAGNE DISTRICT.
A remarkable and picturesque view of the cavalry of our gallant French allies fording a river in the Champagne country.

we were told, of escaping the enemy's fire when undertaking this very gallant action, and while rescuing the officer he sustained about forty wounds from bombs, some of them being very serious. Angus was one of the ten honoured on June 29th.

On June 16th another lance-corporal, Joseph Tombs, of the 1st Battalion the Liverpool Regiment, called also the King's, was near Rue du Bois, where Britons have performed so many gallant deeds. On his own initiative he crawled out of his trench repeatedly, and under a very severe fire from heavy guns and machine-guns, he rescued four wounded men who were lying about a hundred yards from our trenches. One of these rescues was especially noteworthy, for Tombs dragged the man back to safety by means of a rifle-sling placed round his own neck and the man's body. This heroism and devotion undoubtedly

MICHAEL O'LEARY'S HOME AT MACROOM.

saved his life, for he had been wounded so severely that without immediate attention he would have died.

This ends for the present our tale of heroism in France and Flanders. Seventy-two Victoria Crosses were given, but who can say how many were earned ? Many more, we are quite sure. But these—the official ones—which we have here recorded, make up a story of courage and devotion which may perhaps have been equalled, but can never have been surpassed, since man the fighter first emerged from " the dark and backward abysm of time."

Towards the end of April, 1915, Great Britain and France became involved in a second great campaign, the attack on the Gallipoli Peninsula, and before August 4th, 1915, four Victoria Crosses had been awarded for gallantry there, and this was merely a beginning.

The first two were gained on that terrible and unforgettable day, April 26th, 1915, when the British troops made good their landing on the almost impregnable Gallipoli Peninsula; for, as was truly said, by all the precepts of war our men ought never to have got ashore at all. On one of the beaches were a few survivors of the Royal Dublin Fusiliers, Royal Munster Fusiliers, and Hampshires, who had got ashore, but at a frightful cost. Nearly all the senior officers had been killed and wounded, including the general, but with the remnants of the brigade were Lieut.-Col. C. H. M. Doughty-Wylie, C.M.G., C.B., of the Headquarters Staff, and Captain G. N. Walford, a brigade-major of the Royal Artillery, and these two realised that something must be done. Accordingly they organised and led an attack on the hill above the beach, whereon was the village of Seddul Bahr. The Turkish position was very strongly held, was entrenched, and was defended by concealed guns. Nevertheless, the attack succeeded completely, for not only was the village taken, but so were the

V.C.'s won in Gallipoli

Old Castle and Hill 141 beyond it. This was mainly due to the initiative, skill, and great gallantry of these two officers, both of whom were killed in the moment of victory.

In this Gallipoli campaign the Australians took no small part, and it is not surprising that one of them, Lance-Corporal Albert Jacka, of the 14th Battalion of Infantry, early gained there a Victoria Cross. It was for most conspicuous bravery on the night of May 19th-20th, at "Courtney's Post." It seems that Jacka and four other men were holding a portion of a trench when they were heavily attacked and the four were either killed or wounded. Seven Turks then rushed into the trench, but they had not reckoned on Jacka. At once he attacked them and killed the whole seven, shooting down five with his rifle and finishing off the remaining two with the bayonet.

Corporal Jacka's deed of heroism

On July 24th the gallant Australian received the V.C.

In the force which invaded the Gallipoli Peninsula was the 3rd (Special Reserve) Battalion of the Hampshire Regiment, and in this was a young officer, Second-Lieutenant G. R. Dallas Moor, who had only joined the Army in October, 1914. On June 5th, 1915, he was in some fighting to the south of Krithia, when he noticed that a detachment on his left, having lost all its officers, was falling back before a heavy Turkish attack, and so was endangering the safety of the whole line. Promptly realising this, Moor dashed after the retiring men, pulled them up, and then led them

MR. AND MRS. O'LEARY, FATHER AND MOTHER OF MICHAEL O'LEARY, V.C.

forward and recaptured the lost trench. By his personal bravery and presence of mind he saved a dangerous situation, for which service he was awarded the Victoria Cross on July 24th.

We have seen how eighty-two men won the Victoria Cross ; but what about the brave men who helped them, and the other brave men whose deeds of heroism were unnoticed ? In most cases their names are unknown.

To thank them and be grateful to them is our simple duty, but we will refrain from praising them. They do not need it. Words can add nothing to the honour they have won. Better it is to take our farewell of them in the spirit of the words which Sir Henry Newbolt has applied to Nelson and his men :

"Lover of England, stand awhile and gaze,
With faithful heart and lips refrained from praise."

MILITARY FÊTE DAY

CHAPTER LXXXII.

AT PETERHOF.

AN INSIDE VIEW OF RUSSIA IN WAR TIME.

By John Foster Fraser, Author of "Russia To-day," "The Real Siberia," etc.

The Glow of Religious Sentiment over the Whole of Muscovy—The Tsar Crushes the Vodka Peril—Germany Calculates on Revolutionary Trouble, but the Unprecedented Patriotism of all Parties Preserves Russian Union—A War Waged Not by the Russian Government but by the Russian People—Development of Public Opinion Puts Down Official Profiteers—Attitude of the Baltic Province Russians—"Russia for the Russians"—The Fire of Animus against the Germans—How the War Affected Industrial Russia—Neutrals and the Rush for Contracts—Supplies Held Up by Lack of Communications—Warsaw Before its Evacuation—Caring for the Refugees from Galicia—The Imperial Family and Hospital Work—Affection for the Tsar—Russia and Her Allies.

THE TSAR AND THE GRAND DUKE NICHOLAS AT THE FRONT.

In September, 1915, the Tsar placed himself in supreme command of his Army and Navy, and the Grand Duke Nicholas, whose fighting retreat had wrested admiration even from the foe, was appointed "Viceroy of the Caucasus and Commander-in-Chief of the valiant Caucasian Army."

NOTWITHSTANDING the reverses to which her giant Army was subjected, Holy Russia never questioned the result of the war.

France remained animated by a splendid chivalry, and Britain was determined at whatever cost to defend her Empire. It was, however, not so much the spirit of nationality which bound the one hundred and sixty million people of Russia together as a deep-seated abiding belief that their holy country could never be subject to an alien Power.

You have to understand the religious sentiment which permeates the whole of Muscovy to appreciate how the Russians felt in regard to the conflict which was waged on her frontiers. She had her set-backs. Millions of her sons yielded their lives, but the end had to be—the Russian mind was incapable of thinking otherwise — a victory for Holy Russia.

It is this state of thought which made Russia in war time so incomprehensible to the foreigner. The people were moody and emotional, poetical rather than practical, and while bad news depressed them, good news never elated them. They took victories as a matter of course, because they knew they were to come. The Russians are in many ways the most charming people on the earth. They have the simplicity of children. Their hospitality is unbounded. A Russian will go out of his way, and spend much more than the condition of his purse justifies, to give the visitor a good time. He knows perfectly well that men of other countries look upon him as something of a savage, with a considerable tincture of wild Tartar blood in his veins. He is aware that, compared with other lands, he is backward; but he modestly reminds you that Russia, as a great people, has been in existence for not much more than one hundred years.

Yet with all its hindrances, the Russian Empire has widened and extended until the dawn of the twentieth century found it the greatest cohesive nation on the earth. Indeed, it had grown so much, and drawn within its territory so many people of other races, that it may be said to have become fenced around with non - Russian speaking Russians. It was its size, its majesty, which filled the imaginative Russian with the conviction that it had a mighty destiny,

YY   **393**

THE SWORD OF FAITH: RUSSIAN SOLDIERS MAKING THE SIGN OF THE CROSS
AS THEY PASS A WAYSIDE SHRINE.

From the outset of the war the soldiers of the Tsar, by the spirit in which they entered into the conflict with the neo-paganism of Germany, gave a new and deeper meaning to the term " Holy Russia." As they marched to the front their path was marked by many a wayside shrine or cross, and as the troops passed by, each man invariably made the sign of the cross and murmured a prayer·

not to be interfered with by the incursions of German soldiery. We heard a great deal about the numberless millions of men which Russia could put into the field. From the cold regions below Archangel, from the warm lands in the region of the Caucasus, from the prairies beyond the Volga, and from the illimitable stretches of Siberia the Russian was called to arms. He responded, not because he had a thirst to slay Germans, but because he felt it his duty to defend Holy Russia.

Frenchmen and Englishmen proceeded to war laughing and with gay songs upon their lips. Russian **The hymn** soldiers never do that. They go to their **before battle** church and humbly pray before their ikons, the sacred pictures of their particular saints ; they stand with bowed head while the picturesque and long-haired priests sprinkle holy water upon them, and then, singing hymns, they march to their fate, never letting go of the faith that whatever may befall them individually, Holy Russia must be triumphant.

I was in Russia during a considerable part of the first year of the war. The thing that impressed me most of all was the calm confidence of the people. In Petrograd, in Moscow, the ancient capital, in all the great cities, life progressed much as it did in normal times. Business was conducted in the ordinary way. All the entertainments, the theatres, and the pleasure gardens were in full swing. It was only by witnessing hymn-singing battalions of soldiers marching through the streets, or coming across groups of pale-faced wounded fellows hobbling along, that one was reminded that a great war was in progress.

When the alarm was first sounded, the Russian authorities had a mighty difficulty to face. They remembered that during the Russo-Japanese War the efficiency of their men was much impaired by drunkenness. The principal beverage in the country was vodka, a fiery spirit mostly made from rye, the manufacture of which was a Government monopoly, and the effect of which was direful.

Germany calculated that the mobilisation of the Russian troops would be a slow and laborious process. The belief which prevailed in Berlin was, on the outbreak of hostilities, that first a swift blow should be levelled against France, and when France was in the dust, it would be time enough for the hordes of the Kaiser to sweep round and reckon with the soldiers of the Tsar.

But the Emperor William forgot the power of the Emperor Nicholas. The Tsar of All the Russias is the Little White Father to his people. Whatever order he issues is not in the nature of a law, but is a religious ordinance which must be obeyed. Therefore, swiftly grasping the necessity for action, the Emperor Nicholas issued his famous ukase, proclaiming that the Government manufacture of vodka should cease, so that the work of the Army should not be retarded by the drunkenness of the soldiers.

It is generally accepted that the Russian was a drunkard —as a matter of fact, the most drunken person in Europe. This is quite a mistake. The country where the least amount per head of the **Scotching the** population in Europe is expended on **vodka peril** alcohol is Norway. The country which comes next is Russia. Per head of the population, the Russian, in normal times, spends 18s. a year on drink, while in England the amount spent each year per head of the population is 66s. The difference is that, whereas in England the money is disbursed chiefly on so inhocuous a beverage as beer, practically all the money in Russia was spent on this fierce vodka spirit, which did tremendous harm physically, morally, and industrially to the subjects of the Tsar.

Forbidding the State manufacture of vodka did two things. It lopped off a revenue of £67,000,000 a year which went into the Imperial Exchequer, and it shut off the supply to the ordinary civilian. Freedom was given to the Zemstvos (local assemblies) and the municipalities **Obeying the " Little** to follow up the action of the Tsar in **Father's " edict** what way they pleased. With few exceptions, all the authorities throughout the realm, from Archangel to Tiflis and from Moscow to Vladivostok, prohibited the sale and consumption of alcohol in any form. Not only was vodka removed, but the police put seals on cellars, and prevented the consumption of brandy, of wines, and of beer.

Within a few days the whole of Russia, which had been a byword to the world, became teetotal. In a constitutionally governed country such a thing would have been impossible. It was only by the exercise of autocracy that such a revolution could be effected in the land of the Tsar. Because the original command came from the Little White Father, the Russians accepted it without question.

It is not, however, to be assumed that even in these days men with money could not obtain wine and spirits by subterranean means. They could. But, speaking in a broad and general sense, it may be said that after the issue of the ukase ninety-nine per cent. of the people of Russia never touched a drop of alcohol. Drunkards, of course, were distressed, and had recourse to methylated spirit and other beverages. But that means of ministering to the appetite was checked, because even methylated spirit could not be procured except through complicated formalities, which practically put it out of the reach of the former toper.

The thing to be taken notice of is that, without demur, Russia fell in with the new condition of things. Temptation being removed, the artisans of the towns and the moujiks of the steppes, unable to dispose of their earnings as they did formerly, found themselves in possession of more money than ever they had before. They were able to spend it on better food, on giving better clothing to their children, in providing themselves with healthy amusements; and so, although in Russia the cost of living was materially increased in consequence of the war, the people were in every sense much better off than they were formerly.

The soldiers responded to the call of their monarch with greater alacrity than they would have been able to do if they had fuddled their brains in the vodka taverns. The speed with which Russia was able to mobilise was a marvel to the world. In the early weeks of the struggle, when the German armies were engaged in their first great attempt to sweep through the North of France and gain possession of Paris, it was the action of the Russian troops in the north-east, rushing into Prussia, until at one time there was a belief that nothing could restrain them from reaching Berlin, that caused the Kaiser to slacken the pressure on the western front. He required German troops to proceed and contest the progress of the Russians in the north-east.

Not only that, but the abstinence of the nation had a beneficial effect industrially. I have never placed the Russian workman **Russian artisan's** high as an artisan; but the point **efficiency increased** is not to be missed that his efficiency was increased by at least fifteen — some people say twenty-five—per cent. owing to his inability to reach the vodka bottle.

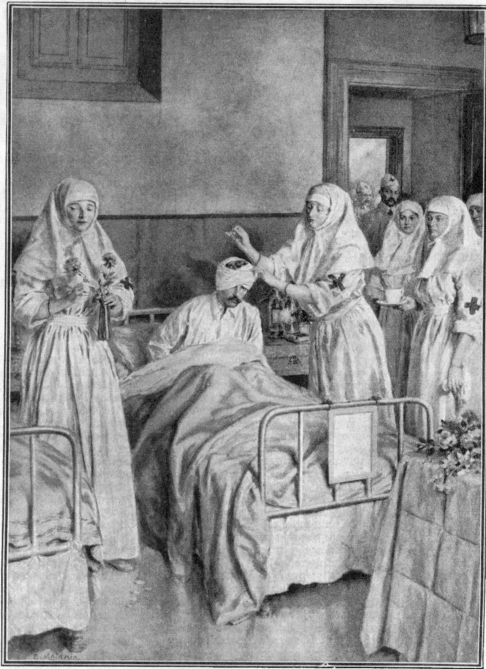

THE EMPRESS OF RUSSIA AND THE GRAND DUCHESSES OLGA AND TATIANA AS NURSES IN THE HOSPITAL AT TSARKÖE-SELO.

The Tsaritza—Alexandra-Feodorovna—is seen in the centre of the group. The Empress' eldest daughter, the Grand Duchess Olga, is on the left of the picture, while a younger daughter, the Grand Duchess Tatiana, is on the right. They attended almost daily at the hospital at Tsarköe-Selo, about fifteen miles south of Petrograd, where two of the Russian Imperial Palaces are situated.

WITH THE RUSSIAN TROOPS IN POLAND: SOLDIERS ENJOYING THEIR TEA IN THE OPEN.

Another great change which the war produced in Russia was the development of public opinion. It is not necessary to remind readers that in old days public opinion, such as it is understood in England, was non-existent in the dominions of the Tsar. The Government was paternal, it was autocratic, it watched over and cared for the people. Those who were irritable under constant surveillance, who hungered for a different condition of government than that which existed, and who gave vent to their views by joining in revolutionary movements, were harshly—and no doubt in many cases cruelly—treated.

One of the things which the German Government cal-culated upon was that, with Russia at war, the various revolutionary parties would endeavour to upset the existing régime, produce internal trouble, and so make Russia all the easier prey to Germany.

Now, for the first time within knowledge, the war was not waged by the Russian Government, but by the Russian people. The war of 1903 between Russia and Japan was regarded by the majority of the Russian people as a dispute between the Government and Japan. When Japan was able to overthrow Russia, the Russians themselves did not feel that their national dignity had been lowered. They accepted that a blow had been struck at the Government. The present war was from its outset different from that. Instead of the struggle on the frontiers providing the revolutionary party with a chance to push their propaganda into effect, it completely obliterated all political dissension throughout the whole of the Tsar's realms, in precisely the same way as political differences were sunk throughout the British Empire.

Patriotism of all parties Doubtless many of the advanced thinkers looked to a change, for what they considered to be the better in the administration of affairs, when the war should be over. For the time being, however, the revolutionaries—the men who had been nurtured on Western ideas, who resented autocracy as out of date, and desired their country to be administered on lines akin to those which we have in England—were just as true and as loyal to their Emperor as were men who had spent their lives within the precincts of the Court. Men who were exiled because of their opinions voluntarily returned to Russia, risking imprisonment, but eager to be of some service to their Motherland.

Such loyalty, which I believe the Russian Government never contemplated, had its effect in another direction. The grip of autocratic administration was slackened. There was a revolution in progress in Russia, but it was all to the good. Men discussed what was happening in the world, and in Russia particularly, with a freedom which twenty months previously would have been impossible. Newspapers criticised Ministers in a manner which, if attempted a little while back, would have landed them in the Fortress of Peter and Paul, or have sent them on a long visit to Siberia. Public meetings were held, especially in Moscow. What was happening in the war was debated with as much **Freedom of public** freedom as in England itself. While at **debate** concerts, I heard songs loudly applauded, and with the police standing by, which would have meant the arrest of the singers, if not of the audience, but a couple of years before.

Russia had some incompetent Ministers. The public knew they were incompetent; they said so in conversation in the cafés; they said so at public meetings. Writers said so in newspaper articles. And the consequence was that a number of these inefficient highly-placed personages were removed.

The war gave birth to healthy public opinion in Russia. I cannot but believe that it will continue after the war, if no steps should be taken to prevent it. And, if it does not run wild—for it is not to be forgotten that the Russians are an emotional and easily led race—it will be for the permanent well-being of the body politic.

During the first year of the war there was a remarkable development of public consciousness that action should be taken—violent, if necessary—to remove the black spots which disfigured the national escutcheon. Nothing pained the high-minded Russian in the past more than the knowledge that in public as well as in commercial life Russia had done what honourable men could not defend. Everyone was aware that little business was transacted without someone taking what he would have called a "commission," but which others would have described as a bribe. Of course, there were officials actuated by as worthy motives as those in any land, and whose hands were clean. But in the past every Russian shrugged his shoulders and was ready to admit that the accomplishment of services was

SERVING AN AMBUSCADED GUN AT AN IMPORTANT POINT ON THE RUSSIAN FRONT IN POLAND.

slow, chiefly because there was someone who needed a little—and occasionally a very large—stimulus to do his duty.

In what is called corruption, Russia is no worse than some other lands which consider themselves enlightened; but the practice of men receiving payment to do their duty was far too prevalent. In great Government contracts there were officials who wanted their commission from the manufacturer before the documents were allowed to go forward to the Minister to sign them. Right down to the humble policeman, badly paid, the same practice was usual. In most ordinary business trans-

Campaign against actions, the straightforward deal was **"commissions"** generally held up by someone who wanted to know what his commission was to be before the negotiations advanced to completion.

That was the state of things before the war. It was the state of things at the beginning of the war. The public, however, soon became acquainted with the fact that even the supply of munitions and war material of all sorts, so necessary for the equipment of the Army, were being retarded in delivery because of the pernicious practice of delay until the commission was arranged.

Then there swept through the nation a feeling of resentment, followed by a vociferous declaration that this sort of proceeding must cease. It would be idle to say that the frank indignation of the populace was the means of purifying public life. The point, however, I am making is that the Russians, who had been in the habit of acquiescing or explaining that the receiving of a reward by an official was an old custom, hard to remove, no longer defended it. It was vehemently denounced. There came forth a zealous belief that Russia was hampering herself by allowing such conditions to continue. There was clamour that certain prominent men, who were supposed to have exploited the necessities of their country to their own advantage, should be shot. The Government took the principal manufacturers into counsel, and all Government contracts had to pass through a special committee, thus preventing the "go-between" from lining his own pockets.

Everywhere I went I came across a vigorous campaign against the old practice. Officials in Russia were not too well paid. The defence often put forward for the niggardly pittance that was handed to them was that they could easily find other means to secure recompense for their labours.

The war not only stirred up the sentiment of the nation, but it moved men's minds to think of the future. One of the consequences of this was to create an ideal Russia in the popular imagination, where officials would be well paid for their labours, and where there would be purity in public life and fair dealing between men, so that the country, instead of being pointed at by other peoples, would be accepted as a model.

Thus it is to be seen that the conflict was not only one waged to overthrow the Germans. It was one between old habits and new ambitions, with the thought ever at the back of men's minds that not only would the unhappy days end by the repulsion of the invaders from Muscovite territory, but in the regeneration of Russia itself.

Another great change which was evolved during the first twelve months of the war was Russia's attitude toward other nations. Easy-going and poetical, visionary and religious, more given to theorising than to working, the Russian people awakened to the fact that in modern matters, commerce particularly, she had slipped under the domination of other races. It was the break with Germany which caused her to appreciate how dependent she had allowed herself to be upon neighbouring countries, particularly Germany.

Now it is to be remembered that a considerable section of Russian territory is comprised in what are known as the Baltic Provinces, where the people are not Slav, like the mass of the rest of the nation, but rather Teutonic in origin, with a part of the **Baltic Province** population speaking German as their usual **Russians** tongue. It is not for me to dispute the loyalty of these Baltic Province Russians. But they have always regarded themselves as superior to the ordinary Russians; which, let it be admitted, they are in commerce and in manufacturing. For while the Slav is a dreamer, the Teuton is a practical man. With a German origin and bearing German names, it is not to be wondered at that many of these people had sympathy with the great progressive neighbouring country of Germany.

The Baltic Province Russians showed business aptitude. Travelling into the interior, establishing commercial concerns, finding that the needs of the country in manufactured

397

articles could not be supplied by the Russians, they let Germany make good the deficiency. For a generation Russia was subjected to a much more drastic invasion than that which took place during 1915. It was a commercial invasion, which percolated throughout the land until it may be said that, from a trading point of view, Russia was but a colony of Germany. More than half the manufactured goods which went into Russia from abroad came from

GENERAL IVANOFF.
In the great Russian rally on the eastern front in September, 1915, General Ivanoff's army captured 70,000 prisoners, 70 guns, and 200 machine-guns.

Germany. A vast proportion of the principal shops in the great cities carried German names. Official life was permeated by German-speaking Russians. So even in Government departments it was no unusual thing to find employees of the State conversing between themselves in the German language.

Beyond this, the war had not been in progress many weeks before the Russians became dimly aware—and ultimately glaringly aware—that subterranean endeavours were being made to swing public opinion in favour of Germany. Stories got about, no doubt ill-founded, that even in the highest circle Germanic influences were at work.

The war compelled Russia to examine her own condition. She was alarmed. She heard rumours that there was a peace party in Russia, and that it was **" Russia for the Russians "** chiefly composed of people of German origin. She found her ears filled with scornful references to France and to Great Britain, and she discovered that the instigators were men with German names. There was a shortage of manufactured goods. There was not a household which was not brought to a realisation how great had been the hold on Russia by Germany.

It required no agitation to rouse the Russian people to a decision that too long had she been subservient to another Power, which had been exploiting them. Accordingly, there flamed into existence a movement which may be described as " Russia for the Russians." The questions were asked: Why should Russia purchase so much from Germany? Why could not Russia make more of the necessaries of life than she did? What was wrong with the skill of Russian working men that they did not produce a

multitude of useful articles for themselves instead of paying Germany for them?

The asking of these questions led to a speedy decision. Russia must wake up, must cease her old-time stupor, must adapt herself to modern manufacturing conditions, must develop her own illimitable resources, must advance in industry without reliance upon other lands, and thus demonstrate to the world that she was not encompassed with a sort of semi-Oriental indolence, but was quick, alert, adaptive, and capable of taking her place alongside any of the Western nations.

That Russia will, within the lifetime of any of us, carry her present desires to the goal she has in vision is not to be accepted ; but the war jogged the national liver, **Hatred toward** it stirred the latent national **the Germans** feeling, and caused Russia to take stock of her own potentialities and capabilities with the purpose of utilising them to the advantage of her own people.

What animated Russia most against the enemy was not so much the invasion of her territory as the bitterness engendered by the fear that Germany might impose her own commercial conditions upon Russia to the retardment of Russian industries. The firm determination to do more

GENERAL PETROFF.
President of the Commission of Inquiry which was appointed in the summer of 1915 to inquire into the supply of Russian munitions.

for herself, and accept less from the foreigner, was one of the direct results of the war.

Hatred towards the Germans developed to such an extent that the German tongue, although it had previously been the commercial language of the country, was prohibited. No one was allowed to talk German over the telephone : there were notices hung over the receivers

LINE OF TRENCHES IN THE BREASTWORK OF
FORT 7 OF THE KOVNO DEFENCES.

threatening terrible punishments if such a thing
were attempted. Hotels which had German
names had to quickly change the description.
In the big hotels of Petrograd, Moscow, and
elsewhere, it was customary for notices to be
hung up in three or four different languages
for the instruction of visitors; but in every
case German was obliterated. If anyone was
heard speaking this language, there was a hue-
and-cry, and frequently the
Hue-and-cry against offender was maltreated at
foreigners the hands of an infuriated
mob. Many people could
not differentiate between German and English,
and quite a number of cases came to my notice
of both English men and English women being
insulted because over-ardent and patriotic Muscovites imagined they were speaking German.
I myself was molested in a tramcar one
morning, because I happened to be speaking English
with a friend. Indeed, it is difficult to realise the intensity
of the hatred toward Germany which grew up and increased
in volume during the war.

I was witness of an explosion of public wrath in Moscow.

As already mentioned, most of the huge
emporiums, though legitimately Russian,
were conducted by men who, to their
misfortune, bore German names. The
folk of Moscow, always more vehement
in their patriotism than the cosmopolitan
population of Petrograd, frequently demonstrated against suspects of any kind being
allowed to remain in the city, and conceived the idea that while the shops
pretended to be Russian, they were in
fact German.

With the breaking of a few windows,
a riot commenced. Shops, dozens of
them, were gutted; millions of roubles'
worth of goods were cast into the streets,
and appropriated or destroyed. Great
clothing stores were reduced to ruins;

TRANSPORTABLE MAILED PROTECTOR FOR RIFLEMEN—TAKEN
FROM THE RUSSIANS BY THE GERMANS.

valuable furniture was smashed to atoms; bookshops had
their contents completely spoilt, and from the upper
windows of music warehouses grand pianos were hurled into
the thoroughfares, and there their demolition was completed.

Under the new law, the wine and spirit vaults were under
lock and key, and sealed; but the mob
broke in and took possession of enormous
quantities of liquor, and in one cellar
where barrels of wine were broken open,
there was a flood four feet deep, and at
least a dozen men, overcome by the fumes,
were drowned. Russians with German
names, but whose families had been in
the country for at least a century, men
whose sons were actually fighting in the
Russian Army, were chased by the crowd,
caught, and some of
them subjected to the **Fire of animus in**
most cruel deaths. The **Moscow**
police apparently did
nothing to check the disorder, not even
when a number of the shops were set on
fire. The best explanation is that the
police seem to have regarded it to be
their duty not to interfere with a patriotic
demonstration.

For two days the rioting continued.
Many were the lives that were sacrificed.
It is right to say, however, that the
Governor-General of the city, who was

CEMENTED TRENCH IN FORT 8 AT KOVNO, WHICH WAS CAPTURED BY
THE GERMANS ON AUGUST 16-17TH, 1915.

THE TSAR AND HIS "VALIANT CAUCASIANS."
Emperor of Russia inspecting the Army of the Caucasus, which inflicted a heavy defeat on the Turks in January, 1915.

under the strain of war. There was a shortage of men's labour, so that in many occupations women had to be employed. A number of female tram - conductors were engaged. Then, owing to the check put upon the importation of manufactured articles, not only was there a scarcity, but prices considerably increased. Food rose to something approaching famine prices, and once or twice to my personal knowledge there was a distinct shortage of beef. This, however, was due not to lack of herds in Russia, but to the Government commandeering so many head of cattle in order to provide beef for the soldiers, who, in their peasant occupations during peace time, could rarely afford such a luxury.

on a sick-bed when he heard of the outrages, sent soldiers into the disturbed districts. A few volleys into the crowd, killing between thirty and forty people, brought a quick cessation of the trouble. There was a Government inquiry, with the result that the chiefs of the police were removed from their offices. I mention this particular case as evidence of how swiftly the fire of animus flamed against the obnoxious Teutons.

It was a little singular that, while the passions of the people could scarcely be restrained against the Germans, comparatively little dislike was displayed toward the Austrians. It was my lot to see many prisoners marched through the streets. While the German soldiers were execrated, and they responded with sullen, scornful looks, a kindly sympathy was extended to the Austrian prisoners. The Germans marched along, black-browed and resentful; but the Austrians generally seemed merry, and exchanged chaffing remarks with the spectators. Most of the Germans were transferred to Siberia; but the majority of the Austrians were drafted into farming districts, where their labour could be utilised in tilling the land.

At Moscow there was little on the surface to suggest that the country was at war. Business proceeded as usual.

War and industrial life It was only by seeing long ambulance trains at the railway - stations, by coming across long processions of wounded in the streets, by seeing the parade-ground within the Kremlin constantly occupied by troops under drill, and the little groups of open-mouthed spectators before the guns which had been captured from the enemy, that one was reminded of what was happening in the history of the world.

A little investigation soon revealed that the nation was

ARMENIANS WHO FOUGHT THE TURKS NEAR VAN.
In the early part of October, 1915, the Turks were defeated by Russian troops near Van, which had been heroically defended by Armenian volunteers, some of whom are seen in our photograph with captured Turkish guns.

I saw much of the Russian Army, and although it was short of many things, the commissariat department was efficient and the transport effective. No soldiers in this dreadful struggle were better fed or better clad than the troops of the Tsar.

It was very much the same in Petrograd, the official capital of the country. Hotel prices are always high in Russia; but they were never so high as during war time. One of the reasons was that the proprietors, deprived of their profits because of the stoppage in the sale of wines, endeavoured to recoup themselves by increasing the prices of everything else. **Russia caught unawares**

Russia, while possessing so enormous an Army, had been rather unpractical in her preparations for the great, inevitable bout between herself and Germany. In many respects she was caught unawares. Germany knew how ill-provisioned she was in munitions. Russia on her part had been casual in taking notice of what the long years of warlike preparation in Germany really meant.

Many of the absolute essentials for war could not be

Before Van could be relieved by the Russian forces it was splendidly defended by the inhabitants, a number of whom, under the command of a Russian officer, are here seen in the trenches

Armenians digging trenches outside the town of Van, in Asia Minor.

Van, in Asia Minor, was threatened with extinction by Kurds and Turks, and but for the determined resistance of the native Armenians the population would have been massacred. In the left-hand photograph some defenders are seen in the trenches outside the town, which was occupied by Russian troops from the Caucasus in May, 1915. At foot, on the right, is a group of the men who defended Van against the Turks and Kurds.

RUSSIAN INVASION OF ASIA MINOR. THE DEFENCE AND OCCUPATION OF VAN.

provided in Russia to equip a fair proportion of her soldiery. She had to seek supplies from abroad. The German market was shut off, and France and Britain were much too busy preparing for their own requirements to offer much assistance to Russia, though they did help in many ways.

The result was that the representatives of big manufacturing concerns in neutral countries descended upon Petrograd in considerable numbers. They were mostly Swedes and Americans. One of the biggest hotels in Petrograd was crowded with Americans who were seeking to secure contracts with the Russian Government. Many of them did. The difficult point was the delivery. War goods could enter Russia without much hindrance by means of the " back door," that is to say they could be landed at Port Arthur or Vladivostok, and brought into the country through Siberia. That, however, was a long and difficult route. The quickest ways were by Archangel and Odessa; but the gateway to Odessa through the Dardanelles had not been forced by the French and British Allies, and an entrance by way of the White Sea was hampered by the Arctic ice, which enclosed Archangel for several months of the year. It was this difficulty of getting absolutely necessary supplies from allied and neutral countries which had much to do with the compulsory retirement of the Russian troops. They were brave enough; but bravery without shells and general munitions did not count for a great deal.

Neutrals and contracts

However, there was great confidence in the ability of the British and French warships and soldiers to knock a way through the Dardanelles, clear the passage of the Bosphorus, and thus provide an open route from the outer world to Odessa. As a preliminary to this, the chiefs of the principal trading firms went to Odessa, furnished offices, and laid the train not only for supplying the soldiers with requisites from England and America, but also for providing the civilian population with goods, which these countries could supply, and for which the people were in need.

Russia was hard put to it to obtain supplies from abroad. During the dark days of winter, the only means through which she could receive help from Britain and France was by way of Sweden. The population of Sweden was not particularly enthusiastic over the cause of the Allies. It could not be said that Sweden put facilities in the way of communication. Sweden had long been under the intellectual spell of Germany, and, while the folk of this part of Scandinavia did not look with a fond eye upon the manner in which German goods were flooding the country, they had, according to their point of view, less to fear from Germany than from Russia, because the Swedes had long nursed a dread that if ever Russia had the power, she would cut a way from Finland across the northern parts of Sweden and Norway, and create for herself a port on the North Sea.

The Swedish attitude was not dictated by any resentment toward Great Britain, although the Swedish trading classes did not like ships being held up by the British Admiralty on the ground that the cargoes, while destined for Sweden, were really intended for Germany.

It was perfectly natural that Sweden should not wish to incur the enmity of Germany. Therefore it can be easily understood that, when she provided the only route between France, Britain, and Russia, her authorities did not go out of their way to help in the conveyance of goods to the enemy of Germany.

I travelled that route—across the North Sea from Newcastle to Bergen, thence to Stockholm, then due north to the real " land of the midnight sun," and to the very edge of Lapland, round the top of the Gulf of Bothnia, and so across the Swedish frontier into Finland and down to Petrograd—a journey occupying eight days.

There was only a single line to the north of Sweden. There was no railway communication with Finland. The Russians laid a temporary line on the frozen earth to a place opposite Karungi, on the Swedish side of the Tornea River; but when this fell into disuse owing to the spring thaw, it was necessary to convey all goods by vehicle a distance of some twenty miles along the frontier, and then ferry across the Tornea River to a point where the Finnish railway could be touched.

Taking goods into Russia by this means in bulk was an impossibility. The Swedes themselves made a very close examination to prevent the transit of medical supplies. The only plan by which articles from France and England could be sent to Russia was through the agency of the parcels post. Thus it was that millions of small packages travelled by means of that circuitous route. I saw train-loads upon trainloads of parcels taking sections of small machinery into the country, where they could be put together. All this was very hampering and most expensive, and will convey to the mind of the British reader to what a pass our Russian ally was put.

But with the coming of spring, although the Karungi route was still available, large articles, such as machinery, had

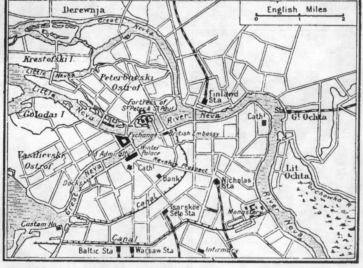

PLAN OF PETROGRAD, SHOWING DELTA OF THE NEVA.

to be taken into Russia by way of the White Sea and Archangel. As soon as the ice broke, fleets of merchant ships made their way to Russia's northern port, although many of them were impeded, or prevented altogether, by the enemy submarines, which were on the watch at the mouth of the White Sea.

The single line from Archangel to the south was in process of being doubled. It was over these metals that Russia got most of her supplies during the summer of 1915. Ordinary merchandise had practically to be ignored, the railway was requisitioned by the military authorities. Mountains of goods were stacked on the quay-sides at Archangel, exposed to damage by reason of the tempestuous weather. Traders also suffered to a considerable extent. The Manufacturers' Association of Moscow, however, did what was best in the circumstances—sent representatives to Archangel, and by the utilisation of the waterways in that part of the world were able to forward much merchandise, though the delay was great. With the prospect of a famine in particular articles, several representatives of the principal Moscow firms made research throughout the Empire, particularly in towns where trade had come to a standstill, and were able to purchase from the retailers many of their goods, and forward them to Moscow and to Petrograd.

Difficulties of goods traffic

The war, instead of reducing the populations of the great cities, increased them. The wealthier classes, who had been in the habit of travelling abroad, principally to German spas, remained at home. They did not even go to Yalta, the beautiful watering-place in the Crimea; nor did many of them take up their abode on their country estates. They were anxious to keep in touch with what was happening in the great drama. They remained in the capital, or took up their residence in Moscow, Kieff, Jaroslav, and other

when there was a rush of people making their escape before the enemy entered the city. Never was railway traffic so congested. Civilians had to be content with travelling under disagreeable conditions in cattle trucks. The journey from Warsaw to Moscow took over two days. Thus Moscow had a larger population than in normal times.

It was the same down at Kieff, the Holy City of Russia. Refugees from the region of Galicia all made for this town. Thousands of them came without any possessions except the clothing in which they stood. It says **The refugees from Galicia** much for the warm-heartedness of the Russians that, although there was little organisation, kindness and hospitality to the unfortunate were abounding, and for fifty miles around there was scarcely a house which did not shelter and care for some family which had been obliged to fly before the invaders. Thus the big towns were well filled, and although prices rose abnormally, trade was brisk.

There were periods when the Russians were depressed. They knew of the sacrifices which they were making, and there was little opportunity for them to learn what their Allies were doing,

GENERAL VIEW OF THE CITY OF MOSCOW.
It is popularly said that Petrograd is the brain and Moscow the heart of Russia.

centres. There was a great inflow of refugees from Poland and from the south-western districts of the country.

For months Warsaw, the capital of Poland, was a hustling military centre. Most of the troops intended to fight the Germans in the north-eastern theatre were sent that way. Endless processions of regiments marched through the streets, unarmed in many cases, for the soldiers were to receive their rifles at the front; which meant that they were to get their weapons from **brother soldiers** who were wounded, or to have them passed on from men who were dead.

Hotels were packed with Russian officers. Though the boom of the guns could be heard,

Warsaw before its evacuation and German aeroplanes frequently flew over the city, life proceeded gaily enough. There was little news of what was taking place at the fighting-line, except that the return of enormous convoys of wounded men indicated that the resistance to the invaders had been stubborn. Weeks before the actual evacuation took place, there were indications of what was going to happen. The treasury was removed; the wives of officials were provided with permits to leave; British residents were given the hint they had better clear out. So matters proceeded until within the last few days,

THE NEVSKY PROSPECT, PETROGRAD.
The principal thoroughfare of the Russian capital. A broad and stately boulevard and one of the handsomest avenues in Europe.

They became somewhat critical. They recalled how, when the French and British were being pressed by the Germans on the western front in the autumn of 1914, the Russians put up a vigorous attack in the north-east in order to draw off some of that pressure, and they asked the question why, when they were being pressed in Poland and Galicia, the French and British Armies did not act vigorously in order to withdraw some of the German pressure on the Russian front? They mourned that the passage of the Dardanelles had not been forced. They grieved that the ammunition which they expected from their Allies was prevented from being delivered. Still, though depressed, they were determined. Always at the back of their thoughts was the conviction that, whatever might be the mishaps, they were temporary, and that the foe must ultimately be decimated or repulsed.

No better proof of the spirit which animated the nation could be found than the way in which the whole of the civilian population recognised what was incumbent upon it. Slowly—for the Russian is incapable of doing things quickly—munition factories were organised, and the people set about producing war material for their troops. Frequently there was such a shortage that the soldiers were obliged to retire long distances before the superior equipment of the Germans. In time that trouble was surmounted. Within their capabilities, not so great as those of England, all the factories of Russia were engaged in turning out munitions of war.

It has been said, and rightly, that the people of Russia, the civilian population, did more than the Government itself. The Government attended to all military matters, the arming and the provisioning of the troops. Everything else was left to organisations and private individuals. For instance, the whole of the nursing of the wounded was left to the Red Cross Society and Russia's innumerable benevolent institutions. The Russian Red Cross Society had been active for many years, because within the scope of its operations was the improvement of the housing of the poorer classes, as well as the care of the sick.

Practically all the ladies of the better classes engaged in hospital work. Each province, every Zemstvo, and every municipality had not only to look after **Activity in hospital** the injured, but also to make provision for **work** the dependents of the fighting men. Representatives of all the local authorities met, and schemes were drawn up whereby each district could do its share in caring for the maimed or sick. Some municipalities could accept a thousand men ; others were only able to look after fifty men. Above this, all private individuals with houses of any size set apart either the whole dwelling or a certain number of rooms, and undertook at their own charge to minister to the wants of the poor fellows. The consequence of all this was that the wounded and the poor were looked after as a result of municipal or private philanthropy.

You could not take a walk in any of the main streets of the big towns, or drive through any of the villages, without constantly seeing the Red Cross flag, indicating the existence of a hospital, great or small. Of course, some of these hospitals were much better equipped than others. But within their means, all sections of the community gave freely. What Russia accomplished in looking after the sufferers should be remembered for all time by those who are disposed to criticise what takes place in the land of the Tsar. The Dowager-Empress was at the head of the Red Cross Society, while the Empress herself and her daughters, the Grand Duchesses Olga and Tatiana, not only made comforts for the wounded, but gave the lead to other ladies by taking their share in hospital nursing.

The love of Russia accentuated affection for the Little White Father. His Majesty ultimately took command of the Russian Army, but long before then he had shown solicitude for his soldiers **Affection for the** by travelling to the seat of war, and by **Tsar** visiting the Cossack soldiers who were fighting below the Caucasus. He went to arsenals, and witnessed the manufacture of implements of war ; he paid informal and quite unostentatious visits to hospitals—arriving often in a simple carriage, and attended by a single aide-de-camp—moving amongst the wounded, talking to them, and addressing the humblest private as " Brother."

All of which goes to demonstrate not only how Russia faced her ordeals, but how the war changed her aspect upon the world in general, and stiffened her in the determination that in the future she would be more worthy of her ideals.

Russia came to appreciate the good qualities of her Allies. For two generations she had had unstinted admiration of British institutions. It would be idle to contend that she could ever graft these on to her Constitution, or adapt them to the peculiar Slav temperament. The war, however, brought the whole body of the Russian people to know more about the British Empire than ever they did before. They were happy in the knowledge that the people of Great Britain were getting a better understanding of Russia, were dropping the old story-book conception of it as a land of bleakness and cruelty, and were coming to realise that, with innumerable drawbacks, it had many phases of life from which other nations might learn much.

A BODY OF STALWART COSSACKS, WHOSE TRADITIONAL INTREPIDITY PROVED ALL BUT UNAVAILING WHILE RUSSIA LACKED GUNS TO PIT AGAINST THE COLOSSAL ORDNANCE OF THE TEUTON FOE.

The crew of H.M. submarine E11.

Cheering the E11 on its return from the Dardanelles.

On Gallipoli : Welcome capture of supplies for the British commissariat.

Sturdy Turkish prisoners under escort on Gallipoli Peninsula.

Ammunition train bringing up food for the guns.

Filtered water, stored in cans and old petrol tins, for the troops on Gallipoli

Bringing up supplies: Animated scene after the British landing at Suvla Bay.

A gully in Gallipoli: British troops returning from the trenches.

THE HEROIC STRUGGLE ON GALLIPOLI PENINSULA AND THE SUVLA BAY BATTLES.

Extraordinary Revelation in Sir Ian Hamilton's Despatch—Dardanelles Operations Muddled by Lack of Order in Embarking Troops—Siege Warfare Begins with a Night Adventure by the Gurkhas—How the French Troops Battled for Haricot Redoubt—Heroism of the Lancashire Territorials—Enver Pasha Tries to Teach Liman Von Sanders and Essad Pasha the Art of Victory—The Men of Anzac Wipe Out Enver's New Army—The Immortal Charge of the Australian Light Horse—New Zealanders and Indian Brigade make a Wonderful Night March—Gurkhas Storm Q Hill and Reach the Mountain Crest—The Decisive Hour in the Dardanelles Campaign—Why the Great Scheme of Operations Failed of Victory—New British Army Lands in Suvla Bay and Advances for Two and a Half Miles—The Irish Division Carries Chocolate Hill—The Collapse at Anafarta Ridge—The Zone of Flame that Checked the British Advance—The Irishmen Take Dublin Hill, and the Suvla Bay Army Connects with Anzac—Magnificent Charge by the Yeomanry Division—Capture of a Commanding Point in Anafarta Valley.

FROM the first despatch of Sir Ian Hamilton, published on July 6th, 1915, it looked as though the naval operations in the Dardanelles had been planned without consulting him. The commander of the Mediterranean Expeditionary Force left London with his Staff on March 13th, and arrived at the island of Tenedos about mid-day on March 17th. He was just in time to witness the series of naval disasters in the Strait on March 18th, and he says he came to the "reluctant deduction that the co-operation of the whole of the force under my command would be required to enable the fleet effectively to force the Dardanelles."

Then followed a surprising revelation by the gallant general. His troops, he stated, had already been brought to the scene of action, and were crowded in troopships by the island of Mudros. But they could not be disembarked for a surprise attack on the Gallipoli Peninsula at a time when the Turkish defences were incomplete, for Sir Ian Hamilton went on to say : "Before doing anything else, I had to redistribute the troops on the transports to suit the order of their disembarkation. The bulk of the forces at my disposal had, perforce, been embarked without

SIR IAN HAMILTON AND GENERAL GOURAUD.
A meeting at Seddul Bahr on June 28th, 1915. General Hamilton brought news of a success at Krithia. Two days later General Gouraud was grievously wounded.

its having been possible to pay due attention to the operation upon which I now proposed that they should be launched. Owing to lack of facilities at Mudros, redistribution in that harbour was out of the question. Therefore, I ordered all the transports, except those of the Australian Infantry Brigade and the details encamped at Lemnos island, to the Egyptian ports. On March 24th I myself, with the General Staff, proceeded to Alexandria, where I remained until April 7th, working out the allocation of troops to transports in minutest detail as a prelude to the forthcoming disembarkation."

There was thus a delay of over a month before the troopships returned to the Turkish coast, and by then all the extremely valuable element of surprise in the military operations had vanished. A great decisive opportunity had been lost owing to the want of proper order in placing the troops in the transports in the early part of the month of March. Sir Ian Hamilton's use in this connection of the strange word "perforce" seemed to show that some Government plan, abruptly conceived and ordered to be carried out hurriedly, was the cause of the troops being put in transports in such a way that they could not be disembarked on the Gallipoli Peninsula. It further appeared from the

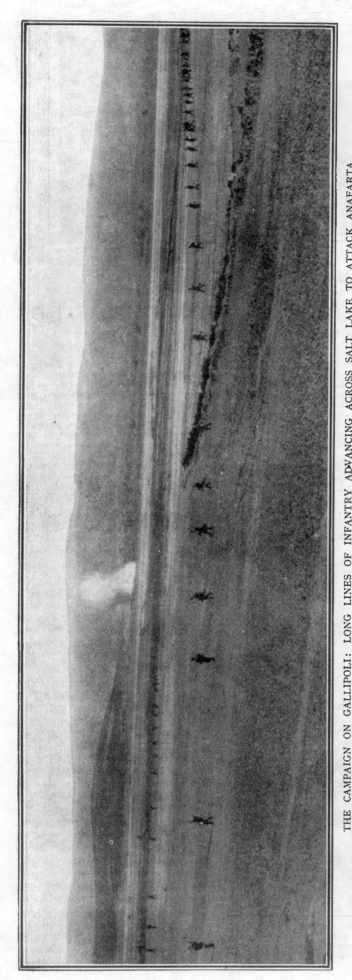

THE CAMPAIGN ON GALLIPOLI: LONG LINES OF INFANTRY ADVANCING ACROSS SALT LAKE TO ATTACK ANAFARTA.

passages cited from Sir Ian's despatch that he did not expect to use the whole of his troops in helping the fleet to force the Dardanelles. Some other military operations in the Mediterranean area were intended, and it was with reluctance that the British commander came to the conclusion that Gallipoli alone would be his field of action.

Apparently we have to go back to the Walcheren Expedition to find a parallel to the circumstances in which the Dardanelles campaign was conceived. For, though the Crimean War was sadly muddled, the mistakes there do not seem to have been so serious as were those which the British, Australasian, and Indian troops were asked to retrieve along the gateway between the Mediterranean and the Black Sea. Sir Ian Hamilton was a commander of experience, and he **Leaders worthy of** was admirably served by subordinate **their men** officers like Generals Sir W. R. Birdwood and Hunter-Weston, of whom it is sufficient to say that they were worthy of the men they led into action. The heroism of the troops was marvellous, and solely by their indomitable tenacity they won a narrow footing along the cliffs below the mountain fortresses, from which the Germans and Turks continued to sweep every landing-place with shell fire.

But after a footing had been won below Krithia and north of Gaba Tepe, the attacking forces could make no further progress of importance. There mustered at first scarcely two army corps of them, including the 29th Division, the Australian and New Zealand Expeditionary Force, the Naval Division, an Indian Brigade, and a French division composed of Zouaves, African troops, and some white battalions. After the losses of the landing battles, Sir Ian Hamilton must have had less than 35,000 bayonets immediately at hand for the desperate work of a thrusting attack at the seat of power of the Ottoman Empire, which could draw upon half a million or more men for the defence of the road to Constantinople. As a matter of fact, the Turco-German commanders concentrated all their principal armies on the defence of the Dardanelles. The campaign against Egypt was discontinued, and the attack on Russia across the Caucasus was reduced to an unimportant defensive battle. Even the comparatively small Indo-British army advancing along the Euphrates up towards Bagdad was only opposed by a single weak Turkish army corps. All the main military resources of one of the greatest warrior races in the world were organised by capable German officers and set in a series of almost impregnable mountain defences, in order to safeguard the channel forts, which prevented the allied fleet from forcing the waterway to victory.

There were never less than 150,000 Turkish soldiers, with thousands of German engineers and artillerymen, holding the entrenched heights between Achi Baba and Sari Bair. It mattered little if our men put more than their number of foes out **Everything against** of action. New Turkish armies poured **our men** down the mainland track to Gallipoli, or were carried across the Sea of Marmora in transports. No wonder our advance was slow and our casualty lists terribly heavy. Everything was against our men. The enemy was deeply entrenched on one of the finest lines of natural fortifications in the world, with guns and howitzers commanding every site occupied by our troops. The enemy could bring most of his provisions and supplies up by road at night, with little or no interference from the fire of our ships, and a huge flotilla of small sailing vessels, plying across the Sea of Marmora greatly assisted in the provisioning of the defending army. There was scarcely any water in that part of the mountainous Peninsula occupied by the attacking troops. Even their machine-guns at times became unworkable through want of water in the jackets to keep the barrels cool. Everything necessary for existence had also to be brought to the

THE TERRACED AND SAND-BAGGED DUG-OUTS OF THE INTREPID AUSTRALIAN TROOPS AT GABA TEPE.

PICTURESQUE VIEW OF THE HILL SO GALLANTLY STORMED BY THE AUSTRALIANS AT GABA TEPE.

SHELLS FROM TURKISH BATTERIES FALLING NEAR
H.M.S. ALBION.
When the Albion went aground in the Dardanelles, the Turks
opened fire on her from the land batteries, and two shells are
seen exploding in the water between the shore and the battleship.

tapioca, and sago—they were still bombarded with boxes of bully beef. There
were times when they rolled the beef tins
into the sea in order to avoid eating the
meat, but the indefatigable and unchange-
able director of food supplies in the
Dardanelles went on throwing ton upon
ton of bully beef at the troops. He was,
it was jestingly said, almost as much of
an annoyance as the German artilleryman on the Asiatic side of the Strait, who
worked the mobile howitzer batteries
which enfiladed our lines.

We have seen that at the end of April,
1915, the allied troops in the southern
end of the Peninsula had forced their way
forward for some five hundred yards
from their landing-places. By this time
both sides showed signs of exhaustion,
but Sir Ian Hamilton resolutely judged
that the troops who could first summon up
spirit to make another attack would win
some hundreds of yards of ground. And
as his own force was crowded together
under gun fire in a very narrow space,
he determined to be the first to strike
out. He therefore brought the 2nd

H.M.S. ALBION REPLYING TO THE FIRE FROM THE
TURKISH BATTERIES.
While the task of refloating the Albion was proceeding the Albion's
gunners replied vigorously to the enemy's fire. Her big guns had just
fired when the above photograph was taken.

bombarded beaches, and thence carried laboriously
by hand through narrow communication trenches
to the men in the firing-line. As summer came on,
the white troops were almost prostrated by the
tropical heat, and plagued by a monstrous number
of flies. It became at last a feat of great
ingenuity to swallow food without eating live flies
also. The Anzacs, as the men of the Australian
and New Zealand Army Corps were called, reverted
to a state of picturesque savagery. They left off
all their clothes, except for one garment around
their loins, and their bare bodies were

The magnificent Anzacs baked to a Red Indian colour, so that
they looked at last, by reason of their
state of nature and their magnificent
physique, more terrifying barbarians than the Turks
opposed to them.

In any other age than ours, the Dardanelles Expedition
would have collapsed in the summer through an outbreak
of deadly pestilence. For those great disease carriers,
flies and vermin, filled our trenches, the flies feeding on
the corpses left between the lines. Happily, since the
South African War, Sir Almroth Wright and his pupils
had made great advances in the science of preventive
medicine, and for both enteric and cholera they had
devised vaccination treatments, which greatly reduced
the mortality from these two dreadful battle pestilences.
The reversion of the Anzacs to a state of nudity was an
excellent protection against the chief vermin-borne
diseases, and it was combined with a system of disinfecting
the clothes of all the troops, which also removed at intervals the agents of pestilence. The water was filtered and
boiled, and the troops supplied with an abundance of good
food. In fact, the Army Service Corps rather overdid
the food supply; for in the heat of the tropical summer,
when the soldiers wanted light food—such as rice,

Australian and New Zealand Infantry Brigades down
from the Sari Bair region, and rearranged the 29th
Division into four brigades, composed of the 87th and
88th Brigades, the Lancashire Territorial Brigade, and the
29th Indian Infantry Brigade. Then with the remnant
of his forces he formed a new composite division, which
he used as a general reserve, after reinforcing the French
division with the 2nd Naval Brigade.

The 29th Division went into action at 11 a.m. on May
6th, when it moved out leftward, on the south-east side of
Krithia. Half an hour afterwards the
French force on the right also advanced **Combined operation**
along the lower slopes of the river **held up**
ridge of the Kereves Dere. The com-
bined operation, however, made little progress. The
British troops were held up outside a pine wood,
which the enemy had transformed into a machine-gun
redoubt; and the French also were checked by a
terrible fire from a strong fieldwork after reaching the
crest of the ridge. The following morning the Lancashire

THE ROYAL NAVAL DIVISION ON GALLIPOLI.
General Sir Ian Hamilton leaving after inspecting the Royal
Naval Division, which is seen in the background.

Territorials charged gallantly up the slope towards Krithia. They were caught by the German machine-guns; but as they retired, another Territorial force, the Queen's Edinburgh Rifles, took the pine wood by a magnificent rush. Besides dislodging the machine-gun parties, they brought down Turkish snipers working from wooden platforms on the trees, and thus cleared the way for the general advance. But just as all seemed to be going well, and the Inniskilling Fusiliers came up to maintain our hold on the pine wood, the Turks, by a gallant charge, won back this clump of trees in our centre. Nevertheless, the Inniskillings

Great charge at Krithia went on and captured three enemy trenches, till in the afternoon all the advance was again held up by an enfilading fire from hostile machine-guns hidden on a ridge between the gully running towards Krithia and the sea. The operation looked like ending in a stalemate; but neither General Hunter-Weston, one of the greatest thrusters in our Army, nor Sir Ian Hamilton, a man with all the fighting temperament of the Highlander, would submit to the check. The commander threw in all his reserves, and ordered a general advance; and despite their weariness and their heavy losses, the men rose with a will, and in a great bayonet charge recaptured the pine wood and advanced nearly all their line some three hundred yards.

THE BRITISH COMMANDER-IN-CHIEF GOING ASHORE.
General Sir Ian Hamilton and General Braithwaite being rowed ashore
in a boat from a warship.

The troops were quite worn out, but Sir Ian Hamilton kept most of them working when darkness fell at the task of consolidating their new position. His airmen had told him that the enemy were receiving reinforcements, and he was resolved to make one more push before the new hostile forces got into position. At half-past ten the next morning (May 7th) he flung out the New Zealand Brigade, and won another two hundred yards in front of the pine trees. Then at half-past four in the afternoon he threw the 2nd Australian Brigade into his front, and sent his whole line forward against Krithia. The sparkle of the bayonets could be seen through the smoke of shells from the ships' guns and heavy artillery, as the attacking troops went forward in a long line stretching right across the Peninsula. The Senegalese sharpshooters were broken by the storm of heavy shells from the ridge by Kereves Dere. But the black troops were rallied by their officers, and sent forward in another rush, supported by a small column of French soldiers. Their figures were seen outlined against the sky on the crest of their ridge just as darkness fell and veiled all the battlefield.

When morning came, Sir Ian Hamilton found that the French had captured the machine-gun redoubt on the ridge, and had entrenched in front of Zimmerman Farm.

Footing gained below Achi Baba   On the right of the British line the 87th Brigade, fighting in the darkness, had taken another two hundred yards of ground ; while the Australian Brigade, though swept by shrapnel, machine-gun, and rifle fire, extended our front for another four hundred yards.

The gain of ground in the three days' battle was only six hundred yards on the right, and four hundred yards on the left-centre. It does not look much on the map, but

WORKING A MACHINE-GUN IN THE TRENCHES ON GALLIPOLI.

in practice it meant life instead of death, for it gave the allied troops just living room on the tip of the Peninsula, enabling them to scatter sufficiently in bivouacs in a network of narrow ditches, to avoid annihilation from the high-placed enemy batteries. Sir Ian Hamilton confesses that it was only on May 10th, 1915, that he felt that his footing below Achi Baba was fairly secure.

General Liman von Sanders, the descendant of an Englishman named Sanders, showed an instant appreciation of the advantages won by the attacking troops. He made a furious attempt in the night to drive the allied line back ; but after a desperate hand-to-hand conflict, the French and British retained all their newly-won position. For the first time for eighteen days and nights the half-shattered but indomitable 29th Division was able to have an ordinary sleep. It was a sleep disturbed by shells, as the men were only drawn back to the dug-outs near the beach, while the newly-arrived 42nd Division took their places in the firing-trench. But even a dug-out with howitzer shell interludes was a place of peace and repose after the adventures of the preceding three weeks.

By this time the weary attacking troops had exhausted all opportunities of surprise and initiative. The enemy was well aware of their numbers and dispositions, and as our men were in possession of the Turks' first line of defence, no more battles in the open were possible. All further advances had to be conducted by the method of siege warfare, in which the ground was very gradually won by local efforts, after slow, methodical preparation. Sir Ian Hamilton prepared this change of tactics by arranging all his artillery under a central fire control, so that all the heavy pieces and most of the light pieces could be switched together by telephone for an intensive bombardment of a short section of the hostile front. The guns of the fleet were similarly placed under a central control by means of wireless stations, and the machine-guns were set in carefully chosen redoubts to strengthen the system of trenches.

Meanwhile the officer commanding the 6th Gurkhas had begun on his own initiative the new method of advancing by local efforts. Between Krithia and the open sea there was a deep, picturesque river bed, known on the map as the Saghir Dere, and known in the camp as Gully Ravine, and crowned seaward by a steep bluff. Below the bluff was Y Beach, where some of the troops had fought their first landing battle. Since then the enemy had transformed the bluff into a powerful fortress, from which a number of machine-guns had continually broken up the left wing of our attacks. To assail the fortified cliff across the gully was madness, but the mountaineers of Nepal worked their way along the shore, and then started in the darkness to crawl up the steep height on their hands and knees. They reached the top, but failed to surprise the enemy, who beat them back with a sweeping fire. The enterprising Gurkhas, however, had shown the way in which the bluff could be captured, and the next day Major-General H. V. Fox, commanding the 29th Indian Infantry Brigade, devised plans for a concerted attack. This was carried out in the evening of May 12th, when the Manchester Brigade made a feint of a storming attack on the right of the enemy's position. The guns of H.M.S. Dublin and H.M.S. Talbot opened fire seaward on the Turkish trenches, while the guns and howitzers of one of the British divisions kept up a heavy shell fire from the land. Evening deepened into night, and the great bluff flamed with bursting shell that kept the Turks below their parapets. Then again in the darkness a double company of Gurkhas crept along the shore, and scaling the cliff, carried the position with a rush. They were followed by their machine-gun section, and another double company of their battalion, and when dawn broke the conquered position had been connected with our main line, advancing our left flank by nearly five hundred yards.

Nothing of much importance was done for another fortnight. During this time the hardest work fell on the sappers, who tried to work up within rushing distance of the enemy's second line by means of winding saps from which the troops could debouch. On May 25th the Royal Naval Division and the 42nd Division were able to entrench a hundred yards nearer the Turks, and four days afterwards the entire British line was helped onward by means of engineers' work. At the same time the French force also progressed and **German submarines** captured a machine-gun redoubt on the **intervene** ridge going down to the Kereves Ravine.

But all this slow movement of approach against the hostile mountain fortress was suddenly complicated by a series of terrifying naval disasters. Some German submarines worked down to the Dardanelles in the third week in May, and all our naval dispositions and transport work were abruptly checked.

We had already lost the Goliath, a useful old battleship, by a destroyer attack delivered by a very enterprising German naval officer. This disaster only entailed greater watchfulness on the part of our scouts ; but the torpedoing of H.M.S. Triumph on May 26th, and the torpedoing of

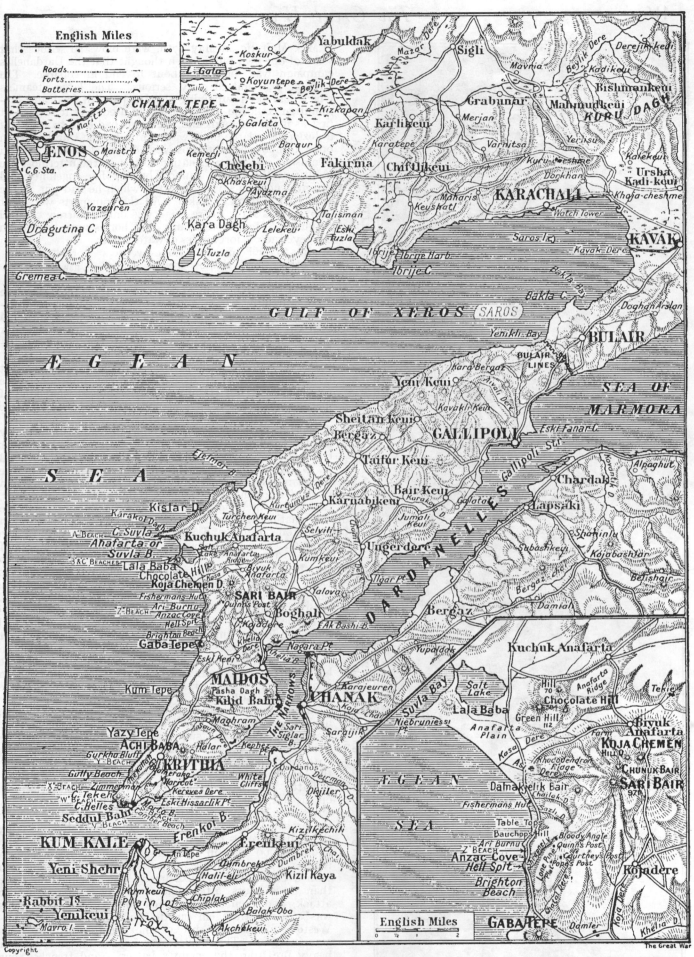

English Miles

Roads
Forts
Batteries

MAP OF THE GALLIPOLI PENINSULA SHOWING THE VARIOUS LANDING-PLACES, WITH
ENLARGED INSET OF THE SARI BAIR REGION.

BATTLE-SCARRED BUT BY NO MEANS DOWNHEARTED: SCENE AT A LANDING-STAGE "SOMEWHERE ON GALLIPOLI."

The terse inscription on the reverse of this official photograph is as follows: "The Dardanelles operations: Wounded British soldiers about to embark for the hospital ship." Officers and men are seen walking side by side, each bearing on his more or less tattered tunic a label setting forth the particulars of his wounds.

H.M.S. Majestic on May 27th, were blows so serious that some of our own public even thought that the Dardanelles campaign was suddenly about to end in collapse. The outlook was indeed very serious. The large steamers which had been supplying the troops with food and ammunition could no longer be safely used, and it seemed at first as if the Germans and Austrians had only to send half a dozen more large underwater craft to the Dardanelles in order to maroon the troops we had landed on the Gallipoli Peninsula. It was a situation to test to the uttermost the ability of the British sailor; but by fine ingenuity and inventiveness he saved the army which he had put ashore with such remarkable skill. All the transports were sent into Mudros Bay, where there was only a narrow channel to guard. Men, stores, guns, and horses were henceforth conveyed across forty miles of water from Mudros to the Peninsula in mine-sweepers **Meeting the** and other small, shallow vessels, which **new menace** did not lie deep enough in the water for a torpedo to strike them at the ordinary depth. Then the large warships, whose guns were very useful, and sometimes of vital value in the military operations, were sheltered near the shore by means of submarine defences, while our destroyers and patrol boats tracked the hostile underwater craft and assailed them in various ways.

During the first phase of the submarine menace, when it remained doubtful if disaster was not impending, the conduct of Sir Ian Hamilton clearly showed what kind of man he was. He at once planned a general attack on the Turkish position. Like all great Scottish Highlanders, danger inspired him to furious effort instead of in any way dismaying him. He was ably seconded by the former commanding officer of the 29th Division, Lieut.-General A. G. Hunter-Weston, who had been promoted to the command of the 8th Army Corps. Hunter-Weston was a man of the calibre of Douglas Haig, a warrior of genius, capable of wielding a great army through his remarkable combination of vehemence and tenacity. He was Sir Ian Hamilton's right-hand man in the southern part of the Gallipoli Peninsula, as Sir W. R. Birdwood was the soul of Anzac. The French Expeditionary Force, brought up to two divisions, with its sphere of action round Kereves Dere, was also controlled by a notable fighting man, the tall, bearded "Lion of the Argonne," General Gouraud. Gouraud had come from the Argonne to replace General d'Amade, one of the conquerors of Morocco, who had fought in France during the retreat from Mons on the right of Sir John French's army. General d'Amade had been wounded during the attack on the Kereves bluff, and he left Gallipoli on May 14th, when the 2nd French Division arrived under General Bailloud, with General Gouraud as Commander-in-Chief.

Almost every night the Turks assailed the allied line, hoping, no doubt, to find that the attacking troops were weakening under the submarine menace. But our positions remained intact, and Sir Ian Hamilton on June 3rd, 1915, made his first deliberate assault on the Achi Baba fortifications. For his line **Hunter-Weston's** of battle he deployed the 29th Division **ruse de guerre** on his left, the 42nd (East Lancashire) Division in his centre, with the Naval Division linking on with the French Army Corps. General Hunter-Weston, directing the British troops on a front of four thousand yards, had about 17,000 men in the firing-line, with 7,000 men in reserve. The action began on the morning of June 4th with a preliminary bombardment which lasted for more than three hours, after which our troops moved out to attack, and then scurried back to their trenches. This was a little stratagem on the part of General Hunter-Weston to draw the fire of the enemy's artillery and machine-guns. The device was successful, and amid a heavy fire from the enemy's batteries and trenches, our artillery renewed its bombardment with increasing intensity, being able to mark more exactly the hostile targets.

GETTING READY TO MEET THE TURK: FRENCH INFANTRY PRACTISING AN ADVANCE.
Some of our Gallic allies putting in a final course of training near Mudros, on the island of Lemnos, which was ceded to Greece by Turkey after the war of 1912-13.

HOW THE GALLANT ANZACS, "STRIPPED FOR THE FRAY," WORKED THE GUNS ON GALLIPOLI.
This remarkable photograph was secured during a fierce artillery duel on the Gallipoli Peninsula at considerable risk to the man with the camera.

TURKISH PRISONERS UNDER GUARD BEHIND THEIR
OWN BARBED-WIRE AT SEDDUL BAHR.

GROUP OF ANATOLIANS RECRUITED BY TURKS AT ISMID FOR
THE CAMPAIGN ON GALLIPOLI.

company of the 6th Gurkhas, the heroes of Gurkha
Bluff, battered their way into the Turkish works,
they had to be withdrawn with the rest of the
brigade in order to avoid being cut off.

While a fresh attack was being organised, the
French corps on our right got also into difficulties.
The 1st French Division carried the opposing enemy
trench, while the 2nd Division stormed in a magnificent spring the strong Turkish redoubt on the Kereves
Ridge, known as the Haricot. But the French left
wing, acting on the right flank of our Royal
Naval Division, was unable to gain any ground, and
this led to a disaster. In the afternoon the Turks,
pouring out through the series of communication
trenches, delivered a massed counter-attack on the
Haricot Redoubt, while their guns prepared the way
for them with a storm of shrapnel and high-
explosive shell. The French lost the
redoubt and fell back, and in so   **Turks' deadly**
doing completely uncovered the right   **counter-attack**
flank of our Naval Division. The men
of the 2nd Naval Brigade were enfiladed and forced to
retire with heavy losses from the position they had captured,
and the Collingwood Battalion, which had gone forward
in support, was almost completely destroyed.

It looked as though the Turks were about to roll up the
whole of our line, for when the Naval Brigade was compelled to retreat across the open, sloping fields under a
terrible fire, the exposed flank of the Manchester Brigade
was in turn caught by Turkish and German machine-guns,
and swept by volleys of rifle fire, and then hammered by
hostile bombing-parties. But the Manchester men—
nearly all of them Territorials—fought with bulldog
courage to hold what they had won. There were places in
which one Lancashire man resisted every force that the
enemy could bring to bear upon him. Company-Sergeant-
Major Hay, having captured single-handed a redoubt near

Precisely at noon our gunners lengthened their fire, and
the entire British line charged with fixed bayonets. Both
the French divisions stormed forward at the same time, so
that the glittering line of bayonets sparkled right across
the Peninsula from the open sea to the closed Strait.

The Lancashire Territorials and the new recruits of the
Anson, Howe, and Hood Battalions of the Naval Division
did extremely well. They captured the first Turkish line
in front of them in from five to fifteen minutes, and then
burst through the second Turkish line in
Naval Division's   another fierce, swift spurt. In less than
brilliant work   half an hour from the time when they
leaped from the trenches, the men of the
East Lancashire Division and the Naval Division had penetrated a third of a mile in the enemy's front, and were
consolidating the conquered ground in a cool, workmanlike
way. The 29th Division was less fortunate, as its left
wing was held up by a wire entanglement, so sited as to
have escaped damage from our shells. It was an Indian
brigade that was checked in this manner, and though a

Krithia, held it for ten hours with four men until he was relieved. Company-Sergeant-Major Alister killed eight Turks and cleared a trench. But probably the best fighter of all was Private Richardson, who fought on alone in a trench south of Krithia for nearly twenty-four hours, and beat back every hostile assault.

The fighting around Krithia in the afternoon of June 4th, 1915, was a matter upon which every Territorial can look back with deep pride. The Manchester Brigade equalled the finest exploits of the old Regular Army. They answered the attack on their flank by throwing back their right wing; and such was their desperate courage that Sir Ian Hamilton could not bear to let them retire. Their position was one of extreme peril, for they were surrounded on two sides, and the Turks were making a sustained and furious effort to drive across the salient and cut off the brigade. So the British Commander-in-Chief formed up the Naval Division, and asked General Gouraud to co-operate in making an attack that should advance the right of our line, and connect and protect the flank of the **Manchesters' great** Manchester men. But the French corps **exploit** was itself still in great difficulties. Twice the attack was postponed at the request of General Gouraud, and at half-past six in the evening he reported that the pressure of the Turkish masses against him was so heavy that he could not advance.

Nothing remained but to withdraw the Manchester men from the second Turkish line which they were holding to the first Turkish line. The troops were very angry, and some of them desired to stay on and die rather than give up any of the ground they had won. But after much persuasion all the East Lancashire Division was extricated from the second line of captured trenches, and placed back in the Turkish firing-line, which they had won in five minutes at the beginning of their attack. The net result of the day's operations was an advance on a depth of two hundred to four hundred yards, along a front of nearly three miles. It was less than had been hoped for, but it was still a very considerable gain. Not only was there a substantial and very useful extension of ground, but the Turks were so severely punished that, though flushed with the victory of regaining their second line, they had not enough spirit

IN THE ENEMY'S TRENCHES: TURKISH PRISONERS

A SILENCED MONSTER: CHEERY CAMERA-PICTURE OF BRITISH SOLDIERS SEATED ON A HUGE GUN CAPTURED FROM THE TURKS AT CAPE HELLES.
In circle: Pile-driving on one of the beaches of the Gallipoli Peninsula.

left to attempt a counter-attack to recover their firing-trenches and forward machine-gun redoubts. Four hundred prisoners were taken, including five German officers, who were the remnant of a machine-gun party from the Goeben. Most of the captures were made by the Lancashire Territorials, whose capable divisional commander was Major-General W. Douglas.

Throughout the month of June the opposing fronts clashed in incessant local attacks and counter-attacks. Many deeds of fine daring and skill were done, such as that which Sergeant Friend, of the 1st Border Regiment, carried out near Krithia on June 9th. At the head of a small party he took a trench at the point of the bayonet and then shattered with hand-bombs the squads of Turks that tried to recover the position. Every battalion on the Gallipoli Peninsula will be able to fill a book with the tale of its adventures during the wearing trench warfare in the broken, mountainous, arid, barren tongue of land which cut off Russia from her western Allies, and prevented the trade in munitions and wheat to the Black Sea ports.

Here we can only mention some of the larger gains made by the allied troops. General Gouraud was not the kind of man to rest under the loss of the Haricot Redoubt. This maze of trenches and communicating saps, with its machine-gun emplacements, commanded the top of the ravine of Kereves Dere, and threw a deadly enfilading fire along the allied front. It had to be cap-

Important French gain

tured. So at dawn on June 21st the French commander launched both of his divisions against the Kereves ridge. The 1st Division, forming the right wing, stormed through a Turkish advanced trench, only to be counter-attacked and driven out ; for the German engineers had arranged a

fanwork of saps by which the Turks could advance safely through shell fire and continually reinforce the fighting-line. Meanwhile the 2nd Division had driven through two Turkish lines and recaptured the Haricot fort. When their comrades on the right retired, the Turks took the victors of the Haricot position on their flank, and got them in a position similar to that in which the Manchester Brigade had been caught. But the French would not give up their Haricot conquest, and while they were hanging on desperately, General Gouraud sent his 1st Division up again in assault after assault.

Turkish division cut up

Just as the sky was shading over at evening, some of the latest recruits of the French Army, striplings of the new drafts, fought their way up the ridge with the impassioned courage of youth, and in ten minutes captured six hundred yards of the enemy's trenches. There were Zouaves and men of the Foreign Legion in the two victorious battalions, but these veterans were the first to praise the lads of the 1915 class. All the night the Turks counter-attacked, and their violent efforts to return into the Haricot Redoubt did not cease till June 23rd, by which time some seven thousand of them lay dead or wounded in front of the French firing-line. The French losses were heavy, amounting to two thousand five hundred men, but they had gained a very important position, and had annihilated the best part of a Turkish division.

After this blow against the Turkish left on the ridge overlooking the Strait, it was the turn of Lieutenant-General Hunter-Weston to hammer at the enemy's right on the cliff overlooking the open sea. The Turks had all along held with great tenacity to the coast, where their position was one of extraordinary strength, owing to the deep ravine running between Krithia and the sea.

"OFFICE" OF THE COMMANDANT OF THE ADVANCED BASE AT SUVLA BAY.
British officers are seen resting under an awning of sand-bags, with which this unconventional "office" had been protected. Overhead, soldiers are passing on to duty along an improvised bridge.

"VIVE LA FRANCE!" ENTHUSIASTIC FRENCH TROOPS ON THEIR WAY TO THE DARDANELLES.

Near the shore the Turks had a formidable system of five lines, prolonged inland by two trenches. The ravine, the famous Gully Ravine, stretching inland in the neighbourhood of Gurkha Bluff and twisting in a north-eastern trend between overhanging hills, was two hundred feet high in places, and covered with thick green undergrowth. There was good water in the ravine, which increased its value. Therefore the Turks held to it with all their might. General Hunter-Weston drew up a scheme of attack, the feature of which was a peculiar pivoting movement, and he put it into action on the morning of June 28th. His design was to hold the enemy at a spot about a mile from the coast, and, on this pivoting point, swing his left flank upwards and through the Turkish positions.

The movement began by the Border Regiment rushing a redoubt known as the Boomerang, when the wire entanglements had been smashed by a brief, intense burst of gun fire. A few minutes afterwards the 87th Brigade stormed three lines of Turkish trenches, while the Royal Scots advanced and took the two trenches in front of them. Then, as this first British wave spread out and flattened over the conquered ground, the 86th Brigade, led by the 2nd Royal Welsh Fusiliers, pushed through the three lines captured by their comrades and bayoneted the Turks out of their last two lines of trenches. It took scarcely more than half an hour for the two brigades—all veterans of the indomitable 29th Division—to carry all the five Turkish lines, and their swift hammer-stroke was consummated by the success of the Indian Brigade, which secured a spur running into the sea from the rearmost

GENERAL SARRAIL.

Commander-in-Chief of the French Army in the Near East. Organised the brilliant defence of the Verdun sector at the time of the Battle of the Marne. Succeeded General Gouraud at the Dardanelles in August, 1915, when that gallant officer was seriously wounded.

Turkish trench. The gully, with its solid hedge of barbed-wire was not attacked until the high ground on either side was won. Then the barbed fence was left uninjured, to hold back the Turks in the ravine, who were hurled down and trapped by their own defences. Altogether the enemy was driven back along the coast for a thousand yards, enabling our left flank to be firmly based high up the coast, and preventing any enfilading fire against our centre. The importance of the advance was seen by the way in which Ali Riza Pasha, the commander at Achi Baba, and his superior Giaour commander, Liman von Sanders, regarded it. For many nights and days they launched the Turkish infantry from Achi Baba in heavy counter-attacks, until the best part of another Turkish division was vainly destroyed.

Enver Pasha became angry at the fruitless results of all the efforts made by the German Commander-in-Chief and the local Turkish pashas. The very violent Young Turk, who was busy arranging for the slaughter of the entire Armenian nation in a manner unknown to the world since the days of the Assyrians, apparently thought that the Christian general in Gallipoli was too sparing of the lives of Turkish soldiers. Enver Pasha had risen to power by a ferocious energy of will which made him a very formidable fighter of the old Turkish school. He was ready to surpass Hindenburg in using up cannon fodder to gain a single tactical point; and on June 29th he made an attempt to overwhelm the attacking troops by weight and pressure of numbers, and to fling them into the sea. Coming into the Peninsula at the head of large reinforcements, he delivered his first blow on the Australian and New Zealand Army Corps. He did not, however, deliver a second blow in the south, as he had designed. The men of Anzac taught him a lesson that made him sympathise at last with the position of Liman von Sanders, Ali Riza Pasha, and Essad Pasha.

Anzacs' offensive defensive The Australasians were perched upon the cliff below Sari Bair, where their immediate purpose was to hold up as large an enemy force as possible, thus lessening the pressure on the Eighth Army Corps and the French Army Corps along the Krithia front. They also kept open the gateway to the vitals of the Turkish positions along the Strait, but the British commander designed this rather as a demonstration than a serious line of attack. As Sir Ian Hamilton remarked in his despatch, the Australians and New Zealanders were not able to fulfil the part allotted to them and play

second fiddle to their comrades round Krithia. Their dare-devil spirit would not let them rest on the defensive, and from the moment they landed they protected themselves by attacking and continuing to attack. Their position round Anzac Cove was a rough semicircle, with a radius of about 1,100 yards. The farthest point was Quinn's Post, consisting of ledges on the brink of a precipice, falling for two hundred feet almost plumb to the valley below. The Turkish line was only a few feet away, and, by a surprise attack, an enemy brigade captured some of the fire trenches on the ledge on May 10th. But the Australians sold the ground dearly, as was discovered later from the diary of a Turkish officer. He wrote that the Turkish losses round Quinn's Post on the day in question were six hundred killed and two thousand wounded. Compared with these figures, an unsuccessful sortie by the Australians at Quinn's Post, **Two Generals** which resulted in seventy casualties, was a **wounded** slight affair, but both Lieutenant-General Sir W. R. Birdwood and Major-General W. T. Bridges were wounded in the fighting in the middle of May. General Bridges died of his wound, but Sir W. R. Birdwood's injury was light, and he went on with his work at the head of the men of Anzac.

At Anzac there was no room to live. The position was far worse than at Krithia, where the two attacking army corps had a large plateau on which to bivouac and shelter. The men of Anzac had only a footing on a single scrubby ridge by the edge of the sea, and their entire position was open to close-range shell fire from the amphitheatre of sombre heights immediately around them. In point of range the Turkish rifles could reach every spot in Anzac ; it was only the lee side of Maclagan's Ridge and of the

TURKISH SHELL BURSTING IN THE VICINITY OF A BRITISH TORPEDO-BOAT.
The missile fell between the torpedo-boat and a transport, happily without doing any harm to either. The smaller view is of a French warship in the Dardanelles.

THE GUNS OF H.M.S. CANOPUS IN ACTION. THIS OFFICIAL PHOTOGRAPH WAS TAKEN JUST AS A 12 IN. SHELL WAS ON ITS WAY TO THE TURKISH BATTERIES ON SHORE.

neighbouring lower fall of cliff by the water's edge that saved the men from direct fire. The enemy's howitzer batteries could pitch their shells everywhere in Anzac, and the Turkish and German guns, operating on the mountains, had an easy plunging fire on nearly all the trenches. As many as 1,400 shells an hour fell at times on Anzac, the calibre of the projectiles ranging from 11 in. high-explosive to 3 in. field shrapnel.

Gun fire, however, could not dislodge the southern pioneer races of the British Empire, so on May 18th General Liman von Sanders came to Sari Bair and used 30,000 troops in an attempt to close the gateway to the Narrows. After a heavy bombardment, lasting twenty hours, the German Commander-in-Chief launched, before dawn on May 19th, a great infantry attack against the left flank and centre of Anzac. Six waves of Turkish infantry were broken by the New Zealanders and Australians by sunrise, and the men on the right flank at Quinn's Post and Courtney's Post, both south-west of **Great enemy attack** the main masses of Sari Bair, also re-**broken** pulsed furious attacks on our right flank.

Then at five o'clock in the morning, when the air cleared, a large additional number of enemy guns, of 12 in. and 9·2 in. calibre, intensified the cannonade, and after four and a half hours of fighting the Turkish infantry on our right flank began to press hard against Courtney's and Quinn's Posts. This vehement attack, however, was so severely handled by the Australians on our right that the column swung away and tried to advance towards the left. But again it was caught by our machine-

gun fire and gusts of shrapnel, and the Turks at last drew back beyond Quinn's Post at eleven o'clock in the morning, and gave way in their crowded trenches under the searching fire from our artillery.

The men of Anzac had only a hundred killed and five hundred wounded, while, plainly visible in front of their trenches, were thousands of dead Turks. They had put out of action at least half the assaulting force, and a few days afterwards the Turks asked for a suspension of arms to remove their dead. Sir W. R. Birdwood was not the kind of man to be tricked in **Treachery well** this manner. He ordered all his trenches **punished** to be strongly manned by way of prepar-ing for the truce, and laid his guns, each with a large store of shrapnel, on the field of slaughter. On the night of May 20th the Turkish stretcher-bearers advanced to collect their dead and wounded, and behind the ambulance men was a line of disarmed soldiers who came forward with upheld arms. Our searchlights played on the extraordinary spectacle, and suddenly the stretcher-bearers drew back; the men who wished to surrender fell flat, all the Turkish artillery opened a furious cannonade, and after several feints the Turkish infantry charged once more on Quinn's Post. But none of them reached it; a curtain of shrapnel descended in front of the Australian position, and no Turk got alive through the rain of death. In the morning the local Turkish commander on Sari Bair, Essad Pasha, renewed the negotiations for the burial of his dead, and in daylight on May 24th some 3,000 Turkish corpses were buried near or removed from the Anzac front, in order

423

BRITISH SUBMARINE E 5 IN THE HANDS OF THE ENEMY : A STRIKING WAR PHOTOGRAPH FROM THE TURKISH SIDE.

While attempting a difficult reconnaissance of the Kephez mine-field in the Dardanelles on the morning of April 18th, 1915, the E15 (Lieut.-Commander Theodore Stuart Brodie) ran ashore on Kephez Point. According to Turkish official accounts, the captain and two others were killed and seven wounded by fire from the shore batteries, but three officers and twenty-one of the crew were rescued and made prisoners of war, the wounded being taken to hospital. The stranded vessel was afterwards torpedoed and rendered useless through a most gallant night exploit by two picket-boats from H.M.S. Majestic and Triumph.

424

to improve the sanitary condition of the ground between the opposing armies.

Fighting went on in the neighbourhood of Quinn's Post for the next five weeks, and then, on the night of June 29th, Enver Pasha arrived at Sari Bair, and endeavoured to show Liman von Sanders and Essad Pasha the way to deal with the men of Anzac. Enver was quite up to date in his artillery tactics. His gunners carefully studied the range of our trenches in daylight, and at **Enver's expensive** the unusual hour of midnight they illu-**impetuosity** minated the mountain-sides and the trenches of Anzac by a sudden bombardment of overwhelming intensity in the Neuve Chapelle and Gorlice manner. Every gun or howitzer was worked as quickly as possible for an hour and a half, and all the Turkish trenches were tipped with darts of flame from the rifles of the infantry, and with the steadier blazes of the machineguns.

Only twelve hours before, during General Hunter-Weston's drive along Gully Ravine, near Krithia, the enemy batteries on Achi Baba had seemed to be short of ammunition; but it was patent that, at Sari Bair at least, Enver Pasha had hurried from Constantinople with large fresh supplies of shells and charges, in addition to his reinforcement of thirty more battalions of new troops. Yet the unexpected bombardment at Anzac did not produce on our well-constructed deep trenches and dug-outs the effect intended. The defect of Enver was that he acted on hearsay, and had none of the practical experience of the man whom he admired. It was Mackensen, with his Grand Phalanx effects, whom the fantastically brutal Young Turk wished to imitate. But he did not control at Sari Bair 2,000 or more guns, he had not 3,000,000 shells accumulated by his batteries, and, moreover, the men of Anzac, with their superb physique and ingenious minds, had been working like navvies of genius for more than two months, making their trenches, communicating ditches, and shelters into a great fortress system.

Enver, merely working on theory in the flame-shot darkness of the tongue of mountain land, packed his troops in German fashion in dense columns and launched them at the New Zealanders and Australians after ninety minutes of blindly vigorous gun fire. The outcome of the Young Turk's generalship, by which he had boasted beforehand that he would sweep all the British into the sea, must have produced a sense of ironic satisfaction in the hearts of Liman von Sanders and Essad Pasha. For each heavy column of Turks was shattered before it reached the Anzac trenches. First the troops under Major-General Sir A. J. Godley knocked a great column to pieces simply by musketry and machine-gun fire. All our guns were laid on their targets, but they did not come at once into operation, as Sir W. R. Birdwood wanted to encourage the enemy to come on and be killed, instead of frightening him away before the battle was fully joined.

It was not until the grand Turkish attack was launched, on a wide, deep front, against both our centre and our left, that our artillerymen gave Enver a striking lesson in the art of stopping infantry. Under the ghostly radiance of our searchlights, the dense formations of Turkish troops were splashed with shrapnel, bursting in starry radiance above their heads, and mowed down in swathes by the sweeping fire of machine-guns, leaving just broken, staggering lines of men to be felled singly by the riflemen of Australia and New Zealand. The conflict scarcely lasted an hour, and by half-past two in the morning of June 30th none of Enver's men remained in the open ground between the trenches. Out at sea our destroyers had caught them with an enfilading fire; our heavy howitzers had torn great holes in the columns, while our field-guns swept the charging multitudes with direct fire.

The Turk displayed remarkable bravery of a characteristically apathetic kind. He came on, tall and vigorous, with fixed bayonet, apparently quite indifferent to death.

On the other hand, little or no organised use was made of this personal attitude of courage of the enemy private. There was no science in the leadership of the company officers. Before each attack the battalions were massed under cover of some rising ground or shrub; but when the mass emerged for the bayonet charge against our position, it seemed more a mediæval swarm of fighting men than a modern military machine. No regular formation was apparent, and no telling manœuvre under fire produced any surprise effect. The men advanced rather slowly, with nothing of the enthusiasm of a dervish charge, and when the mass swayed to one side, the swerving was merely a mob movement along the line of least resistance.

This was not the way in which the Ottoman advanced of old from Asia Minor into the Balkans, overthrowing the Byzantine Empire, conquering Hungary, and laying siege to Vienna. The individual Turk, and in particular the Anatolian peasant and the Mussulman of Macedonia, still proved himself a first-class fighting man. At times he quite enjoyed a man-to-man tussle with the bayonet,

TYPE OF SENEGALESE SOLDIERS WHO FOUGHT WITH THE FRENCH TROOPS IN THE DARDANELLES CAMPAIGN.

having a sturdy build of body that enabled him to stand up to the tall cattlemen and sheep-farmers of Australasia. There were one or two Turkish giants who put up a magnificent fight. The Turk was also a good man with the hand-bomb, which is a weapon that requires nerve and presence of mind in the men who constantly use it. None of our troops despised their opponents. On the contrary, they were often loud in praise of the gallantry of their foes. It was lack of food that had made the Turk seem but a vanishing ghost of himself when the three Bulgarian armies closed upon him in 1912. Even then he had held up the Bulgarians along the Chatalja lines, and in the security of the German-constructed **Fighting qualities** trenches of the Gallipoli Peninsula, in **of the Turks** 1915, he became still more formidable.

Owing to poor training and bad officering, he could not manœuvre efficiently in the open field; but trench warfare, with its sense of security and stability of position, suited the fatalistic temperament of the Turk, and enabled him to display his individual fighting power and laborious energy. He sapped well, like most peasants accustomed from boyhood to the use of the spade, and being guided in his work by brilliant and experienced German engineers, he made the utmost of the tremendous natural advantages he possessed on mountain slopes, with an almost impregnable line of communication behind him.

In front of Krithia and Achi Baba the laborious Turk constructed by the end of June the finest modern fortress in existence. It was a network of trenches and earthwork forts, all protected by barbed-wire, and linked by saps and communication trenches. No infantry could storm the position, because all the works and all the approaches, including the embarkation beaches, were swept by a cross-fire of artillery from the commanding heights of Achi Baba and from mobile batteries working near In Tepe, on the Asiatic shore, close to the buried ruins of Troy.

Sir Ian Hamilton had not sufficient men or sufficient heavy howitzers and high-explosive shell to tear through the lines around Achi Baba. Still less did he possess, in the region dominated by the higher peak of Sari Bair, the means of forcing his way across the five miles of broken rock and dense shrub to the forts guarding the Narrows. His position for the time was one of stalemate, in a case where stalemate meant defeat, and such a defeat as would shake the prestige of British rule in certain parts of the world at a critical moment in our history. Britain, as the greatest of Mohammedan Powers, had chosen to make a diversion from the decisive field of battle with the Germans, and measure in a land campaign a small part of her **A position of stalemate** military forces against the main armies of the chief independent Mohammedan empire in which the Caliphate resided. We had entered upon this tremendously important, and yet only secondary conflict, with a view to accelerating the forward sweeping movement which Russia was making at the time. Meanwhile, Russia had spent all the energy of her spring, and had been thrown back and hammered out of position after position, so that all her power of offensive was destroyed for a considerable time to come. The army which she had intended to land north of Constantinople to co-operate in the allied attack upon the waterway between the Mediterranean and the Black Sea, was unable to carry out its part of the enveloping movement. King Constantine had decided against any participation by Greece in the campaign. Sir Ian Hamilton was left, after three months of fierce, incessant fighting, with a small wasted army, nominally consisting of **Larger force asked for** three army corps, in a desperate, exposed position at the foot of two scientifically-fortified heights, and surrounded by a sea subjected to violent gales likely at times to interrupt communications with the shore.

Sir Ian Hamilton asked for a larger force, and the Dardanelles Committee in Downing Street managed at last to arrange for the despatch of modest reinforcements, which would arrive at Mudros base by about the middle of August. In the meantime the British commander had to keep the enemy in check, and so daunt him by constant attacks as to reduce him to a defensive attitude. In spite of lack of science and skill in Enver Pasha, the brute had the sound instinct of the born fighter. He was a better leader than Nazim Pasha, whom he had assassinated, and his feeling in the matter of the general strategy on the Gallipoli Peninsula was correct. Had he had his way, he would have continually fought us, using up Turkish recruits in ghastly multitudes, with the aim of driving us into the sea. It was the right method, though he tried it in person in a clumsy way. But fortunately for the Allies, the German commander and his Turkish subordinates preferred the prudent and more economical plan

ON THE QUAY AT ALEXANDRIA: PREPARATIONS FOR EMBARKATION.
The transport B.7 and other vessels are seen in the background, while kits and other military impedimenta are being collected by the quayside, in readiness for shipment to the Dardanelles.

Turkish shells bursting among the New Zealanders while the gallant Anzacs were resting behind the trenches on Walker's Ridge.

Two Turkish shells fired from the Dardanelles Strait over the positions occupied by the Australian and New Zealand troops on Gallipoli.

Picturesque view of the dug-outs occupied by men of the Indian Mountain Battery on Gallipoli.

WITH THE HEROIC ANZACS AND INDIAN TROOPS ON BATTLE-SCARRED GALLIPOLI.

427

RED CROSS WAGGONS IN READINESS ON THE EDGE OF SALT LAKE, GALLIPOLI. A PHOTOGRAPH TAKEN BY MR. ASHMEAD-BARTLETT.

of remaining entrenched in a defensive attitude, and letting the British, Australasian, and French troops run the expense of the offensive movements. And as Enver Pasha had failed badly in his own experiment at Anzac, he could not make out a clear case for his instinctive bias towards incessant attack.

While the Turco-German command was debating and hesitating, General Gouraud with the French Army Corps made another leap forward. After the advance on Kereves Dere on June 21st, the enemy had counter-attacked in a desperate fashion day and night for a week, winning only a transient footing between two of the lost trenches. The Turks, who recaptured the lines by a violent night assault, were surrounded at daybreak and either slain or taken prisoners. All the hostile **General Gouraud** effort to recover the ground slackened **badly wounded** completely by June 30th, and at this sign of weakening in his foes, General Gouraud struck out again.

At early morn on June 30th the French left wing charged under cover of massed gun fire and stormed a subterranean fortress at the head of Kereves Dere, known as the Quadrilateral. It consisted of seven deeply-cut lines, connected by shrapnel-proof communications and defended by machine-guns. Some platoons of the Colonial infantry swept over their objective in the vehemence of their movement, and drove some hundreds of yards beyond it. They were encircled, but they fought their way back to the Quadrilateral with but slight loss. In the afternoon came the inevitable Turkish counter-attack against their lost redoubt, but despite the large mass of troops employed by the enemy commander, he won back no ground, and his forces were so severely punished that the customary nocturnal counter-attack was not delivered.

In the evening, however, the allied forces suffered a serious disaster; for General Gouraud was badly injured in both legs by a shell as he came out of his quarters to speak to some of the wounded conquerors of the Quadrilateral. The general had won the high admiration of both French and British troops. He was a noble brother-in-arms to Major-General Paris, the commander of the Naval Division that connected with the left French wing, and to Lieut.-General Hunter-Weston, who directed the operations round Krithia. Sir Ian Hamilton was profoundly perturbed by the serious injuries to the hero of the Argonne battles, who had become, by reason of his driving power and ingenuity in attack, a main pillar of the allied operations. When General Gouraud returned to France, sadly disabled, General Joffre picked out another first-rate commander, General Sarrail, the defender of Verdun, to lead the French Corps in Gallipoli. But, in the meantime, fate again proved unkind to the British Commander-in-Chief, for Lieut.-General Hunter-Weston was incapacitated by illness, and compelled to relinquish the command of the Eighth Army Corps.

In the Turkish camp, where the leaders were sheltered behind the great hills, there were few or no disasters to the directing centres of the armies, such as occurred among the British and French **Turco-German** headquarters at both Anzac and Krithia. **dissensions** But the losses among the Turkish regiments were tremendous, and this led to fierce dissensions among the Turkish and German Staffs. Enver Pasha in turn censured both his Moslem and Giaour military chiefs in the Peninsula, and at the beginning of July, 1915, he made in person another attempt to fulfil his threat to drive the invading forces into the sea. Leaving the invincible men of Anzac to Essad Pasha, Enver went to the south of the Peninsula with ten thousand new levies from Asia, and a great banner was hoisted on Achi Baba to announce his arrival. The local general was still opposed to any attempt to recover the lost ground, and wanted merely to strengthen the trenches and await the next Franco-British advance.

But Enver Pasha would not allow any delay. In his hands were all the threads of Turco-German intrigue in

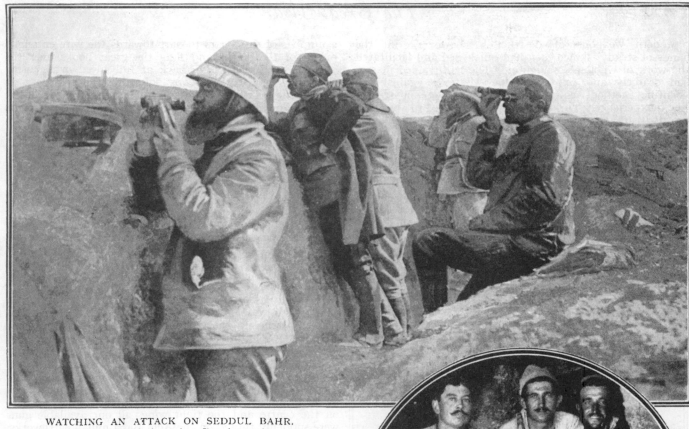

WATCHING AN ATTACK ON SEDDUL BAHR.
Officers on the look-out in a French trench.

FRENCH STAFF OFFICERS IN A ROCK SHELTER.
Three Chiefs of the General Headquarters Staff of the French Army taking part in the Dardanelles operations.

the Balkans, and he badly needed a victory in order to induce Bulgaria to mobilise against Serbia, and open the munitioning route between Berlin and Vienna and Constantinople. The Turks had more men than they could arm, and their supplies of shells and smokeless powder were none too large. The Rumanians were inclined to block the way, and only the Bulgarians were open to a Turco-German alliance. King Ferdinand was convinced that he had nothing to fear from Russia, and he was beginning to think that the Franco-British operations in the Dardanelles region would be sufficiently ineffective to leave

Gallipoli and the Balkans

him free to use his Army, in connection with a large Teutonic force from the Danube, to win the definite mastery of the Balkans. But the old, shrewd, cynical, plotting Coburger of Sofia wanted to feel absolutely certain of success before he launched his thunderbolt. His previous resounding failure against Serbia and Greece in 1913 made him extremely cautious. He was afraid that the Franco-British expedition might achieve enough success to impress the Greek people, or induce the British and French Governments to make another landing near Karachali, and threaten the Turkish railway line running from Constantinople through Sofia, and thence connecting with the Teutonic Empire.

Enver Pasha, therefore, had to show King Ferdinand that the attacking forces in the Gallipoli Peninsula could be driven back with such heavy losses as would maim Britain and France in at least their secondary field of war. The Young Turk delivered his attack from Achi Baba on the night of July 4th, 1915. There was the customary artillery preparation by the batteries on the European and Asiatic shores of the Dardanelles. Fire was opened on the first lines of the British and French troops, and curtained off the support trenches with a rain of shrapnel. The men of Anzac were also kept occupied by a furious bombardment, in which a ship of the Barbarossa class stationed in the Narrows assisted. The battle began about three o'clock in the morning of July 5th, and a squadron of German aeroplanes, with a black Prussian cross marked on their grey ground, joined in the attack by bomb-dropping. But despite this luxury in the preparatory means of

shaking the allied line, the infantry charges that followed were strangely feeble.

There was a desultoriness and a slackness about the Turkish soldiers which were very remarkable. When the men left their trenches and surged forward against the British and French lines, they certainly held together with their old fatalistic stoicism. But in no section did they display the driving power and valour they had shown in previous combats. Possibly it was the raw new Asiatic levies who were thrown out to be slaughtered in the

Raw levies sent to slaughter

hope of wearing our men down. The German Staff, it will be remembered, adopted a similar method round Ypres in October, 1914, when they sacrificed the lives of tens of thousands of inexperienced half-trained recruits, with a view to tiring out our men and enabling their veteran soldiers, held in reserve, to advance at last against the fatigued and sleepy defenders of the British trenches. But, in the event, as it was at Ypres so it was in the Chersonese of Thrace.

Modern weapons of destruction. however, in the hands of steady, skilled men had quickened and facilitated the work of wholesale slaughter. The half-trained masses had scarcely any military value whatever against the scientific methods employed by steady veteran troops. The inexperienced Turkish levies were allowed to approach the British and French trenches, and were shot down almost at point-blank range. Very few of them were able to retire. The chief attack was made at the point where our Naval Division connected with the French Corps

Some fifty Turks gained a footing in one trench, only to be destroyed. The 29th Division wiped out their enemies by musketry and machine-gun fire, and along Gully Ravine, where the Turks massed in great force, they were broken by our naval guns and infantry volleys. By noon the battle ended. Not a single allied position had been seriously menaced, but the Turks lay in swathes in front of our lines. Our casualties were very light, being mainly

A HAPPY INTERLUDE.
A camera-picture that affords a happy relief to the tragic story of Gallipoli. Midshipmen on shore leave off for an afternoon's picnic.

due to a few Turkish high-explosive shells bursting exactly in the trenches. In the evening a large squadron of allied seaplanes circled above Krithia, in spite of the strong wind, and darted over the Strait to the town of Chanak, on the Asiatic shore. There the Germans had built their aerodrome, and the structure was bombed and set on fire as an answer to the bombing sally made by the German airmen early in the morning.

The British submarine factor By this time our submarines, having crept safely through the mine-fields in the Narrows, began to exert an important effect upon the course of operations; for they seriously restricted the transport of troops from the Asiatic coast, and took to shelling the convoys and columns winding down along the road near the shore. Then on Monday, July 12th, Sir Ian Hamilton, pursuing his design to daunt the enemy, delivered another furious assault on the lines round Achi Baba. Our men had invented a new instrument of attack, consisting of an armoured motor-car, with iron hooks attached to short chains. The plan was for

a number of these cars to dart towards the wire entanglements of the Turks and fling the great hooks over the obstacle, and then drive back at full speed, while using the guns against the troops defending the trenches. It was calculated that large gaps could thus be made in the hedges of metal thorns more quickly than the entanglements could be broken with shrapnel by field-guns.

The attack began in the usual way with a terrific bombardment, but, instead of throwing the shells all along the hostile front, the central fire control massed the fire on the enemy's centre, where a Territorial brigade flung out and, smashing through **Great assault** two of the enemy's lines, just reached the **round Achi Baba** third Turkish position. Then the advanced troops were forced back, and as we failed to establish a connection with the French on our right, there was severe hand-to-hand fighting on the exposed flank. Meanwhile the French also stormed two strongly-fortified lines near Kereves Dere, and the combined attack drove the Turks on Achi Baba to a depth of some four hundred yards.

Naturally the Turkish commander concentrated for an attempt to win back the lost ground. As, however, his reserves came up the communicating trenches with their supplies of hand-bombs, our 29th Division rushed into action at an unexpected point. On the left of our front, just by the Achi Baba gully, the Turks had built a powerful rectangular redoubt, perched on the edge of the ravine, down which machine-guns were concealed. At four o'clock in the afternoon, when trench warfare was raging furiously on the centre and the right wing, all our available guns were suddenly turned on the Achi Baba nullah earthworks. Hundreds of high-explosive shells burst into trenches and saps, throwing up masses of earth, sand-bags, and wooden beams. The Turks scurried down the communicating trenches, but our gunners lengthened their fuses and smote the enemy's reserve positions, while a battleship pitched 12 in. shells on the Turkish observation station on the summit of Achi Baba, with the aim of upsetting Ali Riza Pasha's arrangements for directing the operation.

As the smoke was lifting from the battered nullah redoubt, a British brigade charged forward, and the enemy's batteries, which had silently been waiting for this movement, tried to counter it by smashing up the redoubt with shrapnel and explosive shell. The ground about the ravine steamed like an active volcano, but our men leapt through the tornado of death, and capturing the position, found what shelter they could in the twice-battered trenches. There was a considerable number of Turks taking shelter in dug-outs amid the earthworks, and so bravely did they stand their ground, with steel and hand-grenades, that it looked for a moment as if they would keep the position. But the Scotsmen who had made the charge continued their work with the bayonet, and after an underground fight of an hour and a half, all the works were captured.

Our artillery contributed greatly to this success. Throughout the furious combat, it maintained so thick a curtain of shrapnel that the Turkish reserves could not get into the fight. In this manner another four hundred yards of ground was won. In the night the Turks sought in all ways to avoid the anger of Enver Pasha by retrieving their defeat. Orders had been given that officers would be shot if they withdrew from a trench before losing their last man. The Turkish brigadier-generals varied their efforts to counter-attack. Some launched their infantry in bayonet charges, all of which were beaten back; others sent their men creeping up through the low scrub and the saps with girdles of bombs. These bombing parties were the most formidable of the assailants, and at the point where our right wing had advanced too far and got out of touch with the French left, a section of the trenches was recaptured by the Turkish bomb-throwers. But some French gunners swung up their "75's," and, using melinite shell, cleared a path for one of our Naval Brigades. and these keen young land seamen hacked their way into

FINE CAMERA-PICTURE OF A BRITISH TORPEDO-BOAT DESTROYER IN DARDANELLES WATERS.

KEEPING FIT FOR WORK ON SHORE: GENERAL BIRDWOOD, "THE SOUL OF ANZAC," TAKING A DIP IN THE
SEA OFF GALLIPOLI.

the midst of the bomb-throwers and slew them. In order to further occupy the enemy the French general suddenly thrust out his extreme right wing, and made the important tactical gain of all the ground right down to the mouth of the River Kereves Dere, where it runs into the sea.

The Allies' only gain　During these operations the French Corps took two hundred prisoners, and the British Corps two hundred and twenty - two. All these small local successes, however, together with the increasing activity of our submarines, did not have any important effect upon the general position. The loss of men in the Turkish camp was enormous, and throughout the Ottoman Empire recruits of the 1910 class had to be called out to meet the extraordinary wastage. But the

A FLAG OF TRUCE.
Camera record of a dramatic incident during the fighting on Gallipoli. The blindfolded Turk was the bearer of a request for a truce in which his people might bury their dead. The photograph was taken as he was being led by a British officer through the Australian lines. The officer had for the time being taken charge of the flag of truce.

enemy's main works of defence, which protected the forts along the Dardanelles, were as strong as they had been three months before. In fact, their strength had been increased. The only gain to the Allies was that the Turks' ammunition was being exhausted by the heavy fighting, and the contraband trade in munitions through Rumania and Bulgaria was partly checked by the action of the Rumanian Government. It looked as though we should win through owing to the fact that Turkey was an empire of semi-barbaric peasants, whose leaders had lacked the initiative and the intelligence necessary to found the highly-developed technical industries needed in every country that wished to sustain a long war. A thousand or two

skilled German workmen came with their machine tools from Essen to Constantinople to make shells for the defending forces in Gallipoli, but their production was not sufficient to solve the problem of munitions.

It was then that the German Staff altered its main plan of warfare for the third time. It had first aimed at a decisive disruption of the Triple Entente by a swift, overwhelming victory in France. When the French Republican armies proved too strong, Russia was selected as the theatre for the great decision, and at the end of July, 1915, the mighty conflict was still proceeding between the main forces of the Teutonic Empire and the elusive, retreating armies of Russia. It was not at the time clearly apparent what the outcome would be, and in our own country there was some apprehension that, if the Russian resistance seriously weakened, the German Staff would swing a million soldiers westward, and with this huge reinforcement seek again for a decision in France.

But such was not the German scheme. Like Napoleon I., before Sidney Smith dispelled his dream at the Siege of St. Jean d'Acre, the German Emperor had been seduced by a vision of Oriental Imperialism. For many years he had openly displayed an inclination to become the military leader of Islam, and after the Armenian massacres, when the rest of Christendom drew in horror and indignation away from the Turk, the crowned histrionic freethinker, who modelled his conduct upon that of his ancestor, Frederick the Great, journeyed to Constantinople and offered himself as Lord Protector to Abdul Hamid II., the author of both the Bulgarian atrocities and the Armenian massacres. Soon after this Oriental expedition, as has been related in a previous chapter, the German Emperor began to intrigue against British interests in the Persian Gulf, and arranged to link Hamburg to Bagdad and the gulf by a railway system along which the Imperial power of Germany should develop

When Turkey began to weaken against the Franco - British forces, through lack of munitions, the German Emperor suddenly came to the conclusion that he would seek neither east nor west for a final decision in the war, but strike south through Serbia, with a view to fighting for the empire of the world directly with Great Britain. Turkey suddenly became the critical field of the Great War, for the main design of the German Emperor, after establishing direct railway communication with Constantinople through Belgrade and Sofia, was to employ the immense industrial resources of Germany and Austria-Hungary in arming the entire population of the Ottoman Empire, and then **The Kaiser and Islam** conquer Egypt, Tripoli, Tunis, Algeria, Morocco, and the Persian Gulf. If by that time the British Empire were not ready to make peace, there would follow an advance upon India, along the overland route discovered by Alexander the Great. Whispers already ran from mosque to mosque that the German Emperor was ready to adopt the faith of Mohammed, and become another Sword of God for the

[Elliott & Fry.

Lieut.-General Sir W. R. Birdwood, K.C.S.I., C.B., C.I.E., D.S.O., described by Sir Ian Hamilton as "the soul of Anzac." Below: The Marquis of Tullibardine in the trenches on Gallipoli.

Lord Granard in the trenches. Below: Major-General W. P. Braithwaite, C.B., "the best Chief of the General Staff," wrote Sir Ian Hamilton, "it has ever been my fortune to encounter in war."

Prominent members of the British fighting force in the Dardanelles.

Wounded soldiers being conveyed to hospital ships at the Dardanelles.

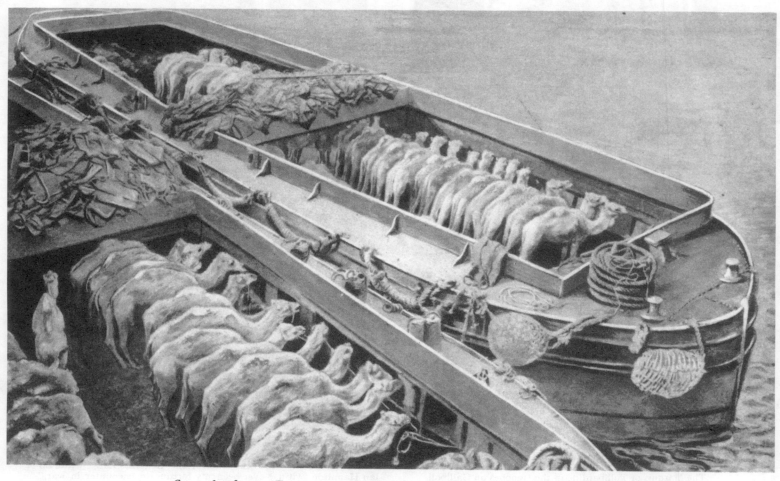

Camels from Egypt on their way to the sands of Gallipoli.

Britain's great battleship, the Queen Elizabeth, leaving Mudros.

"L" Beach, Gallipoli, the landing=place of the 2nd Royal Fusiliers.

Achi Baba, Gallipoli, seen from a point near the French lines.

Activity in Mudros Bay, Lemnos. French troops in the foreground.

advancement of Islam. It was Napoleon's scheme, revived with a larger grasp of detail, and engineered with a longer and more thorough preparation, by which the Caliphate had already been reduced to an instrument of dominion in the hands of the most unscrupulous of all the Hohenzollerns.

Our Dardanelles Committee became anxious about the situation; for it was soon known that the German Emperor, acting largely through Count Tisza, the Hungarian Dictator, had brought about an agreement between Bulgaria and Turkey. This was the most notable stroke of Teutonic diplomacy in the war. Abdul Hamid, who instituted the Bulgarian atrocities, was still living. Barely three years had passed since the Bulgarians in a successful war had avenged themselves upon their ancient oppressors. Yet so strong was the influence of Germany, exercised through the grandson of Louis Philippe of France, who sat on the Bulgarian throne, that at the end of July, 1915, Bulgaria agreed to help Turkey by mobilising against Serbia. Our Dardanelles Committee tried to answer this intricate and far-reaching German move by a sudden violent blow against Turkey. A small new British army of Yeomanry and new recruits was transported to Mudros Bay in the first week of August, 1915, and placed under the command of Sir Ian Hamilton. It was hoped that, with this reinforcement, the Mediterranean Expeditionary Force would be able to carry the enemy's positions on the Gallipoli side of the Narrows and let the Fleet through the Strait into the Sea of Marmora for action against Constantinople.

Sir Ian Hamilton made his plan of operations with notable skill and audacity. He considered that the Achi Baba position was practically impregnable to attack from the Krithia side. The ground there was only to be won by extremely heavy loss to the attacking troops in a direct frontal assault, against line upon line of trenches manned, in German fashion, by an unusual number of machineguns.

Sir Ian Hamilton wanted room for a battle of manœuvre. He selected the apparently impossible region of Sari Bair as the scene of the new operations. The main mass of rock and scrub at Sari Bair was higher than Achi Baba, and the seamed and broken mountain land was neighboured on either side by other difficult summits, running down to plateaus which immediately overlooked the low cliff and ridge where the Australasian Army Corps was entrenched.

The attack on Sari Bair

But in his despatch, Sir Ian Hamilton had already remarked with astonished admiration on the dare-devil spirit of the men of Anzac, and he now resolved that they should be his grand striking force. The task he set them was one to appal and make dizzy any ordinary body of troops. They had to storm and hold Sari Bair. They had to storm a vast mountain mass, fortified by the best military engineers in the modern world, and held in strong numbers by a race of fighting men who had proved themselves magnificent in defence. No operation of war, from the age of Alexander to the age of Napoleon, could compare in difficulty with the attack on Sari Bair; for the numerous and well-handled machine-guns of the defending army, sweeping every slope with a stream of five hundred bullets a minute

constituted a factor of resistance of enormous value. The machine-guns, as employed under the new tactical system by German officers, were more formidable weapons of wholesale slaughter than the quick-firing field-guns, which projected a curtain of shrapnel to stop any infantry charge. All this must be remembered when comparing a modern offensive movement against fortressed heights with the famous attacks on fortified positions made in the days when cannon only fired slowly round shot or case over very short ranges. In a hundred years of incomparable scientific inventiveness, the mechanical instruments of battle had been developed to an inhuman power of general destructiveness. In favourable circumstances a division of 20,000 men might be defeated by ten men with two machineguns. Personal prowess, especially in an attacking force, seemed almost to be reduced to insignificance by the enormously increased importance of the mechanical means of destruction, in the production of which the Germans were for the time supreme.

Sir Ian Hamilton's plan

Everything that science could do for the Turks the Germans had done. They had hedged the mountain slopes with barbed-wire cables of remarkable thickness; they

FRENCH OFFICERS WITHIN THE FORT OF SEDDUL BAHR.
Except for his cap, one of them is wearing a uniform resembling very closely that of a British officer.

had converted the heights into human warrens, to shelter the Turks from both musketry and shrapnel fire; they had provided them with more machine-guns than the attacking force possessed, and had placed a large number of guns and howitzers at the points commanding every uphill field approach. Four months had been spent in fortifying the heights, and any original local weakness in the dispositions had been revealed in twelve weeks' incessant conflict, and thoroughly remedied and again tested. Yet such was the assured confidence of Sir Ian Hamilton in the heroic ability of the men of New Zealand and Australia that, having set them the task of capturing Sari Bair, he took it for granted that they would succeed.

Then on their success he based the second part of his plan.

He first reinforced the men of Anzac with the Indian troops and two divisions from the new army. Then he arranged for troopships, containing the Greek Legion and supporting warships, to make a feint of landing at Karachali, on the mainland of European Turkey, threatening both the railway to Sofia and the Bulair lines.

MAJOR-GENERAL SIR A. J. GODLEY.
Commanded that portion of the Anzac line against which Enver
Pasha launched a great but unsuccessful attack on the night of
June 29-30th, 1915.

Lafayette.

This demonstration was designed to check for a day or two the movement of Turkish reinforcements into the Gallipoli Peninsula, and to lead the enemy to concentrate on Bulair. The real blow then fell in an utterly unexpected manner, in Suvla Bay, only about twelve miles north of the Anzac position. The main body of the new army was thrown into Suvla Bay to storm the Anafarta Ridge, lying close to the heights which the men of Anzac were about to attack in the Sari Bair region. The aim of the operation, as planned by Sir Ian Hamilton, was to compel the Turks to concentrate against the New Zealanders, Australians, Indians, and British supports in a furious battle on the mountain slopes, and then to take the enemy on the flank with the advancing British army from Suvla Bay. It was expected that, if only the men of Anzac could storm and hold Sari Bair, the hostile pressure upon them would suddenly be relaxed by the new army driving down on the Turkish flank. The combined movements from Anzac and Suvla Bay were to form a pair of claws gripping the masses of the enemy about Sari Bair, from which height all the Turkish positions along the Narrows could be dominated and, it was hoped, quickly mastered.

Enver Pasha's third failure While this decisive manœuvre was proceeding, the British Army Corps and the French Army Corps in front of Achi Baba were ordered to make a violent assault upon the Turkish lines, in order to prevent the Turks at Sari Bair obtaining reinforcements from Achi Baba. By a curious coincidence, Enver Pasha was busy, at the time our attack opened, in making preparations for a third attempt to drive the Franco-British troops into the sea. But he entirely miscalculated the point at which the British commander would strike; he sent his large reinforcements to the Achi Baba front, and there he was attacked and held up two days before his own plan of attack matured. The Turkish offensive was designed for April 8th, 1915, being based no doubt on information received from spies concerning the arrival of the new

British army. But the Allies were much too quick and energetic for the enemy, and on August 6th the British and French troops round Krithia made a violent surprise attack which completely defeated Enver Pasha's plan. Though our action around Krithia was only a holding movement, the fighting was of a terrible character, as the advance had to be made against an enemy in superior numbers who was receiving large reinforcements during the struggle. The brunt of the ordeal of courage and endurance fell upon the Territorials of the East Lancashire Division, and in their long and desperate wrestle with death the heroes of Lancashire proved themselves to be men of extraordinary powers.

Terrible fighting around Krithia

Chief among them was a young Manchester

LIEUT.-COLONEL A. S. KOE.
In command of the King's Own Scottish Borderers and the Plymouth
(Marine) Battalion, Royal Naval Division, to whom the landing on "Y"
Beach was entrusted.

Barnett.

master, Lieutenant W. T. Forshaw, who fought in a series of works known as "The Vineyard." He came up with half his company to the post, and there stayed for forty-five hours. He was bomb-throwing continuously for forty-one hours, till through fatigue he lost the use of his arm.

His own detachment was relieved after twenty-four hours, but this magnificent officer volunteered to direct the fresh troops, and with an everlasting cigarette in his mouth, which he used for lighting the fuses of the bombs, he broke down three more Turkish assaults. Towards the end of his miraculous feat of endurance the enemy got over the barricade, but leading his men forward Lieutenant Forshaw shot down the three foremost Turks with his revolver, and the others fled. At the end of the forty-five hours of continual fight the lieutenant was choked and sickened by bomb fumes, bruised by shrapnel fragments, and unable to lift his arm. Yet he said he had never enjoyed himself better in all his life.

By such deeds as this the holding forces round Krithia and Kereves Dere used up Enver Pasha's reinforcements and greatly facilitated the main operations in the Sari Bair region. These Sari Bair operations were also opened by a great movement on the right, which was skilfully devised to draw down the enemy forces and clear the path for the chief attack on the left. The point selected at Anzac for the holding movement was Lone Pine Plateau —an upland some four hundred feet above the level of the sea, extending south-eastwardly from the main mass of Sari Bair towards the promontory of Gaba Tepe, passing

Anzac heroism on Lone Pine

Courtney's Post, Quinn's Post, and Bloody Angle. On Lone Pine Plateau the Turks were dug in with all the science their German directors could command. The deep, narrow trenches in the broken highland of sand and scrub were roofed with great logs against shrapnel, machine-gun fire, and hand-bombs, the upper heavy timber work forming a road, with holes out of which the defending troops could leap for a charge. A row of loopholes in the parapets gave the machine-gun parties and riflemen a large field of fire, while leaving them under cover and safe from everything except a well-placed high-explosive shell.

An Australian Division was given the terrible task of capturing this upland, and the dismounted troopers of the 3rd Australian Light Horse made the great attack. Most of the men were well over six feet in height, and of such magnificent build that it was said, " If these are the Light Horse of Australia, what must their Heavy Dragoons be like ? " They went forward in three lines against Lone Pine at dawn on August 7th. The first line was destroyed by the enemy's fire midway between the trenches. Exactly two minutes after the first regiment, the 8th, cleared the parapet, the second line went forward in turn without hesitation. It fell. For a minute the flag which the Light Horse had carried fluttered in a corner on the Turkish mountain fortress. A few men had got home. Then the flag vanished, and with it one of the very bravest bodies of fighting men the world has seen. Then, ten minutes after the second line disappeared, the third line went over the breastworks, as steady, quick, and straight as the others, but it was stopped by order before reaching the fire zone. The movement was all over in a quarter of an hour. In the darkness of night one or two maimed figures crawled back over the British trenches.

LIEUT. G. D'OYLY HUGHES, R.N. Awarded D.S.O. for swimming ashore in Sea of Marmora and bombing the Ismid Railway line, on August 21st, 1915. [*Photos Russell.*]

COM. ERIC G. ROBINSON, V.C., R.N. Won the Victoria Cross for a conspicuous act of gallantry on February 26th, 1915, when he landed with a demolition party.

CAPT. P. H. HANSEN, V.C., Lincolnshire Regiment. Under heavy fire saved six wounded men from flaming scrub on the Gallipoli Peninsula.

Meanwhile, the 1st Light Horse, attacking from Quinn's Post, had its first advancing line shattered by machine-gun fire, and, after taking a hill along with the Welsh Fusiliers, had to retire with heavy losses.

But those who died did not die in vain ; for the following day the infantry followed the dismounted cavalry, and, after a combat of extraordinary violence, Lone Pine was won. Some of the Australians jumped, with bombs and knives, into the openings in the log roofs, and in a sort of raging madness of battle smashed and knifed the Turks, while the other " White Gurkhas," as the enemy called them, prodded with the bayonet through the roof holes or shot at the heads they could glimpse in the subterranean shadows. Essad Pasha threw down reinforcements from the mountain and hurried out his reserves from the Maidos region. Night and day the furious counter-attacks went on, with every Turkish gun and howitzer within range turned on Lone Pine Plateau. But the Australian Division could not be moved. What they had won they held, and their heroic victorious thrust forward on the left flank of the Anzac position was an operation of the highest value.

For, meanwhile, something was happening on the right flank of Anzac, which should have cleared the Dardanelles of the Turk. A large force of New Zealanders and Indians, with an Australian Division in support, set out on a night march about half-past nine in the evening of August 6th. Preparations had long been going in for this stealthy, nocturnal movement. Huge stores of ammunition and supplies had been secretly conveyed at night through the bush along the coast by Fisherman's Hut and towards the ravine of Asma Dere. The country was so rough, broken, and difficult that the Turkish commander

Momentous night adventure

never dreamt of an advance being made against him from this side. He and his Staff knew the ground intimately and regarded it as hopeless for European troops. At Lone Pine they expected an attack, but at Asma Dere they placed only patrol parties, instead of wasting a large force on lines of connected entrenchments. All this had long since been discovered by the fearless and skilful scouts of Anzac, and the plan of attack had been based on the knowledge thus obtained and on the peculiar

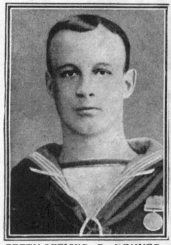

PETTY-OFFICER R. DENYER, Won the D.S.M. on June 4th, 1915, south of Achi Baba.

LIEUT. W. T. FORSHAW, V.C., 1/9th Manchester Territorials. Held a Gallipoli trench for forty-one hours.

PANORAMA OF CHOCOLATE HILL.: SCENE OF A BRILLIANT NIGHT ATTACK BY THE IRISH WING OF THE NEW SUVLA BAY ARMY.

A WELCOME REST: SCENE ON THE SHORE AT SUVLA BAY. A SURPRISE LANDING HERE IN AUGUST, 1915, ANTICIPATED BY TWENTY-FOUR HOURS A PROJECTED ATTACK BY THE ENEMY.

gift of the Australasian and Indian troops for finding their way in the darkness through an unknown wilderness.

The Gurkhas, accustomed in their native Himalayan country to steer their path by the position of the stars, while avoiding the perils of the primeval bush, were at the top of their form. They scouted ahead and silently used their curious knives on the enemy patrols. The expedition worked northward along the coast for a mile and a half, and then turned inland towards a height three miles away. By dawn the column of some six thousand men, under Sir A. J. Godley, had arrived within five hundred yards of the hill. The river course of Asma Dere had been occupied, and out

TROOPS LANDING FROM TRANS-
PORTS AT LEMNOS.
The island of Lemnos was used as a British naval base.

"W" BEACH, GALLIPOLI, WHERE THE LANCASHIRE FUSILIERS LANDED.
H.M.S. Majestic was sunk off here.

at sea were British monitors, linked by wireless with the troops inland, and ready to direct their 6 in. guns on any indicated point of the sombre mountain heights that bent in a crescent round the line of lower sea cliffs.

It was one of the finest surprise movements in modern warfare. The design was to storm the crescent of peaks that blocked all direct advances from Anzac. Instead of attempting the absolutely impossible feat of climbing up the fortified slopes by a frontal attack from the cliffs around the landing beaches, the column had stolen along the coast northward and then swerved inland and opened a furious flank assault on the tremendous

The Turks outmanœuvred

mountain position. The Australian Division on the other flank was making violent sorties from Quinn's Post, Russell Top, and Pope's Post, and fighting desperately on Lone Pine Plateau, with the result that the attention of the enemy was distracted from the vital spot in the Dardanelles system of defence.

By daybreak on August 7th the Australian force forming the left of the secret advance force, was based on Asma Dere, near Suvla Bay, where the new British army had

landed. The Indian Brigade was approaching the vital mountain position of Chunuk Bair, close to the great height of Koja Chemen, and the New Zealand force occupied Rhododendron Ridge. By this time the Turkish commander was fully aware that he had been outmanœuvred and perilously misled. He threw out his reserves in constant local attacks, and the men of Anzac dug themselves in by the scrub awaiting the helping movement of the Suvla Bay army.

Then, at four o'clock in the morning of August 8th, the Australian infantry moved out from Asma Dere towards a hill from which they intended to wheel and storm Koja Chemen Tepe.

But at this point the Turks were in superior force, and by the pressure of numbers they were able to endanger the Australians by an encircling movement.

New Zealanders' splendid charge

The outnumbered attacking troops had to be withdrawn to their Asma Dere position, where they held out against every hostile counter-assault. Meanwhile, the New Zealanders and Indians adopted the best means of relieving the Australians and carrying out the scheme of operations. The New Zealanders clambered up Rhododendron Ridge and, by a magnificent charge over the crest, won the south-western slope of the main peak of Sari Bair. At the same time the Indian Brigade drove upward and extended their ground beyond the farm and on the height known as Hill Q.

The exertion needed in these upward drives was enormous. The ground was so steep and rough that it would have been hard work to climb it without opposition and without a burden. But the troops had to carry kit, rifles, food, and ammunition; they fought in a great heat, and had to go without water, and from every bush and hollow above their heads poured musketry fire or machine-gun torrents of

442 *The Great War*

bullets. Hostile batteries searched the clambering lines of attackers with shrapnel, and fierce, sudden, swooping counter-charges by resolute and hard-fighting Turkish forces forced the New Zealanders and Indians to bunch together in order to meet mass by mass.

By the afternoon of August 8th the energy of the advance was for the time exhausted, and the troops for the rest of the day held to the ground they won, while the work of reorganising the scattered units was undertaken. By nightfall the men were formed into three columns, and at dawn on August 9th, after a rest, in which the reserves came forward and took the strain off the New Zealanders and Indians, the grand attack opened.

Within sight of success

Naval and land guns bombarded Chunuk Bair and Hill Q, that led to the crowning mass of Koja Chemen, some nine hundred and seventy-one feet high. Then the three infantry columns swept out and upwards. The third column was checked by a Turkish force occupying some very difficult ground, but the mountaineers of Nepal, the Gurkhas, were more fortunate. They swept over Sari Bair and reached Hill Q, from which they were able to look down on the Strait. Could the commanding height they won have been held and fortified, the Dardanelles campaign would have been ended, by our guns being brought up to smite the enemy's forts and positions lying below.

Hill Q, however, was suddenly swept by shrapnel, and the Turkish infantry attacked the left column with such weight of numbers that the New Zealanders had to withdraw to the lower slopes of Sari Bair. But throughout the night the hold on Chunuk Bair was maintained, though the men were badly exhausted. Two regiments relieved the New Zealanders, and Sir A. J. Godley, in extreme anxiety, awaited news from Suvla Bay.

The men of Anzac had carried out their part of the combined operations with sublime ardour and incomparable skill. They had almost succeeded in rushing the great central clump of peaks, ravines, and scrubby slopes, with no help but that afforded by the retaining movement of their comrades round Achi Baba. Together, the entire attacking forces in the Achi Baba and Sari Bair regions probably amounted, after their wastage, to less than 60,000 bayonets, while the Turkish armies, with the new reinforcements brought by Enver Pasha, were at least double as strong in men, and placed in commanding positions of extraordinary advantage. Owing to the gift for woodcraft and tracking of the Australasians and Indians, the advantage of position had almost been wrested from the enemy.

A tragic failure

To achieve victory and decide the issue of the war the Suvla Bay force had only to carry out the fairly easy task assigned to it. It was instructed to advance on Anafarta Ridge, the next height of importance north of the Sari Bair, Chunuk Bair, and Koja Chemen masses. By this movement it would threaten the flank and rear of the Turkish forces opposed to the Anzac army and seriously menace their communications. The expected consequence would

THE WAR AGAINST PESTILENCE ON GALLIPOLI: CLOTHING RETURNED FROM THE FRONT IN PROCESS OF BEING FUMIGATED AND CLEANED.

SUBMARINE B11 ALONGSIDE ITS PARENT VESSEL.
The officer on deck with white sweater is Lieut. Holbrook, V.C., who torpedoed the Turkish battleship Messudiyeh in the Dardanelles.

A HERO OF SUBMARINE WARFARE.
Lieutenant Holbrook, V.C., on board H.M.S. Adamant. His right hand is resting almost affectionately on one of the deadly projectiles he used so effectively against the enemy.

be to relieve the pressure against the New Zealanders, Indians, and Australians, and their British supports, and enable the range of heights to be entirely conquered. But, to the extreme and ineffaceable disappointment of the Australasian Army Corps, the movement of co-operation from Suvla Bay did not take place.

At dawn on August 10th the Turkish commander was left free to mass a fresh division on Hill Q and Chunuk Bair, and in successive waves the Turks charged downhill, with a noble contempt of death, and pushed back the two regiments which had taken the place of the outworn New Zealanders. Swept by shrapnel and over-borne by numbers, the small force withdrew further down the slope of Chunuk Bair, and the victorious Turks then charged over the crest into the great gully south of Rhododendron Ridge.

Whoever then was in high command in the Sari Bair region—Essad Pasha, Liman von Sanders, or Enver Pasha — had a daring and glorious inspiration. For the gully led be-tween the advanced lines of the Anzac forces and their base on the beach. Had

A dismaying situation

the daring attack succeeded, there would have been a great British disaster. But Sir W. R. Birdwood, with Sir A. J. Godley and General Baldwin, and other able leaders, were equal to the sudden, dismaying situation. Part of our line on Rhododendron Ridge broke under the desperate valour of the Turk. Every man tried to stop the gap—colonels and generals fought by the side of privates in the ferocious hand-to-hand combats in the scrub. General Baldwin and other commanding officers were killed, but the example they had given was an inspiration to their troops, and by slow, terrible, uphill efforts the Turks were driven back and the ridge recovered.

The great blow was delivered by our naval guns and land artillery. The Turks came on in four lines, the men in each line being set shoulder to shoulder with their fellows. So dense was the formation that the movement was clearly visible from all our warships, and from the neighbouring land batteries. Every gunner threw up on the mountain slope whatever shell was handiest—shrapnel, high explosive, or common shell—and a zone of death was formed in front of our position. But the Turks were so impelled by the momentum of their flying charge down the steep mountain that they could not stop or turn back. They tumbled into the fume and flame and upwhirled earth, and in the explosions some of their bodies could be seen rising as a shell burst and then tumbling into the ravine. There were also ten machine-guns in the Anzac line, and the

12,000 Turks annihilated

TEUTONISED TURKS AT LEMNOS.
Turkish prisoners in charge of a guard of Zouaves on the
island of Lemnos.

GERMAN HUNS IN TURKISH UNIFORMS.
German Marines in Turkish guise engaged in scouting work on Gallipoli.

remnants of choking, half-dazed Turks that got through
the zone of artillery fire were felled by the smoking Maxims.
For half an hour the Maxims were worked for rapid fire, and
scarcely a Turk returned to the hills. Twelve thousand
of them were annihilated in about thirty minutes.

Throughout the rest of the day the enemy continued to
attack, but hour by hour his force slackened, and at nightfall the battle ceased, with the Australian, New Zealand,
Maori, Gurkha, Sikh, and British soldiers holding firmly
to the spurs of Rhododendron Ridge with the farm there,
and the Asma Dere position, extending to Damakjelik
Bair. All our troops were full of soldierly admiration for
their opponents. There were no raw levies in the Sari Bair
heights, but the flower of Ottoman valour. Never did the
Turk fight better in all his warlike history. He was out
to kill; he did not care what became of himself, and

his stark, vehement driving power was such
that the men who slew him praised him.
But who shall praise the men of Anzac?
Mr. Ashmead-Bartlett, our principal authority
in the affair, whose gifts are equal to those
of Kinglake, compares the Battle of Sari
Bair with that of Inkerman. But we
strongly incline to the opinion that there is
no parallel to be found to the entire
operations round Anzac, including the
marvellous nocturnal turning movement
by Asma Dere and the charge of the
Australian Light Horse at Lone Pine, all
crowned by the three-days' battle on the
wild heights, under a tropical August sun,
with no water at hand for men or machine-
guns. In battles of old, men used to fight
for a day, and win or fail. Even at Malplaquet, where
Marlborough in 1702 lost 20,000 men in order to capture
Mons, the attack on the fortified lines of the enemy lasted
less than two full days. The physical and moral qualities
of men in modern warfare are tested in a more severe
manner than they were even in the days of the Crimea.
The condition of the sick and wounded
has certainly improved, but the hale **Operations without**
fighting man in the firing trenches, in the **parallel**
age of magazine rifles, machine-guns,
quick-firing artillery, and aeroplane fire control, has to excel
all his ancestors in the power of both bodily and spiritual
endurance. Naturally, man, in each generation, is inclined
to flatter himself. And in fairness we must admit that our
forefathers at times have, like Sir Richard Grenville in his
single ship action against the Spanish fleet off the Azores,

done things which are incomparable. The clashings of well-matched lines of pikemen or bayonets, stabbing with ferocious skill till their arms tired, have been equally deadly for thousands of years. But the song of the old British Grenadier was true:

> Men talk of Alexander, and some of Hercules,
> Of Hector and Lysander, and such great names as these;
> But of all the world's brave heroes, there's none that can compare
> To the British Grenadier.

To advance, as they did, in front of their companies to the slope of fortressed works, with fuses and hand-grenades, and storm palisade and trench against cannon shot, musketry, and hand-bombs, required a cooler, steadier soul than any hero of Homer ever displayed. And the need for courage of this kind is now combined with the need for moral endurance, amid more dreadful explosive effects, and far longer periods of incessant physical strain, which might appal even the British Grenadier of Marlborough's age. Lieutenant Forshaw, who held a trench in Gallipoli Peninsula by hand-grenade work for forty-one hours, is the modern British Grenadier. As Maurice Maeterlinck justly observed, ours is the greatest of all ages of heroism, and the men of Anzac rank beside the 7th Division, the 29th Division, the Twentieth French Army Corps, and the remnant of the Belgian Army that held the Yser, as the

The heroism of endurance

flower of modern European chivalry. There are some Russian corps, such as the Caucasian, and some Serbian divisions, such as those which regained the Suvovar Ridge, which should be included in the annals of supreme heroism of endurance. But in any event, the men of Anzac will not fail to be mentioned.

Their glorious effort at Sari Bair was deprived of decisive victory through the weakness of part of the co-operating forces that landed in Suvla Bay. The landing on August 6th was a fine piece of generalship, being due directly to the strategy of Sir Ian Hamilton. By feinting with the Greek Legion, composed of Cretan and Hellenic volunteers, at Karachali, the British commander drew the Turks in a

SURVIVORS OF H.M.S. TRIUMPH ARRIVING ALONGSIDE H.M.S. LORD NELSON.
The Triumph was torpedoed by a submarine at the Dardanelles on May 26th, 1915. In the smaller view some of the rescued members of the crew are seen reporting themselves on board the Lord Nelson.

mass at Bulair, and when the new army disembarked at Suvla Bay, there was no fortified line to storm against a large defending force. Disconnected parties of Turkish sharpshooters were quickly driven inland, and by nightfall on August 8th the British position was very promising. One division had swept up northward and occupied the promontory of Karakol Dagh, while the other division swerved round the Salt Lake, and advanced over the plain, wheeling into a strong line in front of Anafarta Ridge. This

Key to Peninsular operations

ridge was the key to all the operations on the Peninsula. At a distance of two and a half miles from the shore, it rose in slopes of low scrub into broken ground some two hundred feet above the sea, and then went upward in hills to the moderate height of four hundred feet, with a large mass behind it, towering to eight hundred and eighty feet. Two miles to the south-west, across a stretch of shrub threaded by a watercourse, were the slopes of Chunuk Bair, Koja Chemen, and other masses of the Sari Bair region. The intervening ground was only a hundred feet high immediately between the Anafarta Hills and the Sari Bair slope. But looking seaward from Hill 100 there

DEBRIS OF BATTLE.
Piles of abandoned arms and accoutrements gathered after one of the battles on Gallipoli, and collected by the side of a shot-shattered barn.

was Hill 112, with its extension Hill 70, and its seaward buttress known as Chocolate Hill, rising between the men on Salt Lake Plain and the Australian Division occupying the Asma Dere position. But by a brilliant night attack on August 8th the Irish wing of the new Suvla Bay army stormed Chocolate Hill, and completed, in an admirable manner, the first linking movement with the battling Anzac force. The new army had swiftly secured a wide front on the eastern side of Salt Lake. The men occupied a large open cup, covered with thick undergrowth, trees, and farmsteads, in which hostile sharpshooters were lodged. There was only about 2,000 yards of thick cover between our line and the Anafarta Ridge, and the Turks had merely a thousand men or so entrenched on the ridge, with a few field-guns behind them. If we had attacked at once, and in great force, it is practically certain that the critical line of heights could have been won. But the Turkish commander was a man of genius, and he outmanœuvred the British generals. He held his trenches with just a skeleton line of troops, and pushed most of his men forward as sharpshooters over the broken ground sloping down to the Salt Lake Plain.

The snipers were mainly local peasants, knowing every nook and ditch, and carrying nothing except their rifles and a large number of cartridges. By their skilful use of the ground, and their rapid movements of concentration towards any point at which our men attempted to advance, they produced the impression of being a force of considerable strength. The result was that the absolutely vital forward movement of an entire British army corps was checked by a small band of Turks on Anafarta Ridge. Then, about noon on August 9th, when the men of Anzac, having been left without help from the Suvla Bay army, were withdrawing from the heights they had won, an unexpected disaster occurred by Chocolate Hill. A strong north wind was blowing at the time, and either by accident from the bursting shells, or by skilful design on the part of the Turks, the scrub caught fire on the height known as Burnt Hill or Hill 70, and the wind-swept flames spread with extraordinary quickness. The blinding, choking smoke and the tongues of fire were driven diagonally across our front, and our infantry were compelled to abandon their advanced positions. For some hours zones of flame and black fume separated the opposing forces, and the low hill which our Territorials had won in the morning, when it was a blaze of green and bright yellow, emerged a smouldering mound of khaki colour. No further advance could be made that day, and in the night all advantage of surprise was lost by the arrival of the Yemen Division to reinforce the gallant and ingenious defenders of the Anafarta Hills. All that could be done on the British side was to extend on the right along the coast, and by the low plain running southward from Chocolate Hill, and connect with the Australian Division. The complete line between Anzac and the newly-landed forces in Suvla Bay was established on Wednesday, August 11th.

All further advances had to be made by the slow, resolute and costly methods of modern siege warfare. On September 15th the Irish Division, which had captured Chocolate Hill, made a charge against the height known as Dublin Hill. The action occurred about four o'clock in the afternoon, and was of a very remarkable character; for, as the Irishmen went out with the bayonet into the saddle between the two crests, the valorous Turks came out to meet them, and there followed a magnificent bayonet fight, in which Irishman and Turk met man to man on equal terms. But the fight did not last long, for in a few minutes the Turks began to give way, and our men captured the crest and shot down their broken, fleeing enemies. Meanwhile, the new army was reorganising for a frontal attack on the Anafarta Hills, after the breakdown on August 10th. Eleven days passed before the work of reorganisation was completed, and in the long interval the Turkish commander was able to bring large fresh forces from the Bulair lines. The enemy strongly entrenched on

Irishman v. Turk

Hill 70 and Hill 112 to protect the flank of their main position on the Anafarta Ridge. The British general brought forward the Yeomanry Division. One brigade was launched at Hill 70, another at Hill 112, while a third brigade was held in reserve to strengthen the attacks. At the same time the troops holding the trenches in the low land

Battery of artillery rattling along the Gallipoli shore into action while a party of infantrymen were availing themselves of a brief respite for a refreshing dip in the pleasant waters of the bay.

Men of an Indian mountain battery on Walker's Ridge, Gallipoli, where, in June, 1915, their position was within seventy-five yards of the Turkish trenches.

Train of donkeys laden with a water supply for the troops in the trenches. The water was carried in a miscellaneous assortment of old petrol tins, which had been cleaned for the purpose.

CAMERA SIDELIGHTS ON EVERYDAY LIFE ON THE GALLIPOLI PENINSULA.

on the south were ordered to rush the hostile positions immediately opposite them, and to wheel northward against Hill 112 in an outflanking, converging movement.

The action began, at three o'clock in the afternoon on August 21st, by a furious bombardment of the two hills by battleships, cruisers, and land batteries. Yet though the heights were blotted out for half an hour by the smoke of the exploding shells, the deeply en-
Our Yeomanry at Hill 70 trenched Turkish riflemen were not seriously disturbed ; for when the Yeomanry charged up Hill 70, many of the Turks left their cover and, standing boldly up on the crest, poured down a rapid fire and then closed on the British with the bayonet. Yet such was the fighting power of the Yeomanry that they still drove on uphill, and, though held up on the north by machine-guns, they reached the southern top and occupied part of the enemy's trench line. But as they

MEMBERS OF RUSSIAN COMMISSION CONVERSING WITH BRITISH OFFICERS AT SUVLA BAY.

were swarming all over the ground just below the crest, a Turkish battery, hidden behind Hill 112, swept the slopes with salvos of shrapnel at a range of twelve hundred yards. Lines of heroic Yeomanry were suddenly destroyed, and the survivors, after retiring down the slope to some slight cover, fell back to their trenches.

Another battalion then moved out to the attack, with the troops that had been held in reserve. As soon as the men came out in open order by Salt Lake, the enemy batteries swept them with heavy shrapnel fire, but the yeomen pressed on steadily without wavering, and at six o'clock in the evening the second attack on Hill 70 opened. This time our shell fire began to tell on the Turks,

and many of them could be seen streaming from the northern knoll, while the Yeomanry, moving forward in a solid mass, formed up under the northern and western slopes. But the attack seemed to hang fire till, as darkness was falling, every yeoman leapt to his feet and the division stormed up the hill at amazing speed and without a single stop. The charging mass reached the crest, bayoneted all the defenders of the trenches, and went down the reverse slopes in pursuit of the fugitives. When complete darkness veiled the scene, it seemed certain that the hill had been won. But there was a knoll on the northern crest, transformed into a machine-gun redoubt, from which the Turks had not been driven ; and they there brought to bear so terrible an enfilading fire that the Yeomanry were compelled to withdraw in the darkness.

The attack on Hill 70 had failed. On the right, the advance against Hill 112 was checked by a solid bank of flame, produced among the shrub by the bursting of shells. The extraordinary fire stopped all further development of the attack. It was a day of disasters, relieved only by the successes of the troops at Anzac, where the Australian infantry drove the enemy from Hill 60, a northern foothill of the Sari Bair clump, and enabled our whole front to be linked up with a trench line in place of isolated posts. The general position was further improved in the last week in August by the capture of an important tactical feature commanding the Anafarta valley to the east and north. But though one of the bitterest German military writers, Captain Persius, was moved to remark at the beginning of September, 1915, that " the English landing at Suvla Bay was carried out with surprising success, and it remains remarkable that the enemy has gained a fast footing on three points of the Peninsula," it must be confessed that, from the British point of view, the new landing did not achieve the results which had been expected.

Of the new troops, the Londoners who fought with the Australasians at Sari Bair won the praise of these veterans of Gallipoli ; and the Irish Division that captured Chocolate Hill and Dublin Hill was composed of men of great valour ; while the Yeomanry Division, though defeated, was glorious even in disaster. On the other hand, there were some new troops that flinched when suddenly thrown into the furnace of battle ; and the genius for leadership, which might have repaired the passing hesitation of untried fresh recruits, was not clearly visible throughout the first and decisive phase of the operations. The battle for Anafarta Ridge must be ranked with that of Spion Kop ; and at Spion Kop the hostile heights were held by a more numerous force than that which defeated our attempt at Anafarta.

The explanation of our failure seems to be that, as the ground was very rough and difficult, the men had to advance in very open order, becoming separated from each other, and losing touch with their officers. It needed troops highly trained **The breakdown at** in skirmishing and very self-reliant, with **Anafarta** each man eager to push on of his own accord towards the objective, without stopping for orders or waiting to see if his comrades were following him. But these requirements were not fulfilled by the unblooded, unhardened new battalions. It is said that in the Anzac region a large reserve was ready to reinforce the troops who had gained the heights, and was waiting only till the Anzac flank was secured from attack by the forward movement of the Suvla Bay army. But the reserve was not thrown into action, when Hill Q and Chunuk Bair were won, because of the peril of a Turkish turning movement round Asma Dere, where an Australian Division had already been almost surrounded and destroyed. The plan of mastering the Dardanelles broke down at Anafarta, after the enemy had been completely surprised, and when he had only a few battalions of gendarmes to oppose the advance of the British army.